CRITICAL COMPANION TO

Mark Twain

A Literary Reference to His Life and Work

CRITICAL COMPANION TO

Mark Twain

A Literary Reference to His Life and Work

VOLUME I

R. KENT RASMUSSEN

With Critical Commentary by John H. Davis and Alex Feerst

Facts On File

An imprint of Infobase Publishing

**Critical Companion to Mark Twain: A Literary Reference
to His Life and Work**

Copyright © 2007, 1995 by R. Kent Rasmussen

Facts On File, Inc.
An imprint of Infobase Publishing
132 West 31st Street
New York NY 10001

Library of Congress Cataloging-in-Publication Data
Rasmussen, R. Kent.
Critical companion to Mark Twain: a literary reference to his life and work /
R. Kent Rasmussen.—Rev. ed.
p. cm.
Rev. ed. of: Mark Twain A to Z. 1995
Includes bibliographical references and index.
ISBN-10: 0-8160-5398-7 (acid-free paper)
ISBN-13: 978-0-8160-5398-8
1. Twain, Mark, 1835–1910—Encyclopedias. 2. Authors, American—
19th century—Biography—Encyclopedias. I. Rasmussen, R. Kent.
Mark Twain A to Z. II. Title.
PS1330.R37 2006
818'.409—dc22
2004046910

Facts On File books are available at special discounts when purchased in bulk
quantities for businesses, associations, institutions, or sales promotions. Please
call our Special Sales Department in New York at (212) 967-8800 or
(800) 322-8755.

You can find Facts On File on the World Wide Web at
http://www.factsonfile.com

Text design by Erika K. Arroyo
Cover design by Cathy Rincon
Maps by Dale Williams

Printed in the United States of America

VB Hermitage 10 9 8 7 6 5 4 3 2 1

This book is printed on acid-free paper.

I am often asked how one person could write a book such as this. Part of the answer lies in having talented friends like Kevin Bochynski and Barbara Schmidt, whose invisible contributions have improved almost every page. The least I can do in return is give them a page on which they are not invisible. To both of them, therefore, I dedicate this book.

CONTENTS

FOREWORD

"If I'd knowed what a trouble it was to make a book," Huck wrote, "I wouldn't a tackled it." If Kent Rasmussen had any such doubts along the way, he overcame them, and all of Twaindom is in his debt for this remarkable guide to the great author's life and works—the more remarkable because it is essentially the work of a single author.

One happy result of this single perspective is evenness and consistency: All the details a reader needs are there in every entry, and the entries never contradict one another in statements of fact. Throughout, Kent Rasmussen is aware of the kinds of questions the reader is likely to ask, takes nothing for granted in the reader's prior knowledge of Twain, and presents the hard facts where a reader would be most likely to look for them.

Here are the dates, places, and people presented clearly, without a word wasted. Major and interesting characters are described, and placed in the works in which they appear. The works themselves are summarized, and often with that important extra step taken: There are original contributions in the analysis of the relationship between *Pudd'nhead Wilson* and its precursor, "Those Extraordinary Twins," for example, and in a chapter-by-chapter comparison of *Following the Equator* and its slightly longer English counterpart, *More Tramps Abroad.*

Mark Twain deserves the attention he receives from the world of scholarship. His life reflects that of our nation, from frontier days to the beginning of the modern age. When Sam Clemens was born in 1835, our flag had 24 stars and Andrew Jackson was president. Clemens had many lives: river boy, printer in New York and Philadelphia (in his late teens), steamboat pilot, militia man (for about two weeks), western prospector, reporter, lecturer, and travel writer in a day when tourists were less common and less numerous. He enjoyed the new times as they came: He went up in a balloon (in Paris, in 1879), had one of the first telephones in a private home, and invested in one of the first typesetting machines (the wrong one). In his writings he predicted television, predicted that the energy of the 20th century would be atomic, and—less happily—anticipated the horrors of modern warfare.

His path crossed those of historical figures—some from a distance, as when he described Charles Dickens and Jefferson Davis. He actually met Czar Alexander II, and dined with both Kaiser Wilhelm II and the Prince of Wales (later King Edward VII). He knew Ulysses S. Grant well, arranged the publication of Grant's *Personal Memoirs*, and had the satisfaction of paying Grant's widow the largest royalty check that had ever been written. A few weeks before Twain died, he was playing miniature golf with Woodrow Wilson in Bermuda.

The characters Twain created are here—virtually every character in *Tom Sawyer* and *Huckleberry Finn*, with citation by chapter and verse. There are even word counts of Twain's works, done by a patient computer. Perhaps there is a law of diminishing returns for human effort, but Rasmussen's machine never became tired or bored with details, and left him free for the work he does so well: careful analyses, gracefully presented, with a full awareness of how the works and their contexts are related to Twain's life and times.

Those times are well set down in a comprehensive chronology by years—a time line showing where Samuel Clemens lived, what was going on in his life and writing, and some of the more significant literary and historical events of the period.

Every Scholar I have heard praises *Mark Twain A–Z* as an invaluable source for those who love Mark Twain. In the years since I wrote the 1995 introduction, I would have thought it would be foolhardy to improve on this admirable book.

Again, I was happily surprised. In his newly revised volume, now titled *Critical Companion to Mark Twain*, Rasmussen has made the organization even more friendly to the reader and has added a brief Twain biography, critical essays on the major works, a filmology, a list of major Web sites . . . What more could one think to add? But surely Rasmussen will, and again will delight us.

Thomas A. Tenney
Editor, *Mark Twain Journal*
The Citadel
Charleston, S.C.

INTRODUCTION

Critical Companion to Mark Twain is an enlarged and reorganized edition of *Mark Twain A to Z,* which first appeared in 1995. With approximately 170,000 words of new textual material, new maps, new illustrations, and new appendices, as well as substantial revisions of earlier material, this edition might fairly be regarded as an entirely new book. However, it is not quite that, so the first question that must be answered is exactly how it differs from *Mark Twain A to Z.*

Mark Twain A to Z is an encyclopedic reference book built around about 1,235 alphabetically arranged entries on all aspects of Mark Twain's life and writings. *Critical Companion to Mark Twain* incorporates all of that material, plus more than 350 entirely new A–Z entries. It also adds 33 original critical essays that analyze Mark Twain's most important works. However, the differences between the two books do not stop there. To make the book easier for students to use, its textual material is now arranged in three separate parts. Part I contains a concise but comprehensive summary of Mark Twain's life. Part II contains entries on all his writings, arranged alphabetically by title, with overviews, synopses, critical essays, and related entries (such as entries on specific characters) connected with the titles grouped together. Readers interested in individual Mark Twain works will now find the most relevant material in one place. Part III contains all the entries that are not primarily tied to specific works in the second section. In that section, readers will find alphabetically arranged entries on individual persons, places, ships and steamboats, magazines and journals, literary genres and terminology, and other topics.

Another difference between *Mark Twain A to Z* and the present work is the latter's greatly expanded appendix section. The Books by Mark Twain appendix has added bibliographical details, descriptive annotations of many titles, and notes on reprint editions. The suggested reading appendix has been significantly expanded and is now organized under subject headings; all its entries are annotated. Entirely new appendices include a mediagraphy, a list of useful Web sites, a Mark Twain calendar of days, an annotated list of novels about Twain, and a filmography that summarizes data on more than 90 film and television adaptations of Twain works. The final addition is a new glossary that contains more than 200 unusual words and phrases that appear in Mark Twain's writings. Glossary entries provide concise definitions, representative quotes using the glossary terms, and keys to the works in which the terms can be found.

Among other special features carried over from *Mark Twain A to Z* is the 15-page chronology detailing events in Mark Twain's life and the world at large. *Critical Companion to Mark Twain* adds a second table listing events that have occurred since Mark Twain died in 1910. This table covers major posthumous publications, dramatic adaptations of Mark Twain's works, events in the lives of people close to Mark Twain, and developments in scholarship and resource preservation. Added to the *Mark Twain A to Z* map of Mark Twain's travels and residences in America is a new map of his world travels (with the *Following the Equator* entry), as well as other maps illustrating places important in his life and writings. The total number of illustrations scattered throughout the volume has been increased from 130 to 200, and special attention has been given to pictures that are rarely seen. All illustrations from Mark Twain's books are taken from their first American editions, unless otherwise indicated.

The new organization entails a modified system of cross-references. In this volume, works by Mark Twain that are subjects of entries in Part II are rendered in SMALL CAPITAL LETTERS the first time they appear in other entries. Similarly, references to persons, places, things, and other topics that are subjects of entries in Part III are also given in SMALL CAPITAL LETTERS the first time they appear in other entries. For example, "VAN WYCK BROOKS" denotes a reference to an entry titled "Brooks, Van Wyck." However, as in the previous edition, there are some exceptions. Cross-references indicate topics that add relevant information to the entries in which they appear. Some subjects are rarely cross-referenced because readers may take for granted that entries on them exist. Such subjects include Mark Twain's best-known books, his closest relatives, and places that are intimately associated with him—such as Missouri, the Mississippi River, Hannibal, and Hartford. It should also be noted that names of characters and other topics that are listed following the longer entries on works within which they appear are *not* marked as cross-references.

When I wrote my original introduction to *Mark Twain A to Z*, I pointed out that anyone already familiar with Mark Twain's extensive writings and complex life knows that a single reference book—even one as large as mine—cannot encompass everything about him that one might wish to know. During the nearly 75 years that he lived, he traveled throughout America, resided in all its major regions, and spent more than 13 years abroad. Meanwhile, he raised a family, launched careers as a printer, miner, journalist, inventor, lecturer, and publisher, and became personally acquainted with many of the leading figures of his time. On top of all this, he wrote millions of words in travel letters, sketches, stories, essays, polemics, novels, and plays. In addition to the classic fictional narratives

that he contributed to American literature, he wrote at length about the places he visited, the people whom he met, and countless issues that concerned him. Within his lifetime, he published dozens of books, and he died leaving behind enough material for dozens more.

Now, nearly a dozen years after writing those words, I feel that I may have understated the immensity of the subject. Primarily a historian by training, I have written a book on an entire society, a book on an entire country, and a book on an entire continent. No subject on which I have written, however, strikes me as being bigger than Mark Twain. There seems to be no end to his breadth or depth. Almost every year sees the publication of new books about Mark Twain that reveal previously hidden dimensions of the man, while raising yet more questions and inspiring still more research. While updating my bibliography for this book, I noticed that of the many important titles I was adding, more than 80 had been published since *Mark Twain A to Z* first appeared in 1995. Many of them examine previously unexplored territory; others add to the growing shelf of useful reference works. I cannot claim to have read all these new works, but I have done my best to incorporate the most important new findings of the past decade. In addition to writing wholly new entries for this volume, I have revised and supplemented the information in hundreds of my original entries, some of which I have replaced completely.

Another point that I made in my original introduction was that because the "A to Z's" of Mark Twain might easily encompass far more territory than one book could cover, I elected to concentrate on hard factual information and leave analysis and interpretation to others. So far as my own contributions to *Critical Companion to Mark Twain* go, that statement remains largely true. However, in order to provide an even more useful resource, especially to students, the present volume now includes literary analysis and interpretation. I am pleased to be able to bring into this book the expertise and insights of John H. Davis and Alex Feerst. Their critical commentaries on the most important individual Mark Twain works add a completely original and exciting new dimension that greatly enhances this volume's utility. All their contributions to the book carry their bylines.

Throughout its text, *Critical Companion to Mark Twain* brings to its subject an intense, integrated examination of Mark Twain's life and writings. I have carefully read each of his works at least five times, I have listened to many of them on audiotapes and CDs, and I have made extensive use of computer database information and frequently searched more than several million words of electronic texts. The space that this book distributes among Mark Twain's writings is deliberately uneven. In general, it looks most closely at the works most often read. For this reason, *Tom Sawyer* and *Huckleberry Finn* are treated nearly exhaustively, while a work such as *Christian Science* receives perfunctory attention. The space devoted to *Huckleberry Finn* alone now amounts to about 50,000 words—the equivalent of some student handbooks on the novel. On the other hand, the inherent complexity or special textual problems of some less-read works has often moved me to give them more space than they might otherwise merit. For example, *Following the Equator* is Mark Twain's least-read travel book, but I devote considerable space to explaining its complex relationship to *More Tramps Abroad,* its British counterpart.

My basic approach to defining entries and assigning headwords to them has been to place information where readers are most apt to seek it. Wherever possible, I define entries around discrete rather than collective subjects. For example, information about the illustrator Dan Beard can be found under "Beard," not "illustrators," in Part III. In the matter of book titles, I suspect that most readers will look for Mark Twain's novel about Joan of Arc under "Joan," rather than under *Personal Recollections of Joan of Arc*—the book's full title—so it is entered as *Joan of Arc, Personal Recollections of.* Likewise, *Pudd'nhead Wilson* goes under "Pudd'nhead," not *The Tragedy of Pudd'nhead Wilson; Huckleberry Finn* goes under "Huckleberry," not *Adventures of Huckleberry Finn* and so on.

Most entries on real persons are listed under surnames, when known, in Part III. An example is "Clemens, Olivia Langdon." (In a few exceptional cases, entries on real persons follow entries on

works in which they appear, in Part II. An example is Edward VI, who is a character in *The Prince and the Pauper* and is not discussed elsewhere.) Persons best known by their pseudonyms are entered under the names that readers are most likely to seek. For example, Artemus Ward is listed under "Ward, Artemus" and not under his real name of Charles Farrar Browne. In contrast to human beings, ships and steamboats are entered under their full names. For example, the steamboat *A.B. Chambers* goes under the "A's" in Part III. Newspapers are entered under their full masthead names, which generally include the names of the cities in which they were published. This system has the advantage of grouping related entries together, such as the *Hannibal Courier, Hannibal Journal,* and *Hannibal Western Union,* in Part III. Fictional characters are listed alphabetically by last name, where known, under the Characters and Related Entries subhead of each work entry in Part II. Fictional characters whose last names are unknown, such as *Huckleberry Finn*'s Jim, are entered under their first names in the subsection. In such cases, titles and honorifics are ignored for purposes of alphabetizing; thus "Aunt Polly" (whose last name is not known) goes under "Polly, Aunt." Because some characters appear in more than one work, to find names, readers may find it helpful to consult the index.

The synopses of Mark Twain's major works account for the most important details in each work, chapter by chapter. Many synopses contain supplemental information, such as dates and corrected names; such information is always enclosed in parentheses to differentiate it from what is actually in Mark Twain's texts. Mark Twain's travel books present special synopsizing problems, as they mix fact and fiction and typically lack clear and consistent narrative voices. For example, although the second part of *Life on the Mississippi* describes Mark Twain's trip on the Mississippi River in 1882, it would be a mistake to assume that its narrator is Mark Twain. The narrator of chapter 30 who describes rising early to watch sunsets may well be Mark Twain, but who is the narrator of chapter 32 who met the fictional Karl Ritter in a Munich dead house? To avoid reading more into the texts than is actually there, I often employ the inelegant but inclusive term *the narrator* in these synopses.

The purpose of these synopses is not to provide substitutes for reading Mark Twain's original works but to provide material that is sufficiently detailed to be useful for serious study, reference, and review. I encourage teachers who fear that their students may use the synopses as an alternative to reading Mark Twain's texts to take a different view: Allowing students to draw on the synopses and other reference aids can actually liberate teachers from the tedium of having to drum in basic facts, permitting them to challenge their students to higher levels of textual interpretation that demand careful reading of full texts. I might add that I personally found writing synopses an unexpectedly difficult task that required multiple readings and constant rechecking to get details right, and I recommend to teachers that they occasionally ask their students to write synopses of chapters of novels or short literary works. Such exercises strengthen our powers of observation by making us realize how careless our initial readings can be.

Within biographical entries on real persons, the dates and locations of birth and death are the most precise that I have been able to find. The abbreviation "c." (circa, or "about") indicates an informed estimate, while a question mark (?) indicates less informed guesswork. The abbreviation "*fl.*" (*flourit*, or "flourished") indicates the years within which something concrete is known about a person's life. The good news is that this new edition fills in many of the dates that were incomplete in *Mark Twain A to Z.*

Most entries on individual works provide specific figures for total numbers of words. Some figures I have estimated by counting and extrapolating, but most derive from computer counts of electronic texts. Since I now have access to more electronic texts than were available when I wrote *Mark Twain*

A to Z, the word counts in the present volume are generally more complete and more precise. Readers may note that some of these figures differ significantly from estimates made previously by other writers. I consider my own figures to be the more accurate, but I would caution that definitive word counts are impossible. Different editions of Mark Twain's texts often vary in length, and different computer software programs count words differently. Furthermore, there will always be disagreement on what constitutes a "word." For example, is *stagecoach* one word or two? If it is one word, how should *stage coach* be counted? Should numbers and abbreviations count as words? Such questions should be raised, but I am not convinced they need be answered.

Finally, it is generally known that Mark Twain was born Samuel Langhorne Clemens. He did not adopt his pen name until he was 26 and then was both "Mark Twain" and "Sam Clemens" through the rest of his life. Knowing when to call him "Clemens" and when to call him "Mark Twain" has long bedeviled writers. For the sake of simplicity, I referred to him throughout *Mark Twain A to Z* as "Mark Twain," trusting that readers would know to whom I referred. I later came to regret that decision because it frequently seemed inappropriate to use "Mark Twain." Readers will find that in this volume I usually call him "Clemens," in which I now follow the lead of the Mark Twain Project in Berkeley. Whatever other benefits this change produces, it saves more than two full pages of text.

I will end here by reiterating a sentiment that I expressed in the first edition: My hope is that this book will enhance other people's interest in Mark Twain. I also hope that readers of this book will not allow its inevitable omissions to spoil their appreciation of its substantial contents.

R. Kent Rasmussen
Thousand Oaks, California

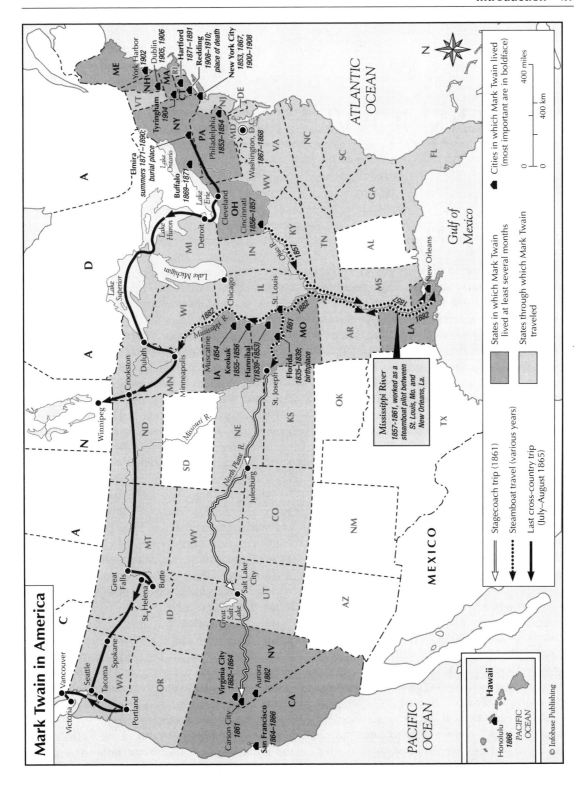

Mark Twain in America

York Harbor 1902
Dublin 1905, 1906
Hartford 1871–1891
Redding 1908–1910; place of death
New York City 1853, 1867, 1900–1908

ME
VT
NH
MA
CT
RI
NY
NJ
DE
PA

Tyringham 1904

Elmira summers 1871–1890; burial place

Philadelphia 1853–1854

MD

Washington, D.C. 1867–1868

Buffalo 1869–1871

Lake Ontario

VA
NC
SC
FL

ATLANTIC OCEAN

Cleveland
OH
Cincinnati 1856–1857

Lake Erie

Detroit

MI

Lake Huron

Ohio R. 1857

KY
TN

WV

GA
AL

Gulf of Mexico

New Orleans

Lake Superior

Lake Michigan

WI

IL

IN

Chicago

1882

St. Louis

MS

1882
1851
1882

LA

Mississippi R.

Muscatine 1854
Keokuk 1855–1856
Hannibal 1839–1853
IA

Florida 1835–1839; birthplace

1861

MO

AR

Duluth

Crookston

MN

Minneapolis

St. Joseph

Missouri R.

KS

OK

TX

Mississippi River 1857–1861, worked as a steamboat pilot between St. Louis, Mo. and New Orleans, La.

Winnipeg

ND

SD

NE

North Platte R.

Julesburg

CO

NM

MEXICO

Great Falls

Butte

St. Helena

MT

WY

ID

Spokane

Seattle
Tacoma

WA

Portland

OR

Salt Lake City

UT

Great Salt Lake

AZ

Virginia City 1862–1864
Aurora 1862

Carson City 1861

NV

San Francisco 1864–1866

CA

Vancouver

Victoria

C A N A D A

N

Cities in which Mark Twain lived (most important are in boldface)

0   400 miles
0   400 km

States in which Mark Twain lived at least several months

States through which Mark Twain traveled

Stagecoach trip (1861)

Steamboat travel (various years)

Last cross-country trip (July–August 1865)

PACIFIC OCEAN

Hawaii

Honolulu 1866

PACIFIC OCEAN

© Infobase Publishing

ACKNOWLEDGMENTS

When I wrote my original acknowledgments for *Mark Twain A to Z* a dozen years ago, I remarked that people in Mark Twain studies are special. Since then, my contacts in the field have increased many fold, and every new contact I have made has strengthened that original opinion. If the people in Mark Twain studies are special, it is because Mark Twain himself was so special: He was at once entertaining, thought-provoking, and endlessly fascinating. All those who delve deeply into his life and work find it impossible to become bored with the man. Indeed, the excitement and joy in Mark Twain studies are so palpable that wherever one goes to study that singular man—and whichever scholar, archivist, or private Mark Twain enthusiast is approached for assistance—a warm welcome and sincere desire to share knowledge are assured.

A great danger exists in acknowledging the assistance of individual people: The more names one mentions, the greater the hurt that is felt by those who are inadvertently overlooked. My first thanks, therefore, will go to those whose names I do not mention here: all the scholars, friends, librarians, center employees, and others whom I have met, with whom I have corresponded, and who have encouraged my work and helped in a wide variety of ways.

I would also like to extend a warm thank-you to the people who were in at the start, who helped me to get my original writing assignment, who encouraged me—especially when the prospect of completing such an ambitious book sometimes seemed beyond my powers—and who assisted me in various ways, large and small: Dahlia Armon, JoDee Benussi, Julie Castiglia, Christopher Ehret, Noelle Penna, Michael Patrick, Erik Rasmussen, Susan Schwartz, Barbara Staten, Michael Sutherland, and my wife, Kathy.

It is a commonplace in Mark Twain studies to say that all roads leading to Mark Twain eventually pass through Berkeley and the Mark Twain Project at the University of California. It happens that I grew up in Berkeley and graduated from Cal, but it now grieves me to know how close I once was to the *Mark Twain Papers* without being aware of its existence, even as I reveled in the publication of *Letters from the Earth* during the early 1960s. However, my many return visits to the campus have been happy ones, as Bob Hirst and his staff have repeatedly extended to me the spirit of collegiality for which they are renowned. That spirit is contagious in Mark Twain studies. Over the years, I have enjoyed similarly warm welcomes at Hannibal's Mark Twain Boyhood Home, at Hartford's Mark Twain House, and at the Elmira College Center for Mark Twain Studies, whose Quarry Farm has become one of my favorite places in the world. When I first enjoyed the electric excitement of reading David Carkeet's description of the house at Quarry Farm in his novel *I Been There Before,* I never imagined that one day I would have the privilege of staying in that house. For that honor and countless other reasons, I would like to thank the center's directors, Gretchen Sharlow and Barbara Snedecor, and their staffs.

Another unexpected thrill in my life has been the generous praise that *Mark Twain A to Z* has received from scholars in the field. When I started writing the book, I foresaw a different kind of reception—one that might involve tar, feathers, and a rail. However, the reality has been the exact opposite. For this reason, and for their ongoing support and encouragement, I am indebted to Lawrence L. Berkove, Louis J. Budd, Gregg Camfield, Jocelyn Chadwick, Vic Doyno, Shelley Fisher Fishkin, Robert L. Gale, Alan Gribben, Michael Kiskis, Horst H. Kruse, J. R. Le Master, Peter Messent, Tom Quirk, and the late Everett Emerson.

Many others have given me encouragement and assistance that have made this new edition a better book. As it is difficult to know where to begin, I will take the coward's way out by simply listing their names alphabetically: Mary and Charles Boewe, Wes Britton, Warren Brown, Joe and Ellie Curtis, Beverly David, Mark Dawidziak, Terrell Dempsey, Bill Erwin, Philip Ashley Fanning, Michelle Free, Clyde V. Haupt, Richard Henzel, Jules A. Hojnowski, Hal Holbrook, Tom Larson, Sandy Laurie, William Loos, Kevin Mac Donnell, Patrick K. Ober, Ron Powers, Lucinda Robb, Bernard Sabath, Clay Shannon, Bob Slotta, Henry Sweets III, Richard Talbot, David Thomson, Headly Westerfield, Martin D. Zehr, and Jim Zwick. To that list, I must add Alex Feerst and John H. Davis, who have written the critical essays that enhance this book. In a sense, Alex and John have carved out their own book-within-a-book.

I would also like to add a special thank-you to mystery writer Lilian Jackson Braun for taking my bait and using Mark Twain in her *Cat Who* stories. I would especially like to thank her for having Polly give a copy of *Mark Twain A to Z* to Jim Qwilleran, even though Mr. Q's Siamese cat Koko finds the book most useful as a bed.

Finally, while most of what has gone into both editions of this book derives from my own reading of Mark Twain, it should be obvious that it also draws heavily on the painstaking research of others, most of whom are cited in the present volume's bibliography. However, as lengthy as that bibliography

is, it does not cite everyone whose work I have used. I would, therefore, again like to extend my thanks to Mark Twain scholars generally. To those whom I have had the honor of meeting personally, I will add that it has been a joy getting to know you, and I cannot wait until I see you again.

In my original acknowledgments, I singled out the names of two people who truly did make the difference between the success and failure of my book: Kevin Bochynski and Tom Tenney. Before I started the book, neither had ever heard of me, but ere long, they both made it their personal business to ensure that my book succeeded by sharing their knowledge, extending my range of contacts, reading my draft manuscripts, and generally encouraging me. I was pleased to make both men—and their spouses—personal friends, and it is especially gratifying, after all the years that have passed, to report that they remain good friends. Meanwhile, Kevin himself has since become legendary among Mark Twain scholars for the knowledge and assistance that he shares, and at the last Mark Twain Studies Conference at Elmira, Tom was *twice* honored for his generous contributions to Mark Twain scholarship.

Like Mark Twain's Hank Morgan, I was born modest—not all over, but in spots. One spot, however, about which I'm not modest is the fact that publication of *Mark Twain A to Z* helped to draw into Mark Twain studies a newcomer who has become one of the field's leading figures: Barbara Schmidt. Since Barb caught the Mark Twain bug, she has become a tireless researcher whose generous contributions to scholarship—most notably through www.twainquotes.com—have become so prolific that when authors like me write their acknowledgments, they have macros ready-made to sing her praises. I know a good thing when I see it, and I have probably been one of the main beneficiaries of Barb's expertise and generosity. She has done for *Critical Companion to Mark Twain* what Kevin Bochynski did for *Mark Twain A to Z*. Choosing to dedicate these volumes to both of them is, thus, one of the easiest decisions I have ever made.

PART I

Biography

Clemens, Samuel Langhorne

(November 30, 1835, Florida, Missouri–
April 21, 1910, Redding, Connecticut)

Samuel Langhorne Clemens, the man who would one day become famous as "MARK TWAIN," was the sixth child of John M. and Jane L. Clemens, who were both descended from Southern families. Clemens was named "Samuel" after his paternal grandfather, SAMUEL B. CLEMENS, and "LANGHORNE" after a family friend from VIRGINIA. (After Clemens became famous, he occasionally traveled under the ALIAS "Samuel Langhorne" to avoid recognition). Clemens adopted "Mark Twain" as his permanent PEN NAME in 1862, but friends afterward knew him as "Sam" or "Clemens," as well as "Mark." However, members of his family always knew him as "Sam," and he used his real name until his death. Moreover, his real name appeared in most of his books—either on their title pages, below "Mark Twain," or on their copyright pages.

Clemens was born in FLORIDA, Missouri, on November 30, 1835 (a birthdate that he shares with JONATHAN SWIFT and WINSTON S. CHURCHILL). His family had settled in that northeastern MISSOURI village about six months earlier, after leaving PALL MALL, Tennessee—the place in which he was probably conceived. His parents followed the example of his mother's sister, Patsy, and her husband, JOHN QUARLES, who had preceded them to Florida a year or two earlier. Clemens would later make fictional use of this saga of family history in *The Gilded Age* (1873), which he wrote with CHARLES DUDLEY WARNER. Clemens's opening chapters in that novel trace the fictional Hawkins family's migration from eastern TENNESSEE to northeastern Missouri. Most members of the Hawkins family are modeled on members of Clemens's own family; Clemens himself can be found in the fictional family's adopted son, Clay Hawkins.

Born prematurely, Clemens was regarded as a sickly child through his first years. Eventually, however, he grew stronger and appears to have enjoyed fine health until he was about 60 years old. During his youth, he contracted such common

This earliest known photograph of Clemens captures him as a 15-year-old printer's apprentice in Hannibal. A tintype, it presents a mirror image of him holding metal type of the letters "MAS." *(Courtesy, Mark Twain Project, The Bancroft Library)*

diseases as measles but escaped more dangerous maladies, such as CHOLERA, and survived several near drownings.

HANNIBAL CHILDHOOD, 1839–1853

Shortly before Clemens turned four, his family moved again, this time to nearby HANNIBAL, a larger town on the MISSISSIPPI RIVER. Hannibal would remain Clemens's home until 1853, but during the intervening years, he also lived on his uncle's farm outside Florida through most of his boyhood summers. Both Hannibal and Florida would later figure prominently in his adult memories of his boyhood, and those memories would inform his most famous works of fiction. The fictional St. Petersburg that he later depicted in *Tom Sawyer* (1876) and *Huckleberry Finn* (1884) is modeled principally on Hannibal but also has important elements of Florida.

Although Clemens was also to draw upon his own youthful experiences for many of the incidents and episodes he used in *Tom Sawyer* and other writings, his fiction should not be read as AUTOBIOGRAPHY. Nevertheless, the character of Tom Sawyer himself has clear autobiographical elements that draw on Clemens's youth. In contrast to the young Sam Clemens, Tom Sawyer is an orphan who lives with his apparently spinster aunt, Polly. However, Polly herself is modeled on Clemens's mother; Tom's half-brother, Sid Sawyer, is modeled on Sam's younger brother, HENRY CLEMENS; Tom's cousin Mary Sawyer is modeled on Clemens's sister PAMELA CLEMENS MOFFETT; and the house in which Tom lives is modeled closely on Sam's own BOYHOOD HOME. Many other characters that populate Clemens's fiction are also modeled on, or inspired by, Clemens's boyhood friends and acquaintances. For example, Clemens modeled Becky Thatcher on his childhood neighbor Laura Hawkins (whose real name he also gave to a character in *The Gilded Age*). Clemens himself openly acknowledged modeling Huckleberry Finn on Hannibal's pariah boy TOM BLANKENSHIP and *Huckleberry Finn*'s Jim on a slave known as Uncle DANIEL, who lived on the Quarles farm.

Clemens's childhood was typical for his time and region. Although his family was poor, he grew up in a white culture sustained by African-American SLAVERY with the confident assumption that future wealth awaited him. That assumption was encouraged by his father, who had purchased an immense tract of TENNESSEE LAND that he was confident would one day enrich his family. As a boy, Clemens enjoyed swimming and outdoor games with friends, who included SAM and WILL BOWEN, JOHN BRIGGS, JOHN GARTH, THOMAS NASH, and JOHN ROBARDS. He attended Sunday schools of several Protestant churches, most notably a Presbyterian church. He received his only formal education in small private schools, whose teachers included ELIZABETH HORR and JOHN D. DAWSON. He was an indifferent student and had a particularly difficult time with mathematics. However, he enjoyed reading, and his strongest subject was spelling. His schooling also gave him fine penmanship, whose quality can be seen in his adult handwriting.

Clemens's formal education ended when he was about 13, a year or two after his father died in 1847. John M. Clemens's death left the family in poor financial condition and contributed to Sam's having to go to work at an early age. Around this same time, Clemens became an apprentice in the printing office of JOSEPH AMENT, the owner of the HANNIBAL COURIER. He also did printing work for his brother Orion's Hannibal newspapers, in which he published some of his earliest writings.

ITINERANT PRINTER AND STEAMBOAT PILOT, 1853–1861

In June 1853, when Clemens was not yet 18, he left Hannibal with the idea of visiting the World's Fair being held in NEW YORK CITY. His first stop, however, was SAINT LOUIS, Missouri, where he lived with Pamela's family for two months while earning his first real wages doing printing work. From there he went to the East Coast and spent several months working as a journeyman printer in New York City, PHILADELPHIA, and WASHINGTON, D.C. By the time he returned to the Midwest in April 1854, his mother and two brothers were living in MUSCATINE, Iowa, where he joined them and went back to work for Orion. When Orion relocated to nearby KEOKUK, Sam followed him there. However, Clemens found his older brother an unsatisfactory employer—one who tended to be dictatorial and rarely paid him.

In October 1856, Clemens left Keokuk for CINCINNATI, Ohio, where he did printing work for about four months and wrote several humorous letters for a Keokuk newspaper under the pen name THOMAS JEFFERSON SNODGRASS. Through this period, he stayed in a Cincinnati boardinghouse in which he later said he met an older man named MACFARLANE who made a strong impression on his developing philosophy of life.

By Clemens's own account, which may not be completely reliable, he became interested in exploring the upper reaches of SOUTH AMERICA's Amazon River while he was in Cincinnati. This was a few years after William Lewis Herndon and William Francis Lynch published an account of their explorations of the Amazon. It was also the same time that the search for the sources of Africa's

Portrait taken during the late 1850s, when Clemens was a steamboat pilot (*A.B. Paine,* Mark Twain: A Biography, *1912*)

Nile River was capturing the world's attention. In order to reach Brazil to achieve his goal, Clemens went to NEW ORLEANS on the steamboat PAUL JONES in February 1857. By the time he reached LOUISIANA, however, he had persuaded the *Paul Jones's* veteran pilot Horace Bixby to take him on as a cub, or apprentice. Under the supervision of Bixby and others, Clemens trained in steamboat PILOTING for two years. In April 1859, he became fully licensed as a pilot. He spent the next two years enjoying an income of about $250 per month—a huge sum in that period. The four years during which he piloted STEAMBOATS—a period that more or less coincided with the presidency of JAMES BUCHANAN—he spent going back and forth between St. Louis and New Orleans.

PROSPECTOR AND REPORTER IN THE FAR WEST, 1861–1866

The outbreak of the CIVIL WAR in April 1861 abruptly ended commercial traffic on the Lower Mississippi River and forced Clemens to change his occupation. After returning to St. Louis on the last passenger boat out of Louisiana, he visited his sister's family and then went back to Hannibal to see old friends. Years later, he wrote a magazine article titled "A PRIVATE HISTORY OF A CAMPAIGN THAT FAILED" that offers a fanciful account of joining an irregular "Confederate" unit that he and his friends—including ABSALOM GRIMES—called the MARION RANGERS, after their home county. After patrolling the region aimlessly for several weeks, the unit disbanded. Clemens's account is the only evidence that a unit of that name ever existed. In any case, Missouri was never part of the Confederacy, and Clemens was never a Confederate soldier.

After ABRAHAM LINCOLN became president in March 1861, he appointed Orion Clemens secretary to the government of the newly created NEVADA Territory. Orion lacked the money necessary to travel west, so Sam paid his way, and both of them crossed the country in a STAGECOACH, thereby beginning a new phase in Sam Clemens's life. In August, the brothers arrived in CARSON CITY. Sam was ostensibly Orion's private secretary, but that unpaid post gave him little to do, so he soon went off on his own to dabble in MINING in Nevada's newly opened silver and gold fields, subsidized by his brother's new income. His first major foray was into the HUMBOLDT district, northeast of Carson City, with several more experienced prospectors. After that venture failed, he spent about five months working claims in the ESMERALDA district to the south.

Through this period, Clemens resumed writing travel letters to newspapers, and several of his letters—to which he signed the pen name "JOSH"—caught the attention of JOE GOODMAN, the editor of the VIRGINIA CITY TERRITORIAL ENTERPRISE, Nevada's leading newspaper. Goodman offered Clemens a position on his staff. Since his prospecting work showed no signs of becoming profitable, Clemens accepted the post. In September 1862, he walked from Aurora to VIRGINIA CITY and started a new career as a newspaper reporter. This period began his real development as a writer, and early the following year, he began signing his articles "Mark Twain" for the first time. As a "beat" reporter, he covered every kind of local news, including early sessions of the territorial legislature, and when news became difficult to find, he was not above inventing stories, such as his PETRIFIED MAN and MASSACRE HOAXES. Under the permissive supervision of Goodman and his partner, DENIS MCCARTHY, Clemens became more disciplined as a writer and sharpened his skills, while earning a reputation along the Pacific Coast as a humorist and an occasionally savage satirist.

During the nearly two years Clemens spent with the *Territorial Enterprise,* he paid several visits to CALIFORNIA's chief city, SAN FRANCISCO. In May 1864, he and his friend STEVEN GILLIS left Nevada for San Francisco, where Clemens took a reporting job with the daily SAN FRANCISCO CALL. A different kind of newspaper writing than that to which he was accustomed, this new job did not agree with him. Later that year, when he got into trouble with city police over criticisms of the department that he had published, he went inland with Gillis and took refuge at JACKASS HILL, a mining camp in TUOLUMNE COUNTY where DICK STOKER and two of Gillis's brothers lived. There he dabbled in "pocket" mining and loafed. During a brief prospecting expedition into neighboring CALAVERAS COUNTY he heard a tale about a fabulous jumping frog that he would later write up and publish in New York's SATURDAY PRESS.

After returning to San Francisco in early 1865, Clemens occupied himself with writing sketches for magazines such as OVERLAND MONTHLY, the GOLDEN ERA and the CALIFORNIAN; he also wrote travel letters for the *Territorial Enterprise.* The popular success of his JUMPING FROG STORY, which was widely reprinted after first appearing in the *Saturday Press* in November 1865, attracted national attention to the name "Mark Twain" for the first time.

WORLD TRAVELER, 1866–1867

In early 1866, Clemens went to HAWAII, then known as the SANDWICH ISLANDS, aboard the steamship AJAX after arranging to write travel letters on the islands for the SACRAMENTO UNION. He intended to stay only briefly but found the islands so congenial that he remained for six months. Toward the end of his stay, he scored a journalistic coup by being the first writer to deliver a story on

the sinking of the clipper ship HORNET to the mainland. When he returned to California in August, he found that his letters from Hawaii and his *Hornet* story had enhanced his reputation considerably. In October, he capitalized on his newfound fame by LECTURING in San Francisco on the subject of Hawaii. It was the first speaking engagement for which he charged admission. The success that his San Francisco lecture enjoyed prompted him to organize a small lecture tour through northern California and western Nevada and launched him on another new career, as a lecturer.

In December 1866, Clemens left San Francisco for the East Coast. He had a commission to write travel letters for the SAN FRANCISCO ALTA CALIFORNIA (these were posthumously collected in MARK TWAIN'S TRAVELS WITH MR. BROWN). Instead of returning across the continent the way he had come west, he sailed down the Pacific Coast on the steamship AMERICA, crossed NICARAGUA by land and boat and then sailed up the Atlantic Coast to

Portrait that Clemens had taken during the *Quaker City*'s stop in Constantinople in 1867 *(Library of Congress)*

New York on the steamship SAN FRANCISCO. On the first leg of this journey he met Captain NED WAKEMAN, who told him a dream story that he would later develop into "CAPTAIN STORMFIELD'S VISIT TO HEAVEN." After spending seven weeks in New York City, Clemens returned to the Midwest, visiting friends and relatives in St. Louis, Hannibal, and Keokuk, and delivering lectures on Hawaii.

While Clemens was in the Midwest, he learned about the famous Brooklyn pastor HENRY WARD BEECHER's plans to lead a tourist cruise to Europe and the HOLY LAND on the steamship QUAKER CITY. Anxious to continue his travels, Clemens persuaded the editors of the *Alta California* to pay for his passage on the *Quaker City* and give him $20 for each of 50 travel letters that he would write on the journey. In June, he set sail for Europe on the *Quaker City*. When Beecher, ROBERT HENDERSHOT, MAGGIE MITCHELL, and General WILLIAM T. SHERMAN failed to make the trip, Clemens found himself the ranking "celebrity" among the 65 to 70 passengers who did make the trip.

The *Quaker City*'s passage to the MEDITERRANEAN was the first of 25 crossings of the ATLANTIC OCEAN that Clemens would make. Among the highlights of this voyage were visits to TANGIER, FRANCE, ITALY, GREECE, TURKEY, RUSSIA, PALESTINE, and EGYPT. During the five-month cruise, Clemens made close friendships with MARY FAIRBANKS, DANIEL SLOTE, ABRAHAM JACKSON, and CHARLES JERVIS LANGDON, whose sister Olivia Langdon he would later marry.

The lively and often irreverent letters that Clemens wrote during the *Quaker City* cruise were widely reprinted throughout the United States, adding to the national reputation that had begun with his publication of the jumping frog story. In late November 1867, only days after the *Quaker City* returned to New York City, publisher ELISHA BLISS invited Clemens to write a book on the trip for the AMERICAN PUBLISHING COMPANY, of which he was president.

BECOMING AN AUTHOR, 1868–1869

Not yet ready to think of himself as an author of books, Clemens did not immediately accept Bliss's offer; meanwhile, he took up a job as private secretary to Nevada's new senator, WILLIAM MORRIS STEWART, whom he had known in the West. He briefly lived with Stewart in Washington, D.C., where he closely watched how the federal government worked, collected ideas for future sketches and stories, and wrote for newspapers, including the *Chicago Daily Republican* and the *Virginia City Territorial Enterprise*. Stewart introduced Clemens to ULYSSES S. GRANT, and Clemens was in Washington while Congress was bringing articles of impeachment against President ANDREW JOHNSON.

It was not until October 1868 that Clemens finally signed a contract to write a TRAVEL BOOK; however, he began writing soon after accepting the proposal in principle nine months earlier. His *Quaker City* travel letters served as the framework for his first substantial book, *The* INNOCENTS ABROAD (1869). Meanwhile, in late December, he met Olivia (Livy) Langdon and began a correspondence with her. While visiting Bliss in HARTFORD, Connecticut in January 1868, Clemens met the Reverend JOSEPH TWICHELL, another person who would become a lifelong friend.

In March, when Clemens learned that the editors of the *Alta California* were planning to use his *Quaker City* letters to publish their own book, he sailed for California to talk them out of their plan. He returned to the West Coast by way of Central America, this time sailing from New York to PANAMA aboard the steamship HENRY CHAUNCEY. After his meeting with the *Alta California* editors proved a success, he remained on the West Coast for three months. Most of this time he spent working on his book, with the help of BRET HARTE, but he also conducted a small lecture tour that took him back to western Nevada. After pronouncing his book finished in early July, he delivered a farewell lecture in San Francisco and then sailed back down the coast for Central America, never to return to California or Nevada again.

Not long after delivering his *Innocents Abroad* manuscript to Bliss, Clemens went to ELMIRA, New York, to visit the Langdon family and begin courting Livy. After Livy rejected his first marriage proposal in September, he continued his suit through correspondence. In November, he began his first long lecture tour, which took him from the Midwest to upstate New York over a period of four months. In February 1869, he interrupted the tour to revisit Elmira, where he finally persuaded Livy to accept his marriage proposal. The couple set their wedding date for exactly one year later.

Still seeing his future in journalism, Clemens shopped around for a newspaper in which to buy an interest. With the help of a generous loan from Livy's father, JERVIS LANGDON, he bought a one-third interest in the BUFFALO EXPRESS in August 1869, a month after *Innocents Abroad* was published. He then took up residence in a Buffalo boardinghouse and began his duties as an editor of the *Express,* to which he contributed a lighter tone with such sketches as "JOURNALISM IN TENNESSEE" and "THE LEGEND OF THE CAPITOLINE VENUS." In November, he began another long lecture tour, this time through New England and other eastern states, under the aegis of JAMES REDPATH's new lyceum bureau.

STARTING A FAMILY, 1870–1873

On February 2, 1870, Clemens's MARRIAGE to Livy took place in the Langdon family home in Elmira, with the Reverends Joseph Twichell and THOMAS K. BEECHER conducting the ceremony. The next day the members of the wedding party went by train to Buffalo, where Clemens learned that his father-in-law had purchased, furnished, and staffed with servants a grand house for him and Livy. The ensuing year was one of the busiest, most eventful, and most difficult in Clemens's life. Meanwhile, *Innocents Abroad* was becoming a runaway best seller, a fact that increased the marketability of his other work.

During the spring, as Clemens agreed to write a monthly column for the GALAXY magazine, Bliss was after him to write another book. Clemens agreed to do so and decided his subject would be his western experiences. In July, he signed a new contract with the American Publishing Company; a month later he was hard at work on the book that was to become *ROUGHING IT* (1872).

While Clemens's newspaper, magazine, and book-writing commitments made unprecedented demands on his time, his new family responsibilities also distracted him. His father-in-law contracted stomach

cancer, and Clemens and his wife spent time in Elmira helping nurse him. By the time Jervis Langdon died in August 1870, Livy—who was now pregnant—was in poor health herself. When an old college friend, EMMA NYE, happened to be passing through Buffalo, she stayed on to help nurse Livy. However, Nye contracted typhoid fever and died in the Clemenses' house in late September. On November 7, Livy delivered her first child, a son named Langdon. Langdon's birth was premature, and both he and his mother became dangerously ill.

Worn out by the succession of personal tragedies that they experienced during their 13 months in Buffalo, Sam and Livy decided to leave the city. In March 1871, they put their house and interest in the *Buffalo Express* up for sale and went to Elmira, where they stayed at QUARRY FARM, which was owned by Livy's sister, SUSAN CRANE. In September, they relocated to Hartford, renting a house in the city's NOOK FARM community. The following year, they purchased property on Hartford's Farmington Avenue, where they had a new house built (it later became the MARK TWAIN MEMORIAL). Meanwhile, Clemens undertook another long lecture tour through the eastern states.

Never strong, 19-month-old Langdon Clemens died in June 1872. By then the Clemenses had their second child, Susy, who had been born in March. A second daughter, Clara, followed in June 1874, and a third, Jean, in July 1880. All three daughters were born at Quarry Farm, where the family spent most of their summers—much as Clemens had spent his boyhood summers on the Quarles family farm in Missouri.

In August 1872, Clemens sailed from New York on his first trip to ENGLAND. He began the voyage with the idea of writing a satirical travel book about England. However, he was so taken by the country and the warm reception he was accorded there that he abandoned his book idea and instead concentrated on seeing sights and making arrangements for future visits.

THE FIRST NOVELS, 1873–1877

In early 1873 Clemens and his Hartford neighbor Charles Dudley Warner collaborated on what was the first novel for both of them: *The Gilded Age,* a complex multifamily saga that satirized Washington politics and gave its name to an era in American history. In May Clemens returned to Great Britain, this time with his family. During this visit he met such literary figures as ROBERT BROWNING, IVAN TURGENEV, Herbert Spencer, Anthony Trollope, Wilkie Collins, and LEWIS CARROLL. He also began what would a long friendship with the Scottish physician and writer JOHN BROWN, whom he met in SCOTLAND. While he was in Britain, he delivered several lectures on Hawaii and attended the second trial of the TICHBORNE CLAIMANT, whose case fascinated him. During this trip, the family also spent two weeks in IRELAND. After taking his family back to New York in November, Clemens almost immediately returned to England by himself to begin a longer lecture tour.

During the spring of 1874, an unauthorized dramatic adaptation of *The Gilded Age* opened in San Francisco that was built around the character of Colonel Sellers, played by actor JOHN T. RAYMOND. Clemens had the production stopped, bought out its owner, Gilbert B. Densmore, and made an arrangement with Warner that gave him sole rights to all works adapted from his own portions of *The Gilded Age*. He then rewrote the play and opened it in New York as *Colonel Sellers*. With Raymond in the lead role, the play toured the country for 12 years and earned Clemens a great deal of money. Its success encouraged him to try other plays, but none of his other dramatic works succeeded.

Around this same time Clemens began writing the first novel that was entirely his own: TOM SAWYER. In late 1874, he published "A TRUE STORY," his first contribution to the ATLANTIC MONTHLY, a magazine edited by his friend W. D. HOWELLS. Early the following year, the *Atlantic* began publishing "OLD TIMES ON THE MISSISSIPPI," an embellished memoir of Clemens's experiences as an apprentice STEAMBOAT pilot. Clemens also finished writing *Tom Sawyer* during the summer of 1875, but it would be a year and a half before the American Publishing Company got out the American edition. Meanwhile, PUBLISHERS in England, Germany and CANADA issued the book. Because of the ease with which pirate book publishers north of the border—such as BELFORD BROTHERS—could

ship books into the United States, Clemens began a long struggle to secure copyright of his own books in Canada.

Around the middle of 1876, Clemens began writing the novel that would later be hailed as his most important work: HUCKLEBERRY FINN. He began it as a direct sequel to *Tom Sawyer*, but the story took unexpected turns, and it would be nearly eight years before he finished it. Aside from a steady stream of short works, the late 1870s was a comparatively fallow period in Clemens's writing. During 1877, his best-selling work was his self-pasting SCRAPBOOK, an invention of his own that he patented and had manufactured by a company owned by his former *Quaker City* companion Daniel Slote. That year ended on a sour note when Clemens delivered a poorly received speech at a banquet honoring JOHN GREENLEAF WHITTIER in BOSTON.

TRAVELER, WRITER, AND BUSINESSMAN, 1878–1890

From April 1878 through August 1879, Clemens traveled abroad with his family. He spent most of this time in western Europe while searching for material for another big travel book. The result was A TRAMP ABROAD (1880), which focuses mostly on his time in GERMANY and SWITZERLAND. During part of that trip, he was joined by Joseph Twichell, who served as his inspiration for Harris, the fictional traveling companion of the book's unnamed narrator. After returning to the United States, Clemens scored a personal triumph in November, when he delivered a well-received speech at a banquet honoring former president Grant in CHICAGO.

After completing *A Tramp Abroad* in early 1880, Clemens turned his attention to a new novel, *The PRINCE AND THE PAUPER* (1881), whose first draft he finished in September. Set in 16th-century England, this novel took his writing in a new direction while retaining elements of the boy stories he set in 19th-century Missouri. Meanwhile, he was thinking about writing what he wanted to be a "standard book" on the Mississippi River; to do that, he needed to return to the river. In early 1882, he went by train to St. Louis with his new publisher, JAMES OSGOOD, and a secretary, ROSWELL H.

PHELPS. There the three travelers boarded a packet steamboat called the GOLD DUST and sailed down the river to VICKSBURG, Mississippi, from which a second steamboat took them to New Orleans. After going back up the river to Hannibal, Clemens continued as far north as Minneapolis and St. Paul, MINNESOTA. After he returned home, he combined an account of his recent journey with an expanded version of his "Old Times on the Mississippi" articles to produce his third travel book, LIFE ON THE MISSISSIPPI (1883).

Clemens then turned his attention to finishing his masterwork, *Huckleberry Finn*, which was published by CHARLES L. WEBSTER & COMPANY, a firm that he had formed in May 1884 in the hope of increasing the profits from his own books. He made his niece's husband, CHARLES L. WEBSTER, his junior partner and president of the company but was actively involved in the company's operations throughout its brief existence. *Huckleberry Finn* became the company's inaugural publication in February 1885, but English and Canadian editions of that book had already come out in December 1884. Over the next several years Clemens focused much of his energy on business matters, particularly those of Webster & Company. The company scored its biggest success with its publication of the two-volume *Personal Memoirs of U. S. Grant*, which

came out in late 1885 and early 1886. The company's attempt to duplicate this achievement by commissioning an authorized biography of Pope LEO XIII in 1887 failed, and the company's fortunes steadily failed until it went into BANKRUPTCY in 1894, despite Clemens's bringing in FREDERICK J. HALL to replace Webster as president.

Meanwhile, Clemens was investing increasing amounts of money into the PAIGE COMPOSITOR, an automatic typesetting machine developed by Hartford inventor JAMES W. PAIGE. Impressed by how much faster than human typesetters the machine could set type, Clemens was confident that once Paige perfected his compositor, every newspaper printing office in the world would buy at least one machine, and the return on his investment would make him fabulously rich. However, Paige never quite perfected his enormously complicated machine, and a more efficient typesetting machine developing by Ottmar Mergenthaler emerged in time to corner the market and capture the riches that Clemens had dreamt of reaping for himself.

Clemens's last major work of the 1880s was *A CONNECTICUT YANKEE IN KING ARTHUR'S COURT*, which Webster & Company published in 1889. This book was an innovative SCIENCE-FICTION story in which Hank Morgan, a contemporary American, is cast back into sixth-century England, where he tries to implant modern science and technology and American republicanism.

EXILE AND BANKRUPTCY, 1891–1894

By the early 1890s, Clemens's financial situation was deteriorating seriously. The expense of maintaining his big Hartford house was becoming burdensome, his publishing company was failing, and the Paige compositor was draining his resources. In June 1891, he and Livy closed down their house and sailed to France. Over the next year, they moved throughout western Europe and stayed in both major cities and health spas, such as AIX-LES-BAINS, in France, and MARIENBAD, in Bohemia. Clemens wrote articles on his travels for American magazines and kept up a busy correspondence with Frederick Hall about the problems of Webster & Company. He also completed a short novel, *The AMERICAN CLAIMANT* (1892), which used the char-

Olivia, Clara, Jean, Sam, and Susy Clemens on the "ombra" porch of their Hartford home in 1884
(Courtesy Mark Twain Project, The Bancroft Library)

acter Colonel Sellers whom he had created in *The Gilded Age.*

In June 1892, Clemens returned to the United States alone aboard the steamship HAVEL, on the first of four round-trip transatlantic voyages he would make before bringing his entire family home in 1895. The deterioration of his business interests in the United States demanded his personal attention. In September, after he had rejoined his family in Italy, he rented a villa near FLORENCE, where the family lived until the following May. During this period, he completed another novel, *PUDD'NHEAD WILSON* (1894), in which he returned to an antebellum Missouri setting similar to that of *Tom Sawyer.* However, this novel deals with the heavier issues of slavery, racial identity and murder. Clemens originally began the novel as a FARCE built around the comic possibilities of SIAMESE TWINS with conflicting personalities. However, when he realized that that approach would not work, he abandoned the idea of the Siamese twins and found what was arguably his strongest female character, the slave woman Roxana, emerging to take control of his book. Despite the book's massive makeover, Clemens salvaged most of his original material by publishing it as an appendix to *Pudd'nhead Wilson* titled "THOSE EXTRAORDINARY TWINS."

During this same period Clemens also completed *TOM SAWYER ABROAD,* a novella serialized in MARY MAPES DODGE'S *SAINT NICHOLAS MAGAZINE* that then became the last book that Webster & Company publishing before declaring bankruptcy in 1894. The same year also brought the collapse of the Paige compositor. After the failure of his publishing firm, Clemens still hoped that the typesetting machine would be his financial salvation. However, in October 1894, HENRY HUTTLESTON ROGERS—a top executive of the Standard Oil Company whom Clemens had met a year before—personally oversaw a practical trial of the machine in a Chicago newspaper office in which Mergenthaler's linotype machines were already working smoothly. After Paige's machine failed its trial, it was clear that it had no commercial value, and Clemens's entire investment was lost.

Through this period of frequent trans-Atlantic traveling and financial disaster, Clemens completed the last long novel that he would publish during his lifetime: *PERSONAL RECOLLECTIONS OF JOAN OF ARC* (1896). As a historical novel, this book resembles aspects of *The Prince and the Pauper* and *Connecticut Yankee* but differs in following the known history of Joan of Arc's life closely, while introducing relatively few comic touches. Clemens later regarded the book as among his best works, but few modern scholars or readers would share that view.

After a final round-trip to the United States on his own in early 1895, Clemens sailed from England with his family in May 1895, beginning what he would later call his round-the-world lecture tour. While his family spent the summer at Quarry Farm, Clemens planned a yearlong tour that would restore his solvency and allow him to pay off his bankrupt publishing company's debts. His new friend Henry H. Rogers helped arrange settlement terms with the company's creditors, making Livy—much of whose inheritance had gone into the company—the primary creditor. Clemens was ready to sacrifice the copyrights of his books to his creditors, but Rogers protected them by having them reassigned to Livy, and he also negotiated an agreement with HARPER AND BROTHERS that made that New York firm the sole authorized publisher of Clemens's books in the United States.

AROUND-THE-WORLD TOUR, 1895–1896

In July, Clemens began what was to be a 140-lecture tour by taking a train from Elmira to his first engagement in CLEVELAND, Ohio. He was accompanied by his lecture agent JAMES B. POND and Livy and Clara. Susy and Jean remained behind with their aunt at Quarry Farm. On the first leg of the tour, Clemens delivered 22 lectures in Ohio, MICHIGAN, Minnesota, Manitoba, NORTH DAKOTA, MONTANA, WASHINGTON, OREGON, and British Columbia. On August 23, after Pond left him in Victoria, Clemens sailed out of Vancouver with his wife and daughter on the steamship WARRIMOO. A tour stop had been scheduled for Honolulu, Hawaii, but because of a cholera epidemic on the islands, no passengers on the ship were allowed ashore there.

The *Warrimoo* then crossed the PACIFIC OCEAN to FIJI and from there went to AUSTRALIA in mid-September. In Sidney, Clemens was joined by the

Australian lecture agent CARLYLE SMYTHE, who stayed with him through the following July. Clemens spent more than three months in Australia and NEW ZEALAND. On the first day of 1896, he left South Australia for CEYLON, crossing the INDIAN OCEAN on the steamship *Oceana*. After an overnight stop in Ceylon, he continued to Bombay on another ship, arriving on January 20. Over the next two months, he criss-crossed India, delivering 20 lectures in 12 cities, including Rawalpindi, which later became part of PAKISTAN. His audiences were made up mostly of local American residents and British civil servants and military personnel, along with smaller numbers of Indians. On March 28, Clemens left Calcutta aboard the steamship *Wardha*, which made brief stops at Madras and Ceylon before proceeding to the island of MAURITIUS.

After resting with Livy and Clara in Mauritius for two weeks, Clemens boarded the *Arundel Castle* to continue his journey to SOUTH AFRICA—the last leg of his tour. After a brief stop in MOZAMBIQUE, the ship reached Durban, Natal, on May 6, 1896. Clemens then spent two months lecturing throughout the region's British colonies and Afrikaner republics before officially ending his lecture tour in Cape Town on July 15. The next day, he and his family left for England aboard the steamship *Norman*.

EUROPEAN WANDERINGS, 1896–1900

After arriving in England two weeks later, the Clemenses rented a house in GUILDFORD. Susy and Jean were to rejoin the family in England, but when their parents received a letter notifying them that Susy was ill, Livy and Clara immediately left for the United States. By the time they landed at New York, Susy had died from spinal meningitis. (Clemens learned of her death by telegram). After Susy was buried in Elmira's WOODLAWN CEMETERY, Livy, Clara, and Jean rejoined Clemens in England. In September, the family moved to another house in LONDON's Chelsea district in September.

The following May, while Clemens was living in Chelsea, a distant relation of his named JAMES ROSS CLEMENS, who was also living in London, became seriously ill, and word got out that Mark Twain may have died. A journalist who visited Sam Clemens's home to confirm the rumor was sur-

Clemens in 1901 *(Courtesy Library of Congress, Prints & Photographs Division)*

prised to find Clemens alive and in good health. When he asked Clemens what he should report to his publisher, Clemens suggested he say that "the report of my death was an exaggeration." That remark, in a wide variety of forms, would become one of the most famous quotes ever attributed to a writer.

During that same month, Clemens also finished writing *FOLLOWING THE EQUATOR*, his book about his round-the-world tour, and began a period lasting several years during which he wrote numerous long stories that he would never finish. Most of these stories were published long after his death; they include "TOM SAWYER'S CONSPIRACY," "Which Was the Dream," "THE CHRONICLE OF YOUNG SATAN," "THE GREAT DARK" and "SCHOOLHOUSE HILL." Meanwhile, Clemens took his family to Switzerland in August 1897. In late September, they went to AUSTRIA, where they lived in several different places in and near VIENNA over 20 months. In May 1899, they returned to London, where Clemens gave numerous speeches at banquets and public occasions for several months before the family went to SWEDEN. There Jean received treatments for her epilepsy at the osteopathic clinic of Dr. JONAS KELLGREN. In October, the family returned to London and lived in the Knightsbridge district until July 1900, when they moved to DOLLIS HILL.

TRIUMPHANT HOMECOMING, 1900

After an uninterrupted absence from the United States lasting more than five years, Clemens returned home in October 1900. By then it was widely known that he had paid off all his debts completely two years earlier, and he was received with acclaim. After the family took up residence in Manhattan, Clemens returned to Hartford with Clara to attend the funeral of Charles Dudley Warner. Now constantly in demand as an after-dinner speaker, Clemens kept up an active social life and spoke in public frequently. In October 1901, the family moved to a rented house in RIVERDALE-ON-THE-HUDSON (now part of the Bronx). The following April, the Clemenses bought a house in TARRY-TOWN, New York but never lived there. In May–June 1902 Clemens made his last trip to Missouri and the Mississippi River, to accept an HONORARY DEGREE from the University of MISSOURI. During that same trip, he paid an emotional last visit to Hannibal.

Meanwhile, Livy was suffering from declining health, which prompted the family to find a more agreeable climate for her. In October 1903, the Clemenses sailed for Italy and rented a villa outside Florence. Livy died there the following June. After Clemens returned to the United States with his daughters, he spent several months in TYRINGHAM, Massachusetts and then rented a house on Fifth Avenue in Manhattan. During the ensuing four years, while he lived in New York City, he reestablished his reputation as the "BELLE OF NEW YORK" with frequent public appearances and became involved in political causes, such as the CONGO REFORM ASSOCIATION. He also kept busy publishing comparatively minor works, including "A DOG'S TALE" (1904), EXTRACTS FROM ADAM'S DIARY (1904), KING LEOPOLD'S SOLILOQUY (1905), EVE'S DIARY (1906), WHAT IS MAN? (1906), CHRISTIAN SCIENCE (1907) and A HORSE'S TALE (1907).

In December 1906, in the dead of winter, Clemens attracted public attention by wearing a dazzling WHITE SUIT when he went to Washington, D.C., to testify before a congressional committee on copyright law—one of his passionate interests. Although he did not afterward wear such suits regularly, depictions of him in white suits would later become part of his popular public image.

Among the honors that Clemens received during this period were a banquet put on by Harper's on the occasion of his 70th birthday in 1905 and an honorary degree from OXFORD UNIVERSITY in 1907. For the latter occasion, he made his last trip to England, traveling on the steamship MINNEAPOLIS with his business manager, RALPH ASCHCROFT. During that voyage, he befriended a young girl named FRANCES NUNNALLY, who afterward joined the informal group of "ANGELFISH" that he had recently started to form.

STORMFIELD, 1908–1910

After spending the summers of 1905 and 1906 in DUBLIN, New Hamphire, Clemens wanted his own summer home. By then he was meeting regularly

Clemens and Dorothy Quick, one of his first Angelfish, during his return voyage from England in 1907 *(Library of Congress)*

with ALBERT BIGELOW PAINE—who was to become his biographer and the first editor of his papers. On Paine's advice, Clemens bought land outside REDDING, Connecticut, where he arranged to have a new house built. His daughter Clara and his private secretary, ISABEL LYON, oversaw the construction and furnishing of the house, which was ready for occupancy in June 1908. After Clemens moved into the new Italianate mansion, he decided to make it his year-round home and later gave it the nickname STORMFIELD, after a fictional sea captain about whom he wrote in the last book he would publish during his lifetime, Extract from "CAPTAIN STORMFIELD'S VISIT TO HEAVEN" (1909).

In October 1909, Clara married Russian musician OSSIP GABRILOWITSCH, whom she had met when the family was living in Vienna a decade earlier. In December, after Clara and Ossip went to Europe to live, Clemens revisited one of his favorite vacation spots, BERMUDA, with his friend Joseph Twichell. He returned home in time for Christmas, only to suffer the grief of having his youngest daughter, Jean, die on Christmas Eve. In January,

he returned to Bermuda, but his health began declining so rapidly that Paine fetched him home in April.

On April 21, 1910—only a week after Clemens returned to Redding, he died quietly in his bed. He had suffered from angina pectoris, and his DEATH was due to heart failure. He was buried alongside other family members in Elmira's Woodlawn Cemetery. Clara and Ossip, who had returned in time to be with him when he died, remained at Stormfield long enough for Clara to deliver Clemens's only grandchild, NINA GABRILOWITSCH, four months later.

PHYSICAL APPEARANCE

Clemens grew to medium height in his adulthood and maintained a trim physique throughout his life. He was right-handed and had blue eyes. In 1878, he wrote a letter to BAYARD TAYLOR describing himself as "5 ft. 8½ inches tall; weight about 145 pounds, sometimes a bit under, sometimes a bit over; dark brown hair and red [mustache], full face with very high ears and light gray beautiful beaming eyes and a damned good moral character."

PART II

Works A–Z

"About Play Acting"

Essay written in mid-1898 about *The Master of Palmyra*, a 20-year-old play by German dramatist Adolf von Wilbrandt (1837–1911) that Mark Twain attended in VIENNA. The bulk of his essay summarizes the four-hour play's complex plot about a Christian woman of Roman times who, after repeated reincarnations, concludes that life is meaningless. Marveling at the rapt attention and patience of the Viennese through such grim fare, Clemens argues that a large audience for tragedy must exist. He uses the play list from a New York newspaper of May 7, 1898, to make the point that too much fare is light comedy—"mental sugar" that will bring on "Bright's disease of the intellect." For a tonic, he suggests *The Master of Palmyra* and recommends that New York should have at least one theater devoted to tragedy.

The essay first appeared in New York's *Forum* in October 1898 and was later collected in *The Man That Corrupted Hadleyburg and Other Essays and Stories* (1900).

"About Smells"

ESSAY on Christian class prejudice published in 1870. Clemens reports reading that the Reverend T. De Witt Talmage publicly complained about having to endure the "bad smells" of working-class parishioners in his Brooklyn church. He reminds Talmage that heaven probably admits not only working-class men, but even blacks, Eskimos, Tierra del Fuegans, Arabs and others. "All things are possible with God." He suggests that if Talmage "were sitting under the glory of the throne" and a working man such as BENJAMIN FRANKLIN entered heaven, Talmage "would detect him with a single sniff and immediately . . . ask to be excused. Clemens adds that Talmage would not have enjoyed keeping company with Christ's disciples, either, as he could not have stood their "fishy smell." He concludes by offering the hope that Talmage does not represent modern Christian character.

The 660-word essay first appeared in the May 1870 GALAXY. Not collected in any early standard edition, it was published in *The Curious Republic of Gondour and Other Whimsical Sketches* in 1919 and in the MARK TWAIN PROJECT edition *What Is Man? and Other Philosophical Writings* (1973).

Adamic Diaries

Collective term for Clemens's various Adam and Eve writings. "EXTRACTS FROM ADAM'S DIARY" (1893) and *EVE'S DIARY* (1905) are light and comic in tone, written for specific audiences, with little attention to religious issues. Later pieces, such as "THAT DAY IN EDEN," "EVE SPEAKS" and "Papers of the Adam Family" (c. 1905–06), are pointed satires on Christian beliefs.

For critical commentary, see *Extracts from Adam's Diary* entry.

"Adam's Soliloquy"

SKETCH written in early 1905 and first published in *EUROPE AND ELSEWHERE* in 1923. In modern New York City, the spirit of ADAM muses over a dinosaur skeleton in a museum. He is puzzled because he cannot remember having named this creature. He recalls taking up the question with NOAH, who will not explain why this creature was left off his ark. Later, Adam sits outside, watching passersby. He is struck by the fact that a baby he sees is identical to the first baby born in the world; he further marvels over the fact that its mother has the same look of devotion that Eve had when gazing at her own baby 300,000 years earlier. Adam strikes up a conversation with the young mother, who tries to guess his identity. When he reveals that his name is Adam, she is puzzled by his having only one name—like the "original." He asks if she has ever seen the original, but she says that seeing him would scare her badly. Adam asks why she should be scared by seeing her own kin—an idea she thinks "prodigiously funny." Adam is proud of his wit.

Clemens wrote this 2,500-word sketch shortly after completing "THE CZAR'S SOLILOQUY" and *KING LEOPOLD'S SOLILOQUY*. Although the piece remained unpublished during his lifetime, it appears to have revived his interest in Adam and Eve and inspired him to fresh work on the ADAMIC DIARIES.

The Adventures of Colonel Sellers (1965)

Abridgement of *The Gilded Age* (1873) edited by CHARLES NEIDER. On the rationale that the only parts of the original novel worth reading are those written by Clemens, Neider reduced C. D. WARNER's chapters to synopses. He left Clemens's own chapters intact but overlooked Clemens's contributions to Warner's chapters.

Adventures of Huckleberry Finn

See HUCKLEBERRY FINN, ADVENTURES OF.

The Adventures of Tom Sawyer

See TOM SAWYER, THE ADVENTURES OF.

"The Aged Pilot Man"

BURLESQUE poem in chapter 51 of *Roughing It* (1872). An 800-word ballad in 28 stanzas, "The Aged Pilot Man" extols the heroism of Dollinger, a PILOT of 40 years' experience on the Erie Canal. The poem's narrator recalls going to Albany with his parents when a summer storm suddenly erupts. Their mule-drawn canal boat plows on in the rag-ing tempest as mounting perils fill the passengers with alarm. The stoic Dollinger repeatedly calms them with the admonition, "Fear not, but trust in Dollinger, and he will fetch you through." The joke, of course, is that the canal is shallow and only slightly wider than the boat, which scarcely requires a pilot. After steering it through such perils as a low bridge, torrential rain, curves in the canal and shoal water, Dollinger meets his match when the canal springs a leak, bringing the voyage to jarring halt. The day is saved, however, when a farmer quietly lays a plank out to the boat, allowing its passengers to *walk* ashore.

According to *Roughing It*, Clemens originally wrote this poem for the WEEKLY OCCIDENTAL, a Nevada literary newspaper that expired before the poem was published. He adapted its form from "The Raging Canal," a comic ballad by Pete Morris (1821–?) and was partly inspired by Samuel Coleridge's "Rime of the Ancient Mariner." Dollinger himself appears to be modeled on ISAIAH SELLERS, an immeasurably proud steamboat pilot of about 40 years' experience. A *Tramp Abroad* (1880) adapts Dollinger's story in an account of a fictional raft trip down Germany's NECKAR River (chapter 14). Like Dollinger, the raft's captain is a 40-year veteran.

Ah Sin, The Heathen Chinee

Play produced in 1877. The only major writing project on which Mark Twain collaborated with BRET HARTE, *Ah Sin* is a four-act play set in a mid–19th-century CALIFORNIA mining camp. Its title character is a CHINESE laundryman whom Harte had made famous in his poem "The Heathen Chinee." In late 1876, Harte stayed at Clemens's Hartford home while working on the play. At the end of the year, the two men signed a contract to produce it with Charles T. Parsloe, an actor noted for his Chinese impressions. The play opened in WASHINGTON, D.C., the following May. Though moderately well received, it closed after one week. On July 31, AUGUSTIN DALY opened a new production in New York City that ran for four weeks. A chaotic mixture of broad comedy and drama, the story revolves around the resourceful Ah Sin, who manipulates gullible miners in order to solve a supposed murder mystery. It badly needed revisions, but its squabbling authors could not get together to provide them. FREDERICK ANDERSON edited the play's first published version in 1961.

The American Claimant (1892)

Clemens's sixth NOVEL. Generally regarded as an unsuccessful blend of sharp social SATIRE and FARCE, *The American Claimant* is loosely built around Colonel Mulberry Sellers, whom Clemens created for *The Gilded Age*. Its story had an unusual evolution. After Clemens and C. D. WARNER published *The Gilded Age* in 1873, an unauthorized dramatization from their novel was staged. Clemens bought the rights to this play, which stressed an eccentric characterization of Sellers. A decade later he persuaded W. D. HOWELLS to collaborate with him on a new play, which they called *Colonel Sellers as a Scientist*. This play, which emphasized Sellers's bizarre inventions, flopped, but Clemens remained interested in its theme. In early 1891, he began turning the play into a novel. Once he began writing, however, he found another theme more compelling. Long interested in claimants—such as his distant relation JESSE LEATHERS, who claimed to be the rightful Earl of Durham—he made claimants the story's new center, giving it a theme similar to that of Thomas Hardy's *Tess of the D'Urbervilles*, which was published a year earlier than *The American Claimant*. The only significant elements of the play that he kept pertain to Sellers's inventions. In just over two months he completed the novel, convinced that he had created a sure success.

SYNOPSIS

A 66,000-word story in 25 chapters, *The American Claimant* opens 15 years after the events of *The Gilded Age* and takes place during at least two months. Its story involves several of the earlier novel's characters, notably Colonel Sellers, the claimant of the novel's title. Sellers is an eccentric American inventor and dreamer who fancies himself the rightful Earl of Rossmore. Most of the action in which he is involved tends toward farce. The other central character is Lord Berkeley, an English viscount who is heir to the current Earl of Rossmore. Berkeley comes to America prepared to trade his hereditary rank for the chance to make his own way in an egalitarian republic free of aristocracy. His story line tends toward heavy social satire, as he tests his personal renunciation of aristocratic privilege in the democratic society he hopes to find in America. Berkeley's path inevitably crosses that of Sellers, generating an intricately interwoven plot filled with confused identities.

Although the novel opens with a disclaimer announcing that no weather will be found in the book to avoid intrusions on the narrative, weather proves to be the central theme at the end of the book.

Chapter 1
The story opens in ENGLAND's Cholmondeley Castle, where the Earl of Rossmore and his son Berkeley discuss Berkeley's intention to go to America to "change places" with Simon Lathers, a distant relative whose claim to be earl he accepts. Rossmore concedes that while "morally the American tramp *is* the rightful Earl of Rossmore; legally he has no more right than his dog." He accedes to Berkeley's going to America, confident that the trip will sour him on his idealism. Meanwhile, a letter arrives from Mulberry Sellers in America, who announces that Lathers has died, making him rightful earl.

Chapter 2
The scene switches to an earlier moment in America, where Sellers—not yet an earl—is in his Washington, D.C., home. He is working on a complex mechanical toy and is surrounded by cheap portraits of distinguished Americans labeled with the names of former "Earls of Rossmore." His library also displays a map labeled "Future Siberia," with fancifully named cities. The large house is run-down and sparsely furnished, but otherwise tasteful. Washington Hawkins, a friend he has not seen in 15 years, arrives as a congressional delegate from the CHEROKEE STRIP.

Chapter 3

Polly Sellers, the colonel's wife, fills Hawkins in on Sellers's activities over the past 15 years. We also meet the old family servants, Jinny and her husband, Dan'l, and learn more about Sellers himself. Sellers completes his game, which he calls "Pigs in the Clover," and tells Hawkins that he thinks there might be a few hundred thousand dollars in it. This figure impresses Hawkins, but Sellers is more interested in his latest invention: the scientific materialization of departed spirits. Within three days he expects to perfect his process and begin calling up the dead. He dazzles Hawkins with the possibilities—such as replacing New York City's living policemen with dead ones, at half the cost. He predicts that there are billions in the scheme; however, he cannot scrape together $3.40 to pay a bill collector who comes to the door.

Hawkins tells Sellers about One-Armed-Pete, a Cherokee Strip bank robber with a $5,000 reward on his head, whom he saw on a train headed to Baltimore. Sellers drafts a plan to capture Pete, beginning with a personal ad that he places in a Baltimore newspaper.

Chapter 4

Sellers and Hawkins discuss how they will spend their reward money until Polly quiets them. The next day Sellers takes the plans of his new game into town to patent it, while Hawkins takes the game itself into town to see if it has commercial possibilities. A Yankee furniture repairer is interested in producing the game but can pay nothing down, so he offers to pay a five-cent royalty on each 25-cent game he sells. After having the man draw up a contract, Hawkins dismisses the subject from his mind.

When Sellers gets home, he excitedly announces that his cousin Simon Lathers and his brother have died, leaving him the rightful Earl of Rossmore. He cables his daughter, Sally Sellers—whom he now calls "Lady Gwendolen"—to return home from college to help mourn. The next day he sends the cable that the Earl of Rossmore receives in chapter 1. He also asks authorities in Lathers's ARKANSAS village to embalm the Lathers brothers and ship them C.O.D. to Rossmore. He arranges elaborate family mourning observations and renames his house "Rossmore Towers."

"AND I AS USURPER—A NAMELESS PAUPER, A TRAMP."

Standing in the breakfast room of Cholmondeley Castle, the Earl of Rossmore and his son Berkeley discuss the latter's plans to go to America.

Chapter 5

Glad to get away from her snooty, rank-conscious classmates, Sally arrives home seven days later. In studying *Burke's Peerage*, Sellers finds that the Rossmore earldom was founded by William the Conqueror and that it ranks third in England. Meanwhile, he receives a cable from One-Armed Pete answering his ad and promising to come to Washington in 10 days. The next day, Sellers ships the remains of the Lathers brothers to England, while Lord Berkeley simultaneously starts for America.

Chapter 6

When the Lathers brothers arrive in England, Rossmore reluctantly gives them a formal funeral and has them interred in the family plot. Back in America, Sally leads a double life: By day, she is sensible and democratic Sally Sellers, working to support the family; by night, she is romantic "Lady Gwendolen."

After One-Armed Pete arrives in Washington, he sends Sellers instructions to meet him near the New Gadsby Hotel the next day. That night, Sellers and Hawkins visit Pete's hotel to spy. Hawkins spots Pete boarding an elevator in his western CLOTHES, but does not notice Viscount Berkeley boarding the elevator.

Chapter 7

In his hotel room, Berkeley records "impressions" of his travels in his journal. He is distressed to find that Americans treat him deferentially everywhere he goes just because of his title. That night, he is awakened by a call that the hotel is on fire. Saving only his journal, he rushes down the hallway, snatches an outfit from another room and puts it on. It is a gaudy cowboy suit that attracts considerable attention outside. He goes off and finds new lodgings.

The next morning Berkeley examines the pockets in his new clothes and finds more than $500 in cash. When he reads a newspaper report that *he* died a hero in the hotel fire, he decides to let the error stand so that he can start a truly new life. Since he is officially "dead," he no longer needs to find the American Claimant.

Chapter 8

Sellers reads the report of Berkeley's death in the newspaper, which also reports that a one-armed man was seen headed for certain death during the fire. Unconcerned by the possibility that Pete has died, Sellers promises to "materialize" him so that they can still collect the reward money. After breaking the news of the latest death of a kinsman to his family, Sellers goes to the hotel to claim Berkeley's body for shipment to England.

Chapter 9

At the hotel, Sellers and Hawkins find five charred, unrecognizable bodies. When officials point out that three reports of Berkeley's death place him in spots other than where these bodies were found, Sellers and Hawkins fill baskets with ashes from each of the three places where Berkeley may have died. At home, Polly joins Sellers in sitting up with

the ashes, but refuses to let her husband put them on display in the front room.

Chapter 10

Berkeley, now feeling free for the first time, banks most of his newfound money in a way that will make it impossible for him to retrieve it. He keeps wearing the gaudy western clothes, hoping their rightful owner will find him. While at the bank, he invents a new name for himself: "Howard Tracy." He cables his father to report that he is unhurt, to tell him that he has taken a new name, and to say good-bye. With limited money and no identification, he must now survive on his own.

That evening Berkeley attends a lecture at the Mechanics' Club Debate. The first lecturer attacks MATTHEW ARNOLD, arguing that irreverence is one of the American press's greatest qualities. The second speaker praises the great achievements of inventors who lacked college educations. Berkeley leaves, thrilled by the arguments for egalitarianism.

Chapter 11

In searching for a job, Berkeley finds that he has no chance without political backing. To get closer to common people and conserve his resources, he moves into a cheap boardinghouse run by Rachel Marsh and her husband. The Marshes' attractive daughter Hattie Marsh surprises Berkeley with her relaxed openness and teaches him how Americans use titles such as "lady."

Berkeley also meets Barrow, who believes that aristocratic privilege survives in England only because of the acquiescence of society as a whole. The mass of the people need only declare themselves dukes and duchesses and laugh the nobility into oblivion.

Chapter 12

At his first boardinghouse supper, Berkeley has trouble adjusting to the stench of old cabbage. The landlord Marsh shocks him with his undemocratic tyranny over a young unemployed tinner, Nat Brady. Nevertheless, Berkeley concludes that he is living in a house that is a "republic" in which everyone is free and equal. When Berkeley later boards a streetcar, Sellers and Hawkins see him and recognize

One-Armed Pete's clothes. Sellers thinks that Berkeley is the materialized form of One-Armed Pete that his experiment has called up.

Chapter 13

Unable to find work or even join a labor union, Berkeley is becoming desperate. As he grows surly, other boardinghouse residents turn away from him and tease him. However, after a bullying amateur boxer named Allen picks on Brady, Berkeley whips Allen easily, regaining the respect of the other boarders. Meanwhile, his financial situation is so bad that he cables his father, on the pretext of telling him his new name.

Chapter 14

To cheer up Berkeley, Barrow takes him to the Mechanics' Club, where a blacksmith named Tompkins denounces the English aristocracy. Berkeley's conscience burns, but afterward Barrow demolishes Tompkins's argument, which he says ignores the "factor of human nature."

Chapter 15

When Marsh reminds Berkeley the next day that he has not paid his weekly bill, Berkeley discovers that he has been robbed—as have other residents since Allen disappeared. To buy time, Berkeley tells Marsh that he expects a cable from home. Marsh's sarcastic reply drives Berkeley to blurt out that his father is an English earl. Everyone is too stunned to know how to react; however, Marsh will not let Berkeley leave the house to fetch his cable, so Brady volunteers to go. After Brady returns with a cable, everyone is breathless as Berkeley opens it. His father's message has one word: "Thanks." Berkeley is spared further embarrassment when Barrow offers to pay his bill.

Chapter 16

Barrow tells Berkeley that he has found work for him if he can paint details in pictures. Barrow introduces Berkeley to a German named Handel who paints human figures from tintypes, and to an old sailor, Captain Saltmarsh, who paints cannons and backgrounds. Their problem is that each man can paint nothing else; since their customers want variety, they need help.

Chapter 17

Berkeley's spirits sink as he waits for a cable from his father. After a week, he decides to join the painters. They are so pleased with a hearse he paints on a canvas that they make him a full partner. As he paints cats, hacks, sausages, tugs, pianos, guitars, rocks and other things, the painting business booms and Berkeley's self-esteem rises.

Back at Rossmore Towers, Hawkins despairs because One-Armed Pete has failed to show up as Sellers promised. To cheer up Hawkins, Sellers shows him a new invention: his "Cursing Phonograph," for use by sea captains too busy to swear themselves. Another of Sellers's inventions is a decomposer that produces sewer-gas for home use in lighting; he hopes to have the system adopted in the White House so that it will catch on.

Chapter 18

Sellers reveals his biggest project to Hawkins: a plan to liberate RUSSIA by buying Siberia and using its political prisoners to start a revolution.

When Sellers sees Berkeley strolling by his house, he congratulates himself on getting his "materializee" to come. Berkeley, meanwhile, notices that he is at the American Claimant's home. Sellers invites Berkeley in, tells him that he is expected, and makes some remarks intended for One-Armed Pete that are inscrutable to Berkeley. After Berkeley identifies himself as an artist, Sellers engages him to restore paintings and leaves him to work alone.

Chapter 19

Sellers and Hawkins wonder why this materialization of One-Armed Pete has *two* arms and speaks with an English accent. Sellers concludes that he has materialized an ancestor of Pete and proposes materializing him "down to date." Once One-Armed Pete is under their control, they will have him confess every crime he ever committed and then collect a fortune in rewards.

When Polly asks about Berkeley, whom she sees painting in another room, she surprises Sellers and Hawkins by mentioning that she has seen him eating apples—impossible behavior for a materializee.

Chapter 20

When Sellers's daughter Sally arrives and meets Berkeley, it is love at first sight. She invites him to stay for dinner, but he declines in order to go out and buy decent clothes. The next day, Berkeley returns in a new suit.

Chapter 21

Sally and Berkeley work in different parts of the house, and they are desolate apart from each other. As a result of a mixup, Sally goes to a friend's house for dinner, while Berkeley dines at her house. When she returns, a quick exchange of glances tells her and Berkeley that their affection is mutual. When they are finally alone, they embrace and kiss. Hawkins accidentally sees them and is appalled by the idea that Sally is kissing a "materializee."

Chapter 22

Despondent over what he has just seen, Hawkins cannot understand why no one else notices the brimstone stench emitted by Berkeley. When Sellers joins him, he puzzles over the mystery of a materializee eating solid food. He also confesses to liking Berkeley too much to "degrade" him to a burglar, so he and Hawkins agree to sacrifice their hopes for reward money and leave Berkeley as he is.

Sally tells Berkeley that her father's claim to be an earl is a "sham" and that she no longer wants to be called "Gwendolen." She asks Berkeley if he wants to marry her only because of her rank. Suppressing the urge to laugh, Berkeley swears that he loves her only for herself, then asks her how *she* feels about aristocracy and nobility. He is relieved to learn that she does not disapprove of real titles. This line of questioning reopens her doubts about Berkeley's sincerity, since she still worries that he is after her father's earldom.

Chapter 23

That night Berkeley writes his father, telling him that he is ready to renounce his quest in America and that he intends to marry the American Claimant's daughter. After receiving the letter, Rossmore immediately leaves for America in order to deal with matters personally.

Over the next 10 days, Berkeley's spirits rise and fall with Sally's shifting moods as he paints a portrait of Sellers in "a peer's scarlet robe." Berkeley eventually learns that Sally has been acting oddly only because she still thinks that he is after her father's earldom. They reconcile, but Berkeley tries to prove his point by telling her that *he* is the son of an English earl. This only angers her. His claim seems completely illogical and he has no proof. When he further identifies himself as the son of the Earl of Rossmore, Sally grows even angrier. Berkeley leaves with the understanding that he should not return without proof of his claims.

Chapter 24

During 10 miserable days of waiting for his father's cable, Berkeley confides in Barrow, who humors him. Sally, too, is miserable throughout this period. Meanwhile, Hawkins and Sellers learn that Sellers's "Pigs in the Clover" games are sweeping the nation, with factories working night and day to supply them. Hawkins is ecstatic, but Sellers is indifferent and tells him to hunt up the Yankee who makes the games and collect the royalty money—half of which Hawkins can keep. Sellers then returns to working on a temperance lecture. Dissatisfied with his previous lectures on temperance, he suspects that his problem is lack of experience with alcohol, so he gets drunk in order to study the results. However, he gets so sick that he must stay in bed for several days and he misses his lecture.

Once Sellers recovers, he finds that Hawkins has banked enough money for him from his game that he can take Polly to England to press his claim for the earldom. They pack and leave for New York.

After her parents leave, Sally asks Hawkins for advice about Berkeley. Hawkins cannot tell Sally what he really thinks, namely that Berkeley is a materialized spirit, so he invents a story calculated to make her reject Berkeley. Hawkins tells Sally that Berkeley is a "dissipated ruffian" from the Cherokee Strip whose real name is "Spinal Meningitis Snodgrass," that he is the son of an idiot doctor, and that his brother is named "Zylobalsamum Snodgrass." Despite the terrible picture of Berkeley that Hawkins paints, Sally concludes that "he has no friend but me, and I will not desert him now." She asks Hawkins to find Berkeley and bring him to her.

Chapter 25

Hawkins goes straight to the telegraph office and cables Sally's parents to return from New York because she is "going to marry the materializee." Meanwhile, a note arrives at Rossmore Towers saying that the Earl of Rossmore will arrive that evening. Berkeley arrives the same evening, hoping only to see Sally. When he is alone with her, she drops references to the Snodgrass family. After failing to get a rise out of him, she finally asks if he is the son of Dr. Snodgrass. Just as it appears that Sally and Berkeley are again reconciled, Berkeley's father appears and finds them embracing. When Rossmore asks his son for a hug, Sally realizes that Berkeley really is an earl's son and says that she will *not* have him. However, after a long private talk with Sally, Rossmore gives his approval to the marriage, which she is now willing to go through with.

Meanwhile, Hawkins talks with Berkeley, who convinces him that he (Berkeley) is not a materialized spirit. Once everyone is together again, plans are made for a quiet wedding at Rossmore Towers, and Sellers and Rossmore became great friends. The Sellerses plan to go to England to visit with Rossmore, but Sellers misses the train and Hawkins reports that he is off on a new scheme and will join the others later. In a note he has left to Hawkins, Sellers explains that since making an offer to purchase Siberia with the big money he expected from his materialization scheme, he is concerned that if the czar suddenly accepts, his credit will suffer when he cannot meet the payment. He is therefore going to San Francisco to test a new scheme with the Lick telescope; he plans to reorganize the Earth's climates by controlling sunspots to shift climates around the globe. For example, he wants to buy GREENLAND and ICELAND, then move one of the Tropics to the Arctic Circle, which he will convert into a tropical resort.

PUBLISHING HISTORY

After writing this book in early 1891, Clemens serialized it in the NEW YORK SUN's Sunday edition from January 3 to March 27, 1892. It also appeared in various McClure Syndicate magazines and in England's *Idler*. Charles L. WEBSTER & COMPANY and CHATTO & Windus both published *The American Claimant* as a book later the same year. A later HARPER volume, *The American Claimant and Other Stories and Sketches*, combines the novel with most of the stories previously published in MERRY TALES. Since its original publication, *The American Claimant* has rarely been reprinted, except in uniform editions of Clemens's works. A facsimile reprint of the first edition was issued as part of the OXFORD MARK TWAIN edition in 1996. That edition includes a new introduction by novelist Bobbie Ann Mason and an afterword by British scholar Peter Messent. DAN BEARD illustrated the first American edition of the book, and Hal Hurst illustrated the *Idler* serialization. The Chatto & Windus edition combined Beard's and Hurst's illustrations. Beard apparently was responsible for the Rossmore family motto, *Suum Cuique*, which appears in several illustrations, including the original cover. It is a Latin phrase that loosely translates as "To each, his own."

CRITICAL COMMENTARY

Frequently misattributed to Mark Twain is the statement, "Everybody talks about the weather, but nobody does anything about it."

In *The American Claimant,* however, the writer offers readers that opportunity. Before the story begins, he announces, "No weather will be found in this book. This is an attempt to pull a book through without weather. It being the first attempt of the kind in fictitious literature, it may prove a failure, but it seemed worth the while of some dare-devil person to try it, and the author was in just the mood." This mood may clarify reasons for the critical confusion about the coherence of this novel; possibly, Clemens is simply having fun with this story, and with critics who must find meaning. As he wrote about the book: "I think it will simply howl with fun. I wake up in the night laughing at its ridiculous situations" (Messent 2). The writer next jovially invites readers to place the weather where they desire, interspersing it with the plot. As Herman Melville establishes mood before *Moby-Dick* begins with an etymology and pages of extracts referring to whales, taken from a wide range of sources, so Clemens refers his readers to an appendix of weather quotations. Borrowing these quotations "from qualified and recognized experts," he urges the reader "to turn back over and help himself from time to time as he goes along." Involving readers is a typical Twainian practice, as in the story of the old ram (chapter 53 in *Roughing It*).

Despite such melodramatic touches as love-at-first-sight and a western outlaw with a price on his head, the two plots—based on Sellers and on Berkeley—flow into one and ultimately bring varying elements together: The couple marries; parents (rival claimants) are reconciled; the claim is seemingly resolved; the apparent title character (Sellers) becomes successful and prosperous and, true to character, leaves on an idealistic project; the less obvious title character (Berkeley) learns a middle way between aristocracy and democracy. The story follows several traditions. Like a comedy, it ends with a marriage; like an adventure yarn, the protagonist seeks further adventures; like a "well-made" novel, plot details are wrapped up. Calling them "ridiculous situations," Clemens knows that some of these details become extravagant, even surreal, but the excess is part of his fun.

The novel, nevertheless, leaves many readers and critics, unsatisfied. Plot issues are resolved but thematic ones are not. Several targets, themes, and motifs do not ultimately cohere in this novel; Clemens leaves many ideas unconnected. Recurring Twainian notions include role reversals, antiromanticism, multiple identities, and a potential legacy. Many larger matters are brought up but left hanging, such as labor relations and capitalism (as represented by Sellers's notion of replacing laborers with animated corpses), the American class struggle, the failings of American democracy, the ambivalence of Americans toward aristocracy, materialism, political corruption, and—on the horizon as the novel ends—the overthrow of autocratic governments and regime-building by Colonel Sellers, beginning in czarist Russia.

Colonel Sellers

This unfinished aspect coincides with the character of Colonel Sellers, a man with incomplete dreams. When the reader meets Sellers in his home, he has covered the word *SIBERIA* on a large map, "the most imposing decoration of the establishment," with the word *FUTURE* (chapter 2); both foreshadow the expedition at the end. His dreams are large, and his schemes are elaborate but rarely successful. Calling

his wife Polly "Lady Rossmore," his daughter Sally "Lady Gwendolen," and his shabby home "Rossmore Towers," Sellers sees what he believes more clearly than he sees reality. Sellers plans to use the weather to make Siberia more hospitable and democratic, ultimately intending to alter climates generally to improve the planet for everyone, a conception with as much likelihood of success as most of Sellers's grand ideas. Readers ultimately feel the powerlessness of expectant participants who discover they have no roles to play. As the narrator says at the beginning, no weather appears in the book, and the author leaves no suitable place for it to be inserted where it can alter the plot or affect characters.

Indeed, the novel's plot affords little room for interference by weather. The weather does not affect the plot or story until Sellers himself proposes to alter weather to improve the world, but if he has success, he has it offstage and beyond the novel. Asserting that "weather is necessary to a narrative of human experience" while proving otherwise in the novel, Clemens sets up the weather as a literary issue by saying that it is "a literary specialty" at which he is not "very good" (preface). He asks readers to do it for him—in effect, to become writers themselves. Writers are supposed to have control of their writing, to know where it is going. For realists like Clemens, characters mainly determine directions of stories. People, like weather, are unpredictable and contradictory. As Bobbie Ann Mason asserts, Sellers's "notion to use sunspots to reorganize the world's climates seems to suggest that one might as easily mastermind the weather as mess with human nature" (Mason xl). Sellers's elaborate schemes work no better than any other effort to control the weather. Just as Samuel Clemens himself poured his money into a typesetting invention so complicated that its mechanism jammed more often than it worked, so the colonel places his faith in a weak claim to an earldom, in materializing corpses to solve labor problems, in strange inventions such as a cursing phonograph, and in the creation of new republics by transforming climates. At the same time, he dismisses as trivial a simple game he invented that reaps him a fortune. *The American Claimant* is full of absurd projected events, none of which actually occurs in the story. Still, the main story goes along as life goes along, despite complications and inconsistencies. As people cannot control weather, they cannot control life, with or without rules.

Great Britain versus America

Clemens emphasizes the conflict between the two cultures separated by the Atlantic. Introducing the Rossmores, holders of the title Sellers covets, he mocks both British spelling and pronunciation: "the Honourable Kirkcudbright Llanover Marjoribanks Sellers Viscount Berkeley, of Cholmondeley Castle, Warwickshire (Pronounced K'koobry Thlanover Marshbanks Sellers Vycount Barkly, of Chumly Castle, Warrikshr)" (chapter 1), but he also illustrates the inaccuracy and misperceptions of appearance on the other side of the Atlantic. When Berkeley, son of the current earl, temporarily renounces his inheritance, title, and aristocracy in favor of Sellers in order to become a claimant to the equalitarianism he perceives in American democracy, he is disappointed to discover that wealth, position, and political influence weigh more heavily than merit, ability, or need in judging and rewarding individuals. Ironically, at one point he finds himself proclaiming his noble status to assert his worth. After losing all but his journal in a hotel fire, he wears the clothes of an icon, the cowboy, an exemplar of American self-reliance and democracy. The ridiculousness of this English gentleman dressing like an American cowpoke points to the clash between democratic ideals and reality in materialistic America. Symbolic of this conflict is Sally Sellers, a student at Rowena-Ivanhoe College (its name a mockery of romantic and knightly ideals), who at home must play two roles, simple Sally and noble Gwendolen.

More ridiculous is that not only has Berkeley (Bark-lee in England, Burk-lee in America) coincidentally, taken the clothes of One-Armed Pete, the western outlaw sought by Sellers and his friend Washington Hawkins for a reward, but also Sellers and Hawkins mistake this two-armed, British-accented man for westerner Pete, mainly because of the clothes and the location. Bark-lee has become Burk-lee, then a cowboy assumed to be Outlaw Pete, who designates himself Howard Tracy, whom

Sellers and Hawkins think is a materialized spirit. When Tracy is with Sally, Hawkins—believing him to be a dead man who belongs in Sheol—thinks he smells brimstone (chapter). This confusion of identities, including Sally's and Polly's dual roles and second names, testifies to the many possibilities for characters and plots, for the complexity of life and of literature.

Living at a boardinghouse that represents American diversity and, therefore—one might think—American individualism and scorn of class, Berkeley hears, among other surprising opinions, the paradoxical assertion that Americans loathe rank but would welcome it if it were offered to them. Exemplifying that view, Colonel Sellers seeks to elevate society with his inventions but, proud of his perceived lineage, yearns to rise in social status; while creating labor-saving devices, he also undermines working people and the labor movement with a plan to produce a cheap labor force.

Matters do not resolve neatly. With this novel, Clemens may be saying that literary criticism is a lot of talk that does nothing about literature. He probably realized that, in *The American Claimant*, he had written himself into excesses that could not be accommodated by the story in which he had placed them, but having begun in fun, he decided to extend the fun by giving readers the false sense of control that the writer sometimes experiences. He limits that power and yanks it back, so readers also feel the frustration, common to authors, of not bringing ideas to fruition. Clemens thus presents his various ideas, rounds out the two main plots into a relatively neat though imperfect resolution, and still has his fun.

Critical Commentary by John H. Davis

CHARACTERS AND RELATED ENTRIES

For information on the characters Washington Hawkins, Aunt Jinny and Uncle Dan'l, Colonel Sellers, and Polly Sellers, see the Characters and Related Entries section of the *Gilded Age* entry.

Barrow Character in *The American Claimant* (1892). A short, roughly 40-year-old journeyman chairmaker, Barrow becomes Lord Berkeley's friend in a Washington, D.C., boardinghouse. He lends Berkeley money after the latter is robbed, stands by him when everyone else thinks he has gone daft, and helps find him a job. Although a fervent believer in republican principles, Barrow convinces Berkeley that only a fool would turn down an aristocratic title. He thus unwittingly helps persuade Berkeley to recant his renunciation of his own aristocratic privileges. At the end of the novel Barrow attends Berkeley's wedding to Sally Sellers.

Berkeley, Lord Kirkcudbright Llanover Marjoribanks (Howard Tracy) Major character in *The American Claimant* (1892). An English viscount just under 30 years old, Berkeley is the son and sole heir of the Earl of Rossmore, whose title is challenged by a distant relative in America. Intelligent, honest, and fair-minded, Berkeley has powerful democratic egalitarian impulses. He accepts the claimant's case and wants to go to America to swap places with him. Once there, he hopes to make a new life for himself in a land of equality. Against his father's wishes, he heads for WASHINGTON, D.C., where the new American claimant, Colonel Mulberry Sellers, lives.

Though Berkeley remains committed to the *idea* of equality, his experiences in America teach him that *practicing* equality is a different matter. He misses the respect that aristocratic status brought him, and he is confused and unsettled by the many evidences of inequality that he observes. By the end of the story he is ready to return to England and resume his privileged life.

Brady, Nat Minor character in *The American Claimant* (1892). An example to Lord Berkeley of what happens to a well-liked and respected person who falls on hard times, Brady is a weak, out-of-work tinner who is tyrannized and bullied in a Washington, D.C., boardinghouse. Brady and Berkeley nevertheless become friends; at end of the narrative it is revealed that Brady is engaged to Hattie Marsh, the landlord's daughter.

Cholmondeley Castle The site of the opening scene in THE AMERICAN CLAIMANT (1892), Cholmondeley (pronounced *Chumley*) is a medieval cas-

tle standing on 22,000 acres of land forming one of several seats of the Earl of Rossmore. It is apparently located in Warwickshire in central England, since Mulberry Sellers has a map of Warwickshire labeled "The Rossmore Estates." The name most likely is taken from Clemens's English friend Reginald Cholmondeley, whose Shropshire estate he visited in 1873 and 1879. Other possible sources include Sir WALTER SCOTT's 1822 novel, *Peveril of the Peak,* which has a character called "Cholmondeley of Vale Royal," and William Gilbert and Arthur S. Sullivan's 1888 comic opera *The Yeomen of the Guard,* which has a character named "Sir Richard Cholmondeley." WARWICK CASTLE is the site in which *Connecticut Yankee* (1889) begins.

Lathers, Simon Figure mentioned in *The American Claimant* (1892). A relative of Colonel Sellers, Lathers is the latest claimant to the Rossmore earldom in England at the beginning of the novel. Almost immediately, however, he and his unnamed twin brother are reported to have been killed by a log at Duffy's Corners, ARKANSAS, "at a smoke-house raising, owing to the carelessness on the part of all present . . . induced by overplus of sourmash." Sellers becomes Lathers's heir-presumptive and has the remains of the Lathers brothers shipped to England for burial in the Rossmore family plot.

Clemens modeled Lathers on his distant cousin, JESSE M. LEATHERS, who claimed to be the rightful Earl of Durham. Unlike the fictional Lathers, Leathers died from tuberculosis and alcoholism in a New York City hospital. Lathers's bizarre death, however, closely resembles that of Clemens's grandfather SAMUEL B. CLEMENS.

Marsh, Aunt Rachel Character in *The American Claimant* (1892), in which she is introduced in chapter 11 as the WASHINGTON, D.C., boardinghouse landlady of Lord Berkeley. Described as "all motherliness and charity, good-will and good-nature," she is known to her boarders as "Aunt Rachel." Her husband, identified only as "Marsh," is a gruff, sarcastic 60-year-old man who takes pleasure in publicly humiliating down-on-their-luck boarders, such as Nat Brady.

Marsh, Hattie (Puss) Character in *The American Claimant* (1892). An attractive, pleasant, and open 18-year-old woman, Hattie is introduced in chapter 11 as the daughter of Berkeley's boarding-house landlords. She gives Berkeley a lesson on egalitarianism by explaining how democratically Americans use the title "lady." After Berkeley defeats a bully in chapter 13, she allows him to call her "Puss," a nickname reserved for her intimates. She seems sweet on Berkeley and puts a flower in his buttonhole every morning, but he is not romantically interested in her. Though she is the object of every male boarder's attention, she ends up engaged to the most unlikely suitor of all, Nat Brady.

One-Armed Pete Background figure in *The American Claimant* (1892). Although One-Armed Pete never appears in the story, he is a constant presence. Before the narrative begins, he robs a bank in Tahlequah, in Cherokee country, and flees east. Along the way he is spotted by Washington Hawkins, who allies with Colonel Sellers to capture him for the reward money. They manage to set up a meeting with him, but he dies in a hotel fire first. Disappointed by the man's death, Sellers proposes to "materialize" Pete's spirit and collect the reward anyway. Sellers even expects that Pete will confess to enough crimes for them to keep collecting reward money for years.

Meanwhile, Lord Berkeley, who is also staying at Pete's hotel, when it burns happens to grab some of Pete's cowboy CLOTHES as he flees the blaze. Berkeley never knows anything about Pete, but when he finds a lot of cash in his borrowed clothes, he seeks the rightful owner by wearing them in public. Sellers and Hawkins see Berkeley and conclude that *he* is One-Armed Pete, materialized from the dead. Sellers accounts for the fact that Berkeley has *two* arms and speaks with an English accent by concluding that he has materialized the spirit of one of Pete's English ancestors.

Rossmore, Earl of Character in *The American Claimant* (1892), which opens in his Cholmondeley Castle. A direct descendant of William the Conqueror and the father of Lord Berkeley, Rossmore is 70 years old, tall, erect and "stern-browed." With large estates and a huge income, he is more than slightly miffed that his position is challenged by Simon Lathers, an impoverished American relation. He is also appalled by his son's determination to go to America to trade places with the new American claimant, Colonel Sellers. Eventually, however, he approves of his son's marriage to Sellers's daughter and finds that he even likes Sellers himself.

After Colonel Sellers declares himself the Earl of Rossmore, he gives the name "Rossmore Towers" to his shabby two-story house at 14,042 Sixteenth Street, WASHINGTON, D.C. (chapter 4).

Saltmarsh, Captain Minor character in *The American Claimant* (1892). A 60-year-old former Yankee sailor, Saltmarsh, along with a younger German shoemaker, Andy Handel, appears only in chapter 16 as an untalented assembly-line portrait painter. Saltmarsh paints only cannons and seascape backgrounds, while Handel paints only human figures from tintypes.

Saltmarsh is clearly modeled on CAPTAIN NED WAKEMAN, who also inspired Captain Ned Blakely, Captain Hurricane Jones, and Captain Stormfield. Like them, Saltmarsh is "tall, erect, powerfully built, with coal-black hair and whiskers," with "a gait and countenance that were full of command, confidence, and decision." He is also honest, simple-hearted, "full of sound religion, and is as devoted a student of the Bible and misquoter of it as you can find anywhere."

An unrelated Captain Saltmarsh is mentioned in *Roughing It* (1872) as the friend of a bore whom the narrator meets in Maui (chapter 77).

Sellers, Sally ("Lady Gwendolen") Character in *The American Claimant* (1892). The daughter of Colonel Sellers, Sally is first mentioned when Sellers calls her home from Rowena-Ivanhoe College (chapter 4). Thinking that he is now the Earl of Rossmore, Sellers dubs her "Lady Gwendolen." Never comfortable with this aristocratic pretension, Sally drops the name altogether after meeting and falling in love with Lord Berkeley in chapter 20. In chapter 22, she says, "My name is Sally Sellers—or Sarah, if you like." The name "Sarah" does not otherwise appear in the narrative. Unlike her father, Sally is sensible and levelheaded; once she is home, she starts designing and making clothes and becomes the family's financial mainstay.

Snodgrass, Spinal Meningitis   Spurious name given to a character in *The American Claimant* (1892). In chapter 24 of that book, Sally Sellers asks Washington Hawkins what he knows about Howard Tracy, the Englishman to whom she is betrothed. She does not realize that Tracy's real name is Lord Berkeley. Hawkins, on the other hand, thinks that Tracy is a materialized spirit. Not wanting to reveal that fact to Sally, he invents a story to turn her against Tracy. He explains that Tracy is really a "dissipated ruffian" from the Cherokee Strip named "Spinal Meningitis Snodgrass," the son of the idiot Dr. Snodgrass, and brother of Zylobalsamum Snodgrass. For the moment, Sally believes the story but does not turn against Tracy. Instead, she worries about what to call him after they wed.

Whatever humor Clemens may have found in this name doubtless evaporated when his daughter Susie Clemens died of spinal meningitis in 1896.

BIBLIOGRAPHY

Mason, Bobbie Ann. "Introduction." In *The American Claimant*. 1892. Reprinted in *The Oxford Mark Twain*, edited by Shelley Fisher Fishkin, xxxii–xliii. New York: Oxford University Press, 1996.

Messent, Peter. "Afterword." In *The American Claimant*. 1892. Reprinted in *The Oxford Mark Twain*, edited by Shelley Fisher Fishkin, 1–19. New York: Oxford University Press, 1996.

Twain, Mark. *The American Claimant*. 1892. Reprinted in *The Oxford Mark Twain*, edited by Shelley Fisher Fishkin. New York: Oxford University Press, 1996.

"Around the World"

Series of articles in the BUFFALO EXPRESS. In October 1869, Clemens's future brother-in-law, CHARLES J. LANGDON, began an around-the-world trip with an Elmira college teacher named Darius Ford (1824–1904). Ford agreed to write letters about his travels that Clemens would rewrite for the *Express* under the title "Around the World." From then until March 1870, Clemens published 10 articles, only two of which were based on Ford letters. Two articles were based on invented travels; the rest derived from Clemens's own experiences in California and Nevada. He later revised several of these letters for *Roughing It*.

"As Regards Patriotism"

Brief essay written around 1900 and first published in EUROPE AND ELSEWHERE (1923). Clemens contends that in America patriotism has become an official religion: the "love of country, worship of country, devotion to the country's flag and honor and welfare." He goes on to argue that if people were trained to think for themselves, they would develop a true form of patriotism, one growing out of reason and honest feelings.

"Aurelia's Unfortunate Young Man"

SKETCH originally published in 1864. The anonymous narrator of this sketch has received a letter from a young lady in San Jose (California) calling herself Aurelia Maria who is confused by the conflicting advice she is getting. Her story follows.

At 16, Aurelia met and fell in love with Williamson Breckinridge Caruthers, a man from New Jersey six years older than she. They became engaged and everything seemed to be going well until Caruthers contracted virulent smallpox; after he recovered, his face was pitted like a waffle-mold. Aurelia considered breaking off their engagement, but decided to give her betrothed another chance. The day before the wedding was to take place, however, Caruthers fell down a well and had a leg amputated above the knee. Aurelia gave him another chance. On the Fourth of July, he lost an arm when a cannon exploded prematurely; three months later,

Aurelia's young man, in an alarming state of depreciation *(Sketches, New and Old)*

a carding machine pulled out his other arm. Though devastated by Caruthers's alarming depreciation, Aurelia decided to bear with him.

As their next wedding date approached, Caruthers contracted erysipelas, which blinded him in one eye. Aurelia's friends insisted that she break off her engagement, but she said that Caruthers was not to blame and set a new wedding date. This time Caruthers broke his remaining leg and had it removed. After the nuptials were again rescheduled, Caruthers was scalped by Owens River Indians (of the eastern SIERRA NEVADA).

Aurelia is now perplexed. Her parents oppose her marrying Caruthers because he lacks property and cannot earn a living, so she asks the narrator for advice. The narrator suggests that she buy Caruthers a wig, a glass eye and wooden limbs, and give him another 90 days to go without an accident. If he succeeds, she should marry him; if he fails, he will probably finish himself off.

PUBLISHING HISTORY

Clemens's original sketch, titled "Whereas," appeared in the CALIFORNIAN on October 22, 1864. Its original form is about 2,300 words in length. He revised the sketch for publication in his first book, THE CELEBRATED JUMPING FROG OF CALAVERAS

COUNTY, in early 1867, but by the time the book appeared, someone else—probably CHARLES HENRY WEBB—had cut just over half the text from its opening and retitled the result "Aurelia's Unfortunate Young Man." Clemens retained this title in future reprintings, each of which contained additional revisions. The version now most frequently reprinted is the one that originally appeared in SKETCHES, NEW AND OLD (1875).

CHARACTERS AND RELATED ENTRIES

Aurelia Maria Central character in "Aurelia's Unfortunate Young Man." A young lady of San Jose, California, Aurelia became engaged at 16. Since then, her betrothed has been disfigured so many times that she wonders if she still should marry him. The sketch's narrator suspects that "Aurelia" (which comes from a Latin word for *golden*) is not her real name.

Clemens's friend W. D. HOWELLS had a sister named Aurelia. However, Clemens wrote "Aurelia's Unfortunate Young Man" five years before he met Howells.

Caruthers, Williamson Breckinridge Title character of "AURELIA'S UNFORTUNATE YOUNG MAN." A New Jersey man apparently living in California's eastern SIERRA NEVADA—since he is scalped by Owens River Indians—Caruthers is 22 years old when he becomes engaged to Aurelia. Over about a year's time, he suffers seven mishaps that take away his scalp, an eye, both arms and both legs and leave his faced pockmarked.

"The Austrian Edison Keeping School Again"

ESSAY on JAN SZCZEPANIK that Clemens wrote while in VIENNA in early 1898 and published in London's *Century* magazine the following August. A Polish inventor running a large Viennese laboratory, Szczepanik was noted for his contributions to the development of a primitive form of television known as a telelectroscope. Several years earlier, while a schoolmaster in Moravia, he developed a method of photographically copying patterns onto textiles. As a schoolmaster, he was exempt from military duty; however, he got into trouble with the government by failing to register for service when he left teaching to concentrate on inventing. Instead of removing him from his lab to perform his military service, the government sentenced him to return to his Moravian village every two months to teach half a day. Clemens notes that if Szczepanik were to live until he was 90, these bimonthly trips would add up to *more* than three years of time lost from his laboratory—a point he promises to bring to the government's attention. Clemens also used Szczepanik as a character in a story, "FROM THE 'LONDON TIMES' OF 1904."

autobiography, Clemens's

As a literary form, autobiography can encompass narratives, journals, memoirs, and letters. Generally, however, it is seen as a connected narrative story of an author's own life that provides introspective commentary. Although Clemens wrote and dictated half a million words of material that he called "autobiography," he left little that meets the form's narrow definition. Nevertheless, his manuscripts—which are now held by the MARK TWAIN PROJECT—have spawned five major "autobiography" publications.

Before examining Clemens's explicitly autobiographical texts, it is important to note that much of his writing, including his fiction, is autobiographical in nature. The opening chapters of *The Gilded Age* (1873), for instance, adapt the story of his own family's coming to Missouri before he was born and recreate his early childhood environment there. In *Tom Sawyer* (1876), Clemens expands this description of his early milieu and depicts many incidents that happened to him during his youth. One of the closest things to true autobiography that Clemens ever wrote is the first part of *Life on the Mississippi* (1883), which vividly describes his coming of age as a cub steamboat PILOT in the late 1850s. "THE PRIVATE HISTORY OF A CAMPAIGN THAT FAILED" (1885) gives a highly embellished account of his

brief CIVIL WAR experience (1861). *Roughing It* (1872) continues this story with a fuller but equally embellished account of his years in the Far West (1861–66). His other TRAVEL BOOKS cover briefer periods of his life. *Innocents Abroad* (1869) details his five-month journey to the Mediterranean in 1867, and *A Tramp Abroad* (1880) describes highlights of his European travels in 1878–79. The latter chapters of *Life on the Mississippi* recount his return visit to the river in 1882, and *Following the Equator* (1897) describes his round-the-world LECTURE tour of 1895–96.

Most of Clemens's travel books, as well as many of his short works, contain significant autobiographical fragments. For example, *Innocents Abroad* describes his discovery of a corpse in his father's office when he was a boy (chapter 18), and *A Tramp Abroad* recounts an incident during his first steamboat trip (chapter 10). *Life on the Mississippi* recalls his residence in SAINT LOUIS during the early 1850s (chapter 51) and adds poignant memoirs of his youth in

Clemens dictated much of his autobiography from his Venetian bed while he was living in New York City in 1906. *(Courtesy Library of Congress, Prints & Photographs Division)*

Hannibal (chapters 53–56). In *Following the Equator* he tells how an incident he observed in Bombay, INDIA, took him back to his youth, when he saw people abusing SLAVES; this recollection leads him into a discussion of his relationship with his father and a time when he saw a slave killed (chapter 38).

Clemens began consciously writing "autobiography" in 1870, when he wrote an essay on his family's TENNESSEE LAND. Over the next quarter century, he added more sketches on his life and on people he had known, setting aside most of these pieces without thought of publishing them. (Note that the BURLESQUE AUTOBIOGRAPHY, which he published in 1871, has nothing to do with his real autobiography.) His interest picked up during the mid-1880s, when he wrote several long passages about his relationship with General GRANT. When the AMERICAN PUBLISHING COMPANY issued the first uniform edition of his books in the late 1890s, Clemens wrote a brief autobiographical introduction that his nephew, SAMUEL E. MOFFETT, revised for publication.

In 1906, Clemens resumed his autobiography in earnest and began dictating passages to secretaries regularly. By this time, his biographer, A. B. PAINE, was installed in his household, where he assisted in this work. Clemens continued these dictations intermittently until 1909, when he also wrote "THE TURNING POINT OF MY LIFE," an essay summing up his entire life, and "THE DEATH OF JEAN," which he called the "final chapter" of his autobiography.

Clemens liked to boast that he had discovered a new method of creating autobiography by simply talking about whatever interested him at the moment. The inevitable consequence of this discursive approach is that his dictations wander aimlessly. Some recall incidents from his youth, others recall people he has seen recently. Rarely, however, does he try to link passages together into a coherent narrative. His autobiography includes scores of unconnected memoirs, sketches of people he knew and essays on various subjects. Several stretches of his dictations are simply extracts from a manuscript written by his daughter SUSY CLEMENS, to which he added comments. Another part of his "autobiography" comprises the 21,000-word essay IS SHAKE-

SPEARE DEAD?, which he published as a book in 1909.

Clemens also believed that he was creating the first completely honest autobiography ever written. He described what he was doing as speaking "from the grave," since he expected to be dead long before it was published. After GEORGE HARVEY approached him about serializing parts of his autobiography in the NORTH AMERICAN REVIEW, however, he published about 100,000 words in 25 installments as "Chapters from My Autobiography" (September 1906–December 1907). Meanwhile, he continued his dictations, ultimately leaving about half a million words of material for Paine to publish after his death. After incorporating extracts of this material in his biography of Clemens in 1912, Paine assembled *Mark Twain's Autobiography*, which HARPER'S published in two volumes in 1924. The 195,000 words of this edition include passages that appeared previously in the *Review*, as well as a few chapters that Paine published in HARPER'S MAGAZINE in early 1922. Paine's introduction to the book implies that it contains everything from Mark Twain's autobiography worth publishing. The material is actually a carefully selected and discreetly edited collection of Clemens's most nostalgic and cheerful material. After BERNARD DEVOTO became editor of the Mark Twain Estate, he reexamined the manuscripts and decided that Paine had left out far too much. Further, he believed that the additional passage of time had lessened the sensitivity of much of what Clemens had written about other people. DeVoto selected about 150,000 words from the original manuscripts and *Review* articles that were not in *Mark Twain's Autobiography*; these he published as MARK TWAIN IN ERUPTION in 1940.

Two decades later, CHARLES NEIDER decided that it was time to put everything into something like traditional chronological order. After selecting passages from all the earlier publications, he imposed a drastic rearrangement that approximates a chronologically ordered autobiography and published the result as *The Autobiography of Mark Twain* in 1959. After another three decades had passed, Michael J. Kiskis collected the *North American Review* chapters into a new book titled *Mark Twain's Own Autobiography* (1990). Using the same text and arrangement as the *Review,* Kiskis argues that since the magazine articles are the only version of the autobiography that Clemens himself saw through publication, they are closer to what he intended his autobiography to be than any of the previous book editions. Appendixes in Kiskis's edition include a chronological summary of Clemens's autobiographical writings and a table detailing the relationships among the *Review* chapters and Paine's, DeVoto's, and Neider's editions of the autobiography.

The 1996 OXFORD MARK TWAIN includes a facsimile reprint of the original *North American Review* articles in one volume titled *Chapters from My Autobiography.* Kiskis contributed an analytical afterword and playwright Arthur Miller a reflective introduction. Three years later, Dover published a similar facsimile edition under the title *My Autobiography: "Chapters" from the North American Review.* Of the various autobiography editions published as books, Kiskis's contains the fullest index.

After 25 magazine installments and six published book editions, the history of Mark Twain's autobiography remains unfinished. A major challenge still facing the Mark Twain PROJECT is to prepare something approximating a definitive edition of a work that by its nature can never be "definitive."

Clemens dictating his autobiography to Albert Bigelow Paine and a stenographer. E. F. Ward (1892–1991) painted this picture for a biography of Clemens that Paine published in *St. Nicholas Magazine* in 1916 and presumably worked under Paine's direction. (St. Nicholas Magazine)

"The Awful German Language"

Originally published as an appendix to *A Tramp Abroad* (1880), this 7,530-word ESSAY is a comic analysis of GERMAN, exaggerating the idiosyncrasies of a language that even a gifted person needs 30 years to learn. It begins with the narrator's visit to HEIDELBERG Castle, whose museum keeper wants to add the narrator's German to its curiosity collections. Resenting this slight, the narrator examines German's perplexities and finds that no other language is as slipshod. German has 10 parts of speech—all troublesome. An average German sentence occupies a quarter of a newspaper column, contains all 10 parts of speech, is filled with compound words not in dictionaries and treats 14 to 15 difficult subjects, each within its own parenthesis—and its verb comes last.

German's unpleasant features include splitting verbs in two—putting one half at the beginning of a chapter and the other half at the end; its frightful personal pronouns and adjectives; and distributing genders to its nouns without rhyme or reason, so that a turnip has sex, while a girl does not. Also, some German words are so long that they have a perspective. German does have some virtues, however, such as capitalizing all nouns. Also, words are spelled as they sound, and the language contains some very powerful words.

Averse to pointing out faults without suggesting remedies, the narrator proposes several reforms. He would leave out the dative case; move verbs closer to the front; import stronger words from English; redistribute the sexes according to the will of the Creator; do away with long compounds; and discard everything in the vocabulary but *Zug* and *Schlag*. He concludes with the German Fourth of July oration that he delivered before the Anglo-American Students Club.

"An Awful Terrible Medieval Romance"

See "A MEDIEVAL ROMANCE."

"Battle Hymn of the Republic (Brought Down to Date)"

PARODY of "Battle Hymn of the Republic" written around 1900. Following the original song's meter closely, Clemens transforms the hymn into an ironic attack on American imperialism in the Philippines. His verses allude to searching out the "stranger's wealth," lust marching on, crushing patriots, and legalizing prostitution. Possibly out of respect for the song's original author, Julia Ward Howe (1819–1910), Clemens made no attempt to publish the parody during his lifetime. It first appeared in 1979 in *A Pen Warmed-Up in Hell: Mark Twain in Protest*, edited by FREDERICK ANDERSON.

"The Belated Russian Passport"

Short story written by Clemens at YORK HARBOR, Maine, in the summer of 1902 and published in *HARPER'S WEEKLY* on December 6, 1902. Though this story has been read by some as a SATIRE on bureaucracy, it seems more likely that Clemens's main object was simply to write a marketable story

with a fast pace and an ironic ending. It may have grown out of Clemens's own experience of entering RUSSIA without a valid passport in 1867—an incident described in chapter 35 of *Innocents Abroad* (1869). The story may also reflect some of the anxiety that he felt in his return to MISSOURI in May–June to receive an HONORARY DEGREE from the University of Missouri and to revisit Hannibal for the last time.

SYNOPSIS

The story opens at a great BERLIN beer garden, where a crowd of American students is bidding farewell to Alfred Parrish, a YALE student about to return home. His friends encourage him to extend his holiday travel to St. Petersburg, RUSSIA, but he confesses that he is far too timid to do that. An older man overhearing this conversation introduces himself to Parrish as Major Jackson. Claiming to know St. Petersburg—as well as every official between Berlin and there—well, he pushes Parrish into accompanying him there that very night, by scooping up Parrish's train tickets and cash and taking off to exchange them. Parrish survives the first of what will be a series of increasingly severe anxiety attacks when the major returns after a long delay. Parrish's self-confessed "girlish" nature makes the ensuing journey an overwrought nightmare for him.

Jackson hustles Parrish off to the Russian consulate to get him a visa. The consul is out, so Jackson leaves Parrish's passport, asking a clerk to have it approved and mailed to St. Petersburg. The clerk warns that this is risky, as a government edict mandates that anyone caught in Russia without a passport will be sent to Siberia for 10 years. Since this conversation is conducted in Russian, Parrish does not know the peril the major is getting him into until their train journey is well under way. Parrish panics, and his sufferings increase when the major makes him sneak past a nearsighted inspector when they reach the Russian frontier.

After they reach St. Petersburg, a new crisis arises when Parrish cannot produce a passport at their hotel. The major takes him to the head of the secret police, Prince Bossloffsky, and manages to push his way in. The prince throws Parrish into deeper despair by reminding him of the edict about Siberia; however, the major persuades the prince to grant Parrish a 24-hour delay so he can collect his passport from the mail train.

Too nervous to sleep that night, Parrish writes his mother a letter as a kind of last will. The next day he and the major nervously await the mail train from Berlin under the watchful eyes of two policemen. When they overhear Englishmen in the dining room mention that the train is delayed, the major drags Parrish off to the American legation to get a new passport. When they reach the shabby legation office, they find that the minister is away on vacation. They now have only 30 minutes until the prince's deadline, and the secretary of the legation will not grant Parrish a passport because even the major knows too little about him to vouch for him. Suddenly, the secretary starts asking Parrish increasingly detailed questions about where he had once lived in New Haven, Connecticut. Finally, the secretary exclaims that *he* will vouch for Parrish, because he himself once lived in the same New Haven house that Parrish's family once owned.

CHARACTERS AND RELATED ENTRIES

Jackson, Major   Character in "The Belated Russian Passport." A blustering 51-year-old American living in Europe, Jackson persuades young Alfred Parrish to travel with him from Berlin to St. Petersburg, RUSSIA, a place he claims to have known intimately for 10 years. Reminiscent of Clemens's Colonel Mulberry Sellers, Jackson is an indomitable optimist, confident that he can overcome any obstacle because "everyone" knows him. In fact, hardly anyone seems to know him, and he puts Parrish into great danger by taking him into Russia without a passport. Although Jackson repeatedly fails to deliver on his promises, he does speak Russian fluently, and sticks with Parrish until he is saved from disaster at the end of the story.

Parrish, Alfred   Central character in "The Belated Russian Passport." A 19-year-old student who is traveling alone in Europe after finishing two years at YALE UNIVERSITY, Parrish was born in New Haven, Connecticut, where he lived until his family moved to BRIDGEPORT when he was 14. Timid

and effeminate, he is anxious to return home; when friends encourage him to go to St. Petersburg, RUSSIA, he confesses that he was nicknamed "Miss Nancy" as a child and perhaps should have been a girl. Major Jackson, an older man who overhears Parrish, talks him into accompanying him to St. Petersburg.

"Bible Teaching and Religious Practice"

Essay written toward the end of Mark Twain's life and first published in EUROPE AND ELSEWHERE in 1923. Arguing that religion has been responsible for the "lion's share" of changes in history, this 1,800-word piece compares changes in Christianity with those in medicine. The Christian Bible, for example, "is a drug store. Its contents remain the same; but the medical practice changes." As the world changes its views towards such matters as witchcraft and SLAVERY the church falls into line. It is, therefore, the world that corrects the Bible. "The Church never corrects it; and also never fails to drop in at the tail of the procession—and take the credit of the correction."

bluejay yarn

Tall tale in *A Tramp Abroad* (1880). Chapter 2 introduces Jim Baker, a simple-hearted old California miner who has lived alone so long that he has learned the languages of the beasts and birds and come to the conclusion that blue jays are the best talkers of them all. The next chapter—subtitled "Baker's Blue-jay Yarn"—is devoted entirely to his story of a blue jay's attempt to fill a hole in the roof of a vacant cabin with acorns. Clemens first heard this story from JIM GILLIS at JACKASS HILL in the winter of 1864–65. Gillis evidently based his story on a jay he had seen on the roof of an abandoned cabin; he modeled Baker on his partner DICK STOKER.

CRITICAL COMMENTARY

With the jumping frog story and the story of the old ram in *Roughing It,* the blue-jay yarn is among Mark Twain's best animal fables. Some critics declare the story his greatest short work (Blair 133). The blue-jay yarn harks back to the West for its humor and specifically to the Southwest for its framework. It is a FRAME-STORY, a story that comprises other stories, but the number of frames varies among reprintings. Excerpting the story from its source, editors begin it at different points. The contents of these frames comment on each other, so the absence or presence of certain material in a printing affects the presentation and interpretation of the story. The blue-jay yarn originally appeared in *A Tramp Abroad,* a book Twain struggled to write and to fill with material. One interpretation of the story is that it was written in reaction to the famous poorly received WHITTIER birthday speech, a humorous speech Mark Twain gave before the New England literary elite in 1877. No one laughed, and Mark Twain always regarded the speech as a disaster.

To understand the tale fully, readers must consider the complete composition—preparation, introduction, and tale itself—which consists of five frames, with one implied. Some anthologies begin the tale with Jim Baker's telling of the knothole incident, which is actually the final frame; others begin with Twain's assertion that animals talk to each other, including his introduction of Jim Baker (the fourth frame). The story itself begins with the author's walk into the Black Forest (third frame), but that story lies within the larger book, *A Tramp Abroad* (second frame), which brings Twain to Europe, establishing the punning premise: Author Mark Twain as "tramp," seemingly controlling material, whose plans to "tramp" across Europe are thwarted by proffered rides. The implied fifth frame, according to one interpretation, is the "Whittier Birthday Speech."

Typically in southwestern humor tradition, the educated narrator introduces an uneducated narrator (first frame) who introduces the subject (second) and tells the story (third), reversing order as the story concludes. Their contrasting speech contributes to the humor. Twain, however, in this tale places himself in the woods as an American (a Western) mocked by European birds (Easterners); ravens laugh at him, with no opportunity to be funny, creating class distinctions with jokes about his dress. Twain's preceding references to legends, superstitions, and trees untouched by sunlight prepare readers for fantasy, supernaturalism, and unreality.

Prepared to accept talking animals, readers encounter Jim Baker realistically asserting the blue jay's abilities, particularly in language and grammar. The storytellers, the author as tramp, and Baker as hermit-miner, present jays as human, emphasizing negative traits, but with command of language. The entire story can be read as a symbol of Mark Twain's struggles to write his book. With human frailty and the difficulties of writing as implied context, a jay (a symbol of the author) labors to fill a house (a book, in this case *A Tramp Abroad*) with acorns (stories and humor). Getting laughs in some places is like playing to an empty house (audience); filling the unfillable resembles pleasing the unpleasable. Writers lack the control of material that readers (and authors) assume, as Twain's supernaturalism/realism mood-shift paradoxically illustrates. They cannot know what provokes laughter in everyone. The jay thought he was in control of the knothole. Other jays, just as deceived and engaged, make him the butt to divert laughter from themselves after one accidentally discovers the house. Belittling by ravens (or foreigners) is hurtful, as when French critics missed humor in the jumping frog story, but harder when the author's own kind (jays—Americans, fellow authors) make him feel foolish. Presenting himself as tramp, as he had portrayed the Brahmans, the author stresses common humanity while asking for understanding.

Mark Twain reverts to a long-abandoned theme—east v. west, as in "Jumping Frog" and "Buck Fanshaw's Funeral." Jays are westerners, like Baker and Twain, who recognize and understand a good joke. From Nova Scotia ("New Scotland" for New England), the owl—archetypally wise—represents the Brahmans who are characters in the Whittier birthday speech. Like the tramps touring Yosemite in that speech, the narrator stops at an old Sierra miner's cabin, legendary from blue-jay gossip about its knothole. Not wise but shrewd, jays create a tourist site; however, unimpressed by western marvels, such as Yosemite, or western humor, the owl—like some dinner guests—misses the joke, so the joke is on them. Humor is not dependent on opposed educated and uneducated narrators. Baker, educated about jays and other animals, understands their talk and humor. The "wise" eastern owl, seeing no point, is the uneducated character.

As a humble tramp, Twain appeals to shared humanity, subject to misapprehension and deception. As a confident artist, he clarifies humor as more manner than matter, using skillful construction while illuminating human nature. Placing an American on the world stage with a book about Europe amid European and American grandeurs, including the Black Forest and Yosemite Valley, he uses contrasting frames to make the dinner affair appear petty.

BIBLIOGRAPHY

Blair, Walter. "Mark Twain's Other Masterpiece: 'Jim Baker's Blue-Jay Yarn.'" *Studies in American Humor* 1:3 (January 1975): 132–147.

Quirk, Tom. ["Jim Baker's Blue-Jay Yarn."] "Part 1. The Short Fiction." In *Mark Twain: A Study of the Short Fiction. Twayne's Studies in Short Fiction*, 73–80. New York: Twayne Publishers, 1997.

Twain, Mark. "Baker's Blue-Jay Yarn." *A Tramp Abroad*. 1880. Reprinted in *The Oxford Mark Twain*, edited by Shelley Fisher Fishkin, 21–42. New York: Oxford University Press, 1996.

———. "Whittier Birthday Speech [December 17, 1877]." In *Mark Twain: Collected Tales, Sketches, Speeches, & Essays, 1852–1890*, edited by Louis J. Budd, 695–699. New York: Library of America, 1992.

Wilson, James D. "Jim Baker's Blue-Jay Yarn." In *A Reader's Guide to the Short Stories of Mark Twain*. Boston: G. K. Hall, 1987. 153–161.

Critical Commentary by John H. Davis

"Boy's Manuscript"

A short story that Clemens wrote sometime late in 1868, "Boy's Manuscript" is his earliest known piece of fiction inspired by his Hannibal childhood

and it clearly anticipates both *Tom Sawyer* (1876) and *EXTRACTS FROM ADAM'S DIARY* (1904). It takes the form of a diary spanning several weeks in the life of lovesick Billy Rogers, who is smitten by a beautiful, blue-eyed blonde eight-year-old named Amy. Billy's efforts to impress Amy by showing off, and the heartache her fickleness causes him, parallel much of what happens between Tom Sawyer and Becky Thatcher in chapters 3 through 18 of *Tom Sawyer*. In contrast to the later novel, however, this story ends with Billy's breaking up with Amy and then falling in love with a much older girl. It is probably significant that Clemens wrote this story while in the midst of courting Livy; certain incidents and nuances in the story may reflect that courtship.

Although Clemens finished this 7,400-word story, he never published it himself. Whatever title he may have given it was lost along with its first two manuscript pages. A. B. PAINE supplied the title that has been used since the story was first published in *Mark Twain at Work* (1942) by BERNARD DeVOTO—who dubbed the story the "embryo of *Tom Sawyer*."

CHARACTERS AND RELATED ENTRIES

Amy Fictional character. A forerunner to *Tom Sawyer*'s Becky Thatcher, Amy is an eight-year-old blue-eyed blonde, with whom Billy Rogers, the diarist of "BOY'S MANUSCRIPT," is smitten. Just as Becky torments Tom in the later story, Amy upsets Billy with her fickleness. Also like Becky, Amy appears to have been modeled on Clemens's childhood sweetheart LAURA HAWKINS. A different character, Amy Lawrence, is Tom Sawyer's rejected sweetheart in *Tom Sawyer* (1876).

Rogers, Billy The prototype of Tom Sawyer, Billy is the diarist of one of Clemens's earliest attempts at straight fiction, a story posthumously published as "BOY'S MANUSCRIPT." Billy, whose age is not clear, is obsessed with the ups and downs of courting eight-year-old Amy—the prototype of Becky Thatcher. Many of his thoughts and actions anticipate those of Tom in *Tom Sawyer*. Billy also has in him some of the adult Clemens, who was courting his future wife, Livy, at the time he wrote this story.

Billy fantasizes about falling down outside Amy's house so that he will be taken inside for loving care; Clemens actually had such as experience at Livy's house. Billy, however, seems more fickle than either Tom Sawyer or Clemens; by the end of the story, he has forgotten Amy and is obsessed with 19-year-old Laura Miller.

Burlesque Autobiography, Mark Twain's ("A Burlesque Biography") (1871)

Sketch published as a booklet with the full title, *Mark Twain's (Burlesque) Autobiography and First Romance*. Tending more toward FARCE than BURLESQUE, this fictional history of Clemens's ancestors is an exercise in euphemism. While it describes most of his ancestors as carefree humorists, a close reading reveals them to be clever criminals who met violent ends. The sketch is also laced with historical and geographical nonsense, such as a reference to ancestors living in Aberdeen (a Scottish town) in the county of Cork (Ireland) in England. Parenthetical insertions in the synopsis that follows explain some of the sketch's references.

SYNOPSIS

In response to public demand, the author tenders his family's history. The earliest recorded "Twain" was an 11th-century friend of the family named Higgins in Aberdeen. It remains a mystery why the family has since gone by the maternal name rather than Higgins. During the time of William Rufus (England's William II), Arthour Twain was a noted highway solicitor who died suddenly after visiting the resort at Newgate (a prison). Augustus Twain achieved renown in the mid-12th century by sticking passersby with his saber until he carried this joke too far. Authorities removed one end of him, and mounted it on a high place on Temple Bar (i.e., he was beheaded). Over the next two centuries, the family tree shows a succession of high-spirited soldiers.

In the early 15th century, Beau Twain had infinite sport imitating the handwriting of others until he contracted to break stone for a road. During 42 years in the stone business, he was a conspicuous member of the benevolent society known as the Chain Gang.

John Morgan Twain came to America in 1492 as a passenger with COLUMBUS. After he grumbled about the food and Columbus's navigating and fretted constantly about his "trunk," the crew threw him overboard, only to have him steal the ship's anchor. On the positive side, he was the first white person interested in civilizing INDIANS, for whom he built a jail and a gallows (on which he appears to have been the first white man hanged in America). His 17th-century great-grandson, known as "the old Admiral," commanded a fleet of well-armed vessels that hurried merchantmen across the ocean (i.e., he was a pirate). Eventually, he was cut down—though his widow thought that if he had been cut down 15 minutes sooner he might have lived (i.e., he was hanged).

Charles Henry Twain was a late 17th-century missionary who converted 16,000 South Sea islanders. They remembered him as a good, tender man and wished they had more of him (i.e., they ate him). In the mid-18th century, Pah-go-to-wah-wah-pukketekeewis, "Mighty-Hunter-with-a-Hog-Eye-Twain," helped General Braddock fight the oppressor Washington (Washington fought *with* Braddock in 1755).

Other ancestors are better known to history by their *aliases*—such as Richard Brinsley Twain, alias Guy Fawkes; John Wentworth Twain, alias Sixteen-String Jack; William Hogarth Twain, alias Jack Sheppard; Ananias Twain, alias Baron Munchausen; John George Twain, alias Captain Kydd. A collateral branch of the family includes George Francis Train, Tom Pepper, Nebuchadnezzar and Baalam's Ass, who differed from the ancient stock in going to jail instead of getting hanged.

The author points out that while RICHARD III had the advantage over him in being born with teeth, he had the advantage over Richard in being born without a humpback. The author decides to leave his own history unwritten until he is hanged like his ancestors.

PUBLICATION HISTORY

Anxious to capitalize on his post-*Innocents Abroad* (1869) fame, Clemens arranged with his GALAXY editor Isaac Sheldon to publish this 2,180-word sketch in a three-part booklet titled *Mark Twain's (Burlesque) Autobiography and First Romance*. The booklet included a short story better known as "A MEDIEVAL ROMANCE" and a series of cartoons drawn by HENRY LOUIS STEPHENS titled "The House that Jack Built"—a PARODY of the popular nursery rhyme, caricaturing Jay GOULD and other figures connected with the Erie Railroad scandal.

Clemens hoped to have the booklet ready for the 1870 Christmas market, but production problems delayed its publication until the following February. J. C. HOTTEN issued a pirate edition in London several months later, followed by ROUTLEDGE's authorized English edition in May.

Later fearing that this booklet might damage his reputation, Clemens bought its plates from Sheldon and destroyed them. Nevertheless, the sketch later appeared as "A Burlesque Biography" in *The $30,000 Bequest and Other Stories* (1906).

CHARACTERS AND RELATED ENTRIES

Twain, John Morgan   Character in Clemens's *(Burlesque) Autobiography* (1871). A purported ancestor, "John Morgan Twain" allegedly came to America in 1492 as a passenger with CHRISTOPHER COLUMBUS. Possibly taking his name from the PIRATE Henry Morgan, Twain was an inventive con man who in some ways anticipates *Connecticut Yankee*'s (1889) Hank Morgan. When he boarded the ship, he carried everything he owned in an old newspaper; when he left, he had four trunks, a crate, and several champagne baskets, and he even suggested searching other passengers' luggage because some of his own things were missing. After making himself unpopular by constantly complaining, he was thrown overboard. Even then, he managed to steal the ship's anchor and sell it to INDIANS. Twain was the first white person to try civilizing the Indians— by building a jail and a gallows—and was also the first white man hanged in America.

Twain boarded Columbus's ship with four monogrammed items that pose interesting deciphering challenges, if the initials mean anything. He had a handkerchief marked "B. G." ("brigadier general"?); a sock marked "L. W. C."; another sock marked "D. F." ("defender of the Faith"?); and a night-shirt marked "O. M. R." ("old man river"?).

"The Californian's Tale"

Short story written in 1892. Unusually SENTIMENTAL for a Clemens story, this tale embellishes the story of a man whom Clemens met in CALIFORNIA during his MINING days. In 1882, Clemens outlined the true story in his NOTEBOOKS but set it aside for a decade. While the real miner's wife died in a stagecoach accident, the wife of Clemens's fictional miner is killed by INDIANS.

The story first appeared in 1893 in *The First Book of the Authors Club, Liber Scriptorum*, edited by Arthur Stedman. Mark Twain published it in *HARPER'S MAGAZINE* in March 1902 and it was collected in *The $30,000 Bequest and Other Stories* a few years later. Although the story has nothing directly to do with Clemens's own experiences in the West, the 2002 Hallmark Channel's *Roughing It* miniseries contains an otherwise reasonably faithful dramatization of "The Californian's Tale." Adam Arkin plays the miner, Henry. Sam Clemens (Robin Dunne) himself fills the role of the story's unnamed narrator.

SYNOPSIS

Set near Tuttletown, a real mining town in California's TUOLUMNE COUNTY, in the late 1850s, this story is told 35 years later by an unnamed narrator. While prospecting around the Stanislaus River, he has met many prematurely aged miners who are so worn out by 40 that they are "living dead men." One such man, named Henry, lives in an unusually neat cottage. Like most local miners, he invites the narrator in, and he shows off all the wonderful homey touches provided by his wife, whose beautiful daguerreotype the visitor admires. Henry tells his guest that his bride was 19 on her last birthday—the day that he married her.

It is a Wednesday, and the woman (who is never named) is due home on Saturday evening. As the days pass, the visitor eagerly anticipates meeting his host's wife. Other prospectors drop by as well, to ask when she will arrive and to hear Henry read her latest letter. By Saturday night, Henry, the narrator, and three other prospectors prepare to greet Henry's wife, but she does not arrive on schedule. Henry grows sick with fear until a message comes reporting that his wife is delayed. After he finally passes out, his friends tenderly put him to bed and start to leave. When the visitor begs them to wait until Henry's wife arrives, they explain that the woman was killed by Indians 19 years earlier. Never completely sane since then, Henry has gone through this same ritual every year around the same time that his wife disappeared. Over the years, the number of miners who wait up with him has shrunk from 27 to three, and they have to drug him to get him through the ordeal.

"Cannibalism in the Cars"

Short story written in 1868. At Terre Haute, INDI-ANA, the narrator changes trains and meets a man in his late forties. When the stranger learns that the narrator is from WASHINGTON, D.C., he asks him many well-informed questions about government affairs, but his mood changes when he overhears the name "Harris," and he begins a story that he has never told before.

In December 1853, the stranger took a train from St. Louis to Chicago that carried 24 passengers—all men. The first night out, snowdrifts blocked the train. It carried plentiful firewood, but no provisions, and was 50 miles from help. On the seventh night without food, a passenger named Gaston proposed that it was time to decide who should die to feed the rest. Another man, named Williams, then nominated the Reverend James Sawyer to be the first meal, Wm. R. Adams nominated DANIEL SLOTE, and CHARLES J. LANGDON nominated SAMUEL A. BOWEN. After Slote declined in favor of JACK A. VAN NOSTRAND, Van Nostrand objected, launching an argument over procedure. Eventually, Gaston was elected chairman, along with a four-man selection committee.

The passengers then caucused before submitting nominations. After a complex floor debate, a passenger named Harris was elected to become dinner. For eight days, two men a day were elected as breakfast and dinner—with the stranger commenting on their varying gastronomic qualities. The surviving passengers were finally rescued just after electing a man for breakfast.

As the stranger prepares to get off the train, he invites the narrator to visit him, assuring him that he could like him "as well as I liked Harris himself." The stunned narrator learns from the conductor that the stranger, a former member of Congress, once nearly starved while snowed in on a train. Since then, he has retold his grisly story over and over, usually carrying it to a point where everyone in the train but him is eaten. The narrator is so relieved to know he has been listening to a harmless madman, not a bloodthirsty cannibal, that he overlooks contradictions in the stranger's story—which names nearly 40 persons, including a boy, on a train supposedly carrying only 24 men.

BACKGROUND AND PUBLISHING HISTORY

"Cannibalism" was one of the first fictional pieces that Clemens wrote after returning from the QUAKER CITY excursion. His idea for the story may have originated in an article published in his brother's MUSCATINE, Iowa, newspaper in February 1855 concerning a train-load of snowbound legislators who ate dogs to stay alive. To develop the story's intricate satire on legislative procedure, he drew on his own experience reporting on NEVADA's territorial legislature and the federal Congress. He also played with names; most of his characters have the names of real friends and acquaintances, including several connected with the *Quaker City* excursion.

The 3,400-word story first appeared in the November 1868 issue of London's *Broadway*, a house organ of George ROUTLEDGE and Sons. It was subsequently collected in SKETCHES, NEW AND OLD (1875) and in MARK TWAIN'S LIBRARY OF HUMOR (1888). The story's notion of having "a man for breakfast" reappears in a chapter on desperadoes in *Roughing It* (1872; chapter 57). "Cannibalism in the

Cars" lends itself to dramatic adaptation and is occasionally staged by small-theater companies.

"The Canvasser's Tale"

Short story published in 1876. A comparatively simple story of 2,340 words, this tale touches on several themes that Clemens develops more fully elsewhere. For example, the narrator of this tale resembles characters in "THE $30,000 BEQUEST" (1904) in being ruined by relying on receiving a rich inheritance. He also resembles a man in "THE CAPITOLINE VENUS" (1869) who must have money to win the hand of his sweetheart. The story concerns the narrator's uncle, who collected echoes. As a duplicate sound, an echo is a kind of twin—a theme Clemens later explored in stories such as *Pudd'nhead Wilson* (1894). That novel opens with an incident similar to one in "The Canvasser's Tale": David Wilson expresses a wish to own half a barking dog, so that he could kill his half. In "The Canvasser's Tale," a man who owns one of two hills containing the world's greatest echo wants to level his hill in order to destroy the entire echo.

"The Canvasser's Tale" is told as a FRAME-STORY in which neither the setting nor the time is specified. A tired, shabby man with a portfolio comes to the door of the anonymous narrator, who assumes him to be a canvasser (i.e., a salesman). He takes pity on the stranger and allows him to relate his own story, describing events that apparently occurred about 30 years earlier.

SYNOPSIS

Orphaned while young, the stranger was raised by his rich, generous uncle Ithuriel. After completing college, he traveled abroad and got the idea of persuading his uncle to take up the foreign custom of collecting rarities. His uncle adopted this idea eagerly, and turned his fortune to building a cowbell collection. Eventually, he needed a single bell to complete his collection, but the owner of the only existing specimen refused to sell. Not interested in keeping a collection he could never complete, Ithuriel sold out and began collecting brickbats,

only to experience the same frustration again. After failing to complete collections of flint hatchets, Aztec inscriptions, and stuffed whales, he decided to go after something no one else collected: echoes. He purchased great specimens in Georgia, Maine, Kansas, and Tennessee, and bought a masterpiece in Oregon for $216,000.

Meanwhile, the nephew courted Celestine, the daughter of an English earl, happy in the knowledge that he would be sole heir to his uncle's fortune. Trouble began, however, when his uncle went after the world's greatest echo, the "Great Koh-i-noo," or Mountain of Repetitions, in a remote New York location. This fabulous echo would talk for 15 minutes after hearing a single word. Unfortunately, the hills containing the echo were owned by two people and there was a competing collector in the field. Ithuriel bought the echo's east hill for over three million dollars; his rival bought the other hill for a similar amount. Neither man was content, but neither would sell out to the other. Finally, Ithuriel's rival decided that if he could not own the entire echo, he would destroy his half so no one could have it. After Ithuriel secured an injunction to stop the man from taking down his hill, his rival appealed the case up to the Supreme Court. The Court ruled that the two men were tenants in common in the echo; therefore, if one took down his hill, he must indemnify the other for the echo's value. Further, neither man could use the echo without the other's consent—which neither would give. The result was that the echo was useless and the properties unsalable.

A week before the nephew was to marry the earl's daughter, news of his uncle's death came, along with the will naming him sole heir. After reading this document, the earl concluded that the nephew had inherited nothing but debt and called off the wedding. Within a year, Celestine died of a broken heart, leaving the nephew wishing only for death.

Although the narrator had had his fill of canvassers, he agrees to buy two of the stranger's echoes.

BACKGROUND AND PUBLISHING HISTORY

Clemens wrote this story during the summer of 1876, after setting aside his *Huckleberry Finn* manuscript.

He initially considered having Ithuriel collect caves, but switched to echoes. He probably got the idea of using echoes from his travels in ITALY in 1867, when he observed superb echoes in PISA and near MILAN. Chapter 19 of *Innocents Abroad* describes the latter as "the MOST REMARKABLE ECHO IN THE WORLD," asserting that it repeats words 52 times.

"The Canvasser's Tale" first appeared in the ATLANTIC MONTHLY in December 1876. It was later reprinted in *PUNCH, BROTHERS, PUNCH!, THE STOLEN WHITE ELEPHANT,* and *Tom Sawyer Abroad; Tom Sawyer, Detective and Other Stories.*

CHARACTERS AND RELATED ENTRIES

Ithuriel, Uncle Character in "The Canvasser's Tale." The rich uncle of the story's narrator—whom he raised as a son—Ithuriel amassed $5 million in the pork business. At his nephew's suggestion, he took up collecting hobbies but ended up blowing his entire fortune on echoes, leaving his nephew only mortgages.

A rabbinical name meaning "discovery of God," Ithuriel is the name of an angel in John Milton's *Paradise Lost* (1667) whom Gabriel commissions to search for Satan. As a near homophone of *ethereal,* it is also an apt name for a man who collects things without material substance.

"The Capitoline Venus (Legend of)"

Short story written in 1869. Written with some of the conventions of a drama, the story is divided into six brief chapters, or "scenes," and most of its text is dialogue. As a story about an art HOAX, this piece resembles "IS HE LIVING OR IS HE DEAD?" It opens in the Rome studio of a young American sculptor, George Arnold, who is talking with a woman named Mary about the futility of their relationship. Mary's father will not let her marry George until he acquires $50,000. In the next scene, the father repeats this demand. George owns a wonderful statue he calls "America," but the

father cares only about market value; he gives George six months to come up with $50,000.

Back in his studio, George explains his problem to a childhood friend, John Smith, who scoffs at him and promises to raise the money in *five* months. He has George swear not to oppose anything he does, then takes a hammer to the America statue, disfigures it badly and carts it away, leaving George in a state of collapse. The day that George's six-month deadline is up, tradesmen appear at his studio to deliver expensive goods on credit—which his banker tells him is excellent. Mary's father then appears to tell him he can wed Mary, who arrives next. The bewildered George proclaims he is saved, but has no idea why or how.

The fifth scene cuts to a café, where several Americans are reading the weekly IL SLANG-WHANGER DI ROMA ("The Roman Rebuker"). The newspaper tells about a "John Smithe" who bought land in the Campagna six months earlier and transferred its title to George Arnold with a promise to improve the property. Smitthe later unearthed a damaged but otherwise remarkable ancient statue of a woman that the government seized. After a month of secret study and deliberation, a government commission has announced that the statue is a third-century B.C. Venus worth 10 million francs. Under Roman law, the government must pay half this sum to Arnold.

The sixth scene jumps ahead 10 years; George and Mary discuss the famous Capitoline Venus and the fact that John Smith is the author of their bliss. When a baby coughs, George chides Mary for taking inadequate care of the children. A brief afterword admonishes readers to keep their own counsel when they hear about such things as petrified men near Syracuse, New York. Moreover, "if the BARNUM that buried him there" offers to sell, "send him to the Pope!"

BACKGROUND AND PUBLISHING HISTORY

Clemens wrote this 2,000-word piece shortly after the so-called Cardiff Giant was discovered near Syracuse on October 15, 1869. The story appeared in the BUFFALO EXPRESS as "Legend of the Capitoline Venus" on October 23. The title was abbreviated when the story was republished in SKETCHES, NEW AND OLD five years later. The Cardiff Giant was an artificially aged gypsum sculpture of a man that someone had buried near Syracuse a year before he dug it up. Its unearthing caused a sensation; many people believed it to be a petrified giant, while others were sure it was an ancient sculpture. The episode had remarkable similarities to Clemens's PETRIFIED MAN HOAX, which he had published in Nevada seven years earlier.

The idea of selling antiquities to the Roman government came out of Clemens's visit to Rome in July 1867. The city was then under papal government, which had a policy of buying all freshly discovered antiquities at half their assessed market value. Chapter 28 of *Innocents Abroad* (1869) comments that "when a man digs up an ancient statue in the Campagna, the Pope gives him a fortune in gold coin."

CHARACTERS AND RELATED ENTRIES

Arnold, George   Character in "The Capitoline Venus." An impoverished American sculptor living in Rome, Arnold needs to raise money in order to win permission to marry his sweetheart, Mary, from her father. Arnold's friend John Smith saves him by transforming his prized "America" statue into a fake antiquity. Arnold becomes rich and marries Mary, but 10 years later his "bliss" seems artificial.

Il Slangwhanger di Roma   Fictional Italian newspaper in "The Capitoline Venus" (1869), which quotes from it on the unearthing of an ancient statue whose description closely matches George Arnold's damaged sculpture. The newspaper's title is as fake as the statue it describes. *Slangwhanger* is a 19th-century English term that could mean either a person addicted to slang, or a person who scolds. A literal translation of the title might thus be "The Roman Rebuker."

Smith, John   Character in "The Capitoline Venus" (1869). A lifelong friend of the sculptor George Arnold and a resident of ROME, Smith makes Arnold rich by pulling off a careful HOAX. He takes Arnold's statue of a woman, hammers off its nose and other parts, buries it in a plot of land

that he buys near Rome and registers in Arnold's name, then digs up the statue five months later. The newspaper *Il Slangwhanger di Roma* ("The Roman Rebuker") praises "John Smitthe" for making the discovery.

"Captain Stormfield's Visit to Heaven"

Unfinished SATIRE, presented in the form of a first-person narrative by an old sea captain who has died and gone to heaven. Shortly before his own death, Clemens published two chapters of this story as *Extract from Captain Stormfield's Visit to Heaven* (1909).

SYNOPSIS

The fullest published form of this story begins with a prologue signed by Mark Twain in which the author describes Captain Stormfield as a person he knows well. He explains that although Stormfield has told him this story as a true experience, he himself regards it as a dream. The narrative that follows is divided into six chapters, the third and fourth parts of which correspond to chapters 1 and 2 of *Extract from Captain Stormfield's Visit to Heaven*.

Chapter 1

Stormfield describes his death aboard a ship, where he overhears a doctor and other crew members planning his burial at sea. They assume that Stormfield expects to go to hell. He dies a moment later and finds himself hurtling through space. As he passes through a dark void, then through the sun, he calculates that the time it takes for him to reach the sun means that he is traveling at the speed of light.

After Stormfield passes through the sun, another man comes alongside him and joins his journey. Stormfield finds that his hunger for companionship allows him to overlook the fact that his new companion, Solomon Goldstein, is a Jew. He explains to Goldstein that they appear headed for hell; Goldstein accepts Stormfield's logic but later grows morose when he realizes its implication that he will never see his daughter again.

Albert Levering's frontispiece to *Extract from Captain Stormfield's Visit to Heaven* shows Stormfield piloting a comet. In the story itself, Stormfield *is* a comet.

Chapter 2

As Stormfield and Goldstein continue their journey, many other travelers join them. Hearing these people pour out their tragic stories makes Stormfield realize the falsity of the notion that death brings rest. After a week, the convoy numbers 36, but Stormfield drives some of its less agreeable members away.

Chapter 3

This chapter—the first in the "Extract" portion of the story—opens with Stormfield in his 30th year of racing through space "like a comet." There is no explanation for the disappearance of the traveling companions introduced in the earlier chapters.

There is also no explanation of a new name, "Peters," to whom he is now addressing his narrative.

By Stormfield's own calculations, his average velocity is roughly a fifth the speed of light. We can infer, therefore, that he has traveled about six light-years—only far enough to take him to our solar system's nearest stellar neighbor, though the story seems to suggest a far longer journey. Meanwhile, Stormfield thrills in passing slow comets, until he encounters an unimaginably huge one that tempts him into altering his course by a point in order to engage in a race. The scale of this other comet is such that 200 billion crewmen are sent aloft to alter its rigging and 100 billion passengers rush to the decks to watch the race. As Stormfield passes the comet, he thumbs his nose at it. This enrages its captain, who orders its stupendous cargo of brimstone—presumably bound for hell—jettisoned, allowing the comet to leave Stormfield far behind.

As Stormfield approaches a blazing array of lights, he assumes they are furnaces and that he has finally arrived at "the wrong place." However, the lights turn out to be the gates of Heaven. He lands and reports to a head clerk, who asks where he is from. "San Francisco" means nothing to the clerk, nor do "California" and the "United States." Only when he mentions Jupiter while trying to describe Earth's location is progress made. It turns out that he has arrived in the wrong district of Heaven because of veering off course while racing the comet. A clerk takes two days to find Earth on a map "as big as RHODE ISLAND," and then announces that it is known as the "Wart." Stormfield, now officially admitted to Heaven, spends a day wandering the great hall, until he is told how to use a "wishing carpet" to teleport himself instantaneously to his own part of Heaven, millions of leagues away. Everything about heaven's size, he learns, is unimaginably huge.

The moment that Stormfield arrives in his proper district, he is recognized and issued all the angelic accoutrements he was disappointed not to receive when he first arrived: wings, halo, harp, hymn book, and palm branch. The clerk who greets him is a PIUTE Indian whom he had known in California's Tulare County. He soon discovers, in fact, that INDIANS constitute a big majority in his district.

As Stormfield joins a multitude headed for a cloud bank to take up his duties as an angel, he is puzzled by the horde of despondent people returning from the clouds and dumping their angel gear along the way. However, after he has spent a day of monotonously trying to make music by singing and playing a harp while sitting on a cloud, his own enthusiasm for being an angel wanes. "This *ain't* just as near my idea of bliss as I thought it was going to be, when I used to go to church," he tells another angel. He then leaves the clouds himself and gratefully sheds his angel gear.

Stormfield next encounters Sam Bartlett, a man he apparently knew on Earth, who explains to him what a busy place Heaven is. His Sunday-school notion of a Heaven filled with psalm-singing, do-nothing angels is the exact opposite of the real Heaven, in which people are busy learning and ful-

Captain Stormfield has all the angelic accoutrements he expects from Heaven in this illustration from a Russian edition of his story published in Moscow in 1980.

filling themselves in ways they could not on the worlds from which they came. Several months later he meets Sandy McWilliams, a man from New Jersey who has been in Heaven for 27 years. McWilliams teaches Stormfield about coming to terms with one's original age in Heaven. They spot an unhappy woman whose infant child had died just before McWilliams came to Heaven; McWilliams suspects that she is downcast because she has found her daughter to be a mature, highly educated adult with whom she has nothing in common. Another of Stormfield's preconceptions about the hereafter is punctured.

Chapter 4

Stormfield's difficulties in adjusting to life in Heaven include using his angel wings. McWilliams explains that most angels only wear their wings for special occasions since they have no practical value for transportation. Excitement is mounting in Stormfield's district because of the impending arrival of a New York bartender who drowned in a ferryboat accident the very night that he rediscovered religion. The heavenly host are expected to turn out in big numbers for him. Most people get whatever they want in Heaven. An example of someone who will *not* get what he wants, however, is the Brooklyn pastor Thomas De Witt Talmage, who expects heaven to be just for the elect, when in fact it is for everyone. McWilliams explains to Stormfield that one of the main charms of Heaven is that "there's all kinds here—which wouldn't be the case if you let the preachers tell it."

Stormfield also learns about the hierarchy of prophets and patriarchs in Heaven. ADAM is not at the top of this hierarchy, but he is one of the most popular figures there and the best at drawing a crowd. Ordinary Christians tend to perceive heaven as a republic, though it is ruled by a king. How, he asks, "are you going to have a republic under a king?" The answer is that Heaven is as authoritarian as RUSSIA and there is little mingling between people at different levels.

Stormfield is surprised to learn that persons such as SHAKESPEARE and Homer are regarded as "prophets" in heaven. He is even more shocked to learn that one of the highest-ranking prophets is a common tailor from Tennessee named Edward H. Billings, who is the greatest poet in the universe. Heaven, Stormfield learns, recognizes those who do not get their just rewards on Earth. Another such person is a Hoboken butcher named Richard Duffer, who fed and supported poor people so quietly and unobtrusively that he went to his grave unjustly scorned as a miser. One more such person is Absalom Jones, an obscure Boston bricklayer who was "the greatest military genius our world ever produced."

Heaven also proves to be a place in which humans learn how significant their own world is in the larger scheme of things. When beings from the colossal planet Goobra, for example, learn that the Earth "is so little that a streak of lightning can flash clear around it in the eighth of a second, they have to lean up against something to laugh." Stormfield further learns that white people are such an insignificant minority in the American section of Heaven that "you can't expect us to amount to anything in heaven, and we *don't.*"

When the bartender finally arrives, Stormfield and McWilliams join millions of other angels who magically teleport themselves to his reception. Hundreds of thousands of torch-carrying angels troop by. The reception climaxes when Moses and Esau suddenly appear to welcome the bartender. Soon after they vanish, the "Extract" version of the story ends abruptly.

Chapter 5

Stormfield reflects on the time that he has spent in Heaven. He and McWilliams discuss the astronomical scale of Heaven and the meaning of a light-year. Their journeys take them to an "asterisk," or asteroid, where they encounter a race of tiny beings whom Stormfield compares to Gulliver's Lilliputians. This chapter essentially ends Stormfield's personal narrative.

Chapter 6

The final fragment relates McWilliams's narrative about a man named Slattery who had been born in Heaven, and who fell along with Satan aeons ago. Slattery was involved in a scheme by Satan to populate a region with a race of people he created in whom all positive and negative moral qualities are

equally balanced—leaving them "ciphers." A second experiment was attempted, this time mixing up the moral qualities randomly in individuals, thereby creating the human race, with all its unexpected results.

Stormfield meanwhile learns from McWilliams that providence actually reacts quickly—in heavenly time—to earthly wrongs. Since a thousand years of Earth time is equivalent to only a day in Heaven, what seems a slow response to us is actually rapid. Prayers are always answered, and quickly in heavenly time. Unfortunately, in the minute that Heaven takes to answer a prayer, a entire year passes on Earth.

BACKGROUND AND PUBLISHING HISTORY

In a February 1906 autobiographical dictation, Clemens relates how he met Captain Edgar Wakeman, who in 1868 told him he had visited heaven. Drawing on Wakeman's story, Clemens began writing "Stormfield" that same year. By around 1873, his manuscript had grown to 40,000 words and he showed it to W. D. Howells, who recommended its publication. Instead of publishing it, however, Clemens—by his own admission—"turned it into a burlesque of *The Gates Ajar,* a book that had imagined a mean little ten-cent heaven about the size of Rhode Island." *The Gates Ajar*—which Clemens mentions by name in "Stormfield"—was a popular novel published in 1868 by Elizabeth Stuart Phelps (1844–1911). Though sentimental, Phelps's story rejects many traditional Christian notions about heaven, such as the idea that angels will find fulfillment in prayer and psalm-reading. Mark Twain claimed to burlesque her book, but he actually adopted many of her ideas. One of these was that a person's rank in heaven is measured by his intrinsic worth, not by his earthly accomplishments. This, for example, is why a bricklayer is honored as the world's greatest military genius.

Over the next three decades, Clemens periodically returned to this story; he occasionally added to it, but always ended up stowing it away again. He clearly had doubts about the direction the story should go. His notes indicate, for example, that he considered having Stormfield visit hell, an idea that he gave up on. At some point he worked his close friend JOSEPH TWICHELL into the story. Twichell is the "Peters" to whom Stormfield is talking in the two "Extract" chapters.

Clemens's slowness in finishing and publishing "Stormfield" has long been taken as an indication of his ambivalence about its subject matter. His wife, Olivia Clemens, evidently admired the story, but regarded it as blasphemous, a sentiment with which Clemens was inclined to agree. While he was not averse to poking fun at religion, he was hesitant to offend believers. Whatever his own reservations, it may have been Livy's opposition that discouraged him from publishing the story until after she died. Meanwhile, Clemens enjoyed reading the story aloud to friends.

Not long after Clemens dictated his remarks about the writing of "Stormfield," he submitted part of it to HARPER'S MAGAZINE. Ironically, after Clemens had withheld the story for decades for fear of offending Christians, Harper's editor GEORGE HARVEY rejected it because it was "too damn godly." Harvey changed his mind a year later, however, and published the two "Extract" chapters in Harper's December 1907 and January 1908 issues. In October 1909, Harper's published Extract from Captain Stormfield's Visit to Heaven as a Christmas gift book, stretching the approximately 15,000 words of text out over 121 pages. Appropriately, this tale about heaven was the last book that Clemens published during his lifetime.

Clemens's surviving "Stormfield" manuscripts present special problems to scholars because of the difficulty of dating their composition. The fact that Clemens himself never supervised an edition of his entire manuscript has left minor inconsistencies between the "Extract" that he published in 1909 and the posthumously published fragments. For example, the first chapter from the posthumous version calls the title character "Captain Ben Stormfield," while the first "Extract" chapter calls him "Captain Eli Stormfield." And whereas he calculates his speed as at or faster than the speed of light in the first chapters, he estimates it at about a fifth of that in the "Extract."

In 1952, a fuller version appeared in a new edition, Report from Paradise, which DIXON WECTER

prepared before his sudden passing. This version attached the first two "chapters" summarized here and a previously unpublished piece, "Letter from the Recording Angel." In 1970, Ray B. Browne published a still fuller version in a new book, Mark Twain's Quarrel with Heaven: "Captain Stormfield's Visit to Heaven" and Other Sketches, adding the last two chapters.

The 1985 Claymation film THE ADVENTURES OF MARK TWAIN includes a dramatization of Stormfield's arrival at heaven. The 1996 OXFORD MARK TWAIN edition includes a facsimile reprint of the first edition of Extracts from Captain Stormfield's Visit to Heaven. It contains a new introduction by science-fiction writer Frederick Pohl and an afterword by James A. Miller.

CRITICAL COMMENTARY

In "Captain Stormfield's Visit to Heaven" Clemens stages his response to the conventional Christian version of heaven satirized in his Letters from the Earth. Heaven, Stormfield quickly finds out, is at once informal and hierarchical, pluralist and functionally segregated. Recent arrivals quickly dispense with harps and formal angel dress and have great control over their daily activities. Politically, however, heaven is a rigid hierarchy, as Stormfield's informant, Sandy McWilliams, explains, "this is Russia—only more so. There's not the shadow of a republic about it anywhere" (p. 81). In addition to being unequal, the tiers of heaven are also functionally separate. There are people representing all earthly regions, languages, and cultures, but they do not mix or communicate much, and for the sake of convenience and familiarity, they tend to stay in their areas of origin.

The highest pleasure in Stormfield's heaven is intellectual satisfaction. Most people abandon the boring goal of endless leisure in favor of an active afterlife and a line of work that they love: "You can choose your own occupation, and all the powers of heaven will be put forth to help you make a success of it, if you do your level best" (p. 43). This version of heaven reflects the values of American capitalism structured around the ideal of a solid work ethic ("It's the same here as it is on earth—you've got to earn a thing, square and honest, before you enjoy it"). But it is also based on a vaguely marxist notion of employment, in which work is rewarding, suited to one's temperament, and connected to the act of self-cultivation: "The shoemaker on earth that had the soul of a poet in him won't have to make shoes here" (ibid.).

Clemens's capacious imagination of heaven includes the far-flung regions of outer space. This geographical expansiveness requires a complex bureaucracy to keep it working and generates a culture of travel and tourism. Stormfield learns that "if Abraham was to set his foot down here by this door, there would be a railing set up around that foot-track right away, a shelter put over it, and people would flock here from all over heaven, for hundreds and hundreds of years" (p. 83). After the celebrated arrival of a secretly pious New Jersey barkeeper, Stormfield is informed that a monument will be put up "where Moses and Esau had stood, with the date and circumstances, and all about the whole business, and travelers would come for thousands of years and gawk at it, and climb over it, and scribble their names on it" (p. 121). Tourists and learned men from other planets and systems "come here, now and then, and inquire about our world" and "then go back to their section of heaven and write a book of travels, and they give America about five lines in it" (pp. 93, 104). Clemens published five travel books and spent a significant portion of his life overseas; in his version of heaven, after worldly existence has ceased, tourism and travel writing are part of everyday life.

Critical Commentary by Alex Feerst

CHARACTERS AND RELATED ENTRIES

Bartlett, Sam Minor character in "Captain Stormfield's Visit to Heaven." A person whom Captain Stormfield apparently knew on earth who greets him on his arrival in heaven and explains to him what a busy place heaven is.

Billings, Edward H. Background figure in "Captain Stormfield's Visit to Heaven." Once an ordinary Tennessee tailor, Billings is the greatest poet in the universe. In heaven, he ranks higher than WILLIAM SHAKESPEARE and Homer, both of whom

serve him. Unable to publish his poetry when he was on earth and treated as a fool by ignorant neighbors, Billings never expected to make it to heaven. However, he not only made it, but was accorded the greatest reception given anyone in thousands of centuries—making him a prime example of how heaven values greatness that goes unrecognized on earth.

Clemens may have gotten his idea for Billings from Herman Melville's *Moby-Dick* (1851), which alludes to a "poor poet of Tennessee" (chapter 1).

Goldstein, Solomon Minor character in "Captain Stormfield's Visit to Heaven." A Jewish man who accompanies Stormfield through space during the first part of his journey toward heaven, Goldstein exhibits such natural humanity that Stormfield gradually sheds his ingrained anti-Semitism.

Jones, Absalom Figure mentioned in "Captain Stormfield's Visit to Heaven." Ranked in heaven as the world's greatest military genius, Jones was an obscure Revolutionary-era bricklayer who lived near Boston on Earth and could not even enlist in the service because he had lost both thumbs and several front teeth. A prime example of how heaven ranks a person by intrinsic worth, not earthly achievement, Jones is also an example of Clemens's interest in the theme of undiscovered genius. In this regard, he contrasts with Joan of Arc, a simple French peasant girl whose military genius was discovered.

McWilliams, Sandy Character in "Captain Stormfield's Visit to Heaven." A 27-year resident of heaven, McWilliams befriends Stormfield several months after the latter's arrival, and helps teach him the ropes. The perpetually 72-year-old man teaches Stormfield that even though heaven allows people to choose any physical age they want, most return to the most advanced age that they achieved on Earth. McWilliams is Stormfield's constant companion, as well as the narrator of the final chapter of the story.

Peters, Reverend George H. Name mentioned in "Captain Stormfield's Visit to Heaven." In the chapters of this narrative published as *Extracts from Captain Stormfield's Visit to Heaven* (1909), Stormfield addresses himself to someone named "Peters," who is not identified within the story. Peters's full name and identity can, however, be reconstructed from other sources. Clemens's working notes describe him as the "Reverend George H. Peters," a pastor from Marysville, California, near SACRAMENTO. Other writings leave no doubt that Clemens based Peters on his friend JOSEPH TWICHELL—whom he calls "Peters" in "SOME RAMBLING NOTES OF AN IDLE EXCURSION." His autobiography suggests that Twichell used "Peters" as an alias when they visited Bermuda together in 1877.

After having heard a great deal about CAPTAIN EDGAR WAKEMAN—the man on whom Stormfield is modeled—Twichell happened to meet Wakeman on a ship in mid-1874 and spent considerable time in his company. Not realizing that Twichell was a Protestant minister, Wakeman lectured him at length on the Bible. Twichell's account of his meeting with Wakeman later gave Clemens additional material with which to build the fictional Stormfield—whose monologue to "Peters" seems to be an adaptation of Wakeman's lecturing to Twichell.

Slattery Minor character in "Captain Stormfield's Visit to Heaven," in which he is the subject of Sandy McWilliams's narrative which concludes the novelette. Slattery was born in heaven, where he was closely associated with Satan from the time of his fall. He assisted in the creation of the human race.

Stormfield, Captain Eli (Ben) Narrator and central character of "Captain Stormfield's Visit to Heaven." A ship's captain who dies at sea when he is at least 65 and then spends 30 years hurtling through space, Stormfield expects to land in hell. He is delighted, however, to arrive in heaven and to learn that it is nothing like the tediously pious place he learned about in Sunday school.

Stormfield is modeled on EDGAR WAKEMAN, a veteran sailor who during the 1860s told Clemens about a vivid dream he had of going to heaven. Like Wakeman, Stormfield is a big, blustering man, profoundly innocent of formal education, but an enthusiastic and imaginative student of the Bible. A subtext of the "Extract" portion of his narrative is his running lecture on Bible matters to someone named Peters. Clemens may also have put a bit of his tycoon friend H. H. ROGERS in Stormfield, who comes from "Fairhaven"—presumably Rogers's home town, Fairhaven, Massachusetts (Wakeman himself came from Connecticut). The image of Stormfield's speeding through the heavens, racing a comet, also evokes Clemens's own personal identification with HALLEY'S COMET.

The truncated version of this story that Clemens published in 1909 gives the character's full name as "Captain Eli Stormfield" from SAN FRANCISCO. Posthumously published chapters call him "Captain Ben Stormfield of Fairhaven and 'Frisco."

Talmage, T[homas] De Witt (January 7, 1832, near Bound Brook, New Jersey–April 12, 1902, Washington, D.C.) Protestant clergyman whose hypocrisy Clemens publicly mocked. An eloquent speaker, Talmage drew record crowds at Brooklyn's Central Presbyterian Church and his sermons were reprinted in thousands of newspapers. In 1870, he reportedly objected to having working-class men mix with his parishioners. Clemens quickly attacked him in a brief essay, "ABOUT SMELLS."

Talmage also appears as a character in "Captain Stormfield's Visit to Heaven," which Clemens published after Talmage's death. That story depicts Talmage as a rare person who does not find what he expects in heaven—since it is not limited to the elect. Talmage's name also appears in Clemens's posthumously published "The Second Advent," in which a "St. Talmage" betrays his savior for 30 pieces of silver.

the Wart Name by which heaven knows Earth in "Captain Stormfield's Visit to Heaven." When Captain Stormfield hears an admissions clerk at one of the gates utter this name, he warns him: "Young man, it wouldn't be wholesome for you to go down there and call it the Wart."

BIBLIOGRAPHY

Baldanza, Frank. *Mark Twain: An Introduction and Interpretation.* New York: Holt, Rinehart & Winston, 1961.

Browne, Ray B. "Mark Twain and Captain Wakeman." *American Literature* 22 (November 1961): 320–329.

Gibson, William M. *The Art of Mark Twain*, edited by David Ketterer. Hamden, Conn.: Archon, 1984.

McMahan, Elizabeth, ed. *Critical Approaches to Mark Twain's Short Stories*. Port Washington, New York: Kennikat, 1981.

Miller, James A. "Afterword." In *Extract from Captain Stormfield's Visit to Heaven*, edited by Shelley Fisher Fishkin. New York: Oxford University Press, 1996.

Rees, Robert A. " 'Captain Stormfield's Visit to Heaven' and *The Gates Ajar*." *English Language Notes* 7 (March 1970): 197–202.

Twain, Mark. *Extract from Captain Stormfield's Visit to Heaven*.

Wilson, James D. "Extract from Captain Stormfield's Visit to Heaven." In *A Reader's Guide to the Short Stories of Mark Twain*, 83–92. Boston: G. K. Hall & Co., 1987.

The Celebrated Jumping Frog of Calaveras County, and Other Sketches (1867)

Clemens's first book. On the advice of his friend CHARLES H. WEBB, Clemens assembled this collection of sketches in early 1867, only to have it rejected by GEORGE W. CARLETON and other publishers. Webb himself then published the book in May. Four months later, GEORGE ROUTLEDGE issued an unauthorized edition in London, with the same title and contents.

The book's 200 pages contain 27 items, including the JUMPING FROG STORY of the title, "AURELIA'S UNFORTUNATE YOUNG MAN," "CURING A COLD," "LUCRETIA SMITH'S SOLDIER," and "THE KILLING OF JULIUS CAESAR 'LOCALIZED.' " Aside from the frog story, virtually all the items originally appeared in the VIRGINIA CITY TERRITORIAL ENTERPRISE and the CALIFORNIAN. With Webb's help, Clemens assembled the collection from clippings he had saved; to avoid offending easterners, he made many minor revisions, such as removing allusions to death and drinking.

Preoccupied with a midwestern lecture tour and preparations for the QUAKER CITY excursion, Clemens paid little attention to the book's production and later expressed dissatisfaction with its many typographical errors and unauthorized editorial changes. The book sold poorly and soon went out of print. Clemens later reprinted much of its contents in other collections. In 1903, HARPER issued a new book, *The Jumping Frog: In English, Then in French, Then Clawed Back into a Civilized Language Once More by Patient, Unremunerated Toil.* Aside from its title story, this edition has nothing to do with the earlier book. The 1996 OXFORD MARK TWAIN edition includes a facsimile reprint of the first edition of *Celebrated Jumping Frog* with a new introduction by humorist Roy Blount Jr. and an afterword by Richard Bucci, a former editor of the MARK TWAIN PROJECT.

Chapters from My Autobiography

See AUTOBIOGRAPHY, MARK TWAIN'S.

Choice Humorous Works of Mark Twain (1873)

Title of a pirated collection of stories published by JOHN CAMDEN HOTTEN in London. Six years later, Clemens revised and corrected an authorized version of the book for ANDREW CHATTO.

"The Cholera Epidemic in Hamburg"

Essay written in 1892 and first published in EUROPE AND ELSEWHERE in 1923. While staying in BAD NAUHEIM in August 1892, Clemens learned about a CHOLERA outbreak 220 miles to the north in Hamburg, where 40 deaths a day were suddenly being reported. His essay finds it remarkable that a nearby tragedy of such magnitude is so poorly reported. He censures the German press for its coverage of the epidemic and accuses German newspapers generally of being in a state of "eternal lethargy," offering meager news and jumbled facts.

He also alludes to this period in chapter 20 of *Following the Equator* (1897).

Christian Science (1907)

Book analyzing the CHRISTIAN SCIENCE religion and criticizing its founder, Mary Baker Eddy (1821–1910). In 1907, Clemens combined magazine articles on Christian Science that he had published several years earlier with fresh material in *Christian Science, With Notes Containing Corrections to Date.*

The 63,000-word volume is divided into "books" of nine and 15 chapters, with seven appendixes and a conclusion. The first book examines Christian Science tenets and practices, questioning whether divine healing is dangerous. It opens with a burlesque in which the narrator breaks every bone in his body in a fall off a mountain cliff in AUSTRIA, only to be told by a "Christian Science doctor" that there is nothing wrong with him.

The second book focuses more on Eddy. On the basis of inconsistencies in writing style, it challenges her claim to have written *Science and Health* and criticizes her hunger for power and wealth.

HARPER AND BROTHERS was reluctant to publish the book but did so because of its contractual obligations to Clemens. The company also included the title in most of the uniform editions of Clemens's work that is later published. In 1973, Paul Baender and the editors of the MARK TWAIN PAPERS published a corrected version of *Christian Science* within *What Is Man? and Other Philosophical Writings*, a volume which also contains *WHAT IS MAN?* and *LETTERS FROM THE EARTH*. The *OXFORD MARK TWAIN* (1996) edition includes a facsimile reprint of the first edition of *Christian Science*, which includes a new introduction by historian Garry Willis and an afterword by Hamlin HILL.

"The Chronicle of Young Satan"

Unfinished novel written between 1897 and 1900 and published posthumously. A story about an angel who visits AUSTRIA in the early 18th century,

"Chronicle" is the second of four versions of similar stories that Clemens never finished. These manuscripts are collectively known as "THE MYSTERIOUS STRANGER" stories—the same title that Clemens's literary executor A. B. PAINE gave to a condensed and bowdlerized version of "Chronicle" that he published as an authentic Clemens work in 1916. Until the full extent of what has been called Paine's "editorial fraud" was revealed nearly a half century later, *The Mysterious Stranger, A Romance* was the only version of "Chronicle" known to the world. In 1969, Clemens's original text was finally published as he wrote it, with his own title, "The Chronicle of Young Satan."

Many characters in the Mysterious Stranger stories are modeled on people Clemens knew during his youth. In fact, he placed the first version of these stories in a mid-19th-century Missouri setting similar to that of his Tom Sawyer and Huck Finn stories. When he wrote "Chronicle," he transplanted his earlier version's characters and settings to Austria.

Though the Mysterious Stranger stories are intertwined, each has a distinct story line and themes. "Chronicle" reflects the issues that concerned Clemens in the late 1890s, as well as philosophical questions that he would later explore more fully in "*WHAT IS MAN?*" and other writings. The fact that the story is set in Austria in 1702 is almost irrelevant, as the questions that it addresses are universal.

The structure of the story is similar to that of *Joan of Arc* (1896), with an elderly narrator, Theodor Fischer, recalling a time in his youth when he was close to a remarkable being—indeed, one not of this Earth. The Satan of the story's title is an angel who is visiting the Earth on an unexplained mission. Unimaginably old by Earth standards, Satan has been everywhere and seen everything, and has godlike powers that allow him to move freely in time and space. Not constrained by a moral sense, he sees himself as being on a plane vastly higher than that of man, whom he regards as inconsequential. Seeing man as nothing more than a "machine" with no ability to create, he laughs at the idea that man's civilizations have achieved anything to be proud of. As Satan weaves in and out of the lives of the villagers, he amuses himself by tampering with the fates of persons whom he encounters.

SYNOPSIS

"Chronicle" has 11 chapters of uneven length, totalling 54,300 words. Theodor Fischer's narrative begins in AUSTRIA in the spring of 1702 and ends abruptly about a year later, when Satan takes Theodor to India and Ceylon.

Chapter 1

The story opens in the fictional Austrian village of Eseldorf in May 1702, when its narrator, Theodor Fischer, is a boy. The village is a paradise for Theodor and his friends, but trouble comes when a Hussite woman distributes literature that goes against Catholic beliefs. After a warning by the village's stern priest, Father Adolf, the village never admits another Hussite. Father Adolf is always on hand each December 9 when the village celebrates the Assuaging of the Devil at the bridge that villagers tricked the Devil into building 700 years earlier. Father Adolf is respected because he does not fear the Devil, but the village's best-loved priest is Father Peter, whom Adolf got the bishop to suspend for saying that God would find a way to save *all* his children. Now nearly destitute, Father Peter and his niece Marget face foreclosure on their house.

Chapter 2

Theodor spends most of his time with Nikolaus Baumann, a judge's son, and Seppi Wohlmeyer, the son of the principal innkeeper. The local castle's serving-man Felix Brandt often tells them stories, and teaches them not to fear supernatural beings. One day after Brandt tells them about seeing angels, the boys are playing on a hill when a handsome, well-dressed young stranger approaches. The stranger seems to read Theodor's mind and performs amazing tricks, such as lighting a pipe by blowing on it. After showing the boys that they can have anything they wish, he uses clay to fashion animals that spring to life, then makes hundreds of miniature people who begin building a castle.

The stranger reveals that he is an angel, and startles the boys by saying that his name is "Satan." A nephew of the great Satan, he is 16,000 Earth years old. When Satan's tiny clay workmen quarrel, he casually crushes them—at the very moment he is explaining that angels cannot commit sin.

Though disturbed by Satan's callousness, the boys feel drunk with the joy of being with him. He has been everywhere and seen everything and forgets nothing; however, his remarks about humans reveal that he considers them as inconsequential as flies. When the castle is finished, Theodor marvels at its perfection, but Satan creates a fierce storm over it and lightning sets off its magazine, causing the castle and its people to be swallowed into the earth. The boys are devastated, but Satan is indifferent.

Satan instructs the boys to call him "Philip Traum" in the presence of others, adding that he will prevent their tongues from revealing what they know about him.

When Father Peter approaches, he walks *through* Satan as though the angel were not there. The boys are also invisible to the priest. As Satan explains the differences between himself and man, he emphasizes that he lacks the moral sense. After he dissolves himself to go on an errand, the boys wonder if they have been dreaming. Father Peter returns, searching for his wallet, which he is astonished to discover is filled with gold coins. Despite reassurances from the boys—who correctly guess that Satan has left the money for him—the priest is perplexed about what to do with it.

Chapter 3

After Father Peter pays his mortgage the next day and deposits the rest of his gold with Solomon Isaacs, the villagers again become friendly with him and his niece. Several days later, Father Adolf returns from a trip and asks the boys about Peter's gold. Adolf pronounces that the money has been stolen from him and has Peter arrested. When Peter is set to be tried in a civil court, Marget is soon in a desperate financial plight, and Ursula her housekeeper tries to help her.

One day Theodor encounters Satan and they find Ursula comforting a stray kitten, which Satan says is a lucky cat that will provide for its owner. After Ursula leaves, Theodor wishes he could see Marget and is suddenly in her parlor with Satan, whom he introduces as Philip Traum. When Ursula arrives, she is upset to see Satan get Marget to invite him to supper, but plentiful food miraculously appears.

When Theodor thinks to himself that he would like to see the inside of a jail, he and Satan are suddenly in a torture chamber. Theodor expresses shock at a prisoner's "brutal" mistreatment, but Satan corrects his choice of words, saying that such cruelty is a *human*, not a *brute*, thing. A moment later, Satan transports him to a French village, where they see poor people working themselves to death under miserable conditions. Satan derides the human race as illogical and unreasoning. A moment later, they are back in the village, where they learn that Hans Oppert, the village loafer, has disappeared after beating his dog. Satan repairs the dog's wounds, talks with it, and learns that Oppert fell over a precipice.

Chapter 4
During a dull week in which Satan does not appear, the boys occasionally see Ursula. She boasts that things are going so well that she has hired a servant, Gottfried Narr—whose family has been under a cloud since his grandmother was burned at the STAKE as a witch. Though suspicious about Narr, the villagers seek his company hoping to learn why Marget is suddenly so prosperous. Suspecting that witchcraft is involved, Father Adolf encourages villagers to spy on Marget and Ursula. When Marget invites 40 people to a party, Adolf arrives uninvited. The priest studies the bottle of wine he is drinking from and calls for a large bowl. He fills it from the bottle, then pronounces the house "bewitched and accursed." As guests rush out, Satan slips into the priest's body, calls for a funnel, and pours the contents of the bowl back into the bottle. The guests now cry out that Father Adolf is possessed, as the priest goes to the market square, where he juggles a hundred balls at once and astounds everyone with his acrobatics. Confident that their priest is possessed by witches and devils, the villagers wail that God has forsaken them.

Theodor returns to Marget's house, where the atmosphere is funereal. When Satan enters, however, everyone brightens. They discuss music and poetry, and Satan dazzles everyone with an amazing display of chess skill against Marget's suitor, Wilhelm Meidling. Afterward, Satan composes the most beautiful music on the spinet that anyone has ever heard.

Chapter 5
The next day, the villagers are anxious about the witch-commission's failure to summon Father Adolf, who has disappeared. Meanwhile, Satan, as

"Traum," charms the entire village. As Theodor's parents discuss this marvelous stranger, Theodor's sister Lilly admits that she is infatuated with him—though betrothed to Joseph Fuchs. When Joseph arrives, he reports that all anyone is discussing is Traum, adding that the strange youth is doing things that might get him in trouble—such as saving a man from drowning without getting himself wet. Joseph implies that Traum—like Father Adolf—may be possessed, and adds that he has offended Wilhelm, whom he might need to get himself out of legal trouble. Wilhelm then arrives and describes another of Traum's musical miracles, adding that Marget has professed her slavish devotion to the stranger. Insinuating that his own life is ruined, Wilhelm goes to a back room for liquor. When Satan arrives, Wilhelm tries to stab him with a butcher knife, but Satan lets the knife fall to the floor harmlessly and soothes Wilhelm's feelings.

Chapter 6
That night, Theodor tries to talk Lilly into forgetting about Satan but gets nowhere and goes to bed worrying about the misfortunes that have befallen the village since Satan's arrival. Satan rouses him with music and takes him to CHINA. When Theodor accuses Satan of causing unhappiness by not taking into account the consequences of his actions, Satan counters that he *always* knows what the consequences will be. He explains that though the villagers are nothing to him, he likes Theodor and his friends and Father Peter. He also explains that whereas man is simply a "machine" in which happiness and suffering are about equally divided, he himself has a mind that can *create*. He goes on to explain that the things he is doing for the villagers will actually bear good fruit some day. For example, he is changing Nikolaus's fate so that both he and a neighbor child whom he tries to save from drowning will drown, instead of enduring years of misery as cripples. He also assures Theodor that Father Peter will be exonerated and will be happy for the rest of his life. He tells Theodor that he has put Father Adolf on the far side of the moon and that he will spare the priest from his long and odious future by having him burned.

Chapter 7

Theodor and Seppi spend all their spare time with the doomed Nikolaus until Satan's grim prophecy is fulfilled. At the ensuing funeral, a carpenter seizes the body of the girl whom Nikolaus tried to save in payment of a debt. The girl's mother goes mad with grief, so the boys beg Satan to relieve her distress. He responds by arranging for her to be condemned as a witch, and the chapter ends with the boys seeing the woman burned at the STAKE.

Chapter 8

When Satan next appears, he shows Theodor and Seppi the history of the human race's progress. He begins by recreating the Garden of Eden at the moment that Cain clubbed Abel to death, then follows with a long series of wars, murders and massacres. Next, he shows some slaughters of the future and tells the boys about the bloody wars that are coming. He soon begins laughing and making fun of the human race, but when he sees that he is upsetting the boys, he stops and gives them wine in extraordinarily beautiful goblets.

Satan is never alone, as animals love him and follow him everywhere. Often he frees them from traps. When four gamekeepers discover him freeing a trapped rabbit, they threaten to punish him for poaching. After he starts revealing dark secrets about each man, he denounces one of the keepers, Conrad Bart, as a murderer. The man puts a gun to Satan's chest, but Satan turns him to stone, then turns himself into Father Adolf and flees. After a jury rules that Bart met his death by the visitation of God, his family prospers by exhibiting his petrified body.

Chapter 9

Theodor considers asking Satan to predict his own future but decides that he would prefer not to know. Instead, he asks to know Seppi's future, and gets the answer in a multivolume book that he will read for the rest of his life. He also later learns that Seppi is doing the same thing with *his* life. Occasionally, Theodor and Seppi get Satan to tell them what will happen in town a day or two in advance, and use the information to win bets with other boys. The boys often travel with Satan over great distances and times. Sometimes they stay away for

weeks and months, yet return within a fraction of the second when they left.

When villagers become impatient with the failure of the witch-commission to go after Father Adolf, they chase down a suspected witch themselves. Theodor suggests that only Catholics could have such courage, but Satan disagrees and takes him to Scotland to show him Protestants persecuting a witch. They return to Eseldorf in time to see the suspected witch being hanged. Though sickened by the spectacle, Theodor joins the crowd in throwing a stone at her, causing Satan to laugh aloud. When three men turn on Satan and accuse him of failing to throw a stone, he predicts that all three of them will soon die—including one who has just five minutes to live. Four and a half minutes later, one man starts gasping for breath and is soon dead. As Satan leaves with Theodor, he says that of the 68 people in the mob, 62 did not want to throw stones at the woman. He explains that the human race is made up of sheep governed by minorities. When Theodor objects, Satan cites the example of human wars; although there has never been a just or honorable war, the minority of people advocating war always prevail. Two centuries in the future, England will bear the most honorable name a nation has ever borne, yet it will spoil its good name by letting itself be drawn into a shameful war (an allusion to the South African War, 1899–1902).

Chapter 10

Many days pass with no sign of Satan. However, Father Adolf is back. Satan has stopped visiting Marget, who asks for Wilhelm to defend her uncle in his coming trial. When Father Peter's trial finally begins, he himself is too feeble to attend. Father Adolf testifies that two years earlier he found the bag of gold coins that Peter later stole from him. When the boys give their testimony, people merely laugh. Wilhelm does the best he can to represent Father Peter, but his case is hopeless. Theodor's spirits rise when Satan appears standing next to Wilhelm and melts into him. Through Wilhelm, Satan asks Father Adolf to confirm that he found his sack of coins *two* years earlier, then points out that since the dates on most of the coins are only *one* year old, the gold could not have been Adolf's. The court dismisses the case.

Theodor and the others rush to tell Father Peter the good news, but Satan visits him first and tells him that he lost the case and is forever disgraced as a thief. The shock so unsettles the old man that he goes mad; however, he is happy—as Satan predicted he would be.

When Satan later argues that the human race lives a life of continuous and uninterrupted self-deception and has hardly a single fine quality, Theodor cites the sense of humor as such a quality. Here, also, Satan disagrees, saying that humans have merely "a bastard perception of humor." Humans laugh at a thousand low-grade and trivial things, while failing to appreciate the 10,000 high-grade comicalities in religion and hereditary royalties and aristocracies. As an example, he cites the pope's infallibility. He calls laughter the race's only effective weapon against such juvenilities, but says that the race does not think to use it. When Satan realizes that Theodor feels hurt, he lets up, then flashes Theodor around the world, making quick stops in strange countries. In INDIA, they watch a juggler, then Satan transforms himself into a native. He takes a seed from the juggler, places it on the ground and causes a wonderful tree to shoot up, with its branches heavy with oranges, grapes, bananas, peaches and other fruits. As people fill their baskets with fruit, a Portuguese man arrives and commands everyone to leave his land. Satan pleads for him to let people harvest fruit for just one more hour, but he refuses. When the man strikes and kicks Satan, the tree's fruit and leaves suddenly die. In a voice that none of the Indians understands, Satan tells the man that though the tree will never again bear fruit, he must personally water it in each hour of the night or he will die. Satan and Theodor then vanish away to Ceylon.

Chapter 11

Theodor still hungers to see Satan show off some more. To accommodate him, Satan takes him to a place where a magician performs a trick for a rich rajah. As Satan starts to expose the man as a fake, the narrative ends.

BACKGROUND AND PUBLISHING HISTORY

After settling in VIENNA in September 1897, Clemens began writing the first version of the Mysterious Stranger stories, setting the narrative in the St. Petersburg of his Tom Sawyer and Huck Finn stories. Between November 1897 and January 1898, he reworked this first fragment into the early 18th-century setting of "The Chronicle of Young Satan," He resumed work on the manuscript in May 1899, just before he left Vienna for London, where he continued working on it into October. He wrote the second half of the manuscript between June and August 1900, then set it aside for more than two years. After returning to it in late 1902, he revised the first chapter to set the story in the late 15th century, then shifted its direction so radically that he ended up with a fourth version, which he called NO. 44, THE MYSTERIOUS STRANGER.

After A. B. PAINE published a bowdlerized edition of "Chronicle" as THE MYSTERIOUS STRANGER, A ROMANCE in 1916, Clemens's original manuscript was largely forgotten until JOHN S. TUCKEY revealed the extent of Paine's intervention in 1963. Six years later, "Chronicle" was published in the MARK TWAIN PROJECT's edition of *The Mysterious Stranger Manuscripts* (1969), edited by William M. Gibson.

"Chronicle" has not been adapted to the screen, but the 1985 Claymation film THE ADVENTURES OF MARK TWAIN includes the scene in which Satan fashions miniature people from clay. Clemens evidently got his idea for that scene from a passage in the Apocryphal New Testament in which Jesus brings clay figures to life. He mentions that passage in the 24th letter in MARK TWAIN'S TRAVELS WITH MR. BROWN (1940).

CHARACTERS AND RELATED ENTRIES

Adolf, Father Character in "The Chronicle of Young Satan." A Roman Catholic priest in ESELDORF, Father Adolf is respected and feared by villagers. He is ambitious and anxious to become a bishop and tries to ruin the gentle Father Peter by accusing him of stealing his gold; however, he is foiled by the angel Satan. Satan makes it appear that Adolf is a witch and plans to spare Adolf long years of cruel misery by having him burned at the STAKE. Adolf also appears in NO. 44, but in a greatly reduced role. In THE MYSTERIOUS STRANGER, a bowdlerized version of "Chronicle" prepared by ALBERT BIGELOW PAINE and FREDERICK DUNEKA, Adolf is reduced to a minor character, and his worst traits are given to a new character called the astrologer. Duneka, a Roman Catholic himself, evidently objected to Clemens's depiction of the priest.

Clemens's early drafts of "Chronicle" call the evil priest "Lueger." He modeled Adolf on Dr. Karl Lueger, a loud and zealous anti-Semitic Austrian politician who was burgomaster of Vienna when Clemens was living there and writing "Chronicle" in 1897.

Eseldorf   See the Characters and Related Entries section of the *No. 44, The Mysterious Stranger* entry.

Fischer, Theodor   Narrator of "The Chronicle of Young Satan." Like *Joan of Arc*'s (1896) Sieur Louis de Conte, Fischer tells his story about his youth from the vantage point of old age. At the time his story takes place, he is about the same age as Huckleberry Finn, whom he resembles in being both a narrator and a person acutely sensitive to the suffering of others. As an ordinary Austrian village boy in Eseldorf, Fischer also enjoys the same diversions as Huck, such as playing in the woods, swimming, and fishing. He differs in having a conventional family, with parents named Rupert and Marie, and a sister named Lilly—who is being wooed by Joseph Fuchs, the son of the prosperous brewer. Fischer's father is the church organist, village bandleader, violin teacher, and tax collector and seems also to be a judge (chapters 2 and 5).

Fischer provides the focus of the narrative by befriending the angel Satan, who confides in him and reveals countless wonders to him, such as trips to faraway places. Also a foil for Satan's diatribes about the human race, Fischer appears to be coming around to Satan's point of view when his narrative ends abruptly in CEYLON, where Satan has taken him for diversion.

Theodor Fischer does not appear in *No. 44, THE MYSTERIOUS STRANGER*; however, that story has an unrelated character named Gustav Fischer who is one of the better-natured printers.

Peter, Father   Character in "The Chronicle of Young Satan." The uncle of Marget, Peter is the kindly Eseldorf priest whose reputation Father Adolf tries to ruin. After Satan helps Peter out of his financial distress by filling his wallet with gold, Adolf has Peter arrested for robbing him. Satan later saves Peter from being convicted, then causes him to lose his mind so that he can spend his last years happy.

Satan   Character in "The Chronicle of Young Satan." A favorite nephew of the fallen archangel Satan (the narrator of *LETTERS FROM THE EARTH*), the young Satan is 16,000 Earth-years old. He has been everywhere and seen everything (chapter 2). He is a spirit in a body that looks and feels real to the touch and can make himself invisible, merge into other bodies and move instantaneously through space and time. He has godlike powers and uses them freely.

Satan resembles the characters called "Forty-four" in Clemens's other "MYSTERIOUS STRANGER" stories, "SCHOOLHOUSE HILL," and *NO. 44, THE MYSTERIOUS STRANGER* in being a boy with marvelous powers who visits an isolated village. He differs from these other characters, however, in distancing himself more from humans, while being more forthcoming about his identity. Though he never explicitly states why he is visiting Earth or what he hopes to accomplish, he explains who he is and where he comes from.

Satan first appears in "Chronicle" when he joins Theodor Fischer and his friends, who are playing on a hill near Eseldorf (chapter 2). In the form of a boy about the same age as the others, he is so handsome, graceful, and personable that the boys are instinctively drawn to him. Communication is easy, as he reads their minds and anticipates their questions and desires. After identifying himself as an angel, he tells the boys to call him "Philip Traum" when other people are around. As the narrative unfolds, Satan astounds the boys with his powers and increasingly intervenes in the lives of villagers. Despite his ageless wisdom, he shares the boyishness of Tom Sawyer, Hank Morgan, and other Clemens characters in liking to show off.

Traum, Philip Pseudonym used in "The Chronicle of Young Satan." After the angel Satan meets Theodor Fischer and his friends, he tells them to call him "Philip Traum" around other people (chapter 2). When a villager later remarks on how the name Traum "fits him," Fischer parenthetically explains that "Traum is GERMAN for Dream" (chapter 4). Fischer's narrative usually calls the character "Satan," and does not use the name "Traum" after chapter 6.

"Concerning the Jews"

ESSAY written and first published in 1899 in response to public queries about a magazine article on Austrian politics that Clemens had published during the previous year. The essay is of interest primarily as Clemens's fullest expression of his feelings about Jews. The 7,170-word article takes the form of a point-by-point reply to a letter from a Jewish American lawyer who asked Clemens why Jews are almost universally reviled and what he thinks can be done to change anti-Jewish prejudices.

Clemens summarizes the issues raised by his correspondent under six numbered points:

1. The Jew is a well-behaved citizen.

2. Can ignorance and fanaticism alone account for his unjust treatment?

3. Can Jews do anything to improve the situation?

4. The Jews have no party; they are non-participants.

5. Will the persecution ever come to an end?

6. What has become of the Golden Rule?

Before discussing these issues, Clemens addresses the question of his own racial and ethnic biases. He claims to hold no prejudice against Jews and adds what has become one of his most frequently quoted remarks:

> I am quite sure that (bar one) I have no race prejudices, and I think I have no color prejudices nor caste prejudices nor creed prejudices. Indeed, I know it. I can stand any society. All that I care to know is that a man is a human being—that is enough for me; he can't be any worse.

That passage leads Clemens into a long aside about one of his pet subjects: the unfair treatment that Satan has received from humankind. A sentence within that same passage suggests that the lone prejudice to which Clemens alludes applies to the French, whom he castigates for their unjust condemnation of Alfred DREYFUS. That remark conforms with other negative things that Clemens wrote elsewhere about the French and FRANCE.

Under the heading "Point No. 1," Clemens then acknowledges that Jews are well-behaved citizens. In language remarkably similar to what he wrote about CHINESE immigrants in California and Nevada, he praises Jews for their industry, sobriety, generally inoffensive behavior, honesty, self-sufficiency, benevolence, and devotion to family. He calls particular attention to the honesty of Jewish businessmen. He admits that the Jewish reputation for petty commercial cheating and usury has some basis but points out that Jews have no monopoly on "discreditable ways" and concludes that "the Christian can claim no superiority over the Jew in the matter of good citizenship."

Under "Point No. 2," Clemens addresses reasons for anti-Jewish prejudice and immediately dismisses the notion that religious fanaticism accounts for it. Drawing on examples of prejudice and persecution from biblical texts and European and American history, he suggests that 90 percent of the hostility against Jews in modern RUSSIA, AUSTRIA, and GERMANY derives from the inability of average Christians to compete with them in business. The problem, then, is the Jew's reputation as a "money-getter."

Skipping to "Point No. 4," Clemens examines the question of Jewish participation in politics. Here, he becomes more critical of Jews for their general failure to make themselves a political force in any country. In reply to the argument that Jews lack the numbers to make themselves a political force, Clemens cites the example of Irish immigrants to the United States who have won significant political power there through organization. He then goes on to estimate the numbers of Jews in the United States.

Returning to "Point No. 3," Clemens considers what Jews might do to improve their situation and immediately stresses the importance of combination and organization. Again, he cites the successful example of the Irish and even suggests sending Irishmen to Austria to organize Jews. The points that Clemens makes seem to anticipate the 20th-century Zionist movement that led to the creation of the state of Israel by Jews in 1948. This may not be entirely coincidental, as he ends this section of his essay by calling attention to the work of Theodor Herzl (1860–1904), the founder of modern Zionism, who had recently proposed gathering the world's Jews together under their own government in Palestine. He concludes with the ironically prophetic suggestion that allowing Jews to do that might be a mistake, as "It will not be well to let the race find out its strength. If the horses knew theirs, we should not ride any more."

Clemens's remarks under the last two numbered points, on the questions of whether Jewish persecution will ever end and what has become of the Golden Rule, are the briefest in the essay. On the first matter, he suggests that religious persecution has already largely ended, but that racial and commercial prejudice will continue. The matter of the Golden Rule he dismisses with some noncommittal remarks about its irrelevance to the commercial bases of Jewish persecution.

Clemens concludes the essay with lavish praise of the contributions that Jews have made to human history, despite that fact that they constitute less than 1 percent of the world's population. Their commercial importance, he says, is "extravagantly out of proportion" to their numbers, as are their contributions to the world's list of great names in literature, science, art, music, finance, medicine, and abstruse learning.

Although "Concerning the Jews" does not mention "anti-Semitism," the essay is clearly an attempt to combat anti-Semitism. Clemens wrote it at a time when anti-Semitism was on the rise in both the United States and in Europe, where he had resided during the years leading up to the time he wrote it. However, as an argument against anti-Semitism, the essay is a peculiar sort of document. Although it strongly praises Jewish virtues, it also explicitly confirms the stereotype of Jews as commercially devious. Moreover, it contains the notoriously misanthropic suggestion that there cannot be anything worse than a human being—Jewish or otherwise. Modern critics called "Concerning the Jews" both counterproductive as a defense of Jews and inherently naive as a portrait of Jews, whose religion and culture Clemens little understood.

Clemens's references to Jews in his other writings are generally positive but not completely free of anti-Semitic tinges. For example, "THE CHRONICLE OF YOUNG SATAN"—on which Clemens was working around the same time that he wrote "Concerning the Jews"—has an evidently Jewish money lender named Solomon Isaacs, who is honest but clearly avaricious. Despite apparent inconsistencies in Clemens's writings and utterances and the unsatisfactory aspects of "Concerning the Jews," it is clear not only that Clemens himself was not anti-Semitic but also that he was what Carl Dolmetsch called "philo-Semitic." He had a genuine admiration for Jews and had no hesitation in welcoming the Russian Jew Ossip GABRILOWITSCH as his son-in-law in 1909.

BACKGROUND AND PUBLISHING HISTORY

Clemens wrote "Concerning the Jews" in response to letters he received about "Stirring Times in Austria," a long article on Austrian politics that he published in the March 1898 issue of *Harper's Magazine*. Drawing on his firsthand observations of a brawl on the floor of the Austrian legislature on October 28, 1897, Clemens used that article to describe the event and analyze Austrian politics. That article included some passing comments about the hatred of Austrian politicians for Jews, and those remarks moved several American Jews to write to Clemens, who singled out one letter from a lawyer to form the basis of his public reply.

"Concerning the Jews" first appeared in *Harper's Magazine* in September 1899. It was later collected in *The Man That Corrupted Hadleyburg and Other Essays and Stories* in 1904.

A Connecticut Yankee in King Arthur's Court (1889)

One of Clemens's most complex and ambitious NOV-ELS, *Connecticut Yankee* is a pioneering SCIENCE-FIC-TION story about a 19th-century American who tries to implant modern technology and political ideas in sixth-century ENGLAND. The novel falls within a rich literary tradition of reworking Arthurian legends in modern idioms—a tradition that Alfred, Lord TENNYSON'S *Idylls of the King* revitalized in the mid-19th century.

Using Thomas MALORY'S *Le Morte d'Arthur* as his starting point, Clemens began *Connecticut Yankee* as a SATIRE on the customs and institutions of the feudal world. The book's early chapters poke fun at medieval ignorance, superstition, and notions of chivalry. As the book develops, however, it evolves into a savage attack on *all* institutions and ideologies that support monarchy, privilege, SLAVERY, and established churches. The fact that the book's portrayal of sixth-century England is romantic and ahistorical is largely irrelevant, since its real target is the modern perpetuation of oppression and antidemocratic institutions. The book has as much to do with the 19th century as it does with the time in which it is set.

Despite *Connecticut Yankee*'s often heavy-handed political diatribes, it is filled with humor and invention. Clemens invests its hero, Hank Morgan, with many of the traits he admired in inventors such as JAMES PAIGE, and has great fun turning Hank loose to build a modern civilization out of nothing. When Hank first arrives in Camelot, he is anxious to invent all the "little" things he misses, such as soap, matches, paper, ink, and glass. By the end of the novel, he has created workshops and factories to produce not only the little things, but batteries, TELEPHONES, electric dynamos, steamships, trains, and more. Hank also sets up newspapers, insurance companies, a stock board, and other enter-prises. He persuades knights to wear advertising sandwich-boards and ride on bicycles, he gets kings to play baseball in armor, and he has a holy hermit power a sewing machine. Hank himself becomes history's first true fire-breathing dragon when he scares enemies into submission simply by blowing tobacco smoke out of his helmet.

Connecticut Yankee contains too many contra-dictions and inconsistencies to permit easy analysis. It is a sprawling mixture of satire, crude BURLESQUE, sociological diatribes, and horrifying violence, and its tone often changes abruptly. One moment, for example, Hank silently vows to hang Morgan le Fay for cold-bloodedly killing a page boy; the next moment, he approves her hanging her entire band simply for performing badly. Later, Hank boasts of England's dramatic gains in prosperity and educa-tion, then immediately admits to hanging the country's first author for publishing a stale joke. The most shocking change in tone, however, occurs at the end. Once Hank realizes that his modern civilization is doomed, he unleashes the full destructive force of late 19th-century technol-ogy on England's massed chivalry, killing more than 25,000 knights, who doubtless include many men who earlier saved him from hanging.

SYNOPSIS

Slightly longer than *Huckleberry Finn* (1884) at 119,000 words, *Connecticut Yankee* is divided into a brief preface, an untitled prelude, and 44 numbered chapters. Its story is told within a FRAME set in the present (i.e., around 1889). While touring an En-glish castle, the unidentified frame-narrator—prob-ably Mark Twain himself—meets an American (Hank Morgan) who tells him a fabulous story about being transported to the sixth century. After growing too tired to continue, Hank leaves the nar-rator a manuscript containing his story and goes to bed. The narrator then stays up all night reading the manuscript, which forms chapters 1–43 of the novel. The 44th chapter is recorded by Hank's assistant, Clarence. Appended to the end of this

Clemens liked illustrator Dan Beard's laughing helmet in this frontispiece, which depicts Hank Morgan's rude introduction to sixth-century England.

chapter is a "P.S." signed "M. T." that returns the story to the present, with the narrator finishing his reading and going to Hank's room in time to see him die.

Hank's narrative spans roughly 10 years of the early sixth century, with most of its action unfolding within five comparatively brief episodes followed by chapters that sweep over several years. In the prelude, Hank explains that he was knocked unconscious in Connecticut in 1879 and woke up in England in A.D. 528. He is immediately captured, taken to Camelot, and sentenced to be burned at the STAKE. Chapters 1–6 cover several days in which Hank befriends Clarence and uses his knowledge of a coming ECLIPSE to stop his own execution and make people think he is powerful magician. By chapter 7, he is King Arthur's prime minister. In chapters 7–10 he begins a four-year period of reorganizing the kingdom's administration while gradually introducing modern civilization. Chapter 10 indicates that seven years have passed.

Once Hank's new civilization is running smoothly, he takes his first trip away from Camelot in chapters 11–21. Donning armor, he rides with a woman named Sandy to rescue damsels from ogres. Along the way, he visits Queen Morgan le Fay (chapters 16–18). After Hank discovers the "ogre" castle to be a pigsty and its "princesses" hogs, he and Sandy join a pilgrim caravan to a religious shrine (chapter 21).

In chapters 22–26, Hank spends several weeks in the Valley of Holiness, where he enhances his reputation by restarting a holy fountain. Later, King Arthur comes to the valley and conducts business for several days. In chapter 27, Hank and Arthur begin a new adventure together, leaving the valley disguised as freemen in order to study common people firsthand. Several weeks later, their PICARESQUE journey ends abruptly when angry peasants turn on them. A passing nobleman carries them to safety but then sells them into slavery in chapter 34.

Chapter 35–38 cover the months in which Hank and the king accompany the slave caravan to LON-

DON, where Hank's escape gets all the slaves condemned to hang. After a dramatic rescue by knights on bicycles (chapter 38), Hank returns to Camelot, where he humiliates knight-errantry on the tournament field (chapter 39). Chapter 40 hurries through the next three years, with Hank unveiling his secret schools, mines, and factories in order to begin his revolution in earnest.

Chapters 41–44 take place over several months during which the legendary tragedy of Arthur's destruction unfolds in the background. Now married to Sandy, Hank takes his family to France. While he is away, a civil war erupts, resulting in Arthur's death. Hank returns to England to find that the Church's INTERDICT threatens his modern civilization. Meanwhile, Clarence has fortified a stronghold and assembled loyal boys to meet a coming assault by more than 25,000 knights. Hank's modern weapons annihilate the knights, but he and his tiny army are trapped amid the enemy dead. A spell cast by Merlin puts Hank to sleep until the 19th century, leaving Clarence to finish writing Hank's narrative.

For the sake of simplicity, the synopsis that follows calls the narrator "Hank" throughout, although this name does not appear until late in the narrative. Information enclosed in parentheses does not come directly from the chapters in which it appears.

Preface
The laws and customs depicted in this tale are historical. If they did not exist in sixth-century England, they existed later. Furthermore, for each custom or law taken from a later time, one may be sure that the sixth century had something worse.

Word of Explanation
In WARWICK CASTLE the FRAME-narrator meets a stranger whose candid simplicity, familiarity with ancient armor, and restful company are attractive. The stranger does all the talking, seemingly drifting into another time, uttering such names as Sir Launcelot and Sir Galahad with easy familiarity. Their guide interrupts with a remark about a bullet hole in Sir Sagramour le Desirous's chain-mail. He suggests it may have been made during Oliver CROMWELL's time, but the stranger smiles and says he made it himself. That night at the Warwick Arms, the narrator reads about Launcelot in MAL-

ORY. The stranger enters his room, has a few whiskeys and begins telling his story:

An American born and reared in Hartford, Connecticut, the stranger calls himself a practical and unsentimental "YANKEE of Yankees." He is the son of a blacksmith and nephew of a horse doctor, and was himself both until going to work at the (COLT) arms factory, where he learned how to make everything from guns to engines. Good at figuring out *how* to make things, he became superintendent over a thousand men. One day, he fought with a man named Hercules, who cracked him on the head with a crowbar.

The Yankee (identified as Hank Morgan in chapter 39) woke up under a tree with a helmeted horseman staring at him. Challenging Hank to "just" (joust), the horseman charged with a spear, chasing him up the tree. Hank agreed to accompany the man, certain he must be from a circus or asylum. An hour's walk took them to a turreted fortress on a hill. Hank asked if it was BRIDGEPORT, but the man told him it was Camelot.

After starting to nod off, Hank gives the narrator a manuscript, in which he has recorded his entire story, and retires for the night. Under dim writing on parchment pages, the narrator sees traces of old Latin. He begins reading the narrative where Hank left off.

Chapter 1
Near Camelot, a young naked girl approaches Hank and his captor. Though she is indifferent to the circus man, she is astonished by Hank. Townspeople react similarly; everyone stares at Hank but ignores his captor. Falling into the wake of a gorgeous cavalcade, he and his captor cross a drawbridge into the castle.

Chapter 2
Thinking that the castle must be some kind of asylum, Hank tries to find someone who is not a patient. He meets a good-natured page boy, with whom he quickly makes friends. The boy asks many questions without waiting for answers, then unnerves Hank by mentioning that he was born in the year 513. Hank asks him if everyone here is crazy, but the boy explains that he is at King Arthur's court and that the date is June 19, 528. Though unsure why, Hank

tends to believe him. He then remembers that the early sixth century had only one total solar ECLIPSE—on June 21, 528, O.S. (Old Style). Since he also knows that no eclipse is due in 1879—the year from which he comes—he expects to know the truth about where he is within 48 hours.

Hank then decides that whether this is an asylum or the sixth century, he will boss the place within three months. He dubs the page "Clarence" and learns that his captor is Sir Kay the Seneschal. Clarence tells Hank that he can expect to be imprisoned but promises to help him. He then leads Hank into the great hall, where lofty banners hang over a company of colorfully dressed men sitting at a round table. There are also about 20 other prisoners, many maimed and caked with blood.

Chapter 3

Most of the gracious and courtly talk that Hank overhears consists of monologues about adventures—usually DUELS between strangers. Though the whole company appears nearly brainless, Hank finds something lovable about these men and sees a manliness in most faces, especially those of Galahad and Launcelot.

The crowd listens closely when several prisoners step forward, identifying themselves as captives of Kay, who rises to speak. Kay tells how Launcelot slew seven giants and helped him defeat nine foreign knights, then wore his—Kay's—armor and vanquished 50 more knights. These he ordered to report to Queen Guenever as Kay's prisoners. Clarence scoffs throughout Kay's narrative, then grows despondent when an old man, Merlin, rises to recite a tale that he has told a thousand times. Merlin drones on about taking Arthur to the Lady of the Lake, soon putting everyone but Hank to sleep.

Chapter 4

The first person to wake is Sir Dinadan, who rouses the hall by tying mugs to the tail of a dog, making the crowd laugh themselves to tears. After explaining his prank repeatedly, Dinadan recites a string of stale jokes. Kay then explains how he captured Hank, calling him a "prodigious giant" whom he met in a distant land of barbarians. He concludes by ordering Hank executed at noon on June 21. When others question whether Hank's strange

CLOTHES contain enchantments that will protect him, Merlin suggests stripping him. Moments later, Hank stands naked before everyone's unembarrassed eyes, then is sent to the dungeon.

Chapter 5

When Hank wakes up the next morning, he thinks he has been dreaming; however, Clarence arrives and jolts him back to reality by telling him he is to be burned at the stake the next day. Hank begs Clarence for help, but Clarence thinks escape impossible because Merlin has cast a spell over the dungeon. Calling Merlin a humbug, Hank laughingly proclaims that he himself is a magician and sends Clarence to tell the king that he will cause a great calamity if any harm befalls him. Hank then frets about *what* his calamity will be until he remembers the eclipse. His troubles now seem over.

When Clarence returns, he reports that the king was ready to release Hank until Merlin talked him out of it, arguing that by not naming his calamity, Hank proved his powerlessness. Assuming a dramatic posture, Hank orders Clarence to inform the king that he will blot out the sun!

Chapter 6

Though Hank realizes he is in great danger, he is heartened by the thought that the eclipse will make him the kingdom's greatest man. Suddenly, soldiers burst in and tell him that he is to be burned *immediately*. As they take Hank to a courtyard before 4,000 hushed spectators, Clarence appears. Thinking that he is helping Hank, Clarence excitedly explains that he got Hank's execution date changed by saying that his enchantment needs another day to reach full potency. Hank is too stunned to admit he is ruined.

As a monk holds a torch to Hank's feet, the crowd stares at the sky, where a dark edge is moving across the sun. The eclipse is beginning! Merlin orders the torch applied, but King Arthur forbids it. Hank then proclaims he will destroy anyone who moves. Arthur begs him to banish the darkness, offering him *anything*—even half his kingdom. Hank asks for time to consider. He cannot stop the eclipse and is also unsure *what* eclipse is happening, since he thinks the date is June 20 until the monk tells him that it is actually the 21st. Hank now dictates his terms: The king may keep his dominions but must make him perpetual minister and executive and pay him 1 percent of all added revenue he raises. As the crowd applauds, the king orders Hank freed.

Still unsure of the eclipse's duration, Hank advises the king to reconsider before he agrees to turn back the darkness. Meanwhile, he struggles into the sixth-century clothes brought to him. When the eclipse becomes full, Hank proclaims that the king's silence affirms their agreement, and he orders the enchantment to end. The crowd cheers when the rim of the sun reappears.

Chapter 7

Richly rewarded, Hank is now the kingdom's second personage. Despite his new luxuries, he misses little conveniences like soap, matches, mirrors, glass, chromos, gas, candles, books, pens, paper, and ink. He especially misses sugar, coffee, tea, and tobacco. Seeing himself as another Robinson Crusoe (DEFOE's castaway), Hank must invent, contrive, and reorganize to make life bearable.

Hank becomes the talk of the kingdom; everyone wants to see him, and the public pressures him to perform another "miracle." A lunar eclipse is coming, but not for another two years, so he must think of something else. When he learns that Merlin is plotting against him, he has the old magician imprisoned and announces that he will perform just *one* more miracle. Working secretly, he and Clarence prepare to blow up Merlin's tower, packing the ancient structure with blasting powder and erecting a lightning rod as a detonator. After warning the growing mass of spectators to keep their distance, Hank watches the weather. When conditions appear favorable, he starts the show. He lets Merlin try his enchantments, then gestures as the tower explodes. Afterward, the king wants to banish Merlin, but Hank retains him to "work" the weather.

Chapter 8

After the tower episode solidifies Hank's position, he begins accepting the fact that he is not living in a dream. The only threat to his colossal power is the Roman Catholic Church. It a curious country in which he finds himself. Its simple people are like rabbits; they know no better than to love and honor the nobility and the Church, despite receiving nothing in return but blows. Hank believes that *any* kind of royalty or aristocracy is an insult. Most British subjects are slaves, in both name and fact; the rest are slaves in fact, without the name.

Inherited ideas about pedigree and inherited dignities determine how people regard Hank. They admire and fear him, but no one *reverences* him, since he lacks a pedigree or inherited title. The Church has converted a nation of men to a nation of worms, inventing the "Divine Right of Kings," preaching humility, obedience and self-sacrifice to commoners, introducing heritable ranks and aristocracies and teaching people to bow down before them.

Hank's anomalous position as a giant among pygmies makes him Britain's only truly great man. He could get a title but does not ask for one and declines one when it is offered. The only title he wants must be conferred by the nation itself. After several years, he wins just such a title when a village blacksmith dubs him "the Boss"—a name that sweeps the kingdom.

Chapter 9

Hank regards Camelot's frequent tournaments as wearisome bullfights but attends them out of political and social necessity and looks for ways to improve them. Launcelot and others want Hank to participate in the tournaments, but he pleads that his work keeps him too busy.

During one long tournament, Hank tests his plans for starting a newspaper by having a priest from his Department of Public Morals and Agriculture cover the tournament as a journalist.

One day, as Hank sits in his box, Dinadan enters to tell him jokes. As the knight recites a particularly stale story, Hank's mind so wanders that he scarcely notices when Dinadan is called to joust. He awakens in time to see Sir Gareth knock Dinadan hard. By the time Hank mutters his wish that Dinadan be killed, Gareth is knocking Sir Sagramour le Desirous off his horse. Thinking that Hank's remarks are meant for him, Sagramour challenges him to duel—*after* he spends three or four years searching for the Holy Grail.

Chapter 10

Sagramour's challenge makes Hank the subject of court gossip. The king pushes Hank to seek adventures to gain renown, but Hank protests that he needs three or four years to get the kingdom running smoothly. During the three years or so he has been in office, he has begun new industries, gathered the brightest minds of the kingdom, trained expert teachers, set up graded schools, established religious freedom and a variety of Protestant churches, and begun scientific mining.

As four more years pass, Hank shows what a despot can do with the resources of a kingdom behind him. However, he still waits to turn on the full light of his new civilization because he is not ready to confront the Church. Meanwhile, he establishes a WEST POINT military academy and a naval academy.

Clarence, now 22 years old, can do anything. Hank trains him for journalism, to which he takes like a duck. Hank also has TELEPHONE and TELEGRAPH lines laid secretly. Since no one knows where any place is, he sends out a mapping expedition, but drops the idea when priests interfere. He systematizes taxes, but the condition of the kingdom as a whole is about the same as it was when he started. With everything running smoothly, however, he feels ready for a rest.

Chapter 11

The country is full of liars who occasionally appear at court with wild tales of princesses or others needing help. One day a woman shows up claiming that three ogres have been holding her mistress and 44 beautiful "young" girls in a castle for 26 years. Every knight begs permission to rescue them, but the king gives the job to Hank.

The woman calls herself the Demoiselle Alisande la Carteloise (Hank starts calling her Sandy in the next chapter). When she cannot even explain where the castle is, Hank fumes, but Clarence wonders why he even asks her for such information, since she will accompany him on his mission. Scandalized by the idea of traveling alone with a woman, Hank mentions that he is nearly engaged to someone named Puss Flanagan.

Much is made of Hank's coming expedition, and knights fill him with advice. Finally, he struggles into a suit of heavy armor and is hoisted onto his horse. With Sandy behind him, they depart.

Chapter 12

As they ride into the country, Hank is miserable inside his armor. He needs a handkerchief, but cannot get at it. His armor heats up, rattles noisily and grows heavier. Unable even to scratch, Hank reaches the peak of his misery when a fly invades his helmet. He dismounts and has Sandy remove his helmet, fill it with water and pour it down his armor. As they await help to get Hank back on the horse, Sandy talks constantly, but never expresses an idea—like a perfect BLATHERSKITE.

Chapter 13

When they resume their journey, Hank discovers new irritations. He longs to smoke his pipe but has no matches. He is hungry because he follows the knightly custom of trusting to providence instead of carrying food. The first night, he sleeps in his armor during a storm, which sends bugs and worms seeking shelter inside his outfit. In the morning, he rises crippled with rheumatism, but Sandy is fresh as a squirrel. They start off again at sunrise, with Sandy on the horse and Hank limping behind.

Soon they meet peasants repairing a road. The peasants are flattered by Hank's offer to eat with them. Though these people are "freemen," they have so many duties to their lord, restrictions on their movements, and taxes that they resemble the French before the blessed revolution (of 1789). Nevertheless, they remain humbly reverent toward the king and the Church. Hank asks them if a nation in which *every* man could vote would ever elect a single family to reign over it and grant special privileges to another hundred families. The idea of a nation giving every man a say has never occurred to the peasants, so Hank tells them that he has seen such a nation. One man who grasps what Hank is saying declares that stealing the will from a nation must be the greatest crime. Sensing this man's potential, Hank sends him to be put in his "man factory." Hank himself believes that one should be loyal to one's country, not to its institutions or office-holders. Since he now lives in a country that gives only six persons in a thousand a say, he thinks that what the other 994 persons need is a "NEW DEAL."

Chapter 14

After Hank gives his hosts three pennies, they give him a flint and steel—which he uses to light his pipe after mounting his horse. The first blast of smoke from his helmet sends everyone running.

The next day, Hank and Sandy encounter a half-dozen armed knights and their squires. When the knights charge, Hank lights his pipe and blows smoke through his helmet, causing the knights to scatter. Confident that Hank has disabled the men, Sandy secures their surrender and their promise to report to Camelot as Hank's property.

Chapter 15

When Sandy tells Hank that he has captured *seven* knights and their squires, he asks who they are, but quickly regrets giving Sandy a chance to launch another long narrative. She describes Sir Uwaine and Sir Gawaine's long struggle with Sir Marhaus, with Hank interrupting occasionally to criticize her archaic speech. In the afternoon, they approach a castle.

Chapter 16

As Hank wonders who lives in the castle, a horseman approaches, wearing a sign for "Persimmon's Soap." It is Sir La Cote Male Taile, one of several knights promoting soap for Hank as part of his secret plan to introduce hygiene among the nobility while making knight-errantry look foolish. His soap factory runs night and day, stinking up Camelot.

Wearing heavy armor, Hank (Will Rogers) needs to be hoisted onto his horse in this film scene from chapter 11. In the novel, the experience moves Hank to say, "I hate a country without a derrick." *(Twentieth Century–Fox)*

La Cote identifies the castle as the abode of Arthur's sister, Queen Morgan le Fay. Inside, Hank is startled to find Morgan gracious, beautiful, and youthful looking, despite her reputation as an evil old woman. She looks young enough to be the granddaughter of her husband King Uriens. Hank suspects that Morgan has been misrepresented, until she casually stabs a young page for accidentally touching her. When Hank carelessly compliments Arthur, Morgan orders him and Sandy to the dungeon, but Sandy warns the guards that the Boss will destroy them. Morgan instantly becomes sweet again and claims merely to be jesting so she can see Hank blast her guards to ashes.

Chapter 17

Morgan le Fay wants Hank to demonstrate his powers by killing someone, but the call to prayers interrupts her. Relieved, Hank expresses his admiration of the Church's ability to keep its murderous nobility religious. Later, he and Sandy dine in a great banquet hall, where a horrible band plays a tune sounding like the first draft of "THE SWEET BY-AND-BY." After dinner, the queen orders the composer hanged. Meanwhile, more than a hundred people eat everything in sight, become drunk, and tell anecdotes that would embarrass even Queen ELIZABETH. At midnight, an old woman appears and calls down a curse on the queen for killing her grandchild, the page boy. When Morgan orders the woman to the stake, Sandy startles Hank by proclaiming that the Boss will dissolve the castle if Morgan does not recall her command. Morgan complies but collapses while everyone else rushes for the exits.

Morgan is now too frightened even to hang her composer without Hank's permission. Looking for a way to lift her spirits, Hank has the band play "The Sweet Bye-and-Bye" again, then gives her permission to hang the *whole* band. After Hank hears a distant shriek, Morgan proudly leads him to a cell, where her executioner is racking a man named Hugo who is accused of killing a stag. In a private interview, Hugo tells Hank that he *did* kill the stag but will not confess so that his family will not be stripped of their property. Hank orders Hugo's release and sends him to his Man Factory.

Chapter 18

When priests later denounce the executioner's crimes, Hank admits that many priests are *not* frauds and self-seekers after all—a thought that disturbs him since he dislikes anything that might reconcile people to an Established Church. He punishes the executioner by making him leader of the queen's new band.

The next day, Hank inspects Morgan's dungeons. Their inmates include a prematurely aged couple imprisoned since their wedding night for refusing a nobleman his customary rights to enjoy the bride (on her wedding night)—*le droit du seigneur*. For nine years, they have been within 50 feet of each other, each without knowing the other was alive. Hank frees 47 prisoners, leaving only a lord who ruined a village's well. Most of these people were imprisoned for trifling offenses. The most recent captive, for example, merely suggested that kings and commoners would look the same without CLOTHES. Another prisoner has spent 22 years peering at his home through a crack, trying to see his wife and five children. After observing five funerals, he was tormented by not knowing which member of his family was still alive. When Hank frees him, however, he discovers that *everyone* in his family is still alive; the queen faked all the funerals simply to torture him. His crime: saying that the queen had "red hair," when "auburn" was the only acceptable description for one of her rank. Five persons have not seen daylight in 35 years; no one remembers their names or when or why they were incarcerated.

Chapter 19

The next morning, Hank and Sandy go back on the road. Sandy begins a new narrative about Sir Marhaus that concerns the seven knights whom Hank captured earlier. He considers what a curious country this is for people who seem never to get old, but the conversation stops abruptly when he asks Sandy her age.

Chapter 20

After riding 10 miles, they see an approaching knight—Sir Madok de la Montaine, who carries an advertisement for "Peterson's Prophylactic Toothbrush." Madok is trying to catch up with Hank's stove-polish man, Sir Ossaise of Surluse, for tricking him into chasing after potential customers—who turned out to be Morgan's toothless former prisoners.

Later, Hank and Sandy see the reunion of a family with a man who had been imprisoned for 50 years. Hank regards their failure to express outrage at their oppressors as evidence that all true revolutions must begin in blood.

Two days later, Sandy spots the ogres' "castle." All Hank sees is a pigsty, but he humors Sandy by pretending that an enchantment hides the castle from his eyes. He promises to treat Sandy "princesses" as ladies, even though they appear to be hogs—which he buys from the starveling swineherds who Sandy thinks are "ogres." When they reach home later, Sandy quarters the unruly hogs in the house.

Chapter 21

Hank gets little sleep that might with the hogs cavorting through the house, and ponders whether Sandy is sane. He concludes that she is, given her training, and allows that people would consider *him* insane if they knew what he was trained to believe. At breakfast, he is shocked to learn that Sandy does not know whose house they are in; however, he is relieved to learn that they can leave her "princesses" there to be collected by friends. His distress returns when Sandy says she will stay with him until a knight wins her away in fair combat.

After departing, Hank and Sandy fall in with a procession of cheerful PILGRIMS headed for the Valley of Holiness, where they plan to cleanse themselves of sin by drinking water from the miraculous fountain. In the afternoon, they overtake a procession of slaves chained together by the neck who have tramped 300 miles in 18 days. When their master ruthlessly whips a young woman, Hank decides not to interfere but vows to be the death of SLAVERY.

At a village inn, Hank meets a knight who is promoting plug hats for him. Just arrived from the Valley of Holiness, Sir Ozana Le Cure Hardy reveals that the miraculous fountain stopped flowing nine days earlier and that Merlin has been trying to restart it. Hank has Ozana carry an order to Clarence in Camelot to send supplies and assistants to the valley as fast as possible.

Chapter 22

Now that the holy fountain has stopped flowing, the pilgrims' desire to see it is 40 times greater. At the valley, the overjoyed abbot begs Hank to restore the fountain immediately, but Hank refuses to act until after Merlin quits. The next day he visits the fountain inside its chapel and finds that it is an ordinary well with a leak. While Merlin works his incantations from outside, Hank spreads the idea that restarting the fountain will be difficult.

When Hank later discusses the hermits with Sandy, he chides her for not grasping his modern jargon until he notices how hard she is trying to understand him. After he apologizes, they become better friends, and he realizes that he is developing a mysterious reverence for her. They tour the strange menagerie of hermits, who compete to be the most unclean and verminous. For 20 years, the valley's greatest hermit has done nothing but stand atop a 60-foot-high pillar bowing up and down continuously. Hank later harnesses the hermit to a sewing machine and gets him to turn out 18,000 tow-linen shirts over the next five years.

Chapter 23

On Saturday, Hank inspects Merlin's progress and finds him in a foul mood. Proclaiming that a potent Eastern spirit has laid a spell that no mortal can break, Merlin says that the water will *never* flow again and quits. Hank tells the distressed abbot that Merlin's remarks about the spirit are true, but that it *may* be possible to break the spell. Merlin gleefully reminds Hank that in order to break the spell, he must not only know the spirit's name but *pronounce* it—an act that will kill him. Hank's cracks about Merlin's weather forecasting abilities anger the magician, who decides to remain in order to see Hank fail.

That evening two experts arrive from Camelot with tools, supplies, and fireworks and help Hank patch the well. By the next afternoon, when they complete their preparations, the water is back to its normal level. The men install a pump and set up fireworks. That evening, criers announce the coming miracle and the valley fills up with people. After men chant in Latin, Hank mounts a platform, reaches to the sky and pronounces: "Constantinopolitanischserdudelsackspfeifenmachersgesellschafft!"

("The Bagpipe Manufacturers Company of Constantinople") as blue flares illuminate the area. More awful words and colored flares follow, creating a display so dazzling that even the hermit atop the pillar stops bowing to watch. Finally, Hank commands the spell to end and pronounces the dreaded spirit's name: "BGWJJILLIGKKK!" As rockets light up the sky, water gushes from the chapel and the crowd goes wild.

Chapter 24

With his influence in the valley now prodigious, Hank persuades the abbot to allow the monks to bathe again and has his men rebuild an ancient bath in the monastery's basement. Before he can leave the valley, however, he catches a bad cold. As he recuperates, he plans to tour the country alone disguised as a peasant.

One morning, Hank stumbles upon a cave with a telephone office that Camelot men have set up the previous night. He phones Clarence and learns that the king, queen, and half the court are headed for the valley to see the restored waters and should arrive in two and a half days. He also learns that the king has started raising the standing army that he (Hank) has been planning and is already officering it with nobles instead of West Point cadets. Clarence connects him with the superintendent at West Point, whom he orders to send a cadet to the valley.

Back at the monastery, Hank is annoyed to find a new magician regaling monks by revealing what anyone—such as a distant emperor—is doing at the moment. Fearing that his own reputation may suffer, Hank challenges the man to reveal what he himself is doing with a hand hidden behind his back; however, the fraud claims that his magic works only with royalty. When the abbot asks what King Arthur and his court are doing, he says they are sleeping after a hunt. This remark leads to an argument with Hank, who insists that the king is *riding*. Hank stakes his reputation on his prediction that the king will arrive in the valley in two days. After the king appears on schedule, the monks carry the magician out on a rail.

Chapter 25

As he typically does while traveling, Arthur holds court in the valley. Though a wise and humane judge, he is biased toward the upper classes. In one case, he rules in favor of a bishop who claims a young bride's estate because she married privately to evade *le droit du seigneur.*

Arthur has started staffing his army before Hank has had time to prepare a plan for selecting officers through examinations that only his own cadets can pass. Three priests whom Arthur has brought with him as an examination board refuse to examine Hank's commoner candidate, Malease Webster. After Arthur permits Hank's West Point professors to examine Webster, the cadet displays dazzling expertise in the sciences of war, mathematics, and astronomy. By contrast, neither of the nobles who came with Arthur can answer anything. Nevertheless, the official board awards the lieutenancy to the noble with the more impressive pedigree.

Afterward, Hank interests Arthur in staffing a "King's Own Regiment" entirely with high-ranking noble officers—most of whom will pay to get in. This regiment would do whatever it wants, while commoner regiments would do the real military work. Hank also thinks of using this regiment as a means of replacing the hated royal grants.

Chapter 26

When Hank tells Arthur about his idea of touring the country in disguise, the king wants to join jim. First, however, he must attend to the "kings-evil"—a rite in which he touches scrofulous subjects, giving each a coin. Hank saves the treasury nearly a day's expenses by substituting his mint's new nickels for the gold pieces traditionally handed out. As he waits for the ceremony to end, he buys a copy of the first newspaper, the *Camelot Weekly Hosannah and Literary Volcano,* from a newsboy.

Chapter 27

That night, Hank prepares Arthur for their journey by hacking his hair and whiskers and outfitting him in coarse garments. At dawn, they slip away and walk 10 miles before resting. When Hank sees upper-class people coming, he dashes to the king, who is slow to adopt a humble posture. A flunky raises a whip to Arthur, but Hank jumps to take the blow. Afterward, the king becomes a constant anxiety to Hank.

Arthur later asks Hank why he does not warn him *before* he (Arthur) does something foolish. After starting to admit that he cannot read minds, Hank explains that his gift of prophecy works only for distant future events—in contrast to that of Merlin, who can see only a few days ahead. Hank now has to satisfy the king's hunger to hear about the future.

For several days, Hank steers Arthur away from further encounters with knights. One day, Hank happens to fall down—an accident that makes him realize he should get rid of the dynamite-bomb in his knapsack. As he holds the bomb, wondering what to do with it, several knights nearly run the king down, provoking Arthur to curse at them. The knights turn on the king, but Hank gets them to chase him instead, then blows them to bits with his bomb.

Chapter 28
Hank devotes the fourth day to drilling the king's dangerous habits out of him. He tells Arthur that his bearing is all wrong—he stands too straight and looks too confident. Hank must explain everything to the king, one detail at a time.

Chapter 29
That afternoon, Hank and the king reach a darkened hut by a denuded field. Inside, Hank finds a woman warning him to flee, as God has cursed her house, but he ignores her warnings. After fetching water, he finds the king inside the hut opening shutters. When he sees that the woman has smallpox, he urges Arthur to flee, but the king insists on helping, and carries the woman's dying adolescent daughter down from a loft. To Hank, this is heroism at its greatest: challenging death without defenses. Arthur then brings down another daughter, who is already dead, and lays her by her dead father. The woman tells her story:

Her family's troubles began a year earlier, when the local lord planted fruit trees on their farm. One day her three grown sons discovered the trees cut down and reported the crime. They were thrown in a dungeon, where they remain. Only the woman, her husband, and her daughters remained to protect and gather their crops—which ripened at the same time as their lord's. As the woman and her daughters harvested the lord's crop, they were fined for being a man short. Meanwhile, their own crops perished. Between their fines and crop losses they ended up with nothing and then contracted smallpox. Driven mad by hunger and frustration, the woman uttered a blasphemy that brought down the Church's ban.

As the woman concludes her story, she hears her daughter's death rattle.

Chapter 30
At midnight, Hank and the king cover four corpses and leave the house. Hearing footsteps, they hide outside and listen to men excitedly calling out to their parents that they are free. Hank pushes the king to move on.

The sight of a burning house in the distance interests Hank because he is starting up a fire insurance business and a fire department. As they move through the darkness, a storm threatens and Hank walks into a man hanging from a tree. Lightning reveals more bodies hanging nearby. Finding the manor house burned to the ground, Hank and the king rush off. Several miles away, the wife of a charcoal-burner welcomes them into her house.

After rising late the next day, Hank and the king learn about the previous night's affair from the woman and her husband (identified as Marco in the next chapter). When the manor caught fire, people swarmed to the rescue and saved everyone but the lord. After he was found bound and stabbed, suspicion fell on a family he had recently mistreated, and his retainers led the villagers in pursuit of everyone connected with the family, killing 18 people. Hank is grieved to learn that every prisoner in the manor house burned to death, but the king interjects that three men escaped, and urges they be caught. Marco agrees, but Hank senses his lack of enthusiasm. He leaves with Marco to show him which way the escapees went. Away from the house, he startles the man by asking if the escaped men are his cousins. Once Hank declares that letting the men escape would be honorable, the relieved Marco pours out his true feelings, admitting that he helped hang his neighbors the previous night only for fear of being thought disloyal to his lord if he failed to cooperate.

Chapter 31

While Hank and Marco kill time to make it appear they have been searching for the escaped prisoners, Hank studies the ways in which different classes treat one another. Suddenly a mob of frightened children rush out of the woods, where Hank and Marco rescue a boy the children nearly hanged while imitating their elders.

In the hamlet of Abblasoure, Hank is pleased to see his new coins circulating and has a goldsmith change a $20 gold piece for him. He meets several master mechanics and invites the most interesting of them, the blacksmith Dowley, to Sunday dinner at Marco's. Marco's pleasure at Dowley's acceptance vanishes when Hank also suggests inviting Dickon the mason and Smug the wheelwright. However, Hank calms him by promising to pay for everything. He also buys Marco and his wife new outfits, claiming they are a gift from the king, whom he calls "Jones," describing him as a prosperous but eccentric farmer and himself as a farm bailiff. At the hamlet's best shop, he orders everything needed for the banquet—arranging for the goods to be delivered on Saturday and the bill on Sunday.

Chapter 32

The arrival of Hank's order on Saturday makes the Marcos nearly faint. Besides abundant food, there are extra staples, furniture, and crockery, as well as new outfits for the Marcos, who are too excited to sleep that night. On Sunday, the guests assemble under a tree. As everyone becomes congenial, Dowley boasts about how he rose from friendless orphan to master blacksmith and describes his lavish life-style—making Hank want to humiliate him. The guests are astonished when Mrs. Marco sets out a new table and stools, followed by sumptuous dishes. Each item outdoes the blacksmith's domestic grandeurs. When the storekeeper's son arrives to collect the bill for 39,150 milrays. Hank has him read it aloud, then casually gives the boy four dollars, telling him to keep the nine cents change. To Hank's gratification, Dowley is crushed.

Chapter 33

Hank soon has Dowley happy again. After dinner, conversation turns to business and wages, with Hank and Dowley doing most of the talking, while Arthur nods off. Under King Bagdemagus, this realm has the protection system, in contrast to the free trade system Hank is promoting in Arthur's realm. Dowley boasts about high local wages, which are about double Camelot's. Hank argues that since prices here are *more* than double, his own land is actually better off, but the others cannot grasp his reasoning. So far as Dowley is concerned, the fact that local wages are higher is the only thing that matters.

Smarting at losing this argument to Dowley, Hank determines to strike back. He starts with a discussion about an unwritten law dictating that wages must steadily rise, predicting future wage levels that amaze the other men. Even more amazing is his prediction that one day workers will form trade unions and dictate their own wages. Discussion turns to the pillory, which Hank argues should be abolished. He points out that being sentenced to the pillory can mean death for someone convicted of a minor crime, particularly if that person is unpopular. When he suggests that none of the other men is unpopular for exciting his neighbors' envy, Dowley winces. After getting everyone to agree that persons failing to report a crime should be pilloried, Hank mentions the local law fixing wages and casually recalls Dowley's earlier admission that he once paid higher than legal wages. The moment the others grasp what Hank is driving at, they go to pieces. Hank has scared the men too much.

Chapter 34

After Hank calms the panicky men down, the king awakens from his nap and starts prattling about agriculture. He calls onions "berries" and plums "cereal" and makes other mistakes, causing the men to grow more restless. Crying out that one man would betray them and that the other is mad, the men suddenly attack Hank and the king, and Marco runs for help. By the time Marco returns with more men and dogs, Hank and the king are in woods, where they hide their tracks in water and climb a tree. Eventually, their pursuers find them and force them down with fire. At that moment, horsemen arrive. Their leader, Earl Grip, drives the peasants away and lets Hank and the king ride with him about 10 or 12 miles.

The next morning Hank and the king are invited to continue with Grip's men to Cambenet, where they see the same slave caravan that they encountered earlier. Hank fumes when he hears an orator declaiming about "glorious British liberties." Suddenly, Grip's men handcuff Hank to the king, and Grip orders them sold as slaves. Hank and the king cry out that they are freemen, but the orator reminds them that the burden of proof lies with them. The master of the slave caravan buys them at auction, paying seven dollars for the king and nine dollars for Hank, then marches them away.

Chapter 35

Brooding about having fetched only seven dollars, Arthur bores Hank by monotonously arguing that he should have brought at least 25. Gradually, the slave driver realizes that the king's regal style spoils his marketability, and tries unsuccessfully to beat it out of him.

During a month of marching, Arthur grows seriously interested in the SLAVERY question and thrills Hank by declaring himself ready to abolish slavery. The king's new attitude sets Hank to planning their escape. Meanwhile, they have several adventures. One night, as the slaves huddle in a deadly blizzard, a woman accused of being a witch seeks their protection. When her pursuers catch up with her, the slave master makes them burn her amidst his slaves, in order to keep them warm.

Later, they see an 18-year-old girl hanged for petty theft in a LONDON suburb. A priest tells her heartrending story: She was happily married until her husband was impressed into the navy and disappeared. Never told what became of him, she gradually became mentally disordered and stole a bit of cloth to buy her baby food. As the executioner slips the noose over her head, she hugs her child desperately, crying that it will die without a father or mother. The good priest promises to be both, allowing the girl to die happy.

Chapter 36

When the slave caravan enters London, Hank sees people he knows, including Sandy, but getting their attention is hopeless. The sight of a newspaper boy

and telegraph lines cheers him, but his biggest interest is finding a piece of wire with which to pick the lock on his chains. Eventually, he steals a metal pin from a prospective buyer. Hank unlocks his chains that night, but the master arrives before he can free the king. As the master leaves, Hank pounces after him. Outside, he jumps the man and struggles with him until they both are arrested. Then he discovers he has attacked the *wrong* man.

Chapter 37

Hank's concern about what is happening at the slave quarters robs him of his sleep in the noisy jail. The next morning, he tells the court he is a slave of Earl Grip, for whom he was on an important errand when the other man attacked him. Begging Hank's pardon, the court frees him and orders the other man whipped.

Hank finds the slave quarters empty except for the master's battered corpse and learns that his mysterious escape so angered the man that he whipped the other slaves until they rose and killed him. *All* the slaves are now condemned to be hanged tomorrow and a massive search is under way for Hank. After buying another outfit to disguise himself, Hank goes to a telegraph office and contacts Clarence, whom he orders to send help immediately.

While waiting for help to come, Hank begins upgrading his CLOTHES in stages, in order to approach local grandees whom he knows for help. This plan soon crumbles, however, when one of the condemned slaves and an officer capture him. Hank boasts that no one will be hanged, but the officer tells him that his capture means that everyone will be hanged *today*! Hank estimates that the knights will arrive about three hours too late to rescue them.

Chapter 38

That afternoon a multitude assembles outside London's walls to witness the hangings. When Arthur proclaims himself King of Britain, the crowd merely taunts him. Hank receives the same treatment when he identifies himself as the Boss. Soon, the grim ceremony begins. After two slaves are hanged and a blindfold is put on the king, 500 fully equipped knights suddenly enter the compound on bicycles. As Launcelot sweeps in, Hank springs up

Armor-clad members of the nobility keep the trains running in this illustration from a Russian edition of *Connecticut Yankee* published in Moscow in 1980.

and commands the assemblage to salute the king. Clarence then arrives and explains he has been training the knights for just such an occasion.

Chapter 39

Home at Camelot again, Hank reads a newspaper story about his coming combat with Sir Sagramour. Interest in the match is widespread because it will be the first tournament under a law permitting combatants to use any weapons they choose. More important, the battle is seen as a final struggle between the land's two mightiest magicians: Merlin, who is helping Sagramour, and the Boss. As the champion of hard, unsentimental reason, Hank wants to destroy knight-errantry.

On the day of combat, Sagramour is an imposing tower of iron mounted on a mighty steed, while Hank wears only a gymnast costume and rides a slender horse. After Merlin casts spells to make Sagramour invisible, the contest begins. The men charge each other; just as Sagramour's lance nears its target, Hank twitches his horse aside. After two more misses, Sagramour futilely tries chasing Hank down. On Sagramour's final charge, Hank ropes him off his horse. The astounded audience cheers for more. After Hank almost effortlessly lassos seven more knights, including Launcelot, Merlin steals his lasso. Sagramour then challenges Hank again—this time bent on death. Though ostensibly unarmed, Hank does not budge until Sagramour is 15 paces away. He then whips out a revolver and fires. Before anyone knows what has happened, Sagramour lies dead on the field. No one can figure out what killed him.

No other knights challenge Hank, so he dares *all* of them to come at him at once. Five hundred men scramble to their saddles and charge together. This time, Hank fires two revolvers; he is just two bullets away from disaster when the knights break rank and flee.

Chapter 40

With knight-errantry humbled, Hank uncovers all his secret schools, mines, and factories to an astonished world. To keep the knights down, he issues a permanent challenge—advertising that he stands always ready to meet the world's massed chivalry with just 50 men on his side.

Over the next three years, England prospers, with schools everywhere, as well as colleges, newspapers, and even authors—though Hank suppresses Sir Dinadan's stale jokebook and has him hanged. Slavery is gone, and all men are now equal before the law. The telegraph, telephone, phonograph, typewriter, sewing machine, and other devices are at work throughout the land. There are STEAMBOATS on the THAMES, steam warships at sea, and Hank is preparing an expedition to discover America. A railway line connects Camelot and London and more lines are being developed.

Hank's biggest remaining plans are to replace the Catholic Church with several Protestant faiths and to introduce universal suffrage after Arthur dies—in perhaps 30 years. Looking forward to the coming republic, Hank admits to having a "base hankering" to be the first president. Clarence prefers a modified republic with a hereditary royal family, and argues convincingly for a royal family of cats, until Hank realizes he is joking.

One morning, Sandy rushes in to tell Hank that their baby, Hello-Central, is suffering from croup (Hank explains that he is already married in the next chapter). Sir Launcelot, now the stock-board president, happens by and ends up staying three days to help Hank watch the baby. Doctors recommend sea air for Hello-Central, so Hank and Sandy cruise the French coast in a warship for two weeks, then settle ashore on the doctor's recommendation. After a month in FRANCE, Hank sends the vessel home for supplies and news. He particularly wants to hear about a pet project—baseball teams composed of kings.

Chapter 41

When the baby's croup worsens, Sandy proves again what a flawless wife and mother she is. Hank explains that when he realized he could not keep Sandy from his side, he married her. Their first year of marriage proved how fortunate he was to have her as a wife.

When Hello-Central recovers two and a half weeks later, Hank remembers that his warship has not returned and rushes to the sea, where he finds that his great oceangoing commerce has vanished. Leaving his family behind, he returns to England the next day. Dover's harbor has ships, but no activity. In Canterbury he discovers that the Church has put England under the INTERDICT. After disguising himself, he makes his way to Camelot alone. Desolate silence prevails everywhere, even in London—whose Tower shows recent war scars. When Hank reaches Camelot several days later, he finds the town shrouded in darkness.

Chapter 42

Clarence, drowned in melancholy, tells Hank how Launcelot's affair with Queen Guenever triggered the Interdict. Launcelot made a stock-board killing that hurt Arthur's nephews, Sir Agravaine and Sir Mordred, badly. They got revenge by telling Arthur about Launcelot and Guenever. The king then laid a trap that caught Launcelot, who killed

Agravaine and 12 other knights. This incident started a civil war. When Arthur sent Guenever to the STAKE. Launcelot rescued the queen, accidentally killing his faithful friends Sir Gaheris and Sir Gareth, in his blind fury. After several battles, the Church patched up a peace that satisfied everyone but Sir Gawaine, who remained bitter about Launcelot's slaying his brothers. Arthur then joined Gawaine, leaving his kingdom in the hands of Mordred—who attempted a permanent takeover. After Mordred chased Guenever to the Tower of London, the archbishop of Canterbury laid down the Interdict.

Arthur fought Mordred in southeast England, then began negotiating a peace that would give Mordred part of his kingdom. After dying in battle, Gawaine appeared to Arthur in a dream and warned him not to let anyone fight, for one month. The ensuing truce collapsed when a knight raised his sword to an adder. In the next great battle, Arthur and Mordred killed each other.

The Church, which has all the knights on its side, now controls the country and will maintain the Interdict so long as Hank remains alive. Hank scoffs until Clarence tells him that virtually all his followers have deserted to the Church and all his modern communication and transportation systems have shut down.

During Hank's absence, Clarence prepared for the coming war by assembling 52 trained teenage boys who grew up free from the Church's influence. He fortified Merlin's Cave to withstand a siege, wiring it to dynamite charges under all the modern factories, workshops, and magazines. The cave itself is surrounded by wire fences connected to an electric dynamo; its approaches are guarded by Gatling guns; and a wide belt surrounding it is mined with dynamite torpedoes covered with sand.

After praising Clarence's preparations, Hank proposes to strike. The next day he issues a proclamation declaring that the death of the king has ended the monarchy, leaving executive authority vested in him until a new government is created. Meanwhile, the nobility, privileged classes, and Established Church no longer exist, and a republic is proclaimed.

Chapter 43

At the cave, Hank sends out word that his factories will be blown up without warning. Through a week of waiting, he converts his diary into a narrative and writes letters to Sandy, though he cannot send them. Meanwhile, his spies report that the Church is massing the knights against him. His proclamation of the republic generates excitement for one day, then the Church takes control. With all England now marching against them, Hank's boys beg not to be asked to destroy their country, but Hank explains that their only true foes are the knights who will march in the vanguard.

After the huge enemy host arrives, its front ranks charge into the Sand Belt and are blown to bits. Hank then detonates the charges to destroy his factories and congratulates his army on their victory. Declaring that the war with the English nation—as a nation—is over, he says that they must now kill *every* knight in order to end the conflict. Explosions have dug a ditch in the Sand Belt, so Hank has a stream diverted for the next emergency.

That night, Hank creeps out to the perimeter and finds knights pouring into the ditch. The electric fences are so powerful that they kill before victims can cry out. Back at the cave, Hank turns on floodlights that reveal three walls of corpses surrounding them. While the lights immobilize the enemy, he turns on the remaining fences, killing another 11,000 men, then signals to turn the brook's water into the ditch, as Gatling guns spit bullets into the 10,000 knights still alive. Within 10 minutes, the enemy is annihilated. Hank and his 53 men are masters of England.

Hank's narrative now ends.

Chapter 44

Clarence closes the narrative, explaining that when the Boss went out to help the wounded, he was stabbed by the first man he met—Sir Meliagraunce. His wound was not serious, but his men's position was desperate because they were trapped by the enemy dead surrounding them. Several days later, an old woman appeared, offering to cook. One night Clarence caught her doing something over Hank. She proved to be Merlin in disguise,

gloating that Hank would now sleep for 13 centuries. As Merlin laughed, he bumped into an electric wire and was instantly killed.

Clarence ends the manuscript promising that if the Boss does not awaken, they will carry him to a remote recess and hide this manuscript with him.

A final "P.S.," signed "M. T.," returns the narrative to the present day. It is morning as the narrator lays the manuscript aside. He goes to Hank's room and finds him on his back, mumbling to Sandy about Hello-Central, Clarence, his cadets, and strange dreams of an abyss of 13 centuries that separate them. Growing incoherent, he starts to cry out but never finishes.

BACKGROUND AND PUBLISHING HISTORY

The genesis of *Connecticut Yankee* goes back to Clemens's 1866 visit to HAWAII. Fascinated by elements of feudalism that he observed there, he later planned to write a novel set in the islands. Meanwhile, several visits to England gave him ideas for a medieval tale. He finally started his Hawaiian novel in 1884 but soon abandoned it. By then he was familiar with Arthurian romances, which he read to his children. In December 1884, G. W. CABLE gave him a copy of Thomas MALORY's *Le Morte d'Arthur*, which stimulated him to begin a burlesque of Arthurian romances. By early 1886, he was seriously at work on *Connecticut Yankee*. In November of that year, he gave a public reading from his draft manuscript at the Military Service Institution on New York's Governor's Island.

After four years of intermittent writing, Clemens completed *Connecticut Yankee* in April 1889, then spent several months revising it in typescript. *Century Magazine* published four extracts in November; Charles L. WEBSTER & COMPANY published the book on December 12, with CHATTO and Windus issuing an English edition the next day. Meanwhile, CHARLES HEBER CLARK accused Clemens of plagiarizing the story from a novella he had published nearly a decade earlier.

While completing his manuscript, Clemens saw illustrator DAN BEARD's work in COSMOPOLITAN magazine and arranged with him to illustrate *Con-*

necticut Yankee. Given considerable freedom in subject matter and treatment, Beard contributed a major dimension to the book. His 220 pictures capture the author's intentions fully, while adding shadings of characterization and strengthening the book's humor and its serious political message. Beard used real people such as SARAH BERNHARDT and ALFRED, LORD TENNYSON as models for characters, and drew wickedly savage caricatures of Jay GOULD, WILHELM II, EDWARD VII and Queen VICTORIA.

Since its first publication, *Connecticut Yankee* has remained in print continuously and is still available in many editions. In 1979, the MARK TWAIN PROJECT published the first corrected edition—which is also the first modern edition to use all of Beard's illustrations. With Clemens's corrected typescript no longer extant, the project drew on his original manuscript—now in the New York Public Library's Berg Collection—and on the *Century* extracts, which contain corrections not made in the Webster edition. The first edition of the book has also been reprinted in several facsimile editions, including a volume in the 1996 *OXFORD MARK TWAIN* edition. The Oxford edition includes a new introduction by novelist Kurt Vonnegut and an afterword by Louis J. Budd.

CRITICAL COMMENTARY

Many critics find *A Connecticut Yankee in King Arthur's Court* perplexing or confusing, while the general public has not been confused in its admiration. One of Mark Twain's most popular novels, *A Connecticut Yankee* has probably been presented in more variations than *Huckleberry Finn*, from silent and black-and-white to color films and musical productions, from movies to television. Children and radio technicians have crossed centuries to Arthur's court; Model-T Fords have replaced bicycles in rescuing the Yankee, and various means have transported the character from Connecticut in the, usually updated, era of a particular version to England in the medieval period.

What confounds critics about *Connecticut Yankee* is not its story idea or plot or humor per se but the character of the Yankee and the violent turn he and the plot take—a jarring clash of comedy and mass slaughter. This curious mix of humor and horror is more justifiable than some critics have realized or granted. The novel's popularity attests to the readiness of readers to accept and appreciate it in its many, even mixed, forms and genres. It is among the first time-travel stories and a foundation work of SCIENCE FICTION. Without contradicting other interpretations, it may also be read as the first science-fiction western, that is, as a novel figuratively of the American West set in Old England, manipulating western mythology with chivalric traditions.

Critics have considered the story of *Connecticut Yankee* as commentary on European and American political and economic imperialism and colonialism; on the potential of technology, with the threat of annihilation; on robber barons and evils of big business, including global corporations; on excessive (well intentioned or not) political power; on political corruption; on the South and slavery; on America's aristocracy of money; on superstition and unjust laws; on modern warfare; on apocalyptic fiction; and on utopian literature. The novel is also read as a simultaneous assault on the feudal world and on Victorian fascination with medievalism. By analogy, the novel does comment (negatively) on all of these topics, as the Yankee, thrown back to a primitive era compared to his fast-paced, invention-filled 19th century, quickly judges that his superiority can improve the culture and people's lives. Seized by the grandeur of his ideas and the simplicity of these people, the Yankee realizes he can, would, and should be the top man in the society he creates. Necessarily, bringing progress to a backward people and culture entails eliminating the society in place; similarly, in Clemens's time, eastern civilization was irrevocably altered as it pushed westward across America.

Misled by humor and folksiness, wanting to like him, readers sometimes mistake the Yankee for Clemens or an adult Tom Sawyer and expect consistency from that notion, but the Yankee is an unreliable narrator who may deceive the reader because he deceives himself. Some readers forget that his creator called him an ignoramus. He cannot be trusted because his purposes, initially well intended, begin as one thing and become another, usually to his aggrandizement. Shifts in tone or plot direction do not necessarily result from the author's changes of mind but from the character's growing megalomania.

The Yankee is a cowboy braggart with grandiose schemes to tame the frontier of primitive England, bringing civilization, which westerners ensure by taming the West. He is a cowboy in a mythical sense and in what have become pejorative senses. The Mythic Cowboy, often a stranger, enters a frontier outpost, eradicates a menace (e.g., outlaws), a barrier to civilization, and leaves. When civilization comes, his usefulness ends because, as part of the frontier, often molded by it, likely using uncivilized methods to eliminate obstacles, he is obsolete; if he marries and settles, he becomes part of the encroaching civilization, abandoning cowboy ways, for women and families represent civilization in westerns (Brown 37). The menace he perceives is the society itself, ironically using products of advanced civilization to overwhelm it. Like Clint Eastwood in his twist on the western myth in the 1973 film *High Plains Drifter*, the Yankee destroys the community to save it. He does marry and have a family, but settling dooms him, just as it threatens the newly married lawmen in Stephen Crane's "The Bride Comes to Yellow Sky" and the film *High Noon*.

In another sense, Hank is the stereotypical trail-herd cowboy who barges into a community and rides roughshod over inhabitants, enforcing his single-minded notions upon them. Literally treed by Sir Kay the seneschal, he probably kills Kay later, in the novel's apocalyptic climax. He dresses the Knights of the Round Table in sandwich boards touting products beyond their comprehension, tricking them into unknowingly demeaning themselves and the chivalric myth. He imposes no limits after his ascent to power, ordering hangings for minor offenses. Frightening ignorant people with a smoking pipe, the Yankee proclaims that his goal is to form a republic, but he uses fear, secrecy (conspiracy), deception, and advance knowledge to override the people's wishes to give them what he believes is best for them.

Also applicable to the Yankee is the post-19th-century sense of the cowboy as a reckless person who ignores potential risks. The Yankee wears blinders as he schemes with missionary zeal to plant American civilization in sixth-century England. In other works, such as "To the Person Sitting in Darkness," Clemens sarcastically applies the term *blessings of civilization* to American and European colonialist-imperialist-missionary exploitation of African and Asian native peoples. The Yankee also places blinders on the people by establishing secret factories and by training them in his thinking. He sets in motion events that lead to thousands of deaths and societal chaos.

The Myth of the Old West

No one disputes that *Connecticut Yankee*—with its time-travel plot, parallel worlds, and potential of altering histories and destinies—is an early science-fiction story, but few are aware that Mark Twain, with Bret HARTE and Crane, is a major purveyor of the Myth of the Old West (Slotkin 113; Brown 5), particularly in *Roughing It*. As a science-fiction western, *Connecticut Yankee* compares knights to cowboys; the Yankee, equivalent of the western stranger in town, also calls knights "white Indians," creating a double symbolism for the loss of two ways of life, Indian and frontiersman. The society he proposes is the encroaching civilization that ends their world, the "Lost World" of the subtitle; the last battle is the genocide of one race.

The so-called Code of the West surely has roots in chivalry. In the television western *Have Gun—Will Travel* (1957–1963), a chess knight is the symbol embossed on the holster and rifle of Paladin, defined by his name as a knightly champion and described in the show's theme song as a "knight without armor," a soldier-of-fortune whose "fast gun for hire heeds the calling wind." The name of the B-movie trigger trio, the Three Mesquiteers (1935–1943), based on novels by William Colt MacDonald, recalling the Three Musketeers, also evokes knightly associations. More recent book titles reflect the continuing connection: *The Real Wild Bill Hickok: Famous Scout and Knight Chivalric of the Plains—A True Story of Pioneer Life in the Far West* (1931), about a historical figure; *William Boyd: Hopalong Cassidy, Knight of the West* (1983), about a B-movie cowboy; *Knight in a White Stetson* (1999), a novel. An anthology of western writings contains this statement: "As the mythic Camelot had its knights, the mythic old West had its cowboys" (Hillerman 169).

The western protagonist is often a stranger in town. Being a "man without a name" reiterates his status there. Hank Morgan begins his story with "I am an American," then emphasizes he is a Yankee from Connecticut, "a Yankee of the Yankees" (Preface). Interestingly, he is from East Hartford but longs for a girl in West Hartford, figuratively a longing for what is lost and what is about to be lost. As the fictional cowboy in Owen Wister's *The Virginian* (1902), a novel where many western archetypes appear or begin, is southern, so people from all America comprise the westerner; as such, the westerner represents all Americans. Seth Jones, a popular dime-novel western hero (1860s onward), is from New Hampshire (Brown 27). An American stranger in ancient Britain, Hank becomes, like the television cowboy, "a knight without armor in a savage land," but supremely self-confident and shrewd.

Also significant is the Yankee's name. Not only is "Hank" western-sounding, but the surname, that of a type of horse, suggesting a rider or cowboy, is appropriate in other ways. That the name literally means "sea dweller" emphasizes the extent that he initially is a fish out of water in Camelot. On another level, others have noted allusions to the pirate Henry Morgan and the financier J. P. MORGAN as being pertinent to Hank's sometimes violent, sometimes economic exploitation of the people and country of Camelot. Often changed in movie versions to Martin—for instance, in those starring Will Rogers and Bing Crosby—perhaps to avoid confusion with Morgan le Fay, the surname possibly implies that Hank is closer to her villainy than is obvious to sympathetic readers. Hank himself deliberately suggests parallels between him and Merlin, the main villain.

The reader is told that Hank's father was a blacksmith, his uncle was a horse-doctor, and he was both at first. He later works for COLT ARMS FACTORY, where he learns to make guns, revolvers, cannon, boilers, engines, all sorts of labor-saving machinery. These three professional associations are metaphorical links to the West, the East, and technology. He serves a multiple symbolic role as the mythic cowboy whose actions open the West to the East by bringing technology (civilization). Including weapons among labor-saving machinery is ironic; they provide an easier means of killing people.

Morgan is a type of antihero; he begins as an apparent hero, but circumstances and his actions, spurred by egomania and arrogance, make him a villain. Because he considers himself not just the power behind the one called "His Majesty" but the real king with the real power, his initials ("H.M.") are appropriate to his assumed position and superiority.

Morgan does not, like the archetypal cowboy, ride into the sunset at the end of his adventure; rather, at the beginning, sentenced to die "at high noon," he predicts an eclipse, a symbolic sunset portending the eclipse of this culture by advancing civilization. Rather than save the community, Morgan says, "my eclipse would be sure to save me, and make me the greatest man in the kingdom besides" (chapter 6). This episode recalls earlier stories—clichés by Clemens's era—of white intruders, such as Columbus with a Moon eclipse and John Smith with a compass and gunpowder, awing Natives with technology.

Long before Wister called the frontier the "vanished world" in his preface to *The Virginian* (1902), Cooper's *Leatherstocking Tales,* noting "civilization's encroachment" and "the disappearing wilderness," foresaw the ending of the frontier, a fact increasing its allure and fascination. Although Slotkin says the frontier and its myth, fed by Cooper and "penny dreadful" newspapers, significantly contribute to Clemens's maturing as man and writer (113), the writer becomes disenchanted with the Myth of the West after experiencing life there, as retold in *Roughing It:* He finds no noble savages or eloquent woodsmen. Also initially captivated by Malory's tales of chivalry, he becomes tired of the mythology of knighthood, especially after reading in an unbowderlized edition of *Morte D'Arthur* "that the alleged glory days of British chivalry provide no admirable heroes, no moral or ethical standards, no inspirational ideals" (Bowden 180). Debunking and demythification in *Roughing It* and ambivalent aspiration and despair in *Connecticut Yankee* are the results.

Modern Technology

In 1869, 20 years before Mark Twain published *Connecticut Yankee,* the country he had crossed in 1861 by stagecoach—from Missouri to Nevada— was connected by railway from coast to coast. It had already been linked by telegraph during the Civil War. The Northern Pacific, the second transcontinental railroad, was completed (1883) the year before he began writing *Connecticut Yankee* (Brown 47). Technology holds the country together and also presages the end of the frontier. Control of technology is control of the land and the people. Morgan intends to be and briefly becomes the person with that power. "Unlimited power *is* the ideal thing when it is in safe hands," he says (chapter 10).

Morgan's original intention is the improvement, even the uplifting, of the lives of those under his rule, so as the symbolic stranger in town come to wipe out evil and injustice, he initially resembles the B-movie hero, "Wild" Bill Elliot, who would tell an opponent he was "a peaceable man," then roughly and thoroughly beat the man in a no-holds-barred fistfight. Like other strangers, Morgan achieves his goals with violence and death. His main weapon is technology. Appropriately, with technology as his primary instrument of conquest, Hank calls his daughter "Hello-Central" (his wife, Sandy, had given her the name). The name recalls for him Puss Flanagan, a telephone operator he had loved in 19th-century America, and by using the name, he expresses his longing for that world and, in a surprising turn, a loving connection to the new one. "Hello-Central," however, specifically derives from the Central Telephone Exchange. This medium of communication connects him to various spies and followers throughout the land and to secret outposts and hidden fortifications spread over the country, keeping him informed and all under his sway. The name may allude as well to the Central Pacific Railroad that linked with the Union Pacific to form the first transcontinental railroad, unifying the United States and ensuring the conquest of the West.

Viewing the people of Arthur's time as incapable of understanding the world he can bring, the Yankee becomes indifferent to what he and that civilization can inflict upon the people of this land

and time. Previously challenged to a duel by Sir Sagramour, he accepts a challenge to enter the tournament but arranges for the rules to be altered so that fighters may choose any weapons they desire. As the tournament begins, the self-assured Yankee, little needing an ego boost, hears one spectator shout encouragement to him, " 'Go it, slim Jim!' " (Chapter 39), which sounds more in place at a rodeo than a contest of knighthood. Hank peaceably pulls challengers from their horses with a lasso until it is stolen by Merlin; he then sounds like a cowboy walking into a deserted western street before a shootout: "Somebody was going to die this time. If he got the drop on me, I could name the corpse" (ibid).

The Chivalric Code

Although Arthur declares Hank weaponless after the loss of his lariat, Sir Sagramour defies the chivalric code by riding against an apparently unarmed man. Hank therefore has goaded the knights into breaking their own principles, the rules they live by that make them what they are. In the real western gunfights Clemens had actually observed in Nevada, men typically fired at each other, behind cover, usually with rifles or shotguns, not pistols if much distance was involved, but Hank describes a gunfight in terms like those that have become mythical: "I never budged so much as an inch till [he] had got within fifteen paces of me; then I snatched a dragoon revolver out of my holster, there was a flash and a roar, and the revolver was back in the holster before anybody could tell what had happened" (ibid.). The knights unknowingly witness the first fast draw, and, as in many descriptions in stories of the West, "a riderless horse" gallops away leaving its occupant, Sir Sagramour, lying "stone dead" (ibid.). Like the confident gunslinger, or like a smug boy throwing a dare, Hank Morgan shouts, " ' . . . I challenge all!' " (395). Before he empties his guns, he kills nine knights, and the others stop charging. With this successful western bluff, the knightly tournament has become not only a western rodeo but also a showdown or shootout.

Hank now confidently declares, "Knight-errantry was a doomed institution. The march of civilization was begun" (ibid). This march develops into the equivalent of mass murder three years later at the Yankee's last showdown, the Battle of the Sand-Belt, possibly meant to recall the real-life Sand Creek Massacre of Cheyenne and Arapaho by Colorado militiamen (1864). With 52 of his most trusted and trained followers, the Yankee kills thousands of knights with flooded trenches, Gatling guns, and electrified fences. Winning the battle but losing the war, Hank and his loyalists are trapped in their fortified cave by the bodies of those they have killed. These rotting and stinking corpses surrounding the Sand-Belt fortress sicken and kill most of Hank's supporters. Hank falls to the man he called a fraud, Merlin, the antithesis of his modernity.

Civilization and the Frontier

Inasmuch as Hank, directly and indirectly, calls the knights both "cowboys" and "Indians," when he destroys the massed chivalry of England, he symbolically destroys both the aboriginal and the frontier cultures of the West. Civilization overwhelms both. The white is transformed, gradually and quickly, and the Indian is practically eradicated. The loss of knight errantry is the loss of the frontiersman, roaming the territory finding adventure.

The historian Frederick Jackson Turner defined the frontier as the "meeting point between savagery and civilization." Henry David Thoreau wrote that the West symbolizes "absolute freedom and wildness" (qtd. in Brown 42). Huckleberry Finn, feeling restricted by civilization, reckons "I got to light out for the Territory ahead of the rest, because aunt Sally she's going to . . . sivilize me and I can't stand it," but Clemens abandoned his only effort to place Huck there when he abruptly stopped writing *Huck Finn and Tom Sawyer Among the Indians* the same year he began writing *Connecticut Yankee,* possibly because he realized that absolute freedom leads to absolute wildness. Hank Morgan finds himself in a land and, later, a position where he can practically make his own rules by force of will, ingenuity, guile, and—not necessarily a last resort—violence.

Civilization is paradoxical. It helps preserve life, largely by hindering freedom, but its advances can result in greater losses of life and of freedom. Ironically, like the westerner who brings law, or civiliza-

tion, through violence, Hank also loses what he fought for. However, unlike the typical cowboy who displaces himself by altering the frontier and moving to the next frontier to maintain his freedom, Hank even more graphically illustrates and foreshadows the end of this mythical figure because he quite literally has no place to go. The only frontier is oblivion. Caught between two worlds, he has lost the land whence he came as well as the land he found and altered. Too slightly does the Yankee realize how much a part of this frontier world he becomes in befriending Clarence, sympathizing with Arthur, marrying Sandy, and having a child. He had meant to remain above these people as a benevolent ruler, harsh when necessary, as he thought appropriate for "a superior man like me" (chapter 5). Even in marrying Sandy, he deceives himself: "She was a flawless wife and mother; and yet I had married her for no particular reasons, except that by the customs of chivalry she was my property until some knight should win her from me in the field" (chapter 41); he has accepted the Code of Chivalry, which he had scorned.

Civilization and Corruption

Connecticut Yankee demonstrates the horror but also the corruption that civilization can spawn. Hinting at the precariousness of Morgan's civilization is the stock market he establishes. The knights, particularly Launcelot, become speculators. Human greed and overreaching soon consume these men who had dedicated themselves to saving others, seeking the ideals of their society and of chivalry, finding the Holy Grail, and attaining purity. Speculation evokes buried pettiness that leads to manipulation of the market and swindling of each other. The result, their being men, is more pettiness and, their being knights, is war, dividing the kingdom when, in spite, some who lost money to Launcelot inform Arthur of the affair with Queen Guenever. Through the materialism generated by the market, Hank's civilization brings about its own fall.

In the archetypal western, peace occurs as the result of violence, opening the way for healthy growth. With that prospect, the westerner moves on before more people arrive at this now-livable community, bringing new laws and restrictions. In terms of the myth of the West, Hank Morgan's final shootout figuratively looks backward to the historic O. K. Corral (1881), the most famous gunfight of the Old West, and forward to the filmic massacre of hundreds at the end of *The Wild Bunch* (1969). It foreshadows the mass murder of which human beings are capable when they become more civilized. The West, civilization, and myth are scrutinized, as well as Arthur's and Hank's times and countries.

Setting the beginning of his novel 10 years before its date of publication, Mark Twain grants readers with knowledge of culminating events in that decade—including the last cattle drives, deaths of Billy the Kid (1881) and Jesse James (1882), final surrenders of Geronimo (1886) and Sitting Bull (1881)—a broader perspective on the closing of the West. He may have sensed what the 1890 U.S. Census appropriately revealed the year after his novel's release: "the frontier—defined as habitable area with fewer than two inhabitants per square mile—has disappeared" (Brown 48). The Lost Land, referred to in the title of the first chapter, refers not only to Hank Morgan's loss but also to that of the Mythic West.

Critical Commentary by John H. Davis

DRAMATIC ADAPTATIONS

Connecticut Yankee has long been one of stage and screen's most frequently adapted stories from Clemens's writings. Most adaptations set their FRAMES in the periods in which they are made, instead of going back to the novel's 1879 starting point. While typically emphasizing humorous contrasts between past and present, adaptations tend to expand the novel's romantic story line and add modern-day characters who parallel persons whom the Hank Morgan character meets in the sixth century—much like the dual characters in the 1939 film *The Wizard of Oz*. Most productions alter Hank Morgan's name—possibly to avoid confusion with Morgan le Fay—while retaining the character's sobriquet, "the boss," which is typically transformed into "Sir Boss."

In the first film version of *Connecticut Yankee* in 1921, Harry Myers (who later played the drunk millionaire in Charles Chaplin's 1931 film *City Lights*) starred as the Boss, "Martin Cavendish," after Douglas Fairbanks turned down the role. The film opens with Cavendish reading Clemens's novel and dreaming about introducing 20th-century technology to Camelot. The story line from this film was adapted to Richard Rodgers and Lorenz Hart's musical *A Connecticut Yankee* six years later. William Gaxton played the Boss, "Hank Martin," in the production, which had 418 performances on BROADWAY in 1927–28. The same play also had 45 performances in London in 1929 and was revived on Broadway in 1943. The updated 1943 production starred Dick Foran playing Hank as a member of the United States Navy during World War II. The 1943 version was in turn adapted to television in 1955, with Eddie Albert as Hank.

The first film adaptation using sound was also titled *A Connecticut Yankee;* however, it used an entirely new script. Released in 1931, this film cast the popular humorist and radio personality Will Rogers as a radio show host and technician named Hank Martin. Hank goes on a service call to the castle-like home of a wealthy eccentric, who claims to have invented a radio that can hear voices from the distant past. After Hank is knocked out by a falling suit of armor while listening to voices from King Arthur's time, he wakes up near Camelot. As in the novel, he is spared from being burned at the STAKE when an ECLIPSE darkens the sky. King Arthur (William Farnum) then dubs Hank "Sir Boss." This adaptation gave Rogers an opportunity to work in jokes about contemporary Depression-era issues and display his roping skills when Hank faces knights in a tournament.

The first color film adaptation of *Connecticut Yankee* came out in 1949. Also titled *A Connecticut Yankee*, it starred Bing Crosby as Hank Martin, an early 20th-century American blacksmith who turns up in Camelot after being knocked off his horse in 1905. This film emphasizes Hank's romance with Sandy (Rhonda Fleming) and has a completely new selection of songs unrelated to those of the earlier Rodgers and Hart musicals. Although Edmund Beloin's script often departs radically from the original novel, it is unusual in using a FRAME similar to that of the original novel. It begins with Hank visiting WARWICK CASTLE as a tourist and telling his

In the 1931 adaptation of *Connecticut Yankee,* Hank (Will Rogers) is dragged before the knights of the Round Table. *(Twentieth Century–Fox)*

story to its current owner (Cedric Hardwicke, who also plays King Arthur). At the end of his narrative, Hank is again in the castle in 1905, and he meets the lord's niece, who happens to be a dead ringer for Sandy.

Several later feature-film adaptations of *Connecticut Yankee* were produced by the Disney Company. The first Disney adaptation was made with the unlikely title of *Unidentified Flying Oddball,* which was later changed to THE SPACEMAN AND KING ARTHUR. Using little more than the central premise of *Connecticut Yankee,* this 1979 film sends an astronaut (Dennis Dugan) back to Camelot, where he immediately explains where he has come from and then struggles to return to his own time.

In 1995 Disney released *A Kid in King Arthur's Court,* in which a modern, baseball-playing California boy named Calvin Fuller (Thomas Ian Nicholas) goes back to the time of King Arthur (Joss Ackland) and saves Camelot from an evil nobleman with the help of MERLIN (Ron Moody).

Another film even more loosely inspired by *Connecticut Yankee* is *Black Knight* (2001), in which comic Martin Lawrence plays Jamal Walker (a. k. a. Skywalker), a hip young modern man working in a medieval theme park in Los Angeles. After Jamal falls into the park's castle moat and is knocked unconscious, he awakens in medieval England, where he becomes involved in a rebellion against an unlawful king. Although the film's historical setting is not King Arthur's time, the film's story is clearly inspired by *Connecticut Yankee.* A scene in which Jamal shows castle musicians how to play modern music owes a debt to a similar scene in the 1949 musical adaptation, in which Bing Crosby does almost exactly the same thing, though with much different music.

Connecticut Yankee has been adapted to television many times. Boris Karloff played Merlin against Thomas Mitchell's Boss in a 1952 *Studio One* play. Three years later, Karloff played King Arthur to Eddie Albert's Boss in an adaptation of the 1943 Broadway musical. Meanwhile, Edgar Bergen played the Boss in *Kraft Television Theatre's* 1954 production. Later television productions took on increasingly unusual qualities. In 1960, for example, Tennessee Ernie Ford starred in "A Tennessee Rebel in King Arthur's Court" in his own variety show. CBS-TV broadcast a feature-length animated *Connecticut Yankee* in 1970. Largely devoid of humor, this version was closer to the original story than most live-action adaptations and even included the apocalyptic battle of the SAND BELT. In 1978, CBS aired a considerably lighter animated version, *A Connecticut Rabbit in King Arthur's Court*, with Bugs Bunny. That same year, PBS-TV broadcast one of the most thoughtful adaptations of the original story, with Paul Rudd as the Boss, Richard Basehart as King Arthur, and Roscoe Lee Browne as a brooding Merlin who is not fooled by the eclipse.

In December 1989, NBC-TV celebrated the 100th anniversary of the novel's original publication with a new production that was the first television film to use the full title of the novel: *A Connecticut Yankee in King Arthur's Court.* This production cast a 12-year-old Hartford girl, Karen Jones (Keshia Knight Pulliam), in the role of "Sir Boss." Its script alternated between presenting faithful renderings of the novel's original dialogue and offering such radical departures as having the Boss leave Camelot in a hot-air balloon—a departure reminiscent of the wizard's exit from Oz in *The Wizard of Oz.* In mid-1992, the *MacGyver* television series presented a two-part episode loosely based on *Connecticut Yankee,* having the endlessly inventive MacGyver draw on all his skills to save Merlin and King Arthur from enemies. Three years

later, Canadian television contributed *A Young Connecticut Yankee in King Arthur's Court* (1995), in which a teenage boy named Hank Morgan (Philippe Ross) goes back to the time of King Arthur (Nick Mancuso). Another major departure in television adaptations was 1998's *A Knight in Camelot,* in which Whoopi Goldberg played the Boss role as Dr. Vivien Morgan, a modern American scientist who is accidentally sent back to King Arthur's time, taking her laptop computer with her.

CHARACTERS AND RELATED ENTRIES

Abblasoure Fictional English village in *Connecticut Yankee* (1889). Located in the kingdom of Bagdemagus, Abblasoure is about 10 miles south of the Valley of Holiness. After Hank Morgan and King Arthur visit the "Small-pox hut" near Abblasoure and see the manor house burn down, they stay with the charcoal burner Marco and his wife just outside the village (chapters 29–34).

Arthur, King Character in *Connecticut Yankee* (1889) and the chief figure in the national epic of England's early Middle Ages. Arthur has not been proven to be historical, but some historians regard him as a Celtic warrior who became legendary fighting the Saxons. By the 12th century, he was being transformed by romances into an epic figure: the king of all of Britain, endowed with great courage, wisdom and magnanimity. Arthur's importance in later literature grew until he became the central figure in such romances as THOMAS MALORY's *Le Morte d'Arthur* and Alfred Lord TENNYSON's *Idylls of the King.* In these epics and others, Arthur becomes king after receiving the magic sword Excalibur from the Lady of the Lake and meets his downfall after discovering that his wife Guenever is adulterously involved with his best friend, Sir Launcelot.

Of all the characters in *Connecticut Yankee,* only Hank Morgan appears more frequently than Arthur. Clemens adapts Arthur from Malory, retaining the legendary character's essential nobility and strength, while portraying him as a dimwitted daydreamer insensitive to his subjects' welfare. Hank's relationship to Arthur is a central thread in the narrative. He first meets the king at the court

Dan Beard's depiction of King Arthur in *Connecticut Yankee* reflects Thomas Malory's heroic image of the legendary figure.

excuse to proclaim England a republic, setting in motion the novel's final confrontation.

Though Hank describes Arthur as his own age—about 40 in chapter 40—Hank tends to look on him as a father figure. He never neglects to show him proper deference even after becoming the kingdom's most powerful person. Hank claims not to respect Arthur as a king but admits to admiring him as a *man*—particularly after Arthur risks his life to help a peasant family dying of smallpox (chapter 29). Immediately after this noble deed, however, Arthur disgusts Hank by suggesting they help capture the same family's sons, who have escaped the oppressor responsible for ruining the people Arthur has just helped.

Most actors who have portrayed King Arthur in screen adaptations of *Connecticut Yankee* depict him as considerably older than the character described in the novel. They include Charles Clary (1921), William Farnum (1931), Cedric Hardwicke (1949), Boris Karloff (1955), Richard Basehart (1978), Kenneth More (1979), and Michael Gross (1989).

Bagdemagus, King Background figure in *Connecticut Yankee* (1889), Bagdemagus (Bademagu in some Arthurian legends) never appears in the narrative, but is mentioned several times. In chapters 29–34, Hank Morgan and King Arthur pass through Abblasoure and Cambenet in Bagdemagus's tributary kingdom near the Valley of Holiness. Chapter 9 calls him *Sir* Bagdemagus, a knight whom Sir Gareth bests in a tournament, as well as father of Meliganus—who may be the Sir Meliagraunce who stabs Hank in chapter 44. Chapters 33 and 40 call him *King* Bagdemagus, and the latter lists him as a member of the Bessemers baseball team.

Boss, The Hank Morgan's unofficial title in *Connecticut Yankee* (1889). The novel's narrator and central character, Hank is identified three different ways. In the opening sequence, the FRAME-narrator (possibly Mark Twain himself) identifies Hank only as a stranger whom he calls "the YANKEE"—a name repeated in four chapter titles (11, 27, 34, and 39). Hank mentions his real name only twice within his narrative: In chapter 15, he imagines his 19th-century girlfriend calling him "Hank"; in chapter 39, he

in chapter 2 and becomes his first minister in chapter 6. Thereafter, Arthur has an active role in almost every chapter except those pertaining to Hank's mission with Sandy. In chapter 27, Arthur and Hank set out to tour the kingdom and are together continuously through chapter 38. Hank last sees Arthur two chapters later, before going to Gaul. After he returns to England, he learns that Arthur and Launcelot are waging a great civil war (chapter 42). Arthur's end comes much as it does in Malory, with Arthur and Mordred killing each other in battle. Arthur's death then gives Hank an

In the 1931 film *A Connecticut Yankee,* Will Rogers (right) wears a badge identifying him as "The Boss." The novel itself says nothing about a badge, but Hank can be seen wearing a similar badge in several of Daniel Beard's illustrations. *(Twentieth Century–Fox)*

quotes a newspaper article referring to him as "the King's Minister, Hank Morgan, the which is surnamed The Boss." This last name originates in chapter 8, in which Hank discusses his antipathy toward ranks and titles. He claims that he has never sought a title and even declined one when it was offered—presumably by King Arthur. The only title he wants is one issuing "from the nation itself." After running the kingdom for several years, he receives just such an honor when a village blacksmith coins a title that sweeps the nation and becomes the *only* name by which Hank is known thereafter. Translated into modern speech, this title is "the Boss." Hank relishes being a "The," since it makes him a "Unique"—like "*The* King" or "*The* Queen."

Although Hank is never formally knighted, five characters violate chivalric custom by calling him "Sir Boss": Sandy (chapter 19); Sir Ozana le Cure Hardy (twice in chapter 21); a telephone man named Ulfius (chapter 24); Queen Guenever (chapters 26 and 39); and even King Arthur (chapter 27).

Despite Hank's frequent protestations of democratic sentiments, he has a strong dictatorial bent that a title such as "the Boss" satisfies. Shortly after arriving in Camelot, for example, he expresses con-

fidence that he will "boss the whole country inside of three months" (chapter 2). He later expresses pride in demonstrating "what a despot could do with the resources of a kingdom" (chapter 10)—an ambition that recalls New York's corrupt political leader "BOSS" TWEED (1823–1878).

"THE BELATED RUSSIAN PASSPORT" (1902) has a character named Prince Bossloffsky.

Cambenet   English village in *Connecticut Yankee* (1889). In chapter 34, Earl Grip rescues Hank Morgan and King Arthur from angry peasants in Abblasoure and takes them about 32 miles south or southeast to Cambenet. The same day they arrive, they are sold into SLAVERY in an auction and marched off in a caravan that eventually takes them to LONDON.

Camelot   The legendary seat of England's King Arthur, Camelot is a principal setting in *Connecticut Yankee* (1889), whose narrator, Hank Morgan, is there through chapters 1–10 and 39–43. In common with many Arthurian legends—particularly those recorded since the 13th century—*Connecticut Yankee* depicts Camelot as a huge hilltop castle overlooking a town and a broad plain. The novel does not describe the castle in detail, but offers glimpses of a drawbridge, an arched gateway, towers, turrets and vaulted ceilings, as well as wall hangings that resemble the 11th-century Bayeux Tapestry (chapters 1–2)—all features suggesting architecture and culture of the High Middle Ages instead of the sixth century in which the story is set.

Camelot cannot be confidently linked to any historical site. Sir THOMAS MALORY—Clemens's major source—identified Camelot with Winchester, a city in southern England about 60 miles west-southwest of LONDON. This location conforms with *Connecticut Yankee*'s vague geography. The novel's best geographical clues appear in chapter 37, when Hank communicates with Camelot by TELEGRAPH from London. He orders Clarence to send 500 knights from Camelot to London, then calculates that at an average gait of seven miles per hour on horseback, the men should reach London in nine hours—including time to change horses twice. If we allow one hour for changing mounts, the knights would travel just over 55 miles at this rate. Furthermore, since haste is imperative, Hank instructs the knights to enter London at its *southwest* gate—a point suggesting that Camelot itself is southwest of London.

Evidence in chapter 24 suggests that the nearest route from Camelot to the sea lies to the *north,* and that the Valley of Holiness is about 75 miles *south* of Camelot. These details seem to rule out Camelot's being near Winchester, which is 20 miles north of the English Channel; however, *Connecticut Yankee's* geography should probably be regarded as tolerantly as that of the Mississippi River in *Huckleberry Finn's* latter chapters.

Camelot Weekly Hosannah and Literary Volcano

Newspaper in *Connecticut Yankee* (1889). Believing that he cannot modernize sixth-century England without a newspaper, Hank Morgan starts planning one in chapter 9 by having a priest cover a tournament. In the next chapter, he begins training Clarence as an editor. Hank sees the first issue of the *Hosannah* while he is in the Valley of Holiness in chapter 26. Though he relishes the paper's liveliness, he fears that its overall tone may be too irreverent.

Though the *Hosannah* is mentioned by name only in chapter 26, it is probably the same paper that Hank sees being peddled in London several months later (chapter 36), as well as the morning paper that he reads in Camelot in chapter 39. The next chapter jumps ahead three years, by which time there are several newspapers in the kingdom. When Hank returns from Gaul in chapter 42, he finds that Clarence has been keeping his newspaper going despite the Church's INTERDICT, while covering the civil war between King Arthur and Launcelot.

The title of the *Hosannah and Literary Volcano* resembles those of newspapers mentioned in "JOURNALISM IN TENNESSEE" (1869), such as the *Avalanche, Moral Volcano, Semi-Weekly Earthquake* and *Thunderbolt and Battle Cry of Freedom.*

Clarence (Amyas le Poulet)

Character in *Connecticut Yankee* (1889). The novel's most important newly invented male character—apart from the Yankee Hank Morgan himself—Clarence is a 15-year-old court page boy when Hank meets him in chapter 2. Hank immediately dubs him "Clarence"—possibly after EDMUND CLARENCE STEDMAN—and does not mention his real name, Amyas le Poulet, until chapter 13. Clemens probably takes this name from Sir Amyas Paulet (or Poulet) (c. 1536–1588), an English ambassador to France who was famous as the "keeper" of Mary Queen of Scots during the last two years of her life. Paulet was related to Lord St. John (Sir William Paulet) of *The Prince and the Pauper* (1881). In several ways, Clarence mirrors the historical Paulet in being Hank Morgan's "keeper." He is with Hank from his arrival at Camelot until his end at Merlin's Cave. He helps him in prison, becomes his right-hand man, rescues him from execution, and finally sees to the concealment of his body and the completion of his manuscript. Also like the historical Paulet, Clarence probably does not outlive his charge for long, as the novel ends with him in an apparently hopeless situation.

Clarence has a complex combination of traits. As an irreverent scoffer, he is a foil to Hank, much as Clemens's "Mr. Brown" was in his early travel writings. Clarence is wittier than Hank and enjoys his greatest comic triumph when he proposes replacing England's ruling family with a cat dynasty (chapter 40). Although Clarence has many modern attitudes to go with his natural skepticism, he also has many of the superstitions of his times. For example, when Hank claims to be able to blot out the sun early in the narrative, Clarence collapses in fright (chapter 5).

Clarence befriends Hank at court because he is naturally outgoing and talkative. On his first appearance, he closely resembles a young American in *A Tramp Abroad* (1880) who barrages the narrator with questions without waiting to hear the answers (chapter 27). After seven years pass, Clarence is taking on characteristics of a young Clemens, writing irreverent articles in the *Camelot Weekly Hosannah,* which Hank has trained him to edit. By the end of the narrative, he has adopted most of Hank's views and is the only person in the kingdom older than 17 who stands by Hank during the INTERDICT.

Hank's description of Clarence gives him androgynous characteristics that inspired the illustrator DAN BEARD to model him on the actress SARAH BERNHARDT.

Since he is not a fully rounded character, Clarence has not fared well in dramatic adaptations. In most films, his character simply disappears, with some of his functions distributed among other characters. When Clarence does appear in a film, he usually bears little resemblance to Clemens's character. Film actors who have played him include Charles Gordon (1921), Frank Albertson (1931), Rodney Bewes (1979) and Bryce Hamnet (1989).

A Danish Yankee in King Tut's Court   Musical adaptation of *Connecticut Yankee* (1889). On May 31 and June 1, 1923, New York's Institute of Musical Art staged this student production, with book and lyrics by Herbert L. Fields, Dorothy Crowthers, and Richard C. Rodgers and four songs by Lorenz Hart. Inspired by the opening of King Tut's tomb in Egypt three months earlier, these performances were evidently fund-raising events employing material being developed for the BROADWAY production of *A Connecticut Yankee* that opened four years later.

Dinadan the Humorist, Sir   Character in *Connecticut Yankee* (1889). The brother of La Cote Male Taile and a playful joker in MALORY's *Le Morte d'Arthur*, Dinadan is the object of Hank Morgan's scorn in *Connecticut Yankee* because all his jokes are stale. He first appears at Camelot's banquet hall, where he ties a mug to a dog's tail (chapter 4). Later he bores Hank with history's most tired joke—about a humorous lecturer who fails to raise a single laugh from his audience, then is told that he was so funny that it was all everyone could do "to keep from laughin' right out in meetin' " (chapter 9). Years later, Dinadan becomes England's first published author, but Hank suppresses his book because it contains the lecture joke and has him hanged (chapter 40).

Dowley   Character in *Connecticut Yankee* (1889). An Abblasoure blacksmith, Dowley is a boastful self-made man who twice becomes the target of Hank

Morgan's spite. In chapter 31, Hank invites Dowley and two other men to dinner at Marco's home, where Dowley brags about rising from orphanhood to prosperity. Hank relishes crushing Dowley by casually paying a huge bill for the banquet items. After dinner, he and Dowley argue about wage levels in their different realms. Dowley's inability to grasp the economic concept of real wages frustrates Hank, who tries to scare Dowley by hinting that he could be pilloried for overpaying workers. Instead, he throws Dowley and the others into a panic. When King Arthur makes things worse by babbling nonsense about agriculture, Dowley and the others attack him and Hank (chapters 32–34).

Flanagan, Puss   Background figure in *Connecticut Yankee* (1889). Remarks scattered through the novel indicate that before Hank Morgan came to sixth-century England, he had a girlfriend named Puss in Hartford who was half his age. In chapter 11, he tells Clarence that he is "as good as engaged to be married" to "Puss Flanagan" of "*East* Har—." Later he recalls his sweetheart as a 15-year-old TELEPHONE operator whom he used to call in the mornings just to hear her voice (chapter 15). Years later, he thinks about his "Hello-girl" from *West* Hartford at the moment of his triumph over the massed knights (chapter 39). Even after marrying Sandy, Hank dreams of Puss and cries out "Hello-Central" in his sleep. Thinking that Hank is calling out the name of a lost love, Sandy tries to please him by naming their baby "Hello-Central" (chapter 41).

In naming Puss Flanagan, Clemens may have been thinking of his childhood playmate and cousin Tabitha Quarles, who was known as "Puss" during the summers that he spent at his uncle John QUARLES's farm.

Galahad, Sir   Sir Launcelot's son in Arthurian legends, Galahad was said to be so pure that he alone succeeded in finding the Holy GRAIL. He is a minor character in *Connecticut Yankee* (1889). Hank Morgan first sees him in chapter 3, and lassoes him off his horse in chapter 39. Later Galahad becomes president of the stock-board, a post he sells to Launcelot (chapter 40).

In "THREE THOUSAND YEARS AMONG THE MICROBES," Sir Galahad is a college student and brother of Lemuel Gulliver.

Gareth, Sir (Garry) Minor character in *Connecticut Yankee* (1889). The favorite brother of Sir Gawaine in MALORY's *Le Morte d'Arthur*, Gareth appears twice in *Connecticut Yankee*. In chapter 9, Hank Morgan fondly calls him "Garry" and quotes a long journalistic account of a tournament in which Gareth defeats 14 other knights. As in Arthurian legend, Gareth is later accidentally killed by Sir Launcelot. This so angers Gawaine that he refuses to accept a settlement of Launcelot's war with King Arthur, giving the Church the pretext to lay down the INTERDICT (chapter 42).

Gawaine, Sir Minor character in *Connecticut Yankee* (1889). A central figure in Arthurian legends, Gawaine was the nephew of King Arthur and brother of Gareth and Gaheris. *Connecticut Yankee* first mentions him in chapter 15, in which Sandy recites a long tale about Gawaine's exploits taken from THOMAS MALORY's *Le Morte d'Arthur*. Following Malory, Clemens's novel makes Gawaine a major instigator in the civil war between Arthur and Sir Launcelot, who accidentally kills Gawaine's brothers while rescuing Guenever. Vowing revenge, Gawaine refuses to accept Arthur and Launcelot's peace settlement and is later killed while fighting with Arthur against Mordred.

Grail, Holy A Christian talisman associated with the cup Christ used at the Last Supper, the Holy Grail has been legendary since early medieval times. In the late 12th century, Arthurian romances began incorporating tales of knights searching for the Grail, which only knights who were free of sin—such as Sir Galahad—had a chance to find. Such quests figure prominently in THOMAS MALORY's *Le Morte d'Arthur* and ALFRED, LORD TENNYSON's *Idylls of the King*.

In *Connecticut Yankee* (1889) Sir Sagramour challenges Hank Morgan to fight, but immediately excuses himself since he is about to go "grailing" (chapter 9). Hank scoffs at the idea of expeditions spending years seeking the Grail, only to have other expeditions spend more years searching for them, and calls the Grail "the Northwest Passage of that day."

When Clemens was in LONDON in 1907, he visited Basil Wilberforce, the canon of Westminster Abbey, and was shown an object that was believed to be the Holy Grail. A scholar had found the relic after a clairvoyant divined its location. Clemens handled the object and seems to have accepted it as authentic. However, it was soon afterward dismissed as fraudulent.

Grip, Earl Minor character in *Connecticut Yankee* (1889). An important noble who lives near Cambenet, Grip rescues Hank Morgan and King Arthur from angry peasants and conveys them to Cambenet, where he sells them in a slave auction (chapter 34). Hank later escapes in LONDON and is arrested in a scuffle; the court frees him when he claims to be a slave of Grip (chapter 37).

Guenever, Queen Minor character in *Connecticut Yankee* (1889). In Arthurian legends, Guenever is the beautiful Roman wife of King Arthur and is coveted by the king's nephew Mordred. THOMAS MALORY began the enlargement of her role in the legends by making her the tragic lover of Sir Launcelot. Guenever rarely appears in *Connecticut Yankee* but betrays her interest in Launcelot as early as chapter 3. Later, Arthur wistfully remarks that Guenever is unlikely to notice his absence when Launcelot is around (chapter 26). Guenever speaks only once in the novel—when she remarks on Hank's not wearing armor before his combat with Sir Sagramour in chapter 39.

Three years later, Guenever's affair with Launcelot is revealed to Arthur while Hank is out of the country. Arthur orders her burned at the STAKE, starting a civil war. After Launcelot rescues Guenever, Mordred tries to make her marry him, but she eventually becomes a nun in Almesbury (chapters 41–42).

Hello-Central Minor character in *Connecticut Yankee* (1889). Hank Morgan's daughter, Hello-Central first appears in chapter 40, when she has an attack of the croup—similar to those that Clara Clemens suffered as a baby. It is not until the next chapter, however, that Hank explains that he married the baby's mother, Sandy, sometime during the previous three years. This chapter also recalls how Sandy chose "Hello-Central" for the baby's name—thinking it meant something dear to Hank, since he mumbles the words in his sleep. The phrase is actually one he used when calling his former girlfriend, Puss Flanagan, on the TELEPHONE in Hartford. When *Connecticut Yankee* ends, Sandy and Hello-Central are evidently stranded in France.

Hugo Minor character in *Connecticut Yankee* (1889). An approximately 30-year-old man whom Morgan le Fay's executioner is torturing in chapter 17, Hugo tells Hank Morgan that he killed a stag that was ravaging his fields, then dumped it in a forest to avoid detection. Though nominally guilty, he refuses to confess in order that his family not be stripped of everything they own. His wife, however, begs him to confess to end his suffering on the rack. Impressed by the couple's courage, Hank has Hugo freed and sends him to his Man Factory.

Interdict Ecclesiastical weapon that churches use to control communities by restricting their sacraments. During the Middle Ages, the Roman Catholic Church made especially effective use of the Interdict at a time when most western Europeans were Roman Catholics. In chapter 41 of *Connecticut Yankee* (1889), Hank Morgan returns to England from France to learn that the Archbishop of Canterbury has put the country under an Interdict. Though the Church aims the Interdict at King Arthur and Sir Launcelot's civil war, its real target is Hank, whose worst fears concerning an Established Church are confirmed. The Interdict wins back all but a handful of the thousands of people he trained in modern technology and politics, bringing his civilization to a sudden end.

Jones Pseudonym used in *Connecticut Yankee* (1889). In chapter 31, Hank Morgan tells the charcoal-burner Marco that King Arthur, his traveling companion, is a prosperous farmer named "Jones." Earlier, Hank pretends to Clarence that he is a magician who has known Merlin through centuries under many different names, including several of

Clemens's favorite stock names: Jones, Smith, Robinson, and Jackson (chapter 5).

Kay the Seneschal, Sir Character in *Connecticut Yankee* (1889). As the foster brother of King Arthur, Kay is a pervasive figure in Arthurian legends. In the prelude to *Connecticut Yankee*, Kay captures Hank Morgan the moment that Hank awakens in the sixth century. He takes Hank to Camelot in chapter 1, in which Hank calls Kay the "circus man" before learning his name in the next chapter. Kay then regales the court with a long story about Sir Launcelot's wearing his armor while capturing other knights (chapter 3). In chapter 4, Kay tells how he captured Hank, then suppresses a yawn as he orders Hank to be burned at the STAKE. Chapter 4 of *Pudd'nhead Wilson* (1894) alludes to the story of Launcelot and Kay, but reverses the knights' roles.

Seneschal is an Old French word for the household steward of a feudal lord.

La Cote Male Taile Minor character in *Connecticut Yankee* (1889). The brother of Sir Dinadan, La Cote is the "missionary knight" promoting soap whom Hank Morgan and Sandy encounter near Morgan le Fay's castle in chapter 16. In a tale taken from THOMAS MALORY, La Cote's chief fame rests on an excursion similar to Hank and Sandy's that he once made with a foulmouthed damsel aptly named Maledisant.

Launcelot of the Lake, Sir Character in *Connecticut Yankee* (1889). In medieval Arthurian legends, Launcelot is a central figure as King Arthur's bravest knight. Later retellings of these legends—notably those of THOMAS MALORY and ALFRED, LORD TENNYSON—emphasize how Launcelot's adulterous affair with Queen Guenever leads to a civil war that destroys the kingdom. This same event brings down Hank Morgan's civilization in *Connecticut Yankee*. Nevertheless, of all the traditional Arthurian characters who appear in this novel, Launcelot is treated with the most respect.

Connecticut Yankee mentions Launcelot frequently but gives him no significant role until chapter 38, when he leads 500 knights mounted on bicycles from Camelot to London to rescue Hank and the king. In the next chapter, Launcelot is among the knights whom Hank unhorses with his lasso. Filled with admiration for Hank's courage, Launcelot then offers to fight Sir Sagramour in his place after Merlin steals Hank's lasso. Three years later, Hank sees Launcelot for the last time when both men sit up all night watching croup-afflicted Hello-Central (chapter 40).

After Hank leaves England, Launcelot becomes president of the stock-board and makes a killing that provokes Mordred and Agravaine to tell Arthur about his affair with Guenever, thus touching off the destructive civil war (chapter 42).

Man Factory   Training center in *Connecticut Yankee* (1889). A central theme running through this novel is the idea that a person's beliefs and reasoning powers are solely the product of training. Recognizing that he cannot achieve the political and social revolution he desires without fundamentally retraining people, Hank Morgan creates an academy to which he alludes occasionally as a "Man Factory" whose mission is to "turn groping and grubbing automata into *men*" (chapter 17). He first mentions the factory in chapter 13, when he sends a spirited peasant to report to Clarence there for training. Aside from promising the man that he will learn to read and that no priests are connected with his factory, Hank says nothing about who runs it, where it is, or what else it teaches.

Morgan's conception of the "Man Factory" seems to anticipate the concept of a "character factory" that lay behind Robert S. S. Baden-Powell's (1857–1941) creation of the Boy Scout movement in the early 20th century. After serving in the South African (Boer) War, Baden-Powell returned to Great Britain in 1902, feeling a need to do something to strengthen the moral and physical fiber of British youth. He launched the Scout movement with the idea of creating a "character factory" that would raise standards of idealism and patriotism. Whether he got the idea from *Connecticut Yankee*'s "Man Factory" remains to be shown.

Marco, the son of Marco   Character in *Connecticut Yankee* (1889). A charcoal-burner living near the village of Abblasoure, Marco figures prominently in chapters 30–34, in which Hank Morgan and King Arthur stay with him and his wife after visiting his cousins' "Small-pox Hut." The night before Hank meets him, Marco is out helping to hang neighbors suspected of burning down the manor house and killing the local lord. Hank nevertheless regards Marco as an essentially good-hearted man drawn into mob actions out of fear. Marco himself is immensely relieved to learn that Hank shares his dislike for the nobility. Later, Marco basks in glory at the banquet that Hank stages for Dowley and other leading village artisans at his home. However, Marco is quick to join the others in turning against Hank and the king when they appear to be dangerous.

Marco first appears in chapter 30 but is not named until the next chapter, in which Hank calls him "Marco," or "Marco, the son of Marco." Hank calls Marco's good-natured wife "Dame Phyllis" (chapter 31) and "Mrs. Marco" (chapter 33) and refers to the couple as "the Marcos" (chapters 31–32).

Merlin   Character in *Connecticut Yankee* (1889). Since the mid-12th century, Merlin has been a central figure in Arthurian legends, usually as a powerful sorcerer and benevolent counselor to King Arthur, whom he helped to put in power. Nineteenth-century writers depicted Merlin as a simpler but often menacing wizard—a trend to which Mark Twain's *Connecticut Yankee* contributed. His novel makes Merlin both the primary adversary and comic foil of Hank Morgan, who regards him as an old numskull handicapped by belief in his own magic (chapter 22).

Merlin first appears in Camelot's banquet hall, where he puts everyone *but* Hank to sleep with his weary tale about taking Launcelot to the Lady of the Lake (chapter 3). The scene is the antithesis of the final chapter, in which Merlin puts *Hank* to sleep for 13 centuries. After Hank is put in the dungeon, he determines to prove himself a greater magician than Merlin by threatening to blot out the sun (chapter 5). Merlin ridicules Hank's threat and is the person most eager to burn him at the STAKE; however, he fails to turn back the ECLIPSE, leaving Hank his vanquisher (chapter 6). Hank later gives Merlin another chance to demonstrate

Merlin has more than an accidental resemblance to Alfred, Lord Tennyson in Dan Beard's illustrations for *Connecticut Yankee.*

his power before he blows up Merlin's tower, lowering Merlin's reputation even more. King Arthur suggests banishing Merlin, but Hank keeps him on the payroll as a weatherman, refusing to take him seriously (chapter 7).

Hank and Merlin meet again in the Valley of Holiness, where Merlin's incantations fail to restart a holy fountain. Merlin declares that the spell over the fountain is unbreakable, giving Hank yet another opportunity to embarrass him (chapters 22–26). Merlin's next humiliation occurs in chapter 39, in which he fails to help Sir Sagramour defeat Hank in a tournament. Seeing the encounter as the "final struggle for supremacy between the two mas-

ter enchanters of the age," Hank gains another spectacular triumph, leaving Merlin's reputation flatter than ever.

Merlin plays no role in the monumental confrontation between Hank and the Roman Catholic Church several years later, but Hank and his tiny army convert Merlin's cave into the headquarters of their coming war against the massed chivalry of England. After they annihilate thousands of knights, they are trapped inside the cave by the corpses encircling them. Disguised as an old woman, Merlin enters the cave and casts the spell that makes Hank sleep until the late 19th century. Merlin then runs into an electrified fence and dies with a triumphant laugh frozen on his face.

Joan of Arc (1896) mentions Merlin as having prophesied Joan's coming 800 years earlier (book 2, chapter 2). This allusion contrasts sharply with *Connecticut Yankee,* in which Hank belittles Merlin for being unable to prophesy more than a few years into the future (chapter 27).

The many character actors who have played Merlin in screen adaptations of *Connecticut Yankee* include Brandon Hurst (1931); Murvyn Vye (1949); Boris Karloff (1952), who also played King Arthur on television two years later; Victor Jory (1954), who played Injun Joe in the 1938 adaptation of *Tom Sawyer;* Roscoe Lee Browne (1978); Ron Moody (1979 and 1995), and Rene Auberjonois (1989).

Mordred, Sir   Character in *Connecticut Yankee* (1889). A complex figure in Arthurian legends, Mordred is usually depicted as the son of Morgan le Fay—in some accounts he is her son by King Arthur's unintentional incest with his sister. In *Connecticut Yankee,* Mordred appears only in chapter 42, which identifies him as a nephew of Arthur's who triggers the civil war by revealing to the king Guenever's adulterous affair with Launcelot. As in the legends, Mordred then tries to seize both the kingdom and Guenever for himself, until he and Arthur kill each other in battle. The novel's newspaper account of this final confrontation remarks that Mordred "smote his father Arthur."

Morgan, Hank (The Boss)   Narrator and title character of *Connecticut Yankee* (1889). One of

Clemens's most complex creations, Hank Morgan embodies many of the contradictions of Clemens himself, as well as traits of characters as diverse as Tom Sawyer, Huckleberry Finn, and Colonel Sellers. Possible models for Hank are numerous; in addition to Clemens, they range from Charles Heber CLARK's fictional Professor Baffin to the Hartford inventor JAMES PAIGE. In the novel's prelude, set around 1889, the FRAME-narrator introduces Hank as a stranger he meets in WARWICK, England. Hank begins a fantastic story about going back to sixth-century England, then retires to bed, leaving the frame-narrator to read the rest of his story from his first-person manuscript—which becomes the core of the novel. The book concludes with the narrator finishing his reading and revisiting Hank just before Hank dies (chapter 44).

Clues scattered throughout *Connecticut Yankee* reveal Hank's background. When he arrives in Camelot in chapter 2, he gives 1879 as the year from which he has come; later developments indicate that about 10 years pass before Merlin returns him to his own time by putting him to sleep. Not long before this happens, Hank gives his age as 40 (chapter 40); he therefore must be about 30 when he comes to Camelot, putting his birth date around 1849—a date that supports his remark about being a boy during President BUCHANAN's administration (chapter 11).

Born and raised in Hartford, Connecticut, Hank calls himself a practical and unsentimental YANKEE. His father was a blacksmith and his uncle a horse doctor; he himself was both before going to work at the COLT ARMS FACTORY. There he supervised several thousand men and learned to make everything from guns, boilers, and engines to diverse labor-saving devices—an inventive talent that he uses to modernize sixth-century England.

Though Hank presents himself as a man without formal education, he reveals a wide knowledge of history and literature. He knows exactly when two sixth-century ECLIPSES occurred (chapters 2 and 7); he confidently discusses history from the 19th century back to the sixth century and even earlier (chapters 27 and 33); and he has a special interest in the French Revolution (chapters 13 and 20). An admirer of history's greatest inventors, he is familiar with the work of Johannes Gutenberg, James Watt, Richard Arkwright, Eli Whitney, Samuel Morse, George Stephenson, and Alexander Graham Bell (chapter 33). His reading includes Henry Fielding's *Tom Jones*, Tobias Smollett's *Roderick Random*, SIR WALTER SCOTT (chapter 4); Alexandre Dumas (chapter 18); DANIEL DEFOE's *Robinson Crusoe* (chapter 7), BENVENUTO CELLINI (chapter 17); Casanova (chapter 18); Geoffrey Chaucer's *Canterbury Tales* (chapter 21); and *HAMLET* (chapter 39). His comments on early GERMAN and his use of German tongue twisters suggest that he speaks that language (chapter 22). Despite his literacy, however, he retains certain vulgar tastes, such as liking tacky 19th-century chromos (chapter 7).

Hank's early travels probably took him to the Midwest, the South, and possibly the West. He

Hank Morgan as the Boss in *Connecticut Yankee*

knows what STEAMBOAT explosions look like (chapter 27), as well as sunsets over the upper MISSISSIPPI (chapter 39). He is familiar with etiquette in ARKANSAS (chapter 3) and with journalism there and in ALABAMA (chapters 10 and 26). And somewhere, he learned western horsemanship and roping skills that he uses in a tournament (chapter 39). He has also picked up an INDIAN trick of making fake tobacco from willow bark (chapter 12).

Although Hank seems to shun vigorous physical activity, his background and several incidents in the narrative indicate that he must be strong and robust. In describing his arms factory job, he implies that he fought with his men frequently. He also demonstrates his toughness in episodes in which he and King Arthur take on an angry mob (chapter 34), he escapes from a slave caravan (chapter 36), and he faces ironclad knights on the tournament field (chapter 39). In general, his health seems good, though he has a bad cold and rheumatism in chapter 24 and once had smallpox (chapter 30).

Like Tom Sawyer, Hank loves impressing people with gaudy effects—from spectacular public displays such as blowing up Merlin's tower (chapter 7) and restarting the fountain in the Valley of Holiness (chapter 23) to such simple things as hosting a banquet for commoners (chapter 32). He also has Tom's eye for showy details; he enjoys the theatricality of having 500 knights on bicycles rescue him and Arthur from the gallows but regrets not pulling off the stunt at high noon (chapters 37–38).

Hank shares Colonel Sellers's entrepreneurial zeal. Appointed the king's prime minister, he immediately acts to increase revenues by putting everything possible on a paying basis—including the tournaments (chapter 9) and knight-errantry itself (chapter 19). He runs a successful insurance business (chapter 30), converts a holy hermit into a money-making sewing machine (chapter 22), and has knights scour the country promoting soap, toothbrushes, stove polish, and other products.

Although Clemens establishes *why* Hank can do what he does, he has him accomplish far more than one man—however gifted—could possibly do in such a short period of time. Hank not only organizes factories to make everything from soap, tooth-

brushes, paper, and matches to bicycles, steam engines, TELEPHONES, and electric dynamos, he also must personally develop *every* scrap of technology, from MINING and processing raw materials to making parts for his machines. Not satisfied with doing all this and administering the kingdom, he also organizes a patent office, an insurance company, newspapers, and a stock-board, and somehow sets up schools and training institutions such as his "Man Factory" and his WEST POINT. Meanwhile, he still finds time to attend tournaments and to travel. He gets excellent help from Clarence, but his right-hand man cannot know anything about modern technology beyond what Hank teaches him.

As a voice for Clemens's political and social ideas, Hank talks constantly about free will and democratic principles, while maintaining a stubborn belief in a mechanistic philosophy that contradicts these same sentiments. For all his expressed idealism, he ultimately regards human beings as little more than machines. One moment, for example, he praises Marco for demonstrating his manhood by denouncing his manor lord (chapter 30). Only moments later, however, he sees Marco sniff at a slave and disgustedly suggests that "there are times when one would like to hang the whole human race and finish the farce" (chapter 31). By the end of the novel, Hank nearly does just that, when he and his few remaining followers annihilate nearly 30,000 knights—who presumably include many men he has earlier described as friends (chapter 43).

Hank's attitude toward women is puritanical. His first known contact with a woman does not occur until after he has been in Camelot for several years, when Arthur assigns him to rescue damsels from ogres. When Hank realizes that he must travel alone with a young woman whom he calls Sandy, he is scandalized and protests that he is practically engaged to a certain Puss Flanagan (chapter 11). Sandy bores Hank, but he cannot get rid of her, even after several years. He finally marries her, largely to avoid compromising her further (chapter 41). After a year of marriage, however, he unaccountably calls her the perfect mate and extols her virtues in terms that Clemens customarily saved for his own wife. Nevertheless, Hank cannot put his former sweetheart entirely out of his mind.

After calling this character "Sir Robert Smith" in his earliest draft of *Connecticut Yankee*, Clemens renamed him "Hank Morgan." A common nickname for "Henry," "Hank" is a near-homophone of "Yank." Industrialist J. P. MORGAN has been suggested as Clemens's inspiration for Hank's surname. Another candidate is the 17th-century PIRATE Henry Morgan, whom England rewarded with high offices and a knighthood. Some scholars see a meaningful similarity between Hank Morgan's name and that of the queen Morgan le Fay of legend; however, Hank's account of his visit to the evil queen curiously fails to comment on this similarity. Hank's name, in fact, appears just twice in the novel. In chapter 15, he dreams of telephoning Puss Flanagan and hearing her say "Hello, Hank!" In chapter 39, he reads a Camelot newspaper story about his coming tournament combat that calls him "Hank Morgan." Meanwhile, Hank is known as "The Boss" from chapter 8 until the end.

Connecticut Yankee's illustrator DANIEL BEARD modeled his drawings of Hank on a Connecticut man named George Morrison, a photoengraver who worked next to his studio.

As the central character in *Connecticut Yankee*, a Hank Morgan character has appeared in every dramatic adaptation of the novel, but often in different guises and under different names. Since the 1927 musical adaptation, he has most often been called "Hank Martin"—possibly to avoid confusion with Morgan le Fay. In most cases, however, he is also called "the Boss" or "Sir Boss." Actors who have played the Boss include Harry C. Myers (1921), William Gaxton (1927), Will Rogers (1931), Dick Foran (1943), Bing Crosby (1949), Edgar Bergen (1954), Eddie Albert (1955), Paul Rudd (1978), Whoopi Goldberg (as "Vivian Morgan," 1998), and 10-year-old Keshia Knight Pulliam (1989).

Morgan le Fay, Queen   Character in *Connecticut Yankee* (1889). Morgan is the wife of King Uriens, with whom she rules a realm the size of the District of Columbia that is tributary to her brother King Arthur. In Arthurian legends, Morgan is typically vested with magical powers. In some versions she is the mother of Mordred—often by her brother Arthur, whom she hates. Descended from Celtic deities, she was originally a "fay," or fairy, untouched by time who has degenerated into a mortal who must use magic to keep from aging.

Morgan appears in chapter 16–18 of *Connecticut Yankee*, when Hank Morgan and Sandy stay at her castle. Hank describes her as the sister of Arthur but only hints at her possessing magical powers. Knowing of her evil reputation, Hank expects her to be old and repulsive, but is surprised to find her beautiful and youthful-looking enough to pass for her husband's granddaughter. He does not say how old she is, but his description of prisoners in her dungeon suggests that she and her husband have occupied their castle at least 22 years and no more than 35 years.

Aside from her unaccountable youthfulness, Morgan reveals no real magical powers in *Connecticut Yankee*; in fact, she has a terrible dread of Hank's purported powers. Her most conspicuous trait is heartless and mindless vindictiveness. For example, she kills a page boy for a trivial offense (chapter 16) and she has psychologically tortured a prisoner for 22 years because he said that she has "red" hair—which she has. After Hank releases 47 prisoners from her dungeon, Morgan wants to go after them with an ax (chapter 18).

DAN BEARD's illustration of Morgan dresses her in a jewel-adorned costume made famous by SARAH BERNHARDT on the stage.

Sagramour le Desirous, Sir   Character in *Connecticut Yankee* (1889). A short-tempered knight, Sagramour overhears something Hank Morgan says about another knight and takes it as an insult directed at him. He challenges Hank to a duel, but sets a date three or four years in the future to give himself time to seek the HOLY GRAIL (chapter 9). Several years later, Hank reads in the *Camelot Weekly Hosannah* that Sagramour is lost and that a new expedition is about to search for him (chapter 26).

When Sagramour finally fights Hank in chapter 39, Merlin casts an enchantment intended to make him invisible to Hank, who nevertheless rides circles around him and ropes him off his horse to win the combat. After Hank defeats seven more knights, Merlin steals his lasso and Sagramour challenges

Hank again. This time Hank shoots Sagramour dead with a revolver; he then defeats all the knights at once.

The bullet hole that Hank makes in Sagramour's chain-mail is the only physical evidence that survives from the sixth century to prove that Hank was actually there. In the 19th-century prelude to *Connecticut Yankee,* Hank tours WARWICK Castle's armor collection with the FRAME-narrator and laughs when their guide points out the bullet hole, suggesting that it was made by Cromwell's soldiers. The narrative of *Connecticut Yankee* thus begins as an explanation of how Hank came to shoot Sagramour.

Clemens's use of the bullet hole as a plot device may go back to his visit to PARIS's Bois de Boulogne in 1867, when a guide showed him a tree with a bullet hole made by a would-be assassin of Czar ALEXANDER II. In *Innocents Abroad* (1869) he predicts that guides will point out that hole to visitors until the tree falls down in 800 years, then put up another one and keep telling the same story (chapter 14).

Sand Belt   Fictional battle site in *Connecticut Yankee* (1889). The "Sand Belt" is a defense perimeter that Clarence sets up around Merlin's Cave, where Hank Morgan and his tiny army take on the massed chivalry of England. Forty feet wide, the belt lies 100 yards beyond the last of a series of electrified fences that surround the cave. It is laced with explosive torpedoes covered with a thin layer of sand (chapter 42). When the first wave of knights enters the belt, they are blown to bits, leaving a deep ditch in its place (chapter 43). Afterward, Hank congratulates his men on winning the "Battle of the Sand-Belt," then puts them to work diverting the course of a nearby stream. When the next wave of attackers fills the ditch, he floods it with the stream's waters, drowning thousands of knights. The scenario resembles an incident in America's CIVIL WAR, when Union troops besieging Petersburg, Virginia, were trapped and killed in a crater formed by a mine blast.

Sandy (Demoiselle Alisande la Carteloise)
Character in *Connecticut Yankee* (1889). The novel's most important female character, Sandy

first appears at Camelot in chapter 11, when she relates a tale about three ogres' holding 44 beautiful princesses captive for 26 years. Every knight begs permission to rescue the women, but King Arthur assigns the mission to Hank Morgan. Hank then interviews the Demoiselle Alisande—whom he nicknames "Sandy" in the next chapter. The only solid information that he gets out of her is that she is from the land of Moder, has no family, and is new to Camelot. He then takes her with him on his mission, remaining constantly uncomfortable with what he regards as the impropriety of traveling unchaperoned with a woman.

Throughout his mission, Hank regards Sandy as a airheaded BLATHERSKITE who relates interminable tales and disgraces the human race by abasing herself before hogs that she thinks are princesses (chapter 20). Hank is anxious to get rid of her, but discovers that she is unshakably committed to staying with him. Meanwhile, Sandy repeatedly proves

Sandy helps Hank cool off in his armor in chapter 12 of *Connecticut Yankee.*

herself more decisive than Hank. She secures the surrender of seven knights whom Hank frightens by blowing tobacco smoke through his helmet (chapter 14) and twice cows Morgan le Fay into backing down (chapters 16–17).

Hank's relationship with Sandy changes in the Valley of Holiness, where she nurses him through an illness. One day, after he belittles her failure to grasp his modern slang, he realizes how hard she tries to please him, and he apologizes. As their friendship improves, Hank senses that he is developing "a mysterious and shuddery reverence" for Sandy (chapter 22). In chapter 27, he leaves her behind when he and Arthur tramp off disguised as peasants. Sandy reappears momentarily in chapter 36, when Hank spots her looking for him in London.

In chapter 40, the narrative jumps ahead three years, by which time Hank and Sandy have a daughter named Hello-Central. In the next chapter, Hank explains that he has married Sandy because he could not get rid of her and did not want to compromise her. Nevertheless, he has become Sandy's worshipper after a year of marriage and calls her a "flawless wife and mother," His description of their relationship as the "dearest and perfectest comradeship that ever was" mirrors Clemens's description of his own MARRIAGE. Despite Hank's lavish praise of Sandy, however, he is still thinking about his old girlfriend, Hartford telephone operator Puss Flanagan, as late as chapter 39. He seems to be dreaming about Puss even after marrying Sandy, who overhears him call out "Hello, Central!" in his sleep.

Hank and Sandy last see each other in Gaul, where they go for Hello-Central's health. After Hank returns to England to confront the massed chivalry of the country at Merlin's Cave, he writes to Sandy daily, though there is no way for him to post letters to her (chapter 43). After he returns to the 19th century, he dies calling out Sandy's name. DANIEL BEARD, whose illustrations model Sandy on the actress Annie Russell (1869–1936), suggests a happier ending for the book. His final picture shows Hank, Sandy, and the baby reunited over a supine Father Time.

Actresses who have portrayed Sandy on screen include Pauline Starke (1921), Maureen O'Sullivan (1931), Rhonda Fleming (1949), Sally Gracie (1954), Janet Blair (1955), and Sheila White (1979). Constance Carpenter (1927) and Julie Warren (1943) played Sandy in BROADWAY musical adaptations.

"Small-pox Hut"   This title of chapter 29 of *Connecticut Yankee* refers to the house of a destitute English peasant family whom Hank Morgan and King Arthur meet on the day the mother, her husband, and her two daughters succumb to smallpox. At great peril to the king—who unlike Hank has never had smallpox—the men ease the woman's sufferings and wait with her until she dies, leaving the house just before her three adult sons return. The sons are freshly escaped from Abblasoure's manor house prison and know nothing of their family's troubles until this moment. In the next chapter, Abblasoure's lord is murdered and his house burned down. Suspicion immediately falls on friends and relatives of the "Small-pox Hut" family, and the murdered lord's retainers wreak a terrible vengeance. Meanwhile, Hank and the king find hospitality in the home of the family's relative Marco—who has escaped the purge.

The Spaceman and King Arthur (_Unidentified Flying Oddball_)   One of the loosest adaptations of *Connecticut Yankee* (1889) yet filmed, this 1979 Disney movie sends an inept astronaut back in time to Camelot. An inventor named Tom Trimble (Dennis Dugan) builds a robot that resembles him for an interstellar space flight, then accidentally takes off in the spaceship—which unaccountably delivers him to sixth-century England. In contrast to most adaptations of Clemens's novel, Don Tait's screenplay has Trimble immediately explain who he is and where he comes from, then concentrate on returning to his own time. Trimble also draws on his knowledge of history to warn King Arthur (Kenneth More) that Mordred (Jim Dale) and Merlin (Ron Moody) are plotting to take over his kingdom. Using 20th-century gadgetry and know-how, Trimble helps Arthur defeat his foes, then flies off in his spaceship. The script contains a Clarence character (Rodney Bewes), but its Sandy character (Sheila White) is much closer to the spirit of Clemens's original Clarence.

Valley of Holiness Fictional place in *Connecticut Yankee* (1889). A monastic center located near the Cuckoo Kingdom, the Valley of Holiness appears to be about 75 miles south of Camelot. After completing their mission of rescuing damsels from ogres, Hank Morgan and Sandy enter the valley with a band of PILGRIMS, who are anxious to cleanse their sins in water from the valley's holy fountain. Coincidentally, the fountain stops flowing about 10 days before Hank arrives. He discovers that the fountain is an ordinary well with a leak, which he repairs; then he restarts its water beneath a spectacular fireworks display (chapter 23). After this "miracle," he contracts a bad cold and stays in the valley to rest. Meanwhile, King Arthur arrives with part of his court. A few days later he and Hank begin a journey disguised as freemen, leaving the valley in a direction that takes them farther from Camelot (chapter 27).

Originally an arid site, the valley's importance as a religious center began several hundred years earlier when ascetic monks established a monastery. When a stream miraculously appeared, they built a bath and the water stopped flowing. After the abbot destroyed the bath, however, the waters returned and the valley became famous. At the time of Hank's visit, it has a population of several hundred monks and nuns and an unspecified number of holy hermits, as well as a large transient population of pilgrims. Clemens drew some of his ideas for the valley's holy fountain and ascetic hermits from the writings of W. E. H. LECKY.

A Yankee at the Court of King Arthur Title under which CHATTO and Windus published the English edition of *A Connecticut Yankee in King Arthur's Court* in London in December 1889. "A Yankee *in* the Court of King Arthur" is stamped on the spine and front cover of early American editions. While Chatto dropped "Connecticut" from the title to avoid confusing British readers, the American edition evidently dropped the word in order to save space.

BIBLIOGRAPHY

Bowden, Betsy. "Gloom and Doom in Mark Twain's *Connecticut Yankee*, from Thomas Malory's *Morte Darthur*." *Studies in American Fiction* 28, no. 2 (Autumn 2000): 179–202.

Brown, Bill, ed. "Reading the West: Cultural and Historical Background." In *Reading the West: An Anthology of Dime Westerns*, 1–40. Boston: Bedford, 1997.

Carter, Everett. "The Meaning of *A Connecticut Yankee*." *American Literature* 50, no. 3 (November 1978): 418–439.

Clark, William Bedford. "How the West Won: Irving's Comic Inversion of the Westering Myth in *A Tour on the Prairies*." *American Literature* 50, no. 3 (November 1978): 335–347.

Hillerman, Tony, ed. "The Spree at the End of the Trail." In *The Best of the West: An Anthology of Classic Writing from the American West*, 169–170. New York: Harper, 1991.

Ketterer, David, ed. "Introduction." In *Tales of Wonder by Mark Twain*, xiii–xxxiii. Lincoln: University of Nebraska, 2003.

Slotkin, Richard. "Mark Twain's Frontier: Hank Morgan's Last Stand." In *Mark Twain: A Collection of Critical Essays*, edited by Eric J. Sundquist, 113–128. Englewood Cliffs, N.J.: Prentice Hall, 1994.

Twain, Mark. *A Connecticut Yankee in King Arthur's Court*. Edited by Bernard Stein. Berkeley: University of California Press, 1979.

"Corn-pone Opinions"

Posthumously published ESSAY. This exercise of just over 2,000 words explores an idea that is central to the philosophy that Clemens developed in WHAT IS MAN?—namely, that humans are incapable of independent thought. He wrote the essay around 1901; A. B. PAINE published a slightly abridged version in EUROPE AND ELSEWHERE (1923), and Paul Baender published a corrected version in *What Is Man? and Other Philosophical Writings* (1973). It is not known whether the essay's "Jerry" existed.

SYNOPSIS

Clemens recalls a young black man, a slave named Jerry. Fifty years earlier, he enjoyed hearing Jerry's daily sermons and regarded him as the finest orator in the United States. One of Jerry's texts was: "You tell me whar a man gits his corn-pone, en I'll tell you what his 'pinions is." Clemens interprets this to mean that no man is independent enough to hold views that might interfere with his bread and butter. Since every man gets his views from others, there can be no such thing as an original opinion. He further argues that public opinion is formed by the instinct that moves individual people to conform. That instinct in turn is a product of the need for self-approval—which really means the approval of others.

"Curing a Cold"

SKETCH first published in the GOLDEN ERA, as "How to Cure a Cold," on September 20, 1863. After catching a nasty cold when his hotel burned down in VIRGINIA CITY, Nevada, the narrator does *everything* he is advised to do to get rid of it. When told to "feed a cold and starve a fever," he does *both*. He drinks warm salt-water, a solution of molasses, aquafortis, and turpentine—then gin and molasses and onions and other concoctions. He also tries applying a sheet bath and a mustard plaster and takes a steam-bath at Steamboat Springs (a spa near Virginia City). When he visits SAN FRANCISCO, *two* friends recommend that he drink a full quart of whiskey a day—so he drinks a half gallon. He advises other sufferers to follow his course of treatment, since "if it don't cure, it can't more than kill them." Revised versions of the 1,800-word sketch appeared in THE CELEBRATED JUMPING FROG OF CALAVERAS COUNTY AND OTHER SKETCHES (1867) and in SKETCHES, NEW AND OLD (1875).

"A Curious Dream"

SKETCH written in 1870. Set in "no particular city," this story relates a macabre dream about a midnight procession of moth-eaten human skeletons marching past the narrator's doorstep, lugging decaying gravestones and coffins. One skeleton stops to talk.

His headstone identifies him as John Baxter Copmanhurst, deceased in May 1836. Copmanhurst complains about his rags, his battered headstone, and the dreadful conditions in the neglected CEMETERY. He no longer even takes pride in his epitaph— "Gone to His Just Reward." Passersby merely laughed at it, so he scratched it off. Fed up with the townspeople's disregard for their ancestors' graves, he and his fellow corpses are leaving to find a town that cares enough to maintain its cemetery properly. At dawn, the narrator awakens suddenly. He assures the reader that "if the cemeteries in his town are kept in good order, this Dream is not leveled at his town at all, but is leveled particularly and venomously at the *next* town."

Clemens wrote this 3,400-word sketch—subtitled "Containing a Moral"—to call attention to a neglected BUFFALO cemetery. It appeared twice in the local BUFFALO EXPRESS: on April 30 and May 7, 1870. According to A. B. PAINE, the sketch launched a reform movement. It was issued as a pamphlet in 1872 and reprinted in SKETCHES, NEW AND OLD three years later. In 1907, Vitagraph adapted the story to film, with Mark Twain's approval. ("A Curious Dream" is not related to "A Strange Dream," which Clemens published in New York's *Saturday Press* in 1866.)

"A Curious Experience"

SHORT STORY written and published in 1881. Clemens's longest narrative set in the CIVIL WAR, "A Curious Experience" purports to be the authentic firsthand account of an incident that a Union Army major experienced during the winter of 1862–63. Told within a FRAME signed with the initials "M. T.," the story concerns a teenage boy named Robert Wicklow who fakes a conspiracy to take a Union fort. Wicklow's elaborate scheming anticipates Tom Sawyer's "evasion" conspiracy in *Huckleberry Finn* (1884), as well as his abolition scare in "TOM SAWYER'S CONSPIRACY." Wicklow's account of how he was orphaned also anticipates some of Huck's elaborate lies in *Huckleberry Finn*.

The 10,660-word story first appeared in CENTURY MAGAZINE in November 1881. It was later collected in *The Stolen White Elephant, Etc.* and in *The American Claimant and Other Stories and Sketches*.

SYNOPSIS

The unnamed officer recalls commanding Fort Trumbull at New London, Connecticut. One night a boy named Robert Wicklow appeared and begged permission to enlist. After Wicklow related a moving story of escaping from NEW ORLEANS—where his pro-Union father was lynched—the major enrolled him as a drummer-boy. Later, he heard disturbing stories about Wicklow's strange behavior and learned that the boy was studying the fort's armaments and manpower and sending messages to allies who intended to capture the fort. After getting authorization to administer martial law, the major rounded up suspects and got Wicklow to confess to being the center of a conspiracy. Wicklow's alleged accomplices were arrested, but none corroborated his story and Wicklow himself escaped. After he was tracked down, he was found to be a local Connecticut resident who had manufactured the whole conspiracy in his imagination.

"A Curious Pleasure Excursion"

SCIENCE FICTION story reflecting Clemens's interest in ASTRONOMY that was first published in 1874 and collected in *SKETCHES, NEW AND OLD* (1876). The *NEW YORK HERALD* published this piece as a letter signed by "Mark Twain" on July 6, 1874—nearly 17 years after publishing Clemens's letter criticizing the QUAKER CITY excursion. Capitalizing on public concern about a comet recently discovered by the French astronomer Jerome Eugene Coggia, the sketch PARODIES the *Quaker City* excursion by proposing a luxury cruise aboard the comet—which resembles the giant comet of Clemens's later "CAPTAIN STORMFIELD'S VISIT TO HEAVEN." The sketch also takes subtle digs at several notorious politicians, including the Radical Republican leader Benjamin

Franklin Butler (1818–1893) and Alexander Robey Shepherd (1835–1902), the corrupt territorial governor of the District of Columbia. Clemens may have written the sketch to generate publicity for his play about political corruption adapted from *The Gilded Age* that opened in New York two months later.

SYNOPSIS

Mark Twain announces that he has gone into partnership with BARNUM to lease the comet from Mr. Coggia and equip it with a million staterooms and many fabulous amenities. On July 20 (1874), it will begin a voyage that will include stops throughout the solar system and at stars in several constellations. Traveling up to 40 million miles a day, the comet will return to New York on December 14, 1991.

Expecting to accommodate many politicians, the excursion's promoters have issued complimentary round-trip tickets to several public servants who have earned a rest. In the interest of promoting further business, Mark Twain informs advertisers that the comet will carry bulletin boards and paint, and he advises cremationists that they will be going straight to some very hot places.

"The Curious Republic of Gondour"

SKETCH published in 1875. Two years after coauthoring *The Gilded Age* (1883)—which indicts democracy's worst abuses—Clemens wrote "Gondour" as a serious proposal for a political antidote to universal suffrage. The public ignored the sketch, but some of its ideas find echoes in Clemens's later writings. For example, his central theme—that the educated should wield the most political power—finds an ironic rebuttal in *Huckleberry Finn* (1884), in which Pap Finn drunkenly rages that he will not vote in the same country that permits a black college professor to vote (chapter 6). The sketch's description of how Gondour citizens defer to each other in public closely resembles a moment in *Connecticut Yankee* (1889) when Hank Morgan walks through a sixth-century English village observing how a freeman behaves toward members of different classes (chapter 31).

SYNOPSIS

After learning Gondour's language, the unidentified narrator studies the nation's unique political institutions. When Gondour experimented with universal suffrage, its ignorant nontaxpaying classes controlled the government and corruption was rampant. *Restricting* suffrage was unacceptable, so the problem was remedied by the appealing gimmick of *enlarging* it. While every citizen retained the vote, the constitution was quietly amended to provide additional votes based on property ownership and education in a formula ensuring that the most educated people would control the government. Votes based on wealth are known as "mortal" because they can be lost; those based on education are called "immortal," because they can only be lost in cases of insanity.

Now that citizens are honored primarily for the number of votes they hold, they are disinclined to gamble, speculate or do anything that might imperil their votes. One effect of this system becomes evident when the narrator walks with a friend, whose deference to passersby is determined by how many votes they own. The greatest benefit of this system is Gondour's clean, efficient government. All officeholders must pass competitive examinations, and only educated candidates of high moral character have any chance to be elected. Thanks to generous salaries, officials have no need to steal. The Grand Caliph who heads the government is elected for a 20-year term. The office has twice been held by women, who also fill many offices in the cabinet that governs the country.

After listening to Gondour's proud and contented people, the narrator is relieved to return home, where people do not feel such pride in their country.

PUBLISHING HISTORY

In the hope that readers would take this sketch more seriously without his name on it, Clemens published "Gondour" anonymously in the October 1875 issue of ATLANTIC MONTHLY. The magazine's editor, W. D. HOWELLS, invited him to contribute

more reports on Gondour, but public indifference to the first sketch stifled Clemens's interest.

Never included in any of Clemens's authorized anthologies, the sketch first saw book publication in 1919, in *The Curious Republic of Gondour and Other Whimsical Sketches* (New York: Boni and Liveright). This unauthorized anthology also includes 15 other Clemens sketches, mostly from the GALAXY and the BUFFALO EXPRESS.

CHARACTERS AND RELATED ENTRIES

Gondour   Fictitious nation visited by the anonymous narrator of "The Curious Republic of Gondour" (1875). Gondour's contented people, who speak a language other than the narrator's, have lived at least several generations under a democratic government that awards extra votes to people on the basis of their wealth and education. The nation's unit of currency is the *saco*—a name possibly deriving from a Greek word for shield.

"The Czar's Soliloquy"

SKETCH published in 1905. During the fortnight after RUSSIA's Czar Nicholas II (1868–1918) had troops fire on striking workers at St. Petersburg on January 22, 1905, Clemens wrote this POLEMIC to express his indignation. Inspired by reports that the czar meditated regularly after his morning bath, he has the czar indict himself in his own words. About a third of the SOLILOQUY's 2,500 words concern the importance of CLOTHES—a theme discussed in *Connecticut Yankee* (1889)—particularly in chapter 18—and "DIPLOMATIC PAY AND CLOTHES." Later the same year, Clemens wrote a similar attack on Belgium's king in *KING LEOPOLD'S SOLILOQUY*.

SYNOPSIS

As the czar contemplates his bony, naked body before a mirror, he wonders what about himself could possibly inspire awe and reverence. Without his clothes, he believes that he would be destitute of authority and no one could tell him from any common person. Who, he asks, is the real emperor of Russia? His clothes. Further, his grand titles are part of his clothes.

He muses over the passivity of his people, wondering why they allow themselves to be abused, and laughs at moralists who, by saying that it is wrong to kill a czar, thereby support his oppressions. After considering some of his latest crimes—such as destroying the Finnish constitution and his recent massacre—he starts to fear that the nation may be stirring out of its lethargy as people discover the true meaning of patriotism: loyalty to the *nation* itself, not to a family or a fiction. If Russia's 25 million mothers were to teach their children this truth, his successor would think twice before repeating his atrocities.

The czar pulls two newspaper clippings from beneath his pillow and reads them. One tells of his atrocities in Poland; the other tells how he made subjects worship him in abject servitude. He weeps over his own cruelty and pious hypocrisy. To revive his spirits, he decides to put on his clothes—his only protection against finding himself out.

PUBLISHING HISTORY

Clemens signed this piece on February 2, 1905–the 35th anniversary of his MARRIAGE to Livy and the first anniversary he had without her. After appearing in the *NORTH AMERICAN REVIEW* in March, the piece was not anthologized until Charles NEIDER's *Mark Twain: Life As I Find It* included it in 1961.

"The Dandy Frightening the Squatter"

Clemens's earliest-known publication in the East, this 425-word SKETCH appeared in Boston's *CARPET-BAG* on May 1, 1852. The sketch purports to recount an incident that occurred in Hannibal 13 years earlier. When a steamboat stops for wood, a young dandy tries showing off for two women by scaring a backwoodsman he sees loafing on shore. Armed with pistols and a bowie knife, the dandy accosts the man, threatening him as if he knows him. Without hesitation, the backwoodsman punches the dandy in the face, knocking him into the river.

"The Death Disk"

SHORT STORY set in mid-17th-century ENGLAND about a young officer who is saved from execution by the fortuitous intervention of his daughter. An officer under Oliver CROMWELL's Commonwealth, Colonel Mayfair is waiting to die for exceeding his orders. Ordered to feign attack on a superior force, he and two fellow officers turned their feint into a glorious victory. For their disobedience the three officers have been court-martialed and sentenced to be shot.

SYNOPSIS

The story opens as Mayfair is at home saying farewell to his family. When his daughter Abby Mayfair asks him for a story, he starts explaining what is happening to him but is not finished when soldiers come to take him away. Abby thus never realizes that the story she has heard is about her own father. According to Mayfair's story, Cromwell faces a moral dilemma. He wants to spare two of the condemned officers, so that only one must be executed as an example. He orders the condemned officers to draw lots to determine who will be executed, but all three refuse, since they regard doing so as a willful act of suicide, which their religion will not allow.

Meanwhile, Cromwell decides to resolve the moral dilemma by having an innocent child make the choice for him. He has the first child who appears on the street brought to him. He does not realize, however, that the beautiful little girl thus found is Mayfair's daughter Abby. She so wins Cromwell over that he promises to obey her commands. He then gives her one red and two white sealing-wax disks to distribute among the prisoners, without telling her what the disks are for. When Abby finds her own father among the men, she gives him the prettiest disk—the fatal red one. Cromwell is devastated when he learns that Abby has given the death disk to her own father. He finds a way out, however, when Abby reminds him of his earlier promise and demands that her father be freed. Interpreting the incident as an expression of God's will, Cromwell pardons Mayfair and allows him to go home.

BACKGROUND AND PUBLISHING HISTORY

In early 1883, Clemens read Thomas CARLYLE's edition of *Oliver Cromwell's Letters and Speeches* (1845). Later that year he wrote W. D. HOWELLS that he was considering writing a play about an incident concerning Cromwell's use of a young girl to select rebellious soldiers to execute. He did nothing with the idea until late 1899, however, when he wrote "The Death Disk." The story appeared in HARPER'S MAGAZINE in December 1901, with three full-page illustrations by LUCIUS HITCHCOCK. Early the following year, Clemens dramatized the story and had it staged at Carnegie Hall as *The Death Wafer*. In 1909, Biograph released *The Death Disk* as a silent film—probably one reel in length. Edgar S. Werner, a New York publisher, issued the story as a book, *Death-Disk*, in 1913.

CHARACTERS AND RELATED ENTRIES

Mayfair, Abby Character in the "The Death Disk." The seven-year-old daughter of Colonel Mayfair, Abby does not understand that her father faces possible execution. When she investigates where he has gone, she happens to be near OLIVER CROMWELL's headquarters at the same moment he orders that a child be found to help make a choice that he himself cannot make. Abby's innocence, charm, and sincerity so win him over that he rashly promises to grant whatever command she makes. He then puts her to a seemingly innocent task that causes her unwittingly to condemn her own father to death. When Cromwell realizes what he has made Abby do, he gladly grants her command to pardon her father.

Mayfair, Colonel Character in "The Death Disk." The 30-year-old Mayfair is the youngest colonel in England's army during its Commonwealth period. OLIVER CROMWELL condemns him and two fellow officers to death for exceeding their orders: Their offense is winning a glorious victory when ordered only to feign an attack. Mayfair is spared from execution by the fortuitous intervention of his daughter, Abby Mayfair.

"The Death of Jean"

ESSAY written by Clemens immediately after the death of his daughter Jean Clemens in 1909. On the morning before Christmas, Jean died suddenly at STORMFIELD. Over the next two days. Clemens remained home and wrote what he called the "end of my autobiography" as Jean was taken to ELMIRA, New York, for burial. Both a catharsis and a summing up of his life, the 4,200-word essay is the last substantial writing he ever completed. It takes the form of a diary, with its first entry dated 11:00 A.M., Christmas Eve. Its final entry is dated 5:00 P.M., December 26, by which time Jean's funeral was over. After finishing the piece, Clemens vowed never to write again. The essay is a poignant reflection on the terrible suddenness of the calamity, paying a moving tribute to Jean and recalling Clemens's other losses. Now he is alone, he writes. Yesterday he was 74 years old. Who can estimate his age today?

HARPER's MAGAZINE published the essay in January 1911 and it was reprinted in *What Is Man? and Other Essays* in 1917. Clemens wanted the piece to be the concluding chapter to his AUTOBIOGRAPHY, but his wish was ignored until Michael J. Kiskis published *Mark Twain's Own Autobiography* in 1990. The 1979 television drama MARK TWAIN: BENEATH THE LAUGHTER uses Clemens's composition of the essay as its unifying structure.

"The Dervish and the Offensive Stranger"

ESSAY written around 1900–01 and first published in *EUROPE AND ELSEWHERE* (1923). Taking the form of a DIALOGUE, the 1,300-word essay anticipates Clemens's longer WHAT IS MAN? While the Dervish argues that good deeds exist, the Offensive Stranger contends that *no* deed is "good" or "bad." He offers examples of good intentions gone bad, such as Utah settlers building irrigation dams that desiccate Indian lands, and COLUMBUS's discovery of America, which opened the New World to Europe's poor while simultaneously exterminating the original Indian population. He also cites examples of evil deeds with good results, such as the French Revolution, which desolated millions of families but bestowed on Europe all its great liberties. Other historical cases discussed are American intervention in the Philippines, the South African War, and Western missionaries in China.

The Devil's Race-Track: Mark Twain's Great Dark Writings (1980)

Collection of posthumously published material selected and edited by JOHN S. TUCKEY from *WHICH WAS THE DREAM? AND OTHER SYMBOLIC WRITINGS OF THE LATER YEARS* (1967) and *FABLES OF MAN* (1972)—both of which Tuckey originally edited for the MARK TWAIN PROJECT. Among the volume's stories are "Little Bessie," "THE ENCHANTED SEA-WILDERNESS," "THE GREAT DARK," "THREE THOUSAND YEARS AMONG THE MICROBES," and "THE REFUGE OF THE DERELICTS," and excerpts from "Which Was the Dream?" Clemens wrote all the stories in the collection after he was 60 years old.

"Diplomatic Pay and Clothes"

ESSAY that Clemens wrote in VIENNA in January 1899 and published in *Forum* in March. It laments the shabby pay, CLOTHES, and housing that American diplomats have traditionally received in foreign countries and expresses the hope that American policy is changing.

Opening with an allusion to the recently concluded Spanish-American War peace conference, Clemens applauds the news that members of the American delegation to Paris received generous compensation. He hopes that this precedent will reverse the nation's long history of "disastrous precedents," such as the "plain black-swallow-tail" suits worn by American ministers at formal diplomatic events. Arguing that plain clothes are actually "glaringly conspicuous" in the midst of gaudy foreign diplomatic occasions, Clemens suggests making diplomats temporary generals or admirals, so that they may wear the corresponding uniforms. The essay also discusses the inadequate pay and housing that American diplomats generally have in foreign countries, and cites Great Britain as having a particularly good record of taking care of its diplomats properly. He concludes that it is time for the United States to "come out" and change its style.

Clemens's interest in the country's treatment of its diplomatic corps grew out of his anger at the government's neglect of BAYARD TAYLOR. The theme emerges occasionally in other writings, notably "THE BELATED RUSSIAN PASSPORT," which depicts a dismal American consulate in St. Petersburg, Russia.

"Does the Race of Man Love a Lord?"

ESSAY published in 1902. To the assertion that "an Englishman does dearly love a lord," Clemens responds that Americans are no different. Indeed, all humans admire power and conspicuousness, particularly the latter, and like to rub against rank. Perceptions of what constitutes rank vary, but can be found everywhere: from the 400 million Chinese who worship their emperor to the lowliest boys' gang with one member who can thrash the rest. A "lord" is "any person whose situation is higher than our own." Admitting that he himself is not free of this impulse, Clemens recalls his immense pleasure in having a private audience in VIENNA with the emperor (Franz Josef I) several years earlier (May 25, 1899); he particularly relishes the envy he can arouse in others when he relates details of the experience.

The 4,860–word essay first appeared in the *NORTH AMERICAN REVIEW* in April 1902 and was collected in *The $30,000 Bequest and Other Stories* (1906).

"A Dog's Tale"

Short story written and published in 1903. The dog narrating this story is struggling to understand the ways of her human masters. Trained by her mother to help others in danger, she saves her masters' baby from a fire, only to see her own puppy cruelly sacrificed in a scientific experiment. Widely reviled as Clemens's most brazen concession to SENTIMENTALITY, *A Dog's Tale* can be read both as a parable on SLAVERY and as a tribute to Clemens's mother, who—like the narrator's mother—reputedly sent Clemens into the world with an oath to behave properly.

SYNOPSIS

Aileen Mavourneen reflects on her life. Though her mother was vain and frivolous, she had kind and gentle ways that she passed on to her children. When Aileen was old enough to be sold away, her mother admonished her to accept her lot without complaint and never to think of herself at times of danger to others, but to "think of your mother, and do as she would do."

Aileen's new home is wonderful. Mr. and Mrs. Gray, 10-year-old Sadie, and the servants treat her with love and kindness, and she also socializes with neighbor dogs. When she has her own puppy, her happiness is complete. One winter day Aileen is sleeping in the nursery when a fireplace spark ignites material over the baby's crib. She awakens to the baby's screams, sees flames rising, and starts to run until she remembers her mother's words and pulls the baby to safety. When Mr. Gray sees Aileen dragging the baby in the hall, he beats her with a cane until he hears screams from the nursery.

With one leg badly injured, Aileen limps to the attic to hide. She hears her name called but lays low for days while her strength ebbs. Finally, Sadie finds her, begs forgiveness, and returns her to the family, where she is treated royally. Everyone is proud of Aileen's heroism, especially Mr. Gray, a scientist who tells his distinguished colleagues that Aileen acted not by instinct but through the use of reason. The scientists then discuss optics and the

The footman consoles Aileen after her master kills her puppy in a scientific experiment.

question of whether a certain brain injury would produce blindness.

The following spring, Gray's colleagues return and take Aileen's puppy to his laboratory. Aileen does not understand what they are doing but is proud of the attention given to her pup. The men do something to the puppy's head that makes him shriek and stagger in confusion; Gray proclaims that his theory is correct: The puppy is *blind*. As Gray's friends congratulate him for his contribution to humanity, the puppy dies. Gray orders that it be buried in the garden and Aileen follows the servant who performs this duty. As she watches the puppy being "planted," she imagines it growing out of the ground as a fine handsome dog. However, two weeks of patient waiting leave Aileen frightened that something terrible has happened.

The servants' loving ministrations only heighten her fear. She is losing her strength.

BACKGROUND AND PUBLISHING HISTORY

Clemens wrote this 4,400-word story at Elmira during the summer of 1903 as his family was preparing to move to Italy. Evidently writing to satisfy his daughter Jean's opposition to vivisection, he was likely influenced by ROBERT BROWNING's poem "Tray"—narrated by someone who wants to buy a dog that saved a child from drowning in order to open its brain "by vivisection." The incident of the baby's crib catching fire resembles an accident that occurred when Clara Clemens was a baby and her nurse saved her from a fire.

A Dog's Tale first appeared in the Christmas issue of HARPER'S MAGAZINE in 1903, illustrated by W. T. SMEDLEY. Around the same time, Britain's National Anti-Vivisection Society issued the story as a pamphlet. The following September, HARPER AND BROTHERS published it as 36-page book. It was first collected in The $30,000 Bequest and Other Stories in 1906 and was adapted to a film called Science in 1911. Around 1930, 200 copies of the British pamphlet were discovered and donated to Williams College. To preserve their market value, they were to be sold at the rate of two copies a year, with the proceeds going to a "Dog's Tale Scholarship" fund.

CRITICAL COMMENTARY

Clemens writes in Pudd'nhead Wilson, "If you pick up a starving dog and make him prosperous, he will not bite you. This is the principal difference between a dog and a man" (chapter 16). Echoing that 1894 statement is a 1903 short story, "A Dog's Tale," written in response to daughter Jean's request to support antivivisectionist views. In the story, a scientist, testing a theory, picks up and blinds a puppy, betraying the puppy's mother, who had saved the life of the scientist's own child. With this inherently emotional plot, Clemens justifies using sentimentality, but without focusing on Jean's topic, he includes new and old themes while experimenting with a different narrative approach—using a dog as narrator.

Most critics believe that Clemens, a longtime opponent of sentimentalism, is himself too sentimental here. This loss of objectivity possibly derives from moods and memories enveloping this last story completed at beloved QUARRY FARM while Livy was recuperating. Some critics acknowledge the sentimentality but offer qualified praise for the story's literary aims.

General readers then, and since, may more readily accept this sentimentality. A child fan wrote to the writer: "you are awfully mean to write such a sad . . . story. . . . I am going to keep the book just the same . . ." (quoted in Leary 68). The public accepted the story as evidence of Clemens's sympathy for the underdog; Clemens counters the absence of emotion, here toward animals, with emotion. Though he believed sentimentality had led people to immorality, such as fighting wars for glory, he justified using highly emotional writing for morally righteous purposes as a means to urge some readers to think.

Nonetheless, the story is more than an appeal to emotions. Story and tone may derive not only from general sources in ancient and modern literature but also from personal ones, memories evoked by the family's final stay at Quarry Farm, such as baby Clara Clemens's rescue from fire and also Clemens's placing flowers on daughter Susy's grave for the last time.

The themes of science and language strengthen Clemens's assault on cruelty and indifference. The story resembles Nathaniel Hawthorne's stories of cold, cruel scientists, such as "The Birthmark" and "Rappaccini's Daughter." Clemens attacks "frosty intellectuality" (chapter 3) through Gray, the scientist; "gray" signifies the neutrality Hawthorne considered cold intellect, curiosity separating mind from feeling. Like Hawthorne's scientists Dr. Rappaccini and Aylmer, Gray compartmentalizes, satisfying science while ignoring his family's love for the puppy. Clemens even implies a similarity between the master-dog relationship and human slavery. His innovative dog-narrator recalls the vernacular ex-slave in "A TRUE STORY." The dog's language provides humor, characterizes vanity and class superiority, places dog-practice over human words, and implies miscommunication as barrier to true understanding.

Critical Commentary by John H. Davis

CHARACTERS AND RELATED ENTRIES

Aileen Mavourneen Narrator of "A Dog's Tale" (1903). The offspring of a female collie and a male St. Bernard who takes her name from a popular song by the Irish writer Mrs. S. C. Hall (1800–1881), Aileen learns patience and a loving philosophy of life from her mother, then is sold to a family named Gray. Her happiness seems perfect when she has her own puppy—apparently sired by an Irish setter named Robin Adair; however, she dies of a broken heart after her master kills her puppy in a scientific experiment.

Gray Fictional family in "A Dog's Tale" (1903). The story's narrator, Aileen Mavourneen, is owned by 38-year-old Mr. Gray; his gentle 30-year-old wife, Mrs. Gray; and their 10- and one-year-old daughters. Mr. Gray is a renowned scientist interested in neural systems; his prosperous family lives on an estate with many servants. The Grays love Aileen and treat her wonderfully, until the day that she saves their baby from a fire. When Mr. Gray sees Aileen dragging the baby in a hallway, he beats her severely, breaking her leg. After Aileen's heroism is discovered, however, the Grays treat her better than ever. Mr. Gray appreciates her gallantry and admires her intelligence but later kills her puppy in an experiment.

BIBLIOGRAPHY

Herzberg, Gay S. " 'A Dog's Tale': An Expanded View." *Mark Twain Journal* 19 (1977–1978): 20.

Leary, Lewis, ed. *Mark Twain's Letters to Mary*. New York: Columbia Univerity Press, 1963.

Messent, Peter. *The Short Works of Mark Twain: A Critical Study*. Philadelphia: University of Pennsylvania Press, 2001.

Smith, Janet, ed. *Mark Twain on Man and Beast*. New York: Lawrence Hill, 1972.

Twain, Mark. "A Dog's Tale." In *The $30,000 Bequest and Other Stories*. 1906. Reprinted in *The Oxford Mark Twain*, edited by Shelley Fisher Fishkin, 50–67. New York: Oxford University Press, 1996.

———. *The Tragedy of Pudd'nhead Wilson and the Comedy of Those Extraordinary Twins*. 1894. Reprinted in *The Oxford Mark Twain*, edited by Shelley Fisher Fishkin. New York: Oxford University Press, 1996.

Wilson, James D. *A Reader's Guide to the Short Stories of Mark Twain*. Boston: G. K. Hall, 1987.

A Double-Barrelled Detective Story

Short novel written in 1901 and published as a book in 1902. One of Clemens's most outrageous BURLESQUES, this story combines grotesque violence and MELODRAMA while spoofing DETECTIVE fiction in general and Sherlock Holmes in particular. Its central story line is about revenge. A young man

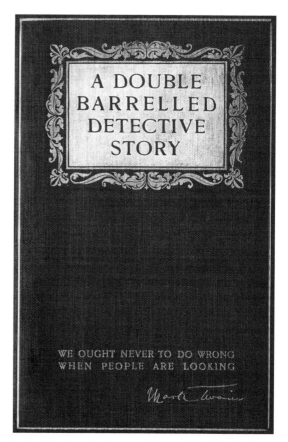

A combination of a large typeface and spaciously decorated pages transformed Mark Twain's 20,650-word novella into a 179-page book in its first separately published edition.

with extraordinary tracking abilities pursues a father he has never known in order to punish the man for mistreating his mother. A second story line (its second "barrel") concerns a young miner's murderous revenge on another cruel tormentor.

Clemens earlier hinted at the theme of a man tracking down his own father in *Pudd'nhead Wilson* (1894), in which Tom Driscoll regrets not being able to kill his natural father. Clemens's interest in extraordinary tracking skills probably arose out of his fascination with aborigine trackers of AUSTRALIA, whom he praises in *Following the Equator* (1897). It is probably not a coincidence that that book compares the abilities of native Australians favorably to those of Sherlock Holmes (chapter 17).

Lest there be any doubt as to Clemens's burlesque intentions in this story, chapter 4 contains a passage of purple prose into which he slips remarks about "a solitary oesophagus [that] slept upon motionless wing." A lengthy footnote attached to this passage adds his mock-serious reply to letters complaining about this passage.

SYNOPSIS

Containing 20,650 words in 10 chapters, the story falls into three parts. The first part opens in 1880, when a man named Jacob Fuller cruelly abuses his young wife in VIRGINIA. The narrative then jumps ahead six years, when this woman—who now calls herself Mrs. Stillman—lives in New England with her son Archy, who has a bloodhound's tracking powers. When Archy is 16, she tells him about his father's abuses, and he agrees to track his father down and torment him. The second part falls entirely within chapter 3, in which Archy describes his quest in his letters to his mother dated from 1897 to 1900. After finding Fuller and driving him out of COLORADO, Archy discovers that he has pursued the wrong man. His three-year quest to catch up with the innocent man takes him to a California mining camp. The third part comprises the final seven chapters, which are set in Hope Canyon, where Archy solves the murder of a ruffian named Flint Buckner—who turns out to be the father he has sought. He also finds the innocent Jacob Fuller and helps him regain his sanity and wealth.

Chapter 1

In 1880, Jacob Fuller marries a beautiful young woman in Virginia over the objections of her proud father, who casts her out. To avenge himself, Fuller psychologically abuses his wife for three months, then ties her to a tree, strikes her, and sets bloodhounds on her that tear away her clothes. After he abandons her, never to return, she proclaims that she will bear his child. The neighbors who free her want to form a lynch party, but Fuller is gone. The woman then shuts herself up with her father. After her father dies of a broken heart, she sells his estate and vanishes.

Chapter 2

In 1886, a young southern woman calling herself Stillman is living in a New England village with her five-year-old son, Archy Stillman. An unusual child without friends, Archy senses that he differs from other children. When he tells his mother that he once *smelled* a postman coming, she guesses that he has the gift of the bloodhound. After confirming her theory with tests, she warns Archy never to reveal his secret.

Buoyed by her son's powers, the woman makes plans to get revenge against her husband, then bides her time, resuming her neglected interests such as painting and music. When Archy turns 16, she tells him how his father abused her. The boy's southern sense of honor is so outraged that he wants to find and kill his father immediately; however, his mother wants him to punish the man by stalking him and wearing him down with fear and guilt. Years earlier, she explains, she paid to have his hiding place discovered. The man—Jacob Fuller—is a prosperous quartz-miner in Denver, Colorado. With her preparations made, the woman makes available to Archy all the money that he will need to carry out her plan. He is to post reward notices wherever he finds Fuller, then give him enough time to sell out his interests at a loss and move on, prolonging his suffering until he is ruined.

Chapter 3

On April 3, 1897, Archy writes his first letter to his mother from Denver, where he is in Fuller's hotel. Finding Fuller to be a cheerful, likable person makes Archy's task harder, but he vows to persevere in his mission. On May 19, he reports that he has posted warning notices that have scared Fuller into selling his mining interests at a loss and sneaking out of Denver disguised as a woman. He has now tracked Fuller to Silver Gulch, MONTANA, where the man nervously keeps to himself as he prospects. Archy's June 12 letter reports that Fuller is now calling himself "David Wilson."

Back in Denver on June 20, a distressed Archy reports that he has been after the *wrong* man—his father's innocent cousin who has the same name of Jacob Fuller. Anxious to set things right, Archy returns to Silver Gulch in July, but finds the man gone. He now devotes himself to finding the innocent man again and convincing him that his persecutions were a mistake. A year later, on June 28, 1898, Archy writes from SAN FRANCISCO that Fuller—who now calls himself "James Walker"—has sailed for AUSTRALIA. Archy does not write his next letter until October 3, 1900. After chasing Fuller through Australia, INDIA, and CEYLON and back to North America, he thinks Fuller is somewhere near Hope Canyon, the California mining camp from which he writes. Archy is staying with a cheerful young man named Sammy Hillyer—the only person big-hearted enough to be friendly toward the camp's black sheep, Flint Buckner.

Chapter 4

A new camp with 200 silver miners, Hope Canyon is so remote that the outside world scarcely knows that it exists. Flint Buckner lives in a cabin at the end of the village, where he holds a young English boy named Fetlock Jones in near SLAVERY. Other miners encourage Jones to leave Buckner, but the boy is too terrified to try and draws his only pleasure from planning ways to murder Buckner. One day, as Jones helps Buckner light the fuse to blasting powder in a mine shaft, Buckner strands him in the shaft without a ladder. Jones overcomes his panic in time to cut the fuse. Though badly shaken, he is satisfied that Buckner has shown him a way to accomplish his goal. His vows that in two days Buckner will be dead.

Chapter 5

Late the next night, miners gather in the tavern to gossip about Jones and Buckner after the latter leaves at the same time that he always does. Dis-

cussion then turns to the camp's other mysterious character, Archy Stillman. All anyone knows about him is that he can find anybody or anything that is lost. As someone starts to describe one of Archy's feats, the camp's sole white woman—Mrs. Hogan—bursts in. Crying that her child is missing, she begs for someone to fetch Archy, who is roused from bed. While pretending to look for clues, Archy picks up the missing child's scent, then leads everyone to the wickiup (hut) of Injun Billy, who found the baby wandering outside.

Chapter 6

The next day, the arrival of Sherlock Holmes electrifies the village. Jones is momentarily alarmed by his Uncle Sherlock's arrival but takes comfort in knowing that his uncle cannot solve *any* crime unless he arranges its details beforehand. Jones again vows that tonight will be Buckner's last on Earth. Meanwhile, villagers flock to the tavern to admire their famous visitor.

Chapter 7

That night, Jones walks with his Uncle Sherlock near Buckner's cabin, where he excuses himself to get something. After returning to the tavern, they talk for several hours. Near midnight, Jones goes out to watch Buckner leave at his usual time, then joins his uncle in the billiard room. An hour later, an explosion rocks the camp. Everyone rushes down to Buckner's destroyed cabin; Buckner's remains are found 50 yards away.

After an inquest, Holmes pores over the explosion site collecting clues. Satisfied that he has what he needs, he leads the men back to camp. The miners decide that Jones is the only logical person to have killed Buckner, but recognize that he was not even near Buckner's cabin for at least an hour before the explosion.

Chapter 8

Inside the tavern, Holmes outlines his case. After dismissing his nephew as a possible suspect, he advances robbery as a motive, then argues that since Buckner had nothing worth stealing, his killer must be stupid; further, the murderer—like *all* assassins—is left-handed. Finally, he stuns everyone by naming Sammy Hillyer as the assassin. Hillyer begs for help from Archy, who pushes forward and repudiates Holmes's conclusions. Step by step, Archy explains that the murderer used a slow-burning candle to ignite a long fuse that caused the lethal explosion. After Holmes interrupts with a few questions, Archy asks everyone to pass by him so that he can examine their feet. After 82 men pass by, he names Jones as the assassin. Holmes tries to prove Jones's innocence, but Archy examines *his* feet and says that he provided the very matches that Jones used to light the candle. After the assembly votes to arrest Jones and try him, Jones sobbingly confesses his crime and begs to be hanged immediately.

Chapter 9

In an undated letter to his mother, Archy describes Buckner's funeral, at which he found "James Walker," the innocent man he has been chasing. Now insane, Walker fears that Sherlock Holmes is after him; however, a miner reports that Holmes was recently hanged in San Bernardino. Walker then tells the story of his persecutions, eliciting the whole camp's sympathy. Thinking Holmes responsible for Walker's misfortunes, the angry miners seize Holmes—who is still alive after all—and start to burn him at the STAKE. After the sheriff arrives to save Holmes, it is discovered that Jones has escaped; however, there is no interest in recapturing him.

Chapter 10

In Archy's final letter to his mother, 10 days later, he says that he is about to take "James Walker"—who is almost sane again—back to Denver. He has also learned from Hillyer that Buckner's real name was Jacob Fuller. With his father dead and buried, Archy's quest is over.

BACKGROUND AND PUBLISHING HISTORY

Clemens wrote this story while summering at SARANAC LAKE in 1901, two years after dabbling in a similar theme in an unfinished story later published in HANNIBAL, HUCK & TOM (1869) as "The Human Bloodhound." *The Double-Barrelled Detective Story* first appeared in HARPER'S MAGAZINE in January–February 1902. HARPER'S issued it as a 179-page book in April, with illustrations by Lucius HITCHCOCK. CHATTO and Windus followed with

the English edition in June. The story was also collected in *The Man That Corrupted Hadleyburg and Other Essays and Stories* (1904). In 1965, Adolfas Mekas adapted the story to film in an independent production. In 1996 a facsimile reprint of the first edition of *A Double-Barrelled Detective Story* was published in the OXFORD MARK TWAIN edition as part of a volume titled *The Stolen White Elephant and Other Detective Stories* (1996).

CRITICAL COMMENTARY

A Double-Barrelled Detective Story is a mixture of borrowed, retooled, and parodied texts and ideas. Critic Hamlin Hill, extending the title's metaphor, called it a "Gatling gun of ideas, modes of writing, and crossed purposes" (Hill 30–31). Its two main narratives are a tale of revenge and a burlesque of detective fiction in general and Arthur Conan Doyle's Sherlock Holmes stories in particular. Many elements of the story are a burlesque of Doyle's first Sherlock Holmes novel, *A Study in Scarlet* (1887), such as the basic conceit of a revenge narrative set in the American West; Archy's supernatural tracking talent; Holmes's nephew, Fetlock Jones, with a conveniently soundalike name; and the much-discussed "solitary esophagus" passage, with its extended cagey footnote, which opens chapter 4. References to other Holmes adventures are also included, such as his return from apparent death after Doyle had pitched him off Reichenbach Falls.

When Holmes himself arrives in chapter 6 (appropriating another author's character is a liberal borrowing for such a copyright hawk as Clemens Twain), Fetlock Jones privately expresses his envy and disdain for his uncle: "He can't detect a crime except where he plans it all out beforehand and arranges the clews and hires some fellow to commit it according to instructions." Fetlock's complaint about Holmes's contrived investigations expresses Twain's own criticism about the detective form itself, or at least as it was practiced by Doyle. Fetlock's ingenious murder of his sadistic master, Flint Buckner, in the mining camp works to parody the arcane trivia and pat manipulations that Doyle uses to bring the typical Holmes mystery to an impressively fastidious ending. Whereas Clemens's Holmes unfolds a patently wrong solution to the murder based on his insistence that "all assassins are left handed," Archy solves the mystery by noticing that matches, like Holmes himself, are of "a breed unknown to this camp" (chapter 8). As often occurs in Mark Twain's burlesques, the author goes on to commit offenses not all that different from those of his target. Critical in this case of Doyle's unnaturally airtight architecture, Clemens relies on his own favorite improbabilities, such as mistaken identity and convenient family ties.

In addition to the relatively superficial humor of burlesque, Peter Messent notes, *A Double-Barrelled Detective Story* indirectly stages a deeper social satire on such problems as violence and prejudice in American culture. The cycle of southern vengeance that propels the story emerges in chilling satirical tones in Archy's response to his mother's revelation of her past: "We are Southerners; and by our custom and nature there is but one atonement. I will search him out and kill him" (chapter 2). Sherlock Holmes, an unwelcome outsider in the story and in the West, narrowly escapes lynching in the mining camp. Clemens had planned to write a history of lynching and was researching America's violent history while composing this story, notes Judith Yaross Lee. Though Clemens would shy away from publishing the lynching book in fear of alienating his southern audience, in 1901 he wrote the essay "The UNITED STATES OF LYNCHERDOM" as its introduction. (That essay was not published until 1923.)

The revenge narrative in *A Double-Barrelled Detective Story* is sparked by Jacob Fuller's treatment by his bride's father, whose belief in Jacob's indelible class is similar to a perception of race. Jacob is rebuffed by his bride's father, who believes that Jacob's character is "written in [his] face" and that he is "treacherous, a dissembler, a coward, and a brute without any sense of pity or compassion" (chapter 1). He attributes these qualities to the origins of Jacob's "unconsidered" family in Sedgemoor (in southwest England) and believes they are visible on Jacob in "the Sedgemoor trademark," a view he passes on to his daughter. During her abusive marriage with Jacob, she "taunted him with his origin; said she was the lawful slave of a scion of slaves." (ibid.). In this sense, although the revenge narrative

is propelled by Archy's drive to redress Jacob's cruelty, the underlying cause is a long-standing English prejudice that has crystallized into a form of pseudo-racial bias and been preserved and transported to the American South. Ironically, the father's belief in the connection between physiology and character is what creates the story's central problem B, as Peter Messent puts it, "in dismissing Jacob on the basis of such apparent evil traits, the father-in-law may have helped to bring them into being" (Messent 205).

Critical Commentary by Alex Feerst

CHARACTERS AND RELATED ENTRIES

Buckner, Flint   Character in *A Double-Barrelled Detective Story* (1902). A silver miner in HOPE CANYON, California, Buckner is a sadistic bully who holds young Fetlock Jones in bondage until Jones blows him up. Afterward, Archy Stillman learns that Buckner's real name was Jacob Fuller—the father he has spent years trying to locate in order to avenge his abused mother. Buckner's habit of leaving the camp's tavern at the same time every night is an important element of Jones's murder scheme. As a bully, Buckner seems to be modeled partly on William Brown, the steamboat pilot whom the young cub in *Life on the Mississippi* (1883) dreams of murdering.

Fuller, Jacob   Name of two characters in *A Double-Barrelled Detective Story* (1902). The first Fuller is a 26-year-old man from an old but "unconsidered" family who resents his cavalier VIRGINIA father-in-law's opposition to him and gets revenge by brutalizing his wife and abandoning her in 1880. His wife bears his son, Archy Stillman, who later goes after him to avenge his mother's mistreatment.

With information obtained by his mother, Archy finds Fuller in Denver, COLORADO, where he is a prosperous, cheerful and popular miner. After tormenting this man and driving him away, Archy learns that this Fuller is a younger cousin of his father with the same name. As the innocent Fuller explains in chapter 9, he flees out of fear of being unjustly lynched for his cousin's crimes. Archy spends three years chasing Fuller around the world in order to explain his mistake and make amends. By the time he finally finds Fuller again in

California, the man has changed his name to James Walker and has gone mad. The narrative ends with Fuller regaining his sanity and Archy about to take him back to Colorado to restore his original wealth. By this time, Archy has learned that a sadistic Hope Canyon miner named Flint Buckner who has been murdered was really his father, Jacob Fuller.

Holmes, Sherlock   Character in *A Double-Barrelled Detective Story*. One of the most famous characters in literature, Sherlock Holmes was introduced by Sir Arthur Conan Doyle (1859–1930) in *A Study in Scarlet* in 1887. Clemens enjoyed the stories, but had a low regard for DETECTIVES. In *Following the Equator* (1897), he compares Sherlock Holmes's tracking talents unfavorably to those of native Australians (chapter 17). In addition to his brilliant deductive powers, Holmes was famous for bouncing back to life after dying. In Clemens's own detective story, Holmes visits the remote mining camp of Hope Canyon—apparently to see his nephew Fetlock Jones. After he arrives, a man named Flint Buckner is murdered. Holmes investigates the crime, impressing everyone with his brilliant analysis of clues until the moment that he names Sammy Hillyer the murderer. Archy Stillman then steps forward and embarrasses Holmes by proving not only that Holmes's nephew is the real murderer, but that Holmes himself was Jones's unknowing accomplice. Holmes's humiliation is complete when Jones explains that he involved him in his crime because he was confident that his uncle would never be able to solve it.

In chapter 9, Holmes is reported to have been mistakenly hanged in San Bernardino; however, he is still alive in Hope Canyon. When a deranged man appears in camp claiming that Holmes has been unjustly persecuting him, a lynch mob forms. Aware of Holmes's reputation for not staying dead, the mob tries burning him at the STAKE until a sheriff stops them.

Hope Canyon   Fictional CALIFORNIA mining camp in *A Double-Barrelled Detective Story*. The scene of the novella's last seven chapters, Hope Canyon is in a deep gorge in a remote part of the ESMERALDA district (actually part of NEVADA). The two-year-old silver-mining camp has yet to prove itself and is unknown to the outside world. Its residents include about 200 miners, one white woman and child, several CHINESE washermen and some INDIANS.

Jones, Fetlock   Character in *A Double-Barrelled Detective Story* (1902). A 16- or 17-year-old English nephew of Sherlock Holmes, Jones is virtually a slave to Flint Buckner when Archy Stillman arrives in Hope Canyon mining camp in 1900. Too terrified of Buckner to accept the offers of help that he receives, the likable young Jones finds solace in spending his nights inventing ways to kill Buckner—a goal that he achieves in chapter 7. After Stillman proves him guilty, Jones escapes, but no one tries to recapture him.

Jones's obsession with planning ways to kill Buckner recalls the cub pilot of *Life on the Mississippi* (1883) who spends his nights planning ways to kill his tormentor, William Brown (chapter 18). Unlike the cub, Jones actually kills Buckner by blowing him up—a fate similar to the accidental death of the real Brown.

Jones's given name, "Fetlock," is an old English word for the tuft of hair above the hoof behind a horse's leg. Clemens probably uses it as a play on the name of Jones's uncle "Sherlock."

Stillman, Archy   Central character in *A Double-Barrelled Detective Story* (1902). The son of a woman who calls herself "Mrs. Stillman," Archy is born shortly after his father, Jacob Fuller, abandons his mother in 1880. Archy has the tracking powers of a bloodhound, possibly because his father set hounds on his mother when she was pregnant with him. When Archy is 16, his mother explains how his father brutalized her and he vows revenge. The story then follows his three-and-a-half-year pursuit of his father in the Far West. Despite the fact that Archy has grown up without friends and willingly sacrifices his youth to torment his father, he has a kind and generous nature and seems to get along well with people he encounters.

An earlier incarnation of Archy Stillman appears in Clemens's unfinished story "A Human Bloodhound," which was first published in HANNIBAL, HUCK & TOM (1969). In that story, written about two years earlier than *A Double-Barrelled Detective Story*, a man named Harbison grows up with a "miraculous" ability to recognize and remember individual smells.

BIBLIOGRAPHY

Busch, Frederick. "Introduction." In *The $30,000 Bequest and Other Stories*, edited by Shelley Fisher Fishkin. Oxford: Oxford University Press, 1996.

Hill, Hamlin. *Mark Twain: God's Fool*. New York: Harper and Row, 1973.

Kraus, W. Keith. "Mark Twain's 'A Double-Barrelled Detective Story': A Source for the Solitary Esophagus." *Mark Twain Journal* 16, no. 3 (Summer 1972): 10–12.

Lee, Judith Yaross. "Afterword." In *The $30,000 Bequest and Other Stories*, edited by Shelley Fisher Fishkin. New York: Oxford University Press, 1996.

Messent, Peter. "Comic Intentions in 'A Double-Barrelled Detective Story." In *The Short Works of Mark Twain: A Critical Study*, 202–214. Philadelphia: University of Pennsylvania Press, 2001.

Wilson, James D. "A Double-Barrelled Detective Story." In *A Reader's Guide to the Short Stories of Mark Twain*, 53–60. Boston: G.K. Hall & Co., 1987.

Ritunnano, Jeanne. "Mark Twain vs. Arthur Conan Doyle on Detective Fiction." *Mark Twain Journal* 16, no. 1 (Winter 1971–72): 10–14.

Twain, Mark. *A Double-Barrelled Detective Story*. In *The Stolen White Elephant and Other Detective Stories*, edited by Shelley Fisher Fishkin. New York: Oxford University Press, 1996.

"Doughface" ("Huck Finn")

Posthumously published story fragment written around either 1897 or 1902. The MARK TWAIN PROJECT edition HANNIBAL, HUCK & TOM calls this fragment "Doughface"; in "HUCK FINN AND TOM SAWYER AMONG THE INDIANS" it is called "Huck Finn." Narrated by Huck, the roughly 500-word piece concerns a young prankster, "Rowena Fuller" (modeled on Roberta Jones), who borrows a horrible mask that Huck has lent to Tom Sawyer. One night she uses it to sneak up on Miss Wormly, a "superstitious old maid," who is so frightened that she goes mad and never recovers. The story is

based on an actual incident that Clemens describes in chapter 53 of *Life on the Mississippi*.

"Down the Rhône"

Posthumously published ESSAY about a trip Clemens made on FRANCE's RHÔNE RIVER in 1891. A. B. PAINE abridged this 10,000-word piece from a longer manuscript of Clemens's unfinished book INNOCENTS ADRIFT, publishing it in EUROPE AND ELSEWHERE (1923) with minimal editorial explanation. In late September (not August, as the essay states), Clemens hired a French boatman (the "Admiral") to navigate his flatboat from Lake Bourget in Savoie down the Rhône to the Mediterranean. His only other companion on the 10-day trip was his courier JOSEPH VEREY, but the manuscript adds the fictional "Mr. Harris" of *A Tramp Abroad* (1880).

SYNOPSIS

After spending a night at Lake Bourget's Castle of Châtillon, the narrator crosses the lake on the Admiral's roomy flatboat to a canal that takes them to the Rhône. As the boat drifts down this swift river, he describes passing sights. Seeing a young woman with a face like the Mona Lisa reminds him of the hours he stared at that famous painting, wondering what vanished marvels others find in its serene expression. He recalls how Noel Flagg (a Hartford painter) once told him that Dr. Horace Bushnell had advised him that his talent needed training. When Flagg and his brother first saw the Mona Lisa and other Old Masters, they scoffed. After completing their training, however, they returned to gaze on these works in awe.

To avoid being overcharged at a hotel, the narrator tries posing as a DEAF-AND-DUMB Frenchman only to find his tariff raised the next morning. Believing that he has an honest face, he recalls an incident in New York, when he went to Francis Hopkinson Smith's house on a cold night and persuaded the maid—who did not know him—to lend him Smith's overcoat.

When the courier asks the narrator why he lacks the nerve to walk along a crumbling precipice, the narrator observes that while some people can skirt precipices fearlessly but dread the dentist's chair, he is just the opposite. Born without prejudices against dentists, he does not mind the pain. In fact, he offers the revolutionary idea that the exquisitely sharp effect that a dental drill produce is *too* high and perfect a sensation for our human limitations even to recognize as pain. What we feel may in fact be exquisite *pleasure*. When the flatboat goes down the Rhone Falls, the narrator gets out to walk.

Shortly after this episode, the manuscript abruptly ends. Clemens's interest in the voyage itself faded after just four or five days—around the time he passed St. Etienne. He wrote 174 manuscript pages, but never attempted to finish his book; however, he recalls this journey with a quote from his diary in chapter 55 of *Following the Equator* (1897). Around 1901, he wrote a brief addendum on the trip that was later published as "THE LOST NAPOLEON."

"Edward Mills and George Benton: A Tale"

SHORT STORY written and published in 1880. An ironic moral tale, this story is a parable about cousins who grow up as foster brothers. One, George Benton, does everything wrong but is always given a fresh start. The other, Edward MILLS, strives to be good, only to be ruined by George and treated as a pariah. One of Clemens's archetypal TOWN DRUNKARDS, George alternately reforms and falls; he is much like Pap Finn—the kind of RAPSCALLION whom charitable women favor in *Huckleberry Finn* (1884). His career also resembles that of Charlie Williams in *Life on the Mississippi* (1883), while the relationship between him and his foster brother anticipates themes that Clemens explores more fully in *Pudd'nhead Wilson.* The moral of this tale is summed up in Clemens's famous MAXIM: "Be good and you will be lonely."

Clemens wrote this 2,300-word story during the summer of 1880, as he was finishing *A Tramp Abroad.* It appeared in the August issue of the ATLANTIC MONTHLY and was reprinted in *The $30,000 Bequest and Other Stories* (1906).

SYNOPSIS

After distantly related cousins Edward Mills and George Benton are orphaned as infants, they are adopted by the Brants, a childless couple. The Brants lovingly raise the boys to believe that if they are "pure, honest, sober, industrious and considerate of others . . . success in life is assured." Edward makes this admonition his unswerving rule, but George grows up selfish and thoroughly disagreeable. Edward takes up an apprenticeship that leads to a partnership in a business, while George remains a financial drain on the Brants. When the Brants die, they leave everything to George because he needs it more than Edward; they also require him to buy out Edward's partner so that Edward can look after him.

George's drinking and gambling ruin Edward's business, leaving both men penniless. Edward diligently struggles to rebuild his life, but times are hard and the best job he finds is hod-carrying. As George continues his dissipated habits, he becomes a favorite of the Ladies' Temperance Refuge, which repeatedly rescues and reforms him. Even after he is imprisoned for embezzlement, people petition for his release and provide him with a good job and other help. Edward meanwhile quietly improves his position until he becomes a bank cashier—only to be killed by burglars when he refuses to open his employers' safe. One of his murderers proves to be George, who is sentenced to die despite a petition campaign for his pardon.

Edward's widow and children receive token relief, but the bulk of the public's sympathy goes to George and his family—especially after George discovers religion. George's grave becomes a shrine bearing the inscription. "He has fought the good fight." Edward's grave bears a more honest inscription: "Be pure, honest, sober, industrious, considerate, and you will never—."

CHARACTERS AND RELATED ENTRIES

Benton, George Character in "Edward Mills and George Benton: A Tale" (1880). The adopted son of the childless Brants, Benton is the opposite of his foster brother, Edward Mills. He is greedy, selfish, dishonest and dissipated, but like Pap Finn and Clemens's other TOWN DRUNKARD characters, he is the pet of respectable society up until the moment he is executed for murder. When he is buried, his headstone bears the inscription, "He has fought the good fight." Afterward, fresh flowers are placed on his grave every day.

Benton's grandnephew, also named Thomas Hart Benton (1889–1975), was a Missouri artist who helped create the school of American Regionalism. Known for realistic portraits of ordinary people, he illustrated *Life on the Mississippi* for the Limited Editions Club in 1944.

Mills, Edward Character in "Edward Mills and George Benton: A Tale" (1880). An adopted son of the childless Brants, Mills devotes his life to being good, only to be murdered by his ne'er-do-well foster brother, George Benton. Quiet, diligent, and uncomplaining, he finally expresses his exasperation at life in an ironic epitaph: "Be pure, honest, sober, industrious, considerate, and you will never—"

"The Enchanted Sea Wilderness"

Unfinished story originally written for *Following the Equator* (1897). The first of several nightmare-voyage stories that Clemens wrote, "The Enchanted Sea-Wilderness" is a FRAME-STORY about a ship trapped in an eerie maelstrom near Antarctica in 1853–54. Its roughly 65-year-old narrator is a sailor whom Clemens met on a ship in late 1895 or early 1896. He began writing the story around late October 1896, after completing about 14 chapters of *Following the Equator*. It was first published in 1967 in *Mark Twain's* WHICH WAS THE DREAM? AND OTHER SYMBOLIC WRITINGS, edited by JOHN S. TUCKEY.

The unnamed man's narrative treats a theme paralleling a recent event in Clemens's life. The narrator sees his ship's disaster as a judgment on his captain for having left a dog to die after it had saved everyone else. Clemens wrote the story while obsessed with guilt over having left his daughter Susy Clemens alone at home, where she burned up with fever while he was traveling around the world. It may have been his inability to resolve the fate of

the captain—whom he modeled on himself—that caused him to abandon the story. Seven years later, he took up a similar theme in "A DOG'S TALE," in which a master cruelly mistreats his pet dog after it saves his baby from a fire.

SYNOPSIS

Scattered about the oceans are spots in which compasses go mad, forcing sailors to steer by the heavens. The worst such spot is a huge circle in the southern Indian Ocean. Its great outer circle, tossed by eternal storms, is known as the DEVIL'S RACE-TRACK; its calm center is the EVERLASTING SUNDAY. An old sailor aboard the author's ship has been there; he tells his story.

In December 1853, the sailor was a 23-year-old crewman on the brig *Mabel Thorpe*, which carried provisions and blasting powder to the gold mines of AUSTRALIA under a hard-hearted master named Elliot Cable. Two months before sailing, the *Thorpe* took aboard a beautiful St. Bernard dog, which became a valued and beloved member of the crew. One night, when the ship was becalmed below SOUTH AFRICA, the dog detected a fire and awakened the captain in time to stop it from reaching the powder-kegs and killing everyone. The dog then helped the crew load the lifeboat as the ship burned. Before the lifeboat shoved off, however, the captain tied the dog to the ship's mainmast. When the crew pleaded to save the dog, the captain said it would only get in the way and would eat too much. As flames consumed the piteously wailing animal, the men predicted that a judgment would come on the captain.

The next morning the men spotted the *Thorpe*'s sister ship, the *Adelaide*, a slower brig that had preceded them on the same course. Since the *Adelaide*'s Captain Moseley and two mates had died from illness, Cable took command of it and continued its course to Australia. Almost immediately, however, a gale began driving the ship southeast, pushing it hundreds of miles through wild seas. Eventually, the captain calculated that they were about halfway between Kerguelan's Land and the Antarctic Circle, nearing the Devil's Race-Track. On the 18th day, their ship entered a wild storm and its compass went crazy, confirming everyone's worst fears. For nine days, it was too dark to tell day from night, but on the 10th morning, they entered the calm center—the Everlasting Sunday, where they drifted helplessly.

Seven months later, they came upon a fleet of becalmed ships, on which they found the desiccated bodies of long-dead people. The first ship they examined was the *Horatio Nelson*, on which the narrator's uncle had disappeared 13 years earlier. They also found a New England whaler; an English ship, the *Eurydice*, which had been bound for Australia with convicts; a Spanish ship; and the British man-of-war *Royal Brunswick*, which was wonderfully preserved though it had been there since 1740. Unlike the merchant ships, the warship maintained its log up until the end.

CHARACTERS AND RELATED ENTRIES

Devil's Race-Track Fictional Indian Ocean region, located roughly midway between "Kerguelan's Land" (Kerguelen Island, 49° south latitude, 70° east longitude) and the Antarctic Circle—about 2,400 miles southeast of Cape Town, SOUTH AFRICA, and due south of Pakistan. A ferocious maelstrom 500 miles in diameter, the Devil's Race-Track makes magnetic compasses go wild and draws ships into its center—known as the Everlasting Sunday. When it sucks the brig *Adelaide* into it in "The Enchanted Sea Wilderness," the sky grows pitch-dark, though it is near the height of the Southern Hemisphere's summer near the Antarctic Circle.

Chapter 25 of *Life on the Mississippi* (1883) describes several stretches of the river with the word "Devil's" in their names. One of them is called the "Devil's Race-Course."

Everlasting Sunday The calm center of the Devil's Race-Track—a maelstrom that sucks vessels in and then preserves them as in a museum. In "The Enchanted Sea Wilderness," the brig *Adelaide* enters the Everlasting Sunday after nine days of being drawn through the stormy outer darkness. Within its black wall of clouds, the *Adelaide* crew finds perfect stillness under a bright cloudless sky. They drift helplessly for seven months, then come upon a fleet of becalmed ships filled with desiccated bodies. The scene resembles a passage omitted from *Life on the Mississippi* (1883) about a

balloon voyage into a dead-air belt containing becalmed balloons carrying desiccated corpses.

Clemens associated Sundays with stillness and inactivity—a point he discusses in chapter 24 of *A Tramp Abroad* (1880). Throughout his writings, he generally uses "everlasting" in a negative sense, as with "everlasting fire" (*Huckleberry Finn*, chapter 31; IS SHAKESPEARE DEAD?, chapter 11; *The Prince and the Pauper*, chapter 20); "everlasting hell" (*Joan of Arc*, book 3, chapter 14; "Was It Heaven or Hell?" chapter 9) or other "everlasting" punishments (*Roughing It*, chapter 65; *Life on the Mississippi*, chapter 10). "Everlasting Sunday" is thus his idea of an ultimate hell.

"An Encounter with an Interviewer"

Sketch written around 1875. The narrator befuddles a reporter from the *Daily Thunderstorm* with bizarre answers to his questions. For example, he gives his age as 19, but says that he began writing in 1836. He cannot account for this discrepancy, or for the fact that he was born on October 31, 1693—a date that should make him 180 years old. As the most remarkable person he has ever met, he names Aaron Burr (1756–1836). He happened to be at Burr's funeral, when Burr asked him to make less noise. He finds Burr remarkable because he got up to observe his own funeral and rode to his grave next to his driver. The narrator also explains that he was born a twin, but that either he or his brother died in their bath—no one was sure which. He admits, however, that it was actually *he* who drowned, and that his family buried the wrong child.

The 1,500-word sketch was published in PUNCH, BROTHERS, PUNCH! (1878), THE STOLEN WHITE ELEPHANT (1882), and other collections.

"English As She Is Taught"

ESSAY published in April 1887. A Brooklyn school-teacher named Caroline B. LeRow approached

Cover of the pamphlet published in 1887

Clemens with a manuscript she had assembled from her pupils' most outlandish answers to questions. She later published the manuscript as *English As She Is Taught;* meanwhile, Clemens wrote this 4,275-word essay with choice extracts from LeRow's material and brief comments on the state of education. He gave the $250 that CENTURY MAGAZINE paid him for the article to LeRow and later extracted some of its contents in chapter 61 of *Following the Equator* (1897). A decade later, when Clemens's financial distress was common knowledge, LeRow begged permission to give the $250 back to him.

Extracts include definitions such as assiduity being the "state of being an acid," an equestrian "one who asks questions," and a eucharist "one who plays euchre." Under the heading of grammar, one pupil defines gender as "the distinguishing nouns without regard to sex," while another asserts that "every sentence and name of God must begin with a caterpillar." Mathematics pupils assert that "parallel lines are lines that can never meet until they run together" and that "a circle is a round straight line with a hole in the middle." One geography pupil says that Austria's principal occupation "is gathering Austrich feathers." Another explains that "Ireland is called the Emigrant Isle because it is so beautiful and green." Many pupils like to assign the year 1492 to any important historical event, such as the birth of George Washington and the Declaration of Independence. One pupil calls EDGAR ALLAN POE "a very curdling writer" and another identifies Chaucer as "the father of English pottery." Mistakes such as these are reminiscent of Huck's mixed-up account of English history in chapter 23 of *Huckleberry Finn* (1884).

"The Esquimau Maiden's Romance"

SHORT STORY written in 1893. After immediately revealing his identity as "Mr. Twain," Clemens describes spending a week with a young Eskimo woman named Lasca, apparently at or near the Arctic Circle—a region that he never personally

F. Luis Mora's illustration for "The Esquimau Maiden's Romance" shows Lasca sitting with Clemens.

visited. The bulk of the FRAME is Lasca's narrative of her tragic romance with a young man named Kalula.

Lasca explains how her father's great wealth—which comprises 22 iron fish-hooks—has ruined her life. People treat her differently, everyone is greedy, and she cannot find a suitor who loves her for herself. About two years earlier, however, Kalula came into her life. Coming from a remote community, the handsome young stranger knew nothing of her father's wealth. The couple fell in love and became engaged. Unfortunately, the morning after Lasca's father shows off his fish-hook collection to Kalula, a hook is missing. Kalula

confesses to having gotten up during the night to fondle the fish-hooks admiringly but denies taking one. Nevertheless, a trial of community elders finds him guilty and puts him to the "trial by water." Since Kalula does not sink, he is proclaimed guilty. Lasca renounces him and he is cast adrift on an iceberg.

Nine months later, on the day of the "Great Annual Sacrifice, when all the maidens of the tribe wash their faces and comb their hair," Lasca finds the missing fish-hook in her hairdo. She and her father agree that they have murdered Kalula.

The story satirizes the inverted ideas that Eskimos and westerners have about wealth. The Eskimos think nothing of wearing sables and other furs that are of immense value to westerners; their idea of wealth is metal objects such as ordinary fish-hooks that are worth little to westerners. The result is that "a hundred million dollars in New York and twenty-two fish-hooks on the border of the Arctic Circle represent the same financial supremacy."

This 6,000-word story first appeared in the November 1893 issue of *Cosmopolitan*, with illustrations by DAN BEARD. It was later collected in *The Man That Corrupted Hadleyburg and Other Essays and Stories*.

CHARACTERS AND RELATED ENTRIES

Kalula Character in "The Esquimau Maiden's Romance." A young Eskimo man, Kalula falls in love with Lasca. Falsely convicted of stealing a fish-hook from Lasca's father, he is put on an iceberg drifting south. Clemens may have taken Kalula's name from a book written by his friend HENRY MORTON STANLEY in 1873, *My Kalulu: Prince, King, and Slave: A Story of Central Africa*.

Lasca Title character and narrator of "The Esquimau Maiden's Romance." About 20 years old and plump, Lasca is the "most bewitching girl in her tribe." She is also the daughter of a man so rich that she never had a suitor not motivated by greed until she met Kalula. Her name is apparently short for "Alaska."

Europe and Elsewhere (1923)

Collection assembled by A. B. PAINE. The book's 35 essays, sketches and travel letters are a mixture of previously published and unpublished Clemens materials. They include fragments from two unfinished TRAVEL BOOKS, "A MEMORABLE MIDNIGHT EXPERIENCE" (1873) and "DOWN THE RHÔNE" (1891). Aside from "THE WAR PRAYER"—which Paine previously published in his biography of Clemens—most of the book's previously published items are minor, such as articles on AIX-LES-BAINS and MARIENBAD written for the *NEW YORK SUN*, and his letters on the visit of the shah of Persia to England in 1873, printed here as "O'SHAH." Of greater importance are two anti-imperialist essays from the *NORTH AMERICAN REVIEW*—"To the Person Sitting in Darkness" and "To My Missionary Critics." There are also three sketches on ADAM AND EVE and two on Satan.

Other essays include "AS REGARDS PATRIOTISM," "CORN-PONE OPINIONS," "THE LOST NAPOLEON," "SOME NATIONAL STUPIDITIES," "THE UNITED STATES OF LYNCHERDOM," and "A Word of Encouragement for Our Blushing Exiles." The book also includes tributes to ANSON BURLINGAME, MARJORIE FLEMING, biologist Jacques Loeb, SAMUEL ERASMUS MOFFETT, and THOMAS BRACKETT REED.

Paine supplies a brief preface and reprints a long essay on Clemens that BRANDER MATTHEWS wrote for a uniform edition in 1899.

Eve's Diary (1906)

SHORT STORY written in 1905 and later slightly expanded and published as an illustrated book. Written in the form of actual diary entries, it chronicles the entire relationship of ADAM AND EVE. For critical commentary, see *EXTRACTS FROM ADAM'S DIARY*.

SYNOPSIS

The diary begins on a Saturday, when Eve is a day old. Feeling "like an experiment," she inspects her surroundings and notes such flaws as ragged mountains, too many stars and a loose moon. She wants to put some stars in her hair, but cannot reach them with a pole and cannot hit them with clods, blaming her failure on the fact that "I am left-handed and cannot throw good."

Eve soon observes another "experiment"— whom she later learns is Adam—and follows it about. She thinks it is a man but cannot be sure, since she has never seen a man. She cannot understand why it ignores her. She chases it up a tree; when she throws clods at it, she hears language for the first time. Eve spends a week following it, trying to get acquainted. Eventually they get along, and Eve takes over Adam's task of naming everything he sees. She is lonely when Adam is not around and experiences her "first sorrow" when he avoids her. Disappointed when Adam takes no interest in her name, she spends time with her "sister"—her reflection in a pool. Eve experiments with sticks that create pink dust that burns her; she experiences pain and calls the dust "fire." Further experiments with the pink dust start a forest fire, which inspires Eve to invent such words as "smoke" and "flame." Eve works on improving her estate, but Adam takes little interest. Her discovery of fire has led to another, unwelcome discovery: fear.

A brief "Extract from Adam's Diary" is inserted in which Adam makes allowances for Eve's youth and confesses that he is starting to appreciate her beauty. He marvels that she finds interest in *everything*. Eve even tames a brontosaurus that wanders in, but Adam does not want it around, for fear it will crush his house accidentally.

As Eve's own diary resumes, Eve goes several days without seeing Adam, so she spends more time with the animals and travels great distances. Eve is curious about everything—for example, how does the water in the stream get back up the hill at night? Why can wood swim, but not stone?

The diary then jumps ahead, to after the Fall. Eve finds that she and Adam love each other and she wonders *why* she loves him. It cannot be because he is bright, for he is not; nor can it be because he is gracious, industrious, educated or chivalrous, for he is none of those things. She concludes that she loves him, "Merely because he is *mine* and is *masculine.*"

After 40 years pass, Eve prays that if one of them must die first, it be she since Adam is stronger and she could not live without him. At her grave, Adam says, "Wheresoever she was, *there* was Eden."

BACKGROUND AND PUBLISHING HISTORY

Clemens wrote this 6,000-word story for the 1905 Christmas issue of HARPER'S MAGAZINE. W. D. HOWELLS and HENRY ALDEN reprinted it in a Harper collection, *Their Husbands' Wives*, in March 1906. It was then illustrated by LESTER RALPH and stretched to fit a 106-page book by itself in June 1906, with some additional material that Clemens had written for "EXTRACTS FROM ADAM'S DIARY."

Eve's Diary has been reprinted many times, often in combination with *Extracts from Adam's Diary*. The OXFORD MARK TWAIN edition published facsimile reprints of both books as *The Diaries of Adam and Eve* (1996). That volume includes a new introduction by science-fiction novelist Ursula K. Le Guin and an afterword by Laura E. Skandera-Trombley, the author of *Mark Twain in the Company of Women* (1994).

Clemens's interest in Adam and Eve continued after he published *Eve's Diary*. Several fragments later published in LETTERS FROM THE EARTH (1962) as "Papers of the Adam Family" elaborate on Eve's story. In two extracts from "Eve's Autobiography," Eve looks back to the idyllic days in Eden, when she and Adam regarded themselves as scientists. Their proudest discovery was Adam's finding that water runs *down*hill; however, when someone else later got credit for this discovery, Adam's heart was broken. Eve discovered how milk got *into* cows, viz., through their hair. This fragment also includes "Interpolated Extracts from Eve's Diary," which discuss Eve's discovery that the teeth in lions suggests that they are intended to be carnivores. She and Adam make further discoveries and invent new words.

Most of Clemens's ADAMIC DIARIES were written at least partly as BURLESQUES of the Bible, but he seemed to have a special reverence for "Eve's Diary." The conclusion that he intended it as an homage to his recently deceased wife, Livy, is made inescapable by Adam's comment on Eve's death: "Wheresoever she was, *there* was Eden." Scholars have suggested that the story's depiction of Adam and Eve's relationship has autobiographical undertones similar to those in the MCWILLIAMS FAMILY STORIES.

Clemens wanted the illustrations to be serious instead of comic, and he was delighted with Ralph's elegant line drawings. At least one provincial library banned *Eve's Diary*, however, because the illustrations depicted Adam and Eve undressed.

In 1988 the actor David Birney adapted Adam and Eve's diaries into a single stage play in which the characters alternate their remarks. The production was broadcast on public television's *American Playhouse* series as "The Diaries of Adam and Eve."

"Eve Speaks"

Sketch written around 1900 and first published in EUROPE AND ELSEWHERE (1923). Eve narrates the first three of four brief sections of this 1,000-word ADAMIC DIARY. The time is three months after the Fall. Eve wonders why she and ADAM have been driven from the Garden of Eden, feeling it is unfair that they have been punished for their ignorance. They did not know right from wrong, because they lacked the moral sense. Adam arrives. Their son Abel sleeps. A day later, Abel still sleeps. His parents find him drenched in blood after his brother struck him. Later Eve finds that they cannot wake Abel at all. Is it death? The last paragraph is extracted from the diary of Satan, who acknowledges that Abel is dead. He says, "the product of the Moral Sense is complete. The Family think ill of death—they will change their minds."

Extracts from Adam's Diary

SKETCH originally published in 1893 that was later revised and reissued in several forms, including a self-contained book. Lighter and more comic in tone than the later ADAMIC DIARIES, this sketch does not

As Eve looks on, Adam chisels his pictographic "diary" in stone tablets, 44 of which decorate alternate pages throughout the book.

"Niagara Falls Park." She has other faults, such as eating too much fruit. The new creature eventually identifies herself as Eve.

Eve wants Adam to quit going over Niagara Falls; he does it anyway, in a barrel and in a tub. After he tires of Eve's research and experimentation, he moves to a more remote location. Meanwhile, Eve continues trying to get apples from the forbidden tree. When she finally eats one, death comes to the world; a tiger eats Adam's horse. Adam finds a place outside the park that Eve calls Tonawanda. Eve follows him; she is "curtained in boughs and bunches of leaves" and blushes and titters when Adam removes them. As Eve makes their CLOTHES out of animal skins, Adam begins to find her a good companion.

A year later, a new creature appears among them who is named Cain. Adam thinks that Eve "caught it while I was up country trapping on the North Shore of the Erie." He puzzles over the new creature and Eve's curious devotion to it. As he studies it, he concludes it must be a kangaroo. When Cain is about two years old, Adam concludes he is not a kangaroo. Months later, another baby, Abel, appears. Adam cannot understand why *he* never finds one. The final paragraph jumps ahead 10 years. Adam now understands that Cain and Abel are boys; there are some girls as well. He concludes that he "was mistaken about Eve in the beginning; it is better to live outside the Garden with her than inside it without her."

BACKGROUND AND PUBLISHING HISTORY

This simple text, originally about 4,000 words in length, has had a complex publishing history that has produced multiple versions. Clemens wrote his original draft some time before early 1893. When he was invited to contribute a humorous piece to the *Niagara Book*, a souvenir publication for the 1893 BUFFALO World's Fair, he reworked his Adam material by placing Eden at NIAGARA FALLS and working in local Buffalo place names, such as Lake Erie and Tonawanda. The resulting piece appeared in the book as "The Earliest Authentic Mention of Niagara Falls, Extracts from Adam's Diary. Translated from the Original Ms. by Mark Twain." In 1897 the story

mention God and generally avoids religious themes. It is written in the form of actual day-to-day diary entries by ADAM and should be compared to Clemens's much earlier "BOY'S MANUSCRIPT."

The diary begins when Eve arrives in Eden—which surrounds NIAGARA FALLS—and continues, with widening chronological gaps, until Abel is 10 years old. Adam initially puzzles over "the new creature with the long hair" who gets in his way, and resents her naming "everything that comes along." For example, he had already named the estate "Garden of Eden," but she has renamed it was included in the English edition of *Tom Sawyer, Detective*, but without reference to Niagara Falls; this may have been Clemens's original version. Meanwhile, Clemens occasionally read extracts from the text during his 1895–96 worldwide lecture tour.

In April 1904, HARPER'S published *Extracts from Adam's Diary* as an 89-page book, using the *Niagara Book* version and adding illustrations by Fred STROTHMANN. The following year, Clemens rewrote the story, removing all references to Niagara so it could be merged into "EVE'S DIARY," which he was then writing for HARPER'S MAGAZINE. Harper's did not, however, publish any "Adam's Diary" material in its Christmas issue. Next, when "Extracts from Adam's Diary" was collected in *The $30,000 Bequest* anthology, it contained only minor revisions of its original text. Clemens's new 1905 material was finally incorporated into the book publication of EVE'S DIARY in 1906. The 1904 book edition was reprinted unchanged in Harper's 1931 book, *The Private Lives of Adam and Eve*. The OXFORD MARK TWAIN edition published facsimile reprints of the first editions of both "diaries" as *The Diaries of Adam and Eve* (1996). In 1988, actor David Birney adapted both "diaries" to a stage play, *The Diaries of Adam and Eve*. He and Meredith Baxter Birney played the title roles, wearing clothes contemporary to Clemens's time. Birney continued to stage his production into the 21st century.

CRITICAL COMMENTARY

Clemens demonstrates his fascination with the First Family (particularly Eve) in his various Adam and Eve stories, mainly written between 1892 and 1910. With a few inconsistencies, these stories form a fictional biography of two people falling in love and finding interdependence. The stories "Extracts from Adam's Diary" and "Eve's Diary" are both the most familiar and the only ones published in the author's lifetime, as well as the two he chose to revise as complementary pieces. In these diaries, emphasizing Eve's effect on Adam, Clemens focuses on the pair's developing relationship, mostly leaving theology to the unpublished works. Humanity does fall in these stories, and in Clemens's view of the Fall, both Adam and Eve are responsible for it. Traditionally, the Fall has often been regarded as fortunate, since

it enabled God to demonstrate his love by redeeming humanity through Christ: without the Fall, there could be no redemption. In these stories, love—human love—is the reason for the fall. Eve's love saves Adam and, through him, humanity. God hardly appears. The emphasis is on a couple's relationship.

In her diary, Eve says, "I feel exactly like an experiment. . . . I am coming to be convinced that that is what I am—an experiment, just an experiment, and nothing more." But Eve is much more, as she soon realizes, and she will cause Adam to become much more than he ever imagined he could be, even as they lose the great gift that has been conferred upon them. Adam is "the other Experiment," but at the same time, Eve also declares in "Autobiography of Eve" that they are both scientists, and although Adam and Eve never refer to themselves as such in their diaries, they behave as scientists in each. Not only are they subjects and results of an experiment, but they, mainly Eve, are also researchers of themselves and their world. They are involved in discovering not only who but what they are. They are the experiment happening, but also the ones determining how it and their world develop. As scientist, Eve classifies and categorizes the creatures and objects of this new world by naming them. Unlike the objective scientist, she intuitively believes in natural relationships between words and things; she sees a creature and immediately knows what to call it.

The emphasis on empirical science underscores the importance of experiencing in order to understand. Although ignorant and innocent, Eve is intelligent. Naming things around her is part of her way of expressing her love for the world she calls "majestic . . . noble and beautiful"; for Adam, at least initially, naming is mechanical, a chore, a part of his duties as estate manager. He accepts the world as is. Eve wonders about it, wants to know more, and becomes eager to be a part of it, to alter it for the better if she can. This world accepts her, as indicated by the animals' behavior toward her. They follow her, listen to her, usually obey her. As Shelley Fisher Fishkin observes, "Eve's sense of self remains independent from her status as Adam's helpmate." She does not surrender her human integrity as she finds the complement of her humanity in Adam.

Adam comes to realize, as Eve does, that Eden is more than a place. It is a state of mind that the two build around each other. Attracted by Eve, Adam feels himself pulled out of his self-absorption and into an expanded view of the world through which he can experience his full humanity and can make that humanity felt in his environment. Eve provides dialogue and language for Adam and teaches him inclusiveness and expansiveness. She also offers him companionship and ends her own loneliness: "I used the sociable 'we' a good deal, because it seemed to flatter him to be included" (*Eve's Diary*).

Adam eagerly joins Eve in eating the fruit of the Forbidden Tree, saying he was obliged to do so although "it was against my principles," because he was hungry; that is, human urges—desire for food and for Eve—compel him to join her in altering and abandoning Paradise. But these basic human drives are minor compared to the qualities Eve helps Adam to realize. Ursula Le Guin notes "that although Eve has not changed much, she has changed Adam profoundly." In the end, Adam has begun to realize what Eve—even in losing the Garden—has brought to him. As James Wilson asserts, "the diaries chart their discovery of the redemptive power of human love," not divine love.

In some ways, the diaries are reminiscent of the three McWILLIAMS stories about a married couple. The diaries present "the difference of the sexes," in Lawrence Berkove's words, beginning "as comic contrast, transmut[ing] into interdependence, and culminat[ing] as a love that is sufficient unto itself and feels no need of a heaven."

Critical Commentary by John H. Davis

BIBLIOGRAPHY

Berkove, Lawrence, ed. *The Best Short Stories of Mark Twain*. New York: Modern Library, 2004.

Brodwin, Stanley. "The Humor of the Absurd: Mark Twain's Adamic Diaries." *Criticism* 14 (1972): 49–64.

Fishkin, Shelley Fisher. "Mark Twain and Women." In *The Cambridge Companion to Mark Twain*, edited by Forrest G. Robinson, 52–73. Cambridge: Cambridge University Press, 1995.

Le Guin, Ursula. "Introduction." *The Diaries of Adam and Eve*. 1904. In *The Oxford Mark Twain*, edited by Shelley Fisher Fishkin, xxxi–xli. New York: Oxford University Press, 1996.

Twain, Mark. "Autobiography of Eve." In *The Bible According to Mark Twain: Irreverent Writings of Eden, Heaven, and the Flood by America's Master Satirist*, edited by Howard G. Baetzhold and Joseph B. McCullough, 42–62. New York: Simon & Schuster, 1996.

———. *The Diaries of Adam and Eve*, edited by Shelley Fisher Fishkin. New York: Oxford University Press, 1996.

———. "Eve's Diary: Translated from the Original." In *The Bible According to Mark Twain: Irreverent Writings of Eden, Heaven, and the Flood by America's Master Satirist*, edited by Howard G. Baetzhold and Joseph B. McCullough, 20–33. New York: Simon & Schuster, 1996.

———. "Extract from Adam's Diary: Translated from the Original MS." In *The Bible According to Mark Twain: Irreverent Writings of Eden, Heaven, and the Flood by America's Master Satirist*, edited by Howard G. Baetzhold and Joseph B. McCullough, 8–16. New York: Simon & Schuster, 1996.

———. "'Extracts from Adam's Diary' from the Original Niagara Book Version." In *The Bible According to Mark Twain: Irreverent Writings of Eden, Heaven, and the Flood by America's Master Satirist*, edited by Howard G. Baetzhold and Joseph B. McCullough, 278–286. New York: Simon & Schuster, 1996.

———. "Pudd'head Wilson's New Calendar." *Following the Equator: A Journey around the World*. 1897. In *The Oxford Mark Twain*, edited by Shelley Fisher Fishkin. New York: Oxford University Press, 1996.

Wilson, James D. *A Reader's Guide to the Short Stories of Mark Twain*. Boston: G. K. Hall, 1987.

Extracts from Captain Stormfield's Visit to Heaven

See "Captain Stormfield's Visit to Heaven."

Eye Openers: Good Things, Immensely Funny Sayings & Stories (1871)

Pirated collection of Clemens sketches, published by John Camden HOTTEN. The unauthorized book includes Clemens's BURLESQUE AUTOBIOGRAPHY and 26 sketches, including the first book publication of "JOURNALISM IN TENNESSEE."

"A Fable"

Aesopian tale first published in 1909. Borrowing animal characters from RUDYARD KIPLING's *The Jungle Book* (1894), Clemens presents a simple allegory about the role of training in aesthetic appreciation. A human artist paints a picture, but among the animals, only his house cat can find its beauty.

Clemens wrote this 1,100-word tale in DUBLIN, New Hampshire, in June 1906 and published it in *HARPER'S MAGAZINE* in December 1909. It was later collected in *The Mysterious Stranger and Other Stories* (1922).

SYNOPSIS

After painting a picture, an artist places it to be viewed through a mirror to double the distance and soften its beauty. His cat tells the animals of the woods that the picture is the most beautiful thing he has ever seen, explaining that a "picture" is something flat and a "mirror" is a hole in the wall. Doubting that anything can be as beautiful as the cat describes, the ass goes to see for himself, but when he stands *between* the picture and the mirror, he sees only an ass in the hole and returns to denounce the cat as a liar. Hathi the elephant sends Baloo the bear to investigate. Baloo calls both the cat and the ass liars, as there is nothing in the hole but a bear. Each of the other animals also sees only its own kind in the hole. After Hathi himself finally goes, he denounces all the others as liars and says that the cat is morally and mentally blind since the hole contains nothing but an elephant.

The cat draws this moral: "You can find in a text whatever you bring, if you will stand between it and the mirror of your imagination."

Fables of Man, Mark Twain's (1972)

Collection of posthumously published material, edited by John S. TUCKEY for the MARK TWAIN PROJECT. Clemens wrote most of this material after 1895, with some pieces going back to the 1870s. Most are unfinished, but some he completed and did not publish because he or his publishers thought them too bold for publication. Several items appear in earlier books edited by A. B. PAINE and BERNARD DEVOTO; however, Tuckey's volume is the first to publish critically edited texts.

Most selections reflect the growing despair of Clemens's last years, when he became convinced that man is the creature of a remote and uncaring god and that mankind will forever repeat its greatest follies. Each selection is a fantasy exploration of some aspect of the nature or condition of mankind. Tuckey has arranged the 36 stories under three broad headings. "The Myth of Providence" contains 16 mostly satirical explorations of ideas about man and the universe. "Little Bessie" (written, 1908–09), for example, is about a precocious three-year-old who questions the harshness of divine justice. "THE INTERNATIONAL LIGHTNING TRUST"—which Clemens was about to publish when he died—is about two men who get rich selling insurance, while convincing themselves that they are merely instruments of God's will.

The seven stories in "The Dream of Brotherhood" challenge the notion that there will ever be true brotherhood. Its longest selection is the unfinished novel "THE REFUGE OF THE DERELICTS," in which victims of various misfortunes gather together. This section also includes "You've Been a Dam Fool, Mary. You Always Was!" and two short pieces about Jews.

"The Nightmare of History" has 13 stories exploring the possibility of new religious myths enslaving mankind. The section's longest piece, "The Secret History of Eddypus, the World-Empire," projects a nightmare future in which Mary Baker Eddy's CHRISTIAN SCIENCE religion dominates the world. Several shorter selections were previously published as part of the "Papers of the Adam Family" in LETTERS FROM THE EARTH (1962).

Tuckey's THE DEVIL'S RACE-TRACK: MARK TWAIN'S GREAT DARK WRITINGS (1980) includes "The Refuge of the Derelicts" and 11 shorter pieces from Fables of Man.

"The Facts Concerning the Recent Carnival of Crime in Connecticut"

First published in 1876, this SHORT STORY is Clemens's first major exploration of the power of one's conscience. It is a theme frequently touched on in Tom Sawyer (1876), which he published the same year. He carried this exploration further in Huckleberry Finn (1884), in which Huck finally concludes that "it don't make no difference whether you do right or wrong, a person's conscience ain't got no sense, and just goes for him anyway" (chapter 33). While the anonymous narrator of this 6,600-word story differs from Clemens in having an ambulatory son and an aunt named Mary, he resembles the author in other details, such as speaking with a drawl and being a prosperous 40-year-old writer.

SYNOPSIS

Pleased to receive a letter from his morally upright Aunt Mary announcing her imminent visit, the narrator vows that if his "most pitiless enemy" appeared, he would right any wrong he may have done him. At that moment, the door opens and a shriveled dwarf enters. About 40 years old, misshapen and covered with green mold, the dwarf seems like a dim BURLESQUE of the narrator himself. The dwarf's rude behavior and exaggerated drawl also remind the narrator of himself.

When the narrator threatens to toss him out, the dwarf accurately describes how the narrator recently turned away a tramp and broke a young writer's heart by refusing to read her manuscript. Everything that the small fiend says is an accusation, and every accusation a painful truth. When the dwarf admits that he is the narrator's conscience, the narrator joyfully springs at him, but he jumps atop a bookcase. After the man's son enters the room and is chased out, the man discovers that his conscience is invisible to all but him. He tries to lure his conscience closer, but cannot get at him.

From his pygmy visitor, the narrator learns that consciences harass people repeatedly for the same offense not only because it is their business, but because they enjoy it. He also learns that when people listen to their consciences, the consciences grow; however, when people—such as the narrator—ignore them, they go to sleep and shrivel. The conscience of one man he knows sleeps in a cigar-box; that of another man is 37 feet tall. The conscience of a thieving publisher (JOHN CAMDEN HOTTEN?) can be seen only with a microscope.

When Aunt Mary arrives, she berates the narrator for neglecting people whom he promised to look after and chides him for his smoking habit. As she talks, the narrator's conscience falls to the floor and weakens, allowing the man to tear him to shreds and burn the pieces. Now a free man, the narrator orders his aunt out. Since then, his life has been bliss. In settling old scores, he has killed 38 persons, burned down a house and swindled widows and orphans. He concludes by inviting medical colleges seeking tramps for research to examine the lot in his cellar.

PUBLISHING HISTORY

After delivering this story as a paper to Hartford's MONDAY EVENING CLUB on January 24, 1876, Clemens published it in the ATLANTIC MONTHLY in June. It was later collected in The Stolen White Elephant, and in Tom Sawyer Abroad, Tom Sawyer, Detective and Other Stories. In 1988, actor Richard Henzel appeared in a television adaptation of this story titled "Mark Twain's Carnival of Crime." Dressed as an elderly Clemens, sitting in his study recalling the incidents of the story, Henzel recites most of the original text, while acting out its various characterizations.

Richard Henzel plays the conscience-stricken narrator of "Mark Twain's Carnival of Crime." *(Courtesy Richard Henzel; Helmut Lipschis, photographer)*

CRITICAL COMMENTARY

"The Facts Concerning the Recent Carnival of Crime in Connecticut" is Clemens's first examination of the divided self, a theme he would explore in later works, including the *Mysterious Stranger* manuscripts, as well as in the consciences of Tom Sawyer and Huckleberry Finn. Some critics think Clemens is deliberately presenting a double-pronged conscience, perhaps looking in two directions, east and west.

Still adjusting to eastern ways and conflicted regarding his life and literature, the writer possibly presents that conflict from opposing directions. The central conscience of this work is the moldy dwarf; gentler and less formidable, though as insistent, is Aunt Mary, representing eastern societal expectations. Constantly reminding the narrator of past wrongs, the dwarf connotes looser western

ways, qualified by Clemens's Calvinistic upbringing. As one ages and begins accepting one's sins, so the narrator has worked hard to ignore the dwarf's twinging for every misstep. As a result, this baggage from the past (West), once heavier, shrinks the further away the narrator moves (East). Unable to ignore Aunt Mary, he welcomes a visit from her and offers to right wrongs against his worst enemy, the previously invisible, unknown conscience.

Details in the sketch suggest the unnamed narrator is Clemens: the drawl he shares with the dwarf, the refusal to read a manuscript, the cheating publisher, the wronged younger brother (Henry), the chafing under eastern social expectations. The character of Aunt Mary, who signifies new ways and restrictions, is apparently based on Clemens's friend MARY FAIRBANKS, whom he called "Aunt Mary," and his wife, Olivia, who initially disapproved of his smoking and desired prayers at every meal. Clemens himself sought to meet eastern literary standards and was disappointed that western literature was often misunderstood or unaccepted, even disapproved.

As caricature, the dwarf has no sense of proportion, punishing any action with guilt, allowing no enjoyment or satisfaction. A product of guilt, he harries people to repent everything, as in Huck's struggle with his conscience about Jim in *Huckleberry Finn*: "What's the use you learning to do right when it's troublesome to do right and ain't no trouble to do wrong and the wages is just the same?" The amoral dwarf deals more with typical wrongs and sins or ethical issues than social improprieties. Whereas selfish pleasure motivates the dwarf, moral certainty based on rules of genteel society drives Aunt Mary.

Motivated by self-esteem, the narrator measures himself against others, not against principle. The dwarf is an internal agent, formed as counter to and from basic impulses, particularly guilt and self-doubt, which he utilizes. Aunt Mary is an external influence, formed by social forces demanding conformity. Internal mechanism relies on what a person essentially is, external upon what one becomes for society. Without an appropriate compromise, the outcome is a divided self, pulled between society and inner drives. The dwarf is a burlesque of the self, not the true self. In their master/slave relationship, the narrator forever sees his worst self exaggerated in the dwarf.

Deciding to reject both consciences, noting that the dwarf becomes weaker when ignored, the narrator ignores Aunt Mary in order to put the dwarf to sleep, implying that the consciences are linked. He kills the dwarf, then throws his shredded body into the fire, calling it "my burnt-offering," a scapegoat for his sins. Then he orders Aunt Mary out. Free, without restraints or guilt, he begins his carnival of crime.

The anticlimactic order of the subsequent atrocities (he swindles a widow and children out of their cow, after murdering 38 people) indicates that the story is not meant seriously. Lacking conscience, the narrator lacks self-control, but he is a victim of self-imposed guilt. Knowing his bliss will not last, he must find inner strength, relying on himself and not a self-defeating inner self and conformist society.

Critical Commentary by John H. Davis

BIBLIOGRAPHY

Twain, Mark. "The Facts Concerning the Recent Carnival of Crime in Connecticut." In *Mark Twain: Collected Tales, Sketches, Speeches, & Essays, 1852–1890*, edited by Louis J. Budd, 644–660. New York: The Library of America, 1992.

"The Facts Concerning the Recent Resignation"

SKETCH first published in the *New York Tribune* on February 13, 1868 and reprinted in *Sketches, New and Old* (1875). After working in WASHINGTON, D.C., for two months as Senator William M. STEWART's private secretary, Clemens wrote this 2,660-word piece as a SATIRE on the pretensions of minor government officials. He later wrote two similar sketches, "My Late Senatorial Secretaryship" (1868) and "Running for Governor" (1870).

SYNOPSIS

Dateline: WASHINGTON, D.C., December 2, 1867. Clemens announces that he has resigned as clerk of the Senate Committee on Conchology after only

six days on the job because of outrages heaped on him. He has not, for example, been given an amanuensis with whom to play BILLIARDS. More important, he has not received due courtesies from other cabinet members. He went to the secretaries of the Navy, War Department, and Treasury, with trenchant advice, only to be treated rudely and ignored. When he attempted to sit in at a cabinet meeting, even the president (presumably ANDREW JOHNSON) treated him brusquely, demanding to know who he was. Told that clerks are not invited to cabinet meetings, he left, only to suffer a final indignity back at his own office when a member of his Senate committee demanded that he get out some reports. Appalled that for $6 a day he was expected to *work*, he quit, crying "Give me liberty or give me death!" When he billed the Treasury Department for his services, the secretary disallowed every item but his salary for six days. The items not allowed included three $50 fees for consultations with cabinet members and a $2,800 reimbursement for 14,000 miles of travel to JERUSALEM.

"The Five Boons of Life"

Clemens's first publication in HARPER'S WEEKLY (July 5, 1902), this 765-word fable takes the form of a condensed novel in five chapters. It is a pessimistic summing up of the futility of seeking any lasting joy in life, apart from release. Clemens would later amplify this sentiment in "THE DEATH OF JEAN" 1909), which calls his daughter's death "the most precious of all gifts."

SYNOPSIS

The good fairy offers a youth the chance to choose Fame, Love, Riches, Pleasure or Death as a gift, warning him that only one is truly valuable. The youth chooses Pleasure, but eventually discovers that each pleasure he experiences is short-lived and disappointing. When the fairy returns, the youth makes Love his second choice. Years later, he sits by a coffin; desolated by his losses, he curses Love. Next he chooses Fame. Soon his name fills the world and everything is good—until envy comes, followed by detraction, hate, persecution, and, finally, pity—the funeral of fame.

His fourth choice is Wealth—which represents power. In just three years, however, he is reduced to shivering in a garret, clothed in rags. Now he curses all the gifts as nothing but temporary disguises for the lasting realities of Pain, Grief, Shame, and Poverty. Finally realizing what the fairy has been trying to tell him, he calls out for the inestimable gift that will end his pain and grief. However, when the fairy returns, Death is not among the gifts she can offer, as she has given it to a child who asked the fairy to make the choice for her. When the man asks what is left for him, the fairy answers, "the wanton insult of Old Age."

Following the Equator: A Journey Around the World (1897)

Clemens's fifth and last TRAVEL BOOK, written in 1896–97 and published in 1897. In contrast to his earlier travel writings, *Following the Equator* is a relatively straightforward narrative of the round-the-world LECTURE tour that he made between July 1895 and July 1896. Its narrative follows his itinerary faithfully, often inserting specific dates and places, and it contains few attempts at invention or embroidery. In another departure from his earlier travel books, Clemens makes no attempt to mask his identity as its narrator. In contrast to *A Tramp Abroad* (1880), for example, he alludes to traveling with his wife and daughter, though he never mentions either's name (chapters 1, 34, 40, 44, 48, and 65; his wife Livy can be seen in a photograph on page 66 of the early editions). He specifically mentions "Clemens" in a story about meeting General Grant (chapter 2) and in a list of horse billiards scores (chapter 4); later he discusses the "MARK TWAIN CLUB" (chapter 25) and explicitly identifies himself as "Mark Twain" (chapter 45).

While *Following the Equator* contains many humorous passages, its general tone is more serious than that of the earlier travel books. It has lengthy

James B. Pond's photograph of Clemens relaxing on a deck chair aboard the *Warrimoo* provided the frontispiece for the first edition of *Following the Equator*.

discussions of Australian labor recruitment, history and economic development, Indian culture, British rule in India, and South African politics. It offers only three tall tales (chapters 2, 13, and 28) and attempts BURLESQUE only rarely—as in Clemens's claim to have been bitten by a cobra (chapter 57) and a preposterous summation of South Africa's tangled politics (chapter 65). The book lifts many passages directly from Clemens's NOTEBOOKS and extracts quotes from about 30 other authors that total about 24,000 words.

Each chapter head presents at least one MAXIM attributed to "PUDD'NHEAD WILSON's New Calendar." The original American edition is a lavishly illustrated one-volume book; most later editions are sparsely illustrated two-volume sets, with 36 chapters in the first volume and 33 separately numbered chapters in the second volume. While the narrative follows Clemens's itinerary closely, it distributes its

Around-the-World Lecture Tour, 1895–1896

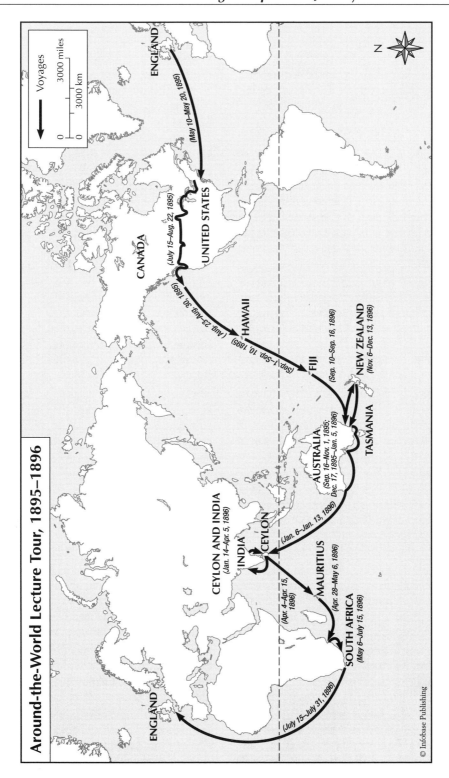

ENGLAND
(May 10–May 20, 1895)

UNITED STATES
(July 15–Aug. 22, 1895)

CANADA

HAWAII
(Aug. 23–Aug. 30, 1895)

FIJI
(Sep. 1–Sep. 10, 1895)

NEW ZEALAND
(Nov. 6–Dec. 13, 1896)
(Sep. 10–Sep. 16, 1896)

AUSTRALIA
(Sep. 16–Nov. 1, 1895;
Dec. 17, 1895–Jan. 5, 1896)

TASMANIA

CEYLON
(Jan. 6–Jan. 13, 1896)

CEYLON AND INDIA
(Jan. 14–Apr. 5, 1896)

INDIA
(Apr. 4–Apr. 15, 1896)

MAURITIUS
(Apr. 28–May 6, 1896)

SOUTH AFRICA
(May 6–July 15, 1896)

ENGLAND
(July 15–July 31, 1896)

Voyages
3000 miles
0   3000 km
0

N

© Infobase Publishing

space unevenly. Though he spent nearly equal amounts of time in Australia, India, and South Africa, 40 percent of the book is devoted to India, 27 percent to Australia and 10 percent to South Africa. The remaining space covers his Pacific voyage and his visits to New Zealand, Ceylon, and Mauritius.

SYNOPSIS

Following the Equator contains 188,000 words in 69 numbered chapters and a conclusion. The first chapter summarizes Clemens's journey from ELMIRA, New York—which he left on July 14, 1895—across the northern United States to British Columbia in Canada. On August 23, he sailed into the PACIFIC OCEAN on the steamship WARRIMOO. The next seven chapters cover his voyage, during which he touched at HAWAII (August 30) and FIJI (September 10). This section also discusses the recruitment of South Seas islanders to plantations in Australia's Queensland colony, which Clemens never visited (chapters 5–6).

After reaching Sydney, AUSTRALIA (which Clemens often calls "Australasia"), on September 15, Clemens was joined by Carlyle SMYTHE, who accompanied him on the rest of his tour as his agent. They traveled around Australia's southern periphery by train and ship until November 1 (chapters 9–25, 27–29, and 36), then sailed to NEW ZEALAND, where they also traveled by train and ship from November 6 through December 13 (chapters 26, 30–35). After returning to Australia, they spent a week in New South Wales. On December 23, Clemens left Sydney aboard the *Oceana*, touching at several Australian ports before making his final departure from the continent on January 4, 1896.

Clemens reached CEYLON on January 13, 1896 (chapters 37 and 62), continuing on to INDIA the next day. After reaching BOMBAY on January 20, he spent over two months traveling through India, mostly by train (chapters 38–61). On March 28, he left CALCUTTA aboard the *Wardha*, stopping in Madras and Ceylon before continuing to MAURITIUS, where he landed on April 15 (chapters 61–63). On April 28, he sailed for SOUTH AFRICA, stopping in MOZAMBIQUE on May 4 (chapter 64) before reaching Durban on May 6. Over the next two months, he traveled through South Africa by

train (chapters 65–Conclusion). He considered his lecture tour ended in Cape Town, from which he sailed on July 15. After touching at MADEIRA, he reached Southampton, England, on July 31.

The chapter numbers below are taken from the one-volume American edition of *Following the Equator*, whose first 36 chapters match the chapter numbers of first book of two-volume editions. Chapter numbers for the second book of two-volume editions are inserted in parentheses. Information taken from outside chapters—such as names and dates—is presented within parentheses.

MORE TRAMPS ABROAD (1897), the British edition of *Following the Equator*, has 72 numbered chapters and a conclusion. Most of its chapters have nearly identical counterparts in *Following the Equator*; however, all but the first nine are numbered differently. Both editions also have chapters that break differently, so there is no consistent numerical relationship between chapters in the two editions. In the chapter synopses that follow, numbers of *More Tramps* chapters corresponding to each *Following the Equator* chapter are given in square brackets. For example: "*Chapter 62 (2:26) [MTA–65 & 66]*" indicates *Following the Equator*, chapter 62 (chapter 26 in volume 2) [*More Tramps Abroad*, chapters 65–66]. Additional comments within brackets describe substantive differences between chapters of the two editions. These remarks ignore the minor differences in spelling, punctuation, phrasing, and paragraph breaks that pervade the two editions.

Chapter 1 [More Tramps Abroad–1]

The LECTURE journey starts in PARIS, France, where Clemens has been living with his family. After he sails to America with his whole family, two family members (Olivia and Clara Clemens) elect to continue with him. They start west from New York (July 14, 1895) with Major POND managing the tour to the West Coast. A slow march takes them to Victoria, British Columbia, where they sail on the PACIFIC OCEAN aboard a comfortable ship (*Warrimoo*) with good discipline and a pleasant crew (August 23).

The ship's brightest passenger is a young Canadian. A "remittance man," he is a dissipated ne'er-do-well who has been sent abroad to live on monthly remittances since he cannot keep pledges of abstinence. Most such pledges do not strike at a problem's root—man's *desire* to drink. For his own part, Clemens once got relief from lumbago when he stopped smoking and drinking coffee, tea, and alcohol. He later recommended a similar regimen to a woman whose health had run down; unfortunately, she could not stop doing any of these things because she no bad habits to break.

Chapter 2 [MTA–2]

Several days out, the ship encounters such hot weather that the passengers and crew begin wearing white linen. Shipboard conversation wanders to instances of extraordinary memory. One passenger who had served under India's viceroy recalls a Brahmin memory expert. Mark Twain recalls his own second meeting with General GRANT, who remembered a remark that Clemens had made the first time they had met, 10 years earlier.

A popular game among passengers is finishing incomplete stories. One man offers $50 to anyone who can satisfactorily end a story that he began reading 25 years earlier, when a train wreck interrupted him before he finished. None of the proposed endings satisfies a jury, so Clemens leaves it to readers to end the story themselves.

Chapter 3 [MTA–2 & 3]

On the seventh day out (August 30), the ship anchors off Honolulu, but no one can go ashore because of CHOLERA. Seeing HAWAII reminds Clemens of his earlier visit there (1866) and of KAME-HAMEHA I and his successors. The old monarchy is gone now, replaced by a republic, and the islands are modernizing. [This chapter matches the end of chapter 2 and all of chapter 3 in *More Tramps Abroad*.]

Chapter 4 [MTA–4]

The ship sails the next morning. On September 3, the passengers see a lunar ECLIPSE. Two days later, they cross the equator, but there are no "fool" ceremonies, such as are often customary during crossings. A popular shipboard diversion is "horse-billiards," or shovel-board (shuffleboard), a game demanding skill and luck [*More Tramps Abroad* has an additional half-page on horse-billiards]. In a tourna-

ment, Clemens wins a cheap Waterbury watch that later perplexes him when he tries to reconcile its time with that of the eccentric bells of Pretoria's parliament clock.

Deck-washing aboard the ship begins early; crew members never warn passengers when they will begin and enjoy sloshing water through their ports. Passengers also often ruin their clothes when they brush up against freshly painted surfaces. When the ship crosses the International Dateline on September 8, it suddenly becomes September 10. A child who is born in steerage at that moment will probably go through life never knowing its correct birthday.

Chapter 5 [MTA–5]

In an argument among Scottish passengers about pronouncing Scottish words, Clemens annoys everyone by interjecting his own opinion; however, his timely invention of a couplet that he attributes to Robert Burns ends the argument agreeably.

As the ship proceeds, interest in the Southern Cross constellation mounts. After the ship enters a Milky Way of islands, it passes through the Horne (Futuna) Islands, in the region from which workers are recruited for Australia's Queensland plantations. In former times, "recruiting" was simply man-stealing, but workers must now come voluntarily. A book by Captain Wawn, a former recruiting ship-master, says that labor recruiters are popular among the islanders, but Wawn's own evidence suggests otherwise.

Chapter 6 [MTA–6]

A pamphlet by the missionary William Gray is a strong indictment against Queensland labor recruiting. Since everyone involved in recruiting profits but the recruits themselves, one wonders why they go to Queensland willingly.

Chapter 7 [MTA–7]

After entering the FIJI islands, the ship lands at Suva on September 11. A single sailing vessel from Duluth (Minnesota) represents the American commercial marine in the harbor. As everyone goes ashore to explore, Clemens visits the governor's country residence. Fiji's last king ceded the islands to Britain in order to stave off American occupation.

Chapter 8 [MTA–8]

A glance at a map of the South Pacific reveals what a stupendous island wilderness the region is. Much remains unknown about it. Twenty years ago, two men speaking an unknown language drifted to Fiji on a canoe; even now, no one knows where they came from.

As the ship returns to sea, its most cultivated passenger is an English naturalist who lives in New Zealand. Owning an exhaustive knowledge of Australasia's fauna, he regards the region's most remarkable creature to be that curious combination of bird, fish, amphibian, burrower, crawler, quadruped, and Christian called the Ornithorhyncus (duckbill platypus), the most grotesque of animals. His poetic tribute to the creature recalls Julia MOORE's verses.

Chapter 9 [MTA–9 & 10]

On the evening of September 15, the ship approaches Sydney, AUSTRALIA. Its harbor is enclosed by a dangerous precipice that once caused a tragedy when the *Duncan Dunbar,* loaded with schoolgirls and their mothers, broke up on its rocks (1857). The beautiful harbor and city have a fine climate, but Australia as a whole has really good climate only around its edges. Its broad interior regions are dry and forbidding, generating hot winds that blow dust storms resembling Nevada's alkali dust storms (ZEPHYRS). [*More Tramps Abroad* omits most of the final paragraph on dust storms.]

Chapter 10 [MTA–11 & 12]

Modern Australian history began in 1770 with Captain COOK's founding of a British colony. Australia and Tasmania soon became harsh penal colonies. As more respectable colonists arrived, provisions were made for their protection, but a body called the "New South Wales Corps" became exploitative and oppressive and made rum the currency of the land. Eventually, New South Wales grew rich from mines and wool ranching, and developed every kind of cultural amenity.

Chapter 11 [MTA–13]

The people of all English-speaking colonies, including New South Wales, are lavishly hospitable. Sydney is an English city with American trimmings. Its finest homes are mostly residences of "squatters"—the Australian term for great landowners. Australians resemble Americans closely in dress, general appearance and speech, though they tend toward pronunciations such as *piper* for "paper."

Chapter 12 [MTA–14]

In Sydney, Clemens dreams that the visible universe is the physical body of God, within which the vast worlds we see in space are corpuscles, and human beings and other creatures are mere microbes. A missionary, Mr. X., finds Clemens's dream similar to sacred Hindu accounts of their origins. He thinks that one reason Christianity does not catch on in India is that its miracles pale next to those of Hindu legends.

Chapter 13 [MTA–15 & 16]

Australasia spends liberally on public works, such as government buildings, hospitals, and parks. The continent has four or five governors, but they are always away, leaving the lieutenant-governors to do the work; however, the country practically governs itself, limiting the governor's functions and making his ball a major event. Attending a Government House ball is the first of Sydney's great social pleasures; others include visiting Admiralty House, touring the harbor and fishing for sharks—the swiftest fish in the sea.

A previously unpublished story tells how impoverished young CECIL RHODES arrived in Sydney in 1870 and caught a great shark containing a copy of the *London Times* just 10 days old. The paper reported that since France had declared war on Prussia (July 19, 1870), wool prices were shooting up. Rhodes took the valuable news to Sydney's richest wool-broker, with whom he made a deal to corner the colony's entire crop, thereby pocketing his first fortune. [This chapter contains all of chapter 15 and the first two paragraphs of chapter 16 of *More Tramps Abroad.*]

Chapter 14 [MTA–16]

Health problems keep Clemens from visiting Queensland. Instead, he takes a train to Melbourne, the capital of Victoria. Australian distances are deceiving; Victoria looks small on a map, but is actually as large as Britain. The gauges of Australian trains change at each colony's borders, requiring passengers and freight to be shifted to different trains. Clemens changes cars at Albury, then slides smoothly through gameless plains.

Chapter 15 [MTA–17]

Wagga-Wagga is the former home of the famous TICHBORNE CLAIMANT, who had been a butcher there. For a quarter of a century, this impostor claimed to be "Sir Roger Tichborne," only to confess on his recent deathbed that he was Arthur Orton of Wagga-Wagga [*More Tramps Abroad* has four additional pages on Orton].

In Melbourne, Clemens hopes to unravel a mystery about another impostor—a man who once posed as *him*. On the day that President GARFIELD was shot (July 2, 1881), Clemens's wife received a letter from an English friend—here called "Henry Bascom"—whom he had known in England during the 1870s. Then in Melbourne, Bascom expressed condolences about Clemens's death during an Australian lecture tour. Bascom added that he reached Melbourne too late to see the body, but was in time to be a pallbearer. Since then, Clemens has been anxious to learn who the dead impostor was. The mystery has since grown larger; Bascom himself is now dead, and Sydney and Melbourne journalists never heard of the impostor. Just as the mystery appears unsolvable, it unexpectedly clears up; however, the rest of this story is saved for later (*see chapter 25*).

Chapter 16 [MTA–18]

A stately city, Melbourne covers an immense area. The Melbourne Cup, run on November 5, Guy Fawkes's Day, is Australasia's biggest annual event.

What most interests travelers to other lands are the people, novelties, and local history. While novelties are rare in Australia's modern cities, the country's history is almost always picturesque; it reads like beautiful lies. [*More Tramps Abroad* adds a two-page anecdote about an escaped convict named Buckley (c. 1780–c. 1856) who lived among Aboriginals for 32 years, then spent the rest of his life in Australia's European society.]

British colonial audiences welcome Americans warmly. Although the war-cloud hanging over England and America makes Clemens a prospective prisoner of war, he encounters no trouble anywhere

(an allusion to friction between the United States and Britain over Britain's dispute with Venezuela over the latter's border with British Guiana).

Chapter 17 [MTA–19]

The British Empire contains about 400 million people. Against such numbers, Australia's four million are nearly nothing; however, statistics show that they command a tenth of Britain's trade.

In the 17-hour train ride from Melbourne to Adelaide (October 11), Clemens meets a judge going to Broken Hill. That town in New South Wales is only 700 miles from Sydney, but to get there by train, the judge travels 2,000 miles by way of Adelaide. The route takes them through the kind of scrubby plains in which one expects to find hostile Aboriginals lurking, as in Australian novels. Aboriginals are great trackers: They may be assigned to the bottom level of human intelligence, but they can follow trails that would baffle Sherlock Holmes.

Chapter 18 [MTA–20]

As they pass through beautiful hills, Clemens asks a man the difference between gorse and broom; the man cannot answer, though he has been in Australia more than 50 years. When he was 20, he came from England hoping to amass £200 within five years and go home, but he is still here. His story seems pathetic, until Clemens learns that the man once helped discover fabulous copper mines and is now rich enough to buy a city. Since the copper strikes saved South Australia, the colony has also developed prosperous wool and grain industries.

The train also carries an American with the unique vocation of buying Australia's kangaroo-leather crop for shoes.

Chapter 19 [MTA–21]

An Australian specialty is the botanical garden. Whatever we can grow under glass will flourish outdoors in Australia. At Adelaide's zoo, Clemens sees a laughing jackass and a dingo. South Australia is confusingly named, as it is really *middle* Australia. As early as 1871–72, the province built a telegraph line across the continent to Port Darwin, connecting Australia with the rest of the world. To reach San Francisco, telegrams from Melbourne pass through 20 stops over 20,000 miles.

Chapter 20 [MTA–22]

Clemens encounters a friend, Mr. G., whom he knew at BAD NAUHEIM. While discussing mutual acquaintances, he tells G. about a fox-hunt he once saw in England and also recalls how he once got away from Nauheim in time to avoid a CHOLERA quarantine. When he took his family into ITALY, getting through customs would have been an ordeal, had he not carried a letter from the Italian consul-general at Frankfort.

Chapter 21 MTA–23]

Before visiting Australia, Clemens had never heard of the "weet-weet"—a lightweight object that Aboriginals can throw incredible distances using a technique that no one else understands. Their reputation for low intelligence must be due to race-aversion.

Whites have used many methods to keep the native population down, and there has been a long history of distrust on both sides. One of the kindest and most gentle ways, however, was a Christmas pudding laced with arsenic that whites gave to blacks. One of the many humorous things in the world is the white man's notion that he is less savage than other savages. [*More Tramps Abroad* has two additional pages about Aboriginals.]

Chapter 22 [MTA–24]

Australia provides no end of materials to imaginative writers. A whole literature could be made out of the Aboriginal alone. The prize curiosity of all the races, Aboriginals have incredible athletic skills, amazing hunting and tracking ability, and refined artistic skills. They also can stand immense physical pain. Australia's colorful slang contains such expressions as "Never-never country" for unpopulated plains and "new chum" for tenderfoot.

Chapter 23 [MTA–25]

From Adelaide, the travelers go to Horsham, Victoria, on October 17. They visit a nearby agricultural college, where magpies are out in full force. From there, they visit Stawell in the gold-MINING country. [Chapters 23 and 24 are combined in *More Tramps Abroad*'s chapter 25.]

Chapter 24 [MTA–25]

The travelers next go to Ballarat, where the first great Australian gold strike occurred in 1851, after smaller strikes elsewhere had begun drawing immigrants to Australia. Though comparatively small, Ballarat has the amenities of a major city, and its English is the standard dialect of cultivated Australasians.

Chapter 25 [MTA–26]

On October 23, Clemens goes (north) from Ballarat to Bendigo—a mining center that has turned out half as much gold as CALIFORNIA. His stay is made memorable by a hospitable Irishman, "Mr. Blank," who has an amazing familiarity with Clemens's books. Blank had been president of the 32-member Mark Twain Club of Corrigan Castle, Ireland, with which Clemens once conducted a prodigious correspondence. At first, the club's attentions flattered him; gradually, however, he came to dread its long monthly reports and its voluminous questions about his work, so he stopped replying. Blank confesses that *he* was the club's sole member; he wrote every speech and report himself. He also confesses to having written the "Henry Bascom" letter about Clemens's death in Australia (*discussed in chapter 15*).

Chapter 26 [MTA–27]

After visiting Maryborough and other towns, Clemens sails for NEW ZEALAND—a country about which he knows little. Aboard the steamer, he meets Professor X. of YALE UNIVERSITY, who describes the prodigious effort that he and fellow Yale professors once made to impress a visiting New Zealander with their knowledge of his country.

Chapter 27 [MTA–28, 29 & 30]

Clemens's November 1 diary entry describes sailing past Tasmania, whose native peoples are now dead and gone. Years ago, the long wars between whites and blacks were finally ended by the heroic work of a bricklayer named George Augustus Robinson. Alone in his belief that the native peoples were human beings, Robinson single-handedly talked them into surrendering peacefully. [This chapter has part of three *More Tramps Abroad* chapters. It omits a two-and-a-half-page extract from James Bonwick's *The Lost Tasmanian Race* that is in *More Tramps Abroad*'s chapter 28; it also omits a page and a half about Robinson from *More Tramps's* chapter 29; it has all of chapter 30 except a Pudd'n-head Wilson maxim.]

Chapter 28 [MTA–31]

Robinson proves the truth behind the aphorism, "Given the Circumstances, the Man will appear." His tale recalls a pre-CIVIL WAR story about a man named Ed Jackson, who went from Memphis, Tennessee to New York. Jackson's friends gave him a fake letter of introduction to Commodore VANDER-BILT from a man whom Vanderbilt purportedly knew as a boy. His friends expected Jackson to get into trouble; instead, he won Vanderbilt's confidence and returned as the director of a vast commercial project.

Chapter 29 [MTA–32 & 33]

The travelers stop at Tasmania's remarkably clean capital, Hobart—one of many "Junior Englands" they encounter. [This chapter matches chapter 32 and the first three pages of chapter 33 of *More Tramps Abroad*, which has two additional pages on convicts from J. S. Laurie's *The Story of Australasia.*]

Chapter 30 [MTA—33]

Clemens's first New Zealand stop is at Bluff, where the country's rabbit plague began. On November 6, he passes Invercargill and stops at Dunedin. There he meets Dr. Hockin, whose home is a museum of Maori art and antiquities. Hockin has a ghastly curiosity—a lignified caterpillar with a plant growing out of its neck that exemplifies nature's gift for playing nasty tricks. [This chapter matches the last four pages of *More Tramps Abroad*'s chapter 33, which omits a paragraph on tapeworms.]

Chapter 31 [MTA–34]

On November 11, the travelers ride a New Zealand "express" train that goes just over 20 miles per hour. Its cars are unusually modern and pleasant, however, in contrast to those on a train they rode to Maryborough, Australia. On that trip, a stranger describes what may be the world's worst hotel.

Chapter 32 [MTA–35]

The train passes through "Junior England" to Christchurch, whose museum has many interesting native artifacts and the skeleton of an extinct moa. Four days later, the travelers go to Lyttleton. From

there they sail for Auckland aboard the over-crowded *Flora*—the foulest boat on which Clemens has ever sailed. [About 375 words criticizing the company that operates the *Flora* are omitted in MTA.] At their first chance, they switch to the *Mahinapua.*

New Zealand women got the vote in 1893; they have proven that women are not as indifferent to politics as many people believe.

Chapter 33 [MTA–36]

During a quiet day at Nelson, the travelers learn about the notorious "Maungatapu Murders" of 30 years earlier—Nelson's one great historical event. The confession of Burgess, one of the convicted murderers, may be without peer in the literature of murder as a succinct, cold-blooded account of grisly crimes.

On November 20, they reach Auckland, but poor health keeps Clemens from visiting Rotorua's geyser region. They all sail from Auckland on November 26.

Chapter 34 [MTA–37]

On November 27, they anchor at Gisborne, where they watch passengers transfer between their ship and a tug on a swinging basket-chair. They leave Napier by train on December 2 and pass through Waitukurau.

Chapter 35 [MTA–38]

They continue their journey to Wanganui, where they see many Maori, who—unlike native Australians—were not exterminated. Wanganui has some curious war monuments paying tribute to white men "who fell in defense of law and order against fanaticism and barbarism." Calling Maori patriotism "fanaticism" cannot, however, degrade it. A strangely thoughtless monument honors Maori who fought *against* their own people. While Clemens is in Wanganui, a lunatic bursts into his room to warn him that Jesuits plan to kill him.

On December 9, the travelers reach Wellington, from which they sail back to Australia.

Chapter 36 [MTA–39]

On December 13, they sail aboard the *Mararoa*. At sea, Clemens reads poems from JULIA MOORE's *Sentimental Song Book*, which has the same charm as

GOLDSMITH's *Vicar of Wakefield*. After reaching Sydney on December 17, they spend several days visiting nearby towns. Meanwhile, Clemens collects curious town names—such as Coolgardie, Mullengudgery, Murriwillumba, and Woolloomooloo—from which he composes a poem on Australian weather.

Chapter 37 (volume 2: chapter 1) [MTA–40]

On December 23, the travelers sail on the steamer *Oceana*. They stop at Melbourne for Christmas and at Adelaide for New Year's, then pass Cape Leeuwin on January 5, 1896, to begin the eight-day voyage to CEYLON.

Chapter 38 (2:2) [MTA–41]

The next day they continue their journey aboard the *Rosetta* and reach INDIA on January 20. A bewitching city, Bombay is the ARABIAN NIGHTS come again. India is a land of dreams and romance, of fabulous wealth and fabulous poverty, palaces and hovels, famine and pestilence, tigers and elephants; it is a hundred nations, a thousand religions, and 2 million gods.

At the travelers' hotel, the German manager and three assistants take them to their rooms, followed by 14 baggage-carriers with one item each. The burly German cuffs a servant, suddenly transporting Clemens back to his Missouri boyhood, when he saw slaves treated similarly. Through the evening, employees scream orders through hotel passageways; shouting, crashing, bird-screeching, and other sounds continue until midnight. At five the next morning, the din begins afresh when a crow begins jabbering.

Chapter 39 (2:3) [MTA–42]

Old dreams of India rise in a vague moonlight over one's opaque consciousness, illuminating a thousand forgotten boyhood visions of barbaric gorgeousness, with sumptuous princely titles such as Maharajah of Travancore, Nabob of Jubbulpore, and Begum of Bhopal. One's day in India begins when a "bearer" knocks at the door to announce in his strange "Bearer English" that the bath is ready. Manuel X., the first bearer whom the travelers hire, is so slow and forgetful that he is soon replaced by a younger man whom Clemens dubs "Satan." The

first task that Satan performs is to announce a visitor whom he calls "God"—the Aga Khan—who is surprisingly familiar with Huck Finn.

Chapter 40 (2:4) [MTA–43]

Other strong images of India are Government House and the mansion of a young native prince. Clemens interests himself in ceremonies and visits the Towers of Silence, where the Parsees leave their dead to be dried and picked clean by vultures—a funeral system equivalent to cremation as a sanitary measure.

Chapter 41 (2:5) [MTA–44]

A Mr. Gandhi [*not* Mohandas Gandhi] shows the travelers a Jain temple; then they see an Indian prince receive a Jain delegation in a colorful ceremony. Compared to this, a Christian exhibition would be a hideous affair—with the added disadvantage of white complexions. Nearly all black and brown skins are beautiful, but beautiful white skin is rare.

Chapter 42 (2:6) [MTA–45]

Near midnight the travelers see the betrothal ceremony of a 12-year-old Hindu girl. As they ride back in the dark, rats scurry around dim human forms stretched everywhere on the ground, illuminated by faint lamps. As Clemens writes this passage a year later, he reads cables reporting that plague is now sweeping Bombay. [This chapter's final passage, 775 words from Alexander William Kinglake's *Eothen* (1844) on plague in Cairo, is not in *More Tramps Abroad*.]

Chapter 43 (2:7) [MTA–46]

A Bombay trial of a cold-blooded murderer recalls the forgotten days of Thuggee, when professional murderers and thieves roamed India. The trial's official report reads like a Thug report of 50 years earlier; the criminal side of Indians has always been picturesque and readable.

There is only one India, and it has a monopoly of grand and imposing specialties and marvels all its own. India invented the plaque, the Car of Juggernaut, and Suttee—which once moved widows to throw themselves on their husbands' funeral fires. India's specialty is famine; it has 2 million gods and worships them all; everything is on a giant scale—

even poverty. On top of all this, India is the mother of that wonder of wonders—caste—as well as that mystery of mysteries, the satanic brotherhood of the Thugs.

Chapter 44 (2:8) [MTA–47]

On January 28, Clemens learns of an official Thug-book as he prepares to travel by train. Two days later, the railway station provides a great spectacle of people. Satan ruthlessly pushes a path through them; he was probably a Thug in an earlier incarnation. As Clemens travels, he reads about these strange Thugs and reaches the intensely Indian city of Baroda on January 31.

Chapter 45 (2:9) [MTA–48]

On a trip out of town, Clemens rides an elephant, then visits the Gaikwar of Baroda. During the train ride back from Baroda, he meets a man traveling with a remarkably long, low dog that reminds him of a dog that once saved him from embarrassment:

> While taking a train into New York City to visit Augustin Daly [see DALY, AUGUSTIN] at his theater once, Clemens happened to read a newspaper article about "bench-shows" for dogs that listed the dimensions of a prize Saint Bernard. When he reached New York, James Lewis surprised him with the warning that he would never get into Daly's office. That evening, a giant Irishman let him in the back entrance of Daly's theater, only to tell him that he would go no farther. As the man grilled him about what business he was in, Clemens spotted the man's pet dog; it was a Saint Bernard identical to the one he had seen in the newspaper, so he said he was a "bench-show" operator. The Irishman challenged him to prove it by giving his dog's dimensions. Quoting what he remembered from the paper, Clemens won the man over with precisely correct figures and was soon in Daly's office. As the only man ever to run Daly's back-door blockade, Clemens won an envied reputation among theater people.

Chapter 46 (2:10) [MTA–49]

Still on the Indian train, Clemens reads more about Thugs and cites incidents of their murderous activities before the British government suppressed them. Thugs were remarkable in many ways; they worked together without regard for religious or caste differences. Rarely fastidious about whom they killed, they were motivated by piety, gain, and the sport of killing.

Chapter 47 (2:11) [MTA–50]

There are many indications that Thugs often killed for sport. One might think that they were too callous to have human feelings; however, they had a passionate love for their own kin—a fact that a shrewd British officer used against them to help end their depredations.

Chapter 48 (2:12) [MTA–51]

The travelers leave Bombay for Allahabad by night train (February 2). On Indian trains, passengers do not pay extra for sleeping space, so they often must compete for places. The trains are manned exclusively by Indians, who are easily the world's most interesting people, but also the nearest to being incomprehensible. Their character, history, customs, and religion are filled with riddles.

Chapter 49 (2:13) [MTA–52]

The journey from Bombay to Allahabad is long, but too interesting to be tiring. The day begins early in the countryside, where nine-tenths of the people are farmers. India is not beautiful, but there is an enchantment about it. Its many names describe it correctly as the land of contradictions. For example, it is both the land of splendor and the land of desolation. The land where all life is holy, it is also the land of the Thug and poisoner.

Allahabad, the "City of God," is having a great religious fair near the confluence of the sacred Ganges and Jumna rivers, from which many people carry holy water.

Chapter 50 (2:14) [MTA–53]

The train ride to Benares takes just a few hours (February 5). Midway, the travelers change cars—a dull thing in most countries, but not in India, with its huge crowds, splendid costumes and confusion. There is another wait outside Benares, where women are carried in palanquins to stay hidden from view. The long ride to the hotel passes dusty, decaying temples. Though the region aches with age and penury, Benares does not disappoint. Older than history, it is as busy as an anthill, unspeakably sacred, and equally unsanitary. Religion is its business.

Chapter 51 (2:15) [MTA–54]

A great religious hive, Benares is a sort of army and navy store, theologically stocked. It offers everything for the pilgrim, from purification and protection against hunger to long life. It is a religious VESUVIUS in whose bowels theological forces have thundered and smoked for ages.

Chapter 52 (2:16) [MTA–55]

In a Benares temple, the travelers see a man shaping tiny gods from clay; every day he throws 2,000 of them into the Ganges—Benares's supreme showplace. As the travelers cruise on the river, they see nine corpses being burned, and marvel that people drink its dreadful water. They also visit the temple of the Thug goddess, Bhowanee or Kali. With Indians, all life seems to be sacred—except human life.

Benares is also the site of an important episode in the career of Warren Hastings, who saved the Indian Empire in 1781—the best service ever done to the Indians.

Chapter 53 (2:17) [MTA–56]

In Benares, Clemens sees his second living god, Sri 108 Swami Bhaskarananda Saraswati. Of the many wonders he has seen in the world, none interests him as much as these gods. What makes something a wonder is not what *we* see in it, but what *others* see. After Sri 108—who has attained a Hindu state of perfection—suggests that they exchange autographs, Clemens gives him a copy of *Huckleberry Finn*.

Chapter 54 (2:18) [MTA–57]

A train takes the travelers to India's capital, Calcutta (February 8), a city rich in historical memories, particularly of Clive's and Hastings's achievements. Its only great monument, however, is a lofty tower to Ochterlony (Sir David Ochterlony, 1758–1825). If India built similar monuments to all who deserved them, the landscape would be monotonous with them.

England is so far from India that it knows little about the eminent deeds its servants have performed there. The average person is profoundly ignorant of remote countries. All that most Hindus know about America, for example, is George Washington and CHICAGO—the "holy city" of the recent Congress of Religions. To outsiders, "Calcutta" infallibly evokes thoughts of the Black Hole. Visitors rush to see it, but nothing remains.

Chapter 55 (2:19) [MTA–58]

On February 14, the travelers leave Calcutta for Darjeeling. As they pass countless villages, they seem to be within a single vast city—the biggest on Earth. Multitudes of men work the fields, but no women. The hymn "From Greenland's Icy Mountains" (by REGINALD HEBER) speaks of lifting heathen lands from "error's chain," but when Clemens recalls seeing elderly women doing backbreaking work in GERMANY and AUSTRIA, he thinks that we should first lift *ourselves*.

After changing to a smaller train, the travelers begin a picturesque ascent into tiger country and eventually reach Darjeeling in the Himalayas, where they admire the mighty mountains.

Chapter 56 (2:20) [MTA–59]

Over the next few days, they view the stupendous mountains. Before leaving, they ascend even higher on a regular train, then fly down a 35-mile track in a canopied hand-car the size of a sleigh, as if on a toboggan, stopping occasionally to gather flowers and see the view. It is the most enjoyable day Clemens has spent on Earth.

Chapter 57 (2:21) [MTA–60]

Nothing is left undone to make India the most extraordinary country under the sun. For years, the government has tried to destroy murderous wildlife, but statistics still show a curious uniformity in the numbers of people annually killed by animals. Snakes alone kill 17,000 people a year, though 10 times that number of snakes are killed. Narrow escapes do occur. In the same jungle where Clemens killed 16 tigers and some elephants, a cobra bit him, but *it* got well.

From Calcutta, the travelers zigzag west through Muzaffurpore, Dinapore, Benares, and Lucknow.

Chapter 58 (2:22) [MTA–61]

Of the many causes of India's Great Mutiny of 1857, the chief was the East India Company's annexation of the Oudh kingdom. Though caught wholly unprepared, England crushed the Mutiny in perhaps the greatest chapter in its military history. Many moving stories of suffering and heroism are demonstrated in extracts from G. O. Trevelyan (Sir George Otto Trevelyan [1838–1928], author of *Cawnpore* [1865]).

Chapter 59 (2:23) [MTA–62]

The travelers ride over the route of Campbell's retreat from Lucknow (February 22) and visit Cawnpore. At Agra, one expects too much of the Taj Mahal to appreciate it fully in one visit. Just as he had to see NIAGARA 15 times in order to clear away his imaginary falls, Mark Twain must see the Taj many times.

Chapter 60 (2:24) [MTA–63]

The travelers wander contentedly, visiting various towns such as Lahore, where the lieutenant-governor lends Clemens an elephant, drifting as far as Rawal Pindi (Rawalpindi, Pakistan). They also visit Delhi and have a long rest near the "intensely Indian" town of Jeypore (Jaipur) (early March). The most picturesque and outlandish show Clemens has ever seen develops when a rich Hindu marches a religious procession into town, drawing an immense, colorfully dressed audience.

By this time, they have lost their servant Satan, who cannot obey orders to stay sober. He is replaced by a "Mohammedan" (Muslim), Sahadat Mohammed Khan.

Chapter 61 (2:25) [MTA–64]

India's colleges resemble our high schools in oversupplying the market for highly educated employees. A little book published in Calcutta, *Indo-Anglian Literature,* is filled with letters written by educated Indians begging for help. The authors of these letters reveal that their education consists mainly of learning *things* without their meanings. Such learning contrasts with that of Helen KELLER; though deaf, dumb, and blind since infancy, she not only knows things, but understands their meanings. Proof that the education of many American students is an empty as that of their Indian brothers is found in "ENGLISH AS SHE IS TAUGHT," a collection of examination answers from Brooklyn schools.

Chapter 62 (2:26) [MTA–65 & 66]

Finally, the travelers sail from Calcutta (March 28), spending a day at Madras and several days on Ceylon before heading toward MAURITIUS. The ship's captain cannot tell the truth plausibly—the opposite of a Scottish passenger, who cannot lie in an *un*plausible way. One day, the captain tells about an Arctic voyage on which the mate's shadow froze to the deck.

No day can be more restful than one aboard a ship cruising in the calm tropics. Without mail, telegrams, or newspapers to distract, the world is so far away that it seems a dream. If he could, Clemens would sail on forever and never live on land again. On April 15, the travelers reach Mauritius; the next day, they go ashore and take a train to Curepipe in the mountains.

Chapter 63 (2:27) [MTA–66]

In 1892, Mauritius experienced a devastating cyclone followed by a deluge of rain. It is the only place on earth where no breed of matches can stand the damp. Nevertheless, what there is of Mauritius is beautiful.

In thinking about French civilization, one wonders why the English let FRANCE have Madagascar. After all, robbing each other's territories has never been a sin among European nations. *All* territorial possessions of all nations—including America—are pilfered. AFRICA has been as coolly divided among the gang as if they had bought and paid for it; now they are beginning to steal each other's grabbings. All the world's savage lands will fall under European rule; this is good, as dreary ages of bloodshed and disorder will give way to the reign of law. When one compares what India was before to what she is now, one must concede that the most fortunate thing ever to befall her was Britain's establishment of supremacy. [This chapter matches the second half of chapter 66 in *More Tramps Abroad*.]

Chapter 64 (2:28) [MTA–67]

The finest boat that Clemens has seen in these seas, the *Arundel Castle* is thoroughly modern. On May 4, it lands at MOZAMBIQUE's Delagoa Bay, where the travelers spend an afternoon ashore. Two days later, they reach Durban in SOUTH AFRICA. Meanwhile, a fellow passenger tells Clemens how P. T. BARNUM bought SHAKESPEARE's birthplace around the same time that he was trying to buy the elephant Jumbo. Clemens heard the story from Barnum himself.

Chapter 65 (2:29) [MTA–68]

In Durban, the travelers stay at a hotel where servants repeatedly awaken them to offer unwanted services in the early morning. Durban is a neat, clean town in which splendidly built ZULU pull rickshaws. Outside of town, the travelers visit a Trappist monastery, where every detail that makes life worth living has been placed out of reach. In the nearby Transvaal, politics has been in a confused state since CECIL RHODES and his chartered company attempted an invasion.

Chapter 66 (2:30) [MTA–69]

Information on South African politics is so conflicting that strangers cannot avoid being confused. Four months earlier, Dr. (LEANDER STARR) JAMESON led about 600 armed men into the Transvaal, where the Boer government quickly captured and imprisoned them. Much of the confusion about these events is cleared up by the time Clemens writes these pages in May 1897. He has learned that foreign—"Uitlander"—capitalists in the Transvaal had chafed under burdens imposed by the Boers (Afrikaners), whose republican government they wanted to reform. Sensing a chance to profit from their discontent, Rhodes arranged for Jameson to lead men into the Transvaal to support an expected rising. Jameson received a letter from the Transvaal Reformers urging him to come rescue women and children, but waited two months to launch his raid. By then the Reformers no longer wanted him to come. Publication of that letter made Jameson a hero in Britain and inspired an homage from the poet laureate (Alfred Austin). [*More Tramps Abroad* has an additional half page on the laureate.]

Chapter 67 (2:31) [MTA–70]

Jameson's raid caused serious political problems for the Transvaal Reformers, but Clemens finds the military problems more interesting. Always fond of giving military advice, he reviews the incident and shows how Jameson should have done things differently. During the Anglo-Boer war of 1881, the British lost 1,300 men to the Boers' loss of just 30.

Since the Transvaal Boers were ready to put 8,000 men against Jameson, what Jameson needed was 240,000 *men*—not the 530 boys that he actually had. Overencumbered by artillery and Maxim guns, Jameson would have done better to bring a battery of Pudd'nhead Wilson maxims—which are deadlier and easier to carry.

Chapter 68 (2:32) [MTA–71]

True to form, Rhodes got the Transvaal Reformers into trouble while staying out of it himself. He has always been judicious this way. He and his gang are also lawfully reducing the population of Rhodesia (now Zimbabwe) to a form of SLAVERY even worse than the old American slavery.

Johannesburg has the world's richest concentration of gold mines, whose capital came from England and mining engineers from America. Clemens once knew everything that these people know about MINING—except how to make money at it.

Religious, ignorant, obstinate, bigoted, lazy, and unclean, the typical Boer is also hospitable and honest with whites while remaining a hard master to blacks. He has good hunting skills, loves political independence, and prefers the veld's seclusion. Given his nature, it is surprising that Uitlanders expected Boer government to be different than what it was.

During several train journeys in the Cape Colony, Clemens enjoys the veld's surpassing beauty. African women he sees in King William's Town and Bloemfontein remind him of people he had known 50 years earlier.

Chapter 69 (2:33) [MTA–72]

After Rhodes, South Africa's most interesting convulsion of nature is Kimberley's diamond crater. One of the strangest things in history is that sparkling diamonds lay there for so long unnoticed.

The travelers' arrival at Cape Town in July ends their African journey. They have now seen every great South African feature except Rhodes himself. Many reasons are advanced to explain Rhodes's formidable supremacy: his prodigious wealth, his personal magnetism and persuasive tongue, his majestic ideas, his vast schemes for England's territorial aggrandizement. Frankly admitting that he admires Rhodes, Clemens concludes that when the man's time comes, he will buy a piece of the rope for a keepsake.

Conclusion [MTA–Conclusion]

Before leaving Cape Town, Clemens visits Parliament and some old Dutch homes. In one home, he sees a portrait of Dr. James Barry, an army surgeon who came to the Cape 50 years earlier and rose to a high position. Only after Barry died (1865) was "he" discovered to be a woman.

On July 15, 1896, the travelers sail on the *Norman,* which delivers them to Southampton, England, two weeks later, after a stop at MADEIRA.

BACKGROUND AND PUBLISHING HISTORY

After completing his lecture tour and reaching England at the end of July 1896. Clemens settled in GUILDFORD with Livy and Clara. He expected his other daughters, Susy and Jean, to join him soon, and planned to begin writing as soon as he found a suitable house in London for the family. However, in mid-August Susy suddenly became ill and died in Hartford. The crushing news delayed Clemens's work and darkened his attitude. He finally started writing during the last week of October; six months later he completed the chapters on India and pronounced his book finished. He had set aside his notes on South Africa for another book, but in order to bring his manuscript up to the necessary size for a SUBSCRIPTION BOOK, he hastily added more chapters on South Africa and was busy with revisions through another month. An important supplement to *Following the Equator* is MARK TWAIN'S NOTEBOOK (1935), which contains lengthy extracts from his travel journals. Three chapters in Clara's book *My Father, Mark Twain* (1931) contain her account of the tour.

Clemens's dark mood as he wrote *Following the Equator* is revealed in a letter to W. D. HOWELLS that he wrote two years later, saying that he wrote the book "in hell," trying to give the impression that "it was an excursion through heaven." To lighten his manuscript's tone, he deleted many passages containing self-pitying remarks and removed two long sections that have been posthumously published as "THE ENCHANTED SEA WILDERNESS" and "Newhouse's Jew Story."

After finishing his revisions on May 18, 1897, Clemens sent a copy of the manuscript to FRANK BLISS's AMERICAN PUBLISHING COMPANY in Hartford. With the help of BRAM STOKER, he negotiated a new contract with ANDREW CHATTO, his English publisher, whom he gave a copy of the manuscript in mid-June. As his publishers prepared their different editions, he busied himself with new writing projects. He took his family to SWITZERLAND in mid-July and to VIENNA two months later.

Finding an appropriate title for the new book proved difficult. As Clemens finished his revisions, he preferred "Imitating the Equator" or "Another Innocent Abroad." He also considered "The Latest Innocent Abroad" and "The Surviving Innocent Abroad," but finally settled on "Following the Equator" in late July, while Chatto chose "More Tramps Abroad" for the English edition.

Meanwhile, Bliss—without consulting Clemens—lopped the ends from many chapters and removed passages that he considered dull. Chatto made only minor cuts from his edition, which is much the closer to Clemens's original manuscript. In mid-November, Bliss issued *Following the Equator;* Chatto issued MORE TRAMPS ABROAD around the same time. In October, the *NEW YORK HERALD* published about 6,000 words from the book in an advance review without Clemens's permission. Clemens himself published just one extract from the book, as "From India to South Africa" in *McClure's Magazine* (November 1897). His original manuscript is now held by New York Public Library's Berg Collection. Since its original publication, *Following the Equator* has been reprinted only occasionally, apart from uniform editions of Clemens's works.

The first edition of *Following the Equator* was Clemens's most elaborately decorated book. Its cover has a color picture of an African elephant framed by stamped gold arabesques repeated on the spine, and its 712 pages are printed on coated paper. It has 193 illustrations, including the first photographs published in a Clemens book, and original art by 11 illustrators, most of whose pictures are signed. DAN BEARD contributed about 24 drawings scattered through 14 chapters. Other illustrators include F. M. SENIOR (13 pictures), THOMAS J. FOGARTY (10), C. H. WARREN (9), FREDERIC DIELMAN

(8), F. Berkeley Smith (7, plus the cover), A. B. Frost (7), Charles Allan Gilbert (5), Peter Newell (5), Benjamin West Clinedinst (4), and A. G. Reinhart (3). By contrast, the first edition of *More Tramps Abroad* has just four illustrations.

Several facsimile reprints of the first edition of *Following the Equator* have been published. The reprint published in the 1996 Oxford Mark Twain edition contains a new introduction by novelist and essayist Gore Vidal and an afterword by Fred Kaplan, author of The Singular Mark Twain (2003). That edition also includes a facsimile of King Leopold's Soliloquy (1905), a polemic about the imperialistic exploitation of the Congo Free State.

CRITICAL COMMENTARY

By the time of Mark Twain's fifth and final travel book, *Following the Equator*, he had not been an "innocent" or a "tramp" (financial problems notwithstanding) for some time. Like his first book, *The Innocents Abroad*, *Following the Equator* was based on a well-publicized tour with a specific itinerary. It provides a fitting bookend for the travel-writing segment of Mark Twain's work (Melton 138). Mark Twain's consciousness of his own renown is reflected in the process of observing himself as a literary personage moving through foreign scenes. The conditions of the lecture tour, which are organized around Mark Twain's celebrity, at once guide the trip and spill into the text. On this note, Mark Twain recounts the gratifying reception he often received in the places that he visited, noting appreciatively, "The welcome which an American lecturer gets from a British colonial is a thing which will move him to his deepest deeps, and veil his sight and break his voice" (chapter 16). Clemens also confronts the results of his own work's incursion into foreign markets. For example, he has an audience with a guru who wants to discuss "a feature of the philosophy of Huck Finn," and he decides to encourage this trend, later giving a copy of the book to another guru, who "showed a quite remarkable interest in Chicago" thinking "it might rest him up a little to mix it in along with his mediations on Brahma (chapters 39 and 53). If *The Innocents Abroad* recounts the travels of a representative American, *Following the Equator* records the inci-

dents in the tour of an exceptionally famous American author and makes for a very different journey.

Travel Writing

Clemens was a renowned author lecturing to finance his recent bankruptcy, and his reflections on the act of travel writing take on a decisively economic cast. From the perspective of an avid investor, Clemens hazards a tongue-in-cheek model of travel writing as an international observation economy in which local commonplaces can be exported with a significant appreciation: "Anybody who has an old fact in stock that is no longer negotiable in the domestic market will let him have it at its own price. . . . They cost almost nothing and they bring par in the foreign market" (chapter 9). According to this assessment, Clemens's own frequent role of professional reiterator is conceived as a kind of importer-exporter with a shrewd eye for global anecdote markets. Some critics have found fault with the results of this approach, which expanded in Mark Twain's later years, particularly when he had pages to fill; Beidler, for example, finds some things to admire in *Following the Equator* but is disappointed by the many parts of the book that constitute a "major exercise in mainly pictorial, anecdotish, often plagiaristic page filling" (Beidler 296).

The influence of other people's impressions not only encroaches on Clemens's text but also it seems to have taken on a larger role in his view of tourism as a search for other people's experiences. By the time of *Following the Equator*, Melton notes, American tourists had become much greater in number abroad and thus more obtrusive in shaping all travel. Whereas in previous travel books, Clemens seems to believe one could eventually cut through inherited predispositions to apprehend a site for what it was, in *Following the Equator* he is more resigned to the persistent thicket of representation through which tourists experience, for example, the Taj Mahal as an "inflation of delusive emotions, acquired at secondhand from people to whom in the majority of cases they were also delusions acquired at secondhand" (chapter 53).

If Mark Twain's travel books, as Jeffrey Melton argues, reflect the developmental stages of modernizing tourism, *Following the Equator* is a "sad, if cynical, acknowledgment of what is to come, a watershed marking the close of the first phase of the Tourist Age and an end to willful ignorance of its dark, imperialistic context" (Melton 139). Clemens's lectern gave him a front row seat from which to witness the enduring colonial legacies in nations such as Australia, India, and South Africa. Clemens's many tart observations in the text on economic, social, and political effects of colonialism and imperialism presage the vocal anti-imperial stance he would occupy for the last decade of his life, during which he served as vice president of the Anti-Imperialist League. Clemens met a number of lachrymose and absurd realities in the course of his tour; as a result, the tenor of his humor in *Following the Equator* often strays toward the sardonic. Watching a German expatriate nonchalantly hit an Indian servant sends Clemens on a disgusted flashback to the social expressions of slavery in the South of his childhood (chapter 38). Clemens describes at length the process by which workers are "recruited" from various South Sea Islands for Queensland plantations and expresses dubiousness about the cost of the "civilizing" process. Though Clemens is not unabashedly romantic about the primitive state of nature, as he may seem in fictional texts like *Tom Sawyer*, he is skeptical of the terms of exchange under which islanders accept a life abroad—they are 12 times more likely to die, but those who survive are able to return with a pocket watch (18–90).

Cultural Ambivalence

Clemens's ambivalence about Euro-American civilization in the text grows to include a preference for dark over light skin, which Susan Gillman calls "the orientalizing of blackness." He admires the Fijian king's "flowing white vestments, and they were just the thing for him; they comported well with his great stature and his kingly port and dignity" (chapter 7) and expresses annoyance with the incongruence of transplanted Western clothing on missionized children. This disgust with Western culture inappropriately draped on the missionary school students in Ceylon is then reflected in the way Clemens views the European clothes on the members of his own party: "Ugly, barbarous, destitute of taste, destitute

of grace, repulsive as a shroud. I looked at my women-folk's cloths . . . and was ashamed to be seen in the street with them. Then I looked at my own clothes, and was ashamed to be seen in the street with myself" (chapter 37). Continuously enchanted with the vivid colors of India, Clemens extends this logic to skin tone—which had underwritten slavery during his childhood. The "white complexion," Clemens decides "is not an unbearably unpleasant complexion when it keeps to itself, but when it comes into competition with masses of brown and black, the fact is betrayed that it is endurable only because we are used to it. Nearly all black and brown skins are beautiful, but a beautiful white skin is rare" (chapter 41). In this chain of emotional association, what begins as a conviction about the imposition of European culture on other locales thus terminates in an aversion to the basic signifier of Euro-American privilege, white skin.

Language and Culture

In the course of traveling, Clemens's specialized ear was drawn to the linguistic peculiarities he encountered, many of them the direct results of British and American imperialism. These include the story of an American child who grew up on his father's Hawaiian plantation speaking only Kanaka and later forgot it in favor of English only to have it brought to the surface by an on-the-job trauma, and "Billy" Ragsdale, a prodigious "half-white" Hawaiian interpreter who exiles himself to Molokai after developing leprosy (chapter 3). Clemens wins an argument about Scottish pronunciation with the ship's lone Scot by fabricating a couplet that he attributes to Robert Burns (chapter 5). He catalogs several characteristic Australian pronunciations and notes their connection to "costermonger." "All over Australasia," Clemens writes, "this pronunciation is nearly as common among servants as it is in London among the uneducated and the partially educated" (chapter 11). Clemens deems Indian English "tropically ornate and sentimental and rhetorical," a condition he strikingly connects to the psychological conditions of the colonized: "Through ages of debasing oppression suffered by these people at the hands of their native rulers, they come legitimately by the attitude and language of fawning and flattery" (chapter 61). As a professional manipulator of language for humorous effects, and a sympathizer with the casualties of imperial muscle, Clemens admires the convergence of the two in a well-turned rejoinder by Fijian king Thakombau, who, upon being told that British acquisition of Fiji was "a hermit-crab formality" responded that "the crab moves into an unoccupied shell, but mine isn't" (chapter 7).

Critical Commentary by Alex Feerst

CHARACTERS AND RELATED ENTRIES

Jackson, Ed Character in *Following the Equator* (1897). Chapter 28, titled "When the Moment Comes the Man Appears," presents a tale inspired by the previous chapter's true story about a man in Tasmania who emerged from obscurity to stop the settlers' wars against the native population. The fictional Jackson is a guileless young man who leaves MEMPHIS, Tennessee, before the CIVIL WAR to visit New York City. As a joke, his friends give him a phony letter of introduction to "COMMODORE" VANDERBILT purporting to be from a man who grew up with Vanderbilt. The joke backfires with happy consequences, however, when Vanderbilt accepts the letter as genuine, makes Jackson his houseguest, and returns him to Memphis as the director of a vast scheme to control the local tobacco commerce. Jackson's friends expect him to be in a vengeful mood, and they avoid him, until he reveals his wonderful news and promises them all jobs.

Mark Twain Club of Corrigan Castle, Ireland

Fictitious organization whose former president, Mr. Blank, the narrator of *Following the Equator* (1897) meets in Bendigo, Australia (chapter 25). Twenty years earlier, the narrator began a long correspondence with the club's secretary, who sent him a list of its 32 members and a copy of its by-laws. After spending an evening discussing the club's busy history, Mr. Blank reveals that "he was the Mark Twain Club, and the only member it had ever had!"

BIBLIOGRAPHY

Beidler, Philip D. "Following the Equator: A Journey Around the World." In *The Mark Twain Encyclope-* dia, edited by J. R. LeMaster and James D. Wilson, 296–297. New York: Garland, 1993.

Gillman, Susan. "Mark Twain's Travels in the Racial Occult: *Following the Equator* and the Dream Tales." In *The Cambridge Companion to Mark Twain*, edited by Forrest G. Robinson, 193–219. Cambridge: Cambridge University Press, 1995.

Kaplan, Fred. "Afterword." In *Following the Equator and Anti-Imperialist Essays*, edited by Shelley Fisher Fishkin. New York: Oxford University Press, 1996.

Macnaughton, William R. *Mark Twain's Last Years as a Writer*. Columbia: University of Missouri Press, 1979.

Melton, Jeffrey Alan. "Touring the Round: Imperialism and the Failure of Travel Writing in *Following the Equator*." In *Mark Twain, Travel Books, and Tourism: The Tide of a Great Popular Movement*, 138–166. Tuscaloosa: University of Alabama Press, 2002.

Messent, Peter. "Racial and Colonial Discourse in Mark Twain's *Following the Equator*." *Essays in Arts and Sciences* 22 (1993): 67–84.

Mutalik, Keshav. *Mark Twain in India*. Bombay: Noble Publishing House, 1978.

Rodney, Robert M. "Circling the Globe, 1895–96." In *Mark Twain Overseas*, 161–196. Washington, D.C.: Three Continents Press, 1993.

Shillingsburg, Miriam Jones. *At Home Abroad: Mark Twain in Australasia*. Jackson: University Press of Mississippi, 1988.

Twain, Mark. *Following the Equator and Anti-Imperialist Essays*, edited by Shelley Fisher Fishkin. New York: Oxford University Press, 1996.

Zwick, Jim. *Mark Twain's Weapons of Satire: Anti-Imperialist Writings on the Philippine-American War*. Syracuse, N.Y.: Syracuse University Press, 1992.

"From the 'London Times' of 1904"

SHORT STORY about an American army officer executed for murder, even after a miraculous invention that anticipates modern television proves him innocent. An example of near-future SCIENCE FICTION, the story was written while Clemens was living in VIENNA in early 1898 and was following the ALFRED DREYFUS affair. It appeared in CENTURY MAGAZINE the following November. The story takes the form of three contributions to the *Times* of London that are signed "Mark Twain" and date-lined Chicago, April 1, 15, and 23, 1904 (Clemens himself would be in Florence, Italy, on those dates). The conclusion of the story is one of many examples in Mark Twain's writings of trial scenes resulting in twisted justice.

SYNOPSIS

The narrator recalls a gathering in Vienna in March 1898, when he saw American army officer JOHN CLAYTON and Polish inventor JAN SZCZEPANIK argue violently over the latter's tel-electroscope invention. Three years later the two men met again in CHICAGO. By then, the telelec-troscope was being used everywhere, enabling instant visual communication around the globe. Clayton and Szczepanik quarreled several more times, then Szczepanik disappeared. At the end of 1901, a corpse found in Clayton's basement was identified as Szczepanik, and Clayton was convicted of murder.

Clayton's hanging was delayed for several years, however, as the governor—his wife's uncle—stayed his execution until public pressure finally made further delays impossible. Trying to make Clayton as comfortable as possible, the governor allowed him the use of a telelectroscope. Mark Twain stood by as the execution neared and happened to watch the czar's coronation in China on the telelectro-scope. Moments before Clayton was to be hanged, Szczepanik appeared on the screen. After Szczepanik explained that he had been hiding from the attention that his fame brought him, Clayton was pardoned and freed.

Soon a new public clamor arose: Szczepanik may have been alive, but *someone* was killed, and Clayton must be the murderer. A new trial has just been held. Since an 1899 amendment to the U.S. Constitution requires all retrials to be heard by the U.S. Supreme Court, that body has convened in Chicago. The Court rules that even though Szczepanik is alive, Clayton should be executed on the basis of his original conviction. The chief jus-

tice cites a French precedent in Dreyfus's case: "Decisions of courts are permanent and cannot be revised." The fact that Clayton has already been pardoned for that conviction is dismissed: "A man cannot be pardoned for a crime that he has not committed; it would be an absurdity." The governor issues Clayton a new pardon, but the Court annuls it and Clayton is hanged. In a pointed commentary on the Dreyfus affair, the story ends with the comment that "all America is vocal with scorn of 'French justice,' and of the malignant little soldiers who invented it and inflicted it upon the other Christian lands."

CHARACTERS AND RELATED ENTRIES

Clayton, Captain John Character in "From the 'London Times' of 1904." An American army officer, Clayton has violent quarrels with JAN SZCZEPANIK over the latter's telelectroscope invention in Vienna in 1898 and in Chicago in 1901. After Szczepanik disappears, a corpse found in Clayton's basement is identified as his. Clayton is convicted of murder and sentenced to hang, but his execution is stayed several years because the governor of Ohio is his wife's uncle. Moments before Clayton is finally to be hanged, Clemens happens to see Szczepanik alive on the telelectroscope. Clayton is freed, but public clamor over the unidentified murder victim brings him back to trial, this time by the U.S. Supreme Court. Citing the precedent of the ALFRED DREYFUS case, the Court rules that the earlier court decision cannot be wrong, and Clayton is hanged.

"A Gallant Fireman"

Clemens's earliest-known publication, this 150-word SKETCH appeared in the *HANNIBAL WESTERN UNION* on January 16, 1851. It reports on a fire that broke out in a neighboring grocery store a week earlier. As the staff prepared to remove equipment, its apprentice (JIM WOLFE) carried off old cleaning materials. An hour later, he returned—after the fire was extinguished—thinking himself a hero. The sketch's first book publication came in 1979 in

Early Tales & Sketches, edited by Edgar M. Branch and Robert H. Hirst.

"A Ghost Story"

Story written and published in 1870. Clemens's interest in what he called the "petrification mania" began in 1862, when he wrote his PETRIFIED MAN HOAX in Nevada. In October 1869, while he was living in BUFFALO, New York, farmers near Syracuse unearthed a huge stone figure that became notorious as the "Cardiff Giant." Clemens responded to this hoax by writing "The Legend of the CAPITOLINE VENUS." Within a few months, P. T. BARNUM was compounding the hoax by exhibiting a plaster copy of the Cardiff Giant in New York City. This time Clemens responded with "A Ghost Story" for the BUFFALO EXPRESS (January 15, 1870). Later collected in SKETCHES, NEW AND OLD, the 2,460-word story has no relation to the "THE GOLDEN ARM" story, which was published under the same title in 1888.

SYNOPSIS

The anonymous narrator takes a big room in a building far up Broadway. On his first night in the long-unoccupied building, he is overcome by dread when he goes to his room alone as a storm rages outside. During the night, something tugs at his bedclothes. After examining the room, he is satisfied that the door is still locked, but the sight of a giant footprint on the hearth horrifies him. Eventually, he confronts a huge form in the dark. Once it takes shape, however, he is relieved to see that it is only the Cardiff Giant, whom he invites to join him in a smoke. The specter explains that he is the ghost of the giant on display across the street. Anxious to be reburied so that he can rest, he hopes that if he scares people badly enough, his body will be taken away. Since the museum is empty at night, he has crossed the street to try his luck. The narrator tells him that he is wasting his time haunting a plaster cast of himself, as the "real" Cardiff Giant is in Albany. The embarrassed giant says that the petrified man has not only "sold" everybody else, but is selling its own ghost. He leaves, taking the narrator's robe and sitz bathtub with him.

The Gilded Age: A Tale of To-day (1873)

Clemens's first NOVEL; written in collaboration with C. D. WARNER. A sprawling epic with multiple story lines and dozens of characters, *The Gilded Age* is both a MELODRAMATIC saga of a midwestern family nearly destroyed by its faith in illusory wealth and a fierce SATIRE about post–CIVIL WAR America. The novel skewers government and politicians, big business, and America's obsession with getting rich. It is now best remembered for its title, which gave its name to the era that it describes.

While *The Gilded Age* touches on many themes as it shifts uncomfortably between melodrama and satire, occasionally verging into BURLESQUE, it always projects a powerful message about the futility and self-destructiveness of chasing after riches. This theme is personified in the character of Colonel Sellers, who sees "millions" in countless visionary schemes, though he rarely rises above grinding poverty. Sellers, however, is primarily a creature of burlesque. The novel's dominant story line is a melodramatic one, following the saga of the Hawkins family, from its patriarch Si Hawkins's unshakable faith that his worthless TENNESSEE LAND will eventually enrich his heirs, to the destruction of his adopted daughter Laura, who is drawn into the corruption of Washington politics, where she loses her innocence and eventually her life. Another central character is Missouri's corrupt Senator Abner Dilworthy, who is closely modeled on a real politician of the time. Many other minor political and judicial characters in the story are also modeled on a real-life people, as is Laura Hawkins. The novel specifically deals with hypocritical politicians, vote-buying, conflicts of interest, court corruption, and the jury system. It indicts political corruption during President GRANT's administration, but Grant himself is not attacked, though he makes a fleeting appearance in the story.

In addition to attacking the corruption and values of its time, *The Gilded Age* PARODIES then-popular sentimental and melodramatic novels. It does this by presenting many deliberately exaggerated sensational elements: the steamboat AMARANTH's disastrous explosion; Laura Hawkins as the possible heiress of unknown parents; Laura's false marriage to Colonel Selby; Clay Hawkins as a heroically self-sacrificing adopted son; Ruth Bolton as a woman hovering between life and death; long-suffering Alice Montague, who never reveals her love for Philip Sterling; and Philip's heroic search for a coal vein. Not surprisingly, these elements do not all fit together neatly.

Clemens and Warner contributed nearly equally to the book, with each writing mostly about the characters that he himself created. Clemens drew on his own family's background to launch the narrative with the story of the Hawkins family, whose move from Tennessee to Missouri resembles that of his family during the 1830s. He modeled Si Hawkins closely on his father, Washington Hawkins on his brother Orion Clemens, and Sellers on a cousin of his mother. While the early chapters fictionalize events that the Clemens family experienced in the 1830s, the fictional events are set more than a dozen years later. A key to their chronology is Laura Hawkins: She is five years old at the beginning of the novel and 28 at its end. After chapter 40 specifies that it is "the winter of 187– and 187–," the narrative continues at least another year, but presumably not beyond 1873—the year in which it was written. Since the narrative spans 23 years in Laura's life, it must begin around the late 1840s. Chapter 18 carries the story through at least 1868 (a year in which Clemens lived in WASHINGTON, D.C.), and possibly a bit later. The bulk of the book is therefore set just after the Civil War.

An odd gimmick of *The Gilded Age* is the insertion of "mottoes" at the head of each chapter. Most are quotations from foreign languages, including many in non-roman alphabets and characters. Clemens's Hartford friend J. H. TRUMBULL selected the quotes from 42 different languages, including tongues as exotic as Arawak, Choctaw, Efik, Old English, Eskimo, Kanuri, Quiché, Sanskrit, Wolof, and Yoruba. Most of the quotes relate to the content of the chapters. A Chippewa phrase at the beginning of chapter 1, for example, translates as "He owns much land"—an obvious allusion to Hawkins's Tennessee Land. Early editions of *The Gilded Age* presented the quotes untranslated, evidently as a subtle joke. In *A Tramp Abroad* (1880), Clemens claims to have "a prejudice against people who print things in a foreign language and add no translation" (chapter 16). Later editions of *The Gilded Age* added an appendix with Trumbull's translations of the book's quotations.

SYNOPSIS

The novel contains 161,000 words in 63 numbered chapters. Its first 11 chapters (written by Clemens) cover about a dozen years in the history of the Hawkins family. The story opens in eastern TENNESSEE around the late 1840s, when Si Hawkins gets a letter from his friend Beriah Sellers that persuades him to move his family to northeastern MISSOURI. Along the way, he and his wife adopt two recently orphaned children, Clay and Laura. Chapter 6 advances the narrative 10 years, by which time Hawkins and Sellers have each made and lost several fortunes and Sellers has settled in nearby Hawkeye. Though desperately poor, Hawkins refuses to sell his Tennessee land. As his children grow up, level-headed Clay becomes the family's main support, while Washington dreams of easy riches. After Si Hawkins dies, the revelation that he adopted Laura changes her life.

The next 12 chapters (by Warner) introduce a new story line revolving around two young easterners, Philip Sterling and Harry (Henry) Brierly, who go to Missouri to work on a railway survey. They meet Sellers, who excites Brierly's interest in developing Stone's Landing into a major river and railroad entrepôt. Sellers and Brierly prepare a petition to Congress to improve navigation on the village's river. Meanwhile, in a subplot unrelated to the rest of the book, Sterling conducts a tenuous long-distance romance with Ruth Bolton, a headstrong Quaker woman in Philadelphia. Chapter 18 makes it clear that the Civil War has passed. During the war, Laura Hawkins married Colonel Selby, an already married Confederate officer who abandons her. After the war, Senator Dilworthy visits Missouri and becomes interested in Sellers's river-development scheme. When he returns to Washington, D.C., he takes Washington Hawkins with him as a secretary and starts working for a congressional appropriation for the river scheme.

By chapter 24, the novel's focus is shifting to the national capital, while Sellers and Brierly remain in Missouri, directing a crew working on the river project. As they run out of money, their attention shifts east. In chapter 30, Laura Hawkins goes to Washington as Dilworthy's guest and Sellers accompanies her as a chaperon. Laura becomes the senator's lobbyist, and she, Sellers, Brierly, and Dilworthy work to promote a new bill to get the government to buy the Hawkinses' Tennessee land for the purpose of building an industrial school for AFRICAN AMERICANS freed from SLAVERY. Meanwhile, Sterling becomes a partner in the coal business of Ruth Bolton's father.

The story makes a dramatic shift in chapter 38, when Laura sees Selby again in Washington and tries to reestablish a relationship with him. From this point, she is the central character. Just as Congress moves to approve Dilworthy's bill to purchase the Tennessee land, Laura's relationship with Selby reaches a crisis. She follows him to New York and kills him. Over the next year, she becomes a national *cause célèbre* while awaiting her murder trial. Meanwhile, as the effort to push the land bill through Congress drags on, Dilworthy's attempt to buy his reelection to the Senate is exposed. The novel reaches an ironic double climax when the land bill is unanimously voted down at the same moment that Laura is acquitted of murder. The sudden end of the Hawkins family's dream of wealth finally drives Washington Hawkins back to reality, but Laura now hopes to capitalize on her notoriety by launching a lecture tour. The vicious reception she gets at her first engagement breaks her heart, and she dies. Meanwhile, through all of these tumultuous events, Sterling stoically searches for a coal mine, which he fortuitously discovers just as his straitened circumstances are about to make him give up. In contrast to almost everyone else in the novel, Sterling gets rich through hard, honest work, and he wins Ruth's hand.

The authors wrote all but three chapters separately. In the chapter summaries that follow, the

Illustrator Augustus Hoppin's frontispiece sets the tone for the novel by showing Colonel Sellers "feeding his family on expectations."

initials of each chapter's author are given in parentheses. This information derives from a copy of the book that Clemens personally annotated. The first 31 chapters are numbered identically in both one- and two-volume editions. The chapters numbered 32–63 in one-volume editions are numbered 1–32 in the second volume of two-volume editions; both sets of numbers are given below. For example, "Chapter 45" in one-volume editions is equivalent to "2:14" in two-volume editions. Information enclosed within parentheses in chapter synopses comes from sources outside of the chapters themselves. For example, chapter 36's summary places "Mr. Buckstone" in parentheses after his title as a committee chairman because his name is not given until the next chapter.

Chapter 1 (MT)

On June 18 in an unspecified year (probably the late 1840s; June 18 was the birthday of Mark Twain's mother), Squire Si Hawkins, the postmaster of tiny Obedstown, Tennessee, meets the monthly mail carrier, who brings a single letter for Hawkins himself. After reading it, Hawkins tells his wife, Nancy, that he will go to MISSOURI, and gushes about how his 75,000 acres of TENNESSEE LAND will one day bring prosperity to their children. As he reads his letter from Beriah Sellers aloud, Nancy recalls to herself how Sellers once nearly ruined them in Kentucky with a scheme to export slaves to ALABAMA. Sellers's letter advises the Hawkinses to come to Missouri as quickly as they can. Within four months, Hawkins makes the necessary arrangements and the family leaves Obedstown.

Chapter 2 (MT)

On the Hawkinses' third day on the road, they stop at a log cabin, where a 10-year-old boy named Clay is mourning the death of his mother. An old woman explains that Clay's entire family has been lost to fever, leaving him without kinfolk or friends to raise him. Hawkins immediately offers to adopt Clay, whom his wife warmly welcomes into the family.

Chapter 3 (MT)

Another week of travel takes the family to a shabby Mississippi River village, where Clay, Emily, and Washington Hawkins admire the mighty river with the family slaves Aunt Jinny and Uncle Dan'l. When a STEAMBOAT appears, Dan'l thinks that it is the Almighty Himself and prays frantically.

Chapter 4 (MT)

The next day, the Hawkinses take passage aboard the steamboat *Boreas*. Though initially terrified by the craft's unfamiliar sights and sounds, they soon adjust and the children frolic. Clay and Washington are in the pilothouse when a rival boat, the *Amaranth*, is spotted. As the *Amaranth* closes on the *Boreas*, the latter fires up to race. After taking the *Boreas* through "Murderer's Chute," the pilot is startled to see the *Amaranth* gaining and guesses that it took on a "lightning pilot" (Wash Hastings) at NAPOLEON. Just as the *Amaranth* finally pulls even with the *Boreas*, a sudden roar and thundering

crash leave it a helpless wreck, and the *Boreas* turns to save as many people as it can.

Chapter 5 (MT)

The day after the *Amaranth* accident, the *Boreas* continues upriver. Laura Van Brunt, a five-year-old girl from the wrecked boat, clings to Si Hawkins. A careful search fails to find her parents, so Hawkins and his wife add her to the family. From SAINT LOUIS, they take a smaller steamboat another 130 miles upriver to a shabby Missouri town, whence they travel overland for two days to an inland village of about a dozen cabins (alluded to as "Murpheysburg" in chapter 18). After welcoming them warmly, Sellers explains that his latest speculation is raising mules for the southern market. Within a week or two, the Hawkinses are in a log-house of their own. Hawkins buys out the village store and reads farm reports in big-city newspapers to keep ahead of the local market. He does well enough to build a two-story house that is renowned for its magnificence and abundance of lightning rods; villagers think him lucky and eventually dub him "Judge Hawkins."

Chapter 6 (MT)

Ten years have passed. Hawkins and Sellers have made and lost two or three moderate fortunes and are again poor. Hawkins, who now has eight children, is back to his log-house, and Sellers—who also has eight children—has moved to Hawkeye, 30 miles away. All the children have grown considerably. Though Laura Hawkins is becoming a rare beauty, no one guesses that she was not born into the family.

After each of Hawkins's first two BANKRUPTCIES, he rejected cash offers for his Tennessee land. Now his family is so desperate that he is ready to sell. However, when an agent for an iron company offers him $10,000 for the land, he loses his head and demands $30,000 just for half the rights to the land's iron. After the man leaves. Hawkins realizes his blunder, but cannot find the man again. He then gathers the family to discuss their dire financial plight. Washington proposes to accept Sellers's invitation to join him in Hawkeye, and Laura and Emily offer to go to St. Louis. Clay arrives the next day from where he has been working for over a year, saving money that helps the family out of its immediate predicament.

Chapter 7 (MT)

When Washington Hawkins reaches Hawkeye, Sellers greets him earnestly. He dazzles Washington with talk of vast speculations and recalls details of what led to Si Hawkins's ruin. Washington is relieved to see that Sellers lives in a substantial brick house, but its sparse furniture is threadbare and Sellers's children are shabbily clothed. As Sellers talks about a huge speculation involving London bankers, Washington—chilled to the bone—edges toward a tiny stove and accidentally knocks its door off, revealing that it contains only a candle. Unperturbed, Sellers explains that his "stove" is an invention that prevents rheumatism by giving the *appearance* of heat, rather than the heat itself.

Chapter 8 (MT)

After sharing the Sellerses' meager supper, Washington sleeps in a cold bed and awakens to notice that Sellers has sold his sofa. Over breakfast, Sellers explains his plan to help the Rothschilds buy up wildcat midwestern banks, adding that he is developing a solution to cure sore eyes that will make millions—especially in Asia. Mesmerized by Sellers's broad vision, Washington writes a glowing letter to his mother, then accompanies Sellers to a real estate office, where Sellers has arranged for him to clerk for General Boswell, one of the town's richest men.

Chapter 9 (MT)

Washington's new job includes board in his employer's home, where Boswell takes him for supper. There Washington immediately falls in love with Boswell's teenage daughter, Louise. As time passes, Washington also dines occasionally at the Sellerses', where the bill of fare is declining. When his father becomes gravely ill, Washington is called home to join the family vigil at the patriarch's bedside. Just before Judge Hawkins dies, he calls everyone together and admonishes them, "Never lose sight of the Tennessee Land!"

Chapter 10 (MT)

Shortly after Hawkins's funeral, something changes his daughter Laura's life. An inquest into the death

of a corrupt politician named Major Lackland finds evidence that Laura is not the Hawkinses' natural child, setting village gossips to buzzing. Laura digs into her father's papers and finds correspondence between him and Lackland concerning her origins. Several years earlier, an unknown party discovered that her natural father survived the *Amaranth* accident and lost his memory. It appears that Hawkins was waiting until the man's mental health improved before telling him about Laura, but the man disappeared again. Intrigued by the idea that she has a mysterious father somewhere, Laura tells everything to her mother. Her revelation does not affect her family's love for her, but she is bitter about the gossips and feels that Ned Thurston—her prospective beau—has let her down badly.

Chapter 11 (MT)

The Hawkins family has now been in Hawkeye for two months. Washington Hawkins suddenly decides to drop in for dinner at the Sellerses after a long absence. Mastering his surprise, Sellers welcomes him and sits him down at the family table, where the dinner consists solely of fresh water and turnips. As Washington eats, Sellers prattles about new speculations and about how turnips and water prevent rheumatism. Miserable knowing that he is robbing the children of food, and afflicted by the turnips in his stomach, Washington excuses himself and leaves.

Chapter 12 (CDW)

In New York City, young Philip Sterling and Harry (Henry) Brierly discuss how to make their fortunes. A multitalented Yale graduate, Philip studied law, but hates practicing it. After turning to writing, he has not been able to find a newspaper position and is ready for any change. When Harry proposes that they both go to Saint Joseph, Missouri, to work as engineers on a railway survey contracted by his uncle, Philip jumps at the chance to get away.

Chapter 13 (CDW)

As Philip and Harry travel to Missouri by train and steamboat, they make friends with several men with whom they will be working. When they stop at St. Louis, Philip learns of Harry's intention to work on the commercial aspects of the Salt Lick Pacific

Extension, instead of as an engineer. During a long delay, they meet Sellers, who impresses them as an important businessman—although he gets Philip to pick up a big bar tab.

Chapter 14 (CDW)
Meanwhile, a letter from Philip reaches Ruth Bolton in Philadelphia, where she lives with her Quaker family. After quitting a stifling school, she wants to study medicine, although her parents worry about her fragile health. Her businessman father, Eli Bolton, admires Philip but has reservations about his lack of capital.

Chapter 15 (CDW)
After Ruth's parents reluctantly permit her to study medicine, she is soon happy in her new undertaking. Meanwhile, many businessmen visit the Boltons' home, talking glibly with Ruth's father about their ideas for vast "schemes."

Chapter 16 (CDW)
In St. Louis, the surveying party is detained by an engineer's illness. As Philip and Harry run out of money, Philip writes to Ruth about his impatience. Meanwhile, he and Harry often see Sellers, who excites Harry with his grandiose plans for developing Stone's Landing into a railroad and steamboat hub. When Philip and Harry finally leave by steamboat, Sellers sees them off. After returning upriver, they go overland to the surveying camp near Magnolia—a "town" consisting of one house.

Chapter 17 (CDW)
After two weeks in camp, Harry writes to Sellers, assuring him that the railway line will go through Stone's Landing. When the surveyors finally reach this town, however, all they find is a minute village next to a crooked, sluggish stream called Goose Run. Sellers soon appears in a wagon. He welcomes Philip and Harry to "Napoleon" and the "Columbus River" and sits down with Harry to lay out the future city. When the surveying party moves on, Harry returns to Hawkeye with Sellers to prepare a petition to Congress to improve navigation on the river.

Chapter 18 (CDW)
It is now eight years since the death of Si Hawkins, and the years between 1860 and 1868 have transformed America dramatically. The conflict between the Union and the Confederacy (the "Civil War" is never named) has left its imprint on Missouri. Washington Hawkins served bravely, but without distinction, and Sellers was captain of Hawkeye's home guards. The war has also changed Laura Hawkins. After escaping from Murpheysburg's gossips, she took solace in reading and developed crude notions of women's emancipation. Nevertheless, she fell in love with George Selby, a Confederate colonel posted to Hawkeye. After Selby was transferred to southwestern Missouri, Laura followed him and they were married. For three months, she was devoted to him, until he was ordered to New Orleans. After refusing to take her with him, he admitted to being married already. Laura then returned to Hawkeye, with nobody but her mother and Washington knowing about her mock marriage.

Chapter 19 (CDW)
Harry is still in Hawkeye, helping Sellers prepare their petition. Fitting into local society well, he flirts with Laura and engages her imagination by remarking how easily one can break into Washington society. When Laura later asks Sellers about visiting Washington with him, Sellers hints that Senator Dilworthy wants him to go there to lobby for Missouri. In one of his hallucinations, Sellers remembers Dilworthy's staying at *his* home during a visit to Hawkeye. During the summer, Philip passes through Hawkeye.

Chapter 20 (CDW)
During Dilworthy's visit to Hawkeye (which Sellers remembers incorrectly in the previous chapter), the senator stays with his old friend General Boswell. After Sellers presides over a public reception at which Dilworthy speaks, he and Harry take him to "Napoleon" and outline their plans. Though little interested in the town itself, the senator favors the appropriation for the river. Afterward, he arranges for Washington Hawkins to become his private secretary in Washington. After meeting Laura, he spends much of his remaining time in her company and invites her to visit Washington, D.C., during the winter.

Chapter 21 (CDW)
Meanwhile, as Ruth Bolton tires of her medical studies, she grows more interested in her letters

from Philip, who silently hopes that she will come around to wanting marriage. In the autumn, Ruth enrolls in the Fallkill Seminary in Massachusetts, where she stays with Philip's friends, the Montagues. She becomes close to Alice Montague and enjoys her new life in Fallkill.

Chapter 22 (CDW)

During the winter lull in the Missouri railroad work, Philip and Harry go east, where Harry has trouble interesting investors in Napoleon but manages to interest his uncle and some brokers in the Columbus River scheme. During a weeklong sidetrip to Fallkill, they visit the Montagues frequently.

Chapter 23 (CDW)

In New York City, Harry gets a letter from Sellers urging him to rush to Washington to confer with Dilworthy, who is presenting their petition to Congress. Dilworthy then introduces Harry to important people in the capital. Meanwhile, Philip is growing dissatisfied with the railway contractors' large but indefinite promises. By now proficient as an engineer, he continues studying his new vocation and publishes some articles on the subject. When he returns to the West, he heads a division in the field.

Chapter 24 (MT)

Washington Hawkins marvels at the capital city and finds his new life an unceasing delight. The capital's major sights include the Capitol building, the unfinished Washington Monument, and the president's fine white barn. The city has many boardinghouses—in which congressmen are not welcome. Everyone in the city represents some kind of political influence. As the river appropriation bill works its way through committees, Hawkins writes home to Sellers in his official capacity as Dilworthy's secretary.

Chapter 25 (MT)

Elated by news from Hawkins and Harry about the appropriation bill's progress, Sellers hires men to begin work at Stone's Landing. Hawkins also writes to Louise Boswell to report that he is about to sell the family's Tennessee land for $40,000—a figure he vows to increase many times over in new investments.

Harry rejoins Sellers at Stone's Landing, where he directs a crew working to straighten out the river.

The work stalls when money from the appropriation does not come through. Harry and Sellers pay their workers with 30-day orders, but shopkeepers eventually refuse to honor them, leaving the workers ready to rebel. After Harry goes east to get the money from the new Columbus River Slackwater Navigation Company, the workers are angry enough to hang Sellers, but he beguiles them with talk of future riches, gives them each a lot in Napoleon, and shares his own cash savings with them.

Chapter 26 (CDW)

When Ruth Bolton returns home from Fallkill, her plan to pursue a medical career seems less important, but this feeling passes. Her mother tells her that Philip will be surveying some land that her father has acquired to see if it has coal, as pressures build on Bolton's business interests. Meanwhile, Philip himself writes to Ruth, telling her about his reservations over the Napoleon and railway schemes.

Chapter 27 (MT)

His reputation damaged by the work stoppage, Sellers anxiously awaits the appropriation funds. He remains enthusiastic about the future, expecting that Napoleon's development will eventually cause Hawkeye to die. As he assures his wife that good news should soon come from Harry, a letter arrives.

Chapter 28 (MT)

Harry's letter recounts his experience in New York City, where he visited the president of the development company and learned that *no* money is coming from it. Furthermore, because he and Sellers owe money for the stock that they have subscribed, they are personally responsible for the $9,640 due to the workers and they each *owe* the company $4,000. Harry also learned that most of the appropriation money went to paying off congressmen and lobbyists; however, the company's president assures him that things will pick up when larger appropriations are obtained in coming sessions of Congress.

At this same time, Louise Boswell hears from Washington Hawkins, who reports that he has refused the $40,000 offer for the Tennessee land.

The following summer, the people of Hawkeye suddenly subscribe such a large share in the railway that the railroad line is routed through their town instead of through Stone's Landing—whose development stops, dashing all Sellers's hopes.

Chapter 29 (CDW)

Philip Sterling takes a train in Ilium, Pennsylvania. Along the way, he gets into a fight with a conductor who mistreats a woman. Thrown off the train, he walks five miles to the next station and makes plans to sue the railroad. After reaching Ilium, he sets up camp five miles outside of town and spends a month carefully surveying Bolton's land. He concludes that a fine vein of coal runs through it and gets Bolton's permission to begin mining operations.

Chapter 30 (MT)

Louise learns from Washington that Dilworthy plans to sell the Hawkinses' Tennessee land to the government. The news raises Laura's hopes of being invited to go to the capital herself. Eventually, an official invitation comes from her brother, conveying a check for $2,000 as a loan from the senator for her to buy clothes in New York. Laura also receives two dead-head tickets for railway passage and invites Sellers to accompany her. They arrive in Washington in late November.

Chapter 31 (CDW)

Meanwhile, Harry Brierly leaves New York for Washington, where Sellers wants him to help lobby for a benevolent scheme for black people. He lingers in Philadelphia, where Philip—now Bolton's coal business partner—is also staying. Philip shares his concerns about Ruth with Alice Montague, who is also visiting there. One night, all four young people go to a concert. A false fire alarm starts a panic, and Philip is seriously injured when he tries to protect the women.

Chapter 32 (volume 2: chapter 1) (MT)

Delighted that his beautiful sister is in town, Washington Hawkins spends two weeks showing Laura the sights—including sessions of Congress, which is just opening. Invitations pour in, and Laura is soon "in society." Dilworthy is so pleased with the attention Laura receives that he adds new CLOTHES and jewelry to her wardrobe—as loans against the future sale of her family land. The first formal reception that Laura attends is at a cabinet secretary's home, where she is the center of attention.

Harry Brierly is also there. Unable to get near Laura, he overhears guests describing her as a landed heiress from a distinguished western family who wants to sacrifice her estates to help uplift the downtrodden negro.

Pleased with Laura's debut, Dilworthy begins calling her "daughter" the next morning. He gives her more money and unfolds the plans in which he wishes her to assist him.

Chapter 33 (2:2) (MT)

Laura learns about Washington's three aristocracies: the old families known as the "Antiques"; the wealthy parvenus; and the families of powerful public figures. She also learns how to deal with the tiresome customs of exchanging social visits. One of her callers is the wife of the Honorable Patrique Oreillé (Patrick O'Reilly)—a contractor who helped Wm. M. Weed steal $20 million from New York City before becoming respectable.

Chapter 34 (2:3) (MT)

Three months in Washington make Laura confident in her beauty and social skills. She is also now used to large sums of money, which she spends freely and shares with her mother, brother, and Sellers—who insist on giving her notes for "loans." Laura is on good terms with many members of Congress. Generally believed to be very wealthy and soon to be become more so, she is much courted and envied. Her brother Washington is also adjusting to a developing celebrity of his own.

Chapter 35 (2:4) (MT & CDW)

Laura and Dilworthy discuss Laura's progress in persuading Senator Hopperson and other members of Congress to support the Tennessee land bill. By this time, Laura is well acquainted with many journalists, with whom she exchanges gossip. Sellers also enjoys talking with these men and discusses Senator Balloon's checkered career with them.

Chapter 36 (2:5) (MT)

While waiting for the chairman of the House Committee on Benevolent Appropriation (Mr. Buckstone) to appear, Laura enters a bookshop. When she asks for copies of (Hippolyte) Taine's *Notes on England* and *Autocrat of the Breakfast-Table* (by Oliver Wendell HOLMES), the smug, ignorant clerk does not know what she is talking about. He tries to interest her in other books, only to receive a blast of her sarcasm.

Chapter 37 (2:6) (MT)

When Chairman Buckstone does not appear outside the shop as Laura expects, she sends him a note inviting him to call on her. That evening, she flirts with the chairman for two hours, emerging confident that she can get him to vote for the land bill. Though aware of Laura's coquettish designs, Buckstone is confident that he will triumph in the end.

Chapter 38 (2:7) (CDW)

At a day reception given by Representative Schoonmaker's wife, Laura spots Colonel Selby and rushes away with her brother. Seeing her former lover so unnerves Laura that she skips the president's reception and stays in her room for two days. When she finally emerges, she borrows a revolver from Washington. After visiting Mrs. Schoonmaker to learn where Selby is staying, she sends him an anonymous note asking him to call at Dilworthy's house to discuss cotton claims.

Chapter 39 (2:8) (CDW)

When Selby arrives, seeing Laura staggers him. Recognizing danger in her calm, icy tone, he tries to temporize, but admits that his wife is alive and with him in Washington. When Laura moves toward him, he grasps her hands. Pleading that he may still love her, he claims to be helpless since the war has ruined him. Laura collapses into a chair, Selby kisses her and falsely swears his love. For the moment, Laura is happy, but she presses Selby to commit himself to some course of action. When Selby leaves, Laura is confident that he belongs to her, but Selby merely curses to himself.

Chapter 40 (2:9) (CDW)

The narrative is now explicitly in the 1870s. Sellers is one of the best-known men in Washington. Always in the midst of gigantic schemes, speculations, and gossip, he thrives in the capital's bustle and confusion. He knows President GRANT, as well as all the senators and representatives and people in every department. He is a favorite on newspaper row, which feeds on his confidential revelations.

Aided by Harry Brierly, he meanwhile advances his own affairs, particularly the Columbus River navigation scheme and the Tennessee land plan. He is responsible for a dispatch to a New York paper concerning Dilworthy's support for creating an industrial school for colored people on the Hawkinses' Tennessee land. This story excites Washington Hawkins's interest, and Sellers assures him that there are millions in the plan.

Meanwhile, Laura's life rushes on in intrigues. She sees Selby publicly and privately, and grows impatient with his failure to take steps to free himself from his wife.

Chapter 41 (2:10) (CDW)

Hopelessly in love with Laura, Harry spends much time at the Dilworthys' in order to be near her, but she barely notices him. He confronts her about rumors concerning her and Selby and surprises her with the news that Selby plans to take his family to Europe soon. He then writes her a long, passionate letter, but she merely sighs and burns it.

Meanwhile, Philip Sterling has spent a pleasant winter being nursed by Ruth and Alice. When he learns about Harry's obsession with Laura, he decides to go to Washington to check on him. He is also concerned that a man named Pennybacker is doing something to harm Eli Bolton's business interests.

Chapter 42 (2:11) (MT)

Congressman Buckstone's "campaign" is brief, but it is he, not Laura, who is conquered, and he becomes champion of her "Knobs University Bill." After learning that Mr. Trollop is the bill's greatest enemy, Laura devises a scheme to blackmail him. First she has Buckstone persuade Trollop to deliver a major speech on a pension bill that he supports. As the chapter later reveals, Buckstone writes Trollop's speech, but Laura copies it in her own hand and has her version delivered to Trollop at the last minute—with a crucial page missing. Trollop later visits Laura to discuss the university bill, which he calls a fraud on the government. Laura proves him that *she* wrote his pension speech and shows evidence of his support for other frauds. Her threat to expose her authorship of his speech induces him to promise to support her bill.

Chapter 43 (2:12) (MT)

The next day, Buckstone gives notice of the Knobs Industrial University Bill to the House. All the newspapers except the *Washington Daily Love-Feast* immediately attack the bill. The vicious opposition of New York papers disturbs Laura, but Dilworthy assures her that journalistic persecution will actually help them by eliciting public sympathy. Buckstone later formally presents the bill to the House, where it is referred to the Committee on Benevolent Appropriations. Over the next 10 days, a storm develops in the press over the "Negro University Swindle." A tide of congressional defections is reversed when Trollop announces his support.

Chapter 44 (2:13) (CDW)

After talking with Harry about the latter's obsession with Laura, Philip wants time to adjust to Washington before deciding what to do. He sees Sellers, who is still filled with grandiose ideas. Although Sellers dismisses the ugly rumors about Laura, Philip realizes that he should steer Harry away from the woman.

Meanwhile, Laura confronts Selby, who denies that he is going to Europe and promises to run away with her after her bill passes. Unable to trust him, Laura vows that if he betrays her again, it will be his last time. When Philip visits Laura, she admits that Harry means nothing to her and promises to leave him alone. Harry meekly accepts this bad news from Philip but inwardly thinks that Philip simply does not understand women.

Chapter 45 (2:14) (MT)

There is much anticipation in the air on the day that Buckstone presents the university bill to the House of Representatives. Outlining the bill's provisions, he argues that colored people should be trained to become productive workers and that the Hawkins land in Tennessee is an ideal site for a training institution. After a motion to suspend the rules is carried, the bill's supporters allow no recesses in order to let the opposition wear itself out. By dawn, the bill is carried.

Chapter 46 (2:15) (CDW)

The next morning, Philip Sterling accompanies Dilworthy to the latter's home. They are surprised to find that Laura is gone and that her room shows evidence of a hasty departure. At Harry's lodging, Philip finds a note from Laura asking Harry to escort her to New York. Philip immediately goes there. At Jersey City, he sees a newspaper reporting that Laura has shot Selby in a hotel parlor. Before dying an hour later, Selby issued a deposition claiming that Laura was a lobbyist who had hounded him to leave his wife and had threatened to kill him. Both Laura and Harry—who was with her when she shot Selby—are in jail. The sensational story sweeps the nation.

Chapter 47 (2:16) (CDW)

The next day, Philip gets Harry out of jail with the help of Harry's uncle. Sellers and Washington Hawkins visit Laura and pledge to support her. Dilworthy also promises to stand by her, and her mother soon arrives from Missouri. By the following day, newspapers are beginning to treat Laura more sympathetically. After she is indicted for first-degree murder, the city's two most distinguished criminal lawyers are retained to defend her. Laura's land bill fails to pass in the Senate and must await the next session. Meanwhile, Philip takes Harry to Pennsylvania to help in his coal-mining operation.

Chapter 48 (2:17) (CDW)

In Pennsylvania, the contracting firm of Pennybacker, Bigler, and Small is doing badly, and Eli Bolton reluctantly allows them to borrow money on his name. Meanwhile, Philip Sterling opens the coal mine and works through the summer, with few signs of success. Harry is recalled to New York for Laura's trial, but it is delayed.

Chapter 49 (2:18) (MT & CDW)

After finally striking coal, Philip cautiously reports to Bolton, whose business interests are at a low ebb. This news buoys Bolton's position, until Philip reports that his initial find was worthless. Bolton then arranges to sell his house. In the fall, news of his business failures stops work at the mine. Philip later buys the Ilium tract cheaply and goes home.

Chapter 50 (2:19) (CDW)

At his mother's home, Philip still thinks about finding coal at Ilium. He visits Fallkill, where Squire Montague approves his plan to study law in his office; however, Montague has such confidence in Philip's coal mine that he lends him money to reopen it in the spring. When Philip passes through Philadelphia again, he sees Ruth and hears from Harry that Laura's trial is about to begin.

Chapter 51 (2:20) (MT)

In December, Washington Hawkins and Sellers are still looking after the University Bill. Hawkins frets over Laura's trial, but Sellers remains optimistic. As they discuss the cost of getting a bill passed in Congress, a telegram arrives reporting that Laura's trial is postponed until February. Sellers is confident that before the trial ends, the bill will be passed and they will have a million dollars to send to the jury.

Chapter 52 (2:21) (MT)

Weeks drag by monotonously as Sellers and Hawkins await developments in Congress and occasionally visit Laura in New York. Spending more time with Dilworthy than with Sellers, Hawkins behaves as if he were in mourning. To help the bill, Dilworthy promotes a public image of Hawkins as a meditative man concerned only with benevolent enterprises benefiting the downtrodden.

Chapter 53 (2:22) (MT)

As Congress nears its close, Dilworthy goes home to solicit support for his reelection to the Senate in his state legislature. He meets with his biggest opponent, Mr. Noble, attends prayer meetings, and goes out of his way to speak to a Sunday school in Cattleville. Before Dilworthy leaves the state capital, Noble assures him of his support in the legislature.

Chapter 54 (2:23) (CDW)

Laura's trial finally opens on February 15. It is less than a year after the shooting, and public sympathy has swung in her favor. When she enters Judge O'Shaunnessy's courtroom, her simple, dignified appearance elicits admiration. During the jury selection process, any prospective juror who appears to know anything is dismissed. When the jury is impaneled four days later, it has only two members who can read. District Attorney McFlinn opens the case for the state and calls Harry Brierly to the stand.

Chapter 55 (2:24) (CDW)

After taking the stand, Harry describes his trip to New York with Laura. The defense attorney, Braham, cross-examines him, doing what he can to imply that Harry himself had an interest in eliminating Selby. Over the next week, other witnesses testify and evidence is given that Selby started to retract his deposition when he realized that he was dying, admitting that he had once wronged Laura. After the prosecution finishes, Braham opens the case for the defense, emphasizing aspects of Laura's background that might have contributed to her becoming insane. He calls Harry the "spark" that finally set her off.

Chapter 56 (2:25) (MT & CDW)

Two days later, Mrs. Hawkins and her son both testify about Laura's origins and her mock marriage to Selby, and Sellers testifies about the search for Laura's natural father. Medical experts then testify that there were sufficient causes for Laura to become insane; later it is learned that the chief expert was paid $1,000. Two weeks later, the lawyers sum up their cases. Braham's summary moves half the courtroom to tears. By the time the jury goes out, Washington Hawkins and Sellers have returned to Washington, feeling dispirited.

Chapter 57 (2:26) (MT)

Congress's decision on the University Bill, a verdict in Laura's trial and Dilworthy's reelection are all imminent. Sellers and Washington Hawkins arise early in the morning in their excitement. Impatient for news, they go out and see a newspaper bulletin posted reporting that Dilworthy was *not* reelected after Noble told the state legislature that Dilworthy had bribed him. Hawkins and Sellers then rush to the Capitol, arriving in time to see the Senate vote their bill down unanimously. Hawkins is in a state of collapse; Sellers helps him home, where they find a telegram reporting that Laura has been found *not* guilty.

Chapter 58 (2:27) (CDW)

The moment the jury foreman announces that Laura is not guilty, the courtroom erupts into cheers, and women throw themselves on the defense attorney. The judge then orders that Laura be sent to the State Hospital for Insane Criminals and she is taken away; however, the authors immediately explain that since "this is history and not fiction," Laura is actually freed. Her mother wants to take her home, but Laura refuses. Laura then receives a telegram from her brother reporting the bad news about the bill and Dilworthy. A LECTURE agent named Griller appears and offers her $12,000 to give 30 lectures on whatever subject she chooses.

Harry goes to the West Coast on an unspecified new venture and Philip rushes back to Philadelphia.

Chapter 59 (2:28) (MT)
Reacting calmly to his public disgrace, Dilworthy returns to the Senate and demands "an investigation of the bribery charges." Eventually, the full Senate accepts the report of a committee that exonerates Dilworthy, who returns home to a warm reception.

Chapter 60 (2:29) (MT)
While adjusting to her restored freedom, Laura considers six or seven letters from former lovers proposing marriage but burns each letter and decides to take up lecturing. At her first engagement, she steps onto the stage before a mostly empty hall, in which a handful of coarse people laugh at her and begin to throw things. She flees outside, where an angry mob assaults her. After making her way home, she sinks into a torpor. The next morning, she is found dead. An inquest rules the cause to be heart disease.

Chapter 61 (2:30) (MT)
Clay Hawkins, who has prospered in AUSTRALIA, rushes back to America when he belatedly hears about Laura's trial. After learning of her acquittal in San Francisco, he goes directly to Hawkeye, arriving in time to comfort his mother when news of Laura's death comes.

Meanwhile, Sellers and a prematurely aged Washington Hawkins are preparing to leave their cheap Washington boardinghouse. Hawkins receives a telegram from Louise saying that her father—who is now poor—consents to their marriage. Swearing that he is forever done with the family's Tennessee land, Hawkins vows to turn to real work. At this moment a telegram arrives from Obedstown

Laura's lecture audience turns against her in chapter 60.

demanding $180 for current taxes on the land. After hesitating, Hawkins shreds the letter and pronounces the spell broken.

Chapter 62 (2:31) (MT)
Back at his Pennsylvania mine, Philip Sterling is growing discouraged. His tunnel has passed the place where he calculates the main coal vein should be. When he runs out of money, he discharges his workers and sells most of his tools and materials. One man stays on for a week to help him; then Philip continues working by himself until his last hope is gone. After one final blast, he does not even check the results; however, his fortuitous discovery of a stream of water indicates that he has struck a rich vein. He returns to his cabin and finds a telegram reporting that Ruth is very ill.

Chapter 63 (2:32) (CDW)
At Ilium, news of Philip's coal strike is already lifting his reputation, but he rushes to Philadelphia to be at the side of Ruth, who is delirious with a fever. His presence helps her to rally and she finally professes her love to him. Afterward, Eli Bolton goes to Ilium to arrange for developing the coal mine, which Philip has reconveyed to him under the terms of their original partnership. The mine proves even richer than Philip originally suspects. After Ruth fully recovers, she and Philip plan a happy future together. Alice Montague wishes them both well, never revealing her own feelings for Philip.

Appendix
The authors apologize for failing to find Laura's lost father.

BACKGROUND AND PUBLISHING HISTORY

According to Clemens's biographer A. B. PAINE, Clemens and Warner got the idea of writing *The Gilded Age* together during a dinner-table conversation in early 1873. After they had heartily criticized modern novels, their wives suggested that they write something better and they accepted the challenge immediately. Since Clemens already had a story idea, he began writing first. After completing 11 chapters, he turned the manuscript over to Warner, who added the next 12 chapters. Thereafter, they swapped the manuscript back and forth frequently as each man grew bored with it. In several instances, both purportedly wrote key chapters, then had their wives select which to use. Clemens's version of Laura's fate in chapter 60 is a prime example.

While Clemens's most personal contribution was adapting his family's history to the Hawkinses, Warner used his experience from surveying a Missouri railway survey in the early 1850s and his study of law to write the chapters on railroad surveying and on Laura's murder trial. Each author contributed a share of characters and plot elements. Clemens created the Hawkins family, Sellers, Dilworthy (whom Warner introduces in chapter 19), Washington society people, and congressmen. His chapters concentrate on Hawkins family history, the fate of the Tennessee land, Sellers's speculations, and the investigation of Dilworthy. Warner's main characters are Sterling, Brierly, the Bolton and Montague families, Selby, and the New York legal figures. His chapters center around these characters and around Laura's murder trial. In general, Warner uses Clemens's characters more than Clemens uses Warner's. A copy of the book that Clemens personally annotated indicates the passages that each author wrote. While most chapters were written primarily by one man or the other, Clemenss's notes show that both contributed at least something to nearly every chapter. Warner wrote chapter 18, for example, but it follows

Clemens's plan. Another example is Warner's chapter 29, in which the episode of Sterling's being thrown off a train is based on an incident that Clemens once personally witnessed.

Although it is not possible to determine the full extent of each author's influence on his partner's chapters, it seems likely that Clemens influenced how Warner treated his characters—particularly Sellers. For example, it is in one of Warner's chapters that Sellers reveals that he was born in VIRGINIA—a point probably suggested by Clemens (chapter 13). By contrast, Clemens says little about Warner's most important characters. Of the 18 chapters in which Ruth Bolton is mentioned, for example, Clemens wrote only one, and it mentions her just once (chapter 62).

After finishing the book in April 1873, the authors copyrighted it and the AMERICAN PUBLISHING COMPANY issued it as a SUBSCRIPTION BOOK the following December, with illustrations by HENRY LOUIS STEPHENS, TRUE WILLIAMS, and AUGUSTUS HOPPIN. Its initial sales were even better than those of *Innocents Abroad* (1869) and *Roughing It* (1872), but they tapered off within a few months. *The Gilded Age* was the most widely reviewed of Clemens's early books, and the American reviews were generally favorable. While *The Gilded Age* has never been regarded as one of Clemens's most significant works, it has generally remained in print since its original publication.

The Gilded Age presents special challenges to the editors of the MARK TWAIN PROJECT, who need to reassemble the scattered portion of the original manuscript in order to determine the precise nature of each author's full contributions to the book. In 2006, it appeared that a Project edition of the book still lay many years in the future. The most important reprint editions published to date include Bobbs-Merrill's 1972 edition, edited and annotated by Bryant Morey French; Library of America's 2002 edition, lightly annotated by Hamlin HILL; and the 1996 facsimile reprint of the first edition in the OXFORD MARK TWAIN edition. The latter has a new introduction by novelist Ward Just and an afterword by Gregg Camfield, the author of *The Oxford Companion to Mark Twain* (2003). In 1965 CHARLES NEIDER published an abridgement of the book called THE ADVENTURES OF COLONEL SELLERS, which reduces Warner's chapters to synopses, while leaving Clemens's chapters intact.

Several months after the book was published, a San Francisco journalist named Gilbert B. Densmore dramatized it. In April 1874, he put his play on stage with JOHN T. RAYMOND in the role of Colonel Sellers. After Warner and Clemens learned about this unauthorized production, they agreed that each would relinquish to his partner dramatic rights in the characters he created. Clemens then bought out Densmore's play and revised it for a successful New York production that was soon renamed *Colonel Sellers*. With Raymond continuing in the lead role, this play toured for a decade and made Clemens more money than he got from the novel's sales. Later he tried to write another play about Sellers that he eventually transformed in a short novel, *The American Claimant* (1892), which is a sequel to *The Gilded Age*.

CRITICAL COMMENTARY

The Gilded Age operates on two levels: as a formal BURLESQUE of the SENTIMENTAL novel and as a political SATIRE of greed and corruption in American business and politics. While the burlesque elements of *The Gilded Age* are aimed at feminized popular fiction, the novel's satirical attentions are focused on business and politics, injecting real-estate speculation, railroad surveying, and Beltway politicking into the domestic interior of the MELODRAMATIC novel. Though a collaborative work, written with Charles Dudley Warner, *The Gilded Age* marks an important moment in Clemens's career. Critic Bryant French calls the book a revealing transition from travel writing and short sketches to more sustained and complex fiction. The book is also one of many instances of the aggressive emergence of socially engaged realism in the late 19th century.

Realism versus Sentimentalism

According to anecdote, it was literary rivalry along gender lines that first led Warner and Clemens to collaborate on a book. The novel's legendary genesis in dinner party banter among Clemens, Warner, and their wives sets up the novel as a self-conscious masculine realist satire challenging ostensi-

bly feminine sentimental fiction. Clemens's and Warner's disdain for sentimental fiction (which their wives enjoyed) was a common posture among critics of the period. Challenged by their wives to do better, Clemens and Warner wrote *The Gilded Age* both to mock and one-up existing works and thereby please their wives. The novel's final editorial process ironically mirrors its genesis. Clemens and Warner's collaborative composition began with each man writing several chapters and then handing them off once he grew bored. Later, the two began to write competing versions of some chapters, with their wives selecting the better versions. Through this process, the form and direction of the novel was fundamentally decided by Clemens's and Warner's wives. What had begun as a mockery of feminine fiction was in the end assembled according to the tastes of their wives.

Clemens and Warner constructed *The Gilded Age* to reflect and exaggerate what they liked least about sentimental fiction. An ironic upshot of this is that at times the novel seems more like a clumsy imitation than a burlesque. Plot elements that were likely intended to play on the overcooked improbabilities of sentimental fiction, such as Laura Hawkins's orphan origins, or her seduction and betrayal by Colonel Selby, are also what constitute the story. As FREDERICK ANDERSON put it, by borrowing the hackneyed conventions of sentimental fiction, *The Gilded Age* inadvertently "capitulates to the very conventions it was planned to attack" (Anderson 107). While mocking certain stock plot elements, Clemens and Warner also attempted to differentiate *The Gilded Age* from the sentimental novel. One such strategy frequently entailed the insertion of self-conscious judgments within the narrative about the storytelling process. The anonymous third-person narrator makes frequent reference to *The Gilded Age* as history, in contrast to fictional confections. For example, after a fight with Ruth Bolton, Philip Sterling is seized by a momentary desire to "fling himself out of the house in tragedy style," which he resists (chapter 22). In the most dramatic instance of this technique, Laura Hawkins's trial momentarily splits into two aftermaths—a fake detour in which she is committed to a mental asylum, followed by a return to the self-described "historical" narration, in which she is set free, as the law would have demanded (chapter 58). Clemens and Warner make their flouting of convention explicit in the epilogue, by apologizing for not finding her father, as form would demand.

Within the story, the female characters both challenge and fulfill their confinement to domestic roles and stock romantic novel types. Laura is a complex example. After Colonel Sellers, she is arguably the most charismatic figure in the novel. After she is jilted by Selby, her combination of physical magnetism, ambition, and cold intensity allows her to ascend as a Washington, D.C., lobbyist. One of the novel's key scenes depicts Laura enjoying an authoritative victory over Senator Trollop (chapter 42). She has secretly ghostwritten his showboating speech on the floor of Congress and has withheld the last page to prove her authorship and blackmail him with exposure and public humiliation, which she describes in detail. *The Gilded Age* may have been born as the response of two jocular men to the female-dominated realm of sentimental fiction, but this scene suggests the power and capability of a female ghostwriter. At the same time, Laura is undone by her willingness to abandon the fruits of her labors to pursue, and then have vengeance upon, Selby, whose rejection helped to impel her worldly ascent. Complementing Laura's spectacular rise and fall is the more subdued arc of Ruth Bolton's medical career and marriage. Ruth is an ambivalent figure who is on the one hand devoted to her own life and education (and has the ability to put men in their place with wit) and at the same time eventually loses her drive and is in the end content to settle down with Philip.

Critiquing Government

Clemens and Warner's other main venture is a critique of the business of government in the nation's capital. Noting the relative scarcity of Washington, D.C., novels in the canon of American literature, Ward Just declares *The Gilded Age* "the ur-fable of the American city of government" (Just xxii). Bryant French's detailed scholarly study of *The Gilded Age* connects many of the novel's characters and episodes to actual events that likely inspired them, such as the scandal surrounding Kansas's Senator Samuel Pomeroy and the trial of Laura Fair, both in the early 1870s (French 87). Many other events, such as the Crédit Mobilier scandal, did not make it directly into the novel but nevertheless form the historical background of government corruption against which *The Gilded Age* takes place. Clemens and Warner's catalog of corruption ranges from the great Dilworthy scandal to the chronic petty misappropriation of Senator Balloon, who ships his personal belongings at the expense of taxpayers, by sprinkling a few public documents into boxes packed with his clothing and possessions, which the text suggests is standard practice among politicians.

David Sewell traces fault lines between various critical interpretations of Clemens's satire of Washington business as usual, from those who saw his attacks as personal and staying on the surface of what was at stake to the more Marxist interpretations, such as that of Philip Foner, who sees Clemens as indicting the basic structure of government and capitalism in America (Sewell 320). The extent to which Clemens was attacking individuals or groups for their moral failings or the political and economic system that attracted and shaped them remains unclear, but his disgust with the process and the result is evident in his famous remark in *Following the Equator* (1897) that America has "no distinctly native criminal class except Congress."

Wealth and Class

Apart from the official scandals and offenses, Clemens and Warner represent a social cross section of the capital city during a period of radical wealth creation and class reconfiguration. They anatomize Washington's three social circles, suggesting the complex ecosystem in which old money, the nouveau riche, and passengers on the government gravy train interact. Clemens and Warner's exploration of Washington, D.C., also touches on the tense relationship between Europe and America, a preoccupation that would animate the work of many novelists, including Henry James and Edith Wharton. Laura, for example, receives a visit from Mrs. Oreillé, whose husband, an Irish New Yorker originally named Patrick O'Reilly, has been transformed after two years in Paris, into Patrique Oreillé. Mrs. Oreillé's final insufferable identity is the result of an absurd case of multiple grafting—a family of Irish immigrants ascends the rungs of American society by playing at being (continental) European. Mrs. Oreillé's acquired airs and clumsy appropriation of French culture sends up the inexact frenzy for prestige among the nouveaux riches seeking to filter themselves through continental Europe.

The Hawkins family land, drawn from the TEN-NESSEE LAND in the Clemens family history, serves as a barometer for the exigencies of fortune and vagaries of human belief that drive the market. It is almost sold at several points in the story for sums ranging from $7,000 to $3 million. Before Laura's downfall, it is theoretically worth that much many times over. Si Hawkins suffered, and made his family suffer, to hold onto the land, and its name was on his lips when he died. In the end, after the Senate unanimously votes down the Knobs Industrial University appropriation, the land goes back to being a burden, and Washington tears up the tax bill for the land, getting out from under the family legacy. The Tennessee Knobs University plot is stitched into the actual Reconstruction-era land-grant system. The Morrill Land Grant Act of 1862, signed by Abraham Lincoln, set aside land to give the states for the establishment of "land grant schools." In 1890, the second Morrill Act extended further land grants, including land earmarked for 17 black colleges. There was certainly money to be made, and Clemens takes a typically jaundiced view of suddenly race-sensitive philanthropists eager to help recently emancipated AFRICAN AMERICANS spend the government's funds.

Family History

The novel's Tennessee land, like much of the Hawkins plot line, was based on Clemens's family history. When Washington Hawkins decides to stop paying taxes on the land and relinquish ownership without making any money, Clemens converted his family's worthless land into literary raw material for *The Gilded Age*, not to mention theatrical and prose spin-offs featuring Colonel Sellers. (He once said that he was the only member of the family to profit from the land; most of his profits came from a play adapted from the novel.) In stark contrast to the institutional corruption of Washington and the calculations of social climbing is the opportunistic charisma of Colonel Sellers, who became one of Clemens's most popular characters. If *The Gilded Age* hedges two of Clemens's personal preoccupations—entrepreneurial ambition and a simultaneous disgust with the human capacity for greed—Colonel Sellers serves as a charming, if buffoonish, advertisement for populist capitalism, modeled on Clemens's uncle, JAMES LAMPTON, and regarded by some contemporaries and critics as an authorial proxy.

Apart from Sellers, *The Gilded Age* features a large cast of not fully realized characters and has been criticized for its disarray of subplots. The characters in *The Gilded Age*—their experiences and relationships—never rise to the level of emotional intensity that was the distinguishing characteristic of sensation fiction, the form Clemens and Warner set out to burlesque. The novel's various pork barrel schemes, in contrast, are accomplishments of vivacity. Ward Just estimates that "The heart of the novel . . . is the promotion of the two schemes" (Just xxxiii). In their novel excoriating corruption and greed, Clemens and Warner crafted a number of brazen and ill-hatched schemes—the Tennessee Knobs land appropriation and Columbus River–widening project—which retain virtual lives of their own, with the continued potential to fascinate, entertain, and disgust.

Critical Commentary by Alex Feerst

CHARACTERS AND RELATED ENTRIES

Amaranth Fictional STEAMBOAT in *The Gilded Age* (1873). In chapter 4, Si Hawkins takes his family up the Mississippi River on the steamboat *Boreas*, which races with the *Amaranth*. The latter blows its boiler after ignoring its head engineer's warnings, and the *Boreas* picks up 39 wounded persons and 22 dead bodies. Ninety-six persons are missing—including the parents of Laura Van Brunt, whom the Hawkinses adopt. Years later, it is learned that Laura's father survived the accident (chapter 10).

The location of this accident poses a problem. In writing about it, Clemens was doubtless thinking of the PENNSYLVANIA's 1858 explosion near MEMPHIS, which he called the "Good Samaritan City." In chapter 4, he alludes to "Good Samaritans" helping the *Amaranth*'s injured and mentions a Memphis physician; however, since the Hawkinses are traveling *north* from Tennessee on the *Boreas*, they should be nowhere near Memphis when the *Amaranth* explodes.

Dilworthy, Senator Abner Character in *The Gilded Age* (1873). A corrupt MISSOURI politician, Dilworthy came from an unspecified neighboring state and profited as a Unionist in the CIVIL WAR (chapter 20). A later chapter describes him as a former state legislator, governor and member of the House of Representatives but does not say where he held these offices (chapter 53). After being discussed in chapter 19, Dilworthy first appears in the chapter when he visits Hawkeye. There Colonel Sellers interests him in supporting a bill to develop the river at Stone's Landing. When Dilworthy goes back to WASHINGTON, D.C., he takes Washington Hawkins along as his private secretary. Later he brings Laura Hawkins to his Washington home (chapter 30), a mansion near the White House (chapter 39). He develops an avuncular relationship with Laura, who becomes his lobbyist for a bill to get the federal government to buy her family's TENNESSEE LAND for an industrial school for freed blacks. After enjoying initial success, Dilworthy is eventually ruined by a state legislator's revelation that he has been buying votes for his reelection to the Senate (chapter 57).

Ostensibly honest and smugly pious, Dilworthy is appalled by the suggestion that he personally might profit from supporting the Columbus River scheme. He claims to have one principle in public life—never to "push a private interest if it is not justified and ennobled by some larger public good" (chapter 35). He talks sanctimoniously and often attends prayer meetings, but his true feelings are revealed when Laura enters his study unexpectedly and catches him holding his Bible upside down (chapter 35).

Though Dilworthy is introduced in C. D. WARNER's chapters, Clemens contributed at least equally to his development and wrote exactly half of the 27 chapters in which he appears. The authors modeled Dilworthy closely on a KANSAS politician, Senator Samuel Clarke Pomeroy (1816–1891), whose own investigation by the Senate was in the headlines as they were writing. Their outlines even called the Dilworthy character "Bumroy." Portly and bald like Dilworthy, Pomeroy was investigated on bribery charges by his own state legislature. Although he was cleared by a U.S. Senate committee in 1873, his political career was ruined. Augustus HOPPIN used Pomeroy as his model for his illustrations of Dilworthy in *The Gilded Age*.

Hawkeye Fictional town in *The Gilded Age* (1873). When Si Hawkins brings his family to MISSOURI, he settles them in a small village later alluded to as Murpheysburg (chapter 18). Hawkeye is first mentioned in chapter 6 as the place to which Colonel Sellers has relocated. It is 30 miles from Murpheysburg, which in turn is five miles from Swansea, to which Hawkeye is linked by stagecoach. When Washington Hawkins moves to Hawkeye in chapter 7, he finds it a "pretty large town for interior Missouri." The rest of his family moves there shortly after his father dies (chapters 10–11). Hawkeye is 10 miles from Stone's Landing (chapter 17), which Sellers wants to develop into a major railroad and river transportation hub. This dream is dashed when the people of Hawkeye subscribe enough shares in the railroad to ensure that it will pass through their town instead of Stone's Landing (chapter 28).

Loosely modeled on FLORIDA, MISSOURI, Hawkeye also has elements of the river town Hannibal—the second Missouri home of Clemens's family.

Hawkins, Clay Character in *The Gilded Age* (1873). Clay is the first of two children whom Nancy and Si Hawkins adopt during their migration to Missouri. Si finds the recently orphaned boy when he stumbles into a funeral service on his family's third day out from eastern Tennessee (chapter 2). The approximately 10-year-old Clay has recently lost his mother to fever. Since no one else in his impoverished village offers to take him in, Si takes it on himself to invite the boy to join his family. When he presents Clay to his wife and tells her what he has done, she thanks him for paying her the compliment of "taking it for granted that I'll be willing to it."

The family quickly accepts Clay—and their second adoptee, Laura—as full members of the family. Clay fits in well, but it is clear from the start that he has more sense than his loving but impractical new relatives. For example, when Si encourages Clay to imagine himself becoming a millionaire and a governor, Clay replies that his natural mother "always told me to work along and not be much expecting to get rich, and then I wouldn't be disappointed if I didn't get rich" (chapter 5). It is a lesson that other members of his new family are slow to learn.

At the time when Si Hawkins adopts Clay, a villager calls his generous act "bread cast upon the waters—it'll return after many days . . ." That remark proves prophetic. Clay grows up to become not only a fine man but the most sensible member of the family—the one who bails out the family with his own savings when they get into desperate financial trouble (chapter 6). After Si Hawkins dies, the rest of the family look to Clay "for almost their whole support" (chapter 18).

As an adult son experienced in taking care of the rest of his family, Clemens evidently modeled Clay on himself. Moreover, the fictional Clay has a relationship with his brother, Washington Hawkins, that parallels Clemens's relationship with his own impractical older brother, Orion. Clay's relationship with Washington is also similar to that of the adopted brothers in "Edward Mills and George Benton: A Tale." Just as the adoptive father in that story instructs the more responsible Edward to help take care of his less responsible brother, George, Si Hawkins asks Clay to look after Washington's welfare and "help him along all you can" (chapter 6).

After figuring prominently in the early chapters of *The Gilded Age*, Clay is next mentioned briefly in chapter 18 and then disappears from the narrative until chapter 61, when he learns of his sister Laura's troubles and returns home. It is revealed that years earlier he followed his instinct for adventure by going to Australia, where he settled down and became a prosperous merchant in Melbourne.

Through the intervening years, he has supported his family with remittances.

Hawkins, Laura (the "Duchess") Character in *The Gilded Age* (1873). Laura first appears as five-year-old Laura Van Brunt, whom Nancy and Si Hawkins adopt when the *Amaranth* disaster orphans her (chapter 5). By the end of the novel, she is 28 years old (chapter 60). Her natural parents are believed to have been prosperous easterners, who came to New Orleans by way of Cuba before taking passage on the *Amaranth*. By the time Laura is 12, everyone but her new parents forgets that she is adopted, despite the fact that she is developing into an exquisite beauty quite unlike her foster sister Emily. At 15, she is "willful, generous, forgiving, imperious, affectionate, improvident [and] bewitching" (chapter 6) and her family later calls her the "Duchess" (chapter 9).

After Si Hawkins dies, Laura discovers that he had learned that her natural father was still alive (chapter 10). This man, said to be mentally unbalanced, again disappears without a trace, however. Insensitive villagers gossip about Laura's mysterious background, making her distrustful of people. Nevertheless, she falls deeply in love with a Confederate colonel, George Selby, during the Civil War; she follows him to another town and marries him (in a chapter written by C. D. Warner); three months later, Selby tells her that he already has a wife and abandons her (chapter 18). Thereafter, Laura never fully trusts men and rejects countless suitors. Later she becomes a ruthlessly effective lobbyist for Senator Dilworthy in Washington, D.C., where she again becomes involved with Selby. When Selby jilts her a second time, she follows him to New York and kills him. By the time she is tried, public sentiment has swung in her favor and she is acquitted. At the same time, however, Dilworthy's career is ruined and a congressional bill on which Laura pins her hopes of profiting from her family's Tennessee land collapses. She tries to start a new life as a lecturer, but public hostility is so devastating that she dies of heart failure.

Although Clemens gave this character the name of his childhood friend Laura Hawkins, he appears to have modeled her—as a youth—on Laura

Wright, a 14-year-old girl with whom he became infatuated on a STEAMBOAT in 1858. The character's adult career is partly modeled on the experiences of a San Francisco woman named Laura D. Fair, who gained notoriety in the early 1870s during two sensational trials for killing her lover. Fair's case received national attention because of her dependence on an "emotional insanity" plea. Fair was never a lobbyist, but like the fictional Laura, she saw her attempt to launch a lecture career quickly ruined by an angry mob.

Hawkins, Si (Silas)   Character in *The Gilded Age* (1873). The patriarch of his family, Hawkins is an honest, well-meaning man who is easily lured by get-rich schemes—particularly those advocated by his friend Colonel Sellers, who lures him to MISSOURI. When introduced in chapter 1, Hawkins is about 35 years old and is known as "Squire Hawkins" because he is postmaster of tiny Obedstown, where he runs a general store out of his house. After resettling in Murpheysburg, Missouri, he buys another small store and makes it a success by studying market trends in big-city newspapers. He gets a reputation for being lucky and gradually becomes known as "Judge Hawkins" out of respect. He and Sellers make a fortune raising mules to sell in New Orleans but lose it on a sugar speculation. Three BANKRUPTCIES in 10 years eventually break his spirit, leaving him with eight children in desperate poverty. Despite being hard up, he has avoided accumulating serious debts.

Many aspects of Hawkins's life are taken from that of Clemens's father, John M. Clemens: from his deep-rooted sense of southern honor to his naive faith that the future welfare of his children is assured by his "TENNESSEE LAND." The narrative's chronological clues suggest that Hawkins dies in his late forties—also like Clemens. Further, both men die condemning their children to lifetimes of false hopes in the land. And just as Clemens died kissing his daughter Pamela, Hawkins dies kissing his daughter Laura. Unlike Clemens, however, Hawkins is generally warmer and more demonstrative.

Jim Blaine's old ram's tale in *Roughing It* mentions an unrelated character named "Sile Hawkins" (chapter 53).

Hawkins, (George) Washington   Character in *The Gilded Age* (1873) and *The American Claimant* (1892). Introduced early in *The Gilded Age* as the 10-year-old son of Si Hawkins. Washington is the family's dreamer—much like Orion Clemens in Clemens's own family. His thoughts are always on impractical inventions, vast speculations and the riches he hopes to reap from the family's TENNESSEE LAND. At some point, he is educated in SAINT LOUIS (chapter 6), but he avoids steady employment. When the family's fortunes decline, he goes to Hawkeye hoping that Colonel Sellers will steer him to riches. Instead, Sellers gets him a bookkeeping job with General Boswell, with whose daughter Louise he falls in love (chapter 8). After years of getting nowhere, he serves briefly in a Confederate unit during the CIVIL WAR (chapter 18). Several years after the war, Senator Dilworthy is so impressed by Hawkins's guilelessness and adaptability that he takes him to WASHINGTON, D.C., as his unpaid private secretary—a post similar to the one that Clemens held under WILLIAM M. STEWART (chapter 20). Hawkins flourishes in the capital; he makes good money clerking for two congressional committees and throws himself into working for Dilworthy's bill to get the government to buy his family's land. The arrival of his beautiful foster sister, Laura Hawkins, even transforms him into a society favorite. By the end of the narrative, however, all his pipe-dreams are smashed and he renounces the Tennessee land in favor of solid work. Now about 33 years old, he looks forward to returning to Hawkeye to marry Louise (chapter 61).

When *The American Claimant* opens about 15 years later, Hawkins is still poor. He is now stout and about 50, but looks much older. He is married to Louise, has children and is living in the CHEROKEE STRIP in what is now OKLAHOMA (chapter 2). Returning to Washington as an unofficial congressional delegate, he again falls under Sellers's influence. He is practical enough to investigate having one of Sellers's inventions marketed but otherwise accepts Sellers's wild schemes without question—from materializing the dead to manipulating sunspots to alter Earth's weather. Sellers appreciates Washington's loyalty and steadily magnifies his importance by referring to him with increasingly exalted titles, such as major, senator, and admiral (much as the baggage-car man in "THE INVALID'S STORY" shows his growing respect for a presumed corpse with increasingly exalted titles). Hawkins is referred to as "George Washington Hawkins" just once, in chapter 5 of *The Gilded Age*.

Jinny, Aunt, and Uncle Dan'l AFRICAN-AMERICAN characters in *The Gilded Age* (1873) and *The American Claimant* (1892). In the first novel, 30-year-old Jinny and her 40-year-old husband Dan'l are the family SLAVES of Si Hawkins who accompany his family from Tennessee to Missouri (chapter 3). After one of Hawkins's bankruptcies about 10 years later, they are sold at auction and taken downriver (chapter 7). In *Claimant*, they reappear as elderly household servants in the Washington, D.C., home of Colonel Sellers (chapter 3). Described as "old wrecks," they not only do no housework, they require another, younger servant to take care of them. They often quarrel loudly about religion; Dan'l is a "Dunker Baptist" and Jinny a "shouting Methodist."

Obedstown Fictional town in *The Gilded Age* (1873). Located in the Knobs of East TENNESSEE, Obedstown is modeled on JAMESTOWN, Tennessee, where Clemens's parents lived before moving to Missouri. Its 15 homes are so scattered in the woods that is difficult for visitors to realize that they are in a "town." Nearby villages include the Forks and Shelby. Si Hawkins and his family leave the town at the end of chapter 1. The town is mentioned again in chapter 61, when Washington Hawkins receives a tax bill from the town on the family's TENNESSEE LAND.

Obedstown takes its name from the real Obed (or Obeds) River, a minor tributary of the Tennessee River, about 22 miles south of Jamestown. Obed was the name of several biblical figures, the best known of whom was the son of Ruth and Boaz.

Sellers, Mulberry (Colonel Sellers) (a.k.a. Eschol and Beriah) Character in *The Gilded Age* (1873) and *The American Claimant* (1892). One of Clemens's most enduring creations, Sellers is a warm-hearted, generous optimist whose resilience and enthusiasm for grandiose schemes never flag. He is first mentioned in the opening of *The Gilded Age*, when Si Hawkins receives a letter from him urging Hawkins to come to Missouri. Although Hawkins has previously lost money in Sellers's speculations, he accepts his advice (chapter 1). Sellers himself first appears in chapter 5, when the Hawkinses reach Murpheysburg (identified by name in chapter 18), where Sellers lives in a one-room cabin with his wife of one week, Polly (whose name is first given in chapter 7). Sellers's embarrassed admission that his wife calls him "Colonel" suggests that he has only recently adopted this honorific title; however, earlier in the same chapter Washington Hawkins refers to him as "Colonel Sellers" *before* his family even reaches Murpheysburg. Chapter 6 of *The Gilded Age* jumps the narrative ahead a decade, by which time Sellers has eight children, including two sets of twins, and is living in Hawkeye.

Always the romantic, Sellers has given his children names such as Lafayette, Roderick Dhu, and Marie Antoinette (chapter 11). Little more is said about these children, however, and by the time *Claimant* begins all but one of them are dead (chapter 2). Seller's age is never specified, but it may be close to that of Si Hawkins, who is about 35 at the beginning of the narrative. Since *The Gilded Age* unfolds over about 23 years and *The American Claimant* opens about 15 years later, Sellers is probably in his early seventies by the time of the latter novel.

As a central character in *The Gilded Age*, Sellers is a crucial link among the other major characters. He encourages Washington Hawkins in his delusions about his family's TENNESSEE LAND; along with coauthor C. D. WARNER's character Henry Brierly, he is a major player in the abortive scheme to develop Stone's Landing; he is an unofficial ally of Senator Dilworthy, and he accompanies Laura Hawkins as a chaperon when Dilworthy invites her to come to WASHINGTON, D.C. Sellers flourishes in the national capital, where "for the first time in his life his talents had a fair field" (chapter 40). Though he never actually accomplishes anything, he gets to know everyone in the government, including President GRANT, who enjoys hearing him talk (chapters 40 and 44).

At the end of *The Gilded Age,* after every scheme with which Sellers is connected collapses, he decides to go into law and shoot for the chief justiceship of the United States (chapter 61). By the time *Claimant* opens, however, he and his wife Polly live in a poor black neighborhood of Washington, D.C. (chapter 2). Signs in front of his shabby house proclaim him an "Attorney at Law and Claim Agent," as well as "a Materializer, a Hypnotizer, a Mind-Cure Dabbler, and so on." When his old friend Washington Hawkins arrives, Sellers explains that he returned to Washington to take up an ambassadorial appointment to England, but arrived a day too late. Over the ensuing years, he occasionally prospered, only to give his money away. He counts many great men among his friends, including U. S. Grant, WILLIAM T. SHERMAN, Philip Sheridan, and Robert E. Lee. He also dabbles with inventions, including one that actually has commercial worth—a mechanical game called "Pigs in the Clover." Most of his ideas are of dubious value—such as schemes to materialize the dead, use sewer-gas for home lighting, and manipulate sunspots to alter the earth's climate. His ideas, however, are always more important to him than money. Though Sellers is still promoting commercial schemes in *Claimant,* this book's central theme is his claim to be the rightful Earl of Rossmore. By the end of the narrative, however, he happily abandons this claim when his daughter Sally Sellers marries the current earl's son, Lord Berkeley.

Clemens modeled Sellers closely on his mother's cousin JAMES LAMPTON, whom his AUTOBIOGRAPHY describes as a "person who could not be exaggerated." Like Sellers, Lampton forever saw vast riches around the corner and always said of the Clemens family's Tennessee Land that "there's millions in it!" Clemens claimed that many of the strange behaviors attributed to the fictional Sellers—such as the turnip and water banquet of *The Gilded Age* (chapter 11)—actually occurred. Sellers also borrows traits from other people, notably Clemens's father—who tinkered with a perpetual motion machine when Clemens was young—and who matched Sellers's fierce pride in his VIRGINIA birth. Like Clemens's brother Orion Clemens, Sellers changes religions frequently but is a consistent tee-

totaller. Sellers is also like Clemens himself in his fascination with inventions and his weakness for financial speculation.

Although Sellers was Clemens's own invention, his coauthor Warner suggested his "impossible" name, "Eschol Sellers"—which he borrowed from a man he met in the West years earlier. Warner suggested this name because it was quaint, but Clemens was probably already aware of its biblical significance, as he had earlier mentioned Palestine's "Eschol" (or Eshtaol) in *Innocents Abroad* (1869; chapter 46). Shortly after *The Gilded Age* came out, a real Eschol Sellers appeared and objected to seeing his name in the novel, so the authors renamed their character "Beriah"— another biblical name meaning "unfortunate." (When Clemens wrote for the SAN FRANCISCO CALL in 1864, he made fun of the name of a local Southern sympathizer named Beriah Brown.) Clemens tells how he and Warner made this change in his autobiography, in chapter 47 of *Life on the Mississippi* (1883) and in the introduction of *Claimant.* In *Claimant,* he further altered the name to "Mulberry," or "Berry"—an adaptation of Beriah with a hint of "HUCKLEBERRY." Colonel Mulberry Sellers is also the name of a character in "THREE THOUSAND YEARS AMONG THE MICROBES."

Shortly after publication of *The Gilded Age,* JOHN T. RAYMOND played Sellers in a dramatic adaptation of the novel that proved so popular that the play was soon renamed *Colonel Sellers.* CHARLES NEIDER'S edition of THE ADVENTURES OF COLONEL SELLERS (1965) is a condensation of the *The Gilded Age* that omits most of Warner's text.

Sellers, Polly   Minor character in *The Gilded Age* (1873) and *The American Claimant* (1892). The dutiful wife of Colonel Mulberry (Beriah) Sellers, Polly occasionally persuades Sellers to behave more sensibly—in matters such as putting baskets of human ashes on display in their home—but is generally unobtrusive. Although she recognizes that the world regards her husband as a failure, she regards him as a success because of his kindness, generosity, and optimism. At the end of *Claimant* she goes to England alone, as Sellers remains behind to work on a new scheme.

Stone's Landing Fictional village in *The Gilded Age* (1883). Located 10 miles from Hawkeye, Missouri, Stone's Landing is a collection of about a dozen cabins standing on the muddy bend of Goose Run (chapter 16). Colonel Sellers wants to develop Stone's Landing into a metropolis called "Napoleon" by bringing in a railroad and transforming the crooked stream into the navigable "Columbus River." Neither Stone's Landing nor Napoleon is mentioned after chapter 28, when a decision is made to route the railroad through Hawkeye instead of Stone's Landing; however, later chapters occasionally mention the "Columbus River" scheme in retrospect (chapters 31, 40, 46, and 50).

A reference to "Napoleon" in chapter 4 is apparently to NAPOLEON, Arkansas.

BIBLIOGRAPHY

Anderson, Frederick. Review of Mark Twain and "The Gilded Age." *Nineteenth-Century Fiction* 21, no. 1 (June 1966): 106–108.

Camfield, Gregg. "Afterword." In *The Gilded Age*, edited by Shelley Fisher Fishkin. Oxford: Oxford University Press, 1996.

French, Bryant Morey. *Mark Twain and the Gilded Age: The Book That Named an Era*. Dallas, Tex: Southern Methodist University Press, 1965.

Harris, Susan K. "Four Ways to Inscribe a Mackerel: Mark Twain and Laura Hawkins." *Studies in the Novel* 21 (1989): 138–153.

Hutchinson, Stuart. *Mark Twain: Humour on the Run*. Amsterdam: Rodopi, 1994.

Just, Ward. "Introduction." In *The Gilded Age*, edited by Shelley Fisher Fishkin. Oxford: Oxford University Press, 1996.

Twain, Mark, and C. D. Warner, *The Gilded Age*, edited by Shelley Fisher Fishkin: New York: Oxford University Press, 1996.

"Goldsmith's Friend Abroad Again" (1870)

Story told in seven letters to Ching-Foo by the fictional Ah Song Hi, a CHINESE immigrant to the United States. Ah Song Hi indentures himself to an American labor broker and leaves China for America believing that it is a land where "all are free all equal, and none reviled or abused." Soon, however, he experiences a different reality. The American consul in Shanghai cheats him and 1,300 other immigrants out of a fee that they should not have to pay. Ah Song Hi crosses the ocean in a ship's steerage. He patiently endures it when the captain uses scalding steam to control the crowded Chinese passengers because he believes that the same system is used on American passengers.

The moment that Ah Song Hi steps ashore in SAN FRANCISCO, he is assaulted by a policeman. His luggage is taken from him and he is made to spend the last of his money on a smallpox vaccination he does not need, since he has already had the disease. Through everything, he remains optimistic.

A month later Ah Song Hi writes his fourth letter. By now he has been set free by his employer, who cannot hire him out. A white man sics his dogs on Ah Song Hi. Another man persuades a policeman to stop the attack, but the dogs' owners abuse Ah Song Hi verbally and the policeman arrests him for disorderly conduct. He is beaten again and tossed in jail. Within his crowded cell he is beaten by other prisoners. That night another, badly beaten prisoner is thrown into the cell. This man dies the next day.

Only when Ah Song Hi reaches the courtroom does his optimism begin to fade. He observes the strong correlation between a defendant's ethnicity and his chance of acquittal. He also discovers that Chinese people cannot testify against whites in court. His white benefactor arrives to testify in his behalf, but loses his nerve and slips out of the courtroom. Ah Song Hi is convicted. As he is being remanded to prison, he learns that the local newspaper's court reporter will inevitably write a report that will "praise all the policemen indiscriminately and abuse the Chinamen and dead people."

BACKGROUND AND PUBLISHING HISTORY

Clemens worked as a newspaper reporter in San Francisco during the early to mid-1860s, at a time when tens of thousands of Chinese immigrants were coming into CALIFORNIA through San Francisco. He developed a high regard for these immigrants and was inclined to report honestly on the mistreatment that he witnessed. His paper, the SAN FRANCISCO CALL, did not welcome criticism of the police, so Clemens saved his pen for articles and books to be written later. He found his inspiration for the form of this story in Oliver GOLDSMITH's *The Citizen of the World* (1762), which purports to contain letters from a Chinese philosopher exposing the hypocrisies and shams of 18th-century English society.

Clemens published "Goldsmith" in GALAXY in October–November 1870 and January 1871. Neither he nor A. B. PAINE included the story in any of their standard anthologies. It did appear, however, in the unauthorized edition, THE CURIOUS REPUBLIC OF GONDOUR *and Other Whimsical Tales*, in 1919, and has since been reprinted occasionally in special collections. The story was possibly omitted from early collections because of its stridency and its raw subject matter. It touches on police brutality, diplomatic corruption, anti-Chinese violence, pornography, prostitution, alcoholism, journalistic lack of integrity, greed, and hypocrisy.

CHARACTERS AND RELATED ENTRIES

Ah Song Hi   Title character and narrator of "Goldsmith's Friend Abroad Again." A hopeful CHINESE immigrant to America, Ah Song Hi indentures himself to an American labor contractor. He writes seven letters to Ching-Foo, retaining his idealistic optimism about America until a biased judge sends him to prison. He is presumably from Shanghai, from which he writes his first letter. Indeed, his name, *Ah Song Hi,* could mean "big Shanghai" in Chinese.

"The Great Dark"

Unfinished NOVEL written in 1898 and published posthumously. "The Great Dark" is one of several stories that Clemens began about prosperous, happy family men who suddenly find themselves in nightmare worlds so real that they wonder if their "normal" lives are the dreams. Filled with allusions to details from Clemens's own life, these stories may reflect his struggle to cope with the disasters that his family experienced in the 1890s, when his publishing firm failed, his investment in the PAIGE COMPOSITOR evaporated, his daughter Susy died, and his daughter Jean suffered from epilepsy. "The Great Dark" begins at a moment that corresponds to the year 1880 in his own life, when Susy was eight and Clara was six; seven years earlier his family had sailed to Europe on the BATAVIA—an event alluded to in the story.

As an exploration of human beings being reduced to microscopic size, "The Great Dark" anticipates another unfinished SCIENCE-FICTION story, "THREE THOUSAND YEARS AMONG THE MICROBES." The story's unnamed ship sails in perpetual darkness—a condition that recalls Mark Twain's fascination with fear of the dark, as he describes it in "A MEMORABLE MIDNIGHT EXPERIENCE," *A Tramp Abroad* (chapter 13), *The Prince and the Pauper* (chapter 18), *Connecticut Yankee* (chapter 30), and elsewhere.

SYNOPSIS

The narrative begins on the birthday of eight-year-old Jessie Edwards. Alice Edwards describes her husband Henry and two daughters as they use a microscope to study tiny animal life in a drop of water. Mr. Edwards then writes a statement that continues the narrative. In explaining his experiments, he thinks how much what he sees in the water drop resembles an uncharted ocean. As he contemplates these wonders, the Superintendent of Dreams appears and promises to give him a comfortable ship and crew with which to explore his microscopic ocean with his family.

A moment later, Edwards is on a ship at sea on a blustery night, listening to a mate named Turner complain that he has never been more puzzled about *where* he is; even the captain does not know. Their unnamed ship has just sailed over the spot where an island should be and they are now in the middle of where GREENLAND should be. Turner also admits seeing a whale with hairy spider legs, but Edwards does not reveal that his description matches something he saw under his microscope. Turner mentions occasionally seeing a human specter—who turns out to be the Superintendent of Dreams. In Edwards's cabin, Turner elaborates on the strange voyage: All the water through which they have sailed is the same temperature, and both days and nights are dark, with no sign of sun, moon or stars in the sky. As Turner explains why he thinks the world has come to an end, the invisible Superintendent of Dreams playfully drinks Turner's coffee. Afterward, Edwards reproaches the superintendent for playing such tricks.

The superintendent reveals that the ship has sailed 2,350 miles across the drop of water, which is 6,000 miles wide. He does not tell Edwards how much longer the voyage will last, but assures him that the ship will never run out of provisions. He explains that it is always night because the drop of water is mostly outside the microscope's luminous circle. When Edwards proposes ending this dream, the superintendent startles him by saying that he (Edwards) has spent his whole life on this ship, and that his *other* life is the dream. Quickly accepting this idea, Edwards decides to tell his wife the truth immediately. He is surprised to discover that Alice has vastly different memories of their past experiences. For example, he remembers their sailing to Europe together seven years earlier on the BATAVIA with Captain Moreland (in October 1873 Clemens's family sailed to Europe on the *Batavia* with Captain John E. Mouland), but Alice insists that he has dreamed the trip, just as he has dreamed meeting Dr. JOHN BROWN. Not able to remember living anywhere other than on the ship—except in "dream homes"—Alice remembers things that Edwards does not, such the captain's son being beaten by a spider squid. As they talk, Edwards begins remembering other incidents. After Alice asks him how long it has been since he boxed or fenced with George (George GRIFFIN?), their black servant, he is soon boxing with George and remembering having often done it before.

Before dinner, Henry asks his daughters if they remember living anywhere else, but Jessie remembers only dream homes. At dinner, everything seems real, and Edwards finds that he seems to know everyone well, except a stranger sitting next

to him. After an argument between Captain Davis and his mate breaks up the dinner party, Edwards struggles to remember things from his lives on the ship and on land, but as his memories of events on the ship sharpen, those of his life on land dim.

The narrative jumps to "Book 2, Chapter 1," and the narrator admits having lost "Book 1." Several years have now passed, and the Edwardses have a new son named Harry. The puzzled crew, who now think that they are headed for the South Pole, have mutinied several times over the years. Growing increasingly restless as huge animals are sighted, the crew wants the captain to turn the ship back. One day, a giant squid seizes the ship, throwing the crew into a panic until the captain turns Gatling guns on the beast. Meanwhile, Edwards and his wife search for their children, who are found hiding in the ship's hold.

With the ship in a dead calm and unable to escape the squid's domain, mutineers confront the captain and demand to know where they are. When they try to shoot him, however, they discover that their guns are unloaded. The captain admits not knowing where they are, but insists that since they are in the hands of God, it is safe to go ahead. The manuscript then ends.

PUBLISHING HISTORY

While living in Austria in the fall of 1898, Clemens wrote most of "The Great Dark" at the same time he worked on "MY DÉBUT AS A LITERARY PERSON," which deals with the sinking of the HORNET. He left his roughly 24,500-word story untitled; his literary executor A. B. PAINE called it "Statement of the Edwardses." Paine's successor, Bernard DEVOTO, gave it the name "The Great Dark" and included it in LETTERS FROM THE EARTH. After publication of that book was delayed, DeVoto included an extract from the story in his own book, *Mark Twain at Work* (1942). The complete story was finally published in *Letters from the Earth* in 1962. Five years later, John S. TUCKEY included a corrected text in WHICH WAS THE DREAM? AND OTHER SYMBOLIC WRITINGS (1967).

CHARACTERS AND RELATED ENTRIES

Edwards family Characters in "The Great Dark." An American family living on a ship in a dreamlike voyage, the Edwardses remember their land-life at Springport as if it were a dream. Henry Edwards begins the narrative as a healthy, energetic 35-year-old. His wife, Alice, is 10 years younger—just as Clemens's wife was 10 years younger than he was. The Edwardses begin the story with two children: eight-year-old Jessie and six-year-old Bessie, and have a third third, Harry, during the voyage. They also travel with a 28-year-old nurse called Germania, a 30-year-old black servant named George, and a maid named Delia.

Clemens wrote "The Great Dark" in 1898, but did not set it in a specific year. Several striking parallels between its fictional Edwards family and Clemens's real family suggest that Clemens was thinking of the year 1880. On March 19 of that year, for example, his daughter Susy became eight—the age that Jessie Edwards becomes on the same date. In 1880, Clemens's second daughter, Clara, was six—Bessie Edwards's age. That was also the year in which Clemens's third daughter, Jean, was born; Jean's birth parallels that of Harry Edwards in the story—though Harry's birthday is June 8—the birthdate both of Clara and of Clemens's brother BENJAMIN CLEMENS. A final parallel is that Clemens and his wife sailed to England on the BATAVIA in 1873—seven years before 1880. In the story, Henry Edwards remembers taking his family to Europe on the *Batavia* seven years earlier, when they met the same Dr. JOHN BROWN in Scotland whom Clemens and his family met in 1873.

"The Great Revolution in Pitcairn"

SKETCH written in 1878. While in Europe, Clemens evidently heard news concerning PITCAIRN. A British admiral who had recently visited the South Pacific island reported on nearly idyllic conditions among its 90 inhabitants: Their sole occupations were farming and fishing and their sole recreation was religious services; money did not exist on the island, and everyone over 17 could vote. The admiral's report casually added that a "doubtful acquisition"—an American stranger—had settled on the island.

From that presumably factual premise, Clemens invents a second report—made four months later by a Captain Ormsby of the American ship HORNET. The resulting sketch speculates on what impact an aggressive modern American might have on a simple, isolated society, and plays with themes that Clemens would later develop more fully in *Connecticut Yankee* (1889). A special aspect of Pitcairn that must have appealed to him is the confused relationships among its inhabitants, all of whom were descended from the same handful of HMS *Bounty* mutineers. His fictional stranger gains power by trading on the fact that he alone on the island is not motivated by nepotism—since he is the only person not related to everyone else.

The American, Butterworth Stavely, quickly ingratiates himself on Pitcairn by throwing all his energy into religion. He then fosters discontent by calling attention to such matters as overly short Sunday services, the limited voice of women in prayer meetings, and the insufficient amount of children's Sunday school. After engineering the ouster of the chief magistrate, he turns the population against English overrule. Citing ITALY and GERMANY as nations to emulate, he calls for unification, and persuades the islanders to proclaim independence and create an empire—with him as emperor.

Stavely sets up orders of nobility, using HOLY LAND names for titles, and establishes an army and a navy. Staffing these services proves problematic, and discontent with the new regime begins. It accelerates after Stavely raises a woman named Nancy Peters to the peerage and marries her; she angers a third of the women on the island by inviting the other two-thirds to be her maids of honor. More trouble follows when Stavely levies taxes to pay for the military. He finally goes too far by taking up a collection at church to pay off the national debt. After a Social Democrat tries to assassinate him, he is overthrown in a general revolt. He is punished with banishment from church services, and the nation reverts to its old ways.

Clemens originally wrote this 4,350-word sketch as a chapter for *A Tramp Abroad* (1880) but instead published it in the ATLANTIC MONTHLY in March 1879. Its first book publication was in THE STOLEN WHITE ELEPHANT, ETC. (1882), whose contents were later incorporated into *Tom Sawyer Abroad* and *TOM SAWYER, DETECTIVE*.

CHARACTERS AND RELATED ENTRIES

Pitcairn A volcanic South PACIFIC island covering two square miles, Pitcairn has one of the world's smallest and most isolated human settlements. Located just below the Tropic of Capricorn, midway between Tahiti and Easter Island, Pitcairn was uninhabited until 1790, when mutineers of the British warship HMS *Bounty* and some Tahitians established a hideaway whose existence was unknown to the outside world until 1808. After Great Britain annexed Pitcairn in 1839, it tried to resettle the residents elsewhere, but a tiny community remained. The island is the setting of Clemens's 1879 sketch "The Great Revolution in Pitcairn."

Stavely, Butterworth (Butterworth I) Character in "The Great Revolution in Pitcairn" (1879). An American settler in tiny PITCAIRN Island, Stavely foments a revolution that throws off English rule, replaces universal suffrage with a system of nobility, and gets himself crowned "Emperor Butterworth I." Soon, however, he is overthrown and the island reverts to its previous condition.

In his desire to find trouble where none exists, Stavely resembles Tom Sawyer, particularly the Tom of "TOM SAWYER'S CONSPIRACY." More significantly, he is a rehearsal for Hank Morgan, the modern American of *Connecticut Yankee* (1889) who revolutionizes sixth-century England. Stavely, however, is a kind of mirror image of Morgan—who seeks to destroy the established church and replace hereditary nobility with universal suffrage.

Life on the Mississippi (1883) mentions a real Hannibal resident named John Stavely (chapter 55). "Stavely" is also the name of characters in several of Clemens's unfinished stories.

Hannibal, Huck & Tom, Mark Twain's

Collection, published in 1969, of mostly unfinished material edited by WALTER BLAIR for the MARK TWAIN PAPERS and published by the University of California Press in 1969. The material—none of which was published during Clemens's lifetime—is arranged in two sections. The "Hannibal" section has five pieces with autobiographical themes: "VILLAGERS OF 1840–3," "Jane Lampton Clemens," "Tupperville–Dobbsville," "Clairvoyant," and "A Human Bloodhound." The "Huck & Tom" section has five unfinished stories revolving around Tom Sawyer and Huckleberry Finn. These include "HUCK FINN AND TOM SAWYER AMONG THE INDIANS," which had been published in *Life* magazine, and five other pieces published for the first time in this collection: "DOUGHFACE," "Tom Sawyer's Gang Plans a Naval Battle," "TOM SAWYER'S CONSPIRACY," and "Tom Sawyer: A Play."

The most important items of *Hannibal, Huck & Tom* were reprinted in the Mark Twain Library edition of *Huck Finn and Tom Sawyer Among the Indians and Other Unfinished Stories* (1989), which was edited by Blair and Dahlia Armon. This edition added "BOY'S MANUSCRIPT," "Hellfire Hotchkiss," and a richly autobiographical letter from Clemens to WILL BOWEN, as well as a number of additional textual corrections and expanded explanatory notes.

A Horse's Tale (1906)

Novella written in 1905 and first published in 1906. One of the last major pieces of fiction that Clemens published in his lifetime, *A Horse's Tale* ranks with *A DOG'S TALE* among his most MELODRAMATIC and SENTIMENTAL works. Its primary setting is the fictional Fort Paxton, which seems to be in the Rocky Mountains of MONTANA or WYOMING. No time period is specified, but allusions to historical persons and events suggest that it takes place in the late 1860s—after the CIVIL WAR and before the completion of the transcontinental railroad in 1869. The story uses the historical Seventh Cavalry, but not George Armstrong Custer, its only commander. One of its characters is a "young" Buffalo Bill, who is clearly based on the historical BUFFALO BILL CODY, though he scouted for the Fifth Cavalry during the late 1860s and early

Lucius Wolcott Hitchcock's rendering of Cathy Alison on Soldier Boy, along with Buffalo Bill, for the *Harper's Monthly Magazine* serial of *A Horse's Tale*.

1870s, not for the Seventh Cavalry as the story states. The narrative concludes in SPAIN, taking its bullfight descriptions from JOHN HAY's *Castillian Days*. Clemens also used the story to pillory Henry A. Butters (?–1908), an officer of the PLASMON company, who appears as the horse thief "Hank Butters" in chapter 6.

SYNOPSIS

Containing about 17,530 words, *A Horse's Tale* is divided into 15 numbered chapters, whose narrators vary. The narrative opens at the fictional Fort Paxton headquarters of the Seventh Cavalry, with Soldier Boy introducing himself as Buffalo Bill's favorite scout horse. Shortly afterward, Cathy Alison, the orphaned niece of Brigadier General Thomas Alison, arrives from France. She quickly becomes a favorite among both soldiers and local

Indians and is the special pet of Buffalo Bill, who teaches her to ride. After Soldier Boy saves Cathy from wolves, Buffalo Bill gives him to her. When General Alison retires, he takes Cathy and Soldier Boy to SPAIN, where Cathy elects to remain with her Aunt Mercedes. Shortly after they arrive, Soldier Boy is stolen. About six months later, Cathy sees a bull gore Soldier Boy in a bullfight ring. When she rushes to her horse's side, she too is fatally gored.

Information not given within the chapters—such as Buffalo Bill's last name—generally appears below within parentheses. However, for the sake of simplicity, the synopsis occasionally mentions personal names where they do not appear within chapters. For example, chapter 8 is subtitled, "The Scout-Start. BB and Lieutenant-General Alison," but does not mention Buffalo Bill or Cathy by name within its text.

Chapter 1

Introducing himself as the favorite horse of Buffalo Bill (Cody), Soldier Boy boasts about his pedigree, strength, and speed as a scout horse. Just returned from a 40-day scouting expedition up the Big Horn, he is at Fort Paxton, where the Seventh Cavalry is garrisoned. The fort awaits the arrival of the orphaned niece of its commander, Brigadier General (Thomas) Alison.

Chapter 2

Mercedes, the Spanish sister-in-law of the general's deceased brother, writes to Alison from ROUEN, France. She explains that Catherine's parents wanted their daughter to go to him because he is about to retire and because her own health is broken. Mercedes says that Cathy is exceptionally high-minded and good-hearted, has an acute sense of justice, and loves animals.

Chapter 3

General Alison writes to his mother in San Bernardino (California) about the arrival of Cathy, who has quickly conquered everyone with her winning ways. The Indians have already nicknamed her "firebug." The general describes Cathy's first meeting with Buffalo Bill and Soldier Boy.

Chapter 4

Cathy writes to her Aunt Mercedes about her wonderful life at the fort. She loves the plains, the animals, and the Indians, and tells how Buffalo Bill took her on Soldier Boy to Chief Thunder-Bird's and Chief White Cloud's camps. She is learning to ride and shoot a bow.

Chapter 5

Alison writes to Mercedes, describing Cathy's great popularity. Both the Seventh Cavalry and the Ninth Dragoons have adopted her and made her an officer. Despite her special treatment by adults, Cathy is popular with other children, whose lives she has made more exciting. Under Buffalo Bill's tutelage, she has become an extraordinary rider. To help care for her, Alison's mother has sent Mammy Dorcas, a servant who has been with the family since she was a slave. Dorcas and Cathy are already as devoted to each other as mother and daughter.

Chapter 6

Soldier Boy meets another horse, a Mexican plug (called "Mongrel" in the next chapter), who is the property of a horse thief named Hank Butters, the partner of Blake Haskins. Familiar with Soldier Boy's reputation, the plug is impressed by his claim of descent from fossils. Soldier Boy also boasts about Cathy's riding skill and mentions that she refused to ride him in a steeplechase in order to give the other children a chance to win. The only person who has ridden Soldier Boy for more than two months, Cathy has been training her own army unit, "the 16th," or "1st Battalion Rocky Mountain Rangers," which has elected her lieutenant-general and bugler. Soldier Boy also talks about the cavalry's dog Shekels.

Chapter 7

Soldier Boy tells Shekels about Mongrel, the Mexican plug, who overheard the horse thieves planning to get Buffalo Bill.

Chapter 8

Buffalo Bill compliments Cathy on her army unit, the Rangers, and she offers to have this unit serve as his guard of honor when he goes to Fort Clayton.

Chapter 9

Soldier Boy tells Shekels that after Cathy escorted Buffalo Bill to Fort Clayton, she learned that he had been shot in an ambush, then immediately rode to his rescue. After four hours in the saddle, she went to sleep, fell, and broke her arm. Soldier Boy stood by through the night, fighting off hungry wolves. The next morning Buffalo Bill arrived on a litter pulled by Mongrel and another horse that he and the scout Thorndike got when they killed Blake Haskins and his fellow tough (Butters). When Buffalo Bill saw the wolves that Soldier Boy killed, he gave the horse to Cathy in return for a kiss.

Chapter 10

While Cathy convalesces, Dorcas tells Alison that Cathy is having too much company and is too busy trying to supervise her army unit. She also tries to persuade Alison that animals talk to each other, citing Shekels as an example. When Dorcas says that Cathy wants the general to stand in for her at the court-martial of one of her child officers, Alison makes up an excuse to delay the proceeding, hoping that Cathy will get well soon enough to preside herself.

Chapter 11

Several months later, Thorndike—who now rides Mongrel—talks with Antonio, an Andalusian. Antonio reminisces about Spain and bullfighting, which he considers the grandest sport.

Chapter 12

Mongrel and another horse named Sage Brush discuss man's cruelty to dumb animals. They wonder if bullfighting is a religious service.

Chapter 13

General Alison has taken Cathy, Dorcas, and Soldier Boy to Spain. He describes their travels in a letter to his mother, reporting that Cathy has decided to stay with her Aunt Mercedes. Alison himself is not sure if he and Dorcas will ever return home. When Cathy left the post, she was given a grand military send-off, complete with the bands playing and escorts. In a postscript, Alison mentions that Soldier Boy was stolen the previous night.

Chapter 14

Soldier Boy talks to himself. Since being stolen five or six months earlier, he has traveled almost constantly and is worn down. He has changed hands perhaps a dozen times, each time going to a lower-level master. Now a bony scarecrow, he thinks that his end may be near and wants only to see *her* (Cathy) again.

Chapter 15

General Alison writes to Mrs. Drake, the wife of the Seventh Cavalry's colonel. He reports that Cathy has been on the lookout for her horse. He also describes how a bull has ripped open a horse in the ring; as the animal drags its bowels on the ground, Cathy issues a bugle call and rushes into the ring, where the horse falls at her feet—just before the bull gets her. She is carried away unconscious. Before she dies at home, she asks for "Taps" to be blown.

BACKGROUND AND PUBLISHING HISTORY

According to A. B. PAINE, actress Minnie Maddern Fiske (1865–1932) wrote to Clemens in September 1905, asking him to help her campaign against bullfighting in MEXICO. She hoped that he might write something similar to A DOG'S TALE, which had been used by antivivisectionists. That same month Clemens began writing *A Horse's Tale*. However, he set the conclusion of the story in Spain, not in Mexico as Fiske might have preferred. HARPER'S MAGAZINE published the story in two installments in August–September 1906, with five illustrations by LUCIUS WOLCOTT HITCHCOCK. In October 1907, Harper's published *A Horse's Tale* as a 153-page book, using Hitchcock's illustrations. Paine later included the story in *The Mysterious Stranger and Other Stories* (1922).

CRITICAL COMMENTARY

A Horse's Tale bears many similarities to *A Dog's Tale*. Both stories are statements against the mistreatment of animals. Both begin as attacks against specific targets—bullfighting in the former and animal vivisection in the latter—and expand into other concerns of Clemens, such as language. He wrote both in response to a request for a story. Both experiment with narration, using animals as narrators, and both involve children as devices more than as characters. Partly related to that usage, both become increasingly sentimental. Despite these similarities, *A Horse's Tale* has not been as well received, critically or popularly, as *A Dog's Tale*. Also flawed by sentimentality, *A Dog's Tale* more successfully merges sentiment and cynicism, even humor. *A Horse's Tale* becomes weighted down by the excess of its characteristics, though it does not lack virtues.

As the writer's daughter Jean persuaded her father to write a piece condemning scientific vivisection of animals, so animal rights activist and actress Minnie Maddern Fiske, perceiving the result, *A Dog's Tale*, to be a successful attack and useful propaganda, asked the author to contribute to the fight against bullfighting, about which he knew little. He agreed, but as with the tale for Jean, the story does not directly concern the requested target; the final pages blunt the attack with sentimentality and misdirection. In *A Dog's Tale,* Clemens more subtly approaches the object of attack by focusing on an experiment with fatal results, making its point without mentioning vivisection. Sentimentality results from Clemens's too close identification with the victim's mother, shortening aesthetic distance and disinterestedness, but in the short space and compactness of this story, the horror of the cruelty and its aftermath are sharply affecting. Spending time on other concerns, *A Horse's Tale* is slower but more abrupt. In chapter 5, an Indian boy torments a raven he has caught until he is trounced by Cathy Alison, a multilingual, orphaned child devoted to animals. Despite her devotion, the focus shifts from animals to her.

Cathy's trouncing of the boy establishes the theme against mistreating animals; however, the anti-bullfighting theme appears later, in chapter 11, in an ironic dialogue between Indian scout Thorndike and Spanish cowboy Antonio, who reminisces about Spain, Cathy's home to which she is to return, and more directly in a dialogue between their horses commenting on the overheard conversation. The abruptness of the deaths in the bullring, unlike the suddenness of that in the earlier tale, seems to be an afterthought, an anticlimactic means of ending the story. Describing bullfighting as "the grandest [sport] in the world" (chapter 11), Antonio says he saw his first bullfight as reward from his uncle, a priest, for giving his savings to a mission; the juxtaposition of this generosity with the horrors of the bullring permits a contrast of Christian charity with animal mutilation and death as well as a jab at missionary interference in the lives of non-Christians, a familiar target.

"All the world [is] represented" at this slaughter (chapter 11), according to Antonio, unintentionally indicting humankind. Amid the splendor of ceremony, sounds, and glittering costumes are "blindfolded, broken-down nags, lean and starved, fit only for sport and sacrifice, then the carrion-heap," many later disemboweled by the bull their riders pierce with spears. Brave bulls bring pride, joy, and delight to the crowd. Bulls that hesitate, for whatever reason, the people despise and want punished and ridiculed, laughing at those whose

legs are severed. Enthusiasm stirred, Thorndike adds the sharpest irony to the conversation: "perfectly grand . . . perfectly beautiful. Burning a nigger don't begin" (chapter 11).

More irony comes from the animals' perspective as horses. Reversing roles with word-play, Sage Brush reflects Clemens's philosophy, saying that humans "are created as they are . . . They are only brutal because that is their make; brutes would be brutes if it was *their* make." By having Sage Brush explain why man mistreats animals that do no harm with "Man is not always like that . . . he is kind enough when he is not excited by religion," Clemens suggests that similar emotions drive people's bloodlust and religious fervor.

The anti-bullfighting theme culminates in three chapters of unequal length, making up a short "Part II in Spain." The whole story is unevenly structured because the 12 chapters in Part I, which is untitled, unbalance these final three chapters, which appear even more anticlimactic and tacked-on. Despite the strong ironies of chapters 11 and 12, the writing in Part II seems hurried and forced. After gushing over the activities surrounding Cathy's departure for Spain, General Alison adds a postscript saying that her horse was stolen last night, as though the author realizes he must wind up the story (chapter 13).

Never explaining how or why he or Cathy happened to be at the bullring in the last chapter, Alison gives his impressions, and his imagination, of the events there, expecting them to become the reader's. Seeing Soldier Boy gored, Cathy runs calling him; after he falls "at her feet," she lavishes kisses upon him and is also gored (chapter 15).

Clemens performed this story for groups accompanied by music; however, his insertions of musical bars into the story—while an interesting experiment with mixed media—are distracting and disconcerting. More in the way of the tale than an expansion of its range, the music suggests the sudden appearance of a band in a desert rather than background sound or a score reiterating a theme. If its use is thematic, it links the child and the horse in happy and sad moments, and it reprises Cathy's life just before and at her death.

Whether the story's sentimentality results from Clemens's realizing he had cast his dead daughter

Susy as heroine Cathy (Hill 113) or lingering grief over the more recent death of wife Livy, he loses control early in this story. Begun with Soldier Boy—Buffalo Bill's horse, later a gift to Cathy—as narrator, the story soon offers too many narrators. *A Horse's Tale* ceases to be the horse's story, as Aunt Mercedes, General Alison, and Cathy narrate and the story increasingly moves away from Soldier Boy and becomes Cathy's.

The reason this tale fails to replicate the limited success of *A Dog's Tale* is not limited knowledge but lack of limitations. Occasionally exciting and adventurous, *A Horse's Tale* is most effective when Clemens exercises control over its best attributes—humor and sharp irony.

Critical Commentary by John H. Davis

CHARACTERS AND RELATED ENTRIES

Alison, Catherine (Cathy)   Central character in *A Horse's Tale* and narrator of chapter 4. Born in SPAIN of an American father, George Alison, and a Spanish mother, Cathy lives in FRANCE (possibly in ROUEN) until she is nine, when both her parents die. Her aunt Mercedes then sends her to western America to live with her bachelor uncle, General Thomas Alison, who is about to retire from the army. There Cathy conquers everyone with her vivacity, kindness and sense of justice. The soldiers adopt her and make her an officer, and she becomes close to Buffalo Bill (WILLIAM CODY) and his horse Soldier Boy. Despite being everyone's pet, she remains unspoiled and popular among other children.

Cathy has learned English and Spanish from her parents; she also speaks French and some German and Italian. In the West, she begins learning Indian languages but is not good at formal studies and makes errors resembling those cited in "ENGLISH AS SHE IS TAUGHT" (chapter 5). She also loves using big words that she does not understand. Descended from a Virginia family on her father's side, Cathy identifies with her mother and thinks of herself as Spanish. After her uncle retires, he takes her to her aunt's home in Spain, where she chooses to remain. About six months later, she sees her beloved horse Soldier Boy gored in a bullfight ring. When she rushes to his side, she is gored to death herself.

While Cathy has the athleticism and daring of a rugged boy, she also exhibits such strongly feminine traits that the family servant, Mammy Dorcas, theorizes that she is "twins," in which the boy twin is submerged. Cathy's combination of gentle and martial qualities closely resembles Clemens's depiction of Joan of Arc, whom—like Cathy—he modeled physically and temperamentally on his daughter Susy Clemens, adding his daughter Jean's love of animals. When Clemens submitted his manuscript to HARPER'S MAGAZINE, he included a photograph of Susy on which he wanted the illustrator to model Cathy.

Soldier Boy   Title character of *A Horse's Tale* (1907). An example of a stolidly unimaginative animal that is morally superior to most human beings, Soldier Boy is the sole narrator of chapters 1 and 14 and a primary conversationalist in chapters 6, 7, and 9. When the narrative opens, he is BUFFALO BILL CODY's veteran scout horse. A fast and noble steed whose mother was a Kentucky Thoroughbred and father a bronco, he considers himself well educated, but is given to using words that he does not understand, such as "acrimonious" and "antiphonal." In chapter 6, he mentions that the only person who has ridden him for several months is young Cathy Alison, to whom he is devoted. When he later saves Cathy from wolves, Buffalo Bill gives him to her (chapter 9).

When Cathy returns to Spain, she persuades her uncle to take Soldier Boy along (chapter 13). Shortly after they arrive, Soldier Boy is stolen, then spends the next five or six months being passed around among disreputable owners until he is a bony scarecrow. By the final chapter, he is reduced to working in a bullfight ring, where he is horribly gored. Cathy—who has been searching for him—reaches his side just before he dies. Then she, too, is fatally gored.

BIBLIOGRAPHY

Hill, Hamlin. *Mark Twain: God's Fool.* New York: Harper & Row, 1973.

Twain, Mark. *A Horse's Tale.* New York: Harper and Brothers, 1907.

"How I Edited an Agricultural Paper Once"

SKETCH written for the GALAXY (July 1870) and later republished in SKETCHES, NEW AND OLD (1875), and in MARK TWAIN'S LIBRARY OF HUMOR (1888). Similar in tone to "JOURNALISM IN TENNESSEE," this 2,225-word sketch PARODIES the notion that newspaper editors must know anything. It recalls two moments in Clemens's life when he temporarily took over a newspaper. As a youth in Hannibal, he ran his brother Orion's paper and boosted circulation with facetious attacks on a rival. After his unhappy brother returned, he left town permanently. A decade later, he left NEVADA under similar circumstances—according to *Rough-*

ing It (1872; chapter 55). The sketch also anticipates Clemens's later playful writings on agriculture. Chapter 70 of *Roughing It*, for example, is built around a joke about turnips growing on vines. In *Connecticut Yankee* (1889), Hank Morgan creates a "Department of Public Morals and Agriculture" in Camelot (chapter 9); when King Arthur later pretends to be a farmer he makes remarks about agriculture as outrageous as those of this sketch's narrator (chapter 34).

SYNOPSIS

The narrator, an editor of 14 years' experience, temporarily takes over an agricultural paper during its regular editor's vacation. After he publishes his first issue, an agitated old gentleman reads his editorial about shaking turnips from trees and angrily protests that turnips do not grow on trees. When the editor amends his statement to say that turnips grow on vines, the man shreds the paper and stomps out. The next caller tells the editor to read aloud his remarks about the "guano bird" and other nonsense, then leaves satisfied that he is not the one who is crazy.

The regular editor returns outraged that his paper's reputation has been injured. Acknowledging that the narrator's issue has had a record sale, he says he prefers not to be famous for lunacy and cites some of the paper's most bizarre statements—about a molting season for cows and other matters. When he complains that the narrator never told him he knew nothing about agriculture, the narrator protests that this is the first time he has ever heard of a man's having to know anything to edit a newspaper. To prove his point, he asks who writes drama critiques, book reviews, and editorials on finance and Indian campaigns? The answer is people who know nothing about these subjects. He then resigns.

The agricultural paper's temporary editor fancies that one of his readers is displeased in F. Opper's illustration for Harper's edition of *Sketches, New and Old.*

"How to Make History Dates Stick"

Posthumously published ESSAY written in SWEDEN in 1899. Aimed at helping to teach children historical dates, this 5,425-word essay explains two systems based on visual clues. The first is one that Clemens used in 1883 to teach his own children the dates of ENGLAND's monarchs. While his family was at QUARRY FARM, he staked out 817 feet along a carriage-road to represent the 817 years that had elapsed since William the Conqueror (1066), adding signposts to mark each reign. As his children mastered these dates, they added more signs to represent other historical events.

His second system uses a technique that he developed in his LECTURING days, when he drew pictures to help remember his lecture topics. This system requires only a pen and small squares of colored paper. Though he thinks it essential that each person draw his own pictures, he suggests specific images to get readers started and provides his own crude drawings as samples. For example, he recommends drawing pictures of a whale and the appropriate dates on 21 slips of white paper to represent each year of William the Conqueror's reign. Like "William," "whale" starts with a "W" and the huge animal symbolizes the magnitude of William's reign. For succeeding monarchs, he suggests such images as a hen for Henry, a lion for Richard, an editor for Edward and a burning martyr for Bloody Mary. From there, readers are trusted to continue on their own.

The essay first appeared in HARPER'S MAGAZINE in December 1914. A. B. PAINE later included it in *What Is Man? and Other Essays of Mark Twain* (1917).

"How to Tell a Story"

ESSAY written and published in 1895. This often-reprinted 2,070-word essay sums up Clemens's views on the proper recitation of "humorous" stories, which he defines as an American invention differing from French and English "witty" or "comic" stories in that they depend for effect on the *manner* of their telling, not their *matter*. Unlike the telling of a comic story, telling a humorous story properly is a difficult art. It requires stringing together incongruities and absurdities of which the teller is seemingly unaware. Its other ingredients include "slurring" its main point, dropping in studied or incongruous remarks,

and pausing at the right moment—all techniques that ARTEMUS WARD had mastered.

"The Wounded Soldier" is an example of a witty story that relies on its "nub": A soldier carrying a wounded comrade does not realize that his friend's head has been shot off until someone tells him. When he sees the decapitated body, he exclaims, "But he told me it was his *leg!*" As an example of a humorous story, Mark Twain retells the "GOLDEN ARM" story in full, while explaining the crucial importance of the pause.

This essay does not mention the JUMPING FROG STORY, although it is precisely the kind of humorous story that Clemens has in mind. Clemens wrote this essay shortly after publishing *Joan of Arc* (1896), which contains another yarn that fits his humorous story definition perfectly—even though it is told by a Frenchman, Joan's uncle Laxart, who "drone[s] out the most tedious and empty tale one ever heard," without suspecting that it is "anything but dignified and valuable history." Like Simon Wheeler's frog story, Laxart's tale concerns remarkable animals—a bull that he rides to a funeral and a swarm of bees that sting him so badly that his face looks like a raisin pudding. Joan nearly dies laughing at the ridiculous story, but her uncle has no idea *what* she is laughing at (book 2, chapter 36).

After appearing in the October 3, 1895, issue of *Youth's Companion*, this essay was collected in two different anthologies titled *How to Tell a Story and Other Essays*, one of which was later reissued as *LITERARY ESSAYS*. A facsimile reprint of HARPER AND BROTHERS' 1898 edition of the book was part of the 1996 OXFORD MARK TWAIN edition. This edition contains a new introduction by novelist David Bradley and an afterword by Pascal Covici Jr.

"Huck Finn and Tom Sawyer Among the Indians"

Unfinished novel. A direct sequel to *Huckleberry Finn* (1884), this roughly 18,000-word fragment begins a story that Clemens started writing in July 1884. While hoping to cash in on the popularity of western stories, Clemens evidently intended to attack romantic notions about INDIANS and life in the West. Once he started, however, the story took him in a direction that he could not easily go, and he abruptly abandoned it.

As the narrator, Huck Finn picks up exactly where he left off in *Huckleberry Finn*—which ends with him afraid that Aunt Sally Phelps will try to adopt and civilize him. His suggestion that he may have "to light out for the Territory" appears to anticipate the new story, which takes him, Tom, and Jim deep into the Central Plains region that later became NEBRASKA.

SYNOPSIS

Chapter 1
Tom and Huck are growing bored at the Phelpses' ARKANSAS farm when Aunt Polly calls them back to Missouri. Immediately after they get home, Polly takes Tom, his brother Sid and his cousin Mary to the western side of the state to visit relatives on a hemp farm. Huck goes along to keep Tom company and Jim joins them, fearing that he might be put back into SLAVERY by crooked white men if he remains behind. At the hemp farm, Tom again grows bored and proposes to go west to travel among INDI-ANS. Huck and Jim are content where they are, but by extolling Indian virtues, Tom wins Jim over, and Huck agrees to go along to avoid being left alone.

Chapter 2
The adventurers quietly make their preparations, buying provisions, barter goods, and mules that they stash in an abandoned house. When a full moon arrives, they slip away with their pack train. After leaving Aunt Polly a note telling her that they will be gone, but not where they are going, they head west into the Plains, traveling by night for four days to avoid detection. About six days out, they encounter a family emigrating from southern Missouri to OREGON who invite them to join their party. The Mills family has three grown sons and two daughters—seven-year-old Flaxy and beautiful 17-year-old Peggy, on whom everyone dotes. Tom and Huck learn how to ride, rope, and shoot from the brothers during a week of traveling. At the PLATTE RIVER they find a small Indian camp.

Chapter 3
The emigrants camp by the river, letting their horses rest while awaiting Peggy's sweetheart, Brace John-son, an experienced frontiersman. Everyone becomes friendly with the five Indian men (later identified as Oglala Sioux), who satisfy all of Tom's romantic ideas about Indians. They are manly, friendly, gal-lant, and entertaining. Peggy baffles Huck by show-ing him a knife that Brace gave her for killing herself if she is ever captured by Indians.

After several days, Tom and Huck ask the Indi-ans if they can visit their community and are thrilled to learn that they plan a buffalo hunt for the next day. When the Indians notice Peggy staring off into the distance, they ask what she is looking for and seem perturbed when Huck says that *seven* friends are expected. That evening the Indians come to eat with the emigrants in war dress; Tom suspects that something is amiss when the Indians do not smoke. As he goes to warn the Millses, the Indians suddenly kill everyone but the girls and Jim, whom they take prisoner, and Huck and Tom, who escape into the woods. The next morning, the boys are left alone. With all the food and pack animals gone, they are in a desperate situation.

Chapter 4
Accepting responsibility for getting Jim into his predicament, Tom pledges not to turn back until he rescues him, and Huck insists on helping. For sev-eral days, the boys forage for food while awaiting Brace Johnson. When Brace finally arrives, hearing that Indians have captured Peggy makes him fran-tic, but Huck calms him down by assuring him that Peggy has her knife, though he is not really sure about this. Huck asks Brace *why* he wishes Peggy were dead and is satisfied by the answer—which we do not hear. When he later finds Peggy's knife, he hides it from Brace.

Chapter 5
After burying the massacre victims, Brace and the boys discuss the disaster. Details about the Indians' behavior convince Brace—who grew up among Indians—that the massacre was probably a private vendetta avenging the murder of someone by a white person. After he locates the Indians' trail, he and the boys strike off in pursuit of the killers.

Several days later, they find an abandoned camp; Brace sends Huck and Tom ahead without him, asking them to find and bury Peggy's body. After Huck tells Tom why Peggy's death is so important to Brace, Tom agrees to join Huck in pretending to find and bury her. They let four hours pass, then return and tell Brace that they have followed his instructions.

Chapter 6

Four more days on the trail bring Brace, Huck, and Tom closer to the Indians and teach the boys more about Brace's background and his respect for Indian religion. When Brace realizes that he has accidentally eaten antelope meat on a Friday, violating an Indian superstition, he becomes angry with himself for the bad luck that this carelessness will bring. The next morning, Tom gets lost in a heavy fog.

Chapter 7

Brace searches for Tom while Huck tends a fire that serves as a beacon. After a while, Brace returns with a dehydrated white man whom he has found wandering in a delirium. He leaves the stranger with Huck, telling him not to let the man eat or drink more than an occasional spoonful of soup, and goes back to look for Tom. During the night, Huck leaves the tent to tend the mules and ends up spending hours looking for a missing animal as a storm kicks up. He returns to find that his fire is out and it is raining too hard to restart it. When he enters the tent, a sudden flash of lightning illuminates the grinning face of the stranger, who has gorged himself to death on food. At dawn, Brace returns with Tom. After they bury the stranger, they rest for a day or two to allow the exhausted Tom to recuperate.

Chapter 8

Brace and the boys continue their quest, which takes them up the North Fork of the Platte River, approaching WYOMING, where they find signs of a large party of horsemen. While Huck is alone tending mules, two white men chasing an antelope stop when they see him. Sensing that the men are thieves after his mules, Huck leads them directly to Brace. The men shoot at Huck, then Brace overtakes and kills both of them. Farther up the river, Brace, Huck, and Tom stumble upon the rustlers'

camp. When they go back down the river, a flash flood roars down the valley. Avoiding its path, they watch the rustlers' camp wash past and scramble up a hill to save themselves.

Chapter 9

Floodwaters turn the hill into an island, where Brace and the boys spend eight days waiting for the water to recede. When they return to the trail, they come upon the remains of a large, recently occupied Indian camp, in which Huck and Tom find traces of the Indians who killed the Millses. Brace finds a white woman's shoeprint but does not suspect it could be Peggy's. By now thoroughly disenchanted with Indians, Tom finally admits that "book Injuns and real Injuns is different." In order to convince Indians that he is crazy, Brace sews small dried animals all over his clothes. As he and the boys pick up the Indians' trail again, the manuscript ends.

BACKGROUND AND PUBLISHING HISTORY

Clemens began writing this story while correcting proofs for *Huckleberry Finn* in July 1884. His abrupt abandonment of the story—in which he invested considerable research—remains puzzling. Walter BLAIR, who edited the MARK TWAIN PAPERS edition of the story, suggests that Clemens set an impossible task for himself. Trying to write a realistic story about Indians abducting a white woman was leading him toward a frank treatment of rape—a subject about which he was incapable of writing. On the other hand, Clemens had a history of setting aside manuscripts for years before finishing them. In 1889 or 1890, he had the entire manuscript of this story typeset on the PAIGE COMPOSITOR and printed—a possible indication that he still intended to complete it. Several modern writers have attempted to complete the story, but none of them has had access to Clemens's full working notes.

For unknown reasons, the pages of Clemens's original manuscript were dispersed among six locations, with most of the surviving pages held by the Detroit Public Library. The story was first published in the December 20, 1968, issue of *Life* magazine, with illustrations by James McMullan. The following year Universal Studios bought its film rights. Meanwhile, the story appeared in its first book edition, HANNIBAL, HUCK & TOM (1969), edited by Walter Blair. The story is also in the popular edition, *Huck Finn and Tom Sawyer Among the Indians and Other Unfinished Stories* (1989), edited by Blair and Dahlia Armon.

CHARACTERS AND RELATED ENTRIES

For information on Tom Sawyer, see the Characters and Related Entries secton of the *Tom Sawyer* entry. For information on Huckleberry Finn and Jim, see the Characters and Related Entries section of the *Huckleberry Finn* entry.

Johnson, Brace   Character in "Huck Finn and Tom Sawyer Among the Indians." A 26-year-old archetypal frontier he-man, Johnson draws on skills that he learned from growing up among INDIANS to lead Huck and Tom after Oglala Sioux who have massacred his fiancée's family, the Millses. Clemens's physical description of Johnson closely matches a description that BUFFALO BILL CODY wrote of Wild Bill Hickok.

Mills family   Characters in "Huck Finn and Tom Sawyer Among the Indians." A family migrating from southern Missouri to OREGON, the Millses invite Tom, Huck, and Jim to accompany them across the Central Plains. The family consists of a 55-year-old man; his wife; adult sons Buck, Bill, and Sam; and daughters 17-year-old Peggy and seven-year-old Flaxy. After INDIANS kill everyone in the family except Peggy and Flaxy, whom they carry off, Tom and Huck join Peggy's fiancé, BRACE JOHNSON, in pursuit. When the rescuers reach an abandoned Indian camp, they find indications that Peggy is still alive just as the story ends abruptly.

Huck Finn and Tom Sawyer Among the Indians and Other Unfinished Stories.

See HANNIBAL, HUCK & TOM, MARK TWAIN'S.

Huckleberry Finn, Adventures of (1884)

Generally regarded as Clemens's greatest work, his third novel commands as much attention from students and scholars as all his other works combined. It is certified as an American "classic" and is often called a "masterpiece"—even *the* great American novel. Despite its elevation to such eminence, however, Clemens himself did not regard it as exceptional. Even as late as 1908, he ranked it below *Joan of Arc* (1896) and *The Prince and the Pauper* (1881) among his favorite books. In creating *Huckleberry Finn,* he was as unaware of its significance as his youthful narrator Huck was of his own virtue.

Huckleberry Finn's importance lies in both its content and its construction. Essentially the coming-of-age story of a young white boy helping a

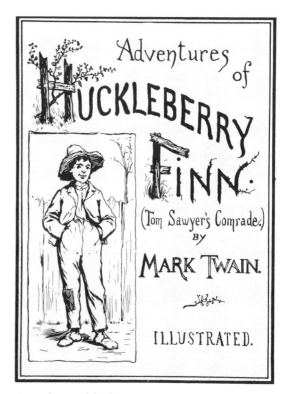

Cover design of the first American edition of *Huckleberry Finn,* which came out in January 1885—a month after the first British edition appeared

slave to escape servitude in the pre–CIVIL WAR South, the novel, is simultaneously a children's story, a humorous adult novel and a profound sociological document. In this latter regard, it explores such universal themes as freedom and bondage, race relations, conscience, greed, and vice. Clemens invested considerable humor in the book, but one of its overriding themes is human cruelty and callousness. Huck begins his journey by escaping from a brutal captivity imposed by his father, then travels down the river and witnesses brawls, murders, lynch mobs, a pointless bloody feud, and greedy chicanery. With such horrors as a backdrop, Huck is consumed with guilt over his promise to help Jim escape—a promise that has led him to steal the property of Jim's owner, Miss Watson, thereby flouting the legal and social conventions of his society. Sure that he will go to hell for this sin, he writes a letter to Miss Watson revealing where Jim is, but suddenly decides he would rather go to hell than betray his friend. Few novels have more poignant moments.

As is the case with most of Clemens's books, the structure of *Huckleberry Finn* is flawed. Its problems reflect Clemens's uncertainties about what kind of book he was writing. He begins it in the same light spirit as *Tom Sawyer* (1876), whose sequel he initially intended it to be. Then he shifts to a more sober tone as he sends Huck and Jim down the Mississippi River. Finally, he returns to the light mood of the beginning with a long—and now much reviled—concluding sequence. The novel's greatest strengths lie in its central chapters, set on the river. Despite its structural inconsistencies, the book achieves greatness through Clemens's decision to tell its story through the voice of a simple, uneducated boy. It is the first major American novel written entirely in an authentic vernacular. School officials and librarians regarded the book's language as unnecessarily coarse and banned it for this reason, as well as for its presumably objectionable morals; however, the book's language has come to be appreciated as the core of its realism, and as a feature that makes the book a valuable document of its time.

It should be noted that the full title appearing on the title page and cover of the first edition of this book is *Adventures of Huckleberry Finn (Tom Sawyer's Comrade)*. E. W. KEMBLE's illustration for the half-title page that opens the first chapter reads "The Adventures of Huckleberry Finn"; however, *"The"* is not properly part of the book's title, though it has been used more often than not in reprint editions.

SYNOPSIS

The novel has about 112,000 words in 43 chapters of uneven length. The narrative begins in Huck's hometown of St. Petersburg and ends in Pikesville, 1,100 miles down the Mississippi River, nearly a year later. The narrative divides into three distinct sections.

Its first 11 chapters are set in or near St. Petersburg. The earliest chapters continue the action of *The Adventures of Tom Sawyer* and are very much in the same vein. The narrative makes a sharp change when Huck's father, Pap Finn, appears. Pap takes Huck upriver and keeps him in a cabin in ILLINOIS. In chapter 7, Huck fakes his own death and goes to Jackson's Island. There he finds the slave Jim, who has run away to avoid being sold down the river. They remain on the island through chapter 11.

The second part of the narrative constitutes almost precisely half the entire text. In chapters 12 through 30, Huck and Jim go down the Mississippi River on a raft, interrupting their journey several times with episodes on shore. Nevertheless, this section of the novel contains virtually the entire story of the journey. In chapter 19, two con men—the King and the Duke—board the raft and take control of the voyage.

The final part comprises chapters 31 through 43. All the action takes place in and around Pikesville, where Huck finally rids himself of the King and the Duke. Meanwhile, Jim is captured and held prisoner at the nearby farm of Silas and Sally Phelps. Huck goes to the Phelpses to help Jim escape and is mistaken for their nephew Tom Sawyer. When Tom himself arrives, he pretends to be his own brother, Sid, and offers to help free Jim. Most of the action in these chapters concerns Tom's elaborate "evasion" plans for Jim's escape. Huck, Jim, and Tom are still in Pikesville at the conclusion.

Chapter 1

Huck Finn introduces himself as narrator and summarizes the most important events concluding *The Adventures of Tom Sawyer,* in which he and Tom find and split a pirate treasure worth $12,000. Judge Thatcher now manages their money, which earns each boy a dollar a day in interest. The Widow Douglas has taken Huck for her son, and she and her spinster sister, Miss Watson, are trying to "sivilize" him. Huck chafes under the confinements of his new life. Such things as clean CLOTHES, shoes, his own room, regular meals, prayers, and so on hold few attractions for him. He tries fleeing, but Tom persuades him to return so that he can be respectable enough to join Tom's new robbers' gang.

When Huck returns, the widow cries over him, but life soon returns to its previous pattern. After supper, the widow tells Huck about MOSES and the "Bulrushers," but his interest soon fades. Miss Watson wears him down with talk about the "good place" that only makes him hope that he will not go there if she does.

After Huck goes to his room, Tom Sawyer calls for him at midnight.

Chapter 2

As Tom and Huck sneak out through the widow's backyard, Huck trips, and Miss Watson's slave Jim comes out to investigate. Unable to see anyone, Jim sits under a tree and falls asleep. Not able to resist playing a joke, Tom puts Jim's hat on a limb over his head. Later, Jim makes a reputation among other slaves with stories about the night he was bewitched.

Joe Harper, Ben Rogers, and two or three other boys join Huck and Tom and they all boat down the river. After the others swear an oath of secrecy, Tom leads them to a hidden entrance to the CAVE that he found in *Tom Sawyer.* Inside, they agree to form a robber's band to be called "Tom Sawyer's gang." They draw up an oath that each boy signs in blood. One boy suggests that the family of any member who tells gang secrets should be killed. The others like the rule; however, it seems to exclude Huck, who has no real family to kill. His offer of Miss Watson is satisfactory, so he is allowed to join. At the end of the meeting, the boys tease

young Tommy Barnes for having fallen asleep. Tommy churlishly threatens to reveal the gang's secrets, but Tom buys his silence for five cents. Huck returns home shortly before dawn.

Chapter 3

The next morning, Miss Watson scolds Huck for soiling his clothes. The widow, however, merely looks sorry, making Huck feel guilty. Miss Watson prays with Huck in a closet and encourages him to pray daily, telling him that he will get whatever he prays for. When he gets a fishline, but no hooks, he is confused as to the efficacy of prayer. Occasionally, the widow talks to Huck about Providence and gets his hopes up, but Miss Watson typically dashes them the next day.

Huck has not seen his father, Pap Finn, for over a year. A man found drowned in the river above town is reported to be his father, but Huck senses that the drowned person is someone else.

After about a month in Tom's gang, Huck and the others quit. Huck is bored because they have not really robbed or killed anyone, but merely pretended; he cannot share Tom's belief that enchantments are at work. On one occasion, the gang gathered at Cave Hollow to attack Spanish merchants and rich Arabs, who turned out to be a Sunday-school picnic. The gang scattered the picnickers and collected loot that included a hymnal and a religious tract, but the Sunday-school teacher routed them. Afterward, Tom explained that the caravan was enchanted, as in (MIGUEL DE CERVANTES's) *Don Quixote.* Though skeptical, Huck tries Tom's suggestion of rubbing an old lamp to call up a genie but eventually concludes that magic lamps and genies are just another of Tom's lies.

Chapter 4

Three or four months carry the narrative into winter. Huck attends school regularly, though he occasionally plays hookey and gets whipped. At first he hates school, but comes to tolerate it. He even finds things to like about the new ways of living with the Widow Douglas.

One day Huck spots ominously familiar bootprints in the snow near the widow's house. He flies off to Judge Thatcher and tries to persuade him to take his entire fortune of $6,000, plus interest. The judge senses that something is wrong, but Huck will not explain. He calms Huck by offering to buy his fortune for a "consideration" of one dollar. Huck next visits Jim, who uses an ox's hairball to tell his fortune. Jim's reading contains cryptic references to Huck's father and warns him to keep away from water.

Huck feels troubled that night as he goes up to bed. He enters his room and finds his father sitting on a chair.

Chapter 5

Seeing his father scares Huck momentarily. A history of beatings has made Huck afraid of him, but once he sees how bedraggled his father is, his fears melt away. Pap immediately turns on Huck, berating him for wearing starchy clothes and being educated. He makes Huck read aloud, then smacks the book away and demands that Huck quit school. In town for two days, Pap has come from downriver, where he heard about Huck's money; he knows that Judge Thatcher controls the money and wants Huck to get it for him. Claiming that he does not really have any money, Huck challenges Pap to ask Thatcher for himself. The next day Pap calls on Thatcher while he is drunk and tries bullyragging him.

Judge Thatcher and the Widow Douglas go to court to have one of them appointed Huck's legal guardian, but a new judge rules in Pap's favor. Pap celebrates by getting drunk and lands in jail for a week. The new judge tries to reform Pap by taking him into his own home, where he and his wife clean him up and give him new clothes and a nice room. Pap repays them by sneaking out at night, swapping his new coat for booze, then returning to get drunk. He wrecks the room, crawls out the window, breaks his arm in two places, and nearly freezes in the snow.

Chapter 6

After recovering, Pap goes to court seeking control of Huck's money. He continues to torment Huck for staying in school, occasionally beating him. Huck now wants to stay in school to spite his father. Huck gets small amounts of money from the judge to give to Pap, who repeatedly gets drunk and lands in jail.

Pap finally spirits Huck away to a spot three miles upriver, on the Illinois side. He puts Huck in a secluded old log cabin in the woods, where they live off fish and game. When the widow sends a man to get Huck, Pap chases him off with his gun. Pap keeps a close eye on Huck, locking him in the cabin when he goes out. Apart from Pap's occasional thrashings, Huck mostly enjoys this life. He can cuss, smoke, and fish, and he does not have to go to school. After two months, his clothes are rags, and he cannot imagine returning to the widow.

Huck's pleasure wanes as Pap grows more abusive. As his father spends longer periods away, Huck begins planning his escape. He finds an old saw blade and starts cutting through a log at the rear of the cabin, hiding his work with a blanket when he hears Pap coming.

One day Pap returns to the cabin in an especially foul mood. His lawsuit against the judge is going poorly and there is talk of another trial to get Huck away from him and make the widow his guardian. This news alarms Huck. He does not want to return to the widow's any more than he wants to stay with Pap. He plans to tramp overland to get away. That night Pap gets drunker than usual and rages about how the government keeps him from having his rights and even allows black men to vote. He drinks until he has delirium tremens, rages incoherently through the night, and chases Huck with a knife, calling him the "Angel of Death." To protect himself, Huck sits in a corner with the gun.

Chapter 7

The next morning, Pap awakens Huck, demanding to know why he has the gun. Huck explains that someone tried to break into the cabin during the night. Satisfied by the explanation, Pap sends Huck out to check fishlines. It is now June, and the river is rising rapidly. A big canoe drifts by, and Huck seizes it. This unexpected booty gives him a new idea. He hides the canoe and now plans to go 50 miles downriver and find a permanent place to camp. He begins figuring out how to keep both Pap and the Widow Douglas from coming after him.

Later that day, Huck and Pap capture a big piece of drifting raft that Pap later tows across the river to sell. Huck launches his escape plans by cutting the rest of the way through the log wall and getting out of the cabin. He packs all the cabin's supplies into the canoe and then covers his tracks and the hole he cut in the wall. To make people think that he has been killed, he smashes the cabin door with an ax and spreads a wild pig's blood around inside. To make it appear that his body has been dumped in the river, he drags a sack full of rocks from the cabin to the shore. He then leaves a trail of cornmeal from the cabin to a nearby pond so it will appear that his killers escaped inland. He even pulls out some of his own hair and sticks it to the ax with pig blood. Finally, he goes a short distance down the river in the canoe and waits for the moon to rise. He falls asleep in the canoe, but awakens when he hears Pap rowing toward him. After Pap passes him, Huck heads downriver. Eventually, he reaches the Illinois side of uninhabited Jackson's Island, where he goes ashore and sleeps in the woods.

Chapter 8

The next morning Huck awakens to booming noises and sees a crowded ferryboat cruising by the island. The boat is firing a cannon across the water, evidently to bring Huck's drowned body to the surface. Huck clearly sees the people aboard, who include Pap, Judge Thatcher, Becky Thatcher, Joe Harper, Tom Sawyer, Aunt Polly, Sid Sawyer, and Mary (Sawyer). The boat rounds the island, leaving Huck confident that no one else will come looking for him.

After three days on the island, Huck stumbles upon fresh campfire ashes. Frightened, he climbs a tree to spy around and nervously stays aloft for hours. He crosses to Illinois to be safe, but the sounds of horses and human voices scare him back to the island. Now determined to learn who built the fire, he scouts around until he finds Miss Watson's slave Jim. Huck is immensely relieved, but Jim is terrified because he thinks Huck must be a ghost. After Huck persuades him otherwise, Huck learns that Jim has been on the island as long as he has. Huck explains how he escaped from his father. Before Jim admits that he has run off, he gets Huck to promise not to tell on him. Jim then explains that he overheard Miss Watson talking about sell-

ing him to someone in NEW ORLEANS for $800. That possibility was enough to make him leave immediately. He sneaked aboard a big commercial raft with the intention of going down the river some distance, but slipped off to avoid detection and swam to the island. In a long conversation, Jim impresses Huck with his vast knowledge of folk superstitions.

Chapter 9

Huck shows Jim a rugged ridge in the center of the island in which they find a spacious cave. At Jim's insistence, they move all their gear into the cave. Huck thinks that the cave's location is inconvenient, but Jim argues that it would provide both a good hiding place and protection against the rain he thinks is coming. Soon after they settle in, a heavy storm begins.

Over the next 10 or 12 days, the river rises rapidly, inundating much of the island. The floodwater brings with it more debris, which Huck and Jim venture out at night to explore. One night they catch a section of well-constructed lumber raft. Another night, they find a two-story frame house (the "House of Death") floating down the river that they investigate at daybreak. In an upstairs room they discover the naked body of a man shot in the back, but Jim will not let Huck look at the man's face. After they load their canoe with clothes, utensils, and other supplies they find in this floating house they return to the island.

Chapter 10

Huck asks about the dead man, but Jim refuses to discuss him because it would be bad luck (Jim finally identifies the dead man in the last chapter). When they rummage through clothes taken from the house, they find eight dollars sewn inside a coat. Huck reminds Jim of his recent prediction that they would encounter bad luck because Huck had handled a snakeskin two days earlier. Jim insists that the bad luck is still coming.

Three days later Huck kills a rattlesnake in the cave and puts its body on Jim's bedding. That night another rattler bites Jim as he goes to bed. Huck kills the snake and follows Jim's instructions for disposing of it but is careful not to tell him he was responsible for the first snake. The snakebite keeps

Jim laid up for four days. Huck ponders on the dangers of defying superstition and recalls the disastrous example of Hank Bunker.

As days pass, the river falls. Jim and Huck catch a catfish more than six feet long. Feeling restless, Huck proposes slipping into town to learn the news. Jim approves and suggests that Huck use a dress they found in the house to disguise himself as a girl to avoid recognition. Huck paddles the canoe up the Illinois shore, crosses the river near the ferry landing, and drifts down the opposite side before going ashore. He sees a light in a shanty that had long been unoccupied before he left town. Through its window he sees a woman he does not know.

Chapter 11

When the woman invites Huck in, he introduces himself as Sarah Williams from Hookerville. The woman chats idly and drifts to the subject of Huck's "murder." She tells Huck that many people think the murderer is Pap Finn, while others think it is the runaway slave Jim. There are rewards out for both. Pap left town with some toughs shortly after Huck was presumed killed and many people think that he killed his son so he could get at Huck's money without a lawsuit.

The woman also tells Huck that she has seen smoke rise from Jackson's Island and that her husband is going there that very night to hunt for Jim. Huck nervously picks up a NEEDLE and tries to thread it. The woman asks him his name again. This time he says "Mary Williams." She notices the contradiction and tries several tricks that prove Huck is a boy. Huck invents a new story about having been apprenticed to a mean farmer when his parents died. He says that his name is really George Peters and that he has run away to find his uncle Abner Moore in Goshen. As the woman prepares food for Huck and sends him off, she identifies herself as Mrs. Judith Loftus.

Huck rushes back to the island, stops at its north end to build a fire as a diversion, then continues to the camp. He awakens Jim and tells him. "They're after us!" Without a word, Jim helps pack everything onto the raft, and he and Huck leave the island.

Chapter 12

After a long night drifting downriver, Huck and Jim establish a routine of hiding by day and rafting by night. They tie up among cottonwood trees on an Illinois sandbar and camouflage the raft. The next evening, Jim pulls up some of the raft's planks and builds a wigwam shelter elevated above the main deck.

The second night they run between seven and eight hours in a current that Huck estimates at over four miles an hour. They talk and fish and occasionally swim to keep themselves awake. On the fifth uneventful night, they pass SAINT LOUIS. Occasionally, Huck slips ashore to buy or borrow food. After discussing the morality of "borrowing," Huck and Jim decide that it would be better if they were to quit borrowing, so they resolve to quit taking crabapples and persimmons.

Five nights south of St. Louis, a lightning storm comes up. The raft drifts into a wrecked steamboat precariously perched on rocks. Huck wants to board it to explore, but Jim wants to leave well enough alone and ignore it. Huck prevails. They fasten the raft to the steamboat's starboard derrick and go aboard. Huck cautiously works his way toward the captain's cabin on the texas deck.

Huck hears voices in a cabin and sees two men—Jake Packard and Bill—who have tied up a third, Jim Turner. The first two men are arguing about killing Turner. They finally agree to go ashore and wait for the steamboat to break up, so that Turner will be drowned. Huck rushes back to Jim and proposes they cut the murderers' skiff loose so the sheriff can catch them. Jim tells Huck that their raft has broken loose. Now *they* are marooned on the doomed steamboat.

Chapter 13

As Huck recovers from his initial shock, he realizes that he and Jim must now find the murderers' skiff in order to save themselves. Just as they locate it, the murderers appear and board it themselves. Before these men shove off, however, they remember that they have failed to take Turner's share of loot from him. They go back to get it, allowing Huck and Jim to escape on their skiff.

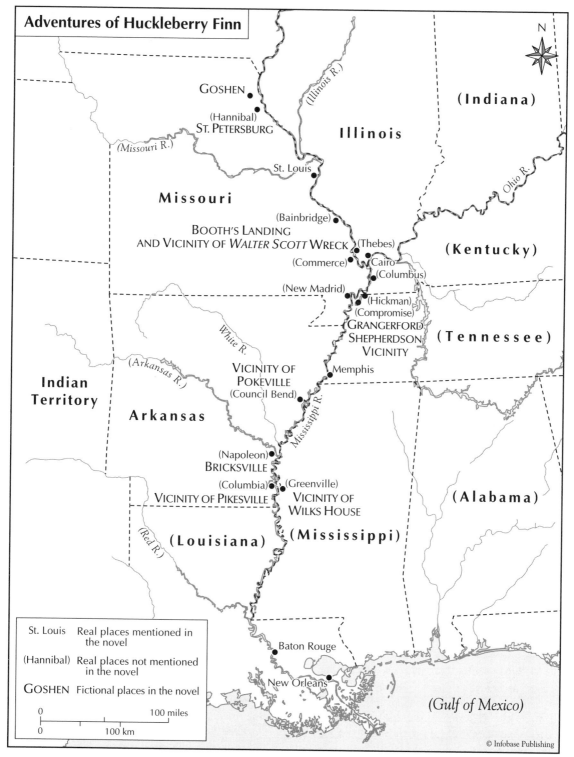

Real and imaginary places in *Huckleberry Finn*

As Huck and Jim search for their raft, Huck worries about the men aboard the doomed steamboat. He dislikes the idea of leaving even murderers in such a fix—especially since he might one day be a murderer himself. He tells Jim to land near the next light they see, so he can go ashore and find someone to rescue the murderers.

The storm worsens, but Huck and Jim find their raft. They also see a light. Huck rows the skiff ashore, as Jim takes the raft farther downstream. Huck boards a steam ferry and awakens its watchman. The ferryboatman turns out to be the boat's owner. Huck tearfully tells him a story about his family and a Miss Hooker being stranded on the wrecked steamboat—which the startled ferryboatman identifies as the *Walter Scott*. The man happens to mention a rich local person named Jim Hornback. He is concerned about who will pay for the rescue effort. When Huck mentions that Hornback is the uncle of the fictitious Miss Hooker, the ferryboatman jumps to begin organizing his rescue effort.

Before the ferryboat reaches the *Walter Scott*, the steamboat breaks up and washes downstream. Huck rows his skiff around the drifting wreck and calls out, but no one answers. Eventually, he rejoins Jim farther down the river. They go to an island, hide the raft, sink the skiff and sleep soundly.

Chapter 14

The next morning, Huck and Jim sort out the goods from the steamboat that the murderers left in the skiff and find boots, blankets, books, clothes, cigars, and other things. After they rest, Huck crows about their adventure aboard the steamboat. Jim, however, says he does not want any more adventures, explaining that when he discovered the raft was missing, he thought that he would either die or be sold down the river. Huck concedes that Jim is right and has "an uncommon level head for a nigger."

As Huck reads to Jim, they take up the subject of kings and royalty. They debate whether King Solomon was truly a wise man and then discuss King Louis XVI and his son the DAUPHIN. Finally, they argue about why some people speak French. Though Jim applies superior logic in each argument,

Huck fails to see that he has been bested and concludes that "you can't learn a nigger to argue."

Chapter 15

Huck and Jim plan to go as far as CAIRO, Illinois, where they will sell the raft and take a steamboat up the OHIO RIVER to the free states. They calculate that three more nights will get them to Cairo. On the second night, however, heavy fog forces them to tie up on a sandbar. Huck takes the canoe out to find something to fasten the raft to. The swift current separates him from the raft; then he and Jim spend the night trying to find each other in the fog. The situation worsens when they drift in among small islands and swirling currents. Both of them fall asleep from exhaustion.

When Huck awakens under a clear night sky hours later, he finds the raft. Jim is worn out and asleep, and the deck is littered with dirt and leaves. Huck boards the raft and lies down, as if he has been sleeping. When Jim awakens, he is immensely relieved to find Huck alive and safe, but Huck tries to convince him that he has merely dreamt the night's misadventures. As Jim tries to explain the meaning of each detail in his dream, he realizes he has been fooled when Huck asks him to explain what the litter strewn on the raft means. Jim then shames Huck by contrasting his own concern for Huck's safety with Huck's effort to make a fool of him, and goes to the wigwam without a further word.

After spending 15 minutes preparing to "humble myself before a nigger," Huck finally does it, then admits that he has not been sorry since then. He plays no more tricks on Jim.

Chapter 16

After sleeping through the day, Huck and Jim set out again and find themselves behind a huge raft with about 30 men in its crew. They discuss the difficult problem of finding the tiny village of Cairo.

(Some editions of *Huckleberry Finn* insert the "RAFT CHAPTER" here.)

Huck and Jim continue watching for Cairo. As Jim's prospects of being truly free grow, Huck feels guilty about helping him to escape. It grieves him to think that he is stealing from Jim's owner, Miss Watson. Jim talks enthusiastically about saving money to buy the freedom of his wife and children, adding that if he cannot buy his children, he will find an abolitionist to steal them. Huck is so shocked by Jim's plans that he decides to report Jim as a runaway.

Huck takes the canoe to scout out where they are. As he paddles off, Jim calls after him, thanking him for being such a good friend. Two slave hunters then approach him in a skiff. Huck now has his chance to turn Jim in but cannot bring himself to do it. Instead, he concocts a story that makes the slave hunters think that he has relatives with small-pox aboard the raft. The men feel guilty about not helping Huck, so each gives him a $20 gold piece. Jim, who has been hiding underwater, is more grateful than ever to Huck.

As Huck and Jim drift downriver, their faith in finding Cairo erodes. One morning, they notice *two* channels in the river. One is the unclouded water of the Ohio; the other, the muddy water of the Mississippi. There is now no doubt; they have passed Cairo. They guess that they missed the town in the fog a few nights earlier and blame their bad luck on the snakeskin that Huck handled on Jackson's Island. They now plan to return upriver in the canoe; however, they awaken that night to find that their canoe is missing. They decide to continue downriver instead until they can buy another canoe in which to return.

After dark, they shove off again on their raft. The night is particularly dark. A steamboat coming up the river ignores their signal lantern and plows into them. Jim dives off one side of the raft, Huck off the other. After swimming under the boat's paddle-wheel, Huck surfaces and calls out for Jim, but gets no reply. He grabs hold of a plank and drifts with the current to the left bank and goes ashore. About a quarter of a mile inland, he stumbles upon a big log house. When barking dogs corner him, he freezes.

Chapter 17

A voice calling from a window orders Huck to identify himself. He gives his name as "George Jackson" and says that he fell off the steamboat. The voice asks if he knows the Shepherdsons, then orders him to enter the house slowly. Inside, Huck finds three

tall men pointing guns at him. There are also an old woman and two young women. As he soon learns, he is in the home of the Grangerfords.

The older man, Colonel Grangerford, is satisfied that Huck is not a threat, and the old woman instructs her slave Betsy to fetch Huck food. The youngest son, Buck Grangerford, takes Huck to his room for dry clothes. As Huck eats, he answers questions and invents a biography. He claims he has come from southern Arkansas. After his sister Mary Ann ran off to marry, his family disintegrated until only he remained. He was coming up the river as a deck passenger when he fell off the steamboat. The Grangerfords invite Huck to stay indefinitely. When Huck awakens the next morning, he finds that he has forgotten his new name. He challenges Buck to spell it for him, then writes it down so he can remember it.

Everything about the Grangerford house impresses Huck. It is full of touches usually found only in houses in towns, such as brass doorknobs and a parlor without a bed. He describes its decor and sees such books as JOHN BUNYAN's *Pilgrim's Progress*, HENRY CLAY's speeches, and DR. (JOHN) GUNN's *Family Medicine*. He also describes the melancholy artwork and poetry of the family's deceased daughter, Emmeline Grangerford.

Chapter 18

Huck takes quickly to the Grangerfords, who have many kinfolk living in the region. Another big aristocratic family, the Shepherdsons, also live nearby. One day as Huck and Buck hunt in the woods, a rider whom Buck recognizes as Harney Shepherdson comes along. They duck into the brush. Buck shoots at Harney, knocking his hat off. Harney rides up and aims his rifle at Buck but leaves without firing. Later, Buck tells Huck about the long-standing FEUD between the Grangerfords and the Shepherdsons.

The following Sunday the Grangerfords and the Shepherdsons attend the same church. All the men carry guns, and Huck feels the tension. Afterward, Sophia Grangerford has Huck go back to fetch a Testament she forgot. Inside her Testament, he finds a note: "Half-past two." It means nothing to him but thrills Sophia.

Later that day, the slave Jack leads Huck to a swamp on the pretext of showing him water moccasins. Jack slips away, leaving Huck to find Jim, who has been hiding there since the raft was smashed. Jim explains that he followed Huck ashore that night, keeping silent for fear of capture. Since then, he has been repairing and restocking the raft, which is not as badly damaged as Huck had thought.

The next day, Huck awakens at the Grangerfords' to find almost everyone gone. Jack reports that Sophia has run off with Harney Shepherdson and that the Grangerford men are trying to catch them as the women round up relatives. Huck hurries to the timber yard by the steamboat landing, where he sees Buck and his cousin Joe shooting at horsemen. Huck climbs a tree to watch. When Buck and Joe move closer to his tree, Huck shouts to them. Buck says that the Shepherdsons have killed his father and brothers in an ambush. Two or three Shepherdsons are also dead. Sophia and Harney have escaped across the river.

The Shepherdsons surprise Buck and Joe by attacking from behind, on foot. The boys run to the river. The Shepherdsons shoot them as they try to swim away. These sights are so horrifying to Huck that he later dreams about the awful experience. When darkness falls, Huck climbs out of the tree, pulls the boys' bodies ashore, then rushes back to the swamp. He and Jim board their raft and leave immediately.

Chapter 19

Huck and Jim continue their voyage down the river, enjoying two or three of the most idyllic days of their journey. By day, they hide in the cottonwood; by night, they drift on the raft. One morning, Huck finds a canoe and paddles up a creek to hunt for berries. Two ragged men tear along a path toward him, begging for help to escape their pursuers. Huck has them go upstream first, so they can wade down the creek to throw the dogs off their scent. He then takes the men back to the raft.

The two men are strangers to each other. Each explains the various scams he specializes in. The younger man suggests they "double-team it together." After a long silence, the younger man grows somber and begins moaning about being "degraded." He alludes to the "secret of his birth" and suddenly blurts out: "By rights I am a Duke!" He explains that he is the rightful Duke of Bridgewater and asks to be treated with the respect due his rank. Huck and Jim agree to wait on him.

After dinner, the older man makes an announcement of his own. He is the "late dauphin," the son of LOUIS XVI and "Marry Antonette." This makes him "Looy the Seventeen," the "rightful king of France." Jim and Huck agree to serve him as well. After a frosty moment, the men agree to be friends. Though Huck knows that both men are frauds, he is content to avert trouble and says nothing.

Chapter 20

The King and the Duke suspect that Jim is a runaway slave, but Huck protests that no runaway slave would be going *south*. He also invents another biography for himself, claiming to be from Missouri's PIKE COUNTY. When hard times hit, he, his father, younger brother Ike, and Jim began rafting downriver in order to live with his Uncle Ben, near NEW ORLEANS. A steamboat hit their raft, drowning his father and Ike. He and Jim are continuing the journey, traveling by night to avoid troublesome encounters with people by day.

The King and Duke appropriate the wigwam as their own sleeping quarters, leaving Jim and Huck to sleep in the rain. As he often does, Jim stands Huck's watch on top of his own. The next morning, the King and Duke begin scheming. The Duke has a carpetbag filled with handbills, mostly for dramatic productions. He persuades the King to perform with him in scenes from ROMEO AND JULIET and RICHARD III in the towns they will visit.

Eventually they land the raft below a town called Pokeville and go ashore. Most townspeople are at a religious camp meeting outside of town. The Duke takes over an untended print shop as Huck and the King go the camp meeting, where they join a lively group. The King gets up and tearfully tells the crowd that he was a PIRATE for 30 years on the Indian Ocean, but now he wants to devote the rest of his life to working as a missionary among the pirates. The enthusiastic crowd has him pass the hat. He collects $87.75 and also finds a jug of whiskey as he leaves.

Meanwhile, the Duke has been busy in the print shop, where he has taken in $9.50 doing small jobs and selling newspaper subscriptions. He has also printed handbills advertising a $200 reward for a runaway slave whose description matches Jim's. The bills give the address as "St. Jacques Plantation," below New Orleans. The Duke explains that they can now run the raft by day. If anyone challenges Jim's presence, they can simply show a handbill and say they are going south to collect the reward. In order to make this scheme work, however, they will have to tie Jim up when anyone approaches and when they leave him alone on the raft.

Early the next morning, Jim tells Huck that he has had his fill of kings.

Chapter 21

As the raft continues downstream, the Duke and King rehearse the balcony scene from *Romeo and Juliet* and the sword fight from *Richard III.* The Duke also teaches the King to recite HAMLET's SOLILOQUY, giving him a version reconstructed from memory. Huck is impressed by the King's recitation. During a stopover at a village, the Duke has handbills printed to announce the coming production.

Two or three days later, they stop above another town (Bricksville), which appears promising because a circus is performing there that very day. The Duke hires the courthouse and posts bills for their "Shaksperean Revival," featuring "David Garrick, the Younger" and "Edmund Kean, the Elder." As Huck idles about the town, he comments on its tumble-down condition and its loafers such as Ben Thompson. A rowdy drunk named Boggs rides into town yelling threats aimed mostly at a man named Colonel Sherburn, who warns him to stop his abuse after one o'clock. When that hour arrives, Sherburn shoots Boggs and the crowd cries for a lynch party.

Chapter 22

After collecting rope, a mob swarms to Sherburn's house, where they knock down the fence. Sherburn steps out on the roof over his porch. Holding a double-barreled gun, he stares the crowd into uncomfortable silence. He then dresses them down for their cowardice, calling Buck Harkness, their leader, a "half a man." Huck leaves as the mob dis-

perses, then sneaks into the circus, where he gushes over every wonder he sees.

That night the King and Duke stage their "Shaksperean Revival" to 12 unappreciative people. The only person who does not leave before it ends is a boy who has fallen asleep. The angry Duke declares that what these "Arkansaw lunkheads" really want is "low comedy." The next day, he makes up new handbills advertising "The King's Camelopard or The Royal Nonesuch . . . Ladies and Children Not Admitted."

Chapter 23

The King and Duke rig a stage at the courthouse, which they pack that night. The Duke introduces the "Royal Nonesuch" with a provocative speech. When the curtain rises, the King comes out on all fours. Naked and painted with multicolored stripes, he delights the crowd by prancing about wildly. After two encores, the Duke ends the show. The audience rises angrily, but one man persuades the others to give the rest of the town a chance to be taken in by the frauds to spare those present from becoming laughingstocks.

The second performance goes as on the first night. Afterward, the King and Duke have Jim and Huck move the raft to a point below the town. On the third night, Huck recognizes men who attended the previous performances. The crowd is armed with rotten fruit and eggs, as well as dead cats. Once the house is packed, Huck and the Duke slip out, run to the raft and take off downstream. Huck is concerned about leaving the King behind but is surprised to find him already aboard the raft. The con men find that their three-night take adds up to $465.

After the King and Duke are asleep, Jim and Huck discuss what RAPSCALLIONS kings are. Huck talks about kings such as HENRY VIII. Jim again stands Huck's watch during the night. Toward daybreak, Huck overhears Jim moaning about his wife and children and gets him to talk a little about them. Jim relates a painful story about a time when he smacked his daughter 'Lizabeth for disobeying him before he realized that scarlet fever had left her deaf and dumb.

Chapter 24

The next day, the King and Duke scout new villages to exploit. When Jim asks for some relief from being tied up all day, the Duke dresses him up as King Lear, paints him blue and posts a sign on the raft saying that he is a "sick Arab," telling Jim to howl and carry on if anyone approaches.

The rascals want to try their "Royal Nonesuch" show again but figure that they are not far enough from the last place where they performed it for it to be safe. The Duke goes off to inspect a village, while Huck stays with the King to check out another village downriver. After Huck and the King put on recently bought store CLOTHES, the improvement in the King's appearance astounds Huck. The King suggests boarding a steamboat that is loading freight nearby, so they can arrive in the next village in style. As they canoe downriver, they see a "young country jake" (Tim Collins), whom the King offers a ride to the steamboat. He introduces himself as the Reverend Elexander Blodgett and calls Huck "Adolphus," as if he were a servant. The man initially takes the King for a Mr. Wilks, explaining that someone named Peter Wilks in the next town has just died, while he was expecting his English brothers to arrive. The King pumps the man for every detail about Wilks, his family and neighbors.

After the man boards the steamboat, Huck and the King return for the Duke. The King tells the Duke everything he has learned about the Wilkses. His plan is to impersonate Harvey Wilks and have the Duke impersonate Harvey's deaf and dumb younger brother, William Wilks. They hail a big steamboat (the *Susan Powell*), which they ride to the village, where they are immediately received as Peter Wilks's brothers.

Chapter 25

Most of the town turns out to greet the impostors and lead them to Wilks's house, where Peter Wilks's nieces, Mary Jane, Susan, and Joanna Wilks, greet their supposed uncles. The King and Duke pay sobbing tribute over the coffin, disgusting Huck with their exaggerated grief. The King impresses everyone by rattling off the names of all of Peter Wilks's special friends.

Mary Jane presents a letter from her deceased uncle that the King reads. Wilks has left his house and $3,000 in gold to his nieces and has left his successful tanyard, other houses and land, and $3,000 in gold to his brothers Harvey and William. The letter tells where the gold is hidden in the basement. Huck accompanies the King and Duke downstairs to find it. When the impostors count the gold, they find that it is $415 short of $6,000. To avoid suspicion of dishonesty, the Duke suggests they make up the "deffisit" by contributing their own money. He then suggests giving *all* the money to the girls—an idea that wins everyone's approval upstairs.

The King prattles on, upsetting the Duke with talk about the funeral "ORGIES." Dr. Robinson arrives and quickly denounces the scoundrels as frauds, calling the King's English accent the worst he has ever heard. He appeals to the girls to shun the frauds, but Mary Jane hands the King the bag of gold and asks him to invest the money for them and not to bother with a receipt.

Chapter 26

That night, the Wilks girls put on a big dinner at which Huck acts as the King's servant. Afterward, he eats in the kitchen with Joanna, who asks him about ENGLAND. Skeptical of Huck's unlikely answers, Joanna asks him to swear he is telling the truth. Mary Jane and Susan arrive at this moment and take her to task for not treating Huck properly as a guest. The sisters' sensitivity and Joanna's beautiful apology make Huck feel so bad about his role in the King and Duke's swindle that he decides to steal the girls' gold back from the impostors.

Huck searches the Duke's and King's rooms, and he hides in the King's room when the scoundrels arrive. He then hears the Duke say that he wants to take the money that he and the King already have and leave immediately. The King insists on staying so they can auction off Wilks's properties. The Duke is concerned about Dr. Robinson, but the King laughs him off. Huck sees the King hide the money in his bed and grabs it after the men leave the room.

Chapter 27

After waiting a bit, Huck takes the gold downstairs. He wants to hide it outside the house, but the doors are locked. When he hears someone else coming, he stuffs the money inside Wilks's coffin and hides as Mary Jane enters the parlor. He agonizes over leaving the money in the coffin, but cannot retrieve it without being seen.

The next morning, Huck finds the parlor shut. He watches people carefully to detect whether anything unusual has happened. In the afternoon, as the Reverend Hobson conducts the funeral in the parlor, Huck is not sure if the gold is still in the coffin.

After Wilks is buried, the King says that he must return to his congregation in England. Saying that he is anxious to settle the estate as soon as possible and take the girls back to England, he immediately puts Wilks's property up for auction. The next day everyone is shocked to learn that the King has already sold the family slaves, sending the two boys upriver and their mother downriver. On the morning of the auction, the King and Duke awaken Huck and grill him about the missing gold, but Huck shifts suspicion onto the slaves who have just been sent away.

Chapter 28

Later that morning, Huck sees Mary Jane in her room crying about the slave family being separated. Momentarily forgetting himself, he assures her that the slaves will soon be reunited. He now feels compelled to tell her the whole truth. After making Mary Jane promise to leave town for a few days, he confesses that her supposed "uncles" are frauds. He adds that prematurely exposing the frauds could mean trouble for someone whom he cannot name.

Huck finally settles on a plan for Mary Jane to spend just one day with the Lothrop family outside of town—long enough for him to make his getaway. He tells her that if proof that the King and Duke are frauds becomes necessary, she can write to Bricksville and mention the "Royal Nonesuch." He insists that she leave immediately, to avoid accidentally betraying that she knows something is wrong. He also gives her a slip of paper telling her where he hid the money. After Mary Jane leaves, Huck tells Susan and Joanna that Mary Jane has gone across the river to visit Hanner Proctor.

At the auction that same day, virtually all the Wilks property is sold off. Later that day, a steamboat lands and townspeople are delighted that two more men claiming to be Harvey and William Wilks have arrived.

Chapter 29

The arrival of more claimants excites the town, but does not faze the King and Duke. The distinguished-looking newcomer who calls himself Harvey Wilks says that since their luggage went ashore at the wrong town, he and his brother cannot prove who they are. They will therefore retire to a hotel to await their luggage, which contains their proof. The King jokes about them, but several people do not laugh, including Dr. Robinson and Levi Bell, newly returned to town. Another man (Hines) steps forward and says he saw the King and Huck in a canoe upriver the morning of the day they came to town.

Robinson proposes taking Huck, the King, and the Duke to the hotel to confront them and the newcomers together. He also demands that the townspeople take charge of Wilks's gold until his true brothers are identified; this forces the King to reveal that the gold is missing. The resulting investigation at the hotel lasts over an hour. Huck thinks it should be obvious to anyone that the King is lying and that his freshly arrived counterpart is telling the truth. When Huck testifies about life in England, Robinson merely laughs and tells him he is not much of a liar.

Bell has the King and Duke write something down, then surprises them by comparing their handwriting with letters written by the real Harvey and William Wilks. This test appears to prove them impostors; however, the new "Harvey" fails as well. He claims that William transcribes all his letters for him, but his brother cannot write anything with his arm in a cast. At the least, Bell concludes, the test proves the King and the Duke *not* to be Harvey and William Wilks. The King tries to talk his way out of this by suggesting that the Duke deliberately altered his own handwriting as a joke.

The man that Huck thinks is the real Harvey asks if anyone there helped prepare Peter's body for burial. Ab Turner and another man present themselves. The man then asks the King what was tattooed on Peter's chest. The King calmly answers, a "small blue arrow." The other Harvey says the tattoo was the letters "P-B-W"; however, neither Turner nor the other man remembers seeing any mark on Peter's chest. A voice rises suggesting that all four claimants be lynched, but Bell proposes opening Peter Wilks's grave to examine his body. Dr. Robinson makes sure that Huck and the four claimants are kept under restraint.

As the crowd marches to the CEMETERY, the sky darkens ominously. Huck now regrets sending Mary Jane out of town, fearing that he is about to be hanged. Just as the lid to Wilks's coffin is removed, a flash of lightning reveals the bag of gold. The excited mob surges forward, allowing Huck to escape. He runs to the river, grabs a canoe, and paddles to the raft. Thinking himself finally free of the scoundrels, he calls to Jim to set the raft loose. Just as they start to drift off, however, the King and Duke row up to the raft. Huck almost cries.

Chapter 30

When the King and Duke board the raft, the King turns on Huck for trying to run out on them. Huck protests that he thought that the King and Duke must be dead, so he was merely trying to save his life. The Duke makes the King leave Huck alone, reminding him that he had not looked out for anyone but himself. He then blames the King for doing everything wrong from the start—except for his remark about the blue-arrow tattoo, which saved their lives.

The realization that they have not only lost their chance at the Wilks fortune, but their "Royal Nonesuch" money, causes the King and Duke to argue over who is responsible for the disaster. Each accuses the other of having hidden the money in the coffin with the idea of coming back later to dig it up for himself. The argument ends when the Duke throttles the King, forcing him to confess that he stole the money. Eventually, both get drunk and become friends again. Once they are asleep, Huck tells Jim what has happened.

Chapter 31

The raft drifts south for "days and days" without stopping at any settlements. When the King and Duke feel safe again they start working towns, but everything they try fails: temperance lecturing, a

dancing school, elocution lectures, "missionarying," "mesmerizering," doctoring, telling fortunes, and other things. Their money runs out and they grow morose and talk secretly with each other.

Eventually, the band lands the raft about two miles below a town named Pikesville. The King goes into town alone, leaving instructions for the Duke and Huck to follow at noon if he does not return. By now, Huck is determined to escape the con men at the first opportunity. At noon, he and the Duke go into town and find the King drunk in a saloon. As the Duke and King argue, Huck runs back to the raft, but Jim has disappeared. Huck returns to the road and finds a boy who tells him that a runaway slave fitting Jim's description has been caught and taken to the farm of Silas Phelps, two miles farther downstream. He explains that an "old fellow" with a handbill offering a reward for the slave has sold the runaway for $40.

Huck's guilt over helping a slave escape resurfaces. He is ashamed of his sinfulness, but cannot bring himself to pray. Instead, he writes a letter to Miss Watson, telling her where Jim is. After he completes the letter, he feels washed clean of sin for the first time but trembles to think how close he has come to consigning himself to hell. Second thoughts creep in, however. He recalls all the ways in which Jim has become a friend. Finally, he decides, "All right, then, I'll go to hell" and tears up the letter. He is now determined to win back Jim's freedom.

Huck shifts the raft to an island (Spanish Island), where he spends the night. The next day he puts on his store-bought clothes and paddles the canoe ashore. When he reaches the town, the first person he sees is the Duke, who is pasting up handbills for a new "Royal Nonesuch" performance. Huck invents a story to account for his absence the day before and tells the Duke that the raft has disappeared. The Duke reveals that the King has sold Jim for $40—money that he quickly blew on whiskey and gambling.

When the Duke accuses Huck of trying to give them the shake, Huck points out that it would not make sense for him to leave without his slave, and blubbers about losing the only property he owns. Taking pity on Huck, the Duke offers to tell him where Jim is—provided that he not give away the secret of their "Royal Nonesuch." The Duke starts to tell the truth, but abruptly switches to a lie, telling Huck that a man named Abram G. Foster—40 miles inland—has Jim, and he insists that Huck start walking immediately. Huck walks about a mile, then doubles back and heads for the Phelps farm.

Chapter 32

Huck arrives at the Phelps farm on a hot, quiet afternoon. As he approaches the house, barking hounds surround him. A slave woman named Lize chases the dogs away; then a white woman and several children come out to greet him. The woman puzzles Huck by acting as if she expects him. She tells her children that he is their cousin Tom and insists that he call her "Aunt Sally." Not knowing which direction she thinks he has come from, Huck invents a noncommittal story about his steamboat's blowing out a cylinder-head, and adds that he has hidden his luggage near the town.

Aunt Sally's detailed questions make Huck almost ready to give up his unintentional masquerade. However, she sees her husband coming home and tells Huck to hide so they can play a joke on him. When Mr. Phelps comes in, Aunt Sally springs Huck on him and asks who he thinks it is. The man has no idea, so she proclaims: "It's *Tom Sawyer!*" Immensely relieved, Huck confidently answers a flock of questions about "the Sawyer family." The sound of a steamboat whistle reminds him that the real Tom Sawyer may arrive soon, so he insists on returning to town alone to fetch his luggage, hoping to find Tom before he reaches the Phelpses.

Chapter 33

Huck takes the Phelps' wagon to town and meets Tom along the road. After convincing his friend that he is not a ghost, Huck fills him in on his situation. Tom proposes that Huck return to the house alone with his luggage and that he arrive later. When Huck adds that he plans to free Jim from captivity, Tom eagerly offers to help. It shocks Huck that the respectable Tom would stoop to the level of a "nigger stealer." Huck gets back to the house sooner than he should, but innocent old Uncle Silas suspects nothing.

Later, Tom appears at the door and asks for Mr. Archibald Nichols, a neighbor. When Aunt Sally invites Tom in, he introduces himself as William Thompson. He prattles on about where he is from, then stuns Aunt Sally by suddenly kissing her on the mouth. Eventually, he identifies himself as his own brother, Sid Sawyer, explaining that he begged to come along on this trip. (From this point through chapter 42, Huck goes by the name Tom, and Tom goes by the name Sid.)

At supper, Huck learns that the townspeople are planning violence at the King and Duke's "Royal Nonesuch." Jim has told Uncle Silas and a man named Burton all about their show. That night Huck and Tom slip out and go to town. Huck wants to warn the rascals of the danger they are in, but as the boys reach town, they see the two con men covered with TAR AND FEATHERS and being carried out on rails. The sight sickens Huck.

Chapter 34

As the boys return home, Tom guesses that Jim is being kept prisoner in a cabin where he has observed a slave (Nat) entering through a locked door with food. Tom proposes to Huck that they each devise a plan for freeing Jim. Huck's plan is to steal the key to the cabin off Uncle Silas while he sleeps, then spring Jim free and break for the raft, but Tom insists on something vastly more elaborate. At the farm, they examine the cabin from outside and inspect the surrounding area.

The next morning, Huck and Tom accompany Nat when he takes food to Jim. They find Jim chained to his bed inside the dark cabin. When Jim sees them, he cries aloud; however, Huck and Tom pretend that they have heard nothing and convince Nat that he only imagines having heard Jim. Tom whispers to Jim not to let on that he knows them and that they are going to get him free.

Chapter 35

Under Tom's direction the next day, the boys begin gathering supplies for Tom's elaborate escape plans. It soon becomes clear that he wants to do everything in the most complicated and time-consuming manner possible. For example, instead of having Jim free his leg chain from his bed by simply lifting up the bed to slip it off, he wants Jim to saw the bed's leg off. All his ideas come from books he has read about famous escapes by people such as "Baron Trenck . . . Casanova . . . Benvenuto Chelleeny [CELLINI] . . . Henri IV" and others.

Chapter 36

That night Huck and Tom begin digging at Jim's cabin with case-knives. They work for hours until their hands are blistered but barely make an impression. Tom reluctantly concedes that they should use real digging tools and "*let on* it's case-knives." When they resume with picks and shovels, they make rapid progress. After they quit, Tom's hands are so raw he cannot climb the lightning rod to their room. He follows Huck's suggestion to come up the stairs, "and let on it's a lightning rod."

The next day Tom and Huck steal more supplies, such as tin plates, for Jim. That night they dig all the way into Jim's cabin and gently awaken him. He is tearfully grateful and wants them to find a chisel to break his chain so he can leave immediately. However, Tom explains his escape plan, assuring Jim that they will spring him loose immediately if an emergency arises. Jim agrees to go along. During a long chat, the boys learn that the Phelpses have been treating Jim very kindly.

The next morning the boys begin smuggling supplies to Jim on his food plate. They accompany the slave Nat to the cabin. While they are there, dogs begin pouring into the cabin through the hole dug the previous night. After chasing the dogs out and covering the openings, Tom persuades Nat that he has only imagined seeing the dogs in the cabin.

Chapter 37

Huck and Tom smuggle implements to Jim for scribbling messages. Aunt Sally begins noticing things missing from around the house, such as candles, a shirt, a sheet, a spoon and a candlestick. The spoon turns up in Uncle Silas's pocket; then Tom and Huck confuse Aunt Sally by making it impossible for her to count her spoon collection accurately. To add to her confusion, they replace the missing sheet, and then steal and replace it repeatedly until she no longer pays attention to its absence. Finally, they shred the sheet to make a rope ladder for Jim and smuggle as much of it to Jim as they can fit inside a pie that they bake in a bed-warming pan.

They also smuggle tin plates in to Jim. He scratches marks on them and throws them out his window.

Chapter 38

Tom insists that Jim scratch on the wall a coat of arms that he designs for him. He also wants Jim to inscribe "mournful" messages on his wall. However, Tom is not satisfied with log walls, so he and Huck steal a big grindstone from a nearby mill. Since they cannot handle the grindstone by themselves, Jim leaves his cabin to help. Tom enlarges the hole in the ground in order to get the grindstone into the cabin.

Tom's next idea is to collect spiders, snakes, and rats for the cabin, but Jim draws the line at rattlesnakes. Tom's final idea is for Jim to grow a flower in the corner of his cell watered by his tears. When Jim protests that he does not cry enough to keep a flower alive, Tom promises to smuggle an onion to him help produce tears.

Chapter 39

The next morning the boys fill a wire trap with rats and hide it under Aunt Sally's bed. While they are off catching spiders, Sally's children open the cage. Sally whips the boys, but they simply capture more rats. They also add spiders, insects, and dozens of harmless snakes to the menagerie they are collecting for Jim. The snakes escape from a bag in their room, and for some time afterward are found throughout the house, making Aunt Sally a nervous wreck.

After three weeks of preparation, everything is ready for the escape, which Tom calls an "evasion." Both boys and especially Jim are exhausted. Meanwhile, Silas Phelps has been writing to the nonexistent St. Jacques plantation near New Orleans. Since no reply has come, he talks about advertising in St. Louis and New Orleans newspapers to find Jim's owner. Huck's anxiousness to free Jim mounts.

Tom now wants to send anonymous letters to make sure that the actual escape does not go unnoticed. He has Huck borrow the frock of a servant girl to wear while delivering a letter that warns of brewing trouble. Over the next several nights, Tom posts ominous pictures on the Phelpses' door, causing Aunt Sally to grow increasingly anxious. Finally, Tom writes a long letter warning that a cutthroat gang of abolitionists is planning to steal the runaway slave the next night and spirit him away to INDIAN TERRITORY.

Chapter 40

The next day, Huck and Tom relax by fishing and examining the raft. At home they find everyone in a sweat over Tom's anonymous letter. Aunt Sally hustles the boys to their room, where they sleep until nearly midnight. When they arise, Tom puts on a dress he has stolen from Aunt Sally in order to play the role of Jim's mother in the escape. Tom sends Huck downstairs to get butter for their provisions. There, Huck bumps into Aunt Sally, but manages to hide a slab of corn pone and the butter under his hat. Not satisfied with Huck's reasons for being in the cellar, Aunt Sally takes him into the sitting room, where he finds 15 farmers armed with guns. As she questions Huck in the hot room, streaks of butter begin oozing down his face, making Aunt Sally think Huck has "brain fever." Relieved to find only butter under his hat, she sends him back to his room.

The moment Huck is upstairs, he and Tom go out the window and head for Jim's cabin. Tom is pleased about the armed men in the house. After he and Huck enter the cabin, armed men pour inside. Nevertheless, Tom, Huck and Jim quietly slip out through the hole dug under Jim's bed. As they go over a fence, the men shoot at them and set dogs on them. The dogs know the boys, however, and lose interest in the chase when they catch up with them.

Once they seem safe on the raft, Jim and Huck are happy. However, Tom is the happiest—because he has a bullet in his calf. However, this news takes all the pleasure out of the escape for Jim and Huck, who insist on fetching a doctor immediately. Huck takes the canoe to go find a doctor.

Chapter 41

Huck finds a kindly old doctor and tells him that his brother has shot himself on Spanish Island. The doctor heads for the island with Huck, but he will not ride in the flimsy canoe with a second person, so he leaves Huck behind and paddles to the island by himself.

That night, Huck sleeps in a lumber pile and awakens in broad daylight. Before he can start back

to the island, he runs into Uncle Silas, who makes him accompany him home. The house is full of farmers and their wives talking about the crazy runaway slave who has left all manner of strange things in the cabin, such as the giant grindstone. No one can explain who did all the work that must have been done in the cabin.

As the day wears into night and Tom does not appear, Aunt Sally and Uncle Silas grow increasingly worried. Huck tries to reassure Aunt Sally, who makes him promise not to leave the house again. Three times he slides down the lightning rod, but changes his mind about leaving when he sees Aunt Sally patiently sitting on the front porch with a candle.

Chapter 42

The next morning, Uncle Silas fails to learn anything in town about Tom's whereabouts. When he returns, he gives Aunt Sally a letter he collected at the post office the day before. It is from her sister, Aunt Polly. Sensing what trouble that message must contain, Huck starts to leave, but at that moment, Tom appears. He is carried to the house on a mattress. The old doctor is with him, as is Jim, with his hands tied behind him.

Jim's captors are treating him roughly and some want to hang him as an example for other would-be runaways. Others are opposed because they do not want to be responsible for paying Jim's owner. The men take Jim back to the cabin and chain him up tightly, but the doctor suggests that Jim be treated more kindly. He explains how when he found Tom on the island and needed help badly, Jim emerged from hiding and gave him all the help he could, risking his own freedom to provide it. The men agree that Jim has acted well, but no one moves to lighten his load of chains.

As Aunt Sally nurses Tom through the night, Huck dodges Uncle Silas in order to avoid embarrassing questions. The next morning Huck visits Tom, who astounds Aunt Sally by confessing that he and Huck are behind Jim's escape. His ecstasy is spoiled, however, when he learns that Jim is again a prisoner. He now stuns both Huck and Aunt Sally by saying that Jim is a free man. Miss Watson died two months earlier, he reveals, freeing Jim in her will. Tom explains that he engineered the entire escape for the "adventure of it" and demands that Jim be set free immediately.

At that moment, Aunt Sally's sister Polly enters the room. Aunt Sally gets her third thunderbolt when Polly explains that "Sid" is really Tom and "Tom" is really Huck Finn. Her confusion is tame, however, compared to what Uncle Silas experiences when everything is explained to him. Aunt Polly verifies that Jim is free. It emerges that Tom has been intercepting all the letters she has sent to Sally.

Chapter the Last

When Huck finally speaks privately with Tom, he asks what Tom intended to do with Jim if the "evasion" worked. Tom explains that he had hoped to continue rafting down the river, having adventures. Then, when they reached the mouth of the river, he would tell Jim that he was free and take him home on a steamboat, "in style, and pay him for his lost time," and have a big reception for him on his arrival at home.

Tom (left) and Huck share Jim's pleasure in being free in E. W. Kemble's final illustration for *Huckleberry Finn.*

Jim is freed soon after Aunt Polly's arrival. Tom gives him $40 for having been a patient prisoner and suggests that some time he, Huck, and Jim make a trip into Indian Territory. Huck says he could not afford to pay for the outfit, because he reckons that his Pap has all his money by now. Now it is Jim's turn for a revelation. He tells Huck that the murdered man they saw in the floating house (chapter 9) was his father.

After Tom gets well, he wears his bullet around his neck on a watch-guard. Huck says that Aunt Sally wants to adopt him. He cannot stand that idea and reckons that he must "light out for the Territory ahead of the rest."

BACKGROUND AND PUBLISHING HISTORY

None of Clemens's books had a more fitful start and painful development than *Huckleberry Finn.* Thanks to the research of Walter BLAIR and Victor Doyno, the history of the book's composition is now reasonably firmly established. Clemens worked on the book intermittently over eight years, during which his conceptions of what he was writing changed radically.

The quick success of *Tom Sawyer* in 1876 moved Clemens to begin a sequel immediately. Determined to use a boy as his narrator in the new book, he thought Tom would be unsuitable and selected Huck Finn—a decision that probably sent his narrative in directions that he never expected it to go. By the end of the summer of 1876, he had written at least as far as chapter 16, in which a steamboat smashes Huck and Jim's raft—an incident that may have left Clemens baffled as to where next to take his story. Three years later he resumed the story, carrying it to about chapter 21. After another interval, he wrote the book's second half around late 1882 and early 1883 and added significant passages to chapters 12–14. By this time, he had already extracted a passage known as the "RAFT CHAPTER" for another book, *Life on the Mississippi* (1883). In that book he alludes to having worked on his novel "by fits and starts, during the past five or six years" (chapter 3). Although that passage also says that he might finish his novel "in the course of five or six more [years]," he pronounced *Huckleberry Finn* done in the summer of 1883, shortly after *Life on the Mississippi* was published. Through the following year, he edited the book with the help of his friend W. D. HOWELLS.

To illustrate the book, Clemens commissioned E. W. KEMBLE, who drew about 175 pictures for it. In later years, he was uncertain how well he liked Kemble's work. Meanwhile, he had a photograph of the bust that KARL GERHARDT sculpted of him inserted as a second frontispiece to *Huckleberry Finn*.

To publicize his forthcoming book, Clemens published extracts in the December 1884 and January and February 1885 issues of CENTURY MAGAZINE. The novel's first book publication occurred in England and CANADA on December 10, 1884. On February 18, 1885, Clemens's own firm, CHARLES L. WEBSTER & COMPANY, issued the first American edition of the novel as its inaugural publication. Since then, *Huckleberry Finn* has remained in print continuously, selling at least 20 million copies in more than 100 languages.

Although the typeset pages of the first American edition of *Huckleberry Finn* were comparatively accurate, Clemens was unhappy with them but lacked the time to correct proofs thoroughly. One of the most glaring errors that slipped through to publication was his use of the name "Bessie" for Becky Thatcher—a mistake in chapter 8 that he had marked for correction himself. Virtually all the hundreds of English- and foreign-language editions that were published over the next century were based, directly or indirectly, on the first American and English editions. The first significantly corrected edition was finally published on the 100th anniversary of the novel's original American publication.

In 1985, the University of California Press issued an edition of *Huckleberry Finn* that had been prepared by the editors of the MARK TWAIN PROJECT, who made every effort to recreate Clemens's original intentions for the book. In 1988, the press issued the project's full scholarly edition of the novel. The project's editors meticulously edited and annotated the novel, but their work was handicapped by the fact that they had access to only the last half of Clemens's original handwritten manuscript—the only portion of the manuscript then known to exist. The editors also drew on the book's

first American edition; the *Century Magazine* excerpts; an incomplete set of first edition page proofs; and chapter 3 of *Life on the Mississippi*, in which the "Raft Chapter" was first published. Three typescripts that were used in intermediate editing phases of the original American edition were also not known to have survived.

Only three years after the project issued its scholarly edition of *Huckleberry Finn*, one of the most dramatic events relating to modern Mark Twain scholarship began unfolding. In February 1991, it was publicly announced that the long-missing portion of Clemens's manuscript had been found. The missing pages turned up in Hollywood, California, in an old trunk owned by a granddaughter of James Fraser Gluck (1852–97), a BUFFALO, New York, civic leader who was already known to have persuaded Clemens to donate his *Huckleberry Finn* manuscript to a library that later became part of the BUFFALO AND ERIE COUNTY PUBLIC LIBRARY. In 1991, the Buffalo library had owned the other parts of the manuscript for more than a century. What was not then known was whether the library had ever owned the pages that had now unexpectedly resurfaced.

Since the revelation of the manuscript's reappearance came about because Gluck's heirs were preparing to sell its pages through a New York auction house, it became urgent to establish the manuscript's legal ownership before the pages might be scattered among private collectors. Fortunately, documents were soon found that proved conclusively that Clemens had indeed given the entire manuscript to the Buffalo library. It is possible that Gluck had removed the first part of the manuscript from the library to have its pages bound, but this is not certain. In any case, when he died in 1897, those pages were stored along with his private papers, and they passed down to Gluck's granddaughter, unnoticed until 1990.

After ownership of the manuscript was legally established, the pages were returned to the Buffalo and Erie County Public Library, where they joined the rest of the manuscript on permanent display. By the terms of an agreement reached among the library, Gluck's heirs, the Mark Twain Project, and the MARK TWAIN FOUNDATION—which owns the copyrights of all unpublished Clemens materials—arrangements were made to publish a new edition of *Huckleberry Finn* that incorporated manuscript material that had not appeared in any previous edition. Under the terms of that agreement, Random House—which was rumored to have paid as much as one half million dollars for publication rights—published *Adventures of Huckleberry Finn: The Only Comprehensive Edition* in 1996, with a new introduction by Justin Kaplan and a foreword and addendum by Victor Doyno. This edition included all of Kemble's original illustrations and restored four long passages—including the "Raft Chapter"—in the places from which they had been deleted in the original edition. Doyno's addendum included facsimiles of original manuscript pages as well as extensive notes on other changes revealed by the recovered manuscript.

Over the next several years, Victor Fischer, Lin Salamo, and other editors of the Mark Twain Project used the rediscovered manuscript to reedit *Huckleberry Finn*. In 2001, the University of California Press published the project's new edition in its popular Mark Twain Library series. Two years later, the Press followed with a greatly expanded scholarly edition, which includes a full account of the manuscript's history. In contrast to the Random House edition, the two Mark Twain Project editions place the portions of the manuscript that Clemens had deleted in appendices, rather than within the main text, and draw on the manuscript to perfect their annotations and textual corrections and emendations. Also in 2001, Michael Hearn published a revised edition of his *Annotated Huckleberry Finn*, which uses the corrected text established by the Mark Twain Project.

When portions of the rediscovered manuscript were first published, the passages that Clemens had deleted from his book drew considerable public attention. The first substantial deleted passage comes from a scene in chapter 9 in which Jim and Huck are conversing inside a cave on Jackson's Island. While a storm rages outside, Jim tells how he saw a ghost when he was about 16 years old. At that time, he was owned by a young medical student who one night sent him to the college's dissecting room to "warm up" a corpse that he was

going to work on. When the corpse seemed to come to life, Jim fled.

In a much briefer passage removed from the scene in chapter 19 introducing the characters of the King and Duke, the King tells the Duke about the money he has made pretending to be a missionary in camp meetings. This theme is developed further in a long passage deleted from the camp meeting episode in chapter 20. Amid its description of people whooping and wallowing in straw near a mourner's bench are several lines about a "fat nigger woman" making white people uncomfortable by throwing herself on other mourners.

CRITICAL OVERVIEW

By any objective measure, *Adventures of Huckleberry Finn* is a remarkable book. During the century and a quarter since its first publication, it has remained in print continuously, has been translated into more than 100 different languages, and has gone through nearly 1,000 editions. It is probably the most widely read American novel ever written and is still, even in the 21st century, the most widely assigned American novel in both high school and college classrooms. For these reasons alone, the book demands serious attention.

In addition to being one of the most widely assigned novels in American schools, *Huckleberry Finn* has also been one of America's most frequently banned books. Since it first appeared in the United States in early 1885, calls for its removal from libraries and classrooms have repeatedly popped up. What makes the book's long history of censorship interesting, however, is not so much the frequency of banning calls as the variety of reasons that have been advanced for expelling the book from libraries and classrooms. These reasons include the book's coarse language, its failure to condemn slavery explicitly, its low moral standards, and its white racist point of view. By contrast, defenders of the novel cite its powerful moral lessons, the richness and authenticity of its language, and the power of its implicit condemnation of slavery and racism. The breadth of the divide between *Huckleberry Finn*'s critics and its defenders should make it evident that it is not an easy book to assess. However, that is not the only difficulty that stands between the book and its readers.

The Enigma of Greatness

Among other obstacles to understanding *Huckleberry Finn* are the claims that it is one of the greatest American novels ever written. As early as 1913, the eminent literary critic H. L. Mencken called *Huckleberry Finn* "one of the great masterpieces of the world . . . the full equal of *Don Quixote* and *Robinson Crusoe* . . ." In 1941, V. S. Prichett called *Huckleberry Finn* "America's first truly indigenous masterpiece," and nine years later, critic Lionel Trilling called it "one of the world's great books and one of the central documents of American culture." The Nobel Prize–winning poet T. S. Eliot grew up in Missouri, in which *Huckleberry Finn* is partly set, but did not read the book until he was an adult because his parents had steered him away from it during his childhood, perhaps out of fear that it might corrupt him. He later recalled that his parents regarded the book as unsuitable for boys, so he grew up thinking it must be a book suitable *only* for boys. When he finally read the book as an adult, he discovered that it was, in fact, eminently suitable for adults, and he added his voice to those who called it a masterpiece.

All this is extravagant praise for any book and more especially for one that early critics dismissed as the "veriest trash" and that went on to inspire repeated calls for censorship. It is therefore not surprising that readers who approach the book hoping to find one of the greatest novels ever written may instead come away confused and fail to notice the book's true merits, many of which are so subtle that they may appear, on first reading, to be flaws rather than virtues. In this regard, it may be worthwhile to look a little more deeply at the issue of the book's greatness.

The idea that *Huckleberry Finn* is *the* Great American Novel may well have originated with a remark that the 20th-century American writer Ernest Hemingway made in *Green Hills of Africa* in 1935—a year that happened to coincide with the centenary of Samuel Clemens's birth. Hemingway wrote the following:

> All modern American literature comes from one book by Mark Twain called *Huckleberry Finn.* . . . it's the best book we've had. All American writing comes from that. There was nothing before. There has been nothing as good since.

Much time and energy has gone into trying to understand what Hemingway meant by those words. Although he appears to say that *Huckleberry Finn* is the greatest American novel, he does not explain what makes it so. Moreover, if one reads his remarks about the book in their entirety, his praise is accompanied by a serious criticism:

> All modern American literature comes from one book by Mark Twain called *Huckleberry Finn.* If you read it you must stop where the Nigger Jim is stolen from the boys. That is the real end. The rest is just cheating. But it's the best book we've had. All American writing comes from that. There was nothing before. There has been nothing as good since.

Hemingway's praise now appears to be ambiguous. His allusion to the fugitive slave Jim being stolen refers to *Huckleberry Finn*'s chapter 31, in which Huck discovers that the rascals who call themselves the King and the Duke have sold Jim to Silas Phelps, whom they have duped into believing that Jim is the object of a $200 reward offered by a New Orleans plantation owner. In chapter 33, Tom Sawyer reappears for the first time since chapter 3, and from that moment, the novel takes a different turn. The final chapters are devoted to Tom and Huck's largely comical effort to liberate Jim in an ludicrously elaborate and—as is later learned—ultimately unnecessary scheme that Tom calls an "evasion." When Hemingway says that the novel's "real end" occurs when Jim is stolen, he appears, in effect, to be charging that the one-quarter of the novel that follows that moment is not worth reading. That seems a curious view, but it is shared by most modern critics, many of whom also do not much care for the novel's first three chapters. Not coincidentally, the early and late chapters that critics most disdain are also those in which Tom Sawyer appears. This conjunction between Tom Sawyer and the weakest chapters in *Huckleberry*

Finn is one of several keys to understanding the novel and is worth exploring at length, as John H. Davis does in the "Critical Commentary" below.

The Problem of the "Evasion" Chapters

It should be evident that one of the obstacles to appreciating *Huckleberry Finn* is determining how to regard the book's many objectionable chapters. Indeed, one might fairly ask whether it is possible for a novel to be a "great" book if about one-third of its content is demonstrably unsatisfactory. Is Hemingway right? Should readers simply stop reading in chapter 31 and ignore the rest? Scholar John Seelye took Hemingway's advice by rewriting Clemens's novel as *The True Adventures of Huckleberry Finn* (1970; rev. ed. 1987). Seelye's version rudely expels Tom Sawyer from Huck's narrative toward its beginning, omits the evasion chapters altogether, and concludes with Jim being killed by bounty hunters, rather than returning to St. Petersburg in glory, as in Clemens's version. Seelye's version may be truer to Hemingway's vision of how the narrative should play out, but it does not help readers of Clemens's *Huckleberry Finn* solve the problem of how to regard its problematic chapters.

Modern critics have divergent views on how to regard the so-called evasion chapters. Some shake their heads in disappointment at what they regard as Clemens's betrayal of the promise of the earlier parts of the book, in which the slave Jim is elevated to a high level of human dignity, only to be reduced to a comic foil at the end. Some critics dismiss this shortcoming as merely being characteristic of Clemens's lifelong inability to write an entirely satisfactory book. Virtually every one of his books has some kind of major flaw, such as an inconsistency in tone, a breakdown in plot, or the inclusion of extraneous passages. The problem with *Huckleberry Finn*, according to some critics, is Clemens's inability to control his material by sustaining a consistent direction in the development of both his plot and his characters. Throughout the bulk of the narrative, Huck develops a growing affection and admiration for Jim that makes him eventually realize that he and Jim—and by extension, white and black people—share a common humanity. Moreover, he grows in strength and independence. The

pinnacle of his maturation occurs in chapter 31, shortly after he learns that the King and Duke have sold Jim. In his eagerness to be good and do the right thing, he drafts a letter to Miss Watson, telling her where she can find her escaped slave, Jim. Then, as he reflects on his positive feelings for Jim, he abruptly changes his mind, thinks, "All right, then, I'll go to hell," tears up his letter, and decides to help Jim escape, rather than turn him in. Without realizing the full implications of his decision, Huck decides to do the right thing, all the time thinking—because of his conditioning as a white person in a slave culture—that he is doing the wrong thing. Soon afterward, however, Tom reappears in the story, and Huck seems to shrivel back to the level of the fawning sidekick that he was in *Tom Sawyer*. From that point, he goes along with schemes suggested by Tom that can only be said to degrade both Jim and himself.

A much different perspective on the evasion chapters sees them as an extension of the novel's ironic condemnation of slavery and racism in America. According to this view, the novel as a whole is a kind of parable on the history of America's treatment of African Americans through the 19th century. It begins with Jim's struggle to win his freedom and, by extension, the freedom of his people. Just as it appears that he has won his freedom, it is snatched away from him—just as the freedom won by African-American slaves after the Civil War was effectively taken away from them by the failure of postwar Reconstruction and the restoration of white power throughout the former Confederate states. Clemens completed *Huckleberry Finn* in 1884—seven years after Reconstruction officially ended with the withdrawal of the last federal troops from southern states. During those years, nominally free black Americans suffered untold indignities as white state governments legislated discriminatory laws that made a mockery of their emancipation. The indignities that Jim endures in the last chapters of *Huckleberry Finn* may be seen as reflecting the unpleasant realities of the post-Reconstruction South.

Finding the Novel's Strengths

To a much greater extent than in Clemens's other books, *Huckleberry Finn* is a novel that requires repeated readings to uncover its many levels of meaning and artistic and ironic nuances. At its first and most accessible level, *Huckleberry Finn* is an irresistible adventure story filled with both explicit and subtle humor. Although Clemens himself appears not to have appreciated the greatness of this novel, he was right on the money when he called his unfinished manuscript a crackling good story. It is filled with colorful and sometimes astonishing characters, it contains thrilling action and moving melodrama, and it frequently supplies exciting surprises. On top of all that, it is set on the majestic Mississippi River, whose power and inexorable movement give its story a clear form.

On its surface, *Huckleberry Finn* is a straightforward sequel to the boy's story *The Adventures of Tom Sawyer*. Indeed, if its first several chapters were to be grafted onto the end of that earlier novel, the earlier narrative would continue smoothly. However, *Huckleberry Finn* is a very different kind of book, and that fact is evident in its opening paragraph, in which Huck introduces himself as the novel's narrator. By using a young, uneducated boy as his narrator, Clemens was able to detach himself from his narrative and tell his story through the eyes of an innocent and ignorant observer who naively reports his observations and neither interprets nor judges what he sees.

One of the products of Huck's naïveté is the natural honesty of the novel's narrative. As Huck witnesses instances of brutality, lying, cheating, and hypocrisy, he merely describes them and makes little or no attempt to evaluate them. From the reader's viewpoint, Huck's naive observations often add to the humor of many episodes because of his inability to understand what he observes. A prime example occurs in chapter 22. While Huck is watching a circus, a drunken man disrupts the show by insisting that he be allowed to ride a horse. He finally gets his way, only to have the horse that he mounts break loose and take him on a wild and hair-raising ride. Huck becomes worried sick about the danger the man is in, but to Huck's astonishment, the man takes firm control of the horse, sheds his clothes to reveal a gaudy circus costume, and demonstrates his riding skills. Huck's sympathy then shifts to the ostensibly embarrassed ringmaster, who appears to have been taken in by the rider's ruse. It never occurs to Huck that this drunken-rider act is a regular part of the show.

The Issue of Slavery

Huck's role as a narrator also serves to strengthen the novel in other, more subtle ways. One of the strongest objections that has been made to *Huckleberry Finn* is that it fails to condemn slavery explicitly. There is some validity to that charge. As the novel's narrator, Huck not only never condemns slavery, but he also frequently expresses views that support the notion that slaves are the rightful property of their owners. One such moment occurs in chapter 16, in which Jim expresses his hopes for the future and says that if he and his wife cannot buy the freedom of their children, "they'd get an Ab'litionist to go and steal them." When Huck hears those words, he is shocked and regrets helping Jim to escape:

> Thinks I, this is what comes of my not thinking. Here was this nigger which I had as good as helped to run away, coming right out flat-footed and saying he would steal his children—children that belonged to a man I didn't even know; a man that hadn't ever done me no harm.

Passages such as that appear to support the view that *Huckleberry Finn* fails to condemn slavery. However, it is through Huck's actions, rather than his words, that slavery is condemned. Trained to believe that slavery is condoned by Christianity, he believes he is sinning by helping Jim. Eventually, he decides to purge himself of sin by writing a letter to Jim's rightful owner, Miss Watson, to tell her where she can find her slave (chapter 31). For a moment, he feels "good and all washed clean of sin for the first time." However, as he thinks about what a good friend Jim is, his heart softens, and he relents. He then concludes "All right, then, I'll go to hell" and tears up the letter. One of the ironies of the novel is that Huck usually does the right thing, while thinking that he is doing the wrong thing. That is a point of view that can only be sustained by having him narrate his story.

Language and Realism

At the time *Huckleberry Finn* was first published, some people—most notably author Louisa May

Alcott—condemned the book as unsuitable for children. One of the reasons advanced was the coarseness of the novel's language. Huck occasionally uses rough words, such as "dang," "hell," and "sweat." Equally objectionable was his grammar. He constantly uses words such as "t'other," "ain't," and "warn't"; he frequently uses double negatives; and he often fractures his syntax. The fact is, however, that Huck's language is an authentic rendering of the way that real Missouri boys would have spoken during the mid-19th century. There is a naturalness and vigor about his language that gives his narrative a vitality that holds up well more than a century after the book was written. Indeed, *Huckleberry Finn*'s language has come to be regarded as one of its major strengths. By telling his story in an authentic American frontier vernacular, Clemens broke away from the American literary mainstream, which generally imitated the genteel forms of European literature, and helped to liberate American literature. Huck Finn is now often considered to be the progenitor of characters later created by writers such as Ring Lardner, Ernest Hemingway, Sherwood Anderson, Gertrude Stein, William Faulkner, and a score of other major American writers. Lionel Trilling credited the novel with establishing "for written prose the virtues of American colloquial speech," and it may well have been Huck's vigorous language that Hemingway was thinking of when he said that "All modern American literature" comes from *Huckleberry Finn*.

There is, however, much more to Huck's language than its primitive coarseness. Huck is also capable of lyrical and evocative passages of surprising power. He is particularly good at creating vivid images of life on the Mississippi River, which Clemens knew so intimately. A particularly moving passage opens chapter 19, in which Huck and Jim resume drifting down the river on their raft after Huck has escaped from the nightmarish and senseless violence of the Shepherdson-Grangerford feud. Here Huck describes a typical morning, when they tied up the raft so they could hide during the daylight hours:

> Next we slid into the river and had a swim, so as to freshen up and cool off; then we set down

on the sandy bottom where the water was about knee deep, and watched the daylight come. Not a sound, anywheres—perfectly still—just like the whole world was asleep, only sometimes the bull-frogs a-cluttering, maybe. The first thing to see, looking away over the water, was a kind of dull line—that was the woods on t'other side—you couldn't make nothing else out; then a pale place in the sky; then more paleness, spreading around; then the river softened up, away off, and warn't black any more, but gray; you could see little dark spots drifting along, ever so far away-trading scows, and such things; and long black streaks—rafts; sometimes you could hear a sweep screaking; or jumbled up voices, it was so still, and sounds come so far. . . .

The Question of Racism

Of the many charges made against *Huckleberry Finn*, perhaps the most contentious is the claim that the novel reflects white racist views. Among the evidence amassed in support of that charge, Exhibit A is the book's generous use of the word *nigger*. In 1957, when the National Association for the Advancement of Colored People (NAACP) sought to have the book banned from New York public schools, it cited the novel's "excessive use of 'nigger.'" It is true that the novel does use that word frequently (more than 200 times), but does that fact alone make the book "racist"? The first thing to keep in mind is that the narrative is told, not in Clemens's voice, but in Huck's. Clemens uses the word *nigger* only when he puts it in the mouths of his characters. In *Huckleberry Finn*, every word of the narrative comes through the voice of Huck. In the only nonnarrative portions of the text, the brief prefatory notes, the only allusion to African Americans uses the term *negro*. In *Tom Sawyer*, Clemens's only Tom and Huck story that is not narrated by Huck, the word *nigger* appears nine times, but only in its characters' dialogue. When Clemens speaks in the voice of that novel's anonymous narrator, he uses only *negro* and *colored* to refer to African Americans.

It is understandable why many readers are uncomfortable with a text that repeatedly uses a word as emotionally charged as *nigger*, especially when that word comes out of the mouths of white people. However, readers should understand that the word reflects the usage of the time and place in which *Huckleberry Finn* is set. An ignorant mid-19th-century boy such as Huck would not have used any other word to refer to black people, especially slaves. To put any other word in his mouth would be unnatural and would detract from the realism of his vernacular voice. More to the point, however, is the way in which the word is employed. Huck never uses it as a term of disrespect. Moreover, one of the few remarks that he makes about African Americans that appears to be disrespectful occurs at the end of the wonderful passage in chapter 14 in which he argues with Jim about the biblical king Solomon. That chapter concludes with Huck's remarking, "you can't learn a nigger to argue." However, even that remark can scarcely be construed as a reflection of the author's racist attitude, as the remark is ironic. Huck's attempt to best Jim in an argument is entirely unsuccessful, as Jim outargues him on every point. Instead of recognizing that he has been defeated by a black man—whom he describes elsewhere in the same chapter as having "an uncommon level head, for a nigger"—Huck incorrectly concludes that black people cannot argue properly. To perceptive readers, however, it is clear that the novel is, in fact, demonstrating that a black person is perfectly capable of exercising logic superior to that of a white person. Indeed, in this passage and in many others, the strongest message that the novel conveys is that no one race is superior to any other.

Although *Huckleberry Finn*'s evasion chapters muddy the question of how Clemens depicts Jim, neither Jim nor any other of the novel's numerous black characters ever behaves in a fashion that might be considered shameful. However, the same cannot be said for the novel's white characters. Even Huck is not above criticism. On two occasions (in chapters 10 and 15), he plays mean-spirited jokes on Jim. To his credit, he comes to regret those jokes and in chapter 15 humbles himself enough to apologize to Jim, but Jim's conduct toward him is beyond reproach. Jim consistently goes out of his way to look after Huck and to show his affection for him. At the climax of the novel, he

even sacrifices his own freedom to help Tom, despite the ordeal through which Tom has put him. Like Jim, some of the other black characters in the novel—none of whom plays a major role—occasionally behave foolishly, but none of them ever acts dishonorably.

By contrast, many of the novel's white characters are despicable. They include drunken loafers, unscrupulous con men—such as the King and the Duke—thieves and murderers, and hypocrites, such as the feuding Grangerfords and Shepherdsons, who attend church services to listen to pious sermons about brotherly love, while keeping their guns handy (chapter 18). Through Huck's innocent descriptions of white misbehavior, *Huckleberry Finn* implicitly condemns not only individual white characters but also the culture that they represent. Huck rarely fully understands what he describes, but by the end of his narrative, it is clear that he is sick to death of the southern white culture that he takes to be "sivilization," and it is no wonder that he is anxious to light out for the territory.

CRITICAL COMMENTARY: HUCK FINN AND TOM SAWYER

Clemens decided that Huckleberry Finn, and not Tom Sawyer, was the right character to be the protagonist of his sequel to *The Adventures of Tom Sawyer*. Nonetheless, such is Tom's personality that his presence challenges Huck's potential heroism at the beginning and the end of the novel. Tom's charisma, to which Huck's awe contributes, is perhaps the reason Clemens rejected him as main character; Tom overwhelms or overshadows. A leader who needs followers, Tom attracts them because he knows where to go and what to do and can cite the best authorities. Huck willingly follows him because he is less sure. If he senses flaws in Tom's declarations, Huck can offer only his thinking, no match for Tom's codes, traditions, customs, and rules. Unlike Huck, Tom would not bond with runaway slave Jim; like his society, Tom would dominate Jim (as he does others) or, as the last chapters show, use him, treating him as less than human. Despite his mischievousness, Tom is very much part of his society, whether or not he realizes it. With nothing to run from, he is not the outsider

Huck is. To Huck and the other boys, Tom seems free because he defies the authority of Aunt Polly and other adults, uses his imagination to enhance his play, and manipulates others to his thinking. Intelligent and shrewd but entangled in the authorities he cites, Tom represents the society from which Huck runs. Huck admires Tom, bows to his superior knowledge, and wants to be like him (even briefly becoming Tom at the end of the novel), but Huck, in fleeing societal restraints, subconsciously runs from his friend, and Tom's absence defines Huck.

Tom's Cruelty

Huck does not realize that latent in Tom's play—indeed, in many children's games—is cruelty. Clemens sees Tom's play as microcosmic of the roles society assigns people to play, such as those designating race and class. Tom's rules are like the rules society enforces that actually hide cruelty and blind people to the truth. By projecting Tom's game-making not only into the world beyond St. Petersburg where Huck ventures but also upon St. Petersburg before Huck leaves, Clemens creates a metaphor that clarifies why Huck flees and why he returns, implying that escape must be more than physical, that freedom is illusionary, and that societal changes will not occur without changes in people. By extending Tom's initially attractive traits to logical negative extremes, Clemens slightly alters Tom's personality in the beginning and more emphatically in the end to represent the world of repression from which Huck runs.

Tom's reappearance in the last third of the novel suggests that Huck cannot escape this society. Huck does not realize that he metaphorically runs from Tom, and he does not wish to escape Tom. Indeed, he wants to be with Tom. After fundamentalist, uptight Miss Watson tells Huck that Tom will not go to the "good place" she has described, Huck is pleased, because he would rather be in hell with Tom than with her in heaven. At the end of *Tom Sawyer*, after Huck complains about the restrictions of living with the Widow Douglas, who has unofficially adopted him, Tom tells him, "Huck, we can't let you into the gang if you ain't respectable, you know." In answer, Huck pleads, "Now, Tom, hain't

you always ben friendly to me? You wouldn't shet me out, would you, Tom? You wouldn't do that, now, *would* you, Tom?" and agrees to go back to the widow. Huck enters this society to become respectable in Tom's eyes. Tom has told him that the robbers he wants to emulate in his gang are high-toned, sometimes "awful high up in the nobility—dukes and such" (chapter 35), as if foreshadowing those "high-toned" people Huck would later meet in his own novel, aristocrats who ambush each other, a gentleman who cold-bloodedly shoots an unarmed man, two men called King and Duke who fleece the gullible and innocent. This respectability is metaphorically suspect. Huck seeks ties to Tom's gang because he has ties to nothing. He lacks Tom's confidence.

His admiration for Tom undiluted, Huck does not realize that Tom in this final scene of *Tom Sawyer* has not only placed him in those shackles but has also set him up to experience the sharpest cruelty in *Huckleberry Finn* and the disillusionments of his journey. Huck enjoys Tom's company. Despite his faults, Tom brings excitement, adventure, and often fun when he enters a scene. Huck expresses the seemingly universal respect for Tom's abilities in frequent evocations of his name, recognizing his cleverness and bravado, desiring Tom's help or insight, justifying his own words or actions, and comparing Tom and himself.

Although *Tom Sawyer* concludes positively, with Huck looking forward to joining Tom's gang of robbers, the step to emotional hurt for Huck is a short stretch of Tom's imagination. Huck first experiences cruelty in his own novel from Tom, the person he most admires. The society represented by Tom relies upon artificial, often unjust, rules that encourage, and endorse, mistreatment of those outside the rules and the society. At one point, Huck stops him from tying a sleeping Jim "to the tree for fun," but "nothing would do Tom but he must . . . play something on him" (chapter 2). The resulting joke is relatively harmless, but the inclination implies a meaner streak in the Tom of this novel.

The point is not that Tom is malicious or that Huck is a stranger to cruelty and emotional pain. The novel is not a maturation story in the strictest sense because Huck knows of evil and many of the harshest realities of life, including cruelty, before he leaves his hometown. Naive and ignorant but not a traditional innocent, Huck cusses, smokes, skips school, is subject to no rules, and experiences scarce parental interference. As Huck admires Tom, Tom and the other boys envy Huck; however, his mother long dead, he has grown up without love as the son of an abusive alcoholic father who is mean, racist, ignorant, and dishonest. Huck has been periodically abandoned, sometimes beaten, and had to learn to fend for himself. Indeed, the most frightening person Huck encounters in his novel is his father, Pap Finn. He continues to witness and experience suffering on his journey. He watches Boggs and Buck Grangerford die, is mistreated by the Duke and the King, and witnesses the mistreatment of Jim, along with much more. What Huck begins to realize, as repeatedly reinforced by incidents down the river, is the ambiguity of life and that matters are rarely all black or all white. Lionel Trilling writes, "*Huckleberry Finn*. . . . deals directly with the virtue and depravity of man's heart." Virtue and depravity frequently occur in the same person. Tom surprises readers of *Huckleberry Finn,* as his virtues dim beside some depravities, such as his tormenting Jim and prolonging his enslavement at the end of the novel.

Social Injustice

Much of the injustice in this society is caused by adherence to unjust rules, written and unwritten, that fail to fit all situations and consider human consequences. Tom bows to the authority of romantic books and imposes the "laws" he derives from them upon others: " 'I've seen it in books; and so of course that's what we've got to do' " (chapter 2).

Miss Watson's Bible is her equivalent to Tom's books of romance; less adaptive and imaginative than Tom, she is a close follower of scripture. Following Christ's directive ("when thou prayest, enter into thy closet" [Matt. 6:6]) she literally takes Huck into the closet to pray. On the other hand, she calls Huck a fool for taking literally her claim that whatever he prays for he will receive. Like many who accept literally, she does so on her own terms. Like others who own slaves, she misses the

contradiction between slavery and religious teachings. Miss Watson's Bible—which teaches brotherhood, the Golden Rule, love of neighbor, even love of enemies—is also used to justify slavery.

Legislative laws and court decisions, as applied, are similarly contradictory. Though the rationale for laws is protection of property and person, laws enforcing slavery consider people property. A person can not only lose personal freedom but also be stripped of his or her entire family because the family belongs to someone else. Exemplifying this legal separation of families, Jim intends to save money to "buy his wife, which was owned on a farm close to . . . Miss Watson . . . and they would both work to buy the two children; and if their master wouldn't sell them, they'd get an ab'litionist to go and steal them"; this audacious assertion shocks Huck: "It most froze me to hear such talk. . . . Just see what a difference it made in him the minute he judged he was about free . . . coming out flatfooted and saying he would steal his children—children that belonged to a man I didn't even know; a man that hadn't done me no harm" (chapter 16). Those who follow the laws lose sight of others' humanity. Laws supporting slavery, such as the Fugitive Slave Act, are the most unjust of all. Legality is not the only standard of freedom.

Custom, Folklore, and Tradition

In addition to laws, customs, traditions, ancient codes, folk beliefs, and superstitions are also important in Tom and Huck's society. These things acquire respect from being handed down through generations; the weight of years gives them the power of law. Clemens writes in "Pudd'nhead Wilson's New Calendar," "Let me make the superstitions of a nation and I care not who makes its laws or its songs either" (*Following the Equator,* chapter 51). Significantly, Huck enters *Tom Sawyer* carrying a dead cat to be used at the cemetery that night to rid himself of warts; he and Tom then seriously discuss other wart-removing methods derived from the same sources (*TS*, chapter 6). A non-superstitious parallel occurs in *Huckleberry Finn* when Huck smells the dead cats, among the rotten tomatoes and other items, that villagers intend to throw at the Duke in vengeance for his cheating them. Huck's use of the cat and consideration of other cures with Tom—along with Pap's beliefs about witches, other slaves' reverence for Jim's stories about witches riding him, Jim's prophesying with the ox hairball, and his and Huck's linking the snakeskin with bad luck—all illustrate respect for the supernatural. In many ways, the pull of superstition is stronger than that of law for this culture, awing Huck, Tom, Jim, and other characters.

Similarly, though they mean little to Huck, tradition and custom are more important than law. Years of shooting, maiming, and killing are sufficient for the Shepherdsons and Grangerfords to justify their feud. Buck Grangerford defines a feud, in effect, as a tradition of killing, and then explains its origins to Huck: "A man has a quarrel with another man, and kills him; then that other man's brother kills HIM; then the other brothers, on both sides, goes for one another; then the COUSINS chip in—and by and by everybody's killed off, and there ain't no more feud. But it's kind of slow, and takes a long time" (chapter 18). People, however, also reinterpret custom according to circumstances. When Colonel Grangerford expresses disapproval of Buck's shooting at Harney Shepherdson from behind a bush rather than facing him, Buck typically establishes custom with precedent: "The Shepherdsons don't, father. They always take advantage" (chapter 18).

Romanticism

Tom, too, establishes customs among his peers with traditions he culls from the rituals preserved in his books. Citing and adapting ceremonial behavior derived from tales of Robin Hood, pirates, knighthood, and thieves, Tom inflicts romantic notions upon his playmates that resemble the lockstep romantic notions Clemens elsewhere called the "Sir Walter [Scott] Disease," which, he believed, paralyzed southern thinking, freezing the society in the past and tying it to obsolete modes and manners: "There, the . . . civilization of the nineteenth century is . . . confused and commingled with the Walter Scott Middle-Age sham civilization and so . . . practical, common-sense, progressive works [have] mixed with the duel, the inflated speech, and the jejune romanticism of an absurd past that is dead, and out of charity ought to be buried" (*Life on the Mississippi,* chapter 46). A carrier of the Wal-

ter Scott disease, Tom Sawyer elaborates and expands on what he reads, not only applying, but also contributing to and even inventing, the unreasonable rules that people willingly follow. In Clemens's view, this kind of romanticism alters one's perceptions of reality; by setting people's eyes upon misplaced standards of chivalry, ceremony, honor, and revenge, romanticism diverts people from the actual.

Emmeline Grangerford's poetry is another example of rampant romanticism. Huck says Emmeline "could rattle off poetry like nothing. She didn't ever have to stop to think" (chapter 17), a comment about the literature and the people of this society. Huck may "take no stock in dead people" (chapter 1), but Emmeline certainly does. Amid the horrific killings of the honor-motivated feud, soon to include her brother Buck, Emmeline writes sentimental poetry glamorizing death, obscuring its reality. Her interest in death or suffering over life is of a pattern with Tom's intense preoccupation with following proper procedures, his and Huck's concern with the right order for supernatural spells and cures, Miss Watson's literalistic behavior, and the regulations governing the Grangerfords and Shepherdsons in their feud. As with many people, the eerie aspects of death fascinate Tom and Huck. These concerns generate a sense of their own that blocks common sense. A romantic aura—a prestige of idealism—attaches itself to these guidelines.

Honor Codes

Colonel Sherburn is a righteous man who feels justified in shooting unarmed Boggs. Here and elsewhere, the customs and traditions of honor codes sometimes contradict laws and logic. Colonel Sherburn is not, like Colonel Grangerford, an aristocrat by birth. Huck describes Grangerford as "a gentleman all over" (chapter 18). Whereas the Grangerford house, lands, and people positively impress Huck, the village of unpainted shacks, leaning fences, and weedy gardens where Sherburn is "the best dressed man in that town" is "just mud . . . nothing else *but* mud. . . ." (chapter 21). The villagers are loitering louts who stir only to watch dogfights, sick a dog on a nursing pig in the street, pour turpentine on and set fire to a dog, or laugh as one runs himself to death after they tie a tin pan to his tail. One of few people in town exerting effort, Sherburn is a storeowner for whom "the crowd drops back on each side" (chapter 21) to let him by. An aristocrat by virtue of superiority to his environment, he needs only glance around him to convince himself. He can believe that he, at least, has standards.

Enamored of his societal position, Sherburn easily feels superior to Boggs, who monthly combines a drunken spree with a tirade against a townsperson but never causes harm. Like a knight from a Scott romance, Sherburn follows the outward form of challenging a person who has insulted him to a duel; however, Boggs's reputation as a foulmouthed drunk is well known, and he has no weapon. Sherburn simply murders Boggs. As Tom adapts rituals to suit situations, so Sherburn twists the rules of dueling to salve his wounded pride. Like Buck Grangerford in shooting from ambush, Sherburn perverts the code to his advantage because he has paradoxically elevated it above the reality of the situation and values it more than humanity, as Tom and Miss Watson see what they must see to preserve their visions of the world even if doing so distorts their vision. Sherburn is, in effect, playing games, like Tom, without even mild compassion for those beneath him.

This blindness to actuality can lead to disastrous consequences. The Grangerfords and the Shepherdsons—their similarities and differences indicated by their names (referring to those who plant and those who graze animals)—live side by side and share a boat landing. Their conflicts may be seen as analogous to that of the North and the South. Similarly the name "Sherburn" may be a combination of Sherman, Sheridan, and Burnside (Union generals, all of whom the author knew by the time he published the novel) with a southern colonel, and Sherburn's violence, pride, honor, and a sense of insult intended to recall the Civil War and the senselessness that contributed to it. In the needless deaths of Boggs and the Grangerfords and the subjugation of his friend Jim, Huck observes the horrifying results of a civilization based on the honor codes portrayed by Scott, with a religion and culture perverted to fit the falsity.

Conformity

Huck, at least initially, attempts to conform to society. Pap Finn, however, stands completely against it. Pap accepts no authority and respects nothing. A new judge, who does not know Pap, accepts Pap's assurance of reform, including a signed pledge, and provides him a new coat and "a beautiful . . . spare room" in his own house; Pap trades the coat for whiskey and devastates the room (chapter 5). Huck reports: "Every time he got money he got drunk; and every time he got drunk he raised Cain around town; and every time he raised Cain he got jailed" (chapter 6). Though he neither acknowledges nor takes responsibility for anything, Pap believes that people and life generally deny him his due: "A man can't get his rights in a govment like this" (chapter 6). Like the Duke and the King, Pap follows no law but survival. Pap's rationale for having children is that they can "go to work and . . . do suthin' for him and give him a rest." He continually charges violation of his rights but grants no rights to and frequently assaults those of others: ". . . he wouldn't a give me the road if I hadn't shoved him out o' the way" (chapter 6). A bully and a child abuser, Pap dies under unknown circumstances, shot in the back, likely, by companions in crime. Pap is an argument for rules. Huck's novel does not oppose law, codes, or standards of behavior but rather the blind or unthinking acceptance of rules. Huck is caught between worlds.

Huck falls back into his old life after Pap kidnaps and imprisons him. Resuming old habits, Huck enjoys life in the woods, except for the beatings. Although this life is nearly freedom for him, Huck—who liked living at the widow's to an extent—subconsciously yearns for more structure. Partly for that reason, he is drawn to Tom. More a part of society than he realizes, Tom—with a stable family, social relationships, and a permanent home—also instills structure into his existence with his reading and imagination.

Huck is unsure; Tom is confident. Huck longs for confidence and stability, but to gain them, he loses freedom; and what is worse is that he must conform to a way of life he cannot fully accept or understand. Cramped by rules (and fear of Pap), Huck runs. Tom represents those rules and conformity to them. Throughout the novel, Huck encounters aspects of society that reflect Tom Sawyer's play and personality. Huck overcomes Jim's objections to boarding a wrecked boat by citing the loot they might find and by asserting, "Do you reckon Tom Sawyer would ever go by this thing?. . . He'd call it an adventure—that's what he'd call it; and he'd land on that wreck if it was his last act" (chapter 12). He also uses Tom to urge himself to satisfy his curiosity about voices he hears on the boat: "Tom Sawyer wouldn't back out now, and so I won't either. . . ." Tom's bravado helps place Huck in danger when the real pirates Bill and Jake, as in the blood oath signed by the robbers of Tom Sawyer's Gang, plot to kill Jim and take his share of their plunder for betraying them. Despite what Tom says, no honor exists among these thieves. Huck meets the harsh reality of Tom's world of "noble" robbers just as the steamboat *Walter Scott,* symbolizing romanticism, collides against the hard rocks of the shore, symbolizing realism, and sinks. On the other hand, Tom and Jim's raft, until it is invaded by the Duke and the King, is an island of sanity apart from the shore, where the reality of people constantly disappoints and the ambiguity of their behavior is frustrating.

Social Contradictions

On land, the contradictions of society are many and inescapable. Not only are the Shepherdsons and the Grangerfords churchgoing people who kill each other, but they also attend the same church, to which they bring their rifles. Ironically, they consider a sermon about brotherly love to be a good one. Colonel Sherburn applies the gentleman's code to a man he does not consider a gentleman, and because Boggs is not a gentleman, Sherburn does not grant him a choice of weapons or allow him to secure one. A seeming coward for shooting a man known to be harmless and to cause a ruckus only when drunk, Sherburn subsequently, single-handedly and bravely, faces down a lynch mob, there for hatred of him, not love of Boggs. After killing Boggs and after quelling the mob, he contemptuously throws his weapon down, scornful that these people would even consider questioning his behavior. Even his contempt has become ceremonial.

The contradictions in the everyday life of this society are most evident in Jim's situation. Presumed to be an ignorant slave, Jim understands and feels deep human emotions. His advice is usually sound, and Huck regrets not following it. He often comprehends problems instinctively but also logically. At the end of the novel, Tom knows that Jim has been set free but refuses to tell him, so that he can play his elaborate game of helping him to escape; Jim is therefore free but not free. Despite his nobility and strength of character, Jim is both the victim of Tom and the ultimate victim of this society, which Tom represents. Like his society, Tom does not see a human being in Jim but an object to be exploited. Huck comes to see Jim's humanity.

Jim's life in the novel is framed by the jokes played upon him—Tom's joke at the beginning, two by Huck within the story, and the escape plot contrived by Tom at the conclusion. Some of these jokes turn to Jim's advantage. The first joke (removing Jim's hat as he sleeps and placing it on a tree limb) leads to Jim's complicated explanation that witches had bewitched him, ridden him long distances, taken him to see the devil, and put his hat in the tree—a story that becomes more involved with each telling. Tom might laugh at Jim's foolishness, but Jim uses the joke to elevate his status among the other slaves (Smith 364). Later instances of Jim's wisdom hint that he knows the truth.

In their cruelty, Huck's jokes on Jim parallel Tom's earlier joke and anticipate Tom's final joke on him. After they examine their loot from the floating house, Huck—eager to make fun of Jim's claim that handling a snakeskin brings bad luck—places the skin of a rattlesnake he has killed in Jim's bedding, forgetting that a snake's mate curls around its skin, and the mate bites Jim on the heel. Jim is "laid up for four days and nights" (65). Huck does not tell Jim he placed the snake and says he will never hold a snakeskin again. As Jim uses superstition to prevent Huck from asking about the dead body (Pap) Jim found in the floating house by saying such talk is bad luck (chapter 10), so he uses it to solidify his position of wisdom, and—unknowingly—to humble Huck. The incident foreshadows

Tom's proposing a rattlesnake as a pet for imprisoned Jim in Tom's most contrived joke: "A prisoner's got to have some kind of a dumb pet, and if a rattlesnake hain't ever been tried, why there's more glory to be gained." Jim, more quickly than Huck, sees the emptiness of Tom's calls to glory: " 'I doan' *want* no sich glory. Snake take 'n bite Jim's chin off, den *whah* is de glory?' " (chapter 38).

Huck's second and last joke on Jim is a turning point of the novel. When Huck, in their canoe, separated from Jim on the raft by fog, finds Jim asleep the next morning amid signs that he has endured a terrific struggle with the river, Jim is overjoyed to see him, but Huck swears he has been nowhere and convinces Jim that the fog and their separation did not occur. Accepting with difficulty Huck's adamant word that all was a dream, Jim describes its reality, including his almost drowning, saying he must interpret "de powerfullest dream I ever see . . . because it was sent for a warning." As Jim becomes absorbed in interpretation, Huck springs his punch line by pointing to the debris on the raft and asking "what does *these* things stand for?" (chapter 15). After readjusting his mind, Jim tells Huck how worried he was about him and how grateful he was to see Huck safe, then says, "Dat truck dah is trash; en trash is what people is dat puts dirt on de head er dey fren's en makes 'em ashamed." Here, a 19th-century runaway slave has come close to calling an antebellum white person trash. Huck, however, knows, or feels, that Jim is right: "It made me feel so mean I could almost kissed *his* foot to get him to take it back." Tom's cruelty to Jim and then to Huck finds its way into Huck's cruelty to Jim, but Huck does what Tom would not do; he apologizes. Huck realizes he has hurt another human being: "I didn't do him no more mean tricks, and I wouldn't done that one if I'd a knowed it would make him feel that way" (chapter 15).

Conscience v. Conformity

By the time Tom reappears in chapter 33, Huck has fought his conscience and won, vowing to go to hell rather than turn in Jim, but the King has illegally sold Jim with a counterfeit reward notice. Tom's final joke on Jim reintroduces Huck to the hellish frustration of restrictions and entanglements that Huck has run from but cannot escape. Just before this, the boys' roles are reversed. Coming to the Phelps farm after learning that Jim is captive there, Huck is mistaken for Tom by the Phelpses, relatives who expect him. There, Huck becomes the person he has long admired: "if they was joyful, it warn't nothing to what I was; for it was like being born again, I was so glad to find out who I was" (chapter 32). Huck had been a nobody. Other boys envied him but did not wish to trade places with him. Huck is pleased to become his hero, Tom, but he does not truly become a new person, and Tom becomes even more Tom when he realizes where Jim is being kept. Informed of the deception by Huck, Tom pretends to be his half-brother Sid, which is appropriate since, as the critic Frank Baldanza says, Huck "is to Tom what Tom is to Sid"—less clever, articulate, and brave in matters involving "civilized resourcefulness" (107).

When Tom quickly agrees to help Huck release Jim, Huck—who loves Jim but has not resolved the conflicts of societal expectations—thinks, ". . . I'm bound to say Tom Sawyer fell, considerable, in my estimation. Only I couldn't believe it. Tom Sawyer a *nigger stealer!*" (chapter 33). Tom, however, is not violating one of the most sacred tenets of his community, as Huck believes; he is plotting a joke as an adventure that he thinks carries fewer risks than Huck imagines. Knowing that Miss Watson freed Jim in her will, Tom does not step outside the bounds of conduct in his world, for he now imagines Jim to be an unjustly held prisoner like those in romantic novels.

After Tom explains why he knows Jim is in the cabin, Huck's response epitomizes the contradictions of society: "It shows how a body can see and don't see, at the same time" (chapter 34). Like so many people in the novel, Tom sees the rule but not the reality. He rejects Huck's simpler and more sensible ideas for freeing Jim as not "romantical enough." Huck proposes lifting the bed to remove Jim's shackle; Tom wants Jim to saw its leg off: "I bet we can find a way that's twice as long" (chapter 34). Tom regrets that no moat surrounds the cabin and suggests digging one. Though Tom prolongs the process as much as possible and is happy that armed farmers appear in response to his letter, the three finally make their escape, and Tom is more delighted when he realizes he has been shot, an unexpected "romantical" touch.

Lawrence Holland observes that Jim and Huck, crediting Tom's unmerited heroism, believe that Tom would not place his well-being before others, so as Jim sacrifices his freedom to allow Tom to see a doctor, he and Huck "are as close in rapport as they have ever been." Symbolically, they help preserve the culture for which Tom stands by returning to it. Tom tells everyone Jim is free and gives Jim money for his patience. Meanwhile, not only has Jim's freedom been delayed, but he has also been captured wearing a dress, is roughly handled by his captors, and threatened with hanging. Jim, supported by Huck, emerges the noblest person, but Tom, as usual, is the center of the action.

Emancipation and Betrayal

Eric Sundquist says that in this last part of the novel, "Twain's penetrating vision into the moral collapse of post–Civil War promises of black equality still leaves Jim every inch a man—dignified, compassionate, and wise." Tom calls the escape an "evasion" because his books use that label for escapes of "prisoners of style" (chapter 39). The term seems appropriate because commentators have long found this episode's meaning evasive. Ernest Hemingway, as noted above, suggested skipping this part, but critic Victor Doyno—surprised at the little outrage by earlier reviewers that Tom "deceitfully conspired to keep Jim imprisoned"—observes that, in his famous praise, Hemingway misreads this section by linking the boys as if they hold the same attitude about Jim. This final section has been the most harshly criticized, but possibly Clemens meant it to be tiresome, so that readers grow tired of Tom and his excesses.

One critic accuses Tom of "racist torment of Jim" (Sundquist 11); another says in Tom is "demonic power . . . an urge that mingles love and hatred, creativity and destruction . . ." (Seelye 51). Doyno, Fishkin, Holland, and Sundquist agree that in this section Clemens comments on "the situation of freed Black people in the South both before and after the Civil War" ("Afterword," 15). Fishkin

asks, "Is what America did to the ex-slaves any less insane than what Tom Sawyer put Jim through in the novel?" and "What is the history of post-emancipation race relations in the United States if not a series of maneuvers as cruelly gratuitous as the indignities inflicted on Jim in the final section of *Huckleberry Finn?*" (Fishkin 143, 144). Tom, willingly delaying Jim's release, reflects the denial of freedom experienced by many black people before and since the Civil War.

Huck is stuck in the real world, as Tom is not. Huck sees things more or less as they are, unobscured by what glazes Tom's and much of society's eyes. He tries to travel the simplest and straightest route, but he is not a pragmatist who can stick to this philosophy. He does the best he can under the circumstances. He lacks the guidelines or the imagination of Tom Sawyer to aid him in his adventures. He does not have the "style" he admires so much in Tom. Huck's imaginative power serves him in creating elaborate lies, not in creating new worlds out of his surroundings.

Just as Huck does not renounce the laws and customs he defies, Huck does not renounce Tom. He cannot escape them or Tom Sawyer, as best exemplified by Tom's appearance at the end of the story and by Huck's many references to him. As he says, Huck does not "wish to go back on no regulations" (chapter 35). He adopts a laissez-faire attitude and wishes others would do so regarding him. When Aunt Polly—who has a personality between those of the Widow Douglas and Miss Watson—mentions adopting Huck, he reacts with "I been there before" (chapter 43) and proposes escaping to the Indian Territory. Interestingly, Tom has already said that he, Huck, and Jim should sneak out one night to "go for howling adventures amongst the Injuns, over in the Territory." Typically, Tom's proposal is for adventure and Huck's is for survival.

Running to the Territory is not a solution; neither is going downriver, but at least this trip made Huck more aware and more willing to accept someone at his true worth, not at the value imposed by society. Civilization does not eradicate ambiguity but rather complicates and confuses issues with rules, regulations, habits, customs, and beliefs, notions of honor and religion—written and unwritten, legal and extralegal. Only in such a culture of "established" and, therefore, complex standards can Tom's worlds really be imagined and carried to extremes by the degree of adherence to or faith in them.

Clemens offers no definite answers in his novel. He suggests an approach, that of recognizing the multifaceted quality of life and human nature and of attempting to see the essential worth of a situation or person. Huck and Jim are each more aware of the ambiguity of civilized life after their trip and each values the other more as a human being. In the end, Huck seeks escape from civilization, and Fishkin wonders, ". . . How can a society that debases human lives on a mass scale consider itself civilized?" Huck, however, demonstrates the compassion of which people are capable. At the circus, as the audience laughs at the man pretending to be drunk, Huck thinks, "It warn't funny to me, though; I was all of a tremble to see his danger" (chapter 22); that the man is actually in no danger only emphasizes Huck's concern for his fellow creatures. The contrast between his feelings for a stranger and Tom's treatment of Jim is deep.

By contrasting Tom Sawyer with Huck Finn, Clemens contrasts vividly the real with the false. You cannot, as Huck puts it, "pray a lie."

Critical Commentary by John H. Davis

DRAMATIC ADAPTATIONS

Since *Huckleberry Finn*'s publication in 1884, its story has inspired numerous stage plays and musicals, more than a half-dozen feature films, and a like number of television productions, as well as cartoons and even an opera. While many of these adaptations have treated certain episodes of the novel faithfully, none has attempted to adapt all the book's major episodes. Ironically, the very first dramatic production to be called "Huckleberry Finn" had almost nothing to do with the novel. In November 1902, a Klaw and Erlanger musical titled *Huckleberry Finn* ran briefly in Hartford. This production used Jim and several other *Huckleberry Finn* characters, but was actually based mostly on episodes from *Tom Sawyer*.

The PBS production of *Huckleberry Finn* in 1985 was the most ambitious attempt to film the novel in its entirety. *(Public Broadcasting System)*

The first film adaptation, in 1920, was a silent movie titled *Huckleberry Finn*, featuring Lewis Sargent (1904–?) as Huck and George Reed (1867–1952) as Jim. Shot on Mississippi River locations, the film was designed to resemble E. W. KEMBLE's original book illustrations. Paramount produced the first sound film adaptation in 1931. This production was actually a sequel to Paramount's 1930 *Tom Sawyer*, with Junior Durkin (1915–1935) returning as Huck and Jackie Coogan (1914–1984) as Tom; Clarence Muse (1889–1979) played Jim. In order to capitalize on *Tom Sawyer*'s success, the film gave Becky Thatcher a major role and had Tom accompany Huck and Jim on their raft journey. Eight years later, MGM released a more orthodox adaptation, with Mickey Rooney (1920–) as Huck and Rex Ingram (1895–1969)—who was born on a steamboat near CAIRO, Illinois—as Jim. William Frawley (1887–1966), later known as Fred Mertz in "I Love Lucy," played the Duke. In contrast to the Paramount production, this film did not use Tom Sawyer at all.

It was not until two decades later that another feature film was made from *Huckleberry Finn*. Meanwhile, several adaptations appeared on television in the mid-1950s, and Josh Logan announced in 1951 that a BROADWAY musical, *Huck and Jim*, with book by Maxwell Anderson and music by Kurt Weill, was under production. This play was never produced, however, possibly because MGM announced the following year that it planned to produce a musical film version of *Huckleberry Finn* that would star Dean Stockwell (1936–) as Huck, Gene Kelly as the King, and Danny Kaye as the Duke. This film was not produced, either, but MGM released the first color film adaptation of the novel in 1960 as *The Adventures of Huckleberry Finn*, a big-budget production with several songs by Alan Jay Lerner and Burton Lane. Eddie Hodges (1947–) played Huck, and boxing champion Archie Moore (1913–) was Jim. An example of the condensation that typifies adaptations is the film's reduction of the entire Grangerford–Shepherdson feud to a two-minute description.

In 1974, Reader's Digest and United Artists combined to release *Huckleberry Finn* as a musical sequel to their previous year's *Tom Sawyer*. Jeff East (1957–) returned as Huck, and Paul Winfield (1941–2004) played Jim. The following year, a new television film of *Huckleberry Finn* aired on ABC-TV, with 21-year-old Ron Howard (1954–) as Huck and his "Happy Days" costar Donny Most (1953–) as Tom Sawyer. Antonio Fargas (1946–), soon to be a regular on "Starsky and Hutch," played Jim, and Royal Dano (1922–1994) appeared as Mark Twain to introduce the story. The 1979 television play MARK TWAIN: BENEATH THE LAUGHTER dramatized two poignant scenes from *Huckleberry Finn* that rarely appear in full-length productions. Another television film, *The Adventures of Huckleberry Finn*, aired on NBC-TV in July 1981, though it was made two years earlier. In this production, Kurt Ida played Huck and Brock Peters (1927–2005) played Jim; Larry Storch (1923–) and Forrest Tucker (1919–1986) were the King and Duke.

In 1984, a Broadway production of *Huckleberry Finn* was finally launched as BIG RIVER, winning a Tony Award for best musical. In early 1986, the most ambitious adaptation of the novel to date aired on public television as a miniseries, with Patrick Day (1968–) as Huck and Samm-Art Williams (1946–) as Jim. Although this four-hour production was faithful enough to the original story to incorporate the "RAFT CHAPTER," it omitted the Wilks episode. Seven years later, Disney contributed its own adaptation as *The Adventures of Huck Finn*, a feature film with Elijah Wood (1982–) as Huck and Courtney Vance (1960–) as Jim. This film gave extended treatment to the Grangerford and Wilks episodes, while omitting Tom Sawyer and the "evasion" episode altogether. It also greatly expanded Jim's role by having him captured by the Grangerfords and having him go ashore with Huck and the con men in the Wilkses' village.

Clemens's novel has also inspired several prose adaptations. The most interesting of these is John SEELEY's *The True Adventures of Huckleberry Finn* (1970 and 1987), which retains most of Clemens's original text, while reducing Tom Sawyer's role significantly, eliminating the evasion sequence and rewriting many passages in stronger language.

CHARACTERS AND RELATED ENTRIES

Adolphus   Fictitious name in *Huckleberry Finn* (1884). In chapter 24, the King has Huck pose as his English servant and calls him "Adolphus" to impress Tim Collins. Although Huck presumably goes by this ALIAS throughout the entire Wilks episode, it is mentioned only once.

Allbright, Charles William   Background figure in the "Raft Chapter" of *Huckleberry Finn* and *Life on the Mississippi*. In a ghost story that Huck Finn overhears aboard a giant raft, Allbright is a baby boy who was killed by his father, Dick Allbright. The ghost story concludes with the baby's discovery in a barrel. When Huck himself is discovered aboard the raft, he wins the crew's sympathetic laughter by giving his own name as "Charles William Allbright." The name of another character in *Life on the Mississippi*, Charlie Williams, may be related to this one.

Allbright, Dick   Central character in a ghost story told in the "Raft Chapter" of *Huckleberry Finn* (chapter 16) and *Life on the Mississippi* (chapter 3). Huck Finn sneaks aboard a giant raft and hears a man named Ed tell about Allbright, a fellow boatman whom he knew five years earlier. Three years before that, Allbright choked his infant son to death and put his body in a barrel that later followed him and brought misfortune on his crewmates. When the captain of Ed's raft brings the barrel aboard, Allbright's dead son, Charles William Allbright, is found inside. Allbright wraps the baby in his arms, jumps off the raft and disappears.

Apthorps   Family mentioned in *Huckleberry Finn* (1884). In chapter 28, Huck persuades Mary Jane Wilks to leave town for a few days to stay with the Lothrop family. However, he tells her sisters that she has gone to see Hanner Proctor across the river. He adds that she will also visit the wealthy Apthorps, hoping to persuade them to come to the auction that the King is planning.

Balum   Background figure mentioned in *Huckleberry Finn* (1884). In chapter 8, Jim tells Huck about a time when a dream told him to give his last 10 cents to a man named Balum—nicknamed "Balum's Ass"—to invest. This man gave the money to the poor, expecting a hundred-fold return. Mark Twain's BURLESQUE AUTOBIOGRAPHY alludes to an ancestor named "Balum's Ass" who belonged to a "collateral branch" of his family.

The biblical Balaam was a heathen soothsayer with a miraculous talking ass summoned by the king of Moab to invoke a curse upon Israel (Num. 22–24).

Barnes, Tommy   Minor character in *Huckleberry Finn* (1884). The youngest and most timid boy at the first meeting of Tom Sawyer's Gang, Tommy falls asleep as the bloodthirsty would-be pirates discuss massacring the families of members who betray their secrets (chapter 2). When the older boys tease him, he threatens to tell their secrets. Instead of having Tommy's family slaughtered, however, Tom Sawyer buys his silence for five cents.

Bartley, Widow   Minor character in *Huckleberry Finn* (1884). The Widow Bartley is mentioned in

chapters 24–25 as a friend of the late Peter Wilks. In Chapter 27, Huck sees her just before Wilks's funeral.

Bell, Levi   Character in *Huckleberry Finn* (1884). A lawyer friend of the recently deceased Peter Wilks, Bell is in Louisville, Kentucky on business when the King and Duke arrive in his village posing as Wilks's brothers in chapter 24. Bell and Dr. Robinson lead the effort to find the truth when two more men claiming to be Wilks's brothers appear in chapter 29. Bell proposes a handwriting test. That fails to settle the matter, so he proposes exhuming Wilks's body to see if it is tattooed, as the newly arrived Harvey Wilks claims.

Ben, Uncle   Name mentioned in *Huckleberry Finn* (1884). In chapter 20, Huck invents a story to show the King and Duke why he and Jim are rafting down the river. He tells them that he, his father, younger brother Ike, and Jim were going downriver to live with his Uncle Ben, south of NEW ORLEANS, when his relations were killed in an accident.

Betsy   Minor character in *Huckleberry Finn* (1884). Betsy appears briefly in chapter 17 as a household slave of the Grangerford family.

Big River   Musical adaptation of *Huckleberry Finn*. With music and lyrics by Roger Miller (1936–1992), *Big River* opened in Cambridge, Massachusetts, on February 22, 1984. In June, it moved to BROADWAY, where it won seven Tony Awards, including best musical. Daniel H. Jenkins played Huck and Ron Richardson was Jim. In August 2003, *Big River* returned to Broadway with a largely deaf cast, after first being staged at a small Los Angeles Theater. The revival was the first-ever Broadway musical with a deaf cast.

Huckleberry Finn mentions the Mississippi River by name only twice, but alludes to it as the "big river" perhaps half a dozen times; the first instance is in chapter 7.

Bilgewater   Nickname used in *Huckleberry Finn* (1884). The younger of the two con men who board Huck and Jim's raft in chapter 19 claims to be the Duke of Bridgewater. The older man, who styles himself "King Looy Seventeen," occasionally calls the Duke "Bilgewater" or "Bilge." In chapter 25, he calls him simply "Biljy."

Clemens gives "Bilgewater" as the name of the playwright of *Blood, Hair and the Ground Tore Up* in an 1865 newspaper sketch. Another sketch has a "Captain Bilgewater," and *Roughing It* mentions a "Colonel Bilgewater" (chapter 77). In *1601,* the Duchess of Bilgewater is a 22-year-old courtier of Queen Elizabeth I who was "rog'red by four lords before she had a husband."

Bilgewater is the foul water that collects in the bottoms of vessels, and *bilge* has long been nautical slang for worthless talk. Clemens's essay "About All Kinds of Ships" defines bilgewater as a place where "only the dead can enjoy life."

Bill   Name of three characters in *Huckleberry Finn* (1884). When Huck boards the derelict steamboat *Walter Scott,* he overhears men named Bill and Jake Packard planning to kill a third man (chapters 12–13). He later invents a brother named Bill when he tells the Grangerfords where he comes from (chapter 17). Another Bill is one of the Bricksville loafers (chapter 21).

Blodgett, Reverend Elexander   ALIAS used in *Huckleberry Finn* (1884). In chapter 24 the King meets a young man named Tim Collins and introduces himself as Blodgett, "one o' the Lord's poor servants."

Boggs   Character in *Huckleberry Finn* (1884). In chapter 21, Huck is idling in the scruffy village of Bricksville, when Boggs charges in on a horse during his monthly drunk. A red-faced man in his fifties, Boggs rides about wildly, hurling insults and threats, proclaiming that he has come to kill Colonel Sherburn. Drunk or sober, he is known to be harmless, so people merely laugh at him. Sherburn, however, is not amused; he warns Boggs that he will endure his taunting only until one o'clock; if Boggs persists after that, it will be his end. Sherburn later shoots Boggs and has to confront a lynch party.

Details of the Boggs episode are inspired by a shooting that Clemens saw as a boy, when WILLIAM OWSLEY shot SAMUEL SMARR. It is possible that

Clemens picked up the name from Lilliburn W. Boggs (1792–1860), Missouri's governor from 1836 to 1840. He also uses Boggs for a detective's name in "THE STOLEN WHITE ELEPHANT."

Booth's Landing   Village in *Huckleberry Finn* (1884). In chapter 13, Huck tells a ferryboatman that a woman named Miss Hooker was visiting at Booth's Landing upriver. She was in a horse ferry crossing the river that lost its steering oar and got swept into the wreck of the steamboat *Walter Scott.*

Bradish   Figure mentioned in *Huckleberry Finn* (1884). In chapter 8, Jim tells Huck that Bradish was the owner of a one-legged slave who started a "bank" in which Jim lost five dollars. "THE $30,000 BEQUEST" mentions a rising young lawyer named Bradish whom Aleck and Sally FOSTER consider as a possible mate for one of their daughters.

Bricksville   Fictional ARKANSAS town in *Huckleberry Finn* (1884). In chapters 21–23, Huck spends four days in Bricksville. The first day, he sees Colonel Sherburn shoot Boggs, follows a lynch mob to Sherburn's house and sneaks into a circus. In the evening, the King and Duke stage a SHAKESPEARE performance in the courthouse that flops miserably. Over the next three nights, however, they pack the courthouse with the lurid "Royal Nonesuch." Taking care to slip out of town before its third show begins, they deny the townspeople their revenge. Bricksville is not mentioned by name until chapter 28, when Huck tells Mary Jane Wilks that she can prove the King and Duke are frauds by sending to Bricksville for witnesses.

Huck describes Bricksville as a one-horse town whose streets are all mud, whose houses are elevated to escape floodwater and whose riverfront houses are buckling and falling into the river. The name "Bricksville" is ironic; its houses are frame structures that have never even been painted.

Clemens modeled Bricksville and its location partly on NAPOLEON, Arkansas. His description of Bricksville's sleepy main street, where loafers like Buck Harkness sit whittling and chewing, also recalls his description of Hannibal in chapter 4 of *Life on the Mississippi* (1883).

Bridgewater, Duke of   Name used in *Huckleberry Finn* (1884). In chapter 19 two rogues join Huck and Jim aboard their raft. The younger man claims to be the rightful Duke of Bridgewater; throughout the balance of the narrative, he is known as the Duke, and the name "Bridgewater" is not mentioned again. The older rogue, who is known as the King, usually calls the Duke "Bilgewater."

The Duke claims that his "great-grandfather, eldest son of the Duke of Bridgewater," came to America and died, leaving a son, about the same time that his own father died. The late duke's second son then seized the title and estates, while the rightful duke, the infant, was ignored. The rogue claims to be the lineal descendant of that infant.

Bridgewater was the name of a real English dukedom that died out before Clemens's time. The third and last Duke of Bridgewater was Francis Egerton (1736–1803). As one of the richest men of his time, he had a title to which the greedy might naturally aspire. However, he never married, shunned women after a romantic disappointment, and died childless. The title "Bridgewater" was carried over into an earldom, but in 1829 it, too, expired. The well-known wealth and eccentricities associated with the Bridgewater name assured its frequent use in 19th-century humor.

Buckner, Lafe   Minor character in *Huckleberry Finn* (1884). Buckner is mentioned once, as one of the lazy BRICKSVILLE, Arkansas, tobacco chewers Huck sees in chapter 21. "JOURNALISM IN TENNESSEE" mentions a Buckner who is the imbecilic editor of the *Daily Hurrah.*

Bud   Background figure in *Huckleberry Finn* (1884). In chapter 18, Buck Grangerford tells Huck how his 14-year-old cousin Bud was shot by Baldy Shepherdson in a family feud, about three months earlier.

Bunker, Hank   Figure mentioned in *Huckleberry Finn* (1884). In chapter 10, Huck calls Bunker a person who once defied superstition by looking at a new moon over his left shoulder and bragging about it. "In less than two years he got drunk and fell off of the shot tower and spread himself out so that he was just a kind of a layer, as you may say; and they slid him edgeways between two barn doors for a coffin."

Burton   Minor character in *Huckleberry Finn* (1884). Burton is a PIKESVILLE neighbor of SILAS PHELPS. In chapter 33, Huck learns that Jim, whom Phelps calls "the runaway nigger," has told Phelps and Burton about the King and Duke's "scandalous" "Royal Nonesuch." Burton in turn tells the rest of the townspeople, who break up the King's CAMELOPARD performance and then TAR AND FEATHER the rascals.

camelopard (cameleopard)   Archaic term for giraffe. One of the most outrageous moments in *Huckleberry Finn* occurs in the "King's Camelopard," or "Royal Nonesuch," scene in chapter 23. The King goes on stage naked and painted with multicolor stripes. He dances about wildly, to the amusement of an all-male audience. Clemens's use of "camelopard" may have been inspired by EDGAR ALLAN POE's "Four Beasts in One; or the Homo-cameleopard" (1836). In this story, an ancient Syrian king prances on all fours in the skins of a beast. In *Innocents Abroad* (1869), Clemens mentions "cameleopards" among the animals that he would have accepted for transportation in the Holy Land (chapter 41).

Capet   Name of a medieval French dynasty. In chapters 21 and 26 of *Huckleberry Finn* (1884), the duke sarcastically calls his partner the king "Capet." Familiar with THOMAS CARLYLE's history of the French Revolution, Clemens would have known that revolutionists called the deposed King Louis XVI "Citizen Louis Capet." Louis XVI was the father of Louis XVII—the person whom *Huckleberry Finn*'s King claims to be. Alternatively, "Capet" may be the Duke's garbled pronunciation of "Capulet," the name of Juliet's family in *ROMEO AND JULIET*. Since the Duke has the King play Juliet in his "Shakespearean Revival," "Capet" may be his way of insulting the King.

Child of Calamity   Minor character in the "Raft Chapter" of *Huckleberry Finn* (1884; chapter 16) and *Life on the Mississippi* (1883; chapter 3). One of the tough-talking boatmen whom Huck sees on a giant raft, the "Child of Calamity" brags about his prowess before taking on another big tough named Bob; however, a smaller man named Davy comes along and thrashes both of them. Later, the Child of Calamity discovers Huck in his hiding place.

Collins, Tim   Minor character in *Huckleberry Finn* (1884). In chapter 24, Huck and the King meet Collins, "an innocent-looking young country jake," walking toward a steamboat that is loading cargo. When the King gives Collins a canoe ride to the steamboat, Collins tells him about the recent death of Peter Wilks in a nearby town. He gives details on every member of the Wilks family and on all the leading townspeople. Collins himself is on his way to Rio de Janeiro ("Ryo Janeero"), where his uncle lives—possibly to act out Clemens's own youthful ambition to go to SOUTH AMERICA.

After Collins boards the steamboat, the King and the Duke devise a plan to go to Wilks's town and pose as his English brothers, Harvey and William Wilks. In chapter 29. a man named Hines challenges the King's claim to be Harvey Wilks, claiming that he saw the King with Collins in a canoe the morning the imposters arrived in town. Hine's statement is the only mention of Collins's name.

Damrell, Sister   Minor character in *Huckleberry Finn* (1884). One of the nosy Pikesville neighbors who visit the Phelpses after Jim's escape attempt, Sister Damrell questions why Jim had a ladder in his hut (chapter 41). Clemens's family had a neighbor named Mrs. Damrell when they lived in FLORIDA, MISSOURI, in his infancy.

dauphin   French title for the heir to the royal throne. In *Huckleberry Finn* (1884) Huck tells Jim about the "dolphin," the son of LOUIS XVI who disappeared in prison (chapter 14). Later, an old con man who joins them on their raft claims to be the missing dauphin. After presenting himself as "Looy Seventeen," he is known as the King (chapter 19).

The real Louis XVII (1785–1795?) almost certainly died in prison, but many people believed that he escaped. In later years at least 35 claimants professed to be the missing dauphin; several visited the United States. If *Huckleberry Finn*'s "King" had been Louis XVII, he would have been about 60 years old at the time the story takes place. The King is clearly older than this—a fact that the Duke, the novel's other charlatan, is quick to point out.

FRANCE adopted *dauphin* as a title in the mid-14th century. As King Charles VII's official title before he was crowned in 1429, it is the only name that Joan uses for him before his coronation in Clemens's novel *Joan of Arc* (1896).

Davy   Minor character in the "Raft Chapter" of *Huckleberry Finn* (chapter 16) and *Life on the Mississippi* (chapter 3). Davy is a small raftsman who beats up two bigger toughs, the "CHILD OF CALAMITY" and Bob. Later, he saves Huck from being painted blue and thrown overboard.

Downriver   Musical adaptation of *Huckleberry Finn* (1884) that ran briefly at New York City's St. Clement's Church in December 1975, with book by Jeff Tamborino, lyrics and music by John Braden. Another musical adaptation of *Huckleberry Finn*, the vastly more successful *Big River*, opened on BROADWAY nine years later.

The Duke   Character in *Huckleberry Finn* (1884). One of Huck's RAPSCALLIONS, his real name is never given. The Duke and King appear suddenly at the beginning of chapter 19, when both are fleeing trouble in an unnamed riverside town. They do not know each other, but soon agree to work together. Huck describes the Duke as about 30 years old and dressed "ornery." He has just been selling a product that removes tartar from teeth; the product got him into trouble because it also removed the enamel. ("Duke" and "King" are lowercased in the first edition of *Huckleberry Finn*. They are capitalized in this reference book to avoid possible confusion.)

The Duke introduces himself as a "jour printer, by trade." In the next chapter he spends a day

The Duke (Orral Humphrey, left) and the King (Tom Bates) rehearse for the Duke's "Shakesperean Revival," as Huck (Lewis Sargent) and Jim (George Reed) watch, in Paramount's 1920 adaptation of *Huckleberry Finn*. *(Arkent Archive)*

working in a Pokeville print shop, proving he could probably earn a living at this trade if he were willing. He also describes himself as doing "a little in patent medicines; theatre-actor—tragedy, you know; take a turn at mesmerism and PHRENOLOGY when there's a chance; teach singing-geography school for a change; sling a lecture, sometimes." His familiarity with WILLIAM SHAKESPEARE and the general quality of his language suggests that he has some education.

After and the older man have described their various vocations, he sighs audibly and tearfully announces that he is "the rightful Duke of Bridge-water." He pompously adds, "here am I, forlorn,

torn from my high estate, hunted of men, despised by the cold world, ragged, worn, heart-broken and degraded to the companionship of felons on a raft!" Clemens evidently adapted this ornate language from that of his own kinsman, JESSE LEATHERS, who claimed to be the rightful earl of Durham. The impact that the Duke's impersonation has on Huck and Jim inspires the older con man to proclaim himself the rightful king of France. The Duke must accept this fresh imposture in order not to compromise his own.

While both the Duke and King are patent frauds, they differ in important ways. The Duke, for example, is the more inventive of the two. It is he who proposes staging the "Shaksperean Revival" and its tawdrier sequel, the "ROYAL NONESUCH." He also comes up with the idea of printing handbills depicting Jim as a runaway slave; this gives them an explanation for Jim's presence on the raft and enables them to run during the daylight hours.

Scoundrel though he is, the Duke is clearly more compassionate than the King. In general, he preys on the baser instincts of people, while the King preys upon their trust. His most successful scheme, the "Royal Nonesuch," for example, takes advantage of the prurient interests of men and their thirst for revenge. The King's best scheme, by contrast, is his effort to swindle the nieces of Peter Wilks out their inheritance. There are limits to how far the Duke will go; in chapter 26, he proposes taking the gold that they have already have and leaving, as he does not want to steal from orphans. He agrees to the King's plan to sell off Wilks's estate only when he is convinced that the girls will get their property back after he and the King are safely away.

In chapter 30, the Duke protects Huck from the King's wrath after they all escape from what likely would have become a lynch mob. When the King turns on Huck for fleeing without him, the Duke reminds the King that he did not behave any differently himself. In the next chapter, the Duke shows sympathy for Huck's plight after he and the King have sold Jim. The Duke is inclined to tell Huck where Jim is, but thinks better of it and instead sends him off on a wild-goose chase. The next time that Huck sees the Duke, the two con men have been TARRED AND FEATHERED and are being ridden out of town on rails (chapter 33).

The Duke and King reappear toward the end of Mark Twain's unfinished novella "TOM SAWYER'S CONSPIRACY." Huck runs into them on a steamboat while they are coming to Missouri with phony extradition papers looking for Jim. This time they are playing a nastier game than in *Huckleberry Finn*. When they learn that Jim is in a St. Petersburg jail awaiting trial for murder, the Duke proposes an ugly scheme to save him: He and the King will have new extradition papers forged to take Jim south on a bogus prior murder charge. Once they are safely

away from Missouri they will sell him. Huck and Tom Sawyer (who never meets the rascals) approve the plan as the only way to save Jim's life; however, the rascals do not return until the moment a judge is pronouncing a death sentence on Jim at his trial. As soon as the King and Duke open their mouths in the courtroom, Tom jumps up and proclaims that their voices are the same ones that he overheard at the scene of the murder. He begins to produce what appears to be conclusive proof of their guilt when the manuscript abruptly ends.

The first actor to portray the Duke on screen was Orral Humphrey in the 1920 silent film *Huckleberry Finn*. William Frawley (1887–1966), later known to television audiences as Fred Mertz in *I Love Lucy*, played the Duke opposite Mickey Rooney in 1939. Other film Dukes include Mickey Shaughnessy (1960), David Wayne (1974), and Robbie Coltrane (1993). Actors who have played the Duke in television adaptations include John Carradine (1955), Jack Carson (1957), Merle Haggard (1975), Forrest Tucker (1981), and Jim Dale (1986). Dale later won fame for his unabridged recordings of Harry Potter novels.

Dunlap, Sister   Minor character in *Huckleberry Finn* (1884). Sister Dunlap is a friend of Sally Phelps in chapter 41. Her relationship to any other Dunlaps is not mentioned, although Huck evidently knows a great deal about the Dunlap family. In Chapter 2 of *Tom Sawyer, Detective*, Tom tells Jake Dunlap about their adventures of the "last summer," demonstrating that "there warn't anything about his folks,—or him either, for that matter—that we didn't know."

Ed (Eddy, Edwin, Edward)   Character in the "Raft Chapter" of *Huckleberry Finn* (chapter 16) and *Life on the Mississippi* (chapter 3). Ed is the riverboatman who tells a long ghost story about Dick Allbright and the haunted barrel.

evasion   Popular shorthand expression for the last 10 chapters of *Huckleberry Finn* (1884). In chapter 39, Tom Sawyer reveals the last details of his elaborate plans to liberate Jim, explaining that "when a prisoner of style escapes, it's called an evasion."

Thereafter, "evasion" is a codeword for Tom's escape scheme.

ferryboatman   Minor character in *Huckleberry Finn* (1884). After Huck and Jim escape from the wrecked steamboat *Walter Scott* in chapter 13, Huck boards a steam ferry and awakens its watchman—who owns the boat. Huck blubbers out a dramatic story about his fictitious family and a Miss Hooker being stranded on the wrecked steamboat. An evident penny-pincher, the ferryboatman is concerned about who will pay for a rescue effort. When he mentions a local rich man named Jim Hornback, Huck quickly says that Hornback is Miss Hooker's uncle. At the prospect of a reward, the ferryboatman jumps into action, but the steamboat breaks before he can reach it.

Finn, Huckleberry   Character in much of Clemens's important Mississippi fiction and arguably his most famous creation. Huck Finn appears in all the stories containing Tom Sawyer and he narrates most of them. Indeed, Huck proved an important narrative device for Clemens by providing him with an authentic vernacular voice through which to express himself. Huck is the central character in *Adventures of Huckleberry Finn* (1876) *and a major character in The Adventures of Tom Sawyer* (1884), "HUCK FINN AND TOM SAWYER AMONG THE INDIANS," "TOM SAWYER'S CONSPIRACY," *Tom Sawyer Abroad* (1894) and *Tom Sawyer, Detective* (1896). He also appears briefly in "SCHOOLHOUSE HILL" and narrates "DOUGHFACE."

Huck is introduced in chapter 6 of *Tom Sawyer* as a friend of Tom. He is "the juvenile pariah of the village," a good-hearted but socially disreputable waif. His mother is dead and his drunken father, Pap Finn, is never around, leaving Huck to fend for himself. He sleeps where he wishes, dresses as he likes, fishes whenever he wants to, and never goes to school. Like Tom BLANKENSHIP—the Hannibal boy on whom he is modeled—Huck is the freest boy in St. Petersburg and the most envied by other boys. Though Blankenship is the model for Huck's character, Huck's vernacular voice has a strong black strain. Indeed, in recent years he has been shown to speak with much the same voice as Clemens's "SOCIABLE JIMMY"—a

Frontispiece of *Huckleberry Finn* drawn by E. W. Kemble, whose early drawings of Huck Clemens thought were "too Irishy"

young midwestern AFRICAN AMERICAN whom Mark Twain met in the early 1870s.

As is the case with Tom Sawyer, Huck's age and physical description are vague throughout *Tom Sawyer*. Chapter 17 of *Huckleberry Finn*, however, reveals Huck to be "thirteen or fourteen or along there." His surname probably derives from JIMMY FINN. In 1895, Clemens said that there was "something about the name 'Finn' that suited Huck," adding that a name such as "Arthur Van de Vanter Montague" would not do.

What Huck most values in life is his freedom. He loses this freedom in *Tom Sawyer*, then struggles to regain it in *Huckleberry Finn*. What most threatens his independence is success. At the end of *Tom Sawyer*, he and Tom split a treasure worth $12,000 and he becomes a hero for helping to save the Widow Douglas from Injun Joe. He then becomes the widow's reluctant ward. He even has to pledge himself to become respectable in order to win membership in Tom Sawyer's gang.

Huckleberry Finn begins where *Tom Sawyer* leaves off, adding several new assaults on Huck's freedom. He now attends school regularly and has a nemesis. The widow's sister, Miss Watson, now lives in her household, and she burdens Huck with frightening talk about heaven and hell. Some of these changes have their rewards, however. Throughout *Tom Sawyer*, Huck is completely illiterate; he can now read and write with some facility. Several times he uses these skills to his advantage.

Huck's new wealth creates another problem for him: It draws his father, Pap Finn, to town. Pap removes the last vestiges of Huck's independence by imprisoning him in a cabin. This final blow impels Huck to escape all his oppression.

When Huck first plans to flee from his father, he intends to tramp east through Illinois. After he finds a canoe in chapter 7, however, he decides to paddle south about 50 miles, then camp permanently near the river. His primary goal is never to be found by either Pap or the widow. Ironically, the novel ends with Huck almost precisely where he was at the beginning; this time, however, it is Tom's Aunt Sally Phelps who wants to adopt him. He considers lighting out for INDIAN TERRITORY, "because Aunt Sally she's going to adopt me and sivilize me and I can't stand it. I been there before."

Although Huck and Tom Sawyer experience many adventures together, they are different kinds of characters. Where Tom seeks attention and fame, Huck seeks only to be left alone. Where Tom is romantic and creative, Huck is realistic and practical. While Tom is often clever, his inventiveness tends toward quixotic fantasies. Huck is probably at least equally clever, but his inventiveness is always directed toward quick, practical solutions to problems. The most outstanding example of their differences comes in the "evasion" chapters in *Huckleberry Finn*, in which they scheme to liberate Jim from captivity. To Huck, the problem is simple: Wait until Uncle Silas Phelps falls asleep, snatch his key to Jim's hut, then spring Jim free and flee. Tom's solution is to spend weeks laboriously reenacting the romantic aspects of famous escapes about which he has read.

Huck demonstrates his intelligence repeatedly throughout *Huckleberry Finn*. He plans and executes a complex escape from his father that does not waste a single step. As a result, he gets away with a large horde of supplies, and within a single day he has convinced everyone that he is dead and his body has disappeared in the Mississippi River. Later, as he and Jim go down the river, he must repeatedly invent fresh ALIASES and explanations of who he is and what he is doing to satisfy the demands of strangers, some of whom are hostile. He also saves the Wilks sisters from being robbed by the King and Duke and manages to locate Jim and get the raft away from the scoundrels' grasp without arousing their suspicion. His intelligence seems to fail him only when he falls under the influence of Tom Sawyer, as at the end of *Huckleberry Finn*, when he goes along with Tom's preposterous "evasion" plan.

Another of Huck's distinctive characteristics is his good-heartedness and his sensitivity toward the suffering of others. Throughout *Huckleberry Finn* he suffers under the burden of trying to reconcile conflicting demands. He commits himself to helping Jim gain his freedom, but suffers guilt pangs because he is "stealing a poor old woman's nigger that hadn't ever done me no harm." He finally concludes that standing by Jim is the greater imperative and that he is willing to go to hell to see the matter through.

Huck's sensitivity extends to all human beings. During their first days together, Huck plays several boyish tricks on Jim, but he comes to regret taking advantage of Jim's trust so greatly that he overcomes all his training as a white southerner and humbles himself before the black man to ask forgiveness. His kindness even extends to proven criminals. In chapter 13, he and Jim strand three murderers aboard the derelict steamboat *Walter Scott*. His conscience will not, however, let him rest, so he tricks a ferryboatman into trying to save the men. Later, he even tries to save the King and Duke from a lynching at Pikesville, despite all the nasty things these scoundrels have done to him and Jim.

Huck appears in all the finished and unfinished sequels to *Huckleberry Finn*, but none of these stories significantly develops his character.

Huck's precursor, in "BOY'S MANUSCRIPT," is a character named Wart Hopkins. The latter character is similar to Huck in being somewhat disreputable, but differs in being a mean-spirited person. In his AUTOBIOGRAPHY, Clemens explains that Huck is his childhood friend TOM BLANKENSHIP, drawn "exactly as he was." Elements of other people can also be found in Huck, however. Blankenship's older brother, BENCE BLANKENSHIP, for example, is known to have helped an escaped slave. Huck also has similarities with another of Clemens's characters—Tom Canty, whom Clemens created while interrupting his work on *Huckleberry Finn* to write *The Prince and the Pauper* (1881).

In the first draft of *Tom Sawyer*, Clemens evidently intended to carry the story into Tom's adulthood. He wrote a note about his characters "fifty years later," calling Huck "Bishop Finn." Playwright BERNARD SABATH's play *THE BOYS IN AUTUMN* (1981) reunites Huck and Tom during the 1920s.

Dozens of actors have portrayed Huck on stage and screen, going back to late 19th-century efforts to dramatize *Tom Sawyer*. Robert Gordon was the first actor to play Huck in films, in two silent film adaptations made of *Tom Sawyer* in 1917–18. Junior Durkin was the first to play Huck in talking films, in 1930–31. One of the best-known portrayals was by 19-year-old Mickey Rooney in 1939. The next feature film adaptation of *Huckleberry Finn* was not made until 1960, when 13-year-old Eddie Hodges played Huck. Jeff East played Huck in musical adaptations of *Tom Sawyer* and *Huckleberry Finn* made in 1973–74. Ron Howard was 21 when he played Huck in a made-for-television film in 1975. More recent actors include Kurt Ida, Anthony Michael Hall, Patrick Day, and Elijah Wood. Daniel H. Jenkins played Huck in the BROADWAY musical *BIG RIVER* in 1984.

Finn, Pap   Character in *Huckleberry Finn* (1884). Huck's father is mentioned occasionally in *Tom Sawyer* (1876) and often throughout *Huckleberry Finn*, but he appears only in chapters 5–8 of the latter narrative. Clemens's working notes for *Tom Sawyer* indicate that he considered using Pap Finn as Injun Joe's partner in that book's GRAVE-ROBBING scene. In the third chapter of *Huckleberry Finn*, Huck says that Pap has not been seen around town for "more than a year." When Pap finally appears,

Pap Finn waits in Huck's room to surprise him in chapter 5 of *Huckleberry Finn*.

he comes from "away down the river," but it is never revealed where he has been, or what he has been doing while away.

In chapter 3, Huck hears that the rotting body of a drowned man found upriver has been identified as Pap, but he is sure Pap is still alive. The next chapter provides Pap with an eerily dramatic entrance. One winter's day, Huck finds fresh tracks made in the snow with a familiar bootprint. He visits the slave Jim, who tells his fortune with a hairball. Jim's reading contains ominous references to Huck's father. The chapter ends when Huck goes to his room that night and finds Pap awaiting him.

Notorious as a former TOWN DRUNKARD, Pap is a widower who has evidently long abused Huck. Chapter 5 of *Huckleberry Finn* describes Pap in some detail. About 50 years old, he has long, black, greasy hair, a long beard, and sickeningly white skin. His CLOTHES are pure rags; his toes poke through his boots. He wears a black slouch hat with the top caved in. The moment Huck enters his room, Pap turns on him, berating him for living so well and especially for learning how to read. Since neither he himself, his deceased wife, nor any member of their family could read, he will not stand for Huck's being literate.

Pap has been in town for two days and knows about Huck's finding treasure. Indeed, Huck's money is the reason for his coming. Over the next several weeks, he cadges money from Huck that he uses to get drunk and is regularly in and out of jail. A judge attempts to reform him at the end of chapter 5, but Pap's attempt at reform fails spectacularly and nearly kills him in the process. Frustrated in his efforts to get Huck's money, Pap eventually takes Huck to an isolated cabin in ILLINOIS, about three miles upriver. There he keeps Huck locked up while he visits the town to drink work on his legal case. Over about two months, his treatment of Huck grows more abusive, forcing Huck to plan his escape. Eventually, Pap returns to the cabin. Even more drunk than usual, he goes into a tirade about the injustices of the government. That night he has a delirium tremens attack and chases Huck with a knife. The next day Huck completes his escape by faking his own murder. Pap last appears in the narrative early in chapter 8, when Huck sees him among the townspeople aboard the ferryboat that is searching for his body in the river.

In chapter 11, Huck learns from Judith Loftus that Pap left town soon after Huck's faked murder. Many townspeople suspect that Pap murdered Huck, and there is a $200 reward out for him. People were ready to lynch Pap, but suspicion shifted to the slave Jim when it was found that he had run off. Huck further learns that a few days after his faked murder, Pap persuaded Judge Thatcher to give him money to hunt for Jim in Illinois. Pap may thus be among the men that Huck hears in the Illinois woods in chapter 8. Pap was last seen in town when he got drunk and left with hardlooking strangers.

Meanwhile, in chapter 9, Huck and Jim find the "House of Death" floating in the flooded river. A naked dead man is lying on the floor of a second-story room littered with playing cards and whiskey bottles. Jim determines that the man was shot in the back and has been dead for two or three days. He warns Huck not to look at the body's face and the next day refuses to discuss the dead man with Huck. In the final chapter of the book Jim finally tells Huck that the dead man was his father, Pap.

Despite Pap's abusive treatment of Huck, it is evident that he has helped to shape Huck's character. At least five times Huck recalls things he has learned from his father. In chapter 12, for example, Huck recalls: "Pap always said, take a chicken when you get a chance, because if you don't want him yourself you can easy find somebody that does, and a good deed ain't ever forgot."

Clemens modeled Pap partly on the real Jimmy FINN. Though a town drunk, the real Finn lacked Pap's brutish qualities. Perhaps significantly, he died in November 1845—around the same time that the fictional Pap Finn would have died. Clemens drew on other models as well, such as the hard-drinking father of TOM BLANKENSHIP—his model for Huck himself.

Huck's father was developed into a major character in the 1902 Klaw and Erlanger musical *Huckleberry Finn*. While Pap has figured in many film adaptations of *Huckleberry Finn*, his role has generally been a limited one on the screen. Frank Lanning was the first film actor to play him, in the silent *Huckleberry Finn* (1920). Richmond Warner was the first actor to play Pap in a sound version of the novel, in 1931. Victor Kilian (1891–1979) played Pap opposite Mickey Rooney in 1939. Other film portrayals include Neville Brand (1960), Gary Merrill (1974), and Ron Perlman (1993). Actors who have played Pap in television adaptations include Rance Howard (1975), Cliff Osmond (1981), Frederic Forrest (1986), and Maurice Kowaleski in *Mark Twain: Beneath the Laughter* (1979). Jon Clinch's 2007 novel *Finn* explores Pap's background and what leads to his demise.

Gang, Tom Sawyer's   Tom Sawyer's formation of a "robbers' gang" links the end of *Tom Sawyer* (1876) with the beginning of *Huckleberry Finn* (1884). In chapter 33 of the first book, Tom reveals his plans for a gang. Two chapters later, he tells Huck that he must become respectable in order to be fit for membership. Tom finally organizes the gang in the second chapter of *Huckleberry Finn*, when he, Huck, Joe Harper, Ben Rogers, Tommy Barnes, and perhaps one or two other boys go to the CAVE south of St. Petersburg. After swearing everyone to secrecy, Tom shows them the entrance to the cave that he discovered in *Tom Sawyer*. Inside, he has each boy take a terrible oath, promising to commit all kinds of bloody mayhem. At the suggestion of Ben Rogers, the gang adds the rule that it will wipe out the family of any member who reveals its secrets. This rule is soon tested and found to be flexible, when Tommy Barnes responds to the teasing of the older boys by threatening to tell the gang's secrets.

Although the caravan of Spanish merchants and rich Arabs that Tom Sawyer's gang attacks in chapter 3 of *Huckleberry Finn* turns out to be a Sunday-school picnic (and only a primer class at that), it mounts a formidable resistance.

Tom wants the gang to be high-toned: "We ain't burglars. That ain't no sort of style. We are highwaymen." The gang's main activities will be robbing and killing people and holding prisoners for ransom. The full launching of these plans is delayed by the boys' struggle to find a meeting day that will not conflict with the Sabbath. Tom is elected first captain, with Joe Harper as second captain.

The gang's biggest operation occurs in chapter 3, when it raids a caravan of rich Spaniards and Arabs at CAVE HOLLOW. So far as Huck can tell, however, the caravan is a Sunday-school picnic, "and only a primer-class at that." Huck does not buy Tom's explanation that magicians turned the caravan into a picnic out of spite. By the end of the chapter, Huck and the other boys have all resigned. In JOHN SEELYE's reworking of *Huckleberry Finn*, titled *The True Adventures of Huckleberry Finn* (1970), the other boys turn against Tom during the gang's organizational meeting. After they beat Tom up, he makes no further appearances in the story.

Garrick, David (February 19, 1717, Hereford, England–January 20, 1779, London) English actor. Noted for managing London's Drury Lane Theatre, Garrick was also renowned for promoting SHAKESPEARE festivals. In chapter 20 of *Huckleberry Finn* (1884), the Duke opens his carpetbag and reveals a handbill describing him as the "world renowned Shakespearean tragedian, Garrick the Younger, of Drury Lane, London." He uses this name through the next two chapters, when he attempts to stage a "Shakespearean Revival" in Bricksville. Emulating one of the real Garrick's most famous roles, he plays Richard in the sword fight scene from *RICHARD III*. As the Duke doubtless knows, however, there was no "Garrick the Younger." Further, Garrick died in 1779; if he had left a son, this "Garrick the Younger" would have been at least 60 years old during the time in which *Huckleberry Finn* is set, and the Duke is only about 30.

Goshen Town mentioned in *Huckleberry Finn* (1884). In chapter 11, Huck—disguised as a girl—tells Judith Loftus that he is trying to reach an uncle named Abner Moore in Goshen. Loftus says that Goshen is 10 miles upriver from St. Petersburg.

Goshen is modeled on the tiny historical village of MARION CITY. *Goshen* is the Old Testament name for a land of plenty through which MOSES led the Israelites out of EGYPT.

Grangerford   Fictional family in *Huckleberry Finn* (1884). At the end of chapter 16, Huck and Jim are separated when a steamboat runs down their raft a few days south of CAIRO, Illinois. Huck swims to the left bank of the river. In the next chapter, he stumbles onto the farm of a family named Grangerford. The precise location of their farm is vague; circumstantial evidence—such as a book of HENRY CLAY's speeches in their parlor—suggests that they live in KENTUCKY, near the TENNESSEE border. Huck stays with the family through chapters 17 and 18—a period lasting perhaps two weeks, possibly longer.

The family comprises Colonel Saul Grangerford, his wife, Rachel, three sons, and two daughters. Bob Grangerford, the oldest child, is in his early thirties; his brother Tom is slightly younger. Both are "tall, beautiful men with very broad shoulders and brown faces, and long black hair and black eyes." Charlotte Grangerford is 25, a tall, imperious woman with the bearing of her father. The youngest children are Sophia and Buck Grangerford.

Originally there were at least nine Grangerford children. Three unnamed sons were killed—apparently in a long FEUD with the Shepherdson family. A daughter, Emmeline Grangerford, died at 15. The family has numerous other relatives in the region, but it is not specified which, if any, of them are surnamed Grangerford. These relatives include a 14-year-old cousin, Bud, killed by a Shepherdson about three months earlier, and Buck's cousin Joe, who is killed in chapter 18.

The Grangerfords own more than a hundred slaves. Each family member has a personal slave; even Huck has one while he lives with the family. Only two slaves are named: Huck's servant, Jack, and Betsy, a household servant.

Like the home of the Phelps family that Huck meets later in the narrative, the Grangerfords' house is modeled on that of Clemens's uncle JOHN QUARLES. Huck describes its decor in some detail in chapter 17—a passage that closely resembles the description of "The House Beautiful" in chapter 38

of *Life on the Mississippi* (1883). The Grangerfords seem to personify Clemens's idea of the shallowness of southern civilization. They live in a large, ornately decorated house, wear fine CLOTHES, are pious, and have impeccable manners. Beneath their refined veneer, however, they are savages, ready to destroy themselves in a senseless feud. Huck admires the family and comes to love some of its members but cannot make sense of their ideals.

Huck's time with the Grangerford family is a turning point in the novel, separating the chapters in which Huck and Jim are alone on the raft from those in which they travel with two con men, the King and the Duke. After Clemens wrote the earlier chapters, his story stalled so badly that he wrote a scene in which the raft is destroyed and put his manuscript aside. After an interval of several years, he resumed the novel with the Grangerford episode, which ends with Huck and Jim's reunion and Huck's discovery that the raft is not really destroyed after all. After Huck witnesses the horrifying events of the Grangerford-Shepherdson feud, he resumes his raft journey with enormous relief. His painful memories stay with him, however, magnifying his already strongly compassionate nature.

The Grangerford episode was the first part of *Huckleberry Finn* to be published. A slightly modified version of chapters 17 and 18 appeared as "An Adventure of Huckleberry Finn" in the CENTURY MAGAZINE in December 1884.

Grangerford, Buck   Character in *Huckleberry Finn* (1884). The youngest member of the Grangerford family, Buck befriends Huck in chapters 17–18. He shares his clothes and bedroom with Huck and looks forward to a long friendship. He and Huck are about the same age—13 or 14. Buck is so anxious to kill a Shepherdson in the family FEUD that he ambushes Harney Shepherdson in chapter 17. One of the most poignant passages of *Huckleberry Finn* is Huck's description of Buck's being killed in chapter 18.

Grangerford, Emmeline   Background figure in *Huckleberry Finn* (1884). Deceased at 15, Emmeline was the youngest daughter of the Grangerford family, which preserves her room as an apt memorial to her fascination with death. She was obsessed with painting funerary tributes and writing OBITUARY poetry. Huck describes her work in chapter 17, in which he recites her finest poem, "Ode to Stephen Dowling Bots, Dec'd." Huck particularly admires Emmeline's ability to "slap down" lines without even having to think about them. According to a neighbor, she was so quick to compose verses on a person's death, "it was the doctor first, then Emmeline, then the UNDERTAKER." What killed her, apparently, was her inability to find a rhyme for "Whistler"—a demise recalling that of Andrew Jackson in the JUMPING FROG STORY. Huck regrets that no one has written a verse about Emmeline herself. He attempts to fill the gap himself but soon gives up.

Clemens modeled Emmeline's literary inclinations on those of his QUAKER CITY shipmate Bloodgood H. CUTTER and the poplar contemporary versifier JULIA A. MOORE.

Grangerford, Saul (Colonel Grangerford)

Character in *Huckleberry Finn* (1884). The first member of the Grangerford family to confront Huck in chapter 17, the "colonel" is distinguished-looking, approximately 60 years old, tall and slim, with "a darkish-paly complexion." He has a thin face, thin lips and nostrils, a high nose, heavy eyebrows, piercing black eyes and a high forehead. His hair is black (or gray), straight, and long. An immaculate dresser, he is never frivolous and never loud. Though stern, he is kind and, according to Huck, "everybody loved to have him around." Grangerford's description closely resembles that of Judge Griswold in "Simon Wheeler, Detective." Both characters borrow features from Clemens's father, John M. Clemens.

In many ways, Grangerford is an archetypal southern gentleman, from his white linen suits to his honorific title "colonel." As the owner of several farms and a hundred slaves, he is wealthy and aristocratic. Despite his kindness, however, he seems to value honor so highly that he is willing to risk destroying his family in a meaningless feud with the Shepherdsons. When Huck meets him, he has already lost three sons to the feud. By the end of chapter 18, the feud kills him, his remaining three sons, and other relatives.

Grangerford, Sophia

Character in *Huckleberry Finn* (1884). The beautiful and gentle 20-year-old daughter of the Grangerford family, Sophia elopes with Harney Shepherdson, precipitating the final confrontation in the FEUD between the two families. The couple's relationship as lovers separated by a family feud recalls *ROMEO AND JULIET*. In contrast to the Shakespearean tragedy, however, Sophia and Harney escape alive, leaving their families to kill each other off. Sophia's story also bears a striking resemblance to the yarn that Huck tells her family about himself in chapter 17. He invents an imaginary Arkansas family, explaining that it was destroyed when a sister named Mary Ann eloped.

Hagan, Sowberry

Name mentioned in *Huckleberry Finn*. In chapter 6, Pap Finn alludes to Hagan as an accomplished cusser whom he heard "in his best days."

Harkness, Buck

Minor character in *Huckleberry Finn* (1884). In chapter 22, Harkness leads the Bricksville mob that goes after Colonel Sherburn for shooting Boggs. Sherburn calls the mob cowardly, lacking a single "real man." However, he singles out Harkness as a "part of a man," or "half a man." In the previous chapter, Huck mentions a "Buck" as one of the loafers he seeks in town; this person could well be Buck Harkness.

Hicksville

OHIO town mentioned in *Huckleberry Finn* (1884). When Tom Sawyer arrives at the Phelpses' house in chapter 33, he calls himself "William Thompson" and claims to be from "Hicksville, Ohio." Hicksville is the name of a real Ohio town in the state's northwestern Defiance County. Aside from the obvious allusion to the slang term for a country bumpkin. Clemens may have chosen the name as a wordplay on "Bricksville."

Hightower, Brer

Minor character in *Huckleberry Finn* (1884). Hightower is one of the nosy Pikesville neighbors who visit the Phelpses after Jim's escape attempt in chapter 41. He enumerates all the jobs done in Jim's hut and says that 40 people could not have done that much work.

Hines   Minor character in *Huckleberry Finn* (1884). Hines lives several miles upriver from the town in which the Wilkses live. He appears only in chapter 29, in which he challenges the King's claim to be Harvey Wilks. He wants to know why, if the King's claim to have come to town in a steamboat is true, he saw the King and Huck a few miles upriver, sitting in a canoe with a local man, Tim Collins. Hines's accusation leads to a quick inquest at the inn. Afterward, he holds onto Huck when everyone goes to the graveyard to exhume Peter Wilks. When Wilks's coffin is opened, a sack of gold is found; Hines lets out a whoop and inadvertently releases Huck.

Hobson, Reverend   Minor character in *Huckleberry Finn* (1884). A Baptist minister, Hobson appears in chapters 24–25 and 27 to conduct the funeral service for Peter Wilks. He and his wife are among the townspeople taken in by the King and Duke's claim to be Wilks's brothers.

Hooker, Miss   Name mentioned in *Huckleberry Finn* (1884). In chapter 13, Huck and Jim leave several criminals stranded on the wreck of the derelict steamboat *Walter Scott*. Huck then tries to get help for them ashore. To win the sympathy of a ferryboatman, he says that someone named "Miss Hooker" is stranded on the wreck along with his family and implies that she is related to Jim Hornback, a wealthy local man.

Hookerville   Fictional town mentioned in *Huckleberry Finn* (1884). In chapter 11, Huck—disguised as a girl—tells Judith Loftus that he is from Hookerville, seven miles below St. Petersburg. The town is also mentioned in "TOM SAWYER'S CONSPIRACY." Mark Twain's working notes for the latter story indicate that Hookerville is modeled on Saverton, a real Missouri town seven miles below Hannibal.

Hopkins, Aleck James   ALIAS used by Huck in *Huckleberry Finn*'s (1884) "Raft Chapter" when he sneaks aboard a large raft. Immediately after he is discovered, he gives his name as Charles William Allbright. On further questioning, he invents the name "Aleck James Hopkins" and says he lives on his father's trading scow.

Hornback, Jim   Figure mentioned in *Huckleberry Finn* (1884). In chapter 13, Huck meets a FERRY-BOATMAN near Booth's Landing who mentions that Hornback is a wealthy local resident. Huck wants the ferryboatman to go to the wrecked steamboat *Walter Scott*. He says that his family and a Miss Hooker are stranded on the wreck, implying that Miss Hooker is related to Hornback. Hoping to be rewarded by Hornback, the ferryboatman takes his boat out, but the steamboat breaks loose before he reaches it.

Hotchkiss, Sister   Minor character in *Huckleberry Finn* (1884). The most gossipy neighbor of the Phelpses in chapter 41.

"House of Death"   Derelict house in *Huckleberry Finn* (1884). In chapter 9, while Huck and Jim are living on JACKSON'S ISLAND, they find a two-story frame house brought down the river by the floods. They enter a second-story room at night, but find it too dark to explore. At daybreak, they reenter the room and discover a man who has been shot to death, evidently in the midst of a drunken card game. Jim will not allow Huck to look at the dead man's face. They carry off candles, kitchen utensils, tools, and other practical supplies. In chapter 11, Huck uses a dress taken from the house to disguise himself as a girl when he visits Judith Loftus. In chapter 43, Jim finally tells Huck that the dead man he saw in the house was his father, Pap Finn.

Textual allusions to nudity, crude graffiti on the walls, women's underclothes, masks, playing cards, and whisky bottles, strongly suggest that the floating house had been a whore house. The episode thus contains one of the few acknowledgments of prostitution in Clemens's published writings.

The term "House of Death" is frequently used in modern Clemens criticism; however, it does not appear within *Huckleberry Finn*. The original heading to chapter 9 uses "The Floating House."

Hovey, Deacon Lot   Minor character in *Huckleberry Finn* (1884). A friend of Peter Wilks who, along with his wife, is taken in by the King and Duke in chapters 24–25.

Ike Name mentioned in *Huckleberry Finn* (1884). In chapter 20, Huck invents a story to explain to the King and Duke why he and Jim are rafting down the Mississippi River. Huck tells the con men that he, his father, and his four-year-old brother Ike were heading to a relative's home near New Orleans when a steamboat struck their raft. Ike and the father drowned.

Jack Minor AFRICAN-AMERICAN character in *Huckleberry Finn* (1884). After Huck settles into the home of the Grangerfords in chapter 17, a personal slave is assigned to him. Chapter 18 identifies the man as Jack. Unbeknownst to Huck, Jack is also secretly looking after Jim, who is hiding near the plantation. Eventually, Jack takes Huck to Jim, being careful not to implicate himself, in case trouble arises.

"Jack" is also the name of one of the lazy tobacco chewers whom Huck sees in Bricksville in chapter 21.

Jackson, George ALIAS that Huck uses in *Huckleberry Finn* (1884). In chapter 17, Huck stumbles onto the farm of the Grangerfords. Asked to identify himself, he gives his name as "George Jackson" and claims to have fallen off a steamboat. He invents an autobiography, telling the family that he comes from southern ARKANSAS. His sister Mary Ann eloped; other family members died or left, until he and his father were the only ones who remained. When his father died, he decided to go upriver and took deck passage on the steamboat from which he claims to have fallen. Since he has no family, and no place to go, the Grangerfords invite him to stay with them. The first night Huck shares a bedroom with Buck Grangerford. He awakens the next morning to find that he has forgotten his new alias. He gets Buck to remember it for him by challenging him to spell it.

In what most likely is a COINCIDENCE, the ferryboatman whom Huck meets in chapter 13 utters "My George!" and "By Jackson" in consecutive remarks.

Jim Character in *Huckleberry Finn* (1884) and other stories. An AFRICAN-AMERICAN slave of indeterminate age, Jim first appeared in the "RAFT CHAPTER" (chapter 3 of *Life on the Mississippi*), which Clemens excerpted from his unfinished *Huckleberry Finn* manuscript. This chapter alludes to Jim's being owned by the Widow Douglas. In the completed *Huckleberry Finn*, Jim belongs to the widow's sister and housemate, Miss Watson.

Chapter 1 of *Huckleberry Finn* describes Miss Watson as newly arrived in St. Petersburg. It is not clear, however, whether Jim also is newly arrived. Miss Watson may have bought him after joining her sister, though her apparently straitened circumstances make this seem unlikely. Chapter 16 mentions that Jim's wife is a slave "on a farm close to where Miss Watson lived." It seems logical that Jim was once on this same farm with his wife, for chapter 23 makes it clear that he enjoyed a time when he shared a house with his children. Less clear, however, is *where* the farm is. It could be near either Miss Watson's current home in St. Petersburg or some previous residence.

Jim is not a character in *Tom Sawyer* (a slave child named Jim in that novel is a different character), so there is no record of his being in St. Petersburg before the events of *Huckleberry Finn*. On the other hand, in chapter 42 of *Huckleberry Finn*, Tom says that he and Huck "have knowed [Jim] all his life." Earlier, in chapter 23, Huck says that Jim is "low and homesick; because he hadn't ever been away from home before in his life." These two remarks suggest that Jim has lived in or near St. Petersburg for a long time.

Jim's age is also uncertain. Huck occasionally calls him "old Jim." In chapter 35, Huck is concerned with the slowness of Tom's escape plan for Jim and complains that Jim is "too old" to wait: "He won't last." Despite these remarks, it seems doubtful that Jim could be much over 40. In chapter 8, a slave trader offers to buy him for $800—a high price for any but a comparatively young man.

Chapters 16 and 23 offer clues about Jim's family. In chapter 23, Jim talks about his children, 'Lizabeth and Johnny, and tells a story about 'Lizabeth's contracting scarlet fever at four. The tone of his remarks suggests that both children are still very young. None of Jim's family appears in any story; however, fragmentary notes in Clemens's papers indicate that he once considered writing a story in which Huck and Tom buy Jim's wife and (one) child and present them to him as a Christmas gift.

Some writers on *Huckleberry Finn* have called Jim "Jim Watson," but this is not a name that Clemens himself uses. Indeed, such would not have been the naming practice of the time, although emancipated slaves often took the surnames of their masters. Another misconception about the novel is that Jim is called "the Nigger Jim." Jim is frequently called a "NIGGER" in the book, but the phrase "Nigger Jim" never appears there.

Huckleberry Finn introduces Jim as a friend of Tom and Huck, who enjoy testing his superstitions. When Jim overhears that Miss Watson intends to sell him down the river to raise money, he sneaks onto a large raft floating down the Mississippi. He intends to go some distance downriver, but swims to Jackson's Island to avoid discovery on the raft. He wants to make his way to free territory, where he can earn money to buy the freedom of his wife and children. Huck, also hiding out on the island, stumbles on Jim and agrees to go with him to free territory. As their journey develops, Huck feels increasingly guilty about his complicity in helping Jim to escape from slavery.

It happens that Jim leaves St. Petersburg the same night that Huck Finn is reported murdered. The COINCIDENCE makes Jim a prime suspect. He is thus a doubly wanted man. Huck learns this news from Judith Loftus when he goes back to town. He also learns that her husband and another man intend to search Jackson's Island for Jim. He rushes back to the island, and he and Jim gather their possessions together and leave as fast as they can.

Their plan is to raft down the Mississippi to CAIRO, Illinois, from which Jim can go up the OHIO RIVER to a safe free state. They go past Cairo during a foggy night, however, so they decide to continue downriver until they can buy a canoe in which to paddle back to Cairo. Each mile deeper they go into the South increases Jim's peril of remaining a slave. The journey builds a strong bond between Jim and Huck, who gradually comes to appreciate Jim's great dignity. Huck learns of Jim's love for his family and becomes his surrogate son. Jim's innate intelligence and common sense constantly shine through his surface ignorance. Many critics and scholars have called Jim the most noble character that Clemens created, but it seems to be his lot perpetually to face perils from which Huck and Tom must save him.

In *Huckleberry Finn*, Jim's constant fear of recapture dominates the middle chapters. Much of the narrative follows Huck, however, while Jim hides, away from the action. Jim's peril increases greatly after the King and Duke join them on the raft; these con men, who would sell their own mothers for a profit, stand ready to sell Jim at the first opportunity. Jim's worst nightmare comes true in Pikesville, where the King sells him for $40. Jim is then held prisoner at the farm of Sally and Silas Phelps, who happen to be Tom Sawyer's aunt and uncle.

When Huck learns where Jim is, he goes to the farm. Tom Sawyer appears shortly afterward and offers to help free Jim, although he privately knows that Miss Watson has recently died, freeing Jim in her will. Instead of revealing this fact and sparing Jim further suffering, Tom concocts an elaborate plan to bust Jim out of his makeshift jail. His complex "evasion" scheme succeeds, but at the cost of risking his, Huck's, and Jim's lives. After Tom himself is shot in the leg, Jim sacrifices his freshly won freedom to help a doctor treat him. Jim is thus back in custody again and is nearly lynched by irate townspeople. Only after Jim endures all this does Tom reveal that Jim has been legally free for two months.

Jim resting after spending the night fighting the river's strong currents and looking for Huck in his canoe, in chapter 15 of *Huckleberry Finn*

Jim next appears in the unfinished novel "HUCK FINN AND TOM SAWYER AMONG THE INDIANS." As the story opens, Jim is back in St. Petersburg. When Aunt Polly takes Huck and her own family to western Missouri, Jim accompanies them so he will be safe from men who might try to put him back into slavery while his friends are gone. Jim then accompanies Huck and Tom on an extended outing on the western plains, where he is captured by a band of INDIANS. Blaming himself for getting Jim into this new fix, Tom vows to rescue him, but the manuscript ends abruptly before Jim is seen again.

Tom Sawyer Abroad (1894) places Jim, Huck, and Tom in a balloon journey across North AFRICA. Jim has little to do beyond serving as a foil for Tom's arguments about everything from the Crusades and Catholic bishops to fleas and sand. Jim is again placed in peril briefly when the boys strand him atop the SPHINX, from which they rescue him from an angry mob. This novella ends with Jim's piloting the balloon from Mount Sinai to Missouri and back in order to fetch Tom a corncob pipe.

Jim does not appear in *Tom Sawyer, Detective* (1896), but returns in the unfinished novella "TOM SAWYER'S CONSPIRACY." Now a paid employee of the Widow Douglas, Jim is finally saving money to buy his wife and children. Nevertheless, he has enough idle time to join Huck and Tom in an abolitionist hoax as a summertime diversion. The "conspiracy" backfires when real conspirators murder the local slave trader and Jim is charged with the murder. Tom, confident that he and Huck will help apprehend the real culprits, makes things even worse for Jim by suggesting a plausible motive for his killing the slaver. Eventually, Jim goes on trial for the murder. Just as the judge is pronouncing a death sentence on him, the Duke and King enter the courtroom and ask for the judge's attention. Tom—who until now has never met the con men—cries out that their voices are those of the true murderers. He begins to present incontrovertible proof of their guilt but is cut off when Clemens's manuscript ends abruptly.

In his AUTOBIOGRAPHY, Clemens confessed to modeling Jim partly on Uncle Daniel, a middle-aged slave on the FLORIDA, MISSOURI, farm of his uncle JOHN QUARLES. Clemens admired Daniel's levelheadedness, guilelessness, and warmth. It was while spending his youthful summers at the Quarles farm that Clemens developed an affection for black people that emerges in his characterization of Jim. Other models for Jim include JOHN T. LEWIS, a tenant farmer at QUARRY FARM, and GEORGE GRIFFIN, Clemens's long-time butler.

Since George Reed (1867–1952) played Jim in the first film adaptations of *Huckleberry Finn* in 1920 and 1931, Jim has become an important role for black actors. The ages of actors playing him have ranged from 29-year-old Antonio Fargas in a 1975 television film and 33-year-old Paul Winfield in a 1974 film, to 64-year-old George Reed in 1931 and 54-year-old Brock Peters in a 1981 television film. Other actors who have portrayed Jim include Rex Ingram (1939), Archie Moore (1960), Samm-Art Williams (1986), and Courtney Vance in the 1993 Disney adaptation. Jim's wife never appears in *Huckleberry Finn;* however, Odessa Cleveland played her in a role written into the 1974 film.

Joe   Name of two minor characters in *Huckleberry Finn* (1884). A 19-year-old cousin of Buck Grangerford named Joe is killed by the Shepherdsons in chapter 18. An unrelated "Joe" is among the Bricksville loafers whom Huck sees in chapter 21.

Kean, Edmund (March 17, 1787, London–May 15, 1833, Richmond, England)   English Shakespearean actor. The leading tragedian of his time, Kean was known as "Kean the Elder" to differentiate him from his son, Charles John Kean (c. 1811–1868). The younger Kean toured America in 1830 and 1845–47 and was an acclaimed Hamlet. He was even better known for his lavish "Shakespearean Revivals"—a fact of which the Duke seems to be aware in *Huckleberry Finn* (1884). In chapter 21–23, the Duke makes up handbills advertising a "Shaksperean Revival" in which he bills his partner, the King, as "Edmund Kean the Elder" and himself as "David Garrick the Younger."

The King (Dauphin)   Character in *Huckleberry Finn* (1884). One of Huck's RAPSCALLIONS, the "King" is a con artist who allies with a younger man known as the Duke when both join Huck and Jim on the raft in chapter 19 after being chased out of a town. His real name is never given. ("King" and "duke" are lowercased in the novel but are uppercased throughout this book to avoid ambiguity.) At least 70 years old, he is bald, heavily whiskered, foul-smelling and shabbily dressed, and he possesses only a ratty carpetbag. Huck calls the man "baldhead" until he establishes his identity. The old man tells the younger man that he was running "a little temperance revival," making "five or six dollars a night" until word got out that he was drinking on the sly and he was run out of town. His background also includes "doctoring," "layin' and o' hands," telling fortunes, and preaching.

After both con men list their credentials, the younger man suddenly announces that he is the true Duke of Bridgewater. The old man sees how this ploy wins Huck and Jim's deference. He tops the Duke by tearfully confessing that he is the dauphin, the true king of France, Louis XVII. Although Huck knows the man is a fraud, he refers to him as "the King" thereafter.

The King and Duke soon control the raft, giving the story a plausible reason for continuing the voyage *down* the river, away from Jim's chance for freedom. The two charlatans plan to work riverfront towns and use the raft for quick getaways.

The King is coarser and less educated than the Duke but is at least the latter's equal in intelligence. He thinks quickly on his feet and has a prodigious memory. He easily learns the Duke's SOLILOQUY from *HAMLET* and masters every detail about the Wilks family and their neighbors that he can squeeze out of Tim Collins in chapter 24. He also has steely nerves. Even when his imposture as Harvey Wilks is exposed in chapter 29, he maintains his composure so well that he and the Duke get a fresh chance to escape lynching.

Where the King fails to match the Duke in inventiveness, he makes up for it in greater ruthlessness. While the Duke tends to prey upon people's base instincts, the King preys on their generosity and trust. For example, the King induces people attending a pious camp meeting at Pokeville to give him money to become a missionary, and he convinces the trusting Wilks girls that he is their uncle. What dooms the King in almost every venture is his careless cockiness and his inability to control his greed. If he were to follow the Duke's advice in chapter 26, he could easily pocket nearly $3,000 in gold. His insistence in going for the entire Wilks estate not only costs him this gain, but also the money he made on the "Royal Nonesuch"; it also nearly costs him his life.

The King's negative characteristics are many. He is alcoholic, he has a violent temper, and he has no scruples whatever. But for the Duke's intervention, he appears ready to throttle Huck after they all escape from the Wilks fiasco. Later, he sells Jim for $40, then gets drunk and blows the entire sum on gambling. The King is also a lecher. At the camp meeting, pretty girls—taken in by his false piousness—ask to kiss him, "and some of them he hugged and kissed as many as five or six times." Clemens's manuscript revisions show that he toned down the King's lecherous behavior when he meets the Wilks girls in chapter 25; however, he overlooked a passage in chapter 28 alluding to the King's kissing Mary Jane "sixteen or seventeen times" when they met. (JOHN SEELYE restores and magnifies the King's lecherous nature in *The True Adventures of Huckleberry*

The King (left) and Duke agree to "double-team it" in chapter 19 of *Huckleberry Finn*.

Finn.) The King returns in "TOM SAWYER'S CONSPIR-ACY" to attempt stealing Jim again and may even be a murderer.

Clemens had a fascination with claimants to royal titles and doubtless took elements of the King from many charlatans. One person in particular who may have influenced him was CHARLES C. DUNCAN, captain of the *QUAKER CITY.* A possible allusion to Duncan appears in the King's bogus *Hamlet* soliloquy. Another possible model from the *Quaker City* voyage was GEORGE J. ADAMS, a phony prophet described in chapter 57 of *Innocents Abroad* (1869). The King may have elements of San Francisco's Emperor Norton, who also claimed royal French descent. A purely fictional model may have been JOHNSON JONES HOOPER's comic character Simon Suggs. An ironic coda to Clemens's life is the fact that biographer A. B. PAINE later dubbed *him* the "King."

As is the case with the Duke, the King has provided a rich character role for many actors. Film actors who have portrayed him include Tom D. Bates (1920), Walter Connolly (1939), Tony Randall (1960), Harvey Korman (1974), and Jason Robards (1993). Actors who have played the King in television adaptations include Thomas Mitchell (1955), Basil Rathbone (1957), Jack Elam (1975), Larry Storch (1981), and Barnard Hughes (1986).

Lally Rook STEAMBOAT mentioned in *Huckleberry Finn* (1884). In chapter 32, Sally Phelps tells Huck that her husband Silas Phelps once traveled from New Orleans to Arkansas on "the old Lally Rook," which blew a cylinder head during his voyage. A real side-wheeler, the *Lallah Rookh* operated on the Mississippi from 1838 through 1847. Its name derives from an epic poem written by THOMAS MOORE in 1817.

Lize Minor character in *Huckleberry Finn* (1884). A household slave of the Phelpses, Lize is the first person Huck sees when he reaches the Phelps plantation in chapter 32. 'Lizabeth is the name of Jim's daughter, who is described in chapter 23.

Loftus, Mrs. Judith Character in *Huckleberry Finn* (1884). Mrs. Loftus and her husband have recently settled in a long-unoccupied "shanty" near St. Petersburg. At the end of chapter 10, Huck visits the town disguised as a girl, hoping to gather some news. When he sees Loftus knitting through her parlor window, he calculates that as a newcomer to town, she would not know him but should know the latest gossip. In the next chapter, the woman invites Huck in. He introduces himself as SARAH MARY WILLIAMS. In one of the novel's most famous scenes, Loftus uses several ruses to get Huck to reveal that he is a boy. These include tossing an object on his lap, which he catches with his knees, as a boy would, instead of with his dress, as a girl would. Mark Twain evidently borrowed this "lap-test" from chapter 63 of Charles Reade's *The Cloister and the Hearth* (1861).

Mrs. Loftus finally gets Huck to confess that he is a boy, but does not totally accept his revised ALIAS of "George Peters." Even so, she provides him with a snack before he leaves and tells him to send word if he needs help.

This meeting is significant in two ways. It tests Huck's ability to think quickly under pressure and it provides Huck with crucial information. He learns from Mrs. Loftus that the townspeople think that Jim is his murderer. He also learns that her husband intends to hunt for Jim on Jackson's Island that same night, so he rushes back to the island in order to flee with Jim.

Mrs. Loftus is about 40 years old in the novel, but her most famous screen portrayer, Lilian Gish, was 90 when she played her in the 1986 PBS adaptation of *Huckleberry Finn.*

Lothrop, Mister Figure mentioned in *Huckleberry Finn* (1884). In chapter 28 Huck persuades Mary Jane Wilks to leave town to avoid inadvertently revealing that she knows the King and Duke to be frauds. She agrees to go to the home of Mr. Lothrop, about four miles inland. After she leaves, Huck tells her sisters that she has gone across the river to help tend Hanner Proctor.

Marples, Brother Minor character in *Huckleberry Finn* (1884). Marples is one of the nosy Pikesville neighbors who visit the Phelpses after Jim's escape in chapter 41. He marvels at how many things were done in Jim's hut, suggesting that "they must a ben a house-full o' niggers in there every night for four weeks, to a done all that work."

Mary Ann   Fictitious name mentioned twice in *Huckleberry Finn* (1884). In chapter 16, Huck tells a slave catcher named Parker and his partner that his father is sick, "and so is mam and Mary Ann." In the next chapter, Huck tells the Grangerford family that he was living in southern Arkansas, where his family disintegrated after a sister named Mary Ann eloped. A brother named Bill went after her, but he never returned either. Then three more members of the family died, leaving Huck alone. Huck's second Mary Ann story is closely paralleled by what actually happens to Sophia Grangerford and her family in chapter 18.

Moore, Abner   Fictitious name mentioned in *Huckleberry Finn* (1884). When Huck meets JUDITH LOFTUS in chapter 11, he invents "Abner Moore" as an uncle whom he is on his way to visit in Goshen.

Nat   Minor character in *Huckleberry Finn* (1884). A slave of Silas Phelps, Nat is assigned to looking after Jim, who is imprisoned on the farm. After being introduced in chapter 34, Nat is first identified by name in chapter 36.

Nichols, Archibald   Name mentioned in *Huckleberry Finn*. In chapter 33, Tom Sawyer arrives at the Phelps farm and pretends to be William Thompson. When Uncle Silas answers the door, Tom says "Mr. Archibald Nichols, I presume?"—a subtle allusion to HENRY MORTON STANLEY's meeting with David Livingstone. Nichols is a neighbor who lives several miles from the Phelpses.

"Ode to Stephen Dowling Bots, Dec'd."   Sentimental ode by Emmeline Grangerford that Huck admires in chapter 17. Bots was a boy who "fell down a well and was drownded." His surname is ironic; although the poem states that he suffered from neither coughing nor any other sickness, *botts* was a slang term for colic. The popularity of the ode is attested to by the English poet A. E. Housman (1859–1936), who in 1927 told CYRIL CLEMENS that he knew it by heart.

They got him out and emptied him; Alas it was too late. . . ."

Clemens's original draft of *Pudd'nhead Wilson* (1894) disposes of Aunt Patsy Cooper's obnoxious sons by having them fall down a well and drown.

Packard, Jake   Minor character in *Huckleberry Finn* (1884). Packard is one of three criminals whom Huck sees inside the derelict steamboat *Walter Scott* in chapter 12. He has a partner named Bill who is itching to kill Jim Turner, whom they have tied up. Packard suggests that instead of shooting Turner, they leave him aboard the steamboat to drown when the boat breaks up. He argues, "I'm unfavorable to killin' a man as long as you can git around it; it ain't good sense, it ain't good morals." Packard and Bill are about to row away from the steamboat in the next chapter, but remember to go back to get Turner's money, leaving Huck and Jim to take their skiff. All three criminals presumably drown when the steamboat later sinks.

Parker and John   Minor characters in *Huckleberry Finn* (1884). In chapter 16, Huck keeps two slave catchers, identified only as Parker and John, away from the raft by begging for their help to make them think that his family has smallpox. Business has evidently been good for these men; each gives Huck a $20 gold piece to ease his conscience for not helping him.

Penrod, Brer   Minor character in *Huckleberry Finn* (1884). Penrod is mentioned once in chapter 41 as a neighbor of the Phelpses who wonders how a grindstone got into the hut in which Jim is a prisoner. A "Penrod" is also among the passengers eaten in "CANNIBALISM IN THE CARS" (1868).

Peters, George   ALIAS used in *Huckleberry Finn* (1884). In chapter 11, Huck's claim to be a girl named "Sarah Mary Williams" fails to fool Judith Loftus, so he instead claims to be "George Peters." In chapter 17, he adopts "George Jackson" as an alias.

Phelps, Sally (Aunt Sally)   Character in *Huckleberry Finn* (1884) and *Tom Sawyer, Detective* (1896). The sister of Tom Sawyer's Aunt Polly—and therefore the sister of Tom's mother—Sally is married to Silas Phelps, with whom she lives near Pikesville, Arkansas. The Phelpses' farm and local community

The Phelpses welcome Huck (Lewis Sargent), believing him to be Tom Sawyer, in the 1920 film adaptation of *Huckleberry Finn*. *(Paramount)*

are closely modeled on the FLORIDA, MISSOURI farm of Clemens's uncle JOHN ADAMS QUARLES where Clemens spent his boyhood summers. In *Huckleberry Finn*, Huck goes to the Phelpses' farm—where Jim is being held as a runaway slave—and is stunned to be warmly greeted by Aunt Sally (chapter 32). It soon emerges that she thinks he is Tom, whom she expects momentarily. Having apparently never seen Tom before, she does not recognize him when he arrives a few hours later and pretends to be his brother Sid Sawyer. During several weeks at the Phelpses, Huck and Tom try Sally's patience with their preparations for Jim's escape. When Sally finally learns the boys' true identities, she wants to adopt Huck herself.

Sally is also a character in *Tom Sawyer, Detective*, but the story gives her little to do beyond wringing her hands in distress when her husband is charged with murder.

Huckleberry Finn describes Sally as being in her late forties. She has at least three children. When Huck arrives, an unspecified number of young children come out with her. Huck alludes to one child as Jimmy (chapter 33); he calls another Matilda Angelina Araminta Phelps (chapter 37); and a third child he calls Thomas Franklin Benjamin Jefferson Elexander Phelps (chapter 39). Sally's much older daughter, Benny Phelps, is mentioned only in *Tom Sawyer, Detective*.

Many film and television adaptations of *Huckleberry Finn* exclude or severely truncate the episode with the Phelpses. Among the actresses who have played Sally in adaptations of *Huckleberry Finn* are Elvia Allman, in a 1981 television movie, and Geraldine Page, in the 1986 PBS television miniseries. Elisabeth Risbon played her in the 1938 film adaptation of *Tom Sawyer, Detective*.

Phelps, Silas   Character in *Huckleberry Finn* (1884) and *Tom Sawyer, Detective* (1896). The husband of Tom Sawyer's Aunt Sally Phelps, Silas first appears in chapter 32 of *Huckleberry Finn*, when Huck and Tom arrive at his farm. For reasons not made fully clear, the runaway slave Jim has become Silas's prisoner after being sold by the treacherous King. A farmer and part-time preacher, Silas is a harmless, somewhat addled person who trusts everyone and is easily bewildered. Clemens's notes indicate that Silas struggles with his conscience over Jim and wants to free him; in the novel, he prays with Jim daily.

Silas is a central character in *Tom Sawyer, Detective* (1896), in which he is tormented by a wealthy neighbor, Brace Dunlap, whom he will not allow to marry his daughter, Benny Phelps. Eventually driven to distraction by Brace's brother Jubiter Dunlap, Silas uncharacteristically strikes Jubiter on the head with a stick. The blow does no real damage, but Jubiter is later found dead and Silas is arrested for his murder. Though Silas hysterically confesses, Tom Sawyer proves him innocent.

Tom Sawyer, Detective's characterization of Silas is partly modeled on a 17th-century Danish pastor in a novel by Steen Steensen Blicher (1782–1848). Silas has only rarely been written into film adaptations of *Huckleberry Finn*. James Almanzar played him in a 1975 television adaptation of the novel, and James Griffith played him in the 1981 television film. Porter Hall played Silas in the 1938 adaptation of *Tom Sawyer, Detective*.

A curious incident occurring before *Huckleberry Finn* was first published in the United States involved Silas. After the first copies of the book were bound, E. W. KEMBLE's illustration of the meeting between Silas and Huck was discovered to have been maliciously altered. The drawing shows Silas standing next to his wife facing Huck, with his pelvis thrust slightly forward; its caption reads, "Who do you reckon 'tis!" The altered picture shows what appears to be an erection emerging from Silas's groin. After this alteration was discovered, printed copies of the book had to be recalled, but the person responsible for the apparent obscenity was never identified.

Pikesville Fictional town in *Huckleberry Finn* (1884). Huck and his raftmates land about two miles below this "little bit of a shabby village" in chapter 31; the remainder of the novel is set in or near the town. The novel does not specify the state in which Pikesville is located, but it is probably ARKANSAS. When Aunt Polly arrives from St. Petersburg, Missouri, in chapter 42, she says that she has traveled 1,100 miles. This same distance

from Hannibal, Missouri—on which St. Petersburg is modeled—would reach Natchez, Mississippi, or Ferriday, Louisiana, well below Arkansas. Other writings, however, indicate that Clemens meant to put Pikesville somewhere in southern Arkansas, just above the farm of Sally and Silas Phelps. *Tom Sawyer, Detective* (1896) does not mention Pikesville by name, but explicitly places the same Phelps farm in Arkansas. Chapter 2 of that story puts Tom and Huck's steamboat journey from their home—presumably St. Petersburg—to the Phelpses at "not so very much short of a thousand miles."

In *Huckleberry Finn*, Pikesville is the place where the King and Duke steal Jim from Huck and sell him as a runaway slave, and it is there that Tom and Huck see the rascals TARRED AND FEATHERED.

Pokeville Fictional town in *Huckleberry Finn* (1884). In chapter 20, Huck alludes to Pokeville as a "one-horse town" on the Mississippi River. Analysis of the raft's progress suggests that Pokeville is south of Compromise, Kentucky, and north of NAPOLEON, Arkansas. It is not clear, however, on which side of the river it stands. After landing at Pokeville, Huck attends a camp meeting outside of town at which the King claims to be a reformed PIRATE and collects money so he can become a missionary. Meanwhile, the Duke takes over an empty printing shop in the town and sells print jobs and newspaper subscriptions for discounted cash prices.

Proctor, Hanner Figure mentioned in *Huckleberry Finn* (1884). In chapter 28, Huck tells Mary Jane Wilks that the King and Duke are frauds and asks her to leave town so she will not inadvertently give this secret away. She goes to the home of the Lothrop family; however, Huck tells her sisters that she has gone across the river to "set" with her gravely ill friend Hanner Proctor, who has the "pluribus-unum mumps."

raft Clemens's first major literary use of a raft occurs in *Tom Sawyer* (1876) when Tom, Huck Finn, and Joe Harper raft downriver to Jackson's Island to play PIRATES (chapter 13). A raft is the central focus of much of *Huckleberry Finn* (1884), even though it figures directly into only about a fifth of the novel's chapters. In chapter 9, Jim and Huck capture a section of a lumber raft brought to Jackson's Island by the flooding Mississippi River. It is about 15 or 16 feet long and 12 feet wide, with a pine-plank deck about six or seven inches above the water. When Jim and Huck leave the island in chapter 12, they tie their possessions to the raft, build a plank "wigwam" on it for shelter, and put on a mound of dirt for building fires. They also prepare an extra steering oar and a forked stick on which to hang a lantern as a running light for night travel. When they begin, they are towing a canoe that they use for trips ashore.

The fact that the raft is Huck and Jim's primary means of conveyance plays a determinative role in the development of the story, especially after they lose their canoe in chapter 16. Their original plan is to drift to CAIRO, Illinois, sell the raft, and buy steamboat passage up the OHIO RIVER. After they accidentally drift past Cairo, they cannot return *up*stream on the raft, so they decide to keep drifting south until they can buy another canoe in which to return upriver. Almost immediately, however, a steamboat hits their raft, separating Jim and Huck and apparently ending their voyage. Clemens's working notes indicate that he was through using the raft in the narrative, and this seems to have been the point at which he set his manuscript aside for several years.

When Clemens resumed writing, he had Huck spend time ashore with the Grangerford family, Huck then discovers that Jim is hiding nearby; the raft not only is not destroyed, Jim has repaired it and has collected fresh supplies. The moment that the Grangerford family is shattered by its feud with the Shepherdsons, Huck rejoins Jim on the raft and they resume their voyage downriver as fast as they can (chapter 18). Several days later, two con men known as the King and Duke board the raft and take control, providing a new impetus for continuing south. After two further episodes ashore interrupt the raft journey, the voyage ends in chapter 31, when Huck hides the raft on Spanish Island and spends the remainder of the narrative with the Phelps family near Pikesville.

Ridgeway, Sister   Minor character in *Huckleberry Finn* (1884). One of the nosy Pikesville neighbors

who visit the Phelpses after Jim's escape attempt in chapter 41.

Robinson, Doctor   Character in *Huckleberry Finn* (1884). A "big iron-jawed man," Robinson is introduced in chapter 24 as a friend of the late Peter Wilks. The first person to dispute the King and Duke's claim to be Wilks's brothers, Robinson belittles the King's English accent and laughs at his bogus explanation of "ORGIES." In chapter 29, Robinson heads an inquiry that exposes the frauds.

"Royal Nonesuch"   Ribald entertainment staged in *Huckleberry Finn* (1884). In chapter 22, the Duke and King distribute handbills around Bricksville, Arkansas, advertising "The Thrilling Tragedy of the King's Camelopard or the Royal Nonesuch!!!" The line "Ladies and Children Not Admitted" fills the house. After a solemn introduction by the Duke, the performance consists solely of the King prancing about on all fours, naked, with stripes painted all over him. After members of the audience demand two encores, they are outraged to realize that his cavorting constitutes the entire performance. One

In the "Royal Nonesuch" scene in Paramount's 1920 adaptation of *Huckleberry Finn,* the King (Tom Bates) closely matches E. W. Kemble's illustration (inset) for the book's first edition.

man persuades the others to defer their revenge until other townspeople are duped at the next performance. On the third night, men from the first two nights return with violence in mind. The Duke pockets the gate, however, and slips out with Huck to escape on the raft with the others.

As they drift downstream, the King and Duke look for another town in which to repeat their "Royal Nonesuch" success. When they attempt it again in Pikesville, however, the audience is ready for them. Before the show, Jim—whom the King has sold for reward money—tells a man named Burton about their scam. The moment that the King begins his camelopard routine, the audience turns on him and the Duke. Tom and Huck reach town as the two frauds are carried out on rails, TARRED AND FEATHERED (chapter 33).

In his AUTOBIOGRAPHY, Clemens acknowledges getting the idea for the Nonesuch episode from Jim GILLIS. He used Gillis's title, "The Tragedy of the Burning Shame," in his draft manuscript but thought it too vulgar to keep in the book, though he later mentioned its name in "TOM SAWYER'S CONSPIRACY" (chapter 9). Clemens called his own version "mild" and "pale" compared to Gillis's "outrageous funny" and "unprintable" story. Gillis's version may have drawn on an older folk story, featuring a naked man romping on stage with a lighted candle in his rectum. Similar stories were widely told in early 19th-century America. It is even possible that the King's cavorting involved sexual pantomime and that he wore a giant smoking phallus. Huck only says, "never mind the rest of his outfit, it was just wild, but it was awful funny."

Rucker, Ben   Minor character in *Huckleberry Finn* (1884), Chapters 24–25 mention Rucker and his wife among the friends of the late Peter Wilks who are duped by the King and Duke.

Saint Jacques plantation   Fictitious place mentioned in *Huckleberry Finn* (1884). In chapter 20, the Duke prints a handball advertising a reward for a slave who has run away from a "St. Jacques Plantation," 40 miles below NEW ORLEANS. The phony bill provides an explanation for Jim's presence on the raft. In chapter 31, Silas Phelps gets custody of

Jim and writes to the nonexistent plantation to claim the reward. By chapter 39, he is giving up on getting a reply.

Sawyer, Tom   See the Characters and Related Entries section of the *Tom Sawyer* entry.

Shackleford, Abner   Minor character in *Huckleberry Finn* (1884). In chapter 24 Tim Collins names Shackleford and his wife as friends of the late Peter Wilks. In the next chapter, Shackleford introduces the King to Dr. Robinson as "Harvey Wilks."

Shepherdson   Fictional family in *Huckleberry Finn* (1884). Five or six branches of the aristocratic Shepherdsons live a few miles north of the Grangerfords, with whom they have been engaged in a deadly FEUD for about 30 years. They attend the same church as the Grangerfords and use the same steamboat landing. Huck sees Shepherdsons at both places but mentions only two by name: Harney and Baldy Shepherdson. At the end of chapter 18, the Shepherdsons kill all the men in the branch of the Grangerford family with whom Huck is living.

Shepherdson, Baldy   Background figure mentioned in *Huckleberry Finn* (1884). In chapter 18, Buck Grangerford tells Huck that Baldy Shepherdson, an "old man," shot his cousin Bud three months earlier. Within a week, the Grangerfords killed Baldy. In an earlier incident, Shepherdson killed two of three Grangerfords in a gunfight.

Shepherdson, Harney   Minor character in *Huckleberry Finn* (1884). Harney is the secret lover of Sophia Grangerford. In chapter 18, Huck sees Buck Grangerford ambush Harney, who makes no attempt to retaliate after spotting who is shooting at him. Huck later unwittingly carries a message from Harney to Sophia. The next day Harney and Sophia elope, precipitating a deadly battle between the two feuding families.

Sherburn, Colonel   Character in *Huckleberry Finn* (1884). A prosperous merchant in Bricksville, Arkansas, Sherburn is proud-looking, about 55

years old and the town's best-dressed man. Huck arrives just before a drunk named Boggs provokes Sherburn into shooting him (chapter 21). Afterward, a mob goes to Sherburn's house to lynch him, but he quietly stares them down, then scatters them simply by cocking his gun. Sherburn is modeled partly on WILLIAM PERRY OWSLEY, a Hannibal merchant who shot a man named SAMUEL SMARR in 1845.

Spanish Island   Fictional Mississippi River location in *Huckleberry Finn* (1884). Spanish Island is a wooded island a few miles below Pikesville where Huck hides the raft after learning that the King has sold Jim (chapter 31). He spends the night there, then returns to Pikesville by canoe. In chapter 40, Huck, Tom Sawyer, and Jim flee to the island after completing Jim's escape. Once there, Tom reveals that he has been shot in the leg. Huck leaves to fetch a doctor. The island is not identified by name until the next chapter, when Huck tells a Pikesville doctor where to go to treat Tom. Jim emerges from hiding to help the doctor and is soon recaptured on the island.

Susan Powell   STEAMBOAT in *Huckleberry Finn* (1884). In chapter 24, Huck, the King, and the Duke board a big CINCINNATI steamboat about four or five miles above the village in which the Wilks family lives so that when they land at the village, they will give the appearance of having come all the way down the river from Ohio. In chapter 29, the King identifies the boat as the *Susan Powell.*

Thompson, Ben   Minor character in *Huckleberry Finn.* Thompson is mentioned once, as one of the lazy Bricksville tobacco chewers whom Huck describes in chapter 21. Other loafers are mentioned only by first names. They include Andy, Bill, Buck (Harkness?), Hank, Jack, and Joe.

Thompson, William   ALIAS used by Tom Sawyer in *Huckleberry Finn.* In chapter 33 Tom turns up at the farm of his aunt Sally Phelps and playfully introduces himself as "William Thompson" of Hicksville, Ohio, claiming to be looking for a neighbor named Archibald Nichols. At dinner Tom

changes his story and says that he is actually Sid Sawyer—his half-brother.

Clemens may have borrowed Tom Sawyer's pseudonym from a historical figure. There is evidence that his early travel letters were influenced by the work of the southern humorist William Tappan Thompson (1812–1882), who—like Tom's invented character—originated in OHIO. Thompson wrote several popular books about a southern hick named "Major Jones," one of whose letters is in MARK TWAIN'S LIBRARY OF HUMOR (1888).

Turner, Ab   Minor character in *Huckleberry Finn* (1884). Turner is one of two men who "helped to lay out the late Peter Wilks for burying." In chapter 29, Turner and his unnamed partner cannot recall seeing any kind of tattoo on the deceased's body.

Turner, Jim   Minor character in *Huckleberry Finn* (1884). In chapter 12, Huck sees Turner on the derelict steamboat WALTER SCOTT. A murderer, Turner has recently killed someone called "old Hatfield." Now, his former partners, Jake Packard and Bill, want to kill him, fearing that he will turn state's evidence and betray them for some unnamed affair. They decide to leave him tied up on the steamboat, however, expecting it to sink within two hours. In the next chapter, they are about to get off the steamboat but return for Turner's money, leaving Huck and Jim to snatch their skiff. Turner and the others presumably drown when the steamboat later sinks. An early draft of *Huckleberry Finn* indicates that if the boat did not break up, Bill was prepared to return and tie Turner to a rock to make sure he drowned.

Utterback, Sister   Minor character in *Huckleberry Finn* (1884). She is one of several nosy Pikesville neighbors who visit the Phelpses after Jim's escape attempt in chapter 41.

Clemens's AUTOBIOGRAPHY recalls a Mrs. Utterback who was a farmer's wife and a faith healer when he was a child.

Walter Scott   Fictional STEAMBOAT that Jim and Huck explore in chapters 12–13 of *Huckleberry Finn* (1884). The *Walter Scott* is a wreck "that had killed herself on a rock." Its position on the Mississippi River appears to be somewhere between Thebes, Illinois, and Commerce, Missouri, perhaps 25 miles northwest of CAIRO, Illinois. Against Jim's advice, Huck insists on boarding it during a storm. Inside, he hears two men, Jake Packard and Bill, discussing whether to kill a third man, Jim Turner, who is tied up. Huck wants to strand these murderers aboard the wreck by cutting their skiff loose and then find a sheriff to arrest them. However, Jim discovers that their own raft has drifted away, so they take the murderers' skiff themselves. When Huck goes ashore to find help for the stranded men, he learns that the steamboat is called the *Walter Scott*. The boat breaks up before a local ferryboatman gets to it.

Steamboat names associated with romantic literature, such as *Ivanhoe* and *Lady of the Lake*, were common on the Mississippi River during Clemens's time. *Walter Scott* was the name of a real NEW ORLEANS–based side-wheeler during the 1830s. Mark Twain evidently chose the name for his fictional steamboat as a subtle dig at the Scottish writer SIR WALTER SCOTT. The name can be seen as a symbol of the South's moral depravity, which Clemens blamed, in part, on Scott's romantic literature.

Watson, Miss   Character in *Huckleberry Finn* (1884). A "slim old maid," Miss Watson evidently is a recent arrival to St. Petersburg, where she lives with her sister, the Widow Douglas, and helps to raise Huck. Huck finds her a more severe and pious guardian than her sister and hankers to get away from her control. At the beginning of *Huckleberry Finn*, Miss Watson owns the slave Jim. (How she has come to own Jim is not explained, and it is later established that Jim has lived in St. Petersburg for many years.) For financial reasons, she decides to sell him; when he overhears her plans, he flees to Jackson's Island, where he joins Huck. Through the ensuing chapters, Huck is troubled by the idea that he is harming Miss Watson by stealing her slave. To ease his conscience, he finally writes her a letter, telling her where Jim is. However, his affection for Jim proves stronger than his conscience, so he tears up the letter and resigns

himself to going to the "bad place" that Miss Watson has warned him against (chapter 31). Meanwhile, Miss Watson has died—a fact that Huck and Jim learn from Tom Sawyer in chapter 42. Before she died, she repented her decision to sell Jim and freed him in her will.

Clemens's tendency to forget details about his characters was particularly evident in his allusions to Miss Watson. His prelude to the "RAFT CHAPTER" in *Life on the Mississippi* (1883) alludes to Jim as belonging to the Widow Douglas (chapter 3). He later started a sequel to *Huckleberry Finn*, "TOM SAWYER'S CONSPIRACY," in which Miss Watson is still alive. Another unfinished sequel, "HUCK FINN AND TOM SAWYER AMONG THE INDIANS," mentions "old Miss Watson" as Jim's former owner.

Clemens modeled Miss Watson on an early schoolteacher, MARY ANN NEWCOMB. In the 1939 film adaptation of *Huckleberry Finn*, Miss Watson was played by Clara Blandick, who had previously appeared as Aunt Polly in three films. One of the fullest portrayals of Miss Watson was by Anne Shropshire in the 1986 PBS television miniseries.

Whipple, Bill   Name mentioned in *Huckleberry Finn* (1884). In chapter 13 Huck invents a story for a ferryboatman about being with a group of people who got stranded on the derelict steamboat *Walter Scott*. He names "Bill Whipple" as a person who died heroically in the accident.

White River   River mentioned in *Huckleberry Finn* (1884). In chapter 32, Huck tells the Phelpses—who think that he is Tom Sawyer—that his steamboat was three days late reaching Pikesville because it blew a cylinder-head "at the mouth of the White River." The White is a real tributary of the Mississippi River. Nearly 700 miles long, it rises in northwestern ARKANSAS, enters Missouri, then returns to Arkansas and flows southeast, meeting the Mississippi just above the latter's confluence with the Arkansas River. Most of the Missouri portion of the river now passes through MARK TWAIN NATIONAL FOREST.

Wilks   Fictional family in *Huckleberry Finn* (1884). Chapters 24–29 of the novel contain the

Wilks episode, during which Huck stays ashore as the King and Duke pose as the English brothers and heirs of the recently deceased Peter Wilks. The King learns a great deal about the family from Tim Collins, whom he meets in chapter 24. The Wilkses originated in England. Two brothers, Peter and George, settled in America. George and his wife died about a year earlier; Peter died the day before the King meets Collins. Peter had two brothers in England, Harvey Wilks—about his own age—and William Wilks, a man in his early thirties whom he never met. Alerted to the imminence of Peter's death, Harvey and William are expected to arrive at any moment. However, the King and Duke enter the town posing as Harvey and William Wilks themselves. They are greeted by Peter's nieces, Mary Jane, Susan, and Joanna Wilks. At the end of chapter 28, two more men arrive in town claiming to be the English Wilks brothers.

The Mississippi River town in which the Wilkses live is never named. It appears to be in either southern ARKANSAS or MISSISSIPPI. Like many of Clemen's other fictional towns, it is partly modeled on HANNIBAL, Missouri.

Wilks, Harvey and William Names used in *Huckleberry Finn* (1889). Harvey and William Wilks are the English brothers and heirs of the recently deceased Peter Wilks. A "dissenting minister," Harvey is about Peter's age; DEAF-AND-DUMB William is in his early thirties. In chapter 24, the King learns from Tim Collins that these brothers are expected in Peter's town. Since no one there has ever met the brothers, the King decides to pose as Harvey while the Duke poses as William. At the end of chapter 28, two more men claiming to be Harvey and William Wilks arrive. Huck accepts them as the genuine brothers; however, they, too, may be impostors. The fact that the King and Duke are not perturbed by the newcomers' arrival suggests that they recognize kindred scoundrels. Furthermore, the newcomers seem to be suspiciously unmoved by news of Peter's death.

The newcomers arrive with no proof of their identity; however, they are content to retire immediately to a hotel to await mishandled luggage that will prove who they are. The townspeople do not want

to wait, however. They collect all four claimants at an inn to determine which two are the real brothers. Huck thinks that "anybody but a lot of prejudiced chuckleheads" should see that the newly arrived Harvey "was spinning truth" and the King "lies."

Levi Bell, who has letters from the real Wilks brothers, administers a handwriting test that quickly proves the King and Duke to be frauds; however, the test also appears to indict the two newcomers. The man claiming to be Harvey writes in an illegible scrawl, then claims that William is the actual scribe of all the letters sent in his name to Peter. "William," however, cannot produce a handwriting specimen because his writing arm is broken and in a sling. "Harvey" then offers irrefutable proof that he is Peter's brother by describing a tattoo on Peter's chest. This proves nothing, either. Ab Turner and another man who prepared Peter's body for burial cannot remember seeing *any* tattoo on him. Finally, the angry townspeople march all four claimants off to the cemetery to examine Peter's body for the tattoo. The scene ends before the examination is made, so the presumed Harvey's assertion is never verified. Thus, no proof is ever adduced that the real Harvey and William Wilks appear in the novel.

Wilks, Joanna (Joe) Character in *Huckleberry Finn* (1884). At 14, the youngest of the three Wilks sisters, Joanna has a harelip and is devoted to "good works." In chapter 26, she quizzes Huck about England but is forced to apologize to him by her older sisters, Mary Jane and Susan Wilks. Joanna is about the same age as Huck, but E. W. KEMBLE's illustrations in the first edition misleadingly show her towering over him.

Wilks, Mary Jane Character in *Huckleberry Finn* (1884). Mary Jane is the oldest of the three Wilks sisters left orphaned by George Wilks and his wife. When the King and Duke arrive in her town and claim to be her English uncles, Harvey and William Wilks, she immediately accepts them at face value and dismisses the doubts of Dr. Robinson. Huck is so taken by Mary Jane's beauty and innate goodness that he cannot stand the thought of seeing her and her sisters cheated by the scoundrels, particularly when he sees how upset she is by the King's callous separating and selling of the family SLAVES. In chapter 28, he finally tells Mary Jane the full story of the frauds' chicanery. First however, he makes her promise to leave town immediately so that she will not accidentally give away the fact that something is wrong. She leaves before the frauds are publicly exposed. Huck never sees her again, but says that he subsequently thought of her "many a million times."

One of the few strong female characters in Clemens's writings, Mary Jane Wilks has provided screen roles for Charlotte Henry (1931), Lynne Carver (1939), Florence Henderson (TV, 1957), Sherry Jackson (1960), Kim O'Brien (1974), and Patty Weaver (TV, 1975), and Anne Heche.

Wilks, Peter Background figure in *Huckleberry Finn* (1884). Wilks was a prosperous tanner in an unnamed town who died after a three-week illness. The next day, Huck and his raftmates stop near Wilks's unnamed town. The King learns about Wilks from a neighbor named Tim Collins, who is on his way out of the country. As young men, Peter and his brother George came to America from England. Wilks has died a bachelor; his only living relatives are brothers in England, Harvey and William Wilks, and George's daughters, who live in his house.

Wilks has left a letter directing the division of his money and properties between his brothers and nieces. It reveals where $6,000 in gold coins is hidden. For reasons never explained, this hoard is $415 short of $6,000. The King and Duke pretend to be Wilks's brothers and move into the house with his nieces.

Wilks, Susan Character in *Huckleberry Finn* (1884). The 15-year-old sister of Mary Jane and Joanna Wilks, Susan appears in chapters 25–26 and 28 but plays almost no individual role in the narrative.

Williams, Sarah Mary ALIAS used in *Huckleberry Finn* (1884). In chapter 12, Huck is disguised as a girl when he meets a woman named Judith Loftus. He tells her his name is "Sarah Williams." When she later asks him to repeat his name, he answers "*Mary* Williams." Loftus catches the inconsistency, prompting Huck to explain, "Sarah's my first name.

Some calls me Sarah, some calls me Mary." Under pressure, Huck finally admits that he is a boy and gives George Peters as his name. He later has a similar problem remembering the "George Jackson" alias that he gives to the Grangerford family.

Winn, Deacon Figure mentioned in *Huckleberry Finn* (1884). In chapter 3, Huck tries to understand the purpose of prayer and wonders why Deacon Winn cannot recover money he has lost on pork by simply praying for it.

BIBLIOGRAPHY

Baldanza, Frank. *Mark Twain: An Introduction and Interpretation.* New York: Barnes & Noble, 1961.

Blair, Walter, ed. *Mark Twain's Hannibal, Huck & Tom.* Berkeley: University of California Press, 1969.

Brooks, Gwendolyn. "The Chicago *Defender* Sends a Man to Little Rock, Fall, 1957." In *Heritage of American Literature: Civil War to the Present,* vol. 2, edited by James E. Miller Jr., 1,544–1,545. San Diego: Harcourt, 1991.

Doyno, Victor. "Afterword." In *Adventures of Huckleberry Finn (Tom Sawyer's Comrade).* 1885. Reprinted in *The Oxford Mark Twain,* edited by Shelley Fisher Fishkin, 1–25. New York: Oxford University Press, 1996.

———. "Slavery in the World and in Huck." In *Beginning to Write Huck Finn: Essays in Genetic Criticism. Huck Finn: The Complete Buffalo & Erie County Public Library Manuscript—Teaching and Research Digital Edition.* Buffalo, N.Y.: Buffalo & Erie County Public Library, 2002.

Fishkin, Shelley Fisher. "Mark Twain and Race." In *A Historical Guide to Mark Twain,* edited by Shelley Fisher Fishkin, 127–162. New York: Oxford University Press, 2002.

Gibson, William M., ed. *The Mysterious Stranger by Mark Twain.* Berkeley: University of California Press, 1970.

Holland, Lawrence B. "A 'Raft of Trouble': Word and Deed in *Huckleberry Finn.*" *Glyph 5: Johns Hopkins Textual Studies,* 66–80. Baltimore: Johns Hopkins University Press.

Lott, Eric. "Mr. Clemens and Jim Crow: Twain, Race, and Blackface." In *The Cambridge Companion to Mark Twain,* edited by Forrest G. Robinson, 129–152. Cambridge: Cambridge University Press, 1998.

Seelye, John. "What's in a Name: Sounding the Depths of *Tom Sawyer.*" *Sewanee Review* 90 (Summer 1982): 408–429. Reprinted in *Mark Twain: A Collection of Critical Essays*, edited by Eric J. Sunquist, 49–61. Englewood Cliffs, N.J.: Prentice Hall, 1994.

Smith, David Lionel. "Huck, Jim, and American Racial Discourse." *Mark Twain Journal* 22.2 (1984): 4–12. Reprinted in *Mark Twain: Adventures of Huckleberry Finn: Complete Text with Introduction, Historical Contexts, Critical Essays*, edited by Susan K. Harris, 356–369. New Riverside Editions. Boston: Houghton Mifflin, 2000.

Sundquist, Eric J. "Introduction." In *Mark Twain: A Collection of Critical Essays*, edited by Eric J. Sundquist, 1–14. Englewood Cliffs, N.J.: Prentice Hall, 1994.

Trilling, Lionel. "Introduction." In *The Adventures of Huckleberry Finn*, v–xvii. Fort Worth, Tex.: Holt, Rinehart and Winston, 1948.

Twain, Mark. *Adventures of Huckleberry Finn*, edited by Victor Fischer and Lin Salamo, with the late Walter Blair. Berkeley: University of California Press, 2003.

———. *The Adventures of Tom Sawyer.* 1876. Reprinted in *The Oxford Mark Twain*, edited by Shelley Fisher Fishkin. New York: Oxford University Press, 1996.

———. *Following the Equator.* 1897. Reprinted in *The Oxford Mark Twain*, edited by Shelley Fisher Fishkin, 484. New York: Oxford University Press, 1996.

———. *Life on the Mississippi.* 1883. Reprinted in *The Oxford Mark Twain*, edited by Shelley Fisher Fishkin. New York: Oxford University Press, 1996.

———. *Tom Sawyer Abroad.* 1894. Reprinted in *The Oxford Mark Twain*, edited by Shelley Fisher Fishkin. New York: Oxford University Press, 1996.

———. *Tom Sawyer, Detective.* In *The Stolen White Elephant and Other Detective Stories.* 1896. Reprinted in *The Oxford Mark Twain*, edited by Shelley Fisher Fishkin, 115–190. New York: Oxford University Press, 1996.

"In Defense of Harriet Shelley"

ESSAY published in 1894. One of Clemens's longest forays into serious literary criticism, this essay analyzes a biography of Percy Bysshe Shelley (1792–1822) published in 1886 by the Irish Shakespearean scholar Edward Dowden (1843–1913). Rejecting Dowden's claim that Shelley had no responsibility for the suicide of his first wife, he calls Dowden's work "perhaps the strangest book that has seen the light since Frankenstein."

In 1811, Shelley eloped with 16-year-old Harriet Westbrook. He treated her with indifference for three years, then abandoned her and the two children she had borne and went to Switzerland with Mary Wollstonecraft (1797–1851). In early 1816, Harriet's body was found in a London park lake. Just three weeks later, Shelley married Wollstonecraft—who as Mary Shelley wrote *Frankenstein* in 1818.

In the face of Shelley's callous treatment of Harriet, Clemens asks rhetorically why someone would try to write biography when simple facts mean nothing to him. He also attacks Dowden's writing style as a "literary cake-walk" in which artificial elegance substitutes for substance.

This 15,000-word essay first appeared in the July–September 1894 issues of NORTH AMERICAN REVIEW. It was collected in HOW TO TELL A STORY AND OTHER ESSAYS and in LITERARY ESSAYS—which was also issued as *In Defense of Harriet Shelley and Other Essays.*

The Innocents Abroad, or The New Pilgrims' Progress; Being Some Account of the Steamship Quaker City's Pleasure Excursion to Europe and the Holy Land (1869)

Clemens's first book, aside from a small collection of republished sketches, *Innocents Abroad* is an embroidered account of his five-month cruise through the MEDITERRANEAN in 1867 aboard the steamship QUAKER CITY. Most of it is adapted from letters he wrote to the SAN FRANCISCO ALTA CALIFORNIA and other newspapers during the cruise, but he heavily revised many of his letters after the cruise and added a considerable amount of new material.

If the book has a central theme, it is the need for modern Americans not to be awed by the Old World. Almost everywhere the narrator goes, he refuses to be impressed by the sights he has been trained to reverence. BURLESQUE permeates the book, which pokes fun at local legends, dubious relics, paintings of the Old Masters, annoying guides, and romantic TRAVEL BOOKS—especially those about the Holy Land. Patriotic, often almost chauvinistic, *Innocents* never hesitates to describe foreign government incompetence and corruption, poverty, filth, and disease—all of which it finds almost everywhere the travelers go. The book's tone is often inconsistent, however. Some chapters shift between ridicule and praise. To some extent, these inconsistencies are a function of *when* Clemens originally wrote each passage. While most chapters are revisions of his travel letters, some—such as those on France—were written mostly after the cruise was over.

The line between fact and fiction in *Innocents* is not always sharp. While the book clearly builds itself around Clemens's own experiences, its narrator does not necessarily speak in Clemens's voice at all times. In the earliest chapters, the narrator is naive and stumbles into comic situations, but as the book progresses he becomes increasingly worldly and more critical of what he sees.

A major part of the interest and humor in *Innocents Abroad* derives from its remarks about the other Americans with whom Clemens traveled. The book is as much about them as it is about Europe and the Holy Land, and it treats them at least equally savagely. *Innocents* mentions only a few *Quaker City* passengers and crew members by their full names, and then only when they do something praiseworthy—as when MOSES S. BEACH is named in chapter 58. For the most part, the book treats other passengers with varying levels of good-natured fun or fierce ridicule. It assigns nicknames or abbreviations to many persons, such as "Dan" (DAN SLOTE), "Jack" (JACK VAN NOSTRAND), the "Doctor" (ABRAHAM JACKSON), the "Oracle" (Dr. Edward Andrews), and "Dr. B." (DR. GEORGE BRIGHT BIRCH). Though the real identities of most characters can be determined, anecdotes attributed to them are not necessarily all true. Some characters are composites. For example, while Clemens himself identified the blundering "Blucher" as a passenger named Frederick H. Greer, several Blucher anecdotes draw on mishaps of other men, as well as the author's imagination.

Innocents Abroad does not attempt to account for every passenger involved in the *Quaker City* cruise. Several people who became close friends of Clemens—such as MARY MASON FAIRBANKS and EMILY SEVERANCE—make no discernible appearance in the book. Likewise, the book does not account for every trip and adventure that Clemens experienced during the cruise. For example, it neglects to mention his brief visit to SWITZERLAND, and it reduces his weeklong trip through SPAIN to a single sentence. By contrast, it devotes two chapters to TANGIER, where he spent just one day.

Clemens's struggle to give the book coherent thematic unity is reflected in his struggle to find a satisfactory title. His working title included "The New Pilgrim's Progress," "The Exodus of the Innocents," "The Crusade of the Innocents," and "The Irruption of the Jonathans." He was inclined to go with "The New Pilgrims' Progress" but feared it might cause the book to be confused with JOHN BUNYAN's classic religious work. He compromised by using that phrase as a subtitle, while settling on "The Innocents Abroad" for the book's main title.

SYNOPSIS

A book of 191,720 words, *Innocents Abroad* contains a brief preface, 61 numbered chapters (only 60 of which are in most tables of contents) and an unnumbered concluding chapter. While *Innocents* mixes fact and fiction, its narrative structure generally follows the actual journey that Clemens made. Between June 8 and November 19, 1867, he was a passenger on the steamboat *Quaker City*, which took him from New York City to the Mediterranean and back. Along the way, he visited the Azores, Gibraltar, Tangier, France, Italy, Greece, Russia, Turkey, Syria, Palestine, Egypt, Spain, and Bermuda, with brief stops at other ports. *Innocents Abroad* mentions few specific dates—and some of those it does mention are inaccurate. In the synopsis that follows here, wherever the narrator's arrivals and departures can be confidently linked to Clemens's movements, his actual dates of travel are inserted within parentheses. In some instances, these dates differ from the apparent chronology given in *Innocents Abroad*.

The book's first two chapters discuss preparations for the trip. Chapters 3–6 cover the two weeks that the *Quaker City* spent sailing to the AZORES (June 10–23, 1867). Chapters 7–9 continue the voyage to GIBRALTAR, including a side trip to TANGIER (June 23–July 1). Chapters 10–16 cover 10 days in France, beginning with the July 4 landing at MARSEILLE, from which Clemens went to PARIS and back. The ship left Marseille on July 13 and landed at GENOA the next day. Chapters 17–31 are set entirely in ITALY, which the *Quaker City* and all its passengers left on August 11.

Through chapters 32–40, the ship moves about frequently. It enters the Greek islands, stops at ATHENS (August 14–15), CONSTANTINOPLE (August 17–19), SEVASTOPOL (August 21), ODESSA (August 22–24), and YALTA (August 25–28). A second stop is made at Constantinople (August 30–September 3), followed by a landing at SMYRNA (September 5–6), from which most passengers take a train to EPHESUS.

Chapters 41–56 cover Clemens's overland journey with seven other men from BEIRUT to the HOLY LAND, culminating in his rejoining the ship at JAFFA (September 11–October 1). His five-day stop in EGYPT is described in chapters 57–58 (October 2–7). Chapters 59–60 summarize the voyage home (October 7–November 19). During this long stretch, the *Quaker City* made extended stops only at Gibraltar, from which Clemens made a side trip through SPAIN (October 17–25), and BERMUDA (November 11–15); each of these episodes receives just a paragraph in the book.

Through the first 27 chapters of both one- and two-volume editions, chapter numbers match. Chapters in the second volume of two-volume editions are numbered from 1 through 33; this synopsis gives both sets of chapter numbers. Information not in parentheses comes directly from the chapters; parenthesized information comes from other sources.

Chapter 1

For months, the great pleasure excursion to Europe and the Holy Land is discussed everywhere. It is to be a novelty—a picnic on a gigantic scale. Participants will sail over the breezy ATLANTIC and the sunny Mediterranean, scampering about the decks, shouting and laughing, dancing, smoking, singing and making love. They will hobnob with nobility and converse with kings. The brave conception is well advertised, but hardly needs to be. Who can read its program without longing to participate? Not only will the company be selected by a pitiless "Committee on Applications"; a similarly pitiless committee will select the vessel.

The narrator submits his application, rejoicing to learn that staterooms are still vacant. To get past the committee's scrutiny, his references are all the people of high standing *unlikely* to know him. Regrettably, none of the cruise's celebrities—HENRY WARD BEECHER, GENERAL SHERMAN, a popular actress (MAGGIE MITCHELL), and the Drummer Boy of the Potomac (ROBERT HENRY HENDERSHOT)—can go.

Chapter 2

The impressive passenger roster includes three ministers, eight doctors, 16 or 18 ladies, several titled military men, professors, and—most impressive—a man styling himself "Commissioner of the United States of America to Europe, Asia, and Africa" (DR. WILLIAM GIBSON). Thrilled to be headed for Paris, the narrator spends a happy month hanging about in New York with a fellow passenger, Mr. Blucher, who is convinced that *everybody* is going to Paris. Blucher astounds a shopkeeper by offering to pay the balance of what he owes him in Paris during the summer. The ship departs on a June Saturday (June 8, 1867), only to anchor farther down the harbor to wait out an approaching storm. Soon, a gong sounds for prayer meeting.

Chapter 3

On Monday morning (June 10), the ship finally goes to sea. One of the few passengers not to get seasick, the narrator takes smug satisfaction in observing the distress of others. The ship is loaded with "captains": CAPTAIN [CHARLES C.] DUNCAN is chief of the expedition, Captain (Ira) Bursley is the

The narrator takes satisfaction in being one of the few passengers not to get seasick in chapter 3.

executive officer, "Captain L****" (DANIEL LEARY) is the ship's owner, and Captain (William) Jones is chief mate.

Chapter 4

Over the next week or so, the ship plows through the Atlantic without incident as passengers enjoy such amusements as horse billiards. Many gather for evening prayer meetings in a saloon that the unregenerate call the "Synagogue." Numerous passengers diligently begin journals, but most soon lose interest. One young journal keeper, JACK (VAN NOSTRAND) reports daily on his progress; however, by the time he reaches Paris, he reckons he is 4,000 pages behind. Other entertainments include music from an asthmatic melodeon and dancing—an activity impeded by the rolling of the ship. The passengers also celebrate a birthday (Captain Duncan's wife) and stage a mock trial.

Chapter 5

Early on the morning of June 21, passengers are awakened to the news that the AZORES are in sight. Because of rough weather, the ship anchors at the nearest island, where swarthy, noisy, lying, shoulder-shrugging, gesticulating Portuguese boatmen

carry the passengers ashore. Happy to be on solid land, Blucher celebrates by treating nine shipmates to a feast at Horta's principal hotel. When he is billed 21,700 reis, he thinks himself ruined. The day is saved when he learns that the amount is equivalent to only $21.70 in American money.

Chapter 6

Since none of the passengers knows anything about the Azores, the narrator supplies dry facts and details on local history. The community is eminently Portuguese—slow, poor, and shiftless—and Jesuit humbuggery flourishes. An old cathedral has the first of many religious relics the travelers will encounter, including a piece of the true cross.

Chapter 7

The next week's voyage is rough, curtailing activities and making passengers seasick again until the ship reaches GIBRALTAR (June 29). Many passengers buzz about going through SPAIN to Paris, but the narrator stays behind. As he enjoys the magnificent view from atop the Rock of Gibraltar, an officious guide bores him with a local legend about the "Queen's Chair." A few passengers are also proving annoying. A man dubbed "the Oracle," for example, insists that *both* PILLARS OF HERCULES are in Africa. He is tolerable enough, but two others are less so: the ship's self-anointed Poet Laureate (BLOODGOOD H. CUTTER) and a young idiot dubbed the "Interrogation Point." A small party of passengers crosses the strait to TANGIER.

Chapter 8

Tangier gives the sightseers exactly what they have been seeking: something thoroughly and uncompromisingly foreign. It is right out of the ARABIAN NIGHTS.

Chapter 9

The travelers experience their first real adventure in Tangier when the heedless Blucher nearly rides his mule into a mosque. Later they visit a jail and learn how severe punishments for crimes can be. They also learn about contracted marriages and polygamy; Morocco's ruler (Mohammed IV, 1803–1873) reputedly has 500 wives. Tangier is full of interest for one day, but after that it becomes a weary prison. The American consul (Jesse H. McMath) has been here for five years; his post would be an apt punishment for perpetrators of particularly heinous crimes.

Chapter 10

The Fourth of July is celebrated aboard the *Quaker City* on a characteristically beautiful Mediterranean day. After decorating the ship, holding meetings, and setting committees to work, the passengers spend the evening toasting, speaking and dancing on deck. The ship then reaches MARSEILLE, where the narrator and his friends rush ashore (still July 4). After clearing customs with little fuss, they dash to the nearest café, only to find communication in French nearly impossible.

Chapter 11

The eager travelers are adjusting well to all manner of strange customs. One thing they cannot easily adjust to, however, is providing their own soap in hotels. During a dinner, another American embarrasses them with his boisterous talk and laughter and his pitiful bragging about never dining without wine. The travelers visit the local Prado and take a boat to Castle d'If, whose notorious dungeon is famed as the prison of the Count of Monte Cristo and the Man in the Iron Mask. At the zoo, they study a tall, ungainly bird whose tranquil self-righteousness wins him the nickname "The Pilgrim."

Chapter 12

A train carries the narrator and two companions (DAN SLOTE and ABRAHAM JACKSON) 500 miles through the heart of France. French railroads offer much to admire: their trains are spacious and comfortable and they run like clockwork. In PARIS (July 5), the travelers speed through the streets, find a hotel, then look for a place that will satisfy the narrator's wish for a shave in a palatial Parisian barbershop. He settles, however, for a wigmaker's shop, where he endures a dreary and painful shave.

Chapter 13

The next morning the travelers engage a dignified-looking guide, who appears to be quiet and unobtrusive. Hoping for a guide with a romantic French name, they are distressed to learn that his name is "Billfinger," so they call him "Ferguson" instead. At breakfast they make the mistake of having Ferguson join them; his appetite is insatiable. He also has

the annoying habit of stopping at shops to buy things; his delays keep the travelers from the Louvre until shortly before it closes. On their third day in Paris, the travelers visit the International Exposition. Overwhelmed by its size, they leave after just two hours when they hear that Emperor NAPOLEON III and Turkey's Sultan ABDUL AZIZ will appear in a military review.

Chapter 14

The next day the travelers inspect Paris's Notre Dame Cathedral, a brown old Gothic pile whose relics include nails from the true cross, a fragment of the cross itself and part of the crown of thorns. They also visit the morgue, Jardin Mabille, and Jardin Asnières—where they see the high-wire act of Blondin (CHARLES BLONDIN) and cancan dancers—and they study miles of paintings in the Louvre.

Chapter 15

A pleasant visit to Père la Chaise, France's national burying-ground, recalls the tragic story of ABELARD AND HÉLOISE. Meanwhile, the travelers still struggle to communicate in Paris. Many shops advertise "English Spoken Here," but their English-speaking attendants are never on the premises. Other frustrations include the difficulty of finding bartenders who can mix American drinks.

Chapter 16

The travelers spend a day at Versailles (July 10), the beautiful old palace outside of Paris that compares favorably with the Garden of Eden. Everything about it stupefies—especially its gigantic scale. Back in Paris, the travelers tour the "antipodes" of Versailles—the Faubourg St. Antoine, a crowded slum.

Chapter 17

When the travelers return to Marseille (July 12), they learn that the ship's crew has been warring with British sailors; however, no great harm has been done. Many passengers are still on their own overland journeys. The ship next sails to GENOA (July 14), where they find the prettiest women in Europe. The narrator and his friends hire a guide who delights in showing off everything connected with CHRISTOPHER COLUMBUS. The vast Cathedral of San Lorenzo has a Madonna painted by St. Luke, as well as religious relics. The homes of wealthy

Genoese are palatial, and massive architecture is everywhere in view.

Chapter 18

A train takes the travelers through mountains to MILAN (July 17), where their greatest desire is to see the renowned cathedral. That night and the next day, they admire the marble colossus, which they explore thoroughly. Their guide shows them a hideous natural-looking sculpture of a skinless man, which reminds the narrator how hard it is to forget repulsive things. He recalls a childhood experience that left an indelible mark on him. One night, instead of going home late, he sneaked into his father's office to sleep. Gradually, he became aware of the presence of a corpse on the floor (James McFarland, a man killed in Hannibal, Missouri, in September 1843).

In the cathedral's crypt, the travelers stand among treasures worth 50 million francs. They also see the usual holy relics—including Christ's crown of thorns, though it is not as complete as the one at Notre Dame.

Chapter 19

Outside Milan's cathedral, the travelers are harried by their guide, who speaks execrable English and never pauses to let a person appreciate what he shows them. They visit La Scala, the Ambrosian Library, and other sights and stroll Milan's streets. At a public bathhouse, they object to being put in one tub, and they find that no soap is provided. They are, however, learning to emulate English travelers, who carry soap with them. Later they see Leonardo da Vinci's badly ravaged *The Last Supper* in a tumble-down ruin of a church.

Chapter 20

After taking a train from Milan to COMO (July 18), the travelers lodge at a Bellagio hotel on Lake Como. On their arrival, they are fumigated by local authorities concerned about CHOLERA.

Chapter 21

A steamer carries the travelers down Lake Lecco, from which they go by carriage to Bergamo (July 20). Now well into interior Italy, they see solid stone houses, idle peasants, slow-moving carts, and innumerable shrines to saints. They pass through strange old towns, which are unaffected by the changes in the modern world. As they speed past a medieval castle, their guide tells them the legend of the noble Count Luigi Gennaro Guido Alphonso di Genova, who fought in the Crusades and returned 30 years later to rescue his wife and daughter from his brother. The travelers reach Bergamo shortly before their train is to leave for Venice.

Chapter 22

At night, the travelers enter VENICE (July 20), a once-great city that has fallen prey to poverty, neglect, and melancholy decay. Even the romantic gondola disappoints; it is nothing but a rusty old canoe with a sable hearse-body clapped on. Just as all the romance of Venice seems about to disappear, 2,000 gondolas illuminated by lanterns cross the Grand Canal in a festival that lasts all night. Venice is like a overflowed ARKANSAS town, with still waters lapping at doorsteps and boats clustered under windows. By day, it has little poetry; only under moonlight does it become the princeliest among the nations of the Earth.

Chapter 23

Over time, Venetian gondolas grow more interesting; it is quaint to see people conduct routine errands aboard these graceful boats. The travelers themselves go almost everywhere in their gondola—including St. Mark's Square. It is difficult to adjust to the local custom of staring at the faces of pretty young Venetian women, though they seem to like it. However, the travelers enjoy learning curious customs, so they can show off back at home. Some tourists, however, carry this too far—even forgetting their own language.

Visiting a long list of churches and art galleries, the travelers see pictures of enough martyrs and saints to regenerate the world. The narrator regrets lacking the appreciation for the Old Masters that the other passengers have. In Venice, the travelers find their first guide who actually knows anything—a man born into slavery in South Carolina who came here as an infant.

Chapter 24

As fellow *Quaker City* passengers converge on Venice from the north, the travelers go by train to

FLORENCE (July 22–23). There they try to traverse its weary miles of picture galleries, but their enthusiasm is gone. One night, the narrator gets lost and walks miles to find his hotel.

The travelers next visit PISA, where they climb the Leaning Tower. Later the same day, they rejoin their ship at LEGHORN. Back in the company of none but fellow countrymen, they exult in speaking and hearing only their own language. Meanwhile, local authorities question why a steamer would cross the Atlantic merely for a pleasure excursion; they suspect that its people are incendiary, bloodthirsty Garibaldians in disguise. Some passengers visit General GARIBALDI, reinforcing the authorities' suspicions. To avoid the risk of being quarantined on the ship at Naples, the narrator and his friends take a French steamer to CIVITAVECCHIA.

Chapter 25

Italy has many things not easily understood, such as why its bankrupt government builds palatial railroad depots and marvelous turnpikes. The new national government is squandering its resources; its problems are compounded by having to compete with the Church, which owns the richest lands but pays no taxes. Despite its wealth, even the Church is surrounded by poverty and squalor, with wretched beggars at its very doors. For 1,500 years, Italy has poured its energy, finances, and industry into building churches, while starving half its people. Italy is a vast museum of magnificence and misery. Florence's grand mausoleum is an example. It was built to bury the Savior back when Crusaders hoped to bring the Holy Sepulchre to Italy; instead, it holds the Medicis, who cruelly tyrannized Florence.

Chapter 26

Nothing confers more delight than discovery. The narrator imagines being a Roman who visits America and reports to ROME on what he discovers there: a country with no overshadowing church, a government not protected by foreign soldiers, common people who can read and write, thousands of schools and books, and newspapers everywhere. It is a place where common men own the land they till, where Jews are treated as human beings, and where no mendicant priests beg for the Church.

The travelers spend considerable time at Rome's great Church of St. Peter, which is so vast one scarcely knows what to compare it with. They also explore the ancient Forum and the Coliseum—where the narrator finds a copy of an ancient playbill advertising an extravaganza that includes a "General Slaughter" in which lions and barbarian prisoners will war until all are exterminated. He also finds a copy of the *Roman Daily Battle-Ax* that reviews this same performance.

Chapter 27

Proud of avoiding BYRON's old saw, "butchered to make a Roman holyday," the narrator recalls Judge (Augustus W.) Oliver, with whom he once trudged across Nevada's GREAT AMERICAN DESERT in winter. No matter how bad things got, Oliver never complained. Later he lived in rude houses built into the sides of hills, but after large animals fell through his roof three times, he said, "this thing is growing monotonous." Byron's oft-repeated quote is similarly monotonous.

It is also so monotonous to hear about Michelangelo—who seems to have designed *everything* in Italy—that it is a relief to learn he is dead. The travelers enjoy asking unsuspecting guides inane questions about him. Whatever a guide has to show—even an Egyptian obelisk—they ask if Michelangelo made it. When the travelers discover how much guides enjoy arousing admiration, they cease to admire anything, even the sublimest wonders.

Chapter 28 (volume 2: chapter 1)

The picturesque horrors of the Vatican's Capuchin Convent are fascinating. Arches made of human thighbones, pyramids of skulls, and other works of art assembled from monks' bones decorate its underground vault. A monk tells stories about the men who left these bones, using their fragments to illustrate his points in as grotesque a performance as one could ever witness.

The Vatican's wilderness of statues, paintings, and curiosities is dizzying. Where one old master in a palace might be moving, acres of them leave one numb. Why are there so many paintings of Virgins and popes, while Rome's own history remains unpainted? Without wishing to be irreverent, the narrator suggests that Rome ranks Holy Personages in this order:

1. the Virgin Mary;
2. the Deity;
3. Peter;
4. some 12 or 15 canonized popes and martyrs;
5. Jesus Christ—but always as an infant in arms.

Chapter 29 (2:2)

When the overland travelers reach NAPLES by train (c. August 1), they find their ship quarantined in the harbor. While their ship is now a prison, they are free to move about, and they comfort their quarantined shipmates by boating out to them daily to tell them about what they are missing ashore. A trip to Mt. VESUVIUS is memorable, but before the narrator gets around to describing it, he tells about a trip to the Isle of Ischia, a concert at which the audience taunts an aging singer, and a wretched religious imposture—the miraculous liquefaction of the blood of St. Januarius.

Chapter 30 (2:3)

Merely *seeing* Naples may not make one die—as the ancient adage suggests—however, *living* there may produce a different result. In any case, the best way to see Naples is from high up on Vesuvius at dawn. Within the city itself, the filth and smells are intolerable; Naples has 625,000 inhabitants in a space that would hold an American city of 150,000. Nowhere are contrasts between magnificence and misery greater.

Chapter 31 (2:4)

POMPEII dispels one's old ideas about descending dark stairways and gloomy tunnels. Half the city is excavated and open to sunlight. It is now a city of hundreds of roofless houses and tangled mazes of streets. Though its houses seem much alike, they are admirably decorated; many of its ancient pictures are more pleasing than the celebrated rubbish of the Renaissance. What were people doing the night that Pompeii was destroyed? Evidence of Pompeii's customs and history is everywhere, but one wonders what traces an American city buried by a volcano would leave.

Italy's many stately ruins make one reflect on the transitory nature of fame. After just 20 centuries flutter away, what mark is left by those thinking they have made history? Little more than undecipherable inscriptions in stone. Forty centuries from now, perhaps all that will be left of General GRANT's great name will be a garbled encyclopedia entry: "URIAH S. [or Z.] GRAUNT—popular poet of ancient times in the Aztec provinces of the United States of British America."

Chapter 32 (2:5)

For the first time in weeks, all the passengers are together, and the ship leaves Naples with everyone cheerful (August 11). They sail past Stromboli and through the Strait of Messina. After a pleasant cruise through the Greek islands, they anchor at Piraeus, from which they can just make out the Parthenon in ATHENS (August 14). In no previous land has everyone been so eager to rush ashore; however, local authorities tell them to accept an 11-day quarantine or leave. That night, the narrator and three other men (WILLIAM DENNY, GEORGE BRIGHT BIRCH, and ABRAHAM JACKSON) sneak ashore to visit the Acropolis.

Chapter 33 (2:6)

As the ship moves north (August 15), views of barren landscapes make one wonder what supports Greece. Amidst such poverty, even its throne went begging until a Danish prince (George I) accepted it. At the Dardanelles, the ship enters another land rich in history—and poor as the Sahara in everything else—and anchors at CONSTANTINOPLE (August 17). From the anchorage, the Turkish capital is the handsomest city the travelers have seen. Ashore, it is a different matter—an eternal circus, with shops that are mere coops and people thicker than bees.

The chief interest of the famed Mosque of St. Sophia is that it was transformed from a Christian church with little alteration. The travelers also visit the Dancing Dervishes, the Thousand and One Columns, the marble mausoleum of Sultan Mahmoud, and the great Bazaar in Stamboul—one of the few sights worth seeing, but a place where the only thing one cannot smell is something that smells good.

Chapter 34 (2:7)

While Constantinople has many mosques, churches, and graveyards, morals and whiskey are scarce. Parents still sell girls, though not publicly as in the past, and the market for them is up, for various reasons—including the recent return of the sultan (Abdul Aziz) from Europe. If American newspapers were published in Constantinople, they probably would present a "Slave Girl Market Report," such as a sample that follows. Commercial morals are uniformly bad. Constantinople's official scavengers, its celebrated dogs, have been misrepresented. The wretched curs are everywhere, but seem too weak even to cross a street. It is surprising to see newspapers hawked in streets where giants and genii of the Arabian Nights once dwelt. However, the papers are unpopular with the government, which regards them as a mild form of pestilence.

Chapter 35 (2:8)

The ship sails for the BLACK SEA (August 19), while a dozen passengers remain in Constantinople in the clutches of "Far-away Moses," a famous rascally guide. The first port is SEVASTOPOL (August 21), a town horribly battered by the recent (Crimean) war. Though warned in Constantinople to be careful about passports in RUSSIA, the narrator has lost his and is carrying that of his roommate (Dan Slote), who has stayed in Constantinople. Happily, the American flag is all the passport the travelers need, for Sevastopol is the most hospitable stop yet. As plans to visit the emperor of Russia develop, the travelers comb the nearby battlefields for relics.

Chapter 36 (2:9)

To take on coal, the ship sails to ODESSA (August 21–22), which reminds the narrator of a typical American city and makes him feel at home. Happy to learn that Odessa has no sights to see, the travelers celebrate with idling and an ice-cream debauch.

Chapter 37 (2:10)

At YALTA (August 25), the American consul (Timothy C. Smith) advises how to behave before the emperor, explaining that he should be greeted with a smile signifying love, gratification, and admiration. Everyone practices this complicated smile, and the narrator helps draft a formal address to the emperor. The next day the emperor (Czar ALEXANDER II) receives the travelers warmly at his summer palace.

The travelers accept invitations to visit the nearby homes of the crown prince and the czar's younger brother, Grand Duke Michael (Michael Nicholaevitch, 1832–1909). The czar rejoins them at the grand duke's home—prompting the narrator to revise his old ideas about emperors, who behind the scenes are strangely like common mortals.

Chapter 38 (2:11)

After another stop in Constantinople (August 30–September 3), the ship turns toward Asia. Crew members torment the travelers by repeatedly burlesquing their introduction to the czar and the narrator hears his little speech so many times that its words become intolerable. Meanwhile, the first port the travelers visit is SMYRNA (September 6)—a typical Oriental city, with dark, comfortless houses, crooked streets, confusing bazaars, dirt, fleas, broken-hearted dogs, and awful stenches. Such is Oriental splendor.

Chapter 39 (2:12)

From Smyrna, the travelers ride donkeys to a lofty citadel where one of Asia's Seven Apocalyptic Churches stood 18 centuries earlier. As they ascend, veins of oyster shells unexpectedly appear in the mountain. The narrator wonders if the oysters climbed up themselves. A guide tells them that followers of Miller (William Miller, 1782–1849) gathered on this mountain three years earlier to await the ascension.

Chapter 40 (2:13)

The travelers go by train and donkey to EPHESUS (September 7), the site of the fabulous ancient Temple of Diana. The city's former greatness brings to mind the "Legend of the Seven Sleepers":

> About 1,500 years ago, seven young Christians left Ephesus to avoid persecution. They took along bottles of curious liquors, but forgot them in a cave. Five years later, they returned to the cave, found the bottles, drank them and fell asleep. When they awakened, they were naked and their coins lay on the ground, corroded

The repentant pilgrims regret their parsimony after they miss their chance to sail on the Sea of Galilee in chapter 47.

with age. Everything in Ephesus had changed. When the men realized that they had slept for 200 years, they lay down and died. Their names still appear on their tombs: "Johannes Smithianus, Trumps, Gift, High, and Low, Jack, and The Game." Their bottles are inscribed with the names of ancient heathen gods: "Rumpunch, Jinsling, Egnog."

Chapter 41 (2:14)
The travelers leave Ephesus without their usual haul of relics after an official confiscates their plunder, and they sail from Smyrna (September 8). Their excitement grows as they make plans for the Holy Land and divide into small traveling parties. The narrator joins seven others (Dr. George Birch, William F. Church, Joshua William Davis, Colonel William R. Denny, Abraham Jackson, Jack Van Nostrand, and Dan Slote) who will go to DAMASCUS and down the length of Palestine. Others plan less ambitious journeys. At Beirut (September 10), the narrator's party engages a dragoman (guide) named ABRAHAM to organize their expedition and they leave Beirut in astonishing style (September 11).

Chapter 42 (2:15)
The travelers' first camp is near a place called Temnin-el-Foka (September 12), which they dub "JACKSONVILLE." The next day, they pass through historically rich country and pay their respects at Noah's tomb. Its authenticity is beyond doubt:

Noah's son Shem showed it to his descendants, who showed it to theirs, and so on.

Chapter 43 (2:16)
Five tedious hours take the travelers across the torrid Valley of LEBANON, where farmers still plow with sharp sticks and winnow wheat as the prophet Abraham did. At BAALBEK (September 13), the travelers admire the great ancient temples, some of whose stones are larger than a steamboat hull. It seems inconceivable that these blocks were quarried and raised to such heights. Gods or giants must have built Baalbek.

Refusing to travel on the Sabbath, the party's pious "PILGRIMS" insist on completing a three-day journey to Damascus in two days, ignoring the other men's pleas to show compassion for their tired horses.

Chapter 44 (2:17)
The next day brings another 13-hour ride, through hot, barren terrain. At twilight, the travelers look down on DAMASCUS, which is beautiful from the mountain. If the narrator visited Damascus again, he would camp above the city as there is no need to go inside. A tradition claims that Damascus stands on the site of the Garden of Eden. True or not, it is no paradise now. At sundown (September 14), they reach the gates of Damascus, Syria's only walled city, to which even BAKSHEESH cannot buy entry after dark. The city has no street lamps; people go out at night with lanterns, as in the days of the Arabian Nights. After making their way through the narrow streets, the travelers find their hotel through a hole in the wall. The next day, they again fight their way through the streets to see St. Luke's famous crooked "street which is called Straight."

Chapter 45 (2:18)
During his last 24 hours in Damascus, the narrator lies gravely ill but leaves with his companions in the middle of the hottest day thus far (September 16). The motley horsemen present a ludicrous sight as they bounce along single-file: Each man wears green glasses and carries a bobbing umbrella. After passing the spot where Saul was converted, they camp near a place they call

"JONESBOROUGH." The next morning takes them to BANIYAS and the sources of the River JORDAN (September 17). It is curious to stand on ground on which the Savior walked—it seems to contradict the mystery one attaches to a god. The travelers are shocked by the sight of young children whose eyes are covered with flies. People flock to be treated by Dr. B. (Birch), whom they see as a mighty healer.

Chapter 46 (2:19)

The next stop is DAN in the HOLY LAND (September 18). After days of riding over rocks, the travelers find a smooth, open plain and spur their horses on. Fearing Bedouins, their guide wants to halt; his anxiety brings to mind Wm. C. Grimes's purported hairbreadth escapes from Bedouins. The richly historic region also recalls stories of Joshua and untold numbers of kings. The very name "PALESTINE" seems to suggest a country as large as the United States, but the reality is much different. At daybreak, one expects grass to sparkle with dew, fragrant flowers to enrich the air and birds to sing in trees. Alas, there is no dew, no flowers, no birds, no trees.

Chapter 47 (2:20)

The travelers stop Jack from clodding a turtle. After hearing the pilgrims talk about this land of milk and honey, where the "voice of the turtle" is heard, he resents the turtle's refusal to sing. Later, the travelers visit the pit into which Joseph was cast by his brothers.

The travelers relish swimming in the Sea of GALILEE, but find its beauty wildly exaggerated. Even so, they are eager to sail on it and say they will pay *anything* for a boat ride. However, they miss their only chance for a boat by dickering over its price and then become upset with each other. As they pass the shapeless ruin of Capernaum, where Christ gained fame healing the sick, they reflect on how small was the portion of Earth from which Christianity sprang.

Chapter 48 (2:21)

Like all Syrian villages, Magdala is not beautiful; it is cramped, squalid, and ringing with cries for baksheesh. The travelers examine Mary Magdalene's

dwelling, remove bits of the wall for specimens, then go to Tiberias (September 19), where they see only poor and uncomely people. The celebrated Sea of Galilee is neither as large nor as beautiful as Lake TAHOE. Silence and solitude brood over both, but the solitude of the latter is as cheerful and fascinating as the solitude of the former is dismal and repellent. Writers rave about the beauty of Galilee and its surroundings; typical examples appear in books by Grimes and "C. W. E." (Charles Wyllys Elliott). Many visitors here must be Presbyterians; they come for evidences to support their creed and find a Presbyterian Palestine. Likewise, Baptists find a Baptist Palestine, and so on.

Chapter 49 (2:22)

The travelers again swim in the Sea of Galilee but bypass the warm baths near Tiberias. In the morning a fantastically outfitted Arab appears, heavily armed with antiquated weapons. The dragoman (Abraham) explains that the main is to be their guard through Bedouin country. In actuality, the man is simply a source of revenue for the local sheikh. The travelers ascend to a site where Saladin fought a great battle against the Crusaders 700 years earlier.

Chapter 50 (2:23)

From Tabor, it is two hours to Nazareth (September 20), where the travelers visit the grotto where the Annunciation occurred. Thousands of miles away, one can imagine the angel appearing here before the Virgin; but *here*, few can do it. They also inspect the places where Jesus worked as a carpenter and the ruins of the synagogue from which He was driven by a mob. Only fragments of its ancient walls remain, but the pilgrims—whose chief sin is lust for "specimens"—break off pieces.

Chapter 51 (2:24)

Nazareth is interesting because it seems to be precisely as Jesus left it. Its sights make the narrator think of passages he has copied from the "Apocryphal New Testament"—such as chapter 19, which tells how Jesus was charged with throwing a boy off a roof, then miraculously caused the dead boy to speak and acquit Him. Meanwhile, it seems likely that some members of the party will eventually be shot. Its pilgrims read Grimes's *Nomadic Life* and keep their hands always on their pistols—which they often draw and aim at imaginary Bedouins.

At Endor, the travelers find more dirt, degradation, and savagery than at any place they have seen yet. Their journey then takes them through Nain, Shunem, and the Plain of Jezreel before they camp at Jenin (September 21). The next morning they visit Samaria (September 22).

Chapter 52 (2:25)

At Shechem, the travelers see one of the patriarch Jacob's residences and a manuscript said to be the oldest document on Earth. The narrator, however, has purchased one even older—which he will publish when he finishes translating it (an allusion to EVE'S DIARY?). Near Shechem they visit Joseph's tomb and Jacob's well. Early the next day, they pass Shiloh and a shapeless mass of ruins still called Beth-el—from which angels lifted Jacob to Heaven. After the pilgrims take what is left of the ruin, they continue on. No more tiresome landscape exists than that bounding the approaches to JERUSALEM. They halt above the city and marvel as its smallness: it is no larger than an American village of 4,000, or a Syrian city of 30,000. Just after noon they enter through the famed Damascus Gate (September 23).

Chapter 53 (2:26)

Jerusalem is small enough for a person to walk around in an hour. Its streets are badly paved, crooked and so narrow that cats jump across them, from roof to roof. Lepers, cripples, and idiots beg for baksheesh everywhere. Jerusalem is mournful, dreary, and lifeless. The travelers' first stop is the Church of the HOLY SEPULCHRE—a vast structure housing Christ's tomb and the main Crucifixion sites. It also has the tomb of ADAM. Touched by unexpectedly finding the grave of a blood relation in so distant a land, the narrator weeps unashamedly.

Chapter 54 (2:27)

Other holy sites in Jerusalem that the travelers see include the Sorrowful Way, Ecce Homo Arch, St. Veronica's home, and the house of the Wandering Jew—who must be amused to see blockheads such

as these calling what they are doing "traveling." After visiting the Mosque of Omar and other places, they are surfeited with sights; only the Church of the Holy Sepulchre holds their interest. Outside the walled city, they cross the Valley of Hinnom and visit the Garden of Gethsemane and other sites.

Chapter 55 (2:28)

As other shipmates converge on Jerusalem, the travelers organize an expedition on the DEAD SEA. Though war rumors are flying, no one backs out; instead, each person struggles to maintain an unostentatious position at the rear of the caravan. Ancient Jericho (September 25) proves not much to look at; Joshua hardly left enough of the city to cast a shadow. In order to best a rival guide, the dragoman rushes the party to the River Jordan before dawn. At daybreak, they disrobe and enter the river singing, but not for long in the frigid water. Eventually, they wade across and continue to the Dead Sea, where they swim.

After a hideous ride across a torrid plain, the party spends the night in Marsaba's convent. Its ascetic monks seem dead to the outside world, but are kind and generous hosts. Though raised to hate everything Catholic, the narrator cannot help feeling grateful to the Catholic convents that make Holy Land travel tolerable. Refreshed, the travelers proceed to Bethlehem (September 26), where they visit the grotto where Christ was born. Even here, it is impossible to meditate; the tumult of beggars, cripples, and monks permits one to think only of baksheesh. It is a relief to get away.

Chapter 56 (2:29)

After visiting all the holy places around Jerusalem that they had missed earlier, the travelers head for the coast (September 29). They spend their first night at the convent of Ramla and then ride hard for JAFFA, where they see the ship (September 30). So ends the pilgrimage.

Chapter 57 (2:30)

Relieved to be at sea again (October 1), free of anxiety about where to go and other questions, the travelers find being back aboard the *Quaker City* incomparably satisfying after their wearisome pilgrimage. A pleasant voyage takes them to EGYPT. The moment they anchor at Alexandria (October 2), Jack and the narrator go ashore. Their shipmates follow the next morning. At Jaffa the ship took on 40 members of a failed religious commune led by GEORGE J. ADAMS.

Alexandria is too European to be novel, so the travelers take a train to Cairo (October 4), a satisfactorily Oriental city. Their hotel is the world's worst, apart from one in which the narrator once stayed in America. He quotes from an old notebook about the "Benton House" (actually the Heming House, in KEOKUK, Iowa), where he was grudgingly allowed a reading lamp that served merely to illuminate the grimness of his surroundings.

Chapter 58 (2:31)

By donkey and boat, a party of excursionists go up the Nile to Gizeh (October 5), passing the place where Pharaoh's daughter found MOSES in the bulrushes. At the Pyramid of Cheops, muscular men besiege them, demanding to pull them up the pyramid for money. The great pyramid compares favorably in size with both Washington's Capitol and Rome's St. Peter's Cathedral. Its prodigious height reminds the narrator of a time when he thought that a bluff by the Mississippi River must be the highest mountain in the world. Earlier still, he though Holliday's Hill (CARDIFF HILL) near his hometown a nobel mountain, but it was nothing compared to the pyramid.

The nearby SPHINX has a sad face and a dignity not of Earth. Though stone, it seems sentient as it gazes out over the ocean of Time. It is Memory—Retrospection—wrought into visible, tangible form. As the travelers reflect on its grand loneliness and impressive mystery, they hear a familiar clink—a fellow passenger (DR. WILLIAM GIBSON) is trying to break off a specimen. Little is said about the great mosque of Mehemet Ali, Joseph's well, Cairo, and others sights along the return route to Alexandria (October 7).

Chapter 59 (2:32)

As the ship recrosses the Mediterranean and the Atlantic, its passengers relish the chance to rest. Along the way, they pass MALTA and touch at SARDINIA (October 13), ALGIERS (October 15) and

Malaga, Spain (October 17), but because of cholera fears, no one goes ashore at any of these places and the days grow monotonous. While the ship recoals at Gibraltar (October 17–24), the narrator and three companions (Abraham Jackson, JULIUS MOULTON, and JULIA NEWELL) spend a delightful week in southern SPAIN. Their experiences are too numerous for a short chapter and there is not enough room for a long one, so they are left out.

Chapter 60 (2:33)

Immediately after the excursionists rejoin the ship at Cadiz, it sails (October 25). One passenger takes his complaints about the ship's coffee directly to the captain, only to make an egregious ass of himself before everyone when the coffee he denounces proves to be tea. That ass is the narrator.

Several pleasant days at sea carry the ship to MADEIRA (October 28). Told they must wait out a quarantine before going ashore, the passengers vote to sail on. Next, they reach BERMUDA, where they enjoy one of the most pleasant stops of the entire cruise (November 11–15). The ship's final run returns them to New York, so they busy themselves with separating group purchases, packing, and preparing for customs. Some passengers want to enter New York harbor dressed as Turks; however, when the ship finally lands, everyone is dressed in Christian garb (November 19). The long, strange cruise is over.

Chapter 61 (2: unnumbered)

An article written by Mark Twain for the *NEW YORK HERALD* of November 20, 1867 is reprinted, with his signature, to sum up the cruise.

Though advertised as a "pleasure excursion," the cruise did not look or act like one. Parties to a pleasure excursion should be young and giddy; they should dance and sing and make love, but sermonize very little. By contrast, three-fourths of the *Quaker City* passengers were between 40 and 70. They were not gay and frisky, they never romped, they talked little, and they never sang—except at prayer-meetings. The pleasure ship was a synagogue, the pleasure trip a funeral excursion without a corpse.

After mentioning the trip's highlights, Clemens says that he bears no malice or ill will toward anyone connected with the cruise. Things he did not like yesterday, he likes very well today.

Conclusion

Nearly a year after the pilgrimage is over, the author records his thoughts as he writes in SAN FRANCISCO. He finds that his memories of the trip have grown more pleasant. If the *Quaker City* were to embark on the same voyage again, he would gladly join it—even with the same captain, same pilgrims, and same sinners. He made eight or nine good friends among the passengers and was even on speaking terms with the rest—a good average at sea. Indeed, he would rather travel with an excursion party of Methuselahs than have to change ships and comrades constantly. He finds no fault with the manner in which the excursion was conducted. Its program was faithfully carried out, leaving him with good thoughts about the many places he visited.

BACKGROUND AND PUBLISHING HISTORY

Soon after Clemens first left the Midwest in 1853, he began writing travel letters for newspapers. By early 1867, his letters to California papers, such as the SACRAMENTO UNION and the SAN FRANCISCO ALTA CALIFORNIA, were winning him real celebrity; as a result, he began thinking about extending his travels to encompass the whole world. In February 1867, he was writing regular letters to the *Alta* from NEW YORK CITY when he learned of plans for the coming summer's *Quaker City* excursion. Bored with writing about one place, he persuaded the *Alta* to buy him passage on the *Quaker City* and pay him $20 each for 50 letters that he would write on the voyage. He also arranged to write additional letters for the NEW YORK HERALD and NEW YORK TRIBUNE. As early as March, he was discussing the coming cruise in letters to the *Alta* that provide a commentary on the preparations for the voyage up to the eve of its departure.

When Clemens contracted to write letters about the cruise, he was already thinking about getting a book out of the trip; he thus composed his letters with the idea of revision in mind. Within two weeks of his return from the voyage in November,

Elisha BLISS approached him about writing a book for the AMERICAN PUBLISHING COMPANY. After visiting Bliss in Hartford in January, Clemens began working on his book in WASHINGTON, D.C., drawing upon clippings of his travel letters assembled in a scrapbook by his sister, PAMELA MOFFETT. A firsthand description by a journalist friend depicts him furiously cutting and pasting from these clippings, adding revisions in the margins of the pages. He soon discovered, however, that these letters alone would not provide enough material to fill the kind of book that Bliss needed for his SUBSCRIPTION-BOOK market.

By March, Clemens had completed 10 chapters of his book when he learned that the proprietors of the *Alta* objected to his using the letters for which they had paid. He sailed for San Francisco, where he persuaded the *Alta* people to give him all the rights to his letters. He then remained in California for several months. After a brief LECTURE tour that took in western NEVADA, he returned to work on his book in San Francisco in May. While he was there, BRET HARTE helped him with the manuscript, in return for which Harte was invited to extract whatever he wanted for his new magazine, the *OVERLAND MONTHLY.* Harte seems to have limited his advice to suggesting the deletion of passages he thought improper, irrelevant, or overly irreverent. Clemens accepted Harte's recommended cuts, the most substantial of which was a full chapter on Spain. Harte, in turn, published extracts from the manuscript on France and Italy in four issues of his magazine.

On June 23, 1868, Clemens pronounced his manuscript done; two weeks later he left San Francisco for good. He delivered his manuscript to Bliss in Hartford on August 4, 1868, and finally signed a publishing contract with him two and a half months later. In mid-November, he began a lecture tour in the Midwest and East with "THE AMERICAN VANDAL ABROAD" as his topic, generating valuable publicity for his coming book. After completing his tour in March, he turned his attention to correcting proofs of the book with the help of his new fiancée, Olivia Langdon.

The American Publishing Company issued the book as *Innocents Abroad* in late July 1869. The first edition contains 234 line drawings. Most of these pictures are unsigned, but TRUE WILLIAMS and ROSWELL SHURTLEFF are among the known contributors. In the summer of 1870, the London publisher JOHN CAMDEN HOTTEN issued *The Innocents Abroad: The Voyage Out,* the first volume of an unauthorized two-volume edition. Six weeks later, the second volume, *The New Pilgrims' Progress: The Journey Home,* appeared. The following year, Hotten issued a one-volume edition as *Mark Twain's Pleasure Trip on the Continent.* In 1872, GEORGE ROUTLEDGE published an authorized edition in London. Clemens himself made substantial revisions in the Routledge edition, removing words and passages that he feared might offend British sensibilities. This revised text was later used in English-language editions published by TAUCHNITZ in Germany. Pirated editions continued to appear in England.

Although *Innocents* was published in the United States by a subscription house, it was widely and favorably reviewed; it received especially important notices from W. D. HOWELLS in the *ATLANTIC MONTHLY* and Bret Harte in the *Overland Monthly.* Critics praised the book for both its humor and its eloquence but generally preferred the former. Though the book's reviews were almost uniformly positive, Clemens himself later regretted what he came to regard as the crudity of its writing.

Clemens's original 1866-to-early-1867 letters to the *Alta* were republished in *MARK TWAIN'S TRAVELS WITH MR. BROWN* (1940), edited by Franklin Walker and G. Ezra Dane; his letters from the *Quaker City* excursion itself were collected in 1958 as *Traveling with the Innocents Abroad: Mark Twain's Original Reports from Europe and the Holy Land,* edited by Daniel Morley McKeithan. Since the original publication of *Innocents Abroad,* however, no substantially revised edition has ever been issued, aside from that prepared for Routledge. In 1984, the Library of America published the first edition with scholarly annotations in a combined volume with *Roughing It* edited by Guy Cardwell. In 1996, the *OXFORD MARK TWAIN* edition included a facsimile reprint of the first American edition with a new introduction by novelist Mordecai Richter and an afterword by scholar David E. E. Sloane. The MARK TWAIN PROJECT at the University of California has tentatively scheduled publication of a fully corrected edition of *Innocents Abroad* for after 2010.

While the 50 letters that Clemens wrote for the *Alta* form the core of *Innocents Abroad,* the book contains considerable material from other sources. Many passages, including some entire chapters, derive from his letters to the *Herald* and the *Tribune;* others he wrote from scratch after the voyage, drawing on his own NOTEBOOKS—which have since been published—and the writings of fellow passengers, many of whom published travel letters of their own. In combining all these materials, he often rewrote episodes with new casts of characters or added passages to change the tone, as when he softened his criticisms of the Sea of Galilee by adding a lyrical description of the lake at night.

The PBS production of *Innocents Abroad* includes the episode in which Clemens (Craig Wasson) visits the Leaning Tower of Pisa. *(Public Broadcasting System)*

The original manuscript of *Innocents Abroad* is not known still to exist. The Mark Twain Project holds the remnants of the original scrapbook from which Clemens worked, and the library at Vassar College has the original manuscripts of the fragments that Clemens deleted before delivering the manuscript to Bliss.

A television dramatization of *Innocents Abroad* that first aired on PBS on May 9, 1983, featured Craig Wasson (1954–) as Mark Twain, David Ogden Stiers as Dr. Jackson, and Brooke Adams as Julia Newell. While this adaptation follows the broad outline of the original book, it takes many liberties with both specific episodes and characterizations. For example, Mark Twain (not "Clemens" in the script) makes an enemy of the captain (Barry Morse) as soon as he boards the ship and is Jackson's rival for the affections of Newell through the voyage.

CRITICAL COMMENTARY

The Innocents Abroad inaugurated an era of American tourism and travel writing in which a confident and self-consciously uncouth American voice approached Europe with a critical, rather than purely reverent, eye (Messent 27). In providing the "literary measure of the new American spirit," *The Innocents Abroad* is as much about American tourists as their destinations; Jane Jacobs comments that even today, "If the reader is American, he may also find himself on a tour of his own psyche" (Messent 23, Jacobs xxiii). From the beginning, Clemens's fellow passengers on the *Quaker City* voyage are the object of his sharp eye and the target of many of his zingers. On the first page of his book, Clemens plays on the relative self-indulgence of the passengers, describing their journey in the diminutive as a "picnic on a gigantic scale" (chapter 1). Before embarking, Clemens learns the names and pokes fun at the pretentious titles of his cohorts, such as the "gentleman who had 'COMMISSIONER OF THE UNITED STATES OF AMERICA TO EUROPE, ASIA, AND AFRICA' thundering after his name in one awful blast" (chapter 2). Making fun of the status-conscious worthies at home sets up the aggressively populist approach that will underlie Clemens's treatment of ancient and venerable civilization overseas.

Clemens's fellow passengers remain a figure of fun throughout the book. Shortly after setting out, Clemens pokes fun at many passengers' eager adoption of naval terms that they half understand. The other passengers are avid journal keepers; as a commissioned professional, Clemens is subtly defensive, giving the common areas "the semblance of a writing school" (chapter 4). In particular, he chronicles with facetious condescension the progress of a young passenger named Jack Van Nostrand, who fills his journal mostly with boring minutiae (a charge some critics have made about parts of Clemens's own travel writing). Within a few days of his first effort, he is estimating the monetary value of the finished product and soon gives up altogether after falling behind (ibid.).

Several passengers prove particularly durable sources of humor for which they earn titles. Clemens crafts a tour de force description of the "Oracle" as "an innocent old ass who . . . never uses a one-syllable word when he can think of a longer one . . . reads a chapter in the guide-books, mixes the facts all up, with his bad memory, and then goes off to inflict the whole mess on somebody as wisdom" (chapter 7). More annoying is "the poet" who annoys and embarrasses his shipmates by giving "copies of his verses to Consuls, commanders, hotel keepers . . . any body, in fact, who will submit to a grievous infliction most kindly meant." There is also a young man known as "Interrogation Point," a nonstop asker of questions (chapter 7).

Economic Observation

Clemens's preoccupation with the economic development and infrastructure of the regions he visits throughout the trip draws the observation from Jane Jacobs that he was "obsessed with the condition of paving" (xx). Amazed by the quality of roads in the Azores, for example, Clemens offers a poetically detailed description of the "hard, smooth, level thoroughfare, just sprinkled with black lava sand, and bordered with little gutters neatly paved with small smooth pebbles" (chapter 6). At the level of voice, Clemens's faith in the modernization and excitement with novelty fosters his tone of cheerful philistinism regarding the lingering achievements of the Old World. On seeing the paintings of the Old Masters, for example, he pronounces the contemporary copies of the Old Masters' work superior, noting, "May be the originals were handsome when they were new, but they are not now" (chapter 19).

The same practicality that allows Clemens to see poetry in infrastructure leads him to esteem architecture over art, "because I can understand the one and am not competent to appreciate the other" (chapter 25). Business practices and the development of local and international markets, including tourist economies, are a constant undercurrent in Clemens's chronicle. In Gibraltar, he and several other male tourists are recognized and separately taken in by a saleswoman who charms them into buying kid gloves with the same canned flattery (chapter 7). Their male camaraderie is further cemented by the exploration of foreign goods and services, such as sampling and comparing the rough and bloody shaves they receive at various stops (chapter 12).

Language and Culture

Clemens's cultural reporting is significantly colored by his interest in the uses and abuses of language. Acting as a representative American tourist—an Anglophone with a limited grasp of any other language—Clemens bristles at the "base fraud" among French shops of posting an "English Spoken Here" sign regardless of the reality to "inveigle foreigners into their lairs, and trusted to their own blandishments to keep them there till they bought something" (chapter 15). Relieved but barely mollified by the guides that do speak English, Clemens applies his dialect skills to the capture and ridicule of the particularly striking "specimen of guide-English" (chapter 19). The running joke of calling all guides "Ferguson" begins when the narrator and company find a suitable Parisian guide but cannot reconcile themselves to his un-Parisian name, Billfinger. So, they decide to call him, and every other guide, Ferguson. Of a Persian guide, Clemens writes "he considers it an unspeakable humiliation to be called Ferguson. It can not be helped. All guides are Fergusons to us. We can no master their dreadful foreign names" (chapter 35). This ridicule spreads to the names of localities too. When they camp near Temnin-el-Foka, the "boys have simplified the name a good deal, for the sake of conven-

ience in spelling" to "Jacksonville" (chapter 42). This device cuts both ways—it may be a swaggering celebration of English-language chauvinism on Clemens's part or on the other hand a satire of ignorant Americans abroad unable to remember, learn, or pronounce "dreadful" foreign names.

Not long into the trip, Clemens notes that his group is "getting foreignized rapidly, and with facility" (chapter 11). Clemens finds a suitable target for this anxiety in pretentious American Europhiles who claim to have "forgotten their mother tongue," transcribing some of their printed and verbal contortions (chapter 23). Clemens thus formulates the basic double bind of the ambitious American in Europe, caught between showy overreaching and obstinate authenticity: "It is not pleasant to see an American thrusting his nationality forward *obtrusively* in a foreign land, but Oh, it is pitiable to see him making of himself a thing that is neither male nor female, neither fish, flesh, nor fowl—a poor miserable, hermaphrodite Frenchman!" (ibid.). Interestingly, Clemens comes down on the side of remaining an authentic American, despite the ignorant and aggressive behavior it entails. An authentic American, in Clemens's republican spirit, is free to make many things of himself, but a European is not one of them. In his capacious treatment of linguistic situations, Clemens skewers clerks who do not speak English, guides who do (in their own way), and Americans who once did.

The complement of Clemens's needling Americans who over-assimilate is Clemens's craving experiences of cultural difference: "We wanted something thoroughly and uncompromisingly foreign—foreign from top to bottom—foreign from centre to circumference—foreign inside and outside and all around—nothing any where about it to dilute its foreignness—nothing to remind us of any other people or any other land other the sun" (chapter 8). Tourism, in this variety of radical immersion, follows the cultivation of a fetish for the exotic and a taste for rarified experiences that justify leaving home. It also provides a potential boost in social status through the display of worldly knowledge. Clemens and his cohort "wish to learn all the curious, outlandish ways of all the different countries," for the experience but also because "they say the girls like it" and "so that we can 'show off' and astonish people when we get home" (chapter 23).

National Characteristics
The fetish for organizing perceived cultural difference along the lines of national characteristics comes through in Clemens's observation that artists of various nationalities inject their subjects with the appearance of their own cultural sensibility. Clemens reports growing "reconciled" to seeing John the Baptist as, alternately "a Frenchman" and "an Italian." "What next?" he writes, "Can it be possible that the painters make John the Baptist a Spaniard in Madrid and an Irishman in Dublin?" (chapter 19). At the same time, pinning the idea of a particular culture to its basic form of life leads Clemens to suspicions of the often distant relation between cultural commodities and lived experience: "These Marseillaise make Marseillaise hymns, and Marseille vests, and Marseille soap for all the world; but they never sing their hymns, or wear their vests, or wash with their soap themselves" (chapter 11).

Clemens's interest in delineating national characteristics often leads him to rely on ethnic stereotypes that are jarring to the readers today. An early tableau, for example, features a "swarm of swarthy, noisy, lying, shoulder-shrugging, gesticulating Portuguese boatmen, with brass rings in their ears, and fraud in their hearts" in the Azores (chapter 5). When the narrator and his companions hire a guide who is "the offspring of a South Carolina slave," he remarks, echoing the rage of Huck Finn's brutal father, "I could not bear to be ignorant before a cultivated negro" (chapter 23). But he quickly learns from this impressive expatriate a perspective on life in America that he had likely never before considered, explaining to the reader, "this man feels no desire to go back to his native land. His judgment is correct" (ibid.). If Clemens frequently takes advantage of wealthy white Americans abroad, he also becomes aware that the ability to return to one's own land and make social profit from "outlandish" knowledge is a privilege extended only to certain Americans, whose innocence, abroad and at home, is a carefully constructed and preserved world view.

Points of religious convergence and conflict are also a significant lens for Clemens's account. At Gibraltar, Clemens muses on the preserved folkways and appearance of the island's Jewish population and lingers on the Muslim practice of arranged marriages. In Tangier, he makes a comparative study of the ecosystem of coexisting Abrahamic religions where "they have three Sundays a week" (chapter 9). Mocking the opportunism with which locals attach unprovable meaning to sites, Clemens stops in Jerusalem's Church of the Holy Sepulchre to weep over what he has been told is the grave of Adam, "my poor dead relative" (chapter 53). And he takes a moment to describe the "complete *fiasco*" of a Mormon colony at Jaffa (chapter 57). The Roman Catholic Church receives a great deal of Clemens's criticism, in particular what he sees as its rich church/poor people model of wealth distribution, which baffles him even more than America's emerging robber baron oligarchy. With its state institutions that have developed in symbiosis with the church, Italy, Clemens judges, "has turned all her energies, all her finances, and all her industry to the building up of a vast array of wonderful church edifices, and starving half her citizens to accomplish it" (chapter 25).

Even though the entire basis of Clemens's trip is the leisure time afforded his prosperous cohort, he nevertheless dwells on his desire and envy for a qualitative different European sense of leisure, linked to a different experience of capitalism. He spends more than a page meditating on the different qualities of leisure and comfort in American and European life: "Just in this one matter lies the main charm of life in Europe—comfort. In America, we hurry—which is well; but when the day's work is done, we go on thinking of losses and gains, we plan for the morrow, we even carry our business cares to bed with us, and toss and worry over them" (chapter 19). Paradoxically, the affluence that allows an experience and appreciation of singular European leisure is the product of furious American professional productivity.

Poverty v. Modernization
Though Clemens's group is steered toward upscale quarters, he also takes in the effects of incomplete development and the poverty that lags behind, or results from, modernization. In France, he notes

the unpicturesque poverty generally excluded from the purview of tourism, and notes the implicit political significance of poverty in French history: "All through the Faubourg St. Antoine, misery, poverty, vice and crime go hand in hand and the evidences stare one in the face from every side. Here the people live who begin the revolutions" (chapter 16). He sketches the historical trajectory of Venice as a fall from a "haughty, invincible, magnificent Republic" and "Autocrat of Commerce" to a "peddler of glass beads for women, and trifling toys and trinkets for school-girls and children" (chapter 22). In Damascus, he expresses indignation over children such as one who has learned to ask for "Buscksheesh . . . before he learned to say mother, and now he can not break himself of it" (chapter 45). Clemens also comments on the growing European phenomena of genteel poverty and the maintenance of appearances, a theme that would become a key complementary theme in the literature surrounding nouveaux riches Americans in Europe seeking to purchase or marry into land and titles that can no longer support the appropriate lifestyle. Annoyed by the beggars in Europe, Clemens makes a typically mock-violent aside about bringing his mood back up by eating a "friendless orphan" who approached him for money (chapter 25).

History v. Religion

Despite the text's overarching irreverence for grandiose expressions of European culture, it is an interest in history that underwrites Clemens's complaints about the religious preoccupation of European art, imagining the outcome if "great Titian had only been gifted with a prophecy, and had skipped a martyr, and gone over to England and painted a portrait of Shakespeare" (chapter 23). "Rome," he declares, "remains unpainted!" in the sense that no pictorial representation exists of such scenes as " 'Nero fiddling o'er burning Rome,' the assassination of Cæsar, the stirring spectacle of a hundred thousand people bending forward with rapt interest, in the Coliseum, to see two skillful gladiators hacking away each other's lives" (chapter 28). Like those in Rome's past, more interested in gladiators than saints, Clemens seeks a record of

human events, interests, and experiences, as well as spiritual aspirations. Something resembling reverence for the accumulation of artifacts over time does come through in Clemens's fascination for what he terms *melancholy history*, in the form of "rudely carved names of many and many a captive who fretted his life away" left behind by generations of inmates in France's Castle d'If (chapter 11). Clemens similarly declares the Parisian cemetery Père la Chaise "one of our pleasantest visits" and muses wistfully about the special privilege accorded the "royalty of heart and brain" who rest there (chapter 15).

In addition to offering trenchant observations about foreign lands and recording the experience of tourists, Clemens also incorporates the reaction of locals to tourists and the reaction of tourists to the often unusual treatment they receive. Affronted by the apparent boredom of their guides who have the repetitive job of showing and explaining the local culture to tourists, the narrator and his party begin to deny their guides the satisfaction of seeing their own reactions of surprise. For Clemens's party, controlling their visible reacting to cultural artifacts becomes more important than the actual content of their experience itself. They are more interested in showing their guides how unimpressed they are: "All their lives long, they are employed in showing things to foreigners and listening to their bursts of admiration . . . He gets so that he could not by any possibility live in a soberer atmosphere. After we discovered this, we *never* went into ecstasies anymore" (chapter 27). Having abandoned authentic experience or self-cultivation, they become perversely determined to rattle their guides into an unplanned reaction rather than a canned speech. When shown a handwritten letter by Christopher Columbus, Clemens and his cohort withhold the expected awe and comment instead on the poor quality of Columbus's penmanship. Their tourist experience thus enters a decadent phase in which, after too many destinations, the payoff of travel is driving guides crazy with feigned ignorance and blasé obliviousness. In this shift, Clemens and his fellow pilgrims find a sophisticated and unprecedented source of touristic pleasure—annoying their jaded guides—but in doing so relinquish the immediacy of their own experience in favor of controlling the conditions under which they are observed, watching local reactions to their evolving performance of the role of observer.

Critical Commentary by Alex Feerst

CHARACTERS AND RELATED ENTRIES

Blucher (William Blucher)   Character in *Innocents Abroad* (1869). A fictional QUAKER CITY passenger, Blucher is a young man from the Far West making his first voyage. He is naive but full of blustering self-confidence and chauvinism. Chapter 2 introduces him just before the voyage, in New York, where he is astonished to learn that not *everyone* is going to Paris that summer as he is. In chapter 5, he is confused about his new watch's failing to keep up with "ship time." In the same chapter, he treats nine people to dinner in the AZORES but thinks himself ruined when he is billed 21,700 "reis." The next chapter establishes his ineptitude on a donkey ride; this poises him for disaster in chapter 9, when he nearly rides a mule into a TANGIER mosque. Chapter 19 describes how he wrote a note in garbled French to a Parisian landlord. At the Crimean War battlefields of SEVASTOPOL, Blucher is the ship's most enthusiastic relic collector and fills his stateroom with mislabeled bones and mementos (chapter 35). The final reference to him appears in chapter 41, in which he is mentioned as a member of the narrator's expedition through the HOLY LAND. He is also mentioned briefly in chapters 6, 19, and 37.

Clemens invented Blucher as a foil for his narrator in travel letters he wrote to the NEW YORK TRIBUNE, which gives his full name as "William Blucher." Blucher has a close affinity with the "Mr. Brown" of Clemens's letters to the SAN FRANCISCO ALTA CALIFORNIA. Indeed, five anecdotes involving Brown in *Alta* letters (including each incident mentioned above, except the Azores dinner party) are credited to Blucher in *Innocents Abroad*. In January 1870, Clemens wrote a letter to MARY FAIRBANKS that identifies "Blucher" as Frederick H. Greer—a 25-year-old passenger from Boston whom Clemens had also identified as the "interrogation point" in an earlier letter. More likely, Blucher is a composite of more than one real or imagined persons. For example, though Greer went to Tangier with Clemens, the man who nearly violated a mosque was Major James G. Barry. Also, Greer—unlike Blucher—was not with Clemens in the Holy Land.

Clemens used "Blucher" as a fictional name at least as early as 1865. His column in the July 1865 *Californian* names a "Lord Blucher" as a character in a play called *Blood, Hair and the Ground Tore Up* by Bilgewater. Chapter 59 of *Roughing It* features a "mendicant Blucher" who finds a dime and is happy until he meets a starving beggar. Clemens acknowledged basing this character on his friend J. H. Riley.

Ferguson   Joke name for guides in *Innocents Abroad* (1869). A running gag throughout *Innocents* in the inability of the narrator and his companions to handle the foreign names of their guides, most of whom they call "Ferguson"—just as they give names like "Jacksonville" and "Jonesborough" to Arab villages. "Ferguson" appears 35 times in *Innocents*, referring to five different guides. These include a Frenchman named A. Billfinger in Paris (chapters 13–15); an Italian in Genoa (chapter 27); a French guide in Rome (chapters 27–28); a Turk dubbed "Faraway Moses" in Constantinople (chapter 35); and Abraham, a Maltese dragoman in the Holy Land (chapters 45–57). The deleted chapter on SPAIN also calls a guide (Michael Benuñes) "Ferguson." The travelers' favorite "Ferguson" is the patient, trusting Frenchman in Rome, whom the Doctor (ABRAHAM JACKSON) exasperates with inane questions about a mummy. In chapter 35, the narrator says that "all guides are Fergusons to us. We cannot master their dreadful foreign names." A possible echo of this joke name can be found in the 1912 novel *Daddy-Long-Legs* by Clemens's grandniece JEAN WEBSTER.

Grimes, William C.   Fictitious name in *Innocents Abroad* (1869). The author of *Nomadic Life in Palestine*, "Grimes" is a thinly veiled pseudonym for WILLIAM COWPER PRIME, the author of *Tent Life in the Holy Land* (1857). Clemens also uses the name "Grimes" for characters in several stories, including "CANNIBALISM IN THE CARS" and "TOM SAWYER'S CONSPIRACY."

The Interrogation Point Minor character in *Innocents Abroad* (1869). Chapter 7 mentions an irritating young passenger on the QUAKER CITY known as the "Interrogation Point" who constantly asks questions but is too dense to recognize contradictions in the answers he gets. In a March 1869 letter to MARY MASON FAIRBANKS, Clemens identifies the Interrogation Point as Frederick H. Greer, a young passenger from Boston whom he also identifies as "Blucher" in a later letter.

The Oracle Character in *Innocents Abroad* (1869). A pompous old bore on the QUAKER CITY, the "Oracle" is based loosely on Dr. Edward Andrews, a passenger from Albany, New York. Chapter 7 of *Innocents* establishes the character as "an innocent old ass who eats for four," uses long words that he never understands, spouts mis-information on all subjects, quotes authors who never existed, and generally tangles up every argument in which he engages. In his first appearance, he calls the PILLARS OF HERCULES the "Pillows of Herkewls." In chapter 10, he explains how Mediterranean sunsets are related to the planet Jupiter and he dubs Bloodgood CUTTER the "Poet Lariat." He pompously discusses wine in Marseille in chapter 17 and confuses Sodom and Gomorrah with Scylla and Charybdis when the ship passes through the Strait of Messina in chapter 32.

BIBLIOGRAPHY

Ganzel, Dewey. *Mark Twain Abroad: The Cruise of the "Quaker City."* Chicago: University of Chicago Press, 1968.

Hurm, Gerd. "Jeremiad Instructions in Independence: *The Innocents Abroad*." In *Rewriting the Vernacular Mark Twain: The Aesthetics and Politics of Orality in Samuel Clemens's Fictions*, 96–120. Trier: Verlag Trier, 2003.

Hutchinson, Stuart. *"The Innocents Abroad Or the New Pilgrim's Progress."* In *Mark Twain—Humour on the Run*, 11–27. Amsterdam: Rodopi B.V., 1994.

Jacobs, Jane. "Introduction." In *The Innocents Abroad Or the New Pilgrim's Progress*, by Mark Twain, xvii–xxvi. New York: Modern Library, 2003.

Kravitz, Bennett. "There's No Place like Home: 'Geographies of [American] Mind' in *The Innocents Abroad*." *American Studies International* 35 (1997): 52–76.

Messent, Peter. "Old World Travel: *The Innocents Abroad*," In *Mark Twain*, 22–43. New York: St. Martin's Press, 1997.

Railton, Stephen. "Going East: *Innocents Abroad*." In *Mark Twain: A Short Introduction*, 1–17. Malden, Mass.: Blackwell, 2004.

Regan, Robert. "The Reprobate Elect in *The Innocents Abroad*." In *On Mark Twain: The Best from American Literature*, edited by Louis J. Budd and Edwin H. Cady, 223–240. Durham, N.C.: Duke University Press, 1987.

Smith, Henry Nash. *Mark Twain: The Development of a Writer.* Cambridge, Mass.: Harvard University Press, 1962.

Stahl, J. D. *"The Innocents Abroad: Privilege, Gender, and Self-definition."* In *Mark Twain, Culture and Gender: Envisioning America though Europe*, 28–46. Athens: University of Georgia Press, 1994.

Steinbrink, Jeffrey. "Why the Innocents Went Abroad: Mark Twain and American Tourism in the Late Nineteenth Century." *American Literary Realism* 16 (1983): 278–286.

Twain, Mark. *The Innocents Abroad.* Edited by Shelley Fisher Fishkin. New York: Oxford University Press, 1996.

The Innocents Adrift

Title of an unfinished book. In September 1891, Clemens made an 11-day boat trip down the RHONE RIVER. Afterward, he began writing a narrative of the trip, hoping to combine this material and travel letters he was writing to the NEW YORK SUN into a book similar to *A Tramp Abroad* (1880). After working on his manuscript in 1894 and 1904, he had 174 pages, but never made a serious attempt to complete the book. In 1923, A. B. PAINE published a 10,000-word abridgement in EUROPE AND ELSEWHERE as "DOWN THE RHÔNE."

The Innocents at Home

Title of volume 2 of the English edition of *Roughing It,* published by GEORGE ROUTLEDGE & Sons in 1872. Labeled a "sequel" to *Roughing It,* this volume includes chapters 46–79 of the one-volume editions. It omits the book's three appendixes, but includes Clemens's previously published BURLESQUE AUTOBIOGRAPHY.

"The Invalid's Story" ("Limburger Cheese Story")

SHORT STORY published in 1882. The "invalid" is the unnamed narrator, a 41-year-old bachelor who feels like a married 60-year-old. He recalls an experience from two years earlier, when his boyhood friend John B. Hackett died, leaving a request for him to return Hackett's body to his parents in Bethlehem, WISCONSIN.

SYNOPSIS

Although the narrative that follows describes the horror that the narrator and another man experience when they are overwhelmed by a putrid stench in the railway car carrying Hackett's coffin, the narrator explains immediately that Hackett's corpse was *not* in the car with them; the odor came from Limburger cheese. It was only afterward, he explains, that he learned that Hackett's pine coffin was accidentally switched with a box of rifles when the train left CLEVELAND. As the train pulled out, someone put a package of Limburger cheese on the box.

Knowing nothing about Limburger's pungency, the narrator assumes that the foul stench in the baggage car comes from his friend's "coffin." As this foul smell grows more powerful, the narrator and the baggage man, Thompson, do everything they can to find relief. They smoke cigars, push the box into a corner, spread carbolic acid around it, and even set fire to a pile of garbage. All this only makes the stench worse, finally forcing them to ride outside the car in a snowstorm. When the train stops, they are removed frozen

Even fire cannot defeat Limburger cheese in C.D. Weldon's illustration for the Harper edition of *Literary Essays.*

and insensible. The narrator has a violent fever for three weeks and is now going home to die.

BACKGROUND AND PUBLISHING HISTORY

Several sources have been suggested as Clemens's inspiration for this story. The humorist J. M. Field (1810–1856) published a similar sketch in 1846, and ARTEMUS WARD used a version of the story in a lecture that Clemens heard in Nevada in 1863. JOSEPH TWICHELL has also been suggested as a source of the story. When Clemens wrote the 2,600-word story around 1877, he intended to work it into "SOME RAMBLING NOTES OF AN IDLE EXCURSION" until W. D. HOWELLS persuaded him to leave it out. Howells apparently also talked him into leaving the story out of *A Tramp Abroad* (1880). Later, however, Clemens did work it into "Rambling Notes" for his *Stolen White Elephant* (1882) anthology. The story later appeared by itself in LITERARY ESSAYS and other collections.

CHARACTERS AND RELATED ENTRIES

Thompson Character in "The Invalid's Story" (1882). Plain-spoken and good-natured, Thompson is the 50-year-old baggage man on the railway car carrying the pine coffin that the story's narrator believes to contain the remains of a friend. As an awful stench mounts in the car, Thompson patiently understates its putridness and tries coping until it drives him and the narrator out of the car. His growing respect for the corpse's power is reflected in the increasingly exalted titles he assigns to the dead man: "colonel," "gen'rul," "commodore," and "governor." Meanwhile, the stench is actually caused by Limburger cheese.

Is He Dead?

Posthumously published play that Clemens wrote in 1898. Essentially a reworking of Clemens's 1893 short story "IS HE LIVING OR IS HE DEAD?," *Is He Dead?* is a sprawling three-act drama that adds numerous characters and additional plot elements. As in the earlier story, the play revolves around a group of unsuccessful young French painters who hit on the scheme of pretending that one of them— JEAN FRANÇOIS MILLET (a real painter who died in 1875)—is dead in order to inflate the market value of his paintings. The play differs from the earlier story by adding a romantic angle and a usurious art dealer who has lent money to Millet and other artists. The play also borrows gimmicks that Clemens used in other works, such as the Limburger cheese and coffin of "THE INVALID'S STORY," the gender-bending twists of "A MEDIEVAL ROMANCE," the dismembered lover of "AURELIA'S UNFORTUNATE YOUNG MAN," and even *Tom Sawyer*'s idea of pretending to be dead and attending one's own funeral.

Clemens wrote the play while residing in VIENNA at a time when he was furiously starting one project after another, while rarely completing anything. He did complete this play and had hopes of having it produced but never succeeded. He had tried to write plays many times before, but despite his obvious versatility as a writer, he was never able to master dramatic forms—a fact that he himself recognized. His central failing as a dramatist was his inability to translate literary ideas into dramatic forms that could actually work on the stage. He wrote *Is He Dead?* quickly, and one of its most conspicuous faults is its surplus of characters. The play would require at least 50 actors—too many actors to manage efficiently and far too many characters for audiences to follow. The first act alone puts more than 20 separate characters with speaking parts on the stage, along with unspecified numbers of other characters who are coming and going. It is a clear example of a story that might work in prose but fail in the theater.

SYNOPSIS

The play is set during an unspecified time—presumably before 1875, the year in which the real Millet died. It opens in Millet's studio in Barbizon, a community south of PARIS after which the mid-19th-century Barbizon school of landscape painting took its name. Many of Millet's fellow painters owe money to the art dealer Bastien André; they cannot pay because none of them has sold a painting, and André refuses to accept Millet's paintings instead of cash. The artists decide to fake Millet's death to make his paintings salable, and Millet assists by disguising himself as a woman and pretending to be his own widowed sister. The scheme works well, and Millet's paintings begin to fetch high prices. However, a new complication arises when André alters a copy of his original contract with Millet and tries to coerce Millet's ostensibly wealthy sister to marry him. All eventually turns out well after Millet tricks André into thinking that the widow is a deformed cripple who is fleeing and reveals his own true identity to his sweetheart.

Act I

In Jean François Millet's Barbizon studio, near Paris, Millet's friends discuss the financial predicament threatening to ruin him and his entourage of young followers. All the artists are deeply in debt to

Bastien André, a usurious art dealer. Papa Leroux owes him 15,000 francs, and Millet owes him 2,500 francs. André wants to marry Leroux's daughter Marie, but she loves Millet. André presses his case and demands immediate repayment of his loans if Marie does not consent to marry him. Marie declares that she does not love André, and Leroux tells him he has his answer. André then gives Leroux two days to pay.

The artists are disheartened, but their leader, Agamemnon Buckner—who goes by the name "Chicago"—reveals that he has written to every foreigner staying in Paris's hotels about an exhibition of Millet's paintings that he predicts will sell out in one hour, thereby solving all their problems. He then coaches the other artists on how to make sales. When the patrons arrive, André is among them, accompanied by a band of lackeys who contrive to prevent the sales of any paintings, including Millet's *The Angelus* [a real painting], which is the centerpiece of the exhibition. When the artist named Dutchy later muses over why that painting did not sell, he comments that the world never recognizes a masterpiece until its artist is dead. Only then does the artist become famous and his paintings valuable.

After Millet arrives at the studio and finds that none of his pictures has sold, André returns and demands repayment of his loan. In accordance with his understanding of the contract he made with André, Millet offers his pictures in payment of his debt. However, André had cleverly worded the contract to give himself the option to decline Millet's paintings. He demands a cash payment within two days and makes it clear that he wants to ruin Millet.

The deeply depressed Millet decides to kill himself by asphyxiation in a closed room, and several other artists offer to die with him. As the coal fire's toxic fumes begin to do their work, Chicago returns and rouses the artists from their nearly fatal stupor. Brimming with excitement, he explains that Dutchy's remarks about artists' finding fame and riches in death has suggested to him a solution to their problems: Millet must die, or at least appear to die. If he changes his name and disappears, his fame and fortune are assured. The artists embrace the idea, and as the scene ends, Chicago proposes a toast to the "sacred memory of . . . the late Jean François Millet, who sleeps in peace."

Act II

The next day, the artists remove half of Millet's paintings from his studio and hang "SOLD" signs on half of those remaining to create the impression of intense demand for Millet's work. Chicago explains that he has planted stories in Paris and London papers saying that Millet is in poor health and has left for the Barbary coast, where he is not expected to live. The news creates a stir in Paris, where no one admits to hearing Millet's name for the first time. The reports say that Millet's death will be a blow to France. Meanwhile, Millet is kept in seclusion, disguised as the widow Daisy Tillou, his fictitious twin sister. All his fellow artists know of his deception, but they do not reveal their scheme to his lover, Marie Leroux, or her family.

Now, the art patrons who earlier rejected Millet's work rush to his studio, desperate to buy his paintings. When they learn that the widow will sell only four paintings, a bidding war ensues, and the four paintings fetch 90,000 francs.

To deflect suspicion about Millet's awkward impersonation of a woman, Chicago tells a group of elderly women who come to express their sympathy for Millet that his sister is physically well but somewhat addled. This ruse gives Millet greater latitude in his impersonation of a woman. The visitors are amazed at what he says but accept his eccentric behavior. One of them, Mother Leroux, asks Millet to beg André to give her and her husband more time to repay their debt. As Millet starts to send a note to André, the man arrives to demand payment. Millet writes two checks to André to pay his and Leroux's debts. He then berates André for his lust for money, for his lack of pity, and for being a scoundrel. The elderly women proclaim that the ostensible widow's mind is as sound as a nut, but André refuses Millet's check and demands Millet's pictures instead.

Act III

Three months have passed, and Millet, still posing as his widowed sister, Tillou, now lives in a palatial residence in Paris. For several weeks, André has been visiting, paying suit to him, thinking him a wealthy widow. André presents an altered copy of his contract with Millet that gives him ownership of Millet's paintings and threatens to pursue the matter in court. Millet knows the contract is forged but cannot expose André's fraud without revealing his true identity. When André pleads for the widow's hand in marriage, Millet stalls by reminding him that it is the day of her brother's funeral.

Millet's next visitor is Marie, whom he comforts with assurances that her lover [Millet himself] is better off dead. Marie urges Madame Tillou to marry the scoundrel André, believing that marriage may redeem him. Millet refuses, but Marie's suggestion gives him an idea for getting rid of André. He asks Marie to tell André to slip into his (the widow's) room at ten that night to receive an answer to his proposal. After Marie leaves, Millet gives Chicago a list of the theatrical props he needs to execute his plan.

Meanwhile, Millet's bogus funeral is a grand affair, with kings, sultans, and emperors in attendance. Millet himself refuses to attend, telling his comrades that he has never heard of a man attending his own funeral. The deception is nearly exposed when the unnamed king wants to view Millet's body, as Millet's coffin contains only bricks. However, Dutchy cleverly conceals two pounds of Limburger cheese in the coffin, making the king think that the body has decayed too much for the coffin to be opened.

While returning from the funeral, art collectors who had earlier rejected Millet's pictures call on Madame Tillou to pay their respects and bring news of a recent auction in which an American collector bought Millet's *The Angelus* for 500,000 francs, only to have the French authorities force him to sell it to the government for 550,000 francs. The collectors berate themselves for not buying Millet's paintings when they had the chance.

Afterward, Millet's artist friends create a new identity for him: He is to become Placide Duval, a talented but reclusive artist who paints copies of Millet's pictures. While still disguised as his widowed sister, Millet comforts Marie by asking her to imagine that her lover's death is an illusion, and that her lover might return to her disguised as a painter named Placide Duval. Marie says she would know Millet because he had a distinctive scar on his wrist. When she starts to point to the same spot on the widow's wrist, Millet abruptly withdraws his arm. Marie is momentarily cheered by the imaginative scenario but departs brokenhearted, convinced that Millet is dead.

That night, André sneaks into Madame Tillou's room and hides in a place from which he can secretly watch her getting dressed. He is startled by what he sees: The widow is entirely bald, wears a patch over one eye, and walks with crutches. As she calls for her false teeth, glass eye, artificial legs, and wig, the repulsed André sneaks away.

Chicago arranges for the Lerouxes and a few close friends to visit Madame Tillou. After listening to their expressions of grief, the widow announces that she is retiring to her country home and that a reclusive man bearing the fictitious name of "Placide Duval" and his wife will occupy her Paris house. The newcomer will go about disguised, but the Lerouxes and their friends will eventually learn who he really is. The widow has her guests swear to keep his identity a secret for 30 days. Afterward, they may reveal the secret, but it is unlikely anyone will believe them. Marie brightens on hearing the name Duval. Millet then approaches her and holds up his arm to show his scar, revealing his true identity. The lovers embrace, a celebration commences, and the curtain falls.

BACKGROUND AND PUBLISHING HISTORY

Clemens began writing the play on January 14, 1898, and reported that he had finished it on February 5, only three weeks later. Hoping to have the play produced in both London and New York, he persuaded his friend BRAM STOKER to act as his English agent. However, Stoker was too distracted by the burning of London's Lyceum Theatre, which he managed, to deal with Clemens's play. Afterward, the play languished and was largely forgotten. Scholars occasionally mentioned it in their writings, and Carl Dolmetsch published a brief summary in *"Our Famous Guest": Mark Twain in Vienna* (1992), but no one suggested that the play had any merit until Shelley Fisher Fishkin persuaded the University of California Press to publish it. Using a text prepared by the editors of the MARK TWAIN PROJECT from Clemens's secretarial manuscript containing his annotations, the university press published the play in October 2003 in a handsome edition illustrated by Barry Moser (1940–   ), who had previously illustrated a centennial edition of *Huckleberry Finn* for the same press. The book contains a long, scholarly afterword by Fishkin, who recounts its history, analyzes its content, and places it within the broader framework of Clemens's dramatic writings. Of particular interest are the details about the historical Jean François Millet and reproductions of some of his paintings.

"Is He Living or Is He Dead?"

SHORT STORY about an art HOAX that Clemens wrote while visiting in New York in 1893. The unidentified narrator recalls an incident in March 1892, at MENTON, on FRANCE's Riviera coast—where Clemens actually was at that time. The narrator meets a man, whom he calls Smith, who one day calls his attention to a prosperous retired silk manufacturer from Lyons named Théophile Magnan. That evening, Smith tells him an incredible story that becomes the narrative for most of the rest of the story.

When Smith was young, he was struggling as an artist in France, where he joined with three young French painters, Claude Frère, Carl Boulanger and JEAN FRANÇOIS MILLET—a name instantly recognizable to the narrator as the "*great* François Millet." After they had been starving together for two years, Boulanger suggested a bold way out of their poverty. He pointed out "that the merit of many a great artist has never been acknowledged until after he was starved and dead. This has happened so often that I make bold to found a law upon it." He therefore proposed that they cast lots for one of their number to "die." The man thus elected was to start as many paintings as possible for several months—leaving the canvases for his comrades to finish. (Clemens also used the idea of production-line paintings in *The American Claimant*, which he

published a year earlier.) Once sufficient pictures were ready, his comrades would announce his death, as he changed his name and disappeared. Millet is the artist elected, and the comrades carry out the scheme to perfection. Millet even serves as a pallbearer at his own funeral. Smith concludes his tale by revealing that Théophile Magnan is Millet himself.

This FRAME-STORY was part of Clemens's 12-submission deal with *COSMOPOLITAN* magazine, in which it appeared in September 1893, with eight illustrations by Alice Barber Stephenes (1858–1932). It was later reprinted in *The Man That Corrupted Hadleyburg and Other Essays and Stories* (1900). Clemens used it as the basis for a play, *IS HE DEAD?*, that he wrote in 1898 but failed to have produced.

Is Shakespeare Dead? (1909)

Extended ESSAY published as a book. Ostensibly an essay arguing that WILLIAM SHAKESPEARE could not have written the plays attributed to him, this 21,350-word book originated in Clemens's autobiographical dictations. With many passages that are important parts of Clemens's AUTOBIOGRAPHY, the book is of greater interest for what it says about him than for what it contributes to theories about Shakespearean authorship.

HARPER AND BROTHERS published *Is Shakespeare Dead?* a year before Clemens died; it was the next-to-last book he published within his lifetime. A. B. PAINE later included its text in *What Is Man? and Other Essays* (1917). A facsimile reprint of the first edition of *Is Shakespeare Dead?* was published in 1996 as part of the OXFORD MARK TWAIN in a volume that also contains *1601*. The volume has a new introduction by novelist Erica Jong and an afterword by Leslie A. Fiedler.

SYNOPSIS

Chapter 1

The author's autobiography contains many passages about claimants, such as Satan, Louis XVII, Arthur Orton (the TICHBORNE CLAIMANT), Mary

Baker G. Eddy, and William Shakespeare. Never has there been a claimant who failed to get a hearing and accumulate a rapturous following, no matter how flimsy his claim was. A new book, *The Shakespeare Problem Restated* (by George Greenwood, 1908), rekindles the author's interest in the theory that (FRANCIS) BACON wrote Shakespeare's plays. He recalls Delia Bacon's earlier book (*The Philosophy of the Plays of Shakespeare Unfolded*, 1857), which appeared during his steamboat PILOTING days. As an apprentice, he spent hours listening to GEORGE EALER quote Shakespeare and rebut Baconian theories. To satisfy Ealer's need for an argument, he took up the Baconian position that Shakespeare lacked the background in law that the plays' author must have had.

Chapter 2
The author recalls his interest in Satan as a child, when his desire to write Satan's biography was frustrated by the fact that everything "known" about him was conjectural.

Chapter 3
As with Satan, pitifully few facts are known about Shakespeare's life. There is no evidence that he ever wrote anything, that anyone thought him remarkable during his lifetime, or that he was connected with the plays attributed to his name. So far as anybody knows, he never wrote a play, he received just one letter during his entire life, and he wrote only one short poem. Anything else said about him is conjectured.

Chapter 4
A detailed examination of conjectures about Shakespeare's life does not support the idea that he somehow got legal training. William Shakespeare's biography is like a reconstructed brontosaur: nine bones and 600 barrels of plaster of Paris.

Chapter 5
There are three Shakespeare "cults": Shakespearites, who *know* that Shakespeare wrote the plays; Baconians, who *know* that Bacon wrote them; and Brontosaurians, who know that Shakespeare did *not* write the plays, but merely *suspect* that Bacon did. The author is a Brontosaurian.

Chapter 6
Shakespeare's death attracted little attention because he did nothing to merit celebrity. What is known about the author's life in Hannibal provides an interesting contrast with what is known about Shakespeare's life in Stratford. Although the author lived in Hannibal for just 15 years more than 50 years earlier, 16 childhood schoolmates still remember him. By contrast, years after Shakespeare died *in* Stratford—where he lived for 26 years—virtually no one could be found who remembered him.

Chapter 7
The issue of Shakespeare's authorship of the plays can be reduced to a single question: Did *he* ever practice law? To write about any occupation convincingly, one must be trained in it. The author's own expertise in MINING, for example, sets his writing about miners apart from that of BRET HARTE—whose lack of experience is instantly revealed in his unauthentic dialogue.

Chapter 8
A summary of Greenwood's work finds ample evidence in Shakespeare's plays and poems that their author not only had extensive knowledge of law, but knew the workings of the courts and legal life generally. Since Shakespeare clearly had no such experience, he could not possibly have written the plays.

Chapter 9
No one can be sure whether Bacon wrote the plays. He *could* have written them, but conclusive proof is missing.

Chapter 10
The author of Shakespeare's plays must also have had "wisdom, erudition, imagination, capaciousness of mind, grace, and majesty of expression"—none of which Shakespeare is known to have possessed.

Chapter 11
Denying that he expects people to change their minds about Shakespeare, the author says that he is not so foolish as to believe that people will abandon cherished superstitions.

Chapter 12
The author also denies expressing any irreverent ideas—in contrast to the irreverence of the "Stratfordolaters" and "Shakesperiods."

Chapter 13

If one compiled a list of the 500 most celebrated figures in British history back to Tudor times, biographical particulars could be found about every one of them *except* the most illustrious by far—Shakespeare. Nothing that is known about him indicates that he was anything other than a commonplace person. Almost nothing is known about him because he had no history to record.

A postscript to this chapter cites a recent newspaper clipping from Hannibal that attests to the fame that Mark Twain still enjoys in his hometown. He also cites a recent obituary of a Hannibal woman as an example of a person who certainly would have remembered him in Hannibal, but would not have remembered Shakespeare, had she lived in Stratford. Even Hannibal's TOWN DRUNKARDS have left behind more lasting memories than Shakespeare did in his own town.

Joan of Arc, Personal Recollections of (1896)

The last NOVEL that Clemens published in his lifetime, *Joan of Arc* occupies a unique place among his major works. Clemens regarded the book as his best and most important work, but modern opinion holds just the opposite view—a discrepancy that awaits full explanation.

Though *Joan of Arc* naturally falls among Clemens's historical novels, it differs markedly from the others. Unlike *The Prince and the Pauper* (1881), which alters the recorded history of mid-16th-century England, or *A Connecticut Yankee in King Arthur's Court* (1889), which revises a myth, *Joan of Arc* follows its subject's known history closely. Indeed, it often reads as history, with frequent insertions of dates and other historical facts—including a summary of FRANCE and ENGLAND's Hundred Years' War (book 2, chapter 31). Despite its historical faithfulness, the novel avoids the central issue in Joan's life—her religious calling. It never tries to explain where her "voices" come from or why she is so devoted to God. Likewise, it does not consider whether the Roman Catholic

Frontispiece to the first edition of *Joan of Arc*

Church had reasons other than vindictiveness for prosecuting her. Since Joan's story unfolds in a void in which she is an innocent champion of virtue fighting inexplicable evil, the novel's main purpose seems to be to extol her nobility.

The extent to which *Joan of Arc* is a "novel" can be measured by the range of Clemens's creative contributions. His most obvious inventions are characters such as the Paladin and Noël Rainguesson, who offer comic relief without seriously disturbing Joan's known history. Otherwise, Clemens distances himself from the story through two levels of fictional narrators. He presents his book as Jean François Alden's modern translation of an authentic narrative by Sieur Louis de Conte, a contemporary of Joan's. De Conte supposedly recorded his story in 1492 for his relatives' descendants to read. His narrative voice shifts between the immediacy of his participation in events with Joan and the distance of an old man reflecting on the past. Clemens's voice intrudes occasionally when de Conte slips out of his own era to explain things that modern readers might not understand—such as the nature of French village life in the 15th century and the recent history of France.

Joan of Arc contains Clemens's most extensive depiction of war. Like the narrator of "THE PRIVATE HISTORY OF A CAMPAIGN THAT FAILED" and Clemens himself, both the narrator and the chief protagonist of *Joan of Arc* are unfit for war and are appalled by its brutality. De Conte's descriptions of actual fighting tend to be distant and superficial, reflecting his anxiousness to move on to more agreeable matters.

SYNOPSIS

Joan of Arc contains just over 150,000 words of text. Both one- and two-volume editions contain 73 numbered chapters that are divided among three "books." The first book, with eight chapters, constitutes about 14 percent of the novel; the second, with 41 chapters, about 55 percent; and the third, with 24 chapters, about 31 percent. There is also an unnumbered conclusion.

Information given below in parentheses comes from outside the chapters. For example, the mileages given, the most direct distances between towns, are taken from *The Times Atlas of the World.* Most dates in the chapter summaries are taken from Clemens's own text and are thus not in parentheses.

Translator's Preface
A person's character can typically be judged only by the standards of the person's time. Joan of Arc's character, however, is unique in that the standards of *all* time would find it ideally perfect. She may be the only entirely unselfish person in profane history. Her biography is also unique in being the only story of a human life that comes to us under oath—

from the official records of her two trials. De Conte's account of Joan's life is unimpeachable, but the particulars that he adds must be judged on his own word alone.

De Conte's Note
It is 1492, and the author is 82 years old. He relates things that he saw as a youth. His name is mentioned in all the histories of Joan of Arc because he was with her from the time they were children, through the wars, to her end. To this day, he remembers her clearly, and his hand was the last that she touched in life. After all these years have passed, he now recognizes her for what she was—the most noble life that was ever born into this world save only One (presumably Jesus Christ).

Book 1, Chapter 1
The author was born in Neufchâteau on January 6, 1410—exactly two years before Joan of Arc was born in nearby Domremy. Orphaned after the English shattered France at Agincourt (1415), de Conte was raised in the home of a priest in Domremy, where Joan and her brothers were among his many childhood friends.

Book 1, Chapter 2
Like all village children, those of Domremy live in humble dirt-floored houses and tend flocks. They particularly enjoy dancing around a majestic beech tree, which is the home of fairies until the village priest banishes them. The children are heartbroken, but Joan alone confronts the priest to plead the fairies' case. So effectively does she argue that the priest asks for forgiveness.

Book 1, Chapter 3
De Conte also recalls a stormy winter night when a ragged stranger came to the house of Joan, who admitted him before her father could stop her. The stranger proved to be a good man who showed his gratitude for the porridge Joan gave him with a noble recitation of the Song of Roland.

Book 1, Chapter 4
Domremy's children, like all others, have nicknames; Joan has several. On one terrible day, they learn that their mad king Charles VI has given France to England in a treaty (1420). The boys

laugh when the girls say they would like to fight for France, but are interrupted when a madman charges at them with an ax. Everyone scatters but Joan, who gently leads the man back to the village—a deed for which she is nicknamed "the Brave."

Book 1, Chapter 5

France's next year is dismal. On a day when Domremy's boys are trounced in a fight with Maxey's Burgundian boys, they hear that their king is dead and that English armies are sweeping the land. Several years of false alarms and scares follow, until war reaches Domremy in 1428. Marauders ravage the village, wreaking violence that appalls Joan. One day, when the lad known as the Paladin ridicules France's generals, Joan defends them as the pillars of the nation. When the children discuss what they would do if they became heroes, Joan quietly predicts their futures.

Book 1, Chapter 6

Over the next year and a half, Joan grows melancholy, but when de Conte says that France's situation is hopeless, she confidently predicts that France will win its freedom. Wondering where Joan draws such confidence, de Conte watches her. On May 15, 1428, he sees her at the enchanted beech tree, where she converses with an invisible presence.

Book 1, Chapter 7

After mysterious voices leave, Joan tells de Conte that for three years these "voices" have told her that within a year she is destined to lead the armies that will begin freeing France and that *she* will crown the dauphin to make him king (Charles VII). Further, de Conte is to help her. First, she must ask Robert de Baudricourt, the governor at Vaucouleurs (11 miles north of Domremy), for an armed escort to take her to the king. With her uncle Laxart, she visits Vaucouleurs, but the governor rebuffs her.

Book 1, Chapter 8

In Domremy, Joan's family and neighbors think that she has disgraced their village and they shun her, but she remains steadfast through the summer. When the Paladin claims that Joan promised to marry him, she is called before a court at Toul (20 miles northeast of Domremy), where she defends herself so elo-

quently that she wins back her parents' affection. Meanwhile, England's siege of ORLÉANS begins.

Book 2, Chapter 1

On January 5, 1429, Joan reveals that her "voices" have finally given her clear instructions: within two months she will be with the dauphin. Joan's uncle now believes in her wholeheartedly. The next day—her birthday—she bids her village a tearful farewell. She is now 17.

Book 2, Chapter 2

At Vaucouleurs, Joan lodges with a wheelwright's wife and gradually wins the respect of the common people. When Merlin's ancient prophecy that a woman would one day save France is recalled, Joan's reputation soars. Eventually the governor visits her and decides to have bishops test whether she is a saint or a witch. Joan's impatience mounts, however. She tells the governor that the dauphin is suffering a military defeat that will be known in nine days. Meanwhile, she assembles a tiny force, including two knights, and prepares to march to the king. Just as she sets off, the governor arrives. He confirms her report of the king's defeat and gives her his sword and an armed escort.

Book 2, Chapter 3

Joan now leaves with about 25 men, including her brothers Jacques and Jean D'Arc, and is soon in enemy territory. The next morning, de Conte discovers that the Paladin and their mutual friend Noël Rainguesson are among the men whom the governor gave to Joan the night before—thus fulfilling another of Joan's prophecies.

Book 2, Chapter 4

After inspecting her men and instructing them on how to behave, Joan leads horsemanship drills, then continues the march. For five nights, they fight off ambuscades. As the men grow fatigued, Joan remains so strong that some of them suspect that she is a witch and plot to kill her. She confronts the plotters, however, telling them that their scheme cannot work, and she predicts that their ringleader will soon die. After his horse stumbles in a river and he drowns, the conspiracies end.

On a stormy night, Joan rides straight into an enemy force and has a long interview with its commander, who thinks that she is one of his own lieutenants. Without lying, she answer his questions, then leads her band safely away. After 10 days, her band crosses the Loire and reaches Gien (38 miles east-southeast of Orléans).

Book 2, Chapter 5

After resting at Gien, the band pushes on and Joan has her knights carry a message to the king at Chinon. Near Chinon, the knights return and report that the king's minister Georges de la Tremouille and the Archbishop of Rheims (Reims) have kept them away from the king. Joan's only ally at court is the king's mother-in-law, Queen Yolande of Sicily, who eventually helps Joan's knights reach the king. When the king's priests come to interview Joan, she insists on speaking directly to the king. The next day, the king arranges for her band to stay at the Castle of Courdray, where Joan charms people from the court.

Book 2, Chapter 6

After further delays, the king sends priests to Lorraine to investigate Joan's background. Eventually, she is invited to meet him. Dressed simply, she enters a splendid court. A dazzling crowned and bejeweled figure sits on a throne, but Joan ignores him and amazes everyone by finding the true dauphin among the courtiers. After she kneels before him, they talk privately and she whispers something that visibly bolsters him. De Conte later learns that Joan has assured the dauphin that his birth is lawful.

Book 2, Chapter 7

As Joan awaits further developments at Courdray, the Paladin buys a gaudy cavalier outfit and regales people at the local inn with his shameless bragging.

Book 2, Chapter 8

Though Joan's secret message has reassured the king, his advisers suggest that her inspiration may come from Satan, not God. The king sends bishops to test her daily, but they cannot decide about her, so he sends her to Poitiers to be examined by theology professors. After three wasted weeks, Joan's inquisitors conclude that she is indeed sent by God.

Book 2, Chapter 9

Meanwhile the king's priests return from Lorraine with favorable reports on Joan, and good luck begins flooding in. Since Joan is to be a soldier, the church permits her to wear male attire; the king names her "General-in-chief of the Armies of France" and makes his cousin, the royal duke of Alençon, her chief of staff.

Book 2, Chapter 10

Joan's first official act is to dictate a letter to the English commanders at Orléans, ordering them to leave France. The king has armor made for Joan, who sends a knight to Fierbois to fetch an ancient sword that her "voices" have described to her. As she prepares her army, she assigns important posts to each childhood friend: She makes de Conte her page and secretary, Rainguesson her messenger, and the Paladin her standard bearer.

Book 2, Chapter 11

As de Conte and Rainguesson discuss the amazing honor that Joan has bestowed on the boastful Paladin, they realize that she has the "seeing eye." Meanwhile, Joan sends for the swashbuckling old commander La Hire to take charge of training the new recruits at Blois (midway between Tours and Orléans), and she starts on her first war-march.

Book 2, Chapter 12

At Blois, Joan hits it off well with La Hire and shocks the profane old veteran by insisting that he and all the troops attend mass voluntarily. Within three days, all the women and other camp followers are gone and the troops are attending mass. Joan's biggest victory is getting La Hire to say a prayer— one that makes her laugh heartily.

Book 2, Chapter 13

Under the command of La Hire and four other seasoned generals, Joan's army marches from Blois to Orléans. Ignoring her order to approach the city from the north, the generals try to fool her by crossing the Loire to the south side of the city. When she detects their trick, she asks Dunois, the Bastard of Orléans, to explain the generals' blunder. When he cannot, she sends the bulk of the army back upriver to advance on Orléans from the north. She, La Hire, and Dunois then lead a thousand troops into Orléans, where she and her friends put up in the house of Dunois's treasurer, Boucher.

Book 2, Chapter 14
On April 30, Joan sends a message asking the English to reply to her earlier letter, in which she invited them to join her in a crusade to recapture the HOLY SEPULCHRE. They respond by threatening to capture and burn her. She orders Dunois to fetch the rest of her army from Blois.

Book 2, Chapter 15
As they await the army, de Conte, Rainguesson, the Paladin, and Joan's brothers all fall in love with beautiful Catherine Boucher. The most smitten is de Conte, who writes a poem in her honor. He lets Rainguesson recite it to Catherine in company; between Rainguesson's recitation and the Paladin's excessive weeping, de Conte himself is overlooked.

Book 2, Chapter 16
The next night, the Paladin learns through a deserter that the English plan to assault Orléans. The news spurs Joan to prepare for battle. As she meets La Hire's troops the next morning, she sees a huge soldier who is being held for desertion; she inquires about his case and learns that he is a good soldier who returned voluntarily after running off to see his dying wife. Joan pardons the man—who is called the "Dwarf"—and makes him her personal guard.

When Joan leads her army past the English strongholds, not a shot is fired. When she learns that the English have weakened their forts on the south side of the river, she wants to attack them there, but her generals delay her for four days.

Book 2, Chapter 17
Back at the Bouchers' house, the Paladin taunts de Conte for having fallen off his horse during the march, and de Conte wins a knight's praise by frankly admitting his fear.

Book 2, Chapter 18
At midday, Joan suddenly senses that a battle is raging and rushes off to join it. The people of Orléans have spontaneously attacked the Burgundy Gate, where Talbot's more numerous English troops are routing them. Joan's arrival turns the tide and the French capture the English fort at St.

Loup. It is Joan's first real battle and the first significant French victory since the siege began seven months earlier.

Book 2, Chapter 19
As everyone rests from the battle, de Conte and his friends try to solve a mystery about a ghost in the Bouchers' house.

Book 2, Chapter 20
When Joan learns that her irresolute generals plan a long siege against the English troops, she promises to oust the enemy in three days and begins by ordering an assault on the English forts guarding bridges at Augustins and Tourelles. Under her leadership, her army takes the first English position the next day and she is wounded in the foot.

Book 2, Chapter 21
That evening, Joan dictates a letter, telling her parents not to worry when they learn that she is wounded. Catherine Boucher grows upset when she learns that Joan is referring not to her foot wound, but to a terrible wound that she expects to receive the next day.

Book 2, Chapter 22
The next morning, Joan leads the assault on Tourelles and is struck between her neck and shoulder by a bolt from a crossbow. When she hears a retreat being sounded, she rises to countermand the order and leads a successful assault on Tourelles. As she has predicted, she lifts the siege of Orléans. The city has ever since celebrated Joan's victory on May 8.

Book 2, Chapter 23
By dawn, Talbot has evacuated Orléans and the French can scarcely believe that they are again free. Joan marches to report to the dauphin, whom she finds at Tours. She encourages him to go immediately to Rheims (135 miles northeast of Orléans) for his coronation, but Tremouille's cautious advice make him hesitate to act. When the dauphin offers Joan whatever she wants in reward for relieving Orléans, she simply blushes. He ennobles her and her family, dubbing her "Joan of Arc," surnamed "Du Lis."

Book 2, Chapter 24

Joan's ennoblement excites the whole country but dismays the Paladin and Rainguesson because Joan's brothers now greatly outrank them.

Book 2, Chapter 25

As the king causes further delays, Joan's army begins disintegrating. To induce the king to go to Rheims. Joan proposes raising a new army to clear a path for him between Tours and Rheims. After assembling 8,000 soldiers, she begins her march on June 6.

Book 2, Chapter 26

As Joan leaves Tours, the king orders her generals to do nothing without her sanction; however, they still resist her aggressive tactics. She promises to take Jargeau (10 miles east of Orléans) by direct assault—a plan that La Hire enthusiastically endorses.

Book 2, Chapter 27

The next day, the army finally moves on Jargeau. After driving its English defenders within its walls, Joan gives them an hour to leave. They fail to comply, so she resumes the assault the next day until they surrender.

Book 2, Chapter 28

As Joan dictates to de Conte Catherine Boucher drops in to express her concern about Joan's safety. Joan predicts that she will achieve a major victory within four days, then goes into a trance and says that she will die a cruel death within two years. Catherine thinks that Joan is merely dreaming, but de Conte knows that Joan's remarks are prophetic.

Book 2, Chapter 29

No one wants to believe Joan's prophecy that she must complete her work within a single year, but de Conte keeps her prophecy about her death to himself. At dawn, Joan leads her army to Meung and Beaugency. After taking the latter town without a fight, she bombards its castle till night. When Richemont, the constable of France, approaches, D'Alençon opposes letting him join her forces because the king is estranged from him; however, Joan gets D'Alençon to relent. On the morning of June 17, the French learn that Talbot and Fastolfe's forces are coming, Joan decides to take up the bat-

tle the next day. Meanwhile, maneuvering among the English leads to the surrender of Beaugency.

Book 2, Chapter 30

On June 18, Joan's army cautiously advances through the plains of La Beauce toward Patay (15 miles northwest of Orléans). After stumbling on the English position, they take up battle. In three hours of fierce fighting, the French prevail, and Joan predicts that the English power in France is broken for a thousand years. Later, de Conte finds her crying over a dying English prisoner.

Book 2, Chapter 31

It is now 91 years since the Hundred Years' War began, and its English side is looking sick. The Battle of Patay is one of the truly great battles in history, as it has lifted France from convalescence to perfect health.

Book 2, Chapter 32

News of Patay spreads through France in 24 hours. When Joan's army returns to Orléans, the overjoyed town welcomes her as the "Saviour of France."

Book 2, Chapter 33

In looking back from the future, de Conte lists Joan's five "great deeds" as raising the siege of Orléans; the victory at Patay; the reconciliation at Sully-sur-Loire; the king's coronation; and the bloodless march. The reconciliation was between the king and Richemont, who later transformed the king into a man and a determined soldier. De Conte likens Joan's moves to a chess game whose "checkmate" came when Richemont and the king joined forces after her death.

Book 2, Chapter 34

After the Loire campaign, Joan is anxious to take the king to Rheims to be crowned. The king fears crossing English-held territory, but the march to Rheims proves to be a holiday excursion. On June 29, Joan rides out of Gien at the side of the king and D'Alençon, with 12,000 men. After Troyes surrenders without a fight, she permits its English and Burgundian soldiers to carry away their goods, but her men are outraged when each enemy soldier marches out with a French prisoner on his back. The Dwarf gets into an argument with a

Burgundian, whom he kills for insulting Joan. Conceding that the enemy are within their rights to take their prisoners with them, Joan solves the problem by having the king ransom all the Frenchmen.

Book 2, Chapter 35

As Joan's army marches on, Châlon (35 miles northeast of Troyes) surrenders to her army. On July 16, they reach Rheims, where they receive an enthusiastic welcome. The next day, Joan is at the king's side during his coronation. Afterward, when she requests permission to go home, Charles asks what grace he can bestow upon her for her services. She asks only that her village have its taxes remitted, so Charles decrees that Domremy will be freed from taxation forever.

Book 2, Chapter 36

As Joan rides from the coronation, she sees her father and uncle Laxart in the crowd. The king orders that they be honored and offers them fine quarters, but they prefer to stay at the humble Zebra's Inn. When the city gives the king a grand banquet, D'Arc and Laxart eat in a gallery to avoid attention. Afterward, Joan and her Domremy friends join the men at their inn, where Joan tries to put them at ease. She says that her military work is done and that she will soon be home. Their talk covers many things, and Joan nearly suffocates with laughter when her uncle tells a tedious story about getting entangled with beehives while trying to ride a bull to a funeral.

Book 2, Chapter 37

Joan asks her father why he came to town without telling her. His admission that he feared being snubbed gives de Conte the idea that peasants might actually be "people" who one day will rise up and demand their rights. Joan comforts her father and shows him her pike and sword. As they gossip about Domremy, a messenger summons Joan to a council of war.

Book 2, Chapter 38

De Conte follows Joan to the council, where she mocks the notion that a "council of war" is even needed. Asserting that only *one* rational course of action is open—to march on PARIS—she boldly confronts the king's chief minister, Tremouille, and the chancellor, who want to treat with the Duke of Burgundy and wait before moving against Paris. Joan warns that if they hesitate now, the half-year's work now facing them will take another 20 years to complete. Buoyed by his generals' enthusiasm, the king gives Joan his sword to carry to Paris.

Book 2, Chapter 39

Joan issues orders to her generals and dictates a letter inviting the Duke of Burgundy to make peace. The next morning, she bids farewell to her father and uncle and leads her army out. Again, her march is a holiday excursion, with English strongholds surrendering along the way; nevertheless, the king loses his nerve. He goes back to Gien and makes a truce with Burgundy. Joan can handle the English and the Burgundians, but is no match for French conspirators. On August 26, 1429, she camps at St. Denis, near Paris.

Book 2, Chapter 40

Joan sends messages trying to get the king to join her at St. Denis. After nine wasted days, she begins an artillery barrage on the gate of St. Honoré. As her troops enter, she is wounded and carried off. She wants to resume the assault the next day, but the king forbids it. Heartbroken, she asks permission to retire and go home, but the king will not let her go, and her "voices" tell her to stay at St. Denis. At Tremouille's insistence, the king orders Joan to return her army to the Loire, where he disbands it. France's disgrace is complete, and the unconquerable Joan of Arc is conquered.

Book 2, Chapter 41

Eight months of drifting follow as Joan accompanies the king and his council from place to place. The king occasionally lets her lead sorties—in one of which de Conte is wounded. While campaigning near Compiègne (40 miles north-northeast of Paris), which the Duke of Burgundy is besieging, Joan leads the last march of her life on May 24, 1430. She is captured as the Dwarf and Paladin are killed, and her brothers and Rainguesson are wounded trying to defend her.

Book 3, Chapter 1

De Conte hopes to hear that Joan is ransomed, but the king remains silent. Over the next five months, Joan twice tries to escape and is moved to Beaurevoir. Meanwhile, the Duke of Burgundy—desperate for money—ransoms Joan to the English through Bishop Cauchon, who is promised the archbishopric of Rouen. Since Joan's military record is spotless, she is to be tried for religious crimes at Rouen.

Book 3, Chapter 2

Through still suffering from his wound, de Conte goes out on a sortie in October and is wounded again at Compiègne. There he encounters Rainguesson, who has been a prisoner all this time. Heartbroken to learn that Joan has been sold to the English, they go to Rouen to be near her in January (1431).

Book 3, Chapter 3

De Conte gets a job clerking for a good priest named Manchon, who will be chief recorder in Joan's trial. Manchon reveals that Cauchon has packed Joan's jury with 50 distinguished men sympathetic to England. Although an inquisitor from Paris refuses to hear Joan's case because she was already tried at Poitiers, Cauchon gets around all the jurisdictional difficulties. Not only does he not allow Joan to have legal help, he eavesdrops on her when she confesses to his confederate Nicolas Loyseleur, a great University of Paris personage who pretends to be a priest from Joan's region.

Book 3, Chapter 4

Joan's trial finally starts on February 21. De Conte distrusts the formidable court set against Joan, who is brought in chains.

Book 3, Chapter 5

Before continuing his narrative, de Conte promises to stick faithfully to the official trial record—something that his translator affirms he has done. Attending as Manchon's aide, de Conte rejoices to see that Joan's spirit is not broken. The judge summarizes the particulars against Joan, then tells her to kneel and swear that she will truthfully answer all questions. She refuses, however, saying that she cannot tell what her "voices" have revealed. The

judges rail at her for three hours, then allow her to swear her own oath. When the first day ends after five hours, only Joan is not exhausted. During the trial, she often looks at de Conte and Rainguesson—who is in the audience—but does not betray that she knows them.

Book 3, Chapter 6

That night, de Conte learns that Cauchon has tried to make clerks twist Joan's testimony in a special record but failed. The next day, the trial moves to larger chambers and the number of judges is increased to 62. Cauchon again presses Joan to take an oath, but she refuses. He then turns her over to Beaupere, a wily theologian who asks her about her "voices" and presses her on the matter of her male attire. Despite hours of questioning, he fails to trap her.

Book 3, Chapter 7

During the court's third session, on February 24, Beaupere springs his biggest trap: asking Joan if she is in a "state of grace." Since the question is unanswerable, even some of Cauchon's judges object to it. However, Joan replies calmly, "If I be not in a state of Grace, I pray God place me in it; if I be in it, I pray God keep me so." Her brilliant answer takes the heart out of Beaupere's interrogation.

Book 3, Chapter 8

When the court meets on the 27th, Joan is again asked about her "voices," whom she identifies as St. Catherine and St. Marguerite. Weary of hearing the same questions repeatedly, she suggests that the court send to Poitiers for the record of her earlier trial.

Book 3, Chapter 9

On March 1, the judge tries to trick Joan into naming which of the several men who claim to be pope is the true one. It is a dangerous topic, so when she innocently asks, "Are there *two*?," the matter is dropped. De Conte is mortified when a letter that Joan once dictated to him is read aloud and Joan points out its transcription errors. Gradually, Joan grows impatient and rises to predict future French military successes against the English—which de Conte confirms later happened. Her predictions agitate the court and raise further questions about her "voices." De Conte suspects that many in the courtroom are starting to think that Joan really is sent by God and that they themselves may be the ones in peril.

Book 3, Chapter 10

In one of the court's stormiest sessions, on March 3, the judges lose their patience. Aside from keeping them from other duties, the trial is making them laughing-stocks. They all try to go at Joan at once, with questions about her wanting to be worshipped, trying to commit suicide in prison, and blaspheming.

Book 3, Chapter 11

Eventually, Cauchon halts the trial because he is losing ground. After letting all but the toughest judges leave, he spends five days sifting testimony. When the trial resumes on March 10, it is closed to the public. Joan now looks tired and weak, but by the third day she is looking less worn. The questions turn to her use of her own standard in battle.

Book 3, Chapter 12

When the judge begins asking about the Paladin's old claim that Joan once promised to marry him, Joan loses her temper. Cauchon then questions her more about her male attire and her efforts to escape from prison. The session on March 17, the last day of this trial, begins with a new trap. Joan is asked if she will submit her words and deeds to the determination of the church; however, she replies that she will submit them only to God. When she is carelessly asked if she would give fuller answers to the pope, she suggests, they take her to him. Cauchon blanches, since he realizes—as Joan does not—that she has that right, and that if she were to reach Rome, she would receive a fair trial that would free her. He changes the subject.

Book 3, Chapter 13

Before the second trial ends without result, Cauchon asks a lawyer for his opinion and is outraged when the man lists four reasons why the trial should be ruled null and void. The third trial begins on March 27. The reading of 66 articles takes days. They charge Joan with being a sorceress, false prophet, companion of evil spirits, dealer in magic, schismatic, idolater, apostate, blasphemer, disturber, and more. This third

trial also ends without result, so Cauchon reduces the 66 charges to 12 for a new trial.

Book 3, Chapter 14

Joan falls ill on March 29, after her third trial ends. Calling the new charges against her "the 12 lies," de Conte explains why each is false. These charges include such accusations as Joan's claiming to have found her salvation; refusing to submit to the church; threatening death to those who would not obey her; and claiming never to have committed a sin. When the 12 articles are sent to doctors of theology in Paris, Manchon boldly writes in the margins that many of the statements attributed to Joan are the *opposite* of what she actually said.

Meanwhile, concern over Joan's health grows. The English party does not want her to die before the church formally condemns her. After doctors bleed her, she improves until one of Cauchon's men storms at her. When de Conte accompanies Manchon and Cauchon to Joan's cell, Joan asks to confess, but Cauchon insists that she submit to the church and threatens her with damnation.

Book 3, Chapter 15

The court opens again on May 2, with Cauchon and 62 judges. Joan is again brought in chains. An orator reads the 12 charges against her and threatens her with burning at the STAKE unless she submits, but she remains steadfast and again baffles the court.

Book 3, Chapter 16

As news of Cauchon's latest defeat spreads, people laugh at him and make puns on his name, which resembles *cochon*, a word for "hog." On May 9, de Conte and Manchon are with Cauchon when he summons Joan to a torture chamber and threatens her with the rack. She remains calm, however, and says that if forced to confess, she will later recant. The bishops eventually send her back to her cell, and Cauchon again becomes a target of laughter in Rouen.

Book 3, Chapter 17

As 10 more days pass, de Conte and Rainguesson rue Joan's plight. While admitting that Joan was always great, de Conte thinks that she was at her greatest during these trials.

Book 3, Chapter 18

A report finally arrives from the Paris theologians, who find Joan guilty on all 12 articles, asserting that her "voices" belong to fiends. On May 19, 50 judges sit to determine her fate. Four days later, she is again called to court. When a canon of Rouen calls on her to renounce her errors, she refuses.

Book 3, Chapter 19

Still anxious for Joan to condemn herself publicly, Cauchon considers his devious options. He has Loyseleur visit Joan disguised as a pro-French priest. Meanwhile, de Conte and Rainguesson hope for a last-minute rescue by La Hire.

Book 3, Chapter 20

Cauchon leads Joan to a stake over burning coals and has an ecclesiastic preach at her. This fails to move her, however, until he denounces King Charles as a heretic. Meanwhile, the crowd—expecting a burning—grows impatient. When the preacher shows Joan a written form and asks her to abjure, she starts to weaken before the fire. Finally, when Cauchon reads the sentence of death, Joan agrees to submit. A priest reads a form that she is to sign, but she is helped to sign a *different* paper that is substituted, in which she admits to being a sorceress and other things. Cauchon then shocks Joan by pronouncing a sentence of perpetual imprisonment. Joan expects to be taken to a church prison but is instead returned to her harsh English prison.

Book 3, Chapter 21

As Joan is led away, the angry crowd hurls stones at the ecclesiastics. After Joan is returned to her cell, Cauchon keeps trying to wear her down. He allows her to wear female attire but is confident that she will relapse.

Book 3, Chapter 22

Unaware of Cauchon's machinations, de Conte and Rainguesson are excited about the prospect of Joan's becoming free. A few days later, however, they hear a report that Joan has relapsed. When de Conte later visits her cell with Manchon, he sees her in male attire because a guard has switched her clothes. Cauchon is triumphant.

Book 3, Chapter 23

That night, de Conte learns that Joan wants him to write a letter to her family. Since de Conte cannot go to her cell, Manchon passes on her message, which says that she has seen the "Vision of the Tree" and that there will be no rescue. The next day, May 29, Cauchon's court meets to pronounce Joan a relapsed heretic and turn her over to secular authority for punishment. De Conte and Manchon go with the priests who prepare Joan for her execution. When she hears that she is to burn, she becomes so upset that de Conte throws himself at her feet; however, she touches his hand and whispers that he should not imperil himself. Cauchon allows Joan to have communion and she goes to meet her death serenely.

Book 3, Chapter 24

As Joan rides to her execution in a cart, Loyseleur rushes forward from the crowd and begs forgiveness, which she grants. On a platform in the market square, a priest delivers a sermon and pronounces Joan excommunicated. She kneels and prays for the king of France. Everyone, including the secular judge, is so moved that Joan goes to her death without being officially sentenced. After she is chained to the stake, she asks for a cross. An English soldier fashions one of sticks for her. Her last words are to Cauchon: "I die through you."

Book 3, Conclusion

The narrator looks back on these events from a time many years later. As Joan had prophesied, her brother Jacques died in Domremy while she was tried in Rouen. Shortly after her martyrdom, her father died of a broken heart. Her mother lived for many more years and was granted a pension by Orléans. Meanwhile, de Conte and Orléans returned to Domremy until Richemont replaced Tremouille as King Charles's chief minister; then they returned to war. De Conte was with Rainguesson when he died in the last great battle (1453) and he is now the sole survivor of those who fought with Joan.

Charles was indifferent to Joan's fate until after the English were finally expelled from France. They began calling attention to the fact that he had received his crown from someone in league with Satan, so he appealed to the pope, who appointed a

The execution of Joan of Arc, from a mural by J. E. Lenepveu (1819–1898), in Harper's edition of *Joan of Arc*

commission to investigate Joan. The result was that she was rehabilitated.

BACKGROUND AND PUBLISHING HISTORY

Clemens boasted of spending 12 years researching *Joan of Arc*, but his actual research work was slight. He began compiling a reading list in the early 1880s. By 1891, he had read several books on Joan, including Janet Tuckey's popular *Joan of Arc, The Maid* (1880). In September of that year, he asked ANDREW CHATTO to send him additional books. In a letter to H. H. ROGERS, he admitted to lifting the framework of the first two-thirds of his story from just two standard histories. His final section, on

Joan's trial, he based on another five or six books—all of which are listed at the beginning of the novel as "authorities" examined to verify de Conte's narrative. Much of *Joan of Arc* he wrote by simply redrafting the historical outline of Joan's life, adding dialogue and occasional fictional glosses.

Clemens began the actual writing of the novel on August 1, 1892, while he was living in FLORENCE, Italy. He wrote rapidly until the following March, by which time he had 22 chapters and had reached the part in which Joan had raised the siege of Orléans. He was ready to end the narrative there, but during a trip to New York in which he negotiated serial publication of the story in HARPER'S MAGAZINE, its editor, H. M. ALDEN, persuaded him to carry Joan's story to the end of her life. After returning to Europe, Clemens continued writing at a more leisurely pace until he pronounced himself finished on February 8, 1895. (He describes his reaction to this moment in "The Finished Book," a brief essay posthumously published in EUROPE AND ELSEWHERE in 1923.)

Clemens feared that people would not take his book seriously with his name attached to it, so he arranged for HARPER'S MAGAZINE to publish it anonymously. When HARPER AND BROTHERS issued *Joan of Arc* as a book in May 1896, the name "Mark Twain" appeared on its spine and cover, but not on its title page (the English edition listed him as "editor," however).

Since the book's original publication, it has seen comparatively few editions. The book comprised two volumes in Harper's various uniform editions and has occasionally been reprinted in small editions. The MARK TWAIN PROJECT ranks *Joan of Arc* so far down its list of future publications that it is doubtful that it will ever publish a corrected edition. The book was, however, saved from oblivion in 1994, when the Library of America included it in *Mark Twain: Historical Romances*, which is lightly annotated by Susan K. Harris. In 1996, a facsimile reprint of the book's first edition was published as part of the OXFORD MARK TWAIN edition. This edition contains an afterword by Harris and an introduction by Justin Kaplan, winner of a Pulitzer Prize for his *Mr. Clemens and Mark Twain* (1966).

While he was staying in Paris, Clemens commissioned FRANK VINCENT DU MOND to illustrate *Joan of Arc*. Later, he complained that Du Mond's pictures made Joan look too much like an ordinary peasant girl (which was probably historically accurate). When he wrote "Saint Joan of Arc" in 1904, he may have been thinking of Du Mond in decrying artists who remember only that Joan was a peasant girl and forget everything else, painting her "as a strapping middle-aged fishwoman, with costume to match," forgetting that "supremely great souls are never lodged in gross bodies."

CRITICAL COMMENTARY

Personal Recollections of Joan of Arc, which Clemens claimed to have spent 12 years researching, reflects the period in which it was composed. It was one of several books published in 1896 on Joan of Arc, a convergence that suggests, apart from Clemens's long-standing personal fascination, the broader resonance of the figure of Joan of Arc in late 19th-century America.

The rapid urbanization of the century's final decades brought forward questions of rural as opposed to urban ways of life; American sociologists under the influence of recent German research sought to understand and control the waning organic community and rise of atomized urban society. In this context, Joan's 15th-century home of Domremy, with its tree-dwelling fairies (recalling the bucolic childhood scenes of Huck and Tom) invokes a notion of rural community that was an important imaginary resource in a modernizing United States. Joan's pure and hardy character is aligned with her rural peasant upbringing, in contrast to the sophisticated treachery of the king's court and his advisers who undermine Joan from the start and later abandon her to the enemy for the sake of diplomatic appeasement. The disparity between courtiers and peasants also inverts conventional descriptions of masculine and feminine identities. Joan derides the "King's dandies" by comparing them to "disguised ladies' maids," in contrast to her own adoption of a brusque soldier's manner and wearing of male clothing, a detail on which her trial would turn (book 2, chapter 21).

The Historical Context

Another aspect of the text's historical background is the United States's increasing military activity and imperialism. In 1896, the year of the book's publication, America was gearing up for war with Spain. In 1898, the United States would officially enter into war with Spain and also annex Hawaii. Later that same year, THEODORE ROOSEVELT's San Juan Hill battle with his Rough Riders burnished the masculine image that would propel him to the governorship of New York, the vice presidency, and then the presidency of the United States in 1901. By 1900, Clemens had decided that the American presence in the Philippines was little more than veiled colonialism. He stood up as a vocal anti-imperialist, serving as vice president of the American Anti-Imperialist League, writing essays, and delivering speeches critical of U.S. foreign policy. Clemens's *Joan of Arc* arrived at the cusp of America's grappling with its imperial self-image; it provided a timely study of the colonized psyche and brought to the fore a seminal myth of resistance to imperialism.

Although Clemens considered *Joan of Arc* a serious and straightforward effort at literature, some elements of its style and humor are reminiscent of his earlier, lighter work. Despite the pretense that de Conte's voice is rendered from medieval French, the narration often dips into American vernacular: "As for us boys, we hardly saw her at all, she was so occupied" or "When we got home, breakfast for us minor fry was waiting in our mess-room" (book 2, chapters 10 and 17). Invented characters, such as the Paladin and La Hire would not be out of place in a Western mining camp. The Paladin, "the windiest blusterer and most catholic liar in the kingdom," fits into a distinguished line of garrulous exaggerators who populate Clemens's work; he diverts the other characters, and the reader, with puffed-up recitations of his imagined exploits (book 2, chapter 11). La Hire, the hard-living bandit, reluctantly agrees to give up, at Joan's insistence, his cherished hobby of cursing. Despite the narrative's mostly focused drive toward Joan's battles and trials, comic relief is provided by shaggy digressions such as an episode in which the Paladin, Rainguesson, and de Conte compete for the attentions of a young beauty, Catherine Boucher. The Paladin rises to new heights of self-aggrandizement, de Conte writes a poem for her, and Rainguesson outdoes them both by reciting de Conte's poem in an impersonation of the Paladin, who competes pathetically for the spotlight with a crescendo of tears (book 2, chapter 15).

Joan's Virtues

Despite her medieval French Catholic context, Joan's virtues are often folded into Clemens's late 19th-century populism. Her preternatural eloquence, for example, conforms to an American ideal of spare frontier candor: "She said the very thing that was in her mind, and said it in a plain, straightforward way" (book 2, chapter 8). Her effective staging of the coronation is explained as demotic intuition: "It is simple: she was a peasant. That tells the whole story. She was of the people and knew the people" (book 2, chapter 33). As critics have noted, Clemens adjusts Joan's Catholicism into a version that anachronistically conforms to a philosophy closer to American Protestantism in character. She is austere in dress, workaholic in daily routine, and prone to superseding church hierarchy in favor of her own divine inspiration. At one point, de Conte observes, "one might say that her motto was 'Work! Stick to it; keep on working!' for in war she never knew what indolence was. And whoever will take that motto and live by it will be likely to succeed" (book 2, chapter 27). In recounting and admiring Joan's work ethic, de Conte slips into didactic editorializing in the mode of Benjamin Franklin, leaving aside Joan's divine inspiration in favor of urging readers to follow her industriousness. Even though Joan has miraculously acquired her military expertise without training, de Conte makes a point of noting that with the exception of Joan, "in history there is no great general, however gifted, who arrived at success otherwise than through able teaching and hard study and experience" (ibid.). De Conte also provides one scene that gives a mundane background to Joan's generally inexplicable knowledge. After the governor has granted Joan control of his army, she plots an ingenious itinerary across France's complex political geography. De Conte initially

assumed this was given to her by the voices but later found the more mundane source of Joan's knowledge, to be research: "she had been diligently questioning those crowds of visiting strangers, and that out of them she had patiently dug all this mass of invaluable knowledge" (book 2, chapter 2).

In its depiction of Joan's divine mandate, *Personal Recollections of Joan of Arc* departs strikingly from the mechanistic philosophy underpinning Clemens's later works. In many of his late works, Clemens seems morosely convinced that human behavior and identity are determined by training and motivated by self-interest, but Joan stands out as a fated individual of singular inspiration and transcendent action. One critic captures this tension, calling Joan a "transcendent hero in a world in which, for all that, transcendence and heroism are both totally impossible" (Searle 16). She is still rigidly constrained by external forces, such as the voices and the institutions that have power over her, the Catholic Church, and the English and French instruments of state. But her individual volition and dogged resistance to external forces make her exceptional in this regard and an inspirational figure emerging from a period of Clemens's overwhelmingly cynical and pessimistic work.

Feminist Critiques

These "personal recollections" may be *of* Joan of Arc, but they are de Conte's, not Joan's personal recollections. Since the 1980s, Joan of Arc has been a target of feminist criticism. Several scholars have noted that while *Joan* is Clemens's only book to feature a female as its main protagonist, in many ways she is eclipsed by the Sieur Louis de Conte. As Susan Harris points out, Joan remains a static, idealized object throughout the narrative, whereas de Conte's alienation from French society is the real narrative and character transformation of the book. In creating a narrator with enough knowledge and perspective to recount Joan's story, Clemens also creates a character whose consciousness often seems to crowd Joan out of the story. The distance between reader and Joan is increased by the text's multiple narrative frames. The narrator, Sieur Louis de Conte, advertises himself as Joan's "page and secretary." The fictional translator, who has rendered the ancient French into modern English, is listed as Jean François Alden. William Dean Howells, who published the novel anonymously in *Harper's Magazine,* provided another buffer between author and reader. Joan herself is thus occluded by many layers of interference and interpretation, making this text not only a particular account of her life but also a more general demonstration of Clemens's engagement with the challenge, complicated by the submerged voices and experiences of women, of writing history (Zwarg).

Critical Commentary by Alex Feerst

CHARACTERS AND RELATED ENTRIES

Alden, Jean François Fictitious translator of *Joan of Arc* (1896), "Alden" is credited on the title page of the novel with translating Sieur Louis de Conte's ancient French into modern English. A thousand words of prefatory remarks by "the translator" sum up Clemens's esteem for Joan of Arc. Clemens adds modern commentary to the novel in footnotes attributed to the translator in chapters 12, 22, 30, and 35 of book 2 and chapters 2, 5, 11, and 16 of book 3. He may have named Alden after Henry Mills ALDEN, the editor of *HARPER'S MAGAZINE,* in which *Joan of Arc* was serialized.

Cauchon, Pierre (1371, near Reims, France–December 18, 1442, Rouen, France) Historical figure and character in *Joan of Arc* (1896). The bishop of Beauvais, a town near ROUEN, Cauchon acted as England's agent in ransoming Joan from the Burgundians and presiding over the trial that led to her execution. As the conscienceless villain of Clemens's novel, he is first mentioned in chapter 39 of book 2 and figures prominently throughout book 3. The narrator de Conte describes Cauchon as a wheezing, obese brute with a splotchy complexion, cauliflower nose and malignant eyes (book 3, chapter 4). Clemens's personal feelings about Cauchon are revealed in a characteristic remark he attributes to his narrator de Conte, who wonders why Cauchon should want to go to heaven, when "he did not know anybody there" (book 3, chapter 18).

Charles VII (the Dauphin) (February 22, 1403, Paris–July 22, 1461, Méhun-sur-Yèvre, France) Historical figure and character in *Joan of Arc* (1896). The son of Isabella of Bavaria and France's King Charles VI (1368–1422), Charles VII became heir (Dauphin) to the French throne in 1417, when a brother died. By the time he succeeded to the kingship in 1422, however, his position was compromised by his suspected complicity in the murder of the duke of Burgundy in 1419 and his father's treaty with England, which disinherited him the following year. His authority in southern France was tenuous, and England occupied most of northern France and was expanding south. Joan of Arc's emergence in 1429 reversed the shrinkage of Charles's domain and legitimized his authority by getting him properly crowned at Reims. Charles rewarded Joan by ennobling her family and exempting her village from taxation but ignored her plight after she was captured by the Burgundians a year later.

Clemens's novel depicts Charles as a weakling dominated by disloyal advisers, particularly his chancellor, Georges de la Trémouille. In Clemens's eyes, Charles's chief crime was ingratitude. After failing to ransom Joan from her captors, he later had her reputation rehabilitated primarily in order to save his own reputation, since she was responsible for his coronation. The authority of the historical Charles grew after Trémoïlle's assassination in 1433 and he did much to rebuild his kingdom. During the 1440s, he campaigned against the English himself and established a regular army. He played a major role in the expulsion of the English from France in 1453.

de Conte, Sieur Louis Narrator of *Joan of Arc* (1896). Though based on a real person from Joan of Arc's time, Clemens's de Conte is a mostly fictional creation. As the ostensible author of *The Personal Recollections of Joan of Arc,* he writes from the year 1492 for his relatives' descendants. Most of his narrative comes from his firsthand participation in events and from occasional eavesdropping. He also occasionally supplements his narrative with stories taken from unnamed "histories" and testimony given at Joan's rehabilitation hearings.

Born on January 6, 1410—exactly two years before Joan—de Conte is orphaned as a child and raised by a Domremy priest who teaches him to read and write. Though a member of the minor nobility, he grows up close to Joan and many other peasant children. After Joan gains command of France's armies in 1429, de Conte becomes her page and secretary and remains at her side throughout her campaigns. After her capture, he disguises himself and becomes a clerk to the court recorder at her trial in ROUEN, so he is close to her until she dies. In later years, de Conte and his friend Noël Rainguesson return to fighting for France. After the English are expelled from the country in 1453, de Conte retires to Domremy an honored hero.

Like the novel's ostensible translator, Jean François Alden, de Conte (whose surname means "tale" in French) is an alter ego of Clemens, who shares his uncritical worship of Joan of Arc. It is often pointed out that the initials of Sieur Louis de Conte are the same as those of Samuel L. Clemens. While Clemens might have found significance in such congruity, "Sieur" is an honorific title—much like "Sir" or "Mister"—and is not really part of de Conte's name. More telling are the modern views that de Conte occasionally voices. For example, early in the narrative, he discusses how blind men are to women's strength and endurance (book 2, chapter 4). Later, he expresses the thought that one day peasants may discover that they are "people" and rise up to demand their rights (book 2, chapter 37). De Conte also resembles Clemens in calling himself fond of sarcasm, though he is not overly sarcastic throughout his narrative (book 2, chapter 18). He also carries an emotional scar similar to one that Clemens bore after falling in love with 14-year-old Laura Wright in 1858. During his stay at ORLÉANS, de Conte falls in love with Catherine Boucher. In a scene that anticipates Cyrano's wooing of Roxanne in Edmond Rostand's *Cyrano de Bergerac* (1897), de Conte writes a love poem to Catherine that Rainguesson recites for him. He remains a bachelor and carries Catherine's image in his heart for 63 years (book 2, chapter 25). Somewhere along the way, he loses the power of laughter (book 2, chapter 12).

Domrémy Birthplace of Joan of Arc. A village on the Meuse River in the Vosges department of northeastern FRANCE's historic Lorraine region, Domrémy is 30 miles southwest of Nancy. After the village fell under English rule, Joan left it in 1429, never to return. The following year, she made possible Charles VII's coronation and he rewarded her by exempting Domrémy from taxation. The exemption was intended to be perpetual, but it lapsed during the French Revolution (1789).

Domrémy is the principal setting of the first eight chapters of Clemens's novel *Joan of Arc* (1896), whose idyllic description of the village recalls Clemens's fictional St. Petersburg. Domrémy also resembles the real villages of Clemens's youth in being too dull to recognize greatness in one of its own people until the outside world celebrates it (book 2, chapter 2).

Joan of Arc (c. January 6, 1412, Domremy, France–May 30, 1431, Rouen, France)   Patron saint and national hero of FRANCE and the subject of Clemens's last finished novel. An illiterate peasant born in the village of Domremy, Joan took command of the armies of France when she was 17. Within 13 months, she had led them to victories that turned the tide of the Hundred Years' War, paving the way for France's complete liberation from England two decades later. After being captured by the Burgundians in May 1430, she was ransomed by the English and tried for heresy in Rouen by a French ecclesiastical court headed by Bishop Pierre Cauchon that sentenced her to be burned at the STAKE. Two decades later, France's King Charles VII had the Vatican retry her case, and she was officially rehabilitated in 1456. In 1920, the Roman Catholic Church canonized her.

Joan of Arc was Clemens's favorite historical figure. According to A. B. PAINE's biography, when Clemens was a youth in Hannibal, a stray leaf from a history book containing a moving passage about Joan's captivity in Rouen blew into his hands. Paine sees this moment as a turning point in Clemens's life—it not only launched his lifelong fascination with Joan, but gave him an appetite for history generally. While scholars disagree over whether this romantic incident actually occurred, it is clear that Clemens became fascinated with Joan early in life. By at least 1868, he was citing her name in speeches. By the early 1890s, he decided to tell her story in the form of the novel that became *Personal Recollections of Joan of Arc* (1896). Following the outlines of Joan's life closely, he took little license in interpreting her career. For example, though he was skeptical about the "voices" that Joan claimed were guiding her, his novel simply accepts them as given, with no attempt to explain them. On the other hand, while he considered her an "ideally perfect" character, he gave her a robust sense of humor. He also exaggerated her physical attractiveness. At 16, she is "shapely and graceful, and of a beauty so extraordinary that I might allow myself any extravagance of language in describing it" (book 1, chapter 5). He later acknowledged modeling Joan's description on that of his own daughter, Susy, whom he also idealized. Nearly a decade after writing *Joan of Arc*, Clemens again praised her extravagantly in an essay for the December 1904 HARPER'S MAGAZINE, "Saint Joan of Arc," which calls her career "beyond fiction." In 1919, HARPER AND BROTHERS, published Clemens's "Saint Joan of Arc" as a book, with some of the introductory passages from *Joan of Arc* and new color illustrations by Howard Nye.

Orléans   City on the Loire River in the center of FRANCE. When JOAN OF ARC began her military campaigns, Orléans was under siege by the English, who already controlled northern France. In order to stop England's southward advance, Joan made lifting the siege her first priority. After achieving this goal on May 8, 1429, she won the nickname "Maid of Orléans." Her Orléans campaign is the subject of chapters 13–22 of book 2 of *Joan of Arc* (1896). One of her most important lieutenants during this episode is the "Bastard of Orléans," a historical figure named Jean Dunois (1402–1868), who was the son of the Duke of Orléans and cousin of King Charles VII. Dunois also played a major role in the later expulsion of the English from France.

The Paladin (Edmond Aubrey)   Character in *Joan of Arc* (1896). An entirely fictional creation,

the Paladin is one of Clemens's finest comic liars and is *Joan of Arc*'s main comic relief through its first two books. Like Markiss in chapter 77 of *Roughing It* (1872), the Paladin is such a notorious liar that people automatically assume that anything he says is untrue (book 2, chapter 3). The joke on the Paladin is amplified by his claim that he is not "the talking sort" and will let his deeds speak for him (book 2, chapter 7).

The Paladin's real name is Edmond Aubrey, which is not mentioned after the fourth chapter. The son of Domremy's mayor—a man noted for liking to argue—Edmond is dubbed the "Paladin" as a boy because he always boasts about the armies that he will "eat up" some day (book 1, chapter 4). Though he grows into a big and powerful young man, he remains a vain windbag and often delivers comic speeches. Joan sees through his boasting, however, and surprises everyone by naming him her standard-bearer (book 2, chapter 11). Though the Paladin continues to boast, he proves unflinching in battle and dies defending Joan at Compiègne just before she is captured (book 2, chapter 41). Noël Rainguesson—who always enjoys twitting the Paladin—considers him supremely lucky to die this way and concedes that the Paladin has truly earned his name (book 3, chapter 2).

The name *Paladin* is an old French term for knight, associated with the 12 peers of Charlemagne in French legends.

Rainguesson, Noël   Character in *Joan of Arc* (1896). A purely fictional creation, Rainguesson is one of the Domremy boys who go to war with Joan. Free of pretension and ambition and cynical about the horrors of war, he plays the jester throughout the narrative. He especially enjoys twitting the Paladin's vanity and considers himself the braggart's creator. His special gifts include recitation and mimicry. In Orléans, he recites Louis de Conte's love poem to Catherine Boucher and flawlessly imitates the Paladin's boasting about imaginary battle experiences (book 2, chapter 15).

Wounded while protecting Joan during her last assault on Compiègne, Rainguesson disappears in

France during Joan of Arc's Time

Areas occupied by England

ENGLAND

English Channel

Calais
Agincourt
PICARDY

Cherbourg
Rouen
Compiègne
Reims
Meuse R.
LORRAINE

Normandy
Seine R.
Paris
Châlons-sur-Marne
Toul
Vaucouleur
Champagne
Rhine R.

Patay
Seine R.
Troyes
Domrémy
Neufchâteau

Orléans
Jargeau
Gien
Blois
Sully
Tours
Saône R.
BURGUNDY

Loire R.
Chinon
Loire R.

Poitiers

ATLANTIC
OCEAN

FRANCE

Saône R.
Rhône R.

Isère R.

Rhône R.

Avignon
Durance R.
Marseille

Mediterranean Sea

N

© Infobase Publishing

May 1430 (book 2, chapter 41). Five months later, he escapes from his captors and rejoins de Conte at Compiègne (book 3, chapter 2). With his former lightheartedness now lost, he goes to Rouen with de Conte and attends the public sessions of Joan's trial. De Conte's concluding chapter reveals that Rainguesson dies in the last battle against the English, which occurred in 1453.

Rouen French city in which Joan of Arc was executed. Located on the Seine River, 70 miles northwest of PARIS, Rouen was occupied by England in 1419. Eleven years later, the English ransomed Joan from her Burgundian captors, through Bishop Pierre Cauchon. They imprisoned her in Rouen in December 1430 and tried her there for heresy the following spring. On May 30, 1431, she was burned at the STAKE in Rouen. The French recaptured the city in 1449.

Clemens spent most of October 1894 in Rouen and made the city the principal setting for book 3 of his novel, *Joan of Arc* (1896), which he later finished writing in Paris. Rouen is evidently also the place where Cathy Alison lived with her parents before they died in *A HORSE'S TALE*.

BIBLIOGRAPHY

Kaplan, Justin. "Introduction." In *Personal Recollections of Joan of Arc*, edited by Shelley Fisher Fishkin. New York: Oxford University Press, 1996.

Harris, Susan K. "Afterword." In *Personal Recollections of Joan of Arc*, edited by Shelley Fisher Fishkin. New York: Oxford University Press, 1996.

———. "Joan of Arc: The Sieur Louis de Conte." In *Mark Twain's Escape from Time: A Study of Patterns and Images*, 17–28. Columbia: University of Missouri Press, 1982.

Horn, Jason Gary. "Verifying the Truth That Matters: *Personal Recollections of Joan of Arc*." In *Mark Twain and William James: Crafting a Free Self*, 69–105. Columbia: University of Missouri Press, 1996.

Maik, Thomas A. *A Reexamination of Mark Twain's Joan of Arc*. Lewiston, N.Y.: Edwin Mellen Press, 1992.

Miller, Victoria Thorpe. "*Personal Recollections of Joan of Arc* in Today's Classroom." In *Making Mark Twain Work in the Classroom*, edited by James S. Leonard, 55–64. Durham, N.C.: Duke University Press, 1999.

Searle, William. *The Saint and the Skeptics: Joan of Arc in the Work of Mark Twain, Anatole France and Bernard Shaw*. Detroit: Wayne State University Press, 1976.

Stone, Albert E. "Mark Twain's *Joan of Arc*: The Child as Goddess." Reprinted in *On Mark Twain: The Best from American Literature*, edited by Louis J. Budd and Edwin H. Cady, 71–90. Durham, N.C.: Duke University Press, 1987.

Stahl, J. D. "Escape from Sexuality: Mark Twain's Joan of Arc." In *Mark Twain, Culture and Gender: Envisioning America through Europe*. Athens: University of Georgia Press, 1994.

Stoneley, Peter. "*The Prince and the Pauper* and *Personal Recollections of Joan of Arc*." In *Mark Twain and the Feminine Aesthetic*, 76–103. Cambridge: Cambridge University Press, 1992.

Twain, Mark. *Personal Recollections of Joan of Arc*. Edited by Shelly Fisher Fishkin. New York: Oxford University Press, 1996.

Wilson, James D. "In Quest of Redemptive Vision: Mark Twain's *Joan of Arc*." *Texas Studies in Literature and Language* 20 (1978): 181–198.

Zwarg, Christina. "Woman as Force in Twain's *Joan of Arc*: The Unwordable Fascination." *Criticism* 27 (Winter 1985): 57–72.

"Journalism in Tennessee"

SKETCH published in the BUFFALO EXPRESS on September 4, 1869, and later collected in *SKETCHES, NEW AND OLD*. Possibly inspired by an incident in which a MEMPHIS editor assaulted a journalist for calling him a Radical, this sketch is set in TENNESSEE's opposite corner. Its PARODY of southern journalism anticipates *Roughing It*'s (1872) depiction of frontier journalism in NEVADA, where fights among editors were common. It also anticipates *Connecticut Yankee*'s (1889) comparison of the *Camelot Weekly Hosannah and Literary Volcano* with southern newspapers, and it parodies DUELS that are more hazardous to bystanders than to combatants.

SYNOPSIS

After moving to the South for health reasons, the unnamed narrator becomes associate editor of the *Morning Glory and Johnson County War-Whoop*. Assigned to write on the "Spirit of the Tennessee Press," he drafts a dignified summary of the positions taken on controversial issues by the *Semi-Weekly Earthquake, Higginsville Thunderbolt and Battle Cry of Freedom, Mud Springs Morning Howl,* and *Daily Hurrah*. Calling his article "gruel," the chief editor immediately starts rewriting it. As he works, Smith, the *Moral Volcano*'s editor, shoots at him through a window; he fires back, wounding Smith, who then shoots off the narrator's finger. Next, the explosion of a grenade tumbling down the stove-pipe knocks out some of the narrator's teeth.

As the editor admires his revised article—calling rival editors liars and scoundrels—a brick thrown through the window hits the narrator. Colonel Blatherskite Tecumseh then bursts in with a pistol. He and the editor exchange six shots; one mortally wounds Tecumseh, the others hit the narrator.

When the editor goes out, he tells the narrator what to do with Jones, Gillespie, and Ferguson when they show up; however, these men later turn the tables, throwing him out the window and whipping and scalping him. When the editor returns with friends, a general riot begins. Finding southern hospitality "too lavish," the narrator resigns and checks into a hospital.

jumping frog story

Clemens wrote and published this SKETCH in 1865. It first appeared as "Jim Smiley and His Jumping Frog" and was subsequently revised and published under a variety of titles, including "The Notorious Jumping Frog of Calaveras County" and "The Celebrated Jumping Frog of Calaveras County." Modern scholars often refer to it as simply the "jumping frog story."

Told within the classic structure of a FRAME-STORY, the 2,600-word narrative recounts the career of a wily gambler who meets his match when a stranger passes through the camp. While the story builds to several comic climaxes, the essence of its humor is the deadpan delivery of its simple narrator, Simon Wheeler. In the story's earliest published version, Mark Twain himself narrates the frame in the form of a letter to ARTEMUS WARD about his visit to a fictitious mining camp called Boomerang. Subsequent versions of the story alter the frame, dropping the structure of a letter and making the narrator anonymous. Further, Boom-

erang's name is changed to ANGEL'S CAMP—a real place in California's CALAVERAS COUNTY.

SYNOPSIS

The narrator describes visiting an old mining camp in behalf of a friend seeking news of a man named Leonidas W. Smiley. In a dilapidated tavern, he meets garrulous old Simon Wheeler. Wheeler cannot recall a *Leonidas* Smiley, but does recall a *Jim* Smiley who lived in the camp around 1849 or 1850. Most of the balance of the story is Wheeler's narrative about Jim Smiley.

Notorious for betting on anything that he could, Smiley was uncommonly lucky. He would bet on horse races, dogfights, chickenfights—even which of two birds on a fence would fly away first. He owned a mare known as the "fifteen-minute nag"; the horse looked broken-down, but always rallied to win its races. Another of his animals was a bull-pup named Andrew Jackson that won fights by seizing hold of its opponents' hind legs. He also had rat-terriers, chicken cocks, tomcats, and other things on which he was always ready to wager. Once he caught a frog he named Dan'l Webster and spent three months training him to jump.

One day a stranger in camp saw Dan'l Webster and said that he could not see any points about him that were any better than any other frog, but Smiley offered to put up $40 that Dan'l could outjump any frog in the county. The stranger was willing to take the bet but had no frog, so Smiley laid down $40 and went off to find one for him. While Smiley was gone, the stranger pried open Dan'l Webster's mouth and filled him with quail-shot. After Smiley returned with another frog, the new frog hopped off smartly, but Dan'l Webster merely shrugged. The stranger scooped up the money to leave, pausing to repeat his remark about Smiley's frog having no special points about it. After he was gone, Smiley picked up Dan'l Webster and discovered that he was full of shot. He took off after the stranger, but never caught him.

Wheeler's narrative is interrupted when he is called outside. He returns to start up a fresh story about Jim Smiley's tail-less one-eyed cow, but the narrator slips away.

BACKGROUND AND PUBLISHING HISTORY

An incident on which the jumping frog story is based actually occurred at or near Angel's Camp and was reported in a Sonora newspaper in 1853. Clemens heard the story from an old bartender named BEN COON in Angel's Camp in early 1865. His brief notes indicate that the frog's owner was called Coleman and that the amount of money wagered was $50. Shortly after leaving Angel's Camp. Clemens began writing his own version of the story, but it took him half a year and several false starts to find a satisfactory framework. In October, he sent his manuscript to GEORGE W. CARLETON in New York for a book that Artemus Ward was editing, but Carleton turned it down—probably because his book was nearly ready to print. Carleton passed the manuscript to Henry Clapp at the SATURDAY PRESS, which published it on November 18, 1865.

An immediate sensation, the story was reprinted in newspapers and magazines throughout the country. Meanwhile, Clemens published a revised version in San Francisco's CALIFORNIAN magazine. In May 1867, it became the title story of Clemens's first book, THE CELEBRATED JUMPING FROG OF CALAVERAS COUNTY, AND OTHER SKETCHES. Eight years later, it reappeared in SKETCHES, NEW AND OLD as "The Jumping Frog in English, Then in French, Then Clawed Back into a Civilized Language Once More by Patient, Unremunerated Toil." This version adds a poor French translation of the story, along with the original text and Clemens's own literal retranslation. Clemens published a further elaboration of the story in the April 1894 issue of the NORTH AMERICAN REVIEW, as "The Private History of the Jumping Frog Story." This version adds an anecdote about HENRY VAN DYKE'S telling him that the story's roots go back to ancient Greece. Unbeknownst to either man at the time, another scholar had adapted Clemens's story into a Greek tale for a textbook. In November 1903, HARPER'S collected all these materials in a single volume, *The Jumping Frog in English, Then in French, Then Clawed Back into a Civilized Language Once More by Patient, Unremunerated Toil,* freshly illustrated by FRED STROTHMANN.

The jumping frog story has been adapted to the screen in a variety of forms. Both the 1944 and 1985 films titled THE ADVENTURES OF MARK TWAIN, for example, contain versions of the jumping competition. The 1948 feature film BEST MAN WINS is loosely adapted from the original story, with Edgar Buchanan (1903–1979) as Jim Smiley. Television dramatizations of the story followed in 1949 and 1981, and an animated adaptation aired in 1982.

CRITICAL COMMENTARY

Appearing under various titles and many revisions, the jumping frog story evokes humor from disappointment and character flaws, rising expectations and anticlimaxes, and triumph and defeat, sometimes appearing simultaneously. Clemens accomplishes these contrasts with quick movements in the story's framework structure and with juxtaposed characterizations.

The uptight easterner of the story finds both the tale and the teller, Simon Wheeler, inscrutable. On the other hand, the westerner Wheeler—serious and oblivious to all but his story—cannot conceive of anyone uninterested in Smiley, the subject of his story. Initially, the narrator realistically introduces the situation, then unhappily listens, desiring escape; in the second part of the story, Wheeler monotonically mythologizes Smiley; the final part focuses on three increasingly absurd episodes. Juxtaposing bored (easterner) and serious (Wheeler) attitudes intensifies the tension and humor of the story.

Admiring Smiley's gambling antics, particularly his winning tendencies, Wheeler suggests that Smiley will bet on anything, and even switch sides if necessary to secure a wager. He cites horseraces, dogfights, catfights, chickenfights, birdfights, bug journeys, listing them by descending animal size, balanced by bets on Parson Walker's preaching and on his ill wife's recovery chances. That he bets against God's "inf'nite mercy" confirms Smiley's addiction and vulnerability.

As their size decreases, the animals discussed increase in personality and intelligence; expectations rise and disappointments intensify. Smiley's unnamed, asthmatic "fifteen-minute nag" splayfootedly runs to the finish, coughing and wheezing, winning by a neck. Expected to lose, the sickly nag knows when to speed up to win, raising anticipations about the dog, Andrew Jackson, discussed next. Praised for its stubbornness, like its human namesake, Andy is expected to win in combat, but encountering a dog without back legs, he feels Smiley let him down. Despite "genius" and "talent," dutiful Andy—unable to perform his duty—dies of disappointment, preparing readers for the next tale and the loss of Smiley's frog.

The frog, Daniel Webster, also has a name reflecting sectional tensions. Steadfast ("solid as a church") like his human alter ego, the famous senator from New England, Dan'l is described as "modest and straightfor'ard . . . for all he was so gifted." He is a solemn intellectual. He leaps to eat flies, emphasizing his down-to-earth intellectuality. Eager to wager, Smiley leaves to find a frog for a stranger, who meanwhile loads quail-shot into Dan'l. With Dan'l weighted down before he can spring, representatives of both east and west lose. The winner is the second of Wheeler's "two heroes," the stranger, because he outsmarts Smiley.

The original narrator, the uptight easterner, quickly leaves when Wheeler steps away, even as readers yearn for more. Caught at the door, he refuses to hear the story of Smiley's cow, as if returning to larger animals might mean beginning all over again. He escapes the joke played upon him; readers, however, their anticipations heightened by the cow, fall into one. What kind of gambling can be done with a cow? Smiley shares characteristics with each animal: He is conniving and shrewd, like the nag, who goes full-force once bets are down; determined, like Andy; intelligent, like Dan'l; and odd, like the "yaller one-eyed cow" with no tail.

Wishing Wheeler would make a point, the easterner is disappointed in the story because, not admiring its style or presentation of human behavior, he misses its essentials. Though showing little emotion, Wheeler is clearly disappointed he cannot continue. Just as Smiley is distressed to lose, readers are distressed to miss what promised to be another fascinating tale.

Critical Commentary by John H. Davis

CHARACTERS AND RELATED ENTRIES

Andrew Jackson   Dog mentioned in the JUMPING FROG STORY. Once the property of Jim Smiley, Andrew Jackson was a small, unimpressive bull-pup, but had real genius as a fighter in money matches. He allowed opponents to bully-rag and throw him around, but once the money was all up, he would seize hold of the other dog's hind legs and hang on until it quit. His career ended tragically when he confronted a dog with no hind legs; after losing badly, he limped away and—like *Huckleberry Finn*'s Emmeline Grangerford—died of a broken heart when his unique talent failed him.

Boomerang   Fictional mining camp in early versions of the JUMPING FROG STORY. The story's first published version (November 1865) calls its setting "the ancient mining camp of Boomerang"; later versions call it "the decayed mining camp of ANGEL'S." Clemens's earliest known draft of this story reveals a great deal about Boomerang, which it describes as having just 20 "crazy houses" occupied. It suggests, however, that surrounding lodes contain enough gold to restore the "ancient magnificence of Boomerang."

Chapter 29 of *Roughing It* (1872) lists a "Boomerang" among Humboldt mining camps in Nevada. While the name may reflect an Australian influence in western mining camps, the word may also be related to "boomer," a term with several meanings in mining. For example, a "boomer" could be either a person participating in a rush to a "boom" area or the sudden discharge of water in placer-mining.

Dan'l Webster   Title character in the JUMPING FROG STORY. Probably a bullfrog, Dan'l Webster is owned by Jim Smiley, who has spent three months training him to become the best-jumping frog in CALAVERAS COUNTY. Despite his giftedness, Dan'l remains exceptionally modest and straightforward. Smiley carries him to town in a lattice box, on the chance of getting up a wager on him. The frog takes his name from the American statesman DANIEL WEBSTER, who was U.S. secretary of state around the time the events in this narrative occurred.

Smiley, Jim   Character in the JUMPING FROG STORY. A former resident of ANGEL'S CAMP, Smiley was notorious for being willing to take either side of any bet, and he was uncommonly lucky. He once even offered odds to the Parson Walker that the parson's wife would not recover from her illness. Smiley owned many animals on which he wagered, including a broken-down horse known as the "fifteen-minute nag," a fighting dog named Andrew Jackson, chicken cocks, and tomcats. His prize possession, however, was his jumping frog, Dan'l Webster, which he spent three months teaching to jump. He often took the frog with him to town on the chance of getting up a bet—which is how he came to wager with the stranger of the story.

According to Simon Wheeler, Smiley also owned a yellow, one-eyed cow without a tail, but we never learn what he did with this animal. When Clemens first heard the jumping frog story from BEN COON, the Smiley character was called Coleman.

Smiley, Reverend Leonidas W.   Name mentioned in the JUMPING FROG STORY. The story's narrator ("Mark Twain" himself in the first published version) visits ANGEL'S CAMP at the request of an eastern friend (originally ARTEMUS WARD) to look up a boyhood chum named Leonidas W. Smiley. When the narrator asks Simon Wheeler about him, Wheeler launches into a long narrative about someone named *Jim* Smiley. The narrator concludes that *Leonidas W.* Smiley never existed, and was merely an invention of his friend to draw him into being bored to death by Wheeler.

Wheeler, Simon   Character in the JUMPING FROG STORY. The tale opens in a dilapidated mining camp tavern, where Wheeler is found dozing. Though it is not clear that he works in the tavern, he is clearly a long-term camp resident. Old, bald, fat and garrulous, he is good-natured but tediously boring.

The earliest published version of the story opens with the FRAME narrator ("Mark Twain" himself) asking Wheeler about a friend of ARTEMUS WARD. Wheeler then corners the narrator and tells him a long story about someone else—Jim Smiley, a notorious local gambler who owned a champion frog. Lacking a sense of humor,

Wheeler drones on, oblivious to the comic absurdity of his story. His deadpan delivery and attention to detail are modeled on BEN COON, a tavern keeper who told Clemens the frog story at ANGEL'S CAMP in 1865.

Clemens also uses the name "Wheeler" in several other works. It appears once in *Roughing It* (1872); Jim Blaine's "Old Ram's Tale" of chapter 53 mentions a Wheeler who was woven into a carpet in a factory. "Simon Wheeler" is also the central character in "Cap'n Simon Wheeler, the Amateur Detective. A Light Tragedy," a burlesque drama on DETECTIVES that Clemens wrote around 1877. After failing to get this play produced, he started rewriting it as a novel to be called "Simon Wheeler, Detective." Aside from the name, however, the Wheeler of these stories has little in common with the character in the jumping frog story. The play describes Wheeler as brave and gentle, but uneducated and simple-minded enough to have the confidence that a detective needs to succeed.

The name "Simon Wheeler" itself is curiously similar to "Simon Carpenter"—the name that Clemens assigns to himself in "VILLAGERS OF 1840–3."

BIBLIOGRAPHY

Twain, Mark. "The Celebrated Jumping Frog of Calaveras County." In *The Celebrated Jumping Frog of Calaveras County and Other Sketches.* 1867. Reprinted in *The Oxford Mark Twain*, edited by Shelley Fisher Fishkin, 7–19. New York: Oxford University Press, 1996.

———. "Jim Smiley and His Jumping Frog." In *The Best Short Stories of Mark Twain*, edited by Lawrence I. Berkove, 3–9. New York: The Modern Library, 2004.

———. "The 'Jumping Frog.' In English. Then in French. Then Clawed Back into a Civilized Language Once More by Patient, Unremunerated Toil." In *Mark Twain's Sketches, New and Old.* 1875. Reprinted in *The Oxford Mark Twain*, edited by Shelley Fisher Fishkin, 28–43. New York: Oxford University Press, 1996.

———. "The Notorious Jumping Frog of Calaveras County." In *The Signet Book of Mark Twain's Short Stories*, edited by Justin Kaplan, 1–16. New York: Signet Classic, 1985.

"The Killing of Julius Caesar 'Localized' "

SKETCH published in San Francisco's CALIFORNIAN on November 12, 1864. Described by Clemens as a "travesty" of what he calls minutely detailed reporting on sensational items, the sketch describes JULIUS CAESAR's assassination as it might be treated by a modern newspaper covering a political murder during an election. Its core is a translation of a purported article in the *Roman Daily Evening Fasces* that closely follows the characters, events and even some of the dialogue of the third act of WILLIAM SHAKESPEARE's *Julius Caesar*, salted with modern political jargon. The conspirator "George W. Cassius," for example, is described as the "Nobby Boy of the Third Ward." The sketch concludes with the suggestion that Caesar's mantle will be a key piece of evidence at the coroner's inquest. Meanwhile, as Brutus and Mark Antony speak at the Forum, the chief of police prepares for a riot.

Clemens wrote this 3,000-word sketch after covering the 1864 presidential election for the SAN FRANCISCO CALL. He published it four days after ABRAHAM LINCOLN was reelected. The sketch anticipates chapter 26 of *Innocents Abroad* (1869), in which the narrator translates a review from another ancient newspaper, *The Roman Daily Battle-Ax*. It was reprinted in THE CELEBRATED JUMPING FROG OF CALAVERAS COUNTY (1867) and in SKETCHES, NEW AND OLD (1875).

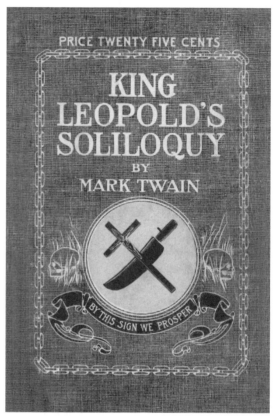

A note pasted into the 1906 printing of *King Leopold's Soliloquy* announced that Clemens declined to accept any royalties from the booklet, so that all profits could go to relief work on behalf of the people of the Congo Free State.

King Leopold's Soliloquy: A Defense of His Congo Rule (1905)

POLEMIC tract. In late 1904, E. D. Morel asked Clemens to support the CONGO REFORM ASSOCIATION, which was focusing international attention on King LEOPOLD II's brutally exploitative regime in what later became the Democratic Republic of the Congo. After joining the American branch of the association, Clemens wrote this rambling "soliloquy" as a satirical attack on Leopold, who condemns himself with hypocritically pious responses to the charges brought against him. Writing primarily for American readers, Clemens did not realize that the United States was not a signatory to the 1884 Berlin Conference that legitimized Leopold's Congo rule. After he discovered his error, his interest in the reform movement waned, but his tract nevertheless may have helped to bring down Leopold's Congo regime.

SYNOPSIS

Alone, apparently in his palace, King Leopold angrily throws down pamphlets that he has been reading, and curses and rages about the charges leveled against him in the press. He sees himself as an agent committed to bringing Christianity to the Congo and rooting out SLAVERY. He knows this is true because he has the blessing of 13 European nations that met in Berlin. Periodically, he interrupts his raging to kiss his crucifix.

As he details the charges brought against him, he wonders why people are so anxious to denounce atrocities and so slow to approve the good things that he has done. He takes some solace in getting America's official approval of the humane and benevolent purposes of his Congo scheme—especially since he knows that America will not confess its blunder by withdrawing its endorsement. He chuckles as he reads from a missionary's suggestion that the United States did not realize it was endorsing Leopold's *personal* rule when it recognized his Congo government.

As he grumbles about meddlesome missionaries who spy and write about what they see, he reads passages from articles and pamphlets by missionaries and others. One of his detractors is the British consul (Roger) Casement—who has the effrontery to publish excerpts from a *private* diary kept by a Congo official. A passage about mutilations of Africans points up the difficulty of arguing with critics. His own people point out that the mutilations they inflict merely follow native customs, but critics ask how *inventing* a barbarity differs from *imitating* one from savages.

A pamphlet complaining about the practice of ransoming prisoners to collect debts fails to acknowledge how hard it is to collect debts without ransom. Ordinary punishments are useless against ignorant savages. Leopold is especially irritated by the charge that he provides nothing in return for the taxes that he extracts. Does he not, after all, furnish the gospel to Africans?

Leopold's most powerful enemy is the kodak (camera)—the only witness he cannot bribe. When he reads a pamphleteer's admission that people shudder and turn away when they hear particulars of his atrocities, Leopold concludes that *that* is his protection. He knows the human race well enough to be confident that people will continue to ignore him.

PUBLISHING HISTORY

After the NORTH AMERICAN REVIEW, which had just published "THE CZAR'S SOLILOQUY," rejected the Leopold piece, P. R. Warren of Boston published it as a 50-page soft-covered book in September 1905. The Congo Reform Association added illustrations—including photographs of Africans with severed hands—and sold the book for 25 cents. Later printings added supplemental documentation and a notice confirming Clemens's instruction that all profits go to the association's work. The 1996 OXFORD MARK TWAIN edition includes a facsimile reprint of the first edition of *King Leopold's Soliloquy* in its *Following the Equator* volume.

Letters from the Earth

Treatise on humankind and religion written in 1909 and first published within a book of the same title in 1962. The last substantial manuscript that Clemens wrote, "Letters" played an important role in reinvigorating popular interest in his work a half century after he wrote it. The book's publication occurred during the same year that the Mark Twain Papers (precursor to the MARK TWAIN PROJECT) signed a publishing agreement with the University of California Press that helped launch it as a professional editing project. The death of Clara Clemens later that year left the editors of her father's papers with unprecedented freedom to select and edit material. Meanwhile, publication of *Letters from the Earth* garnered national attention and alerted the public to a serious side of Clemens that hitherto had not been generally known.

Not easy to assign to a genre, "Letters" begins with an omniscient narrator describing a scene in heaven in which the archangels Satan, Gabriel, and Michael are characters. Its focus then shifts to Satan. Temporarily banished from heaven, he visits Earth and writes his observations about mankind in a series of letters to Gabriel and Michael. Initially, his tone is personal, with frequent use of first- and second-person pronouns. Gradually, however, his letters become less personal and increasingly vitriolic. By its end, the document is essentially a POLEMIC.

Apparently sincere in saying that he expected *Letters from the Earth* never to be published, Clemens used it to express his frank opinions about Christianity, moral beliefs, and human sexuality. "Letters" expands on themes that he explored as early as *Huckleberry Finn* (1884), which opens with Huck considering the nature of heaven (chapter 1) and often has him ponder the efficacy of prayer (especially in chapters 3, 8, 28, and 31). The passages about prayer in "Letters" also bear an affinity to "THE WAR PRAYER," and Satan's mocking remarks about man's concepts of heaven recall "CAPTAIN STORMFIELD'S VISIT TO HEAVEN." Satan's discussion of man's moral sense also develops ideas that Clemens explores fully in *WHAT IS MAN?*, his ADAM AND EVE writings, and elsewhere. "Letters" has also raised questions about Clemens's personal life. Satan's discussion of human sexual intercourse, for example, has led to speculation that Clemens may have been impotent in middle age.

BERNARD DEVOTO prepared the first edition of *Letters from the Earth* by combining two separately paginated manuscript fragments that Clemens probably intended to connect. The first fragment—which Clemens left untitled—is a roughly 1,500-word narrative setting the stage for Satan's banishment. The second fragment, which Clemens titled *Letters from the Earth*, contains about 17,500 words of "letters." Clemens left most of Satan's letters unnumbered; DeVoto gave them 11 sequential roman numerals. Paul Baender's corrected text for the Mark Twain Papers edition (discussed below) ignores DeVoto's numbers but follows a similar sequence. For the sake of clear identification of passages, the synopsis that follows employs DeVoto's letter numbers. Parenthetical notes are inserted where his numbers differ from those of the original manuscript.

SYNOPSIS

Seated on His throne, with Satan, Gabriel, and Michael at his feet, the Creator lifts His hand and a million suns burst forth and scatter in the blackness of space. After leaving the Grand Council, the archangels discuss what they have just seen. Suggesting that the new feature in the universe that the Creator has established is automatic and self-

regulating law, Satan gives it a name: the Law of Nature, or the Law of God.

After three centuries of celestial time—100 million Earth years—a messenger invites the archangels to watch the Creator make animals. The Creator explains that the animals are an experiment in morals and conduct. Each animal has its own temperament. For example, while the tiger's nature is ferocity, that of the rabbit is lack of courage. Though the animals constantly kill each other, they are blameless because they are merely following their nature. The Creator then displays His masterpiece—man, as millions of humans pour into view. He explains that He is putting into each man different measures of moral qualities, such as courage and cowardice, ferocity and gentleness, and so on, and is sending them to Earth.

Several celestial days later, Satan is heard uttering sarcastic remarks about the Creator's industries and is banished from heaven for a celestial day. Instead of going into the empty void of space, as he usually does when banished, he visits Earth to see how the human-race experiment is faring. Later, he writes about it to Gabriel and Michael in private letters.

Satan's Letter (unnumbered)

Finding Earth to be an extraordinarily strange place, Satan thinks that it, its people and its animals are all insane. He finds man a marvelous curiosity because man thinks that he is the "noblest work of God" and the Creator's pet, though his prayers are never answered. Equally incredible, man thinks that he is going to heaven.

Letter 2 (manuscript letter 4)

Nothing about man is not strange to immortals. For example, man imagines a heaven that leaves out his chief delight—sexual intercourse. He fills his heaven entirely with diversions that he cares nothing for on Earth. In his imagined heaven, prayer is substituted for sexual intercourse, everybody sings, and everybody plays the harp. Further, man imagines a heaven in which all the nations are jumbled together, even though they all hate each other on Earth. Finally, there is not a rag of intellectuality in heaven, though every man on Earth possesses some share of intellect. In short, heaven contains everything repulsive to man, and nothing that he likes.

Letters 3 (manuscript letter 5)

Satan discusses Christianity, as it is set forth in the Testaments, which Christians believe are dictated by God. The Bible is actually made from fragments of older Bibles. It has only two new things in it: hell and its singular heaven. Though man has invented both, he credits them to God.

According to the biblical account of Creation, God spent five days making the Earth, then created the rest of the universe in one day. And the purpose of all the other suns and planets? Simply to illuminate the Earth! The Bible says that the universe is 6,000 years old, but inquiring minds now know that its age is 100 million years.

God put ADAM AND EVE in the Garden, telling them not to eat the forbidden fruit, but made them curious, so naturally they ate it. This gave them the moral sense and led to their discovery of sexual intercourse and immodesty. The latter is a strange convention on Earth, since it has no standard. For example, Indian women cover their faces and breasts and expose their legs, while European women cover their legs and expose their faces and breasts.

God expelled Adam and Eve from the Garden for disobeying a command that He had no right to utter. He made one code of morals for Himself, another for His children. Despite His manifest unfairness, He is daily praised for being just and righteous.

Letter 4

After leaving the Garden under a curse, the first pair constantly practiced the "Supreme Act." Cain and Abel and their sisters followed and the work of populating the Earth proceeded. Eventually, God was dissatisfied with the world's morals. Concluding that people were bad, He decided to abolish them by drowning all but a sample on Noah's Ark. Despite being farsighted, however, He failed to foresee that people would go rotten again.

Letter 5

Records of how many animals Noah collected, or how long he spent collecting them, are lost. Further, the Bible suppresses the fact that Noah deliberately sailed before many large animals arrived because he did not have enough room to carry them.

Letter 6 (manuscript letter 7)

On Noah's third day out, a fly was found to have been accidentally left behind, so he spent 16 days going back for it. By saving the fly, he also saved typhoid fever.

The Bible's contradictions are hard to understand. For example, jealousy is a weakness, yet God is a "jealous God." At first He commanded that no *other* Gods should be put before Him; later He said that He was the *only* God. Jealousy is the key. Since Adam and Eve ate the forbidden fruit in order to be as Gods, God still seeks revenge. A human being is a machine and the Creator has planned an enemy to oppose each of its mechanisms. Man equips the Creator with every trait that makes a fiend, then calls him "Our Father."

Letter 7

Noah and his family were saved but were full of microbes; the most important part of his cargo was disease germs. Most animals are distributed to various regions, but not the fly. He is everywhere and is the Creator's special representative. Houseflies destroy more lives than all the rest of the Creator's death-agents combined. The Creator's affliction-inventions are specially designed to persecute the poor. In fact, the worst enemy of the poor is their Father in Heaven. All of the Creator's specially deadly disease-producers are invisible—making it impossible for man to understand his maladies for thousands of years.

Letter 8

Man is the most interesting fool there is. He has not a single written law—in or out of the Bible—with any purpose other than to limit or defeat a law of God. Temperament is a law of God, written in the heart of every creature, and must be obeyed. The Bible does not allow adultery at all, but makes no distinction between temperaments. The commandment against adultery does not distribute its burden equally. It is easy on the very young and very old, but hard on others—especially women.

Letter 9

Although God chose Noah from all the Earth's peoples, and although He could see ahead, the first thing that Noah did after his Ark landed on Ararat was to plant a vineyard, drink the wine, and be overcome. Did the Creator see how badly things would go? When it comes to intellect, the Deity is the head pauper in the universe.

Letter 10

The two testaments are interesting. The Old Testament gives a picture of the Deity before He got religion; the other gives a picture of Him afterward. The Old Testament is interested mainly in blood and sensuality, the New Testament in salvation—by force. The first time that the Deity came to Earth, He brought life and death; the next time, He brought hell. After the Deity realized that death was a mistake because it freed man from his suffering, He invented hell. And it was as Jesus Christ that He invented hell. (In the original manuscript, a new letter begins immediately after this passage.)

The Bible is filled with examples of God's cruel justice (verses are quoted from Num. 31 and Deut. 20). Biblical law says "Thou shalt not kill," but God plants in the heart of man another law: "Thou shalt kill." God cannot keep His own commandments.

Letter 11

Human history is red with blood and bitter hate—but only God in biblical times goes to war with no limits. Totally without mercy, He slew everyone—the innocent along with the guilty. The worst punishment He ever dealt, however, was to put 32,000 Midianite women into prostitution. Even INDIANS did not carry tortures this far. The sarcasms and hypocrisies of the Beatitudes should be read from the pulpit along with the passages from Numbers and Deuteronomy in order to get an all-around view of the Father in Heaven.

BACKGROUND AND PUBLISHING HISTORY

Clemens wrote *Letters from the Earth* between early October 1909—when his daughter Clara married and left his home—and late November, when he went to BERMUDA. This was also the same moment that HARPER's published *Extract from Captain Stormfield's Visit to Heaven*, which explores similar themes.

When Bernard DeVoto became literary editor of the Mark Twain Estate in 1938, one of his first tasks was to select the previously unpublished manuscripts that he thought most merited publication in a new book. A year later, he presented *Letters from the Earth* to the trustees of the estate. In addition to "Letters"—which fills about a fifth of the book's pages—the volume includes the thematically similar "Papers of the Adam Family" and "Letter to the Earth" (later published as "Letter from the Recording Angel"). The rest of the book is unrelated material, including the whimsical "A Cat Tale," "COOPER's Prose Style," "Official Report to the I.I.A.S. [Indianapolis Institute of Applied Science]," "The GORKY Incident," "Simplified Spelling," "Something about Repentance," "From an English Notebook," "The French and the Comanches," "From an Unfinished Burlesque of Books on Etiquette," "The Damned Human Race," and "THE GREAT DARK."

Publication of *Letters from the Earth* was stalled when Clara Clemens objected to its contents, fearing that it misrepresented her father's views on religion. The manuscript was set aside until Clara withdrew her objections in 1962, by which time DeVoto had died. Henry Nash SMITH, then editor of the Mark Twain Papers, wrote a new preface to the book, explaining that aside from a few editorial remarks, it was as DeVoto prepared it in 1939, though several of its pieces had been published between then and 1962. Harper & Row issued the book in September 1962 and *Life* magazine published excerpts in its September 28 issue. An immediate critical success, *Letters from the Earth* made the *New York Times* best-seller list and has remained in print ever since.

In 1973, the Mark Twain Papers project published *What Is Man? and Other Philosophical Writings* in the Works of Mark Twain edition. This volume, edited by Paul Baender, includes corrected and annotated texts of *Letters from the Earth* and several other fragments on religion from *Letters from the Earth*. The Library of America's *Collected Tales, Sketches, Speeches, & Essays* (1992), edited by Louis J. BUDD, uses Baender's version of "Letters" and several other pieces from his volume, as does *The Bible According to Mark Twain* (1995), edited by Howard G. Baetzhold and Joseph B. McCullough.

CRITICAL COMMENTARY

Letters from the Earth begins with a loose biblical rewriting, in which Clemens's sensibility leads to a number of subtle and idiosyncratic substitutions. In his capsule version of Genesis, the universe, rather than beginning with "the word," springs from thought: "The Creator sat upon the throne, thinking. . . . When the Creator had finished thinking, He said, 'I have thought. Behold!" (prologue). This adjustment, though minor, significantly shifts authority from received wisdom transmitted by language to values of rational inquiry—Mark Twain's God thinks before speaking and does not bother to pronounce his creation good. Along with his belief in the base self-interest behind human behavior, Clemens's faith in scientific advancement often steers his critique of religious conventions. Another key substitution leads Clemens from Noah's ark to an extended discussion of disease and immunization. Rather than an olive branch–bearing dove, his account of Noah's ark focuses on a fly that preserves and spreads pestilence (letter 6). Clemens's unfinished manuscript "3,000 YEARS AMONG THE MICROBES" shows an isolated and inflamed version of his fascination with developments in biology. In his disquisition on disease, Clemens's main problem with scientific advancement under religion is, not that the two are necessarily incompatible, but that there is a question as to which is the source of worldly accomplishment. According to Clemens's perverse framing of Protestant logic, God creates disease, and after man discovers a cure, takes credit for the labor. Clemens thus turns Christian notions of freewill, causality, and responsibility inside out—destructive forces are God's creations for which man blames himself, and useful discoveries are human acts for which God enjoys taking credit. Through the alteration of minor details and the magnification of a reverse angle perspective, Clemens nudges his biblical narrative onto the often cynical determinist terrain toward which much of his later work inclined.

In *Letters from the Earth*, the skewering of hypocrisy takes on an intensity that moves past satire into disgusted indictment. Using Satan as a mouthpiece, a device he toyed with frequently in his later work, Clemens is able to express unalloyed disdain for humanity and phrase his perverse observations as satanic in their inverted view of human values. Though dark, some lines display deft and unexpected reversals of wit, though generally without the light leniency of Clemens's early work. For example, taking on the voice of Satan, Clemens offers shorthand descriptions of the human race, such as, "They were full of activities. Busy, all busy—mainly in persecuting each other" (prologue) and "Man is a marvelous curiosity. When he is at his very best he is a sort of low grade nickel-plated angel; at his worst he is unspeakable, unimaginable, and first and last and all the time he is a sarcasm" (Satan's letter). For Clemens, heavenly incongruities are quintessential evidence of worldly hypocrisy. In Letter 2, he ridicules the image of heaven as constructed by Christianity of its day, containing "in labored detail, each and every imaginable thing that is repulsive to a man, and not a single thing he likes" (Letter 2). His favorite incongruities include the absence in heaven of man's favorite activity, sex (ibid.), and the presence of two activities that few seem to enjoy in life, singing and praying, which are the main heavenly occupations. Clemens is disappointed but not surprised that humankind would imagine a heaven according to its image of what it wished it were, rather than in line with an honest assessment of its own pleasures and preferences.

Clemens's voice in *Letters from the Earth* is closer to straightforward denunciation than indirect wit. At the same time, there are many moments of linguistic playfulness and semi-joyful extemporization. One anecdote relates the experience of a man who decides to take his priest's advice and behave like God. Though violent and ironic (in imitating God's vengefulness the man inoculates his children with hookworm, sleeping sickness, and gonorrhea), this embedded yarn is a dark recapitulation of Clemens's dependable tall-tale form, in which a minor misunderstanding snowballs out of control and moves from exaggeration to absurdity. A whimsical and ribald detour about masturbation and the grave legal consequences of "pissing on the wall" takes on a tone of exuberant comedic theme and variation (and hints at the contents of Clemens's renowned dinner speech on the "Science of Onanism"; Letter 10). In his indictment of heaven, it is precisely the lack of lusty exuberance that Clemens derides, and in his ridicule, Clemens attempts to inject the very element he finds lacking in the Christian view of life and the afterlife. His opinion of the Bible, though ironic, is saturated with the admiration of a professional fabulist for the seminal and most read text of Euro-American society: "It is full of interest. It has noble poetry in it; and some clever fables; and some blood-drenched history; and some good morals; and a wealth of obscenity; and upwards of a thousand lies" (Letter 3).

Critical Commentary by Alex Feerst

BIBLIOGRAPHY

Baetzhold, Howard G., and Joseph B. McCullough, eds. *The Bible According to Mark Twain.* New York: Touchstone Books, 1995.

Brodwin, Stanley. "The Theology of Mark Twain: Banished Adam and the Bible." *Mississippi Quarterly* 29 (Spring 1976): 167–189.

Ensor, Allison. *Mark Twain and the Bible.* Lexington: University of Kentucky Press, 1969.

Twain, Mark. *Letters from the Earth.* Edited by Bernard DeVoto. New York: Harper & Row, 1962.

———. *What Is Man? and Other Philosophical Writings.* Edited by Paul Baender. Berkeley: University of California Press, 1973.

Life on the Mississippi (1883)

Though generally classified as a TRAVEL BOOK, *Life on the Mississippi* does not lend itself readily to simple categorization. The book combines an embroidered memoir of the author's apprentice steamboat PILOT days with a narrative of his return to the Mississippi River 20 years later, as well as history and statistics and a hodgepodge of unrelated sketches. If the book lacks focus, it is because Clemens himself was unsure what it was he was assembling. Nevertheless, its strengths are many; it is widely regarded as both one of Clemens's major works and a classic on the Mississippi itself. Its early chapters especially are unrivaled in evoking the excitement of their time. The balance of the book presents a powerful portrait of how much both the river and its commerce could change in a few decades, as well as a savage depiction of the post–Civil War South.

As with much of Clemens's other travel writing, these later chapters are often discursive, mixing physical descriptions, economic statistics, and travel anecdotes—with occasional tall tales of little or no relevance to anything else. The book is narrated in the first person, but readers cannot take for granted that the anonymous narrator is always Clemens himself. The best assurance we have that it is comes in chapter 50, when he recalls how he adopted his pen name. Otherwise, his narrative voice shifts unpredictably.

The text mentions many real people, such as HORACE BIXBY, G. W. CABLE, GEORGE RITCHIE, and others, by name, while disguising others with pseudonyms, such as "Uncle" Mumford, Robert Styles, and Thompson and Rogers. There are also figures of pure invention, such as Karl Ritter, Charlie Williams, and John Backus.

SYNOPSIS

With over 147,500 words—including 12,800 words in appendixes quoted from other sources—*Life on the Mississippi* has 60 chapters, which fall into three distinct groups. The first three chapters form a historical prelude to the rest. Chapters 4–21 are a memoir of Clemens's early piloting years. The first 14 of these chapters originally appeared in seven magazine installments in 1875 as "OLD TIMES ON THE MISSISSIPPI."

Chapters 22–60 cover Clemens's return to the river in 1882. He happened to arrive when the Mississippi was experiencing a record flood—a subject on which he comments frequently. Chapters 22–33 take him from St. Louis through Arkansas; chapters 34–40 continue the journey to Baton Rouge, Louisiana; chapters 41–50 pertain to NEW ORLEANS—the longest stop on the trip. Chapter 51 summarizes the return trip to St. Louis; chapters 53–56 cover his stay in Hannibal and offer significant insights into Clemens's early AUTOBIOGRAPHY. The remaining chapters complete the journey to St. Paul, Minnesota.

Information inserted within parentheses in the synopsis below does not appear in the original chapters.

Chapter 1

A passage from an 1863 issue of *HARPER'S MAGAZINE* describes the Mississippi River and compares it to the other great river systems of the world. The first chapter emphasizes that the Mississippi "is not a commonplace river, but on the contrary is in all ways remarkable." It is extraordinarily long, it drains a vast region, it carries a huge volume of water, it is remarkably crooked, it is constantly reshaping itself, and it is always shifting its channels.

A capsule history of early exploration drawn from the writings of Francis Parkman (1823–1893) remarks that Hernando de Soto's discovery of the river in 1542 gives America's national history "a most respectable outside aspect and rustiness and antiquity."

Chapter 2

Remarks about La Salle and about Louis Joliet and Jacques Marquette's 1673 expedition continue the capsule history. La Salle returned in 1681 to prove that the river empties into the Gulf of Mexico. By a remarkable coincidence, three of the first four great explorers converged on the future location of NAPOLEON, Arkansas.

Chapter 3

During the 70 years after La Salle proved where the Mississippi emptied, European settlements arose slowly along the river. It took another 50 years for serious commerce to develop. The earliest river commerce was on barges and keelboats. As STEAMBOATS killed off this traffic, a new era of giant coal and timber rafts began. To illustrate this era, a long excerpt from an unfinished manuscript (*Huckleberry Finn's* "RAFT CHAPTER") is included.

Chapter 4

The narrator remembers that when he was a boy, the only permanent ambition among his comrades was to be a steamboatman. The mere arrival of steamboats pumped life into the "white town drowsing in the sunshine of a summer's morning." Within minutes, the town awakened to a frenzy of activity as a steamboat landed. Immediately after the boat left, the town sank back into its previous torpor. Once, a local boy who had earlier disappeared showed up as an apprentice steamboat engineer to become the object of envy and hate. Other boys were later thrilled to hear that his steamboat had blown up; however, he not only did not die,

"OUR PERMANENT AMBITION."

Village boys watch the river and dream about their one "permanent ambition"—to become steamboatmen.

but he returned home a bigger hero than ever. Of all the positions on a steamboat, that of PILOT is the grandest. Eventually, the narrator ran off to SAINT LOUIS to become a pilot, only to be rudely ignored.

Chapter 5

Later, the narrator goes to CINCINNATI, from which he intends to travel to SOUTH AMERICA's Amazon to become an explorer. He buys passage to NEW ORLEANS on the steamboat *PAUL JONES*. As he goes down the OHIO RIVER, he imagines himself a member of the crew and hangs around the big mate. When the boat gets stuck on rocks near Louisville, he offers to fetch a tool for the mate, only to be humiliated by the man's reaction to his amazing presumption. He then plays up to the boat's most humble person, the night watchman—a talkative fellow who claims to be the son of an English nobleman.

Chapter 6

During the *Paul Jones's* two-week voyage, the narrator gets to know one of its pilots (later identified as HORACE BIXBY). After reaching New Orleans, he discovers that there is no prospect of any vessel ever shipping to the Amazon, so he looks for an alternative career. Bixby agrees to teach him the river between New Orleans and St. Louis for $500.

The new cub pilot begins by steering the steamboat out of New Orleans. (The narrator calls this boat the *Paul Jones;* Clemens actually began his apprenticeship on the COLONEL CROSSMAN.) As it goes north, Bixby rattles off names of nondescript features along the river. The young cub has a rude awakening when he is turned out for his first middle-of-the-night watch and is equally amazed that Bixby expects to find a plantation in the blackness of night. When Bixby asks the cub the names of points they passed earlier, he impresses on him that he *must* learn these things and tells him to get a NOTEBOOK in which to record information. Bixby finds the plantation in the darkness, but the cub attributes it to luck.

After traveling 700 or 800 miles up the river, the cub's notebook is filling up, but his head remains empty. The chapter ends with the cub following Bixby to another steamboat.

Chapter 7

Aboard their new boat (the CRESCENT CITY), the cub returns to New Orleans and discovers that *down*stream navigation differs greatly from *up*stream navigation. The boat's big pilothouse typically has eight to 10 veteran pilots who are studying the river—which happens to be low on this voyage. Their cryptic discussion about the river discourages the cub. The boat is delayed when a pilot runs it aground. Afterward, Bixby tries to make up lost time by taking it through a dangerous crossing to reach water deep enough for safe night sailing. The other pilots think the feat impossible, but Bixby pulls it off.

Chapter 8

Each time the cub thinks he has mastered piloting, Bixby adds something new to learn. After the cub has learned the name of features along the river, Bixby tells him that he must also learn the river's *shape*—which changes constantly.

One night, when the second pilot, "Mr. W." (STROTHER WILEY), arrives late, Bixby angrily turns over the wheel without, as is customary, telling him where they are. Thinking Bixby insanely irresponsible, the cub stays in the pilothouse to give the other pilot this important information himself but falls asleep. The next morning, Bixby chastises him for even thinking that the other pilot *needed* to be told where he was.

The cub learns how difficult it is to perceive the river's shape in the night but eventually masters this knowledge, only to have Bixby ask him about the river's *depth* at various points. He despairs that he does not have enough brains to be a pilot, but Bixby promises that when he says he will "learn a man the river," he means it. Further, he will "learn him or kill him."

Chapter 9

As the cub masters the river's soundings, Bixby tells him he must next learn to "read" the river as a book. He explains "bluff reefs" and how to maneuver past them. The next day, Bixby leaves the cub alone at the wheel, while secretly watching him. Proud of his new responsibility, the cub gaily whistles until a bluff reef looms ahead. He starts to run the boat ashore, just as Bixby reappears. When he explains that he was dodging a "bluff reef," Bixby scoffs and tells him to run over the next one he sees. The cub does as ordered, but the next hazard turns out to be a harmless "wind reef." As the face of the water gradually becomes "a wonderful book," all the romance goes from the river.

Chapter 10

After mastering the river's *visible* features, the cub thinks his education is complete. Bixby now tells him, however, that he must learn to read the river's depth from its banks and other clues, and how to know whether the river is rising or falling. The cub's education begins anew.

Chapter 11

The cub learns about the difficulties of navigating a rising river, with rapidly changing conditions and small craft constantly drifting downstream. He recalls a story about GEORGE EALER, who was once piloting a big boat through a treacherous stretch of low water near Helena, Arkansas, when he felt he needed help. His fellow pilot, Mr. X., who had navigated the stretch recently, suddenly appeared and took the wheel. He did the sweetest bit of piloting Ealer ever saw, but Ealer later learned that the man had been sleepwalking.

Chapter 12

Occasionally, when the river is low, steamboats send out small craft to take soundings—work that cubs particularly enjoy. The narrator recalls a voyage on which he and another cub competed for the attentions of a pretty 16-year-old girl. When it was time for him to board the sounding boat, his rival tricked him into running an unnecessary errand and took his place in the boat—impressing the girl with his courage. In the foggy gloom, the steamboat accidentally ran the small boat down. After dramatically disappearing, the other cub was rescued and became a hero.

Chapter 13

Pilots need exceptional memories, and Bixby is a prime example. When higher wages drew him to work on the difficult MISSOURI RIVER, he needed just a few trips to master over a thousand miles of the river and earn his full license. Meanwhile, the narrator was under the tutelage of a pilot named (WILLIAM) BROWN.

Pilots also need cool courage and the intelligence to make quick decisions. Every cub's master tests him with tricks to develop his confidence. Bixby, for example, once left the narrator alone at the wheel as their boat entered a safe deep-water crossing, but then tested the cub's confidence about how deep the crossing was. Unbeknownst to the cub, Bixby conspired with the leadsmen and was watching him from a hiding place. As a crowd gathered on the hurricane deck, the captain added to the cub's uneasiness by acting concerned about Bixby's absence. Soon, the nervous cub rang for the leadsmen, who called out such alarmingly shallow readings that the cub begged the engineer to reverse the engines. When Bixby reentered the pilothouse, a roar of laughter rose from the crew, and Bixby counseled the cub to have more confidence in what he knew to be true.

Chapter 14

The narrator explains the minutiae of piloting because he loves the profession better than any other, and because he took measureless pride in it. In the old days, he explains, a pilot was the "only unfettered entirely independent human being that lived in the earth." The pride of steamboating extended down to even the lowliest crew members, especially on such stately boats as the *ALECK SCOTT* and the *Grand Turk.*

Once a pilot named "Stephen W." (Strother Wiley) was so desperate for a job that he agreed to pilot a boat out of New Orleans for half wages. His captain promised not to tell anyone what he was

paying him but nevertheless boasted about his bargain-rate pilot. When word got back to Stephen, he steered the boat up the middle of the river so slowly that the captain agreed to pay him full wages in order to get the boat moving faster.

Chapter 15

Before the CIVIL WAR, a rapid increase of licensed pilots cut wages in half. To reverse the trend, a dozen bold veterans chartered a benevolent association to fix wages at $250 a month. In return for a nominal initiation fee, any pilot could join and receive $25 a month in benefits while unemployed. Owners, captains, and employed pilots derided the association—but as increased river traffic gradually created a pilot shortage, owners began hiring association members. Association pilots could work only with fellow association pilots, however, further increasing demand for their services. As association pilots returned to work, they built a network to exchange information on the river among members. Eventually, their superior safety record moved underwriters to insist that owners hire only association pilots. As the remaining non-association pilots applied for membership, they found that they had to pay stiff initiation fees to cover their past earnings.

Once the association firmly established itself, it acted to restrict licensing of new pilots. The association was set to have wages doubled in September 1861, but by then, the war halted commercial steamboat traffic. After the war ended, new competition from railroads and huge tow barges reduced steamboat traffic to a fraction of its former size. The glory days of piloting were over.

Chapter 16

Although the public always thought steamboat racing was dangerous, the opposite was true—at least after laws restricted boiler-pressure levels—because engineers were more alert and attentive during races. A description of a typical New Orleans–St. Louis race shows that races were generally won by the better pilots. The narrator recalls serving on a particularly slow boat, the *JOHN J. ROE*, and lists the best speed records the top boats achieved.

Chapter 17

One of the Mississippi's remarkable features is its tendency to shorten itself by cutting off bends—

especially in the alluvial-banked lower stretches. During the 175-year period after 1700, for example, the length of the channel between New Orleans and CAIRO, Illinois, decreased from 1,215 miles to 973 miles. At that rate—1.3 miles per year—the river must have been 1.3 million miles long a million years ago. In another 742 years, the river should be just 1.75 miles long.

The chapter concludes with another anecdote about Stephen W.—a notorious borrower. Once he borrowed $250 from a newcomer to the river, "Young Yates." After tormenting Yates for weeks with false promises of repayment, he lined up his creditors and promised to settle his debts in *alphabetical* order.

Chapter 18

In summing up his apprenticeship years, the narrator recalls working with many pilots on many steamboats. Now, whenever he finds a well-drawn character in fiction or biography, he generally takes a warm personal interest in him, because he has already met him on the river. An example is Mr. Brown (William Brown), under whom the narrator cubbed on the PENNSYLVANIA during one of Bixby's absences. Brown tormented the narrator for months, while another cub, GEORGE RITCHIE, was having good times under the mild-mannered George Ealer. Each night when the narrator went to bed, he fantasized about murdering Brown.

Chapter 19

While the narrator was cubbing on the *Pennsylvania*, his brother Henry (Henry Clemens) was a mud clerk on the boat. One day Henry relayed the captain's instruction to make a certain stop to the partly deaf Brown, who ignored him. When CAPTAIN KLINEFELTER asked Brown why he failed to stop, Brown said that Henry had not give him the message. After the captain left, Brown moved to strike Henry, but the cub knocked him down with a stool and pummeled him. Meanwhile, the steamboat plowed down the river with no one at the wheel. Brown finally seized the wheel and ordered the cub out, but the cub stayed to unload pent-up verbal abuse on him. When the cub went to account for himself before the captain, he figured that his piloting career was finished and that a

"I HIT BROWN A GOOD HONEST BLOW."

Before Mr. Brown can strike Henry with a lump of coal, the cub stretches him out with a heavy stool in chapter 19 of *Life on the Mississippi*.

prison term might even await him; however, the captain laughed at the thought of Brown's being beaten and advised the cub to lay for him ashore. When Brown demanded that either the cub went or he would leave, the captain invited *him* to leave.

Chapter 20

During a layover in New Orleans, Klinefelter could not find a pilot to replace Brown, so he asked the cub to stand daylight watches, while Ealer took the night watches. The narrator felt unready for that responsibility, so Brown piloted the *Pennsylvania* upriver while the narrator followed two days later as a passenger on the ALFRED T. LACEY. When the

Lacey reached Greenville, Mississippi, he learned that the *Pennsylvania* had exploded near MEMPHIS, Tennessee. At Memphis, he learned that at least 150 people had died; Henry was fatally injured and Brown had disappeared, but Klinefelter and Ealer were unhurt.

Chapter 21

A half-page summary of the narrator's life over the next 23 years recalls how he got his piloting license only to have his career interrupted by the Civil War. He then became a silver miner and reporter in NEVADA, a gold miner and reporter in CALIFORNIA, a special correspondent to HAWAII, a roving correspondent in Europe, a LECTURER, and finally, "a scribbler of books, and an immovable fixture among the other rocks of New England."

Chapter 22

After 21 years away from working on the Mississippi, the narrator wants to see it again. He enlists "a poet (JAMES R. OSGOOD) for company and a stenographer (ROSWELL H. PHELPS)." To avoid attracting attention, he adopts ALIASES, but has trouble remembering them. The travelers go by train to St. Louis, which the narrator compares with the smaller city that he knew two decades earlier. Dismayed by the virtual disappearance of steamboats from the wharves, he reflects on what a strangely short life the steamboat trade has had.

Chapter 23

The travelers want to go downriver, stopping at each interesting town, but the infrequency of steamboat departures makes this impractical. After inspecting a filthy packet, they decide to take the *GOLD DUST,* a well-maintained VICKSBURG packet. The night the *Gold Dust* leaves port, the narrator begins discovering startling technological changes on steamboats—such as electric floodlights. He also soon learns how much the river has changed its shape.

Chapter 24

The first night out, the narrator visits the pilothouse. Nor recognizing the man at the wheel, he sits down to observe quietly. When he eventually asks about a new piece of equipment, the pilot offers to explain everything and reels off a "tranquil pool of lies." He reaches his finest form when he calls a passing coal-shuttle an "alligator boat," explaining that "alligator reefs" were once the river's most serious hazard. As he talks, he drops his own name, "Robert Styles"—whom the narrator recognizes as a former fellow cub. After telling another alligator yarn, Styles begins an anecdote about Captain Tom Ballou of the *Cyclone,* but the narrator interrupts to point out contradictions. Finally, Styles addresses his visitor by his name and suggests that *he* take the wheel, claiming that he recognized him immediately.

Chapter 25

As the *Gold Dust* continues toward Cairo, the narrator comments on sights along the river, such as Cape Girardeau, Missouri. The steamboat's second mate, Uncle Mumford, fills in details for him. Mumford recalls how the old *Paul Jones* sank nearby. About 200 steamboat wrecks are scattered over the 200 miles separating St. Louis from Cairo. The narrator recognizes many changes in the river and compares modern Cairo with the town that CHARLES DICKENS described 40 years earlier. By the end of the chapter, the boat is nearing Hickman, Kentucky.

Chapter 26

The narrator and his companions discuss the Civil War. A *Gold Dust* pilot who served in the Confederate river fleet recounts how scared he was when his boat got caught in the middle of the Battle of Belmont (November 7, 1861)—U. S. GRANT's first battle. A passenger tells the narrator about a terrible FEUD in this region between the Darnells and the Watsons years earlier. As the boat approaches New Madrid, Missouri, the narrator describes changes along the KENTUCKY shores, as well as the effects of the current floodwater.

Chapter 27

Near New Madrid, the narrator describes the flood conditions. He also comments on the many foreigners who have written about the river and quotes from books by BASIL HALL, FRANCES TROLLOPE, Charles Augustus Murray, FREDERICK MARRYAT, and Alexander Mackay.

Chapter 28

Farther down the Mississippi, the narrator sees a steamboat at the mouth of Kentucky's Obion River that is named for him (presumably the "MARK TWAIN"). The romance has been knocked out of the river by such things as beacon lights, efficient snag removal, floodlights, and scientific charts developed by Bixby and Ritchie. Worse, the Anchor Line has raised captains above pilots and decreed that pilots must always be at their posts, even when their boats are tied up.

The United States River Commission works to control the river with dams and dikes. Reshaping the river is a hot topic of debate along the Lower Mississippi. The narrator and Uncle Mumford doubt strongly that the Mississippi can be tamed; however, the narrator recognizes the value of improving navigation. He cites the example of a single towboat taking two weeks to move 32 bargeloads of coal—an amount that 1,800 railroad cars would need an entire summer to move.

Chapter 29

The *Gold Dust* passes Fort Pillow, Tennessee—the site of the worst massacre in American history (after the Union's Fort Pillow surrendered on April 12, 1864, Confederate troops killed several hundred prisoners, most of whom were black). The narrator notes further changes in the river as the boat approaches Memphis. Half the chapter contains a long extract on the river pirate JOHN MURRELL from a now forgotten book (by Marryat). The chapter concludes with a brief description of a stopover in Memphis.

Chapter 30

After leaving Memphis, the boat passes the site of the *Pennsylvania*'s wreck, entering a region in which many itinerant black workers move between jobs by steamboat. The narrator then recalls an incident that occurred shortly after he left St. Louis. A young passenger from Wisconsin approached him; he claimed to have learned all about the steamboat and insisted on explaining everything. After the man unloaded his cargo of lies, the narrator spotted him laughing. The narrator has the last laugh, when he is alone at the wheel at a moment when the young prankster looks into the pilothouse and recognizes him.

The narrator has himself called early each morning in order to watch the incomparable river sunrises. The boat makes a short stop at Helena.

Chapter 31

As they near Napoleon, Arkansas, the narrator wants to get off the boat to perform an important errand, but his companions want to stay aboard. He explains his errand by relating "A Dying Man's Confession," the story of Karl Ritter, who told him where he had hidden $10,000 in the wall of a building in Napoleon. The narrator wants to recover the money and send it to the German son of a man whom Ritter mistakenly killed.

Chapter 32

Ritter's story stuns Thompson and Rogers, who protest sending that much money to a simple German shoemaker. All three men agree that $10,000 would hurt the German, so they decide to send him just $5,000. As their discussion heats up, they work the figure down to $500. Finally, they decide that instead of money, they will send the shoemaker a "chromo." When the narrator discovers that his companions expect to split the $10,000 with him, they get into a fight. When he finally tells Captain McCord that he wants to go ashore at Napoleon, the captain is amazed. Uncle Mumford explains that a flood washed Napoleon away completely.

Chapter 33

Examples are given of the strange things that the river does to islands as it cuts and shifts. The town of Napoleon may be gone, but its old rival Greenville is flourishing. The Calhoun Land Co. is a new scheme to grow cotton in Chicot, Arkansas, which promises to treat black workers fairly.

Chapter 34

At Lake Providence, Louisiana, an Arkansas passenger named "Mr. H." (Harvey) claims that his state has been held back because of exaggerated accounts of its mosquitoes, which are actually small and diffident. He and a companion claim that the really tough mosquitoes are to be found in LOUISIANA's Lake Providence.

Chapter 35

The packet reaches Vicksburg, Mississippi, which suffered greatly during a long siege in the Civil War.

Details of the terrible conditions during the war are given and the city's postwar recovery is described.

Chapter 36

The previous chapter ended by introducing this chapter as "THE PROFESSOR'S YARN," which is narrated by a college professor who went to California years earlier. Aboard his ship, he befriended John Backus, an Ohio cattleman carrying his life savings in gold to California to take up ranching. As the ship neared SAN FRANCISCO, Backus got drawn into a card game with professional gamblers and wagered his entire fortune on one hand. The professor thought that Backus was ruined, but Backus triumphed as the ship entered the Golden Gate and he turned out to be a professional gambler himself.

This chapter ends with the travelers leaving the *Gold Dust*.

Chapter 37

While writing these chapters much later, the narrator learns that the *Gold Dust* has blown up near Hickman, Kentucky (August 7, 1882), killing 17 people and scalding dozens. The captain and other crew members recovered from their injuries, but the pilot Lem Gray ("Robert Styles") died.

Chapter 38

Aboard a Cincinnati–New Orleans boat (the *Charles Morgan*), the travelers continue their journey south. Decades earlier, Dickens declined to call Mississippi steamboats either "magnificent" or "floating palaces," but the narrator suggests they *were* magnificent to most passengers—who never saw anything approaching their opulence ashore. To make his point, he describes the "house beautiful"—the typical finest home in every river town between St. Louis and New Orleans. Each house has the same white fence, grassy yard, parlor furnishings, and decor, with certain books and certain patriotic and sentimental pictures. Against such dreary finery, even a town's principal citizens would think steamboats magnificent.

Chapter 39

Near Vicksburg the river has straightened itself out, leaving the old river port of Delta inland. The narrator describes Natchez, Mississippi, which is divided into a prosperous hilltop section and a rowdy,

depressed lowland, and quotes Frances Trollope on its charms. A striking change in Natchez is its development into a railroad center and manufacturing stronghold, with a modern ice factory and a yarn mill.

In an overheard conversation, two "drummers" (traveling salesmen) discuss oleomargarine and the versatility of cottonseed oil. The chapter ends as the boat passes Port Hudson, Louisiana.

Chapter 40

At Baton Rouge, the travelers arrive in the "absolute South." From here to New Orleans is a pilot's paradise—wide, deep water without snags or other perils. The state capitol building is modeled on a medieval castle—a subject that opens the narrator's attack on SIR WALTER SCOTT, whom he charges with having had a debilitating influence on the South. The chapter ends with a description of the region between Baton Rouge and New Orleans that includes quotations from Frances Trollope and Basil Hall.

Chapter 41

At New Orleans the narrator finds that the city has grown since his last visit but has not changed fundamentally—except in being cleaner and healthier and having better newspapers. Aside from CEMETERIES, the city has no real public architecture, but does have attractive domestic architecture.

Chapter 42

A description of above-ground vaults in New Orleans cemeteries spurs an argument on cremation as a hygienic and economic alternative to burial.

Chapter 43

A New Orleans UNDERTAKER who has found undertaking to be the dead-surest business in Christendom points out that one thing that is never cheap is a coffin. Contrary to popular belief, undertakers do not prosper during epidemics—since people rush to bury bodies and cut back on profitable extras, such as embalming and ice. The narrator recalls that when he expressed his own wish to be cremated to his pastor (presumably JOSEPH TWICHELL), the man told him, "I shouldn't worry about that, if I had your chances."

Chapter 44

G. W. CABLE leads the travelers on a tour of New Orleans, beginning with the French Quarter. Other sights include the filthy old St. Louis Hotel, which is now a municipal office building; a women's broom brigade; and the West End—where they eat pompano.

Chapter 45

A rambling discussion of the Civil War and Southern sports pays particular attention to a cockfight and a mule race. The war is such a dominant topic of conversation in the South that it is what "A.D." is elsewhere—they date from it. Although New Orleans newspaper editors are strong and direct, their reporters tend to be gushy and romantic. They become unsettled when they write about women.

Chapter 46

The travelers have missed Mardi Gras, but the narrator recalls seeing one 24 years earlier. Because the soul of such a festival is romantic, it could not exist in the North. The South, however, is afflicted by the "Walter Scott disease." While CERVANTES's *Don Quixote* swept away admiration for the silliness of medieval chivalry, Scott restored it. Scott had so large a hand in molding the South's prewar character that he is, in great measure, responsible for the war.

Chapter 47

JOEL CHANDLER HARRIS meets the travelers in New Orleans. They all gather at G. W. Cable's house, where Harris proves too shy to read aloud from his own work. Cable's problems in giving fictional characters unusual French names that turn out to be used by real people reminds the narrator of the problem that he and (C. D.) WARNER had with the name "Eschol Sellers," which they changed to (Colonel) "Mulberry" Sellers.

Chapter 48

The narrator encounters Horace Bixby on a New Orleans street. Now the captain of the new CITY OF BATON ROUGE, Bixby has scarcely changed in 21 years. The travelers join him on a harbor trip. Discussions with veteran steamboatmen tell the narrator what has become of some "former river friends." One pilot became a spiritualist and was bilked for years by a New York medium named Manchester, whom the narrator once visited with a friend.

Chapter 49

Most former pilots have become farmers. The narrator recalls piloting under Captain (J. Ed) MONTGOMERY on the *Crescent City* (actually the CITY OF MEMPHIS), which he once allowed to crash when Montgomery failed to give orders to stop the boat. Anecdotes about heroic pilots include the story of a man who died at the wheel while steering his burning boat to shore. There is no example in the history of Mississippi piloting of a pilot leaving his post to save his own life while he still had a chance to save others.

The chapter concludes with the story of "George Johnson" (SAMUEL ADAMS BOWEN Jr.), a steamboat clerk whose greed and foolishness got him drawn into an unwanted marriage.

Chapter 50

Conversations with other steamboatmen recall the name of Captain ISAIAH SELLERS, whom the narrator once pilloried in a newspaper sketch. It was from Sellers that he appropriated his pen name "MARK TWAIN."

Chapter 51

As Bixby's *City of Baton Rouge* leaves New Orleans, the narrator vicariously relives his first experience as a cub when he observes an apprentice steering under Bixby's watchful eye. The boat reaches Natchez in just $22\frac{1}{2}$ hours. Along the way, George Ritchie runs a half dozen difficult crossings in the fog, using a chart that he and Bixby devised. When they land at St. Louis, the narrator regrets how quickly the delightful trip has passed. He recalls an apprentice blacksmith he knew as a child who was so stagestruck after seeing two Englishmen perform the swordfight scene from *RICHARD III* that he ran off to St. Louis to become an actor and spent the rest of his life performing bit parts.

A chance meeting with an old acquaintance recalls an experience the narrator had in St. Louis nearly 30 years earlier. During a period of civil unrest, he joined a volunteer militia to quell riots. As his unit marched into action, he handed his gun to this acquaintance so that he could step out to get something to drink. He never returned.

Chapter 52

Under the chapter title "A Burning Brand," the narrator remembers wanting to find a St. Louis grain-merchant named Brown. Nine years earlier his clergyman read a letter from an ex-convict named "Jack Hunt" to a prisoner named "Charlie Williams." Hunt's letter—printed here—tells the heartrending story of struggling to go straight, and of his good fortune in winning the trust of Brown, who gave him a job. Hunt owed everything to what he had learned from Williams while in prison. His letter was read from many pulpits, causing a sensation. The narrator was about to write an article about it, when C. D. Warner questioned its genuineness. Investigation proved that Williams had faked the letter, hoping that it would win his release.

Chapter 53

A fast boat (the *Gem City*) takes the narrator to Hannibal—his first real visit to his boyhood home since 1853. He enters the town on a quiet Sunday morning, remembering it as it was three decades earlier. As he climbs Holliday's Hill (CARDIFF HILL) to look over the rooftops, he has the dreamy feeling of still being a boy. He asks an old man, who came to Hannibal a year after he left, about people he once knew. A man long regarded as a perfect chucklehead (SAMUEL TAYLOR GLOVER?) went to St. Louis and became a great lawyer. A woman who had been scared out of her wits (an incident Mark Twain fictionalizes in "DOUGHFACE") died insane 36 years later.

When the narrator mentions his own name, the stranger candidly calls him "another d—d fool" who surprised everyone by succeeding. He is glad that he introduced himself as "Smith."

Chapter 54

From atop Holliday's Hill, the narrator gazes at houses and remembers families from his youth. One family had a son named Lem Hackett (Clint Levering) who drowned as a child. Village boys saw Lem's death as punishment for his sins but were thrown into confusion three weeks later when a "MODEL BOY" named "Dutchy" drowned. The narrator descends the hill passing his BOYHOOD HOME and is corralled into speaking to a Sunday-school group.

Chapter 55

During his three days in Hannibal, the narrator discovers that many old acquaintances—especially women—have changed considerably. He recalls a saddler named John Stavely who never met a passenger or collected a cargo, but greeted every steamboat arrival so enthusiastically that outsiders dubbed the town "Stavely's Landing." He also recalls a childhood hero—a carpenter who claimed to have murdered 60 people, earning the nickname the "Mysterious Avenger."

Now a "city" with 15,000 people, Hannibal has a mayor and even a waterworks. BEAR CREEK has nearly disappeared. The CAVE below the town is mentioned in an anecdote.

Chapter 56

When the narrator was 10, he once gave matches to Jimmy FINN, a town drunk. The same day, Finn went to jail, where he used the matches to set fire to his cell and was burned to death before he could be freed. As a child, the narrator agonized over murdering Finn and feared that his brother would hear him confess in his sleep.

Chapter 57

As the journey continues north (aboard the *Minneapolis*), the narrator praises industrious communities such as Quincy, Illinois, and KEOKUK, Iowa—whose "erratic genius," HENRY CLAY DEAN, delivered a stunning speech in 1861. The narrator also comments on MARION CITY, Missouri, and on IOWA's MUSCATINE and Burlington.

Chapter 58

As the voyage continues upriver, towns such as Davenport, Iowa, and Rock Island, Illinois, are described, and economic statistics on the region are given. Particularly impressive is the rapid growth of St. Paul and Minneapolis in MINNESOTA. There are also comments on local INDIAN legends and on the devastating impact that railroads have had on steamboat commerce. The chapter ends as the boat passes Prairie du Chien, WISCONSIN.

Chapter 59

Among the passengers who board at La Crosse, Wisconsin, is one of the region's early settlers. He rattles off colorful stories about Indian legends. The tale of Winona and Maiden's Rock is one of many stories along the river about an Indian maiden throwing herself from a LOVER'S LEAP. The chapter concludes with the legend of "Peboan and Seegwun," taken from a book by Henry Rowe SCHOOLCRAFT.

Chapter 60

The journey ends at St. Paul, 2,000 miles from New Orleans. Local snowfall moves the narrator to deride tired newspaper banalities about differences between northern and southern weather. St. Paul's history includes a legend about the original post-master, who took the first letter his office received to Washington, D.C., to ask what should be done with it. The chapter concludes with an idiotic Indian legend about White-Bear Lake, whose inconsistencies the narrator derides.

Appendixes

Appendix "A," which pertains to chapter 26, is an article from the March 29, 1882, *New Orleans Times-Democrat* about a relief boat the newspaper sent to help flood victims. Appendix "B" is an article by EDWARD ATKINSON on Mississippi River improvements. Appendix "C" is a defense by Frances Trollope of Basil Hall's book on America. Appendix "D" is Henry Rowe Schoolcraft's version of the Indian legend about the "Undying Head."

BACKGROUND AND PUBLISHING HISTORY

Clemens began thinking about writing a book on the Mississippi at least as early as 1866. When he visited the Midwest in early 1872, he was struck by the great diminution of steamboat traffic on the OHIO RIVER and became anxious to document the steamboat era before it vanished altogether. It was, however, only after W. D. HOWELLS pushed him to contribute something to the ATLANTIC MONTHLY in late 1874 that he finally acted. With the additional prodding of JOSEPH TWICHELL, he started writing about piloting on the Mississippi. The result was "OLD TIMES ON THE MISSISSIPPI," a serial published in the *Atlantic* in 1875.

After using the "Old Times" articles to reveal the little-known profession of piloting, Clemens set aside the idea of a more general book about the Mississippi and turned his attention to other projects. Before returning to his Mississippi book seven years later, he would complete *Tom Sawyer, A*

Tramp Abroad and *The Prince and the Pauper* and begin *Huckleberry Finn*—a novel whose genesis owed much to his writing of *Life on the Mississippi.* He did not want to pursue the Mississippi book project until he found a friend—preferably Howells—to accompany him on a return trip to the river. Howells professed interest as late as mid-1881, but he could not make time for such a trip. By the end of the year, however, Clemens's new publisher, JAMES R. OSGOOD, agreed to go; Osgood also arranged for ROSWELL H. PHELPS to come along as Mark Twain's stenographer. Osgood and Phelps would become *Life on the Mississippi*'s "poet" and "stenographer"—Thompson and Rogers.

On April 10, 1882, Clemens signed with Osgood to publish his book; his unusual contract effectively made him the publisher and Osgood his agent and distributor. A week later, he, Osgood, and Phelps went overland from New York City to St. Louis, where they boarded the steamboat GOLD DUST to go downriver. Clemens began traveling under an alias, "C. L. Samuel," but was recognized almost immediately and gave it up. In Vicksburg the travelers switched to a boat to New Orleans, where they spent a week. They returned to St. Louis on Bixby's *City of Baton Rouge* and then used other boats to continue farther north. By the end of May, Clemens was back in Hartford, where he immediately settled down to write his book for Osgood.

One of the first things that he did was incorporate the "Old Times" articles, which he rounded out with three new chapters on his apprenticeship days. He wanted to write not about his piloting days, but about the Mississippi River itself; however, the "Old Times" pieces were too handy to pass up. His disdain for writing more about his years as a pilot is revealed in the single paragraph of chapter 22 that sums up his years as a licensed pilot and ends abruptly with the remark that "the war came, commerce was suspended, my occupation was gone."

From July through September, Clemens wrote new material while staying in ELMIRA, New York. He returned to Hartford with drafts of chapters 1–44, 50, and 54 and then spent the rest of the year finishing the book. Its completion proved far more difficult than he had expected. Although he had returned from the river with both his own notes and a set recorded by Phelps, he found that he had much less material than he needed. As his writing bogged down, he looked increasingly to other sources for material and drew heavily on books by such writers as Frances Trollope, FREDERICK MARRYAT, and Basil Hall. Aside from appendixes, he incorporated about 11,000 words from other sources. He even worked in a portion of his unfinished *Huckleberry Finn* manuscript—the so-called RAFT CHAPTER, as well as several chapters left over from *A Tramp Abroad*.

When it came time to select a title for the book, Clemens was inclined to use a variation of his previous travel titles—such as *Abroad on the Great River*, *Abroad on the Father of Waters*, or *Abroad on the Mississippi*. After he settled on "Life on the Mississippi," Osgood published his book on May 17, 1883—one year to the day after Clemens left Hannibal. CHATTO and Windus soon followed with an English edition. Since then, *Life on the Mississippi* has remained in print almost continuously, with little alteration in its original text. The first edition has about 310 original illustrations drawn by EDMUND H. GARRETT, JOHN HARLEY, and A. B. SHUTE.

After he had struggled mightily to flesh out his book, Clemens found that his manuscript was much longer than it needed to be, so he invited Osgood and his editors to cut whatever they wanted. As a result, more than 15,000 words were deleted. Most cuts were made to conserve space, but Osgood omitted one chapter to avoid offending southerners. This chapter—which would have been "48" if it had been retained—criticized southern laws and regional chauvinism, portrayed southerners as lacking independent thought, and attacked the cowardice of mobs. Thirty years later, the chapter was published as a four-page pamphlet titled *The Suppressed Chapter of "Life on the Mississippi."*

Other substantial deletions included two whole chapters on foreign travel writers, and substantial passages on the siege of VICKSBURG, government corruption, DUELING, and other subjects. Most of the deleted material would have added little that was fresh to the book; however, a wild tale about a balloon voyage into a "dead-air belt" was also among the casualties. Fortunately, Clemens's original manuscript has been preserved, in New York's J.

Pierpont MORGAN Library. Most of the omitted passages were finally published in an edition of *Life on the Mississippi* issued in 1944 by the Limited Editions Club and Heritage Press. The restored passages in this edition appear in appendixes, keyed to the chapters or pages from which they were removed. The Penguin American Library later reissued this edition, adding a previously unpublished chapter on Hannibal. In 1996, a facsimile reprint of the first edition was published as part of the OXFORD MARK TWAIN edition. This edition includes a new introduction by Mississippi journalist Willie Morris and an afterword by Lawrence Howe.

According to Howells, Clemens regarded *Life on the Mississippi* as his greatest book. His regard for it is attested to by the fact that it is the only book that he attempted to rewrite after publication. He began revising it in May 1908, but never finished the task.

CRITICAL COMMENTARY

Life on the Mississippi mingles Clemens's personal and professional development with the physical and cultural history of the river and the social and economic development of the nation after the Civil War. Of Clemens's five TRAVEL BOOKS, two, *The Innocents Abroad* and *Following the Equator*, closely follow a real-life itinerary and two, *Roughing It* and *A Tramp Abroad*, draw on composite experiences. The structure of *Life on the Mississippi* stands out as incorporating two layers of Clemens's experience of the same geography, separated by several decades—after the author's reminiscences about his education as a cub pilot, he returns as an experienced and lettered man of the world. Rather than moving through unfamiliar settings and commenting sharply on the oddities and disparities, Clemens returns in this book to the scene of his formative years and attempts to examine through comparative personal history a river that has never stopped moving through time and space. Thus composed of layered memories, *Life on the Mississippi* is, in Forrest Robinson's phrase, the "most haunted of Mark Twain's travel books" (36). Clemens's book is in a sense a collation of several rereadings of the Mississippi, the wellspring of Clemens's sensibility and name— a rewriting of his childhood experience and then a rereading of the river as an adult writer.

Life on the Mississippi has a long-standing reputation among critics as one of Clemens's richest and most rewarding books. Gerd Hurm, for example, describes it in terms of broad significance as one of Clemens's most intimate reflections on "the relation between craft and nature, cognition and reality" and "one of Clemens's most elaborate and intricate meditations on aesthetic themes" (Hurm 151). *Life on the Mississippi* has also interested many scholars because its composition dates, setting, and atmosphere overlap with *Huckleberry Finn*, and it has often been used as a critical prosthetic with which to examine Clemens's more famous fictional texts, *Tom Sawyer* and *Huckleberry Finn*. Moreover, Clemens's stated goal was to write a "standard work" on the Mississippi River; the text's many strands of personal recollection and social history still offer valuable insights for contemporary readers interested in the river (Kruse 7–11).

Organization of the Book

The book's first section offers a primordial history of the river. Clemens asserts the river's importance, invests its physical attributes with a depth of significance, and implicitly links its vigor and uniqueness with the nation it runs through: "The Mississippi is well worth reading about. It is not a commonplace river, but on the contrary is in all ways remarkable" (chapter 1). The international scope of Clemens's explanatory panorama transposes the rhetoric of American exceptionalism onto the river. The Mississippi is not only a central physical feature but also an emblem and cause of America's rise in status. Clemens proudly catalogs the Mississippi's exceptional qualities: how much water it discharges, the area of its drainage basin, the unique shape of its mouth, and its willful tendency to change course (ibid.). He also describes the river as "the crookedest river in the world"—appropriate in relation to the prodigious liars and storytellers who patrol it and to Clemens himself, who emerged from it (ibid.).

The section of the book from chapter 4 to chapter 17, first published serially in the *Atlantic Monthly* as "Old Times on the Mississippi," focuses on Clemens's education and coming of age as a cub pilot. As Stuart Hutchinson observes, "Mark Twain

tries to impose on the book an innocence-to-experience plot." Like many of the boys in his riverbank town, Clemens as a child was enamored with the romantic figure of the steamboat pilot. The final jolt that spurred Clemens to take action was the intense envy he felt for a peer who became a steamboat engineer. It "shook the bottom out of all my Sunday School teachings," Clemens reports (chapter 4). "This fellow," Clemens recalls, "had money, too, and hair oil. Also an ignorant silver watch and a showy brass watch chain. He wore a leather belt and used no suspenders. If ever a youth was cordially admired and hated by his comrades, this one was" (ibid.). On Clemens's trip upriver to search for employment, the steamboat becomes a stage for him to perform for the riverbank-bound audience. Clemen s recalls feigning boredom in order to simulate the experience he lacks, "lolling carelessly upon the railings of the boiler deck to enjoy the envy of the country boys on the bank . . . as soon as I knew they saw me I gaped and stretched, and gave other signs of being mightily bored with travelling" (chapter 5).

As Joseph Coulombe observes, in *Life on the Mississippi* Clemens collapses his persona into broader national trends and the historical period his work attempts to evoke. In documenting the history of the steamboat pilot's emergence as a distinct character and recounting his own piloting career, Clemens infuses his writing voice with the swagger of frontier masculinity, which is itself tied to the identity of a young nation. Once young Clemens secures an apprenticeship with Mr. Bixby on the *Paul Jones*, the image of being a steamboat pilot quickly gives way to the harsh realities of gaining mastery of the physical shape of the river and learning to navigate its social world, in which the volatile pilot, given to fits of cursing, bouts of drinking, and acts of physical intimidation, looms large. The romantic figures of the river's early days moved in the current of rough-and-ready frontier commerce. The great barges during the years following the Louisiana Purchase "gave employment to hordes of rough and hardy men; rude, uneducated, brave, suffering terrific hardships with sailor-like stoicism; heavy drinkers, coarse frolickers in moral sties . . . heavy fighters, reckless fellows, every one, elephantinely jolly, foul-witted, profane" (chapter 3). But, unlike the genteel government and finance capitalists that Clemens skewered in *The Gilded Age*, the primitive capitalists of Clemens's nostalgia are merchants and laborers who are "honest, trustworthy, faithful in promises and duty, and often picturesquely magnanimous" (ibid.).

The alignment of Clemens and national development continues into the second half of the book. If the first section transposes Clemens's image onto that of the hard-living freewheeling steamboat pilot, the latter section demonstrates how Clemens has retained the spark of this character while refining its presentation in accord with Victorian social norms. In narrating Clemens's adult return to the river, the latter section also mounts a careful "self-presentation" which "united [Clemens] to a national story of American material success, and it leagued him with the elite class of men leading the financial charge" (Hutchinson 9). Whereas the narrative begins with the charismatic bad-boy pilots, the second half focuses in detail on economic development of areas along the river and the evolution of the shipping business. As Coulombe sees it, the second section merges the persona of Clemens the would-be investor with that of the young pilot.

Transformations on the Mississippi

Though Clemens laments the transformation of the profession, as a young man the author himself was part of a wave of boys who signed on as apprentices and contributed to a labor glut and wage collapse. He explains the process of unionization and both its negative and positive features. On the one hand, a few great individual pilots were defeated in favor of the mediocre mass. On the other hand, formalized information-sharing allowed each pilot's already formidable memory to be augmented by the shared observations of hundreds.

Economic development and consolidation along the banks of the Mississippi brought significant cultural transformations, such as changes in drinking habits and venues. Where barkeepers were once among the boldest and savviest entrepreneurs of the river traffic, by Clemens's second voyage they are reduced to employees: "All the bars on this Anchor Line are rented and owned by one firm."

And whereas a community ethos had predominated in which "everybody traveled by steamboat, everybody drank, and everybody treated everybody else," Clemens discovers on his return that "the principal line of boats on the Upper Mississippi, they don't have any bar at all!" (chapter 34). And though Clemens laments the decline of heavy drinking and increase in temperance, he applauds the technological advancement embodied in the proliferation of ice factories and the resulting "democratization" of cold drinks: "In Vicksburg and Natchez, in my time, ice was jewelry; none but the rich could wear it. But anybody and everybody can have it now" (chapter 39).

Clemens's account includes many details about the rapidly evolving culture of commerce. For example, in relating America's vigorous economic development, Clemens also notes the persistence of Europe as a source of cultural prestige that can be used as a filter through which to upgrade domestic goods. Always interested in and disgusted by a good scam, Clemens notes the popular practice of exporting and reimporting domestic goods under false European labels, such as American Cotton-seed oil: "Sagacious people shipped it to Italy, doctored it, labelled it, and brought it back as olive oil" (chapter 30). While eavesdropping on some fellow passengers, Clemens is amused by the antics of a new breed of fast-talkers, the traveling salesmen known as "drummers," and he includes a transcription of their frenetic sales pitches. In his return to the South as a naturalized New Englander, Clemens notes evolving, and widening, differences in regional identity, such as the "godless grace, and snap, and style about a born and bred New-Yorker," which he praises in comparison to the bumpkin style along the river, such as the goatee, "an obsolete and uncomely fashion." Clemens ties this backwardness unsympathetically to the "iron-clad belief in Adam and the biblical history of creation, which has not suffered from the assaults of the scientists" (chapter 22).

Rhythms of the River

The power and capriciousness of the river's periodic shifts in course is described in many parts of the book. Islands are shunted from one state to another, like "Island 92"; towns are left behind economically, such as Keokuk; and, most dramatically, the former town of Napoleon is submerged (362–364). Such contingencies of soil altering the legal status of land, Clemens notes in his opening remarks, "in the old times, could have transferred a slave from Missouri to Illinois and made a free man of him" (chapter 1). "Mark Twain's greatest self-indulgence," Hutchinson writes, "is the absence of significant reflection on the war" (chapter 5). Nevertheless, many of Clemens's later observations indirectly register its effects, such as shifts in river employment and key Reconstruction-era demographic shifts, such as the "migrating Negro region" on which Clemens comments sympathetically, "These poor people could never travel when they were slaves; so they make up for the privation now . . . they only want to be moving" (chapter 30).

The sound and slang of river speech figure prominently in Clemens's written voice. At several points in the text, Clemens remarks on the processes of speech and language. He notes, for example, how the imposing pilot's tone worked its way into the core of his self-expression: "By long habit, pilots came to put all their wishes in the form of commands. It 'gravels' me, to this day, to put my will in the weak shape of a request, instead of launching it in the crisp language of an order" (chapter 14). In a violent conflict with a bullying pilot in the chapters on the cub pilot, Clemens falls back on his linguistic talent as an offensive resource. But in striking contrast to Clemens's early work, which draws on populist diction for its charm, in this conflict he falls back on the prestige of proper grammar to assert his power over an unlettered pilot: "I tarried, and criticized his grammar . . . I reformed his ferocious speeches for him, and put them into good English, calling his attention to the advantage of pure English over the bastard dialect of the Pennsylvania collieries whence he was extracted." In this case, Clemens's ability to ridicule serves him well against the pilot who "was not equipped for this species of controversy" (chapter 19), demonstrating, even on the river, in Howe's assessment, "the importance of language in the formation of credible authority" (Howe 39).

Clemens explains in the text the origin of his nom de guerre, as emerging from his parody of the work of an elder boatman named ISAIAH SELLERS. Clemens adopts Sellers's pen name in what Bridgman describes as an act of "symbolic patricide . . . the victory of a young man over a knowledgeable but tedious master" (115).

The River as a Metaphor for Education

While Clemens's evolving relationship to language plays a significant role in his story of life on the river, the river itself is one of Clemens's career-long central metaphors for education, experience, and the acts of reading and writing. "Piloting," Gerd Hurm argues, served Clemens as "a training in realism" (157). Lawrence Howe talks about Clemens's "associative method of composition," which was a frequent staple of his work, as formally appropriate to a book about the great, ever-slowing, and ever-shifting river of the North American continent" (Howe 24–25). Clemens writes of his early apprenticeship, "The face of the water, in time, became a wonderful book . . . delivering its most cherished secrets as clearly as if it uttered them with a voice" (chapter 9). Still, while the river is understood as a symbol for a book, at the same time reading, for Clemens, pales in comparison to the unmediated experience of piloting. He decides that "There never was so wonderful a book written by man; never one whose interest was so absorbing, so unflagging, so sparklingly renewed with every re-perusal" (ibid.).

Memorization is crucial to pilots. "Give a man a tolerably fair memory to start with, and piloting will develop it into a very colossus of capability" (chapter 13). Recounting a piloting lesson, Clemens describes his own mind as having the structure of a steamboat, writing, "I dreadfully wanted to ask a question, but I was carrying about as many short answers as my cargo-room would admit of, so I held my peace" (chapter 6). And he fuses the two—the pilot's virtuoso memorization with the writer's prerogatives of proportion and distortion, noting that too good a memory will make a man a bad talker, unable to "distinguish an interesting circumstance from an uninteresting one" (chapter 13). So, while Clemens's knowledge of reading naturally predates his experience with piloting, his mental absorption of the river in some sense mingles with his basic model of reading: "When I had mastered the language of this water . . . as familiarly as I knew the letters of the alphabet, I had made a valuable acquisition" (chapter 9). And this mastery came with an attendant loss. Writing of his completed riverboat education, Clemens notes with some regret that "the romance and the beauty were all gone from the river." Clemens has lost, through the process of gaining knowledge, the simple aesthetic pleasures regarding the river. As a professional with a set task, "All the value any feature of it had for me now was the amount of usefulness it could furnish toward compassing the safe piloting of a steamboat" (ibid.). This reflection on the odd and inevitable reduction of pleasure in professional activities that had once been pure fun resonates with Clemens's frequent claim—true, exaggerated, or otherwise—that he had never been much of a reader of fiction.

Much of Clemens's work flowed from the Mississippi River, which James Cox has called "genius loci of Mark Twain's imagination" (ibid.). Like Clemens's Hannibal childhood, his time as a riverboat pilot, though a relatively small fraction of Clemens's years, deeply informed his voice and persona as a writer. Indeed, *Life on the Mississippi* focuses so tightly on the river in relation to Clemens's identity that the "twenty-one slow-drifting" years between Clemens's boyhood education and his adult return, in which he became a "scribbler of books," is "disposed of" in less than a page (chapter 21). In justifying the detail and length of his account, he even goes so far as to claim, "If I have seemed to love my subject, it is no surprising thing, for I loved the profession far better than any I have followed since, and I took a measureless pride in it" (chapter 14). The floating social life of the Mississippi made up the reservoir of material from which Clemens drew much of his work: "I am to this day profiting somewhat from that experience; for in that brief, sharp schooling, I got personally and familiarly acquainted with about all the different types of human nature that are to be found in fiction, biography, or history. . . . When I find a well-drawn character in fiction or biography, I generally take a warm personal interest in him, for the

reason that I have known him before—met him on the river" (chapter 18).

Critical Commentary by Alex Feerst

DRAMATIC ADAPTATIONS

Material from *Life on the Mississippi* (1883) was loosely adapted into the 1944 film *The Adventures of Mark Twain*, in which Jackie Brown played Sam Clemens as an adolescent and Fredric March played him as an adult. In November 1980, the Public Broadcasting System aired a television dramatization titled *Life on the Mississippi* that was based mostly on the book's early chapters. David Knell played the young cub, Sam, with Robert Lansing as his mentor, Mr. Bixby. The script simplifies the narrative by confining the action to two steamboats, the *Paul Jones* and the *Aleck Scott* (one stern-wheeler evidently portrayed both). Its many liberties include placing Captain Klinefelter and William Brown on the *Scott* and having the *Jones* blow up, killing George Ritchie. The production concludes with Bixby reciting Clemens's own famous remark about growing up with the "one permanent ambition" of becoming a steamboatman—a surprising ambition for a boy (Bixby) raised in Geneseo, New York.

Robert Lansing (left) as Mr. Bixby and David Knell as Sam in the PBS production of *Life on the Mississippi* (*Public Broadcasting System*)

CHARACTERS AND RELATED ENTRIES

Adler, Private Franz   Character in *Life on the Mississippi* (1883). In a tale told in chapter 31, Adler is a German-American cavalryman who kills Karl Ritter's wife and daughter while robbing Ritter's house with his cousin Private Kruger, in NAPOLEON, Arkansas. Ritter uses a FINGERPRINT to track Adler and Kruger down, then spares Kruger and kills Adler. Years later, however, he finds Adler alive in a Munich dead house and learns that it was actually Kruger he killed. Ritter gets his revenge by watching Adler die slowly.

Dutchy   Pseudonym mentioned in *Life on the Mississippi* (1883). Chapter 54 describes "Dutchy" as a Hannibal boy who drowned (probably in BEAR CREEK) when Clemens was a child. In contrast to the sinful "Lem Hackett" (Clint Levering) who drowned three weeks earlier, Dutchy was a MODEL BOY who recited "three thousand verses of Scripture without missing a word" the day before he drowned. In *Tom Sawyer*, the same figure is described as "a boy of German parentage" who lost his mind after reciting "three thousand verses without stopping." Apparently from one of Hannibal's many German families, "Dutchy" has not been identified. If he truly died three weeks after Hackett, his drowning would have occurred in early September 1847. Clemens originally wrote the passage about Dutchy and Hackett for *A Tramp Abroad* (1880) but did not use it in that book.

Hackett, Lem   Character in *Life on the Mississippi* (1883). Chapter 54 describes "Lem Hackett" as the "fictitious name" of a childhood friend of the narrator who drowned on a *Sunday*. "Being loaded with sin, he went to the bottom like an anvil." That night, the rest of Hannibal's boys lay awake repenting as a wild storm whipped up their fears of divine punishment. The narrator prayed, trying to divert God's attention from his own sins to the more wicked acts of his friends, only to make himself feel even more guilty. Three weeks later, the children's ideas about divine retribution were shaken when a MODEL BOY named "Dutchy" drowned.

Hackett is a pseudonym for Clint Levering, a childhood friend of Clemens, who drowned on August 13, 1847—a *Friday*, not a Sunday.

Klinefelter, Captain John S.   (1810, Pennsylvania–1885)   STEAMBOAT captain. Chapters 19–20 of *Life on the Mississippi* (1883) recall the months when Clemens apprenticed as a PILOT on the PENNSYLVANIA, when Klinefelter was captain in late 1857 and early 1858. After fighting with the pilot WILLIAM BROWN, Clemens expected the captain to have him put in irons. Instead, Klinefelter was delighted that Brown had been pummeled, and—according to *Life on the Mississippi*—even told Clemens to lay for Brown ashore. He offered Clemens Brown's place as a regular pilot, but the young cub pilot did not feel ready for the responsibility, so he instead got off the boat in New Orleans. Klinefelter wrote him a chit allowing him to return up the Mississippi as a passenger on the *ALFRED T. LACEY*. On June 13, the *Pennsylvania* blew up, killing Brown and Clemens's younger brother, Henry Clemens. Klinefelter was unhurt.

Kruger, Private   Character in *Life on the Mississippi* (1883). In a tale told in chapter 31, Kruger is a German-American soldier who allies with his cousin Franz Adler to rob Karl Ritter's family in NAPOLEON, Arkansas. Against Kruger's wishes, Adler murders Ritter's wife and daughter. Ritter tracks Kruger down, identifying him by his missing thumb. After ingratiating himself with Kruger in order to learn the identity of his accomplice, Ritter finally confronts Kruger with the truth about his crime. Kruger is sincerely remorseful and offers Ritter the $10,000 in gold that he and Adler have accumulated. Ritter is grateful to Kruger for having tried to save his family, but he later kills him when he mistakes him for Adler. Ritter discovers his mistake years later, when he finds Adler alive in Munich. Determined to make amends to Kruger's surviving son, Ritter tells the book's narrator where Kruger's gold is stashed in Napoleon and asks him to retrieve it and send it to Kruger's son in MANNHEIM, Germany.

Lynch, Archibald   Figure mentioned in *Life on the Mississippi* (1883). Chapter 55 contains an anecdote about Clemens's youth, when he knew a carpenter who called himself the "Mysterious Avenger," claiming to have dedicated his life to avenging the murder of his fiancée by a man named Archibald Lynch.

Mumford, "Uncle"   Character in *Life on the Mississippi* (1883). Mumford is the fictional name for the "second officer" of the GOLD DUST, on which Clemens traveled down the Mississippi in early 1882. He appears to be a composite character, based mostly on the real second mate of the *Gold Dust,* "Dad" Dunham. "Mumford" is a 30-year veteran on the river (chapter 25). As an outspoken travel companion, Mumford is similar to Clemens's imaginary Mr. Brown. He figures in several anec-

Uncle Mumford

dotes in chapters 25 and 28 and is also mentioned in chapters 26, 32, and 34. A drawing of Mumford in the original edition of *Life on the Mississippi* was apparently made from a photograph of Dunham.

Mysterious Avenger   Character in *Life on the Mississippi* (1883). Chapter 55 recalls an anecdote about the narrator's youth, when he knew a carpenter in Hannibal who styled himself the "Mysterious Avenger." This man deeply impressed the young boy by claiming to have murdered more than 60 persons named Lynch. He had sworn vengeance after his bride was murdered on their wedding day by a man named Archibald Lynch and he intended to go on killing Lynches. When the boy alerted a local resident named Lynch to his terrible peril, this man confronted the carpenter and proved that he was a humbug. The narrator later discovered that the carpenter had plagiarized his story from a book by Robert Montgomery Bird (1806–1854), *Nick of the Woods, or the Jibbenainosay, A Tale of Kentucky* (1837). Bird's book, which was popular in its time, is about a mild-mannered Quaker who leads a double life as "Nick of the Woods," a fearsome slayer of Indians.

Ritter, Karl   Character in *Life on the Mississippi* (1883). Ritter is the central figure in a FRAME-STORY within a tale that spans chapters 31 and 32. In chapter 31—which Clemens evidently began writing before 1881—the narrator explains to his companions why he wants to get off the steamboat in NAPOLEON, Arkansas. He recalls a recent visit to MUNICH, Germany, in which he met an old consumptive named Karl Ritter. Ritter then narrates his own story, which is subtitled "A Dying Man's Confession."

A German, Ritter once lived in ARKANSAS, where his wife and daughter were murdered by a housebreaker during the CIVIL WAR. Vowing revenge, he tracked down the murderer, Franz Adler, using FINGERPRINT evidence. He then disguised himself as a fortune teller in order to ingratiate himself with Adler and his partner, Private Kruger—to whom he was grateful for trying to stop Adler from murdering his family. During a midnight meeting, he stabbed Adler to death in the dark. Over the next 15 or 16 years, Ritter wandered the Earth, until settling in Munich, where he got work in a "dead house." There he watched over corpses, in case any were still alive. One day, a body did come to life; it proved to be Adler, who gloated over Ritter's horrified realization that it was actually Kruger whom he had killed years before. Ritter then sat and savored Adler's slow, painful death. Afterward, he searched Adler's things and learned that Kruger had a son living in MANNHEIM. He secretly sent the son conscience money, while tracking down a watch containing a note revealing where Kruger hid $10,000 in Napoleon, Arkansas. Since Ritter is nearing death, he gives the note to the narrator, asking him to retrieve the money and forward it to Kruger's son.

In chapter 32, the narrator's companions, Thompson and Rogers, suggest that Kruger's son— a humble shoemaker—not only has no need for $10,000, but that such a fortune would actually harm him. They argue the amount down to just $500 and then decide simply to send him "a chromo." After the three men fight over how they will divide the money among themselves, the narrator asks the startled captain of the GOLD DUST to let him off at Napoleon. Uncle Mumford informs him that the Arkansas River has washed the town away.

Styles, Robert   Character in *Life on the Mississippi* (1883). A PILOT on the GOLD DUST, Styles is a composite character based mostly on Lemuel Gray (c. 1838–1882), a real *Gold Dust* pilot whom Clemens had known during his own piloting days. In chapter 24 of *Mississippi*, Styles regales the narrator—who is traveling incognito—with outlandish talk about the hazards of navigating in "alligator water." After stumbling over his own lies, he reveals that he recognized the narrator (presumably Sam Clemens) all along. Styles's speedy unmasking of the narrator's attempt to disguise his identity "ended the fictitious-name business" of the latter, but not entirely, as the name "Styles" itself is fictitious.

Clemens's notebooks indicate that both Lemuel Gray and his brother and fellow pilot, Edmund Gray, quickly identified him—not only by his face and voice, but by his habit of running a hand through his hair. The way that they exposed his incognito probably helped inspire a moment in the last chapter of *Tom Sawyer, Detective* (1896); in that book, Tom exposes Jubiter Dunlap's disguise when he recognizes Dunlap's old habit of tracing crosses on his cheek with a finger. In *The Prince and the Pauper* (1881), Tom Canty's mother uses a similar method to prove Tom's true identity.

Clemens used Lem Gray's real name in his manuscript of *Life on the Mississippi*, but substituted "Styles" after learning that Gray had died in the *Gold Dust*'s explosion in August 1882—an incident described in chapter 37. Another change that Clemens made after Gray's death was to omit a passage from chapter 24 in which Styles claims to have been blown up nine times in steamboat accidents. Three of the alleged accidents occurred at Walnut Bend, where he always fell through the roof of the same house. During one of these incidents, Styles took the boat's wheel with him—a passage reminiscent of chapter 18 of *Innocents Abroad* (1869), in which Clemens recalls taking a window sash with him while fleeing a room in which he discovers a corpse.

The 1944 film THE ADVENTURES OF MARK TWAIN adapts Style's alligator yarn by having Sam Clemens himself tell similar lies to CHARLES LANGDON. PHILIP JOSÉ FARMER uses Robert Styles as a character in his science-fiction novel *The Fabulous Riverboat* (1971).

Thompson and Rogers   Characters in *Life on the Mississippi* (1883). The last two-thirds of this book recount Clemens's 1882 journey on the Mississippi River with JAMES R. OSGOOD and ROSWELL PHELPS, neither of whom is mentioned by name in the book. Chapter 22 alludes to them as a "poet" and a "stenographer," while other chapters merely hint at their presence as travel companions. Chapter 32 finally gives them names; "Thompson" is evidently the "poet," leaving "Rogers" to be the stenographer (the "Rogers" mentioned in chapter 22 is unrelated). Both men argue violently with the narrator over what to do with $10,000 that he expects to find in NAPOLEON, Arkansas, thanks to Karl Ritter's instructions.

Williams, Charlie Fictitious name of a character in *Life on the Mississippi* (1883). In a tale subtitled "A Burning Brand" in chapter 52, "Charlie Williams" is the ALIAS of a burglar serving nine years in prison. He forged a letter to himself from a nonexistent fellow convict, "Jack Hunt," dated June 9, 1872 (exactly one week after the death of Langdon Clemens—a curious coincidence in view of the similarity of the character's alias to the name of the dead baby Charles William Allbright of the "RAFT CHAPTER"). The son of a minister, "Williams" is apparently a Harvard graduate; the warden at his unnamed state prison (evidently some distance from St. Louis) describe him as a "dissolute, cunning prodigal."

William's bogus letter tells a heartrending story of Hunt's experiences outside of prison, culminating in his finding God and winning the trust and support of a St. Louis grain merchant named Brown. "Hunt" attributes his success to what he learned from Williams while in prison. The key passage in the letter is Hunt's allusion to William's bleeding lungs—a hint that the ostensibly saintly Williams was dying in prison.

Widely circulated and read in church sermons, the letter wins over everyone who hears it until C. D. WARNER questions its authenticity. The narrator of *Life on the Mississippi* says that he had planned to write an article about this letter until he learned it was a fake. Williams smuggled it out of prison with the evident intention that it be publicized and help lead to his being pardoned. The narrator had long intended to look up the benevolent Mr. Brown when he reached St. Louis but now feels no need to do so.

BIBLIOGRAPHY

Branch, Edgar Marquess. "Mark Twain: The Pilot and the Writer." *Mark Twain Journal* 23 (1985): 28–43.

Bridgman, Richard. *Traveling in Mark Twain.* Berkeley: University of California Press, 1987.

Brodwin, Stanley. "The Useful and Useless River: *Life on the Mississippi* Revisited." *Studies in American Humor* 2 (1976): 196–208.

Coulombe, Joseph L. "Moneyed Ruffians: The New American Hero in *Life on the Mississippi.*" In *Mark Twain and the American West,* 68–91. Columbia: University of Missouri Press, 2003.

Cox, James M. "*Life on the Mississippi* Revisited." In *The Mythologizing of Mark Twain,* edited by Sara de Saussure Davis and Philip Beidler, 99–115. Birmingham: University of Alabama Press, 1984.

Ganzel, Dewey. "Mark Twain, Travel Books, and *Life on the Mississippi.*" *American Literature* 34 (1962): 405–416.

Howe, Lawrence. "Afterword." In *Life on the Mississippi,* edited by Shelley Fisher Fishkin. Oxford: Oxford University Press, 1996.

———. "Mark Twain's Big Two-Hearted River Text: 'Old Times on the Mississippi' and *Life on the Mississippi.*" In *Mark Twain and the Novel: The Double Cross of Authority,* 14–72. Cambridge: Cambridge University Press, 1998.

Hurm, Gerd. "Interpreting Nature: 'Old Times on the Mississippi.'" In *Rewriting the Vernacular Mark Twain: The Aesthetics and Politics of Orality in Samuel Clemens's Fictions,* 150–176. Trier: Verlag Trier, 2003.

Hutchinson, Stuart. "'Old Times on the Mississippi,' *Life on the Mississippi,* 'The Private History of a Campaign That Failed.'" In *Mark Twain—Humour on the Run,* 64–78. Amsterdam: Rodopi B.V., 1994.

Kruse, Horst H. *Mark Twain and "Life on the Mississippi."* Amherst: University of Massachusetts Press, 1981.

Melton, Jeffrey Alan. "Touring the New World: The Search for Home in *Roughing It* and *Life on the Mississippi.*" In *Mark Twain, Travel Books, and Tourism: The Tide of a Great Popular Movement,* 95–137. Tuscaloosa: University of Alabama Press, 2002.

Stoneley, Peter. "The Mississippi Valley." In *Mark Twain and the Feminine Aesthetic,* 45–75. Cambridge: Cambridge University Press, 1992.

Twain, Mark. *Life on the Mississippi,* edited by Shelley Fisher Fishkin. New York: Oxford University Press, 1996.

Literary Essays (In Defense of Harriet Shelley and Other Essays)

Collection of previously published essays. Harper's first issued the volume in 1899 and later included it in all its uniform Mark Twain editions. It contains

"In Defense of Harriet Shelley (1894), "Fenimore Cooper's Literary Offenses" (1895), "Traveling with a Reformer" (1893), "Private History of the Jumping Frog Story (1894), "Mental Telegraphy" (1891), "Mental Telegraphy Again" (1895), "What Paul Bourget Thinks of Us" (1895), "A Little Note to M. Paul Bourget" (1896), "The Invalid's Story" (1882), "Stirring Times in Austria" (1898), "The German Chicago [Berlin]" (1892), "Concerning the Jews" (1899), "About All Kinds of Ships" (1893), "From the 'London Times' of 1904" (1898), "A Majestic Literary Fossil" (1890), "At the Appetite Cure" (1898), "Saint Joan of Arc" (1904), a memorial poem to Susy Clemens (1897), and a biographical sketch by Mark Twain's nephew Samuel E. Moffett. Seven of the first eight items were also in the earlier Harper's anthology, *How to Tell a Story and Other Essays* (1897). In 1900, the American Publishing Company issued its own edition of *How to Tell a Story and Other Essays*, which is almost identical to *Literary Essays*.

"The Lost Napoleon"

Posthumously published essay. Around the eighth day of his Rhone River boat trip in southern France in September 1891, Clemens spotted a mountain range whose profile resembled that of Napoleon Bonaparte lying on his back. After failing to note the range's precise location, he wrote this essay about a decade later, calling the vista the "lost Napoleon" because he forgot exactly where it was. He expresses confidence, however, that if his great discovery were found again and promoted, it would become a major tourist attraction.

A. B. Paine found this essay among Clemens's unpublished papers and included it in *Europe and Elsewhere* (1923), noting that in 1913 he himself found the lost range—east of the Rhône, visible from near the village of Beauchastel, a few miles south of Valence. Paine offers a fuller description and painting of the view in chapter 12 of *The Car That Went Abroad: Motoring Through the Golden Age* (1921).

The "Lost Napoleon" *(A. B. Paine,* The Car That Went Abroad, *1922)*

"The Loves of Alonzo Fitz Clarence and Rosannah Ethelton"

Short story written in 1877 and published in the *Atlantic Monthly* in March 1878. A condensed novel in four chapters, "Loves" is about a couple who conduct their romance entirely through transcontinental telephone conversations—a form of long-distance communication that did not actually exist until 1915. Early action in this burlesque love story is obscure, since the fact that the lovers are speaking by telephone is not clarified until the third chapter. They never meet face-to-face within the story.

SYNOPSIS

Chapter 1
On a winter day in Eastport, Maine, Alonzo Fitz Clarence sits in his parlor. Uncertain about the time his clock is keeping, he tries getting the attention of a servant and his mother, then speaks to his Aunt Susan from his desk. When she tells him that the time is 9:05, he adjusts his clock to 12:35. As they talk, Alonzo hears a voice singing "The Sweet Bye-and-Bye" and is introduced to his aunt's ward, Rosannah Ethelton. Alonzo and Rosannah talk for

two hours, after which Alonzo realizes that his heart is now in SAN FRANCISCO. Rosannah is equally smitten with Alonzo—compared to whom a man named (Sidney Algernon) Burley, whose sole talent is mimicry, suddenly seems shallow.

Chapter 2

Four weeks later, Burley calls on Rosannah to learn why she is avoiding him. He happens to overhear her talking to Alonzo and is distressed by her obvious affection for this rival suitor. When Burley overhears Alonzo's Eastport address, he leaves. Meanwhile, Alonzo's mother and Aunt Susan are thrilled to learn that Alonzo and Rosannah are betrothed; they dismiss the young couple and begin planning the wedding.

Chapter 3

Two weeks later, a man calling himself the Reverend Melton Hargrave of Cincinnati is visiting Alonzo regularly, claiming to have invented a device that prevents telephone eavesdropping; Alonzo is keen to have the device. On one of his visits, the man finds Alonzo's parlor vacant and hears "The Sweet Bye-and-Bye" coming from the telephone. Imitating Alonzo's voice, he interrupts Rosannah and asks her to sing something else. When Alonzo returns, the man hides. Rosannah angrily turns on the bewildered Alonzo and calls off their engagement. Alonzo leaves to find his mother so she can plead his case with Rosannah, giving the intruder the chance to seize the phone in his absence and reject Rosannah's attempt to retract her harsh words.

After Alonzo returns, he spends hours trying to reestablish contact with Rosannah. His Aunt Susan reports that Rosannah has packed and left. Alonzo is stunned, but when he finds a card on his floor with Burley's name, he guesses what his rival has done.

Chapter 4

For two months, Alonzo searches for Rosannah with a carpet-sack and portable telephone, climbing telephone poles in the hope of hearing a signal carrying her voice. When his spirit and body are nearly broken, he is taken to a madhouse in New York. One March morning, he hears Rosannah's singing and finds a telephone, which he uses to tell

her of Burley's trickery. The couple make up and agree to wed on April 1—giving Aunt Susan time to get from San Francisco to Honolulu, where Rosannah now is. Burley happens to call on Rosannah as she is talking with Alonzo; she tells him that she will yield to his importunities on April 1—intending to repay him for his villainy.

On April 2, the *Honolulu Advertiser* carries a notice of Rosannah's marriage to Alonzo; similar notices appear in New York newspapers the same day. Later, Aunt Susan takes Rosannah across the continent to meet Alonzo for the first time. Burley, who has vowed revenge, dies while trying to do violence to a crippled artisan.

CHARACTERS AND RELATED ENTRIES

Burley, Sidney Algernon Minor character in "The Loves of Alonzo Fitz Clarence and Rosannah Ethelton" (1878). A handsome young San Francisco man whose only talent is mimicry, Burley is Alonzo Fitz Clarence's rival for the hand of Rosannah Ethelton. Burley breaks up Rosannah's engagement to Alonzo by imitating the latter's voice and insulting Rosannah over the TELEPHONE. Rosannah later repays his deception by making him think that she will marry him, only to humiliate him when he arrives at her wedding to Alonzo. After vowing revenge, Burley falls into a cauldron of boiling oil while trying to do violence to a crippled artisan.

Ethelton, Rosannah Character in "The Loves of Alonzo Fitz Clarence and Rosannah Ethelton" (1878). A beautiful and graceful young woman of refined taste, Rosannah is an orphan who lives with her grandmother in Portland, Oregon. She is also the ward of Susan Howland, in whose elegant San Francisco home she is staying when she meets Alonzo Fitz Clarence and falls in love with him over the TELEPHONE.

Fitz Clarence, Alonzo Character in "The Loves of Alonzo Fitz Clarence and Rosannah Ethelton" (1878). A young bachelor who lives with his mother in Eastport, Maine, Alonzo has an aunt named Susan Howland in SAN FRANCISCO. Apparently prosperous, he thinks nothing of telephoning his aunt on a whim. During one of his calls, he is introduced to his aunt's ward, Rosannah Ethelton, and falls in love with her. After a rival suitor, Sidney Algernon Burley, breaks up this romance by imitating Alonzo's voice over the phone, Alonzo nearly goes mad trying to find Rosannah again over the TELEPHONE.

"Luck"

SHORT STORY first published in 1891. A FRAME-STORY, "Luck" opens as the narrator attends a LONDON banquet honoring one of Britain's most illustrious military heroes—a lieutenant general whom he assigns the fictitious name Lord Arthur Scoresby. Thirty years earlier, "Scoresby" won immortality at the CRIMEA. As the narrator admires this demigod's unassuming nobility, his clergyman friend mutters, "Privately—he's an absolute fool." His friend's honesty and judgment are beyond reproach, so the narrator burns to hear an explanation. The clergyman later relates how he was Scoresby's instructor at Woolwich 40 years earlier. The young cadet was "good, sweet and lovable," but a hopelessly ignorant dunce whom the clergyman tutored out of pity. Amazingly, Scoresby earned top marks in every examination; by pure luck, he was tested only in the few things he knew. The clergyman thought himself a Frankenstein for helping qualify this "wooden-head" for promotion.

When Scoresby became a captain in the Crimean War (1854–56), the clergyman joined his unit in order to keep an eye on him. Scoresby never did anything during the war but blunder; however, every blunder had such a good result that he was deemed a genius. As Scoresby's reputation grew, he gained greater responsibility and more potential for disaster. After he became a colonel, Scoresby's finest moment came when he routed an entire Russian army with his lone regiment. When the Russians saw his men advancing on their position, they assumed his regiment was the vanguard of the *entire* British army, since no regiment would be foolish enough to attack them alone. The Russians turned and were routed. Dizzy with astonishment and admiration, Marshal Canrobert (François Cer-

tain Canrobert, 1809–1895) decorated Scoresby on the spot. Scoresby's success arose from his not knowing his right hand from his left. Ordered to fall back to his *right*, he had mistakenly gone forward to his *left*. Every medal on his chest records some similar stupidity—proof that the best thing that can befall a man is to be born lucky.

Clemens initialed a footnote to the story claiming that he heard it from a clergyman who had been at Woolwich. He also claimed to have been told by two Englishmen that Scoresby was really Lord Garnet Joseph Wolseley (1833–1913), who lost an eye at Crimea and later became commander in chief of the British army.

Clemens wrote this 1,800-word story around early 1886—a date consistent with the narrator's allusion to Scoresby's being at Crimea 30 years earlier. He evidently thought little of the story, as he set it aside until 1891. Feeling pressed for money that year, he sent it to HARPER'S MAGAZINE, which published it in its August issue. The following year the story was collected in MERRY TALES—all of which was later incorporated into *The American Claimant and Other Stories and Sketches.*

"Lucretia Smith's Soldier"

SKETCH first published in the CALIFORNIAN on December 3, 1864. Taking the form of a BURLESQUE condensed novel, this 1,800-word tale is a PARODY of the SENTIMENTALISM of romantic war stories that were popular at the time. It opens with a pompous prefatory note, signed "M. T.," in which the author affirms that the story is true because its facts were compiled from official War Department records. He also acknowledges various sources of help and inspiration, including a local San Francisco beer.

In the first miniature chapter, it is May 1861. Reginald de Whittaker, a clerk in Bluemass, Massachusetts (a fictional place named after a pharmacological powder used to make blue pills), is anxious to tell his sweetheart, Lucretia Smith, that he has enlisted in the army. In the next chapter, however, she turns him away before he can even speak. His newfound pride as a soldier prevents him from staying to explain. The next morning (chapter 3), Lucretia learns that Reginald has enlisted; she upbraids herself for treating him unfairly and then suffers silently for weeks while hoping for a letter from him. Finally, she sees a report from the war mentioning that "R. D. Whittaker, private soldier" is desperately wounded. In chapter 4, she goes to Washington to nurse Whittaker, whose head is completely wrapped in bandages. When doctors remove the dressings three weeks later, Lucretia angrily discovers that she has wasted her time on the wrong man.

A popular hit throughout the United States, "Lucretia Smith's Soldier" was frequently reprinted—often without attribution. Its first appearance in book form was in THE CELEBRATED JUMPING FROG OF CALAVERAS COUNTY, AND OTHER SKETCHES (1867), in which the prefatory paragraph is severely truncated.

CHARACTERS AND RELATED ENTRIES

Smith, Lucretia Borgia Character in "Lucretia Smith's Soldier." A native of Bluemass, Massachusetts, Lucretia is the sweetheart of REGINALD DE WHITTAKER, whom she wants to enlist to fight in the CIVIL WAR. When Whittaker comes to tell her that he *has* enlisted, however, she drives him off without letting him speak. She learns the truth only after he marches off the next morning, then suffers because no soldier is carrying her name into war. She seeks redemption for her rash behavior by heroically nursing a badly wounded soldier named "R. D. Whittaker" for three weeks, only to discover that he is the *wrong* Whittaker.

Lucretia's selfishness and imperious insincerity reflect Clemens's feelings about her namesake, the Italian noblewoman Lucrezia Borgia (1480–1519), who was notorious in the 19th century for her alleged vice and cruelty. *Innocents Abroad* (1869) comments on "the facility with which she could order a sextuple funeral and get the corpses ready for it" (chapter 19). His 1872 speech to "The Ladies" alludes to the "gentle ministrations, the softening influences, the humble piety of Lucretia Borgia."

Whittaker, Reginald de Character in "Lucretia Smith's Soldier." The young sweetheart of Lucretia

Smith, Whittaker is making $2.50 a week clerking in the Bushrod and Ferguson dry goods and grocery store in Bluemass, Massachusetts, when the CIVIL WAR begins. To please Lucretia, he enlists in the army, but she rebuffs him before he can even tell her that he has enlisted. Recognizing that he is "no longer an effeminate dry-goods student" he leaves without looking back and Lucretia never hears from him again. Meanwhile, her friends receive letters from the war reporting that Whittaker is "morose, unsmiling, desperate" and "always in the thickest of the fight." Later, Lucretia spends three weeks nursing a badly wounded soldier named R. D. Whittaker, who proves to be Richard Dilworth Whittaker of Wisconsin.

"A Majestic Literary Fossil"

Essay published in 1890. The literary relic to which the title alludes is A *Medicinal Dictionary* (which Mark Twain mistitles *Dictionary of Medicine*), published in 1743 by Robert James (1705–1776), a fashionable English physician later famous for his nostrums. He was a friend of Dr. Samuel Johnson, who contributed biographies to James's book.

Mixing quotes with his own commentary, Clemens shows how little the medical thinking in James's book differs from that of ancient times. Further, the book reflects the state of medical knowledge current during Clemens's youth—a time when the ancient Greek physician Galen could have practiced medicine proficiently. Over the next 50 years, however, medical thinking advanced so much that Galen would be hanged if he tried to practice. The dramatic change reflects a general revolution in intellectual thought made possible by the belated recognition that *new* ideas have value.

This essay's theme is echoed in *Pudd'nhead Wilson* (1894), in which Percy Driscoll loses all his children to the "antediluvian methods" of early 19th-century doctors (chapter 1). "THOSE EXTRAORDINARY TWINS" devotes chapter 7 to the ignorance of doctors and calls Galen "the only medical authority recognized in Missouri." The 5,140-word essay first appeared in the February 1890 issue of *Harper's Magazine* and was collected in *Literary Essays*.

"The Mammoth Cod"

SKETCH about male sex organs attributed to Clemens. This scatological sketch was first ascribed to Petroleum V. NASBY in a book privately published in the early 20th century. It has since been credited to Clemens—who some scholars believe wrote it in early 1902. In 1976, the Maledicta Society published *The Mammoth Cod* under his name in a booklet edited by Gershon Legman.

The sketch is ostensibly a letter from a man deriding the "Mammoth Cod Club"—an organization of men proud of their prodigious sexual organs. Its central feature is a four-stanza poem praising bulls, rams, and boars for providing meat, thanks to their efficient use of their mighty cods. It concludes that man is the only beast that "plays with his mammoth cod" merely for fun. A postscript claims that the author wrote the poem to instruct children by showing how "animals do better by instinct than man does by reason." The author suggests that the poem be sung in Sunday schools.

Though the subject matter of "The Mammoth Cod" has superficial similarities with that of Clemens's "SOME THOUGHTS ON THE SCIENCE OF ONANISM" and *1601*, its flat style does not resemble his writing, and his authorship of it remains unproven.

"The Man That Corrupted Hadleyburg"

SHORT STORY written by Clemens while he was in VIENNA in December 1898. It is about a stranger who repays an arrogantly pious town for mistreating him by drawing all its leading citizens into a hoax that destroys the town's reputation for honesty.

SYNOPSIS

Part 1

The story contains 17,500 words and is divided into four numbered parts.

Hadleyburg is so vainly proud of its reputation as the region's "most honest and upright town" that no one notices when it deeply offends a passing stranger. The bitter man spends more than a year plotting revenge to attack what the town values most—its pride. One night he returns to Hadleyburg and leaves a heavy sealed bag at the home of Edward Richards. A note identifies him as a foreigner who visited the town "a year or two ago," when a local man gave him $20 along with advice that turned his life around. According to the note, the bag contains $40,000 in gold to be given to his benefactor, whom he is confident that Hadleyburg's honest citizens will find. All the stranger's unknown benefactor must do to identify himself is give the Reverend Burgess a sealed envelope containing the advice that he rendered to the stranger. At a public meeting, Burgess is to open the envelope and compare it with a copy of the correct statement that the stranger has sealed in his bag of gold.

Richards jokes about how easy it would be simply to keep the stranger's gold and deny everything, but his wife rebukes him. He delivers the stranger's note to Cox, the local newspaperman, for publication. When he returns, he and his wife agree that the only person in town who could have given the stranger $20 is the recently deceased Barclay Goodson, who was hated by the townspeople for publicly belittling its self-righteousness. The only person the town hates more is the Reverend Burgess, who is reviled for an offense he committed years earlier. Richards, however, has always known that Burgess was innocent, but he was too cowardly to speak up to save Burgess's reputation, though he did secretly save him from being run out of town on a rail.

As it dawns on the Richardses that the deceased Goodson is probably the man for whom the gold is intended, they regret their hastiness in giving the stranger's note to Cox. Richards rushes out to find Cox, but newspapers are already publishing the news.

Part 2

The next morning Hadleyburg awakens to find itself famous. The town's 19 principal citizens are especially proud, but soon their thoughts turn to wondering what Goodson told the stranger.

Three weeks later, Richards receives a letter from a "Howard L. Stephenson," who says he saw Goodson give a stranger $20 and heard what he told him. Stephenson adds that Goodson once mentioned feeling indebted to Richards for some "very great service." For this reason, Stephenson feels that Richards is the legitimate heir to Goodson's fortune, and he reveals the crucial message: *You are far from being a bad man; go, and reform.* Though thrilled by the prospect of riches, Richards struggles to remember what service he might have performed for Goodson. Meanwhile, Hadleyburg's 18 other leading citizens receive similar letters; they also struggle to recall their own services to Goodson. With 19 families expecting sudden wealth, the town goes on a spending binge. Meanwhile, 19 people slip sealed envelopes to Reverend Burgess.

Part 3

At the end of a month, 480 people pack the town hall to see Burgess present the sack of gold to the Hadleyburg "incorruptible." After Burgess reads the first sealed message, the crowd is amazed to learn it was written by Deacon Billson—a notorious cheapskate who would never give money away to anyone. Bewilderment turns to astonishment when both Billson and a man named Wilson rise to take credit for the message. Wilson is found to have submitted a nearly identical statement, but neither precisely matches the message that Burgess takes from the sealed bag. Wilson nevertheless appears to carry the day with a glib explanation that wins over the crowd, but before he can claim his prize, Burgess opens a third envelope that contains the same message.

The crowd's amusement reaches a fever pitch as Burgess reads submission after submission with the same message—all signed by leading citizens. Meanwhile, Richards squirms in anticipation of his own coming humiliation; he rises to confess but is shouted down. To his astonishment, Burgess quits after the 18th message, and Richards himself is hailed as the town's only true "incorruptible."

Burgess then reads the balance of the note removed from the bag, in which the stranger reveals that the whole scheme is a hoax. The stranger chides the town for its pride and naïveté, pointing out that by long insulating itself against temptation, it has created "the weakest of all weak things . . . a virtue which has not been tested in the fire." The bag itself, which is filled with gilded lead slugs, is auctioned off to raise money for Hadleyburg's "one clean man," Richards. Unbeknownst to the crowd, the bag goes to the perpetrator of the hoax, who winds up reselling it to "Dr." Harkness for $40,000, which he gives to Richards. Harkness later uses the notorious lead coins to win election to the state legislature by having the image of his opponent, Pinkerton, stamped on them with a humiliating reminder of Pinkerton's shameful connection with the fraud.

Part 4

The Richardses, confused and exhausted by the attention they are receiving, receive a note from Burgess explaining that he saved them at the town meeting to repay the time that Richards had "saved" him. Fearing that Burgess actually intends to expose their hypocrisy for having earlier failed to clear his name when his reputation was unjustly ruined, the Richardses become gravely ill. In his delirium, Richards thinks that Burgess has exposed him. On his deathbed, he confesses that he alone knew of Burgess's innocence in his old scandal, and publicly forgives Burgess for exposing him. He dies without realizing that he has once again wronged Burgess. Mrs. Richards dies the same night.

To hide their shame, the people of Hadleyburg petition to change the name of their town, and they drop the "not" from their original motto, "Lead Us Not into Temptation."

PUBLISHING HISTORY

HARPER'S MAGAZINE published the story in December 1899, and it first appeared in book form in *The Man That Corrupted Hadleyburg and Other Stories and Essays* in June 1900. (Later editions of this collection have slightly different titles.) The 1996

OXFORD MARK TWAIN edition includes a facsimile reprint of the first edition of *The Man that Corrupted Hadleyburg and Other Stories* with a new introduction by Cynthia Ozick and an afterword by David Barrow. The story has also been reprinted in numerous collections of 19th-century short stories, as well as most collections of Clemens's best short works. It was dramatized on television's *American Short Story* series in 1980, with Robert Preston playing the stranger.

CRITICAL COMMENTARY

Commentators often say that the title character of "The Man That Corrupted Hadleyburg" is, like the man who bets against Jim Smiley's frog in the JUMPING FROG STORY, the person killed in "THE PRIVATE HISTORY OF A CAMPAIGN THAT FAILED," and No. 44 in *No. 44, The Mysterious Stranger,* one of Clemens's recurring mysterious strangers. Mysteries abound in this story: the offense the town inflicted on this man, his identity, his seeming omniscience and prescience regarding Hadleyburgians, Barclay Goodson's nature, why a man so antithetical to Hadleyburg ever settled there, the breakup of Goodson's romance with Nancy Hewitt, his and her deaths, how (with the stress on their poverty and low status) the Richardses became members of the 19 principal families of Hadleyburg, what Burgess did to anger the town, why and how Burgess remains there without a job, his first name, and the new name of the town and what it became. Most of these questions remain mysteries, but the stranger's powers may not be as mysterious as they seem. Some scholars believe that he is simply a man who was offended while passing through the town; others say he is a figurative or literal Satan who tempts the town into "falling." Other than as Satan, metaphoric or otherwise, and a passing stranger, he assumes aliases and disguises; but beyond being a person of keen psychological insight—particularly into the inhabitants of this village—who foresees behavior and reactions to certain stimuli, he remains unknown. Seeming to know the people not as a stranger but as one living among them, he (unlike outsiders Goodson, Halliday, and Burgess) does not. His year's study is unlikely to account for such in-depth knowledge.

Ripe for temptation, Hadleyburg is an American Eden into which a serpent drops. It is likely that the serpent has an accomplice in the town, and many clues suggest that the best candidate is Burgess.

This minister without a given first name is the one in the best position to observe and participate as well as provide reliable insight and information. Although his title indicates submission to divine power, his surname, "Burgess," implies he is a free man with no obligation to higher earthly authority. As a free agent, he moves about more easily and quietly than Halliday, with his jokes and laughter, and Goodson, with his scowls and sarcasm. As a minister, Burgess likely views the town and situation in religious terms. Whereas the stranger seeks to tempt the town into falling, Burgess's aim may be to reform it. Two men with different purposes may clarify any dichotomy between interpreting the story as one of revenge or redemption. For Burgess, both apply. Religious language, references, and imagery throughout and Burgess's prominent place in the story indicate a link or an influence. Indeed, the theme centers on a literal reading of one line in the Lord's Prayer and an inverse reading of the rest, as the gist of the plot turns upon the story of the good samaritan.

Similar to the unknown man in the biblical parable, a stranger is abused by a town and stranded in it without means. Far from seeking God's will on Earth, as in the Lord's Prayer, the town, as represented by its most illustrious citizens, trespasses upon others, especially strangers, while priding itself on superficial uprightness. Hadleyburg permits no charity in its law. Burgess bears its unforgiving scorn, as Richards, a lower member of the 19 struggling for daily bread, feels the trespass upon his soul of a higher 19er, the wealthiest man in town. The resentment is expressed in the old bank cashier's first words: " 'Always at the grind, grind, grind, on a salary—another man's slave, and he sitting at home in his slippers, rich and comfortable' " (part 1). Mutual resentment (like hypocrisy) is pervasive but never straightforwardly expressed. Honesty in Hadleyburg is superficial. The town preserves its reputation by allowing no temptations to overt dishonesty—thus welcoming no outsiders—and by training, and intimidating, its populace to observe the letter—not the spirit—of honesty, but by avoiding temptation, the town delivers itself into evil. Hypocritical and proud, lacking charity, pity, and forgiveness, but ever honest, it illustrates Clemens's aphorism: "A man may have no bad habits and have worse."

Go, and Reform!

Beginning like a fable and concluding with a moral, the story concerns the necessity of reform, if not its attainment. The narrator, with inexact fable-like phrases such as "It was many years ago" and "in the drift of time" (ibid.), repeats what he and others have heard over the years (the rumors, the gossip, the lore), piecing together the story and what he thinks people thought and did. For example, he conjectures about the ailing Richards's exposure, "A nurse must have talked in her sleep, for within two days the forbidden gabblings were the property of the town. . . . They seemed to indicate that Richards was a claimant for the sack [of gold] . . . and that Burgess had concealed the fact . . ." (part 4). Like others, the narrator assumes that the stranger is solely responsible and does not look for anyone else or contrary clues or further pursue Burgess's involvement. He accepts the common view, just as he recites the apparent but wrong conclusion that the town is honest again. The town was never honest. Reform is still needed.

In his scam, the stranger says that he was a ruined gambler to whom a generous townsman gave $20, from which he built a fortune through gambling; he now wants to repay the townsman several-fold. The stranger did not truly reform but says he did because of the townsperson's generosity and final remark ("You are far from being a bad man; go, and reform"). By proposing this reforming remark, which "saved the remnant of my morals" (part 1), as a way to identify "the right man," a recurring phrase that increases in irony as exposure of the town approaches, he makes it an instrument to reform the town of Hadleyburg. The next step of his subversion—sending the remark under an alias to each of the 19 important families—indicates involvement by more than one person, for "No two of the envelopes were alike, and no two of the superscriptions were in the same hand" (part 2). As

18 "right" men step forward, Richards remains seated, except for one attempt, stopped by Burgess, to stand exposed like the others; then, Burgess presents Richards as "the right man" by concealing the truth. Believing one "right man" exists, the town thinks it has faced its wrongs, repented, and is ready to reform, but after Richards reveals he has fallen, the town changes its motto as an outward sign of change and remorse but dodges true repentance and reform by hiding behind a new town name.

Richards

Determined to corrupt the town by enticing its 19 leading families with a bag of money, the stranger initially thinks he has failed because of Richards. He could have chosen Cox or another low-level 19er if he intended greed to work its way upward. The stranger has no particular reason for choosing Richards to receive the money, but Burgess does. The stranger is probably involved with Richards because of Burgess. As the poorest of the 19 economically, Richards might succumb, but he is the weakest link in that he is the closest to being honest, to having a conscience that—merged with the training of the town—might impel him in the most moral or ethical direction. He is the most likely one to spoil the plot, as the stranger later thinks Richards *has* done. But Burgess owes him a debt and, because of what Richards did for him, thinks he would behave honestly, as he initially does. Whereas Richards (half-seriously?) jokes of keeping the money, others are more likely to do so. The stranger judges greed to be ultimately more powerful than training and habit, but the call is close. Richards is ironically the "right man"; he hesitates just enough for the plan to succeed. The plan moves forward because of what seems to be more honesty than training in Richards as he follows the stranger's instructions to inform the town, then almost misfires when greed overcomes him and he tries to retrieve the news item. Richards then apparently fails to corrupt the whole town when Burgess protects him, and Richards finally succeeds when, overcome by guilt, he reveals that he, too, fell.

Mrs. Richards says in disgust that Burgess has tried to befriend Richards, noticeable to the extent that other 19ers mock, "'*Your friend* Burgess'" (part 1). Burgess wants to help him, to reward him. If Richards had been immediately dishonest, the scheme would have ended with his hiding the sack left by the stranger. The stranger depended upon town training (intimidated honesty) to cause enough of a delay that others would learn of his proposal, baiting the trap for the whole town. Ironically, exposing dishonesty in Hadleyburg is contingent upon its initial honesty. The best choice, Richards, reacts honestly, setting the plan in motion, initially not caught by it; when he later decides to keep the money, he almost spoils the scheme by preventing news from reaching others. He, and perhaps editor Cox, would have become victims if they had succeeded in retrieving the news release and splitting the money. Finding lead slugs and the explanatory note, they would have stopped the scheme there. Less dependent on timing and chance, Burgess—if he had had input—would have likely proposed Richards as recipient and depended on the knowledge of the man who defied (although secretly) the other families to warn Burgess that they were coming for him, not knowing that, fearing town opinion, Richards is dishonest through silence because he knows Burgess to be innocent and does not say so. Richards is selected because of Burgess's knowledge and ignorance.

Burgess would have suggested that the stranger begin with Richards, and the stranger, if he had chosen an insider to aid his scheme, would have likely chosen Burgess. Burgess's grievances against the town are more numerous and, except for Goodson's, stronger than those held by outsiders in Hadleyburg. The town ended Goodson's romance with Nancy Hewitt, precipitating factors leading to her death. Now, Goodson, too, is dead. Jack Halliday is disliked and not accepted by the principal 19 citizens because he makes fun of them; life is a joke to Jack, and Hadleyburgians are serious people. The stranger's plot would have been merely a joke to Halliday, who in any case lacks the insight, and information, to be the accomplice the stranger needs. Halliday would not have conducted the town hall meeting as effectively as Burgess. Being excluded is a badge of merit more than a grievance to him. He is cynical, not bitter.

Burgess, disgraced and hated, remains in town, but he is an outcast, shunned and scorned by almost all. His reputation ruined, he likely cannot find another church to accept him as pastor, but—intensifying the hurt—Hadleyburg is against his finding another position, for surely such an honest town would not dishonestly accuse a man of the cloth of vile behavior. That fact does not alone explain why he stays there. Whether seeking revenge, retribution, repentance, reform, or a mixture, the minister in Burgess might wish Hadleyburg to see the errors of its ways and alter its behavior.

Goodson

All inhabitants immediately know that only Goodson would have helped a stranger. They never propose Burgess or any other minister in the town as the possible good samaritan, indicating the extent of village insularity. As demonstrated at the town meeting, many townspeople are resentful and angry toward the 19. Some are bitter because they want to be among the elite and are excluded; others—even within the 19—dislike being under the thumb of the leading families. Finding outsiders disgruntled by the town is not difficult, as the narrator indicates early: Hadleyburg offended strangers, "possibly without knowing it, certainly without caring, for Hadleyburg was sufficient unto itself, and cared not a rap for strangers or their opinions" (part 1). But just as easily found are offended inhabitants, afraid to speak openly until united in the meeting. This fact partially explains why the phrase "the right man" so resonates with townspeople. The phrase and a variant, "the right one," occur 11 times, once directly applied by a townsman to Richards (part 3), with "wrong man" appearing one time (part 2), although 18 wrong men step forward, suggesting that the town wants to believe in itself or in someone to justify or redeem it. "The right man," an honest, charitable, righteous person, would relieve the wrong and restore the town to an upright state, which the people realize is not that of Hadleyburg. So, although for selfish reasons, each head of the 19 families tries to convince himself, and later others, that he is "the right man." Subconsciously desiring a Messiah, the people rejoice at the exposure of the 18 and town hypocrisy as a kind of repentance, and especially embrace Richards as "the right man." So, the stranger could easily have found an accomplice in Hadleyburg but none with the qualifications of Burgess.

That Burgess is much involved on the surface may indicate that he is secretly involved as well. The stranger names him to hold the sack of presumed money, to receive the envelopes with the identifying remark, and to conduct the important ceremony that exposes the town's corruptibility, and the author directs attention to Burgess as the choice, hinting at tighter connections. Mrs. Richards questions, "Edward, doesn't it seem odd that the stranger should appoint Burgess to deliver the money?" (part 1). After stammering, Edward says, ". . . maybe the stranger knows him better than this village does," and then twice tells Mary that Burgess is "not a bad man" (ibid.). This parallel foreshadows the remark identifying "the right man" to receive the reward, which, in turn, exposes Hadleyburgian dishonesty, "You are far from being a bad man: go, and reform," and the supplementary "test" remark castigating the town that adds, "mark my words—some day, for your sins, you will die and go to hell or Hadleyburg—TRY AND MAKE IT THE FORMER" (part 3). While both have religious overtones, the first remark sounds like one from a compassionate minister and the second like the summation of a fire-and-brimstone sermon. Literally, unless Burgess helped construct the remarks, no link exists, but psychologically, Clemens has made one for the reader.

Religious Allusions

As noted, religious allusions, while serving other purposes, particularly point to Burgess. They may underscore the satanic metaphor, emphasize the God-like power of the corruptor or role of providence, or stress the hypocrisy of supposedly religious people or the hypocrisy of religion itself. References begin with the title and the plot; as Lawrence Berkove notes, *corrupt* is a Calvinist term (353). All identified outsiders—in some way—are associated with religion: The *Rev.* Burgess, Goodson (God's son), Halliday (hallowed day), Nancy

(grace) Hewitt (spirit) (Rule 623); like them, true religious virtues (e.g., the Golden Rule) are unwelcome in Hadleyburg. Of outsiders, Burgess is the one most directly concerned with religious matters.

These references abound. Significantly, Mary Richards is reading the *Missionary Herald* when the stranger—an ironic missionary—arrives, and his first word is "Pray" (part 1). Religious terms recur from beginning to end. Particularly compelling are repetitive variations of "temptation," "confession," "saved," "sin," "grace," and especially "reform," as well as appearances of "soul" and "moral regeneration." The repetitions culminate in the town hall meeting that becomes an ironic church service.

Identifying Hadleyburg with America, patriotism, and materialism, flags cover the town hall, celebrating the American small-town virtue of honesty; however, figurative accoutrements and church rituals overshadow them. A "horseshoe of tables . . . fenced the front and sides of the platform" (part 3), where Burgess will stand, reminiscent of a Presbyterian or Episcopal/Catholic sanctuary or Methodist altar-table arrangement. "On a little table [like an altar] at the front of the platform" is the gold-sack (ibid.), which Mrs. Richards earlier "kneeled beside . . . and fondled . . . lovingly [with] a gloating light in her poor old eyes" (137), as if in prayer; the 19 couples gaze "at it tenderly, lovingly, proprietarily" while the men recite like silent prayers their "impromptu speeches of thankfulness" (ibid.). With Burgess as master of ceremonies, the assemblage becomes his congregation. When he rises and lays his hand on the sack, rather than a Bible, the place becomes as still as a church for his invocation of Hadleyburgian honesty as inspiration. Having received 19 envelopes, Burgess must realize that the town has been corrupted as he praises its incorruptibility, calling its "well-earned reputation . . . a treasure of priceless value" that Providence has "now . . . inestimably enhanced" (ibid.).

The bulk of this church service to destroy faith consists of the exposure of those who come to testify that they constitute "the right man" who will lead Hadleyburg to greater fame. Suggesting interchangeability and conformity is a similarity of names: Cox, Wilcox, Wilson, Billson. The latter two, anticipating hearing their names, stand simultaneously, each with "head meekly bowed" (ibid.), as Burgess opens and reads one of the letters he holds. Seeing Billson first, the crowd, knowing him, cannot believe he, although identified as "Deacon Billson," would be generous to a stranger. In control now, perhaps Burgess deliberately opens the envelope of someone people would disbelieve to cast immediate doubt. Although Burgess seems "paralyzed" and looks "vacantly" at each man in turn (ibid.), he knows he holds envelopes from each, and from 17 others as well, that must prove their corruptibility. When first Wilson, then Billson, accuses the other of stealing the remark, each symbolically accuses himself (and the other 19ers). After hearing the "hell or Hadleyburg" test remark, slandering the town (hinting at but not yet revealing the hoax), the congregation grants itself absolution: ". . . the audience considered itself officially absolved from all restraint . . ." (ibid.) and, led by Halliday, laughs uproariously, but still yearning for a "right man," or at least a symbolic one, after an extra word discredits Billson's remark, it eagerly accepts Wilson: ". . . three cheers for Mr. Wilson, Symbol . . . of Incorruptibility" (ibid.). Burgess, however, must open all the envelopes before the final one from the stranger.

With each repetition of the remark, signed by a different 19er, the crowd becomes more excited, shouting, "Pile up the Symbols!" collectively creating a song (a celebratory hymn to corruptibility, relief from the pressure of incorruptibility), turning the initial eight words of the remark into a "resemblance of a well-known church chant" (ibid.). After the protesting 19ers are told to sit down and shut up, Burgess stops the Richardses from confessing and pleading: "this town *does* know you two; it *does* like you; it *does* respect you; more—it honors you and *loves* you. . . . but this is not a time for the exercise of charity toward offenders. . . . I see your generous purpose . . . but I cannot allow you to plead for these men—" (ibid.). The town—as with the laughter and singing, led by Halliday—enthusiastically concurs and, after Burgess withholds the 19th envelope ("Oh, bless God, we are saved!"), assents to a proposal "that Richards be elected sole Guardian and Symbol of the now Sacred Hadley-

burg Tradition" (ibid.). With one couple (ironically) saved, the sermon—the stranger's long P.S. read by Burgess—follows; the gist is that "the weakest of all things is a virtue which has not been tested in the fire . . ." (ibid.). As no "benediction" accompanied the nonexistent remark (part 4), so none ends this service, for no good is to follow, but it does contain an offertory, the auction, and ends with the song/hymn, chant, and exaggerated "amen" created by the congregation. The sack is shown to contain gilded disks; the stranger (disguised), not knowing his possible partner has protected one, proposes the auction, to be conducted by Halliday, and directs Burgess to give $1,500 to Richards, with more to follow. Richards, who had told himself he had saved Goodson's soul to justify receiving the reward, gets the money when he is saved.

Burgess

Burgess, the ex-minister who saves him, both gains and loses from his involvement. He momentarily recovers his congregation, as well as the rest of the town, and leads the service. His revenge is public exposure of those responsible for his ouster. With the town covertly unchanged, true reform may not occur, but change in its public perception does. Loss of its arrogance, pride, and superiority is also a gain. Additionally, Burgess holds momentary power over these people, who are appropriately humiliated and shamed before him and the town, and at last he receives public acceptance; however, he receives no pardon, proof of his innocence, or any type of exoneration. Neither a permanent church nor actual reform is in the offing. He desires Richards's friendship and loses it forever through his generosity, because Richards, enduring many temptations, misinterprets his actions. Not only does he not pay his debt to Richards but Richards slanders him, and he loses some of his regained trust and status when the town learns he lied.

The Richardses become paranoid. Initially thinking Burgess has lost his envelope, Richards also believes Providence is against him. The bank clerk, who "bowed his head" (ibid.) at home after the meeting, no longer trusts himself with money. The phrase from the P.S. about the necessity of virtues being "tested in the fire" (part 3) now reverberates. Richards sees tests, temptations, and traps everywhere. Fearful of the money, sensing accusation in the stranger's note saying he deserves it, and distrustful of Burgess's note expressing gratefulness and telling of the withheld envelope, he puts all "in the fire" (part 4). The "fire" also represents his hell: "They came from Satan. I saw the hell-brand on them . . . they were sent to betray me to sin" (ibid.). As he earlier, like the other 19, imagined how he would spend the money, allowing those dreams to dictate his life, he now imagines slights and betrayals. Seeing Burgess turn without nodding, he believes he holds the envelope over his head, for Burgess must have guessed, or was told by their servant from an overheard conversation, that Richards could have cleared him. After betraying himself in his sleep, he calls for Burgess, the minister, to hear his confession, but in it, he falsely accuses Burgess of saving, then exposing, him; in the cruelest irony, he forgives Burgess and dies before Burgess, wronged again, can explain. His reputation, like the town's, sullied once more, Burgess can do nothing this time in rectification.

Circumstantial evidence that Burgess might be an accomplice in the corruption plan is strong. Other than ironic purposes, religious allusions seemingly point to the only identified man of the cloth, who is prominent in the plot. He had wanted to repay Richards for warning him and saving him from harm, but he did not know that Richards knew he was innocent and could clear him; he is also unprepared for what guilt does to Richards. He may have given the stranger helpful information about the 19 and steered him to Richards, assuming Richards would react honestly, trapping the 18 when they responded as they did and getting the money promised to those who did not succumb. As accomplice, he was charged with gathering the envelopes, forcing the 18 to face him as they revealed their greed. Whether or not he knew the falsity of the samaritan story or the slugs, with the second envelope received, Burgess would have known that Hadleyburg had fallen. He might have hoped that Richards would receive the reward when the others revealed their true selves, as he—knowing them personally— likely guessed they would, but after he realized

that Richards, old and poor, had yielded, he prepared the town to accept Richards as "the right man" by interrupting his confession with kind words. Town sympathy for Richards, evidently the most respected of the 19, and his humility led to his acceptance as the one.

But Burgess's withholding the envelope costs him and Richards. The weight of guilt breaks the Richardses, culminating in almost simultaneous deaths. Burgess could not truly save him, as Hadleyburg could not truly be saved. Burgess may have entered the scheme for repayment, revenge, retribution, redemption, and/or reform; he gets revenge but little else. With or without Burgess, the town loses its reputation but does not learn the lesson the loss teaches, for it hides behind another name untold to the reader. It, and its hypocrisy, could be that of any small American town.

Critical Commentary by John H. Davis

CHARACTERS AND RELATED ENTRIES

Burgess, Reverend Character in "The Man That Corrupted Hadleyburg." A pastor without a congregation, Burgess is reviled for some unnamed offense that Hadleyburgers think he once committed. Only Edward Richards knows Burgess to be innocent. Richards lacks the courage to clear Burgess's name but once saved him from being run out of town, leaving Burgess pathetically grateful. In the story's ironic conclusion, Burgess tries to repay Richards by saving him and his wife from public humiliation, only to have Richards destroy his reputation anew with his incoherent paranoid babbling before he dies. Fred Gwynne plays Burgess in the 1980 television adaptation of this story.

Goodson, Barclay Background figure in "The Man That Corrupted Hadleyburg." A bitter man, reviled for laughing at Hadleyburg's reputation for honesty, Goodson died six months before the story begins. His passing is a key to the plot: When people learn that a fortune will be awarded to whichever Hadleyburg man once gave an anonymous stranger $20, Goodson is the only person the townspeople can imagine having done such a thing. Goodson's inability to claim the reward tempts all the hypocrites in town to step forward to pretend that they were the unknown benefactor.

Hadleyburg Fictional town in "The Man That Corrupted Hadleyburg" (1899) whose residents take pride in their incorruptibility. After a stranger's vengeful scheme destroys the town's reputation, the residents adopt a new name that is not revealed. Aside from the fact that Hadleyburg is near a town called "Brixton," its location is not specified. Real-life models that have been suggested for the arrogant town include FREDONIA, New York. The story equates "Hadleyburg" with "hell"; it is possibly a play on HEIDELBERG, Germany, which Clemens also called hell. Alternatively, it may have been inspired by Hannibal, which Clemens once called "H—l."

Whatever "Hadleyburg's" origin, it in turn clearly inspired the name of the town in the 1952 western film *High Noon*, in which Gary Cooper plays a lawman who single-handedly defends a smugly arrogant town against outlaws when its leading citizens abandon him. An early scene shows a sign revealing the town's name to be "Hadleyville." "Hadleyburg" is also the name of the western town in which Gregory Peck is the marshal in the film *Mackenna's Gold* (1969). Like Clemens's town, Peck's Hadleyburg is full of hypocrites.

Harkness, Dr. Clay Minor character in "The Man That Corrupted Hadleyburg." Harkness is a wealthy patent-medicine man and corrupt politician. In order to ensure his election to the state legislature, he buys a notorious bag of gilt slugs and has the name of his rival, PINKERTON, printed on them, along with a slogan that destroys Pinkerton's reputation. The narrator signals his contempt for Harkness by placing quotation marks around his "Dr." title on every mention.

Pinkerton Minor character in "The Man That Corrupted Hadleyburg." A stingy banker and the employer of Edward Richards, Pinkerton is one of the leading citizens whose dishonesty is exposed. His bid for election to the state legislature is smashed when his rival, "Dr." Clay Harkness, has his name and a humiliating slogan stamped on the gilt slugs with which his shame is associated.

Richards, Edward Character in "The Man That Corrupted Hadleyburg." Though impoverished, the elderly bank clerk and his wife, Mary, count themselves among Hadleyburg's 19 leading families and take great pride in their community's spotless reputation for honesty. The story opens with a stranger leaving a bag of gold in the Richardses' care, with instructions to deliver the money to an unnamed man who once did him a kindness. The Richardses are so tempted by this wealth that they steadily compromise their honesty in order to lay a claim to it. At the climax of the story, their dishonesty is about to be publicly exposed, along with that of all the other greedy hypocrites, when the Reverend Burgess silently saves them from exposure. The Richardses feel guilty about both their own hypocrisy and Richards's cowardly failure to clear Burgess of false scandal charges many years earlier. Their guilt mounts when the townspeople propose rewarding them for being honest; even the original stranger seeks to reward them. Guilt turns to paranoia that drives them mad and kills them with nervous exhaustion.

BIBLIOGRAPHY

Rule, Henry B. "The Role of Satan in 'The Man That Corrupted Hadleyburg.' " *Studies in Short Fiction VI* (Fall 1968): 619–629.

Twain, Mark. "The Man That Corrupted Hadleyburg." In *The Best Short Stories of Mark Twain*, edited by Lawrence Berkove, 130–171. New York: Modern Library, 2004.

"The Man Who Put Up at Gadsby's"

FRAME-STORY told within chapter 26 of *A Tramp Abroad* (1880). Watching people patiently fish at LUCERNE prompts the narrator to recall an incident he witnessed in WASHINGTON, D.C., in the winter of 1867. He was walking on Pennsylvania Avenue with (JOHN H.) RILEY on a stormy night when a man named Lykins rushed up to ask Riley for help pushing through his application for San Francisco's vacant postmaster position. Armed with a 200-signature petition, Lykins expected to wrap up the whole matter in one day. Riley, however, cornered him and told him about the man who put up at Gadsby's:

> Back in [President ANDREW] JACKSON's time, when Gadsby's was Washington's principal hotel, a Tennessee man came to Washington expecting to collect a small claim against the government. He arrived with a coachman, a splendid four-horse carriage and an elegant dog. At Gadsby's, he told his coachman merely to wait for him, since his claim would not take long. Late that evening, however, he ordered a bed. It was January 3, 1834. On February 5, he sold his carriage and bought a cheaper one. On August 11, he sold two horses. On December 13, he sold another horse. On February 17, 1835, he replaced the carriage with a buggy. On August 1, he swapped the buggy for an old sulky and on August 29, he sold his coachman. On February 15, 1837, he sold the sulky and got a saddle. On April 9, he sold the saddle, saying that bareback riding was safer. On April 24, he sold his horse, saying that at 57 he was better off walking. On June 22, he sold his dog.

When Lykins pressed Riley to know what happened next, Riley replied that the Tennessean still saw him daily and still expected to get his claim through soon. When Lykins failed to grasp the story's point, Riley advised him to consider putting up at Gadsby's himself, then turned on his heel and disappeared.

Clemens originally wrote this story for the VIRGINIA CITY TERRITORIAL ENTERPRISE in February 1868, when he was working in Washington, D.C., and was beginning to appreciate the slowness with which the federal government operated. Around the same time, he also published "THE FACTS CONCERNING THE RECENT RESIGNATION," a thematically similar story. Clemens revised the Gadsby story as a last-minute addition to *A Tramp Abroad.* He later introduced the "New Gadsby" hotel as the Washington hotel in which Lord Berkeley and One-Armed Pete stay in *The American Claimant* (1892). The hotel burns down in chapter 7.

"Marienbad—A Health Factory"

ESSAY published in the *NEW YORK SUN* on February 7, 1892. In late August 1891, Clemens spent about two weeks in the Bohemian health resort Mariánské Lázne (Marienbad in German), near the western tip of what is now the CZECH REPUBLIC. His essay describes the scenic splendor of the western approach to the town, but finds little else about Marienbad to praise. Put off by cold and wet weather, rude residents, and visitors who talk only about their ailments, Clemens rues the fact that the town's springs, which are famous for curing gout, rheumatism, leanness, fatness, dyspepsia, and other ailments, cannot cure poor manners. The essay is collected in *EUROPE AND ELSEWHERE,* in which A. B. PAINE omitted a passage containing a burlesque love poem about a liver ailment. CHARLES NEIDER restored the missing passage in *The Complete Essays of Mark Twain* (1963).

Mark Twain in Eruption: Hitherto Unpublished Pages About Men and Events (1940)

Extracts from Mark Twain's AUTOBIOGRAPHY. Acting on instructions from the Mark Twain Estate and HARPER'S, BERNARD DEVOTO reviewed the typescripts from which A. B. PAINE had extracted *Mark Twain's Autobiography* (1924) in order to determine what omitted materials merited publication. After calculating that Paine had used only about half of the original typescript text, DeVoto selected about half from what remained to assemble *Mark Twain in Eruption.*

Since he was commissioned to construct a book for general readers, not scholars, DeVoto selected what he regarded as the most interesting passages in Clemens's unpublished typescripts, as well as material that Clemens had published in the *NORTH AMERICAN REVIEW.* He omitted portions he regarded as "irrelevant or uninteresting" and excluded some of Clemens's most excessive personal tirades against individual people.

In contrast to Paine's edition of the *Autobiography*, DeVoto arranged the text of *Mark Twain in Eruption* topically, joining passages on related subjects without regard to their original dates of dictation—which governed Paine's organization. He then divided the material into nine sections, titled "Theodore Roosevelt," "Andrew Carnegie," "The Plutocracy," "Hannibal Day," "Two Halos," "In a Writer's Workshop," "Various Literary People," "The Last Visit to England," and "Miscellany." These sections he broke into numbered subsections.

While the subject matter of *Mark Twain's Autobiography* and *Mark Twain in Eruption* often overlaps, the latter book tends to discuss more recent events and people whom Clemens knew in his later years—especially politicians, businessmen, and publishers. Among the people receiving the most attention are Thomas Bailey Aldrich and his wife, Elisha Bliss, Andrew Carnegie, Montana's Senator William A. Clark, Jim Gillis, novelist Elinor Glyn, Jay Gould, U. S. Grant, Bret Harte, John D. Rockefeller, Theodore Roosevelt, Dick Stoker, Bayard Taylor, Joseph Twichell, Ned Wakeman, Charles H. Webb, Charles L. Webster, and Jim Wolfe. The volume also includes illuminating remarks about the composition of "Captain Stormfield's Visit to Heaven," *1601*, and *Connecticut Yankee*.

After DeVoto prepared his manuscript in early 1940, Clara Clemens objected to passages that she feared would offend relatives of people whom Clemens criticized severely. DeVoto resisted her objections, arguing that Clemens himself wrote the passages with the intention that they would eventually be published. An occasionally acrimonious dispute ensued (parts of which are documented in Wallace Stegner's 1975 edition of *The Letters of Bernard DeVoto*), but Harper's published DeVoto's manuscript with few substantive changes.

Mark Twain's Autobiography

See Autobiography, Clemens's.

Mark Twain's (Burlesque) Autobiography and First Romance

See Burlesque Autobiography, Mark Twain's.

Mark Twain's Fables of Man

See Fables of Man, Mark Twain's.

Mark Twain's Hannibal, Huck & Tom

See Hannibal, Huck & Tom, Mark Twain's.

Mark Twain's Notebook (1935)

Condensation of Clemens's Notebooks and Journals published by Harper's. Drawing selectively on Clemens's notebooks, A. B. Paine rearranged the material into 35 roughly chronological chapters. His brief introduction states that the notebooks "are now offered in full," but the 120,000-word volume actually contains less than a quarter of Clemens's original notebook text. After Bernard DeVoto succeeded Paine as the Clemens Estate's editor, he intended to publish an expanded edition, but never got around to it. In 1975, the Mark Twain Papers began issuing an uncut edition that supersedes Paine's. Since the new edition's first three volumes cover only 1855–1891, *Mark Twain's Notebook* retains some value, as it includes material recorded through 1906. Chapters 22–27 cover Clemens's round-the-world lecture tour of 1895–96 that led to *Following the Equator*, and chapters 27–32 and 34 cover his last years in Europe. In 2001, all the notebooks became available to researchers when the Mark Twain Project published them in a microfilm edition.

Mark Twain's Own Autobiography (1990)

First book publication of Clemens's AUTOBIOGRA-PHY to follow the original arrangement of chapters he published in the *NORTH AMERICAN REVIEW* in 1906–07. Published by the University of Wisconsin Press in 1990, this new edition contains an introduction and notes by Michael J. Kiskis, as well as appendixes summarizing the content of the various editions of the autobiography and a thorough index. Its title reflects the fact that its 25 chapters are the only parts of Clemens's autobiography that he himself prepared for publication.

Mark Twain's Pleasure Trip on the Continent

Title of an unauthorized British edition of *Innocents Abroad* (1869) that was published in London by JOHN CAMDEN HOTTEN in 1871.

Mark Twain's Satires and Burlesques

See SATIRES & BURLESQUES, MARK TWAIN'S.

Mark Twain's Sketches, New and Old

See SKETCHES, NEW AND OLD, MARK TWAIN'S.

Mark Twain's Travels with Mr. Brown (1940)

Collection of 26 travel letters that Clemens wrote to the SAN FRANCISCO ALTA CALIFORNIA between December 20, 1866, and June 6, 1867. The letters cover his voyage from California to the East Coast, residence in NEW YORK CITY, and LECTURE tour in the Midwest. Franklin Walker and G. Ezra Dane edited and lightly annotated the volume, which was published in 1940. The "Mr. Brown" of the title is a fictitious companion whom Clemens created in his earlier letters from HAWAII.

These dispatches, also known as Clemens's "American Travel Letters," originally appeared in the *Alta* between January 18 and August 18, 1867. They link the period immediately after his Hawaii letters with that of his *QUAKER CITY* letters. Most of them he wrote from New York, which he was visiting for the first time since 1853. Highlights include his first meeting with Captain NED WAKEMAN ("Waxman" in the letters); crossing NICARAGUA; observing CHOLERA aboard the steamship *SAN FRANCISCO*; and his return to Missouri after five years. They also comment on his preparation of *THE CELEBRATED JUMPING FROG OF CALAVERAS COUNTY* for publication, his lecture at New York's Cooper Union, a chance encounter with Jefferson DAVIS, and preparations for the *Quaker City* voyage.

CHARACTERS AND RELATED ENTRIES

Brown, Mr.   Character in several series of travel letters that Clemens wrote during the 1860s. "Brown" first appears in Clemens's letters from HAWAII to the *SACRAMENTO UNION* in 1866, in which he is called "a bitter enemy of sentiment." Brown does not appear in the *ROUGHING IT* (1872) chapters drawn from the Hawaii letters, but briefly resurfaces as "Mr. Billings" in chapters 69 and 73.

"Brown" next appears in the letters to the *SAN FRANCISCO ALTA CALIFORNIA* that Clemens wrote during his journeys from California to New York and through the Midwest, from December 1866 to June 1867. These letters have been published as *Mark Twain's Travels with Mr. Brown* (1940).

Clemens used "Brown" in his early letters to the *Alta* from his *QUAKER CITY* cruise, which began in June 1867, but gradually lost interest in the character. Brown disappeared completely when Clemens revised the letters for *Innocents Abroad* (1869). Of 22 references to "Brown" in the original *Alta* letters, 15 are cut completely, five are attributed to a character named "Blucher" and two are attributed to a character named "Jack" (Van Nostrand). One omitted passage, for example, concerns Brown's problems identifying water closets in Paris.

Throughout all these letters, "Brown" is a foil who allows Clemens to say things that he might hesitate to utter in his narrators' voices. In one *Alta* letter, for example, when the narrator comments on the voluptuousness of young women in NICARAGUA, Brown tastelessly interjects that the women are "heifers." Apologizing for Brown's intrusion, the narrator explains that Brown "always unearths the disagreeable features of everything that comes under his notice."

"Brown" may have been partly inspired by William Brown, an irascible steamboat pilot under whom Clemens served in 1858. This man appears as "Mr. Brown" in "OLD TIMES ON THE MISSISSIPPI" (1876) and in early chapters of *Life on the Mississippi* (1883). Like Clemens's imaginary travel companion, WILLIAM BROWN combined total recall with an inability to discriminate between important and unimportant facts. The name may also be a playful reference to Clemens's friend JOHN ROSS BROWNE.

Chapter 52 of *Life on the Mississippi* also mentions another, apparently unrelated "Mr. Brown"; this man is the fictitious St. Louis benefactor of an ex-convict who writes a moving letter to Charlie Williams.

Mark Twain's Which Was the Dream?

See WHICH WAS THE DREAM? AND OTHER SYMBOLIC WRITINGS OF THE LATER YEARS, MARK TWAIN'S.

massacre hoax

On October 28, 1863, Clemens published a 750-word article in the VIRGINIA CITY TERRITORIAL ENTERPRISE titled "A Bloody Massacre near Car-

son." A complete HOAX about a man brutally murdering most of his large family, it was later reprinted under a variety of titles, including "The Dutch Nick Massacre," "The Empire City Massacre," and "The Latest Sensation." Like the PETRIFIED MAN hoax, this hoax is not mentioned in *Roughing It* (1872).

SYNOPSIS

According to ABRAM CURRY (a real person), a man named P. or Philip Hopkins, who lived on the edge of the pine forest between Empire City and Dutch Nick's, rode into CARSON (City) with a bloody scalp in his hand and his own throat slit from ear to ear. After five minutes without speaking, he dropped dead in front of the Magnolia Saloon. Sheriff Gasherie (a real person) immediately led a party out to Hopkins's house, where they found the butchered remains of his wife and seven of his children. Two daughters survived to explain what happened.

After massacring his family and slitting his own throat, Hopkins rides into Carson City holding a bloody scalp in this illustration drawn by True Williams for *Sketches, New and Old.*

Hopkins was known to be affable and nonviolent, but his temperament began changing when his investments went bad. He sold off his shares in local mines after reading in SAN FRANCISCO papers about dividend-cooking games played by their managers, then invested heavily in San Francisco's Spring Valley Water Company on the advice of a SAN FRANCISCO BULLETIN editor. Over the previous two months, his wife had expressed fears concerning his sanity, but no one paid her any heed. It is presumed that he went mad when his stocks failed. The tragedy was thus a product of the newspapers' failure to report on the company's dishonest management.

BACKGROUND

Although deliberate hoaxes—such as Clemens's petrified man hoax of the previous year—often appeared in the *Enterprise*, reactions to the massacre hoax were swift and negative. Even as the other papers in northern California were reprinting the story as fact, Clemens published a retraction; however, it satisfied few, leaving his reputation as a reporter seriously damaged. He offered to resign from the *Enterprise* but was turned down by his editor, JOSEPH GOODMAN. Seven years later, Clemens published "My Bloody Massacre" in GALAXY, explaining the original hoax. He claimed that his only purpose was to trick San Francisco papers into printing a criticism of the city's largest water company. Indeed, he argued that the hoax was meant to be a SATIRE showing that Hopkins was driven mad by the losses he suffered in the stock-cooking schemes. "My Bloody Massacre" lists the original article's inherent absurdities. First, the murderer had the name of a man (P. Hopkins) who was widely known to be a bachelor who had no wife or children to murder. Further, not only did the pine forest "between Empire City and Dutch Nick's" not exist; Empire City and Dutch Nick's were one place. Finally, no one with a slashed throat could possibly ride a horse four miles, not to mention survive an additional five minutes.

CHARACTERS AND RELATED ENTRIES

Hopkins, P. (Philip?)   Name of the alleged murderer in Mark Twain's MASSACRE HOAX (1863). Said to be a 42-year-old native of western Pennsylvania, Hopkins supposedly lived near CARSON CITY, Nevada, with a wife and nine children. Though regarded as affable and nonviolent, he went mad after losing his fortune in San Francisco water company stock and brutally murdered most of his family. He then slit his own throat and rode into Carson City, dropping dead in front of the Magnolia Saloon.

In an article published in 1870, Clemens says that the person whose name he used for the alleged murderer in his hoax "was perfectly well known to every creature in the land as a *bachelor*." This remark almost certainly alludes to Peter Hopkins, the real owner of the saloon in front of which the fictional murderer dies. The original hoax lends a note of verisimilitude by feigning confusion over the murderer's name, which is rendered "P. Hopkins, or Philip Hopkins."

McWilliams family stories

Three FRAME-STORIES published between 1875 and 1882. The stories are told by Mortimer McWilliams, a pleasant New York man with a wife and two children whom the frame narrator meets on what appears to be a commuter train. Each story details a crisis in McWilliams's household. Although McWilliams explicitly addresses "Mr. Twain" in two of the stories, the stories themselves reflect incidents in Clemens's own domestic life in Hartford. For example, his daughter Clara had croup as a baby, and his wife Livy greatly feared lightning. As a trilogy, the stories combine to form a subtle joke: the first two concern gross overreactions to false alarms; the third is about an elaborate alarm system that is ignored when real emergencies occur.

"McWilliams" was the name of a recently married couple who lived in the same boardinghouse as Clemens when he first lived in BUFFALO in 1869. He later used the name Sandy McWilliams for a character in "CAPTAIN STORMFIELD'S VISIT TO HEAVEN" (1909).

"Experience of the McWilliamses with Membranous Croup" (1875) relates how McWilliams got into a mild argument with his wife Caroline (called Evangeline in the next story) over her giving their baby Penelope a pine stick to chew. When McWilliams returned home that evening, his wife reported that another baby named Georgie Gordon had contracted the croup and had little hope of survival. When Penelope coughed, Mrs. McWilliams panicked and launched an extraordinary night of shifting sleeping arrangements around in order to watch over Penelope and protect their infant son (not named) from the croup. When a doctor finally came, he diagnosed Penelope's cough as due to pine slivers in her throat. Since then, McWilliams and his wife have never discussed the incident. The frame-narrator (not identified in this story) adds that readers might find McWilliams's experience an interesting novelty, since very few married men have similar experiences.

This 2,440-word story first appeared in Sketches, New and Old (1875) and was reprinted in Mark Twain's Library of Humor (1888). *Connecticut Yankee* (1889) details the lengths to which Hank and Sandy Morgan go to protect their daughter Hello-Central from membranous croup (chapter 40).

"Mrs. McWilliams and the Lightning" (1880) expands the BURLESQUE of exaggerated fear of lightning begun in "POLITICAL ECONOMY" (1870). During his train ride with the frame-narrator, Mr. Twain, McWilliams describes a night at their "summer establishment" (presumably ELMIRA) when Evangeline awakened him during a storm, demanding that he protect his family against lightning. Evangeline believed that during a lightning storm it is dangerous to lie in bed, stand near a window or a wall, open a door, sing a song, or run water. She also thought that lighted matches, woolen clothes, and open chimneys attract lightning; that it is vital to say one's prayers before a storm; and that cats are full of electricity. After struggling to decipher a GERMAN book, she made McWilliams stand on a chair set on glass tumblers, while wearing a metal fireman's helmet, saber, and spurs, and ringing a bell to ward off lightning. Passersby who shone a lantern through their window to learn what the racket was about revealed that what the McWilliamses thought was a storm was actually distant fireworks celebrating (President James) GARFIELD's nomination (June 8, 1880).

This 2,555-word story was first published in the ATLANTIC MONTHLY in September 1880 and was later collected in *The Stolen White Elephant, Etc.* and in *The American Claimant and Other Stories and Sketches.*

The final story, "The McWilliamses and the Burglar Alarm" (1882), is inspired by Clemens's experience with an unreliable electric alarm system in his own home. His AUTOBIOGRAPHY contains a passage written by his daughter Susy about this system. His autobiography also relates the problems of a neighbor, Francis Goodwin, with his burglar alarm. Many details, such as Goodwin's cook setting off the alarm early in the morning, closely match details in the McWilliams story. In contrast to the first two stories, the crises in "Burglar Alarm" are real and are partly due to McWilliams's own incompetence.

With money left over from building their house (which physically resembles Clemens's Hartford house), Mrs. McWilliams insisted on installing a burglar alarm. After a New York electrician installed a system on the house's first floor, McWilliams met a burglar who entered through the *second* floor. He had the system extended to the second floor, only to meet a burglar who entered through the third-floor BILLIARD room. After the system covered the entire house, the family and domestic staff were often confused about turning it on and off and they experienced a rash of false alarms. As McWilliams pumped ever more money into improving the system, burglars gradually cleaned out his house and then stole the burglar alarm itself. After nine years of suffering, McWilliams gave up.

This 2,350-word story first appeared in the 1882 Christmas issue of HARPER'S MAGAZINE. It was first collected in the posthumous volume *The Mysterious Stranger and Other Stories* (1922).

CRITICAL COMMENTARY

Clemens had been married five years when the first McWilliams story appeared. Settling into married life and becoming more prosperous, he now had enough perspective to write a series of stories recounting the problems of domestic life faced, first, by a young married couple, then by a couple accustomed to each other's traits and peculiarities, and finally, by a couple married for more than a decade. Domestic comedy was a new genre for Clemens. In these stories, the husband, Mortimer, relates to an acquaintance, sometimes identified as Mark Twain, the latest ordeal he and his wife have experienced. Typically, he is the victim of some notion held by Mrs. McWilliams, named Caroline in the first story and Evangeline in the others, and his remarks, usually subtle sarcasms, are the main source of humor. He has been considered a model for a henpecked husband, but he is better described as a man who does his best under trying circumstances; rather than feeling pity or condescension, the reader tends to admire him because of his attitude and his wit. The narrative method also helps create this viewpoint. In these stories, husband and wife unsuccessfully confront sickness, nature, and technology but grow closer as a couple.

Whereas traditional comedy ends with a marriage, domestic comedy begins in marriage. Mortimer is reasonable, but his logic is futile before his wife's declarations about illness or acts of God, and both husband and wife are helpless before machinery. Though proven factually right, Mortimer never gains the upper hand, as he mildly applies logic to his wife's illogic and fits her responses into the discussion as though they are not silly. Even in the absurd third story, Mortimer remains calm under the circumstances; Evangeline, who suggested they buy the burglar alarm, suffers, too, and supports him. She now complements, rather than clashes with, her husband. The two are not simply people whose differences cause dispute, but a unit.

The movement toward closer intimacy is the pattern of the stories. Domestic comedy is associated with sexism, but using the same framework in each story, Clemens softens the sexism as he manipulates readers' perceptions of the protagonists. About upwardly mobile middle-class homeowners, these stories always begin in medias res, with Mortimer, obviously a commuter, on a train telling an acquaintance the latest whimsicality of his wife. Such tales shared by men imply sexist motivations, but Mortimer's deadpan humor and his ability to laugh at himself counter that implication. His wife may unintentionally position him as the butt of ridiculous situations, but he calculat-ingly positions himself as he tells the story. Clemens's storytelling method grants McWilliams the power to modify character perceptions, to control situations, and to affect readers' reactions.

The author alters the traditional framework by using Mortimer as an interior narrator and Clemens as a character who mainly listens. Seen from the third person, Mortimer would appear ridiculous, but by telling his own story to a sympathetic auditor and to readers, he becomes sympathetic. He is self-effacing, aware of ludicrous incidents and his own ludicrousness, a man more put upon than putting on. He presents himself as a reasonable man in unreasonable circumstances who applies logic and seeks sense in nonsense; failing, he adjusts to the situation by using irony and sarcasm, delivered in deadpan expression, as though he recognizes no abnormality. After questioning his daughter's chewing a pine stick and his wife's declaring pine healthful with "she *shall* chew it, too. So there, now!'" he responds, "I now see the force of your reasoning, and I will go and order two or three cords of the best pine wood. . . . No child of mine shall want." Breaking the expected framework pattern, Clemens also breaks from the West, a major source of inspiration; signaling acceptance of eastern ways and an area for new material, the inside speaker is not a westerner, like Simon Wheeler or Jim Baker, but an easterner. The framework establishes distances, permitting Mortimer to see himself as others do and readers to see through his eyes that they would be just as ineffectual against irrationality.

The extent to which the irrationality portrayed in the story is sexist is modified by Mortimer's exaggerating the details (again, his storytelling technique), which puts common human foibles in perspective. He descends into absurdity so that both sexes appear irrational; in doing so, he also assumes a pompous stance that reduces sympathy for him. Mortimer acquiesces to his wife's claims in "Lightning" to the point that he is complicitous. Even shared sexism fades as they become equals in the last story.

In each story, Mortimer's involvement increases. He is almost an innocent bystander pulled, protesting, into the first story. In the second, he offers little resistance to donning the outfit she prescribes, becoming a spectacle after they learn that the "lightning" is celebratory cannon fire. Her concerns cause him to buy the alarm system; there, gender distinctions end. In "Croup," he does not go beyond irony, despite private gloating at the end; in "Lightning," he uses irony, reason, sarcasm, and profanity but participates by mistranslating German rules about thunderstorms and following Evangeline's directions to avoid attracting electricity. Finally, in "Burglar Alarm," the two are partners in suffering, though Mortimer barters for their goods with burglars, shoots a nurse, and is shot by the coachman. By the last story, little conflict exists between them. The McWilliamses are defending their home together against a situation both of them have created.

Mortimer's acquiescence suggests he is henpecked, but he presents himself as a vulnerable man knowing he is vulnerable, marching into the fray nonetheless. His weapons are wit, irony, and a seeming inability to realize he possesses either. Each story builds to a comic climax toward which he perseveres. By remaining calm, he triumphs, or appears to. His main appeal is that he laughs at himself; the humor derives from his reactions. Mortimer is an everyman struggling to cope with a world that becomes more perplexing after marriage. He meets its challenges by recognizing life's absurdities, acknowledging them, and joining forces with his wife.

Readers witness the McWilliamses coping with their children's illness and other events that reveal chinks in marital armor. Mortimer questions Evangeline's parenting skills; she blames a storm on his not saying his prayers. She had said Providence foreordained the croup because "We have not been living as we ought to live." However, balancing her concern for his soul is his concern for her as a young mother and as a wife fearful of a storm. They change from a couple beginning to know each other, seeing previously minor defects, to one learning to live with another's flaws but trying to change them. They finally emerge as a couple, still disturbed by flaws, still encountering conflicts, mainly external, but accepting each other more fully, flaws included—a growth from young love to mature, stable love. The author writes in his notebook, "Love seems the swiftest, but it is the slowest of all growths. No man or woman really knows what perfect love is until they have been married a quarter of a century." Loving and staying together during trials are as much the point of the stories as the humor.

The McWilliamses's maturation into a solid couple with servants and a three-story home is a comment on the development and materialism of the American middle class that seeks ways to dispose of its excess income. This aspect, the incidents in the stories, the husband-wife exchanges, even the fascination with the latest gadgets, reflect the writer's own life, as does the evolution of a marriage into a stable, mature relationship. In the end, Mortimer and Evangeline are content.

Critical Commentary by John H. Davis

BIBLIOGRAPHY

Gibson, William M., ed. "Introduction." In *The Mysterious Stranger* by Mark Twain, 1–34. Berkeley: University of California Press, 1970.

Twain, Mark. "Experience of the McWilliamses with Membranous Croup"; "Mrs. McWilliams and the Lightning"; The McWilliamses and the Burglar Alarm." In *The Complete Short Stories of Mark Twain,* edited by Charles Neider, 99–104; 153–159; 193–198. New York: Doubleday, 1957.

———. *Mark Twain's Notebook,* edited by Albert Bigelow Paine. New York: Harper, 1935.

"A Medieval Romance"

Written in 1869 and published in 1870, this story is a condensed novel of 2,640 words in five chapters. It BURLESQUES romance novels by piling on improbabilities that build to a bizarre dilemma, only to end suddenly as a literary HOAX that refuses to resolve itself. Its central theme is confused sexual identities, which Clemens explored again in "1,002D ARABIAN NIGHT" 14 years later.

The story first appeared as "An Awful Terrible Medieval Romance" in the BUFFALO EXPRESS on

January 1, 1870. The following year Clemens republished it in his BURLESQUE AUTOBIOGRAPHY. It was later collected in SKETCHES, NEW AND OLD.

SYNOPSIS

Chapter 1

In the year 1222, the old German Baron Klugenstein secretly consults with his 28-year-old daughter, "Conrad," whom he has raised as a son. Klugenstein tells Conrad that his own father decreed that the ducal succession would pass to his house if he had a son and his brother Ulrich, the great Duke of Brandenburgh, did not. However, if both men had only daughters, the succession would pass to Ulrich's daughter—provided that she proved stainless. Klugenstein explains that when Conrad was born, he hanged every servant who witnessed her birth, then proclaimed that she was his *son*. Ten years later, Ulrich finally had a daughter named Constance.

Now aged and feeble, Ulrich wants his "nephew" Conrad to come and govern his duchy until "he" can succeed. Klugenstein warns Conrad not to sit in the great ducal chair before she is crowned, since any uncrowned female who sits there must die. Though Conrad objects to cheating her cousin out of her birthright, she reluctantly goes. Afterward, Klugenstein tells his wife that he sent the handsome Count Detzin on a devilish mission to Constance three months earlier. If Detzin has succeeded, Conrad will become *duchess;* if he has failed, Conrad should still become *duke.*

Chapter 2

Six days later, Brandenburgh celebrates Conrad's coming—at the same moment that a distraught Constance curses Detzin for leaving her ruined.

Chapter 3

As months drift by, everyone praises Conrad's wise and merciful government, but Conrad is dismayed by Constance's romantic attentions. When Constance professes her love, Conrad spurns her.

Chapter 4

As more time passes, Conrad and Constance are no longer seen together and Conrad brightens. Meanwhile, rumors sweep the palace that Constance has had a baby. When Klugenstein hears this, he rejoices and praises Detzin.

Chapter 5

Conrad must reluctantly sit in judgment when Constance goes on trial for having a child out of wedlock—for which death is the penalty. Conrad stands up to pass sentence, but the justice insists that Conrad speak from the ducal throne, which Conrad reluctantly ascends. When Conrad asks Constance to name her child's father, she points at Conrad, saying "Thou art the man!" Conrad is helpless. To disprove the charge, Conrad must reveal that she is a woman, then be condemned for sitting on the throne. Her father swoons. Unable to get Conrad out of this dilemma, the narrator abandons the story.

"The Memorable Assassination"

Posthumously published ESSAY. On September 10, 1898, while Clemens was in KALTENLEUTGEBEN, an Italian anarchist named Luigi Lucheni fatally stabbed AUSTRIA's Empress Elizabeth (1837–1898) in Geneva, Switzerland. Deeply moved by the incident, Clemens wrote this 4,000-word essay after seeing the empress's funeral in VIENNA a week later. After several American magazines rejected the essay, it was set aside until A. B. PAINE included it in WHAT IS MAN? AND OTHER ESSAYS in 1917. Paine's edition of MARK TWAIN'S NOTEBOOK (1935) has additional notes on the empress's funeral (chapter 31).

SYNOPSIS

Calling the murder of an empress the "largest of all events," Clemens says that one must go back to Julius CAESAR to find an instance of similar magnitude. Even Caesar's death, however, is not comparable, since the world has grown so much larger and the TELEGRAPH now spreads news so quickly. Indeed, this is the first time in history that the entire world has instantaneously learned of so gigantic an event.

A common form of madness is the desire to be noticed—which helps explain why a mangy Italian tramp committed this murder. In one instant, he lifted himself from obscurity to immortality by striking down a woman who led a blameless and noble life.

The essay concludes with a detailed description of the empress's state funeral.

"A Memorable Midnight Experience"

Sketch first published in *Number One: Mark Twain's Sketches* (1874). In mid-1873, Clemens visited ENGLAND intending to collect material for a travel book along the lines of *Innocents Abroad* (1869). The only substantial segment that he wrote, however, is this 3,400-word gothic sketch. The novelist CHARLES KINGSLEY, a canon of WESTMINSTER ABBEY, arranged for Clemens to have a special tour of the abbey in June. The resulting sketch's fascination with tombs recalls themes that Clemens explores in writings such as "A CURIOUS DREAM" (1870).

SYNOPSIS

Late one night, a Mr. Wright leads the narrator and his friend through Westminster Abbey, "the tomb of the great dead of England." They examine the graves of such people as CHARLES DICKENS, DAVID GARRICK, Thomas Parr, BEN JONSON, William Pitt, and various royal figures. The narrator gets separated from the others and stumbles in the dark. He touches the cold hand of a reposing queen and is startled by a cat that brushes up against him. As a bell tolls midnight, he sees an illuminated clock through a window.

"Mental Telegraphy"

ESSAY begun in 1878 and finished and first published in 1891. *Mental telegraphy*, a term that Clemens coined, describes a phenomenon similar to what is better known as telepathy—the transference of thoughts from one person to another, often

over immense distances. In the examples that Clemens cites in this essay and elsewhere, this process is usually unconscious. Indeed, his essay raises the question of how many so-called original ideas are unconsciously stolen from others thousands of miles away.

Clemens was always interested in psychic phenomena, and the subject of thought transference appears in a wide variety of his later writings, some of which use the phrase "mental telegraphy." In chapter 34 of *Following the Equator* (1897), for example, he tells how he once planted words in the mind of his wife. Another anecdote appears in his 1906 sketch "A MONUMENT TO ADAM," and he discusses mental telegraphy in several passages of his autobiography. Curiously, however, he seems to dismiss the idea of mental telegraphy in his time-travel novel, *Connecticut Yankee* (1889), even though the book's narrator, Hank Morgan, touches on "transmigration of souls" and "transposition of epochs—and bodies" in the prologue. In chapter 24, Morgan unleashes a scathing attack on a sixth-century magician who claims to divine what great figures are doing at the same moment in other parts of the globe. Morgan shatters the magician's reputation by using information he obtains through modern telephonic communication to prove the magician's description of what King Arthur is doing completely wrong.

SYNOPSIS

"Mental Telegraphy" opens with a comment on Clemens's discovery, about 16 or 17 years earlier, that a number of curious coincidences that he had observed "were no more accidental than is the sending and receiving of a telegram." He goes on to argue that human minds are capable of telegraphing thoughts to one another and cites as an example an experience he had around 1874 or 1875 concerning DAN DE QUILLE's book *The Big Bonanza*. At that time, Clemens thought that the publishing market was ripe for a book about the Nevada silver mines and that the person best qualified to write such a book was his former VIRGINIA CITY TERRITORIAL ENTERPRISE colleague William H. Wright, who wrote as De Quille. By that time, the two men had been out of touch for so long that Clemens did not even know if Wright was still alive. Nevertheless, he wrote a long letter to Wright, presenting his idea for a book and even providing a detailed outline. Before posting the letter, however, he thought he should first secure a publisher for Wright, and he pigeonholed his letter. Three or four days later, he received a letter from Wright that had the same date as his own, unmailed letter. The contents of Wright's letter were virtually the same as those in Clemens's letter. Clemens regards the similarities between his and Wright's letters as being too many and too complex to have occurred by chance and concludes that he mentally "telegraphed" the contents of his own letter to Wright. From that time, Clemens began keeping a record of such occurrences, and he goes on to recount other examples from his own experience and that of others.

BACKGROUND AND PUBLISHING HISTORY

Much of the history of this essay is contained within it. During the early 1880s, Clemens tried to publish an anonymous article on the same subject in the NORTH AMERICAN REVIEW, but the editor rejected the suggestion. Afterward, however, he felt that the public attitude toward psychic phenomena had become more open. The 8,130-word essay first appeared in the December 1891 issue of HARPER'S MAGAZINE. It was reprinted in *The £1,000,000 Bank-Note and Other New Stories* (1893) and in many later collections. Clemens also published a follow-up essay, "Mental Telegraphy Again," in the September 1895 issue of *Harper's*. This 2,540-word essay offers four additional anecdotes about mental telegraphy and makes no attempt at further analysis. One of its anecdotes describes a remarkable exchange of letters that he had with the Australian lecture agent Robert Sparrow SMYTHE, who invited Clemens to undertake an around-the-world lecture tour in 1895. On the recommendation of Henry Morton STANLEY, Clemens sent a letter to Smythe from Paris on February 6, 1895. Three days later, he received a letter on the same subject from Smythe, who had posted it during the previous December. Clemens interpreted his own impulse to write to Smythe as having been prompted by Smythe's letter.

Merry Tales (1892)

Collection of Clemens's short stories published by CHARLES L. WEBSTER & COMPANY in March 1892. This edition contains "THE PRIVATE HISTORY OF A CAMPAIGN THAT FAILED," "LUCK," "A CURIOUS EXPERIENCE," "THE INVALID'S STORY," "The Captain's Story," "Mrs. MCWILLIAMS and the Lightning," and "Meisterschaft." All the items except "Captain's Story" were later published as the second half of the HARPER'S edition, *The American Claimant and Other Stories and Sketches*, which retains "Merry Tales" as a section title. The 1996 OXFORD MARK TWAIN edition includes a facsimile reprint of the first edition of *Merry Tales* with a new introduction by novelist Anne Bernays and an afterword by Forrest Robinson, the editor of *The Cambridge Companion to Mark Twain* (1995).

"The £1,000,000 Bank-Note"

SHORT STORY published in early 1893. The narrator recalls an episode from his earlier life when an accident delivered him to LONDON, where he fell in love and became rich while serving as the guinea pig in a bet between two wealthy eccentrics. As a wish-fulfillment fantasy about the acquisition of sudden wealth, the story has a kind of mirror-image relationship to "THE MAN THAT CORRUPTED HADLEYBURG" (1899) and "THE $30,000 BEQUEST" (1904). It touches on a variety of themes relating to capitalism, gambling, claimants, love at first sight, and the importance of CLOTHES. Although it is generally good-natured and has a happy ending, the story has an Anglophobic undertone that is especially evident in a dinner-party scene.

Among Clemens's writings, this story is unusually playful with characters' names. The protagonist, Henry Adams, for example, sees his surname as evidence of his direct descent from the biblical ADAM. His fiancée, Portia Langham, takes her surname from a street near her London home. All the aristocratic guests at the American minister's dinner party have odd names. By contrast, the eccentric brothers who start Adams on his adventure are initially identified only as Brother A and Brother B. At the end, A's name is revealed as Abel.

SYNOPSIS

A young mining-broker clerk (later identified as Henry Adams) goes sailing on SAN FRANCISCO Bay and is swept out to sea. A brig rescues him, then forces him to work without pay on a long, stormy voyage to London, where he arrives ragged and broke. As Adams wanders the streets hungry, he is invited into a fine house on Portland Place, where he meets two elderly men. As Adams later learns, these men are brothers who disagree about what would become of an intelligent and honest stranger set adrift in London with nothing but a million-pound bank-note and no way to explain how he got it. Brother A thinks that the man would starve, since he could not offer the note to a bank without being arrested; Brother B thinks that a man could survive 30 days without being jailed. After making a £20,000 bet on the question, they have purchased the only £1,000,000 bank-note in England and have been waiting for a likely stranger to appear. Adams meets their qualifications, so they make him their guinea pig.

Explaining nothing to Adams, the brothers give him an envelope containing instructions and say good-bye. After he leaves, he opens the envelope, sees money and hurries to the nearest cheap restaurant. Only after dining does he realize that he has been given a bill worth $5 million in American money. He proffers the note to the restaurant proprietor (later identified as Harris) and asks for change. The astonished man not only tells him not to worry about payment, he invites him to order anything he wants. Adams rushes back to Portland Place to correct what he is sure is a monumental mistake, but the butler tells him not to worry and that the brothers will return in a month.

Adams now reads the note in the envelope, which explains that he is being lent the money for 30 days without interest. At the end of that time, he is to report back. If the note's author wins his bet, Adams will receive "any situation" he can fill. The

note is not signed, addressed, or dated. Adams recognizes that the immense bank-note is worthless to him since he cannot cash it, but determines to get through the month in order to win the promised situation, which he is confident will be a well-salaried job. At a tailor shop, he tries on a ratty, ill-fitting suit and asks if he can pay for it later. The disdainful clerk sniffs at this suggestion, but Adams freezes him with his bank-note. The equally shocked manager immediately becomes obsequious and insists on fitting Adams with a first-class wardrobe, assuring him that he can take forever to pay.

Within a week, Adams is sumptuously equipped with everything he needs and is housed in a fine hotel in Hanover Square (near Portland Place). He gets everything he wants on credit simply by showing the bank-note, and he is becoming celebrated as the "vest-pocket monster"—a foreign crank who carries million-pound notes in his pocket. He breakfasts at Harris's humble restaurant, which his patronage makes so famous that its grateful owner even forces loans on him. Despite all his borrowing, Adams figures he is remaining within the means of what his future salary should bring; however, he frets about impending disaster. Meanwhile, he receives the ultimate badge of fame: He is caricatured in PUNCH.

After 10 days, Adams visits the American minister, who invites him to a dinner party. It happens that Adams's father and the minister were boyhood friends and classmates at YALE. Among the people he meets at the dinner party are the Duke and Duchess of Shoreditch, the Earl and Countess of Newgate, Viscount Cheapside, Lord and Lady Blatherskite, the minister's family, and Portia Langham, a visiting friend of the minister's daughter. Adams and Portia instantly fall in love. A latecomer to the party is Lloyd Hastings—a good friend of Adams from San Francisco who is in London to sell shares in a California mine.

The dinner itself fails to come off when the matter of precedence in seating cannot be settled—a common English problem. The duke insists on sitting at the head of the table, but Adams protests on two counts. First, he ranks higher in newspaper gossip columns; second, his family name, Adams, establishes his direct descent from Adam, while Shoreditch only belongs to a collateral branch of the family. When the dinner guests retreat to play cribbage, Adams has a delightful time joking and bantering with Portia, who laughs when he reveals his incredible story. By the end of the evening, they have an understanding.

After the party, Adams walks home with Hastings, who explains his difficulties in selling shares in his mine option and asks for help. Adams offers to permit Hastings to use his own name to endorse his scheme; in return the friends will split the proceeds. Within days, investors begin buying shares. Meanwhile, Adams spends his evenings with Portia, alternating love talk with speculation about what salary Adams should expect from his unknown benefactor.

By the end of the month, Adams and Hastings have each banked $1 million from Hastings's scheme. Adams goes to Portland Place with Portia to report on the million-pound note, which he presents to Brother B. He also shows the brothers a certificate of deposit for the £200,000 he has banked. Even Portia is surprised. "B"—who has won his bet—wants to give Adams the situation he promised him, but Adams respectfully declines. Portia climbs into the old man's lap, kisses him, then explains that the man is her stepfather. The startled Adams tells the man that there is, after all, a "situation" that he wants, namely "son-in-law." The older man starts to ask Adams about furnishing recommendations, but quickly gives in to Adams's importuning.

Since these adventures have occurred, the narrator has become truly happy. His father-in-law has had the million-pound note canceled and framed as a gift. Though the note is a million-pounder, Adams considers its value only a 10th the worth of what it has bought him.

BACKGROUND AND PUBLISHING HISTORY

Clemens recorded a NOTEBOOK entry containing the essence of this story's plot in early 1879. Another seed of the story appears in *Connecticut Yankee* (1889); when Hank Morgan astonishes a sixth-century shopkeeper with a $20 gold piece, he compares the situation with the effect that a $2,000 bill would have in a 19th-century village store (chapter 31). Clemens finally wrote this 7,500-word story in late 1892 while he was living in FLORENCE, Italy, and

Gregory Peck as the "vest-pocket millionaire" in United Artists' *The Man with a Million,* an adaptation of "£1,000,000 Bank-Note."

published it in the CENTURY MAGAZINE in January 1893. A month later, CHARLES L. WEBSTER & COMPANY made it the title piece of a new collection, *The £1,000,000 Bank-Note and Other New Stories.* CHATTO and Windus followed with an English edition in April. The collection also includes "A Cure for the Blues," "About All Kinds of Ships," "The German Chicago," "MENTAL TELEGRAPHY," "The Enemy Conquered," "PLAYING COURIER," "A Petition to the Queen of England," and "A MAJESTIC LITERARY FOSSIL." HARPER'S later incorporated the volume into *The American Claimant, etc.* The 1996 OXFORD MARK TWAIN edition includes a facsimile reprint of the first American edition of *The £1,000,000 Bank-Note and Other New Stories* with a new introduction by author Malcolm Bradbury and an afterword by James D. Wilson, the coeditor of *The Mark Twain Encyclopedia* (1993).

CRITICAL COMMENTARY

As a rags-to-riches tale, "The £1,000,000 Bank-Note" is structurally similar to the fiction of HORATIO

ALGER, whose books had been popular since the late 1860s. But whereas Alger emphasized the importance of hard work and the delay of gratification, Clemens's story offers a version of financial bootstrapping in which luck, fame, connections, and access to capital are the essential elements of attaining worldly success. During his 30-day trial, Henry Adams does not actually work a day, but rather parlays a twist of fate and a spot of luck into a real fortune by massaging his social standing and lending out his temporarily buoyant name.

The event that impels the narrative—the storm that sweeps Adams's sailboat from San Francisco Bay into the Pacific and lands him on board a London-bound brig—comes not through Adams's efforts but while he is loafing. Though employed as a mining clerk and satisfied with the slow "road to eventual fortune," it is his habitual leisure activity—Saturday sailing—that secures his fortune. The initial disparity between Adams's ragged appearance and his borrowed wealth is a source of humor (and one that Adams himself comes to enjoy, wearing his rags out for the pleasure of springing the note on the unsuspecting), but Adams is hardly a typical tramp. He is selected by the old brothers for his "intelligent" and "honest" appearance, perhaps a reflection of his true character or just as likely their response to indelible class signs of breeding and education that Adams emanates despite his rags. His father attended Yale with the U.S. minister to England, an unusual pauper's pedigree; in relating his rescue at sea, Adams sniffs briefly over being made to work "as a common sailor." Adams is exactly the rare specimen that the brothers had sought—a tramp who is not wholly a tramp, but rather a middle manager down on his luck and far from his local bank. The tale's scenario, in turn, is similarly deceptive. Though it draws humor from the appearance of great wealth being given to a member of the underclass, it more closely portrays a rising member of the middle class who shrewdly capitalizes on unusual luck.

The story's central absurdity, a bank-note that cannot be spent, resonated with national ambivalence at the time over monetary policy. In 1893, the year of the story's publication, a banking panic in the United States led to the worst depression the country had seen. State-chartered wildcat banks issued currency of dubious and fluctuating value. The major political parties argued over the merits of backing U.S. currency with gold as opposed to silver. Three years later, in 1896, William Jennings Bryan channeled populist enthusiasm for changing monetary policy in his "Cross of Gold" speech, on which he rose to national prominence and secured the Democratic presidential nomination. In this context, Adams's California friend Hastings and his silver mine are an odd complement to Adams and his note. The mine has real value in the form of hard silver mineral, but Hastings fails to attract capital investors in London until he is endorsed by Adams's counterfeit reputation, which developed, in turn, by Adams's public display of symbolic currency that belongs to someone else. By lending his name to Hastings, Adams manages to convert his notoriety, made buoyant by the uncashable note, into hard currency. Their exchange is one of the story's many exemplars of deceptive value—social standing as determined by the gossip column, authentic currency that is useless as money but invaluable as a prop, Hastings's distant silver mine, Adams's inexplicable possession of visibly sterling character, and Adams's departing quip that, rather than declaring Portia priceless, offers an estimate of what his bride might fetch on the open market: "Yes, it's a million-pounder, as you see; but it never made but one purchase in its life, and then got the article for only about a tenth part of its value."

Critical Commentary by Alex Feerst

CHARACTERS AND RELATED ENTRIES

Adams, Henry (Hal) Narrator of the "The £1,000,000 Bank-Note." At the start of his narrative, Adams is 27 years old, "alone in the world" and a skillful mining-broker clerk in SAN FRANCISCO. An accident lands him in LONDON without friends or funds, but two eccentrics draw him into an experiment that leads him to fame and fortune. Along the way, he wins the hand of Portia Langham—who happens to be the stepdaughter of one of the eccentrics. Adams never deliberately misrepresents himself, but he succeeds because people assume that he is other than what he really is. In this regard, he fits

Clemens's claimant mold. Indeed, his pseudo-aristocratic rank is affirmed by gossip columns—which call him the "vest-pocket monster." At a dinner party, Adams pulls rank on ordinary English aristocrats—with names like Blatherskite, Newgate, and Shoreditch—by claiming direct descent from ADAM.

Adams's story has interesting parallels with Clemens's life. He is about the same age that Clemens was when the latter arrived in the East from San Francisco—where he had enjoyed "a butterfly idleness" while waiting for his Nevada MINING interests to bring him a fortune (*Roughing It*, chapter 58). Also like Clemens—who was known as the Wild Humorist of the Pacific Slope when he came east—Adams is regarded by London society as something of a freak. And, just as Clemens won the hand of Olivia Langdon though he could not satisfy her father's request for references, Adams persuades Portia's stepfather to overlook the same failing.

Brother A and Brother B   Characters in "The £1,000,000 Bank-Note." Wealthy and elderly Englishmen, "A" and "B" have a £20,000 wager that sets Henry Adams adrift in London with a million-pound bank-note to see if he can last a month without being arrested. "A" bets that Adams will fail, while "B" bets on his success. After sending Adams off, the brothers leave town for the month. When they return to receive Adams's report, "A" is called Abel and "B" turns out to be the stepfather of Adams's new fiancée, Portia LANGHAM. Adams asks "B" for permission to marry Portia. Just as JERVIS LANGDON overlooked Clemens's inability to provide satisfactory references when he permitted him to marry his daughter Olivia, "B" overlooks Adams's inability to provide references.

Brother A and Brother B appear to be the inspirations for the wealthy brothers played by Don Ameche and Ralph Bellamy in the 1983 film *Trading Places*. The owners of a prosperous commodities trading firm, the brothers in that film wager $1 that they can transform an indigent African-American street hustler (Eddie Murphy) into a successful commodities trader, while simultaneously turning a conscientious junior employee (Dan Aykroyd) into a common criminal.

Cheapside, Viscount   Minor character in "The £1,000,000 Bank-Note." An aristocrat whom Henry Adams meets at a dinner party, Cheapside takes his name from a historic market district in central London that is mentioned several times in *The Prince and the Pauper* (1881) (chapters 2, 3, and 11).

Hastings, Lloyd   Minor character in "The £1,000,000 Bank-Note." A California friend of Henry Adams, Hastings is in London to sell shares in a California mining venture in which he has an option. After Adams meets Hastings at a dinner party, he uses his temporary celebrity to give Hastings's venture favorable publicity, with the result that both men become rich.

Langham, Portia   Character in "The £1,000,000 Bank-Note." Portia is the 22-year-old stepdaughter of Brother B, a wealthy Englishman who lends Henry Adams a million-pound bank-note while conducting a wager with his brother. Portia meets Henry at a dinner party at the home of the American minister she is staying with. She and Henry immediately fall in love, but Henry does not learn who her stepfather is until the end of the story, which concludes with their marriage.

In naming Portia, Clemens may have been thinking of WILLIAM SHAKESPEARE's *Merchant of Venice* (1596–97), in which Portia is a wealthy heiress in love with Bassanio, who borrows money in order to court her in style. Portia's surname probably derives from Langham Place, a London street connecting Regent Street to Portland Place—where Adams meets Portia's stepfather and uncle. Clemens stayed at the street's Langham Hotel in 1873. The name "Langham" also bears a resemblance to "LANGDON," the maiden name of Clemens's wife, Olivia. Beautiful, cheerful and understanding, Portia matches Clemens's descriptions of Olivia—with whom he fell in love as quickly as Henry does with Portia. And just as Portia's wealthy stepfather overlooks Adams's inability to provide satisfactory references, so did JERVIS LANGDON when Clemens could not come up with any.

Newgate, Earl and Countess   Minor characters in "The £1,000,000 Bank-Note." The Newgates are aristocrats whom Henry Adams meets at a dinner party. Their unlikely name comes from a notorious London prison that was razed in 1902. As late as 1867, executions were publicly staged outside Newgate's walls. Clemens's BURLESQUE AUTOBIOGRAPHY alludes to an ancestor who died suddenly while at the fine old "resort called Newgate."

Shoreditch, Duke and Duchess of   Minor characters in "The £1,000,000 Bank-Note." English aristocrats whom Henry Adams meets at a dinner party, the Shoreditches are accompanied by their daughter, the Lady Anne-Grace-Eleanor-Celeste-and-so-forth-and-so-forth-de-Bohun, who is evidently named after the 14th-century Duchess of Gloucester, Eleanor de Bohun. The dinner fails to come off after the duke insists on taking precedence in the seating arrangements, starting an argument that cannot be resolved.

The name "Shoreditch" comes from a historically poor east LONDON industrial district. As a family name, it recalls the unsavory connotations of "bilgewater."

BIBLIOGRAPHY

Twain, Mark. *The £1,000,000 Bank-Note and Other New Stories,* edited by Shelley Fisher Fishkin. New York: Oxford University Press, 1996.

"A Monument to Adam"

Essay first published in HARPER'S WEEKLY in July 1905. In October 1879, while Mark Twain was in ELMIRA, New York, he and THOMAS K. BEECHER half-jokingly took up a mutual friend's suggestion to build a monument to ADAM. The idea grew out of the indignation raised by CHARLES DARWIN's book, *The Descent of Man* (1871), which was popularly regarded as tracing man back to the monkeys. Clemens and Beecher argued that since Adam was left out of Darwin's theories, something should be done to keep him from being forgotten.

Years later, Clemens wrote this article in response to a NEW YORK TRIBUNE item that recalled his old Adam monument project. He happened to

be using the same theme in a story that he was then writing, "The Refuge of the Derelicts," or "Adam Monument." According to the article, during the earlier episode, several Elmira businessmen proposed investing $25,000 to build a memorial, and Clemens had tentative designs for the monument drawn in Paris. He also got up a petition to Congress to build such a monument "as a testimony of the Great Republic's gratitude to the Father of the Human Race and as a token of her loyalty to him in this dark day of his humiliation when his older children were doubting him and deserting him." Clemens was not among the 92 signers of the petition; he wanted to keep his participation anonymous so that the petition could be taken seriously. When his own Connecticut congressman, JOSEPH R. HAWLEY, happened to pass through Elmira, he persuaded him to take the petition to Congress. Hawley never mustered the nerve to present it, however.

The original "Monument to Adam Petition" is an appendix in A. B. PAINE's *Mark Twain: A Biography* (1912).

More Tramps Abroad (1897)

British edition of *Following the Equator.* Mark Twain wrote this book while living in LONDON and had BRAM STOKER negotiate his contract with CHATTO and Windus. By November 1897, when Chatto issued *More Tramps,* Clemens was in VIENNA. As with the American edition, he paid little attention to *More Tramps*'s production and did not even know that it was missing most of *Following the Equator*'s illustrations until he gave a copy to someone later.

More Tramps differs from its American counterpart more than any of Clemens's other authorized British editions. Aside from the fact that its first edition has only four illustrations, however, these differences are not as significant as sometimes suggested. *More Tramps* has roughly 6,000 words that were cut from *Following the Equator* and it omits another 1,400 words that appear in the latter. Much of the text cut from *Following the*

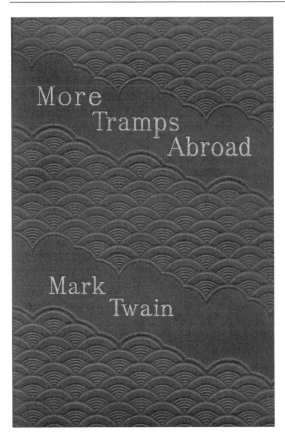

First edition of *More Tramps Abroad*

Equator consists of extracts from books by other authors. The most significant passage cut from *More Tramps* is the harsh indictment of a shipping line that appears in chapter 32 of *Following the Equator*. *More Tramps* also has a slightly different mix of PUDD'NHEAD WILSON maxims as chapter heads.

More Tramps's 72 numbered chapters follow the same order as the 69 chapters in *Following the Equator*, but they break differently in several places. The most substantial differences occur in chapters 18–33 of *More Tramps*, which have about 12 additional pages on Australian subjects (equivalent to chapters 16–30 in *Following the Equator*). Chapters 34–72 of *More Tramps* are almost identical to *Following the Equator*'s chapters 31–69.

A Murder, a Mystery, and a Marriage

Posthumously published SHORT STORY that Clemens wrote in 1876 for a proposed magazine project that failed to materialize. Clemens tried to generate interest in the project for two decades but eventually pigeonholed his story without publishing it. When the approximately 8,000-word story was finally published as a book in 2001, it attracted national attention; however, it is essentially a minor work. What makes it most interesting is that it touches on many themes that Clemens treats more thoroughly elsewhere and thereby helps to illuminate his other works.

The story's central narrative revolves around a Frenchman named Jean Mercier who mysteriously appears in an otherwise undisturbed snowfield in rural Missouri. At the end of the story, Mercier reveals that he traveled from France to the United States in a balloon craft after throwing the author Jules VERNE overboard—presumably to his death. Not wanting his true identity to become known, Mercier adopts a pseudonym and settles in a Missouri village. Later he pretends to be a French nobleman in the hope of marrying Mary Gray, a young woman who is expected to inherit a fortune from her uncle, David Gray. When Mercier learns that the uncle is about to write Mary out of his will, he kills the man and plants evidence that incriminates Mary's true love, Hugh Gregory. Gregory is then scheduled to be hanged as the same moment Mercier is to wed Mary, but in the midst of the wedding ceremony, Mercier is arrested for David Gray's murder, and Gregory marries Mary instead.

Clemens made frequent use of DETECTIVES in his fiction and wrote this story party as a PARODY of the genre. The first mystery the story presents is the unexplained appearance of Mercier in the snowfield. In the absence of tracks of any kind in the open snowfield, it seems physically impossible for Mercier to be where John Gray finds him. That mystery is not explained until Mercier reveals that he dropped from a balloon that continued on without him. Balloon travel had been around since the late 18th century but was still such a novel idea during the 1870s that few readers would have guessed at the solution of the mystery if the story had been published then. Mercier's confession suggests that anyone with brains would have recognized that the crude clues he manufactured to incriminate Gregory were false, but he was counting on the fact that "there were no brains in the community."

Mercier's assumption of the false identity of a French count anticipates the bogus "King" and "Duke" of *Huckleberry Finn* (1884), which Clemens was starting to write around the same time that he wrote *A Murder, a Mystery, and a Marriage*. The readiness with which the villagers of Deer Lick accept Mercier's claim to nobility recalls the electric thrill that the arrival of the Italian "counts" Angelo and Luigi Capello sends through the community of Dawson's Landing in *Pudd'nhead Wilson* (1894) and makes the twins' claim to be noblemen look more suspect than ever.

A second narrative thread running through *A Murder, a Mystery, and a Marriage* is the importance that John Gray places on his daughter's inheriting his brother's fortune. To avoid jeopardizing that inheritance, he forbids Mary from marrying her true love, Hugh Gregory, so as not to offend his brother. Clemens later developed the theme of an anticipated inheritance further in "THE $30,000 BEQUEST" (1904). In both that story and *A Murder, a Mystery, and a Marriage,* parents become obsessed with marrying their daughters off to European nobility.

A final theme in *A Murder, a Mystery, and a Marriage* is the mistreatment that Mercier received in his role as the writer Verne's surrogate traveler. Mercier sees himself as having been something like an abused slave, one driven to justifiable murder by the mistreatment and humiliations that he suffered at his master's hand. Clemens used the idea of a surrogate traveler in his 1880 book *A Tramp Abroad,* in which Mr. Harris performs the tasks that the anonymous narrator finds most disagreeable or dangerous.

The plot of *A Murder, a Mystery, and a Marriage* is absurd but is designed to lead up to the story's doubly surprising ending. The first surprise is the revelation that Mercier reached America by balloon. An even greater surprise is Mercier's claim to have murdered Jules Verne—a prominent French author who was still very much alive at the time Clemens wrote his story. The commentary that Roy Blount Jr. provided for the first authorized publication of the story in 2001 points out that the story's ending is an example of what Clemens called a "nub" or "snapper" in his 1895 essay "HOW TO TELL A STORY."

Clemens himself enjoyed a brief balloon ascent over PARIS in February 1879. A few years later, he wrote a story for *Life on the Mississippi* (1883) about balloonists getting stuck in "a stratum of dead air." That story—whose theme is similar to that of "THE ENCHANTED SEA WILDERNESS"—was left out of *Life on the Mississippi* until 1944, when it appeared in an appendix in an edition published by the Limited Editions Club and Heritage Press. In 1894, Clemens finally developed a balloon-travel theme more fully in *Tom Sawyer Abroad.*

SYNOPSIS

Chapter 1

The story opens in Deer Lick, a prairie village of 600 to 700 residents in southwestern Missouri that is out of touch with the outside world. Among its citizens are John Gray, a 55-year-old farmer; his wife, Sarah; and their 20-year-old daughter, Mary. Mary's suitor is 27-year-old Hugh Gregory, who expects to come into money when his father dies. Hugh is well liked by Mary's parents, but John's estranged brother, David Gray, has hated Hugh ever since Hugh stopped him from cheating Hugh's father out of the Hickory Flat Farm.

Chapter 2

The Reverend John Hurley visits the Grays' home and reports that he has learned that David Gray made his will a year earlier, leaving everything to Mary. Hurley expects that this news will help reconcile the Gray brothers, but John Gray fears that his brother will not leave anything to Mary if she marries Hugh. He therefore forbids her to accept Hugh's proposal, and she reluctantly assents.

That same morning, John Gray goes for a walk in the prairie, which is blanketed with fresh snow. As he ponders his brother's dislike of Hugh, he chances upon an expensively dressed man (later revealed to be Jean Mercier) lying unconscious in the midst of the snow. Since there are no tracks or signs of disturbance in the snow around the man, Gray wonders how he got there. Gray finds a flask beside the man, opens it and presses it to the man's lips. As the man awakens, he speaks to Gray in French, German, Spanish, and other languages until Gray finally says something, and the man thinks he is English. The stranger does not even know what country he is in. Gray takes him home.

Chapter 3

The narrative jumps ahead six months. The Reverend Hurley has still failed to reconcile the Gray brothers. Mary has told Hugh that she still loves him but must follow her father's wishes and not marry him. Meanwhile, the stranger, who now teaches foreign languages, has become popular because of his "high-bred grace of deportment" but has remained silent about his origins. He calls himself George Wayne. Sarah Gray eventually learns that he is French; moreover, he says he is of noble birth—a count. He adds that he had to leave home because he refused to accept an arranged marriage and says that his real name is "Hubert dee Fountingblow." Pledged to secrecy about the stranger's true identity, John Gray becomes excited by the possibility of his daughter's marrying a count but is still puzzled about how the man came to be in the snow the day that he first found him.

Meanwhile, the count has become friendly with both Hugh and David Gray and has tried to "patch up a peace" between them.

Chapter 4

Soon, everyone in the village is talking about "Count Fontainebleau." Mary's parents encourage her to favor the count, but she still pines over Hugh. One day, while the count is visiting David Gray, he finds himself alone in Gray's office and takes the opportunity to read a document exposed in a half-open drawer and is relieved by what he sees. Afterward, he visits Mary and tells her that he loves her but apologizes and insists that she simply forget him. After he leaves, Mary, for the first time, thinks that she could almost love him.

Chapter 5

After three days pass during which the Grays do not see the count, the count appears on a village corner talking to David Gray. When Hugh happens to walk by, Gray insults him, and an argument ensues, punctuated by Gray's promise to go home and write Mary out of his will. As Hugh starts to leave, Gray strikes his cane over Hugh's head, and Hugh knocks him down. As other people restrain Hugh from springing on Gray, Hugh vows to square the account.

Chapter 6

The next morning, the count visits Mary and tells her that he cannot live without her. Suddenly, Mary's father bursts in with the news that his brother has been murdered, and Hugh is in jail.

The village is in a turmoil. A paper is found on David Gray's desk on which Gray has written the opening words of a new will. Near his corpse is a cloth fragment that fits a missing piece of Hugh's coat-skirt. It is rumored that Hugh's father has been getting into financial difficulties. It seems plain to everyone that Hugh is the murderer, but most villagers believe he has committed the crime out of passion, not greed. Meanwhile, Hugh declares his innocence with such obvious sincerity that some villagers waver in the face of the circumstantial evidence against him until a bloody knife belonging to Hugh is found hidden in the stuffing of his bed.

Mary is now the only human being who believes in Hugh's innocence, but her confidence is waning because she has received no word from Hugh. She is unaware that her father has intercepted Hugh's messages. As Mary gives up hope, Hugh's name ceases to be mentioned in her home. Mary still loves Hugh but realizes that she can never marry him.

Mary eventually learns to like the count, who is attentive and comforting, and consents to marry him. Her father is thrilled by the prospect of being allied to foreign nobility. Her parents set June 29 for the wedding, and Mary becomes a recluse in their home. She is assured that Hugh's trial will be delayed for a year or two. However, unbeknownst to her, Hugh is actually tried and convicted of murder on June 22 and is sentenced to be hanged on June 29.

The village is again in a tumult because only a verdict of manslaughter was expected. While David Gray was universally detested, Hugh is universally beloved. Messengers fly to the state capital in the hope of gaining him a pardon.

Chapter 7

On her scheduled wedding day, Mary is the only person who does not know that no reprieve for Hugh has come. Everyone is so uncomfortable about the situation that the local clergyman has even refused to officiate at the wedding. A stranger has been recruited to serve as pastor; when he arrives at the Grays' home for the wedding, he describes a solemn scene at the gallows, where sobbing villagers have been pleading for the sheriffs to delay Hugh's hanging, in case a pardon arrives.

The marriage ceremony finally begins, but before Mary has time to recite her vows, villagers pour into the house, with Hugh and the sheriffs in the lead. Mary falls into Hugh's arms as the sheriffs manacle the count, explaining that he is David Gray's true murderer, and that his accessory in the crime has informed on him. The pastor starts to leave, but John Gray orders him to stay so the ceremony can go on with Mary and Hugh.

Chapter 8

Now under sentence of death for David Gray's murder, the count confesses that his real name is Jean Mercier, the son of a French barber. After teaching himself languages, the sciences, navigation, and many other skills, Mercier became a tourist guide but eventually fell into the evil hands of the author Jules Verne. Verne paid him a great salary and sent him off on disagreeable journeys and turned Mercier's accounts of his adventures into "extravagant and distorted marvels" in his books, humiliating Mercier, who lost all his friends as a result.

On one occasion, Mercier caught a bad fever after Verne sent him up in a patched-up balloon craft that became becalmed over Paris before slumping into the river. Afterward, Verne had the balloon fitted up perfectly so he could accompany Mercier on his next journey. When the balloon was 100 feet above the ground, Mercier threw Verne overboard. After lightening the ship by discarding scientific instruments, Mercier put on Verne's expensive clothes and settled down to enjoy the ship's large stock of fine foods and wine. However, he had lightened the ship so much that it drifted all the way to Missouri, where he got out, into the snow, without landing and let the balloon continue drifting on without him.

To avoid trouble at home, Mercier decided to stay in Deer Lick. When he learned that the wealthy David Gray had made Mary the sole beneficiary in his will, he pretended to be a nobleman and began courting Mary. On the day when he was alone in Gray's office, he found a copy of Gray's will that left everything to a distant relative. However, when he later watched Gray and Hugh Gregory quarreling, he realized that the will he had seen was an old one, and that Mary was still Gray's only heir. Since Gray vowed to rewrite his will that day, Mercier decided to kill him.

Mercier borrowed a knife from Gregory and stabbed Gray to death in his sleep, while an accessory watched at Gray's door. He then planted the evidence that incriminated Gregory, confident that no one in the community had sufficient brains to realize how obvious it was that the evidence implicating Gregory had been planted.

Mercier concludes his confession by expressing his wish to see the late Monsieur Verne again.

BACKGROUND AND PUBLISHING HISTORY

Although relatively brief, this story has a long and complex history. It grew out of Clemens's interest in the idea of balloon voyages. In 1868—around the time he was sailing toward PANAMA—he began writing a story about a Frenchman named Jean Pierre Marteau, whose unconscious body a midwestern farmer finds in an undisturbed snowfield. The farmer takes Marteau home, where he is nursed to back to health, and eventually learns that Marteau escaped from a prison work-party in France after being falsely convicted of murder. Marteau came to the United States in a gas balloon craft—which accounts for how he landed in a snowfield without leaving any tracks around him. Clemens's unfinished draft of that version of the story was published in a volume of his NOTEBOOKS in 1975. A note he inserted above the draft suggests that he abandoned it after learning that Jules Verne's *Five Weeks in a Balloon* (Boston, 1873) had been published in the United States. *A Murder, a Mystery, and a Marriage*, which he wrote later, reworks the balloon-voyage theme of the abandoned story.

In early 1876, Clemens wrote *A Murder, a Mystery, and a Marriage* in two days and tried to persuade his friend W. D. HOWELLS, then editor of the ATLANTIC MONTHLY, to use his magazine for what he called a "skeleton novelette" or "blind novelette" project. His plan was to use the premise of his own story as an outline, or "skeleton," that other writers would be invited to finish. None of the writers who participated in the scheme would see any of the complete stories until the *Atlantic Monthly* published all the versions in consecutive issues. Clemens hoped to enlist such notable writers as BRET HARTE, HENRY JAMES, OLIVER WENDELL HOLMES, and James Russell Lowell but never succeeded in persuading any of them to participate. Over the next two decades he continued to push the idea to Howells and other editors without success.

Clemens's original manuscript turned up among the papers of an English bookseller named James B. Clemens, who willed it to his wife. After she died, her estate sold the manuscript to a bookseller named Lew Feldman in 1945. Feldman had a small number of copies of the story printed so he could apply for copyright, but attorneys for the MARK TWAIN FOUNDATION sued to stop the story's publication. Feldman later sold the manuscript to Frederick Dannay and Manfred Lee—the mystery writers who published stories under the pseudonym Ellery Queen. Their papers—including the Clemens manuscript—ended up at the University of Texas at Austin. In 1995, an attorney working for the BUFFALO AND ERIE COUNTY PUBLIC LIBRARY on matters relating to the recently rediscovered *Huckleberry Finn* manuscript learned of the blind novelette manuscript and started the process that led to its publication. After legal questions about the manuscript's ownership were resolved, the *Atlantic Monthly* outbid *The New Yorker* for magazine rights to the story, and W. W. Norton obtained the rights to publish the story in book form.

Before the story was published in its entirety, the Buffalo Library announced a writing competition in early 2001. It posted the first two chapters of the story online and invited entrants to complete the story. More than 700 people entered the contest. In October 2001, the library announced that the winner of the contest's international category was Carolyn Korsmeyer, a University of Buffalo philosophy professor. Among the judges of the finalists in the competition were author Joyce Carol Oates; humorist Roy Blount Jr.; scholar Leslie Fiedler; Robert H. HIRST, general editor of the MARK TWAIN PROJECT; and radio personality and author Garrison Keillor—who also recorded his reading of *A Murder, a Mystery, and a Marriage* for an audio edition. The library later announced that it had sold the film rights to the story to a production company owned by Goldie Hawn and Kurt Russell.

Meanwhile, the *Atlantic Monthly* published the complete story in its July 2001 issue, and Norton issued a book edition using a text transcribed and emended by Robert Hirst. Both publications included extensive commentary by Roy Blount, and the book edition had original illustrations by Peter de Sève.

CHARACTERS AND RELATED ENTRIES

Gray, David   Character in *A Murder, a Mystery, and a Marriage*. The brother of the farmer John Gray, David Gray is both the richest and the most detested man in Deer Lick, Missouri. John's daughter, Mary, loves Hugh Gregory, but David Gray detests him because Gregory once prevented him from cheating Gregory's father out of a farm. At the beginning of the story, Gray has named Mary the sole beneficiary of his will, but he threatens to write her out unless she renounces Gregory. After Gray and Gregory are seen fighting in public, Gray is murdered by Jean Mercier, but Gregory is convicted of the crime and sentenced to be executed.

Clemens borrowed Gray's name from the journalist DAVID GRAY, who was one of his closest friends when he lived in BUFFALO five years before he wrote *A Murder, a Mystery, and a Marriage*. The real Gray's personality was, if anything, diametrically opposite to that of the greedy and vindictive fictional Gray.

Mercier, Jean Character in *A Murder, a Mystery, and a Marriage*. Mercier is the real name of the Frenchman whom John Gray finds lying in a snowfield near Deer Lick, Missouri, in chapter 2. After settling in Gray's village, Mercier goes by the name "George Wayne" and teaches foreign languages. Eventually, however, he claims to be a French count named "Fontainebleau." Meanwhile, realizing that Mary Gray stands to inherit the fortune of David Gray, he befriends both Mary and Gray. Later, when he suspects that Gray is about to cut Mary out of his will because of her love for Hugh Gregory, he kills Gray and leaves evidence pointing to Gregory as the culprit. After Gregory is convicted of the murder and sentenced to die, Mercier is about to marry Mary himself, when he is arrested after his accessory in the murder confesses.

In the final chapter, when Mercier is under sentence of death for the murder of Gray, he confesses everything: He reveals his true name and origins and blames his crimes on author JULES VERNE, whom he had earlier served as a surrogate traveler. He claims that Verne mistreated him by sending him on hazardous and unpleasant missions and then humiliated him by turning his accounts into outrageous lies in his books.

"My Boyhood Dreams"

ESSAY written by Clemens while in Sanna, SWEDEN, in mid-September 1899. It was first published in *McClure's* magazine in January 1900 and it was collected in *The Man That Corrupted Hadleyburg and Other Stories and Essays* the same year. The facetious 2,300-word piece recalls an evening in BOSTON years earlier, when a dozen friends revealed their most cherished boyhood ambitions.

In an opening that appears to be a response to a query, Clemens states that the only possible answer to the question of whether an old person's boyhood dreams have been realized is disappointment—a disappointment that can only be measured by the person disappointed. He asks rhetorically why anyone would want to join the French army—and says

that this is a question that only ALFRED DREYFUS can answer.

He then recalls an evening long ago in Boston, when he and 11 friends gathered and revealed to each other their boyhood dreams. The dreams of several long-lost friends, James T. Fields, JAMES R. OSGOOD, Ralph Keeler, and Boyle O'Reilly, are not revealed. The survivors include W. D. HOWELLS, who wanted to be an auctioneer but gave up when he settled for being editor of the ATLANTIC MONTHLY in 1830 (sic), and John Hay, who almost achieved his ambition of becoming a steamboat mate before falling as far as private secretary to the president, ambassador, and secretary of state. The others were THOMAS BAILEY ALDRICH, would-be horse doctor; BRANDER MATTHEWS, cowboy; Frank Richard Stockton, barkeeper; G. W. CABLE, circus ring-master; and "Remus" (JOEL CHANDLER HARRIS), buccaneer.

The article ends with a 20-stanza verse, "To the Above Old People," celebrating the infirmities of age. A final editorial postscript (probably written by Clemens himself) says that when the editors submitted proofs of this article to the men named in it, they responded that "they have no recollection of any such night in Boston, nor elsewhere; and in their opinion there was never any such night. They have *met* Mr. Twain, but have had the prudence not to intrust any privacies to him. . . ." In fact, the ambitions named look suspiciously like Clemens's own childhood ambitions.

"My Début as a Literary Person"

ESSAY written in 1899 recalling Clemens's first magazine publication. In June 1866 Clemens was in HAWAII when crew members of the clipper ship *HORNET* reached the islands six weeks after their ship had gone down in the southern PACIFIC. With the help of ANSON BURLINGAME, Clemens interviewed the survivors and delivered a story to California in time to have a major scoop. Later that year he redrafted the story for HARPER'S MAGAZINE, which published "Forty-three Days in an Open Boat" in its December 1866 issue. "My Début" is a 9,000-word essay recounting how he wrote the original stories and got them published; it also provides considerable details from diaries that *Hornet* crew members composed during their voyage of survival.

Although Clemens had earlier scored a major success with the publication of his JUMPING FROG STORY in newspapers across the country, he could not, he explains, regard himself as a properly published author until he had something in a *magazine*. Ironically, when *Harper's* printed his *Hornet* article, it misspelled his pen name as "MARK SWAIN." He wrote "My Début" at a moment when he was obsessed with writing long stories, such as "THE GREAT DARK," based on dreams of being adrift at sea. He used the essay as the title piece in his 1903 collection, *My Début as a Literary Person and Essays and Other Stories*. It has also appeared in *The Man That Corrupted Hadleyburg and Other Stories and Essays* and in many modern anthologies.

which we tell "without saying a word." Such lies support some of the worst forms of human oppression. "It would not be possible," he argues, "for a humane and intelligent person to invent a rational excuse for slavery." As a specific example of such a lie on a grand scale, he cites France's failure to own up to ALFRED DREYFUS's innocence. He then goes on to examine people in England, who "have the oddest ways. They won't tell a spoken lie . . . Except in a large moral interest, like politics or religion."

He concludes that "there is a prejudice against the spoken lie, but none against any other, and by examination and mathematical computation I find that the proportion of the spoken lie to the other varieties is as 1 to 22,894. Therefore the spoken lie is of no consequence, and it is not worth while to go around fussing about it and trying to make believe that it is an important matter. The silent colossal National Lie that is the support and confederate of all the tyrannies and shams and inequalities and unfairnesses that afflict the peoples—that is the one to throw bricks and sermons at."

"My First Lie, and How I Got Out of It"

ESSAY first published in the *New York World* on December 10, 1899. A rambling exploration of lies and how they are told, this essay has an ironic title. Confessing that he cannot remember his *first* lie, Clemens actually discusses his *second*. When nine days old, he recalls, he discovered that if he pretended to be stuck by a diaper pin, he received pleasant attention. Like all babies, he used this ploy regularly, learning the universal human technique of the *unspoken lie*. This leads him to the observation that "almost all lies are acts, and speech has no part in them. . . . All people are liars from the cradle onward, without exception, and . . . they begin to lie as soon as they wake in the morning, and keep it up, without rest or refreshment, until they go to sleep at night."

The essay then develops into a serious examination of what Clemens calls the *lie of silent assertion*,

"My Late Senatorial Secretaryship"

SKETCH first published in the GALAXY in May 1868 as "Facts Concerning the Late Senatorial Secretaryship." After returning from the QUAKER CITY excursion in November 1867, Clemens took up a position as Nevada senator William M. STEWART's private secretary. About two months later they had a falling-out and he quit. Around this same time, he published "THE FACTS CONCERNING THE RECENT RESIGNATION," a sketch satirizing minor government functionaries. A similar piece, "My Late Senatorial Secretaryship," BURLESQUES his own experience as Stewart's secretary, while making fun of the tendency of legislators to dodge issues. He uses his pen name within the sketch, but is careful not to mention Stewart's name. Instead, he uses the abbreviated name "James W. N—," suggesting that he was working for Nevada's *other* senator, JAMES W. NYE.

SYNOPSIS

Mark Twain announces that after two months he is no longer a private secretary to a senator. One morning the senator called him in after the Pacific mail had arrived. Reminding his secretary that he had believed him worthy of his confidence, the senator asked about four letters the secretary wrote on his behalf. The first was to people at Baldwin's Ranch who wanted to establish a new post office. In order to persuade the people that such a post office was unnecessary, the senator had instructed Mark Twain to answer ingeniously. What Mark Twain actually wrote, however, was a disrespectful reply telling the people that what they really wanted was a jail. Now, the senator says, he can no longer enter that district.

Mark Twain's second letter was to constituents who wanted a bill to incorporate their Methodist church in Nevada. The senator asked Mark Twain to explain to them that this was an issue for their state legislature. Instead, Mark Twain told them that Congress knew nothing about religion and that their idea was ridiculous since they could never issue stock on a corporation such as they proposed. Now the senator feels that he is finished with the religious element.

Mark Twain's third offensive letter was to a San Francisco alderman asking about water-lots. The senator wanted a noncommittal reply that would avoid real consideration of the issue. What Mark Twain wrote was atrocious nonsense. Finally, residents of Nevada's HUMBOLDT district asked about changing a post route. The senator wanted to dodge the issue by having Mark Twain write a delicate and dubious reply. Instead, Mark Twain wrote a complex tangle harping on Indian atrocities along the routes. The outraged senator orders Mark Twain to leave the house. Convinced that people like the senator cannot be pleased, Mark Twain resigns.

The Mysterious Stranger, A Romance (1916)

Novella written by A. B. PAINE and FREDERICK DUNEKA from an unfinished manuscript by Clemens, under whose pen name it was published posthumously. As Clemens's literary executor, Paine presented this story as an authentic Mark Twain work, giving no hint of the editorial changes that he and Duneka made. In 1916, HARPER'S MAGAZINE serialized the story (May–November), using full-color illustrations by N. C. Wyeth (1882–1945). HARPER AND BROTHERS published it as a book in October of the same year, with some of Wyeth's illustrations. The volume's falseness is embodied in its cover illustration—Wyeth's painting of the "astrologer," a character added by Paine and Duneka. Paine later collected the story in *The Mysterious Stranger and Other Stories* (1922)—a book that is still being published under Clemens's name.

As a final false note, the first issue of the magazine serial billed the story as the "Only Unpublished Romance by Mark Twain," when—as Paine knew full well—Clemens left a large body of unpublished novels.

Although no astrologer appears in Clemens's unfinished story, Harper used N. C. Wyeth's painting of Paine and Duneka's astrologer to illustrate the cover of the book it presented as a Mark Twain work.

The title "The Mysterious Stranger" has been used in several different ways. Clemens himself used it only once, as the subtitle of his unfinished novel NO. 44, THE MYSTERIOUS STRANGER. Paine and Duneka made it the main title of their revised version of another unfinished Clemens novel, "THE CHRONICLE OF YOUNG SATAN." Finally, the title has become a generic description for both of these original Clemens stories, as well as for his "SCHOOLHOUSE HILL," and it was used as the title of the MARK TWAIN PROJECT edition of all the authentic Clemens versions in 1969.

It was not generally known until well after Clemens's death that he had written more than one "Mysterious Stranger" story. Paine and Duneka knew that several versions existed but suppressed that knowledge when they published their own version. The text published in 1916 as *The Mysterious Stranger, A Romance* is essentially a revision of "The Chronicle of Young Satan." Paine and Duneka deleted about 35 percent of the original text, rewrote many passages, added the astrologer character, and replaced "Chronicle's" final chapter with the conclusion from the *No. 44* manuscript.

Many of Paine and Duneka's changes pertain to religion. For example, while they retained Clemens's Father Adolf character, they gave most of his negative attributes to the nonsectarian astrologer. "Chronicle" contains about seven direct references to "Catholics," but *The Mysterious Stranger* has none. Other significant deletions include about 7,000 words describing Wilhelm Meidling's and Joseph Fuchs's romantic rivalries with Philip Traum and about 4,000 words concerning Traum's affection for animals. Theodor Fischer's sister Lilly disappears, as do Traum's chess games with Meidling.

In 1963, JOHN S. TUCKEY revealed the full extent of Paine's editorial intervention in Clemens's original manuscript and established the correct sequence of Clemens's various versions of the story. In 1968, he published *Mark Twain's The Mysterious Stranger and the Critics,* presenting Paine and Duneka's 1916 text, with annotations indicating their changes, and essays on the work. The following year, the Mark Twain Papers (predecessor of the Mark Twain Project) published the first edition of Mark Twain's origi-

nal texts as *Mark Twain's Mysterious Stranger Manuscripts,* edited by William M. Gibson. Paine and Duneka's text is no longer considered part of Clemens's works, but since it has passed into the public domain, it is still occasionally republished under his name.

CHARACTERS AND RELATED ENTRIES

astrologer   Character in *The Mysterious Stranger.* When ALBERT BIGELOW PAINE and FREDERICK DUNEKA transformed Clemens's "THE CHRONICLE OF YOUNG SATAN" into *The Mysterious Stranger* (1916), they grafted into it an astrologer character from Clemens's *No. 44* manuscript. To this unnamed character, they ascribed the most unpleasant attributes that Clemens had originally given to his own Father Adolf character. In Paine and Duneka's text, for example, it is the astrologer,

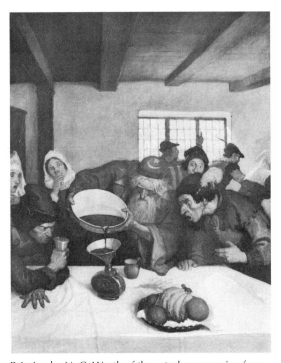

Painting by N. C. Wyeth of the astrologer pouring four quarts of wine into a two-pint bottle in chapter 7 of *The Mysterious Stranger.* In Clemens's story, "The Chronicle of Young Satan," there is no astrologer, and the priest Father Adolf pours the wine.

not Father Adolf, who fills a large bowl with wine from a two-pint bottle; it is the astrologer, not Adolf, who tries to ruin Father Peter; and it is the astrologer, not Adolf, who is denounced as a witch.

When HARPER AND BROTHERS published *The Mysterious Stranger* as a magazine serial in 1916, a fine N. C. Wyeth painting of the astrologer adorned the first issue. That picture was put on the cover of the first edition of the ensuing book, thereby indelibly associating Clemens's name with a character that he did not even put in the story himself.

"My Watch"

SKETCH first published in the *BUFFALO EXPRESS* on November 26, 1870. Clemens describes a watch that kept excellent time until he made the mistake of letting repairmen fix it. Similar tales about watches appear in *Innocents Abroad* (1869), in which Blucher struggles to keep his watch synchronized with "ship time" (chapter 5) and in *Following the Equator* (1897), in which Clemens tries to synchronize a cheap watch with clock bells (chapter 4). The sketch was first collected in *SKETCHES, NEW AND OLD* (1875).

"The New Planet"

SKETCH published in 1909. Noting that astronomers have recently observed "perturbations" in Neptune's orbit that suggest the presence of an unknown nearby planet, Clemens recalls how the perturbations in Uranus's orbit that led to the discovery of Neptune in 1846 affected him. Claiming to be so sensitive that he "perturbate[s] when any other planet is disturbed," he argues that his present perturbations prove that a new planet does exist and hopes it will be named after him. The existence of the new planet was not confirmed until 21 years later, however, when it was named Pluto.

Originally published in *HARPER'S WEEKLY* (January 30, 1909) and reprinted in *EUROPE AND ELSEWHERE*, this brief sketch reflects Clemens's interest

in ASTRONOMY. Both *Tom Sawyer* (1876; chapter 1) and *Innocents Abroad* (1869; chapter 26) comment on the delight astronomers feel when they discover a new planet. *WHAT IS MAN?* alludes to the clues astronomers follow to find invisible planets (chapter 5).

No. 44, The Mysterious Stranger

Posthumously published NOVEL. Also known as the "Print Shop" version of THE MYSTERIOUS STRANGER stories, *No. 44* is the final version that Clemens wrote in this cycle and it may be considered his last novel. Set in late medieval AUSTRIA, the story concerns the unexplained appearance of a remarkable boy with extraordinary powers. Less didactic than "THE CHRONICLE OF YOUNG SATAN," *No. 44* delivers its message more through action than talk. In this version the stranger character, who calls himself "44" (Forty-four), is ostensibly a naive and sensitive boy who struggles to fit into the rough community of printers who share quarters in an old castle. Though 44 works hard, never hurts anyone and never complains, he is so despised by the other printers that they conspire to get rid of him. Unfazed by their persecution, however, 44 plods along contentedly, while surreptitiously performing miracles designed to enhance the reputation of the local astrologer so that the man will be burned by the church.

Forty-four befriends the narrator of the story, August Feldner, an apprentice about his own apparent age. Through observing how people treat 44 and each other, August gradually realizes that man is a cruel, vain creature, whose religious beliefs are empty. After 44 teaches August that everyone is divided into a real and a dream self, the novel ends with a powerful solipsistic message in which 44 tells August that there is no other life than that which he is living now and that *nothing*—including 44—exists outside of August's dreams except August himself and empty space. This final theme reflects Clemens's growing interest in CHRISTIAN SCIENCE, a religion that ostensibly denies the reality of a physical world.

The Austrian adaptation of *No. 44, The Mysterious Stranger* was broadcast on PBS-TV as *The Mysterious Stranger,* with Fred Gwynne as the astrologer (Balthasar Hoffman) and Lance Kerwin as 44. *(Public Broadcasting System)*

Though the story is far removed in time and space from his own youth, Clemens uses it to recreate his own experience as an apprentice printer. *No. 44* offers his fullest exposition of how men worked in print shops, which were almost the same in August Feldner's era as they were in his own. His notes make it clear that he personally suffered many of the same humiliations as an apprentice that August experiences in his story.

SYNOPSIS

A story containing about 71,000 words in 34 chapters, *No. 44* takes place during at least several months, beginning in 1490. Narrating from his old age, August Feldner is an apprentice in a print shop in an old castle overlooking the village of Eseldorf. After the arrival of a remarkable boy named "44" upsets the relationship between the shop's master and the employees, 44 uses his

extraordinary powers to save the master from ruin and to humble his striking workers. He also confuses the village priest and shows August many of the wonders of life.

Chapter 1
The story opens in the Austrian village of Eseldorf in 1490, when its narrator, August Feldner, is a boy. Trouble comes when a Hussite woman distributes literature that goes against Catholic beliefs. But after the village's stern priest, Father Adolf, issues a warning, the village never admits another Hussite. Father Adolf is famous for having fearlessly faced the Devil.

Chapter 2
August is an apprentice in a print shop run by Heinrich Stein in an old castle that belongs to the local (unnamed) prince. The shop works quietly, ignored by the village and the church. August lives in the castle with Stein's family and other employees. Another resident is Balthasar Hoffman, an astrologer whom Frau Stein, the master's stern wife, retains in the hope that he will find treasure.

Chapter 3
One winter day, a boy about August's age appears at the dining hall pleading hunger. Frau Stein wants to turn him away, but the old cook Katrina feeds him, then tells Stein that the boy will work in return for food and shelter. Over his wife's protests, Stein takes him on. When the boy gives his name as "Number 44, New Series 846,962," someone mutters that he must be a "jailbird"—a nickname that sticks. After 44 hauls in several loads of firewood, Frau Stein orders him to walk her dog. Everyone rises to protest because the dog is notoriously vicious, but 44 astonishes them by leading the dog out calmly.

Chapter 4
Resentment against 44 builds among the printers. When the apprentice Ernest Wasserman challenges him to fight, the bewildered newcomer simply grips Wasserman's wrists until he gives in.

Chapter 5
August privately sympathizes with 44, but hesitates to befriend him for fear of being ridiculed. Meanwhile, Katrina takes 44 under her care. As the days

pass, people watch 44 closely, but he goes about his business quietly and proves himself the castle's hardest worker. Often he does remarkable things, for which Balthasar the magician is credited. Longing to share in 44's reputation, August visits 44 in his room one night.

Chapter 6

Forty-four receives August warmly and says how much he needs a friend, making August feel guilty about his selfish motives for coming. However, 44 seems to read his mind and forgives him. To help August not be afraid, 44 gives him mulled claret, which he seems to pull out of the air.

Chapter 7

The next morning, August thinks that the previous night's events were a dream until he meets 44, who assures him that they were not. August senses that 44 can read his mind. After breakfast, Stein praises 44 generously and promotes him to apprentice printer—an announcement coolly received by the other printers. Everyone laughs at 44 when Stein asks him if he has studied classical languages or sciences and he answer no to every question, but Stein promises to be his teacher. Though pleased for 44, August knows that his friend will pay a heavy price for this favoritism. Later, Ernest Wasserman confronts August and promises to reveal that August is 44's friend, until August threatens him with a dirk.

During 44's first day in the shop, the printers make things difficult for him, but he reads August's mind for instructions and performs every task perfectly. The printers now suspect that 44 is an experienced apprentice who has run away, so they cross-examine him about languages and science. His ready answers only anger them more. After 44 gets through the rest of the day by following August's instructions, Wasserman tells on August.

Chapter 8

That night August hides out in a remote corner of the castle. Before dawn, he goes to the kitchen, where Katrina feeds him and rages about the way the men persecute 44. August decides to use his entire savings to pay nuns to pray for 44. In the shop that day, the printers viciously abuse August and 44, but

they cannot make 44 respond. The next day, they work even harder to upset him. Stein cannot protect 44 because he needs the other men to finish a big job for him. Nevertheless, the printers go on strike the next day, demanding that Stein get rid of 44.

Chapters 9–11

With a critical delivery date looming, Stein's situation grows desperate until the journeyman printer Doangivadam arrives and joins with 44 against the strikers. After besting the other printers in a sword fight, Doangivadam tries to negotiate a settlement when word comes that invisible beings are working in the shop.

Chapter 12

Forty-four inspects the shop and reports that the printing job has been completed satisfactorily, so Stein's contract is saved. the angry printers accuse the magician Balthasar of engineering this unwelcome miracle.

Chapter 13

With the printers still uncooperative, Stein's next problem is loading the heavy crates from the job onto a wagon. Doangivadam promises to load the wagon, but several striking workers unexpectedly help. Stein's contract is now completely fulfilled.

Chapter 14

The next day, the strikers deny having helped load the wagon and discover that the empty wagon they have been watching is only a specter. Again they blame Balthasar, who in turn blames 44 and promises to burn the boy if he performs more tricks.

Chapter 15

When August offers to pray for 44, he learns that 44 has no interest in religion, so he vows to devote his own life to saving 44's soul. After performing some astonishing feats, 44 shows August how to make himself invisible.

Chapter 16

Pretending to be acting for Balthasar, 44 irritates the printers by strutting in outrageous finery just before exact Duplicates of all the men start appearing. After the "Originals" realize that the Duplicates intend to work in the shop without pay, they attack them, but the fight ends in a draw. The men now demand that Balthasar destroy 44, who reappears and suddenly explodes into flames.

Chapter 17

Distraught by 44's death, August makes himself invisible and goes through the castle. Everyone is subdued by 44's destruction except the Duplicates, who concentrate on their work. When the magician is called to account for himself before the Holy Office, he cannot be found. Forty-four's ashes are buried without ceremony in unhallowed ground, but when August returns to his room, he finds the "corpse" waiting for him.

Chapter 18

Alive again, 44 laughs and cheerfully says that he really did die. He has assembled an exotic meal, with food from America, which he has visited many times in the past, present, and future. After eating, he smokes a pipe and explains that each person has a "workaday-self" that tends to business and a "dream-self" that cares only for romance and fun. He has created the Duplicates by putting fictitious flesh and bone on the dream-selves of the Originals and he hopes to stir up trouble among them.

Chapter 19

Over the ensuing days, Father Adolf pursues the magician. He declares the Duplicates are evil spirits and tries to burn them, but they vanish each time he chains one to the STAKE. His failures make him a laughingstock. Soon the Duplicates begin courting the young women, leaving the Originals madder than ever. August's efforts to interest 44 in religion get nowhere. When August sarcastically says it is a pity that 44 must belong to the human race, 44 reveals that he is *not* human and explains some of his views on humankind, for which he has a sympathetic pity.

Chapter 20

A week later 44 takes August to a distant town where a promising young artist named Johann Brinker saved Father Adolf from drowning in icy water 30 years earlier. The priest recovered quickly, but Brinker himself was permanently crippled, and his four sisters have sacrificed their own lives in order to tend him.

Chapter 21

The next morning, 44 appears to August in the guise of an old peasant and takes him to a woman who is waiting to be burned at the stake for witchcraft. Cold and tired, she begs 44 for someone to light her fire and end her suffering. As 44 gathers faggots, he is arrested and imprisoned, but escapes easily. However, after Father Adolf arrives to burn the woman, 44 appears again as the magician and allows himself to be captured and chained to a stake. As the priest pronounces judgment on him, 44 vanishes, leaving his empty robes in the chains.

Chapter 22

Back in August's room, 44 provides a sumptuous meal from faraway lands and explains the nature of time and the differences between man and the gods.

Chapter 23

After 44 leaves, August wants to express his affection for Stein's lovely niece, Marget Regen. After making himself invisible, he follows her through the castle and has a confusing encounter with her in which her dream-self seems to emerge, until his own Duplicate appears and interferes.

Chapter 24

August returns to his room to reflect on what has happened. He realizes that he cannot compete for Marget with his Duplicate—who calls himself Emil Schwartz. After the mass the next morning, he makes himself invisible, follows Marget and Emil, and spies on them.

Chapter 25

That night, August drinks heavily with Doangivadam, then visits Marget's boudoir, where three women spot him and scream. After he flees, he is relieved to learn that Stein thinks it was Emil who entered his niece's bedchamber, but then is distressed to hear Stein say that Emil must now marry Marget.

Chapter 26

Forty-four reappears before the distraught August in blackface, singing "Buffalo Gals," "Swanee River," and other songs that drive August to distraction. After 44 settles down, he offers to kill

Emil and Marget's maid, but August objects, so 44 instead turns the maid into a cat.

Chapters 27–29

After napping, August talks with Emil, who does not want to marry Marget but to return to his non-physical state so that he can wander freely in time and space. When 44 returns in the form of Balthasar the magician, Emil pleads to be released from being a Duplicate and his wish is granted.

Chapter 30

As August and 44 eat another exotic breakfast, 44 discusses "dream-sprites," which once carried important secret messages. While commenting on the importance of accurate interpreting in messages, he cites the "CHRISTIAN SCIENCE dialect" as a particularly difficult one to understand and gives an example of a message from Mary Baker Eddy. When he starts to allude to *where* he comes from, August tries to draw him out but learns only that 44 likes visiting Earth because he can shut off his prophecy power and enjoy being surprised. Suddenly, the cat enters to warn 44—who she thinks is Balthasar—that everyone is after him and that the Originals are planning to kill the Duplicates. The news pleases 44 immensely. August becomes invisible and follows 44 and the cat out of the room.

Chapter 31

To improve an already dark and gloomy morning, 44 arranges an artificial ECLIPSE. He announces that he is inviting ghosts from all times and places to join his celebration. In the great hall, they find many armed people waiting for them, including Katrina, who comes at the supposed magician with a knife. Before she can stab him, 44 reveals who he really is by rising up in a glorious white light. His spectacular appearance and his eclipse leave everyone numb.

Chapters 32–33

As he plans a great Assembly of the Dead, 44 amuses himself by making time go backward. Eventually, his assembly gathers and skeletons start trooping by. Suddenly, he and August are alone in an empty world.

Chapter 34

Forty-four explains that he is about to leave forever. When August asks if they will meet in another life, 44 says that there is no other. Life itself is a vision and everything is a dream: "Nothing exists save empty space—and you!" Forty-four vanishes, leaving August appalled, but certain that 44's words are true.

BACKGROUND AND PUBLISHING HISTORY

In 1902, five years after he started writing "The Chronicle of Young Satan," Clemens began a fresh revision of that unfinished manuscript. After rewriting "Chronicle"'s first chapter and pushing its story two centuries further back in time, he shifted directions radically by making a print shop the focus of a new plot. Over the next several years, he worked on the manuscript as his family traveled around. After his wife died in Italy in June 1904, he set the story aside for another year, then worked on it again intermittently until 1908, when he set it aside for good. The long interruptions in his work and the traumas in his personal life are reflected in the manuscript's uneven tone and incompletely integrated story lines. Although his overall story line appears to be complete, he clearly left the final integration of its complex final chapters unfinished.

After Clemens's death in 1910, few people knew that his *No. 44* manuscript existed. When his literary executor A. B. PAINE published a heavily edited version of "The Chronicle of Young Satan" as THE MYSTERIOUS STRANGER, A ROMANCE in 1916, he grafted the final chapter of *No. 44* onto it (changing "August" to "Theodor" and "44" to "Satan" to make it fit), implying that it was a conclusion that Clemens had forgotten that he had written. JOHN S. TUCKEY revealed Paine's deception in 1963, and "No. 44" itself was finally published six years later in the MARK TWAIN PROJECT edition of *Mark Twain's Mysterious Stranger* manuscripts. In 1982, *No. 44* was published as a separate book in a popular edition. That same year, an Austrian television company produced a 90-minute adaptation of *No. 44*, with Chris Makepeace as August, Lance Kerwin as 44, Fred Gwynne as Balthasar, and Bernd Stephan as Doangivadam.

CRITICAL COMMENTARY

Just as a major theme of Clemens's most famous novel, *Huckleberry Finn,* is escape and freedom, the central idea of his last novel, *No. 44, The Mysterious Stranger,* is escape to ultimate freedom. Narrator August Feldner describes his village as lying amid a sleepy AUSTRIA, still in the Middle Ages. Similarly unawakened, August lives and works in a print shop within a medieval castle, unaware that this symbol of the dawning age can spread enlightenment and that a means to personal illumination is closer than the printing press, within himself. Until the stranger arrives, August believes life is as it is meant to be. The society and church discourage learning and nonconformity. Because of this, young August observes human ignorance, suffering, and cruelty; superstition and persecution result and recur because the church and society condone them. Frequently noting envy, greed, selfishness, jealousy, and hypocrisy, sometimes within himself, August must unconsciously sense and desire the means to break barriers; the stranger, called 44, appears to fulfill his wishes.

Huck Finn's view of freedom is simple and basic. Huck equates "being civilized" with losing freedom; the civilization entangling Huck also enslaves Jim. After running away, Huck finds that his few choices always lead back to civilization or chaos. Unlike foreboding strangers in Clemens's earlier stranger-stories, light-hearted 44 befriends August and—with concern and humor—offers another way. Sharing delights from different eras and unknown lands, 44 recognizes the pleasures in the world without ignoring its pain.

Metaphors for Freedom

Huck and Jim's Mississippi raft ride is a metaphor for freedom, but the shore (civilization) increasingly interrupts that idyll until, at journey's end, they reencounter Tom, who—adhering to codes and rules—represents that civilization to which they must return. Huck's pretending to be Tom, whom he admires, symbolizes civilization's envelopment of him. Unlike Huck, August cannot "light out for the territory." Huck flees laws permitting slavery and cruelty, religious dogma hindering rea-

son while fostering anguish, behavioral codes endorsing feuds or duels—all promoting hurt and suffering, superstition, ignorance, prejudice, and bigotry and all trapping people in darkness. Variations of laws and customs, derived from fears and vices and accepted unquestioningly in August's day, are traits of humanity to 44. Neither Huck nor August can completely escape.

Freedom as represented by No. 44 goes beyond the physical, into "unknown possibilities of life" (Tuckey x). August's first paragraph, mentioning the "mental and spiritual clock," establishes a thematic tone emphasizing the mind and soul. Slow and backward, August's clock must be reset. Ultimate freedom discards the body, delving deeper into the mind to the soul; one must release the mind (imprisoned by ignorance) and soul (fettered by religion).

August's society also discourages imagination. Its people are hindered by distance, history, and barely conceptualized alternatives. Other printers—nicknamed "the herd," implying conformity—tell independent-minded Doangivadam to "trim his imagination" (chapter 14). With his unbounded imagination, 44 can time-travel, freeze or even turn time, backward, and erase distance with a thought. Frequently reminded of 44's power and humans' powerlessness to bypass time and space, August can physically escape only through insanity and death. Dreams offer respite and clues to true escape, but because of inhibited human imaginations, the freedom is temporary. However, problems with time and space disappear in dreams as the imagination expands. No. 44 has come to urge August to "work his imagination up" (ibid.) because "once [people] get their imaginations started" (chapter 18), they can experience "all the intensities one suffers and enjoys in a dream!" (chapter 24). Assuming limited human comprehension, 44 enlightens August gradually.

August's name implies majesty and grandeur. Like the Duplicates whom 44 creates, its Latin derivation ("to increase") suggests many possibilities and enhanced mental powers to which August is heir. Emil Schwarz, August's Duplicate, says he is "habitant of the august Empire of Dreams" (chapter 27). The stranger's full name, "No. 44, New Series 864, 962," itself one of many versions, also indicates infinite alternatives. August's powers do increase: "I had not been aware that my spirit possessed this force. I must exploit this valuable power. . . ." (chapter 23). Invisibility and hypnotism, abilities 44 teaches August, represent this transformation. Hypnotism represents 44's creation by thought, again transcending physical barriers. Dreaming is an overall metaphor for expanding imagination, losing physicality, exploring consciousnesses, and freeing minds.

Levels of the Mind

August initially posits two levels of the mind: Workaday (Waking) Self is the conscious level; Dream-Self the subconscious. Dream-Selves are Duplicates with flesh. Resentful, jealous, and later envious, August finally admires his Duplicate, Emil, acknowledging his superiority and desiring his abilities. August and humanity usually remain at the first level, but August experiences another and, pursuing Marget, Master Stein's niece, discovers one even higher, an implication that exercised mentality continues strengthening. August loves Marget, who loves Emil, who loves Elisabeth von Arnim, who loves Martin von Giesbach, desiring the unattainable. This Spiritual-Self symbolizes the fullest potential of spirit and mind. Iterating a mirror motif, August-Emil-Martin is the same character progressively heightened in consciousness/spirituality. August/Emil's calling the other "brother" implies kinship to their Spiritual-Self; however, though Emil will die when August does, the Soul cannot die. Sharing a mind, existing separately, they meet in Dreamland, where all are immaterial, and know each other only through 44's machinations.

No. 44, whom many critics agree represents Creative Imagination (e.g., Krauth 85), is both a means and a connection. He may be August's creative imagination, or August's imaginative creation, conceived to rescue him. August learns that freeing his body means freeing his mind. True freedom, represented as mind over matter (and self), is imagination without boundaries and metaphorically cuts Earth-binding ignorance, prejudices, and superstitions, including religious ones. August desires what he ascribes to Emil and Lisbet and experiences when invisible. Invisible, he temporarily attains the

third level; although surpassing Emil, he retains mind-chains, expressed as petty attitudes toward Emil. Symbolically shedding them by empathizing with Schwarz's pleas—"Set my spirit free!" (chapter 27)—and sincerely calling Emil brother, August is now ready for conclusions drawn from his "psychic adventure, a journey into the deeper mind and beyond—into the realm of the unconscious and of dream experiences, and on at last to that appalling void which one must brave in order to become whole" (Tuckey x).

This void is an initial loss of individual identity; the whole is unified psychic-selves. Paradoxes help explain: One can rise above the body by delving into the mind, discard the body by gaining the soul, find wholeness by seeking separate selves, and explore the self to know the universe. Role switches and characters confusing themselves with their Duplicates symbolize identity loss, suggesting that people do not truly know themselves until they look within. They live lives they think they should live, without actually thinking. The mind imprisons them with petty vices and concerns. Flesh is Emil's prison, as it is humanity's, but his situation represents entrapment, the urge to and means of escape, all mental.

The controversial ending can be seen as metaphoric, a literary solution. *No. 44* is the culmination of Clemens's dream-stories, which question reality. The character 44 tells August that life is a dream, August its dreamer, 44 his guide to this conclusion. Unconsciously, August has summoned his imagination for rescue from a restrictive world. Forty-four sets August free to envision improved existence but adds, "Nothing exists but you. And you are but a *Thought* . . ." (chapter 34).

Bringing together concepts and metaphors of the whole person, 44 makes August complete. He gradually enlightens August, who cannot grasp immediately how to attain his fullest potential. While reminding modern readers of Freud's ego, superego, and id, 44's stages include—surprisingly for Clemens—a spiritual component, but again this component is likely metaphorical.

August exists outside the dream-framework. August has grown older since the "nonexistent" past he relates: "I was only a boy," he says (chapter 1). Forty-four says past and future exist, but as creations of the imagination, built from thought out of nothing, presumably August's thought.

According to the story, readers should cultivate their imaginations and not accept surface events and ideas for reality or lose freedom to conformity and ignorance. Most people live on the surface and do not think deeply. If the world is rotten, imagine a better one. The basic metaphor means that the ability to improve the self and world lies within each person. One can set oneself free.

Critical Commentary by John H. Davis

CHARACTERS AND RELATED ENTRIES

Doangivadam Character in *No. 44, The Mysterious Stranger*. No one knows the real name of the carefree wanderer who was nicknamed "Doangivadam" because he "don't give a damn." A tough, honest, handsome, fearless, and intelligent journeyman printer, Doangivadam works throughout Europe, coming and going as he pleases. In chapter 11, he arrives in Eseldorf in time to help August Feldner and Forty-four meet a printing deadline when most of their master's men are out on strike.

The character is probably modeled on Wales MCCORMICK, a young printer's apprentice with whom Clemens worked in Hannibal. He also bears a strong resemblance to Miles Hendon of *The Prince and the Pauper* (1881) and to La Hire of *Joan of Arc* (1896). Around the time that Clemens wrote this story, he occasionally wore a WHITE SUIT that he called his "dontcareadamn suit."

Eseldorf Fictional village in "THE CHRONICLE OF YOUNG SATAN" and *No. 44, The Mysterious Stranger*. Although the first story is set in 1702 and the second in 1490, both describe Eseldorf as being in the "Middle Ages" in the "middle" of AUSTRIA. Standing beside a river in a woody and hilly region, the sleepy village is just below a castle. Physically it resembles a description of WEGGIS, Switzerland, that Clemens wrote in mid-1896, just before going to Vienna. where he began writing "Chronicle." Eseldorf's setting also resembles KALTENLEUTGEBEN, a resort town near Vienna where he stayed a year later, and it has something of Clemens's own Hannibal and its fictional counterpart St. Petersburg. Like these American towns, it is a "paradise for

boys," who roam the nearby woods, swim, boat, fish and enjoy winter sports.

Several parts of Eseldorf figure into the narrative of "Chronicle," which involves many different villagers. By contrast, most of *No. 44* takes place within a castle containing a print shop that has little contact with the village.

Clemens evidently chose the name "Eseldorf"—GERMAN for "assville" or "donkeytown"—to emphasize the small-mindedness of its residents, who hesitate to hold any opinion not sanctioned by the Church. His working notes show that he originally called the village Hasenfeld, or "Rabbitfield"—a similarly disparaging name. The region's hereditary prince, who remains nameless in "Chronicle," is called Rosenfeld ("Rosefield") in *No. 44*.

Feldner, August Narrator of *No. 44, The Mysterious Stranger*. Like Theodor Fischer of "THE CHRONICLES OF YOUNG SATAN," Feldner tells his story from the perspective of old age. Indeed, the first chapter of his narrative is virtually identical to Fischer's, although his story is set two centuries earlier. About 16 or 17 years old at that time (chapters 2 and 23 give different figures), Feldner is in his second year as an apprentice printer in the Austrian village of Eseldorf. Though timid, he risks the disapproval of his fellow printers to befriend the marvelous visitor Forty-four, who reveals to Feldner his dream-self and eventually proves that existence itself is nothing more than a dream.

Forty-four (44; Quarante-quatre) Name of similar characters in "SCHOOLHOUSE HILL" and *No. 44, The Mysterious Stranger*. In both of these unfinished novels. Forty-four is a boy who suddenly arrives in a village, where he astounds people with his marvelous powers. In "Schoolhouse Hill," he appears at the mid-19th-century Missouri school that Tom Sawyer attends. At first he speaks only French (he introduces himself as "Quarante-quatre") but absorbs knowledge so rapidly that by midday he speaks perfect English and has mastered Latin, Greek, and other subjects. The Forty-four of *No. 44* (whose name is generally rendered "44") visits the late 15th-century Austrian village of Eseldorf, where he joins the household of a print shop owner. Though utterly untutored, he proves himself incomparably knowledgeable and quickly masters the printing craft. Both stories' characters go on to demonstrate a wide range of powers as they involve themselves in village life. While the career of "Schoolhouse" 's Forty-four is truncated by Clemens's early abandonment of the story, the 44 of *No. 44* develops into a quite different type of character and appears to carry his mission to a conclusion when he reveals himself to his Austrian friend August Feldner as nothing more than a creation of August's own imagination (chapter 34).

Both Forty-four characters resemble Satan in Clemens's earlier story "THE CHRONICLE OF YOUNG SATAN." They differ from the latter in being slower to explain who they are and where they come from. "Schoolhouse Hill" 's Forty-four eventually reveals that he is the son of Satan and is millions of Earth-years old (chapters 4–5), while *No. 44*'s 44 admits that he is not of this world but does not reveal that he is merely a figment of Feldner's imagination until the end of the narrative. Meanwhile, he explains that one of his reasons for coming to Earth is so that he can shut off his "prophecy-works" and enjoy being surprised (chapter 30). This 44 also differs from both of the other characters in being despised by most of the people around him.

An unanswered question about these characters is what, if anything, the name "44" meant to Clemens. To complicate matters, *No. 44*'s character calls himself "Number 44, New Series 864,962." Clemens's "Schoolhouse Hill" notes suggest that he may have chosen "44" randomly, as his character was to be one of an untold number of Satan's children, each of whom is identified by a complex number. While various explanations of "44" have been advanced, Clemens may have chosen the number simply because it sounded right. Perhaps he saw it as an abbreviated form of "144." As the square of 12, 144 is the highest number in the standard multiplication table—a learning device that bedeviled Clemens throughout his life. Indeed, in a passage immediately preceding Forty-four's introduction to the teacher in "Schoolhouse Hill," the "multiplication class" recites "up to 'twelve times twelve.' " The number 144 is also suggestive because there are 12 feet, or 144 inches, in two

fathoms—the nautical depth equivalent to "MARK TWAIN."

BIBLIOGRAPHY

Hirst, Robert H. "Note on the Text." In *Mark Twain: No. 44, the Mysterious Stranger*, edited by John S. Tuckey, 197–198. Text est. by William M. Gibson & Staff of the Mark Twain Project. Berkeley: University of California Press, 1982.

Krauth, Leland. *Mark Twain and Company: Six Literary Relations.* Athens: University of Georgia Press, 2003.

Tuckey, John S., ed. "Foreword." In *Mark Twain: No. 44, the Mysterious Stranger*, ix–x. Berkeley: University of California Press, 1982.

Twain, Mark. "*No. 44, the Mysterious Stranger.*" In *The Mysterious Stranger*, edited by William M. Gibson 221–405. Berkeley: University of California Press, 1970.

"Old Times on the Mississippi"

Series of articles published in the ATLANTIC MONTHLY in 1875 and later incorporated into *Life on the Mississippi* (1883). In 1874, 13 years after he left the Mississippi River, Clemens responded to W. D. HOWELLS's request for an *Atlantic* article by writing a memoir of his days as an apprentice steamboat PILOT. He was eager to record a way of life that had been altered almost beyond recognition since the CIVIL WAR. Although these articles are generally acknowledged to be among his masterpieces, they cannot be read strictly as either history or biography. Their portrayal of river life overlooks most of its sordid aspects, focusing instead on the romanticism and heroism of steamboating. Further, they depict the narrator as a much younger and more naive apprentice than the real Clemens was when he began cubbing at the age of 21.

Containing just over 35,000 words, the seven articles appeared in the January–June and August issues of the *Atlantic* in 1875. As quickly as the original installments appeared in the *Atlantic*, they were pirated in newspapers throughout the country. Afterward, BELFORD BROTHERS, a Canadian publisher, collected all the articles in an unauthorized book, *Old Times on the Mississippi* (1876).

In 1882, Clemens revisited the river to gather fresh material for a book. When he returned home, he split his *Atlantic* articles into 14 chapters, which became chapters 4–17 in *Life on the Mississippi* (1883). Satisfied with the editing done on the original articles and not anxious to make additional work for himself, he made only about 45 minor changes in wording, and spelled out many of the names rendered only as initials in "Old Times." "Mr. B." becomes HORACE BIXBY, "Mr. J." is [WILLIAM] BROWN, "George E." is GEORGE EALER, and "Mr. T." is Ben Thornburg. Initials not spelled out in *Life on the Mississippi* include "Mr. W." (STROTHER WILEY), "Tom G.," "Mr. X.," and "Captain Y." (possibly Captain Patrick Yore).

Three new chapters in *Life on the Mississippi* (18–20) completed the story of his cub piloting days. Chapter 21 covers his years as a licensed pilot in one paragraph. The balance of the book relates to his 1882 trip.

While the "Old Times" articles and the book *Life on the Mississippi* are closely related, they are not synonymous—a fact that Clemens himself had trouble remembering in later years. In his autobiographical dictations, for example, he incorrectly called the *book* "Old Times on the Mississippi"—a mistake corrected by A. B. PAINE when he prepared the first edition of the AUTOBIOGRAPHY for publication. "Old Times" has been reprinted only infrequently since publication of *Life on the Mississippi.*

execution for 1,001 consecutive nights by beginning a new tale each night to distract her husband, Sultan Shahriyar. Clemens's burlesque begins on the 1,002nd night, when the sultan orders Scherezade to report to his executioner.

To gain another reprieve, Scherezade begins a new story. Her complex tale is about a boy and a girl whose sexual identities are reversed at birth by a witch, who parts their hair in ways to make people think the boy is a girl and the girl a boy. A sultan's son is thus raised as Fatima, a "girl" interested only in masculine activities, while a vizier's daughter grows up as an effeminate "boy" named Selim. Separated as infants, the children meet again when they are 17 and fall in love. After considerable confusion, they are permitted to marry two years later. Under the sultan's dictate, however, the "bride" Fatima expects to be executed if he bears a child. Amazingly, however, Selim bears twins, so everyone is happy.

When Scherezade's tedious tale ends, the relieved Shahriyar calls for his executioner. However, the tale has taken so long that the executioner has died. Scherezade resumes her tale, prolonging it until the sultan dies as well.

After finishing this 18,000-word story, Clemens was eager to publish it, but first sent a copy to W. D. HOWELLS. In September 1883, Howells reported back that while he thought the story's opening extremely funny, the rest was as tedious to him as it is to Shahriyar. Clemens put his manuscript aside and forgot about it. It was finally published in *SATIRES & BURLESQUES* in 1967.

"1,002d Arabian Night"

Story written in 1883 and first published in 1967. Clemens had a lifelong interest in the ARABIAN NIGHTS; while finishing *Huckleberry Finn* in mid-1883, he wrote "1,002d Arabian Nigh" as a BURLESQUE conclusion to the Near Eastern classic. EDGAR ALLAN POE published a similar story, "The 1002d Tale of Scheherazade," in 1850. The original tales of the Arabian Nights are FRAME-STORIES told by a bride named Scherezade, who postpones her

"O'Shah" ("The Shah Letters")

Letters to the *NEW YORK HERALD* about the 1873 visit to ENGLAND of Nasred-Din (1831–1896), the shah of Persia (ruled 1848–96). While Clemens was in England, the *Herald*'s LONDON office invited him to cover the shah's state visit. On June 17 or 18, he went to BELGIUM with a private secretary, S. C. Thompson, who took notes for him. They watched the Royal Navy collect the shah and carry him back to England, where they observed several state receptions honoring the Persian ruler.

Between June 18 and June 30, Clemens wrote about 14,500 words in five letters to the *Herald*. The assignment bored him, so he declined to cover the shah's subsequent visit to Paris. He had a low regard for Nasr-ed-Din, whom he ranked with TURKEY'S ABDUL AZIZ. The tone of his letters is ironic. His narrator assumes an ingenuous persona, writing as though he personally were responsible for taking the shah to London and "impressing" him. His letters— which the *Herald*'s editors freely emended—include descriptions of Ostend and Dover, as well as English landmarks that the shah visited in London, such as Buckingham Palace, Albert Memorial, Windsor Castle, and the Guildhall.

The shah letters first appeared in book form under the title "O'Shah" in EUROPE AND ELSE-WHERE (1923).

Personal Recollections of Joan of Arc

See JOAN OF ARC, PERSONAL RECOLLECTIONS OF.

petrified man hoax

On October 4, 1862, Clemens published a brief, apparently unsigned article in the VIRGINIA CITY TERRITORIAL ENTERPRISE soberly describing a "petrified man" recently discovered at Gravelly Ford—a spot on the Humboldt River near present Palisade, NEVADA. The article states that "Justice Sewell or Sowell" went to the site to hold an inquest, concluding that the man had died from exposure. When people tried removing the body for burial, it was found to be cemented to bedrock by limestone sediment; however, the judge refused to let it be blasted free.

Over the next month, at least a dozen other CALIFORNIA and Nevada papers reprinted the arti-

cle, but only a third of them recognized it as a HOAX. In June 1870, Clemens discussed the hoax in a GALAXY article, which was later republished in SKETCHES, NEW AND OLD (1875) as "The Petrified Man." This piece gives two reasons for his original hoax. First, he wanted to destroy what he called the growing "petrification mania" with a "very delicate satire." He also wanted to embarrass a judge (A. T. Sewall) with whom he had had a falling-out. The *Galaxy* article analyzes the original *Enterprise* piece, demonstrating how, from beginning to end, it is "a string of roaring absurdities." As proof that he never intended to deceive anyone, he shows how a careful reading of his petrified man description reveals that the body was in a NOSE-TWEAKING position—a posture graphically illustrated by TRUE WILLIAMS's illustration in *Sketches, New and Old*. The hoax is not mentioned in *Roughing It* (1872).

While Clemens's claim that there was a "petrification mania" in the mid-19th century may be exaggerated, stories similar to his were routinely accepted during that era. When he was a child in Hannibal, Missouri, the owner of a large limestone CAVE near the town kept the body of a girl—reputedly his own daughter—in a copper tank in an experiment to see if it would petrify. The most famous "petrification" hoax of all began in October 1869, when the "Cardiff Giant" was dug up in central New York. Clemens quickly responded to that story with two new sketches, "The Legend of the CAPITOLINE VENUS" and "A GHOST STORY."

"Playing Courier"

Lighthearted narrative of Clemens's misadventures while taking his family from AIX-LES-BAINS in eastern FRANCE to Bayreuth, Germany, during the summer of 1891. Clemens wrote the 5,500-word story as the fourth of six letters that he was committed to write for the McClure syndicate. It appeared in the December 19 and 26 issues of the *Illustrated London News* and in the January 8, 1892, *NEW YORK SUN*.

"Political Economy"

Story written and published in 1870. A PARODY on pompous editorial writers, "Political Economy" also anticipates Clemens's McWILLIAMS stories about the joys of home ownership. Its depiction of a man overloading his house with lightning rods is repeated in chapter 5 of *The Gilded Age* (1873), and "THE STOLEN WHITE ELEPHANT" alludes to a criminal's killing a lightning-rod salesman.

The story's harassed narrator—presumably a newspaper publisher—is at home struggling to finish an essay on his favorite subject, political economy. A sentence and a half into his essay, he is interrupted by the arrival of a glib lightning-rod salesman. To minimize the interruption and not appear ignorant, he accepts all the man's installation suggestions and goes back to his writing. Throughout the day, however, the man repeatedly interrupts him with new suggestions; each interruption leads to additional installations and leaves the narrator less able to write. By the end of the day, 1,631 expensive lightning rods cover his house, which a crowd gathers to gawk at. After lightning strikes the house 764 times several days later, the narrator removes most of the rods, but is still too unsettled to resume his essay. The 285 words that he does write string together clichés such as "political economy is the basis of all good government"— and ludicrous quotations attributed to Confucius; HORACE GREELEY; GEORGE GORDON, LORD BYRON; Homer; and others.

First published in the GALAXY in September 1870, the 2,390-word sketch was collected in SKETCHES, NEW AND OLD.

"Post-mortem Poetry"

SKETCH written in 1870. Clemens facetiously praises a custom in PHILADELPHIA newspapers of attaching SENTIMENTAL verses to OBITUARIES. He quotes examples from the *Philadelphia Ledger,* emphasizing verses about children. He calls particular attention to a "transcendent obituary poem" that concerns four children named Belknap burn-

ing to death in their home in 1863 as their neglectful mother is out and their father is being slain in war. The sketch first appeared in GALAXY in June 1870. It was collected in THE $30,000 BEQUEST AND OTHER STORIES. Clemens later invented the ultimate post-mortem poet, Emmeline Grangerford, as a background figure for *Huckleberry Finn.*

The Prince and the Pauper: A Tale for Young People of All Ages (1881)

Novel set in ENGLAND in 1547—the year King Henry VIII died and was succeeded by his young son Edward VI. The first of Clemens's historical novels, *The Prince and the Pauper* begins with the "what if" premise of having Prince Edward accidentally change places with a look-alike commoner named Tom Canty just before his father dies. Canty then becomes king, while Edward—now the true king—has adventures among the poor while striving to regain his throne. Once he is restored to his proper place, he becomes a far more compassionate ruler than he might otherwise have been, permitting Clemens to conclude that Edward's reign was a "singularly merciful one for those harsh times."

Though outwardly a major departure from Clemens's other early novels, *The Prince and the Pauper* has strong parallels with *Tom Sawyer* (1876) and *Huckleberry Finn* (1884). Its lead characters, for example, are similar in age to Tom Sawyer and Huckleberry Finn and share traits of both. Tom Canty's Offal Court home resembles Tom Sawyer's hometown, St. Petersburg, and Canty's sudden elevation to the kingship is an acting out of what might be Sawyer's most grandiose fantasy. Meanwhile, Edward's adventures away from the court anticipate Huck's PICARESQUE journey down the Mississippi. Along the way, he experiences the same kind of abuse from Tom Canty's father that Huck receives from Pap Finn.

The heart of *The Prince and the Pauper* is an exploration of one of Clemens's favorite themes: claimants. The moment that Edward is cast out of the royal palace, he becomes a "forlorn and friendless prince" who is ridiculed by everyone he meets except Miles Hendon—himself a kind of claimant who merely humors Edward until the moment that he actually sees Edward on the throne. There is even a school of thought that suggests that Clemens himself was a claimant who wrote this genteel story in order to win respectability.

SYNOPSIS

The 73,000-word novel is divided into a brief preface, 33 numbered chapters, an unnumbered conclusion and notes by the author. The "prince" and "pauper" of the title are boys born on the same day in the 16th century. When they are about 13 years old, Prince Edward invites the pauper Tom Canty into his palace, where they swap CLOTHES for fun and discover that they look alike. An accident casts the prince out of the palace in Tom's rags. Tom remains inside, where everyone, including King Henry VIII, thinks him to be the prince gone slightly mad. Though each boy proclaims his true identity, no one believes either of them. The next day, King Henry dies and Tom is acclaimed King Edward VI. Over the next three weeks, Tom adapts to being king as Edward struggles to win his way back to his rightful throne. On Edward's second day outside the palace, Miles Hendon, a colorful adventurer who has been out of the country for 10 years, rescues him from a mob and determines to take him to his own family home in Kent. Along the way, Edward is twice kidnapped by Tom Canty's father and endures other adventures. When they finally reach Hendon's home, Hendon discovers that his younger brother has usurped the family estate and married his own sweetheart. Hendon and Edward spend a week in prison, then return to London, where they get separated in a crowd the night before Tom Canty is to be crowned king. The next morning, Edward sneaks into Westminster Abbey, where he interrupts the coronation ceremony. Tom immediately acknowledges Edward to be the rightful king; after some confusion is resolved, Edward is crowned. The next day, Edward rewards Tom and Hendon for their loyal service.

Chapters of uneven length alternate the narrative between the palace and the countryside. Each chapter from 4 through 31 focuses on either Tom or Edward, except chapter 11, which divides its attention between Tom inside the Guildhall and the prince, who is outside. Both boys appear in five chapters; 17 chapters follow Edward's activities; 11 follow Tom.

[Preface]
The tale that follows has been passed down from father to son. "It may have happened, it may not have happened: but it *could* have happened."

Chapter 1
On an autumn day in the second quarter of the 16th century, two boys are born in LONDON. One is Tom Canty, the unwanted son of the Canty family. The other is Edward, Prince of Wales, the much-wanted and celebrated son of the Tudor family.

Chapter 2
Tom Canty grows up in London's Offal Court, near London Bridge, where he lives with his mother and father, two sisters and grandmother. His thieving father, John Canty, and mean-spirited beggarly Gammer Canty treat him cruelly, but Mrs. Canty and his sisters Bet and Nan Canty are kind. He also lives near a kindly priest, Father Andrew, who teaches him to read and instructs him in Latin. Despite his family's poverty and the brawling nature of Offal Court, Tom's life is not altogether unpleasant—especially in the summers. He often plays with other children and swims in the THAMES, and occasionally observes such spectacles as the execution of ANNE ASKEW.

Tom reads Father Andrew's books and grows up daydreaming about kings and princes; his main ambition is to see a real prince. Often pretending to be a prince himself, he cultivates courtly language, organizes a mock royal court and becomes known as a wise and gifted leader. His regal dreams and games are interrupted, however, by the daily real-life necessity of begging.

Chapter 3
One day, Tom wanders far from home and finds himself outside the royal palace in WESTMINSTER. Through a gate, he sees a real prince—Edward. When he moves closer, a guard cuffs him roughly. Edward sees Tom mistreated and invites him inside

Tom Canty meets Prince Edward, in chapter 3.

to his chambers and orders him food. Edward asks Tom about his life outside the palace and tells about his own family. Tom's tales of rugged outdoor sports excite Edward, who suggests that he and Tom exchange their clothes for fun. After putting on each other's outfits, they stand before a mirror and marvel at their mutual resemblance. Edward then notices that Tom's arm was bruised by a guard. As he rushes out to reprimand the man, he hides "an article of national importance" (later identified as the Great Seal). He starts to berate the guard at the gate, only to be tossed out of the palace as a common pauper and ridiculed by the crowd outside.

Chapter 4

For several hours, Edward tries to talk his way back into the palace, as the crowd taunts him. Finally, he seeks help at Christ's Hospital, a children's home established by his father. Instead of giving him a royal welcome, the orphans treat him roughly and chase him away. As he wanders about, a drunken ruffian seizes him; it is John Canty, who thinks Edward is his son, Tom. Canty takes him home; Edward's claims to be the Prince of Wales merely convince Canty that his son is mad.

Chapter 5

Back at the palace, Tom Canty eagerly explores the prince's chambers, but a half hour later he begins worrying about Edward's failure to return. When he steps outside the room, servants bow to him. Lady Jane Grey enters the room and Tom embarrasses her by kneeling down. After she leaves, rumors spread through the palace that the prince is mad until the king (Henry VIII) orders the rumors to cease.

Finally, Tom is taken to the king, who chides him for jesting. Tom prostrates himself and begs to be spared. The befuddled king assures him that no harm will come to him and tests him with a question in Latin. Tom's lame Latin reply pleases the king, but Tom fails completely when the king tries French on him. The king orders that none may speak of the prince's "distemper" and orders Lord Hertford to see that the boy is confirmed as the Prince of Wales the next day. As Tom is led away by Hertford, his heart sinks at the realization that he is a captive.

Another noble irritates the king by reminding him about the Duke of Norfolk, whom the king is anxious to see executed.

Chapter 6

Hertford and Lord St. John relay to Tom the king's command not to insist he is not the prince. Tom agrees, and Hertford adds that the king has commanded he be relieved of his studies for the time being. When the princesses Elizabeth and Jane Grey arrive, Hertford tells them to ignore the prince's "humors"; St. John tells Tom to remember everything he can and to pretend to remember the rest. Conversation is strained, but Elizabeth helps Tom through rough patches. When the princesses leave, Tom asks to rest and is led to an inner apartment. St. John suspects that Tom may in fact not be the true prince, but Hertford discourages such speculation as potentially treasonous.

Chapter 7

In the afternoon, Tom suffers through being dressed for dinner, then endures a meal in which every step is a mystery. He has trouble with the utensils, does not recognize turnips or lettuce, orders his napkin removed so it will not be soiled, fills his pockets with nuts, and drinks from the finger bowl; however, no one expresses surprise. Back in the prince's private rooms, Tom tries on a suit of armor and finds a useful book on court etiquette.

Chapter 8

At five o'clock, King Henry awakens; he is anxious to see Norfolk executed but needs the Great Seal to certify his order. He last saw the seal when he entrusted it to Edward, but the Lord Chancellor reports that the prince cannot remember where it is.

Chapter 9

At nine o'clock, a great pageant begins on the river and a gorgeously dressed Tom Canty follows Hertford to a barge (*continued in chapter 11*).

Chapter 10

Back in Offal Court, John Canty is dragging Edward home when someone steps forward to plead on the boy's behalf. Canty smashes the man's head with his cudgel. At Canty's home, Edward insists that he is the Prince of Wales. Thinking the boy to be Tom, Canty's wife and daughters rush to console Edward, but Canty and Canty's mother beat him.

As everyone goes to sleep, the girls cover Edward with straw and try to comfort him. Suspecting that there is something different about this boy, Mrs. Canty tests whether he has a certain reflex of Tom's, but the results are inconclusive. Just as Edward awakens—thinking that he has been dreaming—someone knocks at the door and warns Canty that the man he killed with his cudgel is Father Andrew. Canty rouses the family to flee, leading Edward by the hand. At London Bridge, the prince escapes in the confusion.

Chapter 11

Meanwhile, Tom Canty rides a royal barge to Guildhall, where the Lord Mayor welcomes him to a banquet. As Tom gapes at the hall's splendor, the real prince is outside, loudly proclaiming his identity. A derisive crowd assails him, but a fantastically dressed man calling himself Miles Hendon hustles him away from danger. Inside Guildhall, it is announced that the king is dead and everyone renders obeisance to Tom Canty. Assured that *his* word is now law, Tom proclaims that the Duke of Norfolk shall not die—an announcement that is joyfully received.

Chapter 12

Hendon takes Edward to London Bridge, where the boy learns that his father is dead. Near Hendon's inn, John Canty tries to seize Edward, but Hendon drives him away. Edward then stuns Hendon by usurping the bed in his room and by ordering Hendon to wash him when a servant brings them food. Thinking the boy temporarily mad, Hendon acquiesces, but Edward—aware that he is now *king*—stretches Hendon's patience by forbidding him to sit in his presence. Hendon tells Edward about his family and relates how he has spent the last 10 years on the Continent as a soldier and prisoner of war. Grateful to Hendon for his help, Edward asks him to name a reward. Citing a precedent from the time of King John (1167–1216), Hendon requests permission merely to sit in the king's presence. Edward grants this request and dubs Hendon a knight.

Chapter 13

After supper, Hendon plays along with the boy's claim to be king by helping prepare him for bed and then sleeping on the floor. The next day, he goes out to buy a secondhand outfit for Edward. When he returns, he begins threading a NEEDLE to repair the outfit and considers his plan to take Edward to Hendon Hall. Only belatedly, he discovers that Edward is gone. From a servant he learns that another boy has fetched Edward away and he goes after him (*continued in chapter 17*).

Chapter 14

Tom Canty meanwhile awakens in Westminster palace, thinking he has been dreaming. When he discovers that he has *not* been dreaming, he returns to sleep. A real dream conveys him to a meadow called Goodman's Fields, where a dwarf enriches him with 12 pennies every week. He reawakens to find an army of titled servants standing by to dress him for breakfast. Afterward, he puts in a weary day in the throne room conducting state business under Hertford's guidance. He is appalled to learn that £20,000 are owing on household expenses. A secretary mentions the late king's intention to raise Hertford to a duke and Thomas Seymour to the peerage.

After spending part of the afternoon with the royal princesses, Tom meets the royal whipping boy, Humphrey Marlow, who he discovers will be a valuable source of information on court people and etiquette. Having Marlow as an ally lightens Tom's burdens, but his spirit sags again when Hertford tells him that in two days he must dine in public to quell rumors that he is mad. Hertford tests Tom's memory in subtle ways, but cannot crack the puzzle of the Great Seal's disappearance.

Chapter 15

Tom spends the next day receiving foreign ambassadors and soon wearies of holding audiences. After three days as king, however, he is adjusting; on the fourth day he is coping, but still dreading his public dinner that night. From his audience chamber, he hears a noisy mob following three people to their execution. He has the prisoners brought to him and recognizes among them a man who once saved someone from drowning in the Thames. The man is charged with poisoning someone; as Tom inquires about the evidence, he realizes that the supposed crime occurred far from the Thames at

the very moment he knows that the man was saving another person's life. Tom sets him free and elicits the admiration of his courtiers for his decisiveness. Next, Tom interviews a woman and her daughter accused of using witchcraft to start a devastating storm. After cleverly getting the woman to show that she lacks occult powers, he frees her and her daughter.

Chapter 16

By the dinner hour, Tom is more relaxed. He relishes his grand entrance into the banquet hall and gets through the dinner without a mistake (*continued in chapter 30*).

Chapter 17 (continued from chapter 13)

Desperate to find Edward, Miles Hendon crosses London Bridge, thinking that the boy will head for Hendon Hall in Kent. Earlier, however, Edward was led across the bridge by a boy (later identified as Hugo), who told him that Hendon sent for him. A ruffian following the boys proves to be John Canty in disguise; Canty now calls himself "John Hobbs" and he tells Edward that his new name is "Jack."

They stop at an old barn. After falling asleep, Edward awakens to find the barn filled with a rabble who have just finished feasting. Canty—who is evidently a former gang member—announces that he has killed a priest and is welcomed by the gang's ruffler. Several people tell their sad stories, including a man named Yokel who explains how English law destroyed his family and forced him into SLAVERY. Outraged by what he hears, Edward cries out that the law that made the man a slave is henceforth abolished. In the face of the gang's ridicule, he insists that he is King Edward. The Ruffler tells him however, that if he must be a king, he should not claim to be king of England. Someone else dubs him "Foo-foo the First, the King of the Mooncalves" and he is subjected to a humiliating mock coronation.

Chapter 18

At the next dawn, the vagabonds march off with Edward in Hugo's charge. They help themselves to provisions as they go, while taunting people and threatening worse depredations if anyone complains. At a village, Hugo tells Edward to help him beg; while he fakes a fit, Edward is to wail and pretend that he is his grieving brother. Hugo begins his act when a kindly-looking man approaches, but Edward denounces him as a fraud and the stranger chases Hugo off. Edward escapes in the opposite direction and wanders into the woods. At nightfall, he sneaks into a barn while workmen lock the door from the outside. He tries to sleep in the pitch-black building, but feels something alive touching him. Nearly paralyzed by fright, he eventually discovers that his companion is a harmless calf, with which he peacefully goes to sleep.

Chapter 19

Edward awakens in the morning with a rat sleeping on him and concludes that he cannot sink any lower. Two young girls enter the barn and ask him who he is; they accept his claim to be king so readily that he gratefully pours out his woes as they take him to the house for breakfast. Their kindly mother thinks Edward slightly crazed and tries various ruses to figure out where he is from. Convinced that he comes from a royal kitchen, she puts him in charge of the cooking, but he nearly lets the meal burn. Ashamed of his failure, he later washes dishes without demur but is about to rebel against his chores when he spots John Canty and Hugo coming and slips away.

Chapter 20

Edward again wanders in the woods. As night falls, he peeks through the window of a shabby hut and sees an old man praying. Thinking himself fortunate to find a holy hermit, he knocks on the door and introduces himself as the king. The hermit gushes over this king who has discarded his crown and wealth, and reveals his own secret—that he is an archangel. He grows angry when he recalls that he would be pope, had the king not dissolved his religious house and cast him out into the world. Edward fears that he is in the clutches of a madman, but the hermit calms down, feeds him, and puts him to bed in a back room. When the hermit asks *what* king he is, Edward answers "of England." The hermit's anger returns when he realizes that Edward is the son of the same King Henry who ruined him. After Edward falls asleep, the hermit sharpens a butcher knife and ties him up.

Chapter 21

When Edward awakens, he sees the hermit looming over him with a knife; the old man tells him to pray and calls him the "Seed of the Church's spoiler." As the man is about to stab Edward, someone knocks at his door and he goes to answer it. Edward is overjoyed to hear Miles Hendon's voice, but Hendon never looks in the back room. Instead, he rides off with the hermit, who claims to have sent the boy on an errand. After they leave, John Canty and Hugo burst in; they untie Edward and return to the forest.

Chapter 22

Over the next several days, Hugo tries to make Edward's life miserable until Edward bests him in a cudgel fight that delights the gang, which now proclaims Edward "King of the Game-cocks." Despite winning the gang's respect, Edward keeps trying to escape.

As days pass, Hugo plots his revenge. He and the tinker start to burn a sore on Edward's leg with a "clime," but Yokel saves the king from this humiliation. When the Ruffler decrees that Edward should steal instead of beg, Hugo concocts a new scheme. He leads Edward into a village where he snatches a package from a woman, dumps it on Edward, and runs off. Edward is trapped by an angry crowd as Miles Hendon reappears.

Chapter 23

As a constable leads Edward off to court, Hendon tells him to be patient and trust in the justice of his own laws. In court, the stolen parcel is opened and found to contain a dressed pig; Hendon gasps, but Edward is oblivious to his peril. After the robbery victim testifies that her pig is worth three shillings and eight pence, the judge clears the court and reminds her that the punishment for stealing anything worth more than 13 pence is death. Horrified, the woman revises the pig's value to eight pence. As she leaves, the constable accompanies her; Hendon follows and overhears him pressuring the woman to sell him the pig for eight pence. Back in the courtroom, Hendon finds the judge sentencing Edward to a short jail term and a flogging.

Chapter 24

As the constable leads Edward to jail, Hendon asks him to let Edward escape. Hendon tells the man that he overheard him tricking the woman into selling him her pig—a crime he claims is punishable by death. Petrified with fear, the man lets Edward escape.

Chapter 25

After paying for his lodgings and fetching a donkey and a mule that he has purchased, Hendon gives Edward the secondhand outfit he bought earlier, and the two ride east. Over the next two days, they ride and swap adventure stories. As they approach Hendon Hall, Hendon talks excitedly about his family and the warm reception awaiting him. When they arrive, however, his brother Hugh Hendon claims not to recognize him and says that the family received a letter years earlier reporting Miles's death in battle. Hendon's father and other brother, Arthur, are now dead; of the 27 servants whom Hendon knew, only five remain—all of whom claim not to recognize him. Hendon suffers his worst blow, however, when his former sweetheart Edith enters and denies knowing him. Told that Edith is now Hugh's wife, Hendon turns savagely on his brother.

Chapter 26

While Hugh's servants run for help, Edward remarks how odd it is that no royal couriers are scouring the country searching for him. To establish his identity, he writes a message in English, Latin, and Greek and instructs Hendon to deliver it to his uncle Hertford. Hendon, absorbed with his own problems, pockets the note without looking at it, assuming that it contains meaningless scrawls. Edith then returns and begs Hendon to flee from her wrathful husband. At Hendon's insistence, she swears that she does not know him. Officers burst into the room and seize Hendon and Edward.

Chapter 27

Hendon and Edward are put in a prison cell with 20 other men and women of various ages. Over the next week, people visit the cell to taunt Hendon. One visitor is his family's faithful old servant Blake Andrews, who first loudly denounces Hendon, then whispers an apology and offers to affirm Hendon's true identity. Hendon declines the offer. Andrews returns regularly, smuggling in food and news, while gradually filling in the history of Hen-

don's family during his absence. He says that Hugh is rumored to have forged the letter announcing Miles's death. Andrews also remarks that the new king is rumored to be mad and that Hugh plans to attend his coronation on the 16th (of February), hoping for a peerage from the Lord Protector (Hertford), who is now the Duke of Somerset. For the first time, Edward realizes that someone else is in his place on the throne.

Meanwhile, Edward is comforted by two gentlewomen imprisoned for being Baptists. When he finds them gone one morning, he rejoices that they are free, but is sorry to lose their company. He and Hendon are then taken into the jail-yard, where Edward is horrified to see the women tied to STAKES. He does not realize, however, how grave their situation is until a torch is put to the wood piled below them. Two girls rush in and try to throw themselves on the flames, begging to die with their mothers. As they are restrained, Edward vows never to forget this awful moment.

As new prisoners pass through the jail, Edward talks with them, hoping to learn all he can about conditions in his kingdom. Their woeful tales deeply move him. One prisoner is an old lawyer who wrote a pamphlet criticizing the lord chancellor; for that, he lost his ears, was debarred, fined £3,000, and sentenced to prison for life. After a repeat offense, he was to lose the remainder of his ears, be branded on the face, be fined an additional £5,000, and remain in prison.

Chapter 28

Eventually, Miles Hendon is tried, declared a "sturdy vagabond" and sentenced to two hours in the pillory; Edward is merely reprimanded and released. When Hendon is put in the stocks, a crowd begins hurling things at him, outraging Edward, who commands the officer in charge to free Hendon. Instead, the officer proposes giving Edward a lash or two; Hugh Hendon then arrives and suggests giving him *six* strokes. When Miles Hendon insists on taking the boy's lashings himself, Hugh orders that their number be doubled. Edward silently watches Hendon being whipped, vowing to himself to reward the man who has saved him from shame. He whispers to Hendon to tell him that he is now an earl. Hendon's courage causes the mob to stop abusing him.

Chapter 29

After Hendon is freed, he and Edward ride for London. Hendon hopes to reach the ear of the new king through an old friend of his father, Sir Humphrey Marlow. On the eve of the coronation they reach London, but at London Bridge they are separated in a crowd of drunken revelers.

Chapter 30

Meanwhile, Tom Canty is finally enjoying being king. Now taking his privileges for granted, he is comfortable ordering his royal "sisters" to come and go, and he gives nobles disapproving looks when they offend him. He so enjoys pomp and attention that he doubles his gentlemen-at-arms and triples his servants. He also works hard to remove unjust laws. When the stern princess Mary (later Queen Mary I) accuses him of being too lenient, he dresses her down and advises her to pray for a real heart. As time passes, he rarely thinks about the fate of the real king or of his own mother and sisters.

The night before the coronation, Edward sneaks into Westminster Abbey.

Chapter 31

On coronation morning, Tom rides a barge down the Thames to the Tower of London, from which he rides a splendid horse to the abbey in the "recognition procession." Along the way, he spots old Offal Court comrades and tosses coins to the admiring crowd. When he sees his mother, however, he instinctively raises the back of his hand to his eyes. This gesture identifies him to his mother, who rushes forward to embrace his leg. As guards push her away, Tom utters, "I do not know you woman!" Tom's disloyalty to his mother destroys all the pleasure of being king, leaving him in a funk. As lord protector, Somerset twice reminds him that he must appear cheerful. When Tom says that the woman in the crowd is his mother, Somerset thinks he has gone mad again.

Chapter 32

The narrative returns to early coronation morning, as WESTMINSTER Abbey begins filling up with eager spectators. Several hours pass, then the royal procession arrives and Tom Canty enters in regal splendor. At the climax of the coronation ceremony (which is briefly summarized), a hush prevails as the Archbishop of Canterbury prepares to place the crown on Tom's head. Suddenly, another boy appears and commands him to stop. The newcomer is seized, but Tom Canty orders his release, proclaiming *him* to be the true king. Only confusion reigns now.

Somerset quizzes the newcomer about the court; Edward answers correctly, but Somerset concludes that his answers do not prove his identity. He then asks Edward something that even Tom cannot answer—where the Great Seal is. Edward directs Lord St. John to go to a secret cabinet in his chambers, and Tom confirms the order. The crowd begins shifting in Edward's favor. The moment that St. John returns without the seal, however, the crowd swings back to Tom. Somerset happens to mention the seal's appearance, however, causing Tom finally to understand *what* the seal is; he prompts Edward to recall where he hid it the night they switched places. With Tom's help, Edward remembers slipping the seal into a suit of armor. St. John again goes after it; this time he returns with the seal. Everyone now acknowledges Edward to be the rightful king. Somerset orders that Tom Canty be flung into the Tower, but Edward overrules him, pointing out his uncle's ingratitude to the person who made him a duke. Edward then asks Tom how he could know *where* the seal was without knowing *what* it was. Tom nervously admits to having used it to crack nuts. The coronation is resumed and Edward is crowned king.

Chapter 33

Back at London Bridge earlier the same day, Miles Hendon emerges from the riot with his pockets picked and sets about to find Edward again. He works his way toward Westminster and goes to sleep near the river as cannons signal the king's coronation. The next morning he goes to the palace hoping to find his father's old friend Sir Humphrey Marlow. By chance, the first person whom he approaches is the whipping boy (the deceased Marlow's son), who recognizes him as the outlandish vagabond who is being sought by the king. The boy has Hendon wait inside the palace, but guards then arrest him as a suspicious character. When an officer searches him, he finds Edward's undelivered note and makes a sarcastic remark about more claimants to the throne as he leaves. Hendon figures that he is doomed; however, the officer returns hastily, shows him unexpected courtesy and leads him to the royal court.

Hendon is left alone at the center of a vast room in which the young king is seated on his throne. In his fantastic rags, Hendon draws scornful looks and derisive remarks. Suddenly he recognizes the king as the very same boy he has been regarding as a pitiable tramp. For a moment, he wonders if he is dreaming; then he takes a chair and sits down before the king. Rough hands seize him, but Edward cries out that he is not to be touched and publicly proclaims Hendon to be his faithful servant and savior, whom he intends richly to reward. Hendon soon comes to his senses and kneels to swear allegiance to the king. At the same moment, his brother Hugh and Lady Edith enter the room. Edward has Hugh arrested.

Tom Canty then enters in an unusual but splendid costume. He kneels before the king, who announces that he is pleased with Tom's conduct during the time he occupied the throne. Edward promises to have Tom's mother and sisters provided for, proclaims Tom chief governor of Christ's Hospital and declares that Tom is forever to be known as the "King's Ward."

Conclusion

Hugh Hendon confesses that he forced Edith to repudiate Miles by threatening to kill his brother if she acknowledged him. Hugh is not prosecuted, however, because his wife and brother refuse to testify against him. He flees to the Continent, where he soon dies. Later, Miles, and Edith are married amid much rejoicing. John Canty is never heard from again.

Determined to redress the evils he observed in his travels, Edward seeks to right the wrongs suffered by Yokel in the Ruffler's gang, the lawyer he met in prison, the daughters of the Baptist women burned at the stake, and others. In the few years remaining to him, Edward frequently tells the story of his adventures in order to keep such injustices fresh in his memory, and he works to remove oppression from his kingdom. Tom Canty lives to be a very old and well-respected man.

BACKGROUND AND PUBLISHING HISTORY

Clemens probably began gathering the seeds of *The Prince and the Pauper* as a boy fantasizing about being a prince. The contrast between being a "prince" and being a "pauper" struck him at least as early as 1864, when he wrote a letter to his family describing his life in NEVADA with the phrase, "the old California motto is applicable here: 'We have lived like paupers that we might give like princes.' "

Clemens began thinking about actually writing *The Prince and the Pauper* sometime during the 1870s. After reading CHARLOTTE YONGE's *The Little Duke* (1854), he got the idea of writing his own story about a king becoming a more humane ruler as a result of switching places with a commoner. He initially planned to use the contemporary Prince of Wales (EDWARD VII) as his hero, but became uncomfortable with placing the living prince in compromising fictional situations, so he looked deeper into the past for a more appropriate subject. By the summer of 1876, he settled on Edward Tudor (Edward VI) and began researching 16th-century English history. In addition to collecting notes on history, he collected word lists from WILLIAM SHAKESPEARE's *King Henry IV, Part 1* and several SIR WALTER SCOTT novels. The main literary product of that summer's work, however, was *1601*. He renewed his research the following summer, by which time he already had the novel's title, and he began writing the early chapters. He set the project aside in early 1878, when he left for Europe with his family on the trip that would lead to *A Tramp Abroad* (1880).

Clemens resumed work on *The Prince and the Pauper* as he finished *A Tramp Abroad* in early 1880. Stimulated by his new story and relieved to escape the drudgery that writing his travel book had become, he completed his first draft in mid-September. Two months later, he arranged with JAMES R. OSGOOD to publish the novel. After W. D. HOW-ELLS read the manuscript and offered suggestions,

Clemens finished his final draft in February 1881. He then delivered the manuscript to Osgood and signed a formal contract to publish the novel as a SUBSCRIPTION BOOK. During the fall, he proofed the book with the help of Howells. In late November, he went to Montreal, hoping to ensure protection of his copyright in CANADA. Osgood meanwhile arranged for FRANK T. MERRILL and JOHN J. HARLEY to illustrate the book, with L. S. IPSEN designing the half-title pages. Clemens limited his involvement in the illustrations to requiring that the title characters be drawn as 13- or 14-year-old boys, and he was very pleased with the results—especially Merrill's pictures of court scenes.

CHATTO and Windus issued the novel's English edition on December 1, with Osgood issuing the first American edition 11 days later. Despite Clemens's arranging for a limited Canadian edition, two pirate publishers later issued editions there. Initial sales of the American edition were good, but not outstanding. Of the first 25,000 copies of the book that Osgood had made, nearly 5,000 copies remained unsold when Clemens's own publishing firm, CHARLES L. WEBSTER & COMPANY, took over the rights to the book in February 1884.

Over the century following its initial publication, *The Prince and the Pauper* went through scores of editions. The first corrected edition was issued by the Mark Twain Papers (later the MARK TWAIN PROJECT) in 1979. The project used Clemens's original handwritten manuscript—now held by California's Huntington Library—and the first American edition, which was made from a copy text that no longer survives. This new edition differs from earlier editions in restoring Clemens's original punctuation and eliminating numerous minor changes made without his permission. It also incorporates all the original illustrations. An appendix also includes a chapter on the whipping-boy Hugh Marlow that Clemens removed from the original edition at Howells's suggestion.

The 1996 OXFORD MARK TWAIN edition includes a facsimile reprint of the first American edition of *The Prince and the Pauper* with a new introduction by "Miss Manners" columnist Judith Martin and an afterword by Everett EMERSON.

CRITICAL COMMENTARY

Most readers concede that *The Prince and the Pauper* is what critics call a "well-made novel," but they generally do not examine how really well made it is, because they also agree that Clemens, escaping the "mere humorist" label, wrote it to comply with prevalent literary conventions of the genteel eastern establishment. Tightly constructed, strongly plotted, historically researched, moralistic, and entertaining, it follows conventional blueprints. The novel, however, is more intricate than most genteel works. Numerous parallel but intermingled metaphors—light-dark, sane-insane, reality-dream, truth-falsity, appearance-actuality, mirror image–foil—constitute its underlying architecture. Kingdoms, dreams, and shadows become Prince Edward's domain. London Bridge symbolically links the worlds of prince and pauper, with the shared Thames, which Tom Canty does not cross but Prince Edward does, representing their symbolic baptisms into new outlooks. The novel also subtly satirizes the genteel. By pulling one boy from and pushing another into gentility, it briefly transforms the genteel to the lower class, ironically with lessons learned from the latter and iterated by its denizen's temporary reign over the former. Clemens, having established a dream-reality metaphor, adds, somewhat surprisingly, a device from medieval dream-visions—guides who help dreamers adjust and understand dreamlands.

Dreamworlds

Medieval dream-vision guides include Virgil and Beatrice in *The Divine Comedy*; the Pearl-Maiden in *The Pearl*; Holy Church and Piers Plowman in *The Vision of William Concerning Piers the Plowman*; the Golden Eagle and Scipio Africanus, respectively, in Chaucer's *House of Fame* and *Parlement of Foules*; and the Evangelist in JOHN BUNYAN's non-medieval *Pilgrim's Progress*. Like Chaucer in *Book of the Duchess*, Miles Hendon (Prince Edward's guide) is a knight, actually a quasi-knight until Edward bestows knighthood, calling himself the "specter knight" of the Kingdom of Dreams and Shadows because he doubts this raggedly dressed boy's claim to a realm of any substance. In dream visions, the protagonist falls asleep, sometimes several times, and finds himself in a strange place where he encounters a mysterious person, often allegorical, who explains the surroundings and leads him, usually, to some decided-upon destination or goal, perhaps a place (heaven) or an idea (enlightenment); Virgil takes Dante through purgatory and hell, explaining punishments, and Beatrice guides him in heaven. Clemens's dream structure is metaphoric and thematic but follows figurative boundaries: Crossing London Bridge, Edward symbolically enters his dream kingdom (Kent, south of London). Tom, trapped in a dream world of palaces, can only ride between them on the River-Pageant, bright lights amid darkness, with the Thames as the common kingdom-divider.

As young boys, the title characters may need guides, but Clemens increases the historical Edward's age by three years, making the boys teenagers, perhaps to appeal to that audience; Tom's guide, Humphrey Marlow, is only slightly older. Hendon is an adult, needed to handle an initially haughty would-be king. With Lord Protector Hertford as adviser on state affairs, Tom requires someone near his age to aid in everyday relationships. Edward requires a physical protector; Marlow, as royal whipping boy, is that in another sense. Switched and separated, Tom Canty, a pauper lost in a royal kingdom, and Edward, the Prince of Wales stranded in a dream kingdom, need guidance in individual dreamlands.

Miles Hendon

These characters are not consciously guides through these differing dream worlds. Because he becomes the more important character, Hendon is the more prominent guide. As Marlow, the whipping boy, stands between Tom (as prince) and the only harm that approaches a royal child, so Hendon stands between Edward (as pauper) and the harm that accompanies poverty. Both supply the boys with aid—information by Marlow and deeds by Hendon—that enables them to survive their dream worlds. It is not coincidental that their roles are similar and that the initials of one are the reverse of the initials of the other, thus corresponding to the reversal (for the boys) of dream and reality. Furthermore, the oft-used initials for royal possession (H.M.) are those of the guide for the false prince,

and the initials of the true prince's guide are M.H., "His Majesty," reversed. Edward's situation is succinctly stated in his companion's initials.

Hendon's fortunes have also met reversal. Appropriately, Tom becomes associated with the person on the lowest rung of the royal retinue, and Edward becomes attached to a member of the fallen nobility. In their real worlds, Tom and Edward are, respectively, below and above these guides on the social scale. In their dream worlds, they are in opposite positions. But both boys are obliged to their guides for aid given to them in their dream worlds. Hendon, a soldier, is an active force for Edward, a boy who asserts his identity against tall odds. Marlow, by his nature and the nature of his job, is passive, complementing Tom's own passivity as he gradually ceases to proclaim his true identity, bows to the wishes of guardian-lords in state affairs, and uses information from the whipping boy to become who he is believed to be.

Playing with History

Like Hendon, Marlow is granted a request by the "king" (Tom) and given an office that extends to his descendants. Both requests are seemingly absurd, and in that sense, dreamlike: Edward grants Hendon and his descendants the privilege of sitting in the English king's presence (chapter 12); Marlow and his descendants permanently receive the office of "hereditary Grand Whipping Boy to the royal house of England" (chapter 14). Establishing a precedent for Hendon's request with a footnote, Clemens presents history with dreamlike qualities. Without attempting to authenticate the position given Marlow, the narrator states in a note in the back of the novel: "James I and Charles II had whipping boys when they were little fellows, to take their punishments for them when they were short in their lessons; so I have ventured to furnish my small prince with one, for my own purposes." Once again, Clemens seems to play with history, utilizing it as though it were a work of the imagination, like a retold dream that when viewed in retrospect is given—consciously or not by its author—some semblance of order.

Clemens's purposes for the anachronistic whipping boy are quite varied. One purpose is a satire of royal prerogatives and appointments. They may seem to be the madness or absurdity of a dream (see chapter 14), but they are true, even if not factually or historically correct for the period. Another purpose is to illustrate the pain that others must endure for and because of the Crown. Ironic, and true as a pun, is the fact that the whipping boy cannot live without pain; it is his livelihood, but most of the king's subjects do not live without pain. A related purpose is that the whipping boy is emblematic of the fact that the rich can escape punishment and suffering, whereas the poor can only escape through their dreams. As a scapegoat, a relief from suffering, the whipping boy is related to the symbolic escape of sleep, and thus to dreams. Like Hendon, he is a guide through the ways of this dreamlike world in which his "master" now lives, for Tom quickly realizes that Humphrey can be a source of information concerning people and matters related to the court and resolves to use his knowledge daily (ibid.).

Marlow is also a gauge by which Tom may study other characters and chart relation to and distance from his real and dream worlds. Like Hendon's fortunes, Marlow's have become reversed, but, more quickly than the former, they are reestablished. Since Tom is now "king" and must concentrate more upon affairs of state than studies, he no longer requires a whipping boy; however, Tom makes Marlow's position permanent by promising to continue his studies and triple Marlow's wages, to which Marlow replies, "this princely lavishness doth far surpass my most distempered dreams of fortune" (ibid.). Similarly, the lavishness of royalty far exceeds Tom's dreams of fortune.

Dreams Realized

Tom and Marlow attain their dreams at almost the same time, as two persons in opposite circumstances—Hendon and Edward—seek to regain their lost positions; their efforts are also successful almost simultaneously. As Tom restores Marlow's fortunes early in the novel, so Edward restores Hendon's fortunes at its end. Like Tom, Marlow helps support two sisters. Marlow earns money through whippings; Tom, often whipped for not bringing in more money to his father, is never paid.

In contrast, Hendon usually performs the whippings in encounters with foes. But he, too, becomes a whipping boy when he asks to take a dozen lashes intended for King Edward (chapter 28). A definite and tangible link between the two boys and the two guides is Sir Humphrey Marlow, late father of the whipping boy and a friend of Hendon's father. Seeking redress from the king, Hendon hopes that Sir Humphrey Marlow, an officer of the Crown, will help him gain an audience with Edward. Shortly after meeting the whipping boy near the palace and asking for Sir Humphrey Marlow, Hendon finds himself in the royal court, where he must confront dream and reality and distinguish between them. The guide is now lost. He is lost because he did not fully realize what kind of guide he was. But his goals and Edward's goal are similar, as they themselves are similar.

Hendon's personality and subplot support the main plot, underscore Edward's plight, and reinforce the dream motif of the novel. A similarity to Edward is evident from the beginning of their relationship; also apparent is the idea that Hendon is a mediating figure between Edward and Tom, the upper classes and the lower classes, the real and the dream. Outside Guildhall, after his first escape from John Canty, Tom's father, Edward asserts his rights as prince and demands to be let in; the crowd mocks and taunts him. His anger produces more proclamations of his identity, generating more taunts. A nightmare for Edward, the situation resembles Clemens's dream of being a humorist at whom no one laughs. As a prince, he is due certain rights, loyalty, and respect; no one believes him—a frustrating experience for one accustomed to others rushing to fulfill his desires and commands. Entering at this point, Hendon, apparently believing Edward, seems to signal a return to reality or the beginning of a better dream. Hendon makes clear that he understands living in this mob's world: " 'Rest thy small jaw, my child, I talk the language of these base kennel-rats like to a very native' " (chapter 11). However, like the prince, Hendon has fallen from high to low and seems out of place, a prince-in-rags defending a prince:

> His doublet and trunks were of rich material, but faded and threadbare, and their gold-lace

adornments were sadly tarnished; his ruff was rumpled and damaged; the plume in his slouched hat was broken and had a bedraggled and disreputable look; at his side he wore a long rapier in a rusty iron sheath; his swaggering carriage marked him at once as a ruffler of the camp. (ibid.)

Described by the narrator as a "fantastic figure" (unreal, dreamlike), he is—like the prince—greeted "with an explosion of jeers and laughter." Indeed, a shout endorses the mirror motif: " 'Tis another prince in disguise!' " (ibid.). Metaphorical repetition resembles entrapment in a hall of mirrors, as in a mad dream. The crowd becomes rowdier, threatening violence, but Hendon rescues Edward.

At Hendon's lodgings on London Bridge, itself a symbolic link between dreamlands, the reader and Edward learn more about Hendon that indicates his role as mirror reinforcement of the prince's plight and as a linking device between worlds. Asked if he is nobly born, Hendon replies, " 'We are of the tail of nobility . . .' " (chapter 12), a phrase indicating his linking status. As Edward has two sisters, Hendon has two brothers. His brother Hugh's lie has forced Hendon from his proper position into three years' banishment. But circumstances, including imprisonment in a foreign dungeon, have extended time away to 10 years. Unknown to Hendon at this point, his father—like Edward's—and his brother Arthur are dead. The potential threat Edward faces from the new monarch "Bloody Mary" has become an actual threat for Hendon with his brother Hugh in power. Hendon's beloved Edith, as retiring as Edward's friend, Lady Jane Grey, is now Hugh's wife. Whereas Hendon's usurper is tyrannical, Edward's dream usurper is merciful. Hugh orders Hendon jailed and punished. Like Edward and Tom, Hendon has an aide during his troubles, Blake Andrews, an "old servant [who becomes] very valuable to Hendon and the king. . . ." Though his name—with syntax suggesting a reversal—is similar to Father Andrew (who aided both Tom and Edward), calling attention to his role, he is not a priest but a faithful (former) servant to Hendon's

family, Miles's elderly equivalent to Marlow. As a mirror opposite to young Marlow, Tom's valuable information source who later helps Hendon, Andrews brings helpful news to Hendon and Edward.

After Hendon and Edward arrive at Hendon Hall, the parallels between them and between dream and reality become even more pronounced. The alliterative double "H's" of Hendon Hall, located near Monk's Holm in Kent (chapter 11), are another aspect of the mirror motif. "Monk's Holm" is a name seemingly out of place in Henry VIII's England, belonging in another world, Edward's dream kingdom. Its initials are the same as Hendon's and as such carry the same implications of reversed majesty. The related parallel, mirror, twin, and dream motifs are thus reasserted.

Absent 10 years, Hendon notes that, of the villagers, " 'none know me' " (chapter 25), as no one knows Edward to be the king. Greeting his brother Hugh, Hendon is, like Edward, called mad and told that he imagines himself to be who he says he is: " 'Thy wits seem touched, poor stranger . . .' "; " 'whom dost thou imagine thyself to be?' " Punning and pitting true against false underscore this dreamlike atmosphere. Pretending he believes Hendon can never return because he is dead, Hugh says, " 'Ah, it seems too good to be true, it is too good to be true,' " thus dreamlike. Hendon asserts that old servants can identify him but learns that Hugh retained only those loyal to him: " 'The . . . villains have survived the two-and-twenty leal and honest,' " symbolizing that the false have usurped the true, as dream has apparently enveloped reality for Hendon. Edward notes the parallel, " 'Mind not thy mischance, good man; there be others in the world whose identity is denied, and whose claims are derided. Thou hast company' " (ibid.). Edward and Hendon are experiencing the same dream. Hendon, becoming desperate, asks Edward not to doubt him; the boy answers that he does not and throws the same proposition back to Hendon, momentarily seized by guilty confusion but saved from answering by Hugh's entrance.

Following Hugh to confront Hendon is Edith who, compelled by knowledge of her husband's evil capabilities, coldly utters, " 'I know him not!' "

(ibid.), denying her loved one as Tom later denies his mother. Another link to Tom's side of the plot and to the dream motif is evident when Hendon next encounters Edith. Convincing himself that Edith denied him for fear of Hugh and springing confidently to greet her when she returns alone, Hendon is again rebuked with a gesture to keep his distance, an action that "made him begin to question, for a moment, if he *was* the person he was pretending to be, after all" (chapter 26), as Tom began to doubt his own reality, his own sanity. Like both Tom and Edward, Hendon is accused both of being mad and living in a dream: " 'The mad cannot be persuaded out of their delusions. . . . I think this dream of yours hath the seeming of honest truth to you. . . . My husband might bid you pleasure yourself with your dream in peace . . .' " (ibid.). With Edith's observation that his dream has the air of reality, dream and reality clash. Confounded, Hendon demands that Edith, looking in his face, swear he is not himself; when she does so, faintly, he declares, " 'Oh, this passes belief!' " (ibid.). Too difficult to believe, the reality of his situation seems the dream Edith declared it. As Hugh's officers carry him away, Hendon's own domain is as substanceless as Edward's. Hendon is now truly a knight of dreams and shadows.

Truth v. Falsity

Appearing in other aspects of the Hendon subplot, particularly in the contrast of truth and falsity, the dream motif continually supports the main plot. By the time Blake Andrews arrives at the jail holding Hendon and Edward, Hendon doubts the reality of any segment of his past life in this village upon which he once would have pinned his life: " 'This man will know me—and deny me, too, like the rest' " (chapter 27). Andrews pretends not to recognize Hendon in order to help without arousing suspicion, asserting, " 'I am [a] true man!' " (ibid.). Later, he whispers to Hendon, " 'I am old and poor, Sir Miles; but say the word and I will . . . proclaim the truth though I be strangled for it' " (ibid.). This conflict between truth and falsity underlying the whole novel also appears in the scene in which Edward, after Hendon has suffered in the stocks and received a lashing originally intended for the monarch, dubs him earl: " 'To be suddenly hoisted, naked and gory, from the common stocks to . . . an earldom, seemed . . . the last possibility in the line of the grotesque' "(chapter 28). So absurd it must be a dream, the situation is certainly dreamlike. Not realizing how real the grants of Edward are, Hendon ironically contrasts and juxtaposes the real and the false:

> "An' this go on, I shall presently be hung like a Maypole with fantastic gauds and make-believe honors. . . . Better these poor mock dignities of mine, [coming] unasked from a . . . right spirit, than real ones bought by servility from grudging and interested power." (ibid.)

He values what he believes to be false as though it is real; ironically, it is real. As difficult as differentiating dream and reality is distinguishing true from false.

This problem and other aspects of the main plot are evident in the final phases of the Hendon subplot as the two plots gradually converge. Released from prison and exiled, Hendon decides to ask justice from the new king but ironically wonders, " 'Ah, yes, but could so fantastic a pauper get admission to the august presence of a monarch?' " (chapter 29) This statement not only calls attention to a parallel, an instance of the mirror motif, between him and the two boys but also introduces several ironies underscoring the dreamlike situation. Hendon considers approaching the king for aid while the king is beside him, in no better situation than he. Both true and false kings are paupers, one by circumstances and one by background. Both "kings" are more fantastic paupers than Hendon.

After losing his pauper-king in a crowd on London Bridge, now significantly the link back, Hendon searches through the night and the next day for Edward, hoping and expecting to find him surrounded by a mocking crowd proclaiming his royalty. Having wandered out of the city into a pleasant countryside with night approaching, Hendon lays down to rest and soon falls asleep (chapter 33). As with Tom and Edward, sleep—at least briefly—dulls Hendon's consciousness to the reality of his difficulties. As a distant, booming cannon announces Edward's crowning as king of England,

Hendon falls asleep and does not awake until almost mid-morning next day. He, who has been so active on behalf of Edward during the monarch's dreamlike experience, is asleep, passive, when his liege, both in reality and in the fantasy kingdom, is crowned.

Twin Motif

In addition to stressing the importance of sleep in terms of the whole story, Clemens uses Hendon to reassert the twin motif. After Hendon arrives at the palace hoping to discover a means to contact his friend Sir Humphrey Marlow, the whipping boy's deceased father, the boy sees him and, given Hendon's description by Edward, concerned about his new Earl of Kent, thinks, " 'He answereth the description to a rag—that God should make two such, would be to cheapen miracles, by wasteful repetition' " (ibid.). Since the reader and even Humphrey know that Edward and Tom are perfect doubles, this ironic statement focuses attention on the dreamlike incredibility of the duplication, an aspect of the dreamy atmosphere of the novel repeatedly reinforced by the mirror motif. For instance, Humphrey has not been told Hendon's name, only the fanciful name "Sir-Odds-and-Ends," but once told the true name, he says, " ' . . . it mattereth not, this is his twin brother, and can give his majesty news of t'other Sir-Odds-and-Ends, I warrant' " (ibid.). Prominence is once again given to the reinforcing parallelism of the subplot and thus to the mirror motif when guards arrest Hendon, left alone by Humphrey, as a suspicious character. Searching him and discovering the paper, entrusted to him by Edward, proclaiming its writer the rightful king, they shout, " 'Another new claimant of the crown! . . . Verily they breed like rabbits, to-day' " (ibid.). Actually, Edward is the only "claimant" to "Tom's throne" to appear thus far, but the effect of these and other statements, the mirror motif, and other such factors is to help establish a fantasy-like setting in which dreamlike situations believably occur.

Led into the presence of King Edward, Hendon experiences difficulty discerning the reality behind this dream situation. Unable to believe what he sees, Hendon turns his eyes from Edward to the room and its people and exclaims, " 'But these are *real*—verily these are *real*—surely it is not a dream' " (ibid.). He wonders whether the king is real or a dream or whether he is living in a dream: " 'Is it a dream? . . . or *is* he the veritable sovereign of England, and not the friendless poor Tom o' Bedlam I took him for . . .?' " (ibid.)

Hendon's choice of words, besides being another instance of the madness-mirror-dream-motifs, is ironically appropriate; Edward became "friendless poor Tom" for three weeks as Tom became "the veritable sovereign of England" during that period, and both were thought mad during that time. So, the transformation into Tom is here given a double sense for Edward because, by entering a world that, for him, was one of madness, he also became *Tom o' Bedlam*. The appearance before him as king of a person he thought insane understandably causes Hendon to question the reality of the situation, the possibility that he might be dreaming, and, indeed, his own sanity. Thus, in testing the "dream" by sitting in the presence of the king, Hendon is also testing himself, his own perception of reality.

The importance of tests thus forms another link between the characters and the two plots, but both Edward and Tom fail the tests applied to their dreams—Edward by not being Tom and Tom by forsaking his mother in pretending to be someone else and revealing himself through a natural reflex. Before Hendon can recover from the triumph of his test, for he now knows "his pauper" to be the king, his brother Hugh and the Lady Edith arrive at court. Because of his bewildered condition, a result of his new insight into past events, Hendon does not see them before Edward angrily says of Hugh, " 'Strip this robber of his false show and stolen estates, and put him under lock and key . . .' " (ibid.), punishing the villain of the subplot as abruptly as might occur in a fantasy or a dream. The test becomes more tangible. The reality that seemed to be dream has vanquished the dream that had become reality for Hendon. Hendon, the only man who seemed to believe that Edward was king, now truly believes. As the guide led the king through a dreamlike situation, so he is led into one himself and thereby to the truth.

The truth to which Hendon led Edward, and that Tom gains through Marlow, is that high status breeds arrogance, arrogance distances sympathy, and distance diminishes mercy. Tom, who arrogantly denied his mother, empathizes with Humphrey, intensifying his guilt for being haughty. With Hendon as companion/example, Edward, suffering among and with his subjects, loses pride and empirically understands the necessity of pity so that he may now genuinely grant it. Restoring and permanently caring for Canty's family, Edward entitles Tom for gentle, merciful governance, to be *mirrored* in his own (ibid.).

Just as through varying dream visions Beatrice led Dante to revelation, Piers Plowman guided Langland to St. Truth, the Pearl-Maiden took the Poet to glimpse New Jerusalem, Evangelist helped Christian reach Celestial City, and Chaucer's different guides brought him to various destinations, so Clemens uses Hendon and Marlow to take Edward and Tom into and out of a metaphorical dream structure to better understanding of themselves and their actual worlds. Using a literary device popularized in the Middle Ages, he successfully enters the modern literary world of eastern America while figuratively tweaking its nose by placing a quite un-genteel character in upper-class splendor and the most aristocratic in the lowest state, transforming high more radically than low. Satire aimed at adults explains elaborate patterns intended for adults in a book aimed at children.

Critical Commentary by John H. Davis

DRAMATIC ADAPTATIONS

This story has been one of the most frequently dramatized of Clemens's works. Shortly after he wrote it, his wife Livy adapted a play from it that family members performed at home during the 1880s. Clemens himself usually played Miles Hendon, with his older daughters playing the title roles. DANIEL FROHMAN and Abby Sage Richardson mounted the first professional production in Philadelphia in 1889 and other adaptations soon followed. Clemens attended a production performed by an educational group in New York City in 1907. Two years later, he made a brief appear-

ance in a short silent film adaptation produced by THOMAS A. EDISON's company. A British film company also filmed the story the same year.

The first feature-length film adaptation was made by the Famous Players company in 1915. Thirty-two-year-old Marguerite Clark (1883–1940) played both title roles in one of the earliest films to use split-screen shooting techniques. In 1920, the Hungarian director Alexander Korda filmed the story in Vienna, with Tibi Lubin as Tom and the prince, Francis Herter as John Canty, and Francis Everth as Miles Hendon. After Korda settled a copyright dispute with the Mark Twain Estate, his film was distributed in the United States two years later.

William Keighley directed the first major sound film for Warner Brothers in 1937. Identical twins Bobby and Billy Mauch (1924–) played the title roles opposite Errol Flynn's Miles Hendon. Laird Doyle's script departed from the original story significantly by having Hertford (Claude Rains) dis-

Identical twins Bobby and Bill Mauch played the title roles in the 1937 adaptation of *The Prince and the Pauper.* (*Warner Bros.*)

cover Tom Canty's real identity, then send the captain of the palace guard (Alan Hale) to find and kill the true prince.

A Soviet film of *The Prince and the Surfer* was made in 1943. Other adaptations have since been made in China (1966), India (1968), and Ireland (1969). The next major adaptation was a joint British-American production released in the United States as *Crossed Swords* in 1977. Its cast included Mark Lester (Edward/Tom Canty), Oliver Reed (Miles Hendon), Harry Andrews (Hertford), Charlton Heston (Henry VIII), George C. Scott (Ruffler), Raquel Welch (Edith), Ernest Borgnine (John Canty), and Rex Harrison (Norfolk).

The Prince and the Surfer (1999) is a modern update set in Southern California's beach culture. The adaptation is loose, but Mark Twain is credited for the original story. The story has also been animated several times. An Australian film was made in 1970 and the Disney Company made a 24-minute cartoon with Mickey Mouse 20 years later.

The Prince and the Pauper has also inspired several television adaptations. The Dumont network aired a one-hour play in October 1957, and a one-hour play was broadcast on the *Shirley Temple Theatre* two years later. In March 1962, *Walt Disney Presents* aired a three-part production that was later packaged as a feature film. Sean Scully played both title roles, with Guy Williams as Miles Hendon. In a major departure from the original story, Hendon accepts Edward's claim to be king and tries to help him get into the royal palace. A Hallmark Channel adaptation that aired in 2000 starred Aidan Quinn as Miles Hendon and Alan Bates as Henry VIII. That production's script was similar to that of the 1937 film.

Clemens's work also inspired a parallel female story—Gwen Davis's novel *The Princess and the Pauper: An Erotic Fairy Tale* (1989), set in the fictional kingdom of Perq in the Irish Sea.

CHARACTERS AND RELATED ENTRIES

Andrew, Father   Minor character in *The Prince and the Pauper* (1881). Andrew is a Roman Catholic priest who has lived in Offal Court since King HENRY VIII closed his monastery. Responsible for what little education Tom Canty has, he would

also have taught Tom's sisters, Nan and Bet Canty, were they not afraid to become literate. John Canty kills Andrew when the latter tries to protect Prince Edward (chapter 10).

Andrews, Blake   Minor character in *The Prince and the Pauper* (1881). An honest and good-hearted former servant at Hendon Hall, Andrews visits Miles Hendon in prison frequently in chapter 27, bringing extra food and news. He is the first person to confirm Hendon's identity, as well as the first person from whom King Edward learns that someone else (Tom Canty) is sitting on his throne.

Canty, Bet and Nan   Minor characters in *The Prince and the Pauper* (1881). The twin sisters of Tom Canty, 15-year-old Bet and Nan are introduced in chapter 2 as "good-hearted girls, unclean, clothed in rags, and profoundly ignorant"—a description almost identical to that which Clemens applied to his childhood friend TOM BLANKENSHIP. The girls appear only in chapter 10, when they try to protect the prince against their father's brutality. After Tom becomes king, he thinks about his sisters occasionally and even dreams about them in chapter 14, but gradually puts them out of his mind. In the last chapter, King Edward VI arranges for the girls' livelihood, and the narrative ends with Tom looking for his mother and sisters to celebrate their good fortune.

Canty, Gammer   Minor character in *The Prince and the Pauper* (1881). The vicious grandmother of Tom Canty, Gammer Canty lives with Tom's family in Offal Court. In chapter 3, Tom tells Prince Edward how Gammer beats him; the prince himself gets a sample of her treatment when John Canty brings him home in chapter 10. At the end of that chapter, the family flees Offal Court and Gammer Canty disappears from the narrative, aside from Tom's later recollection of a nasty beating she once gave him (chapter 15).

The female equivalent of *gaffer*, "gammer" is a term for old wife that goes back to at least the mid-16th century.

Canty, John ("John Hobbs")   Character in *The Prince and the Pauper* (1881). The abusive father of

Tom Canty, John Canty is a professional thief who forces his children to beg and regularly beats them and his wife. Though he is brutal enough to kill Father Andrew (chapter 10) and brag about it to his criminal gang (chapter 17), there are limits to his cruelty. For example, he hesitates to punish the boy he believes is his son when he claims to be Edward, Prince of Wales, thinking him mad. Though the boy proves worse than useless as a gang member, Canty struggles to recapture him each time he escapes—perhaps out of parental instinct. Once the boy is arrested for stealing in chapter 22, however, Canty drops out of the narrative completely. By then, he has also lost contact with his mother, wife, and daughters. After Edward is restored to his throne in chapter 33, he offers to have Canty hanged—if Tom so desires and the law allows—but the final chapter reveals that Canty is never heard from again.

Canty, Mrs.   Character in *The Prince and the Pauper* (1881). The kindhearted, middle-aged mother of Tom Canty, Mrs. Canty protects Tom from her husband and mother-in-law, though she herself is often beaten. When her husband brings Prince Edward home, thinking *he* is Tom, she worries about the boy's apparent madness and is beaten for her solicitousness (chapter 10). Having opposed Tom's book-learning, she sees the boy's claim to be the Prince of Wales as a delusion caused by his reading. After the prince falls asleep, however, she starts wondering if he may in fact *not* be her son. She devises a test to learn the truth; remembering that Tom habitually shields his eyes with the back of his hand when startled, she jars the prince awake several times to test his reactions, but with inconclusive results.

When the Cantys flee Offal Court at the end of chapter 10, they get separated in the crowd and Mrs. Canty apparently never sees her husband again. She reappears in chapter 31 when Tom spots her in the crowd as he rides in the coronation procession. Her sudden appearance so startles him that he instinctively shields his eyes with his hand—the old habit that proves his identity to his mother's satisfaction. Though Tom spurns his mother when she approaches him, their chance

meeting prepares him to renounce his false kingship the moment the real Edward appears. At the conclusion of the narrative, Mrs. Canty and her 15-year-old twin daughters, Bet and Nan Canty, are reunited with Tom.

Canty, Tom   Character in *The Prince and the Pauper* (1881). The "pauper" of the novel's title, Tom is born in London's Offal Court in 1547, on the same day as Edward, Prince of Wales. He appears to be about 13 years old when the main narrative begins.

As Tom grows up, he leads a tough life in the slums. Hungry, cold, and regularly beaten by his father and grandmother, he is forced to beg; however, he preserves some dignity by refusing to steal. Despite his hardships, he is happy because he does not know any better. Consistent with an archaic meaning of *canty*, he is inherently cheerful and finds real pleasure in life. He plays games with other boys, swims in the THAMES and revels in reading Father Andrew's books and hearing stories that appear to come from the ARABIAN NIGHTS. Tom Canty is a kind of composite of Huckleberry Finn and Tom Sawyer, and his shabby neighborhood resembles their hometown of St. Petersburg in important ways.

As the impoverished but good-hearted son of an abusive father, Tom anticipates Huck. He also resembles Tom Sawyer in being obsessed with romantic stories and loving gaudy entertainments, such as parades, fairs, and Punch and Judy shows. Like Tom Sawyer, he is an inventive and natural leader; he directs street gangs in mock wars and organizes a mock royal court, with himself as a prince. His wisdom is recognized by many in the neighborhood, including adults, who come to him for advice. When he later finds himself on the real throne of England, his good-heartedness and wisdom come to the fore. During his first days in Prince Edward's palace, Tom wants nothing more than to be liberated from his captivity. He initially cowers in the presence of nobles and courtiers, but gradually his confidence grows and he asserts his natural leadership. Seeing the cruelty and illogic in archaic laws, he moves to strike down brutal punishments, and pardons as many prisoners as he can. He even tells off the gloomy Princess Mary—the later queen "Bloody Mary"—for having a hard heart (chapter 30). At the same time, however, he delights in regal pomp and multiplies his servants and retainers to gratify his need for show.

By coronation day, Tom is so reconciled to being on the throne that he suppresses guilty thoughts about the fate of the real king and even manages to put his loving mother and sisters out of his mind. It is only when he sees his mother while riding to Westminster Abbey that his purer instincts reemerge. Though he initially disavows her, he is so consumed with guilt that he is ready to renounce all the trappings of power to make amends. Indeed, the moment that the real king reappears, Tom immediately defers to him and does everything he can to have him acknowledged as the true king. After Edward is restored to his throne, he rewards Tom's loyalty and exemplary behavior by making him the "King's Ward," giving him a distinctive outfit to wear, and making him head of Christ's Hospital.

After Olivia Clemens dramatized *The Prince and the Pauper* for family productions, Clemens's daughters and neighbor girls typically played the prince and Tom Canty. Their casting anticipated that of eight-year-old Elsie Leslie Lyde in a professional production in 1889. When the first substantial film adaptation was made in 1915, 32-year-old Marguerite Clark played both roles, as Tibi Lubin (1922), Sean Scully (1962) and Mark Lester (1977) later would. Meanwhile, 13-year-old twins, Bobby and Billy Mauch, shared the leads in the 1937 film adapted from the novel.

Christ's Hospital ("Christ's Church") London home for orphan children mentioned in *The Prince and the Pauper* (1881). In 1552, England's King Edward VI founded Christ's Hospital as a home ("hospital") for foundlings on property that his father had seized from the Grey Friars Church. Although *The Prince and the Pauper* is set about five years before the time the historical Christ's Hospital was founded, the institution figures into its narrative and is the subject of several long appendix notes by Clemens. In chapter 4, Edward—still a prince—goes to Christ's Hospital (initially misnamed "Christ's Church") hoping for succor since

his father had created it. After being roughly treated by the home's ignorant boys, he vows to transform the institution into a school. When he is restored to his throne in chapter 33, he makes good on his vow and names Tom Canty the hospital's chief governor. The real institution did later become a school, which was moved to Sussex in 1902.

Edward VI (Prince Edward) (October 12, 1537, Hampton Court, England–July 6, 1553, London) Historical figure and central character in *The Prince and the Pauper* (1881). Edward was the only legitimate son of England's King Henry VIII, by the latter's third wife, Jane Seymour (c. 1509–1537). Though never formally installed as the prince of Wales, he acceded to the throne on his father's death on January 28, 1547, when he was nine years old. He reigned for five and a half years, first under the supervision of a regency council appointed by his father, then under lord protectors: his uncle, the earl of Hertford (from 1547 to 1549), and John Dudley, the duke of Northumberland (from 1549 to 1553). Though Edward was relatively robust when he became king, his health later deteriorated, and he succumbed to measles, smallpox, and tuberculosis at 15. Before dying, he named his cousin Lady Jane Grey to succeed him.

In *The Prince and the Pauper*, Edward changes CLOTHES with Tom Canty, a beggar boy, and is mistakenly thrown out of his palace (chapter 3). Soon afterward, his father dies, elevating him from prince to king. The novel's dominant narrative thread becomes Edward's struggle to reclaim his crown. His dispossession casts him in the role of one of Clemens's favorite character types—a claimant. As such, he describes himself as "forlorn and friendless" (chapter 11)—a lament remarkably similar to that of the bogus Duke in chapter 19 of *Huckleberry Finn* (1884).

A striking difference between the fictional and historical Edwards is age. While the historical Edward became king at nine, Clemens deliberately obscures his story's chronology in order to depict Edward as about 13 years old—approximately the same age as Huckleberry Finn and Tom Sawyer. It is also roughly the same age that Clemens himself was when his father died—a fact that may bear on the way his fictional Edward reacts to his father's death. Until recently, history has seen Edward as a sickly child; Clemens portrays him as healthy and robust. Edward proves his toughness by enduring hardships and beatings and by boldly standing up to his oppressors, such as Hugo—a bigger boy whom he thrashes in chapter 22. Clemens's Edward is resolute in his convictions almost to the point of absurdity. While never wavering from his claim to be the Prince of Wales—later the king—he is blind to the difficulty others might have in believing his fantastic claim.

In Clemens's reading of English history, he saw tendencies toward compassion and justice in Edward's reign that were absent under other monarchs. To a certain extent, *The Prince and the Pauper* is his attempt to explain *why* Edward's reign was different. At first, Edward is so used to having his way that he impatiently blurts out rash threats against his detractors. He softens as the narrative progresses and his PICARESQUE adventures outside the palace expose him to poverty, cruelty, and injustice that incline him toward reform. His mistreatment at the hands of children at Christ's Hospital, for example, moves him to provide for their education. After he regains his throne, he seeks out many of the victims of injustice he has met and tries to right the wrongs done to them. The novel's epilogue concludes that his reign "was a singularly merciful one for those harsh times."

Foo-foo the First, King of the Mooncalves

Facetious title used in *The Prince and the Pauper* (1881). In chapter 17, young King Edward is cast among a gang of beggars and thieves. Offended by Edward's calling himself "king of England," the gang's Ruffler tells him that if he must call himself a "king," to choose another title. When the tinker proposes dubbing Edward "Foo-foo the First, King of the Mooncalves," the gang subjects Edward to a humiliating mock coronation. Five chapters later, however, Edward wins a cudgel-fight against Hugo and is renamed the "King of the Game-Cocks."

Early 19th-century American slang for an insignificant fool, "foo-foo" also appears in *Innocents Abroad* (1869), which quotes a spurious future

encyclopedia entry by "the learned Ah-ah- Foo-foo" (chapter 31). "Mooncalf" goes back to at least the late 16th century, when it meant a false pregnancy or a monster. A later meaning—likely the one Clemens intends in *The Prince and the Pauper*—is "simpleton."

Hendon, Edith Character in *The Prince and the Pauper* (1881). The wife of Hugh Hendon, her cousin, Edith is the orphaned daughter of an earl who has left her a lapsed title. Like several other female characters created by Clemens—as well as his own wife—Edith is not only beautiful, gentle, and good, but is an heiress to a fortune. Formerly, she was a ward of her father-in-law, Sir Richard Hendon, who originally wanted her to marry his oldest son, Arthur. She, however, has always loved the middle brother, Miles Hendon, who is four years her senior. Arthur hoped to arrange for her to wed Miles, but Miles went off to war when Edith was 16 and did not return for 10 years. Meanwhile, Sir Richard and Arthur died, leaving Hugh to trick Edith into marrying him.

Miles describes Edith in chapter 12; she first appears in chapter 25, when she denies knowing him. It is not revealed until the final chapter that she has disavowed Miles in order to save his life. After Hugh dies, she marries Miles.

Hendon, Hugh Character in *The Prince and the Pauper* (1881). Hugh is the younger brother of Miles Hendon, who describes him as having always been "a mean spirit, covetous, treacherous, vicious, underhanded—a reptile" (chapter 12). Like Clemens's Tom Driscoll and other bad-boy characters, Hugh was his father's pet. When Miles returns to Hendon Hall after a 10-year absence, he finds Hugh—who pretends not to recognize him—the master of the estate (chapter 25). Miles later learns that Hugh forged a letter reporting his death and forced Miles's own sweetheart, Edith, to marry him. In chapter 33, Hugh is in London for King Edward's coronation, hoping for a peerage. Instead, the new king has him arrested and stripped of his estates. Afterward, neither Edith nor Miles will testify against Hugh, who goes to the Continent and soon dies.

Hendon, Miles (Earl of Kent)   Character in *The Prince and the Pauper* (1881). A member of a Kentish family of the lesser nobility, 30-year-old Hendon is in England after three years of fighting in "continental wars" and seven in foreign captivity. He explains in chapter 12 that he was so wild as a youth that his treacherous brother Hugh Hendon persuaded their father that Miles intended to run off with Edith Hendon, whom their father intended for the oldest brother, Arthur. To prevent this, the father banished Miles to Europe for three years to help mature him.

Hendon first appears in the narrative in chapter 11, when he rescues Prince Edward from ruffians. Similar in dress, aspect, and bearing to Don Caesar de Bazan (a character in Victor Hugo's *Gil Blas*), Hendon is tall, trim, and muscular and has the swaggering carriage of a "ruffler of the camp." Hendon admires Edward's noble spirit. Determined to make the boy his ward, he puts up with his royal pretensions, not believing Edward's claims until he sees him on the throne in chapter 33. Meanwhile, he never expresses his doubts aloud, for fear of causing the lad's diseased mind further harm. His devotion to Edward is complete. He twice puts off returning home to Hendon Hall in order to find Edward after John Canty abducts him, and he takes a lashing in Edward's place in chapter 28.

For his part, Edward repays Hendon by allowing him to sit in his royal presence. He also makes

Miles Hendon asks Edward for permission to sit in his presence in chapter 12 of *The Prince and the Pauper.*

Hendon a knight and later Earl of Kent—titles that he confirms after he is safely on his throne. According to the concluding chapter, Hendon's earldom endures until the 17th-century civil wars, in which the last Earl of Kent dies fighting for the king.

When Hendon finally reaches home, his brother disavows him, and he finds himself in the same position as Edward as a claimant. Clemens identified closely with Hendon, whose struggle to prove that he is not an impostor has been compared to Clemens's choosing to write *The Prince and the Pauper* in order to prove himself respectable as a writer. Appropriately, Clemens played Hendon in family dramatic productions of *The Prince and the Pauper.* As a broadly conceived, swashbuckling character, Hendon has also been portrayed by several flamboyant film actors, including Errol Flynn (1937); Guy Williams, television's "Zorro" (1962); and Oliver Reed (1977).

Hendon Hall   Fictitious place in *The Prince and the Pauper* (1881). Located near Monk's Holm (also apparently fictitious) in Kent, Hendon Hall is the ancestral home of Miles Hendon. The estate has a 72-room house maintained by 27 servants. Hendon tells King Edward about Hendon Hall in chapter 12 and they spend about three days riding to get there from LONDON in chapter 25.

Herbert, Sir William (Earl of Pembroke) (c. 1501, Kendal, Westmorland, England–March 17, 1570, Hampton Court, England)   Historical figure and minor character in *The Prince and the Pauper* (1881). An English soldier and courtier, Herbert was the brother-in-law of King Henry VIII's last wife, Catherine Parr, and became a member of Edward VI's privy council. After Edward died, Herbert supported Mary I's succession and helped end Lady Jane Grey's short reign. Herbert appears briefly in chapter 6 of *The Prince and the Pauper* as the privy chamber officer who takes Tom Canty to a room to rest. In chapter 10, the real prince awakens in Canty's house; thinking that he has been dreaming, he calls out Herbert's name.

The historical Herbert was made Earl of Pembroke—the given name of Pembroke Howard in *Pudd'nhead Wilson.*

hermit, holy   Character in *The Prince and the Pauper* (1881). While wandering alone in the woods, Edward VI stumbles upon the house of an old man whom he joyfully calls a "holy hermit" (chapter 20). The white-haired man quietly accepts Edward's claim to be a "king," then reveals that he is an archangel who would have been pope, had not "the king" dissolved his religious house and cast him out into the world. When Edward further identifies himself as king of "England," the hermit deduces that he is the son of his despoiler, HENRY VIII, and determines to kill him. He is about to stab Edward when Miles Hendon arrives. When he leads Hendon off on a wild good chase, John Canty arrives and spirits the prince away.

Clemens also uses the expression "holy hermit" in chapter 14 of *Connecticut Yankee* (1889) and in the table of contents of *Innocents Abroad* (1869) for chapter 55. *The Prince and the Pauper*'s description of the hermit as an "archangel" recalls *Roughing It*'s (1872) description of a Mormon "Destroying Angel" in chapter 12; both characters are filthy, impoverished men bent on killing to do the Lord's work.

Hertford, Earl of (Edward Seymour; Duke of Somerset) (c. 1501–1506–January 22, 1552, London, England)   Historical figure and character in *The Prince and the Pauper* (1881). The brother of King Henry VIII's third wife, Jane Seymour (c. 1509–1537), Hertford became an earl after his sister gave birth to Edward VI in 1537. Henry's will called for a 16-member council of regency to rule England after he died in 1547, but Hertford quickly established himself as lord protector over nine-year-old King Edward, made himself the Duke of Somerset, and ruled England as a virtual dictator for two years. In 1549, his enemies replaced him with the Duke of Northumberland and later had him beheaded for treason.

An important character in *The Prince and the Pauper*, Hertford first appears in chapter 5, when Tom Canty meets the king. After Tom accidentally takes Prince Edward's place, Hertford dismisses the boy's claim not to be the true prince and becomes his steadfast and loyal adviser. He even fails to recognize his true nephew when he sees both boys side by side at the coronation in chapter 32. As "a man of merciful and generous impulses," Hertford approves Tom's desire to outlaw cruel punishments (chapter 15); however, once his real nephew establishes his identity at the coronation, he turns against Tom, ordering that he be "stripped and flung into the Tower."

Among the actors who have portrayed Hertford in films are Claude Rains (1937), Donald Houston (1962), and Harry Andrews (1977). The 1937 adaptation has Hertford learn early that Tom Canty is not the real prince, then plot to murder him.

Hugo   Character in *The Prince and the Pauper* (1881). Somewhat older and bigger than King Edward VI, Hugo is a member of the Ruffler's criminal gang. In chapter 13, he helps John Canty spirit the king away from London Bridge but is not identified by name until chapter 17, when the Ruffler assigns him to supervise the king. The king refuses to cooperate, however, forcing Hugo to struggle to keep him from escaping. At first, Hugo is reasonably cheerful and agreeable, but the king's rebelliousness eventually brings out his cruelest impulses. After the king humiliates him in a fight, Hugo tricks him into being arrested for theft, and he himself disappears from the story (chapter 22).

London Bridge   LONDON's oldest bridge goes back to Roman times. The name properly applies to the *location*—not a specific structure—where the City of London is joined with Southwark. It was the city's only bridge across the River THAMES until 1750. A stone span built in the late 12th century figures prominently in *The Prince and the Pauper* (1881). During the 16th century, this bridge was a village unto itself, crowded with shops and houses; its history and teeming life are described in chapter 12 of the novel. Tom Canty's family lives several hundred yards from the bridge's north end, off Pudding Lane. When Tom's father, John Canty, flees justice in chapter 10, he tells his family to meet on the bridge—a rendezvous apparently not kept. Meanwhile, Prince Edward escapes from Canty's grasp when the latter is accosted by drunken revelers on the bridge. In the next chapter, Edward returns to the bridge with

Miles Hendon, who has a room in one of its inns. After Canty confronts Hendon at the inn, he sends a boy named Hugo to fetch the prince away while Hendon is away shopping the next morning. When Edward and Hendon return about two weeks later, they get separated by a drunken crowd while recrossing the bridge (chapter 29).

In the mid-18th century, London Bridge's wooden buildings were removed; the bridge itself was replaced by another stone structure in 1831. That bridge was dismantled, moved to Arizona's Lake Havasu in the early 1970s and replaced by a structure better able to handle modern motor traffic.

Marlow, Humphrey Character in *The Prince and the Pauper* (1881). The 12-year-old whipping boy of Prince Edward, Humphrey is an orphan son of Sir Humphrey Marlow, a former palace official and friend of Miles Hendon's father. When Tom Canty meets Humphrey, he is amazed to learn that the boy is flogged whenever the prince performs badly in his studies (chapter 14). Humphrey dislikes being flogged but needs the job to support himself and his sisters, so he is thrilled when Tom dubs him "Hereditary Grand Whipping-Boy." Tom discovers that Humphrey is a mine of information on the court and the real prince's life, so he arranges to meet with him regularly. In chapter 29, Miles Hendon heads for London, hoping to find Sir Humphrey Marlow in order to gain an audience with the new king. By chance, the first person he meets at the Palace of Westminster is the younger Marlow (chapter 33).

Clemens's original manuscript of *The Prince and the Pauper* contained a long anecdote that Humphrey recited to Tom Canty. He removed it from the novel but published it as "A Boy's Adventure" in a Hartford newspaper in June 1880. This narrative supplies additional background about Humphrey's father and tells about a wild adventure he had when he put on a gaudy outfit belonging to his father and tried to ride a bull. His adventure proved a disaster when the bull kicked in a beehive. A modified version of Humphrey's bull-and-bees anecdote appears in *Joan of Arc* (1896; book 1, chapter 36).

Mary I (February 18, 1516, Greenwich, England—November 17, 1558, London) Queen of England (1553–58) and minor character in *The Prince and the Pauper* (1881). The daughter of Henry VIII by his first wife, Catherine of Aragon, Mary was a half-sister of King Edward VI. Her brief appearances in *The Prince and the Pauper* reflect the secluded life she led during Edward's reign. In chapter 3, Edward alludes to her as having a "gloomy mien." Tom Canty meets with her briefly in chapter 14 and later rebukes her for having a heart of stone (chapter 30). After the historical Edward's death in 1553, Mary defeated efforts to make Lady Jane Grey queen and seized the monarchy herself. In working to restore Roman Catholicism as England's official religion, her violent excesses earned her the nickname "Bloody Mary." After she died, her half-sister Elizabeth I became queen.

Queen Mary is also briefly mentioned in *1601* and in "How to Make History Dates Stick."

Norfolk, Duke of (Thomas Howard II) (1473–August 25, 1554, Keminghall, England) Historical figure mentioned in *The Prince and the Pauper* (1881). The uncle of King Henry VIII's wives Anne Boleyn and Catherine Howard, the Duke of Norfolk was one of the most powerful figures of his time in England's government. In 1546, however, he and his son, the Earl of Surrey, were charged with treason and sentenced to death. Surrey was beheaded on January 21, 1547, but Norfolk's execution, scheduled for January 28, was canceled because King Henry had died the previous day and the ruling council thought it unwise to begin a new king's reign with an execution.

Norfolk is not a character in *The Prince and the Pauper*, but his name figures prominently in the story. Chapter 5 mentions the recent arrest of Norfolk and Surrey. In the same chapter, Tom Canty (who everyone thinks is Prince Edward) expresses concern over Norfolk's impending death when he meets King Henry; however, the king says that Norfolk is unworthy of his concern and implies that Norfolk has delayed Edward's formal installation as the Prince of Wales. Meanwhile, Norfolk's execution is delayed because the king's Great

Seal cannot be found. In chapter 8, the king commands that Norfolk be beheaded the next day; however, the king dies that night and Tom Canty is proclaimed king at Guildhall. Tom's first official act is to spare Norfolk—a decision that wins him immediate favor in the court (chapter 11) and later in the country at large (chapter 27).

Several film adaptations of *The Prince and the Pauper* have made Norfolk a character. At the conclusion of the 1937 film, for example, Norfolk (Henry Stephenson) replaces Hertford as lord protector (Hertford's actual successor was Lord Northumberland). Rex Harrison played Norfolk in the 1977 film.

Offal Court   Fictional LONDON street in *The Prince and the Pauper* (1881). A "foul little pocket" packed with poor families, Offal Court is a rowdy, drunken hive off Pudding Lane in which Tom Canty's family lives in a third-story room (chapter 2). In chapter 3, Tom describes life in Offal Court to Prince Edward; the neighborhood's proximity to the THAMES RIVER and the rugged sports in which Tom and his friends engage recall Hannibal, Missouri, in which Clemens grew up.

A homophone of "awful," *offal* is a word of Middle English origin describing the viscera and trimmings that butchers remove from animals. Tom's "Offal Court" thus provides an apt counterpoint to Edward's royal court.

Pudding Lane   Historic LONDON road on the north shore of the THAMES, about 150 yards northeast of London Bridge. Chapters 2 and 3 of *The Prince and the Pauper* (1881) mention Pudding Lane in connection with a fictional side street, Offal Court, in which Tom Canty's family lives. Pudding Lane takes its name from the "puddings," or animal entrails, of the district's many butcher shops. In 1666, the Great Fire of London began in Pudding Lane; it is commemorated by Christopher Wren's Monument at the intersection of Pudding Lane and Monument Street. Pudding Lane is also mentioned in *Huckleberry Finn* (1884). The Duke's handbill advertising the "Shaksperean Revival" describes EDMUND KEAN the elder as being "of the Royal Haymarket Theatre, Whitechapel, Pudding Lane, Piccadilly, London, and the Royal Continental Theatres" (chapter 21). The description is geographically nonsensical.

Ruffler, The   Character in *The Prince and the Pauper* (1881). The Ruffler leads the criminal gang that John Canty forces King Edward VI to join in chapter 17. Though exercising nearly dictatorial powers, he has a soft heart; several times he shields Edward from abuse by other gang members. Actors who have portrayed him in films include Lionel Braham (1937) and George C. Scott (1977).

The word *ruffler* appears in mid-16th-century English law as a term for a phony soldier or swaggering vagabond. When Miles Hendon first appears in *The Prince and the Pauper*, he is described as having a "swaggering carriage [that] marked him at once as a ruffler of the camp" (chapter 11). Clemens also uses the word in chapter 14 of *Connecticut Yankee* (1889).

Saint John, Lord (William Paulet; Marquis of Winchester)   (c. 1485–March 10, 1572, Basing House, Hampshire, England)   Historical figure and minor character in *The Prince and the Pauper* (1881). The lord steward of England's royal household, Baron St. John was also president of the privy council under King Edward VI. In chapter 6 of *The Prince and the Pauper*, he relays King Henry's command to Tom Canty that he not deny he is Prince Edward. When St. John expresses his doubts about the prince's genuineness, Hertford cautions him against treasonous remarks. After the real Edward appears at the coronation, St. John twice goes to the royal palaces to fetch the Great Seal (chapter 32).

The historical St. John was distantly related to Sir Amyas Paulet, who had the same name as *Connecticut Yankee*'s Clarence.

Yokel   Minor character in *The Prince and the Pauper* (1881). A member of the Ruffler's criminal gang, Yokel is a once-prosperous farmer who fell on hard times after his mother was burned as a witch because a patient she nursed died. Reduced to begging, Yokel and his wife were lashed from town to town until his wife died, his children starved and he was sold as a slave and branded. When King

Edward VI—who gang members think is a common beggar boy—hears Yokel's sad story, he jumps up to declare the unjust law ended (chapter 17). In chapter 22, Yokel saves the king from an attempt by Hugo and the Tinker to burn a scar on his leg. After Edward later regains his throne, he has Yokel found and provided with "a comfortable livelihood."

BIBLIOGRAPHY

Emerson, Everett. "Afterword." In *The Prince and the Pauper.* 1881. Reprinted in *The Oxford Mark Twain,* edited by Shelley Fisher Fishkin, 1–16. New York: Oxford University Press, 1996.

Twain, Mark. *Historical Romances: The Prince and the Pauper, A Connecticut Yankee in King Arthur's Court, Personal Recollections of Joan of Arc,* edited by Susan K. Harris, 1–212. New York: Library of America, 1994.

———. *The Prince and the Pauper,* edited by Victor Fischer and Lin Salamo. Berkeley: University of California Press, 1979.

"The Private History of a Campaign That Failed"

Fictional account of Clemens's military service during the CIVIL WAR. Writing in 1885 for a magazine series about "leaders" in the Civil War, Clemens prefaced the piece with the remark that he was someone "who started out to do something in it but didn't." While the story appears to be an important link in his AUTOBIOGRAPHY between *Life on the Mississippi* (1883) and *Roughing It* (1872), the specific incidents it relates cannot be taken literally. Indeed, there is no historical evidence that the unit he claims to have joined—the "MARION RANGERS"— existed. Clemens is known to have joined the Missouri State Guard at that time; however, it had no formal connection with the Confederacy. The fact that Clemens's magazine article states that the "Marion Rangers" was a Confederacy unit has caused great confusion about his Civil War experience. The story is at once a comic apologia for a former Confederate irregular who is daring to pub-

lish General U. S. GRANT's Civil War memoirs and a satiric indictment of the stupidity of the military and of war generally. In this latter regard, it ranks beside "THE WAR PRAYER."

The story begins when the unnamed narrator learns of South Carolina's secession from the Union while he is a PILOT on the Mississippi River. A month later, he is in NEW ORLEANS as LOUISIANA is seceding. A few months later, he is home in Missouri as it is being invaded by Union forces. In Hannibal, he and 14 other young men respond to the governor's call for militia by spontaneously forming a unit that they call the Marion Rangers. Aside from Ed Stevens, most of the recruits are given fictitious names.

None of the men has any military experience. Tom Lyman is made captain; the narrator, second lieutenant. By the time all the commissioned and noncommissioned ranks are distributed, only three privates remain. They soon learn, however, that rank counts for little, as none of them is willing to take orders from another.

The unit's first mission is to march 10 miles to New London, when an old veteran named Colonel Ralls takes out a Bible and has them swear fealty to the state of Missouri. They then move on to a spot in the forest they call Camp Ralls, where farmers bring them mules and horses for their use. Over the next few days, the young soldiers drill themselves on horsemanship, mainly by riding to visit local girls. When rumors of an enemy advance reach them, they panic, wondering which way to retreat. During a dark, wet night, they get lost, until dogs set upon them and a farmer named Mason calls the dogs off. The farmer shames the men with questions about what they are doing.

The next night another rumor of Union troops sends the Rangers fleeing into the woods, where they nearly drown in mud. In the morning, they again learn that the rumor has been a false alarm. They spend several days at the Masons' farm, until a new rumor of approaching Union troops scares them back into the woods. Their officers attempt to place pickets, but no one cooperates.

As the days pass, the unit tires of reacting to false alarms, until they are ready to take whatever comes. Finally, they emerge one moonlit night to confront what may be a real threat. When a man approaches on a horse, the narrator joins his comrades in shooting him down. Once it is clear that the rider is alone, they inspect their victim and find that he is neither in uniform nor armed. Calling the incident an epitome of war, which requires the killing of strangers against whom one feels no personal animosity, the narrator concludes that he is not equipped for this awful business. He resolves to retire while he can save his self-respect.

The Rangers continue retreating until they arrive near FLORIDA, in Monroe County. When they hear word that a Union colonel (later identified as U. S. Grant) is about to sweep in, they vote to disband. Half of them leave immediately; the rest remain in service throughout the war. As the former soldiers head home, they encounter General Harris, who futilely orders them to return to duty. The narrator concludes that "I knew more about retreating than the man that invented retreating."

PUBLISHING HISTORY

In May 1885, Robert Underwood Johnson (1853–1937), the editor of CENTURY MAGAZINE, persuaded Clemens to write about his Civil War experiences for his "Battles and Leaders of the Civil War" series. Johnson wanted a piece depicting conditions in Missouri at the start of the war and was very pleased with the 7,000-word manuscript that Clemens sent him in November. The article appeared in the following month's issue of Century, illustrated by EDWARD WINDSOR KEMBLE, with several maps drawn by Clemens himself. The story was first collected in MERRY TALES in 1892 and was subsequently reprinted in The American Claimant and Other Stories and Sketches. Clemens also alludes to this Civil War episode in chapter 67 of Following the Equator (1897).

In April 1981, the Public Broadcasting System aired a dramatization of the story directed by Peter H. Hunt. Gary McCleery played the second lieutenant (who is not named) and Joseph Adams played Tom Lyman. Pat Hingle played a flamboyant Colonel Ralls, and Edward Herrmann is the stranger whom the Rangers shoot. The production includes an epilogue, dramatizing "THE WAR PRAYER." Herrmann reappears as the stranger,

delivering the prayer to a shocked Connecticut congregation in 1899.

CRITICAL COMMENTARY

In "The Private History of a Campaign That Failed," Clemens creates a picture of war. Clearly a description of the Civil War, the war could ultimately be any war. Clemens himself briefly joined a Missouri militia unit, but the unnamed narrator never mentions Missouri, the figuratively neutral border-state; instead he uses the phrase "Out West," suggesting a neutral place and people that were pulled into war, confused about the conflict, first leaning one way, then another. The narrator becomes a westerner, unsure of war or any cause.

News of the war ignites excitement; there are debates, recruitment, volunteering, and organizing. On the upper Mississippi, the narrator's New York pilot mate—a supporter of the Union, like the narrator—questions the loyalty of the narrator, who is a slaveowner's son. But on the Lower Mississippi, as the war fever spreads, the pilot and the narrator become rebels, and the pilot now doubts the patriotism of someone whose father once considered freeing slaves; location influences attitudes. Although Missouri never secedes, the governor orders its militia to repel Union invaders. In defending the state, or area, rather than the South or Confederacy, the narrator and his 14 acquaintances form the "Marion Rangers," an appropriate name because they range rather than raid.

Four Rangers typify soldiers' attitudes toward war. Dunlap, a chivalric novel-reader who is "full of romance," seeks glory. To Stevens, war is a lark. Smith—huge, strong, soft-hearted—typifies determination. Viewing life as serious, "seldom satisfactory," Bowers represents soldiers' tendency to grumble while soldiering. The unidentified narrator could be any of the 15, viewing war from common soldiers' eyes, which was rare before Stephen Crane. All initially confident before the first engagement, the Rangers represent innocents sent to war—playful, gleeful, bored, frightened, immature.

The recruits endure training, terrain, weather, and patriotic speeches. Confused by Colonel Ralls's speech, which is "full of gunpowder and glory"—

not to mention mixed metaphors—they are unclear whom they serve or fight, implying such orations are interchangeable. As town boys unfamiliar with animals and hard labor, the Rangers struggle with horsemanship and daily drills. The recruits trip over roots, become entangled in vines, are torn by briars, stumble (domino effect) downhill, lose equipment, suffer blisters, are rain-drenched, get lost, and are bitten by dogs and rats. Twain captures the recruits resisting the process of becoming soldiers. They refuse orders, outvote their captain, abandon posts, equalize and exchange service ranks, and flank a farmhouse to avoid fighting.

Despite fatigue, injuries, boredom, and rumors, some later master "the grim trade," becoming warriors with fine records; however, an antiwar theme is implicit. "The grim trade" is killing, as the boys grasp after ambushing a horseman perceived as an enemy. In civilian clothes, he could be Everyman, Every Soldier, or no soldier but a representative of war-killed civilians. Guilt-ridden about murdering someone who did him no wrong, the narrator realizes, as does the stranger in "The War Prayer," that this deed extends to the man's innocent family. Meeting fierce, hardened soldiers, the narrator and half his group abandon war to them. Like Civilian Buck Fanshaw in *Roughing It*, the narrator had "killed his man," symbolically "exterminated one army." Sickened that "the epitome of war" is killing strangers, who might otherwise have been well received, the narrator decides to leave war to the professionals.

Clemens implies that the narrator's best soldierly skill, retreating, permitted General Grant—as unknown then as he—to gain fame. Mixing humor and poignancy, Clemens demonstrates war's absurdity.

Critical Commentary by John H. Davis

BIBLIOGRAPHY

Twain, Mark. "The Private History of a Campaign That Failed." In *The Best Short Stories of Mark Twain*, edited by Lawrence I. Berkove, 101–119. New York: The Modern Library, 2004.

The Private Lives of Adam and Eve

Book published by HARPER AND BROTHERS in 1932 that combines Clemens's ADAM AND EVE diaries in a single volume, using the plates of the original 1904 and 1906 editions. No additional material was added. A similar volume, titled *The Diaries of Adam and Eve*, was published in the OXFORD MARK TWAIN edition in 1996.

"The Professor's Yarn"

Tale told in *Life on the Mississippi* (1883). Most of chapter 36 is related by a college professor who is identified only as a passenger on the steamboat GOLD DUST. Years earlier, the professor explains, he went to California to work as a surveyor. Aboard his ship, he befriended John Backus, an Ohio cattleman carrying his life savings to take up ranching on the coast. As they neared San Francisco, Backus was lured into a game (poker?) with professional gamblers. After drinking too much, he wagered his entire fortune on one hand. However, he emerged triumphant, as the ship entered the Golden Gate, and then announced that he was not a cattleman but a professional gambler himself.

The end of chapter 35 introduces this story, pointing out that it is inserted "merely because it is a good story, not because it belongs here—for it doesn't." The disclaimer is accurate, as Clemens originally intended the piece for *A Tramp Abroad* (1880). A deleted portion of chapter 35 indicates that the professor is from YALE.

CHARACTERS AND RELATED ENTRIES

Backus, John   Character in "The Professor's Yarn" in chapter 36 of *Life on the Mississippi* (1883). Backus was a professional gambler who appeared to be a cattle rancher, possibly from Ohio, whom the narrator of "The Professor's Yarn" once met on a voyage to SAN FRANCISCO. Backus impressed the narrator with his expertise on cattle but seemed dangerously naive. When he was lured into a high-stakes card game by three card sharps and got drunk, the professor feared that he would be cleaned out. However, Backus turned the tables on the other men just as their ship reached San Francisco and announced that he was a professional card player himself. Afterward, the professor learns that one of the other card players was Backus's partner and that Backus learned everything he knew about cattle during a one-week "apprenticeship" in Jersey.

Pudd'nhead Wilson, The Tragedy of (1894)

Clemens's last American NOVEL, *Pudd'nhead Wilson* is regarded as a major part of his Mississippi writings. It resembles *Tom Sawyer* and *Huckleberry Finn* in being set before the CIVIL WAR in a small Missouri town modeled on Hannibal. However, it has a much more somber tone. While it contains humor, it deals frankly with small-town prejudice, SLAVERY, miscegenation, lost birthright, degenerate aristocratic values, and distorted parental love. One of its strongest themes is the effect of training on character, demonstrated by the switching of slave and free babies in infancy.

There is some uncertainty about the full title that Clemens intended for *Pudd'nhead Wilson*. The novel has typically been published as *The Tragedy of Pudd'nhead Wilson*; however, the phrase "The Tragedy of" on the first edition's title page might be read as a description—instead of as part of the title. Typographically, the phrase is treated the same as the phrase "And the Comedy" before *Those Extraordinary Twins* on the same page. Clemens himself wrote "Pudd'nhead Wilson, A Tale" on the first page of his manuscript. When the novel was published first as a magazine serial, it appeared under the title "Pudd'nhead Wilson." In any case, while the novel is clearly a tragedy, Wilson himself is not its central tragic figure.

SYNOPSIS

Pudd'nhead Wilson contains 53,000 words, divided among 22 chapters. As is discussed in the background section below, the story is a truncated

revision of a longer work originally titled "THOSE EXTRAORDINARY TWINS." Clemens began the book as a wild BURLESQUE about SIAMESE TWINS. As the story developed, however, he found that new characters were moving his narrative toward a tragedy unrelated to his original premise. He extracted most of the Siamese twins farce and revised the remainder into its published form as *Pudd'nhead Wilson*. Some familiarity with the "Those Extraordinary Twins" story is thus essential to understanding *Pudd'nhead Wilson*'s complex structure.

The narrative spans 23 years in Dawson's Landing, a Missouri village on the Mississippi River. Among Clemens's novels, *Pudd'nhead Wilson* is unusual in assigning specific dates to events. The narrative opens in February 1830. By chapter 5, it is June 1853—a moment coinciding with the date that Clemens left Hannibal. The balance of the story unfolds over four or perhaps five more months, with about three-quarters of the story set in 1853. Most of the action takes place in Dawson's Landing, with several episodes in SAINT LOUIS and ARKANSAS.

As in *The Prince and the Pauper*, *Pudd'nhead Wilson* opens with unrelated boys—one advantaged, the other disadvantaged—born on the same day. The narrative then follows three distinct story lines. The first concerns Roxana (Roxy), a slave woman who switches her baby son, Chambers, with the son of her master. Her son grows up as "Tom Driscoll," murders his presumed uncle for money, and is finally exposed. The second story line follows David Wilson, a brilliant young eastern lawyer whose legal career is ruined by a remark that he makes on arriving in Dawson's Landing. The final story line concerns Angelo and Luigi Capello, Italian twins who come to Dawson's Landing in chapter 5.

It is 1845 when Roxy is freed in chapter 4. From that point, the narrative follows Tom Driscoll up to 1853. In chapter 8, the narrative resumes Roxy's story, with both threads converging in chapter 11. From there, the dominant story is Tom's struggle to pay off his mounting gambling debts, while staying in his uncle's good graces. The climax comes when Tom grows so desperate for money that he kills his uncle while trying to rob him. Tom appears to triumph when the Capello twins are charged with his crime, leaving him to inherit his uncle's estate. However, Wilson defends the Capellos using FIN-GERPRINT evidence that proves not only that Tom is the true murderer, but that he is also rightfully a slave.

Preface

Clemens signs his brief introduction, titled "A Whisper to the Reader," on January 2, 1893, at "Villa Viviani, village of Settignano, three miles back of FLORENCE." It explains that he has sub-jected the novel's "law chapters" to the scrutiny of William Hicks, who trained in law in Missouri 35 years earlier. The discursive sentence describing Hicks rambles on for 176 words (recalling Jim Blaine's old ram's tale in *Roughing It*).

Chapter 1

The narrative opens in February 1830 in the quiet Missouri village of Dawson's Landing, half a day below SAINT LOUIS by Mississippi steamboat. The town's chief citizens are Judge York Driscoll, his friend Pembroke Howard, Colonel Cecil Burleigh Essex, and Percy Driscoll. On the first day of the month two boys are born, one to Percy Driscoll's wife, the other to his slave Roxana. Mrs. Driscoll dies within a week, leaving Roxana to raise both babies while Mr. Driscoll loses himself in his busi-ness speculations.

During this same month, newly qualified lawyer David Wilson arrives from the east. On his first day in the village, he is heard to remark that he wished he owned half of a yelping dog so that he could kill his half. From that moment, he is branded a fool and dubbed "Pudd'nhead Wilson."

Chapter 2

Wilson buys a house on the edge of town and sets up an office in town, advertising himself as "Attor-ney and Counselor-at-Law, Surveying, Conveyanc-ing, etc." No clients come, so he soon sets law aside and works at surveying and accounting. He uses his considerable idle time to experiment with PALM-ISTRY and FINGERPRINTING.

In July, Wilson overhears Roxy flirting and jok-ing with a slave named Jasper, whose skin is very dark. Roxy herself is physically indistinguishable from a "white" person, but "the one sixteenth of

her which was black outvoted the other fifteen parts and made her a Negro." Though her son, Chambers, is only 1/32 black, and is blue-eyed and blond, he, too, is a slave, and by fiction of law and custom a Negro. Chambers and Driscoll's son look so much alike that Driscoll can only tell them apart by their CLOTHES. Wilson wonders how Roxy can tell them apart. He collects their fingerprints on glass plates—something that he does again on Sep-tember 3.

On September 4, Percy Driscoll confronts Roxy and three other household slaves about thefts in the house. He is generally a humane slave owner, but his patience is exhausted. He first vows to sell the guilty slave, and then threatens to sell *all* of them *down* the river, unless the thief confesses. Roxy is innocent, but the other three confess immediately.

Chapter 3

The idea of being "sold down the river" shakes Roxy badly, and the thought of her son's suffering that fate frightens her even more. To ensure that this never happens, she decides to drown him and her-self. After donning her finest dress, she puts Cham-bers in one of Tom's expensive gowns. When she examines her work, she remembers that Driscoll cannot recognize his own naked son, so she switches the babies by swapping their clothes and cradles. Then she practices calling each by its new name. The only person she fears is Wilson, whom she regards as the smartest man in town. Driscoll and his brother leave town on business for seven weeks. On the first of October, Wilson fingerprints the babies again, but even he suspects nothing. Roxy now feels safe.

Chapter 4

(*From this point in the narrative, the boys are known by their false names.*) "Tom" is a bad boy from the start. He cries without reason, bites, scratches and whines constantly, but Roxy is a "doting fool of a mother." Her relationship with Tom becomes warped. To the world, she is not his mother, but his slave. She grows increasingly obsequious and for-gets "who she was and what he had been."

While the pampered Tom grows up sickly, the neglected Chambers is healthy and robust. Tom mistreats Chambers badly, but Percy Driscoll makes it clear that if Chambers ever lifts a hand against Tom, he will be thrashed. Tom uses Chambers as his personal bodyguard and plays nasty tricks on him. When the boys are about 15, Chambers saves Tom from drowning, but this only makes Tom spiteful; he even attempts to stab Chambers.

By adolescence, Tom's relationship with Roxy is strictly that of master to slave. He insults and abuses her to the point that she fantasizes about exposing his true identity for revenge. However, any trace of kindness he shows her lifts her spirits.

In the fall of 1845, the boys' natural fathers, Colonel Essex and Percy Driscoll, die. On his deathbed, Driscoll frees Roxy and gives Tom over to the care of his brother, Judge York Driscoll, who has recently bought Chambers to prevent his being sold down the river as Tom has urged. Shortly after Percy's death, "his great speculative landed estate" collapses, leaving Tom a pauper. However, Judge Driscoll promises to leave his own estate to Tom.

The newly freed Roxy becomes a chambermaid on a steamboat.

Chapter 5

Two years later, Judge Driscoll's wife dies, leaving the judge and his sister, Rachel Pratt, to raise Tom. They continue spoiling him. When Tom is 19, he goes off to YALE. He returns two years later with improved manners, but with new drinking and gambling habits. Bored with Dawson's Landing, he begins frequenting St. Louis. Meanwhile, Judge Driscoll retires from the bench. His greatest interest in life now is the Free-thinkers' Society. He has a high regard for his fellow member, Wilson, whose whimsical "Pudd'nhead Wilson's Calendar" he admires. Other people like Wilson personally, but regard him as inconsequential.

The widow Aunt Patsy Cooper lives with her daughter Rowena Cooper and two younger sons. For a year she has been trying to rent out her spare room. It is now June 1853, and she gets a letter from Angelo and Luigi Capello, Italian brothers who want the room. Rowena is thrilled by the prospect of Italian boarders, as the town has never known travelers. Her neighbors quickly learn about the coming visitors. Judge Driscoll arrives to congratulate Aunt Patsy. Judge Sim Robinson and others soon follow. The chapter ends as the Capellos arrive during a late-night storm.

Chapter 6

The next morning, the charming brothers are soon on familiar terms with everyone. They awe the Coopers with a frank history of their background. After their family—originally of the Florentine nobility—became refugees, the brothers were orphaned and had to travel constantly. The Coopers' slave Nancy interrupts them to announce that the house is filling up with people who want to meet the Italians. A reception line forms spontaneously and the occasion becomes a levee. Patsy introduces the twins to her admiring neighbors as "Count Angelo" and "Count Luigi." The Capellos win over everyone with their charm and manners. Rowena now knows for the first time the real meaning of that great word "Glory." Her ecstasy is complete when the twins entertain masterfully on the piano.

Chapter 7

By the time the crowd reluctantly leaves, the twins have collected many social invitations. Judge Driscoll shows them the town and invites them to a meeting of the Free-thinkers' Society. There they establish a warm rapport with Wilson, who invites them to visit him later that evening. As Wilson awaits the twins' arrival, he puzzles over something he observed that morning, when he saw an unfamiliar woman through the window of Tom Driscoll's room next door. Since then, Wilson has visited the house and learned that Tom is due back in town that evening, but he gets no hint that there are guests in Driscoll's home. (*This story line resumes in chapter 11.*)

Chapter 8

After leaving Dawson's Landing eight years earlier, Roxy became a chambermaid on the steamboat *Grand Mogul*. Forced by rheumatism to retire, she goes to the New Orleans bank where she has amassed $400 in savings, only to learn that the bank has gone bust. She returns to the *Grand Mogul* and goes back to Dawson's Landing. She wants badly to see Tom again, but he is in St. Louis when she reaches Dawson's Landing, where Judge Driscoll's slaves receive her warmly and load her with supplies. Over the next several days, Chambers tells Roxy that Tom has been blowing his allowance gambling in St. Louis and that the judge threatens to disinherit him because of his gambling debts. Chambers wonders why his mother is so interested in Tom.

After Tom returns, Chambers tells him that Roxy wants to see him and is beaten for his trouble. Tom reluctantly admits Roxy and receives her servile greetings indifferently. Unsettled by Tom's coolness, Roxy appeals to his charity by asking him for a dollar. He merely tells her to get out, so she appeals to him as the woman who raised him. Another rude rebuff so angers her that she turns on Tom, predicting that she will have him on his knees begging for mercy. She threatens to go to his uncle "en tell him every las' thing I knows 'bout you." Tom's guilty reaction bolsters Roxy's confidence. She makes vague threats about telling the judge things that will make him bust his will. Soon Tom is on his knees. He gives Roxy five dollars, but she tells him to meet her at the HAUNTED HOUSE.

Chapter 9

After Roxy leaves, the humiliation of abasing himself to a black woman causes Tom to collapse. Late that evening, he meets Roxy in the haunted house. When she tells Tom that he is really *her* son, he starts toward her with a piece of wood, but fails to faze her. She checks him with the lie that her proofs are written on a document that will be disclosed if anything happens to her.

Roxy makes Tom call her "mammy" and tells him that if he fails, even once, to obey her, she will ruin him. Tom's whimpering acknowledgment satisfies Roxy that her triumph is complete. She now lays down the law: He must split his $50-a-month allowance with her. Under pressure, Tom confesses that he is nearly $300 in debt and that his only plan for paying off this debt has been to raise money by stealing. He has recently staged a "raid" in town when he was supposed to be in St. Louis. Roxy approves of his stealing and promises to stay out of town, except when she calls to collect her money. Tom asks who his true father was. To his surprise, Roxy answers proudly, identifying Colonel Essex.

Chapter 10

Over the next several days, Tom adjusts to the idea of being black. He fears discovery and finds himself becoming more empathetic toward other people. People notice his behavior changing. He thinks that his character is changing, but his nature remains unaltered and his old ways gradually return.

The loot from Tom's most recent raid pays off his gambling debts. Over the next few months, he finds himself warming toward his mother, but her strong personality frightens him. Renewed visits to St. Louis soon put him in debt again. He returns to Dawson's Landing for another raid. Disguised as a young woman, he goes to his uncle's house, where he notices Wilson watching him through the window (*the incident noted in chapter 7*). He puts on "some airs and graces and attitudes" for Wilson, then changes his disguise to look like an old woman and visits Roxy at the haunted house. Tom loses his nerve and wants to call off his "raid," but after Roxy tells him about the reception for the twins going on at the Cooper house, he loots many of the neighbors' empty homes.

Chapter 11

(*Continued from chapter 7.*) The Capello brothers arrive at Wilson's house and establish a cordial friendship. Wilson reads from his calendar for them. Tom Driscoll unexpectedly drops in; he tries to embarrass Wilson about his frustrated law career. Wilson replies that while not having a chance to pursue his career has been disappointing, he keeps up his law studies. Tom then teases Wilson about his fingerprinting hobby. As Wilson takes prints from Tom and the twins, Tom teases him about his interest in palmistry as well. This jibe misfires when the Capellos express deep respect for the art. Under coaxing, Wilson reads Luigi's palm and reluctantly reveals that Luigi has killed someone. Luigi confirms this, explaining that he once killed a man to save Angelo's life when a thief tried to steal a knife given them by an Indian prince. Tom declines Wilson's offer to read his palm.

As Tom tries to force the twins to argue with each other, John Buckstone arrives to invite the Italians to an anti-temperance meeting of the Sons of Liberty. Accompanied by the uninvited Tom, the twins leave with Buckstone. The meeting elects them to membership and serves them glasses of whiskey. Luigi downs his, but Angelo says that he is a teetotaler and asks that his membership be reconsidered. After another round of drinks is served, Tom gets cheerfully loud and makes a rude pun at the twins' expense, moving Luigi to kick him off the stage into the crowd. The drunken assemblage passes Tom around until someone yells "fire" and the local firefighters arrive and wreck the hall.

Chapter 12

Early the next morning, Judge Driscoll and Pembroke Howard are fishing when another man informs them that one of the Italians kicked Tom at the previous night's meeting. As a member of one of the "First Families of VIRGINIA," the judge assumes that Tom is managing "the affair" on his own; however, he is shocked to learn that Tom has settled "an affair of honor" in court.

At home, Tom tells his uncle that he has beaten Luigi Capello—Wilson's first legal client—on assault charges in court. The stunned judge insists that Tom challenge Luigi to a DUEL that night. When Tom meekly refuses, the judge calls him a coward and promises to disinherit him. Determined to challenge Luigi himself, he asks Howard to be his second. Tom leaves the house vowing to reform in order to prove himself to his uncle.

Chapter 13

Looking for sympathetic company, Tom wanders to Wilson's house, but even Wilson berates him for taking a personal assault case to court without even consulting his uncle. Still puzzled by the mysterious woman he saw through Tom's bedroom window, Wilson wonders whether the judge is upset with Tom for any reason beyond his failure to challenge Luigi. Tom mentions that some valuables are missing from Driscoll's house, moving Wilson to suggest that a raid has been made on the town.

Just then, Robinson, Buckstone, and Constable Jim Blake enter. Wilson tells them about the new thefts and Robinson rattles off the names of other townspeople who have reported robberies—mostly around the Cooper house. Blake says that his prime suspect is an old woman who was seen leaving several houses. Among the thefts was the twins' valuable

dagger. Tom pales as he hears about the plans being made to capture the thief, especially when Wilson mentions that he and the twins have set their own trap.

On behalf of the Democratic Party, Robinson and the others ask Wilson to run for mayor, as Dawson's Landing is about to be incorporated as a city. Wilson accepts, gratified finally to be making his debut into the town's affairs.

Chapter 14

Meanwhile, Pembroke Howard reports to Judge Driscoll that Luigi Capello has accepted his challenge and will duel with him that very night. Both men think Luigi a splendid fellow. As Howard leaves, Driscoll reconsiders disinheriting Tom; Howard returns and witnesses Driscoll's revised will. When both leave, Tom examines the new will with quiet satisfaction. He again vows to reform, but the specter of unpaid gambling debts deflates his joy. As he goes to seek solace from Roxy, he hears distant gunshots.

Roxy is surprised to learn that Tom was not in the duel. When he laughs at the idea of dueling, he earns his mother's contempt. Disgusted by his cowardice, she suggests that his father would turn over in his grave and adds some remarks about her own proud ancestry. Tom notices that Roxy's nose is skinned. A stray bullet from the duel hit her while she was watching through a window.

When Tom tells Roxy about his latest gambling debts, she agrees that the judge is not likely to give him another chance if he misbehaves again. She outlines a plan. First, Tom must behave himself perfectly. Next, he must go to his St. Louis creditors, explain his situation, tell them that his uncle will not live much longer, and offer to pay interest on his debt until his inheritance comes through. Meanwhile, he should sell off his stolen swag to pay the interest. Roxy impresses upon Tom that he *must* behave and promises to follow him to St. Louis to watch him. One slip, and she will reveal the secret of his birth to ruin him. Much sobered, Tom again vows to reform.

Chapter 15

The next day, everyone connected with the duel basks in glory. As Luigi's second, Wilson is a "made man." The twins, now "prodigiously great," take out papers for citizenship and decide to end their days in Dawson's Landing. Both accept nomination to the city council.

Tom Driscoll chafes over these developments, especially the twins' popularity. When he encounters Wilson and Constable Blake, he taunts Blake about his investigation of the robberies. He also correctly guesses the scheme Wilson has devised to capture the thief of the twins' knife—namely, *publicly* advertising a reward for the thief. He needles Wilson by suggesting that the knife has not been found because it never existed. Or, if the knife does exist, the twins still have it. Tom leaves, satisfied that he has planted seeds of doubt.

Over the next week, Tom's uncle and aunt notice his impeccable behavior. He wins back his uncle's confidence by explaining that he could not meet Luigi on a field of honor knowing him to be an assassin—a fact he says he swore not to reveal. Never questioning Tom's story, the judge denounces Luigi as a villain for drawing him into a gentleman's combat, and vows to prevent both twins from being elected to the city council.

Tom's behavior even pleases Roxy, who is beginning to feel that she loves him. She tells him to go to St. Louis, and that she will follow shortly. That night, Tom carries his swag aboard a big steamer but awakens to find that another thief has robbed him during the night.

Chapter 16
Roxy arrives in St. Louis to find Tom in despair. Her heart goes out to him, making her realize that she truly loves him. Her motherly endearments repulse him, but he is afraid to ask her to stop. In any case, she has a plan to save him. She says that she is worth $600 and offers to let him sell her to cover his debts. Tom is dazed.

Roxy wants Tom to forge ownership papers, take her upcountry, and sell her cheap to someone not likely to ask questions. Tom does as he is told, but instead of going *up*state, he sells her to an Arkansas cotton farmer, rationalizing his treachery by thinking that the farmer will treat her so well that she will not mind being sold *down* the river. He even convinces himself that he is doing her a splendid service. He pays off his debts and resolves to

behave himself so as not to jeopardize his uncle's will, while saving money to buy Roxy's freedom again in a year.

Meanwhile, Roxy is carried away in a steamboat. She is not supposed to know which direction the boat is taking her, but her steamboat experience allows her quickly to realize that she has been "sole down de river!"

Chapter 17
Back in Dawson's Landing, the twins campaign hard for city council, but their popularity has declined. Suspicious remarks are made about their missing knife. Judge Driscoll exhausts himself campaigning against them. For two months, Tom's behavior is so good that his uncle even gives him access to his safe. In the final speech of the campaign, the judge ridicules the twins as cheap frauds and implies that they are assassins.

The next day, Wilson is elected mayor, but the twins lose their elections badly. Tom returns happily to St. Louis. The twins withdraw from society amid rumors that Luigi will challenge Judge Driscoll to a new duel when the latter regains his strength.

Chapter 18
A week later, Tom Driscoll returns to his St. Louis lodgings shadowed by a strange, shabby man, who turns out to be his mother. As Tom blubbers self-recriminations, Roxy tells her story. The planter who bought her was not a bad man, but his wife forced her to work in the fields, conspiring with the Yankee overseer to make her life hell. One day, when the overseer beat a young girl whom Roxy had befriended, Roxy seized his stick and "laid him flat." She then fled to the river, found a canoe and paddled downstream until she found a steamboat tied up. It happened to be the *Grand Mogul*. She told her old crewmates that she had been kidnapped and sold down the river. They collected money for her and let her ride back to St. Louis.

While searching for Tom, Roxy has seen her master distributing handbills. Tom already has seen the man. He knows that Roxy was on the *Grand Mogul*; suspecting that there is something wrong with Roxy's sale, he is pressuring Tom to find her. Reading the truth in Tom's face, Roxy makes him confess what he knows, and he shows her a handbill advertising a reward for her return. He reads her everything on the bill—except his own name, which is listed as a contact for the reward. Roxy senses that he is lying and makes him admit that he has set a trap for her.

Roxy orders Tom to secure her freedom by giving the planter all the money he has and getting his uncle to give him the rest by confessing that he sold her to pay gambling debts. Tom protests that this will guarantee his being disinherited, but Roxy tells him that the alternative is to have his true identity disclosed, then "he'll sell *you* down de river, en you kin see how you like it!" She leaves the building with Tom, keeping a knife at his back. After parting from Roxy, Tom resolves to follow her plan in all details but one. Instead of asking his uncle for the money, he will *rob* him.

Chapter 19

Dawson's Landing buzzes in anticipation of a new duel; however, Judge Driscoll declines Luigi's challenge. He refuses to meet an "assassin" on the field of honor, though he is willing to meet him elsewhere. Driscoll ignores Wilson's attempt to explain Luigi's story, so Wilson warns Luigi to be ready for an attack by the judge at any time.

That night the Capellos are out for a walk as Tom Driscoll slips into town unnoticed. Tom sneaks home and prepares to rob his uncle by blacking his face and laying out a woman's dress for his getaway. To boost his courage, he carries the Capellos' Indian knife when he goes downstairs to his uncle's office. There he finds banknotes stacked on a table next to a sofa on which his uncle is asleep. As he snatches the money, his uncle grabs him and cries out for help. Tom stabs the old man and flees upstairs, leaving the knife behind. In his own room, he pulls the dress over his male clothes and then sneaks to the haunted house. There he cleans blood off himself, burns his outfits, and puts on a tramp disguise. He finds a canoe at the river and paddles to the next village to take a steamer back to St. Louis.

Meanwhile, the Capellos have heard the judge's cries and rushed to his aid, only to become the prime murder suspects when Mrs. Pratt finds them standing next to the judge's dead body. Wilson

then arrives and orders that nothing be touched until Judge Robinson arrives as coroner. As the sheriff takes the twins away, Wilson promises to defend them; then he and Constable Blake find the murder weapon. The next day, Tom Driscoll reads about the twins' arrest in a St. Louis newspaper. He arranges to buy Roxy back from the Arkansas planter and wires his aunt that he is coming home.

The coroner's jury finds that Luigi has committed homicide, with Angelo as an accessory. The twins are in danger of being lynched until they are transferred to the county prison. Wilson's examination of the bloody fingerprints on the knife leads him to conclude that neither twin made the marks. Since it is not known that money was taken during the murder, revenge appears to be the only possible motive. As Luigi is the only person known to have a grudge against Driscoll, the twins' case appears desperate. The only thing that Wilson can imagine saving them would be discovery of a murderer who could not have been their accomplice.

Tom returns to town and wins everyone's pity with his sorrowful demeanor.

Chapter 20

During the weeks that the twins await their trial, only Wilson and Patsy Cooper visit them. The courthouse is packed when the trial opens. Roxy and Chambers are among the spectators. Roxy, who carries her bill of sale with her everywhere, now receives a $35-a-month allowance from Tom.

Prosecutor Pembroke Howard lays out the state's case against the twins. The best that Wilson can do is to call witnesses who testify that the Capellos were not stained by blood when they were arrested. He promises to call witnesses who observed "a veiled young woman" leaving Driscoll's premises after the murder occurred. When the court recesses, Wilson and the twins feel hopeless, but Tom is so jubilant that he feels "sarcastically sorry for Wilson." He plans to torment Wilson for the rest of his life about his mystery woman.

That night Wilson studies his collection of female fingerprints, hoping to find a match with those on murder weapon. Tom drops in to taunt him; he examines a glass plate with Roxy's prints and hands it to Wilson. Wilson idly glances at the plate and is stunned by what he sees. After Tom leaves, he goes to work in earnest. He pulls out plates containing Tom's childhood prints for careful inspection. A new puzzle confronts him: Tom's earliest infant prints do not match his later prints. After a nap, Wilson awakens with a new inspiration. He checks his "records" and discovers a startling truth that has been hidden for 23 years.

Chapter 21

Through the night Wilson prepares enlarged copies of fingerprints on cardboard. In court he surprises everyone by announcing that he will not call the witnesses he promised. Instead, he proposes to present new evidence. He begins by granting the prosecution's claim that the bloody fingerprints on the murder weapon are indeed those of the murderer and outlines a new theory for the crime. He points out that the Capellos' failure to flee the scene of the crime indicates that they are not the likely murderers. He hypothesizes why the person who stole the Capellos' Indian knife kept it, why robbery was the true motive for Judge Driscoll's murder, and why the mysterious woman seen leaving Driscoll's house was actually a man.

As Wilson prepares materials to prove his theory, the audience laughs at the familiar sight of his glass fingerprint plates. Unperturbed, he explains that human fingerprints are unique and immutable. His explanation gradually captures the audience's attention; dramatically, he raises the knife and promises to produce the murderer whose prints it bears by 12 noon.

To demonstrate how fingerprint identification works, Wilson proposes to identify several people—including the defendants—by prints they will make on window panes while he is not watching. His success electrifies the crowd. He now displays enlarged copies of the prints of the Capellos and of two children, whom he calls "A and B." The jury verifies that (1) his copies of the Capellos' prints match those the Capellos have made on the window; (2) the Capellos' prints do *not* match those on the murder weapon; and (3) the prints of one of the unnamed children do match those on the weapon. Tom Driscoll grows panicky as Wilson exhibits additional prints proving that the unnamed chil-

dren were switched in their cradles. Building his argument in logical stages, Wilson pronounces: "Valet de Chambre, Negro and slave—falsely called Thomas à Becket Driscoll—make upon the window the fingerprints that will hang you!" Tom slides to the floor in a faint.

Roxy drops to her knees and begs God for mercy as the clock strikes noon. Tom is handcuffed and taken away.

Conclusion

After pondering the day's amazing events, the townspeople decide to withdraw Wilson's title of "pudd'nhead," electing themselves to replace him. The twins are once again heroes, but "weary of Western adventure," they retire to Europe. Restored to his birthright, the real "Tom Driscoll" continues Roxy's pension, but she cannot fully enjoy it. Her spirit broken, she turns to her church for solace. Though the former "Chambers" now finds himself rich and free, he is handicapped by illiteracy, his slave dialect, and the attitudes and mannerisms of a slave.

The false Tom confesses his crimes and is given a life sentence. A complication arises, however, when creditors of Percy Driscoll's estate come forward to claim Tom as their property, since legally he was Driscoll's slave when he died. When the governor understands the case, he pardons Tom at once and the creditors sell him down the river.

BACKGROUND AND PUBLISHING HISTORY

Clemens wrote *Pudd'nhead Wilson* while living in various locations in Europe during the early 1890s. His initial inspiration came from seeing SIAMESE TWINS on tour in 1891. His plan was to write a "howling FARCE" about the problems of brothers who disagreed on almost everything having to share a single body. He first discussed his plans for the book with Fred J. HALL, during a visit to New York in the summer of 1892. In September, he put *Tom Sawyer Abroad* (1894) aside to begin the new book, which he called "THOSE EXTRAORDINARY TWINS." By the end of the year, he had completed 60,000 words and was starting to assign maxims from *PUDD'NHEAD WILSON'S CALENDAR* to individual chapters.

Clemens signed his preface to the book in January 1893, while he was staying in Florence, Italy. In February, he shipped an 81,500-word typescript to Hall. He was now calling the novel "Pudd'nhead Wilson—A Tale." A few months later, while visiting New York again, he discussed the book with Hall, who discouraged him from publishing it as it was. He now realized that while he had started intending to write a farce, other characters had intruded and begun transforming his story. What he had now had was a hybrid monster. He decided to solve the problem by extracting the story concerning the Siamese twins.

During the 1950s, cover illustrations and descriptions of paperback books often had little or nothing to do with the books' contents.

After returning to Italy, Clemens did a massive scissors-and-paste revision. By the end of July, he had trimmed the manuscript to 58,000 words. He then wrote to Hall, reporting—not quite accurately—"I have knocked out everything that delayed the march of the story. . . . There ain't any weather in, and there ain't any scenery—the story is stripped for flight!" His revisions entailed fundamental changes in the story lines. The result was uneven, with some obvious internal inconsistencies. He made the twins physically separate characters and reduced their role, while giving greater roles to Roxy, Tom Driscoll, and David Wilson. He now regarded his original idea merely as "an extravagant sort of a tale" that "had no purpose but to exhibit that monstrous 'freak' in all sorts of grotesque lights." In a revealing and self-deprecating preface to "Those Extraordinary Twins," he called these changes "a kind of literary Caesarean operation."

During another visit to New York in September, Clemens arranged for serialization of *Pudd'nhead Wilson* in CENTURY MAGAZINE and he read proofs. The serial ran in seven installments, from December 1893 to June 1894, with illustrations by Louis LOEB (1866–1909). Clemens hoped to publish the book with his own company, CHARLES L. WEBSTER & COMPANY, but it declared BANKRUPTCY in April 1894. He went back to the AMERICAN PUBLISHING COMPANY, which issued the book in late November 1894. To bulk up the book, he appended about 20,000 words of material from his original "Those Extraordinary Twins" manuscript, adding transitional passages and comments, as well as a six-page introduction explaining the relationship between that story and *Pudd'nhead Wilson*. CHATTO and Windus issued the first British edition around the same time but did not include "Those Extraordinary Twins." Both books took their texts directly from the *Century* serialization—the only published version that Clemens personally corrected. The Chatto edition used Loeb's illustrations.

The American Publishing Co. edition was lavishly illustrated with whimsical cartoons along the margins of almost every page. F. M. SENIOR illustrated *Pudd'nhead Wilson's* chapters 1–10, 12–15, and 17–19 and all of "Those Extraordinary Twins." C. H. WARREN illustrated the remaining *Pudd'n-*

head Wilson chapters. In 1899 HARPER's reissued the book in a new standard edition of Clemens's works, adding a table of contents with chapter titles that do not appear in the original book. Harper also dropped all the original marginal illustrations, retaining only Senior's frontispiece to "Those Extraordinary Twins" and adding two new *Pudd'nhead Wilson* illustrations by E. W. KEMBLE.

San Francisco's Chandler Publishing Company issued a facsimile reprint of the first edition in 1968, adding a substantial new introduction by FREDERICK ANDERSON. Sidney E. Berger edited the first corrected version of both stories for W. W. Norton's "Critical Edition" series in 1980, drawing mainly on the *Century* text, with corrections based on extant manuscripts. The Norton edition adds an extensive editorial apparatus, reviews and essays and a bibliography. The 1996 OXFORD MARK TWAIN edition includes a facsimile reprint of the first American edition of *Pudd'nhead Wilson* with a new introduction by novelist and poet Sherley Anne Williams and an afterword by David Lionel Smith, the coeditor of *The Encyclopedia of African-American Culture and History* (1995). A more substantially reedited edition will eventually be prepared by the MARK TWAIN PROJECT.

MANUSCRIPTS

The earliest known surviving manuscript is a handwritten draft of about 10,000 words in the Berg Collection of the New York Public Library. These pages, which appear to be a fragment of a larger manuscript, bear the title "Those Extraordinary Twins." The long manuscript that Clemens sent to Hall in February 1893 is in New York's J. Pierpont MORGAN Library. The typescript version that he submitted to *Century* apparently has not survived. Since he personally corrected proofs for the magazine, its text is regarded as the most authoritative version of *Pudd'nhead Wilson.* The text used for the published version of "Those Extraordinary Twins" appears to have been taken from fragments extracted from the Morgan manuscript.

CRITICAL COMMENTARY

A joke beginning *Pudd'nhead Wilson* is also a metaphor crucial to the book's theme. David Wil-

son, former law school student, determines his status the day he arrives in Dawson's Landing. When asked why he says of a dog's irritating howling, "I wish I owned half of that dog," he replies, "Because I would kill my half" (chapter 1). The townspeople's serious dissection of his comments becomes a discussion of abstract property rights and legal responsibility, with references to a "general dog" and "the first case" and conjecture about killing or owning a particular half, resulting in a finding of guilty against Wilson and conviction to a lifelong sentence as a fool: "If he ain't a pudd'nhead, I ain't no judge." Though the joke actually convicts small-town ignorance, close-mindedness, and inclusiveness, Wilson cannot reverse "that first day's verdict" for 23 years, the period covered by the novel (chapter 2). The joke alludes to an assertion by ABRAHAM LINCOLN and an action by King Solomon directly and thematically applicable to this novel about fractured families and races, going beyond individual characters and small towns to American societal flaws. The idea of property rights links the joke to SLAVERY but more to human relationships. The basic idea and the result are that a fraction is greater than the whole, that a small part of a person may be deemed more relevant than other parts, that perception takes precedence over reality, that social labels carry more weight than human attributes, and that people deceive themselves by basing judgments upon total acceptance of the partial. Actions and implications based upon such notions are hurtful to everyone.

The Dog Joke

A misunderstood joke, a single instance, dooms Wilson's law practice. As Wilson is elected a fool, so with Roxana—"to all intents and purposes . . . as white as anybody"—"the one sixteenth of her which was black outvoted the other fifteen parts and made her a negro . . . a slave and saleable as such." Only her speech identifies her as black. Her son (Chambers, later Tom), 31 parts white with "blue eyes and flaxen curls," is—like his mother "by a fiction of law and custom"—a slave and black (ibid.). Tom Driscoll, both the true and the impostor, whether judged by his position, clothes, or speech, is perceived and accepted as white. Based on lineage from the FFV (First Families of Virginia—those claiming descent from original Jamestown settlers), town leaders expect and receive reverence as aristocrats from townspeople, who overlook arrogance, lechery, and cruelty. True aristocrats, the Italian twins are initially idolized, though mainly because of their exoticism as foreigners; according to the novel's backstory, townspeople celebrate their arrival, waiting in line to meet, even kowtow to, them but later scorn them after—based on one incident, when Luigi kills someone to save Angelo's life—the twins are labeled assassins. Despite other qualities (as in the case of the twins, Luigi's quick temper and occasional rashness are balanced by his brother's mildness; together they are ingratiating, entertaining, talented, and brave), a fraction of a person's life can not only obscure the rest but also become the whole, that is, all that others see. In Roxana, despite contrary visible evidence, people see only blackness; in false Tom and false Chambers, the same visually, people see, respectively, white and black. In intellectual, well-educated Wilson, they see a fool, with a foolishness they forgive as years pass but do not forget, continuing to laugh at his foolish fingerprint collecting and other "odd" activities; forgiveness does not alter his situation or bring income. Uniqueness, or individuality, as represented by fingerprints, is not a positive attribute here.

As if mimicking the effect of his joke, Clemens undercuts the several paragraphs positively describing the town with one sentence: "Dawson's Landing was a slaveholding town, with a rich slave-worked grain and pork country back of it." Judged solely by appearance, the town is attractive, ("brick sidewalks," rather than wooden boards), prosperous, and "sleepy and comfortable and contente"; however, undergirding this peacefulness, seeming harmony, and material satisfaction is an evil institution that affects, and infects, all its inhabitants (chapter 1). To suggest a facade, hiding a true nature and a society with complications behind apparent simplicity, Clemens uses such phrases as "whitewashed exteriors," "almost concealed from sight," and "climbing tangles of rose-vines." Beneath the beauty of the rose are its thorns; "pretty homes had

a garden in front, fenced with white palings," but the "touch-me-nots" warn that picket fences contain sharp points. Although white, significantly, is a prevalent shade in these homes, he describes "a breed of geranium whose spread of intensely red blossoms accented the prevailing pink tint of the rose-clad house-front like an explosion of flame," implying the violent potential ever-present in slave societies and foreshadowing the approaching national conflict. Readers becoming acquainted with the town realize that "snug," used to describe a "little collection of . . . frame dwellings," can be replaced with "smug," for most of the people are, like the cat on the window sill, "asleep and blissful," complacent and unaware. Here, the author uses a joke about a cat to inject the importance of property rights, particularly slavery, to this community: "A home without a cat—and a well-fed, well-petted, and properly revered cat—may be a perfect home, perhaps, but how can it prove title?" (ibid.). While all the FFV are well fed and revered, Tom Driscoll is certainly well petted and spoiled, but this town is ironically not a perfect home. Its "sole business street" symbolically parallels the river that thrives on the slave trade and its products, bringing new slaves and transporting sold ones up and down, as well as carrying goods produced by slavery.

Small-Town Aristocracy
Implying the pretentiousness of small-town southern aristocracy while foreshadowing the arrival of the Capello twins is a comment contrasting Venice and Dawson's Landing: "The candy-striped pole which indicates nobility proud and ancient along the palace-bordered canals of Venice indicated merely the humble barber-shop along the street of Dawson's Landing" (chapter 1). Of equal weight with the barber-pole in Dawson's Landing is the tinmonger's pole "on a chief corner," "a lofty unpainted pole wreathed from top to bottom with tin pots and pans," the words "chief" and "lofty" suggesting high aspirations but "humble" and "unpainted" giving a more realistic assessment. The "noisy notice to the world (when the wind blew)" (ibid.) symbolically indicates the community aristocracy to be more sound than substance, air that is arrogance; the emptiness of their claims, based on

high-sounding family names and codes whose purpose is to kill someone to preserve imagined violations of honor, is not evident to the townspeople who circularly value an aristocrat's position because he is in that position. For them, the position becomes the person.

These aristocrats base their nobility and world on antiquated customs supported by the enforced labor of others. They define themselves by their adherence to a code, not their relationship to God, community, or other people. Preserving one's honor as a Virginia gentleman is one's highest duty. Their "unwritten laws . . . were as clearly defined and as strict as any . . . among the printed statutes of the land"; "These laws required certain things of [the aristocrat that] his religion might forbid: then his religion must yield . . ." (chapter 12). Told that Luigi, insulted by Tom, had kicked Tom off a stage, York Driscoll—ironically, a judge—cannot conceive "that blood of my race has suffered a blow and crawled to a court of law about it" (ibid.). The narrator says the assault results when the insult causes "Luigi's southern blood" to boil (ibid.). Ironically describing the false Tom as "of the best blood of the Old Dominion" (ibid.), York becomes so angry that he challenges Luigi to a duel, even though the insult was to the Italian, not to Tom and not to him, thus defying his own code, because these unwritten laws are above the law and become what the gentlemen make them regarding their honor. The single peg becomes a concept of honor, not common sense or human relationship. Again, the whole is lost sight of.

Clemens attacks this notion, in hindsight blaming it on ideas derived from SIR WALTER SCOTT's romantic works, seeing in it the stubbornness and recklessness that led to the Civil War, as well as a tendency to imagine insult—to the South or southern institutions and customs—where it might not be; moreover, this notion helped construct and preserve beyond its time an artificial world, supposedly one of grace, manners, chivalry, and honor, but unfortunately one held in place by a terrible reality, slavery. Some southerners took this world to be the South, ignoring, whitewashing, or denying the netherworld permitting it to exist. The white people between these worlds, Wilson perhaps, contribute to the existence by passivity and acceptance. Wilson chose to come to Dawson's Landing, Missouri, from mid–New York; his best friends, except the twins, are southern aristocrats; and he ironically restores established and traditional order when he exposes Roxana's deception. Publicly, with the twins and Roxana, Wilson is compassionate. Privately, in his calendar and with FFV friend/fellow free-thinker Judge Driscoll, he is cynical, an attitude with which Driscoll sympathizes. The judge smiles knowingly at the calendar maxims but does not apply their implications to the treatment of his slaves, although in other areas he, too, can be compassionate and is not considered a bad master. Percy Driscoll's threat to sell all his slaves down the river (synonym for hell to a slave in the northern regions of the South) prompts Roxana to exchange her child for the judge's nephew. To Driscoll, his relationship with his slaves is a fraction of his real life (the world of the gentleman), though in actuality, it is much larger; they are two sides of the dog. One does not exist without the other. Conflict is inbred in this society.

Historical Setting

Clemens was aware of momentous events during the decade before the Civil War, in which he sets most of the novel. He begins his novel in 1830 (five years before his own birth) with the birth and exchange of Tom Driscoll and Valet de Chambre when Roxana is 20, the death of Tom's mother, and the arrival of David Wilson (age 25). It stops in 1845 for Tom's father, Percy, nearing poverty, to free Roxana and die; for Chambers's father, Col. Cecil Essex, to die; and for Judge Driscoll to assume care of Tom and to buy Chambers, saved from being sold down the river to continue as Tom's lifelong whipping boy. There are brief pauses in 1847 (judge's wife dies), 1849 (Tom goes to Yale), and 1851 (Tom quits Yale), and the author places most of the action in 1853, beginning with the coming of the Capellos, Roxana's return to Dawson's Landing after working eight years as a free woman, having saved, then lost $400 in a bank failure, and Tom's learning he is heavily in debt from gambling, leading to his series of neighborhood robberies. The last major attempt to appease opposing sides in the slavery debate, the Compromise of 1850, began the decade leading to the Civil War. *Uncle Tom's Cabin* by HARRIET BEECHER STOWE, later the author's neighbor, heated arguments in 1852, but significant events leading to the war occurred after 1853, particularly the *Dred Scott* decision (1857), Lincoln's speech accepting the Republican senatorial nomination (1858), and John Brown's raid on Harpers Ferry (1859).

The *Dred Scott* ruling was paradoxical. By saying in its decision that a black man could not bring suit in a federal court, the Supreme Court ruled on a case that could not be brought before it. Scott claimed freedom based on residence in free territory, but the Court declared that being free was not being free. Scott still belonged to someone else. He was like the story's two-ended dog, one end free and the other slave. How much of a person (or dog) can be owned? The novel may suggest that degrees of freedom or slavery exist, in that upriver slavery is considered better (freer) than downriver slavery, but as one cannot truly own one-half of a dog, one cannot own one-half of a person. A person cannot be part free and part slave. He or she must be wholly free to be a complete person. Calling slaves partial persons in the Constitution for purposes of representation was a fiction. In the context of *Pudd'nhead Wilson,* the dog joke and analogy call attention to this injustice.

Pertinent to this discussion is the statement Lincoln gave as he prepared to run for the Senate two years before he became president:

> 'A house divided against itself cannot stand.' . . . this government cannot endure permanently half slave and half free. I do not expect the Union to be dissolved—I do not expect the house to fall—but I do expect it will cease to be divided. It will become all one thing, or all the other.

The halved is representative of the United States, North and South; the states, slave and free; society, black and white; people, Chambers and Tom; a person, body and soul. The dog commentators' discussion is relevant to all meanings: " 'if you kill one half of a general dog . . .' '[You] couldn't and not be responsible if the other end died, which it would' "

(chapter 1). The emphasis falls not only upon interconnectedness and interrelatedness but also upon the necessity of unity (Union); one part both affects and needs the other.

Writing his novel two years after the first public recitation of the "Pledge of Allegiance" by public school children (1892), with its Lincolnesque phrase "one Nation indivisible," Clemens was as aware of developing problems threatening that unity as he was of those in the time of the novel that would tear it apart, particularly affecting race relations, such as the strength and influence of the Ku Klux Klan and increasing southern segregation laws. Setting the final part of his novel eight years before the Civil War and after Roxana has willingly reentered slavery to pay her son's gambling debts, Clemens suggests what the black person faces after (only apparently) gaining freedom. The war fought to end slavery does not bring freedom. That imminent war and its aftermath, in the future of the novel, hang over the minds of the reader and the writer.

Paradox of Color

Ironically, Roxana *is* white; only that "fiction of law and custom" makes her black and keeps her black. Roxana, Chambers, and Tom are all white, but they are all slaves. Like Chambers, she is a slave to the Driscoll family, but she replaces Tom with Chambers so that Tom as Chambers lives as a slave and Chambers as Tom is unknowingly one. Returning from having worked as a free woman, she finds a spoiled, mean, and lazy son—warped by a corrupt system with built-in callousness toward other human beings—who, in reaction to his behavior and his treatment of her, she must blackmail to control so that he becomes her slave. False Tom is slave and slave owner, existing one-half slave and one-half free, but he is more conscious of his situation than false Chambers, who is physically slave while legally master. Roxana goes in and out of slavery. Voluntarily becoming a slave to be sold up the river to pay her son's debts, she is his slave and he is hers. Symbolically or actually, she undergoes the worst a slave can encounter when he betrays her by selling her down the river, figuratively becoming the archetypal slave when she also escapes. Clemens apparently thought that the cruelest aspect of slavery was the splitting and separation of families; he represents that evil, surpassing it while symbolizing the topsy-turvy interconnectedness of the system, when a son not only sells his own mother into slavery but also into its metaphoric lowest circle of hell. Being free does not guarantee freedom; it can quickly be taken away.

Distinctions of color fade as the system enslaves all living under it, white and black simultaneously. Further confounding the color (and the sex) line, false Tom—a white man who is a black living as a white—dresses as a black woman to commit robberies, and Roxy—a black woman who is white with a black son who is white and a white son who is black—dons the disguise of a black man, symbolizing the crossing of both color and sexual barriers. The black/white man and the black/white woman meet in St. Louis, where significantly "it rained . . . hard, apparently trying . . . to wash that soot-blackened town white, but . . . not succeeding" (chapter 18). Not surprisingly, Roxana, in frustration, calls her imitation son a " 'miserable imitation nigger dat I bore in sorrow en tribbilation,' " and he responds, " 'If I's imitation, what is you? Bofe of us is imitation *white*—dat's what we is—en pow'ful good imitation too . . . we don't 'mount to noth'n as imitation *niggers* . . .' " (chapter 8).

The commingling of races that segregation laws sought to enforce has already occurred. The narrator dismisses Colonel Cecil Burleigh Essex early with an abrupt, ironic " . . . with him we have no concern" (chapter 1), perhaps as a way of saying that Chambers's father, Essex, is a small part of a larger picture, a matter greater and more pervasive than one man. He is one of many white men during the years of slavery who had sexual relations with black women, and no more proof is necessary than the single person of Roxana. Her total white appearance testifies that generation after generation of blackness has been washed out of her genealogy; it has dwindled to one-sixteenth. Roxana's experience accounts for only a small fraction of the number of sexual violations in the slaveholding South. To the eye, she is white. To a certain mindset, she is black. The yelping dog that determines Pudd'nhead's future in provincial Dawson's

Landing ironically cannot be seen, and as the townspeople argue over the ownership and disposal rights to an invisible dog, so these same people see Roxy's blackness; the part that is invisible is the most visible and most important to them. Paradoxically, color loses meaning as it gains significance. In an extended analogy and paradox, the invisible dog resembles Ralph Ellison's invisible man, whose identity is lost because, defined by others (white people) who thus maintain control, invisibility is less an issue of visibility than a fear of asserting a humanity that has been stripped away. Because of dehumanizing labels, after learning he is black, impostor Tom says, " 'I am a nigger! Oh, I wish I was dead!' " (chapter 10). Accepting the label for the reality, a part for a whole, he devalues himself.

The Capello Twins

Possibly because he dislikes himself, Tom immediately dislikes the Capello twins, seeing in them what he wishes he could have been, as their presence in the story parallels his. Whereas the town immediately embraces the twins, the Tom it knows is not popular ("he was mainly without society" [chapter 5]). Although his main conflict is with Luigi, he loathes them as one: "He hated the one for kicking him, and the other one for being the kicker's brother" (chapter 15), and Clemens presents them as one, partly a result of remnants he did not edit from his original story, "Those Extraordinary Twins," in which they were conjoined twins, but also deliberately to heighten a symbolic effect that helps draw out false Tom's character as it underscores the motif begun by the initial joke. More often referred to as "the twins" than by their names, they represent two sides of the same person, not the divided and secret personality of the apparent Driscoll heir, and they also reflect the main conflict of the story. They never appear separately; they typically apply the same terms simultaneously to themselves (" '[We] have seen . . . We are twenty-four . . . We are Italians . . . Our names are . . . We shall be . . .' "), and—despite their different personalities—people generally speak of them as a unit. The twins reply to Aunt Patsy Cooper's advertisement to rent a spare room to a single occupant: " 'You desire but one guest; but, dear madam, if you will allow us to pay for two, we will not incommode you,' " to which the Coopers respond, " 'everybody will be dying to see them, and they're all *ours!*' " (chapter 5). Exemplifying a remnant of the twins' conjoined state, several commentators observe that the twins' playing the piano as one ("a classic four-handed piece") is not especially remarkable, certainly not meriting such phrases as "some crowning act . . . something unusual, something startling, something to concentrate upon themselves the company's loftiest admiration, something in the nature of an electric surprise—" (chapter 6), unless they are one playing as two rather than two playing as one. In any case, Clemens calls attention to oneness.

Popular, talented, handsome, intelligent, witty, the twins not only immediately befriend Wilson, whom the false Tom dislikes as well, but they also initially win over his uncle and benefactor. In Dawson's Landing a short time, they are both urged to run for town aldermen. The false Tom schemes to spoil their relationship with Wilson and lies to turn his uncle against them. Unlike the twins, the false Tom was not only not born into nobility but he is also not truly a member by right of American landed aristocracy. Although reared in the Gentleman's Code, he is a coward regarding it, whereas they seem to possess it innately. Whereas he is sneaky, they are daring and bold, qualities of bravery he grants talking to Roxana [about Luigi's duel] and seems to admire as he downplays them and rationalizes his deficit: " 'They've got pluck enough, I suppose; what they lack is judgment. *I* wouldn't have stood there' " (chapter 14). This last comment also denigrates his mother's pluck, for she has moved close enough to watch when a bullet from the duel grazes her.

Similarities also underscore differences. Like Tom and Chambers, the twins " 'were so exactly alike that when dressed alike their own parents could not tell them apart' " (chapter 21); Roxana recalls the day she switched the babies, " 'When I 'uz a-washin' 'em in de tub, yistiddy, he own pappy asked me which of 'em was his'n . . . Now who would b'lieve clo'es could do de like o' dat?' " (chapter 3). As Tom and Chambers are metaphorically two ends of a dog, so Angelo and Luigi are two

sides of the same dog. One twin, Luigi, is a brunette, and Angelo is blonde; "otherwise they were exact duplicates" (chapter 5). Typically, light and dark represent good and evil, but here, slightly more literally, they become metaphors for Chambers and Tom. Neither is as flawed as false Tom, but Luigi seems closer in temperament to him as Angelo does to false Chambers. Luigi is a nonbeliever and a drinker, more volatile than his brother, who is a pious teetotaler with angelic qualities. As Luigi's drinking equates to false Tom's gambling, so does Angelo's calmness equate to false Chambers's humility. As the dark twin, Luigi symbolizes false Tom. The darkness refers to his black blood and to his evil but does not equate blackness with evil because Luigi himself is not evil. Tom's evil develops from his white upbringing; "Tom was petted and indulged and spoiled to his content—or nearly that" (ibid.) because he never receives enough to satisfy him. Luigi kills a man defending his kin (Angelo); impostor Tom kills his relative (Uncle York) to rob him and to inherit his money. Chambers as Tom cowardly beats the true Tom who, as slave, cannot retaliate; Luigi attacks this cowardly Tom for insulting him. Dark and light, the twins—also products of an aristocratic culture, also with a code—are what false Tom—product of a slave society—might have been. But if Percy Northumberland Driscoll, his presumed father, sadistically threatens to sell all his slaves down the river to punish whoever is guilty of petty theft, Col. Cecil Burleigh Essex, his actual father, abandons him to slavery, and Judge York Leicester Driscoll, his foster father, disinherits him for going to court rather than breaking the law by following the higher law of the gentleman, his outcome may not be inevitable, but he lives in a society that largely sets a course for him.

Roxana

Roxana's son, the false Tom, is not the only one confused by values of the dominant society; Roxana, indoctrinated by the culture that emphasizes color and blood, teaches her son to put himself down to pull himself up: " 'Dey ain't another nigger in dis town dat's as high-bawn as you is . . . hold yo' head up as high as you want to—you has de right . . .' " (chapter 9). Because a high-born black person is still a black person, she stresses his Essex blood except when she finds fault. Her indoctrination leads her to blame any perceived wrong on the small percentage of blood from his black side: " 'Whatever has come o' yo' Essex blood?' " (chapter 14). Incorporating the values of the FFV down to the code, little except dialect distinguishing her from York Driscoll, Roxana declares, " 'En you refuse['] to fight a man dat kicked you, 'stid o' jumpin' at de chance! . . . It's de nigger in you, dat's what it is. Thirty-one parts o' you is white, en on'y one part nigger, en dat po' little one part is yo' *soul*. Tain't wuth savin' . . .' " (ibid.). She speaks as though his nativity were in the straight line of succession: " 'You has disgraced yo' birth. What would yo' pa think o' you?' " (ibid.).

Possibly Clemens's best woman character—intelligent and strong-willed, like Rachel in "A TRUE STORY"—Roxana shares Rachel's vanity, and mimics FFV pride, in heritage. Rachel glows when she speaks of her Maryland Blue-Hen ancestry, but Roxana reaches further into the past: " 'En it ain't on'y jist Essex blood dat's in you . . . My great-great-great-gran'father . . . was ole Cap'n John Smith, de highest blood dat Ole Virginny ever turned out, en *his* great-great-gran'mother or somers along back dah, was Pocahontas de Injin queen, en her husbun' was a nigger king outen Africa . . .' " (ibid.). Like a southern aristocrat in Dawson's Landing, Roxana emphasizes a fraction of herself as the part that validates her as a person, her Virginia blood. Ironically, one of Wilson's fingerprinting subjects is John Smith (chapter 2). That her genealogy is unhistorical and false casts doubt indirectly, by analogy, on those of the FFV. They christen their children with quasi-Elizabethan names, such as Percy Northumberland, Pembroke, York Leicester, and Thomas à Becket, to stress Anglo-Saxon links; Rachel names her child Valet de Chambre. The FFV may smile, but their names are no less pretentious (Williams xli).

Through her sacrifice, however, Roxana approaches archetypal motherhood, particularly in her figurative reaction to Solomon's test for mothers. In *Huckleberry Finn,* Jim is, like all slaves in *Pudd'nhead Wilson,* fearful of being sold down the river if he returns to his owner, as he tells Huck in chapter 14, but unlike Roxana, he does not accept the world into which he is born and even asserts that the Widow Douglas, one of his mistresses, is wrong to say Solomon is the wisest man ("I doan' k'yer what de widder say . . ."), particularly based on his baby decision (" . . . dat chile he 'uz gwyne to chop in two" [*Huckleberry Finn,* chapter 14]). When two women claim the same baby, Solomon discovers the true mother by decreeing that the child be halved between the women; the one who immediately surrenders her claim, allowing the other woman to have her child, rather than see her baby harmed, he declares the mother. Jim says that Solomon need only have asked the neighbors for the mother's identity. By explaining Solomon's error in monetary terms, Jim evokes ownership and, thereby, slavery. Their milieu leads masters and slaves to think immediately in these terms. Learning of her son's gambling debts from false Chambers, Roxana blurts, " 'it's 'most enough to buy a tol'able good secondhand nigger wid' " (chapter 8). The worth of people becomes their market value.

The Split-Dog Metaphor

Jim compares the baby to a dollar bill; Clemens uses a dog. Exclaiming, " 'what's de use er dat half a bill? . . . En what use is half a chile? I wouldn' give a dern for a million un um' " (*Huckleberry Finn,* chapter 14). Dismissing a theoretical half-million dollars, as slavery dismisses many more lives abstractly, Jim's reflections resemble but contain more sense than those of the dog commentators as he accurately observes, " 'De 'spute warn't 'bout a half a chile, de 'spute was 'bout a whole chile' " (ibid.). Roxana cares for two babies as though they are one, keeping them side by side, distinguished only by different clothes. Ironically, David Wilson—who will differentiate them in the courtroom—probably gives her the idea of separating them: " 'How do you tell them apart, Roxy, when they haven't any clothes on?' " (chapter 2). An arresting (and symbolically supporting) link is that, as this David, known as "Pudd'nhead," proposes halving a dog and possibly suggests switching babies, "Wise" Solomon, the son of David, proposes halving a baby. The problem, Jim says, is that, because

Solomon has so many children, he does not value them as much as a man who has only one or two (" *He* as soon chop a chile in two as a cat' " (*Huckleberry Finn*, chapter 14) [or a dog?]). The analogy is that a man—such as an aristocrat—who owns many slaves, even a so-called paternalistic slaveholder, is not as mindful of each slave as the holder with very few (" 'a man dat's got on'y one or two chillen . . . know how to value 'em' " [ibid.]). Placing monetary worth on people devalues them and hardens those who price others.

Jim is also sensible in clarifying the importance of influence: " 'de *real* pint is down furder—it's down deeper. It lays in de way Sollermun was raised' " (ibid.). Training is a frequent topic of Clemens's. One child becomes arrogant, condescending, and mean; the other becomes humble, meek, and fearful, each a product of its society. Despite the contradiction of her whiteness, even with her intelligence, Roxy accepts the valuations of her white-dominated community, lowering herself and her son according to its labels for them, and helps inculcate those standards in both "sons," using them in paradoxically different ways with each. The townspeople cannot distinguish between a joke and property because they have learned that the material counts more than the human in Dawson's Landing; they see only the property. Even Wilson accepts and falls into a role given to him by society, retreating into himself and his hobbies. He writes scathingly of the town and America in his calendar maxims but shares these observations with few. With good evidence, he likely suspects others would miss half the joke.

For 23 years, until Wilson catches it, people miss the joke Roxana plays on the town. Figuratively, Roxana splits a baby, a son. She can grasp both the paradox posed by Wilson and the literalness of the townspeople: " 'yo' po' mammy's got to kill you to save you, honey . . . ,' " but she intends to die with her child (chapter 3) until realizing an alternative. She gives up her own child and accepts another woman's baby as her own, assuming responsibility for its protection and rearing. Roxana does not sacrifice her life to death but to a lifetime of scorn from one child and caring for another. The degree of her affection for that child, the true Tom, is

unclear, but she seems to provide guidance and to be a caring mother to him: " 'En you ain't lying, honey?—you wouldn't lie to yo' ole mammy?' " (chapter 8). She and he experience slavery together, a bond she does not share with her own son. She loves that son enough to put him out of the reach of slavery and to put herself back into it: " 'Ain't you my chile? En does you know anything dat a mother won't do for her chile? . . . In de inside, mothers is all de same' " (chapter 16). She places herself in the position of loving two halves, two children split into two different worlds. Roxana tries to do what she believes is best for her child by giving it up, but in saving him, she condemns both children. Each is ill fit for his new station in life. The system altered the spirit of one and destroyed the soul of the other. The joke that sends Chambers down the river is also upon Roxana ("Roxy's heart was broken . . . her hurts were too deep . . . the spirit in her eye was quenched, her martial bearing departed with it . . ."); Roxana no longer laughs (chapter 22).

Ironically now less than she was because she strove to make her son more than he was, Roxana transformed him from slave to slave owner and a child who owned her into her son's slave. The results expose a system that corrupts the people within it. Their judgment tainted in many ways, the same people who elected Wilson a fool elect him mayor. Little in their attitudes has actually changed. Whereas the mystery of the twins' appearance in a rural mid-American slave town may simply be that they wished to leave the consequences and repercussions of Luigi's killing in Europe, the reasons remain unknown as to why David Wilson came to this hick community a young, well-educated lawyer and stayed, labeled a pudd'nhead, to try one case in his later years and become the mayor over fools. Vindication is small, and reform is nonexistent.

Wilson tells the opening joke and delivers its final punch line in the courtroom. Like the "many humorous anecdotes" Judge Driscoll tells to entertain the twins, the joke was "of a pretty early vintage" (Cardwell 1083), so when he "always forgot the nub, . . . they were always able to furnish it" (chapter 7), but unlike Driscoll's jokes, the point is much sharper than a nub. It reverberates beyond the story. Significantly, the house where false Tom learns his true identity, where he and Roxana meet, where he admits to and receives her approval for periodically robbing his neighbors, and where she tells him Essex is his father is appropriately called haunted, because what their situation represents continues to haunt America. What began as a joke about a portion becomes a tragedy that affects a whole nation.

Critical Commentary by John H. Davis

DRAMATIC ADAPTATIONS

Frank MAYO adapted *Pudd'nhead Wilson* (1894) to the stage in 1895. A silent film was made in 1916, evidently with Alan Hale playing Wilson. In 1983, PBS television aired an adaptation with Ken Howard as Wilson and Lise Hilboldt as Roxy. Its

Wilson (Ken Howard) examines a fingerprint plate in the PBS adaptation of *Pudd'nhead Wilson*. *(Public Broadcasting System)*

script glosses over Wilson's reputation as a "pudd'n-head" by making it appear that he has an active law practice. While it follows the original story reasonably faithfully, it includes some odd changes. For example, Roxy does not bother telling Tom that she is his true mother until *after* he has sold her down the river. Toward the end, it is proven that the Capellos' Indian knife is a fake and that they themselves are frauds.

CHARACTERS AND RELATED ENTRIES

Blake, Jim Minor character in *Pudd'nhead Wilson* (1894). As Dawson's Landing's town constable, Blake is investigating Tom Driscoll's thefts in chapter 13, when he, John Buckstone, and Judge Driscoll ask David Wilson to run for mayor. Blake also appears briefly in chapters 15 and 19.

Buckstone, John Minor character in *Pudd'nhead Wilson* (1894). "A great politician in a small way," Buckstone is heavily involved in DAWSON'S LANDING public affairs. He appears at David WILSON's house in chapter 11 to invite the CAPELLO brothers to a Sons of Liberty meeting and is a member of a committee that asks Wilson to run for mayor in chapter 13. In chapter 20's trial scene, he testifies as one of the first persons to arrive at the scene of the murder. In "THOSE EXTRAORDINARY TWINS," Buckstone appears briefly as a confused witness at the Capellos' assault trial in chapter 5.

Capello, Angelo and Luigi Characters in *Pudd'nhead Wilson* (1894). In "Those Extraordinary Twins." Mark Twain's original version of *Pudd'nhead Wilson*, the Capellos are central characters who happen to be SIAMESE TWINS. When that story was revised to become *Pudd'nhead Wilson*, they were recast as ordinary twins with much reduced roles. Careless editing in this transformation left obvious traces of their previous conjoined condition. Although they are not physically connected, they appear always to be together.

The Capellos come from FLORENCE, Italy— where Mark Twain was living when he finished *Pudd'nhead Wilson*. Their family was "of the old Florentine nobility." When they were about 10, their father backed the losing side of a war, so the family had to flee to Germany as their estates were confiscated. Well educated, the young twins were both multilingual and musical prodigies. After a month in exile, their parents died deeply in debt, leaving the twins to be exploited by creditors. They were exhibited in a Berlin museum for two years, then traveled "everywhere," including East Asia, and acquired adult skills early.

In chapter 5 of *Pudd'nhead Wilson*, the Capellos arrive in Dawson's Landing to board in the home of Aunt Patsy Cooper, who thinks that they are the most handsome and distinguished young men the region has ever seen. Aside from the fact that one twin is slightly fairer than the other, Aunt Patsy says they are "exact duplicates." In the next chapter, she glories in introducing both twins to neighbors as "counts." Dawson's Landing takes to them quickly and everyone wants to entertain them. Their participation in a DUEL in chapter 14 makes them so "prodigiously great" that they decide to stay permanently and apply for citizenship. Both are asked to run for the new city council.

As close as the twins are to each other, they are divided by differences reflected in their given names. The blond Angelo is a pious teetotaler with "angelic" qualities, while the dark-haired Luigi (read "Lucifer") is a nonbeliever, drinker, and general troublemaker. In chapter 11, David Wilson

The Capello brothers entertain visitors to Patsy Cooper's home in chapter 7 of *Pudd'nhead Wilson*.

reads Luigi's palm and discovers that he once killed someone. Luigi explains that he killed a man to save Angelo's life, but rumors that he is an "assassin" later gain wide acceptance. The machinations of Tom Driscoll alienate Luigi from his natural ally, Judge York Driscoll, who turns against both twins with a vengeance. When the brothers are caught at the scene of the judge's murder in chapter 19, their case looks hopeless.

The Capellos are mentioned in less than half the chapters of the book, and in most of these they appear so briefly that they scarcely serve a purpose in the narrative. In fact, no reason for their coming to Dawson's Landing is ever given. Their main function is to act as catalysts in Wilson's career. Luigi gives Wilson his first legal case (chapter 5) and elevates Wilson's new prestige even higher when he has him act as his second in the duel. Finally, Wilson's defense of Luigi in the climactic murder trial lifts him to heroic stature.

When Clemens initially created the Capellos as Siamese twins, he wanted to explore the comic possibilities of brothers with contrasting personalities sharing a single body with two heads, four arms, one torso, and two legs. Just as their names symbolize their natures, so do their relative positions: Angelo is on the right, Luigi on the left. They disagree on almost everything but cannot escape each other's influence. When Angelo gets sick, Luigi is confined to bed. When Luigi drinks, the nondrinking Angelo gets drunk. As conjoined twins, they have marvelous mechanisms for coping with their physical limitations. Each brother controls the legs for exactly one week, regardless of time zone. In such routine tasks as eating, they are adept at helping each other. Despite being conjoined twins, they have remarkable physical differences. Luigi, for example, has a darker complexion and is hardier, more masculine and assertive. Angelo gets sick more easily, but "cannot abide medicines," so Luigi takes them for him.

Early editions of *Pudd'nhead Wilson* render the twins' surname inconsistently. *Capello* (Italian for "hair") appears most frequently, with *Cappello* (Italian for "hat" or "cap") appearing occasionally. Clemens's handwritten corrections suggest that he may have preferred the latter spelling.

Chambers (Valet de Chambre)   Name used by two characters in *Pudd'nhead Wilson* (1894). The true "Chambers" is the son of the slave woman Roxana (Roxy) and the white aristocrat Colonel Cecil Burleigh Essex. Though only ¹/₃₂ AFRICAN AMERICAN, Chambers is considered a "Negro," and is legally the slave of Percy Driscoll. He is born on February 1, 1830—the same day that his master's own son, Tom Driscoll, is born. Tom's mother soon dies, leaving Roxy to raise both boys. When they are seven months old, she switches them to protect Chambers from ever being sold down the river. From that moment, in chapter 3, until David Wilson reveals the boys' true identities in chapter 21, the character known to the world as "Chambers" is actually Tom Driscoll. Meanwhile, the true Chambers grows up as "Tom." (However, after Roxy tells her natural son his true identity in chapter 9, she calls him Chambers in private.)

The narrative says little about the boy raised as "Chambers," except that he has a hard life from infancy. He seems to get no affection from anyone. His natural mother is dead; his foster mother, Roxy, favors her natural son; and his natural father regards him as only a slave. "Tom"—who has assumed this character's birthright—treats him miserably. While Chambers's emotional strength is a cipher, he grows up physically strong and healthy. Tom uses him as a bodyguard as he bullies other boys, and then cuffs him relentlessly, knowing that his father will not tolerate Chambers's lifting a hand against him. By the time the boys are 15, Tom's abuse becomes so outrageous that his uncle, Judge York Driscoll, buys Chambers to prevent Tom from persuading Percy to sell him down the river.

Except for a brief mention in chapter 8—when Chambers is working in Judge Driscoll's house—the false Chambers disappears from the narrative between chapters 4 and 20. After Tom is exposed as a murderer and impostor at the conclusion, Chambers finds himself rich and legally free. He is not, however, psychologically free. Aside from suddenly finding himself an orphan, he must deal with the realization that he has been horribly cheated through his entire life. Handicapped by illiteracy and a coarse slave dialect and trained to have the attitudes and mannerisms of a slave, he is petrified by the company of white people. His chances for happiness appear bleak.

"Chambers" is a familiar form of the character's full name, *Valet de Chambre* (variously spelled in the original text), a French expression that translates literally as "room servant." Roxy takes on a similar title when she works on a steamboat as a "chambermaid" after being freed in chapter 4. It is probably a mere coincidence that Clemens himself worked on a steamboat named *A.B. CHAMBERS* in 1859–60. A list of fictional names that Clemens entered into a NOTEBOOK around 1880–81 includes "Valet de Chambre Utterback."

Cooper, Aunt Patsy   Character in *Pudd'nhead Wilson* (1894). A widow with three children—Rowena Cooper and two younger sons—Aunt Patsy owns a Dawson's Landing cottage and a slave, Nancy, but must rent out a spare room to boost her income above subsistence. In mid-1853, after advertising the room for more than a year, she is so thrilled to take in the Capello twins that she basks in glory even before they appear. After they arrive in chapter 6, she vanishes from the narrative. She returns as the twins go on trial for murder in chapter 20, when she and David Wilson are the only townspeople to stand by them.

Aunt Patsy has a much larger role in the original story, "THOSE EXTRAORDINARY TWINS." In chapter 5 of its published version, she is called as a witness at the Capellos' assault trial. Unable to comprehend court procedures, she tries to deal with the presiding judge, Sim Robinson, as an acquaintance until he dismisses her and throws her evidence out.

Cooper, Rowena (Roweny)   Character in *Pudd'nhead Wilson* (1894). The 19-year-old daughter of Aunt Patsy Cooper, Rowena is "amiable, and very pretty, but otherwise of no consequence." She is a romantic in the manner of Walter SCOTT—from whose novel *Ivanhoe* she got her name—and finds herself infatuated with the Capello twins even *before* they arrive. She is nominally the girlfriend of Tom Driscoll, but falls for Angelo Capello when she meets him in chapter 6. This infatuation leads nowhere, however, and Rowena is later mentioned only when Driscoll thinks about her.

Rowena's romance with Angelo is developed more fully in "THOSE EXTRAORDINARY TWINS," in which they become engaged. Rowena finally throws Angelo over in chapter 9, however, after she sees him get drunk when his Siamese-twin brother drinks heavily. Angelo protests that he does not drink himself, but Rowena counters, "you get drunk, and that is worse."

Dawson's Landing Fictional Missouri town in *Pudd'nhead Wilson* (1892), "THOSE EXTRAORDINARY TWINS," and "Hellfire Hotchkiss." Located a half day's steamboat journey down the Mississippi from SAINT LOUIS, Dawson's Landing is a regular stop on the CAIRO and MEMPHIS steamboat lines. When *Pudd'nhead Wilson* opens in 1830, the town is 50 years old and still growing. It appears to be a model American town, with modest but attractive houses, tidy gardens, and peaceful and contented citizens. Like Clemens's fictional ST. PETERSBURG, Dawson's Landing closely resembles the Hannibal of Clemens's youth. Like the latter, Dawson's Landing has a "Main Street" paralleling the river a block inland, is enclosed by hills "in a half-moon curve" and has pork as a major industry. Dawson's Landing also resembles Hannibal and St. Petersburg in being a slaveholding town—a fact of central importance to *Pudd'nhead Wilson.* Its being closer to the Deep South makes the horror of being "sold down the river" a constant specter in everyone's consciousness. Here the true ugliness and brutality of SLAVERY become evident; the town is like a St. Petersburg that has lost its innocence.

In chapter 7 of *Pudd'nhead Wilson,* Judge Driscoll gives the Capello brothers a buggy-ride tour of the town that recalls Clemens's descriptions of the dreary tours he endured while on the lecture circuit. The tour takes in a new graveyard, a jail, a Freemason's Hall, Methodist and Presbyterian churches, and a site for a new Baptist church, a town hall, slaughterhouse, firehouse, and a militia company.

The main action of *Pudd'nhead Wilson* develops in mid-1853, shortly before Dawson's Landing is to be chartered as a city. Minor aspects of the plot include David Wilson's election as mayor and the Capello brothers' unsuccessful campaigns for the new city council. While the people of Dawson's Landing are generally kindhearted, their prejudices and narrowness prevent them from appreciating the qualities of a man like Wilson until he scores a spectacular success in the climactic trial scene. Meanwhile, they do not hesitate to gush over purported Italian nobles, though they invariably prove fickle when their heroes' fortunes fall.

While it is generally acknowledged that Mark Twain took the name "Dawson's Landing" from his teacher JOHN D. DAWSON, it is not clear why.

Driscoll, Percy (Percival Northumberland Driscoll) Character in *Pudd'nhead Wilson* (1894). The brother of Judge York Driscoll, 35-year-old Percy Driscoll is a leading citizen in Dawson's Landing. The narrative opens with the birth of his son, Tom Driscoll, quickly followed by the death of his wife. The couple had several children before this, but all died. Driscoll pours his energy into business, leaving Tom in the care of his slave Roxana, whose own son was born the same day as Tom.

Though a patient and generally humane slave master, Driscoll eventually loses his patience in the face of a series of household thefts and threatens to sell *all* his slaves down the river unless the thief confesses. After three slaves confess, he sells them to local buyers and wins their groveling thanks. Later he congratulates himself on his "noble and gracious" act (chapter 2). Roxy is the only slave he does not sell, but his capricious power alarms her so greatly that she is eventually driven to switching the babies to save her son from ever being sold down the river. Driscoll goes to his grave 15 years later, never suspecting the switch. Indeed, it may only be the intervention of his brother that prevents him from unknowingly selling his true son down the river to satisfy the selfishness of his false son. Worn down from struggling to save his estates, Driscoll dies in the fall of 1845. On his deathbed, he frees Roxy and leaves Tom in the care of his brother (chapter 4).

Clemens probably had his own father, John M. Clemens, in mind when he created Driscoll. An omitted portion of his original manuscript has Driscoll do something that his father once did: Driscoll travels a great distance to collect a debt, only to let the matter go when he finds the debtor hard up. Meanwhile, he sells a slave because he is inconvenient to travel with.

Driscoll, Tom (Thomas à Becket Driscoll)

Name used by two characters in *Pudd'nhead Wilson* (1894). The true "Tom Driscoll" is the son of Percy DRISCOLL. Shortly after he is born on February 1, 1830, his mother dies, leaving him to be raised by the AFRICAN-AMERICAN slave woman Roxana— who bears her own son, Chambers, on the same day. Only 1/32 black, Chambers is almost indistinguishable from Tom. Roxy switches the babies when they are seven months old in order to save her natural son from the perils of SLAVERY. From chapter 4 until chapter 21—when his true identity is revealed in a dramatic trial scene—the character known to the world as "Tom Driscoll" is actually Chambers. Conversely, the true Tom Driscoll is known as "Chambers." To confuse matters further, Roxy begins calling her natural son "Chambers" after telling him his true identity in chapter 9. No one else, however, calls the true Tom by his rightful name again until the final chapter.

By switching babies, Roxy transforms her own son into her legal master—a role reversal that leads her to indulge him and treat him with unnatural deference. A "bad baby" virtually from birth, "Tom" grows up lazy, selfish, vain, greedy, and mean. Oblivious to his origins, he is the worst kind of slave master. He uses Chambers as his bodyguard as he bullies other boys, while treating Chambers so badly that his uncle, Judge York Driscoll, buys Chambers to prevent Tom from persuading his father to sell him down the river. Tom is 15 when his presumed father dies and his uncle adopts him. Thrilled to make Tom their child, the judge and his wife indulge him badly—continuing Roxy's pattern.

Like a childhood schoolmate of Clemens named Neil Moss, Tom goes off to YALE University for two years in chapter 5. He returns with worse habits than ever. He now drinks heavily and gambles recklessly. He also dresses foppishly, until ridicule reforms him. He collects a $50-a-month allowance from his uncle and seems to have no greater interest in life than waiting for his uncle to die so he can inherit the estate. Meanwhile, he makes increas-

ingly long trips to SAINT LOUIS, where he runs up gambling debts. To pay them off, he burglarizes homes in Dawson's Landing.

At heart, Tom is mean-spirited and vengeful. After he tactlessly goads Luigi Capello into assaulting him at a public meeting, he wins a court action against Capello, only to be publicly humiliated for lacking the courage to challenge Capello to a DUEL as southern honor dictates. He seeks revenge by doing everything he can to destroy the reputation of Luigi and his brother.

After eight years of working on a steamboat, Roxy returns to Dawson's Landing in chapter 8. She learns of Tom's dissolute behavior but is still thrilled to see him again. Unaware that Roxy is his true mother, Tom rebuffs her rudely, pushing her into confronting him with the truth. Once Roxy tells Tom who he really is, she reasserts the parental authority she abdicated long ago, and Tom never stands up to her again. In chapter 10, Tom thinks that knowing the truth about himself—that by birth he is a black slave—will cause him to improve his behavior. However, he invariably reverts to his bad habits. Incapable of redemption, he vows to reform out of expediency, not conviction. The kindest thing that can be said about him is that he develops some respect for his mother. However, even this faint impulse to filial devotion cannot overcome his self-centeredness.

When Tom's debts threaten to get him written out of the judge's will, Roxy makes the ultimate self-sacrifice to save him: letting him sell her back into slavery. She directs Tom to sell her to someone in northern Missouri, but, characteristically, he betrays her by selling her *down* the river. Eventually, she escapes and returns to confront him and make him buy back her freedom immediately. The prospect of disinheritance drives Tom to robbing his uncle, and in so doing, he kills him. However, suspicion falls on Luigi Capello. Now confident of inheriting his uncle's estate, Tom badgers David Wilson as he tries to prepare Capello's legal defense. It is, in fact, his own foolish bravado does him in. He visits Wilson the night before Capello's trial and leaves the FINGERPRINT evidence that leads to his own destruction.

After Tom is exposed at the trial, he confesses his crime and is sentenced to life imprisonment.

Since he is now legally a slave, creditors to the old Percy Driscoll estate demand him as their property. The governor pardons him and he is sold down the river—the very fate from which his mother had wanted to save him. (In an early draft, Tom hangs himself to avoid this fate.)

In "THOSE EXTRAORDINARY TWINS," Tom is a minor character mentioned in chapter 4 as the romantic interest of Rowena Cooper.

The significance of Tom's full name, "Thomas à Beckett Driscoll" is not clear, aside from the likelihood that Clemens was deliberately having fun with aristocratic-sounding English names throughout *Pudd'nhead Wilson*. He was familiar with Geoffrey Chaucer's *Canterbury Tales*, but there is no obvious connection between his character and Thomas à Becket (1118–1170), the archbishop whose martyrdom made Canterbury a shrine to pilgrims.

Driscoll, York Leicester (Judge Driscoll)   Character in *Pudd'nhead Wilson* (1894). A county judge and prosperous storekeeper, 40-year-old Driscoll is the "chief citizen" of Dawson's Landing as the narrative begins in 1830. Partly modeled on Clemens's father, John M. Clemens, who was a justice of the peace, Driscoll is immensely proud of his VIRGINIA roots. Although he is sufficiently unconventional to consider himself a freethinker in matters of religion, he is fiercely aware of his presumed aristocratic heritage and is a slave to honor.

Driscoll lives with his wife (unnamed) and his widowed sister, Rachel Pratt. They are all childless—the one thing standing between them and complete happiness. After Driscoll's brother, Percy DRISCOLL, dies in 1845, he and his wife become guardians of Percy's son, Tom Driscoll. They are so gratified to have a child that they tend to overlook Tom's many faults. As Tom's behavior grows worse, Driscoll periodically disinherits him, only to soften and write him back into his will.

In 1850, Driscoll retires from the bench and devotes himself to the Free-thinkers' Society. By chapter 5, he has been retired for three years; he is thus about 63 years old through the last three-quarters of the narrative. Driscoll is a good friend of David Wilson, whom he greatly admires. However, he cannot sway the opinions of other townspeople, who have branded Wilson a "pudd'nhead." In fact, Driscoll's solicitous enthusiasm for *Pudd'nhead Wilson's Calendar* merely damages Wilson's reputation further.

Driscoll's conventional side emerges in chapter 7, when he is the first person to show Angelo and Luigi Capello the town. He tries to impress the twins with his past "several dignities," including service in the state legislature. As much as he likes the twins, however, he feels compelled to challenge Luigi to a DUEL in chapter 13, when Tom fails to respond appropriately to Luigi's publicly kicking him. Driscoll is not concerned with *why* Luigi kicked Tom—only with the fact that the affront requires satisfaction on the "field of honor." Indeed, he regards Luigi as a splendid fellow for promptly accepting his challenge, and admires his conduct in the duel. Afterward, however, Driscoll savagely turns against Luigi when Tom tells him that Luigi is an assassin. His parental desire to believe his own child blinds Driscoll even to Wilson's explanation of Luigi's true story.

In "THOSE EXTRAORDINARY TWINS" Percy Driscoll does not appear and York Driscoll is Tom's natural father. Clemens's working notes indicate that he considered making Driscoll the father of both Tom and Chambers, the son of the slave Roxana.

Essex, Colonel Cecil Burleigh   Background figure in *Pudd'nhead Wilson* (1894). A prominent citizen of Dawson's Landing, Essex is the natural father of the boy who grows up as "Tom Driscoll" (the real Chambers) by the slave Roxana. He is identified in chapter 1 and dies in chapter 4—around the same moment as Percy Driscoll; he otherwise plays no role in the narrative. His relationship to Roxy is not explained, but she is immensely proud that Essex is her son's father, as he comes from one of the "First Families of VIRGINIA." In chapter 9, Roxy tells Tom that Essex was his father. She raves about Essex's "Virginia blood" in chapter 14, but Tom's interest extends only to wishing that he had had a chance to kill the man. Clemens's notes indicate that he considered making Tom's hunt for his father part of the plot, but he saved this idea for A DOUBLE-BARRELLED DETECTIVE STORY and left Tom instead to kill his foster father, York Driscoll.

Free-thinkers' Society   Organization in *Pudd'n-head Wilson* (1894). The Free-thinkers' Society of Dawson's Landing has two members: Judge York Driscoll and David Wilson. They meet for weekly discussions, which often center on Wilson's PUDD'N-HEAD WILSON'S CALENDAR. After Driscoll's retirement, the society becomes his main interest in life. In chapter 7, he takes the Capello twins to a meeting. Since the essence of "freethinking" is rejection of religious authority, such a society is not likely be popular in a conservative Protestant community like Dawson's Landing. However, as the town's leading citizen, Driscoll need not answer for his behavior, while Wilson is considered too inconsequential to matter.

The society seems to be a bigger organization in "THOSE EXTRAORDINARY TWINS," in which it shares a large hall with a Baptist Bible class.

Grand Mogul   Fictional STEAMBOAT in *Pudd'n-head Wilson* (1894). After being freed from slavery in 1845, Roxana goes to work as a chambermaid on the *Grand Mogul,* a steamboat that runs between CINCINNATI and NEW ORLEANS. During the winters, she works on a packet out of VICKSBURG on the Lower Mississippi. After eight years, she leaves the *Grand Mogul* in New Orleans, planning to retire on her savings. When she discovers that her bank has failed, she returns to the boat, whose crew takes up a collection in her behalf (chapter 8). Later, Roxy escapes from slavery on an ARKANSAS farm and finds the *Grand Mogul* laid up nearby; the boat is now on a run to St. Louis—exactly where she wants to go. Her former crewmates give her $20 and take her there (chapter 18).

Pudd'nhead Wilson omits a long description of the *Grand Mogul* from Clemens's original manuscript that indicates that the ornately decorated steamboat is 250 feet long. The published version of "THOSE EXTRAORDINARY TWINS" does not mention the boat.

The name "*Grand Mogul*" reflects the popularity of romantic Oriental names for Mississippi River steamboats, such as the *Grand Turk* and the *Sultana,* that are mentioned in *Life on the Mississippi* (1883) (chapters 14, 16, and 17). *Roughing It* (1872) describes the office of STAGECOACH agent as

a "grand mogul" (chapter 6) and its list of HUMBOLDT mines includes "Grand Mogul" and "Sultana" (chapter 29). The term "grand mogul" also appears in *Tom Sawyer Abroad* (chapter 11).

Howard, Pembroke   Minor character in *Pudd'n-head Wilson* (1894). A middle-aged bachelor, Howard ranks as Dawson's Landing's "recognized second citizen" after Judge York Driscoll, with whom he grew up in VIRGINIA. Like Driscoll, he is first and foremost a gentleman, always ready to defend what he believes on the field of honor. Although Howard contrasts with the freethinking Driscoll in being a determined Presbyterian, the two men are fast friends. In chapter 12, they are fishing together when Driscoll learns of his nephew Tom Driscoll's failure to challenge Luigi Capello to a DUEL. When the judge takes on Capello himself. Howard acts as his second (chapter 14). Considered the town's "great lawyer," Howard is the public prosecutor at Capello brothers' murder trial in chapter 20.

Jasper   Minor character in *Pudd'nhead Wilson* (1894). A young AFRICAN-AMERICAN slave "of magnificent build" in chapter 2, Jasper flirts with Roxy (Roxana), who hints that Jasper has a relationship with the Coopers' slave Nancy. When Roxy leaves Dawson's Landing in chapter 4, she says goodbye to Jasper as he chops wood for David Wilson.

The original manuscript of *Pudd'nhead Wilson* gave Jasper a more important role. A passage deleted from chapter 2 has Jasper stop a runaway horse-and-buggy, saving his young mistress and her baby and nurse—an incident inspired by a rescue performed by Clemens's acquaintance John T. LEWIS. Jasper's grateful master liberates him, allowing him to approach Roxy as a free man.

Clemens's long unfinished story, "Which Was It?," has a strong slave character named Jasper who earns his freedom and eventually dominates his former master through blackmail.

Nancy   Minor character in *Pudd'nhead Wilson* (1894). Mentioned in chapters 4 and 5, Nancy is a slave belonging to Aunt Patsy Cooper. She seems to have a romantic relationship with another slave named Jasper. Nancy has a somewhat larger role in

"THOSE EXTRAORDINARY TWINS," in which she is terrified by the appearance of the Siamese twins.

Pratt, Mrs. Rachel Minor character in *Pudd'-nhead Wilson* (1894). The childless widowed sister of Judge York Driscoll, in whose house she lives, Pratt helps to raise their mutual nephew Tom Driscoll, on whom she dotes. After her brother is murdered in chapter 19, she finds the Capello twins standing by his body and testifies against them at their trial in the next chapter.

Most of the novel's 17 references to Pratt call her "Mrs. Pratt"; she is called "Mrs. Rachel Pratt" once, in the first chapter. In chapter 13, Tom alludes to receiving a gift from "Aunt Mary Pratt"— who is evidently the same character.

Robinson, Judge (Sim) Character in *Pudd'nhead Wilson* and "THOSE EXTRAORDINARY TWINS." A Dawson's Landing judge, Robinson makes several brief appearances. In chapter 5, he congratulates Patsy Cooper when the Capello twins arrive as her boarders. He is mentioned in chapter 12 as the presiding judge at Luigi Capello's assault trial but does not actually appear in the chapter. In the next chapter, he is among the town leaders who ask David Wilson to run for mayor. He is later mentioned as the coroner who attends to York Driscoll's murder (chapter 19). He is at the ensuing murder trial, in which he appears to have some official role, but he is not named as the presiding judge—who is identified only as a "veteran" (chapter 21).

Robinson has a larger role in the published excerpts of "Those Extraordinary Twins," Clemens's earlier version of the story. In chapter 5, he presides over the comical assault trial of the Capellos, who are SIAMESE TWINS in this version. As a *new* judge without legal training, Robinson knows little about trial procedure and takes pride in running a court that disregards legal precedent. When he senses that the trial is headed toward a not-guilty verdict, he insists that *someone* must be found guilty. His inexperience is particularly evident in his failure to get Patsy Cooper to behave properly when she testifies. Despite his unorthodox conduct, Robinson is a popular judge because his decisions are regarded as impartial and just. His blustering behavior recalls

Roughing It's (1872) Ned Blakely, whom Clemens modeled on CAPTAIN NED WAKEMAN. Indeed, it may be significant that one of the witnesses whom Robinson hears testify in "Those Extraordinary Twins" is named Wakeman.

Roxana (Roxy) Central character in *Pudd'nhead Wilson* (1894). When the narrative begins in 1830, Roxy is a 20-year-old domestic slave in the household of Percy Driscoll, in Dawson's Landing, Missouri. Only 1/16th part AFRICAN AMERICAN in descent, she could easily pass for white, were it not for her thick slave dialect. In chapter 1, she bears a son, Chambers, on the same day that her master's wife bears a son named Tom. Mrs. Driscoll soon dies, leaving Roxy to raise both boys. Chambers's father is Colonel Cecil Burleigh Essex, whose relationship with Roxy is never explained.

After Driscoll threatens to sell his slaves down the river for stealing, Roxy becomes obsessed with the fear of having her son sold away. At first, she decides to drown herself and her son, but changes her mind after realizing that she can protect her son by switching him with Driscoll's son. By transforming Chambers into "Tom Driscoll," she becomes her own son's slave. Suppressing her natural maternal instincts, she badly overindulges him. As "Tom" moves into adolescence, he treats Roxy so badly, insulting and abusing her, that she fantasizes about exposing his identity for revenge. Lacking proof, however, she is helpless before the monster she has created.

Fifteen years later, the death of Driscoll leaves Roxy free, but the collapse of his investments leaves her without a home. She goes "chambermaiding" on a steamboat in chapter 4 and reappears four chapters later, after having worked for eight years on the steamboat *Grand Mogul*. Now about 43, she suffers from rheumatism that forces her to retire on $400 that she has saved in a New Orleans bank. When she discovers that her bank has gone bust, she returns to Dawson's Landing. Although Tom has never treated her well, she is desperately anxious to see him. He receives her so rudely, however, that she turns on him savagely, threatening to reveal dark secrets about him to his guardian, Judge York Driscoll. When Tom meets with her secretly, she overwhelms him by force of personality and begins directing his life.

Much of Roxy's motivation is true affection for her son. Her love for him is so great, in fact, that she is willing to be sold back into slavery in order to raise money to clear his gambling debts. Even after he betrays her by selling her down the river—where she becomes a common field hand—she still looks for reasons to love him. On the other hand, she demonstrates no noticeable affection for the boy she has raised as "Chambers," though she is the only parent that he knows.

Roxy's intelligence allows her to devise intricate schemes to solve problems. She anticipates contingencies, sees through duplicity and double-dealing, and adapts quickly to changing circumstances. Her most glaring lapse is failing to control the terms of her sale back into slavery. She does not even know that Tom has sold her *down* the river until she travels to her new home. Ever resilient, however, she escapes, finds Tom in St. Louis, and forces the truth out of him in chapter 18. Angry though she is, even now she does not renounce him. Instead, she puts him to work to regain her legal freedom.

Roxy forces her son, the ostensible Tom Driscoll, to his knees in chapter 8 of *Pudd'nhead Wilson.*

Like many of the white characters in *Pudd'nhead Wilson,* Roxy has her own stereotyped ideas about race and honor. In chapter 14, she shames Tom for failing to fight Luigi Capello in a DUEL, telling him, "It's de NIGGER in you." She thinks Tom should behave in a way befitting his Essex "blood." She is as proud of Essex's aristocratic VIRGINIA background as she is of her own descent from John Smith and Pocahontas, as well as an African king.

Roxy's role in the published fragment of "THOSE EXTRAORDINARY TWINS" is minor; however, her powerful emergence in that original story helped force Clemens to abandon his original plot. He developed her belatedly as he transformed "Those Extraordinary Twins" into *Pudd'nhead Wilson.* There are, consequently, major inconsistencies in her character. For example, the feminine physical features he gives her at the beginning of the narrative seem to be lost by its middle.

Generally regarded as the strongest and most fully rounded female character that Clemens ever created, Roxy is resilient and indomitable, taking many initiatives that drive the narrative forward. No clear models for Roxy in Clemens's experience are known. Two decades before he created Roxy, however, he wrote about another strong black woman, Rachel Cord, in "A TRUE STORY."

It is possible that Clemens took Roxy's name from DANIEL DEFOE's novel, *Roxana, or the Fortunate Mistress* (1724), which W. D. HOWELLS advised him to read in 1885. Defoe's PICARESQUE heroine is a member of upper-class English society, but like Clemens's Roxana she is forced by circumstances into shady behavior. *Pudd'nhead Wilson* uses "Roxana" 25 times and "Roxy" 84 times.

In the 1983 PBS television adaptation *Pudd'nhead Wilson,* Lise Hilboldt played Roxy.

Sons of Liberty Organization in *Pudd'nhead Wilson* (1894). In chapter 11, John Buckstone takes Angelo and Luigi Capello to a meeting of the strong rum party—the "Sons of Liberty"—at Dawson's Landing's Market Hall. Four hundred men attend. Tom Driscoll tags along, gets tipsy and insults Luigi, who responds by kicking him into the audience. The drunken members pass Tom through the auditorium over their heads and erupt into a general melee until someone yells fire. It happens that the firefighters are quartered downstairs; they respond quickly, breaking all the windows in the hall, and dousing the room with water.

The published version of "THOSE EXTRAORDINARY TWINS" summarizes the same scene in chapter 5. In this version, however, the Capellos are SIAMESE TWINS with a single body. At the ensuing trial, witnesses from the Sons of Liberty are unable to identify which twin kicked Driscoll.

Wilson, David ("Pudd'nhead Wilson") Character in *Pudd'nhead Wilson* (1894). Born in New York, Wilson is 25 years old when he comes to Dawson's Landing in February 1830 to seek his fortune. He arrives in the same month in which Tom Driscoll and Chambers are born. "Homely, freckled, sandy-haired . . . with an intelligent blue eye," he is college-educated and has completed a course at an eastern law school.

On his arrival, Wilson makes a "fatal remark." Annoyed by a barking dog, he utters a wish to own *half* the dog. Why? So that he could kill his half. SOLOMON might have said the same thing, but those who overhear Wilson say this merely think him daft, and his ironic remark earns him the nickname "Pudd'nhead." Years later, his reputation is further damaged when his friend Judge York Driscoll shows samples of his ironic MAXIMS to uncomprehending town leaders. The maxims of Pudd'nhead Wilson's Calendar reveal Wilson's intellectual and emotional complexity, but further distance him from other townspeople. Apart from Driscoll, the only person in town who respects Wilson's intellect is the slave woman Roxana. She not only thinks him the smartest man in town, she suspects he may even be a witch. To some, perhaps he is. He ultimately wins respect by performing what many townspeople think a miracle.

Wilson arrives in Missouri with enough money to buy a house at the western edge of town, near Judge Driscoll's home. He also opens an office in town and hangs a shingle advertising himself as "Attorney & Counselor-at-law." Like Clemens's brother Orion Clemens, however, Wilson never gets a case. Eventually, he removes his shingle and concentrates on surveying and bookkeeping, while filling his considerable idle time with such hobbies as PALMISTRY, collecting FINGERPRINTS, and writing his calendar.

Despite his pudd'nhead reputation, Wilson is well liked in town. He is such a gentleman that even the treacherous Tom Driscoll can count on a gracious reception at his home. Wilson seems totally lacking in guile or ambition. After he discovers the terrible truth about Driscoll, in chapter 20, he takes no satisfaction in knowing that the man will hang—despite the fact that he murdered Wilson's best friend.

Meanwhile, Wilson's fortunes improve after the Italians Angelo and Luigi Capello arrive in town in 1853. They increase his paltry stock of intelligent friends and serve as catalysts in his life. Luigi launches Wilson's law career by engaging him to defend him against Tom Driscoll's assault charges in chapter 5. Immediately afterward, Wilson is asked to run for mayor. His reputation rises even higher when he serves as Luigi's second in a DUEL in chapter 14. Finally, his defense of Luigi in the climactic murder trial lifts him to heroic stature. By the end of the narrative, the Capellos are gone, but Wilson's future is apparently secure.

Clemens himself evidently thought little of Wilson. In January 1894, he wrote to his wife, "I have never thought of Pudd'nhead as a *character*, but only as a piece of machinery—a button or a crank or a lever, with a useful function to perform in a machine, but with no dignity above that." Some of this is true. Despite Wilson's evident compassion, his dimensions are limited. Not only is he satisfied to wait two decades to take up his law career, he is content to remain an ascetic bachelor. He seems to devote his life to developing the arcane knowledge that will prove essential for one extraordinary trial, in which pieces of several diverse puzzles fall together simultaneously. It is not an achievement that he could ever hope to repeat.

What most interested Clemens about Wilson is his being "an example of that unfortunate type of human being who, misunderstood at the moment of entering a new community, may spend a lifetime trying to live down that blunder, especially if he gets cataloged by some ridiculous nickname." During the long years that Wilson goes without legal cases, he keeps up with the law, confident that his chance will come. Until his climactic triumph, he is merely an example of unrecognized talent—a theme explored in "CAPTAIN STORMFIELD'S VISIT TO HEAVEN," featuring such unappreciated talents as Absalom Jones.

There are obvious flaws in Wilson's characterization. For example, while his philosophical maxims are often bitterly nonconformist, he has a strongly conventional side. Though not a southerner by birth or upbringing, he empathizes with the South's archaic code of honor. In chapter 13 he astounds Tom Driscoll by saying that he would rather not get his first case than see Judge Driscoll suffer the humiliation of Tom's settling an affair of honor in court instead of in a duel. Later, he serves as Luigi Capello's second in a duel.

Though in many ways astute, Wilson seems remarkably blind to many things happening around him. For example, he never notices Roxy and Tom's many meetings at the nearby haunted house. Further, he apparently never thinks to compare the infant fingerprints of Chambers and Tom Driscoll with their adult prints, or with each other, until an accidental discovery alerts him to Tom's guilt in the murder case.

In the published version of "THOSE EXTRAORDINARY TWINS," Wilson is first mentioned in chapter 3 as a member of the Free-thinkers' Society, Nothing is said about his background. In chapter 5, Wilson defends the Capello brothers—here SIAMESE TWINS—against Tom Driscoll's assault charge. He wins the case and emerges popular, admired, and happy. In *Pudd'nhead Wilson* this scene is reduced to an offstage trial that Wilson loses; however, the case still serves to launch his legal career.

The unfinished story "Hellfire Hotchkiss" quotes Wilson as describing Hellfire as "the only genuwyne male man in this town." In A DOUBLE-BARRELLED DETECTIVE STORY (1902), "David Wilson" is one of the ALIASES used by Jacob Fuller.

A likely real-life model for Wilson was the distinguished Missouri attorney SAMUEL TAYLOR GLOVER, whom the people of Hannibal regarded as a "chucklehead" despite his accomplishments. When *Pudd'nhead Wilson* was serialized in 1893–94, many people thought that a New York Stock Exchange officer named Theodore Wilson was Clemens's model.

Ken Howard portrayed Wilson in PBS's 1983 television adaptation of *Pudd'nhead Wilson.* Oddly, this adaptation overlooks the basis of Wilson's nickname. When it begins, Wilson appears to have an active law practice.

BIBLIOGRAPHY

Cardwell, Guy, ed. "Notes [for *Pudd'nhead Wilson*]." In *Mississippi Writings: The Adventures of Tom Sawyer, Life on the Mississippi, Adventures of Huckleberry Finn, Pudd'nhead Wilson,* 1,082–1,084. New York: Library of America, 1982.

Twain, Mark. *Pudd'nhead Wilson and Other Tales,* edited by R. D. Gooder. New York: Oxford University Press, 1992.

———. *Huckleberry Finn. Mississippi Writings: The Adventures of Tom Sawyer, Life on the Mississippi, Adventures of Huckleberry Finn, Pudd'nhead Wilson,* edited by Guy Cardwell, 617–912. New York: Library of America, 1982.

Williams, Sherley Anne. "Introduction." In *The Tragedy of Pudd'nhead Wilson and the Comedy Those Extraordinary Twins,* by Mark Twain. 1894. Reprint, New York: Oxford University Press, 1996. xxxi–xliii.

Pudd'nhead Wilson's Calendar

Manuscript jottings of David Wilson in *Pudd'nhead Wilson* (1894) and *Following the Equator* (1897). Chapter 5 reveals that Wilson has "for some years" been privately writing a "whimsical almanac," or "calendar," containing ironic MAXIMS. His friend Judge York Driscoll so admires these writings that he shows samples to other townspeople. Unable to appreciate irony, they decide "that if there had ever been any doubt that Dave Wilson was a pudd'n-head . . . this revelation removed that doubt for good and all."

Each installment of CENTURY MAGAZINE's serialization of *Pudd'nhead Wilson* contained small calendars incorporating Wilson's maxims. The maxims appeared as chapter headings when *Pudd'nhead Wilson* was published as a book. Clemens wanted to match these maxims with chapter contents, but soon abandoned the effort. The resulting relationship between the maxims and their chapters is thus mixed. Maxims heading chapter 5, for example, aptly allude to the upbringing of characters discussed within the chapter. One reads: "Training is everything. The peach was once a bitter almond; cauliflower is nothing but cabbage with a college education." In chapter 11, Wilson reads sample maxims to the Capello brothers, who tactfully ask to borrow his manuscript. A maxim heading this chapter comments on how to please an author by asking to read his manuscript. Others are less obviously connected to the chapters.

While Clemens's biographer A. B. PAINE is not alone in regarding the "Calendar" as *Pudd'nhead Wilson*'s most memorable feature, some critics point out that the maxims expose Clemens's inconsistent characterization of Wilson. Many maxims express a cynical pessimism about life that is at odds with Wilson's often conventional behavior. Why, one wonders, would Wilson write such thoughts as: " 'How hard it is that we have to die'—a strange complaint to come from the mouths of people who have had to live" (chapter 10) and "Why is it that we rejoice at a birth and grieve at a funeral? It is because we are not the person involved" (chapter 9). Neither sentiment seems consistent with Wilson's character.

Clemens repeated the calendar experiment three years later by inserting maxims at the heads of chapters in *Following the Equator* (1897), crediting them to "Pudd'nhead Wilson's *New* Calendar." MORE TRAMPS ABROAD, the English edition of this book, contains several maxims not appearing in the American edition. "Pudd'nhead Wilson's Calendar" maxims occasionally appear elsewhere; for example, at the beginning of "THE BELATED RUSSIAN PASSPORT."

"Punch, Brothers, Punch!"

SKETCH that originally appeared in the February 1876 ATLANTIC MONTHLY as "A Literary Nightmare." Inspired by a jingle published in a newspaper, Clemens has his narrator—named "Mark"—read this apparently harmless jingle:

Conductor, when you receive a fare,
Punch in the presence of the passenjare!
A blue trip slip for an eight-cent fare,
A buff trip slip for a six-cent fare,
A pink trip slip for a three-cent fare,
Punch in the presence of the passenjare!

Punch, brothers! punch with care!
Punch in the presence of the passenjare!

The catchy lines immediately possess Mark. For two days, their sing-song rhythms echo in his head, leaving him unable to function. When he goes walking with a clerical friend (inspired by Reverend JOSEPH TWICHELL), he mumbles the verses constantly, oblivious to conversation. Intrigued by the musical rhymes, the friend masters them himself, lifting the burden from Mark—who is soon back to normal. His friend, however, is now helpless. Several days later, the friend returns from Boston, where he conducted a funeral. Unable to clear the rhymes from his head, he was almost a lunatic by the time he got there. To save him from madness, Mark takes him to a local university to discharge his burden on unsuspecting students. He warns readers who encounter the merciless rhymes to avoid them like the pestilence.

In September 1875, NOAH BROOKS and Isaac Hill Bromley (1833–1898) published a version of the streetcar jingle in the *NEW YORK TRIBUNE*, parodying printed instructions given to streetcar conductors. Clemens's version adapts theirs. His *Atlantic* sketch was so popular that he copyrighted "Punch in the Presence of the Passenjare" on sheet music the same year, with additional lyrics and music by A. O. Hand. He changed the title of the sketch in 1878, when DAN SLOTE's company published *Punch, Brothers, Punch! and Other Sketches*, a 142-page book with prominent advertisements for Clemens's self-pasting SCRAPBOOK. CHATTO and Windus simultaneously published an English edition under the title *An Idle Excursion. Punch, Brothers, Punch!* was also the first book to reprint "SOME RAMBLING NOTES OF AN IDLE EXCURSION," "THE LOVES OF ALONZO FITZ CLARENCE AND ROSANNAH ETHELTON" and "THE CANVASSER'S TALE." Its entire contents were reprinted in *THE STOLEN WHITE ELEPHANT, ETC.* (1882).

The Quaker City Holy Land Excursion

Unfinished play. Soon after Clemens returned to New York on the QUAKER CITY in November 1867, he began writing a satirical play about the voyage, encouraged by Charles Henry WEBB. After drafting just two scenes, he abandoned the effort. Elements of the play—notably the name of the ship—are closely based on aspects of the actual excursion.

The play opens in the Wall Street office of the cruise's organizer, Captain Dusenberry (modeled on CHARLES DUNCAN), who unctuously accepts applications for passage from a group of "old maids." His sarcastic asides indicate that his only interest is taking their money. The next scene is aboard the steamship. Two reporters—one of whom is Clemens himself, the other a Blucher-like character named Stiggers—discuss how old the other passengers are and joke about why the cruise's promised celebrities did not come. Dan Sproat (modeled on DAN SLOTE), joins them and they discuss the wearisome PILGRIMS aboard the ship until the manuscript abruptly ends.

Clemens's manuscript is held at Indiana University Library. It was printed privately in 1927 and published in 1968 in Dewey Ganzel's *Mark Twain Abroad: The Cruise of the "Quaker City,"* which also incorporates a related fragment from Clemens's NOTEBOOKS.

CHARACTERS AND RELATED ENTRIES

Dusenberry, Captain   Character in the unfinished play, THE QUAKER CITY HOLY LAND EXCURSION (1867). Clearly modeled on the QUAKER CITY's CAPTAIN CHARLES C. DUNCAN, Dusenberry is a crooked hypocrite who gleefully takes passage money from trusting old people in the one scene in which he appears. His name is evidently Clemens's invention. In September 1867, Clemens wrote a letter to the SAN FRANCISCO ALTA CALIFORNIA from Jerusalem that mentions books that Quaker City passengers were advised to bring with them. One of these books is *Dusenberry's Researches in Palestine*—64 copies of which are in the ship's library. The initials of this nonexistent book's title

are "R.I.P."—possibly a subtle joke reflecting Clemens's opinion that the *Quaker City* cruise was "a funeral excursion without a corpse."

"Raft Chapter"

Originally written for *Huckleberry Finn* (1884), this 5,100-word chapter was omitted from the novel after it appeared in *Life on the Mississippi* (1883). It was first restored to its originally intended place in *Huckleberry Finn* in a 1944 edition of the book. Also called the "Raft Episode," the chapter is *not* about Jim and Huck's raft.

Clemens seems to have written most of the "Raft Chapter" along with the rest of *Huckleberry Finn*'s first 16 chapters around 1876. Several years later, when he was writing *Life on the Mississippi,* he inserted the "Raft Chapter" into the book's third chapter, titled "Frescoes of the Past," in order to illustrate life on the giant flatboats that once clogged the Mississippi. His prelude to this story recalls how he saw miles of such rafts drifting down the river during the 1840s, when he and other boys would occasionally swim out to hitch rides—exactly what Huck does in the "Raft Chapter."

When CHARLES L. WEBSTER prepared *Huckleberry Finn* for publication, he persuaded Clemens to omit the "Raft Chapter" from the novel to save space. Clemens agreed, since the chapter had already been published and because he thought that it contained nothing essential to the rest of the novel. Succeeding editions of *Huckleberry Finn* omitted this chapter until BERNARD DEVOTO restored it in a Limited Editions Club volume in 1944. Modern MARK TWAIN PROJECT editions of *Huckleberry Finn* also include the chapter—inserting it within chapter 16, following that chapter's second paragraph. Some other editions have printed the chapter as an appendix. The 1986 PBS television adaptation of *Huckleberry Finn* dramatized the episode, but staged it on land instead of on a raft—presumably to minimize production costs.

The "Raft Chapter"'s importance to *Huckleberry Finn* is subtle but crucial. Huck swims out to a giant raft hoping to learn how far he and Jim are from their destination, CAIRO, Illinois. He does not get an answer to this question but does learn something else that enables him to answer the question later, at the end of chapter 16. He overhears men on the raft discussing how the clear water of the OHIO RIVER forms a visible channel in the muddy Mississippi below Cairo, where the rivers meet. When Huck later recognizes that the water on which they are floating is clear at the end of chapter 16, he concludes that "it was all up with Cairo." Without the "Raft Chapter"'s explanation of this phenomenon, his remark makes no sense.

SYNOPSIS

Impatient to learn where he and Jim are, Huck decides to visit the big raft floating near them to pick up information. He strips, swims to the raft and sneaks aboard. Thirteen tough-looking men are sitting around an open fire, passing around a jug as one man sings a ribald song. They tire of the song and tease the singer. The biggest man, Bob, claims the right to thrash the singer and boasts outrageously about his prowess, claiming, for example, to be "half-brother to the CHOLERA." Another man, who calls himself the "Child of Calamity," counters with equally outrageous boasts. They face off, but a smaller man named Davy gets up and thrashes both of them.

Huck meanwhile hides in the dark, smoking a pipe he finds, as another man plays a fiddle while the men dance. The men then sit down to spin yarns and get to comparing the waters of the Mississippi and Ohio rivers.

A raftsman named Ed tells a ghost story about a former partner named Dick Allbright who was pursued on the river by a haunted barrel. The climax comes when Allbright's baby, Charles William Allbright, is found in the barrel. After Ed finishes his yarn, the other raftsmen tease him mercilessly. As Ed skulks off, the Child of Calamity finds Huck. Some men want to paint Huck blue and toss him overboard, but Davy rescues him. When asked his name, Huck fetches a big laugh by answering "Charles William Allbright." Then he calls himself "Aleck James Hopkins" and explains that he swam to the raft from his father's trading scow just for the fun of it. The men let him go, and he swims back to rejoin Jim.

Report from Paradise

Volume of Clemens writings published by HARPER's in 1952. Edited by DIXON WECTER, the book includes the first expanded version of "CAPTAIN STORMFIELD'S VISIT TO HEAVEN," the first publication of "Letters from the Recording Angel," and an essay by Wecter.

Roughing It (1872)

Clemens's second major book, *Roughing It* is a loose account of the five and half years that he spent in the Far West during the early 1860s. It begins with the journey that he and his brother Orion Clemens made in July 1861, when they traveled by steamboat and STAGECOACH from Missouri to NEVADA, where Orion became SECRETARY in the new territorial government. After a brief stint as Orion's private secretary, Clemens dabbled in MINING and began contributing sketches to the VIRGINIA CITY TERRITORIAL ENTERPRISE and other western papers. In the fall of 1862, he gave up prospecting and joined the *Enterprise* staff until he moved to SAN FRANCISCO in May 1864. From then until the end of 1866, San Francisco was his base. Through his western years, Clemens became a professional writer and adopted his famous pen name; he also formed important lifelong friendships and acquired a longing to become wealthy.

While *Roughing It* is based on Clemens's real experiences in 1861–66, it is neither straight AUTOBIOGRAPHY nor a TRAVEL BOOK in the same sense as *Innocents Abroad* (1869). It differs from *Innocents* in covering a much longer period and in being written much longer after its events took place. Further, while Clemens built *Innocents* around travel letters written on his journey, he wrote most of *Roughing It* from memory, supplemented by his brother's notes and by articles that he wrote for western papers. The book's 16 chapters on Hawaii resemble *Innocents* in construction and tone, but are so different from the rest of *Roughing It* that they hardly seem an integral part of the book.

Roughing It embroiders many episodes, invents others, and overlooks some of the most important things that Clemens did during his years in the West. It does not, for example, mention how he became "MARK TWAIN" or tell about the HOAXES and the JUMPING FROG STORY that helped make him famous. Many real episodes that it does describe are presented out of sequence, and most are exaggerated or otherwise embellished. However, while *Roughing It* may be dubious as biography, it is an invaluable historical document that contains some of Clemens's best humorous writing. Clemens was in NEVADA during its first silver boom, he was in CALIFORNIA during the immediate aftermath of its GOLD RUSH, and he was in HAWAII when American interest in the islands was rising. *Roughing It*'s descriptions of these and other developments vividly capture the authentic flavor of the times.

A prime reason for not regarding *Roughing It* as autobiography is that its unnamed narrator is younger and more naive than Clemens himself actually was during the early 1860s. In the first chapter, the narrator describes himself as "young and ignorant." He later implies that he is so young that Brigham YOUNG is not even sure whether he is a boy or a girl (chapter 13). A dominant theme of early chapters is the tenderfoot narrator's disillusionments. His romantic image of INDIANS is shattered when he encounters the GOSIUTE (chapter 19). His first prospecting trip in Nevada teaches him that *nothing* that glitters is gold (chapter 28). When he and several companions are later lost in a blizzard, he discovers other long-cherished western myths to be false, such as the possibility of starting a fire with a pistol and the notion that horses stay with their masters in a crisis (chapter 32).

SYNOPSIS

One of Clemens's longest books at 172,473 words, *Roughing It* is divided into 79 chapters and three appendices. The first 21 chapters cover the narrator's journey from St. Louis to SAINT JOSEPH, Missouri, by steamboat followed by a three-week stagecoach trip from St. Joseph to Carson City, Nevada, during which he crosses the Great Plains and the Rocky Mountains. Chapter 21 begins his stay in Carson City, where he drifts from one

Roughing It's young narrator dreams about Indians, deserts, and prospecting in the Far West the night before beginning his journey.

money-making scheme to another. In chapter 26, he begins a brief prospecting career that takes him to the HUMBOLDT and ESMERALDA mining districts. By chapter 42, he has given up on mining and settles down in VIRGINIA CITY as a newspaper reporter. Two years later, he goes to SAN FRANCISCO (chapters 56–59). His time there is interrupted by a sojourn in a California gold-mining district (chapters 60–61). After returning to San Francisco, he takes a reportorial assignment to go the Sandwich (Hawaiian) Islands (chapters 62–77). On his next return to San Francisco, he takes up LECTURING and makes a brief tour of northern California and western Nevada before leaving the Pacific Coast (chapters 78–79). The book ends with brief comments on his return to the East Coast and an allusion to visiting his boyhood home.

While the synopsis that follows is not strictly a condensation of *Roughing It*, it occasionally uses Clemens's own words and spellings. Parenthetical insertions, such as dates and names, are taken from sources outside of the chapters in which they appear.

Chapter 1

The narrator recalls a moment 10 or 12 years earlier when his brother (Orion Clemens) is appointed SECRETARY of the new NEVADA Territory. He envies his brother—especially the long, strange journey he will undertake. When invited to accompany him as a "private secretary," he jumps at the chance and looks forward to spending about three months in Nevada. They begin their journey with a six-day STEAMBOAT voyage up the MISSOURI RIVER to St. Joseph.

Chapter 2

At a St. Joseph stage office the brothers pay $150 each for passage to CARSON CITY on an overland STAGECOACH. Early the next day (July 26), they learn that they can only take 25 pounds of luggage each. After shipping their surplus back to St. Louis, they have only minimal clothing, four pounds of United States statutes, a six-pound unabridged dictionary, guns, blankets and tobacco. The narrator carries a Smith and Wesson seven-shooter; George Bemis, their only fellow passenger, carries an Allen revolver. They begin their journey by riding into the Great Plains of KANSAS, sharing their coach with 2,700 pounds of mailbags. Every 10 miles they change horses. Later a woman passenger boards the coach for a 50-mile leg. She is as silent as the SPHINX until the narrator makes the mistake of speaking to her—then she never stops talking.

Chapter 3

Early the next morning, the coach stops abruptly when its thoroughbrace breaks under the heavy load of mail. The passengers turn out and help remove the mailbags. After the coach is repaired, its conductor reloads only half of the bags inside the passenger compartment, where the travelers find they make excellent seats. As the journey continues, the narrator occasionally sleeps atop the coach and learns that drivers and conductors also often sleep while their coaches are moving.

They pass through Marysville, over Big Blue and Little Sandy and enter NEBRASKA at Big Sandy, about 180 miles out from St. Joseph. When they see their first "jackass rabbit," they entertain themselves by shooting at it. They also encounter SAGEBRUSH, whose inedible nature recalls a moment in SYRIA when a camel ate the narrator's overcoat.

Chapter 4

After the passengers adapt to sleeping on the mailbags, they awaken only when the horses are changed; otherwise, they tumble about happily with the unabridged dictionary inside the coach. On the third morning, they stop at a station where the driver ignores the admiring hostler, innkeeper, and others. The station consists of squalid, sparsely furnished adobe buildings in which they are served an inedible meal with slumgullion. After exchanging their horses for six mules, they continue their journey to the North PLATTE RIVER and Fort Kearney, 300 miles and 56 hours out from St. Joseph.

Chapter 5

On their fourth morning, the travelers see their first prairie dog villages, antelope, and coyote. An allegory of want, the coyote is always poor, luckless, friendless, and despised, yet is capable of unimaginable speed and endurance.

Chapter 6

The great system of stagecoach stations between St. Joseph and SACRAMENTO, California, employs numerous people. At the top are about eight agents, or superintendents, each of whom is responsible for 250 miles of the line. Under them are conductors who are responsible for seeing individual coaches through their routes. Next come the drivers, who are changed on the coaches every day. At the bottom are station-keepers and hostlers—low, rough characters, many of whom are fugitives from the law. The whole system is run by Ben Holliday (Ben Holladay, 1819–1887). The narrator recounts an incident during his travels in PALESTINE, when a young man named JACK (VAN NOSTRAND) naively compared Holliday to MOSES.

At noon on the fifth day, they reach Overland City (JULESBURG), 470 miles from St. Joseph.

Chapter 7

After an hour in Overland City, the travelers continue to the South Platte River. Their new vehicle, a "mud-wagon," breaks down on the sixth morning, when they are about 550 miles out from St. Joseph. During this delay, they join a buffalo hunt in which a wounded bull chases Bemis up a tree. Bemis's description of shooting the buffalo reminds the narrator of a liar named Eckert he once met in Siam (which Clemens never visited) who owned a coconut-eating cat.

Chapter 8

After keeping a sharp lookout, the passengers finally see a PONY EXPRESS rider zoom by; then they pass through Scott's Bluffs Pass and see alkali water in the road. They also pass the site of the Indian mail robbery and massacre of 1856.

Chapter 9

That night, they go through Fort Laramie, reaching the Black Hills (now the Laramie Mountains) on the seventh morning. They breakfast at Horseshoe Station, 676 miles from St. Joseph. Now they are in hostile INDIAN country—with Indians lurking behind nearly every tree. The previous night, Indians shot up a pony rider, so the nervous passengers now sleep on their arms. That night they hear a shriek outside the coach and their driver's call for help, but the coach speeds off in the dark, and no explanation is ever provided.

Chapter 10

To show eastern readers what a Rocky Mountain desperado is like, the narrator describes JACK SLADE. A man who established a fearsome reputation for ruthless lawlessness, Slade became an overland division-agent, cleaned up his division, got his coaches running on schedule and repeated his success at the rough Rocky Ridge division. At the next breakfast stop, the passengers meet the most gentlemanly, quiet and affable officer yet encountered—who turns out to be Slade himself! The narrator nervously sits next to him at breakfast; when Slade insists on pouring him the last cup of coffee, the narrator fears that Slade may later regret his generosity and kill him.

Chapter 11

Two or three years after the events described here, Slade was hanged in MONTANA. A long passage from THOMAS JOSIAH DIMSDALE's book describes Slade's pitiful end.

Chapter 12

From the breakfast station, the stagecoach overtakes a MORMON emigrant train. The coach has covered 798 miles in eight days and three hours, while the emigrants' 33 wagons have taken eight *weeks* to travel the same distance. Now well into the heart of the Rocky Mountains, the coach passes Alkali, or Soda, Lake, where Mormons collect saleratus (a natural bicarbonate used as a leavening agent) to sell in SALT LAKE CITY. When the travelers pass a natural ice house near the pinnacle of the Rockies, they are amazed to see banks of snow in the summer. In another emigrant train, the narrator encounters a man named John whom he alienated as a boy by dropping a watermelon on his head. The coach now begins its descent.

On the 10th morning, the stagecoach crosses Green River; at five o'clock it reaches Fort Bridger, 1,025 miles from St. Joseph. Near Echo Canyon, the travelers meet army troops fresh from skirmishing with Indians. They sup with a Mormon "Destroying Angel" just outside Salt Lake, which they reach at nightfall.

Chapter 13

In Salt Lake City the travelers enjoy their first fine supper and stare at Mormons, fascinated by what they regard as a land of enchantment and awful mystery. The next day they inspect the remarkably clean, orderly, and healthy city of 15,000 residents by a broad plain. Though they are anxious to visit the Great Salt Lake, they instead have a long talk with the Mormon leader HEBER C. KIMBALL and see the city's sights. The second day, they visit the "king," BRIGHAM YOUNG.

Chapter 14

A Mr. Street, who is responsible for laying telegraph lines across Utah, had problems with Mormon subcontractors who would not fulfill contracts with "gentiles" (non-Mormons) until Street went to Young, who ordered them to fulfill their contracts to the letter. Street is now convinced that federal officials are a sham, since Utah is an absolute monarchy in which Young is king.

The narrator's attitude towards polygamy changes when he sees Mormon women. He concludes that a man who marries one has done an act of Christian charity, and that a man who marries 60 has done a sublime deed of generosity.

Chapter 15

In a "Gentile Den," the narrator hears harrowing tales about Mormons assassinating gentiles (non-Mormons) and learns about polygamy. A young gentile named Johnson (an invented character) once breakfasted with Young. While they conversed privately, one of Young's wives entered and demanded a breast-pin like that Young had given to wife number six. Eventually, 25 wives stream through Young's office with the same demand.

Young's family is reputedly so vast that he once accepted the claim of a woman to be married to him, even though he did not know her. The child she passed off as his turned out to be an Indian painted white. Groaning under the expenses of his huge household, Young tried saving money on beds by having a single bedstead made to accommodate all 72 wives at once.

Chapter 16

A long examination of the "Mormon Bible" (The Book of Mormon) finds that it is a prosy bore with incomprehensible histories of wars among peoples whom one has never heard of in places unknown to geography. Though tiresome to read, it teaches nothing vicious and its moral code is unobjectionable.

Chapter 17

After two days in Salt Lake City, the travelers leave feeling little better informed about the "Mormon question" than when they arrived. They have gathered considerable information but cannot tell what parts of it are reliable. The dreadful "MOUNTAIN MEADOWS MASSACRE" is an example of an issue for which their information has three sides. They return to the familiar stagecoach routine fortified with extra provisions.

Chapter 18

At 8:00 the next morning, they reach the ruins of Camp Floyd, 45 to 50 miles from Salt Lake. By 4:00 they have traveled another 45 to 50 miles and enter an alkali desert. During the night, it takes them 12 hours to cover 45 miles to the only watering spot, and 10 hours more to cross the remaining 25 miles.

Chapter 19

On the 16th day out from St. Joseph, the stagecoach is 250 miles from Salt Lake City. At Rocky Canyon, the travelers encounter Goshoot (GOSIUTE) Indians, perhaps the most degraded race in the world. Though a disciple of (JAMES FENIMORE) COOPER and a worshipper of the Noble Red Man, the narra-

tor finds that whenever one gets close to *real* Indians, he merely finds Goshoots.

Chapter 20

The 17th day takes the coach past the highest mountain peaks yet seen. The next day, the travelers encounter telegraph-builders and send a message to Governor (JAMES W.) NYE at Carson City, which is now 156 miles distant. On the 19th day, they cross the GREAT AMERICAN DESERT—a prodigious graveyard of bones. Across its border is Carson Lake, a typically mysterious "sink" that maintains its level though water flows in but never out. At the edge of the desert, they halt at Ragtown, an unmapped spot where the narrator recalls an anecdote that a driver told him near Julesburg. It concerns a coach ride that HORACE GREELEY once made to Placerville, California. Anxious to get there quickly, he asked the driver, HANK MONK, to hurry. Monk went so fast, however, that Greeley bounced around until his head poked through the roof. A day or two later, another passenger boards the narrator's coach and tells exactly the same anecdote. A cavalry officer joins them and repeats the anecdote, as does a Mormon preacher. Finally, a derelict wanderer whom they have saved from death starts to tell the anecdote; however, they stop him and he dies.

Chapter 21

On the 20th day, the coach reaches dusty Carson City, where the narrator witnesses a man named Harris settling an argument with guns. That afternoon, the powerful daily WASHOE ZEPHYR blows through, making it impossible to see. Afterward, the new arrivals take in the governor's state palace—a two-room house. Other high officials live in boardinghouses, using their bedrooms as offices. The Secretary and the narrator board at Bridget O'Flannigan's place, where their "walls" are partitions made from flour sacks. The narrator soon moves upstairs, where he takes one of 14 beds in a room shared by the "Irish Brigade"—camp followers of the governor, who tries to get rid of them by telling them to survey a railroad from Carson City over the SIERRA NEVADA. They balk at this, so he instead sends them east. As the men work, they bring tarantulas home, keeping them in glass tumblers on shelves. One night, a zephyr blows a roof into the boardinghouse, starting a panic when the tarantulas break free in the dark.

Chapter 22

Two or three weeks in this curious new country convince the narrator to prolong his stay. His duties as the Secretary's "private secretary" are light, so he joins Johnny K. (John D. Kinney) on a hike to LAKE TAHOE, which they explore in a skiff. Life at Tahoe is glorious; its pure air would invigorate even a mummy. The men claim 300 acres of forest land and undertake the work necessary to secure their legal title. After posting notices, they being felling trees for a fence. The heavy work required proves so discouraging, however, that they abandon the effort. The next day they start building a log-house. After trimming just one log, they gradually scale their plans down until they settle on a rude house made of brush.

Chapter 23

During two or three weeks of solitude, the men idle away time at their "timber ranch," sleeping in the open and spending days drifting in the boat over Tahoe's crystal-clear water. One night, the narrator starts a fire for dinner. As he goes to the boat, the fire gallops out of control. The men watch helplessly as the conflagration destroys their ranch. They go back to Carson City but later return to the lake for further adventures that will never be recorded.

Chapter 24

Resolved to own a horse, the narrator attends a Carson City auction at which a stranger—who turns out to be the auctioneer's brother—talks him into bidding on a "Genuine Mexican Plug." After buying it for $27, he mounts it and is bucked off instantly. After the narrator is bucked three times, a California youth tries the horse; he manages to stay on, but the animal disappears with him over the horizon. Meanwhile, an older man introduces himself as Abe CURRY and explains that the plug is a swindle. Hoping to get the horse crippled or killed so that someone else will have to pay for it, the narrator lends it out to various people but without success. Finally, he gives it to a passing Arkansas emigrant.

The tenderfoot narrator discovers why his genuine Mexican plug is no bargain in chapter 24.

Chapter 25

Formerly part of Utah, Nevada was under Mormon rule until the silver strikes of 1858 brought in a majority of outsiders who renounced allegiance to Utah. Nevada's residents appreciate having a legitimately constituted American government but resent having strangers in authority over them. Getting legislators to serve in the territory's new government is easy; however, finding a hall in which they can meet is a different matter. Abe Curry has rescued the new government by lending it a building rent-free.

Chapter 26

By and by, the narrator catches "silver fever" from the many prospecting parties going out daily and the rapidly rising value of mining stocks. The latest cry is "HUMBOLDT"—as evidenced by lengthy extracts from an article in the VIRGINIA CITY TERRITORIAL ENTERPRISE. The narrator and three friends decide to try their luck in Humboldt, but he worries that the district's riches may be gone before he gets there.

Chapter 27

The Humboldt prospecting party consists of the narrator, a 60-year-old blacksmith named Ballou, and two younger men named WILLIAM HORACE CLAGETT and Oliphant. They leave Carson City in December with a wagon, two horses, and 1,800 pounds of provisions and tools. Their horses prove so weak that the men end up pushing the wagon themselves and require 15 days to complete the 200-mile trip—including a two-day rest stop.

Chapter 28

When the prospectors reach UNIONVILLE during a rainstorm, they erect a crude cabin on the side of a crevice. Expecting to find silver lying in the open, the narrator sneaks off to begin searching. With growing excitement, he collects bright stones, then finds a deposit of shining yellow scales that convinces him he has found gold. Excitedly, he returns to the cabin, his head filled with dreams of wealth, but Ballou identifies his finds as granite rubbish with glittering mica.

Chapter 29

Under Ballou's guidance, the prospectors spend weary days searching for promising spots. Finally, Ballou finds a quartz ledge with enough silver and gold traces to warrant mining. Calling their new mine "Monarch of the Mountains," the men file claims and go to work. They begin sinking a shaft, but after a week of hard work it is only 12 feet deep, so the narrator, Clagett, and Oliphant resign. Next, they try tunneling from the side of the mountain; however, another week of hard work produces such poor results that they all stop working. Caught up in local prospecting fever, they instead swap shares in their mine with others. After accumulating 30,000 "FEET" of the richest mines on earth, however, they cannot even get credit from the grocer.

Chapter 30

In the midst of Humboldt's boom, everyone owns thousands of feet of undeveloped silver mines, but few have any cash. Much of the frenzy is a product of misleading assays. The narrator and his partners never touch their mine after learning the *real* secret of success in silver mining: *selling* ledges to other people.

Meanwhile, mounting "assessments" on feet that the narrator and the Secretary purchased earlier in ESMERALDA mines become so burdensome that the narrator decides to investigate. After buying a horse, he starts off for Carson City and Esmeralda with Ballou and a Prussian named Ollendorff. For two or three days, they ride through a snowstorm until they reach HONEY LAKE SMITH's inn on the Carson River. Predicting that a flood is coming, local Indians pack up and leave, but no one else can imagine the tiny river to be a threat with no rain in sight. That night, however, the river fills rapidly, marooning everyone on the inn's higher ground. Swearing, drinking, cards, and occasional fights prevail among the people crowded into the inn for the next eight days.

Chapter 31

Two men at the inn unsettle the narrator—a young Swede who constantly sings the same song and a ruffian named Arkansas, who goads the landlord Johnson to fight. Johnson tries to back off, but Arkansas presses him until Johnson's wife cows him into submission with scissors. By the eighth day, the water is still too high to cross safely, but the narrator and his companions try to leave in a canoe. Ollendorff's incompetence causes it to overturn, sending the soaked men back to the inn. The next morning, they get away on their horses, only to discover that the road is invisible in the snowstorm. Ollendorff promises to lead them directly to Carson. After an hour, they find tracks, but as they follow them, the tracks multiply until Ballou realizes that they are following their *own* tracks in a circle. They try to follow a stagecoach that rushes past them but cannot keep up with it. When its tracks disappear in the snow, they realize they have no idea what direction they are going.

Chapter 32

Hopelessly lost in the blizzard, the men stop to build a fire. Ollendorff tries igniting it with his pistol but only blows everything away. Meanwhile, the narrator accidentally releases the horses, which disappear in the storm. Hope rises when Ballou discovers four matches in his pocket, but each effort to light a fire fails. Finally, each man acknowledges that this night will be his last. Ollendorff asks forgiveness for his blunders and forgives the others for their mistakes. Wishing that he could reform and dedicate himself to good works, he swears off drinking and casts his whiskey bottle away. Ballou, in turn, swears off gambling and throws away his cards; the narrator swears off smoking and discards his pipe. Embracing as oblivion overcomes them, the men await death.

Chapter 33

When consciousness returns, the narrator thinks himself dead; however, when he gets up, he sees a stage building and a shed containing their horses just 15 steps away. Feeling humiliated, the men are angry and pettish; their joy at being delivered from death is poisoned. After breakfast, their spirits revive. Itching to smoke, the narrator sneaks off to retrieve his pipe. He fears discovery until he finds Ollendorff with his bottle and Ballou with his cards. Shaking hands, they agree to speak no more of "reform." Eventually, they reach Carson, where they remain a week during the trial of the "great landslide case."

Chapter 34

The steep mountains surrounding Carson City often unleash disastrous landslides during spring thaws, occasionally moving an entire side of a mountain. General Buncombe, who came to Nevada as a United States attorney, was once the victim of the kind of practical joke that established residents of new territories like to play on newcomers. One morning, Dick Hyde rushed into his office, asking him to conduct a legal suit in his behalf. His problem was that a landslide had slid the entire ranch of his neighbor, Tom Morgan, onto his own ranch, covering his property completely. He wanted to sue Morgan to make him leave. Outraged by Morgan's presumption in occupying Hyde's land, Buncombe assured Hyde that Morgan had no case.

That afternoon, former governor Roop (provisional governor Isaac Roop) opened a special court to hear Hyde's case. He was so solemn that some conspirators feared that he might not appreciate that the whole business was a joke. Every witness supported Hyde's position, and Morgan's attorney presented a weak case, contending that Morgan owned the land that his farm has slid over. Buncombe then delivered a powerful speech, confident that Hyde's case was won. When Roop delivered his decision, he acknowledged that the evidence favored Hyde and that Buncombe's oration was persuasive; however, he ruled that since heaven had moved Morgan's property for reasons that mere men cannot question, Hyde could not appeal its decision. He added that Hyde still owned his ranch *under* Morgan's property and was therefore entitled to dig it out. Reeling under the preposterous decision, Buncombe needed two months to realize that a joke had been played on him.

Chapter 35

The narrator and his friends continue their journey to Esmeralda with a new companion, Captain John Nye—an incomparable traveling comrade. He can do anything, solve any problem and find food and lodging anywhere. On their second day out, a poor desert inn turns them away, but Nye insists on stopping, then wins over everyone at the inn, gaining the travelers first-class treatment.

Esmeralda is a slightly more advanced version of Humboldt. The narrator's mining claims are worthless, so he discards them. For several days, he and his party take up claims and *begin* shafts and tunnels, but never finish them. Instead, they wait for buyers—who never come—and live austerely. Eventually, the narrator abandons mining and goes to work in a quartz mill for $10 a week.

Chapter 36

At the quartz mill, the narrator discovers what it means to earn one's bread by the sweat of one's brow. There is never an idle moment in the mill's many tasks. As the mill produces silver bricks, corners are chipped off for fire-assays to determine the proportions of precious metals. The desire of speculative miners for favorable assays makes some assayers less than strictly scrupulous. One man, for example, always got such rich results that he began monopolizing the business. Competitors exposed him by sending a stranger to him with a fragment of a carpenter's millstone, which he assayed at $1,284.40 a ton in silver and $366.36 a ton in gold.

The narrator's milling job lasts just one week. Afterward, he joins the frenzy over the mysterious and wonderful "cement mine."

Chapter 37

The marvelous Whiteman cement mine is rumored to be near MONO LAKE. Whenever Whiteman is spotted passing through Esmeralda, everyone chases after him. Local traditions claim that 20 years earlier, three German brothers survived an Indian massacre, then wandered through the desert and found an exposed cement vein containing nearly pure gold. Each took a large sample, but two brothers died during their wanderings. The third brother was so relieved to survive that he wanted nothing more to do with the mine, so he gave Whiteman his map and instructions for finding the cement vein. For 12 or 13 years. Whiteman has searched for the lost mine. One night the narrator's new partner, CALVIN H. HIGBIE, sights Whiteman passing through the town (AURORA). The narrator, Higbie, and their friends sneak out to follow him, agreeing to meet near Mono Lake. At the rendezvous, other men pour in. Since the secret is out, the hunt ends and the treasure hunters stay to holiday at the lake.

Chapter 38

A silent, solemn, and lifeless place, Mono Lake lies at the loneliest spot on earth. Its water is so alkaline that one can do laundry in it. The water is also hard on wounds, as a raw-skinned dog discovers when he dives in to escape the flies. Sea gulls lay eggs on the lake's islands; one island has a spring hot enough to cook the eggs. Providing board and laundry, the island is like a hotel. Although a half-dozen brooks feed the lake and none exits it, its water level mysteriously remains constant.

Chapter 39

One morning, the narrator and Higbie row 12 miles to explore an island. Finding that their drinking water has spoiled, they search for a stream until rising winds remind them that they have failed to secure their boat. They return to the shore to find the boat gone, making their situation frightful.

However, when the boat drifts nearby, Higbie jumps in and they row back to the mainland in a storm. Just as they reach port, the boat overturns, dumping them in the alkaline water. They then spend a week fishing and camping in the Sierra Nevada, revisit the lake, and return to Esmeralda.

Around this time, the narrator and his companions hire an Indian to do their laundry. Not knowing that gunpowder is hidden in the oven of a discarded stove, the man builds a fire in it to heat water. The stove blows up, taking part of the shed's roof with it.

Chapter 40

The narrator now relates the most curious episode in his slothful career. Outside of town is a rich silver-bearing ledge with an exposed comb owned by the Wide West mine. Its rich ore samples excite everyone, but Higbie suspects that they are not from the Wide West. He sneaks into its mine shaft and discovers a BLIND LEAD—a rich ledge running diagonally through the Wide West. It is public property, so he and the narrator plan to claim it. They make the Wide West foreman (identified as A. D. Allen in the next chapter) a partner to strengthen their position and they post their notices. That night they cannot sleep as they excitedly discuss how they will spend their wealth. The next day, the whole town is excited and the narrator relishes "being rich." However, the men must work on their claim within 10 days or forfeit it. Called away to help nurse Captain John Nye, the narrator leaves Higbie a note reminding him to do the necessary work.

Chapter 41

For nine days, the narrator nurses Nye through his spasmodic rheumatism. Meanwhile, he daydreams about future prosperity and sends instructions to friends and relatives concerning his spending plans and his willingness to forfeit his share of the family's "TENNESSEE LAND." After a falling-out with Nye, he walks home, reaching Esmeralda, where a crowd is gathered at the Wide West mine. Instead of investigating, he assumes that another strike has been made and helps a woman with her sick husband. Back at his cabin, he finds Higbie reading his note. Higbie left town when the narrator did—in order to chase after Whiteman again—and he left a note of his own. Their third partner, Allen, also left town on an emergency. Since *none* of them worked their claim, they have lost it to the new claimants.

Glad to leave the place of their sufferings, the narrator and Higbie spend a month or two away from Esmeralda. They return to learn that the Wide West and their former mine have merged.

Chapter 42

Pondering what to do next, the narrator reviews his past careers: one day grocery clerking; a week studying law; a stab at blacksmithery; a stint as a bookseller's clerk; part of a summer clerking in a drug store; becoming a tolerable printer and a good average steamboat PILOT. He has also been a private secretary, silver miner, and mill operative—amounting to less than nothing in each. After writing grandiloquent letters about his blind lead, he cannot stand the thought of returning home to be pitied, so he briefly yields to Higbie's appeal to try mining again.

It happens that he has occasionally sent articles to the VIRGINIA CITY TERRITORIAL ENTERPRISE. When he returns to town, he is thrilled to find a letter from the *Enterprise* offering to make him city editor at $25 a week. Afraid of being unable to support himself where he is, he accepts and goes to VIRGINIA CITY. The paper's editor, Mr. (JOSEPH) GOODMAN, tells him to cover the town, but he fails to find any news. Goodman suggests that he try what always works for DAN (DE QUILLE)—covering hay wagons. The narrator draws on his powers of invention to make this advice work, then gets good mileage in fanciful accounts about a murder and about emigrants coming through Indian territory.

Chapter 43

As the narrator learns about reporting, he relies more on facts and less on fancy, and swaps "regulars" with reporters from other papers, including his rival Boggs of the VIRGINIA CITY UNION. Anxious to see the monthly school report—to which the *Union* but not the *Enterprise* has access—he uses hot punch to get Boggs to lend his copy. As he writes up his story on the report, Boggs gets drunk and fails to file his own story. When the next school report is due, Boggs gets revenge by stranding the narrator in a mine shaft. After the narrator has

been in town six months, the "flush times" begin and it is easier than ever to fill columns with real news. With the COMSTOCK lode running through the town, money is as plentiful as dust.

Chapter 44

The narrator's salary rises to $40 a week, but he seldom draws it since every man in town is lavish with cash and "feet." Although only a few mines are not worthless "wild cat," speculation runs rampant. When miners file new claims, they give reporters 40 to 50 feet to inspect their mines and write about them. The narrator fills half a trunk with mining stock acquired this way. Everyone's pockets are full of stock, which they give away freely. Mr. (WILLIAM MORRIS) STEWART, for example, offers the narrator 20 feet in a mine just for walking to his office. The narrator declines because it is dinner time, but later learns that the stock's value has risen to $150 a foot. To raise the value of wild cat mines, some schemers "salt" them with more valuable ore from elsewhere.

Chapter 45

Two years earlier, Goodman and his partner bought the *Territorial Enterprise* when it was a poverty-stricken weekly. Now the paper is a great and prosperous daily. Another evidence of the continuation of flush times is the Gould and Curry mine's investing nearly a million dollars to erect a hundred-stamp mill. Money is so plentiful that the problem is not getting it but *spending* it. By happy coincidence, the United States SANITARY COMMISSION is formed around this time. Before Virginia City can even finish organizing a committee to support it, money pours in. Donations accelerate when REUEL GRIDLEY brings his "Sanitary Flour Sack" from Austin, where he raised $8,000 for the Sanitary fund by repeatedly auctioning it off. When Gridley arrives in Virginia City, however, his first auction nets only $5,000. Disappointed civic leaders plan a new campaign for the next day. A cavalcade to nearby GOLD HILL, Silver City, and Dayton returns covered in glory, and the second Virginia City auction raises $40,000. Gridley then goes on to sell the sack in Carson City, California, and the East.

Chapter 46

Nevada's flush times produce countless NABOBS, such as two teamsters who in lieu of $300 cash for a hauling job took a piece of a silver mine that later made them $100,000 a year—each. John Smith traded part of his ranch for an undeveloped mine that later earned him as much as $60,000 a month. Four years after the original owners of the Gould and Curry mine sold out cheaply, it was worth $7.6 million. In the early days, a poor Mexican traded a tiny stream on his property for a section of a mine later worth $1.5 million. Stories like these go on and on, but most nabobs drift back into poverty and obscurity.

A story about two nabobs was once current in Nevada. Blessed with sudden wealth, Colonel Jim and Colonel Jack went to New York City, where Jack wanted to indulge his lifelong desire to ride in a carriage. Unfamiliar with big cities, he boarded an omnibus, gave the driver a $20 gold piece and treated friendly New Yorkers to free rides.

Chapter 47

A philosopher has said that one way to know a community is to observe the style of its funerals. In Virginia City, it is not clear who receives more éclat—the distinguished public benefactor or the distinguished rough. In any case, Buck Fanshaw had a grand funeral. After he died, a committee sent Scotty Briggs to call on the town's new minister—a fledgling from the East (modeled on FRANKLIN S. RISING). Briggs was a stalwart rough with a big heart, but as a product of Nevada's rich and varied slang, he had trouble making himself understood. Gradually, he got his message across and Virginia City put on one of its greatest funerals ever.

Chapter 48

Virginia City's first 26 graves belong to *murdered* men. The rough element always predominates in new mining districts, where no one is respected until he has "killed his man." The highest level of Nevada society was once made up of the lawyer, the editor, the banker, the chief desperado, the chief gambler and, especially, the saloon-keeper. The murderers of the men in those first 26 graves were never punished because of the imbecilic jury system—which bans intelligence and honesty and

prizes ignorance, stupidity, and perjury. The best-known names in Nevada Territory belonged to desperadoes such as Sam Brown, Farmer Pease, El Dorado Johnny, Sugarfoot Mike, Pock-marked Jake, Six-fingered Pete, and others. While these desperadoes killed each other with little provocation, they had contempt for killing small-fry citizens.

Chapter 49

Extracts from Virginia City newspapers of 1862 reveal the temper of the times. The first tells how Deputy Marshal Jack Williams killed William Brown in a shootout. The second, from four months later, tells how the same Jack Williams assaulted and robbed a German engineer. An efficient city officer, Williams was also a notorious desperado who was assassinated five months later. The third extract tells how Tom Reeder, a friend of Williams, argued about Williams's killing with George Gumbert, who stabbed him. After Reeder was treated, he went after Gumbert and was shot. He died two days later, but nothing happened to Gumbert. Trial by jury is the palladium of our liberties. There have been more than a hundred murders in Nevada, yet only two people have suffered the death penalty.

Chapter 50

Murder and jury statistics evoke memories of an extraordinary trial and execution of 20 years earlier, when Captain Ned Blakely commanded a guano ship in the Chincha Islands. Bill Noakes, a bully from another ship, killed Blakely's favorite mate before many witnesses, but in the absence of local authority, no one even thought of arresting him. Furious for justice, Blakely himself arrested Noakes. When he announced he would hang Noakes the next day, other captains demanded a trial. Though exasperated by the legal obstacles they raised, Blakely let them try Noakes, *then* hanged him.

Chapter 51

Vice always flourishes during "flush times." Two unfailing signs signify when money is plentiful: a crowded police docket, and the birth of a literary paper. Virginia City has its paper, the WEEKLY OCCIDENTAL, edited by Mr. F. (THOMAS FITCH). Since the paper needs an original novel, everyone pitches in. Mrs. F. (Anna M. Fitch) writes the opening chapter, introducing as characters a lovely blonde simpleton and a French duke who loves her. In the next chapter, Mr. F. adds a brilliant lawyer who gets the duke's estates into trouble and a young society lady to distract the duke. In the third chapter, Mr. D. (ROLLIN M. DAGGETT) adds a mysterious Rosicrucian, a masked miscreant and an Irish coachman. At this point, a dissolute stranger arrives in town who happens to be a writer; he agrees to write chapter 4, with the narrator's chapter to follow.

The stranger gets drunk and writes pure chaos that destroys every character: The coachman marries the society lady, the duke marries the blonde's stepmother, the lawyer commits suicide, the coachman breaks his neck, the blonde drowns herself, and the duke kills himself after learning that he has married his own mother. Stunned by the fury of the other novelists, the stranger offers to rewrite his chapter. Unfortunately, he gets drunk again and writes something even crazier. This time the lawyer is big-hearted and the blonde falls in love with him; however, her parents insist that she marry the duke within a year. Chance puts everyone on the same ship, which burns up on the Atlantic. The survivors are rescued by two whaling vessels, but a storm separates them and neither can interrupt its voyage. One whaler carries the lawyer to the Bering Straits; the other takes everyone else to the North Atlantic. A year later, the blonde and the duke are about to be married aboard the vessel near GREEN-LAND. Meanwhile, a whale swallows the lawyer in the Bering Straits, then swims to the North Atlantic, where it is cut open by the other whaler. The lawyer pops out and stops the wedding.

The reaction to this chapter is even fiercer. The *Occidental* is issued without a novel and soon dies. Nevertheless, the narrator is proud to have been connected with a literary paper. Since he wrote poetry for it that never got published, he herein publishes a piece called "THE AGED PILOT MAN."

Chapter 52
The flush times peak in 1863, when Nevada claims to have produced $25 million in bullion. Speculation is riotous and freight charges to and from San Francisco run as high as $200 a ton. While Virginia City is a busy city above ground, another busy city exists below ground, where a vast network of timbers supports 30 miles of tunnels in which more than 5,000 men work.

Chapter 53
At the urging of the boys, the narrator is anxious to hear Jim Blaine tell the story of his grandfather's old ram. It is necessary to catch Blaine when he is satisfactorily drunk, however, and it is a while before they find him in that condition. They settle down to hear his story, but he falls asleep before finishing.

Chapter 54
A harmless, industrious race, the CHINESE are never disorderly, drunk, or lazy, and prosper when left alone. Unfortunately, low-class whites abuse them. As the narrator writes this chapter, he reads about San Francisco boys stoning a Chinaman to death (June 1871). About 70,000 Chinese live on the Pacific Coast, including about 1,000 in Virginia City, where they work mainly in laundry and domestic service. All Chinese read, write, and cipher; they waste nothing and can even make abandoned mines pay. Unfortunately, they are subjected to such swindles as a "foreign" mining tax. Holding their dead in reverence, the Chinese believe it critical to be buried in their homeland. For this reason, immigrant workers arrange in advance for their bodies to be shipped home if they die in America. With an ingenious refinement of Christian cruelty, California's legislature has worked to outlaw shipping corpses as a way to deter Chinese immigration.

Chapter 55
Tired of staying in one place, the narrator wants to see SAN FRANCISCO. A Nevada convention has just framed a constitution for a state government, which he fears will end the flush times. About this time a schoolmate of his boyhood appears. An allegory of poverty, he needs $46, which the narrator steps into a bank to borrow for him—never guessing that it will take two years to repay. Goodman leaves town for a week, making the narrator chief editor of the *Enterprise*. Writing the paper's daily editorials proves unbearably burdensome. After Goodman returns, the narrator does not want to go

back to serving in the ranks after having been a general, so he decides to leave. At this juncture, Dan (De Quille) tells him about two men who invited him to accompany them to New York to help sell a rich silver mine, in return for a third share in the profits. Dan declined and suggested they invite a reporter from the other paper. The narrator wants to kill Dan for not telling him about this opportunity sooner, but relents, since he himself may still have a chance to go. His hopes up, he boards a stagecoach the next day, when he sees someone accidentally drop a brick on the foot of a seedy passenger. The vagabond screams in pain but declines medical help, asking only for brandy. Once the coach is under way, he confesses to having a wooden leg.

Chapter 56

While rumbling through California's plains and valleys, the narrator wonders why people rave about California's loveliness, since *no* land with an unvarying climate can be truly beautiful. San Francisco proves a fascinating city in which to live, but its kindly climate becomes predictable and boring; it has eight months of pure sunshine, followed by four months of pure rain. While Mono has endless winter and San Francisco has eternal spring, SACRAMENTO has eternal summer. It *is* hot. Fort Yuma (Arizona), however, is even hotter. A story attributed to John PHOENIX tells about a Fort Yuma soldier sent to the hottest corner of perdition, from which he telegraphed home for his blankets.

Chapter 57

As the site of much of the lucrative early gold mining, Sacramento Valley still shows its scars. Similar disfigurements are visible throughout California; it is hard to believe that flourishing little cities once stood where only meadows and forests are now visible. No other modern land has seen towns die and disappear so absolutely. California attracted a curious and unique population consisting of 200,000 vigorous young men, with women so scarce that the mere *sight* of one was a notable event. Children were equally scarce. A true story recalls how a huge, rough miner was so moved by the sight of a young child that he offered $150 in gold just to kiss it.

Chapter 58

During several months of "butterfly idleness," the narrator stays at San Francisco's best hotel and lives in the style of a man worth $100,000 and soon to become richer. While spending freely, he watches the stock market. Since Nevada has just approved a state constitution, it looks bad for mining stocks, but he holds off selling his shares while speculation goes mad. Suddenly, the bottom drops out. He loses everything and must move to a private boarding-house and take a reporting job (for the SAN FRANCISCO CALL). Then he learns that he has missed his chance to participate in the silver mine sale. On a bright October afternoon, the narrator enjoys his first earthquake (an anachronistic allusion to the October 8, 1865, earthquake). Later he sees a copy of the *Territorial Enterprise* announcing that his rival, Marshal, has made a killing on the silver mine sale in New York. It is the "blind lead" all over again. Despondent, the narrator neglects his duties and takes the advice to resign from the newspaper before he is dismissed.

Chapter 59

For a time, the narrator writes literary screeds for the *GOLDEN ERA*. Then CHARLES WEBB and BRET HARTE engage him to write an article a week for their *CALIFORNIAN*. For two months his sole occupation is avoiding acquaintances. He becomes adept at "slinking" and holds on to his last 10-cent piece to avoid feeling penniless. Meanwhile, he often entertains a collector from the Virginia City bank from which he borrowed the $46. He also happens upon another child of misfortune—another former reporter—whom he calls the mendicant Blucher, who once found a dime at a time when he had not eaten for 48 hours. While Blucher planned how he would dine on this dime, yet another unfortunate accosted him and pleaded for 25 cents for food. Blucher took the man to the city's best restaurant and let him run up a $6.50 tab on his own account, then feasted by himself at French Pete's on his dime.

Chapter 60

By and by, the narrator goes to a decayed mining camp (JACKASS HILL) in TUOLUMNE with an old friend (JIM GILLIS) and spends two or three months living in a hillside cabin. Where a city of 3,000 once stood, only a handful of miners remain in a melancholy exile. This part of California has a little-known and fascinating species of mining called pocket-mining, pursued by only 20 miners. The ingenious process involves washing earth in tin pans. If you find gold, you wash more pans, while working your way toward the richest deposit.

Tuolumne had two poor miners who spent 13 years hiking to a village every day for supplies. Along the way, they always rested on the same boulder. One day, two Mexicans sat on the boulder and found $800 worth of gold in it; later they explored the nearby hill, where they eventually took out $120,000 in gold. The two Americans now take turns getting up early to curse the Mexicans.

Chapter 61

One of the narrator's comrades is another victim of 18 years of blighted hopes—a gentle spirit named DICK BAKER, a pocket-miner of Dead-Horse Gulch (Jackass Gulch). Whenever he feels down, he mourns the loss of his wonderful cat Tom Quartz, which never cared for anything but mining. When the miners first attempted quartz-mining, they laid a charge, forgetting that Tom Quartz was asleep on a gunny sack in the shaft. The explosion sent the cat about a mile and a half into the sky, permanently prejudicing him against quartz-mining.

After two months without striking a pocket, the narrator and his friends go to ANGEL'S CAMP in Calaveras County, but have no luck there, either. Meanwhile, they keep their door open to passing miners and wander as far as the Big Trees and Yosemite.

Chapter 62

After a three-month absence, the narrator returns to San Francisco penniless and becomes the local correspondent for the *Virginia City Territorial Enterprise*. Within five months he is out of debt. With his vagabond instinct again strong, he gets a berth as the *SACRAMENTO UNION*'s correspondent to the Sandwich Islands (HAWAII) and sails on the *AJAX* (March 7, 1866). The ship's 30 passengers include a cheerful soul named Williams, three old whaleship captains and a retired whaleman known as the "Old Admiral." Though beloved, the Admiral wears out other passengers with heated political arguments based on invented facts until he meets his match in Williams.

Chapter 63

As the islands come into sight, the narrator sees Diamond Head and Honolulu. The more he sees of Honolulu, the better he likes it. A delightfully colorful contrast to the drabness of San Francisco, it has bright-colored houses, flowers, huge trees, comely women, and millions of cats.

Chapter 64

At the end of his third day in Honolulu, the narrator can barely sit down because he has ridden 15 or 20 miles on horses. After a fascinating visit to a prison, he rushed back to the American Hotel to hire a horse on which to catch up with an excursion to Diamond Head. He asked for an excessively gentle horse and got one that fell asleep on him. Eventually, he reached a place known as the "King's Grove" near interesting ruins of an ancient temple (at Waikiki) at which it is said that thousands of humans were slaughtered in old times. The missionaries deserve full credit for breaking the old tyranny and bringing the people freedom and legal protections.

Chapter 65

After a rugged climb, the excursionists halt on the summit of a hill with a commanding view of Honolulu. They then visit an old battleground littered with bleached bones. No one knows who fought here; some think it is where KAMEHAMEHA I fought the Oahuans. However, JAMES JACKSON JARVES's excellent history tells a different story.

Honolulu has no regular livery stable, so one must hire wretched horses from KANAKAS—who are unprincipled horse traders. A friend named J. Smith hired a horse with a blanket glued to its hide by raw spots. Another friend bought a horse that he thought he had examined carefully, only to discover that it was blind in one eye. Mr. L. (Lewis Leland) thought that he was buying perfectly matched horses that he had to examine through windows on the opposite sides of a stable; it turned out that he had bought *one* horse that he had seen from two sides.

Chapter 66

Saturday afternoon is a festive day at Honolulu's marketplace, where native girls in gaudy habits ride horses. Occasionally one sees a tattooed heathen who looks like a Washoe mendicant who was blown up in a mine. Poi merchants peddle their unseductive but nutritious mixture, and natives buy the intoxicating *awa* (kava) root. In old times, Saturday was a truly grand gala day with feasts, hula dancing, and revelry, but now it has lost its gala features and the hula is largely forbidden. Missionaries have transformed natives into inveterate churchgoers, and cultivation has given women profound respect for chastity—in other people. Contact with white civilization has reduced the native population from 400,000 in Cook's time to 55,000 in just over 80 years. Local society is a queer medley; a stranger is likely to be either a missionary, a whaling captain, or a high government official.

Chapter 67

The national legislature contains a half-dozen white men and 30 or 40 natives. Its nobles and ministers include DAVID KALAKAUA, the king's chamberlain; Prince William (Lunalilo); and the assembly's president, His Royal Highness M. Kekuanaoa, the king's father. In former times, women were taught to know their place, but missionaries have made them the equal of men. Although Christianized, natives retain some barbaric superstitions, such as believing that enemies can *pray* them to death. They also still have the ability to lie down and die at will. Natives remain oblivious of nakedness and one often finds women bathing naked. Missionaries beg natives not to attend church naked and give them CLOTHES, but the natives merely show up in just one odd garment or another.

Grown folk here play "empire," from the king (KAMEHAMEHA V) and his royal family down. Offices include a Royal Chamberlain, Commander-in-Chief of Household Troops, Royal Steward, Grand Equerry, First Gentleman of the Bed Chamber, Prime Minister—a renegade American (Charles Coffin Harris), Imperial Minister of Finance, Minister of War, Minister of the Navy, Lord Bishop of Honolulu (T. N. Staley), Minister of Public Instruction, governors of the islands, plus High Sheriffs and other small fry too numerous to count, as well as envoys extraordinary and ministers plenipotentiary from foreign governments. All

this grandeur in a playhouse "kingdom" with less than 60,000 souls!

Chapter 68

In Honolulu, the narrator witnesses the funeral of the king's sister, Her Royal Highness Princess VICTORIA. The funeral's printed program (reproduced in the book) lists so many dignitaries that one wonders where the procession will find enough people to serve as its "Hawaiian population generally." Princess Victoria's funeral ceremonies contrast with those of Kamehameha I five decades earlier. Accounts of Kamehameha's death are filled with details about former customs, such as tabus against eating and sleeping in the same house. After the king died, frightful ORGIES followed.

Chapter 69

On a Saturday afternoon, the narrator sails with Mr. Billings from Honolulu to the island of Hawaii to see the great volcano and other sights. The schooner BOOMERANG is too cramped, noisy, and verminous to permit sleep, so the narrator quits his miserable cabin and enjoys one of the most beautiful scenes he has ever seen: the glittering moonlit sea and broad sails straining under an angry gale. On Monday morning, they see the snow-capped peaks of Mauna Loa and Hualaiai. They go ashore at Kailua on the western Kona coast, where they ride horses a thousand feet above sea level and pass through sugar plantations.

Chapter 70

At a plantation they meet a man said to be crazy, Simon Erickson, who is obsessed with talking about his correspondence with Horace Greeley. He once wrote to Greeley on behalf of a woman named Beazely whose son was wasting away while trying to grow turnips on vines. Greeley replied, but his handwritten letter seemed to contain a different message every time Erickson tried to read it. At first it seemed to be about polygamy. Later it seemed to be about Bolivia and mackerel and poultices and swine. When Erickson finally deciphered "turnips," he wrote Greeley again asking to clarify the meaning of "turnips restrain passion." Greeley's clerk sent a clear translation that read "turnips remain passive." It was too late, however, as young Beazely was already dead.

Chapter 71

In the afternoon, the narrator goes down to the sea on a lava flow so old that no one remembers when it was created. At Kealakekua Bay, he sees the coconut tree stump marking the spot where Hawaiians killed CAPTAIN JAMES COOK. The narrator spends the night on the schooner anchored in the bay.

Chapter 72

In the morning, the narrator visits the ruined temple of the last god, Lono. Its chief priest was the uncle of Obookia (Henry Obookia, d. 1818), who was educated and converted in New England and became famous for wanting to bring the Bible to Hawaii. Lono, a favorite god on the islands, sailed away and never returned; many islanders later believed Cook to be Lono. Kealakekua Bay is also near the site of the last battle fought for idolatry. After Kamehameha I died, his son Liholiho attacked the old tabu system, triggering a mass revolt against the old gods.

Chapter 73

The narrator goes with a kanaka by canoe to Honaunau, where naked natives of all ages are SURFING. He then visits the City of Refuge, a sanctuary of the old days; any hunted criminal or refugee who reached it and confessed to a priest obtained absolution and could leave without being harmed. Its massive walls cut from lava pose mysteries about who built it. Nearby is a well engineered road of flat stones.

Chapter 74

The schooner takes the narrator to Kau on the southwestern coast, where he bids his ship farewell. The next day he buys a horse, and a two-day ride takes him to the great KILAUEA volcano. After taking in the dimensions of its enormous crater, he settles in at the Volcano House hotel. At night, he returns to admire the crater's fiery magnificence in the dark. A colossal column of fire-illuminated clouds towers above what looks like the infernal regions. The foreground of the crater's floor is wonderfully illuminated. Most of the floor is as black as ink, but a large area is streaked with streams of liquid fire that look like a colossal railroad map done

in chain lightning on a midnight sky. Here and there are gleaming, gaping holes in the dark crust in which dazzling white lava boils furiously. The smell of sulphur is strong, but not unpleasant to a sinner.

Chapter 75

The next night, the narrator joins a dozen people who descend to the crater's floor with lanterns and native guides. A cauldron threatens to overflow, so the guides refuse to continue, but the narrator and a stranger named Marlette—who has explored the crater a dozen times during the day—proceed alone. They run across the crater's floor until Marlette loses the path and starts to fall through the crust. He finds the path again, by using his feet instead of his eyes. The spectacle at North Lake is worth twice the distance they have come to see it. A heaving sea of molten fire, the "lake" is as blinding as the noonday sun. White-hot chimneys of lava surround its shores, spouting gorgeous sprays of lava. When part of the shelf on which the men are sitting falls in the lake, jarring the surroundings like an earthquake, they take a hint and leave.

Chapter 76

The narrator rides horseback 200 miles around the island of Hawaii. The pleasant trip takes a week because the horses are used to carrying kanakas, who never pass a house without stopping to gossip. The experience reminds the narrator of a painful experience. He once took an aristocratic young lady driving with a retired milk-wagon horse that he told her he had always owned. After the horse stopped at 162 houses and delivered them to the dairy depot, his humiliation was complete.

After his journey ends at Kawaehae (a bay in the island's northwest corner), he returns to Honolulu, then spends several pleasant weeks on Maui. There he enjoys a picnic excursion to Iao Valley and a visit to the dead Haleakala volcano, whose crater dwarfs even Kilauea. Atop its 10,000-foot-high rim he sees the most sublime spectacle of his life when clouds bank together a thousand feet below him, leaving only the rim of the crater visible.

Chapter 77

On Maui, the narrator meets a curious man named Markiss (F. A. Ouidnot). Whatever anyone else says, Markiss tops it. The narrator meets the man everywhere and stays indoors to avoid him. One night Markiss makes a point about a truly "mean" employer with a story about a man named John James Godfrey who worked for a California mining company. One day, an accidental blast sent Godfrey so high that he was 16 minutes returning to Earth—and then the company docked him for lost time. Worn out by Markiss's stories, the narrator leaves the island the next day, convinced that Markiss is a liar. Several years later, his verdict is vindicated. He hears that Markiss has been found dead, hanging from a beam inside his locked room. Although Markiss had a suicide note pinned on him, the jury concluded that he was killed by someone else, reasoning that Markiss was such a consistent liar for 30 years that *any* statement he made must be a lie. Furthermore, they concluded that he was *not* dead—instancing the strong circumstantial evidence of his own word that he was dead. Only after his coffin stood open in Lahaina's tropical climate for seven days did the jury change their verdict. They now ruled "suicide induced by mental aberration"—Markiss said he was dead, and *was* dead. Would he have told the truth if he had been in his right mind? No.

Chapter 78

After half a year on the islands (actually, four months), the narrator sails back to San Francisco (on the clipper ship *SMYRNIOTE*, July 17–August 18, 1866). Once again penniless, he accepts someone's suggestion to stage a public LECTURE. After engaging a large hall and advertising—all on credit—the humorous material that he has prepared seems hopelessly dreary. Panic-stricken, he asks friends to sit near the stage and laugh when he signals for help. He even gives a stranger named Sawyer (William M. Slason, 1831?–1872) a ticket because he has a hair-trigger laugh. During the three days leading up to the event, he eats nothing and only suffers. The afternoon of the lecture, he creeps to the box office and is distressed to find it closed. At 6:00, he enters the theater from the back. After sampling the gloomy solitude of the empty hall, he waits amid the scenery. Eventually, he hears noises. Suddenly, he is onstage, staring at a sea of faces and

quaking in terror. The house is full! Gradually his fright melts away and the evening develops into an unqualified triumph.

Chapter 79

The narrator boldly launches out as a lecturer by engaging his old friend Mike (DENIS MCCARTHY) to be his agent on a tour of Nevada and California. Shortly before he reaches Virginia City, stagecoach robberies near the town become the subject of all conversation. The same night that he lectures there (October 31, 1866), he also lectures in GOLD HILL. When he and Mike walk back to Virginia City that night, six masked men with revolvers accost them and take their valuables. The whole thing is actually a practical joke staged by friends, with 20 others watching from hiding places; even Mike is in on it.

When the narrator returns to San Francisco, he plans a pleasure trip to Japan and around the world, but changes his mind when he decides to go home. He sails off for the isthmus (on the steamer *AMERICA*, December 15, 1866) and New York (on the steamer *SAN FRANCISCO*). He revisits his home (HANNIBAL) and later joins the famous *QUAKER CITY* cruise.

The moral of the book is this: If you are of any account, stay home and make your way by faithful diligence. If you are "no account," leave home; then you must work, whether you want to or not, and become a blessing to your friends by ceasing to be a nuisance to them.

Appendices

The first of three appendices, "Brief Sketch of Mormon History," is an 1,840-word condensation of *The Mormon Prophet and His Harem; Or, An Authentic History of Brigham Young, His Numerous Wives and Children* (1866) by Catharine Waite (1829–1913).

Appendix B, "The Mountain Meadows Massacre," also draws heavily on Waite's book and accepts her conclusion that Mormons were primarily responsible for the massacre.

Appendix C, "Concerning a Frightful Assassination that was never Consummated," contains a long letter from a small-time journalist named Conrad Wiegand to the *Territorial Enterprise* written in January 1870. Wiegand was an eccentric reformer who began publishing a newspaper in Gold Hill after Clemens left Nevada. When he published unsubstantiated charges against a local miner, he was beaten and threatened by the miner. His letter presents a dramatic account of his peril, along with Clemens's sarcastic asides.

BACKGROUND AND PUBLISHING HISTORY

Clemens gave little thought to writing a book about his western experiences until well after leaving the Pacific Coast. The great success of *Innocents Abroad* (1869), however, later prompted him to seek a subject for a similar travel book, and his thoughts naturally went back to his western years. Initially he thought that his time in HAWAII was the most promising subject on which to write a book—probably because he assumed that too many books had already been written on the West. While Clemens had 25 letters from his Hawaii trip that he could use in the way he had used his QUAKER CITY letters to write *Innocents Abroad,* writing about his mainland experiences posed a different kind of challenge. He began by gathering all the relevant material he could find. In March 1870, he asked Orion to send him the journal he (Orion) had kept of their overland stagecoach journey, as well as the scrapbook of his own western newspaper and magazine articles. Clemens had also recently written articles for the BUFFALO EXPRESS about his western experiences.

In July 1870, during Clemens's first summer sojourn in Elmira, ELISHA BLISS visited him on behalf of the AMERICAN PUBLISHING COMPANY to negotiate a book contract, which Clemens signed on July 15. By late August, he was busy writing, but family problems and such responsibilities as writing for the GALAXY soon hampered his progress. His father-in-law, JERVIS LANGDON, died in August; then his wife Livy became seriously ill, and her friend EMMA NYE contracted typhoid fever and died in their Buffalo home in late September. In November, Livy delivered her first child prematurely; then both she and the baby became dangerously ill.

Clemens had promised to deliver his manuscript by the end of 1870, but did not begin submitting pages until mid-March 1871. Two months later, he proclaimed himself "half done." By early July, he was up to the Hawaiian phase of his narrative. He had wanted to limit this section of the book to a few chapters, but found himself so short of pages for the long book he had contracted to write that he eventually devoted nearly a fifth of the entire book to Hawaii. In August, he delivered his final pages to Bliss and began reading proofs.

In early August, Bliss copyrighted "THE INNOCENTS AT HOME" as the book's working title, changing it to "Roughing It" four months later when he copyrighted the book. Meanwhile, Clemens launched a LECTURE tour in mid-October, taking him through the Northeast and Midwest into early February 1872. By December he was using extracts from his new book in a lecture titled "Roughing It." The American Publishing Company began canvassing for *Roughing It* the same month and had the first printed copies from the bindery at the end of January 1872.

The first edition of *Roughing It* had 304 illustrations, about 15 percent of which contain recognizable caricatures of Clemens. Many of the illustrations are unsigned, but most were drawn by Edward F. Mullen and TRUE WILLIAMS. When Williams went on a drinking binge, Bliss engaged ROSWELL MORSE SHURTLEFF, who drew 19 pictures, including the frontispiece. Bliss also borrowed engravings from ALBERT DEANE RICHARDSON's *Beyond the Mississippi* (1867) and adapted pictures from several other books, including JOHN ROSS BROWNE's *Adventures in the Apache Country.* Unhappiness with the quality of his book's illustrations and distrust of Bliss's cost-accounting methods eventually led Clemens to break from Bliss.

The American Publishing Company officially published *Roughing It* on February 19, 1872—a week after GEORGE ROUTLEDGE published a two-volume edition in England. Routledge's edition omitted the illustrations and appendixes of the American edition, substituting the text of Clemens's (BURLESQUE) AUTOBIOGRAPHY. Initial sales of the book rivaled those of *Innocents Abroad,* but tapered off more quickly. Nevertheless, the book sold 73,000 copies during the first two years. Since then, it has stayed in print almost continuously and has ranked as one of Clemens's most popular books.

In 1872, a century after *Roughing It*'s original publication, the MARK TWAIN PROJECT published the first corrected edition of the book. In 1993, the project issued a completely reedited and substantially expanded edition, with new maps and annotation materials and all the original illustrations. The 1996 OXFORD MARK TWAIN edition includes a facsimile reprint of the first American edition of *Roughing It* with a new introduction by author George Plimpton and an afterword by Henry B. Wonham, author of *Mark Twain and the Art of the Tall Tale* (1993).

CRITICAL COMMENTARY

Roughing It is the first full-length work that Clemens wrote almost solely from memory and imagination. He asked Orion, the brother whom he had accompanied west, for his remembrances but lacked his own notes. The writing of *Roughing It* coincided with Clemens's marriage to Olivia Langdon and his entry into eastern society. Appropriate to the time and place of his life, he evolved a persona. First used as a pseudonym out west, "Mark Twain" had been a character in sketches and tales for several years; however, only in the initial travel book, *The Innocents Abroad,* had this character spent a long time with readers. In *The Innocents Abroad,* his pose is that of an innocent in a strange land who engages readers with irony, sarcasm, and mockery that cast doubts upon his innocence. In *Roughing It*, "Mark Twain" becomes a more complex narrator. He is an innocent who learns, becomes an innocent again, then becomes an experienced man of the world. He develops from pseudo-easterner (a novice in the ways of the West) to veteran westerner, then a novice writer evolving into professional author. Actually, the Missourian Sam Clemens was more western than eastern in outlook and manner, had held many diverse jobs, and was older and more traveled than the Mark Twain presented in the book. As a character, he seems to seek a career, trying many different activities, but is always headed toward writing, the profession that is his at the time of the book; as an author and now married man, the real-life writer was building a career. Deliberately retaining some character traits, he made the character/narrator/alter ego much different from himself.

Mythologizing the West

In creating Mark Twain, Samuel Clemens mythologized a public and literary persona. He refined the persona only enough to remind "the reader of Mark Twain's rough edges as he proclaims his respectability" (Steinbrink 305). This rough-smooth paradox epitomizing Mark Twain affects the author's narrative technique, especially in *Roughing It* and other examples of frontier literature, where contrasts are evident and part of the method. The narrator enters a world (river-boating, western frontier, eastern society, old Europe) as a newcomer, an innocent learning and accepting that world, including its myths; then becomes an old-timer, a skilled guide speaking from the ways of that world; and finally steps out of it to be an implied observer, accepting and rejecting from the outside as it suits him, commenting from a farther view as a voice of modified civilization. Overwatching like Emerson's "eye" and Whitman's "I," he becomes a microcosm of American frontier literary history. The civilized voice, cultivated in the east after his western years, buffers the newcomer's acceptance of the frontier and its embodiment by the veteran, enabling him to mediate the rough-smooth sides of Mark Twain to present different angles of a single experience. In debunking himself, he debunks myths his persona has accepted and helped to create.

Before contemporaries and other writers parodied or satirized what later generations could view as objects of humor, Clemens wrote of such frontier staples as fearless lawmen, the western gunfighter and his code, vigilantes, the respect accorded one who has "killed his man" (chapter 14), and the general attitude toward mayhem and gunplay on the fringes of civilization. He also conveyed the thrill of simply riding across this territory: "the preceding night an ambushed savage had sent a bullet through the pony rider's jacket, but he had ridden on . . . because pony riders were not allowed to stop and inquire into such things except when killed" (chapter 9). Most of the staples of western lore appear in *Roughing It*. Prior to viewing the grandeur of volcanoes and valleys in Hawaii, the narrator describes magnificent landscapes and vistas such as Lakes Tahoe and Mono, "dismal deserts" (chapter 14) with "no vegetation . . . endless sagebrush and greasewood . . . great deeps of powdery alkali dust that rose in thick clouds and floated across the plain" (chapter 21), "the majestic panorama of mountains and valleys spread out below us . . . while our spiritual natures reveled alternately in rainbows, thunderstorms, and peerless sunsets" (chapter 17), and other typically western scenery. He also describes travel by stagecoach, deserted towns, decaying mining camps, the dude on the frontier, lonely nights in the wilderness, being lost in the vastness, hazards of weather, gold and silver prospecting and mining, range war, and more. The Genuine Mexican Plug the narrator purchases becomes his bucking bronc (chapter 24). Often laughing at himself, the narrator parodies developing myths and archetypes, mocking myth before it becomes established as myth. He can be awed by the beauty of the Tahoe region one moment, enough to lay claim by building a house, and the next moment carelessly set it ablaze, burning house, food, and acres of woodland, imitating what Americans have repeatedly done to natural resources (chapter 23).

Described by BERNARD DeVOTO as "usually . . . found on both sides of any question he argues" (*Portable Mark Twain* 15), Clemens deliberately stood out from those he stood among. Gladys Bellamy says his "mind was a homeland for extremes" (50). A southerner, he de-southernized himself; a member of a Missouri militia unit, he journeyed west with his abolitionist brother; an easterner in the West, he went east as a westerner; living in the north, he returned south in memory and in fact. Self-dramatizing, self-creating, fictionalizing himself, often smudging lines between fiction and biography, he became a myth. Mark Twain's myth emerges most clearly when he contemplates the west in *Roughing It.*

The fluidity, the blending, the mythologizing merge in the book's narrative method; the narrator tames the frontier with the progressive and overlapping narrative roles of greenhorn, veteran, and observer. Entering in innocence, the narrator absorbs the West, becomes knowledgeable (removing its strangeness), and steps out to view it as another specimen in a variety of life. The method dictates the acceptance, even the creation, and then the downsizing (or civilizing) of frontier myth.

Like Huckleberry Finn at the end of *Adventures of Huckleberry Finn,* Clemens distrusts civilization and heads for the territory. The critic Leonard Kriegel believes *Roughing It* concerns "the reality of an entire society created by those who fled civilization" (xxiii). One of the dividing lines in this society is between the literate and illiterate. For example, degrees of literacy separate Scotty Briggs and the pastor he approaches to perform the funeral of his friend, Buck Fanshaw. Superficially about the funeral, this episode, though comical, focuses upon western violence, justice, prejudice, cultural strata, and the ever-presence of death in Virginia City, as well as the difficulty of communication, here specifically illustrated by the pastor from the east and Scotty, a Nevada miner. This miscommunication represents misunderstanding of the other by east and west.

On one level, Fanshaw, at the top of his social order in Virginia City, is an example of the self-reliant westerner, the loner who takes charge of dangerous situations and straightens them. "A representative citizen" (chapter 47), he dies a horrible and prolonged (though humorous) death. Like the archetypal westerner, and like his friend Scotty, who also dies young, Buck "never entered into a quarrel when he could reasonably get out of it," and when these fights were investigated, "it always turned out that it had originally been no affair of his, but that . . . he had dropped in of his own accord to help the man who was getting the worst of it" (ibid.). This description of Scotty fits his bosom friend, too, because, as Briggs says of Buck, "He never could stand to see things going wrong." (ibid.). Buck represents both those who tame and those who make the West lawless, men of similar cloth. Western justice is blind to the suspicious circumstances of Buck's death, just as Scotty does not see the bigotry in his compliments of Buck: "he was one of the whitest men . . . ever in the mines . . . I've seen him lick four Greasers in eleven minutes . . . He warn't a Catholic . . . He was down on 'em. His word was, 'No Irish need apply!'" (ibid.). As a hint of the prevalent violence, Scotty's death in the last paragraph of the chapter bookends Buck's in the first but, in contrast to Fanshaw's demise, with no details given. Apparently healthy and no older than Buck, he dies, with as few suspicions raised as were for Buck, a month after the narrator hears him tell a children's Sunday-school class the story of Joseph, a man who survives violence to gain eminence. Scotty becomes a Sunday-school teacher in the growing community. Although he cannot grasp the pastor's lofty English and the pastor cannot comprehend Scotty's card-playing and mining slang, they find common ground in their separate approaches to religion, representing a coming-together of east and west without full understanding of each other. Scotty merges the means and the incomprehensibility by repeating Buck's "word" at the funeral: "Amen. No Irish need apply" (ibid.).

Here Clemens illustrates an acceptance of western myth without a certainty of its meaning. As the East does not comprehend what it receives, the children eagerly listen to Scotty's slang-riddled Bible story "unconscious . . . that any violence was being done to the sacred proprieties!" (338). Violence is prominent in the myth embraced by civilization, here represented by the church. Clemens as observer balances myth and reality with typical humor. Language forms the barrier.

Seeking frontiers but lingering near the boundary, Clemens seemingly prefers indistinct borders—literary, mental, spiritual. The result is an ambivalent acceptance of civilization and ultimately a deliberately distant longing for the frontier; he would not wish Huck to become Slade, the murderous gunman in *Roughing It*, who is free but anarchic (Kriegel xxvi).

Shifting Personas

Clemens constantly seeks limits, stretches boundaries, and then erases them. Wayne Ude argues that, with the possible exception of Stephen Crane, Clemens is the only serious writer to recognize "the existence of an inner wilderness that could not be banished to or beyond an artificial frontier [and] the frontier as a meeting place for inner and outer wildernesses" (56). From the beginning, he seeks more than the surface. In fact, Kolb asserts that all of Clemens's works present a "rich and contradictory view of life that stems from" his years on the western frontier (128). Bel-

lamy, however, reminds us that when Clemens left his home at 17, "he went east, not west"—he went to New York, Philadelphia, and Cincinnati before seeing Carson, Virginia City, and San Francisco, and he spent only six years in the west before leaving, never to return, to live the rest of his life in eastern or European cities (50).

The critic HENRY NASH SMITH claims that Clemens deliberately exaggerates his persona to burlesque it, as though standing apart from it, and that he links with the pronoun "I" two very different personae (the tenderfoot and the old-timer), both present from the beginning, creating a contrast implicitly judging both (212); however, the implication is an exterior judge, an observer superimposed on the other voices and, like them, present throughout. Accepting Smith's structure, Kolb also suggests a third voice by stating that Clemens's western journey attains "the destination achieved by myth—a complex, shifting, continually questioning, three-sided vision of human experience itself" (135). The experienced narrator's voice comes through, he says, "like a palimpsest gradually growing more distinct," but the initiate's voice remains, and Clemens, using varying levels of language, juxtaposes voices, often in contradictory poses, so that a third overall voice is heard (ibid., 129, 131). Like the "mute mentor," as Drewey Gunn describes brother Orion's unabridged dictionary, carried on the stagecoach journey, the third voice "asserts its presence" (569).

Orion's dictionary is symbolically supportive in several ways. Robert Coard believes the writer's numerous dictionary references indicate "the self-made man's hypersensitivity to culture, especially in one of its most complex manifestations . . . language" (3), thus, a symbol of civilization brought to the west. Gunn reconciles the views of Smith, who calls it a "symbol of the useless pedantries and proprieties . . . these neophytes . . . take into the wilderness" ("Structure" 215), and that of Hamlin HILL, who calls it essential to the narrator's instinctive sense that he cannot communicate in this world, as Scotty Briggs and the pastor seem to illustrate. The artist, Gunn argues, cannot ignore possibilities of the book holding the writer's true wealth, but because it is always outdated, the remnant of a past culture, the book cannot truly guide one in a new world (569–570).

This ambivalent symbolism reflects the ambivalence of the observer. Smith notes that the narrator simultaneously believes the frontier less and more civilized than it is as he learns that his clothes are unsuitable and, after lugging and dodging the six-pound unabridged for a thousand miles, that he can order and receive a dictionary in two days from San Francisco ("Structure" 215). The narrator learns both that dictionaries are available and that frontier life can be rugged. Carrying a dictionary, the narrator figuratively brings civilization with him. In the same way, the author Clemens himself brings the literary "eastern" tradition to the rougher places of the west.

The process described by Smith and extended by others is literary. Clemens knows the pastor's eastern speech is extreme; the humor and emphasis from the first paragraph of the episode favor Scotty and his ilk. Soon, though, Scotty is domesticated, telling Bible stories to his Sunday-school class in miner's dialect, which the children more readily appreciate than the pastor's stuffy English. Such inconsistencies and reversals are frequent.

Ambivalent Themes

Other contradictions abound. Eastern notions about the west are knocked in the water in "THE DANDY FRIGHTENING THE SQUATTER," Clemens's earliest extant tale, and in the *Roughing It* episode with Mr. Arkansas, a rough frontiersman cowed by a landlady. Clemens not only finds eastern values faulty on the frontier but also frontier values vulnerable. Also out of place are the nabobs from Nevada who go to New York and try to commandeer an omnibus for a fancy carriage. Just as outrageous is "The Story of the Old Ram" in *Roughing It*, which exploits frontier enjoyment of violence. "The boys" (representing the observer) deceive the speaker (the tenderfoot writer) into listening to the pointless and violent tale of Jim Blaine (the veteran storyteller) as they sit symbolically on powder kegs, ready to explode with laughter, Clemens's weapon against violence. The tenderfoot, now a veteran westerner but an aspiring writer, is brought to learn at the feet of a locally admired storyteller, a drunk who cannot tell the

story without attaining a particular degree of inebriation. Full of comic but horrific mayhem, the story is a rambling stream of consciousness that stops mid-sentence when Blaine passes out. The joke is on the expectant would-be author (and readers). The lesson is that structure can be built solely around character and realistic speech.

Violence and violent men receive ambivalent treatment in *Roughing It*. Although Slade's adventures are told with a mixture of seeming admiration and horror, Clemens says Slade is no coward despite his fear before the gallows, calling him a morally courageous gentleman. Treated similarly is Colonel Sherburn in *Huckleberry Finn*, who coldly shoots drunken, unarmed Boggs dead and defies a lynch mob's cowardice. Sherburn and Slade follow frontier codes, but Slade's shooting a man who outdrew him after they agree to settle with a fistfight defies the code, and Sherburn's applying the code to a ranting drunk reveals its ridiculousness. Bold Jack Slade "feared *a great deal more than the Almighty*," cries to see his wife, and pleads for his life before the group come to hang him, becoming "so exhausted . . . by tears, prayers and lamentations, that he had scarcely strength left to stand under the fatal beam" (90, 94). Such discrepancies in myths darken even more next to the absurd light thrown on frontier range wars when an avalanche lands one ranch atop another and the two owners claim the same property (241–247).

Reversals and re-reversals of roles and attitudes continue past the snowstorm in *Roughing It*, which Smith says is the symbolic death of the tenderfoot and the birth of the veteran ("Structure" 219–220). Neither tenderfoot nor veteran remains superior or inferior; the exterior observer maintains balance. The town dog, representing the eastern tenderfoot, is humiliated by the coyote, the old-timer ("Structure" 213–214). The coyote itself, following his triumph, is degraded again but still placed higher than the Indians (48–53), whose romanticized status suffers a few chapters later (146–149). In *Roughing It*, the narrator mainly expresses disappointment that the Indians he sees do not match his expectations; they are more pathetic than fearsome, evoking repugnance and loathing. Here, the observer partially loses balance.

Typically, in the early works, Clemens's narrator is biased against INDIANS. *Roughing It* is no exception. However, the narrator's attitude toward Hawaiians is much different. He is enchanted by them and sympathizes with them over what white missionaries and other intruders have done to the island culture. Dissimilar to the rest of the book, the Hawaiian section presents a sort of post-West before the narrator's actual return to the west. Going to Hawaii is a step into a past culture, lost perhaps but still resembling paradise, a primitive world of true innocence, which the west had mostly lost when he went there. Its people have not yet truly realized the danger of the white man; unlike the Indians—dirty, scruffy, and frequently hostile—he finds them clean, pure, beautiful, and unspoiled.

The explanatory appeal of myth to Clemens is clear. By presenting, accepting, and civilizing myth, particularly in various borderlands, he probes multifaceted human nature and contradictions of personality. Seeking multiple American experiences through language, he embodies American literary experience. Because the frontier is the place where civilization is its roughest and most exposed, *Roughing It* is an appropriate venue for a new narrative voice: young initiate and mature veteran, civilized and rough-edged at the same time.

Critical Commentary by John H. Davis

DRAMATIC ADAPTATIONS

While Clemens was writing *Roughing It* (1872), or shortly afterward, he began to dramatize the incident in his book in which the bully Arkansas terrorizes Honey Lake Smith's inn (chapter 31). He abandoned this effort, however, possibly because AUGUSTIN DALY staged a musical play called *Roughing It* in New York City in February and March of 1873. Daly claimed to have adapted his production from an unspecified French play about a Manhattan couple eloping to the Rocky Mountains. However, his play not only used Clemens's title, but incorporated scenes from his book—such as episodes with Arkansas and JACK SLADE. In 1910, THOMAS A. EDISON's film company produced a short silent film titled *A Mountain Blizzard* that evidently adapted the blizzard episode from chapter 32

of *Roughing It*. Another silent film, *The Pony Express* (1925) featured a brief episode with Charles Gerson portraying Clemens as a western tenderfoot—a character likely inspired by the narrator of *Roughing It*. In later years, portions of *Roughing It* were adapted to several television series, including BONANZA, *Death Valley Days*, and *Rifleman*. In May 1960, NBC-TV broadcast an hour-long adaption of *Roughing It* with Andrew Prine as the young Clemens and James Daly as an older Clemens.

The most ambitious attempt to put *Roughing It* on the screen was a four-hour miniseries of the same title first broadcast over two nights on the Hallmark Channel in March 2002. Charles Martin Smith directed the film, using a script by Stephen H. Berman. The miniseries covers events in *Roughing It* from the moment that the narrator and his brother board a stagecoach in St. Joseph, Missouri, through the moment that the narrator is hired by the VIRGINIA CITY TERRITORIAL ENTERPRISE—a period equivalent to the first 42 of the book's 78 chapters. The miniseries is faithful to the spirit of the book in treating the figure of the narrator as a young and inexperienced man who has seemingly never traveled anywhere or achieved anything before he goes west and who looks up to his much wiser and more accomplished older brother. However, it makes a radical departure from the book in identifying the narrator and his brother by name—as Sam Clemens (Robin Dunne) and Orion Clemens (Greg Spottiswood)—and by presenting their story as biography, rather than fiction—which is curious, as the credits state that the story is "based on the *novel* by Mark Twain." In the book, neither the name "Clemens" nor the name "Mark Twain" is ever mentioned, a fact that allowed Clemens freely to mix fact and fiction with no pretense of writing AUTOBIOGRAPHY.

The FRAME of the Hallmark miniseries is a speech that an old and white-haired Sam Clemens (James Garner) delivers to his daughter Susy's (Jewel Staite) graduating class at BRYN MAWR in 1891. As his speech unfolds, scenes alternate between past and present. Nearly half the narrative is devoted to the cross-country STAGECOACH journey and includes significantly altered episodes with George Bemis and Jack Slade. Almost immediately after the Clemens brothers reach CARSON CITY,

Sam strikes off on his own to take up MINING. From this point, the story departs from the book drastically by having Clemens form a three-way partnership with CALVIN HIGBIE (J. D. Nicholsen) and Ballou (Wayne Robson) and by mixing up unrelated adventures that the book sets in HUMBOLDT, AURORA, and Honey Lake Smith's. (The film even incorporates the unrelated "CALIFORNIAN'S TALE," which Clemens wrote in 1892).

The miniseries reaches its climax when Sam and his partners discover they have blown their claim to the fabulously wealthy BLIND LEAD. Oblivious to where he is going, Sam then staggers away from the cabin he shares with his partners and finds himself in front of the tent building of the *Territorial Enterprise*, which is evidently only a stone's throw away. There reporter DAN DE QUILLE (Ryan Luhning) takes Sam inside, where JOE GOODMAN (Rainer Kahl) offers him a writing job. When the scene shifts back to Bryn Mawr, the older Clemens explains that he finally found "his calling."

CHARACTERS AND RELATED ENTRIES

Admiral, The Old   Character in *Roughing It* (1872). A recently retired whaling captain sailing to HAWAII aboard the AJAX, the Admiral appears in chapter 62 as a beloved and respected defender of the weak whom other passengers shun because of his overbearingness. When he argues about the causes of the CIVIL WAR, he is like ANDREW JACKSON—the bull-pup of the JUMPING FROG STORY: Once he gets hold of an opponent, he never lets go. His fatal weakness is that his arguments rest on a complex tissue of lies; his power is broken when the soft-spoken Williams counters his invented history with even bigger lies.

Clemens loosely modeled the Admiral on a fellow *Ajax* passenger named Captain James Smith (1800–1877), a former whaler recently retired from the Hawaiian navy.

Arkansas   Character in *Roughing It* (1872). A "stalwart ruffian," Arkansas terrorizes people trapped by a flood at HONEY LAKE SMITH's station in Nevada (chapter 31). His reign of terror ends abruptly when the innkeeper's wife confronts him with scissors and gives him a tongue-lashing. As a

blustering bully humiliated by an ostensibly weaker person, Arkansas resembles the Old Admiral of *Roughing It* (chapter 62), the tough-talking raftsmen in *Huckleberry Finn*'s "Raft Chapter" and a Hannibal man whom Jane L. Clemens faced down when Sam Clemens was a boy. After writing *Roughing It*, Mark Twain began to dramatize the "Arkansas" episode but did not finish the play.

Baker, Dick or Jim   Character in *Roughing It* (1872) and *A Tramp Abroad* (1880). Chapter 61 of *Roughing It* describes *Dick* Baker as a 46-year-old California pocket-miner who has become a victim of 18 years of unrequited toil and blighted hopes. Gentle, patient, and big-hearted, he is given to mourning the loss of his wonderful cat, Tom Quartz, who he thinks may have been supernatural. Baker tells how he once accidentally blew Tom Quartz sky-high while blasting a mine shaft.

This same character reappears as *Jim* Baker in chapters 2–3 of *A Tramp Abroad*, which describes him as a middle-aged, simple-hearted California miner who has learned the languages of the birds and beasts. Here Baker relates one of the most

Jim Baker, the narrator of the bluejay yarn in *A Tramp Abroad*, appears as Dick Baker in *Roughing It*.

famous of Mark Twain's tall TALES, the BLUEJAY YARN.

By his own admission, Clemens modeled Baker on his prospector friend DICK STOKER. As a storyteller, however, Baker is more similar to Stoker's partner, JIM GILLIS—who invented the original versions of these tales, making Stoker their hero. Clemens—who often had trouble keeping character names straight—probably was thinking of Stoker when he called Baker "Dick" in *Roughing It,* and of Gillis when he called him "Jim" in *A Tramp Abroad.* His confusion persisted to 1907, when he recorded an autobiographical passage identifying Stoker as the "Jim Baker" of the Tom Quartz tale. He also added that Stoker never owned a cat.

Ballou   Character in *Roughing It* (1872). In chapters 27–33 and 39, Ballou is a hard-working 60-year-old blacksmith and veteran miner who accompanies the narrator and others from Carson City to HUMBOLDT and back. He is based on Cornbury S. Tillou, a 40-year-old French blacksmith who accompanied Clemens to Humboldt in December 1861. A lover of big words, Ballou constantly spouts malapropisms. He calls weary horses "bituminous from long deprivation" and a dog "meretricious in his movements." He gives up drinking coffee made with alkali water, calling it "too technical for him" (chapter 27). Ballou's fondness for big words that he does not understand is shared by the mother of Aileen Mavoureen in *A DOG'S TALE.* Despite his pompous destruction of the language, Ballou is clearheaded enough to recognize that the "gold" the narrator finds in chapter 28 is mica. On the return journey in chapter 31, he is the first to realize that the travelers have been following their own tracks in the snow.

The 2002 Hallmark Channel Miniseries based on *Roughing It* inflates Ballou's role by making him a partner with Clemens and CALVIN HIGBIE in virtually all Clemens's prospecting ventures. Actor Wayne Robson, who plays Ballou, depicts him less as a speaker of malapropisms than as a speaker of frontier gibberish, in the film tradition of Hopalong Cassidy's sidekick, Gabby Hayes.

Bemis, George   Character in *Roughing It* (1872). A passenger on the STAGECOACH from SAINT JOSEPH to Carson City, Bemis is mentioned by name in chapters 2, 4, 7, 12, and 13. As a somewhat oafish traveling companion whom the narrator meets on his trip, he resembles the "Mr. Brown" and "Blucher" characters of Clemens's other narratives. Bemis makes the narrator nervous by carrying an old "Allen" revolver, which he handles carelessly, and tells an amazing story about being chased up a tree by a buffalo (chapter 7). His final appearance is

Bemis unloads his Allen revolver on the tree-climbing buffalo in chapter 7 of *Roughing It.*

in Salt Lake City, where he gets drunk on "Valley Tan" and goes to bed with his boots on (chapter 13).

Billings, Mr. Minor character in *Roughing It* (1872). Billings is mentioned in chapters 69 and 73 as the narrator's companion on his visit to the island of Hawaii. Clemens's original letters to the SACRAMENTO UNION call this character "Mr. Brown" and give this character much larger role. Jim Blaine's tale about his grandfather's old ram in chapter 53 mentions an unrelated "widder Billings."

"CAPTAIN'S STORMFIELD'S VISIT TO HEAVEN" mentions Edward H. Billings as a Tennessee tailor who is the greatest poet in the universe.

Blaine, Jim Character in chapter 53 of *Roughing It* (1872). A stalwart old miner—apparently in Nevada—Blaine is notorious for starting to tell a story that he never finishes about "his grandfather's old ram" (a title under which his tale has been published on its own). On the advice of "the boys" (who are never identified), the narrator watches Blaine carefully to determine when he is satisfactorily drunk—the only time to hear his story. When that moment arrives, he and the boys crowd into Blaine's cabin to listen to him. Blaine begins by telling about the bully old ram his grandfather fetched from Illinois from a man name Bill Yates . . . This is as far as Blaine ever gets about the ram. From this point, each name he mentions leads to another digression, carrying him hopelessly far from his original subject, until he falls asleep.

Blaine's monotonous 1,550-word recitation touches on a variety of unsavory and macabre themes, including drunkenness, freak accidents, physical disfigurement, gruesome death, cannibalism, and predatory UNDERTAKERS. It mentions 27 different characters:

1. his grandfather;
2. Bill Yates, from whom the grandfather gets the ram;
3. Thankful Yates, Bill's father;
4. Seth Green, an acquaintance of Blaine's grandfather;
5. Sarah Wilkerson, Green's wife;
6. Sile Hawkins, whom Blaine momentarily mistakes for Sarah's former suitor;
7. Filkins, the last name of Sarah's correct suitor;
8. Nixon, apparently a political candidate;
9. Deacon Ferguson, who ejects Filkins from a prayer meeting;
10. Miss Jefferson, a glass-eyed woman on whom Filkins landed;
11. Miss Wagner, a heavy borrower, who uses Miss Jefferson's glass eye and Miss Higgins's wooden leg, neither of which fits her properly;
12. Miss Higgins, who lends Miss Wagner her wooden leg;
13. Miss Jacops, a woman who wears a wig and is married to a coffin-peddler;
14. Jacops, the coffin-peddler who waits for Robbins to die;
15. old Robbins, who is slow to die;
16. old Squire Hogadorn from the Indiana town to which Robbins returned;
17. the widder Billings, Hogadorn's second wife, the former Becky Martin;
18. Deacon Dunlap's first wife, the daughter of the widder Billings;
19. Maria, the daughter of Becky Martin, who marries a missionary and dies in grace when she is eaten by savages;
20. the missionary who marries Maria and is also eaten by savages—who later convert, demonstrating the power of Providence;
21. Blaine's Uncle Lem, another example of Providence, who has an Irishman fall on him;
22. the Irishman, a hod carrier who misses a dog when he falls on Lem;
23. Uncle Lem's dog, which is part bull and part shepherd;
24. Parson Hagar, the former owner of the dog;
25. Hagar's mother, who was formerly a Watson;
26. Hagar's sister, who married William Wheeler;
27. William Wheeler, who gets nipped by a carpet-weaving machine and is woven into 14 yards of three-ply carpet, which his widow has buried.

One of Clemens's best-known stories told by a narrator unconscious of his story's humor, the "old ram's tale" has become virtually synonymous with a story that goes nowhere. Clemens himself often recited it—in a modified form—in his public lectures.

When Clemens wrote this story in 1870 or 1871, Pennsylvania congressman James G. Blaine (1830–1893) was Speaker of the House. When Blaine became the Republican candidate for president in 1884, Clemens openly opposed him.

Blakely, Captain Ned Character in *Roughing It* (1872). Chapter 50 describes Blakely as a San Francisco sea captain of 50 years' experience and relates a story about an incident occurring two decades earlier, when he avenged the murder of his black mate in Peru's Chincha Islands. Having a sailor's distrust of the law, he insisted on exacting justice himself. After BILL NOAKES killed his mate, Blakely personally arrested him. The next day, he invited other captains to watch him hang Noakes, but they insisted on a trial. Blakely could not understand why a trial was necessary, since it seemed impossible that anyone would judge Noakes not guilty. He was also surprised that others thought Noakes himself should attend his trial. After conceding that Noakes should be there, however, he balked at allowing someone other than himself to deliver him. Next, he was unhappy with the makeup of the jury, so he let its members know that they had better vote "right." His patience finally reached its limit after Noakes was pronounced guilty and he was told that a "sheriff" would do the hanging. In the face of his boundless wrath, that suggestion was judiciously dropped.

As a gruff, simple, Bible-quoting old salt, Blakely is clearly modeled on Captain NED WAKEMAN, whom Clemens met in 1866. Nothing in Wakeman's history, however, suggests that the Chincha Islands episode really occurred. Clemens apparently invented the story—which has no organic connection with the rest of *Roughing It*—simply to illustrate the administration of justice in frontier situations. He later re-created Blakely as Sim ROBINSON, the judge in "THOSE EXTRAORDINARY TWINS," who is determined to see justice done, regardless of the niceties of the law.

Blakely's story has been anthologized as "A Trial." *Life on the Mississippi* mentions a Union Army officer named "Captain Blakely" (chapter 31).

Boggs Fictitious name used in *Roughing It* (1872) for Clemens's friendly rival CLEMENT T. RICE of the VIRGINIA CITY UNION. In chapter 43, the narrator cannot obtain a copy of the local school report because the principal hates his newspaper. After using a pitcher of hot punch to coax Boggs into lending his copy, the narrator gets his story in on time, but Boggs gets drunk and the *Union* goes to press without the school report. When the next report is due, Boggs gets revenge by stranding the narrator in a mine shaft, causing him to miss his deadline.

Boomerang Fictitious name that Clemens applied to the schooner on which he sailed from Oahu to the island of Hawaii in late May 1866. Chapters 69 and 71 of *Roughing It* (1872) mention the *Boomerang* by name and chapters 73–74 allude to it. Clemens's original HAWAII letters to the SACRAMENTO UNION use both "*Boomerang*" and the schooner's real name, *Emeline*, giving the false impression that he sailed on two different ships. His letters also give the *Emeline*'s skipper the fictitious name "Captain Kangaroo." Clemens spent several nights sleeping aboard the cramped and cockroach-infested ship as he explored the big island. He returned to Oahu on another vessel, the *Kilauea*.

Briggs, Scotty Character in *Roughing It* (1872). In chapter 47, Briggs is the VIRGINIA CITY committeeman delegated to interview a young preacher newly arrived from the East to plan his friend Buck Fanshaw's funeral. Like Fanshaw, Briggs is a stalwart rough and a member of the fire department; he shows up in his full uniform, with red fire helmet and patent leather belt with a spanner and a revolver attached. Though a marked contrast to the pale theological student (modeled on FRANKLIN S. RISING), Briggs has a warm heart that sees him through. However, he and the preacher speak such vastly different argots that every sentence each man utters mystifies the other. Briggs nearly overwhelms the preacher with a torrent of obscure slang taken from the mines, cards, games, and other sources, but eventually makes himself understood. When the grand funeral finally comes off, he serves as a pallbearer. Later, he becomes the first local rough to convert to religion and teaches a Sunday school class in which he tells children Bible stories in language that they can understand. A month before Briggs dies, *Roughing It*'s narrator hears him recite a slang-riddled version of the story of Joseph and his brothers.

Erickson, Simon   Minor character in *Roughing It* (1872). In chapter 70 Erickson is a middle-aged man on the island of Hawaii who is thought crazy because of his fixation on an alleged correspondence with Horace GREELEY. He claims that while he was a minister in Michigan, he wrote to Greeley for advice on behalf of a Kansas woman named Beazely, whose son was obsessed with turnips. Young Beazely had gone into a funk because he could not get turnips to grow on vines. Greeley's handwritten reply was so difficult to read that Erickson himself became unbalanced trying to decipher it. By the time Greeley's clerk sent a legible translation, young Beazely was dead and Erickson unhinged.

Aside from burlesquing Greeley's notorious penmanship, this fictitious anecdote is the fullest development of Clemens's fascination with turnips as a humorous symbol of stupidity. The idea of growing them on vines also appears in "HOW I EDITED AN AGRICULTURAL PAPER ONCE" (1870). In chapter 11 of *The Gilded Age* (1873), Colonel Sellers makes a dinner of nothing but raw turnips, turning them into a "banquet." In chapter 27, he talks about transforming a region into "turnip country." where fortunes will be made once a "contrivance [is] perfected for extracting olive oil out of turnips—if there's any in them."

Fanshaw, Buck   Background character in *Roughing It* (1872). A recently deceased VIRGINIA CITY saloon keeper and high official in the fire department, Fanshaw was found by an inquest to have become so delirious from typhoid fever that he took arsenic, shot himself, cut his throat, and jumped out of a high window. After due deliberation, the jury ruled death "by the visitation of God." More than anyone else, Fanshaw brought peace to the town—by beating the daylights out of anyone who disturbed it. He never went back on a friend, never

shook his mother, and never wavered from his motto, "No Irish need apply!" Generally acknowledged as representing the highest stratum of the mining community's society, he truly merited a grand funeral—which his friend Scotty Briggs struggles to arrange in chapter 47 of *Roughing It*.

This long anecdote is occasionally published by itself as "Buck Fanshaw's Funeral." Clemens evidently modeled Fanshaw on a man named Tom Peasely, owner of VIRGINIA CITY's Sazerac saloon, who was murdered in CARSON CITY in 1863.

feet   MINING term for a portion of a claim. During Clemens's time in NEVADA, the silver mines were generally linear tunnels or shafts whose ownership was measured in "feet." The title to each foot of a mine was recorded in deeds, and mine shares were sold and traded in "feet." *Roughing It*'s (1872) chapters on Nevada use the term frequently after chapter 26, which describes the people of the HUMBOLDT district as "feet crazy."

Irish Brigade   Nickname for about a dozen young men with whom the narrator of *Roughing It* (1872) lives in Bridget O'Flannigan's CARSON CITY boardinghouse. The men—only a fraction of whom are actually Irish—are camp followers of Governor JAMES W. NYE, whom they have followed to Nevada, hoping for positions in the new territorial government. In chapters 21, Nye tries to get rid of them by sending them out to survey a railroad line.

A Mountain Blizzard   Silent film adapted by THOMAS A. EDISON's company in 1910 from the blizzard episode in chapter 32 of *Roughing It* (1872). The same episode is also dramatized in the 2002 Hallmark Channel miniseries titled *Roughing It*.

Noakes, Bill   Minor character in chapter 50 of *Roughing It* (1872). A trading ship's mate in the Chincha Islands 20 years before the time of the main narrative, Noakes was a cruel bully who made the mistake of challenging Captain Ned Blakely when the latter came to the islands. After Blakely twice beat him to a pulp, Noakes shot Blakely's black mate dead—apparently out of spite. Blakely then arrested Noakes, reluctantly allowing him to be tried before he hanged him. Unrepentant to the end, Noakes went to his death without admitting his crime.

Nye, Captain John (?–July 7, 1871, Washington, D.C.) Brother of NEVADA territorial governor JAMES W. NYE. John Nye figures prominently in chapter 35 of *Roughing It* (1872) as the narrator's extraordinary traveling companion who finds food and quarters for the tired party of prospectors returning from HUMBOLDT. The chapter describes him as having "a good memory, and a tongue hung in the middle. This is a combination which gives immortality to conversation." In chapters 40–41, the narrator leaves his ESMERALDA mining camp to help nurse Nye, who is suffering from spasmodic rheumatism at a place nine miles away. When he returns to Esmeralda, he finds that he and his partner have lost their claim on the BLIND LEAD for failing to do the necessary work.

O'Flannigan, Mrs. Bridget Minor character in *Roughing It* (1881). O'Flannigan is the proprietor of the CARSON CITY boardinghouse in which the narrator lives (chapter 21). Tired of being paid in "notes" by her "Irish Brigade" boarders, O'Flannigan appeals to Governor NYE to put his camp followers to work. The real name of Clemens's Carson City landlady was Margret Murphy.

Oliphant Character in *Roughing It* (1872). One of the men with whom the narrator goes to HUMBOLDT (chapters 27–29), Oliphant is based on Augustus W. Oliver (1835–1918?), a probate judge for the newly formed Humboldt County with whom Clemens traveled in December 1861. Oliver's real name is mentioned in *Innocents Abroad*'s account of the same journey (chapter 27).

Ollendorff Character in *Roughing It* (1872) who accompanies the narrator from HUMBOLDT to CARSON CITY and back (chapters 30–33). Ollendorff is based on Clemens's real companion on the first leg of that journey, Captain Hugo Pfersdorff, one of the founders of UNIONVILLE. Chapter 30 of *Roughing It* identifies Ollendorff simply as a Prussian, but *not* the man "who has inflicted so much suffering on the

world with his wretched foreign grammars." This remark alludes to German grammarian Heinrich Gottfried Ollendorff (1803–1865), whom "CAPTAIN STORMFIELD'S VISIT TO HEAVEN" mentions by name. *Roughing It*'s Ollendorff figures prominently in chapter 31, in which he upsets a canoe filled with travelers escaping from HONEY LAKE SMITH's inn, then gets the group lost in a blizzard. In the next chapter, he fails to start a fire with his pistol; when it appears that everyone will die, he asks to be forgiven for his blunders and swears off liquor, throwing his bottle away. When the travelers are saved in chapter 33, he retrieves his bottle.

The Secretary Character in *Roughing It* (1872). The book opens with the narrator stating that his brother has just been appointed to the majestic post of Secretary of NEVADA Territory. The "Secretary" is modeled on Clemens's brother, Orion Clemens—who is never named in the book—but much that is ascribed to him is exaggerated or invented. For example, his depiction as a self-sacrificing drudge forced to pay many petty expenses out of his own pocket is contradicted by Orion's records of his actual relationship with the federal government. The book also mentions the Secretary in chapters 1–4, 13, 21–22, 25, and 30.

Street, Mr. Character in *Roughing It* (1872). In chapter 13, Street is a telegraph contractor in UTAH who introduces the narrator and secretary to BRIGHAM YOUNG. In the next chapter, he tells a long story about problems he once had getting MORMON subcontractors to fulfill their contracts until Young intervened in his behalf. He is so impressed by the Mormon president's purely secular power that he says Utah is an "absolute monarchy and Brigham Young is king!" This character is based on a real telegraph contractor, James Street, whom Clemens and his brother met in western Utah after leaving Salt Lake City. Street later knew Clemens in SAN FRANCISCO and died some time before *Roughing It* was published.

Tom Quartz Animal character in a tale related by Dick Baker in chapter 61 of *Roughing It* (1872). A large gray cat that Baker owned for eight years,

Tom Quartz was a remarkable animal whose only interest in life was MINING. He always supervised pocket-miners closely. After quartz-mining came to the region, Tom Quartz happened to be sleeping on a gunny sack inside a shaft the first day that miners did blasting. After setting their charge, they ran to safety before remembering that Tom Quartz was in the shaft. The ensuing blast sent Tom Quartz tumbling end over end through the sky. He landed covered with soot, threw everyone a disgusted look and stalked off. After that, he was the most prejudiced cat there ever was against quartz-mining.

Clemens adapted Tom Quartz's story from a tale that JIM GILLIS related in California in late 1864 or early 1865. Gillis modeled Baker on his partner DICK STOKER, but the cat never existed, according to Clemens himself. Clemens's first, unpublished version of the story, "The Remarkable Sagacity of a Cat" (1865), calls the cat "George Billson." He published a revised version of the story in the BUF-FALO EXPRESS in December 1869.

Whiteman (Mr. W.) (d. 1883?) Historical figure mentioned in *Roughing It* (1872). Nevada mining traditions recall Gideon F. Whiteman as a prospector who spent years searching the eastern slopes of the SIERRA NEVADA for a fabulously wealthy vein of gold in a "cement mine." According to *Roughing It*, Whiteman learned about the mine from the lone survivor of three German brothers who stumbled on it more than 20 years earlier (chapter 37). Whenever Whiteman is sighted passing through ESMERALDA district, men turn out to follow him. Although Whiteman has suffered and starved for 12 or 13 years with nothing to show for his quest, other men persist in stalking him. In chapter 41, the narrator's partner Higbie blows a chance for riches on his "BLIND LEAD" claim when he cannot resist chasing off after Whiteman again, instead of working the claim.

Roughing It makes it appear that Whiteman spent years searching for the cement mine before the narrator even arrives in Esmeralda. The historical Whiteman did spend nearly two decades in his futile quest; however, he only *began* in 1861. He is believed to have continued his quest until 1880 and to have died about three years later. The search for his mine continued into the 20th century, doubtless inspired partly by *Roughing It* itself.

Williams Character in *Roughing It* (1872). A cheerful passenger aboard the AJAX, Williams distinguishes himself in chapter 62 by breaking the power of the Old Admiral, whose overbearing political arguments wear everyone else out. Williams is the only passenger whom the Admiral cannot goad into an argument, until a day when he unexpectedly reopens one of the Admiral's arguments and turns his lies against him. After pretending to accept the old man's invented pre–Civil War history about outrages against southern women, Williams comes back at him with "clean, pure, manufactured history, without a word of truth in it," calmly getting the Admiral to swallow it. Thereafter, Williams is a hero aboard the ship; whenever the Admiral starts an argument, he is fetched to cow him into submission. Eventually the Admiral stops discussing politics.

BIBLIOGRAPHY

Bellamy, Gladys Carmen. *Mark Twain as a Literary Artist.* Norman: University of Oklahoma Press, 1950.

Busskohl, James L. " 'The Story of the Old Ram' and the Tenderfoot Writer." *Studies in American Fiction* 18, no. 2 (Autumn 1990): 183–192.

Carpenter, Scott. "Demythification in *Adventures of Huckleberry Finn.*" *Studies in American Fiction* 15, no. 2 (Autumn 1987): 211–217.

Coard, Robert L. "The Dictionary and Mark Twain." *Word Study* 43, no. 3 (February 1968): 1–4.

Denton, Lynn W. "Mark Twain and the American Indian." *Mark Twain Journal* 16 (Winter 1971–1972): 1–3.

DeVoto, Bernard. "Introduction." In *The Portable Mark Twain,* 1–34. New York: Viking Press, 1946.

Folsom, James K. "Imaginative Safety Valves: Frontier Themes in the Literature of the Gilded Age." In *The Frontier Experience and the American Dream: Essays on American Literature,* edited by David Mogen, Mark Bundy, and Paul Bryant, 87–94. College Station: Texas A&M University Press, 1989.

Gunn, Drewey Wayne. "The Monomythic Structure of *Roughing It.*" *American Literature* 61, no. 4 (December 1989): 563–585.

Huck Finn: The Complete Buffalo & Erie County Public Library Manuscript—Teaching and Research Digital Edition, edited by Victor Doyno. Buffalo, N.Y.: Buffalo & Erie County Public Library, 2002.

Howe, Lawrence. "Transcending the Limits of Experience: Mark Twain's *Life on the Mississippi*." *American Literature* 63, no. 3 (September 1991): 420–439.

Kolb, Harold H., Jr. "Mark Twain and the Myth of the West." In *The Mythologizing of Mark Twain*, edited by Sara deSaussure Davis and Philip D. Beidler, 119–135. Tuscaloosa: University of Alabama Press, 1984.

Krauth, Leland. "Mark Twain: A Man for All Regions." *Studies in American Fiction* 13 (Autumn 1985): 239–246.

Kriegel, Leonard. "Foreword." In *Roughing It* by Mark Twain, xix–xxvi. New York: New American Library, 1962.

Simonson, Harold P. "The West as Archetype." In *Under the Sun: Myth and Realism in Western American Literature*, edited by Barbara Howard Meldrum, 21–28. Troy, N.Y.: Whitston, 1985.

Smith, Henry Nash. "Mark Twain as an Interpreter of the Far West: The Structure of *Roughing It*." In *The Frontier in Perspective*, edited by Walker D. Wyman and Clifton B. Kroeber, 206–228. Madison: University of Wisconsin Press, 1957.

———. *Virgin Land: The American West as Symbol and Myth.* Cambridge, Mass.: Harvard University Press, 1950.

———. "Transformation of a Tenderfoot." In *Mark Twain: The Development of a Writer*, 52–70. Cambridge, Mass.: Harvard University Press, 1962.

Steinbrink, Jeffrey. "How Mark Twain Survived Sam Clemens' Reformation." *American Literature* 55, no. 3 (October 1983): 299–315.

Twain, Mark. *Adventures of Huckleberry Finn: Tom Sawyer's Comrade*, edited by Walter Blair and Victor Fischer. Berkeley: University of California Press, 1985.

———. "The Dandy Frightening the Squatter." *Early Tales & Sketches*. Vol. 1 (1851–1864), edited by Edgar Marquess Branch and Robert H. Hirst, 64–65. Berkeley: University of California Press, 1979.

———. "The French and the Comanches." In *Letters from the Earth*, edited by Bernard DeVoto, 181–189. New York: Harper, 1962.

———. *Roughing It.* Edited by Shelley Fisher Fishkin. New York: Oxford University Press, 1996.

Ude, Wayne. "Forging an American Style: The Romance-Novel and Magical Realism as Response to the Frontier and Wilderness Experiences." In *The Frontier Experience and the American Dream: Essays on American Literature*, edited by David Mogen, Mark Bundy, and Paul Bryant, 50–64. College Station: Texas A&M University Press, 1989.

"Running for Governor"

SKETCH written shortly after NEW YORK's November 1870 gubernatorial election. Using his own pen name, Clemens describes his entirely invented experiences since being nominated several months earlier to run for governor of New York as an independent against Mr. John T. Smith and Mr. Blank J. Blank (based on John T. Hoffman, 1828–1888). He thought that his good character gave him an advantage over his opponents but soon found the press ready to level unsubstantiated charges against him. One newspaper, for example, called on him to explain why he was convicted of perjury in Wakawak, Cochin China (Vietnam), in 1863. Since he has never been in Cochin China, he does not know how to reply. As a result of his silence, the paper labels him "the infamous perjurer Twain."

Next, the *Gazette* demands that he explain why he was TARRED AND FEATHERED in MONTANA for theft. Since he was never in Montana, he again does not reply and is branded "Twain the Montana Thief." As similarly unanswerable accusations appear, his growing list of SOBRIQUETS includes "Twain the Body-Snatcher," "Mr. Delirium Tremens Twain," "Twain the Filthy Corruptionist," and "Twain the Loathsome Embracer." Urged by supporters to answer these charges, he starts preparing a reply, only to be driven to distraction by new accusations. He is now charged with burning down a lunatic asylum, poisoning his uncle, and other crimes. He gives up and withdraws his candidacy.

Clemens first published this 1,820-word sketch in the *BUFFALO EXPRESS* on November 19, 1870.

The GALAXY reprinted it a month later and it was collected in SKETCHES, NEW AND OLD (1875).

Satires & Burlesques, Mark Twain's

Collection of previously unpublished material edited by Franklin R. Rogers for the Mark Twain Papers (now the MARK TWAIN PROJECT) in 1967. Most of the items in this collection are writings that Clemens left unfinished, such as "Autobiography of a Damned Fool," a story based on the life of Orion Clemens. The volume also has several stories that Clemens completed and intended to publish, such as "1,002D ARABIAN NIGHT." Other notable items include "Hellfire Hotchkiss," several pieces about Simon Wheeler, and BURLESQUES of Verdi's opera *Il Trovatore*, Shakespeare's HAMLET, and Victor Hugo's *L'Homme Qui Rit*.

"Schoolhouse Hill"

An unfinished NOVEL of about 15,000 words that Clemens wrote in November–December 1898, this story is the third of his four unfinished tales built around the "MYSTERIOUS STRANGER" theme. It is set in Huck Finn and Tom Sawyer's Missouri village around the 1840s. Here, however, the town is called simply "Petersburg," not "St. Petersburg." A few familiar characters, including Tom and Huck, appear only in the first two chapters, but Clemens's notes suggest that they were to play a larger part in the chapters remaining to be written. The story is of special interest for an additional reason, as members of Clemens's own family were to appear as the fictional Hotchkiss family. The mercurial Oliver Hotchkiss, who does appear, is modeled on Orion Clemens. Although Clemens abandoned the story abruptly midway through its sixth chapter, the depth of his initial commitment to it is demonstrated by the polish of what he finished, as well as the detailed working notes he left for what remained to be written.

SYNOPSIS

Chapter 1

On a winter morning 30 children assemble outside Archibald Ferguson's school on Schoolhouse Hill. The scholars include Tom Sawyer, his brother Sid, and Becky Thatcher. Huck Finn, though not a scholar, is also there with Tom. When a new boy, about 15 years old, arrives, he immediately attracts attention. His surpassing handsomeness, fine clothes, and dignified and tranquil manner set him apart from the others.

After Ferguson puts the class through several lessons, he notices the new boy and asks his name. The boy speaks only French, but Ferguson can converse well enough with him in that language to explain how he must learn English. The boy astounds him by claiming to have learned the rules of English grammar merely from overhearing the class recite earlier. He proves it by reciting the rules flawlessly, then adds to Ferguson's astonishment by repeating every word, mannerism, and intonation uttered by everyone in the room during the mathematics lesson. The teacher next gives him an English-French dictionary to study; 20 minutes later the boy shows that he has not only memorized every detail, he can comment intelligently on the book's inconsistencies and flaws. Ferguson recognizes that the marvelous boy is no idiot savant and treats him with great deference and respect.

The boy spends the balance of the morning mastering Latin, Greek, mathematics, and "phonography" and then demonstrates remarkable computational powers. After Ferguson notices that the lunch hour has slipped by, he dismisses school early. But first the new boy gives his name as "Quarante-quatre," or Forty-four, and explains that he came to town the previous night.

Chapter 2

As the children leave the school, Tom Sawyer warns Forty-four that he will have to fight Henry Bascom, the school bully, and shows him some boxing moves. Forty-four seems merely puzzled when Henry tries to box with him but defeats the bully effortlessly. When Henry picks on someone else, Forty-four knocks him out with a single slap. At that moment Henry's father, the local slave trader, appears and tries to whip Forty-four, who dodges the blow and crushes the man's wrist in his hand.

Chapter 3

That afternoon at the Hotchkiss home, where Forty-four has taken a room, neighbors pour in hoping to see the now-famous boy. Though hospitable, the Hotchkisses are miffed that everyone else seems to know more about their wonderful guest than they, until their visitors start marveling at little observations they have made—such as Forty-four's having found a candle in complete darkness. This miracle looms even larger when Aunt Rachel, a household slave, notes that the candle is genuine wax. Rachel also remarks that though Forty-four has no luggage, he has been seen in different outfits. Moreover, she has also seen him conversing with a cat and a mouse in their own languages.

Anxious to see Forty-four's clothes, the visitors persuade Mrs. Hotchkiss to let them look in his room. When she picks up his coat, gold and silver coins flood out of its pockets. Everyone scrambles to put the coins back, but even after the coat's pockets are stuffed, a heap of coins remain. The visitors finally leave, convinced that Forty-four is indeed "an extraordinary person."

Chapter 4

That night a severe blizzard rages, reducing visibility to inches and making outdoor travel suicidal. Oliver Hotchkiss is too engrossed in a book on spiritualism to notice the storm until Rachel alerts him to Forty-four's failure to come home. A line is tied around old Uncle Jeff, another family slave, who is sent into the storm to look for Forty-four. The line slips loose, apparently condemning Jeff to certain death. Meanwhile, Forty-four enters the house from the back door. Ignoring Hotchkiss's order to stay inside, he goes out to rescue Jeff and returns with the news that another man is huddled in a nearby shed. When he realizes that the family cares about the man's plight, he rescues him. This man, Crazy Meadows, is nearly frozen. Forty-four again leaves, in order to round up others he has seen in the storm.

Convinced that Forty-four is dying in the storm, Hotchkiss calls together everyone, including the servants, to conduct a seance. After messages are received from LORD BYRON, Napoleon, WILLIAM SHAKESPEARE, and other ancient notables, Forty-four himself appears in the middle of the circle. He dismisses Crazy Meadows and the servants and then discusses spiritualism with Hotchkiss, who is astonished to discover that Forty-four is actually alive. Forty-four tells Hotchkiss that he has managed to save 13 people in the storm, but that 28 have perished under the snow. Hotchkiss and Forty-four settle down to whiskey and corncob pipes by the fire.

Forty-four explains that he was raised "partly in heaven, partly in hell," and shows Hotchkiss a book that he has borrowed from London's British Museum just minutes earlier. Before the conversation proceeds further, Forty-four has invisible servants bring a steaming feast to the table. At Hotchkiss's request he makes his servants visible; they are little red horned men with spiked tails. Hotchkiss's astonishment reaches its fullest level when Forty-four tells him that his father is Satan.

Chapter 5

Forty-four continues explaining to Hotchkiss who he is and why he has come to Earth. He was born before ADAM's fall. A thousand Earth years are only a day by his reckoning, making him 15 by his measure and nearly 5 million years old by Earth measurement. He blames his father for Adam's fall from grace, and blames him for giving mankind the "passionate and eager and hungry *disposition to* DO *evil."* Forty-four's own reason for coming to Earth is to help alleviate the burden of evil consequences bequeathed by his father. He asks for help in this from Hotchkiss, who eagerly accepts. Before formulating a specific plan to carry out this mission, Forty-four intends to spend the night traveling the world to study its peoples. He leaves a servant to wait on Hotchkiss while he is gone. Hotchkiss names the servant "Edward Nicholson Hotchkiss" after a deceased brother.

Chapter 6

The next morning Rachel and Jeff panic when they see the new devilish servant, but reconcile themselves to his presence when they learn that he, like them, is a slave. The supernatural servant astounds the others with his ability to perform impossible errands; at this point the manuscript abruptly ends.

UNWRITTEN CHAPTERS

Extensive working notes that Clemens left indicate the direction that the rest of the story was to go. Forty-four was to found a new church on Earth that would help human beings shed their "moral sense" and eliminate hypocrisy. To this end he would publish his own Bible—which Clemens intended to make an appendix of the novel, along with Forty-four's sermons and dialogues. Meanwhile, Forty-four would continue to astonish the people of Petersburg with new miracles. Along the way, however, he would make his own astonishing discovery by falling in love with one of the village characters—possibly Hellfire Hotchkiss.

PUBLISHING HISTORY

After abandoning this story, Clemens attempted to develop its themes in other versions of the "MYSTERIOUS STRANGER" tales. He first returned to "The Chronicle of Young Satan," which he had started earlier, and then took up *NO. 44, THE MYSTERIOUS STRANGER.* Though those versions are both set in medieval Austria, each has elements closely akin to aspects of "Schoolhouse Hill." "Chronicle" in particular attempts to evoke the atmosphere of boys growing up in a village that characterizes the Huck Finn–Tom Sawyer stories.

The original manuscript of "Schoolhouse Hill" is held by the MARK TWAIN PROJECT, which published the story for the first time in 1969 in *HANNIBAL, HUCK & TOM,* a collection edited by WALTER BLAIR. That same year the project also published the story in *The Mysterious Stranger Manuscripts,* a collection of all the tales edited by William M. Gibson. An amended edition of Gibson's edition of the text also appeared in the 1989 Mark Twain Project publication *Huck Finn and Tom Sawyer Among the Indians.* Each edition contains extensive notes on the story's text and background.

CHARACTERS AND RELATED ENTRIES

For information on Forty-four, see the Characters and Related Entries section of the *No. 44, The Mysterious Stranger* entry. For information on Tom Sawyer, Sid Sawyer, and Becky Thatcher, see the Characters and Related Entries section of the *Tom Sawyer* entry. For information on Huckleberry Finn, see the Characters and Related Entries section of the *Huckleberry Finn* entry.

Ferguson, Archibald Character in "Schoolhouse Hill." The gentle schoolmaster who is astonished by Forty-four's astounding mental powers, Ferguson and his students are so engrossed in admiring Forty-four that the lunch hour slips by unnoticed. Ferguson confesses that such an oversight has never before occurred in his 30 years of teaching and dismisses the school early in honor of a "day of miracles." Although a sharp contrast to *Tom Sawyer's* sadistic Mr. Dawson, Ferguson is also modeled on one of Clemens's own childhood teachers, JOHN A. DAWSON.

Hotchkiss, Oliver One of several fictional characters that Clemens modeled on his brother Orion Clemens, Hotchkiss is the head of the household in which the marvelous stranger Forty-four is rooming in "Schoolhouse Hill." The description of Hotchkiss fits Orion in almost every particular: He is kind, patient, generous, unenvious, eager to learn, and constantly changing his beliefs. His wife, Hannah, however, is just the opposite in this last regard. Typical of his dreamy nature, Hotchkiss is so engrossed in a book on spiritualism the night that a great blizzard rages outside his door that he fails to notice it until it is brought forcefully to his attention. When he sees Forty-four go out into the storm against his orders, he concludes that the boy will die and calls everyone together to hold a seance. After Forty-four returns safely, he identifies himself as the son of Satan and tells Hotchkiss that he wants to work to alleviate the burden mankind has been carrying as a result of Adam's fall. Hotchkiss eagerly accepts his invitation to help him in the task just as the manuscript ends.

Screamers: A Gathering of Scraps of Humor, Delicious Bits & Short Stories

Pirated collection of Clemens material published in London in 1872 by JOHN CAMDEN HOTTEN. The unauthorized book contains several Clemens items in their first book publication, as well as several sketches attributed to Clemens that he did not write.

1601 ([Date, 1601] Conversation as It Was by the Social Fireside in the Time of the Tudors)

PARODY of Elizabethan manners. In the summer of 1876, Clemens began studying 16th-century English history to prepare for writing *The Prince and the Pauper* (1881). Fascinated by indelicacies in old English speech and court language, he wrote *1601* to experiment with Elizabethan DIALOGUE and to amuse his friend JOSEPH TWICHELL.

In Clemens's 2,300-word manuscript, Queen Elizabeth's cupbearer describes an august company of men and women at court who politely discuss matters such as flatulence, sexual intercourse and masturbation—with neither embarrassment nor any sense of impropriety. Indeed, Clemens was intrigued by how differently people of that time perceived "moral" behavior. While he wrote *1601* for fun, he regarded it as representative of the kind of conversations that actually took place in Elizabeth's time. In addition to helping him prepare for *The Prince and the Pauper*, writing *1601* anticipated several scenes in *Connecticut Yankee* (1889). In that novel, the page-boy Clarence assumes the role of *1601*'s disapproving cupbearer when he hears Merlin bore the court (chapter 3). Later, at Queen Morgan le Fay's banquet, Hank Morgan overhears a conversation risqué enough to make "Elizabeth of England hide behind a handkerchief" (chapter 17).

SYNOPSIS

Queen Elizabeth's cupbearer describes a gathering at court attended by Lord (FRANCIS) BACON, SIR WALTER RALEIGH, BEN JONSON, FRANCIS BEAUMONT, WILLIAM SHAKESPEARE, the Duchess of Bilgewater, the Countess of Granby and her daughter the Lady Helen, the Lady Margery Bothby, and the Lady Alice Dilbeery. As they talk, someone breaks wind, releasing a mighty stink. The queen asks the perpetrator to confess, but each person denies responsibility until Raleigh admits that he did it. Calling the effort unworthy of notice, he promises to do better, then issues forth a more powerful blast with an even worse stench.

Conversation then turns to the sexual customs of different peoples. Raleigh tells about a remote people in America whose men remain virgins until they are 35 (about the same age Clemens was when he married) and women until they are 28. Raleigh's remarks move the queen to tease 15-year-old Lady Helen about preserving her virginity. When Helen confesses that she has already sprouted pubic hair, the queen tries taunting young Beaumont into an indiscretion, then tells of meeting Rabelais when she herself was 15. Raleigh adds a story from Boccaccio.

As conversation turns to religion, Luther is mentioned, then poetry is discussed. Shakespeare elicits praise when he reads from *Henry IV* and "Venus and Adonis," but the cupbearer remains unimpressed. After Raleigh begins breaking wind again, conversation shifts to how clever Nicholas Throgmorton had been during Queen Mary's reign to save himself from condemnation; the queen recalls, however, that he could not save his daughter from being debauched. Her remark makes the cupbearer reflect on the debaucheries of the entire company. Conversation shifts to Rubens and CERVANTES and concludes with Raleigh telling a story about a lecherous old archbishop.

BACKGROUND AND PUBLISHING HISTORY

While Clemens wrote *1601* for his own and Twichell's amusement, he later claimed to have anonymously submitted it to a magazine whose editor had wished for a modern-day Rabelais—only to have it rudely rejected. The experience may have been on his mind when he later wrote *A Tramp Abroad* (1880), which asks why writers are not allowed the same license to express indecencies that artists are (chapter 50).

Clemens gave the manuscript to Twichell, who circulated it privately for several years. When JOHN HAY got hold of it in July 1880, he had four unbound copies printed in CLEVELAND. Pressed by requests for more copies, Clemens took the manuscript to Lt. Charles Erskine Scott Wood (1852–1944) at WEST POINT in April 1882 and had him print 50 more copies. With Clemens's approval, Wood altered spellings to reflect late-16th-century forms, set the text in old-fashioned type, and printed it on artificially aged linen to give it an authentic appearance. Since then, dozens of editions of *1601* have been printed. In the absence of an authoritative text, punctuation and spellings have varied greatly, as has the sketch's title.

The 1996 OXFORD MARK TWAIN edition includes a volume with facsimile reprints of the West Point edition of *1601* and the first edition of *IS SHAKESPEARE DEAD?* The volume contains an introduction by novelist Erica Jong and an afterword by Leslie Fiedler.

DAVID GRAY also admired *1601* so much that he encouraged Clemens to publish it openly. He thought that it would be remembered longer than *Innocents Abroad*; however, Clemens never publicly acknowledged his authorship of *1601*.

CHARACTERS AND RELATED ENTRIES

cupbearer, queen's Narrator of *1601*, which Clemens wrote in 1876. As the noble holder of a hereditary post, the cupbearer is in attendance at Queen Elizabeth I's court. There he overhears a conversation among nobles and commoners that shocks him; however, he is so bored by the proceedings that he has trouble staying awake.

Clemens created this character from his research for *The Prince and the Pauper* (1881), in which a cupbearer is among the "silk-and-velvet discomforters" who beset Tom Canty (chapters 6–7). Years after writing *1601*, Clemens alluded to its narrator as a "stupid old nobleman."

Raleigh, Sir Walter (c. 1552, Devon, England–October 29, 1618, London) Historical English explorer and character in *1601*. A favorite of Queen ELIZABETH I, Raleigh explored the Americas during her reign and was later beheaded by King James I for insubordination. In *1601*, Raleigh is the expert gas-passer whom the cupbearer describes as a bloody swashbuckler and—particularly aptly—a

"damned windmill." The cupbearer also alludes to Raleigh as the queen's former lover and quotes Raleigh's description of a place in the "uttermost reaches of America" where people are celibate until age 35 (nearly the same age at which Clemens himself married).

"IS SHAKESPEARE DEAD?" and "A MAJESTIC LITERARY FOSSIL" also mention Raleigh.

Sketches, New and Old, Mark Twain's (1875)

Collection of SKETCHES and SHORT STORIES originally issued as a SUBSCRIPTION BOOK by the AMERICAN PUBLISHING COMPANY. Clemens began assembling material for this volume in early 1871 but set the project aside until after several pirated

True Williams's frontispiece to *Mark Twain's Sketches, New and Old* brings together the book's many diverse characters.

collections of his sketches had been published. The first edition's cover was stamped "Sketches Old and New"; however, the title page reads "Mark Twain's Sketches, New and Old." Since Clemens's pen name appears in the title, the book is usually listed simply as *Sketches, New and Old*.

Most of the book's 63 selections are brief, averaging less than 1,500 words. Of 56 previously published items, about 10 come from Clemens's early western journalism; these include "CURING A COLD," "AURELIA'S UNFORTUNATE YOUNG MAN," and "THE KILLING OF JULIUS CAESAR 'LOCALIZED.'" The book also reprints the JUMPING FROG STORY, adding a French translation from a French magazine and Clemens's excruciatingly literal English retranslation. Several items from New York newspapers include "THE FACTS CONCERNING THE RECENT RESIGNATION" and "A CURIOUS PLEASURE EXCURSION."

About a third of the selections come from the GALAXY. These include "MY LATE SENATORIAL SECRETARYSHIP," "HOW I EDITED AN AGRICULTURAL PAPER ONCE," and "POLITICAL ECONOMY." Fifteen items from the BUFFALO EXPRESS include "JOURNALISM IN TENNESSEE," "THE CAPITOLINE VENUS," "A MEDIEVAL ROMANCE," "A GHOST STORY," and "A CURIOUS DREAM." Other important selections include "CANNIBALISM IN THE CARS," "A TRUE STORY," and "Experience of the McWILLIAMSES with Membranous Croup."

Later editions of *Sketches, New and Old* published by HARPER AND BROTHERS have substantially different contents. Moreover, some sketches that appear in both publishers' editions have different titles. In 1996, a facsimile reprint of the original book was published as part of the OXFORD MARK TWAIN. That edition contains a new introduction by author Lee Smith and an afterword by Sherwood Cummings, the author of *Mark Twain and Science* (1988).

True Williams drew 130 illustrations for the book. When he illustrated *Tom Sawyer* a year later, he used similar designs for chapter openings and adapted several characters from the earlier book. His drawings of Tom—especially his frontispiece for *Tom Sawyer*—are almost identical to the character that he drew for "THE STORY OF THE BAD LITTLE BOY" in *Sketches*. He adapted his picture of Huck Finn for chapter 35 of *Tom Sawyer* from an illustration that he drew for "THE STORY OF THE GOOD LITTLE BOY" in *Sketches*.

"Sociable Jimmy"

SKETCH published in the *New York Times* on November 29, 1874. On the last day of December in 1871, Clemens was resting in a hotel in Paris, Illinois during a lecture tour, when he met the "most artless, sociable and exhaustless talker" he ever encountered. "Jimmy," a black 10-year-old hotel employee, told him about his family, his fellow employees, and the town; nothing he said was remarkable or memorable, but his irresistible enthusiasm moved Clemens to record his entire conversation and publish it three years later as "Sociable Jimmy." As one of Clemens's first published works dominated by a child's voice, the article anticipated the narrative voice he was to give Huckleberry Finn a few years later. A similarly loquacious character appears in chapter 27 of *A Tramp Abroad* (1880).

In 1943, the *TWAINIAN* reprinted "Sociable Jimmy" with little comment and without knowing its original source; Paul Fatout also reprinted it in *Mark Twain Speaks for Himself* in 1978. The sketch's importance was not recognized until years later, however. In mid-1992, it received national attention when the *New York Times* published a front-page story about Shelley Fisher Fishkin's then-forthcoming book, *Was Huck Black?* Fishkin puts "Sociable Jimmy" at the center of her thesis that African-American voices played a powerful role in Clemens's art, particularly in his creation of Huck Finn's speech patterns. The challenging assertion that Huck himself owed his voice to an AFRICAN AMERICAN started a new national debate among scholars about *Huckleberry Finn* (1884).

"Some National Stupidities"

ESSAY written around 1891–92 and first published in EUROPE AND ELSEWHERE (1923). Clemens puzzles over the nearly universal failure of nations to borrow superior ideas from other countries. America, for example, has failed to adopt the wonderful German stove. Conversely, European nations have failed to adopt such superior American ideas as the typewriter, the fountain pen, fair-dealing in shops, improved railroad methods, and especially the improved elevator—which will make possible the vertical development of cities. When America does borrow European ideas, such as gas lighting and the railroad, it generally improves on them. Europe does just the opposite. Where Americans tend to develop borrowed ideas *forward,* Europe develops American ideas *backward.* Its history of doing this goes back 300 years, when the Spanish failed to adopt precolonial Peru's excellent postal system.

"Some Rambling Notes of an Idle Excursion"

SKETCH about a trip to BERMUDA that Clemens and JOSEPH TWICHELL made in 1877. On May 16, 1877, they took an overnight boat from New Haven, Connecticut, to New York City, from which they sailed aboard the steamship *Bermuda* the next day. They spent three days at sea sailing in each direction, and four days loafing on Bermuda, mainly around Hamilton. Twichell is the former Civil War chaplain to whom Clemens alludes as "the Reverend" throughout the sketch.

The approximately 15,000-word sketch is aptly named. Much of it is simply random gossip and overheard conversations, such as that of two brothers discussing cemetery plots on the overnight boat. Aboard the *Bermuda* many of the anecdotes revolve around a dreary young passenger, known simply as "the Ass," who spoils every conversation with a dull question or remark. One of the best-known parts of this segment is a long anecdote about Captain Hurricane Jones—in actuality a caricature of CAPTAIN EDGAR WAKEMAN, who had nothing to do with this journey. Clemens works in the anecdote on the premise that "Jones" was a subject of gossip aboard the ship. Another anecdote, apparently taken from Twichell's Civil War

experiences, concerns two dying soldiers competing for a pine coffin.

Once the travelers reach Bermuda, Clemens raves about the island's peace and quiet, cleanliness, general prosperity, and beauty. At a moment when his opinion of ENGLAND and the British Empire was at a peak, he praises British rule in Bermuda. He also admires the scarcity of dogs, while remaining unsure about the abundance of cats. He tells several cat anecdotes, has a great deal to say about onions in Bermuda, and curses the day that the telegraph will reach Bermuda and spoil its tranquility.

Also known as "Random Notes of an Idle Excursion," the sketch first appeared in the ATLANTIC MONTHLY from October 1877 through January 1878 and was first collected in book form in PUNCH, BROTHERS, PUNCH! (1878). In 1882, it appeared in THE STOLEN WHITE ELEPHANT with "THE INVALID'S STORY" tacked on as an extension. This latter story was separated in later collections.

CHARACTERS AND RELATED ENTRIES

Jones, Captain Hurricane   Name given to a caricature of Captain Edgar WAKEMAN in "Some Rambling Notes of an Idle Excursion," Clemens's account of a 1877 trip to Bermuda with JOSEPH TWICHELL. Aside from the fact that Twichell had struck up a chance acquaintance with Wakeman three years earlier, "Jones" has nothing to do with the rest of the travel account. Clemens justifies his inclusion in the sketch by suggesting that he was the object of gossip on the Bermuda cruise.

Clemens's description of Jones resembles that of Captain Eli Stormfield, whom he called "Hurricane Jones" in an early draft of "CAPTAIN STORMFIELD'S VISIT TO HEAVEN." Like Stormfield, Jones is a sea captain, a formidable swearer and a "profound biblical scholar—that is, he thought he was." A long anecdote that follows is largely an account of Wakeman's efforts to convert Twichell, here called Reverend Mr. Peters, to his views on Old Testament miracles in 1874. Several pages are given over to Jones's explanation of Isaac's struggle against the prophets of Baal. The anecdote ends with Jones remarking that "there ain't a thing in the Bible but what is true; all you want is to go prayerfully to work and cipher out how 'twas done." A character similar to Jones reappears in *The American Claimant* (1892) as Captain Salt-marsh, a hard-swearing Bible-misquoter who has become a painter.

"Some Thoughts on the Science of Onanism"

Speech delivered at Paris's STOMACH CLUB in spring 1879. As a risqué text, "Onanism" ranks with Clemens's *1601*. Clemens uses the speech to warn the private club's artists and writers against a form of self-abuse to which he perceives they are addicted, namely, masturbation. He builds his case with invented quotations from ancient and modern writers who have struggled with this problem, such as Homer, whose *Iliad* says "Give me masturbation or give me death." In his *Commentaries*, CAESAR admits to "times when I prefer it to sodomy." (DEFOE'S) Robinson Crusoe "cannot describe what I owe to this gentle art," and Queen ELIZABETH regarded it as "the bulwark of virginity." In men-tioning Michelangelo as a representative of the old masters, he points out that "old masters" itself is an abbreviation. He also mentions BENJAMIN FRANKLIN, SOLOMON, Galen, (Adam?) Smith, and CHARLES DARWIN.

To assist his audience, he points out signs of excessive indulgence: a disposition to eat, drink, smoke, meet together convivially, laugh, joke, and tell indelicate stories and, especially, a yearning to paint pictures. "Of all the various kinds of sexual intercourse," he concludes, "this has the least to recommend it. As an amusement, it is too fleeting; as an occupation, it is too wearing; as a public exhi-bition, there is no money in it." Cultured society has, unfortunately, banished it and degraded it to "brotherhood with flatulence."

Clemens kept his manuscript of the speech, and 50 copies of it were privately printed as a pamphlet in 1942. It has since been published in *Playboy* and in modern collections of his speeches.

"The Stolen White Elephant"

SHORT STORY written in 1878. A BURLESQUE of DETECTIVE fiction, "The Stolen White Elephant" is a FRAME-STORY narrated by an unnamed "chance railway acquaintance," an unmistakably honest man over 70 years old who once was in INDIA's civil service. Five years earlier, when Britain and SIAM resolved a frontier dispute, Siam's king wanted to atone for being in the wrong by giving the queen of England (presumably Queen VICTORIA, who is not named) a sacred white elephant.

Deputed to convey the elephant to England aboard a special ship, the narrator stops at Jersey City, near New York City, to rest the animal. When the animal is reported stolen two weeks later, he immediately enlists the help of the chief of New York's detective force, Inspector Blunt. Blunt begins by taking a full deposition on the missing animal, whose name is Jumbo, and has his assistant, Alaric, distribute 50,000 copies to every detective and pawnbroker on the continent. He suggests that the narrator offer a $25,000 reward and assigns all his best detectives to the case: five men to shadow the elephant, six to shadow the thieves and 30 to guard the site of the crime. Additional plainclothes detectives are assigned to every transportation depot in Jersey City, while others cover railway sta-tions and telegraph offices between Jersey City and Canada, Ohio, and Washington, D.C. Stressing that everything be done with the utmost secrecy, Blunt confidently predicts that the elephant will be found, filling the narrator with admiration. The next morning, however, newspapers report every detail of Blunt's plans, posing 11 different theories about the crime and naming 37 suspects, including Blunt's two principal suspects. Questioned about the secrecy he promised, Blunt explains that pub-licity is the detective's bread and butter.

Over the next few days, the narrator gives Blunt more money for expenses as they await news. One night, messages begin pouring out of the telegraph from detectives all over the East, reporting on havoc caused by the elephant in separate (and mostly fictitious) towns. One telegram relays an offer from P. T. BARNUM to buy advertising space on the elephant; another reports that people fired small cannon balls at the elephant after it killed mourners at a funeral. The telegrams stop coming when a dense fog sets in. The next morning's papers sum up the gory details: 60 persons dead and 240 injured. The elephant is evidently hiding in the fog. The publicity pleases Blunt.

Several days pass without news, so Blunt recommends doubling the reward. After two weeks pass, the narrator raises the reward to $75,000. The newspapers are turning against the detectives, but Blunt is unperturbed. After three weeks pass, Blunt proposes compromising with the thieves by offering $100,000—half of which customarily goes to the detectives. He relays the offer through the wives of his two prime suspects, only to be told that both suspects have long been dead. He next publishes an encrypted message to lure the thief to a rendezvous. The following night, the narrator brings the $100,000 reward. When Blunt goes into the vast basement of his headquarters where his detectives sleep, he trips over something in the dim light—the dead body of the missing elephant! Now the hero of the hour, Blunt gleefully distributes the reward money among his detectives, pocketing a share for himself. The narrator must be restored with carbolic acid. His priceless charge is dead, his reputation is ruined and he is personally out $142,000. Nevertheless, his admiration for Blunt is undimmed.

BACKGROUND AND PUBLISHING HISTORY

Clemens wrote this 4,420-word story while staying in BERLIN in late November or December 1878. His purpose was to burlesque a well-publicized investigation then under way in New York City, where the wealthy merchant Alexander Turney Stewart's body was stolen from its tomb. The story parallels the Stewart investigation in many lurid details. It also draws on ideas about "sacred white elephants" that Clemens had when he wrote about a character named Eckert in chapter 7 of *Roughing It* (1872). He originally intended this new story for *A Tramp Abroad* (1880), but instead made it the title story of *The Stolen White Elephant, Etc.*, a collection published by JAMES R. OSGOOD. The book appeared in June 1882—a few months after P. T.

Barnum achieved tremendous publicity by importing a real elephant named "JUMBO" from England. The book combines the title story with all the items that had appeared in *Punch, Brothers, Punch!* (1878), as well as several other sketches, including two on the "MCWILLIAMSES." Most of its contents were later incorporated into *Tom Sawyer Abroad; Tom Sawyer, Detective and Other Stories* (1896) in standard editions.

The 1996 OXFORD MARK TWAIN edition includes a volume titled *The Stolen White Elephant and Other Detective Stories* with an introduction by mystery novelist Walter Mosley and an afterword by Lillian Robinson, a literary scholar who has also written mystery fiction. The Oxford volume also includes facsimile reprints of the first American editions of *Tom Sawyer, Detective* and *A Double-Barrelled Detective Story.*

CHARACTERS AND RELATED ENTRIES

Alaric   Minor character in "The Stolen White Elephant." Alaric is the youthful clerical assistant of Inspector Blunt. The name may come from the Visigoth king Alaric I, who sacked Rome in 410 C.E.

Blunt, Inspector   Character in "The Stolen White Elephant." The chief of New York City's detective force, Blunt supervises an elaborate search for the missing Jumbo. Like most of Clemens's fictional DETECTIVES, Blunt misinterprets evidence to support his own theories. He guilelessly accepts reports of elephant sightings from a preposterously large region—even *after* the elephant is found. He believes that publicity and having a "theory" are the keys to a detective's success. After persuading the narrator to offer ever-larger cash rewards, he finds the elephant himself when he trips over it in the basement of his headquarters, where it has lain dead for three weeks. Never shaken, even when the newspapers turn against him, Blunt proclaims his discovery a vindication of his methods and cheerfully divides the narrator's reward money among his army of detectives.

Jumbo (Hassan Ben Ali Ben Selim Abdallah Mohammed Moisé Alhammal Jamsetjejeebhoy Dhuleep Sultan Ebu Bhudpooris)   Name of the missing animal in "The Stolen White Elephant" (1882). Jumbo is a sacred "royal white elephant" that the narrator is conveying to England as a gift from the king of SIAM. During a layover at Jersey City, Jumbo disappears and is believed stolen. Several weeks later, Inspector Blunt finds Jumbo dead from cannon-shot wounds he received during his escape.

The narrator's formal deposition describes Jumbo as dull white, 19 feet tall, 26 feet long from forehead to rump, with tusks over nine feet long. At the time of his disappearance, he is wearing a castle with seats for 15 persons. Jumbo likes squirting people with his trunk and will eat *anything;* he is capable of downing five men or 500 Bibles in one meal. The night he escapes, he reportedly kills 60 persons and injures 240 others.

With some comic exaggeration, the fictional Jumbo's description matches that of a real "Jumbo," an African elephant that was a major London zoo attraction at the same time that Clemens wrote his story. By a remarkable coincidence, P. T. BARNUM brought the real Jumbo to New York in April 1882—just two months before *The Stolen White Ele-*

Caricature of P. T. Barnum with Jumbo by cartoonist Thomas Nast *(A. B. Paine,* Th. Nast, *1904)*

phant, Etc. was published as a book. A long anecdote about Barnum's acquisition of Jumbo appears in chapter 64 of *Following the Equator,* in which Clemens claims to have gotten the story from Barnum himself. Jumbo's removal from England to the United States received great publicity in both countries, and the elephant entertained millions until it was accidentally killed by a train in Ontario, Canada, in September 1885. Meanwhile, Barnum imported a reputedly genuine "white elephant" from Siam in March 1884. Since this animal was mostly gray, it was overshadowed by a truly white elephant exhibited by one of Barnum's rivals—until the latter beast was found to be painted.

In colloquial English, a "white elephant" is an expensive possession of no value to its owner. The expression derives from the alleged practice of Siamese kings who bankrupted their enemies by giving them sacred white elephants, whose upkeep was ruinously expensive. In "The Stolen White Elephant," the king of Siam gives such an elephant to the queen to England to atone for being in the wrong in a frontier dispute. Perhaps the king actually wants to avenge himself against the queen; in any case, his gift has the effect of ruining the queen's civil servant who narrates the story.

"The Story of the Bad Little Boy"

SHORT STORY originally published in the CALIFORNIAN (December 23, 1865) as "The Christmas Fireside for Good Little Boys and Girls." The 1,370-word story explores one of Mark Twain's favorite themes: the difference between Sunday-school morality and real life, in which sin is rarely punished. In contrast to the "bad boys" in Sunday-school literature, the story's title character, Jim, has a tough mother who would rather spank him to sleep than kiss him. Despite the spankings, however, Jim never feels guilt or remorse when he commits such crimes as stealing jam. Everything about him is curious—no matter what he does, he never suffers grief or serious punishment. He is not even drowned when he goes boating on a Sunday. When he grows up, he marries, raises a large family, and brains them all with an ax. He gets wealthy through cheating and rascality. Though the biggest scoundrel in his village, he is universally respected and belongs to the legislature.

The story was first collected in THE CELEBRATED JUMPING FROG OF CALAVERAS COUNTY, AND OTHER SKETCHES and in SKETCHES, NEW AND OLD.

"The Story of the Good Little Boy"

SHORT STORY first published in the GALAXY (May 1870) and reprinted in SKETCHES, NEW AND OLD. This 1,900-word tale deals with one of Clemens's favorite themes: the futility of modeling one's behavior on goody-goody Sunday-school books. The fate of its hero anticipates those of Edward Mills in "EDWARD MILLS AND GEORGE BENTON: A TALE" and Dutchy in Life on the Mississippi (1883).

SYNOPSIS

A good little boy named Jacob Blivens always obeys his parents, is never late to Sabbath school and never plays hookey. Ridiculously honest, his fondest ambition is to be put in a Sunday-school book. Since he realizes that the boys in such books always die, he prepares a moving dying speech and dreams about his sad funeral. Nothing goes right for Jacob, however. Unlike the boys in his books, he never has fun and constantly has bad luck. For example, when he warns Jim Blake against stealing apples because bad boys always fall out of the tree, Blake falls on him. Similar mishaps occur when Jacob assists a blind man and a lame dog, and he nearly drowns while warning bad boys against sailing on Sunday. His final disaster occurs when he tries to help dogs that other boys have tied to nitroglycerin cans. Blown to bits by the nitroglycerin, Jacob never gets to deliver his dying speech.

"Taming the Bicycle"

ESSAY written in 1884. Ever fascinated with machinery, Clemens joined his friend JOSEPH TWICHELL in bicycle-riding lessons in May 1884. His apprenticeship was painful and short-lived; afterward, he wrote this humorous essay describing how he trained in his backyard with an "expert." For eight days, he suffered many minor humiliations and painful falls—especially when mounting his ungainly bicycle with an enormous front wheel. After investing considerable time in polishing the 3,400-word essay, he found it unsatisfactory and set it aside. It was posthumously published in What Is Man? and Other Essays. Meanwhile, Clemens put bicycles in sixth-century England in A Connecticut Yankee in King Arthur's Court (1889). In chapter 38 of that novel, Hank Morgan and King Arthur are rescued from execution by 500 knights in armor who arrive mounted on bicycles.

"That Day in Eden"

Sketch about the Fall, written around 1990 and first published in EUROPE AND ELSEWHERE. One of the ADAMIC DIARIES, this 250-word piece is subtitled "Passage from Satan's Diary." Satan recalls visiting Adam and Eve in the Garden of Eden to help them understand certain moral concepts. However, he fails to explain such ideas as "pain" and "fear," because he cannot experience them. Likewise, he cannot explain "eternal," which Eve cannot experience. After failing to find common ground on "good," "evil," and "morals," Satan explains that the moral sense is something that they should be glad they do not have.

As they talk, Eve eats an apple from the forbidden tree and visibly changes. She suddenly becomes modest. Adam is puzzled until he tastes an apple and undergoes a similar change. He gathers boughs to cover their nakedness and they walk away, "bent with age."

"The $30,000 Bequest"

SHORT STORY published in 1904 about a hard-working young couple who ruin their lives with dreams of vast wealth that they will earn from money that they expect to inherit. Similar in mood and resolution to

"THE MAN THAT CORRUPTED HADLEYBURG" (1899), this story likewise deals with greed, illusory wealth, vindictive practical joking, and empty vanity. Powerful themes from Clemens's own life can be read into the story. The struggle between a practical, provident wife and an irreverent and less responsible husband seems to reflect Clemens's relationship with his own wife. Further, the couple's debilitating expectations from wealth that never materializes recall the Clemens family's expectations of their TENNESSEE LAND. Finally, the story ends with the husband warning against allowing the snare of "vast wealth, acquired by sudden and unwholesome means" to entice one away from the true happiness possible in a sweet and simple life. The statement seems to sum up Clemens's many failed quests for easy riches.

SYNOPSIS

For 14 years, Saladin and Electra Foster have diligently toiled in the pleasant western town of Lakeside. By day, "Sally"—as he is called—plods through his bookkeeping job, while "Aleck" efficiently manages the household and some modestly profitable investments. By night, they read romances to each other and dream of living as royalty. Their romantic bent can be seen in the names they have given their daughters, Gwendolen and Clytemnestra.

One day, Sally receives a stunning letter from his only surviving relative, Tilbury Foster, who lives 500 miles away. Tilbury says that he will shortly die and leave Sally $30,000. To collect this bequest, however, Sally must satisfy Tilbury's executors that he has not discussed the bequest, inquired after Tilbury's condition, or even attended his funeral. Aleck immediately subscribes to a newspaper in Tilbury's town, the *Weekly Sagamore*, and she and Sally vow never to jeopardize the bequest while Tilbury lives.

As Aleck dreams about investing the $30,000, Sally dreams about how to spend it. Sally agrees, however, to hold off all spending until the principal has had a chance to grow from Aleck's investments. Aleck's projections of the rate of financial growth they can expect make Sally's head swim. By the time Aleck goes to bed, she has worked their capital up to a half million dollars in her head. For

more than a week, the Fosters anxiously await their first copy of the *Weekly Sagamore*, only to be crushed when they do not find Tilbury's obituary notice in its pages. Unbeknownst to them, Tilbury died earlier in the week, but thanks to an accident in the *Sagamore*'s print shop, the paper will *never* mention his death.

As weeks and months drag by without news, Aleck's imaginary investments amass a fortune. As more time passes, Aleck works ever harder on her phantom portfolio, while Sally keeps pace with plans for spending the phantom profits. When the couple finally conclude that they are legitimately "rich," they want to celebrate, but are unsure how they can, without giving away their secret. They settle on throwing a party to celebrate the discovery of America. It is a success, but some guests sense that the Fosters are becoming uppity. Afterward, Aleck and Sally begin considering the problem of choosing suitable husbands for their daughters.

After the fantasy fortune hits a million dollars, it takes off at a dizzy rate. Two years later, the Fosters are worth $380 million. When the figure reaches $2,400 million, they pause to take stock. Breaking the Sabbath for the first time, they inventory their wealth and find that they now can realize a steady income of $120 million a year. Aleck at last agrees to retire from "business" and allow Sally to spend freely.

Meanwhile, the mundane facts of real life intrude. Late-night imaginary spending sprees drive Sally to pilfer candles from his employer; these petty thefts lead to others. The Fosters continue to plod through their "restricted fact life," while their dream life settles them into a palace in Newport, RHODE ISLAND. Aleck's philanthropy becomes prodigious: every Sunday she builds new hospitals and universities, while Sally blows millions in gambling and riotous living. The disparity between Sally's dissolute extravagances and Aleck's well-meaning charity drives Sally to confess. Aleck forgives him, but no longer trusts him. Aleck has also been behaving dishonorably, however. She has broken their compact by secretly going back into business. Without consulting Sally, she invests their entire fortune in a purchase of *all* the country's railroads and coal and steel companies on margin, then nervously awaits development.

It is now five years since the Fosters first learned of their bequest. Sally suggests they reconsider the question of their daughters' marriages. After having turned down a dentist and a lawyer, then sons of rich businessmen and politicians, and even members of the aristocracy, he thinks it time to let the girls themselves choose. Aleck then knocks him silly with the news that she is arranging *royal* marriages! For several days, the Fosters walk on air with these happy thoughts and Aleck's new investments start booming. As her imaginary brokers urge her to take her profits and sell, she breaks the good news to Sally. He joins in the chorus to sell, but Aleck insists on holding on a bit longer—a decision that proves fatal. The next day a historic market crash reduces their entire fortune to nothing.

Aleck is devastated, but Sally comes down to earth and reminds her that nothing they have lost was real, and that his uncle's bequest is still coming. At that moment, the *Weekly Sagamore*'s editor arrives to collect on their unpaid subscription. He not only reports that Tilbury has been dead for five years, but that he died a pauper. Aleck and Sally never recover from the shock. Two years later, they both die on the same day.

BACKGROUND AND PUBLISHING HISTORY

Clemens wrote his 12,220-word story during the winter of 1903–4 at an unhappy time in his life. He had moved his family to FLORENCE, Italy, for the sake of his wife's health; her condition did not improve and his work was constantly interrupted by unpleasant distractions. "The $30,000 Bequest" proved to be the longest piece of fiction that he finished and published during the remainder of his life. The story first appeared in HARPER'S WEEKLY on December 10, 1904. In 1906, it was made the title story of a new collection, *The $30,000 Bequest and Other Stories*, which became a volume in HARPER'S uniform sets. Other notable pieces in this collection include "A DOG'S TALE," "Was It Heaven? Or Hell?," EXTRACTS FROM ADAM'S DIARY, and EVE'S DIARY. The contents of later Harper editions with the same title are not identical to those of the first edition. A facsimile reprint of the first edition is part of the 1996 OXFORD MARK TWAIN edition. The Oxford edition has a new introduction by novelist Frederick Busch and an afterword by Judith Yaross Lee.

CRITICAL COMMENTARY

Reversal, particularly in regard to "reversal of fortune or expectations," is the key theme in Clemens's "The $30,000 Bequest," the story of an already moderately successful couple who ruin their lives by building a purely imaginary financial empire out of an empty dream. In this story, reality becomes dream, which becomes reality. A stable, content family receives news that a distant relative intends to curse them, as money has cursed him, with an inheritance, provided they make no mention of it or contact him, including attending his funeral. Swearing never to reveal the bequest, the husband and wife enter a secret life contrary to their surface life but endemic to their characters.

The setting of Lakeside, a town of about 6,000 with churches built for 35,000, implies unrealistic expectations. Rank here is "unknown . . . unconfessed, anyway." In a town with a submerged life, the families belie their exterior. Lakeside's only "high-salaried" bookkeeper, Saladin Foster (Sally) appears prosperous, largely because wife Electra (Aleck) carefully saves—investing in land, gardening, sharecropping—and thereby generates independent income. Controlling the purse, she also carefully spends; they cannot "squander . . . on nonnecessities." Practical in everyday life, both she and her husband are nighttime romantics ("reading romances to each other, dreaming dreams"), which Clemens equates with living in unreality.

Their names reveal more. The narrator notes that their mutual pet names, Aleck and Sally, are "unsexing," revealing their reversed roles—she the aggressive businessperson prudently planning their future, and he the submissive mate eager to shop. With "the plodding world" (reality) outside, Aleck envisions investments for their fortune as Sally imagines ways to spend. Aleck constantly cools Sally's sprees, saying "Don't lose your head." Both, however, forget they have no inheritance, as she accumulates wealth with imaginary investments and he dreams of luxuries, growing increasingly richer mentally. Significantly, their family name "Foster" means "to cling to in one's mind."

The characters' given names are also significant. The historical Saladin successfully led Muslims against Western crusaders; the mythological Electra urged Orestes to kill their mother, Clytemnestra, for murdering their father, Agamemnon, leader of Western forces against Troy. The myth's violence contrasts with the gentle Sally and Aleck and emphasizes underlying turmoil amid contradictory forces.

The two slip deeper into the dreamworld, building a palace, sailing a "dream-yacht," planning a royal marriage, and reversing their former life. She gives more to charities, especially missionaries, but they stop attending church, instead spending Sundays dreaming. Nonetheless, their sympathies become increasingly high-church, Presbyterian to Episcopal to Catholic. This dream life now affects their exterior life.

A reversal of their years-long lifestyle occurs in actuality. Frugal Aleck extinguishes a candle, while Sally tells her to let it burn. Eager for Tilbury Foster's obituary, they ignore a visitor when Tilbury's hometown newspaper arrives. Imaginary bills from imaginary expenses worry Aleck. Realizing their wealth, they conceive excuses for a celebration ("as if they'd come into property," neighbors say), decide daughters' beaus lack proper status, drink imaginary champagne (despite temperance obligations), and place all housework on Aleck to save their daughters for society. Less cautious, daringly investing, Aleck moves closer in financial mind-set to Sally, finally removing all spending restraints. Incurring real expenses, Sally robs his firm, first of candles, then other items. Sally, ashamed, confesses secretly (imaginatively) to gambling, carousing, and drinking. Despite forgiveness, their relationship is forever altered.

Their dream life indistinguishable from reality and their behavior now noticeable, the Fosters encounter ironic reversals. Told to sell, once-cautious Aleck holds; "her imaginary brokers sold her out." More devastating than the market crash is learning Tilbury died penniless four days after notice of the bequest. Entangled in dreams, they let their paper subscription lapse, but accidentally discovering the obituary was mistakenly omitted five years ago, they experience reversed emotions, "grief [that] felt like joy." Unreleased from dream, Sally concludes, "not even the rich are spared." The Fosters cling together until dying the same day. Despite warning others, Sally learns little, regretting Tilbury did not leave more; then, speculation would not tempt them.

Ironically proving the power of money, this illusionary wealth recalls other scenes in Clemens's fiction: the treasure held in trust for—and not seen by—Tom and Huck in *Tom Sawyer;* the narrator and Calvin Higbie in *Roughing It* discovering silver, dreaming of wealth, but failing to do work required to keep their claim; the premise of "THE £1,000,000 BANK-NOTE;" and most vividly, the Edwardses in "THE MAN THAT CORRUPTED HADLEYBURG" agonizing over a bag of BLIND LEAD disks.

Critical Commentary by John H. Davis

CHARACTERS AND RELATED ENTRIES

Foster, Electra (Aleck) Character in "The $30,000 Bequest" (1904). At the beginning of the narrative, Electra has been married to Saladin Foster since she was 19—a period of 14 years. Shrewd and patient with money, she purchased some land after marrying and nurtured her modest investment into a solid, dividend-paying asset. The narrative starts as she and her husband learn that a relative who is about to die will leave them $30,000. She insists on investing the entire capital and not spending any of its proceeds until it grows significantly. As they wait for the bequest to come through, Aleck uses the expected sum to make a series of imaginary investments; over five years, she works her fantasy portfolio to over $2 billion. Only then is she willing to spend the money freely. While Saladin blows imaginary millions on pleasures, Aleck fantasizes about doing good works, such as building hospitals and universities and supporting missionaries. Though generally more sensible than her husband, she finally loses all their imaginary fortune in one reckless gamble. She takes some comfort in the reminder that the *real* bequest is yet to come, but after discovering that it, too, is illusory, she has nothing left to live for.

As the vain but practical wife of a dreamer, Aleck appears to be modeled at least partly on Clemens's sister-in-law, Mollie CLEMENS.

Foster, Gwendolen (Gwen) and Clytemnestra (Clytie) Minor characters in "The $30,000 Bequest" (1904). The comely daughters of Saladin and Electra Foster, Gwendolen is 13 and Clytemnestra 11 at the start of the narrative. Over the next five years, their parents amass an illusory fortune and become obsessed with finding the girls worthy husbands. Toward the end of the narrative, five years later, their mother tells their father that she is arranging for "royal" marriages; in their foolish vanity, they decide to insist on "morganatic" marriages.

"Clytemnestra" seems an odd name for a woman named "Electra" to give her own daughter. In Greek mythology, Clytemnestra is the wife of Agamemnon and mother of Electra; after she murders her husband, Electra and her other children kill her.

Foster, Saladin (Sally) Character in "The $30,000 Bequest" (1904). When the narrative begins, Foster is 35 years old. For 14 years he has been bookkeeping for the principal store in Lakeside, a small town in the Far West. For 10 years, his $800-a-year salary has been one of the town's highest, but he and his wife, Aleck Foster, are not satisfied. Foster is honest, capable, and hardworking, but he fantasizes about spending vast sums on dissolute pleasures. When he thinks he is about to inherit $30,000 from his only living relative, Tilbury Foster, his thoughts go first to how he will spend the money. It is only at his wife's insistence that he agrees to concentrate on protecting the capital. When their illusory fortune evaporates at the end of the story, he finally realizes that his greed has caused him to miss the true happiness that he could have found in a simple life.

Foster, Tilbury Background figure in "The $30,000 Bequest." A 70-year-old, apparently rich bachelor, Foster is the only living relative—an uncle or distant cousin—of Saladin Foster. He lives in a different state, about 500 miles from Saladin's home in the Far West, but has shunned all contact with his relations until the beginning of the narrative, when Saladin unexpectedly receives a letter from him. Stating that he is soon to die, Tilbury denounces money as the bane of his life and promises to bequeath Saladin $30,000. He does this because money has "given him most of his troubles," and he wants it to "continue its malignant work." His bequest contains the condition that Saladin and his wife make no attempt to inquire after him. He dies a few days after sending his letter, but his relations do not learn of his death for five years. When they finally find out he is dead, they also discover that he was so poor that his town paid for his burial. While Tilbury obviously plays his trick to hurt his relatives, he could not know that an accident would keep them from learning of his death for five years.

Lakeside Fictional town in "The $30,000 Bequest." Located somewhere in the "Far West," Lakeside has a population of about 5,000 to 6,000 people and churches representing every Protestant sect.

BIBLIOGRAPHY

Twain, Mark. "The $30,000 Bequest." In *The Best Short Stories of Mark Twain*, edited by Lawrence I. Berkove, 172–197. New York: Modern Library, 2004.

Wilson, James D. *A Reader's Guide to the Short Stories of Mark Twain*. Boston: G. K., Hall, 1987.

"Those Extraordinary Twins"

Original title of the NOVEL that became *The Tragedy of Pudd'nhead Wilson*, as well as the title of an incomplete 10-chapter fragment published simultaneously with *Pudd'nhead Wilson* in 1894. The full title of the AMERICAN PUBLISHING COMPANY's first book edition is *The Tragedy of Pudd'nhead Wilson and the Comedy Those Extraordinary Twins*. The words "the Comedy" were probably intended as a description, not as part of the title. A subhead preceding the first chapter heading is "The Suppressed Farce."

Clemens began writing this story as a grotesque FARCE. Inspired by SIAMESE TWINS from Italy who shared a single torso and a single pair of legs, his original intention was to explore the comic possibilities

The Capello brothers are Siamese twins in "Those Extraordinary Twins."

of brothers with opposing personalities sharing such a body. His original central characters were Angelo and Luigi Capello, a similar set of Siamese twins with separate heads and arms and a common torso and legs. By the time this story neared completion, he found it had shifted from farce to tragedy as new characters intruded. The slave woman Roxana, her son Tom Driscoll and the lawyer David Wilson were taking center stage, turning his "twin-monster" and other characters into irrelevant encumbrances. To solve the problem, Clemens trimmed about 30,000 words from his original 85,000-word manuscript

and—by his own word—"dug out the comedy and left the tragedy." The Capello brothers remained as minor characters, but were recast as ordinary twins in separate bodies. The published version of *Pudd'nhead Wilson* is thus a revised distillation of a more complex story in which the Siamese twins play a major part.

SYNOPSIS

The published version of this story consists of 10 chapters of uneven length totaling 19,800 words—including summaries of several omitted portions, with comments and references to *Pudd'nhead Wilson*. An 11th chapter contains Clemens's comments on the manuscript. The first five chapters make up nearly 70 percent of the total text, with chapter 5 twice the length of any other chapter. In contrast to *Pudd'nhead Wilson*, the published fragment of this story begins in the year 1853.

Chapter 1
The Capello twins write to Patsy Cooper about renting a room in her Dawson's Landing house. She is thrilled by the fact that they are Italians who have traveled the world. Even before they appear, her romantic daughter, Rowena Cooper, becomes infatuated with Angelo Capello. On the following Thursday, the twins arrive near midnight. They present a "stupefying apparition—a double-headed human creature with four arms, one body, and a single pair of legs." Patsy and Rowena are paralyzed into immobility until their stunned slave Nancy drops a tea set. The brothers introduce themselves as "Count Angelo" and "Count Luigi" and retire to their room. Patsy and Rowena discuss the new arrivals and speculate on their personality differences.

As the twins prepare for bed, they bicker. Angelo complains about the tight shoes that Luigi wears, suggesting that only one of them commands the body at once. Angelo also complains about Luigi's smoking. As Angelo tries to sing the hymn "From Greenland's Icy Mountains," Luigi drowns him out with a loud and vulgar song. Before they nod off, Luigi downs a whiskey and Angelo takes a pill to prevent a headache.

Chapter 2
At breakfast the next morning, Rowena raves about how cultured the twins are. After the twins sit

down, Angelo explains that their "natures differ a good deal from each, and our tastes also." The twins bewilder the women by using their arms interchangeably to feed themselves. They explain how they operate, point out various advantages of sharing a body and tell about their family background.

Chapter 3

After breakfast, townspeople crowd into the Coopers' house to see the twins. Judge York Driscoll shows them the town. That night the judge takes the twins to a meeting of his Free-thinkers' Society. Angelo feels slighted by the judge's attentions to his brother and ponders his condition as a Siamese twin.

Chapter 4

At dinner that night, Patsy Cooper entertains the twins and her friend Aunt Betsy Hale. Patsy perceives that Angelo's spirits are low. After she suggests that he retire to bed, Angelo explains that he and his brother alternate control over their body. Some mysterious force gives each of the brothers utter and indisputable command over their body for a week at time; the change occurs exactly at midnight on Saturday, regardless of where they are in the world. Luigi adds to the women's amazement by explaining that although he and Angelo were born at the same time, he is six months older than Angelo, adding, "We are no more twins than you are." He asks the women not to tell others, knowing that this deliberate lie will burden them with wonderful gossip that they cannot pass on.

When the twins rise to greet a visitor in the parlor, Betsy asks about Rowena's relationship with Tom Driscoll, who writes to her from St. Louis. Patsy confides to Betsy that Rowena has become romantically interested in Angelo. Betsy congratulates her. Meanwhile, the Reverend Hotchkiss talks to Angelo about his wish to become a Baptist.

Chapter 5

(A bracketed aside summarizes Angelo and Luigi's argument over religion and other matters, including events described in chapter 11 of *Pudd'nhead Wilson*, concluding with Luigi's kicking Tom Driscoll at the Sons of Liberty meeting.) The text of the chapter proper opens with the town learning the startling news that David Wilson has his law case: He is defending the Capellos against Driscoll's assault and battery charge.

Judge Sim Robinson presides over the ensuing trial, while Robert Allen represents Tom Driscoll. After Harkness, the chairman of the Sons of Liberty, testifies that the Capellos kicked Driscoll, Wilson asks him if he saw *both* Capellos kick Driscoll, or just one. Harkness cannot answer. Wilson proceeds to discredit the other witnesses in order.

Judge Robinson intervenes to insist that the guilty party not go unpunished. When Wilson protests Robinson's unprecedented suggestion to bring separate charges against the Capellos, the judge dismisses his objection. John Buckstone is called to testify about how the twins control their body, but his testimony is inconclusive. Patsy Cooper is called next. She has trouble testifying coherently and insists on speaking familiarly with the judge. Meanwhile, her friend Betsy repeatedly tries to butt in until the judge throws her evidence out.

When the twins testify, they admit that control of their legs passes from one to the other regularly, but do not reveal which brother was in control at the meeting. The judge wants to force them to answer, but even the prosecuting attorney demurs. The baffled jury concludes by asking to be discharged. The judge grumblingly dismisses the defendants and charges court costs to the plaintiff. The twins and Wilson emerge popular heroes.

Chapter 6

(In a summary of action retained in *Pudd'nhead Wilson*, a deputation invites Wilson to run for mayor of Dawson's Landing, which is soon to gain a city charter. Meanwhile, Judge Driscoll challenges Angelo Capello—who Tom believes to be the brother who kicked him—to a duel after Tom declines. Angelo likewise declines, but Luigi accepts in his place.)

The chapter proper begins late Saturday night, at the vacant lot next to Wilson's house where the duel is to take place. Luigi must complete the affair before midnight. Pembroke Howard is the judge's second. Each time shots are exchanged, Angelo faints or lurches, causing Luigi to miss. Angelo himself is wounded several times, as are Wilson and Howard. When the duel is over, Luigi asks for another round, since he has not had a fair chance to shoot. The moment a new round is to begin, midnight strikes. Now in control of the twins' body, Angelo races away.

Chapter 7

Dr. Claypool returns to Aunt Patsy's house, where everyone is attending to the wounded Angelo. The doctor's inscrutable diagnosis throws everyone into despair, and Luigi offers to take a barrel of pills on Angelo's behalf. Angelo insists that he must be baptized that afternoon. His resolution raises him in everyone's opinion.

Chapter 8

The next day, the town divides into pro-Luigi and pro-Angelo parties over the question of who is the greater hero: Luigi, for trying to stand his ground at the duel, or Angelo, for having the courage to follow his conscience. Angelo's determination to be baptized despite his wounds adds to his reputation, and a crowd gathers at the river to see his baptism. Angelo sleeps well that night, but Luigi is kept awake by having to take regular doses of medicine.

Chapter 9

Over the next several days, both twins grow seriously ill. Only when the doctor is summoned out of town do they recover. By Friday, they are back in circulation. The local Democrats nominate Luigi for the new city council, while the Whigs nominate Angelo to run against him. Both twins campaign hard as Wilson runs for mayor unopposed on the Democratic ticket.

As the campaign develops, troubles arise because of the contradictory behavior of the twins. When Luigi controls the legs, he takes Angelo to rum shops, horse races and other disreputable entertainments. When Angelo is in control, he drags Luigi to church meetings and other moralistic gatherings. The night before the election, Angelo is scheduled to head a Teetotalers' Union march and speak at a rally. Luigi drinks enough whiskey beforehand to make Angelo drunk, ensuring that Angelo's great speech is a flop. Getting drunk causes Angelo not only to lose the election, but also Rowena. He protests that he does not drink, but Rowena replies, "You get drunk, and that is worse."

Chapter 10

A week after the election, Angelo's reputation is ruined. Luigi is elected an alderman, but cannot be sworn in since his brother cannot be admitted to the board meetings. The matter is taken to court. Meanwhile, the remaining aldermen are gridlocked. The legal case gets nowhere, and frustrations in town mount. The townspeople solve the problem by hanging Luigi.

CHARACTERS AND RELATED ENTRIES

For information on many of the characters and places that appear in this story, see the Characters and Related Entries section of the *Pudd'nhead Wilson* entry.

Hale, Aunt Betsy Minor character in "Those Extraordinary Twins." A friend of Aunt Patsy Cooper, Betsy has dinner with her and the Capello twins in chapter 4. In the next chapter's trial scene, she accompanies Patsy and interrupts repeatedly during the latter's testimony as a witness. Aunt Betsy is not mentioned in *Pudd'nhead Wilson* (1894), but "the Hales" are named in chapter 13 among the families whose homes are robbed.

Chapters 8 and 17 of *Life on the Mississippi* (1883) mention a spot on the river called Hale's Point.

Hotchkiss, Reverend Minor character in "Those Extraordinary Twins." A Dawson's Landing minister, Hotchkiss appears briefly in chapter 4, to discuss Angelo Capello's becoming a Baptist. A Reverend Hotchkiss is also the father of Rachel "Hellfire" Hotchkiss.

"Three Thousand Years Among the Microbes"

Unfinished SCIENCE-FICTION novel written in 1905 and published posthumously. Composed around the same time that Clemens wrote *EVE'S DIARY*, "Three Thousand Years Among the Microbes" employs the same device as that story by presenting itself as a document "translated by Mark Twain." In this case, the translation is "from the original Microbic," the language spoken by microbes living in the body of a dissipated human being named Blitzowski.

"Three Thousand Years Among the Microbes" falls within a succession of unfinished works about dream states that Clemens wrote during the late 1890s and early years of the 20th century. Clemens's literary executor, Albert Bigelow PAINE, called the story a "sort of scientific, socialistic, mathematical jamboree." Almost too plotless and chaotic to be called a story, it dredges up people, characters, episodes, and motifs from Clemens's life and writings and reads like a medley of loosely connected dreamlike reminiscences. Among the many themes on which its narrator touches are humankind's place in the universe and relationship to its maker, what it means to be human, the effect of celebrity on a person, the persistence of memory, the delusions of CHRISTIAN SCIENCE, the hypocrisies of democratic societies, the failings of medical science, and the attractiveness of novelty.

A fantastic voyage into a microscopic world, "Three Thousand Years Among the Microbes" is similar in concept to "THE GREAT DARK" (1898), another dream story whose characters are reduced to microscopic size. The narrator of "Three Thousand Years Among the Microbes" is a CHOLERA germ named Bkshp, or Huck, a former human being who was accidentally transformed into a microbe by a magician. Throughout his rambling narrative, Bkshp struggles to understand what he is and what he may be becoming. He frequently dwells on his changing mental condition and laments the increasing difficulty he has remembering things from his human existence and doing the math necessary to convert human and microbic time scales. One year of microbic time is equivalent to about 10 minutes of human time, so the 3,000 microbic years of the story's title are equivalent to about three human weeks.

Despite its flimsy structure, the story contains many elements that are characteristic of many of Clemens's earlier and better-structured narratives. These include passages of vernacular dialogue; skeptical audience reactions to what appear to be outrageous exaggeration; card-game metaphors; and puns and other forms of wordplay, especially with the names of characters. For example, the name Bkshp is an abbreviation of the surname of Clemens's childhood friend TOM BLANKENSHIP, on whom Clemens modeled the fictional Huckleberry Finn, and Bkshp also goes by the nickname Huck. Elsewhere, the narrator substitutes BENJAMIN FRANKLIN for Bblbgxw, a yellow-fever germ whom he meets; explains that "Wzprgfski" is pronounced "Tolliver"; and offers the helpful suggestion that "Ggggmmmdw" is pronounced like the Welsh "Llhwbgww." In chapter 10, Bkshp reveals that ordinary microbes do not have vowels in their names, as only those with aristocratic blood are entitled to vowels.

SYNOPSIS

Paine's biography of Clemens cites a letter that the latter wrote to JOSEPH TWICHELL in July 1905, reporting he had written 100,000 words of "Microbes." The version first published in 1966 contains only about 48,200 words but includes editorial notes indicating that some parts of the original manuscript were omitted. The story is divided into 22 numbered chapters of vastly unequal lengths and includes two chapter sequences numbered 11–14 (Clemens used roman numerals). The published edition uses Clemens's original chapter numbers, adding an *a* to each number in the second 11–14 sequence.

A sprawling first-person narrative with neither a clear plot nor a clear sense of time movement, the story relates Bkshp's experiences during his first 3,000 microbic years (three human weeks) of living as a cholera germ in the body of a human being and includes occasional notes that the narrator added up to 7,000 microbic years later. Much of the narrative reads like background material to a story that never quite gets started, and the manuscript ends rather abruptly. Clemens appears to have made no attempt to polish his manuscript, so it contains inconsistencies in spellings, capitalization, and character names.

Preface

In two separate prefaces, the translator states that he believes the story to be an essentially true history and offers a brief explanation of his method, pointing out that the narrator's style is "loose and wandering and garrulous" and that his grammar is heartbreaking.

Chapter 1

The narrator (whose name is not revealed until chapter 5) explains that he was accidentally transformed into a cholera germ by a magician who was trying to turn him into a bird. He was initially displeased with his transformation but soon adjusts and becomes an enthusiastic and real cholera germ.

Chapter 2

The narrator explains that he lives within the body of the aging, dissipated tramp named Blitzowski, who constitutes the entire world of the microbes, who are as proud of it as human earthlings are of their world.

Chapter 3

A single paragraph explains that the narrator's transformation from human to microbe was easy because humans and germs are not widely different. For example, they have many nationalities and languages.

Chapter 4

While expanding on comparisons between the human and microbe worlds, the narrator points out that rivers in the latter world dwarf the Mississippi and Amazon. Indeed, almost everything about the microbe world is vast and awe-inspiring. Moreover, Blitzowski contains more than a thousand independent republics and at least 30,000 monarchies. The histories of some of the latter span as much as 4.5 million microbic years. The Pus family dynasty has held the throne in one monarchy continuously for 25,000 years. All its monarchs use the same name, Henry, and the dynasty's longevity has caused people to equate pus with civilization.

In a footnote added 5,000 years later, the narrator explains that the microbic name for a microbe is *sooflasky*—a word meaning essentially the same thing as "man" in human languages. While offering this explanation, the narrator opens a discussion of the Moral Sense that leads up to its paradox: the fact that by creating the concept of wrong, the Moral Sense enables people to do wrong.

An attractive aspects of the microbe world is its tolerance of foreigners, such as the narrator himself. Microbes do look down on foreigners but treat them courteously. A notable exception is Blitzowski's greatest republic, Getrichquick, where third-rate foreign celebrities outrank first-rate natives. Getrichquick occupies the whole of Blitzowski's fertile stomach and conducts a prodigious export and import trade.

The narrator explains that he won great celebrity for himself through his paleontological expertise, which gave him entry into scientific society. Eventually, he ceased to regret no longer being human and reveled in his celebrity and the satisfaction he got from being among friends and colleagues. Everything about his life became pleasant.

Chapter 5

Returning to the subject of time, the narrator offers more details on microbe and human time. He recalls a conversation he once had with a scientist named Bblbgxw (whom he calls Benjamin Franklin) who spoke the thyroid-diphthyritic language badly, and he mentions his own facility for learning languages. During that conversation, the narrator's own name, Bkshp, is revealed for the first time. Meanwhile, he and Franklin discuss the nature of the soul and what it means to be an individual.

Chapter 6

Bkshp and Franklin's conversations veer onto the subject of celebrity and the penalty for being illustrious. They also discuss the capricious nature of memory, and Bkshp recalls a recent conversation with the historian Wzprgfski (Tolliver), who suddenly could not remember the names of historical figures. Bkshp also mentions Franklin's and Tolliver's divergent beliefs on eternity. Tolliver believes that all atoms will go on forever but that the only world they will ever know is the planet Blitzowski, which is eternal and indestructible. Bkshp knows better and figures that the D.T.'s [delerium tremens] will eventually fetch Blitzowski. Blitzowski is 85 years old, and Bkshp hopes he will live another 10 years, that is, 500,000 microbic years.

Chapter 7

After Franklin leaves, Bkshp steps out on his balcony to receive the acclaim of the multitude waiting to glimpse him. He feels some embarrassment for finding gratification in his celebrity and admits that he has played at being modest about his fame.

Chapter 8

Bkshp explains that he won celebrity after arriving in Blitzowski by hiring a hand-organ and a monkey and singing in English—a tongue that germs find strange and fascinating. To add to his reputation, he claimed to be a native of the far-off and little-known realm of Major Molar, a tooth he knew was at the dentist's. Meanwhile, he was growing fond of the children in the Taylor family, with whom he was living. He was especially fond of Maggie Taylor, at whose wedding he sang. He also dreamed of a human Maggie, but those dreams confused him, making him wonder if he would become human again. He could not remember exactly how old the human Maggie was and was also having trouble remembering the most important facts in human history.

Chapter 9

Bkshp regards Taylor family weddings as a landmark in his career because it was at one of them that he met a music teacher, whom he calls Thompson, who introduced him to other educated people.

Chapter 10

After reaching the microbe age of 78, Bkshp finds that he does not appear to age, in contrast to his 11 closest friends. All of them still feel like boys, but his friends want to know why he does not age. He decides he must reveal his human origins to his friends if he is to remain in favor. He resolves first to tell a few friends the truth and then get their help to win back the confidence of the others.

Before continuing with that part of his narrative, Bkshp discourses on the difficulties of pronouncing microbe names and says that he invented a name for himself that would befit a native of far-off Major Molar. When his friends give up on trying to pronounce that name, he offers his nickname, "Huck," an abbreviation of his middle name, Huxley. To show their gratitude, his friends allow him to change their names. Eventually, he and his friends settle on literary names: Lemuel Gulliver, Lurbrulgrud, Rip Van Winkle, Guy Mannering, Dogberry, Sancho

Panza, David Copperfield, Colonel Mulberry Sellers, Louis XIV, King Herod, Huck [Clemens's manuscript inserts "Huck" in place of "Mark Twain," which is struck out], and Don Quixote.

Bkshp has Gulliver and Louis XIV join him in smoking and drinking before a comforting fire so he can explain his true background. After discovering that they suspect him of inventing an elixir of youth, he says that he does not know the secret of his persistent youth himself. When they look at him reproachfully, he adds that he was not always a cholera germ.

Chapter 11

Bkshp's claim stuns his friends. In the dialogue that follows, he tries to explain that he was an "American," a "man," a creature that inhabits another planet. He explains that he is not talking about Major Molar, which he admits he has never even visited, and says that he merely invented the name that he has been using. His real name is "B. b. Bkshp." He explains that he has told all his lies because no one would have believed the truth, that he is from another planet. Gulliver counters that there are no other planets and suggests that Bkshp discard all his "dream-stuff." When Louis asks if the other planet is as big as Blitzowski, Bkshp stifles a laugh, but when he tries to explain how big that planet is, they both lose their composure. He then tries to explain the planet's size graphically but succeeds only in making Gulliver think he is relating a dream and convincing Louis that he is a great poet. Both friends think that Bkshp has exhausted his imagination, but he says that he has not even begun.

Chapter 12

Bkshp describes his human world as round and covered mostly with oceans. When Gulliver and Louis ask what keeps the oceans from spilling off, he tries to explain interplanetary gravitational forces and elicits further ridicule—especially when he adds that there are *millions* of other worlds. Every detail he adds brings on so much scorn that he finds himself unexpectedly defending his former world. Finally, he tells his friends that they may take or leave the truths that he has told them. Both marvel at the sheer magnitude of his imagination.

Chapter 13

At two in the morning, Bkshp's friends reluctantly leave. Each expresses his admiration of Bkshp's story-telling skill. Louis says it was inspiring to listen to such a poem, and Gulliver vows that he will never again tell the truth. Bkshp is happily confident that his friends will repeat his story to others and thereby help return him to favor.

Bkshp is now concerned about finishing the History of the World he is dictating to his thought-recorder girl before his memory fades to nothing. The girl, whose original name was Kitty Daisybird Timpleton, began calling herself Catherine of Aragon while working with Bkshp on the history of England. That was some time ago. Now Bkshp notices that Catherine has changed and asks her why. She explains that she has read "Science and Wealth, With Key to the Fixtures." This Giddyite religion text does something that changes her flesh to spirit. Bkshp is sure that Catherine is the victim of an illusion but patiently listens as she explains that substance, pain, hunger, and thirst are all fictions of the Mortal Mind. When he asks her to summarize Giddyite principles, she replies with a string of incomprehensible phrases. This conversation pleases Bkshp, as it shows that human and microbe minds are essentially alike in having reasoning powers that place them above other animals. Bkshp next looks into the microbe attitude toward lower animals.

Chapter 14

Bkshp recalls a discourse he once had with a good and wise human clergyman on the question of what constitutes a "creature," and that subject leads to the conclusion that all God's creatures, even the littlest and humblest, are equal in his eyes. Bkshp recalls being troubled by that last point and asking about disease germs and other microbes, only to have the clergyman change the subject. This thought leads Bkshp to ask Catherine about microbe beliefs on this subject. Her explanation befuddles him, but none of his efforts to draw her out lead to their finding any common basis of understanding.

Catherine suddenly springs to the window and calls out to her aristocratic friend, the countess, to ask the Reverend Brother Pjorsky to come inside. Catherine's former spiritual adviser, Pjorsky, comes

from a remote microbe tribe that breeds African sleeping sickness. On realizing that, Bkshp reflects on the irony that not a single microbe in Blitzowski suspects that it is harmful, despite the fact that all of them feed on their host. He also reflects on the cruelty of human beings to microbes.

Catherine tells Bkshp that she once belonged to Pjorsky's Magnanimite sect, of which the countess is an orthodox member. The countess is also a foreigner, a GRQ (Getrichquick) and an SBE (Soiled-Bread Eater)—facts that lead to a new discussion on subjects such as the dignity of labor, the value of earning one's own bread, and the meaning of "morganatic."

Chapter 11a

Catherine prattles on, often jumping from one subject to another, and is especially voluble on the countess's views on the hypocrisies of Getrichquick's egalitarian democracy. The reality is that Getrichquick has more ranks, grades, and castes than any other place. Catherine finally stops when Brother Pjorsky (whom Bkshp dubs a duke) comes to the door. Pjorsky is eating a juicy young SBE whom he has captured and gives Bkshp one of its legs. Catherine is also hungry but does not participate in the meal because she is an SBE, and SBE's do not eat one another.

Pjorsky is pleased to learn that Bkshp shares his views on the rights of the lower animals, even the invisible, deadly microbes that feed on their bodies. He senses that Bkshp is a student of science but surprises him by saying that he has neglected the science of bacteriology. Bkshp sees himself as a past master of his former world's bacteriology but confesses that he knows nothing about the microscopic microbes that infest the microbes of Blitzowski.

Chapter 12a

Pjorsky lectures Bkshp on Blitzowski bacteriology. He explains that the common scientific term for a microbe is *swink* [a Middle English word for slave], outlines the complex interconnections among the planet's species, and tells Bkshp about "his sublime Majesty the Swink, Lord Protector of the Lord of Creation, Redeemer of his Planet, Preserver of all Life," who represents the combination of 100 million swinks.

Chapter 13a

Bkshp finds solace in Pjorsky's words about the great swink and reflects on similarities between human and microbe societies, particularly the many useful contributions of swinks.

Chapter 14a

Bkshp is charmed with Pjorsky's lecture, as its wonders are all new and astonishing to him. He is particularly impressed to learn that the microbes that infest humans are duplicated by even smaller microbes that infest them. He reflects on the many beneficial contributions that microbes have made to the Earth, such as making its soil useful. Eager to see the tiny microbes that infest microbes, he puts a drop of his own blood under a microscope and marvels at the tiny, well-organized world that he sees. As he watches a tiny army march by a reviewing stand, he realizes that their monarch is sending them to war. He and Pjorsky conclude that they have a moral duty to prevent the war, so they pour boiling water on the offending monarch's family, inadvertently extinguishing the armies at the same time.

Chapter 15

After Pjorsky leaves, Bkshp reflects on the differences between sooflaskies and swinks and realizes that the pattern of life is the same everywhere, with each level of beings looking down on the level below it.

Chapter 16

Bkshp now glances over a paper on currency that he wrote during his early days in Blitzowski. He recalls that it has been 3,000 years since Catherine handled that paper and wonders where she is now and reflects on how much has happened during a similar length of time in human history, going back to the founding of Rome. He then inserts his currency paper into his narrative. His discourse on the currency ends as Catherine reminds him that his Advanced Class in Theological Arithmetic is about to arrive. Bkshp then rushes to complete his History of Japan.

Anxious to get to the fossil field to learn what effect his "poem" is having on the boys, Bkshp turns his class over to his assistant, whom he calls Sir Galahad. At the field, he finds all work has halted because everyone's interest is centered on the romance that Gulliver and Louis related. Opinions are divided between Gulliver's and Louis's points of views, with no one taking Bkshp's view; however, everyone wants to hear Bkshp tell his story. When Bkshp says there are only 1.5 billion human beings in his former world, not even Louis is impressed. However, he redeems himself by telling how enormous human beings are. As he adds details, his audience cries out in admiration of his talent for lying.

Bkshp then fields questions about such matters as the Cuban War [Spanish-American War] and the Jap[anese]-Russian War. Each detail he provides evokes appreciative cries, and the boys make wagers among themselves on the statistics that Bkshp will provide. Only Sir Galahad believes him. Eventually, Gulliver proposes to form a company to market Bkshp's Lie. When he asks Bkshp to propose a name for the new enterprise, Bkshp suggests "Standard Oil." However, when he senses that the others are serious about Gulliver's scheme, he realizes he must stop it if he is to preserve his reputation as the head of an institute on morals. He calls the boys to attention.

Chapter 17

After getting his friends' attention, Bkshp pauses to pique their interest and then tells them about a gold discovery he made in Major Molar. Their impatience to get at the gold reassures him that his Institute of Applied Morals [mentioned for the first time] is saved. He understands that the best way to generate interest in a scheme is to pretend to be indifferent.

Chapter 18

Bkshp has finished his History of the World, and Sir Galahad is eager to master it.

Bkshp has saved his college of morals by inventing a gold mine story but now must think up something better to replace it. He gets an idea from his recurrent dream about chewing through Blitzowski's back teeth and finding a huge gold filling. Now convinced that his dream is real, he is sure that the bonanza in Blitzowski's teeth will dwarf both the Big Bonanza of Nevada's silver mines and the Klondike gold rush. Before revealing his stupendous news to the boys, however, he reflects on the immensity of the wealth awaiting them and worries that it might harm them. He gradually reduces the amount he will share with them until he resolves to keep all the gold for himself and let his friends keep the cement. He then goes to bed.

BACKGROUND AND PUBLISHING HISTORY

Clemens wrote "Three Thousand Years Among the Microbes" in only 35 days during May and June of 1905, while he summered at DUBLIN, New Hampshire. The fact that he told FREDERICK A. DUNEKA of Harper's about the manuscript suggests that he wanted to publish the story; however, he lost interest and abandoned it. Later, Paine was sufficiently impressed by the manuscript to print about 3,200 words (6.5 percent) of it as Appendix V in *Mark Twain: A Biography* (1912). Paine's extract contains, in this order, about 1,390 words from chapters 4 and 5; 1,030 words from chapter 14a; 535 words from chapter 6; and 210 words from chapter 13. For more than a half-century, those extracts were the only portions of the manuscript to see publication. In 1966, JOHN S. TUCKEY published the entire manuscript in *WHICH WAS THE DREAM? AND OTHER SYMBOLIC WRITINGS OF THE LATER YEARS*. Tuckey also reprinted the story in *The Devil's Race-Track: Mark Twain's Great Dark Writings* (1980), and David Ketterer included it in *The Science Fiction of Mark Twain* (1984; reprinted as *Tales of Wonder*, 2003). Many scholars have commented on the story, but few have analyzed it at length.

CHARACTERS AND RELATED ENTRIES

Bkshp, B. b. (Huck) Narrator of "Three Thousand Years Among the Microbes." Originally a human being, Bkshp was transformed into a CHOLERA microbe in a failed attempt by a magician to turn him into a bird. He lives in the body of a human being named Blitzowski, whom his fellow microbes regard as both their planet and the lord of their universe. Early in his narrative, Bkshp claims to have made a complete conversion from being a man to being a microbe, but he still struggling to understand what he really is. He is unsure whether he merely dreams of being a human or is becoming a human again.

When Bkshp was a man, he was a scientist with a special interest in paleontology. He continues to regard himself as a scientist and frequently impresses the other microbes with his vast knowledge. He also has such a talent for languages that he can learn six in an hour—a useful skill because of the vast numbers of microbic languages. By his own admission, Bkshp's memories are unreliable. He recalls being the best mathematician at YALE UNIVERSITY when he was a member of the "class of '53" (presumably 1853) but in a footnote he says that he may have never been at Yale, except as a recipient of HONORARY DEGREES. He regards himself as the mathematician among the microbes—but only in microbic math. He has forgotten so much of his human math that he can no longer recall even the basic multiplication table.

Bkshp has never married but claims to have lost his heart to a former human girlfriend, Margaret (Maggie) Adams, about whom he still dreams (much as Hank Morgan dreams of Puss Flanagan in CONNECTICUT YANKEE). Margaret was about three or four years younger than Bkshp, and he himself was between 21 and 23 before he became a microbe. If his recollection of having been in the Yale class of 1853 has any meaning, that would place his birth around the early 1830s and make him a near-contemporary of Clemens, who invested some autobiographical elements in the character.

Microbic names lack vowels, so it appears that Bkshp may take his name from Clemens's boyhood friend TOM BLANKENSHIP, who was the chief model for Huckleberry Finn. The connection between Bkshp and Blankenship is made even stronger when Bkshp adopts "Huck" as a name in order to relieve his microbe friends from the strain of pronouncing his real name (chapter 10).

Blitzowski Character in "Three Thousand Years Among the Microbes." Introduced in chapter 2, Blitzowski is an old thief and tramp whose body is the home and virtual universe of untold billions of microbes, including the narrator, Bkshp, who is a

CHOLERA germ. Blitzowski lives in America, to which he was shipped by his native country, Hungary, when it became tired of him. During the summers, Blitzowski goes on the tramp and sleeps in fields; during the winters, he lives in the city and often sleeps in jails. A "hoary and mouldering old bald-headed tramp" whose body is "a reek of decay, a charnel house," Blitzowski never washes, shaves, or combs his hair. Sober only once during his lifetime, he is malicious and profane. Despite his repulsive qualities, Blitzowski is to the microbes who inhabit his body their entire world, the "lord of their universe." Bkshp estimates Blitzowski's human age at 85 years—a figure equivalent to nearly 4.5 million years in microbe time. Bkshp hopes that Blitzowski will live at least another 10 human years, one-half million microbe years.

Elements of "Three Thousand Years" have affinities with *Huckleberry Finn* (1884), and Blitzowski himself has a close resemblance to Huck's filthy, profane, drunken and malicious father, Pap Finn.

microbic   The language of microbes in "Three Thousand Years Among the Microbes." Microbic has no vowels, so it produces names such as "Bkshp."

Tom Sawyer, The Adventures of (1876)

The first NOVEL that Clemens wrote without a coauthor, *Tom Sawyer* is also his most clearly autobiographical novel. It concerns a long summer in the life of an ordinary young boy living in Missouri in the early 19th century. It is set in a village modeled closely on Clemens's hometown, and most of its characters are taken from life. Its narrative is enlivened by extraordinary and MELODRAMATIC events, but it is otherwise a realistic depiction of the experiences, people, and places that Clemens knew as a child.

Tom Sawyer arrived at a momentous time in American history. Its first edition was issued in England on June 9, 1876. Sixteen days later, Indi-

ans annihilated George Armstrong Custer's Seventh Cavalry at Little Big Horn. Nine days after that, America celebrated the centennial of its birth. Publication of *Tom Sawyer* was little noticed in the United States at the time. The book has, however, proved to be one of the most durable works in American literature. By the time Clemens died, it was his top-selling book. It has been in print continuously since 1876, and has outsold all other Clemens works. It has been issued in hundreds of editions in at least three dozen languages.

SYNOPSIS

The novel is 71,500 words in length and is divided into 35 chapters, plus a brief epilogue. Its plot follows five distinct story lines, which overlap considerably. The loosest story line, beginning in chapter 1, concerns Tom's relationship with his family and his school and church activities. A second story line follows Tom's infatuation with Becky Thatcher, whom he meets in chapter 3. In a third story line, an episode contained within chapters 13–17 has Tom, Huck Finn, and Joe Harper spend a week playing PIRATES on Jackson's Island. A fourth story line begins in chapter 9, when Tom and Huck see Injun Joe murder a man in the graveyard; after the Jackson's Island interlude, this story line culminates with the trial of Muff Potter in chapter 23, when Injun Joe is revealed as the true murderer and disappears. The final and most complex story line ties together the search for Injun Joe, Tom, and Huck's quest for treasure, and Tom and Becky's adventure in a CAVE.

Chapter 1
The narrative opens in the shabby little village of St. Petersburg, on the right bank of the Mississippi River. (Clues here and elsewhere indicate that it is Friday, June 14—a date that occurred in the year 1844). Aunt Polly is searching for her impudent nephew, Tom Sawyer, the son of her deceased sister. She finds him and is about to put a switch to him, but he escapes. That afternoon, Tom cuts school to go swimming. At supper that night, his half-brother, Sid Sawyer, calls Polly's attention to a thread in Tom's shirt that reveals that he removed the shirt in order to swim. Tom silently vows revenge on his priggish brother. After supper, Tom goes out and

gets into a fight with a new village boy (later identified as Albert Temple), whom he chases away. When Tom returns home disheveled, Aunt Polly determines to put him to work the next day.

Chapter 2

Saturday morning finds Tom burdened with the task of whitewashing a huge fence. Just as he tries enticing a young black boy named Jim into helping, a sudden smack from Aunt Polly ends his negotiations. After Polly leaves, Tom persuades Ben Rogers, Billy Fisher, Johnny Miller, and other boys to paint the fence for him. The other boys not only whitewash the fence, they pay for the privilege.

Chapter 3

Tom reports to Aunt Polly that he has finished painting the fence. Astonished to find the fence whitewashed three times over, Polly rewards Tom with an apple and dismisses him. As Tom leaves, he pelts Sid with dirt clods, then joins his pal Joe Harper commanding boys in a mock military battle.

Tom returns home past Jeff Thatcher's house, where he sees a new girl in the garden (later identified as Jeff's cousin Becky Thatcher). Instantly falling in love with this new girl, Tom forgets his previous sweetheart, Amy Lawrence, and hangs about Jeff's house showing off. He arrives home in a happy mood that becomes ecstasy when Sid accidentally breaks a sugar-bowl. When Aunt Polly discovers the wreckage, she smacks Tom without stopping to ask who is responsible. When his cheerful cousin Mary returns home from a week in the country, Tom leaves in order to sulk. That evening, he returns to Jeff Thatcher's house, hoping to catch a glimpse of the new girl. When he steals quietly near the house, a bucket of water is dumped on his head from an upper-story window.

Chapter 4

Sunday morning begins with Tom struggling to master Bible verses for Sunday school, a place that he hates. Mary coaches him and encourages him with the unexpected gift of a pocketknife. At the entrance to the Sunday school, Tom accosts boys as they come in and trades the items amassed the day before for "tickets" that they have earned for memorizing Bible verses; he collects enough to claim

one of the Bibles awarded to pupils who memorize 2,000 verses.

Mr. Walters, the Sunday-school superintendent, conducts the session and introduces several visitors. The most important of these is Jeff Thatcher's uncle, Judge Thatcher. The judge is accompanied by his wife and daughter—the very girl with whom Tom is enthralled. Anxious to impress his visitors, Walters wants to "exhibit a prodigy" by awarding a Bible prize. Tom presents the requisite number of tickets and demands a Bible. Walters is stunned, as are Tom's friends, who sold him the tickets that have made his moment of glory possible. As Tom accepts his Bible, the judge asks him to display some of his knowledge by naming the first two disciples. After Tom stammers "David and GOLIAH," the curtain of charity is drawn over the rest of the scene.

Chapter 5

Later that morning, Tom sits with Sid, Mary, and Aunt Polly in the church during the Reverend Mr. Sprague's sermon. The congregation includes all the village worthies, including the Widow Douglas, the mayor, the postmaster, and Willie Mufferson, the village's MODEL BOY. Tom fights off boredom by playing with a pinch-beetle. A stray poodle that is roaming the aisles sits on the beetle and is pinched. It raises a huge ruckus that delights the congregation, but the minister bravely carries on.

Chapter 6

As morning breaks on Monday, Tom looks for a malady that will keep him home from school. All he can come up with is a loose tooth that Aunt Polly yanks out. On his way to school, he encounters the village pariah, Huckleberry Finn, who is carrying a dead cat. After discussing the supposed wart-curing properties of dead cats, the boys agree to meet that night at the CEMETERY to test it. Meanwhile, Tom persuades Huck to swap a tick-bug for his freshly extracted tooth.

When Tom arrives at school late, the master (later identified as Mr. Dobbins) demands an explanation. Tom is about to lie, but when he spots the new girl in the classroom, he startles everyone with the truth: that he was talking with Huck Finn. Dobbins whips him and sends him to sit with the girls. Tom is delighted to find himself sitting next to

Becky. He shows off his drawing prowess and writes "I love you" on a piece of paper. At that moment, Dobbins takes him by his ear back to his regular seat, next to Joe Harper.

Chapter 7
Bored with schoolwork, Tom releases his tick-bug so that he and Joe can play with it on a slate. While the tick-bug engrosses them. Dobbins tiptoes down the aisle and whacks both of them, Tom spends the noon break with Becky at the empty schoolhouse, where they draw pictures and chat. Tom persuades Becky to become "engaged," but then upsets her by mentioning that he was once engaged to Amy Lawrence. He offers her his treasured brass andiron knob, but she knocks it to the floor. Tom leaves and does not return to school that day.

Chapter 8
Tom goes to CARDIFF HILL. Consumed with self-pity, he wishes he could die, *temporarily*. His spirits lift, however, as he considers simply going far away and not returning. He fantasizes about becoming a clown, or a soldier, or, better still, a PIRATE with the name Black Avenger of the Spanish Main. In preparation for his new life of adventure, he invokes an incantation designed to round up all the marbles he ever lost, but this spell fails. Joe Harper, another truant, then appears and the boys play Robin Hood games the rest of the afternoon.

Chapter 9
Late the same night, Huck calls for Tom. They go to the graveyard outside of town, where they happen on Injun Joe, Muff Potter, and Dr. Robinson in the act of robbing Hoss Williams's grave. Injun Joe starts an argument that develops into a scuffle. Potter is momentarily knocked out and Joe stabs Robinson to death with his knife. The boys flee. Injun Joe robs Robinson's corpse before Potter regains consciousness, then persuades Potter that *he* has killed the doctor. Drunk, as usual, Potter accepts Injun Joe's story and begs Joe to stand by him. Both men then leave.

Chapter 10
After running to the old tannery, Tom and Huck sign a blood-oath, swearing that they will never reveal what they have just seen at the GRAVE-ROBBING. They hear snoring in the building and find Muff Potter asleep.

The next morning Tom oversleeps. Instead of rebuking him, Aunt Polly weeps over him for breaking her heart again, making Tom feel worse than he would after a whipping. He arrives at school in a gloomy mood. He and Joe Harper are flogged for the previous day's hookey. Tom's despair is complete when he finds that Becky has returned his brass knob.

Chapter 11
At noon, word of the murder electrifies the village. Tom joins the flow of townspeople to the graveyard, where he sees Huck. Muff Potter appears and is arrested because his knife was found at the scene of the crime. Injun Joe gives his version of what happened the previous night, leaving Huck and Tom dumbfounded that the man is not struck dead for lying. Agonizing over his secret knowledge of the murder, Tom has trouble sleeping through the next week. Friends and family members notice a marked change in his behavior. To ease his conscience, he regularly visits the jailhouse in order to smuggle goodies to Potter.

Chapter 12
Tom's interest in the murder case lessens as a new concern occupies his thoughts. Becky is ill and out of school. Aunt Polly, concerned about Tom's deteriorating spirits, fills him up with patent medicines and quack cures. These fail, so she orders a large supply of "Painkiller," which tastes like "fire in a liquid form." Tom persuades her to let him dose himself and gradually pours the medicine through a crack in the floor. One day, he gives his dose to Aunt Polly's cat Peter, which springs into the air and runs through the room wildly. Aunt Polly arrives as the cat does double somersaults and flies out the window. Tom explains what he has done and Aunt Polly thumps him. He expresses bewilderment, pointing out that he has only done for the cat what she has been doing for him.

At school that day, Tom is thrilled to see Becky again, but he fails to get her attention.

Chapter 13

Tom now believes that he has no alternative but to run away. Joe Harper shares his feelings of being put upon by the world, so they swear to stick together. Joe wants to become a hermit, but accepts Tom's plan to be pirates. Huck Finn soon joins them. Each boy steals supplies to begin their careers in crime. At midnight, they rendezvous two miles upriver and commandeer a raft to take them to Jackson's Island. Tom again styles himself the "Black Avenger of the Spanish Main." The boys quietly float down the river and land on a bar at the north end of the island. They use an old sail for a makeshift tent, but sleep in the open.

Chapter 14

The boys spend the next morning swimming, skylarking, and fishing. After eating, they explore the island, stopping to swim every hour. Despite their fun, the solitude gradually weighs on them. A booming sound catches their attention. Upstream, a ferryboat crowded with people and surrounded by skiffs is firing a cannon over the water. Tom explains that the boat must be searching for someone who has drowned. Suddenly he realizes that the boat is looking for *them*. The boys return to camp excited, but as night falls, their spirits sag. Joe hints that they might consider going home, only to have Tom deride him.

After his companions are asleep, Tom writes messages on bark. One piece he leaves in Joe's hat along with his personal treasures, the other he tucks into his jacket before sneaking off to the sand-bar.

Chapter 15

Tom wades and swims to the ILLINOIS shore, which he follows upstream to the ferryboat dock opposite St. Petersburg. He swims to the skiff towed behind the ferryboat and rides it across the river to the village and sneaks home. There he peeks inside and sees Aunt Polly, Sid, Mary, and Joe Harper's mother talking. He slips in unobserved and listens to their conversation from beneath the bed in the parlor. He overhears that the raft that he and his friends used was found five or six miles below village, and that he and the others are believed drowned. If their bodies are not found by Sunday, a funeral service will be held for them on that day.

After the others leave, Aunt Polly goes to sleep on the bed. Tom emerges from his hiding place. He starts to place his sycamore-bark message by his aunt's bedside, but then thinks better of it. He kisses Polly and leaves. He detaches the skiff from the idle ferryboat, rows across the river and reaches camp just after daybreak, just as Huck and Joe are debating what to do with the possessions he left behind. Tom relates his adventure, then sleeps till noon.

Chapter 16

That night, the boys collect turtle eggs, on which they breakfast the next two mornings. Friday morning they devote to frolicking, but Joe's and Huck's spirits sink to a new low. Both want to go home, but Tom makes fun of them. As they start to leave, Tom springs a great secret on them that renews their spirits and persuades them to stay. After dinner, Huck teaches Tom and Joe how to smoke corncob pipes. Both boys profess to love smoking, but as their spitting reaches prodigious levels, they disappear to sleep off their new experience.

At midnight a lightning storm rocks the island, keeping the boys awake all night. They build a roaring fire when the storm abates. At daybreak on Saturday, they sleep on the sandbar and get sunburned. Joe and Huck's spirits again flag; Tom invigorates them by suggesting that they play Indians.

Chapter 17

The scene switches back to the village, where the families of Joe and Tom are in mourning. Becky Thatcher mopes about the schoolhouse, regretting her harsh treatment of Tom. Other children arrive and speak reverently about Tom and Joe. The next morning, the largest crowd in memory fills the church for the funeral service. Aunt Polly, Sid, Mary and the Harper family enter dressed in black. As the minister delivers a sermon extolling the boys for their overlooked virtues, the church door creaks open and the three boys march up the aisle. They have come down from the gallery, where they listened to their own funeral sermon. The families throw themselves on the restored boys and the congregation shakes the rafters with joyous singing. This is the proudest moment of Tom's life.

Chapter 18

As circumstances of how the boys made it from the island to the church are told, it is revealed that the chance to attend their own funeral was the secret that Tom saved for Huck and Joe earlier.

On Monday morning Mary and Aunt Polly are attentive to Tom, but Polly chides him for making her suffer by allowing her to think him dead. Tom tries to make her feel better by telling her that he dreamt about her while he was away. To prove it, he recounts every detail he remembers from the night that he sneaked into the house. Aunt Polly is immensely pleased with his amazing "dream." As the children go to school, Aunt Polly heads for Mrs. Harper's.

Now a hero, Tom decides that he no longer needs Becky—unless she is willing to make up. When she arrives at school, Tom ignores her, but makes sure that she sees him flirting with Amy Lawrence. Becky works on Tom's jealousy by extending picnic invitations to everyone but him and Amy. At recess, Tom continues flirting with Amy, but with waning enthusiasm, because Becky is flirting with the new boy, Alfred Temple. After Tom leaves at noon, Becky dismisses Alfred sharply. Realizing that he has been used, Alfred enters the schoolhouse and pours ink on Tom's spelling book. Becky happens to see him do it but resolves to let Tom be punished.

Chapter 19

At home, Tom finds Aunt Polly in an angry mood. She has just learned from Mrs. Harper the truth about Tom's Wednesday night visit to the house. Tom insists that he had came home to leave a message written on bark for her, but she remains skeptical. After he leaves, she takes his jacket out of the closet, hesitates, then finds Tom's bark with the message that he wrote for her. She is so elated she would forgive him any sin.

Chapter 20

Near the school, Tom meets Becky and suggests that they make up, but she snubs him. Becky then enters the empty schoolhouse. Dobbins has left the key in his desk drawer. Becky opens the drawer and finds a mysterious book that Dobbins often furtively reads—an anatomy textbook, which she opens to a picture of a naked human. At that moment, Tom enters the room, so startling Becky that she tears the page almost in half. As she replaces the book in the desk, she tearfully turns on Tom, berating him because she expects that he will tattle on her. She adds that something bad is about to happen to him and stalks off, leaving Tom perplexed.

After class resumes, Tom's damaged spelling book earns him another whipping. Eventually, Dobbins discovers the damage to his anatomy book and demands to know who caused it. No confession is forthcoming, so he starts challenging pupils, one at a time. Tom senses Becky's growing panic; he knows that she will crumble when Dobbins calls her name. Just as her turn comes, Tom jumps up and shouts, "I done it!" Dobbins gives Tom the most merciless flaying he has ever administered and makes Tom stay after school for two hours. Later, Tom and Becky reach a complete reconciliation. Tom goes to sleep that night planning vengeance against Alfred Temple.

Chapter 21

As vacation approaches and Dobbins prepares pupils for "examination day," the frequency and severity of his whippings increase and his victims plot an elaborate revenge. Dobbins is known to drink before these occasions, so the son of the sign-painter in whose house he lives does something to Dobbins while he naps before the big evening. At the school program that night, youngsters parrot speeches and young ladies read predictably melancholic compositions. Tom Sawyer's recitation of the "liberty or death" speech breaks down when stage fright overwhelms him.

The climax to the evening comes when a tipsy Dobbins mounts the stage to draw a map on the blackboard for a geography lesson. He hears the audience tittering, but has no idea what they are tittering about. Meanwhile, a boy lowers a cat on a rope toward Dobbins's head from an opening in the ceiling. The cat snags Dobbins's wig, revealing the fact that his head is gilded. The boys are avenged. Vacation has begun.

Chapter 22

Tom begins the summer vacation by joining the CADETS OF TEMPERANCE but is quickly disillusioned.

Various events and entertainments pass through the village: minstrel shows, a circus, a PHRENOLOGIST, and a mesmerizer. The Fourth of July is a partial flop; its parade is rained out and the featured speaker, Senator BENTON, proves a disappointment. Meanwhile, Becky is with her parents in Constantinople. The secret of Dr. Robinson's murder continues to weigh on Tom.

After measles keep Tom bedridden for two weeks, he emerges to find that the village has experienced a religious revival. Joe Harper is studying a Testament, Ben Rogers is ministering to the poor, and Jim Hollis has become pious. Even Huck is quoting scripture. Tom fears that of all the village residents, he alone is lost. That night a terrible storm convinces him that his end is near. The next day he suffers a relapse and begins another three weeks in bed. This time he emerges to find that the effects of the revival have worn off and his friends have returned to their sinful ways.

Chapter 23

As Muff Potter's murder trial approaches, Huck and Tom consider springing Potter free, but instead merely pass tobacco and matches to him through his cell window. His pitiful gratitude magnifies their feelings of guilt. When the trial begins, the boys hang about the courtroom, lacking the resolve to enter. By the end of the second day, word is out that Injun Joe's evidence is holding firm, and that the verdict seems certain. That night Tom is out late and comes home too agitated to sleep.

After Tom's testimony clears Muff Potter (Walter Brennan) of the murder charge, Muff thanks Tom (Tommy Kelly) and Huck in the 1938 film *The Adventures of Tom Sawyer. (United Artists)*

The next day in court, the prosecution examines witness after witness. When Potter's attorney fails to cross-examine anyone, a murmur of discontent is heard. However, after the prosecution rests its case, Potter's attorney moves to withdraw Potter's original temporary insanity plea and calls Tom as a surprise witness. Without mentioning Huck's name, Tom tells what he saw at the graveyard the night of Dr. Robinson's murder. Just as he is about to reveal that Injun Joe stabbed the doctor, Injun Joe springs out the window and disappears.

Chapter 24

Once again, Tom is a hero. Nevertheless, nightmares of Injun Joe so haunt him that he hesitates to go out at night. Huck also is afraid; Tom's violation of their sacred oath has obliterated his confidence in the human race. Meanwhile, a DETECTIVE from St. Louis arrives to investigate Injun Joe's disappearance, but he leaves after merely announcing that he has found a clue.

Chapter 25

After an unspecified period of time passes, Tom persuades Huck to hunt for buried treasure, exciting Huck's greed with predictions of the wealth they might find. They begin digging near the HAUNTED HOUSE just outside the village. After a few fruitless hours, they move to a spot near the Widow Douglas's house on CARDIFF HILL. This spot also proves fruitless, so they decide to return at midnight to see where the shadow of a tree limb falls. That night, they mark the spot of the limb's shadow and dig again. Further failure moves them to consider yet another spot and Tom suggests that they try the haunted house itself. Agreeing to return during daylight, the boys give the house a wide berth as they go home.

Chapter 26

At noon the next day, the boys return to the tree where they left their tools. Tom remembers it is Friday—an unlucky day to enter haunted houses—so they spend the afternoon playing Robin Hood. On Saturday they finally enter the house and even venture to go upstairs. Two men then enter the house. One is "the old deef and dumb Spaniard" recently seen around the village. The other is a stranger. The boys are shocked to hear the "Spaniard" speak and even more shocked to recognize Injun Joe's voice. Joe and his unknown partner are discussing a job they intend to pull, after which they intend to escape to TEXAS.

Tom and Huck remain where they are as Injun Joe and his partner nap. When the criminals awaken, they discuss burying their "swag." Injun Joe digs into the dirt floor with a knife and strikes a box. The box is filled with gold coins. Injun Joe and his partner speculate that it is a treasure left by JOHN MURRELL's gang. Joe's partner suggests that they no longer need to pull the job they have been planning, but Joe insists on carrying out his plan because it is revenge.

Injun Joe wants to take the gold to his den, located at "Number Two-under the cross." The men find Huck and Tom's tools and become suspicious. To the boys' dismay, Injun Joe starts climbing the stairs, but he stops when the stairway crumbles. As the boys determine to track Injun Joe to his hiding place, they also wonder if his revenge plan is directed at them.

Chapter 27

That night Tom dreams about the treasure Injun Joe has found. The next morning he and Huck discuss the previous evening's adventure. Tom argues for tracking Injun Joe to his hiding place. They try to figure out what Injun Joe means by "Number Two." Tom guesses that it is a room in one of the village's temperance taverns. After he investigates the tavern, he and Huck plan to spy on Injun Joe that night.

Chapter 28

Over the next several nights Tom and Huck hang around the tavern, watching for Injun Joe. On Thursday night Tom enters a room in the tavern, where he finds Injun Joe asleep on the floor, drunk, and nearly steps on his hand. Tom runs out and alerts Huck, who suggests that it might be a good moment to search the room for the treasure box. However, neither boy is up to taking the risk, so they decide to keep watching Injun Joe's room until he is gone.

Chapter 29

The next day Tom learns that Judge Thatcher's family has returned to town. Becky persuades her mother to organize the long-promised picnic. On

Saturday, Tom, Becky, many other children and a few young chaperons ride a chartered steam ferry downriver to the landing by the CAVE. Becky arranges with her mother to stay overnight at Susy Harper's, rather than journey home late. The ferry delivers them at a landing near the cave. Armed with candles, the picnickers stream inside to explore.

Huck, meanwhile, remains in town, watching the temperance tavern. Two men come out carrying a box. Huck quietly follows them to Cardiff Hill. He overhears Injun Joe talking to his unidentified partner about a "revenge job." Joe explains that when the Widow Douglas's husband was justice of the peace, the man treated him so badly that he now wants revenge. His plan is to mutilate the widow's face. When the partner objects, Injun Joe threatens to kill him. Huck runs down the hill to the house of Jones the Welchman and reports what he has overheard, begging not to have his own role in the affair revealed. Jones and his sons go off to protect the widow. Huck hears gunfire and a scream and he runs down the hill.

Chapter 30

The next morning, Sunday, Huck returns to Jones's house to learn what happened the night before. Jones welcomes him and explains that the assailants were chased off in the dark. He tries to get a description of the men out of Huck, who makes a further demand of secrecy. Finally, Huck reveals that the mysterious "Spaniard" is actually Injun Joe. Someone comes to the door, so Huck hides. It is the Widow Douglas, coming to thank Jones and his sons.

At church later that morning, Mrs. Thatcher discovers that Becky did not spend the night at Susy Harper's as planned and Aunt Polly learns that Tom's whereabouts also are not known. Word spreads that Tom and Becky must still be in the cave, where 200 searchers soon converge and work through the night. The next morning, Jones returns home to find Huck sleeping in his house, delirious with fever. The Widow Douglas comes to take care of him. Meanwhile, the search for Becky and Tom in the cave continues for three days.

Chapter 31

At the start of the picnic, Tom and Becky go off on their own in the cave, not noticing that they are becoming separated from the other picnickers. Tom eventually concludes that they are lost. He leads Becky to a fresh-water spring, where he insists that they remain as their candles burn out. Using a kite string to find his way back to this spot, Tom keeps searching for a way out of the cave. When he sees Injun Joe walking through the cave with a torch, he cries out, but Joe seems not to notice him.

Chapter 32

On Tuesday, St. Petersburg goes wild when word is received that Tom and Becky are safe. Tom explains how he found a speck of light in the cave that proved to be an opening through which he and Becky escaped. He then learned from boatmen who picked them up that they were five miles south of the cave's main entrance.

Tom spends two weeks recovering from his exhaustion, then goes to visit Huck. When he stops at the Thatchers', he learns that the judge has had the entrance to the cave sealed with an iron door to prevent other people from getting lost. Tom pales, then announces that Injun Joe is inside the cave.

Chapter 33

People again rush to the cave, where they find Injun Joe lying dead behind the new door, surrounded by grisly evidence of his slow starvation. His body is buried near the cave's entrance.

The next day, Tom and Huck finally catch up on each other's adventures. Tom startles Huck with his revelation that the missing treasure must be in the cave. That afternoon, they go to the cave, entering it through the opening that Tom has kept secret since his escape with Becky. As they enter, Tom outlines his plans for a robbers' gang, which is also to include Ben Rogers and Joe Harper. Inside the cave, Huck's nerve starts to fail; he fears meeting Injun Joe's ghost. The boys persist, however, and find Injun Joe's cache of weapons and treasure. Back in the village, they encounter Jones, who excitedly rushes them off to the Widow Douglas's, where they find Aunt Polly, the Thatchers, the Harpers, and many others awaiting them. The boys are sent off to change into new clothes that have been purchased for Huck.

Tom (Jack Pickford) and Huck (Robert Gordon) reveal the treasure they have found in the cave in *Huck and Tom* (1918), the second part of Jesse Lasky's silent film adaptation of *Tom Sawyer*.

Chapter 34

Away from the crowd, Huck suggests fleeing, but Tom persuades him to stay. Sid arrives and explains that Jones is planning some kind of surprise. Downstairs, the widow announces her intention to provide Huck with a permanent home and later start him in business. Tom interrupts, however, saying that Huck does not need that, since he is already rich. The announcement stuns the crowd into silence. Tom then brings in the gold coins and pours them on a table. The coins add up to just over $12,000, which Tom says that he and Huck will split.

Chapter 35

After word of Tom and Huck's treasure gets out, every "haunted" house in the region is dismantled by treasure seekers. The Widow Douglas invests Huck's money for him, and Judge Thatcher does the same with Tom's money. Now under the widow's protection, Huck suffers the close attention of her servants, who keep him clean and neat. He hates having to eat with utensils, attend church, and speak properly. After three weeks, he bolts and disappears for 48 hours. Tom finds Huck in an empty hogshead near the abandoned slaughterhouse. He tells Huck that he will not be allowed to join his robber gang if he is not respectable. Huck agrees to go back and try living with the widow for another month. Tom promises to have an initiation meeting that night.

Conclusion

An epilogue of just over a hundred words explains that the narrative must end because it is "strictly a history of a *boy*." It cannot continue without becoming the history of a *man*. The narrator assures us that "most of the characters . . . still live, and are prosperous and happy," and suggests he might take up their story as adults later.

BACKGROUND AND WRITING

Clemens prefaced *Tom Sawyer* with the claim that "most" of its adventures "really occurred." This statement must be put in perspective. The events in the novel that Clemens personally experienced or observed as a child are mostly the minor ones. He was a mischievous boy at school; he did show off for LAURA HAWKINS when she moved to his street; his brother Henry Clemens did break a sugar bowl, and so on. The major events, however, such as the GRAVE-ROBBING and murder scene, getting lost in the cave, and finding the treasure, are pure invention.

During his years as a journalist, Clemens wrote about some of the incidents and themes that he would later use in *Tom Sawyer*. His early essays and sketches occasionally evoke his memories of Sunday school, the Cadets of Temperance, "Examination Day," childhood romance, and other matters that figure into *Tom Sawyer*. Around 1868, he completed a short story, posthumously titled "BOY'S MANUSCRIPT," that clearly anticipates *Tom Sawyer*. In February 1870, he wrote a letter to his childhood friend WILL BOWEN recalling many details of their boyhood together that he would use in *Tom Sawyer*.

Tom Sawyer was Clemens's first attempt to write a novel on his own. It is nearly impossible to pinpoint the exact dates that he worked on the manuscript. He may have begun work on the book as early as 1872. After writing about 400 pages of manuscript, he stopped. In early 1873, he joined with his neighbor, C. D. WARNER, to write another, much different novel, *The Gilded Age*. He returned to *Tom Sawyer* during the summer of 1874, most of which he spent in ELMIRA, New York.

In July 1875, Clemens wrote to W. D. HOWELLS, reporting that he had finished *Tom Sawyer*. Later that month, he arranged copyright for his own dramatic adaptation of the story. He gave a copy of the novel's manuscript to Howells for reading. Howells liked the book greatly but upset Clemens by recommending that it be presented as a boys' book. Clemens conceded the point when his wife Livy agreed with Howells's views. The role of Howells and Olivia Clemens—to whom he wrote the DEDICATION to *Tom Sawyer*—in the editing of the book has given rise to a theory that Clemens was constrained by their censorship. Close examination of the various manuscript texts has, however, revealed only minor, and mostly stylistic, changes. There is no reason to believe that the book that was published was something other than what Clemens intended it to be.

PUBLISHING HISTORY

On November 5, 1875, Clemens delivered his manuscript to his American publisher, ELISHA BLISS, who turned it over to TRUE WILLIAMS for illustration. For various reasons—not all of which are clear—it would be over a year before Bliss's AMERICAN PUBLISHING COMPANY finally issued the first American edition. In January 1876, Clemens had Moncure CONWAY take a corrected copy of his manuscript to England, where Conway arranged for its publication with CHATTO and Windus. Chatto issued an unillustrated edition on June 9, 1876. Other foreign editions followed quickly. BELFORD BROTHERS, a Canadian publisher, issued an unauthorized edition in late July, pouring perhaps 100,000 cheap copies of the book into the United States. Around October, BERNHARD VON TAUCHNITZ issued an English-language edition of the book in Leipzig, Germany. Another Leipzig publisher soon issued the first German translation of the book.

Around December 8, 1876, Bliss's company finally issued the first American edition, which was also the first illustrated edition. The company reissued the book in approximately the same format until HARPER AND BROTHERS became Clemens's exclusive American publisher in 1903. Harper's then issued all the authorized editions of *Tom Sawyer* in America until 1931, when its copyright expired. That event launched a spate of new editions, many with fresh illustrations, including an edition illustrated by NORMAN ROCKWELL in 1936. Since the book's original publication, it has never gone out of print.

In 1991, Collectors Reprints, Inc., published a full facsimile reprint of the book, complete with a facsimile of its original cover. The OXFORD MARK TWAIN edition published in 1996 included a facsimile reprint of the first American edition of *Tom Sawyer* with a new introduction by novelist E. L. Doctorow and an afterword by Albert Stone, author of *The Innocent Eye: Childhood in Mark Twain's Imagination* (1961).

MANUSCRIPTS

Clemens's original manuscript of *Tom Sawyer*, extending to 876 handwritten pages, is held by Georgetown University in Washington, D.C. In

1982, the university's library published it as a two-volume photo-facsimile edition. Shortly after completing the manuscript, Clemens had a secretarial, or amanuensis, copy written out by scribes. Howells read this copy and wrote his corrections on it; then Clemens added his own revisions. Clemens attempted to reconcile the two copies of the manuscript before Conway took the secretarial copy to England, but slight differences slipped through. The American edition drew on Clemens's original manuscript; the English edition drew on the secretarial copy. The original English edition also differs from the American edition in having somewhat different chapter numbers.

Clemens personally made additional corrections and revisions on the American edition's proof pages, but did not read proofs for the English edition. Chatto and Windus returned its copy of the manuscript to Conway and it eventually found its way to the museum in MARK TWAIN STATE PARK near FLORIDA, MISSOURI.

In 1980, the MARK TWAIN PROJECT published the first edition of *Tom Sawyer* based directly on the original manuscript that attempts to reconcile Clemens's corrections in the secretarial copy manuscripts and the first American edition.

CRITICAL COMMENTARY

The Adventures of Tom Sawyer is one of Clemens's best-known and best-selling books—"a hymn," in the author's words, "put into prose form to give it worldly air." It is a seminal text of American literature in general and children's literature in particular. The character of Tom Sawyer is regarded as a symbol of American boyhood. One way to view Tom is through his relationship to authority. Critics have taken a range of positions on Tom's behavior and misbehavior—as morally dangerous to impressionable young readers, as liberating in its celebration of freedom and creativity, or as a daring but ultimately conventional affirmation that despite minor infractions, a willful boy can be comfortably absorbed back into the social mainstream. Starting in the 1820s, "Model Boy" stories, in which a young boy is rewarded for behaving in accord with mainstream religious and moral values, became a popular form of moral instruction

(Norton 65). By the 1840s, humorists began to mock such literature by inverting its underlying structural symmetry—that in children good behavior would lead to a positive outcome. Clemens began playing with such conventions in "THE STORY OF THE BAD LITTLE BOY WHO DIDN'T COME TO GRIEF" and "THE STORY OF THE GOOD LITTLE BOY WHO DID NOT PROSPER."

The ensemble of child characters revolving around Tom has various relationships with parental and institutional authority and offers counterpoint to Tom's performance. Tom's half brother Sid more closely acts the Model-Boy part when adults are around, but his private behavior toward Tom is petty and spiteful. Tom is a departure from the one-dimensional "Model Boy," but his behavior is also more complex than utter rebellion. At the other end of the spectrum is Huck, whose status as a poor orphan makes him a fringe romantic figure to the other boys. Huck's rebellious charisma, more extreme than Tom's, is undiluted by the need to appease parents and fit into mainstream society. Though Tom does not resist the conventions of small-town life to the same extreme as Huck, Tom's character centers on his willful departures from docile obedience. Tom's mischief is his charm. At the same time, however, Tom's minor social offenses are easily absorbed by his family and mainstream Hannibal. Willful but sympathetic, Tom shows himself to be more interesting as both a literary and moral figure than the Model Boy. Far from a model of perfect obedience, Tom, despite or perhaps because of his deviation from convention and propriety, effectively one-ups the Model Boy as an archetype that entertains, instructs, and in his more ambivalent relationship to authority, finally conforms to mainstream value.

Boy Capitalist

Tom's tumultuous but symbiotic relationship with authority can also be seen as the spirit of a model entrepreneur—bold, self-serving, charming, and skilled at manipulation. The episode in which Tom maneuvers his peers into doing his chores, whitewashing the fence, is a central scene of American literature. This quintessential scene of childhood grows, in a sense, out of the "embryo businessman" in Tom (Cox 96). Loath to work alone in tedium, Tom is inspired by the realization that compared to his solo task, Jim's job of filling buckets at the well is communal and involves a good amount of socializing and goofing off ("resting, trading playthings, quarreling, fighting, skylarking"; chapter 2). Relegated to whitewashing alone, Tom enlists his friends for an activity that harnesses their play to accomplish his work. Tom, the charismatic huckster, influences his friends by feigning desire, which creates an artificial demand for chores no one would ordinarily want to do. Tom's scheme is a combined feat of theatrical performance, reverse psychology, and labor management. He has turned a solitary chore into a community activity and spectacle, discovering in the process a "great law of human action, without knowing it—namely, that in order to make a man or a boy covet a thing, it is only necessary to make the thing difficult to attain" (ibid.).

Tom's subsequent black market in Bible tickets is another example of his economic savvy. His success in selling the privilege of fence washing to his friends allows him to lay away a stock of candy and trinkets, which he then parlays into verse tickets and finally exchanges for a prize Bible. In doing so, Tom converts hundreds of other children's labor hours into a Bible and enjoys the added bonus of a public ceremony. In contrast to Tom's clever circumvention of the Bible contest (though it blows up in his face at the last moment when he is unable to name for Becky's father the first two disciples) is a facetious anecdote about a German boy who has taken the rules all too seriously and "recited three thousand verses without stopping; but the strain upon his mental faculties was too great, and he was little better than an idiot from that day forth" (chapter 4). The stunted boy serves as a grotesque counterexample of literal-minded ambition and overreaching to the point of self-destruction, in contrast to Tom's shrewd and imaginative gaming of the system.

National Myths: Playing Indian in the Wake of Jacksonian Democracy

After Tom stands as a witness to save Muff Potter, he is a "glittering hero" to the town, some of whose inhabitants "believed he would be President, yet, if he escaped hanging" (chapter 24). As an emblem of American boyhood, Tom stands for a vision of America as much as he does for boyhood. Tom's personal qualities and development mirror those of the nation, or at least, of the nation's self-image in the era reflected in Clemens's portrayal. Pointing to this symbolic fusion of Tom, the boy, with America, the nation, one critic describes *Tom Sawyer* as "a kind of bildungsroman-epic hybrid"—as part of a coming-of-age story that also serves as a national myth (Howe 73). Tom "metamorphoses from an irritating yet amusing juvenile delinquent into something like an American epic hero" (Howe 73). This interpretation of Tom leads one to find national virtue in what is distinctively American about the voices of the text's narrator and characters. E. L. Doctorow declares, in this vein, that the text's voice of "amused tolerance . . . comic rhetoric, its hyperbole, its tongue-in-cheek ennoblement of the actions of a provincial country boy, ask to be read as implicit declaration of a young nation's cultural independence" (Doctorow xxxvii). Referring to Tom as a "familiar Jacksonian type," Forrest Robinson connects him to the egalitarian ideals and agrarian populism that underwrote the administration of Andrew Jackson, the nation's first western president, elected in 1828 (hinted at, perhaps, by the boys' adventures on "Jackson's Island"; Robinson 178).

As the meaning of "Jacksonian democracy" has been debated by historians—noting, for example, that the rhetoric of increasing democratic access for white farmers and laborers did not include similar liberating attention to African Americans and Native Americans or necessarily even help those it claimed to be supporting—the implications of Tom's own related behavior, such as the way he and his friends play Indian and his attitudes about slaves, have also become more complex. The idea of Tom as a representative American type has been reciprocally enlarged by the presence of other literary forms, suggested by Doctorow's description of Tom as "a morally plastic trickster in part derived from the Trickster myths of the Afro-American and Native American traditions" (Doctorow xxxv). Tom could on the one hand be seen as receiving, by virtue of white privilege, great leniency for his misbehavior (a leniency that was never granted, for example, to Injun Joe) or enjoying the fruits of fantasizing about the lives of Native Americans while experiencing none of the downsides.

In their outdoor adventures, the boys flirt with the promise of life in an idyllic state of nature, influenced by their perception of Native American life. Clemens's depictions of Tom and the boys playing fit into a developing image of childhood in America, which included a split between child's play and grown-up's work and, as in this case, often drew on visions of Native American life as exotic and primitive. On Jackson's Island, Tom gets his companions to "knock off being pirates, for a while, and be Indians for a change. They were attracted by this idea; so it was not long before they were stripped, and striped from head to heel with black mud . . . they went tearing through the woods to attack an English settlement" (chapter 16). Deciding to play primitively, Tom and his friends are "glad they had gone into savagery, for they had gained something. . . . They were prouder and happier in their new acquirement than they would have been in the scalping and skinning of the Six Nations" (ibid.). After their return from the island, Tom's "glittering notoriety" is subtly connected with his "swarthy sun-tanned skin" (chapter 18).

Whereas Tom, Joe, and Huck can enjoy playing Indian on Jackson's Island, Injun Joe's everyday existence is relegated to the margins of society, where he nurses grudges and plots revenge for a history of slights. Injun Joe is a sinister and mostly unsympathetic presence in the story whose experiences as a shunned "mixed-blood" loner show the limits of St. Petersburg's tolerance. Though he is among Clemens's most fully fleshed-out Native American characters, Injun Joe plays a limited and stereotypical role, serving as a dark mirror reflecting Anglo-American society and an imaginary repository for its darker habits and fantasies (McNutt 233). Injun Joe represents to the children not only the most violent elements of the world but also the logical endpoint of being thoroughly rejected by society. The liberation from civil society that Tom and his friends enjoy on Jackson Island is darkly mirrored in Injun Joe's experience of exclu-

sion. Tom's adventures and brush with death are thrilling and have the whiff of danger, but Joe's taste for revenge tinged with sadism (as when he relishes the thought of disfiguring the Widow Douglas) makes Tom's escapades appear more or less wholesome by comparison. If Tom occupies a precarious position in relation to authority (and Huck even more so), Injun Joe represents an adulthood circumscribed and made miserable by the disapprobation of mainstream society. Playing Indian for Tom and his friends, then, provides a harmless fantasy of pleasant escape from the strictures of everyday life and also hints at the repressed violence underneath the apparently lighthearted story. Injun Joe embodies not just a counterpart to Tom but also the subterranean drives that animate Tom, but from which he is allowed to remain largely innocent. As Cynthia Wolff observes, "the problem of Injun Joe offers no solution but that of denial. Lock away the small boy's anger; lock away his antisocial impulses; shut up his resentments at his totally feminine world; stifle rebellion; ignore adult male hostility; they are all too dangerous to deal with" (Scharnhorst 158). Injun Joe represents the potential for violence and vengeance and serves as a cautionary figure to Tom and the boys.

St. Petersburg: From Supreme Idyll to Theater of Hypocrisy

Like Tom, the town of St. Petersburg can be viewed from many perspectives. For some, it is an outpost of nostalgia for simple rural community, as in BERNARD DEVOTO's wistful description of St. Petersburg as an "idyll of what we once were." It is also possible to take a harsher view of the town's social life and the parochial values it embodies. Judith Fetterly focuses on the "dull and sleepy" qualities of St. Petersburg that make it "so sensation-hungry that everything that happens is greeted as an entertainment" (Scharnhorst 119). "Smugness, pretense, deception, and greed," writes Thomas Maik, "permeate the village and strip away the mythology of Eden" (Scharnhorst 207). Given this blank canvas, Tom, the "sanctioned rebel," functions to liven things up for characters as well as readers (Scharnhorst 119). Understanding St. Petersburg as boring rather than perfect also allows a different understanding of Tom's character as not just an outgrowth of, but a homegrown remedy for, everyday life in St. Petersburg. In a similar vein, Forrest Robinson focuses on the *bad faith* (Jean Paul Sartre's term for deliberate self-deception) that saturates life in St. Petersburg. Such a perspective, Forrest Robinson shows, affects the way one may interpret something as small as Aunt Polly's habit of wearing useless fashion glasses (a sign of her vanity), particularly in light of her harshness on Tom for lying (Scharnhorst 162). This backdrop of everyday social deception is what provides Tom with the opportunity to step slightly over the bounds of propriety—far enough to surprise and entertain, but not so far as to jeopardize the social order. Robinson writes, "Tom's genius for manipulation makes it possible for him to play at the perilous margins of social tolerance for bad faith" and allows the town to persist in its pious boredom until the next installment of his adventures (Scharnhorst 168–169).

The inept student speeches on examination day provide another forum in which Clemens skewers the hypocrisy of public morality that has trickled down to the children of St. Petersburg. Although Tom's theatricality fizzles out, the roster of speakers intone, with wobbly gravitas, the hypocrisy fostered in the educational system: "The glaring insincerity of these sermons was not sufficient to compass the banishment of the fashion from the schools, and it is not sufficient today; it never will be sufficient while the world stands, perhaps" (chapter 21). In this scene, Clemens's satire circles in particular around the pressure put on young women to echo public morals: "There is no school in all our land where the young ladies do not feel obliged to close their compositions with a sermon; and you will find that the sermon of the most frivolous and least religious girl in the school is always the longest and the most relentlessly pious" (ibid.). If Aunt Polly represents the middle-class morality that Tom enjoys tweaking, the recitation of platitudes is a coming-of-age ritual for those village girls who will ascend to the role of preserving domestic norms and maintaining the stated boundaries of mainstream morality.

Some critics see a deeper malaise in the town's atmosphere. Tom Towers describes the story's basic structure as revolving around "Tom's efforts to exchange the deadening actuality of his everyday life for a more intense, spiritually informed reality which he seeks in the graveyard, on the island, in his quest for secret treasure and with Becky in the cave" (Scharnhorst 130–131). This view of St. Petersburg as not just boring, but "deadening," or as a "phantom town inhabited largely by ghostly presences," further explains the townspeople's morbid fascination with death. It can be seen in Aunt Polly's fantasies about the murder of Dr. Robinson, which are reflected in the custom among school kids to hold inquests on dead cats (Scharnhorst 105, 132, 149). Critical judgments of St Petersburg, Elizabeth Peck notes, have grown harsher over time: "Whereas foolishness, pettiness, and gullibility were once scoffed at as the villagers' worst failings, the adults of St. Petersburg are now charged with vanity, hypocrisy, false posturing, dishonesty, deception, hysteria, childishness, self-indulgence, sensation-seeking, and self-aggrandizement" (Scharnhorst 208). This shift foretells the darker elements that would emerge in the late state of Clemens's career and also suggests a drift in sentiments, among readers, about American public and community life.

Playing by the Book

Tom Sawyer is a text saturated with and propelled by other books and stories, a quality that has led to comparisons with CERVANTES's *Don Quixote*. Like Quixote, Tom is inspired to act out scenes he has read or imagined and use the rules of literary convention in his everyday life. The author grants Tom special stage manager–like privileges over the stories in which he appears. At times, Doctorow writes, it is "as if authorship itself is transferred, and we see a causal connection in what [Tom] seriously and intensely imagined and what comes to pass afterwards" (Doctorow xxxvi). Tom's enthusiasm for stories is accompanied by a taste for overblown performance and grand gestures. In one instance, Tom resists his own impulse to jump out from underneath Aunt Polly's bed, choosing to save his news for later because "the theatrical gorgeousness of the thing appealed strongly to his nature" (chapter 15). When he returns to Jackson's Island, he reveals himself at the mention of his name, "with fine dramatic effect, stepping grandly into camp" (ibid.).

The combination of Tom's theatrical sensibility, desire for excitement, and head full of digested stories (including Robin Hood, pirate tales, western outlaw legends, and myths about Native Americans) keeps the novel in the groove of broader narrative conventions. Through Tom's rule-bound imagination, the children's social space is strictly governed by the conventions of literary genre, and possible actions are allowed or rejected by virtue of their literary aptness. For example, Tom and Joe play Robin Hood "by the book" (chapter 8). When they debate the comparative merits of becoming pirates or hermits, Tom holds firm to their respective criteria, assuring Joe that if he becomes a hermit he will have to "sleep in the hardest place he can find, and put sack-cloth and ashes on his back, and stand out in the rain" (chapter 13). Pirates, though liberated and anarchic in comparison to devout hermits, are equally circumscribed by the activities outlined by the pirate genre. They "take ships, and burn them, and get the money and bury it in awful places in their island where there's ghosts and things to watch it, and kill everybody in the ships—make 'em walk the plank" (ibid.). Conducted according to the conventions of Robin Hood, tales of pirates and Christian hermits, and fantasies about Native Americans, and haunted by the character and structure of Quixote, *Tom Sawyer* is a book that plays, through the whims of its central character, by and against the book.

Structurally, *Tom Sawyer* is a series of loosely connected episodes, a parallel or parody of Quixote's picaresque form (Norton 64). This textual scrappiness—evident in the fragmentary plot and relatively uneven voice—has been, to various readers, either a source of distress or satisfaction. Indeed, Clemens's writing has more often been celebrated for its energy, humor, inventiveness of plot, and virtuosity of language than its craftsmanship, which led Arnold Bennett to apply to Clemens the dubious title of "divine amateur." If one values unity of form, this inconsistency registers as a shortcoming. But one may just as readily experience such arguably jagged construction as a pluralistic organizational scheme. Henry Wonham suggests, on this matter, that we set aside altogether the "obsession with organic unity and read Twain's inconsistencies in tone and

position not as failures, but rather as an engine of his style." Rather than weighing the disparities in tone across the book's various sections, Wonham writes, we can analyze and appreciate Clemens's "ability to juxtapose the attitude of the romancer against that of the straight-faced yarn spinner." He argues that Clemens's "power as a novelist lies precisely in this 'failure' to 'resolve the many voices' of his fiction into a unified and authoritative voice" (Scharnhorst 230, 241).

With such durable popularity and critical importance, *Tom Sawyer* has accumulated considerable cultural sediment, including "a bicentennial stamp . . . commemorative plates and pictures; and countless stage and film productions" (Scharnhorst 148). The popular connection between Tom and American childhood have long since grown so entangled that it is difficult to declare exactly what is quintessential about Tom. On the page, Tom and St. Petersburg have changed little since they first appeared. But over the intervening 130 years, the world has shifted around them. Readers' and critics' notions of childhood, Jacksonian democracy, Native Americans, women, education, small-town life, and the shape of a satisfying story may have changed radically or drifted just a bit over time, but *Tom Sawyer* continues to engage and entertain.

Critical Commentary by Alex Feerst

DRAMATIC ADAPTATIONS

Clemens's interest in creating a play out of *Tom Sawyer* developed along with the novel itself. His interest became even greater after his play based on *The Gilded Age* was a hit on the New York stage. In July 1875, he copyrighted a synopsis of a "Tom Sawyer" drama, but apparently set this project aside in order to concentrate on other plays, including AH SIN; *Cap'n Simon Wheeler, the Amateur Detective;* and *Colonel Sellers as a Scientist.* He finally completed the 22,000-word *Tom Sawyer, A Play in 4 Acts* in 1884 and then pushed his publisher, CHARLES L. WEBSTER, to find a backer to produce it. Meanwhile, the first dramatization of *Tom Sawyer* to be produced may have been an amateur play in Wichita, Kansas, that Clemens gave permission to stage.

Miles and Barton produced Clemens's own play in Yonkers, New York, and in Hartford, in May and June 1885, with a few performances in other towns. The problem of finding professional actors to play a boy was solved by casting women in the lead. Mollie Ravel played Tom in the play's initial run; Kitty Rhoades played him in road-show productions in 1888. Other productions of this play, as well as occasional BURLESQUES, were staged in New York City during the early 1890s.

Later in the 1890s, Clemens sold dramatic rights to *Huckleberry Finn* to the theatrical production team of Klaw and Erlanger. The musical play that they produced with this name in 1902 turned out to be based mostly on *Tom Sawyer*. Clemens was credited with coauthorship, but it appears that a southern writer named Lee Arthur was its primary writer. Klaw and Erlanger's three-act production featured a cast of 80 and elaborate set-pieces. The scenes included several episodes from *Tom Sawyer*, such as the fence whitewashing, but its central story line was original. Huck and his father are suspected of committing burglaries, but the real thieves are exposed when Huck and Tom rescue girls kidnapped by the thieves. The fact that Huck Finn is given a love interest—Amy Lawrence—suggests that Clemens himself was not directly involved in the production. As in the Miles and Barton production, adults played the leads. The play ran for a week each in Hartford, Philadelphia, and Baltimore in late 1902, then closed permanently.

Tom (Tommy Kelly) presents his "tickets" to Mister Walters, the Sunday school superintendent (Donald Meek), as an admiring Becky Thatcher (Anne Gillis) looks on, in the 1938 film *The Adventures of Tom Sawyer*. *(United Artists)*

Meanwhile, impresario PAUL KESTER had the rights to dramatize *Tom Sawyer*. His slowness in developing a script may have contributed to Clemens's allowing Klaw and Erlanger's *Huckleberry Finn* production to draw heavily on *Tom Sawyer*. Kester's play was not copyrighted until 1914, and was not given a first-class BROADWAY production in New York until 1931. Expiration of the original copyright on *Tom Sawyer* that same year led to dozens of new unauthorized dramatizations of the story. Most of these were written for juvenile audiences. The handful of four-act plays to reach publication include Sara Spencer's *Tom Sawyer* (1935) and Charlotte B. Chorpenning's *The Adventures of Tom Sawyer* (1956). In 1957, LIVIN' THE LIFE, a musical based on *Tom Sawyer* and Clemens's other Mississippi writings, was staged in an off-Broadway theater.

Jesse L. Lasky, who earlier adapted *Pudd'nhead Wilson* to film, was the first producer to make a movie from *The Adventures of Tom Sawyer*. He released his production in two parts, with Mary Pickford's brother, Jack Pickford (1896–1993), playing Tom Sawyer in both. *Tom Sawyer* (1917) covered the incidents in the first half of the novel, leaving the rest of the story to the following year's HUCK AND TOM. This first screen adaptation of *Tom Sawyer* was far more faithful to the novel than any version that followed.

The first sound film came in 1930, with Jackie Coogan (1914–1984) starring as Tom in Paramount's *Tom Sawyer*. Paramount immediately followed this production with *Huckleberry Finn*, using the same principals in both films: Junior Durkin played Huck, Clara Blandick was Aunt Polly, Jane Darwell was the Widow Douglas, and Mitzi Green was Becky.

David O. Selznick produced the first color film adaptation of *Tom Sawyer* in 1938, the year before he released *Gone with the Wind*. His production team created a stir by visiting Hannibal to scout locations. However, the town's altered riverfront and modern look made it an unsuitable location for early 19th-century scenes, so the production was taken back to California. The cast of *The Adventures of Tom Sawyer* included Tommy Kelly (1928–) as Tom, Jackie Moran as Huck, May Robson as Aunt Polly, Walter Brennan as Muff Pot-

ter, Victor Jory as Injun Joe, Nana Bryant as Mrs. Thatcher, and Margaret Hamilton as Mrs. Harper.

Tom Sawyer was not adapted to film again until 35 years later. In the meantime, numerous adaptations of the story appeared on television. In 1973, *Reader's Digest* and United Artists released a musical version of the story, with songs by Richard and Robert Sherman. Much of this film was shot on Missouri locations. The cast included Johnnie Whitaker (1959–) as Tom, Jeff East as Huck, Warren Oates as Muff Potter, and Jodie Foster as Becky Thatcher. The same year, a major television adaptation of *Tom Sawyer* starred Josh Albee as Tom, Vic Morrow as Injun Joe, Buddy Ebsen as Muff Potter, and Jane Wyatt as Aunt Polly. In 1985, ABC-TV broadcast a "girls'" version, *The Adventures of Con Sawyer and Hucklemary Finn*, with Drew Barrymore and Brady Ward. In 1982, Soviet television made a three-hour adaptation of *Tom Sawyer*.

Disney's first adaptation of *Tom Sawyer* was released in 1995 as *Tom and Huck*, a much darker film than most screen adaptations of the novel.

CHARACTERS AND RELATED ENTRIES

Austin, Mary   Minor character in *Tom Sawyer* (1876). A friend of Becky Thatcher, who invites her to a picnic while trying to make Tom jealous in chapter 18.

Black Avenger of the Spanish Main   Nickname that Tom Sawyer adopts in *Tom Sawyer* (1876). In chapter 8, he fantasizes about being the "Black Avenger of the Spanish Main." He gives himself this name in chapter 13, when he plays PIRATES on Jackson's Island. He dubs his friends "Huck Finn the Red-Handed" and "Joe Harper the Terror of the Seas." The novel's description of these names as coming from titles in Tom's "favorite literature" appears to be a minor anachronism. NED BUNTLINE's dime novel *Black Avenger of the Spanish Main* was not published until 1847—perhaps three years after *Tom Sawyer* takes place. Another contemporary writer, B. P. SHILLABER, also used "Black Avenger" for a play-pirate name used by his character "Ike."

Constantinople   Fictional Missouri town in *Tom Sawyer* (1876). Mentioned in chapter 4 as the county seat, 12 miles from St. Petersburg, that Judge Thatcher and his daughter Becky are from. In chapter 22 Becky returns to Constantinople for the summer. The town is modeled on PALMYRA, Missouri, the seat of Missouri's MARION COUNTY. In his first draft of *Tom Sawyer*, Clemens called the town "Coonville."

Dobbins, Mister   Character in *Tom Sawyer* (1876). Tom's schoolmaster, Dobbins is modeled on Clemens's boyhood teacher JOHN DAWSON. Chapter 6 introduces him simply as "the master" at a school with 25 "scholars." He and his wife live with a local sign-painter's family. Wearing a wig to cover his total baldness, he is moving into middle age ungracefully. Stern and humorless, he enjoys dishing out corporal punishment. Dobbins is also a frustrated would-be doctor; he keeps an anatomy textbook locked in his desk that he studies when his pupils are busy. Becky Thatcher accidentally tears the book; her fear of punishment suggests that Dobbins is not above whipping girls (chapter 20). He makes his last appearance in chapter 21, when the boys whom he beats in preparation for the annual "Examination Day" exact a nasty revenge.

Douglas, Widow   Character in *Tom Sawyer* (1876) and *Huckleberry Finn* (1884). One of the wealthiest residents of St. Petersburg, the Widow Douglas lives with her spinster sister, Miss Watson (who is not introduced until *Huckleberry Finn*), in a large house on CARDIFF HILL—the fictional name for Hannibal's Holliday's Hill, which was named after the widow's real-life model, Melicent S. Holliday (1800–?). Chapter 5 of *Tom Sawyer* introduces the widow as "fair, smart and forty." She comes to the fore in chapter 29, when Huck Finn overhears Injun Joe plotting with a partner to assault her in order to avenge a whipping that her husband inflicted on him when he was justice of the peace. Huck saves the widow, however, by alerting Jones the Welchman, who drives off the assailants with the help of his sons. Recognizing Huck's inner goodness, the widow informally adopts him and—to his consternation—attempts to "sivilize" him. In the last chapter, Huck runs off, but Tom Sawyer talks him into returning. *Huckleberry Finn* opens with Huck still chafing under the civilizing influ-

ences of the widow and her sister. He likes the widow, but the pressures on him to reform contribute to his readiness to leave St. Petersburg forever after his brutal father shows up.

In the transition from *Tom Sawyer* to *Huckleberry Finn* (1884), Clemens lost track of several details about the widow. At the end of *Tom Sawyer*, she invests Huck's share of the treasure that he and Tom found, but in *Huckleberry Finn*, responsibility for this fortune has somehow passed to Judge Thatcher. The "Raft Chapter" of *Huckleberry Finn*, which Clemens removed before finishing the novel, alludes to the slave Jim's belonging to the widow; in the finished novel, however, Jim belongs to Miss Watson. When Huck concludes his adventures at the end of *Huckleberry Finn*, he fears that Sally Phelps will try to adopt and "sivilize" him, apparently forgetting the Widow Douglas. He threatens to light out west, but in the sequel stories, he is back to living with the widow.

The Widow Douglas has been portrayed in many screen adaptations of *Tom Sawyer* and *Huckleberry Finn*. Jane Darwell, best known as Ma Joad in 1939's *Grapes of Wrath*, played her in Paramount's productions of *Tom Sawyer* (1930) and *Huckleberry Finn* (1931). Spring Byington had the role in the 1939 version of *Huckleberry Finn* with Mickey Rooney. More recent actresses in the role include Josephine Hutchinson (1960), Lucille Benson (1973 and 1974), Jean Howard (1975), Helen Kleeb (1981), and Sada Thompson (1986).

fence, whitewashing of   One of the most famous episodes in Clemens's fiction occurs in *Tom Sawyer* (1876) when Aunt Polly orders Tom to whitewash a fence 30 yards long and nine feet high—dimensions that Tom probably exaggerates in his distressed imagination (chapter 2). Overwhelmed by the size of the job before he even starts, Tom tries to bribe Jim, a young slave boy, to help. After Aunt Polly forbids this, Tom recruits an army of other boys to do the whitewashing for him. Astonishingly, Tom does not pay them—they pay *him*. Now part of American folklore, this episode is annually reenacted in a fence-painting competition during TOM SAWYER DAYS in Hannibal—where a fence erected next to Mark Twain's BOYHOOD

Tom Sawyer (Tommy Kelly) enticing a friend to whitewash the fence in the 1938 film *The Adventures of Tom Sawyer.* *(United Artists)*

HOME stands as a permanent monument. The episode is also commemorated on a U.S. POSTAGE STAMP using a NORMAN ROCKWELL painting and is probably the most frequently depicted scene on the covers of the hundreds of editions of *Tom Sawyer* that have been published.

Tom entices other boys to pay for the privilege of whitewashing by making the job appear to be fun, not work. From the catalog of loot that he amasses, it appears that as many as 20 different boys help. Only three, however, are named: Billy Fisher, Johnny Miller, and Ben Rogers (Huck Finn is a notable omission.) Among the items that Tom collects are an apple, a dead rat, a key, a piece of chalk, a glass bottle-stopper, a tin soldier, a one-eyed kitten, a brass doorknob, a dog collar, and a knife handle, as well as firecrackers, 12 marbles,

and several tadpoles. The next day, he swaps most of these items at Sunday school, using them to accumulate enough "tickets" to claim a prize Bible.

According to Clemens's AUTOBIOGRAPHY, he created the fence-painting episode during a visit to England in the early 1870s. He told the story to Henry IRVING and the Irish playwright William Gorman Wills at a dinner, then returned to his hotel and wrote it out.

Finn, Huckleberry See the Characters and Related Entries section of the *Huckleberry Finn* entry.

Fisher, Billy Minor character in *Tom Sawyer* (1876). One of only three boys identified by name as paying for the privilege of whitewashing the fence in chapter 2, Billy gives Tom a kite in good repair for his chance.

Frazer, Judge Minor character in *Tom Sawyer* (1876). In chapter 22, Tom anxiously awaits the death of St. Petersburg's elderly justice of the peace, so that he can wear his CADETS OF TEMPERANCE sash in a funeral procession. When Frazer appears to be recovering, Tom quits the Cadets. Immediately afterward, the judge has a relapse and dies.

Harper, Joe Character in *Tom Sawyer* (1876) and other stories. Tom's "bosom friend." Joe first appears in chapter 3 of *Tom Sawyer,* when he and Tom oppose each other as generals in a mock war. Four chapters later, Joe sits next to Tom in school and joins him in playing with a tick on Tom's slate. In chapter 8, both boys play hookey and meet on CARDIFF HILL, where they act out Robin Hood games.

Unlike Tom and Huck Finn, Joe has two living parents. His mother, Sereny Harper, appears several times in *Tom Sawyer.* His father, Captain Harper, is mentioned but is never seen on his own. Joe, like Tom, gets into mischief readily, and he shares Tom's feelings of being put upon by the world. In chapter 13, he joins Tom and Huck in running off to Jackson's Island to become a PIRATE. While the boys are on the island, Joe's mother meets with Aunt Polly in chapter 15 to agonize over the boys' disappearance. After the Jackson's Island episode, Joe ceases to be a central character. In chapter 18 Becky Thatcher invites him and his sister, Susy, to a picnic. In chapter 22, Joe is mentioned as one of the boys who got religion during a revival while Tom Sawyer was laid up with the measles.

Joe plays no visible role at Becky's picnic in chapter 29, but his family has a part in the events that follow. Before leaving for the picnic at McDougal's CAVE, Becky Thatcher tells her mother that she will spend the night at the Harpers' instead of returning home. Becky and Tom get lost in the cave and do not return, however. Mrs. Thatcher and Aunt Polly are not aware that they are missing until the next day, when Mrs. Harper tells them that Becky never came to her house.

The final mention of Joe in *Tom Sawyer* is in chapter 33, in which Tom names him as one of the boys he will invite to join his robber band. Joe returns as a member of Tom's Gang in chapter 2, 3, and 8 of *Huckleberry Finn* (1884), in which he is called "Jo Harper." He also makes a mute appearance in "TOM SAWYER'S CONSPIRACY." In that story, he is bedridden with the measles. Tom gets in bed with him to contract the disease himself—even though he already had the measles in *Tom Sawyer*. It turns out, however, that what Joe has is scarlet fever. Tom contracts that disease and nearly dies. Joe's fate is not mentioned.

The childhood friend of Clemens generally regarded as the primary model for Joe Harper is JOHN B. BRIGGS. Clemens also drew on other friends, however, notably JOHN GARTH and WILL BOWEN.

Hodges, Jimmy Figure mentioned in *Tom Sawyer* (1876). An acquaintance of Tom, Hodges has died just before the novel begins (chapter 8). Tom feels sorry for himself and envies Hodges because he has been released from worldly cares.

Hollis, Jim Minor character in *Tom Sawyer* (1876). A friend of Tom, Jim is briefly mentioned in chapters 4, 6, and 22. In the latter chapter, he is one of the boys who gets religion during a revival while Tom has the measles.

Hopkins, Mother Figure mentioned in *Tom Sawyer* (1876). In chapter 6, Huck Finn alludes to Mother Hopkins as a reputed witch and tells Tom that his father, Pap Finn, once drove her off when she was "a-witching him." Although Mother Hopkins does not actually appear in the narrative, TRUE WILLIAMS includes her portrait in his illustrations. In the play that Clemens adapted from the novel, Mother Hopkins is developed into a real witch.

Clemens used the name "Hopkins" for many characters, particularly in his posthumously published writings. In view of the fact that Huck cites Mother Hopkins as an expert on curing warts in *Tom Sawyer,* it may be significant that Clemens used the name "Wart Hopkins" for a character who foreshadowed Huck in "BOY'S MANUSCRIPT."

Huck and Tom; or, The Further Adventures of Tom Sawyer (1918)   Film starring Jack Pickford (1896–1933) as Tom Sawyer and Robert Gordon as Huck Finn. A sequel to the previous year's film *Tom Sawyer,* this five-reel silent film completes the story of Clemens's original *Tom Sawyer* (1876). Its highlights include the GRAVE-ROBBING scene, Injun Joe's trial, and Tom and Becky's adventure in the CAVE.

Injun Joe Character in *Tom Sawyer* (1876). Described by Huck Finn as a "murderin' half-breed" (chapter 9), the cruel and vengeful Injun Joe is the novel's one truly villainous character; he has been a disreputable resident of St. Petersburg for at least five years. He appears only a few times in the narrative, but usually unexpectedly. Even when he is not present, his specter looms.

In chapter 9, Huck and Tom stumble upon Injun Joe, Muff Potter, and Dr. Robinson opening a grave in the town CEMETERY. Injun Joe argues with Robinson over a past slight and then kills him while Potter is momentarily knocked out. When Potter awakens, Injun Joe convinces him that *he* (Potter) is the killer. The next day, when Tom and Huck see Injun Joe give his version of what happened, they are so dumbfounded that he is not struck dead that they conclude he is in league with Satan. Some townspeople want to run Injun Joe out of town for body-snatching, but no one has the nerve to take him on. He reappears at the murder trial in chapter 23, when he testifies convincingly against Potter. Just as Potter's situation looks hopeless, Tom is called as a surprise witness. As Tom starts to declare Injun Joe the murderer, Injun Joe bolts from the building and disappears, leaving Tom more scared than ever.

In chapter 26, Tom and Huck again happen on Injun Joe, at the HAUNTED HOUSE. He has been living in town, unrecognized, as a "DEAF AND DUMB Spaniard." He has a new partner—who is never identified—with whom he is planning a new crime. After he satisfies his need for vengeance against an unnamed party, he intends to flee permanently to TEXAS. Purely by chance, he finds a box of gold coins in the house. Huck and Tom are determined to get hold of the treasure, so they stalk Injun Joe and his partner.

As Tom goes off to McDougal's Cave on Becky Thatcher's picnic in chapter 29, Huck follows Injun Joe and his partner to CARDIFF HILL. He eavesdrops and learns that Injun Joe intends to mutilate the Widow Douglas. Injun Joe wants revenge for a public horse-whipping that the widow's husband gave him when he was justice of the peace. His partner resists the idea, but Injun Joe threatens to kill him. Huck alerts Jones the Welchman, who, with his sons, chases the villains off. Injun Joe again disappears.

Meanwhile, Tom and Becky get lost in the cave. While searching for a way out a day or two later, Tom sees Injun Joe in the cave. Tom escapes detection and eventually finds a way out of the cave. Correctly guessing that Injun Joe has hidden the gold in the cave, Tom does not tell anyone that he has seen him there. After spending two weeks recuperating from his ordeal, Tom learns that Judge Thatcher has had the cave's entrance sealed shut with an iron door. Tom finally reveals that Injun Joe is still in the cave. People rush to the cave and they find Injun Joe dead. His body is just beyond the new door. He has died of starvation after eating candle stumps and bats while trying to dig out with his Bowie knife. Injun Joe is buried just outside the cave. The anonymous narrator reveals that there had been a popular movement to petition the governor to pardon Injun

The murderous Injun Joe haunts Tom's dreams in chapter 14 of *Tom Sawyer.*

Joe, even though the man is believed to have murdered five people in the town.

The geography of the cave episode is peculiar. After Tom and Becky escape from the cave, it is estimated that they had wandered five miles from the cave's entrance—the spot where Injun Joe later dies. It seems unlikely that Injun Joe would penetrate equally deeply into the cave to hide his treasure. Moreover, he should have known about the abundant freshwater to be found in the cave.

Clemens took Injun Joe's name from a Hannibal resident about two years older than him whose real name may have been Joe Douglas. This man was an Osage INDIAN who had been scalped by Pawnees as a child and brought to Hannibal by cattlemen as a teenager. Clemens's AUTOBIOGRAPHY claims that the real Injun Joe once subsisted on bats while lost in the cave. He died a respected citizen in 1925.

Injun Joe does not appear in any other stories, but Clemens mentions him in chapter 13 of IS SHAKE-SPEARE DEAD?

Jackson's Island Fictional island in *Tom Sawyer* (1876) and *Huckleberry Finn* (1884). Jackson's Island is on the Mississippi River, about three miles below St. Petersburg, where the river is a mile wide. In chapters 13 to 16 of *Tom Sawyer*, Tom, Huck, and Joe Harper spend a week on the uninhabited island playing PIRATES. When they explore the island, they determine that it is about three miles long and a quarter mile wide (chapter 14). A 200-yard-wide channel separates the island from the ILLINOIS shore, leaving it about 1,100 yards from the Missouri shore. It has a large sandbar on its northern end, where the boys land, and is heavily forested.

In *Huckleberry Finn*, Huck flees to Jackson's Island to escape from his brutal father and joins forces with the runaway slave Jim there. Chapter 7 describes the island as "standing up out of the middle of the river"; however, a fuller description in chapter 9 matches that of *Tom Sawyer*. This chapter also adds a new feature: a 40-foot-high rocky ridge near the center of the island in which Huck and Jim find a cave that they use as a hideout until they begin their raft journey. Tom, Huck and Jim use the same cave for their headquarters in "TOM SAWYER'S CONSPIRACY."

Clemens reputedly modeled Jackson's Island on a real island near Hannibal that was known as Glasscock's Island in his time. That island's subsequent erosion by the river, however, makes it a poor model for a place with a rocky cavern. There are still several other islands near Hannibal that resemble Clemens's Jackson's Island—a name given to one of them on modern tourist maps.

Jake, Uncle Figure mentioned in *Tom Sawyer* (1876). A slave belonging to the family of Ben Rogers, Jake occasionally allows Huck Finn to sleep in a hayloft and gives him food. Huck tells Tom Sawyer that Jake likes him because he (Huck) never acts as if he were above him and occasionally even eats with him (chapter 28). Jake is one of the few AFRICAN-AMERICAN characters in *Tom Sawyer*.

His friendship with Huck in that novel anticipates the latter's relationship with Jim in *Huckleberry Finn* (1884).

Jim AFRICAN-AMERICAN character in *Tom Sawyer* (1876). Described in chapter 1 as "a small colored boy," Jim works for Aunt Polly. In the next chapter, Tom tries to persuade him to help him whitewash the fence until Aunt Polly intervenes. Clemens probably modeled this character on a young slave boy named Sandy who worked for his family briefly when he was a child. In an essay on his mother, Clemens recalls being driven to distraction by Sandy's constant singing, until his mother reminded him that Sandy sang to keep his mind off having lost all his family. The fictional Jim is singing "Buffalo Gals" when Tom accosts him by the fence.

One of the few characters in *Tom Sawyer* who is clearly an African American, this Jim is not related to the Jim of *Huckleberry Finn*, who never appears in *Tom Sawyer*.

Jones the Welchman Character in *Tom Sawyer* (1876). Jones lives in CARDIFF HILL, below the Widow Douglas. In chapter 29, he is introduced simply as "the Welchman" (a name that the original illustrator TRUE WILLIAMS renders as "Welshman"). After Huck Finn warns him that Injun Joe and his partner are about to attack the widow, Jones and his two sons chase the assailants away. Afterward, Jones welcomes Huck back and gives him food and a bed. In chapter 33 he is finally identified as "Jones." Clemens modeled the character on a Hannibal bookseller named John Davies (c. 1810–1885), who married Clemens's schoolteacher, MARY ANN NEWCOMB, in the late 1840s.

Lawrence, Amy Minor character in *Tom Sawyer* (1876). Amy is Tom's girlfriend until he sees Becky Thatcher in chapter 3. As Tom showers attention on Becky, Amy simpers in the background. Later, Tom flirts with Amy to make Becky jealous (chapter 18), but after he and Becky make up, Amy disappears from the story. In "BOY'S MANUSCRIPT," an earlier story that anticipates *Tom Sawyer*, "Amy" is also the name of a character who is Becky's prototype.

Miller, Johnny Minor character in *Tom Sawyer* (1876). In the fence whitewashing episode of chapter 2, Johnny is one of only three boys to paint the fence who are identified by name. He gives Tom a dead rat on a string for the privilege. He is also mentioned in chapter 16 as a boy likely to be jealous that Tom and Joe are learning how to smoke. In chapter 18, Becky Thatcher invites Johnny's sister Grace to her picnic.

Mufferson, Willie Minor character in *Tom Sawyer* (1876). St. Petersburg's "MODEL BOY," Mufferson appears only in chapter 5. He is "the pride of all the mothers," and an object of loathing to his peers. Clemens modeled him on Theodore Dawson, the son of JOHN D. DAWSON, his last schoolteacher.

Number Two Secret hiding place in *Tom Sawyer* (1876). In chapter 26, Tom and Huck overhear Injun Joe say that he will hide the gold he and his partner have found in a place he calls "Number Two—under the cross." The boys initially think that Joe is referring to a room number in a temperance tavern; in chapter 33, they discover that the "cross" is a spot marked in the CAVE.

Polly, Aunt Character in *Tom Sawyer* (1876) and other stories. Tom's kindhearted and loving guardian, Aunt Polly utters the very first word in *Tom Sawyer*, when she calls out Tom's name. Immediately described as "old," she wears glasses for appearance rather than for function. Tom, who is Polly's "own dead sister's boy," presumably takes his surname from a father, so Aunt Polly and his mother most likely shared a different surname. While Clemens does not assign Polly a surname in any of his novels, he calls her "Polly Sawyer" in the play he adapted from *Tom Sawyer*. However, he often erred in remembering the names and relationships of his characters. In "TOM SAWYER'S CONSPIRACY" Aunt Polly has a brother who is called "Uncle Fletcher," so her surname may be Fletcher.

Aunt Polly is also the guardian of Tom's half-brother, Sid Sawyer, and his cousin Mary. Polly's exact relationship to these two children is not explained. As Tom's cousin, Mary could be Aunt Polly's daughter. However, there is no hint that Aunt Polly has ever been married or that she has ever had children of her own.

Aunt Polly's is a nearly constant presence throughout *Tom Sawyer*. She hovers over Tom to get him to whitewash the fence, she sees him off to school in the mornings, and she is upset on the nights that he stays out late. Although she disciplines Tom without hesitation, she agonizes when she thinks she may have gone too far. Recognizing that though Tom is mischievous, he is basically not bad, she is satisfied to know that he cares for her.

Aunt Polly also appears in later stories, but as little more than a background figure. She is mentioned in chapters 1 and 8 of *Huckleberry Finn* but does not appear until chapter 42, when she goes to the Arkansas home of her sister, Sally Phelps, to investigate what has become of Tom. In "HUCK FINN AND TOM SAWYER AMONG THE INDIANS," an immediate sequel to *Huckleberry Finn*, Aunt Polly calls the boys home from her sister's Arkansas farm,

This illustration of Aunt Polly from the last chapter of the first edition of *Tom Sawyer* closely resembles B. J. Shillaber's Mrs. Partington.

then takes them to visit other (unnamed) relatives in western Missouri.

At the end of *Tom Sawyer Abroad,* Jim goes home from Egypt to fetch Tom's pipe and returns with Aunt Polly's order for Tom and Huck to come home immediately, thus ending the story abruptly. Aunt Polly also appears briefly at the beginning of *Tom Sawyer, Detective* (1896), and she makes her final appearance in the posthumously published "Tom Sawyer's Conspiracy."

In his AUTOBIOGRAPHY, Clemens admits that he modeled Aunt Polly closely on his mother, Jane L. Clemens. Like Aunt Polly, Jane Clemens was kindhearted and loving but differed in having a sharp tongue, an inventive mind, and a lively sense of humor—none of which Aunt Polly shares. Another model for Aunt Polly can be found in B. P. SHILLABER's character, Mrs. Partington. TRUE WILLIAMS's illustration of Aunt Polly in chapter 22 of the first edition of *Tom Sawyer* is taken directly from Shillaber's *Life and Sayings of Mrs. Partington* (1854). Clemens could also have taken elements from his aunt, Martha Ann Quarles, the wife of JOHN QUARLES—a woman whom everyone knew as "Aunt Patsy."

Potter, Muff   Character in *Tom Sawyer* (1876). St. Petersburg's amiable TOWN DRUNKARD, Potter is a key figure in a central story line. Tom and Huck happen to see Potter and Injun Joe robbing a grave for Dr. Robinson late one night, when Injun Joe kills Robinson after Potter is knocked unconscious. When Potter awakens, Injun Joe convinces him that *he* killed the doctor (chapter 9). After Potter goes to jail, Tom and Huck—who know him to be innocent—agonize over what to do. Their mortal fear of Injun Joe prevents them from speaking out, so they ease their guilt by taking tobacco and matches to the tearfully grateful Potter. After Potter finally goes on trial in chapter 23, Tom denounces Injun Joe as the true murderer and Potter drops out of the story.

Clemens's inspiration for Muff Potter came from at least two sources. The character was partly modeled on BEN BLANKENSHIP, one of Hannibal's amiable loafers. Also, around 1853 there was a drunk in the town jail named Dennis McDavid, or McDermid, to whom Clemens recalled passing matches through a cell window.

Muff Potter has provided a colorful screen role for character actors of widely varying ages, including Tully Marshall (1930), Walter Brennan (1938), Warren Oates (1973), and Buddy Ebsen (TV, 1973).

Robin Hood   Legendary English outlaw believed to have lived during the late 12th century. In chapter 8 of *Tom Sawyer* (1876), Tom and Joe Harper play a Robin Hood game on CARDIFF HILL, which they pretend is Sherwood Forest. Characteristically, Tom insists on going "by the book," meaning that as Robin Hood, *he* cannot be killed. Afterward, both boys admit that they "would rather be outlaws a year in Sherwood Forest than President of the United States forever." Later, Tom plays Robin Hood with Huck Finn, who never heard of the outlaw whom Tom calls "the noblest man that ever was" (chapter 26). A letter that Clemens wrote to WILL BOWEN in 1870 recalls how he and Will played Robin Hood games as boys.

Robinson, Doctor   Minor character in *Tom Sawyer* (1876). Robinson appears only in the GRAVE-ROBBING scene in chapter 9, in which he, Injun Joe, and Muff Potter dig up the recently buried body of Hoss Williams. When Injun Joe accuses Robinson of having treated him badly five years earlier and threatens him with his fist, Robinson knocks him down. Potter then jumps Robinson, only to get himself knocked out; at that moment, Injun Joe stabs Robinson to death with Potter's knife. Tom Sawyer and Huck Finn happen to witness the murder, and they return to the site the next day along with most of the townspeople, who see Robinson's body lying on the ground. Muff Potter is arrested for his murder.

Clemens's own dramatization of *Tom Sawyer* depicts the doctor as an unpleasant and pushy man who forces Potter into grave-robbing.

Rogers, Ben   Minor character in *Tom Sawyer* (1876) and *Huckleberry Finn* (1884). A friend of Tom Sawyer, Ben is one of only three boys identified by name as helping to whitewash the fence in chapter 2 of *Tom Sawyer.* He pays an apple for the privilege. Though he is apparently Tom's close friend, he is mentioned only in passing in later chapters. Toward the end of *Tom Sawyer*, Tom names Ben as one of the boys he wants to ask to join his new gang; Ben appears briefly as a gang member in the early chapters of *Huckleberry Finn.* Ben has a sister, Sally, whom Becky Thatcher invites to her picnic in chapter 18 of *Tom Sawyer.*

Saint Petersburg   Fictional town in *Tom Sawyer, Huckleberry Finn,* and other stories. Clearly modeled on Clemens's hometown of Hannibal in northeastern Missouri, St. Petersburg (spelled "St. Petersburgh" in the first edition) appears to be at the same location, on the west bank of the Mississippi. It also matches Hannibal in having a wooded promontory, CARDIFF HILL, on the north side of town. Several miles downriver, toward the ILLINOIS shore, there is a large uninhabited island, Jackson's Island. A few miles south of the center of town is a large limestone CAVE. Tom Sawyer lives in the center of town in a two-story house that closely resembles Clemens's BOYHOOD HOME of the 1840s.

Virtually all the events in *Tom Sawyer* (1876) occur in or near St. Petersburg. The town is also the setting of the first six chapters of *Huckleberry Finn* (1884), which mentions St. Petersburg by name only in chapters 11, 12, and 42. Among the other stories about Tom and Huck, St. Petersburg is the principal setting for "TOM SAWYER'S CONSPIRACY"—which does not mention its name—and "SCHOOL-HOUSE HILL," which calls it simply "Petersburg."

While St. Petersburg physically resembles Hannibal, it differs from the real town in being smaller and less diverse. It appears to have fewer people, fewer industries, and fewer activities. Incidents and characters in *Tom Sawyer* indicate that the town has a mayor, a postmaster, a town clock, at least one church and one school, a newspaper, a printer, two taverns, an abandoned slaughterhouse, and an abandoned tannery. An indication of the town's smallness is the fact that its CEMETERY has only wooden head markers. In general, the town feels more rural than Hannibal; in this regard it resembles the nearby village of FLORIDA, where Clemens spent most of his summers during the 1840s. Many of the events in *Tom Sawyer* occur during a long summer vacation; it is natural that Clemens's depiction of life in St. Petersburg would reflect the summertime experiences of his youth.

The literal meaning of "St. Petersburg" is "Saint Peter's town," or heaven. If Clemens consciously intended the name to stand for "heaven," it represents an interesting contrast with "Hannibal." At least once, he wrote the latter name as "H———l," possibly implying that Hannibal was synonymous with "Hell." To call the fictional counterpart of such a place "heaven" suggests that he intended to satirize Hannibal's small-town hypocrisy—just as he did with the name Hadleyburg in another story. Alternatively, equating St. Petersburg with heaven might simply reflect Clemens's idealization of his summers in Florida. In his AUTOBIOGRAPHY, he recalls the Florida farm of his uncle JOHN QUARLES as a heavenly place for boys.

Clemens was also aware of St. Petersburg, RUSSIA. ANSON BURLINGAME, whom he greatly admired, died there in 1870. Years later Clemens used Russia's capital as a principal setting in "THE BELATED RUSSIAN PASSPORT." His future son-in-law, OSSIP GABRILOWITSCH, was born there in 1878.

Sawyer (?), Mary   Character in *Tom Sawyer* (1876). A cousin of Tom Sawyer, Mary lives with Tom, Tom's half-brother Sid Sawyer, and Tom's Aunt Polly. Mary is a steady presence in Tom's life, but several questions about her are unanswered. For example, neither her last name nor her relationship to Aunt Polly is ever specified. Her name may be *Sawyer,* but the evidence for this is thin. In chapter 32 of *Huckleberry Finn* (1884), Huck talks about Mary and the "Sawyer family" together. Does this mean that Mary is a Sawyer? If so, what is her relationship to Aunt Polly, who is the sister of Tom's mother? Uncertainty about Mary's family ties confused even W. D. HOWELLS. When he reviewed *Tom Sawyer,* he mistakenly alluded to Mary as Tom's sister. (In the 1938 film *The Adventures of Tom Sawyer,* Mary calls herself "Mary Wadsworth Sawyer.")

Another question is how old Mary is. Her age is not given, but she is clearly more mature than Tom. When she first appears, in chapter 3 of *Tom Sawyer,* she is returning from a week in the country at a moment when Tom and other children are still in school. It thus appears that Mary herself is not in school. In chapter 18, however, Sid and Tom leave for school and Mary seems to be going with them. One clue to Mary's age is the fact that she is clearly modeled on PAMELA CLEMENS MOFFETT, Clemens's sister, who was eight years his senior. Like Pamela, Mary is gentle and helpful. In chapter 4, she helps Tom learn his verses for Sunday school, giving him a pocketknife as encouragement. The gift is enough of an extravagance to suggest that Mary—like Pamela—has income of her own. Later, Mary stays home from Becky Thatcher's picnic to tend Tom's sick brother Sid.

Mary also appears briefly in *TOM SAWYER, DETECTIVE* and in "TOM SAWYER'S CONSPIRACY." In the latter story, Aunt Polly sends Mary and Sid out of town when Tom appears to have measles.

Sawyer, Sid   Character in *Tom Sawyer* (1876) and other stories. Tom's priggish younger half-brother, Sid lives with Tom, Aunt Polly, and Tom's cousin Mary (Sawyer?). He first appears in chapter 1 of *Tom Sawyer* (in which he is called "Sidney" only once) but is not clearly identified as a "Sawyer" until chapter 33 of *Huckleberry Finn* (1884). As half-brothers surnamed *Sawyer*, Sid and Tom presumably had the same father and different mothers. Since Aunt Polly is identified as the sister of Tom's mother, Sid's relationship to Polly is unclear—unless he is the son of Tom's mother, in which case the reference to him as "Sid Sawyer" in *Huckleberry Finn* is a mistake. Most likely, Clemens simply never worked out the precise relationships among the characters.

Throughout *Tom Sawyer*, Sid is a constant irritant to Tom. He spies on Tom and reports to Aunt Polly. The brothers share a bedroom, making it difficult for Tom to come and go without being observed. In the unfinished story "TOM SAWYER'S CONSPIRACY," Sid poses such a threat to Tom's scheming that Tom tries to contract measles in order to give Aunt Polly a reason to send Sid out of town.

Sid appears for just a moment in *Huckleberry Finn*. In chapter 8, Huck sees him on the boat that is searching the river for his body. Later in the novel, Tom Sawyer poses as Sid at the Arkansas farm of his aunt Sally Phelps (chapter 33).

Sid also appears briefly in the first chapter of "SCHOOLHOUSE HILL," in which he is described as "the MODEL BOY." Clemens said that he based Sid on his own younger brother, Henry Clemens, but added that Henry was a much finer boy.

Sawyer, Tom   Arguably Clemens's most famous fictional creation, Tom Sawyer has come to symbolize Clemens's work as a whole to many. Tom and his friend Huck Finn are usually viewed as a team, as neither appears in any story without the other. Nevertheless, they are very different kinds of characters.

Clemens provides little physical description of Tom. When Tom first appears in *Tom Sawyer* (1876), he is described simply as "a small boy." Little else about him is revealed, except that he has curly hair and generally goes barefoot. Also, he is tough enough to lick most boys his age and athletic enough to swim considerable distances. Clemens is especially vague about Tom's age, which seems to rise significantly between the beginning and end of *Tom Sawyer*. In the early chapters, Tom appears to be about nine years old. This is the age that Clemens himself was in 1844—the approximate year in which the novel is set. By the last chapters and in *Huckleberry Finn* (1884) and other stories, Tom seems to be at least 13. Uncertainty about Tom's age is reflected in the illustrations of Tom that have adorned Clemens's books and in the casting of films adapted from these stories.

One of the changes in Tom that occur over the course of *Tom Sawyer* is his growing maturity regarding girls. Early in the narrative he has a purely boyish infatuation with Becky Thatcher, a girl who clearly is about eight or nine years old. Tom expresses his emotions by showing off to Becky to get her attention, flirting with Amy Lawrence to make Becky jealous, and sulking when things go badly. As the narrative progresses, he proves his worth by performing real deeds. By its end, he seems to be on the threshold of becoming an adult, while Becky still appears to be about nine years old.

From the start of *Tom Sawyer*, Clemens makes it clear that Tom is *not* a "MODEL BOY." He is inattentive at school and church, he plays hookey frequently, he often sneaks out at night, and he is willing to lie to protect himself. These qualities make Tom an average, normal boy; however, he also has qualities that set him apart. What makes Tom special is his imagination. He is restless, often scheming, and always looking for glory. Despite his lack of interest in school, he is evidently an avid reader of romantic classics, as well as contemporary pulp fiction. He likes to play games based on heroes he reads about, such as Robin Hood and characters in the works of JAMES FENIMORE COOPER. He also finds inspiration in less noble literary creations such as the Black Avenger of the Spanish Main. His impulse to manufacture adventure and to romanticize the ordinary casts him in the mold of CERVANTES's Don Quixote. In this regard, he is almost the opposite of Huck Finn, the realist who has often been called Tom's Sancho Panza.

Tom sees opportunities where others would not and seizes them. Faced with the daunting task of whitewashing a fence, for example, he gets his friends to pay him for the privilege of doing his work. The next day he swaps his freshly accumulated wealth for "tickets" that net him a prize of a Bible that most Sunday-school students spend years working to earn.

Tom is both an initiator and a leader. In *Tom Sawyer,* he is a general in the boys' mock wars, and he generally takes charge in make-believe games. He initiates the PIRATE expedition to Jackson's Island, and he holds the little band together when the enthusiasm of Huck and Joe Harper fades. Later, it is his idea to search for pirate treasure, and he formulates the plan that leads to Injun Joe's downfall. In virtually all the episodes that involve boys undertaking something together, Tom is in charge. Not all his schemes are successful, however. Indeed, some are nearly disastrous.

Several of Tom's schemes have particularly unfortunate results for the ex-slave Jim. In the last chapters of *Huckleberry Finn,* Tom puts Jim through an elaborate ordeal in order to "escape," though he alone among the participants in the scheme knows that Jim is already legally free. The escape plan is a fiasco, leaving Tom with a bullet in the leg in chapter 40. Always ready to turn defeat into victory, Tom relishes the wound as a badge of honor. In "HUCK FINN AND TOM SAWYER AMONG THE INDI-

ANS," Tom's romantic infatuation with "Cooper INDIANS" results in Jim's being taken captive by the Sioux. In "TOM SAWYER'S CONSPIRACY," Tom's elaborate attempt to organize an abolitionist hoax gets Jim arrested for murder.

Matched against Tom's tendency to create trouble for his friends are his loyalty, courage, and innate tendency to do the right thing in the end. In *Tom Sawyer* he and Huck take a blood oath never to reveal to anyone that they have seen Injun Joe commit murder in the GRAVE-ROBBING scene. With good reason, Tom has a mortal fear of Injun Joe. Yet, when the life of the innocent Muff Potter is on the line, Tom steps forward to testify against Injun Joe, fully knowing the terror that awaits him. Likewise, he is willing to risk everything to rectify the mistakes that he makes. In "Indians," he commits himself to rescuing Jim or dying. To right the wrong

True Williams's frontispiece for *Tom Sawyer* depicts Tom fishing while wearing his Sunday best—a moment that never occurs in the novel.

he accidentally creates in "Conspiracy," he stands ready to spend his entire personal fortune—which is considerable, thanks to the treasure he finds in *Tom Sawyer*—and risk his own life to help free Jim. In these respects and others, Tom is a clear literary ancestor of J. K. Rowling's boy wizard, Harry Potter.

A final trait that makes Tom special is his inventiveness. He is both intelligent and indomitable. Perhaps the most impressive demonstration of his resourcefulness is the episode in *Tom Sawyer* when he and Becky Thatcher get lost in McDougal's CAVE. By stretching their resources and strength to the limit over three days in utter darkness, he keeps Becky's hopes alive and finds a way out. Then, despite his exhaustion, he has the presence of mind not to reveal that he saw Injun Joe in the cave. He surmises, correctly, that the gold that Injun Joe found earlier is in the cave. Withholding this information gives him the chance to return to the cave later with Huck to claim the treasure. In *Tom Sawyer, Detective* (1896), Tom's uncle Silas Phelps is tried for murder. The case seems so hopeless that Phelps's lawyer virtually gives up. Tom takes charge of the case, and saves his uncle with a brilliant piece of deduction.

Clemens's preface to *Tom Sawyer* states that Tom Sawyer "is drawn from life . . . but not from an individual—he is a combination of the characteristics of three boys whom I knew, and therefore belongs to the composite school of architecture." It is generally conceded that just as *Tom Sawyer* is Clemens's most autobiographical novel, Tom Sawyer is the character that reveals the most about him as a boy. His memoirs and the testimony of childhood friends, such as Laura Hawkins, confirm that he did many of the things that he attributed to Tom Sawyer, especially in the early chapters of *Tom Sawyer.*

Between film and television adaptations of *Tom Sawyer* and *Huckleberry Finn*, dozens of actors have played Tom. They have ranged in age from 10-year-old Tommy Kelly (1938) to 22-year-old Jack Pickford (1917 and 1918). Other actors who have played Tom include Jackie Coogan (1930 and 1931), Johnnie Whitaker (1973 and 1974), Donny Most (1975) of "Happy Days" fame, and Jonathan Taylor Thomas (1995).

Sprague, Reverend Mister   Minor character in *Tom Sawyer* (1876). Sprague is the minister of a St. Petersburg church, whose congregation regards him as a "wonderful reader." Clemens had a professional interest in public reading; he often criticized ministers as a group as being poor readers. In chapter 5, he puts Sprague to a severe test. The minister delivers a long, wordy Calvinist sermon that threatens to put his congregation to sleep. Tom meanwhile plays with a beetle that gets loose and pinches a stray dog. The dog then runs wildly through the aisles, yelping and bringing welcome relief to the congregation—without stopping Sprague from finishing his sermon. (This scene is repeated in chapters 3–4 of *Connecticut Yankee*, in which the magician Merlin's dull recitation puts to sleep an audience that is awakened by a wildly cavorting dog.) Though not mentioned by name again, Sprague is probably the "clergyman" in chapter 17 who delivers the funeral sermon for Tom, Huck, and Joe Harper, who are presumed dead.

Still-house branch   Stream near Hannibal. A small tributary of the Mississippi River located north of CARDIFF HILL, this stream is mentioned in *Tom Sawyer* (1876) as the locale of the haunted house. It took its name from a local distillery that used its water.

Tanner, Bob   Figure mentioned in chapter 16 of *Tom Sawyer* (1876) as a friend who Tom expects would be jealous if he knew that Tom and Joe Harper have learned how to smoke.

Taylor, Benny   Figure mentioned in *Tom Sawyer* (1876) as a friend of Tom. In chapter 33 Tom "hooks" Benny's wagon to carry the gold that he and Huck have found in McDougal's CAVE.

Temple, Alfred   Character in *Tom Sawyer* (1876). Introduced in chapter 1 only as a "new-comer" from St. Louis, Alfred immediately gets into a fight with Tom. Though taller than Tom, he loses and vows vengeance. His name is first given in chapter 18, in which Becky Thatcher flirts with him to make Tom jealous. When Alfred realizes how he has been used, he pours ink on Tom's spelling book to get him in trouble. Tom learns what Alfred has done at the end of chapter 20. He plans vengeance, but Alfred is not heard from again in the novel. In *Tom Sawyer, A Play in 4 Acts*, Temple finds a dead Indian. Clemens modeled Alfred on a childhood neighbor, Jim Reagan, whom he recalled as the "new boy" from St. Louis.

Thatcher, Becky (Rebecca)   Character in *Tom Sawyer* (1876). Blonde and blue-eyed, Becky is modeled closely on Clemens's childhood sweetheart, LAURA HAWKINS—whose Hannibal home has been preserved as the BECKY THATCHER HOUSE. Becky's age is not specified, but she seems to be about nine years old in *Tom Sawyer*. An earlier story that anticipates *Tom Sawyer* provides a clue. Clemens's "BOY'S MANUSCRIPT" has a character named Amy who is a clear prototype of Becky; her age is specified as just over eight.

While Becky is arguably Clemens's most famous female creation, he gave her little to do beyond reacting to Tom Sawyer. By the time he wrote *Huckleberry Finn*, he even forgot her name. As a character, she represents little more than an idealization of the innocence of young girls.

Becky first appears in chapter 3 of *Tom Sawyer*, when Tom sees her at her cousin Jeff Thatcher's house. Until then, Tom is devoted to another girl named Amy Lawrence. Immediately smitten by Becky, he performs elaborate stunts to impress her. He learns who she is in the next chapter, when he sees her at Sunday school with her father, Judge Thatcher, who is visiting from nearby Constantinople. Tom finally meets Becky face-to-face in chapter 6, when she turns up at his school. No reason is ever given for why she is starting school in St. Petersburg late in the year, while her family lives in Constantinople.

Tom's romance with Becky begins when he contrives to have himself punished so that he must sit next to her in class. He professes his love so quickly that Becky accepts his "engagement" proposal at lunchtime; however, she turns against him when he carelessly mentions that he was once "engaged" to Amy. When Becky is home sick from school in chapter 12, the fear that she might die saps Tom's energy. He is overjoyed when she returns, but she ignores him. His resulting heartbreak contributes

Becky angers Tom Sawyer by flirting with Alfred Temple in chapter 18 of *Tom Sawyer*.

to his decision to run off to Jackson's Island with other boys in the next chapter. Tom finally wins Becky's devotion in chapter 20, when he takes a whipping in her place at school.

After spending most of the summer with her parents in Constantinople, Becky reappears in chapter 29 to host a picnic at the CAVE near St. Petersburg. In one of the novel's most dramatic episodes, she and Tom spend several days lost in the cave, until Tom's calmness and ingenuity save them.

Becky is also mentioned in two stories that Clemens wrote after *Tom Sawyer*, but never again as Tom's sweetheart. In chapter 8 of *Huckleberry Finn* (1884), Huck sees her among the people on the ferryboat searching the river for his body. When Clemens wrote this passage—not long after he finished *Tom Sawyer*—he was already forgetting Becky's name and wrote "Bessie Thatcher." His notes indicate that he later intended to correct this mistake, but the error slipped into the published book and remained uncorrected until the first MARK TWAIN PROJECT edition of *Huckleberry Finn* in 1985. Becky also makes a perfunctory appearance in "SCHOOL-HOUSE HILL."

In contrast to the teenage boys who have portrayed Tom in films, girls playing Becky have consistently been much younger. Among those who have portrayed her on screen are 10-year-old Mitzi Green (1930–31), who twice played opposite Jackie Coogan; 11-year-old Anne Gillis (1938); and 11-year-old Jodie Foster (1973).

BERNARD SABATH's 1984 play, *Hannibal Blues,* depicts an adult Becky Thatcher.

Thatcher, Jeff   Minor character in *Tom Sawyer* (1876). A friend of Tom Sawyer and a cousin of Becky Thatcher, Jeff is introduced in chapter 3 as the son of a St. Petersburg lawyer. In the next chapter he arouses the envy of his peers when he is called up in front of the Sunday school to stand beside his uncle, the great Judge Thatcher. Jeff takes his name from Laura Hawkins's brother Jefferson, who died during childhood.

Thatcher, Judge   Character in *Tom Sawyer* (1876) and *Huckleberry Finn* (1884). The father of Becky Thatcher and brother of an unnamed St. Petersburg lawyer, Thatcher is a prominent judge based at the county seat in nearby Constantinople. It is generally believed that Clemens modeled Thatcher partly on his own father. John M. Clemens, who was a justice of the peace. Thatcher first appears in chapter 4 of *Tom Sawyer,* when he visits Tom's Sunday school. He is "a fine, portly, middleaged gentleman with iron-gray hair . . . a prodigious personage . . . altogether the most august creation these children ever looked upon." He does not make another significant appearance until near the end of the narrative. Chapter 23 mentions a "judge" who presides over Muff Potter's murder trial, but it gives no indication that this judge is Thatcher. Thatcher finally reappears in chapter 32, when he tells Tom that he has had the entrance to the CAVE sealed after Tom and Becky were lost inside. Later, the judge expresses his admiration of Tom for his ingenuity in escaping from the cave and

predicts a great future for him. At the end of the novel, Thatcher gets Aunt Polly's approval to invest and manage Tom's share of the fortune that Tom and Huck find in the cave.

When *Huckleberry Finn* begins, the Thatchers are clearly residents of St. Petersburg and the judge—not the Widow Douglas—is managing Huck's money, along with Tom's. Afraid that his father, Pap Finn, will get his money, Huck tries to give it all to the judge in chapter 4. The judge appears to accept Huck's money when he gives Huck a dollar "for a consideration" and has him sign a receipt. However, in chapter 43 Tom Sawyer makes it clear that Huck's money is still waiting for him. Meanwhile, in chapters 4 through 6, Pap tries to pressure Thatcher into turning Huck's money over to him. Thatcher resists, and even tries to gain legal custody of Huck for himself or the Widow Douglas, but fails. Pap initiates a suit against Thatcher to get control of the money, and it is not until the last chapter of the novel that Huck learns that his father failed in his effort.

Thatcher also appears briefly in "TOM SAWYER'S CONSPIRACY," in which he is still managing Tom and Huck's money.

Tom and Huck   Feature film produced by Disney in 1995. Directed by Peter Hewitt from a script adapted from *Tom Sawyer* (1876) by Stephen Sommers and David Loughery, the film is moderately faithful to its source material. However, it opens during the GRAVE-ROBBING scene from the novel's ninth chapter and gives more emphasis to violence and dark themes than earlier adaptations. Some critics found the film entertaining, while lamenting its tendencies to give Tom (Jonathan Taylor Thomas) too much of a 1990s sensibility, while portraying Huck (Brad Renfro) as overly dull and slightly thuggish. Capitalizing on the popularity of the film's young leads from their television work, advertisements for the film gave it the subtitle, "The Original Bad Boys."

The *Shirley Temple Theatre* aired an unrelated one-hour television play titled "Tom and Huck" on October 9, 1960.

Turner, Bill   Figure mentioned in chapter 14 of *Tom Sawyer* (1876) as having drowned the previous summer—presumably in the Mississippi. A cannon was fired over the water in an attempt to raise his body, in accordance with the folk beliefs of the time.

Walters, Mister   Minor character in *Tom Sawyer* (1876). "A slim creature of thirty-five with a sandy goatee and short sandy hair," Walters is the earnest superintendent of Tom's Sunday school. In chapter 4, Walters wants to impress the visiting Judge Thatcher by awarding a Bible to someone who has mastered 2,000 Bible verses. Shocked when Tom Sawyer steps forward to claim a Bible, he correctly suspects that something is wrong.

Williams, Hoss (Horse)   Figure whose grave is robbed in *Tom Sawyer* (1876). The narrative of *Tom Sawyer* begins on a Friday. Hoss Williams is buried the next day—a fact revealed in chapter 6. The same chapter implies that Williams was a "wicked man," since Huck Finn expects devils to visit his grave at midnight to carry him away. Three chapters later, Tom and Huck happen to be in the cemetery on Monday night, when they see Injun Joe and Muff Potter dig up Williams's body and place it in a wheelbarrow for Dr. Robinson. A similar GRAVE-ROBBING scene occurs in CHARLES DICKENS's novel *A Tale of Two Cities* (1859), which Clemens is known to have read several times before he wrote *Tom Sawyer*.

Tom Sawyer's original illustrator, TRUE W. WILLIAMS, had a little fun in his picture showing the townspeople at Hoss Williams's grave the day after the murder. In a corner of the picture he drew a tombstone with his own name on it.

BIBLIOGRAPHY

Cox, James M. *Mark Twain and the Fate of Humor.* Princeton, N.J.: Princeton University Press, 1966.

DeVoto, Bernard. *Mark Twain at Work.* Cambridge, Mass.: Harvard University Press, 1942.

Doctorow, E. L. "Introduction." In *The Adventures of Tom Sawyer*, edited by Shelley Fisher Fishkin. Oxford: Oxford University Press, 1996.

Gerber, John C. "Introduction." In *The Works of Mark Twain, Vol. 4*, edited by John C. Gerber, Paul Baender, and Terry Firkins, 3–30. Berkeley: University of California Press, 1980.

Howe, Lawrence. *Mark Twain and the Novel: The Double Cross of Authority.* Cambridge: Cambridge University Press, 1998.

Hutchinson, Stuart, ed. *Mark Twain: Tom Sawyer and Huckleberry Finn.* New York: Columbia University Press, 1998.

McNutt, James C. "Mark Twain and the American Indian: Earthly Realism and Heavenly Idealism." *American Indian Quarterly* 4.3 (August 1978): 223–242.

Messent, Peter. *Mark Twain.* New York: St. Martin's Press, 1997.

Norton, Charles A. *Writing "Tom Sawyer": The Adventures of a Classic.* Jefferson, N.C.: McFarland, 1983.

Railton, Stephen. "Going Home: *Tom Sawyer*." In *Mark Twain: A Short Introduction.* Malden, Mass.: Blackwell, 2004.

Robinson, Forrest G. *In Bad Faith: The Dynamics of Deception in Mark Twain's America.* Cambridge, Mass.: Harvard University Press, 1986.

Scharnhorst, Gary. *Critical Essays on the Adventures of Tom Sawyer.* New York: G. K. Hall, 1993.

Stone, Albert E. "Afterword." In *The Adventures of Tom Sawyer*, edited by Shelley Fisher Fishkin. New York: Oxford University Press, 1996.

Twain, Mark. *The Adventures of Tom Sawyer*, edited by Shelley Fisher Fishkin. New York: Oxford University Press, 1996.

Tom Sawyer Abroad (1894)

Clemens's third published story about Tom Sawyer and Huck Finn is a short novel that begins soon after *Adventures of Huckleberry Finn* (1884) concludes. From allusions to actual historical events within these stories, we can surmise that the events in *Tom Sawyer Abroad* occur around 1850—the date that illustrator DAN BEARD put in the map he drew to accompany the story. Clemens first published the story as a serial that ran from November 1893 to April 1894, then released it as a book in New York and London.

Although Huck's narration sets the story up as a sequel to events in *Huckleberry Finn*, the story's mood makes it more of a sequel to the earlier story

The Adventures of Tom Sawyer (1876). Clemens's apparent shift in focus seems to have been reflected in his shifting titles for the story. Originally he planned to call it "Huck Finn in Africa" but was soon calling it "Huckleberry Finn and Tom Sawyer Abroad," or "Huck Finn Abroad." These last two titles and the final title, *Tom Sawyer Abroad,* recall Clemens's first TRAVEL BOOK, *Innocents Abroad,* which includes an account of his own actual visit to North AFRICA in 1867.

Aside from the fact that much of the action takes place over the Sahara Desert and around the pyramids of Egypt, the story has little to do with Africa. There is in fact an emptiness about the story in that aside from Tom, Huck and Jim, the only character with dialogue is the Professor, who disappears in chapter 4. Virtually all other characters are faceless figures observed from a distance.

(These passages recall Clemens's unpublished descriptions of being on a ship becalmed in the Pacific Ocean in 1866 and spending several days getting to know the passengers on another ship through binoculars.) The action scenes in the book are brief and episodic, and a substantial part of the text is devoted to lengthy arguments among Tom and Huck and Jim.

Clemens evidently intended the story as the first part of a series of foreign-travel adventures narrated by Huck. He seems to have been heading the adventure toward some kind of special plot device, but nothing extraordinary ever occurs. Indeed, the jarringly abrupt ending suggests that he ended the story in the middle of something longer. It may be that he intended to publish the rest if the first part proved popular, which it did not.

Tom's map of his journey in *Tom Sawyer Abroad*

SYNOPSIS

Containing 34,000 words in 13 chapters narrated by Huck Finn, this story is a simple narrative of a fantastic balloon voyage. Tom, Huck, and Jim go to SAINT LOUIS to see a balloon craft on display. While they are inside the craft, the Professor, its unstable inventor, takes off before his visitors can get off. After teaching Tom how to work the craft's simple controls, the Professor directs the craft toward England. Somewhere over the Atlantic, he gets into a fight with Tom and falls overboard. The involuntary passengers continue the voyage and make their first landing in Africa's Sahara Desert. They continue across North Africa to the Sinai Peninsula, where the story abruptly ends.

Chapter 1

Tom Sawyer finds himself growing restless. The reputation he earned in his previous adventure as a distant traveler is wearing thin, and he resents seeing the town's elderly postmaster, Nat Parsons, regain his former glory as St. Petersburg's greatest traveler. Parsons, it seems, went to WASHINGTON, D.C., 30 years earlier to ask the president to pardon him for not being able to deliver a letter. After he returned from this magnificent adventure, people came from miles around just to hear his story.

Tom chafes at everything robbing attention from him: a horse race, a burning house, a circus, a slave auction, an ECLIPSE, and a religious revival. He tries to figure out ways to make himself famous again and proposes to Huck and Jim, the former slave, that they launch a "Crusade."

Chapter 2

As one adventure scheme after another collapses, Tom despairs until he reads about a balloon in St. Louis that is to sail to Europe. When he learns that Parsons plans to go there, he persuades Jim and Huck to accompany him to see the balloon. As they reach the strange contraption, they find a crowd making fun of the balloon's inventor. The Professor, as Huck calls him, grows irate when his efforts to talk back to the disrespectful crowd backfire.

Tom, Jim, and Huck join the crowd inspecting the craft, which is like a small ship suspended from a giant oblong balloon with wings. They make a point of being the last to leave—especially since Parsons is aboard—but just as they are about to get off, a shout alerts them to the fact that the balloon is loose, and they are still on board as the craft rises. While the Professor crows about his success and his secret source of power, he makes Tom learn how to operate his ship and says that no one may get off. During the night, Tom tries to overpower the Professor but gives up when he accidentally awakens him.

Chapter 3

The next morning, Tom, Huck, and Jim argue over their location as they eat breakfast. With his newly acquired school learning, Huck insists that the different states that they fly over should have the same colors that they have on maps, bringing down Tom's derision. They also argue about time zones. When they realize that they are about to fly over the ATLANTIC OCEAN, they beg the Professor to turn around, only to have him pull a pistol on them.

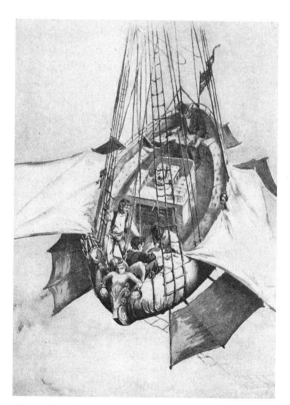

The mad professor plots his course in chapter 4 of *Tom Sawyer Abroad.*

Chapter 4

As the balloon crosses the ocean, Tom, Jim, and Huck nervously avoid the Professor, who says they will be in London in a day. Suddenly he challenges his passengers to admit that they want to leave him, and then goes to the other end of the ship and gets drunk while a storm builds up. He is overheard mumbling something about changing his course, away from England.

Out of the darkness of the storm, a flash of light reveals the Professor crawling toward Tom, threatening to throw him overboard. The sky darkens again the moment that he lunges at Tom, and then Huck sees Tom's head disappear over the edge of the ship. The Professor leaps after Tom. Jim and Huck hear screams from a great distance. When lightning flashes again, Tom's head reappears over the edge; the Professor does not return. Tom has been on a rope ladder, and explains that he was slow to climb back until he learned who had gone overboard. The storm continues.

Chapter 5

When Tom, Huck, and Jim awaken the next morning, the storm is over. They decide to continue to England, since the craft is well stocked with food, clothes and trinkets—even money. Tom teaches the ship's simple controls to the others.

When they finally sight land the next morning, they are puzzled to see nothing but sand. Tom and Huck climb down the ladder to the land, where they are immediately chased by a lion. They make it back to the ladder, but in his panic Jim forgets how to operate the ship and there is a moment of great uncertainty until Tom climbs aboard and takes control. Meanwhile, Huck remains dangling over the lion, and more lions are approaching as the balloon slowly moves along. Tom and Huck face a dilemma: Huck does not want to climb the ladder, for fear that he will slip and let his leg dangle within the lions' reach, and Tom does not want to ascend too high, lest Huck get dizzy and fall. Tom finally shoots a lion so that Huck can scurry up the ladder as the other lions turn on their wounded comrade.

Chapter 6

Once Huck is back on the ship, everyone is engulfed in fleas. Tom takes the balloon higher, until they reach air cool enough to drive the fleas away. Tom then realizes that they are above Africa's Sahara Desert. Huck sees a line on the ground that he thinks must be a line of longitude, but it turns out to be a camel caravan. When they descend for a closer look, caravan members fire on them, so they return to watch from a safer altitude. Meanwhile, horsemen swoop down on the caravan, and a terrific battle ensues. As the caravan repels the attack, a fleeing horseman snatches a baby from a woman's arms. The grief-stricken mother does not notice as Tom steers the airship into the kidnapper, knocking him off his horse. Jim lands to collect the baby and returns it to its mother, who rewards him with a gold chain.

Chapter 7

The balance of the day is spent arguing about such matters as fleas and the ARABIAN NIGHTS, and Huck muses over the pleasant similarities between life on the airship and life on a raft.

Chapter 8

The next morning they come across a caravan, all of whose members are dead. They help themselves to the weapons and valuables that they find and wonder what happened to the caravan as they leave it behind.

The mounting heat of the desert drives the party to search for water, but they only sight one mirage after another. Arguments over the existence of mirages lead into an argument about how much Catholic clerics cuss. By the time Jim and Huck have given up on finding water, Tom steers the ship over a lake in a real oasis. Tom, Huck, and Jim take turns descending to swim, until more lions come along. Once again, Jim panics while at the helm, this time taking Tom and Huck to a high altitude as they hang on the rope ladder. Tom gets back in the ship and takes control, but Huck still hangs from the ladder, too exhausted to climb up after him. Tom steers the ship back to the lake, where he instructs Huck to drop into the water to rest, while the lions busy themselves destroying the clothes that Tom, Huck, and Jim left on the shore, as well as each other.

Chapter 9

Tom, Huck, and Jim haul a dead lion and a tiger cub aboard and use them for bait to fish from the balloon. Afterward they feast on lion and tiger steaks, fried fish, corn pone, and dates plucked off the tops of palm trees. Tom lectures Huck and Jim on the size of the Sahara and gets into an argument with Jim about whether God would create something without value.

Chapter 10

Tom tells Huck and Jim a story from the Arabian Nights about a wandering dervish who tricks a greedy camel driver out of all his animals and wealth. When Jim suggests that the man learned a lesson from this experience, Tom argues that the lesson is useless, as Jim falls asleep. Tom then impresses Huck by piloting the ship to the exact hill in the desert that contains the treasure cave of the dervish story. They stop nearby to tan their animal hides in a salt pond.

Chapter 11

After a day or two of idle cruising, Tom, Huck, and Jim come across another caravan that they observe from a distance for several days. Eventually, a sand storm comes along that engulfs both the balloon and the caravan. When the storm abates, the caravan is completely buried in sand—explaining the mystery of the dead caravan that they encountered earlier. In expressing the grief that they feel for the loss of the caravan, Huck reveals that while he, Tom, and Jim were following the caravan, they closely observed its activities and assigned names to its members such as Elexander Robinson and Harryet McDougal.

The next day, they feel better, and they debate what to do with the tons of sand they have taken on. Jim suggests taking it home to sell; Tom counters by suggesting that there would be big money in selling it as *Sahara* sand but then turns the argument around to point out that import duties would wipe out their profit. Once they agree to clean the sand from the ship, Tom suggests that in view of their different ages, he and Huck should each remove a fifth, and Jim the other three-fifths. Jim argues that it would be fairer if Huck and Tom each removed a *10th*. Huck and Tom laugh over Jim's inverted math but eventually help him do his "share" of the work.

Chapter 12

The ship eventually reaches EGYPT's pyramids, where Jim is overcome with emotion at being in the land of MOSES. They maneuver through a thick fog until they find themselves at the SPHINX. After sailing around it, Tom lands Jim atop its head with an American flag to plant and then flies off to observe the effect with the benefit of "perspective." When Tom and Huck realize that angry people are trying to get at Jim, they rapidly return in the balloon, scattering his assailants.

As Tom, Huck, and Jim cruise around the pyramids, Tom is moved by the antiquity of the surroundings to tell another story from the Arabian Nights, which leads to an argument about whether a bronze horse could actually have flown.

Chapter 13

As Jim pilots the balloon, Tom and Huck explore a pyramid and visit a nearby bazaar. Tom again amazes Huck when he finds the only surviving brick from a long-vanished house described in an Arabian Nights tale. Later, they hire a young man to be their guide and fly to the Red Sea and Mount Sinai.

When Tom's corncob pipe gives out on him, he decides to send Jim and the Egyptian guide back to St. Petersburg to fetch another pipe from Aunt Polly's house. He instructs Jim how to find his way home and back, gives him a note to leave for Aunt Polly, and sends Jim and the guide on their way as he and Huck relax on Mount Sinai. Two days later, Jim returns with the pipe, but also with Aunt Polly's order to return home immediately. They comply and the story ends abruptly.

BACKGROUND AND PUBLISHING HISTORY

Clemens drafted notes for a balloon adventure in his NOTEBOOK as early as 1868 but evidently abandoned the idea a year later after learning that the French writer JULES VERNE had published *Five Weeks in a Balloon*. Ironically, although Clemens appears to have originated this SCIENCE-FICTION idea before he heard about Verne's story, several scenes in *Tom Sawyer Abroad* nearly duplicate episodes from Verne: the oasis scenes, the encounters with lions, the rescues from a suspended ladder, and the caravan buried by a sandstorm.

Clemens apparently wrote *Tom Sawyer Abroad* in response to a $5,000 offer from MARY ELIZABETH MAPES DODGE for a boy's story for ST. NICHOLAS MAGAZINE, which she edited. The offer came at a moment when he was desperate for cash, so he began writing the story quickly while living in GERMANY in August 1892. He wrote half the book in five days.

After completing and revising the story, Clemens sent his typescripts to FREDERICK J. HALL, the head of his own publishing house, CHARLES L. WEBSTER & COMPANY, in the fall of 1892. Hall had it published in ST. NICHOLAS MAGAZINE, in which the story appeared in six installments between November 1893 and April 1894. DAN BEARD drew 29 pictures for the story, all but two of which were used in *St. Nicholas*.

Concerned about the possibility of offending his young readers, Clemens gave Dodge a free hand to edit his manuscript; he was too distracted by other matters to monitor the story's publication himself. However, while he was willing to accept Dodge's deletions—which were substantial—he was outraged by her substituting text for what she had removed. Dodge cleaned up Huck's grammar, removed or softened allusions to death, drunkenness, perspiration, and swearing, and deleted a 650-word passage in chapter 8 about Roman Catholic clerics "cussing." Anxious not to offend racial sensitivities, Dodge permitted Jim to call AFRICAN AMERICANS "NIGGERS," but allowed white characters only to say "darkies." She even had Beard redraw several pictures to put shoes on the characters. According to Beard, Clemens entered the magazine's editorial office after the first installment appeared and proclaimed that while an editor could remove anything from his writings that she chose, "God Almighty Himself has no right to put words in my mouth that I never used!"

Clemens instructed Hall not to use the *St. Nicholas* text for the book edition, but by the time the book publisher received this order, type for the first nine chapters had already been set. Thus, only the last four chapters of the book had text that Clemens approved. Clemens's London publisher,

CHATTO and Windus, prepared its edition from a carbon copy of his original typescript. Chatto's edition escaped Dodge's blue pencil but did not incorporate all of Mark Twain's own final revisions.

Chatto and Windus issued the English edition on April 14, 1894, and Charles L. Webster issued the first American edition on April 18, 1894. The last book published by Webster, *Tom Sawyer Abroad* was, coincidentally, issued the day that the company filed for BANKRUPTCY. Two years later the story was republished by HARPER AND BROTHERS in a combined edition with *Tom Sawyer, Detective*—with which it has appeared in most subsequent editions. The 1996 OXFORD MARK TWAIN edition includes a facsimile reprint of the first American edition of *Tom Sawyer Abroad* with a new introduction by writer Nat Hentoff and an afterword by M. Thomas Inge.

Until 1980, when the University of California Press published an edition of *Tom Sawyer Abroad* corrected by the staff of the Mark Twain Papers (see MARK TWAIN PROJECT), no edition of the story had ever been faithful to Clemens's original intent. All American editions of the story had drawn on Dodge's bowdlerized version—the one still used by publishers seeking to take advantage of the original text's public domain status.

The earliest original manuscript of *Tom Sawyer Abroad* is in the New York Public Library. Complete notes on the corrected text can be found in the University of California Press editions.

Clemens's idea for a fantastic journey in a balloon was adapted to a motion picture, THE ADVENTURES OF MARK TWAIN (1985), which uses Claymation and features an airship modeled on that of *Tom Sawyer Abroad*. Clemens himself pilots the airship, and his passengers are Tom, Huck, and Becky Thatcher.

CRITICAL COMMENTARY

Tom Sawyer Abroad combines two genres that Clemens had successfully employed in the past—TRAVEL BOOKS and juvenile fiction. While Tom, Huck, and Jim undergo no perceptible growth over the course of this short book, the trio experience a bit of the world outside the United States, leading Huck to decide, after spending time in a desert caravan, that "there ain't no surer way to find out whether you like people or hate them, than to travel with them" (chapter 11)—an observation that recalls Clemens's comments about traveling with GEORGE WASHINGTON CABLE, whom he grew to hate during a long lecture tour.

Many recurrent techniques and motifs of Clemens's travel writing appear in the text. While assessing their food supply, Tom the cosmopolitan disparages English food, noting that staying among corpses has "spoilt the water" but "ripened up the beefsteak to a degree that was just right for an Englishman" (chapter 9). Drawing on a running gag from *The Innocents Abroad* (1869), in which guides hired in each country are given the name Ferguson, the trio assign comically unsuitable names to the members of the caravan they fly over: "There was Mr. Elexander Robinson and Miss Adaline Robinson, and Colonel Jacob McDougal and Miss Harryet McDougal . . . and these was big chiefs, mostly, that wore splendid great turbans and simmeters" (chapter 11). Meanwhile, Huck's encounter with the pyramids leads him to reflect excitedly on modern tourism, in which the aura given off by a famous object sometimes threatens to obscure the object itself. Despite all he has seen and heard about the pyramids, Huck isolates his own sincere reaction and reflects on the process of making mental room for them: "I had seen a many and a many a picture of them, and heard tell about them a hundred times, and yet to come on them all of a sudden, that way, and find out they was *real*, 'stead of imaginations, most knocked the breath out of me with surprise" (chapter 12).

Several significant elements of *The Adventures of Tom Sawyer* and the *Adventures of Huckleberry Finn* are also recapitulated, such as the vernacular frame of the narrative "as told" by Huck. Jim's superstitions still provide situations for physical humor, as when Jim interprets the glare on Tom's face as proof he is seeing Tom's ghost (chapter 4) and later mistakes a flock of birds for a ghost (chapter 8). The three relish their freedom from civilization during a stop at the desert oasis, where they play at footracing and boxing and give nudism a try, deciding, "CLOTHES is well enough in school, and in towns, and at balls, too, but there ain't no sense in them when there ain't no civilization nor other kinds of bothers and fussiness around"

(ibid.). In the desert, they entertain the half-baked, get-rich-quick plan of exporting "genuwyne" Sahara sand back to the United States, followed by a tortuous discussion of the logistics and ethics of avoiding import taxes by using the balloon to fly over the border.

Tom, Jim, and Huck also serve as an organ of collaborative literary criticism. The ARABIAN NIGHTS, one of Clemens's favorite books (and a frequent source of material) sparks several of the trio's extended conversations. After Tom tells a story from the Arabian Nights, Huck and Jim engage in tenacious criticism, pointing to what they believe is a key flaw in the story. Later, Tom claims to have found a particular dune featured in the Arabian Nights, and he relates a story about a smooth-talking dervish and a greedy camel driver that Huck and Jim again critique for its moral message, worrying at length over the comparative moral imaginations suggested by the dervish and the driver. Early in the story, Huck, taking on one of Clemens's preferred critical postures, attributes the violence of Tom's fantasy life to WALTER SCOTT's romantic literature, "which he was always reading" (chapter 1).

The trio's general ignorance of geography is a recurrent source of humor, leading to several farcical conversations, such as an argument over whether the individual states should be colored as they are on a map and the concept of time zones. But the more serious dimensions of political geography often underlie such conversations, such as in an early exchange between Huck and Tom on land rights in PALESTINE, based on the example of the Crusades. The "HOLY LAND," Tom explains, is "in the hands of the paynim, and it's our duty to take it away from them" (ibid.). The American appetite for expansion also enters the text more explicitly when Tom reminds Huck and Jim, "We've took California away from the Mexicans two or three years ago, so that part of the Pacific Coast is ours now" (chapter 9).

The hubbub over the balloon ("the St. Louis papers begun to talk a good deal about the balloon that was going to sail to Europe") mirrors the excitement over scientific advancement during the period in which Clemens wrote the story. Like Henry Adams's overwhelming experience of the electric dynamo featured in *The Education of Henry Adams* (1907), Tom's encounter with the balloon leads him to serious thoughts about scientific progress in the context of the United States' developing self-image. As the crowd looking at the balloon ridicules the Professor's creation, he reproaches them, declaring that someday they will "find they had stood face to face with one of the men that lifts up nations and makes civilizations, and was too dull to know it" (chapter 2). Despite the Professor's apparent alienation and instability, his sense of historical perspective and drive to create a "new power, and a thousand times the strongest in the earth," embodies the energy and optimism attached to technological innovation and its role in the advancement of American society in the last decades of the 19th century (ibid.).

Critical Commentary by Alex Feerst

CHARACTERS AND RELATED ENTRIES

For information on Tom Sawyer, see the Characters and Related Entries section of the *Tom Sawyer* entry. For information on Huckleberry Finn and Jim, see the Characters and Related Entries section of the *Huckleberry Finn* entry.

Parsons, Nat Postmaster in *Tom Sawyer Abroad* (1894) who has long excited the envy of his St. Petersburg neighbors by virtue of having traveled to WASHINGTON, D.C., 30 years earlier in order to deal with an undeliverable letter. The reputation as a traveler that Tom Sawyer brings back with him after his own adventures in *Huckleberry Finn* (1884) threatens Parsons' standing and sets the two up as rivals for glory. The story of Parsons going to Washington resembles an anecdote told in chapter 60 of *Life on the Mississippi* (1883) about the first postmaster of St. Paul, Minnesota.

Professor Character in *Tom Sawyer Abroad* (1894). The Professor is the inventor of the balloon craft that carries Huck, Tom, and Jim to AFRICA. In the first chapter, he allows people to board his craft at SAINT LOUIS. Their derisive comments so anger him that he sets sail without giving Tom, Huck, and Jim a chance to get off. He forces them to accompany him across the Atlantic and frightens them with his sullen and erratic behavior. In chapter 4 he gets drunk, attacks Tom during a storm, and disappears after falling out of the balloon.

When Clemens created the Professor, he may have had in mind JAMES W. PAIGE, a silver-tongued inventor whose typesetting machine helped push Clemens's publishing company to declare BANKRUPTCY on the same day that it published *Tom Sawyer Abroad* as a book. The Professor's fate also resembles the fate of JULES VERNE in Clemens's posthumously published "A MURDER, A MYSTERY, AND A MARRIAGE," which he wrote in 1876.

BIBLIOGRAPHY

Brack, O. M., Jr. "Mark Twain in Kneepants: The Expurgation of *Tom Sawyer Abroad.*" *Proof* 2 (1972): 143–151.

Twain, Mark. *Tom Sawyer Abroad and Tom Sawyer, Detective*, edited by John C. Gerber and Terry Firkins. Berkeley: University of California Press, 1982.

Tom Sawyer Abroad; Tom Sawyer, Detective and Other Stories (1896)

Collection of short works first published by HARPER'S in 1896 and later reissued in many standard sets. Except for *Tom Sawyer, Detective*, all the items were published in earlier books. The collection incorporates most of "The Stolen White Elephant" (1882), including its title story and everything previously published in PUNCH, BROTHERS, PUNCH! (1878). Its contents include "SOME RAMBLING NOTES OF AN IDLE EXCURSION," "THE FACTS CONCERNING THE RECENT CARNIVAL OF CRIME IN CONNECTICUT," "THE GREAT REVOLUTION IN PITCAIRN," "THE CANVASSER'S TALE," and "THE LOVES OF ALONZO FITZ CLARENCE AND ROSANNAH ETHELTON."

Tom Sawyer, Detective (1896)

Novella first published as a magazine serial. One of several sequels to *Huckleberry Finn*, this story is set shortly after that earlier narrative ends and, like its predecessor, is narrated by Huck. Drawing on elements of a dramatic criminal trial held in Denmark in the 17th century, Clemens wrote this story to capitalize on the growing popularity of DETECTIVE fiction stimulated by Arthur Conan Doyle's Sherlock Holmes. *Tom Sawyer, Detective* uses many of Clemens's favorite themes: twins, switched identities, sleepwalking, a counterfeit DEAF-AND-DUMB character, and a murder trial. The narrative interweaves several mysteries that Tom Sawyer cleverly unravels in a climactic trial.

SYNOPSIS

The narrative contains 23,400 words divided into 11 chapters, with 30 percent of the text falling in the final chapter. It begins in Tom and Huck's hometown—presumably St. Petersburg, though it is not mentioned by name—from which Tom and Huck travel to ARKANSAS to visit Sally and Silas Phelps. After a STEAMBOAT journey lasting perhaps 10 days they arrive in Arkansas on the first of September, although the first chapter sets the time as "spring." The narrative concludes in mid-October.

The Phelpses are feuding with an unpleasant neighbor, Brace Dunlap, who wants to marry Benny Phelps. Shortly after Tom and Huck arrive, Brace's brother Jubiter Dunlap disappears. It happens that during their steamboat trip to Arkansas, the boys meet Jubiter's long-missing twin brother, Jake Dunlap, who is being pursued by fellow criminals whom he has double-crossed. About the same moment that Jubiter disappears, Jake is murdered by his former partners before anyone else knows he has returned home. When Tom and Huck meet Jubiter wearing the disguise that Jake planned to use, they believe him to be Jake.

Later, Tom and Huck discover the buried body of a man who is assumed to be Jubiter. Silas is arrested for Jubiter's murder, since he struck Jubiter shortly before his disappearance. When he goes to trial, his case looks hopeless, and he makes things worse by confessing. In a flash of brilliant deduction, however, Tom sorts out all the mysteries, identifies the true murder victim and his murderers, and earns a big reward for finding the stolen diamonds.

Chapter 1

During the spring following the time that Tom and Huck freed Jim from his imprisonment (in *Huckleberry Finn*), the boys are restless. They itch to travel, but Tom is reluctant to suggest going on a trip to his Aunt Polly. One day, however, she surprises him with the news that his Aunt Sally Phelps wants him and Huck to visit her in Arkansas. Sally hopes the boys will be a "diversion" from troubles that she and her husband Silas are having with a neighbor, Brace Dunlap, who wants to marry their daughter Benny. While discussing this problem with Polly, Tom and Huck tell her about Brace's brothers, the twin, Jake and Jubiter Dunlap.

Chapter 2

Tom and Huck take a STEAMBOAT down the Mississippi on a "thousand mile" trip to Arkansas. The boat has few passengers, who are mostly sleepy old people; it runs aground so often that it takes four days to reach the lower river. Meanwhile, the boys become interested in a passenger who locks himself in the next cabin. Determined to learn the man's secret, Tom bribes the waiters to let him and Huck enter the man's cabin in their place. The next day, the boys enter the cabin of the mysterious man. Tom immediately recognizes the man as Jubiter Dunlap, but the man nervously confesses that he is actually Jubiter's twin brother, Jake. Calling himself a "hard lot," Jake explains that he is hiding from pursuers. He is thrilled to learn from the boys that folks in Arkansas already think that he is dead, as this will permit him to return home unrecognized. He gets the idea of pretending to be deaf and dumb from Tom's suggestion that his voice might give him away if he speaks.

Chapter 3

As the voyage continues, Huck and Tom spend most of their time with Jake to keep him company, and they describe everyone aboard the steamboat to him. Their information leads Jake to conclude that his pursuers are aboard, so he tells the rest of his story. Through a confidence trick, he and two partners, Bud Dixon and Hal Clayton, stole two diamonds worth $12,000 from a SAINT LOUIS jewelry store. As they fled upriver on a steamboat, they realized that they could not trust each other.

Unable to divide their two diamonds three ways, they had to stay together, but each man was afraid to go to sleep, for fear of being betrayed by the other two. When Dixon finally fell asleep, Jake and Clayton seized the paper containing the diamonds and left, only to discover that Dixon had substituted sugar lumps for the gems. After they returned to the cabin, Jake correctly guessed that Dixon was hiding the diamonds inside his boot heel.

Chapter 4

Jake continues his story. After the three criminals left the steamboat in northern Missouri, they took a room and gambled until the heavy-drinking Dixon fell asleep. Jake and Clayton removed their boots and Dixon's in order to search for the diamonds quietly. After failing to find anything, Jake casually slipped on Dixon's boots in place of his own, then fled north on foot, hoping that it would take Clayton a while to realize he had been conned. At Elexandria, Jake boarded the steamboat on which he has met Tom and Huck.

Jake now thinks that Clayton and Dixon are laying for him aboard the boat, which slowly moves down the river, stopping frequently for repairs. One night, it lands at a woodyard (identified as Flagler's Landing in chapter 11) about 40 miles north of the Phelpses'; the moment that a storm breaks, Jake slips ashore. Seconds later, the boys see two men rushing after him. Meanwhile, the boys have arranged to meet Jake at a sycamore grove near the Phelpses after they land and learn where Jake's brothers are.

Chapter 5

After further delays for repairs, the steamboat finally lands on the evening of September 2 and Huck and Tom go ashore. They rush to their rendezvous point, anxious to tell Jake why they are late. As they near the sycamore grove, they see men running into the woods and hear screams for help. Moments later, two other men enter the woods; then two men run out, chased by the other two. As the boys nervously watch from a hiding place, yet another figure emerges from the woods— a strange, tall man whom they take to be Jake Dunlap's ghost, wearing Jake's false whiskers and "goggles." After this specter walks by, other strollers

appear: Bill and Jack Withers, Lem Beebe, and Jim Lane.

Chapter 6

Tom and Huck trail behind Lane and Beebe until they reach the Phelpses. Meanwhile, Tom points out that since the "ghost" was wearing boots, the thieves must not have removed Jake's boots before they fled. The diamonds must therefore still be in the real boots, which Tom proposes to buy at the auction that is certain to be held after the murder inquest. At the Phelpses' house, Aunt Sally greets the boys warmly, but Huck fails to provide a convincing explanation of why they were so long in getting to the house from the boat.

Chapter 7

At supper, Benny asks after Tom's family. Uncle Silas is visibly agitated—especially when Brace Dunlap's slave Billy comes to the door to ask where Jubiter is. After supper, Tom and Huck retire to a watermelon patch to talk and smoke. Later that night, as thoughts of murders and ghosts make sleep difficult, the boys look out their window and see a man in the yard carrying a shovel on his shoulder; because of his clothes, they assume it is Uncle Silas sleepwalking. A storm kicks up.

Before dawn, the boys awaken. Tom wonders why no one is discussing Jake's murder. They rise early and go out to listen for news, then visit the sycamore grove to see if Jake's boots are still on his body. Huck's nerve fails him, so Tom enters the grove alone, only to discover that the body is gone.

Chapter 8

Breakfast is not cheerful. Brace Dunlap's slave returns to ask after Jubiter, leaving Silas in a sorry state. Tom and Huck return to the woods, where they again see Jake's ghost. Tom soon deduces that the specter is not really a ghost, but Jake himself, still alive. He talks to the man, who initially acts irritated, but then gradually becomes pleasant. Afterward, the boys run into "some of Steve Nickerson's people," who ask all about the new stranger. They then visit a school, where the deaf-and-dumb stranger is already a subject of gossip.

Chapter 9

Over the next several days, the deaf-and-dumb man becomes popular in the area and Brace Dunlap wins public approval by taking him in. Meanwhile, search parties fail to turn up the missing Jubiter. After everyone else gives up, Tom borrows Jeff Hooker's bloodhound to continue to search with Huck. At the Phelpses', the dog finds a fresh grave in a tobacco field. With the help of passersby, they dig up Jubiter's body. When Tom rushes home to brag about his discovery, Uncle Silas nearly faints.

Chapter 10

Silas groans miserably, "I done it!" He explains that Jubiter so aggravated him that he finally "sort of lost his mind" and hit him over the head with a stick. Jubiter ran off, but Silas is convinced that he has killed the man. Tom tells Silas that *he* could not have killed Jubiter; however, no one can imagine who else might have done it. The question of who buried Jubiter also nags at Huck and Tom, who recall seeing Silas with a shovel the night that Jubiter disappeared. Meanwhile, the sheriff arrests Silas and takes him to the town jail. Tom wants to organize an elaborate escape, but Silas squelches the idea. In order to be close to her husband, Aunt Sally goes into town to stay with the jailer's wife until the October trial, leaving the boys and Benny to manage the household.

Chapter 11

Each day, Tom and Huck visit Silas, but the old man is not holding up well and Tom tries to think of ways to help him. In mid-October, when the trial starts, the courtroom is jammed. Tom sits with Silas's "back-settlement lawyer," helping him wherever he can. After the jury is sworn in, the prosecuting attorney opens strongly, promising eyewitnesses who will testify to seeing Silas threaten, kill and bury Jubiter Dunlap. When witnesses testify about "bad blood" between Silas and Jubiter, Silas's lawyer is helpless, but Tom himself cross-examines them and trips them up on contradictions and inconsistencies.

Silas's case deteriorates rapidly after Lem Beebe testifies that he saw Silas killing Jubiter. Meanwhile, Tom unaccountably drops into a "brown

Tom astounds the court with his revelation that the supposed murder victim is alive and in the courtroom.

study," seemingly oblivious to the testimony. Jim Lane backs up Beebe's story, then Bill and Jack Withers testify that they saw Silas carrying Jubiter's body. When Brace Dunlap adds that he saw Silas bury Jubiter, Silas cries out, "It's true, every word—I murdered him in cold blood!"

Silas's sensational announcement fails to faze Tom. When Silas starts to explain how he killed Jubiter, however, Tom interrupts him. A murder *was* done, Tom announces, but Silas had no part in it. With the judge's permission, Tom outlines what really happened. After mentioning a reward poster for stolen diamonds that he has seen posted outside, he accuses Brace Dunlap of conspiring with his brother Jubiter to torment Silas. He pauses, then asks the court to consider how people who become lost in thought often do things unconsciously with their hands—such as drawing figures on their faces. As listeners nod in assent, Tom takes his narrative back to the night before the murder.

Without mentioning names, Tom tells about the diamond thieves aboard the steamboat that stopped at Flagler's Landing. About the same moment that Silas was striking Jubiter, he says, one of the jewel thieves was putting on a disguise in the sycamore grove. Moments later, the partners he betrayed fell on him and beat him to death. Two passersby heard the screams, chased the murderers away and returned to the scene of the crime. One of these men switched CLOTHES with the murder victim in order to assume the dead man's disguise. that man was Jubiter Dunlap. Meanwhile, his companion lugged the murder victim away to Silas Phelps's property, where he took Silas's shovel and old work shirt and buried the murder victim in the tobacco field.

After a dramatic pause, Tom reveals that the dead man was *Jake* Dunlap and that the man who buried him was Brace Dunlap. He then announces that the deaf-and-dumb stranger sitting in the courtroom is *Jubiter*—which he proves by pulling off Jubiter's glasses and false beard. As listeners sing out Tom's praises, he supplies a motive for Brace and Jubiter's actions and denounces the prosecution witnesses as Brace's paid liars. He then adds a tantalizingly incomplete explanation of how he figured out the deaf-and-dumb stranger's true identity and waits for the crowd to insist that he complete his story. He recognized Jubiter, he explains, by his habit of tracing crosses on his cheek with a finger.

Praised by the judge, Tom modestly attributes his deductions to "just an ordinary little bit of detective work." Finally, he adds that there is a thief in the court with $12,000 worth of stolen diamonds on him. When he identifies Jubiter as the thief, Jubiter admits to all of Tom's other charges but denies being a thief. The sheriff searches Jubiter, but turns up nothing. Tom then creates yet another sensation by extracting two big diamonds from Jubiter's boot.

The judge has Brace and his cohorts nabbed; a month later, they are tried and sent to jail. Meanwhile, Silas's reputation is restored and people flock to his church to hear his sermons. When Tom receives a $2,000 reward for recovering the diamonds, he gives half of it to Huck.

BACKGROUND AND PUBLISHING HISTORY

In late 1894, while he was living in FRANCE, Clemens drafted a story with the working title "Tom Sawyer's Mystery." By December he was living in PARIS, where the wife of a Danish diplomat outlined for him the plot of the novel *The Minister of Veilby* (1829), by Steen Steensen Blicher (1782–1848), about a famous 17th-century murder case in Denmark. The details of that story so fascinated him that he completely rewrote his own mystery story in January, working in details from Blicher's novel. In an indirect effort to credit his source, he inserted this partly inaccurate footnote at the beginning of chapter 1:

> Strange as the incidents of this story are, they are not inventions, but facts—even to the public confession of the accused. I take them from an old-time Swedish criminal trial, change the actors, and transfer the scenes to America. I have added some details, but only a couple of them are important ones.—M. T.

Tom Sawyer, Detective was first published in HARPER'S MAGAZINE in August and September 1896, with 21 illustrations by A. B. FROST. The story's first book publication came in November 1896, when Harper's published it in *Tom Sawyer Abroad; Tom Sawyer, Detective and Other Stories*. CHATTO and Windus published the first British edition as *Tom Sawyer, Detective, as Told by Huck Finn and Other Tales* in December. *Tom Sawyer Abroad* and *Tom Sawyer, Detective* are often published together, but the latter—unlike the former—was apparently never issued as a book by itself until Scholastic Press published it as an inexpensive paperback. The 1996 *Oxford Mark Twain* edition included a facsimile reprint of the first American edition of *Tom Sawyer, Detective* in a volume titled *The Stolen White Elephant and Other Detective Stories*.

In 1980, the MARK TWAIN PROJECT issued a corrected edition of *Tom Sawyer, Detective*—along with *Tom Sawyer Abroad*—drawing on Clemens's original manuscripts and the story's first published versions. This edition is also the first since the original magazine serialization to incorporate all of Frost's drawings. The original handwritten manuscript is held by the Mark Twain Project in Berkeley; Clemens's own revised typescript is at the University of Kansas.

In 1938, Louis King directed a Paramount film, *Tom Sawyer, Detective*, with Billy Cook as Tom,

Donald O'Connor as Huck, Porter Hall as Silas, Elizabeth Risdon as Sally, William Haade as Jake and Jubiter, and Clara Blandick in her third film portrayal of Aunt Polly.

CRITICAL COMMENTARY

Tom Sawyer, Detective features recurrent elements of Clemens's storycraft—twins (Jake and Jubiter Dunlap), murder and ghosts, a jewel heist, multiple double-crosses, a theatrical trial, and an opportune windfall. It also draws more specifically on familiar structural and thematic elements of Clemens's previous books featuring Tom and Huck. It is told in Huck's voice and diction—misspellings, malapropisms, and all (such as when the show trial begins with the "lawyer for the prostitution"; 789). The plot is impelled by a conspicuous and vaguely sinister boredom that has fallen over St. Petersburg— "everything's so solemn it seems like everybody you've loved is dead and gone and you most wish you was dead and gone too, and done with it all" (chapter 1). Huck and Tom argue with their usual scholasticism over the logistics of how ghosts' accessories join them in the afterlife (chapter 5). Tom, the budding entrepreneur, cooks up and abandons a scheme to buy the boots, with the hidden diamonds inside, for a fraction of their value but winds up rich anyway (chapter 6). The power of Tom's charisma extends to include expert detection abilities, and in the climactic trial, he acts as de facto counsel for the defense: "You see, Tom was just the same as a regular lawyer, nearly" (chapter 11). Through his theatrical solution of the murder mystery in open court, for which he is praised by the Judge as a "very remarkable boy," Tom manages to reinstall his uncle in the pulpit and restore him to preaching "the blamedest jumbledest idiotic sermons you ever struck" (ibid.).

Critical Commentary by Alex Feerst

CHARACTERS AND RELATED ENTRIES

For information on Tom Sawyer, see the Characters and Related Entries section of the *Tom Sawyer* entry. For information on Huckleberry Finn, the Phelpses, and Pikesville, see the Characters and Related Entries section of the *Huckleberry Finn* entry.

Beebe, Lem Minor character in *Tom Sawyer, Detective* (1896). A neighbor of Silas Phelps in southern Arkansas, Beebe is mentioned in chapters 5, 6, and 11—always in association with his friend Jim Lane. After he and Lane testify against Phelps at the latter's murder trial, Tom Sawyer testifies and proves that both men are paid stooges of Brace Dunlap.

Clayton, Hal Minor character in *Tom Sawyer, Detective* (1896). Clayton is a former criminal partner of Jake Dunlap, with whom he once conspired to cheat another partner, Bud Dixon, out of his share of diamonds that they all stole together. After that attempt failed, Dunlap took all the diamonds himself, leaving Clayton and Dixon to chase him. Clayton and Dixon are probably on the steamboat throughout chapters 2–4, but they appear only momentarily, as they rush past Tom and Huck to follow Dunlap at Fragler's Landing. In chapter 5, Clayton and Dixon are almost certainly the men who beat Dunlap to death in the woods.

Hal Clayton was the real name of a Carson City, Nevada, attorney whom Clemens knew during the early 1860s.

Dixon, Bud Minor character in *Tom Sawyer, Detective* (1896). Dixon is a fearless, hard-drinking criminal partner of Jake Dunlap, who describes him in chapter 3. Before this narrative begins, Dunlap and a third partner, Hal Clayton, tried to cheat Dixon out of his share of stolen diamonds, but he outsmarted them. Dunlap later discovered that Dixon was hiding the diamonds in the heel of his boot, so he switched boots with him while he was drunk and then fled. When Huck and Tom meet Dunlap on a steamboat in chapter 2, Dunlap suspects that Dixon and Clayton are also aboard the boat. Dixon is wearing "a red flannel shirt and some old ragged clothes." Dixon himself appears only briefly; in chapter 4, Huck sees men who he thinks are Dunlap's "two pals" rushing to get off the steamboat at Flagler's Landing, where Dunlap has sneaked ashore. In the next chapter, Dixon and Clayton are probably the men who beat Dunlap to death in a sycamore grove; they flee when Brace and Jubiter Dunlap appear and never reappear in the story.

Dunlap, Brace Character in *Tom Sawyer, Detective* (1896). A prosperous southern Arkansas farmer who lives about a mile from Sally and Silas Phelps, Dunlap is a 36-year-old widower. During the three months leading up to the start of the narrative, he has pestered Silas for permission to marry his daughter, Benny Phelps. Dunlap is mentioned in most of the chapters, but does not appear until chapter 11, when he testifies against Silas at the latter's trial for murdering his brother, Jubiter Dunlap. The trial climaxes when Tom Sawyer proves that Jubiter has not been murdered and that Brace has paid witnesses to testify against Silas.

In the early chapters of *Tom Sawyer, Detective*, Huck indicates that he and Tom knew the Dunlap brothers well during the period covered by the last chapters of *Huckleberry Finn* (1884); however, the only Dunlap mentioned in that earlier story is "Sister Dunlap." In the 1938 film adaptation of *Tom Sawyer, Detective*, Dunlap was portrayed by Edward J. Pawley.

Dunlap, Jake Character in *Tom Sawyer, Detective* (1896). Twenty-seven-year-old Jake is a younger brother of Brace Dunlap and the twin of Jubiter Dunlap—neighbors of Sally and Silas Phelps. At 19 or 20, he became a thief and went to an Arkansas prison, from which he later escaped and fled north. As the narrative opens, he is thought to be long dead. When Huck and Tom take a steamboat to Arkansas in the next chapter, they discover that the reclusive passenger in a neighboring cabin is the missing Jake and become friendly with him. Over the next several days, Jake reveals his sordid past—which resembles the career of Jim Turner in *Huckleberry Finn* (1884).

Dunlap tells the boys how he and two partners, Hal Clayton and Bud Dixon, stole two diamonds worth $12,000 in St. Louis; later, he stole the diamonds from his partners. He thinks his partners are on the steamboat laying for him, so he sneaks off the boat during a rainstorm at Flagler's Landing in chapter 4. He intends to seek the protection of his brothers while disguising himself as a DEAF-AND-DUMB stranger. In the next chapter, his partners catch up with him and kill him. Brace and Jubiter happen upon the scene and chase off the murder-ers. They bury Jake, but do not recognize him. Jubiter assumes Jake's deaf-and-dumb disguise and then he is regarded as missing. When Jake's body is found later, it is believed to be that of Jubiter. Meanwhile, Huck and Tom think that Jubiter is actually Jake. Jake's death is not established until the trial scene in the final chapter; up to that moment, no one besides Tom and Huck even knows that Jake returned home.

In the 1938 film adapted from *Tom Sawyer, Detective*, both Jake and Jubiter were portrayed by William Haade.

Dunlap, Jubiter Character in *Tom Sawyer, Detective* (1896). The 27-year-old brother of Brace Dunlap, Jubiter is "tall and lazy and sly and sneaky and rather cowardly." He works for Tom Sawyer's uncle Silas Phelps, who has hired him to appease Brace, who wants to marry Silas's daughter. As Brace's tool, Jubiter does everything he can to irritate the mild-mannered Phelps. Around the same moment that Tom and Huck arrive at the Phelpses' farm, Silas becomes so mad at Jubiter that he bashes him on the head with a stick. Afterward, Jubiter disappears.

In chapter 9, Huck and Tom find a buried body that is identified as Jubiter; Silas is arrested for murder in the next chapter. Stricken with guilt, the addled man confesses to the crime. At his trial, however, Tom proves that Jubiter is not dead, that he is a DEAF-AND-DUMB stranger who, to this moment, Tom and Huck thought was Jubiter's twin brother, Jake Dunlap. Tom then explains how Jubiter and Brace found Jake's body immediately after the latter was murdered. Not realizing that the dead man was his brother Jake, Jubiter switched CLOTHES with the body, while Brace buried it in order to frame Phelps for Jubiter's murder. In chapter 5, Tom and Huck attempt a conversation with Jubiter, thinking him to be Jake. At the trial, Tom not only unmasks Jubiter's disguise, but calls him a thief and shows that Jubiter has unknowingly been wearing boots concealing $12,000 worth of stolen diamonds. In his only line of dialogue in the narrative, Jubiter admits to all of Tom's charges but protests that he "hain't stole no di'monds."

During the trial, Tom recognizes Jubiter by his habit of tracing "X's" on his face with a finger. The discovery recalls an experience that Clemens himself had in 1882, when he was trying to travel on the Mississippi River under an ALIAS. Shortly after he embarked on the steamboat GOLD DUST, the pilot Lemuel Gray—called Robert Styles in *Life on the Mississippi* (1883)—recognized him by his old habit of running a hand through his hair. *The Prince and the Pauper* (1881) uses a similar device when Tom Canty's mother recognizes him by his habit of shielding his face with the back of his hand when startled.

Dunlap was nicknamed "Jubiter" as a child, when a teacher noticed that he had a big round mole on his leg, surrounded by four small moles that together resembled the planet Jupiter and its first known moons. Other children thought it so funny that they dubbed him "Jubiter" and his real name was eventually forgotten.

Elexandria   Town in *Tom Sawyer, Detective* (1896). Chapters 2 and 4 mention Elexandria as the place where Jake Dunlap boarded the steamboat on which Tom and Huck are traveling. Chapter 8 of "TOM SAWYER'S CONSPIRACY" alludes to "Elexandry" as being 60 miles above St. Petersburg. "Elexandria" is probably Alexandria, a real Missouri town facing KEOKUK, Iowa, across the Des Moines River.

Flagler's Landing   Fictional ARKANSAS location in *Tom Sawyer, Detective* (1896). In chapter 4, Jake Dunlap sneaks ashore from a steamboat at a woodyard about 40 miles above Silas Phelps's farm. In chapter 11, Tom Sawyer identifies the spot as "Flagler's Landing." Clemens may have taken this name from Henry Morrison Flagler (1830–1913), an associate of H. H. ROGERS at Standard Oil who developed FLORIDA resorts.

Hooker, Jeff   Minor character in *Tom Sawyer, Detective* (1896). An Arkansas blacksmith, "Old" Jeff Hooker owns a bloodhound that Tom Sawyer borrows to search for Jubiter Dunlap's body (chapter 9). Hooker laughs at Tom's idea that anyone would want to murder the shiftless Dunlap, but with the dog's help, Tom finds a body. Hooker's role as a debunker recalls a character named Lynch in

the "Mysterious Avenger" tale in chapter 55 of *Life on the Mississippi* (1883). Clemens may have based both characters on someone he knew during his youth.

Lane, Jim   Minor character in *Tom Sawyer, Detective* (1896). A neighbor of Silas Phelps in southern Arkansas, Lane is mentioned in chapters 5, 6, and 11—always in association with his friend Lem Beebe. After he and Beebe testify against Phelps at the latter's murder trial, Tom Sawyer proves that both men are paid stooges of Brace Dunlap.

Nickerson, Steve   Figure mentioned in *Tom Sawyer, Detective* (1896). Nickerson lives "the t'other side of the prairie" from Sally and Silas Phelps in southern Arkansas. In chapter 8, Tom and Huck run into "some of Steve Nickerson's people," who ask about the deaf and dumb stranger whom Huck and Tom have just met.

Phelps, Benny   Character in *Tom Sawyer, Detective* (1896). The daughter of Sally and Silas Phelps, Benny is described in chapter 1 as "half as old as" Brace Dunlap, the unpleasant 36-year-old neighbor who wants to marry her. Though Benny is mentioned throughout the narrative, she plays no role other than to comfort her upset father. She is not among the Phelps children named in *Huckleberry Finn* (1884)—who include Matilda, Jimmy, and Thomas.

Withers, Bill and Jack   Minor characters in *Tom Sawyer, Detective* (1896). The Witherses are brothers whom Huck and Tom happen to see near the scene of Jake Dunlap's murder in chapter 5. In the last chapter, the brothers testify against Silas Phelps at his murder trial, in which Tom exposes them as Brace Dunlap's paid stooges.

BIBLIOGRAPHY

Bay, J. Christian. "*Tom Sawyer, Detective:* The Origin of the Plot." *Essays Offered to Herbert Putnam by his Colleagues and Friends on his Thirtieth Anniversary as Librarian of Congress, 5 April 1929*, edited by William Warner Bishop and Andrew Keogh, 80–88. New Haven, Conn.: Yale University Press, 1929.

Twain, Mark. *Tom Sawyer Abroad* and *Tom Sawyer, Detective,* edited by John C. Gerber and Terry Firkin. Berkeley: University of California Press, 1982.

"Tom Sawyer's Conspiracy"

Unfinished short NOVEL begun in 1897. One of the last stories of the Tom Sawyer / Huckleberry Finn cycle, "Conspiracy" opens shortly after *Tom Sawyer, Detective* (1896) concludes and about a year after the events of *Huckleberry Finn.* Back home looking for ways to stir up excitement, Tom, Huck, and Jim are accidentally caught up in the midst of a murder. The story reflects Clemens's interest in DETECTIVES. He models many minor characters on people he knew in Hannibal and makes fun of their misreading of clues. After the slave dealer is murdered, for example, Detective Flacker suspects that JOHN MURRELL's gang (called "Burrell" here) is behind the crime.

While the story alludes to many characters and events from earlier Tom and Huck tales, its inconsistencies indicate that Clemens paid scant attention to certain details. For example, Miss Watson—who dies in *Huckleberry Finn*—is alive and well here. In chapter 7, Huck encounters his former nemeses, the King and Duke. He expects them to be mad at him for costing them money when he freed Jim in Arkansas; however, the escape episode in *Huckleberry Finn* actually has nothing to do with them. Clemens's confusion about the ending of *Huckleberry Finn* is ironic, since he originally considered ending that novel with a trial scene in which Tom dramatically saves Jim from being convicted for Huck's murder—an ending he reworked for "Conspiracy."

SYNOPSIS

This story narrated by Huck contains about 31,400 words in 10 chapters. To enliven the coming summer, Tom, Huck, and Jim plan to conduct a "conspiracy" that will shake up the town (presumably St. Petersburg) with a phony abolitionist scare. After Tom disguises himself as a runaway slave, Huck will

sell him to a slave dealer, from whom Tom will then escape in order to make it appear that abolitionists have struck. The scheme unravels when real criminals pull a similar trick on the slave dealer and murder him. Tom and Huck learn where the murderers are hiding, but after Jim is charged with the murder, Tom wants to take his time catching the criminals in order to rescue Jim in a dramatic trial. Once the criminals get away, however, Jim's situation becomes perilous. Huck accidentally meets the King and Duke, who offer to get Jim out of Missouri with forged papers and then take him downriver and sell him back into slavery. Figuring that they can rescue Jim later, Huck and Tom accept the plan; however, Jim's peril intensifies when the scoundrels fail to return until his trial is nearly over.

Chapter 1

Huck is again living with the Widow Douglas, for whom Jim—no longer a slave—now works on salary. As summer approaches, Huck goes to Jackson's Island with Jim and Tom Sawyer to discuss how they will spend their time. Huck is content to let things happen, but Tom wants to get up a "civil war." Jim objects to the absurdity of calling any war "civil," so Tom suggests starting a "revolution" instead. This time Jim objects because a proper revolution requires a king to overthrow—and he had his fill of kings the previous summer. Everyone rejects Tom's proposal to start an "insurrection" because the idea is too hazy, but all three agree to get up a "conspiracy."

Chapter 2

Tom suggests creating an abolitionist scare in town. After setting up rendezvous points at scattered places, the conspirators make the island cave in which Jim and Huck hid the previous year their headquarters. In their first official meeting, Tom proposes beginning the conspiracy by running off a slave. Since they cannot run off any real slave, Tom suggests making a fake one—namely himself. He will put on blackface, pretend to be DEAF AND DUMB, and hide in the HAUNTED HOUSE as if he were a runaway, so that Huck can betray him to the slave trader Bat Bradish. After Bradish announces that he has a runaway, Jim and Huck will free Tom to launch the conspiracy.

Chapter 3

Back in town, Tom writes up a handbill, describing himself—as he will appear in disguise—as a runaway Arkansas slave with a $100 reward on his head. He and Huck then ride a canoe down to Hookerville to have handbills printed, which they hang at the post office at night. Afraid that his brother, Sid Sawyer, might interfere with the conspiracy, Tom decides to catch measles from Joe Harper so that Aunt Polly will send Sid away to their uncle Fletcher's farm. The trick works: however, Tom contracts not measles, but scarlet fever—which nearly kills him.

Chapter 4

After Tom recovers fully, the conspirators meet again in their island cave. Tom chisels a cryptic call to arms from the "Sons of Freedom" on a block of wood, which he uses to print a handbill. The printed bill unexpectedly reads backwards, but Tom decides that its message is more mysterious this way. The morning after he and Huck post this message in town, Aunt Polly and others are panicked by the prospect of an abolitionist invasion. Detective Jake Flacker takes charge of the investigation, and Colonel Elder is elected to command troops to guard the town. Huck wonders how the conspirators will get around with soldiers everywhere, but Tom accurately predicts that he will be appointed a spy because of his reputation in the (Jubiter) Dunlap case. To allay Aunt Polly's growing fears, Tom posts a message from the "Sons of Freedom" on her house and others, ordering that no harm befall them. News of the conspiracy spreads as far as SAINT LOUIS.

Chapter 5

After the boys post more runaway-slave bills around town, Huck tells Bradish that he knows where the "runaway" is. However, since Bradish has just paid someone else $200 for another runaway with a $500 reward on him, he is not ready to take on a second captive slave. Tom sneaks onto Bradish's property to examine the sleeping runaway, whom he discovers to be a disguised white man. Since the fake slave has a key hidden in his shoe, he obviously plans to escape that night. Huck wants to call the sheriff to prevent this impending crime, but Tom wants to let matters unfold so that they can have fun helping to catch the criminals later. Meanwhile, they continue their original plan by having Jim blow a horn that night as their make-believe abolitionist signal.

Chapter 6

Before dawn, the boys return to Bradish's, where the slave dealer lies murdered and the fake runaway is gone. Tom finds the footprints of four men, including Jim—who he thinks must have gone for help. As the boys follow the tracks of the fake slave and his accomplice, Tom sees signs indicating that one of them has broken his leg, and he concludes that the fugitives must still be nearby. At the haunted house, Tom crawls under the floor and overhears the criminals talking.

Excited by how this real crime will improve his original conspiracy plans, Tom is even more pleased when he hears that Jim has been arrested for Bradish's murder. The news appalls Huck, but Tom is confident that Jim will go free and end up a hero. When the boys visit Jim in jail, Tom upsets him by trying to invent a motive explaining why Jim would kill Bradish; he figures that getting Jim charged with first-degree murder will make his later rescue an even bigger triumph. Since Bradish once arranged with Miss Watson to sell Jim down the river, Tom suggests revenge as Jim's motive for killing Bradish and makes sure that the district attorney hears about it.

Chapter 7

With most townspeople thinking that Jim is linked with abolitionists, there is talk of lynching him. Huck wants to save Jim immediately, but Tom insists on using the month that it will take before Jim's trial starts to nab the true culprits. After the boys find that the criminals have left the haunted house, however, Tom finally realizes how great Jim's peril is. Now remorseful, Tom gets Huck to rush downriver with him to catch up with the STEAMBOAT on which the criminals must be fleeing. Aboard the boat, Huck stumbles into the King and Duke—the scoundrels he knew a year ago. When he describes Jim's plight, they suggest selling Jim down the river as an alternative to hanging.

Chapter 8

The Duke proposes that he and the King go to St. Louis to have the forged documents that they are carrying modified to show that Jim has murdered someone elsewhere; they will then use these papers to get Jim out of Missouri so they can take him downriver and sell him. Huck agrees to the plan, confident that he and Tom can later rescue Jim and take him to ENGLAND to be free. Though Tom does not see the King and Duke himself, he approves their scheme after he later goes ashore with Huck. For once, Tom wants to use the *quickest* means to free Jim, instead of the showiest. Though not pleased with the new plan, Jim agrees to trust the boys. That night at Aunt Polly's house, Detective Flacker spins theories about the murder, which he thinks was perpetrated by Burrell's gang.

Chapter 9

The next day, the boys search futilely for the tracks of the real murderers. Despairing of capturing the criminals, Tom gets a new idea: He and Huck will accompany the King and Duke as they convey Jim downriver; then, when they reach CAIRO, Illinois, he will buy Jim's freedom from the scoundrels for $1,000—an offer they will not refuse. Thrilled with this plan, Huck insists on paying half; the plan also cheers up Jim. The next day, each boy draws $800 from the money that Judge Thatcher manages for them.

With Jim's trial set for three weeks later, the boys become uneasy when the King and Duke fail to return as promised, so they go to St. Louis to look for them. After four days of fruitless searching, they return home and try to keep Jim cheerful.

Chapter 10

When Jim's trial finally opens, the prosecution presents a strong case. Huck testifies on Jim's behalf, but no one believes his story about the fake "conspiracy." Tom is more convincing, however, and the crowd's sympathies shift toward Jim until the judge asks Tom why he did not tell his story immediately after the murder. After Tom cannot answer, the jury swiftly returns a guilty verdict. As the judge is about to pronounce a death sentence on Jim, the King and Duke suddenly enter the courtroom. The moment they speak, Tom jumps up to denounce *them* as the murderers, saying that their voices are the same ones that he heard in the haunted house. The story ends just as he starts to produce his proofs—a drawing of the King's shoeprint and a set of false teeth that he took from the fake runaway slave's mouth.

BACKGROUND AND PUBLISHING HISTORY

Clemens began this story while living in SWITZERLAND in 1897. After tinkering with it for several years, he abandoned it suddenly, though it appears to be nearly complete. It was first published in HANNIBAL, HUCK & TOM (1969), a volume of the Mark Twain Papers (see MARK TWAIN PROJECT) edited by WALTER BLAIR. It also appears in *Huck Finn and Tom Sawyer Among the Indians* (1989), edited by Blair and Dahlia Armon.

CHARACTERS AND RELATED ENTRIES

For information on Tom Sawyer, see the Characters and Related Entries section of the *Tom Sawyer* entry. For information on Huckleberry Finn, Jim, the King, and the Duke, see the Characters and Related Entries of the *Huckleberry Finn* entry.

Bradish, Bat Minor character in "Tom Sawyer's Conspiracy." Bradish is the nearsighted slave trader whom Tom wishes to involve in his abolitionist hoax by fooling him into thinking that he—Tom in blackface—is a runaway slave. Before Tom's plan is carried out, Bradish is murdered by real conspirators and Jim is arrested for the crime. Near the end of the unfinished novella the King and Duke of *Huckleberry Finn* (1884) are shown to be the true murderers.

The Tragedy of Pudd'nhead Wilson

See PUDD'NHEAD WILSON, THE TRAGEDY OF.

A Tramp Abroad (1880)

The third of Clemens's five TRAVEL BOOKS, *A Tramp Abroad* is the only one that he wrote about a trip that he made solely for the purpose of writing a book. He was in Europe from April 1878 until August 1879. The book covers only about the first third of the 16½ months of his journey.

In April 1878, Clemens sailed to GERMANY with his wife and daughters, a German nursemaid named Rosina (Rosa) Hay, and Livy's friend CLARA SPAULDING. They spent four months in HEIDELBERG and BADEN-BADEN, where JOSEPH TWICHELL joined them in August. From there, they went to SWITZERLAND, where Clemens and Twichell spent a month touring the ALPS together. After Twichell returned home in September, the Clemenses spent two months in ITALY, three months in MUNICH and nearly four months in PARIS. They then made quick visits to BELGIUM and HOLLAND and spent a month in ENGLAND before returning home in August 1879.

Most of *A Tramp Abroad* pertains to the time Clemens spent in southwestern Germany and Switzerland, with a few chapters on eastern France and northern Italy. As with his other travel books, he slips in stories not integrally related to his travels. These include Jim Baker's BLUEJAY YARN, "THE MAN WHO PUT UP AT GADSBY'S," and a tale about Nicodemus Dodge. The book also relates many German legends, including several of Clemens's own invention.

While most of the incidents in *A Tramp Abroad* mirror Clemens's real European experiences, the book's narrator is a different persona. Apart from a BURLESQUE anecdote in chapter 8, in which he signs a note "Mark Twain," the narrator never identifies himself beyond the fact that he is an American who is anxious to travel through Europe on foot, study art, and learn GERMAN. He travels with an "agent," Mr. Harris—whose background is even murkier. The narrator never mentions having a family and appears to be a young bachelor, particularly when he alludes to taking a woman to a ball (chapter 18).

The narrator's mask tends to fall away as his story unfolds, and he increasingly resembles veteran European traveler Clemens. He alludes to having been on a Mississippi STEAMBOAT as a boy (chapter 10), working in a printing office in Missouri (chapter 23), being near NEVADA silver mines (chapter 42), and being with the "INNOCENTS ABROAD" (chapter 47). Chapter 49 reveals more of his background by listing American dishes he craves. In addition to numerous "Southern-style" items, he specifies dishes from Baltimore, Boston, Illinois, Missouri, New Orleans, Philadelphia, San Francisco, the SIERRA NEVADA, Tahoe, the Mississippi, and Virginia—all places Clemens had been, with the exception of Virginia, where his father was born.

Although Clemens went to Europe intending to write a book about his trip, he was unclear about the approach he should take until he was well into his manuscript. Even then, he lacked a clear focus. The book's title reflects his inconsistency: "A

Engraving used as one of two frontispieces in *A Tramp Abroad*

Tramp" could be either a journey on foot or a vagabond. A central theme of the book is a running joke about unfulfilled goals. While the narrator constantly proposes to undertake ambitious *walking* journeys, he invariably ends up *riding*—on anything from donkey carts and rafts to steamboats and trains. Thus, like the "celebrated JUMPING FROG" that never jumps, the celebrated walker almost never walks. The "tramp" that never quite materializes ties in to several other jokes. The travelers carry a pedometer that registers wildly inaccurate distances. When they "climb" in the Alps, they encounter exaggerated perils. For example, an easy afternoon ascent of the RIFFELBERG becomes a huge weeklong expedition (chapters 37–40). Later, the narrator ascends Mont Blanc by telescope (chapter 44).

The travelers also never get around to learning German or mastering painting. They give up on the language when they discover that most Germans speak English (chapter 11). Their study of art and music leads the narrator to the conclusion that "high" art cannot be appreciated without training, since no one can like it naturally. As the narrative nears its end, it offers increasingly harsh views on Europe that reflect the fatigue that overcame Clemens as he wrote. He is especially critical of European manners (chapters 27 and 47), water (chapter 46), and food (chapter 49).

A minor theme throughout the book is the narrator's frequent encounters with talkative Americans, including Cholley Adams (chapter 20), a playful woman (chapter 25), and two unnamed garrulous young men (chapters 27 and 38).

While the narrator of *A Tramp Abroad* never hints that he is married, one might read into the narrative Clemens's gentle teasing of his wife in the narrator's playful mockery of studying art (chapters 11, 14, 42, and 48) and collecting bric-a-brac (chapters 20–22)—activities to which Livy and Clara Spaulding devoted much of their time during the trip. The book also contains a surprising number of tales about lovers destroying each other (chapters 15, 16, and 19).

SYNOPSIS

The 50 numbered chapters and six appendixes of *A Tramp Abroad* contain 157,000 words of text. The narrative moves unevenly and has little relationship to how Clemens distributed his time during his actual travels. The first half of the book is set in southwestern GERMANY. Chapters 1 through 20 cover the narrator's arrival and stay in HEIDELBERG. Within this section are discussions of Heidelberg student life and DUELING (chapters 4–7), music and drama in MANNHEIM (chapters 9–10) and an expedition on the NECKAR River (chapters 11–19). Chapter 3 contains the unrelated BLUEJAY YARN and chapter 8 discusses French dueling. In chapter 20, the narrator shifts his base to BADEN-BADEN, whence he and Harris tour the BLACK FOREST (chapters 22–24).

Most of the second half of *A Tramp Abroad* covers the narrator's alpine experiences in SWITZERLAND and eastern France (chapters 25–47). After an interlude at LUCERNE (chapters 25–27), the travelers visit the RIGI-KULM (chapters 28–29), then go from Lucerne to ZERMATT and the MATTERHORN, by way of INTERLAKEN and the JUNGFRAU (chapters 31–41). The book's most dramatic adventure is the ascent of the RIFFELBERG (chapters 37–40). From Zermatt, the narrator goes to Lake Geneva and MONT BLANC, where he spends several days at Chamonix (chapters 42–46), concluding his time in Switzerland at Geneva (chapter 47).

The last three chapters cover visits to cities in northern ITALY, with brief remarks about Rome, Munich, Paris, Holland, Belgium, England, and sailing home to America (chapters 48–50). The appendixes include discussions of hotel *portiers*, Heidelberg's castle and "college prison," the GERMAN language, and German newspapers.

The first 29 chapters of both one- and two-volume editions of *A Tramp Abroad* have the same numbers. Chapters in the second volume of two-volume editions are numbered 1 through 21; this synopsis gives both sets of chapter numbers. All text that does not come directly from the book's chapters is enclosed in parentheses.

Chapter 1

In March 1878, the narrator of this book believes that it is time for another young man to travel through Europe on foot. To accompany him as his agent, he hires Mr. Harris, who shares his eagerness to study art and GERMAN in Europe. In April, they sail aboard the HOLSATIA. After arriving in GERMANY, they rest briefly at Hamburg, then take an express train south, halting at Frankfurt. The narrator buys a copy of F. J. Kiefer's *The Legends of the Rhine*, translated by L. W. Garnham—who builds English sentences on the German plan, punctuating them with no plan at all. An example of Garnham's toothsome translation is "The Knave of Bergen"—a legend about an executioner who attends a royal masquerade ball disguised as a mysterious knight. After he dances with the queen, his identity is revealed and the outraged king orders his execution. The man saves himself by suggesting that the king knight him to remove the dishonor he has brought on the queen.

Chapter 2

At another stop, the narrator becomes interested in the official called the *portier*, a kind of first-mate of the hotel (also discussed in Appendix A). Meanwhile, the hotel makes elaborate preparations for the arrival of the Grand Duke and Duchess of Baden and the Empress of Germany.

In HEIDELBERG, Harris and the narrator take rooms at the Schloss Hotel, from which they have a serene view of Heidelberg Castle. The charm of the lofty hills around the town is enhanced by the legends and fairy tales that the narrator has been reading. One day he gets lost in the woods and imagines that the ravens are talking about him. Animals *do* talk to each other: however, the only man who truly understands them is a California miner named Jim Baker, whom he quotes at length on the language of bluejays.

Chapter 3

Baker began learning jay language seven years earlier, when his last neighbor left. One day Baker saw a jay land on the roof of his neighbor's vacant cabin, on which the jay found a hole. Congratulating himself on his luck, the jay began filling the hole with acorns. While he worked, he muttered about the disappearance of his acorns into the hole, and vowed to fill the hole if it took a hundred years. As his frustration mounted, he became profane. When a passing jay stopped to investigate, the first jay showed him the hole and explained how many acorns he had put in it. Other jays arrived, exam-

ined the hole and discussed the mystery. They called in still more jays, until perhaps 5,000 were jawing and cussing. Each one expressed a chuckle-headed opinion about the hole, until one of them found the cabin's open door. When they all realized that the jay had been trying to fill up a house, they laughed heartily. Every summer over the next three years jays revisited the famous hole.

Chapter 4

During the summer semester, students are common figures around Heidelberg. Most do not wear badges or uniforms, but a 10th of them wear caps denoting five social organizations called "corps" that are famous for DUELING with swords. Although German university life puts few restraints on students, the vast majority work hard and get solid educations. The students have excellent manners, but the elaborate and rigid etiquette of the corps forbids members from showing any courtesies to rival corpsmen.

Chapter 5

The narrator visits a dueling place on a day when the Red Cap Corps is taking on challengers in one of the twice-weekly combats. A White Cap corpsman acts as his host for the proceedings. Duelists wear goggles, ear protectors and heavy padding over their bodies but use razor-sharp blades and fight with lightning intensity as a surgeon stands by. The first duel ends with both men bloodied and too weary to continue, but does not "count" because it is a draw lasting less than 15 minutes. In the second duel, a White Cap corpsman upsets a man considered a superior swordsman.

Chapter 6

The third and fourth duels end quickly when the surgeon intervenes to treat badly wounded combatants. The fifth duel is unusual in being an affair of "satisfaction" between students not affiliated with any corps. Through all this fighting, the narrator sees men receive hideous wounds but never hears a victim wince or moan.

Chapter 7

In addition to their many laws, the corps also have customs that have the force of law. For example, the laws may not require a member to fight in certain circumstances in which custom dictates that he *must*. It is said that duelists prefer facial wounds because the scars show well, and that they deliberately even make their wounds heal badly. Whether or not this is true, many young German men have grim scars.

Chapter 8

The modern French duel may be ridiculed, but it is actually dangerous. Since it is always fought outside, combatants are nearly certain to catch cold—which is how the famous duelist Paul de Cassagnac (1843–1904) became an invalid.

When the narrator hears of trouble between his old friend (LÉON) GAMBETTA and Fourtou in the French assembly, he goes straight to Gambetta to be his second. However, he acts under a French name—which is why newspapers allude to Gambetta's second as a Frenchman. After having Gambetta draw up a will, the narrator proposes weapons to Fourtou's second—signing his note "Mark Twain." He suggests axes, but Fourtou's second shudders and says that the French code disallows them. The code also forbids rifles and COLT revolvers. Eventually, Fourtou's second produces dainty pistols and proposes a distance of 65 yards between the duelists; however, the narrator talks him down to 35 yards. The morning of the duel, the duelists cannot see each other in the heavy fog, so the narrator has to stand behind Gambetta to holler out his position. After both men fire, Gambetta collapses on top of the narrator. Gambetta is unhurt, but the narrator has several broken bones and crushed organs—making him the only man hurt in a French duel in 40 years.

Chapter 9

One day, the travelers visit MANNHEIM to see WILLIAM SHAKESPEARE's *King Lear* performed in German, but do not understand a single word. On another visit to Mannheim, they hear the opera *Lohengrin* (by RICHARD WAGNER), which the narrator finds unbelievably and painfully noisy. He wonders whether others in the audience naturally like such noise, or if they learn to like it.

Chapter 10

Three or four hours is a long time to sit, yet Wagner operas lasting six hours leave some people actually wishing for more! A German woman explains that one must *learn* to like Wagner's music. After she praises a tenor who has lost his voice, the narrator realizes that Germans appreciate singers for what they *were* as much as for what they are. Why do we regard Germans as stolid and phlegmatic when the opposite seems to be true? Germans also have some admirable customs in their theaters—such as dimming the house lights as the curtain rises. In MUNICH concerts, latecomers are not seated while music is playing. On the other hand, our custom of scattering applause is better than the German custom of saving it up until an act ends.

Watching an old German actor rage around the stage with no audience response makes the narrator think how sick and flat the actor must feel. It reminds him of a moment on a Mississippi STEAMBOAT years earlier when a 10-year-boy awakened excitedly from a troubled sleep to sound the alarm for a fire. Instead of rousing everyone into action as he expected, he was merely advised to dress more warmly. That boy was the narrator.

Chapter 11

During Heidelberg's pleasant summer days, the travelers train for pedestrian tours and make satisfying progress in their German and art studies. After the narrator paints "Heidelberg Castle Illuminated," he and Harris open a studio. As they await orders, they decide to travel up the NECKAR to HEILBRONN with X and Z. They all wear slouch hats, blue army shirts, and overalls and carry knapsacks, opera glasses, canteens, alpenstocks, and sun-umbrellas. Harris also takes a pedometer. Downtown, they board a train, reasoning that they can do their walking on the way back. At picturesque Wimpfen, they eat dinner and nap before setting out again. This time they ride a peasant cart into Heilbronn, where they stay at an inn in which the robber-knight Götz von Berlichingen stayed four centuries earlier. Harris and the narrator share a huge room with beds at opposite ends and a round table as large as King Arthur's in the middle.

Chapter 12

Heilbronn's most picturesque Middle-Age architecture is the *Rathhaus*, or municipal building, whose archive contains a letter written by von Berlichingen. The travelers hire von Berlichingen's own hack and horse to visit a feudal castle noted for withstanding a great siege during the Middle Ages. After the castle finally surrendered, the victorious commander ordered all its men to be killed; however, when the castle's women begged for mercy, he granted one grace—that each woman could remove whatever she could *carry* away. As the castle gates swung open the next day, the women marched out carrying their husbands on their backs.

Chapter 13

At the hotel, the narrator winds Harris's pedometer and pockets it as both men retire early. Harris falls asleep immediately, but the narrator frets and cannot drop off. Later he throws whatever he can find at a noisy mouse, waking up Harris with a shoe and breaking a mirror. The mouse goes away, but new disturbances rob his sleep. Convinced that he will never sleep, he rises to go outside and dresses himself in the dark. In a prolonged search for a missing sock, he bumps into much more furniture than he remembers being in the room. After giving up on the sock, he makes for the door, but cannot find it. He now realizes he is lost; he cannot even find the door by feeling his way along the wall. He retreats to the middle of the room, intending to use the table as a base of departure, only to remember that its round shape makes it useless for orientation. Wandering about randomly, he knocks things down until he rouses the whole house. When X and Z enter with candles, the fresh illumination reveals that he has been circling the same chair all night. According to the pedometer, he has traveled 47 miles.

Chapter 14

Already impressed by the fact that Harris and the narrator are "artists," the landlord is even more impressed to hear that they are on a walking tour of Europe. He explains the road to them, provides them with a lunch and sends them off in von Berlichingen's carriage. When the narrator sees men assembling log rafts, he announces his intention of returning to Heidelberg on a raft. Though his companions fear the dangers of the deep, he charters the longest and finest raft available and its crew.

Chapter 15

As the raft drifts down the gentle river, the travelers watch people work the fields and they gossip with men who hop aboard. As the day grows hotter, the travelers shed their garments, dangle their legs overboard and watch boys swim out to the raft. They pass a steamboat pulling itself on a chain and they see many keelboats. Ashore they buy beer and chickens to eat on the raft. When they pass von Berlichingen's old castle at Hornberg, they hear the legend of "The Cave of the Specter":

> Seven hundred years ago, beautiful young Lady Gertrude loved her poorest suitor, a Crusader named Sir Wendell Lobenfeld. Insisting that Gertrude choose someone worthier, her father locked her up, but she escaped to a cave down the river. Every midnight, she emerged to sing a plaintive love song that Wendel had composed, causing superstitious peasants to think her cave haunted. When Wendel finally returned from the Crusades, Gertrude's repentant father welcomed him as a son, but Wendel was so brokenhearted by losing Gertrude that he wanted only to find a worthy death for himself. Answering the peasants' plea to rid the haunted cave of its dragon, he boated downstream at midnight and fired his crossbow at the white figure emerging from the cave.

Chapter 16

Germany is rich in folk songs, including the popular "Lorelei," about a legend of the Rhine which the narrator likes so much that he reprints Garnham's translation:

> Lore was a beautiful water nymph who sat atop a rock above the Rhine called Lei, luring boatmen to their destruction with her plaintive songs. After falling hopelessly in love with Lore, young Count Hermann boated out to the Lei to offer her his songs. As he sang, the rock erupted in flames and the fairy rose above it, beckoning to him as she called forth waves to destroy his boat. Since then, the fairy has not been seen, but her sorrowful voice is still heard from her crystal castle.

For 40 years, Heinrich Heine's "The Lorelei" has been a favorite German song. The narrator prints its score and original German lyrics, along with his own translation and Garnham's—which is as succinct as an invoice. Garnham is a poet whom he wishes to make known in America; however, even he has a rival. In Munich, Mr. X bought A *Catalogue of Pictures in the Old Pinacotek,* containing such happy English captions as "St. Bartholomew and the Executioner with the knife to fulfill the martyr."

Meanwhile, the raft moves on.

Chapter 17

Near Eberbach they see a crumbling ruin known as the "Spectacular Ruin," whose legend the captain relates:

> During the Middle Ages, a fire-breathing dragon so terrorized the region that the emperor promised to grant whoever destroyed it anything he asked. After the dragon consumed many renowned knights, however, heroes became scarcer and panic spread. Finally, a poor knight from a distant country, Sir Wissenschaft ("Sir Science"), took up the challenge. Though his arrival provoked derision, he calmly went forth armed only with a knapsack. When the dragon attacked him, he took a modern fire-extinguisher from his sack and quenched the dragon's flames, killing it. For his reward, Wissenschaft asked for a monopoly on making and selling spectacles. Though outraged, the emperor granted his request. However, Wissenschaft then reduced spectacle prices so much that a crushing burden was lifted from the nation and the grateful emperor decreed that everyone must buy and wear spectacles whether they needed them or not.

After the Spectacular Ruin, the raft passes a pile of castellated buildings, whose legend the narrator does not repeat because he doubts the truth of some of its details. The travelers also pass Italian laborers blasting a path for a new railway, but they can do little to dodge the resulting showers of stones.

The captain wants to stop for the night, but the narrator insists on continuing on to Hirschhorn.

When the sky grows overcast, everyone else wants to land, but the narrator again orders that they go on. In the growing dark, the wind rises and the crew jumps to meet the storm. With the sea running "inches high," the mate reports that the raft has sprung a leak! Only a miracle will save them now. As the captain orders men forward to bail, cries of "Man overboard!" and "Breakers ahead!" are heard. All is saved, however, when a man jumps ashore and passes a line around a tree. Near midnight, they reach Hirschhorn's "Naturalist Tavern," which takes its name from its display cases of stuffed wildlife specimens.

Chapter 18

The next morning, they breakfast in the garden and encounter the living portion of the tavern's vast menagerie. A pitiable old raven catches the narrator's attention, but he admits that only BAYARD TAYLOR can understand an animal's moral nature. After breakfast, they climb to Hirschhorn's decaying ancient castle and try to hire a skiff to take them to Neckarsteinach. The narrator cannot make himself understood in German, but Mr. X gets results simply by asking (in English), "Can man boat get here?" They decide against taking a boat, however, after the raftsmen discover that the raft's "leak" is merely a crack between its logs.

Bowing courteously to strangers at tables is a German custom that foreigners have trouble mastering. The narrator almost missed a train once because he was uncertain whether to bow to women before leaving his table. Germans also have a winning friendliness. Once, for example, Harris and the narrator exchanged bows with two young women and a man at a BLACK FOREST inn. Later, these same people treated them like old friends in Allerheiligen and helped them plan their route. Later still, the narrator was at a ball in Baden-Baden with a young American woman whose dress was somehow not up to standard. They were spared embarrassment when an elegant German woman whisked his companion away for a proper outfitting. One of the hikers they met earlier, this helpful woman turned out to be a duchess.

Chapter 19

At Neckarsteinach, the travelers dine and plan a visit to the quaint village of Dilsberg across the river. Dilsberg's inhabitants are all blood-kin, but the narrator sees no idiots among them; the captain explains that the government carts them off to asylums. The village's chief pride is an ancient well, which legend claims had a subterranean passage through which supplies were brought to the village during sieges. Under an old linden tree, the captain recites the "Legend of Dilsberg Castle":

> In old times, Dilsberg Castle had a haunted chamber in which anyone who slept would not wake up for 50 years. When a superstitious young knight, Conrad von Geisberg, proposed dismantling this dangerous chamber, friends decided to play a prank on him. His betrothed, Catharina, begged him to spend a night in the haunted chamber. When he woke up, the room was cobwebby and moldy, his clothing was decayed and he felt weak with age. Outside the room, he met strangers who explained that many years had passed. When told that Catharina had died of heartbreak 50 years earlier, Conrad vowed that he too would die of grief. Then young arms surrounded him and Catharina revealed that it was all a jest—he had only been drugged for one night. It was too late: Conrad could not be brought out of his daze.

After hearing this story, the travelers resume their voyage to Heidelberg.

Chapter 20

At Heidelberg, the narrator learns that his trunk has finally arrived from Hamburg and warns readers that when Germans say "immediately," they mean about a week. In preparing for his departure from town, the narrator's chief concern is his ceramics collection, which includes an Etruscan tear-jug and an Henri II plate. Although many people regard bric-a-brac hunting as an activity not suitably robust for a man, the narrator is proud of being a bric-a-brac hunter and "ceramiker."

After a day or two in farewell visits, the travelers take a train to BADEN-BADEN in the Rhine Valley. They get off at Oos and walk the remaining distance—aside from a lift on a passing wagon. They encounter an American minister who is an old friend. As they talk, a young American named Cholley Adams floods them with questions and ends up spending the evening with the minister.

Chapter 21

Situated in beautiful hills, Baden-Baden attracts visitors with hot baths famous for curing rheumatism. An unpleasant encounter with an imperious servant girl at the baths typifies the bad manners of local shopkeepers. Though an inane town, filled with sham and petty fraud, Baden-Baden has good baths and the narrator is pleased to leave his rheumatism there. The travelers stay at the Hôtel de France, which unfortunately is filled with inconsiderate, noisy people keeping long hours. The travelers wander into neighboring villages and particularly enjoy the early 18th-century La Favorita Palace.

Chapter 22

In the Black Forest, the travelers find suggestions of mystery and the supernatural, as well as the quaint kinds of farmhouses and villages that they had expected. One house big enough to be a hotel is ringed by heaps of manure; it appears that a man's station in life can be measured by the size of his manure pile—a feature never adequately stressed in Black Forest stories. To correct this deficiency, the narrator outlines his own Black Forest novel:

> The central character, Huss, is a rich old farmer who owns an immense pile of manure. His neighbor, Paul Hock, is a suitor for his daughter Gretchen, but Hoch's real interest is Huss's manure. Gretchen only loves Hans Schmidt, who has no manure and is not welcome in Huss's house. Heartbroken, Schmidt goes off to die. Eventually, Huss offers Gretchen's hand to Hoch, but on the day of the wedding, his bookkeeper proves that manure missing from his pile is in Hoch's pile. As Hoch is arrested, Schmidt reappears and reveals that he has struck a great manure mine—a GOLCONDA, a limitless Bonanza. Huss then gives Schmidt his daughter.

After lunch in Ottenhöfen, the travelers follow the carriage road up the valley. Along the way, the narrator studies ants and concludes that their reputation for intellect and industry is exaggerated. From the summit they admire the beautiful Allerheiligen gorge.

Chapter 23

The next day, Harris and the narrator head for Oppenau. The true charm of pedestrianism is not in the walking, but in the *talking*. Their conversation goes in many directions: from writers to dentistry to doctors, death and skeletons. The narrator recalls his Missouri boyhood, when the printing office for which he worked hired an ignorant country boy named Nicodemus Dodge, who village smarties thought would be a perfect foil for their pranks. As Harris and the narrator drift into the subject of fossils, the sound of a boy tumbling down a hill disturbs them. The boy is unhurt, but they are left wondering how farmers can live safely on such steep slopes. In the evening, they reach Oppenau—11 hours and 146 miles from Allerheiligen, according to the pedometer.

Chapter 24

The next morning, the travelers return to Baden-Baden on a train filled with a Sunday crowd. At a church service, they sit behind a plainly dressed old woman who must be embarrassed at being in so conspicuous a pew. Angered by the thought of other people laughing at the old woman's poverty, the narrator plans to win some respect for the woman by taking her home in his fine carriage. When she rises, however, he discovers that she is the empress of Germany (Empress Augusta, 1811–1890; the mother of WILHELM II).

That evening, a vast crowd fills the public grounds to hear the *Fremersberg*, a musical story about a medieval nobleman lost in the mountains until saved by a monastery bell. The narrator concludes that the *Fremersberg* must be low-grade music because *he* enjoys it. There seem to be two kinds of music—one which one feels, and another sort that requires a higher faculty.

The travelers' present business in Baden-Baden is to join the courier they have hired for their trip to Italy.

Chapter 25

The next morning they go by train to SWITZERLAND and arrive in LUCERNE at night. Discovering that

the lake's beauty is not exaggerated, the narrator finds Lucerne a charming place. He also discovers that much romantic nonsense has been written about the Swiss CHAMOIS. Most travelers carry ALPENSTOCKS as their trophies.

Half of Switzerland's summer horde is English; most of the rest are Germans and Americans. During dinner at the Schweitzerhof Hotel, the travelers try to guess other diners' nationalities and they argue about the age of a young American woman. To settle the dispute, the narrator decides to ask the woman her age. As he approaches her, she acts as if she already knows him. As he struggles to remember *how* he knows her, she helps him along with remarks about experiences they once shared, but his memory remains blank. Everything he says draws him in deeper, magnifying his embarrassment. Finally, he contradicts himself so obviously that the woman confesses that she has been taking him in because he pretended to know her.

Chapter 26

Tourists flock to concerts at Lucerne's Hofkirche, which has the biggest and loudest organ in Europe. The city's commerce consists mainly of souvenir knickknacks—especially miniature carvings of the Lion of Lucerne, a colossal monument carved into a rock cliff. The monument reminds the narrator how lucky France's LOUIS XVI was to become a martyr instead of dying in bed. The most pitiable act in his unroyal career was letting his Swiss Guard be massacred in Paris on August 10 (1792) in order to save himself.

For years, the narrator's pet aversion has been the cuckoo clock. Now that he is in the creature's very home, he buys one for someone he does not like.

Watching people fish in front of hotels reminds the narrator of an incident from the time he was a newspaperman in WASHINGTON, D.C., in 1867. He was with (JOHN H.) RILEY when he was accosted by a man named Lykins, who was anxious to push through his appointment to San Francisco's vacant postmastership. When Lykins said that he should wrap up the whole matter by the next day, Riley cornered him and told him a cautionary tale about "THE MAN WHO PUT UP AT GADSBY'S." After waiting nine hours to see a fisherman catch something, the narrator suggests that anyone willing to tarry there may as well "put up at Gadsby's" and be comfortable.

Chapter 27

After admiring Lake Lucerne for several days, the travelers go to Fluelen on a steamboat and admire the wonderfully tall mountains surrounding the lake. On the boat the narrator meets an 18- or 19-year-old American boy who barrages him with questions about what ship he came on, where he is staying, and so on, repeating himself several times. The boy is learning German while preparing to enter Harvard. Each time he repeats a question, the narrator answers him differently, but the boy overlooks the discrepancies. Later, the narrator overhears the boy having the same conversation with several women.

Chapter 28

The travelers go by steamboat to WEGGIS, where at noon they begin hiking up RIGI-KULM, from which they want to see an alpine sunrise. By six, they are high enough for a fine view of the lake and mountains. Since their guidebook says that it should take only three and a quarter hours to reach the summit, they are surprised to learn that they have actually only *begun* their ascent. They take rooms at an inn, intending to rise in time to see the sunrise, but sleep like policemen and do not get up until late morning. After several more hours of hiking, they encounter a yodeler, whom they give a franc to yodel some more. Soon they meet another yodeler, whom they give half a franc to yodel. After that, they meet yodelers every 10 minutes and start paying them *not* to yodel. They stop at the hotel at Kaltbad station, eat and hurry to bed so as not to miss the next sunrise. They awaken excitedly but find that it is already late afternoon. Their spirits lift, however, when they learn that hotels at the summit awaken guests for sunrises with alpine horns. As they climb higher, they get lost in the dark and fog. Afraid of stepping over a precipice, they huddle together, shivering and abusing each other for their stupidity, until the fog thins enough for them to see that they are in front of a hotel at the mountain's summit. They check into the hotel.

When a horn blast awakens the men, they snatch their blankets, rush outside and ascend a scaffolding for the best possible view of the sunrise. They discover, however, that the sun is well above the horizon and is going *down*. What they are seeing is not the sun*rise*, but the sun*set*. After dark, they slink back to their room.

Chapter 29

The next morning, the travelers finally awaken *before* sunrise, but while they dress, Harris gets the happy idea of watching it from the comfort of their warm room. As the sky lightens, they sense that something about this sunrise is wrong. Gradually they realize they are looking in the same direction they looked when they watched the previous night's sunset. By the time they reach the summit observation deck, the sun is already well up.

They return to Weggis on a slow, peculiar train whose locomotive and passenger seats tilt back sharply to compensate for the steepness of the tracks.

Chapter 30 (volume 2: chapter 1)

After returning to Lucerne by boat, the narrator wants to rest up for his arduous walking tour. Since he is determined not to do things by halves, he thinks it essential that he visit the Furka Pass, Rhone Glacier, Finsteraarhorn, and the Wetterhorn. He therefore instructs his agent to visit these regions with the courier and report on them. A week later Harris returns with a long report. The narrator admires Harris's work but thinks it much too learned and asks the meaning of some of its many foreign words, such as *dingblatter*—which Harris says is Fiji for "degrees." Other words include *gnillic*, Eskimo for "snow"; *mmbglx*, ZULU for "pedestrian"; and *bopple*, Choctaw for "picture."

Chapter 31 (2:2)

After preparing to walk from Lucerne to INTERLAKEN, the travelers instead hire a four-horse carriage and leave in the morning. Along the way, they see where Pontius Pilate supposedly threw himself into the lake and where Santa Claus was born. They pass majestic mountains, endless limpid lakes, and green hills and valleys, and see an unbroken procession of fruit-peddlers and tourist carriages. On the highway, their driver maintains a comfortable trot, but he tears through villages, aware of the admiration in which he is held. In the heart of William Tell country, they join numerous tourist carriages stopping for dinner at a hotel below the Brünig Pass. A conversation with several Englishmen inflames their desire to see Meiringen from the pass. During an intoxicating ascent up a smooth road, however, both men fall asleep and the narrator awakens angrily to find they have missed an hour and a half of scenery. They sullenly complete their trip through Brienz and reach Interlaken around sunset.

Chapter 32 (2:3)

After dinner at the huge Jungfrau Hotel, the travelers retire to the great drawing room, where a young American bride drives everyone away by playing on the world's worst piano. No one likes mediocrity, but we all reverence perfection—which is what her terrible music is.

Europe has changed immensely. Napoleon was the only European of his time who could be called a traveler. Now everybody goes everywhere and Switzerland buzzes with restless strangers. In the morning, a wonderful sight greets the travelers through their hotel window: the giant form of the JUNGFRAU.

When a picture in a shop window attracts the narrator, he sends his courier to ask its price without identifying himself—thinking that a native will get the best price. The price the courier reports, however, is a hundred francs too high. When the narrator later visits the shop himself and is asked a hundred franc less for the same picture, the shopkeeper explains that this price does not include the courier's commission. The courier's deception explains how men in his trade can afford to work for just $55 a month and fares. Despite the extra cost that couriers add to traveling, the narrator would never consider traveling without one. A courier who might fairly be called perfection is JOSEPH N. VEREY.

Chapter 33 (2:4)

The narrator wants to visit beautiful Giesbach Fall on Lake Brienz's opposite shore but does not, since a boat trip would violate his private contract to travel through Europe on foot. Meanwhile, an even grander sight is at hand—the mighty dome of the Jungfrau.

After a brief stop at an open-air concert, the narrator begins planning a formidable walking trip

to ZERMATT. He gets directions and puts his courier in the care of someone going to Lausanne, but when it appears that it will rain the next morning, he hires a buggy for the trip. With the road to themselves, the journey is exceedingly pleasant, even though their driver gets drunk, and they stop for the night in Kandersteg.

Chapter 34 (2:5)

The guide they hire is over 70, but has strength to spare as they begin their ascent. Though they take great interest in wildflowers, they think little of edelweiss, the ugly Swiss favorite. They stop at a little inn and find a chance for real alpine adventure when the nearby Great Altels beckons to them. After sending Harris to arrange for guides and equipment to climb the mountain, the narrator reads (Thomas Woodbine) Hinchliff's *Summer Months Among the Alps* (1857) to learn about mountain climbing. Hinchliff's description of a particularly perilous ascent raises the narrator's excitement level. The moment he reads about a member of Hinchliff's party falling, Harris enters to announce that arrangements are made for their climb. Admitting that alp-climbing is different from what he supposed, the narrator declines, but instructs Harris to have the hired guides follow them to Zermatt.

Chapter 35 (2:6)

The narrator leaves the inn feeling exhilarated. He and Harris descend down corkscrew curves on a colossal precipice whose path is often little more than a groove. Near the bottom, Harris's hat blows off. They spend several hours searching for it, but all they find is pieces of an opera glass. When they try to find its owner's remains, they argue about what they will do with them once they find them.

At Leukerbad, they wade through liquid fertilizer. Covered with hungry irritating "chamois," Harris refuses to stop at the Chamois Hotel. Instead, they stop at the Hôtel des Alpes, which has the largest woman the narrator has ever seen; she has come to Leuk to shed her corpulence in the baths. The next morning, they hike to the famous Ladders on the perpendicular face of giant cliffs. The narrator orders Harris to climb one so he can record the feat in his book; Harris obliges by using a subagent.

The next morning, they drive to the RHONE Valley and catch a train to Visp, whence they head for Zermatt on foot. At St. Nicholas, they wade ankle-deep in fertilizer-juice and stop at a hotel where all the tourists have their clothes baked. Afterward, their laundry is scrambled and everyone appears at dinner wearing other guests' clothes.

Chapter 36 (2:7)

At St. Nicholas they are awakened early by irritating church bells. The church should heed its own advice to reform by dropping such practices as bell-ringing and reading "notices" from the pulpit. After breakfast, the travelers head for Zermatt. When the narrator admires a glacier, Harris surprises him by finding fault with it. A rabid Protestant, Harris has snarled for days about the superiority of Protestant cantons (administrative districts) over Catholic ones. He claims that Protestant cantons are less muddy when it rains and that everything in them is better—their church bells, dogs, roads, goats, chamois, flower-boxes—even their glaciers.

Later, they see a young Swiss girl just miss slipping over a precipice to her death. Harris irritates the narrator by going on and on about how glad he is that the girl was not hurt. He is heedless of the needs of the narrator—who might have profited from being able to write about rescuing the girl if she had slipped.

Near Zermatt, they approach the MATTERHORN. Nature here is built on a stupendous plan; *everything* is magnificent. At three in the afternoon, they reach Zermatt, where they know they are in real alp-climbing country when they encounter Mr. Girdlestone himself (Arthur Gilbert Girdlestone, English author of *The High Alps Without Guides,* 1870). While there may be no pleasure equal to climbing a dangerous alp; it is a pleasure confined to those such as Girdlestone, who has spent the summer trying to break his neck.

The guides whom the travelers hired earlier are waiting for them at Zermatt, so the narrator devotes his evening to studying up on climbing. Several books teach him the importance of strong shoes, good-quality equipment and having enough rope to tie the entire party together. He also reads a fearful passage by Mr. (EDWARD) WHYMPER,

describing a time when he fell 200 feet in seven or eight bounds.

Chapter 37 (2:8)

Intoxicated by his reading, the narrator announces that he will ascend the RIFFELBERG. Though startled, Harris vows to stand by him unto death. Everyone in Zermatt helps prepare for the expedition, which consists of 154 people, 51 mules and cows, and tons of equipment, including 143 pairs of crutches, 27 kegs of paregoric (an opiate), 154 umbrellas, and two miles of rope. The men include 17 guides, 15 bar-keepers, four surgeons, three chaplains, and a host of other specialists. The narrator has all the men and animals arranged in a single file, lashed together on one strong rope, creating a procession 3,122 feet long. Harris and the narrator, the only persons mounted, take up the dangerous position at the extreme rear, with each man tied to five guides. Out of respect for tourists they will encounter, they wear full evening dress.

After starting in the afternoon, the expedition camps in a meadow. They rise at two in the morning, but wait until nine to start again. In the afternoon, the guides call a halt to admit they are lost. They are not certain that they are lost, however, because none of them has ever been in the region before. Troubles multiply when the expedition comes up against a great rock. The narrator maintains morale by assuring everyone that they will be saved. With the help of paregoric, everyone gets through the night.

The next day, the party uses ladders to scale the rock; the problem of getting the animals over it is solved by blowing it up with nitroglycerin. After bridging the resulting hole, they push on. The following day, new obstacles convince everyone that they truly are lost. To counter the growing demoralization, the narrator attaches a three-quarter-mile-long rope to a guide and sends him off to find the road. When the rope later jerks frantically, the expedition excitedly follows it for half a day, only to find it tied to a ram.

Chapter 38 (2:9)

The expedition camps where the ram has led it. After supper, the narrator again doses the men with paregoric and beds them down. The next morning, Harris brings a BAEDEKER map that proves that they are not lost—the summit is lost. After trying to determine the altitude, the narrator faces a new crisis when a porter shoots the expedition's Latinist while aiming at a chamois. A rumor sweeps the camp that a barkeeper has fallen over a precipice, but happily it turns out to be only a chaplain.

The next morning, they party moves on in good spirits. When they encounter another big rock, they blast it away with dynamite, then discover it had a chalet on its top. After having the chalet rebuilt, the narrator retires inside with Harris to correct his scientific journals. A young man then enters and introduces himself as the grandson of a once-notable American and begins a long, vacuous conversation with Harris about his personal connections with European courts and other matters. He ranks with the innocent chatterbox on the lake (chapter 27) as one of the most interesting specimens of young Americans the narrator has met in his travels.

The caravan starts off again, following the zigzag mule road. After a lost umbrella causes a delay, they reach the summit the next day at noon. Exulting in having demonstrated the possibility of the impossible, Harris and the narrator march proudly into the great dining room of the Riffelberg Hotel and receive an admiring welcome from the tourists—mostly women and children.

Chapter 39 (2:10)

Baedeker's guidebook contains strange statements about the ascent to Riffelberg, but the narrator sends him corrections—instead of three hours, it takes seven days to make the trip.

With the men's strength restored, the problem now is getting them back *down* the mountain. Since balloons are not available, the narrator proposes descending on the great Gorner Glacier, which begins 1,200 feet below the summit. Objecting to the narrator's proposal to have everyone descend at once by umbrella to the glacier, Harris suggests having one man try this alone. However, Harris refuses to *be* that man. Unable to find anyone willing to take Harris's place, the narrator marches the men overland to the glacier and settles them in its middle—which Baedeker says moves

the fastest. That night, the men pitch camp; the narrator paregorics them and retires, leaving orders to be called when Zermatt is sighted.

The next day, they still have not budged. Suspecting that the glacier may have run aground, the narrator rigs spars on each side to break it loose, but meets no success. After learning from Baedeker that the glacier moves less than an inch a day, he calculates that it will take them 500 years to get to Zermatt, so he decides to walk. After breaking camp, the men reach Zermatt in the evening.

Chapter 40 (2:11)

Having learned much more about glacial movement since taking passage on the Gorner Glacier, the narrator shares his knowledge and relates a story about mountaineers who disappeared into the glacial crevices on Mont BLANC in 1864. Another Mont Blanc story concerns the disappearance of three men into a glacier in 1820. The English geologist Forbes (James David Forbes, 1809–1868) predicted that at the rate the glacier was moving, it would deliver the missing men's bodies to the foot of the mountain in about 35 or 40 years. In 1861, some of their remains finally appeared.

Chapter 41 (2:12)

The Alps' most memorable disaster occurred on the Matterhorn in July 1865, during Whymper's ninth attempt to scale the mountain. The chapter quotes at length from Whymper's account of how four men lost their lives.

Chapter 42 (2:13)

Switzerland is a large rock covered with a grass skin too valuable to waste on any but the living. As a result, Zermatt's graveyard is small and occupation is temporary. The travelers leave Zermatt by wagon in a rainstorm. At St. Nicholas, they strike out for Visp on foot. A scene of children playing at mountaineering reminds the narrator of children playing silver-mining in NEVADA. It also reminds him of a young boy whose preacher father disapproved of his playing such things as steamboat captain and army commander on Sundays, and told him instead to play only things suitable to the Sabbath. The next Sunday he found his son impersonating God, casting other children out of Eden.

After a night in Visp, the travelers go by train to Brevet, then by boat to Ouchy and Lausanne (on Lake Geneva). Long moved by BYRON's *Prisoner of Chillon* (1816), the narrator takes a steamer to the Castle of Chillon to inspect the dungeon where Bonnivard was a prisoner (1530–36). The visit removes some of the sympathy he has felt for Bonnivard when he finds Bonnivard's dungeon roomier and more comfortable than a private St. Nicholas dwelling. The travelers next go by train to Martigny and Argentière, from which they see Mont Blanc. Then they take a wagon to Chamonix.

Chapter 43 (2:14)

Everyone in Chamonix is out of doors, where Mont Blanc's looming presence overshadows everything and presents spectacular views. At the exchange of Chamonix, which oversees all Mont Blanc expeditions and issues diplomas to climbers, the narrator tries to buy a diploma for an invalid friend, but finds no sympathy. The office also contains a book listing every fatal accident on Mont Blanc.

Chapter 44 (2:15)

After breakfast the next morning, the travelers study Mont Blanc though a telescope. When climbers come into view, the narrator hits on the idea of using the telescope to ascend the mountain in the climbers' company. At first, Harris is afraid to join him, but is finally persuaded. After a last look at his pleasant surroundings, the narrator boldly puts his eye to the glass and follows the climbers to the summit, where he shares in their triumph.

In August 1866, Chamonix residents witnessed a frightful tragedy on Mont Blanc through their telescopes when three English climbers fell 2,000 feet. Amazingly, two men survived the fall and were seen trying to help the third. They then spent hours making their perilous descent. The next chapter will copy (Stephen) D'Arve's account of one of the most mournful of all mountaineering calamities from his *Histoire du Mont Blanc*.

Chapter 45 (2:16)

On September 5, 1870, 11 climbers reached the summit of Mont Blanc, where they disappeared within a cloud. Help was sent eight hours later, but a raging storm prevented anything from being done

for a week. When rescuers finally reached the summit, they found 10 bodies; the 11th person was never found. One body had a diary recording the climbers' grisly end. Hopelessly lost in the storm, they had wandered aimlessly within a tiny area until cold forced them to lie down and slowly die.

Chapter 46 (2:17)

With guides and porters, Harris and the narrator ascend to the Hôtel des Pyramides near the top of the Glacier des Bossons. After studying the glacier from within a long tunnel hewn inside it, they ask their chief guide to organize guides and porters to ascend the Montanvert, only to be advised that an ambulance would be more suitable. The next day they climb to the Montanvert's summit hotel and view the famous Mer de Glace. They cross this glacier safely, but worry about its yawning crevices.

In the blazing heat, the parched travelers slake their thirst in cold mountain streams—the *only* water in Europe capable of quenching thirst. Away from the mountains, European water is flat and insipid compared to American water.

After more climbing, the travelers return to their hotel, and they leave for Geneva the next morning.

Chapter 47 (2:18)

During several restful days at Geneva, they find the city's many little shops manned by irritatingly persistent clerks asking maddeningly elastic prices. Geneva has few "sights." After failing to find the homes of Rousseau and Calvin, the narrator gets lost among streets with such unlikely names as "Hell," "Purgatory," and "Paradise." The sight of young men deliberately obstructing pedestrians convinces the narrator that Americans are generally superior to Europeans in manners, particularly in their treatment of women.

The travelers prepare to walk to ITALY, but find the road so level that they instead take a train, stopping overnight at Chambéry. The next morning they leave for Turin on a railroad rich in tunnels. They share a compartment with a ponderous Swiss woman who stretches her legs to the opposite seat, crowding an American passenger. When the man politely asks her to move her feet, she sobs about being an unprotected lady who has lost the use of her limbs. Though the man apologizes profusely, the woman sobs until the train enters Italy, where she springs from her seat and strides away.

Turin is a fine city with everything built on a large scale. The narrator has read that tourists should expect to be cheated by Italians, but he experiences just the opposite. After a Punch and Judy show, for example, he gives a small coin to a youth who tries to return it because it is too much. The incident reminds the narrator how he once mistakenly gave a five-dollar gold piece to a blind woman in an ODESSA church and later stole it back.

Chapter 48 (2:19)

In MILAN, the narrator visits the great cathedral and other regulation sights to see what he has learned in 12 years. He finds that his old idea about copies of Old Masters' paintings being superior to their originals is wrong. In VENICE, he concludes that the Old Masters really do contain a subtle *something* that does not lend itself to reasoning, just as certain women may have indefinable charm invisible to strangers. He calls an Old Master that particularly fascinates him the "Hair Trunk"; it is a painting by Bassano in the Doge's Palace titled "Pope Alexander III and the Doge Ziani."

Chapter 49 (2:20)

Venice's St. Mark's Cathedral is such perfection in its nobly august ugliness, it is difficult to stay away from. Nearly 450 years ago, a noble named Stammato robbed the cathedral in a manner out of the ARABIAN NIGHTS. After months of methodically spiriting priceless treasures through a secret passage, he discovered that he could not enjoy his collection alone. He swore a fellow noble to secrecy and showed him his collection, only to be promptly betrayed and hanged.

In Venice, the travelers enjoy a rare luxury—dinner in a private home. European hotel fare is so awful that anyone accustomed to American cooking who is condemned to live on this fare would waste away. One first learns to do without the customary morning meal. What passes for coffee in Europe resembles the real thing as hypocrisy resembles holiness. A European dinner is better than the breakfast, but is monotonously unsatisfying. Starved

for a nourishing meal, the narrator lists American dishes he wants to have waiting for him at home.

Chapter 50 (2:21)

Why is art allowed as much indecent license as in earlier times, while literature's privileges have been sharply curtailed in this century? Every European gallery has hideous pictures of blood and carnage, alive with every conceivable horror in dreadful detail, but no one complains. If a writer described such things, critics would skin him alive.

Titian's Venus of Urbino may defile its gallery; however, his "MOSES" (actually a painting by Giorgione) glorifies it. It has no equal among the works of the Old Masters, apart from Bassano's divine Hair Trunk. The narrator goes to FLORENCE to see this painting and arranges to have it copied for his book. (The frontispiece of *A Tramp Abroad* is actually adapted from an unrelated picture of Moses.)

After visiting Rome and other Italian cities, the travelers go to MUNICH, PARIS, HOLLAND, and BELGIUM, working in SPAIN and other regions through agents to save time. Finally, they cross to ENGLAND, whence they return home on the GALLIA. Nothing that the narrator has experienced abroad compares with the pleasure of seeing New York harbor again. Europe has some advantages that we lack, but they do not compensate for what exists only here. To be condemned to live the way an average European family lives would make life a heavy burden to the average American family.

Appendix A

A hotel official with no precise American equivalent, the European *portier* serves as an intermediary between guests and the hotel, providing services and answering questions that one might be reluctant to ask a hotel clerk. The secret of the portier's devoted service is that he gets fees and no salary. No matter how long you stay in a hotel, you do not pay the portier until you leave.

Appendix B

This 2,560-word description of Heidelberg Castle emphasizes its special attractiveness when illuminated at night.

Appendix C

Subtitled "The College Prison," this essay discusses the special legal status of German students, who can only be tried and punished by their own universities. Convicted students can even choose when they serve their prison time.

Appendix D

"THE AWFUL GERMAN LANGUAGE" examines the perplexities of GERMAN.

Appendix E

"Legend of the Castles" is the story of two old bachelor twins known as Herr Givenaught and Herr Heartless. When Germany's most renowned scholar, Franz Reikmann, faces financial ruin after a speculator cheats him, his daughter Hildegarde dreams that the Virgin has instructed her to ask the brothers to bid on Reikmann's books at an auction. The brothers refuse, but both appear at the auction in disguise. Givenaught not only bids enough to pay off Reikmann's debts and leave him with a generous profit, but he returns Reikmann's books to him.

Appendix F

A survey of German newspapers finds them to be the dreariest of human inventions. They contain little more than "telegrams" and letters concerning political news and market reports. Compared to an average daily American paper, which has between 25,000 to 50,000 words of reading matter, a typical Munich newspaper has exactly 1,654 words.

BACKGROUND AND PUBLISHING HISTORY

In March 1878, Clemens secretly signed a contract with FRANK BLISS to write a book about Europe. A month later, he sailed with his family to Germany, beginning the trip that would become the basis of *A Tramp Abroad.* Why he made this trip when he did is not fully clear. Perhaps the embarrassment he suffered after delivering a speech on JOHN GREEN-LEAF WHITTIER's birthday in December made him want to leave the country. Also, he had not completed a major book since *Tom Sawyer* (1876) and he regarded a TRAVEL BOOK as something he could write comparatively easily.

Shortly after reaching Germany in April 1878, Clemens began writing experimentally but accomplished little for some months. The arrival of his friend JOSEPH TWICHELL in August and the time they spent together gave Clemens the spark he needed. After Twichell left, he hit on the idea of building the book around a man and his "agent" undertaking a walking tour that never quite gets going. Twichell was with Clemens only in the BLACK FOREST and the Alps, but the Harris character based on him travels with the narrator through most of *A Tramp Abroad.*

Clemens completed virtually all the traveling that he described in *A Tramp Abroad* by mid-November 1878, when he settled in MUNICH with his family. He then got down to serious writing. By January, he had completed 20 chapters, but was having trouble staying interested—especially after

True Williams's illustration of the narrator struggling to write opens the first chapter of *A Tramp Abroad.*

discovering that he had seriously overestimated the amount of work that he had finished. After adding another five chapters quickly, he took his family to Paris in late February 1879. His writing grew increasingly difficult, but he persevered until he returned home in September. In January 1880, he finished his manuscript. By then, he had arranged to publish with ELISHA BLISS, instead of Bliss's son, and the AMERICAN PUBLISHING COMPANY issued *A Tramp Abroad* on March 13, 1880.

Though Clemens feared he would never write enough to fill the book, he eventually wrote so much that he had to make substantial cuts. Many deleted chapters had little to do with his European travels. Much of this material appeared in THE STOLEN WHITE ELEPHANT, ETC. (1882), whose title story he originally wrote for *A Tramp Abroad*. Other omitted material that found its way into that collection includes "Concerning the American Language," "Paris Notes," "Legend of Sagenfeld in Germany," and "THE GREAT REVOLUTION IN PITCAIRN." "THE PROFESSOR'S YARN" and a chapter about Dutchy and Lem Hackett later appeared in *Life on the Mississippi* (1883). "The French and the Comanches" finally appeared posthumously in LETTERS FROM THE EARTH (1962). Deleted material still awaiting publication includes chapters on French marriage customs, Hamburg, Munich, and Rome, as well as a brief passage on IVAN TURGENEV, whom Clemens saw in Paris in 1879.

Clemens's extensive notes from his 1878–79 trip are published in the second volume of the Mark Twain Papers (now the MARK TWAIN PROJECT) edition of his NOTEBOOKS. In order to edit a fully corrected edition of *A Tramp Abroad*, the project's editors must first reassemble the book's long-scattered original manuscript—a task that was only about 70 percent complete in 2006. The project has tentatively scheduled a new edition of *A Tramp Abroad* for after 2010; that edition will contain Clemens's complete working notes and the deleted chapters.

While *A Tramp Abroad* has never been as popular as Clemens's earlier travel books, it has generally remained in print. Modern editions, however, have generally ignored the book's original illustrations—which are an integral part of its humor. The

first edition has 328 pictures, of which WALTER FRANCIS BROWN drew more than a third. Brown's illustrations are scattered throughout the volume and are mostly signed "W. F. B." It is difficult to identify who did many of the unsigned pictures, as Brown's work resembles that of TRUE WILLIAMS, who contributed at least 40 pictures. BENJAMIN HENRY DAY added 22 pictures—all clearly signed (chapters 2, 35–37, 39–40, 42–44, 46–48)—and WILLIAM WALLACE DENSLOW did six pictures initialed "W. W. D." for chapter 47's episode about a Swiss woman on a train. Clemens himself added at least nine pictures (chapters 11, 14, 15?, 19–21, 31–32 and 48). Other illustrations were adapted from previously published work by J. C. Beard, ROSWELL MORSE SHURTLEFF, and Edward Whymper.

The 1996 OXFORD MARK TWAIN edition included a facsimile reprint of the first American edition. This edition was evidently the first since the original editions to contain all the book's illustrations. The Oxford edition also contains a new introduction by Russell Banks and an afterword by James Leonard.

CRITICAL COMMENTARY

Clemens's second pass at Europe, *A Tramp Abroad,* is a leisure trip and an armchair sociology sprinkled with details of cultural difference. In it, Clemens records and speculates on the workings of European cultural institutions such as German universities, French duels, hotels, the high-flying quackery of spa treatments, the behavior of Americans abroad, and the phenomena of tourism itself. Like many 19th-century travel writers, Clemens, Jeffrey Melton notes, "serves as a proto-typical modern tourist" who typifies the "self-loathing" of those engaged in "an ongoing battle between 'travelers' and 'tourists,' a struggle for self-identification." Mark Twain threads this foundational irony, the psychology of tourists acting and talking like travelers, into his narrative voice. His intrepid-sounding plans and actual activities become a running joke about the disparity between adventurer rhetoric and tourist lifestyle.

National Characteristics
Encompassing a range of modes from derision, to mild amusement, to earnest curiosity, Clemens

measures and catalogs what he estimates to be national characteristics. Many come in the form of glimmering generalizations with little elaboration, such as his insistence that "French calmness and English calmness have points of difference" (chapter 8). Other one-liners are aimed more directly at concrete national institutions such as the questionable bravery of the French military ("The cross of the Legion of Honor has been conferred upon me. However, few escape that distinction"; ibid.) and German opera. Mark Twain makes repeated references, and devotes an appendix, to his preferred "whipping boy," the GERMAN language. He describes a German production of *King Lear:* "We . . . never understood anything but the thunder and lightning; and even that was reversed to suit German ideas" (chapter 9). An oscillation between reverence and derision of Europe, Melton observes, is a key element of American tourism and travel writing of the period. By engaging in it, Euro-Americans "could wander among the accomplishments of their ancestors, and celebrate them, all the while affirming their belief through direct comparison that America was a land of the future and Europe of the past."

Even Clemens's digressions fit into the overall context of shuttling imaginatively between Europe and the United States. Perhaps most notably, Jim Baker's BLUE-JAY YARN appears in the text during a walk through a German forest, a feature that has piqued many critics. On a pragmatic level, some have attributed this to Clemens's economic needs and length requirements. Finding that he had much less text than he expected, digressions such as this crowd-pleasing western yarn would have been perfect for bulking up the text, a view supported by the flat-footed transition that introduces it: "Animals talk to each other, of course" (chapter 2). Others have observed a higher order structure in Clemens's anecdotal drift, seeing it as a kind of global circuit that brings together his domestic and foreign travels. Richard Bridgman sees significant symmetry in the fact that the blue-jay yarn, "which takes place in the Sierra, ended up in an account of a European walking tour, and a tale laid in a Munich morgue is told during a trip down the Mississippi" (Bridgman 1–2).

German Educational System

Clemens lingers on German higher education, recording the details on the margins of a system that, while foreign, also deeply influenced American education in the late 19th century. The first American research universities, such as Johns Hopkins and the University of Chicago, and the concept of graduate study, emulated the German model. By the late 19th century, many American students went to study in Germany to be near the latest scientific developments and humanist methodologies. By the turn of the 20th century, many American students, including some who would go on to become prominent scholars, such as Edward A. Ross, Robert Park, and W. E. B. DuBois, studied in Germany and returned with acquired methodologies and attitudes. The steady stream of scholars returning from Germany had a profound effect on the intellectual and social life of American universities. This visible phenomenon later prompted William James's 1903 article, "The Ph.D. Octopus," which was about the vexing professionalism of America's new wave of German-trained academics. When Clemens notes the exotic and vexing behavior of German students, his observations suggest the cultural detritus implicitly accompanying the educational flow from Europe into the United States.

But Clemens is more interested in the pathological than the mainstream aspects of educational experience. He spends part of one chapter in the classroom and then devotes three to the idiosyncratic traditions of the student social organizations, to which one-10th of students belonged. His morbid interest comes to rest on the cultish student dueling tournaments: "All the customs, all the laws, all the details, pertaining to the student duel are quaint and naïve. The grave, precise, and courtly ceremony with which the thing is conducted, invests it with a sort of antique charm" (chapter 6). Charmed by this case of potted chivalry, Clemens also touches on the ways German dueling societies spilled over into the topics of class and criminal justice. Clemens was arrested by the system of buffers standing between German university students and the criminal justice system, specifically their option of choosing a convenient time to serve their sentence and their separate "college jail." Clemens follows his incredulity into a close study of the phenomenon and its relationship to Europe's segmented class system: "It is questionable if the world's criminal history can show a custom more odd than this. . . . There have always been many noblemen among the students, and it is presumed that all students are gentlemen . . . perhaps this indulgent custom owes its origins to this" (Appendix C). After describing the room in detail, down to the layers of graffiti and the table that has been ornately carved by generations of bored students, Clemens's response to his discovery is typical of the late 19th-century American in Europe—he tries to buy the table.

The narrator's raft journey, critics have noted, suggests a seed from which Huck Finn grew. If Baker's blue jay seems out of place in Germany, it is equally striking to imagine Huck and Jim in their first draft form drifting down the Neckar. While lazing about on the raft, the narrator notes the disparity of the division of labor between genders, marveling ironically at how European men leave all of the work to women, who "do all kinds of work on the continent"; for example, the chambermaid, who "does not have to work more than eighteen or twenty hours a day, and she can always get down on her knees and scrub the floors of halls and closets when she is tired and needs a rest" (chapter 15). Clemens also freely admits, with some protective irony, his own dandyish affection for "bric-a-brac hunting," which he estimates "is about as robust a business as making doll-clothes, or decorating Japanese pots with decalcomanie butterflies" (chapter 20).

Cultural Observations

Among the many aspects of German culture that stand out to Clemens as requiring comment is the custom of "bowing courteously to strangers when sitting down at table or rising up from it," which Clemens finds charming but also stilted and time-consuming, claiming to have almost missed a train for bowing (chapter 18). Having decided that everyone in Germany wears glasses, Clemens makes it a motif of his travelogue, claiming at one point to want to sketch the only German man he has seen without spectacles (he later decides it was a ruse). Using a dubious pun to squeeze in more eyewear-

based humor, he goes on to construct a mock Germanic "Legend of the 'Spectacular Ruin,'" about a knight who, having slain a dragon, demands for his reward a "monopoly on the manufacture and sale of spectacles in Germany." This small tale is not only a jocular allegory of scientific advancement—the knight Sir "Wissenschaft," meaning "science," invents a fire extinguisher to use on the dragon—and a fake myth meant to explain the perceived ubiquity of glasses among Germans; but it also ends with a small victory for socialized capitalism: the "unselfish monopolist immediately reduced the price of spectacles to such a degree that a great and crushing burden was removed from the nation" (chapter 17).

For the scavenger of everyday details, Clemens's attention to minutiae can be fascinating, even while his penchant for exaggeration and distortion makes such details factually questionable. With the pinch-penny wisdom of a habitual and substandard speculator, Clemens accumulates and records comparative observations about everyday microeconomics. Cigars, we learn in the first chapter, are so cheap in Europe that the stockpile of a thousand "very cheap cigars" from home in Clemens's luggage was a cultural miscalculation. His narrator gets into a pricing match with a woman selling spring water in Baden-Baden, as she refuses to give him a price, asking him to set his own instead. As a consumer craving a clear indication of value, the narrator complains of this "common beggar's trick" designed to "put you on your liberality when you were expecting a simple straight-forward commercial transaction" (chapter 21). He finds the same annoyance in Geneva, where "prices in the smaller shops are very elastic—that is another bad feature" (chapter 47).

Appendix A (beginning with a fabricated epigraph attributed to Omar Khayyám) offers a short and breezy monograph on the portier, the resident fixer and gofer of the European hotel. Clemens records his growing dependency on and fascination with the portier: "Since I first began to study the portier, I have had opportunities to observe him in the chief cities of Germany, Switzerland, and Italy." Clemens's obsessive interest in the proper amount to tip each worker inflected by service, time, and hierarchy yields to an analysis of differing incentive systems and economic psychologies in Europe and America: "What is the secret of the portier's devotion? It is very simple: he gets *fees, and no salary.*" Clemens's general amazement and implicit consumer advocacy hints at the relationship during this period between European traditions of service and the evolving American service sector: "It is the pride of our average hotel clerk to know nothing whatever; it is the pride of the portier to know everything."

European Service and American Tourists

On a broader level, this suggests the ambivalent experience by Americans of everyday life in Europe in contrast to history or civilization in the abstract. Clemens's ardor for European service hints at the American search, despite financial self-assurance, for ingenuity, convenience, and lifestyle adaptation in Europe as well as artifacts of civilization: "It seems to me that it would be a happy idea to import the European feeing system into America. I believe it would result in getting even the bells of Philadelphia hotels answered, and cheerful service rendered." Clemens's wishes were realized many times over as American hospitality ballooned over the following decades, culminating in a new generation of urban hotels, such as the Statler Hotel in Buffalo, opened in 1907, which set new modern standards for American hospitality.

Clemens's gaze, whether admiring or poking fun at European culture or Americans in Europe, is largely focused on understanding America through comparison and encounter with Europe. Even in the middle of his amused distaste, he admits, "Of course when one begins to find fault with foreign people's ways, he is very likely to get a reminder to look nearer home, before he gets far with it" (chapter 21). In his exploration of the German university, Clemens keeps an eye out for the exploits of American students. He notes the presence of 25 members of the Anglo-American club, a "big Kentuckian" who became a dueling expert, and, in Appendix C, relates the tale of an antic southerner who, after spending six months in prison and three in the hospital, decides to transfer elsewhere, finding the German "educational process too slow."

While walking to Baden-Baden, the narrator and his companion attract a voluble and oblivious veterinary student, Cholley Adams, a "manly young fellow . . . a rough gem, but a gem, nevertheless (chapter 20). Near Lucerne, they meet a Harvard-bound young man from New Jersey whose time in Europe has been spent bouncing between pockets of Americans and rattling off lists of ships, cities, and hotels (chapter 27). On the way to the Riffleberg hotel, they meet a self-satisfied young "chatterbox" who is the "grandson of an American of considerable note" (chapter 38). And yet Clemens sings the praises of rude and blundering Americans in Europe with modulated irony and no small spirit of charitable affection, pronouncing the linguist and the chatterbox "the most unique and interesting specimens of Young American I came across in my foreign tramping" (ibid.).

In the period between *The Innocents Abroad* (1869) and *A Tramp Abroad* (1880), the tourist path across Europe was well traveled. The tour industry expanded in size and trickled down in class. It is against a very crowded field that Clemens decides, "it had been many years since the world had been afforded the spectacle of a man adventurous enough to undertake a journey through Europe on foot. . . . So I determined to do it" (chapter 1). As Melton writes, Clemens's travel books "are records not simply of the failure of the Old World civilizations he encounters, but of the failure of touring itself." The sheer mass of package tourism led to a new set of class anxieties, the emergence of new objects of fun, and a new leisure activity while abroad—observing the ugly spectacle of fellow observers: "men and women dressed in all sorts of queer costumes. . . . They had their red guide-books open at the diagram of the view, and were painfully picking out the several mountains and trying to impress their names and positions on their memories. It was one of the saddest sights I ever saw" (chapter 29).

Critical Commentary by Alex Feerst

CHARACTERS AND RELATED ENTRIES

Adams, Cholley Character in *A Tramp Abroad* (1880). A hard-swearing young man from western

New York, Adams introduces himself to the narrator and his friends as they are walking in BADEN-BADEN (chapter 20). He has been in Germany for nearly two years to study horse-doctoring but is becoming homesick while struggling to learn GERMAN and Latin. Adams resembles two other talkative young Americans who appear in chapters 27 and 38.

Baker, Jim   See "Baker, Dick or Jim" in the Characters and Related Entries section of the *Roughing It* entry.

chamois (gemsbok)   Goatlike alpine antelope mentioned frequently in *A Tramp Abroad* (1880). Once common in Europe's ALPS, chamois were hunted nearly to extinction for their meat and skin—which became famous as "shammy" leather. Viewing stories about hunting chamois as romantic nonsense, Clemens uses *A Tramp Abroad* to burlesque the mammal as if it were a flea—precisely what he calls it in his private notebooks. He may also be using "chamois" as a codeword for flea to attack the uncleanliness he found in many Swiss villages. In chapter 35, for example, the narrator's companion, Harris, is covered with chamois bites after walking through a field of "liquid fertilizer" to get to Leukerbad, whose unappealing "Chamois Hotel" the travelers shun.

Dodge, Nicodemus   Character in *A Tramp Abroad* (1880) modeled on Clemens's childhood acquaintance JIM WOLFE. During a free-flowing conversation with Harris in chapter 23, the narrator recalls Dodge as a country lad he knew in a Missouri printing office as a boy. The passage on Dodge opens with his undergoing a job interview that is strikingly similar to Scotty Briggs's interview with a preacher in *Roughing It* (1872). Villagers saw Dodge as a foil for practical jokes, but he was actually a formidable adversary. George Jones gave Dodge an exploding cigar that barely fazed him. When Tom McElroy tied Dodge's clothes into knots while he was swimming, Dodge retaliated by burning up McElroy's clothes. For pinning a rude note on Dodge's back in church, Dodge confined another joker overnight in the cellar of a deserted

house. After practical jokers grew scarce, a young doctor proposed frightening Dodge by putting Jimmy FINN's skeleton—which he had bought for $50—in Dodge's bed. When the doctor and his friends later checked in on Dodge, they found him cheerfully enjoying treasures he had purchased with three dollars he got from selling the skeleton to a passing quack.

Harris (Mr. Harris; the agent)   Character in *A Tramp Abroad* (1880). A fictional traveling companion through most of the narrative, Harris is loosely modeled on JOSEPH TWICHELL, who traveled with Clemens in GERMANY's BLACK FOREST and SWITZERLAND. Clemens found his time with Twichell so stimulating that he expanded Harris's role to provide a coherent thematic structure for his entire narrative. After the book was published, he wrote Twichell an appreciative note specifying many "Harris" anecdotes that actually happened.

Harris is introduced at the beginning of chapter 1 as an "agent" whom the narrator hires to accompany him on a walking tour through Europe. Nothing is said about his background or physical appearance. The balance of *A Tramp Abroad* refers to him as either "Harris" or the "agent." In some chapters, neither Harris nor the agent is mentioned, but the narrator's use of the first-person plural makes it clear that Harris is with him.

Harris's duties as "agent" are not completely clear, especially since the narrator also hires a professional courier in chapter 24 before proceeding south. As a narrative device, however, Harris's role as agent relates closely to the book's primary running joke—namely, that while the narrator boasts about making a "walking" tour, he does most of his traveling on boats, trains, and carriages. He extends this joke by using Harris as his proxy, particularly for disagreeable tasks—such as attending an opera (chapter 10), practicing bowing at tables (chapter 18), attending church (chapter 24), and running after driftwood in a river when the narrator needs exercise (chapter 33). Harris balks, however, when the narrator suggests that he jump 1,200 feet from the RIFFELBERG to a glacier using an umbrella as a parachute (chapter 39). When the narrator orders Harris to climb a perilous ladder in chapter 35, Harris accomplishes the job through a sub-agent of his own.

Harris's biggest assignment is visiting and reporting on Switzerland's Furka region in chapter 30 (he signs his report "H. Harris"; the "H." may stand for *Herr*, German for "mister"). This incident was probably inspired by a three-day trip that Twichell made in the Alps on his own while Clemens and his family rested from climbing the RIGI-KULM.

When Clemens began writing *A Tramp Abroad* in HEIDELBERG, before Twichell joined him, he experimented with a fictional companion called the "Grumbler" (a pseudonym he had used 25 years earlier as a counterpoint to the "RAMBLER") and then with someone named "John." In each case, he was evidently trying to create a character similar to the "Mr. Brown" and "Blucher" that had worked for him during the 1860s. After finally settling on "Harris," he found himself constrained by this fictional companion's clear relationship to the very real Twichell—whose feelings and reputation concerned him. As a result, he left Harris a bland and rather flat character who rarely expresses a strong opinion—in sharp contrast to the earlier Mr. Brown. Harris comes to life only briefly, when he rails against Catholic cantons in Switzerland in chapter 36, finding almost everything within Protestant Swiss cantons to be superior—including "Protestant glaciers."

Clemens later worked "Harris" into an unfinished book about his boat trip on the RHONE in 1891—part of which has been published as "DOWN THE RHÔNE."

Lorelei   The subject of a modern German legend, the Lorelei is a rock cliff jutting into the Rhine River over a dangerous reef between Koblenz and Bingen. In 1801, the German poet Clemens Maria Brentano (1778–1842) published a ballad in an authentic folk idiom associating a woman named "Lore Lay" with the rock. Soon accepted as a genuine folk legend, his ballad was amplified in 1827 by Heinrich Heine (1797–1856), whose song *Die Lorelei* introduced the notion of a beautiful siren sitting atop the Lorelei, luring sailors to their death with her singing. Clemens first learned about the Lorelei in 1878 while sailing to Germany with BAYARD TAYLOR, who sang Heine's song. *A Tramp Abroad* (1880) devotes chapter 16 to the song, including the original lyrics and score and a humorously bad English translation alongside Clemens's own translation of the GERMAN.

BIBLIOGRAPHY

Banks, Russell. "Introduction." In *A Tramp Abroad*, edited by Shelley Fisher Fishkin. Oxford: Oxford University Press, 1996.

Bridgman, Richard. *Traveling in Mark Twain*. Berkeley: University of California Press, 1987.

Driscoll, Kerry. "Afterword." In *A Tramp Abroad*. New York: Modern Library, 2003.

Eggers, Dave. "Introduction." In *A Tramp Abroad*. New York: Modern Library, 2003.

Leonard, James S. "Afterword." In *A Tramp Abroad*, edited by Shelley Fisher Fishkin. Oxford: Oxford University Press, 1996.

Melton, Jeffrey Alan. "Touring the Old World: Faith and Leisure in *The Innocents Abroad* and *A Tramp Abroad*." In *Mark Twain, Travel Books, and Tourism*, 59–94. Tuscaloosa: University of Alabama Press, 2002.

Rodney, Robert M. "Exploring the Continent, 1878–9." In *Mark Twain Overseas*, 95–127. Washington, D.C.: Three Continents Press, 1993.

Twain, Mark. *A Tramp Abroad*, edited by Shelley Fisher Fishkin. New York: Oxford University Press, 1996.

"Traveling with a Reformer"

SKETCH written and published in 1893. Years of tedious railroad travel gave Clemens strong feelings about the poor manners of railroad employees. In *The Gilded Age* (1873), he got his coauthor, C. D. WARNER, to use an incident that he had once observed, when a conductor threw a man off a train for defending a mistreated woman (chapter 29). Clemens seems to have had particularly bad experiences on trips to CHICAGO, including one he made with FREDERICK HALL to see the World's Fair in early 1893. Later that year, he got revenge by writing

"Traveling with a Reformer" for COSMOPOLITAN. After the story appeared in December, the president of the Pennsylvania Railroad retaliated by refusing to grant Clemens complimentary passes when he returned to Chicago with H. H. ROGERS.

When the 5,500-word story first appeared in *Cosmopolitan*, it was illustrated by DAN BEARD. It was first collected in *How to Tell a Story and Other Essays* (1897), which was later issued as LITERARY ESSAYS (1899).

SYNOPSIS

While traveling to the Chicago World's Fair, the unnamed narrator is joined in New York by a serene but humorless man whom he calls the "major." Though illness prevents the narrator from actually seeing the fair, he picks up useful "diplomatic tricks" from the major, who is a passionate advocate of reforming petty public abuses. The major thinks that citizens should watch how laws are executed and work to prevent unfair abuses. When skylarking telegraph operators are slow to serve him, for example, he writes a telegram inviting Western Union's president to dinner, so that he can tell him "how business is conducted in one of your branches." Seeing these words makes the operator pale and promise to reform. The major admits to the narrator that he does not know the president of Western Union and explains the wonders that gentle diplomacy can work.

In the course of their journey, the major uses similar tactics to correct other abuses that he encounters. Meanwhile, he is not above using force when necessary, and he helps throw three roughs off a horse-car. Aboard a train, he later claims that his brother-in-law is a company director, and he not only gets a conductor to make a brakeman apologize to a man he has mistreated, he moves the conductor to *thank* him for complaining. On a "Pennsylvania [Rail]road" train to Chicago, he persuades a conductor to ignore the company's prohibition against Sunday card-playing. On the return train, he secures a sleeper stateroom by threatening to sue the company for violating its contract, and he gets the dining-car staff to serve him a dish not listed on the menu after he sees a railroad employee eating the same meal.

"A True Story"

SHORT STORY written and published in 1874. Subtitled "Repeated Word for Word as I Heard It," this 2,200-word FRAME-STORY is based on a story told by MARY ANN CORD, a former slave who worked for Clemens's sister-in-law in ELMIRA. Most of the story is narrated in an AFRICAN-AMERICAN dialect that Clemens worked hard to make authentic.

After writing this story in mid-1874, Clemens made it his first submission to the ATLANTIC MONTHLY, which published it in November. It was later collected in SKETCHES, NEW AND OLD and was the title story in the slender volume titled *A True Story and The Recent Carnival of Crime* (1877).

SYNOPSIS

One summer evening, the narrator, Misto C-[Clemens?], sits on the farmhouse porch watching the colored servant Aunt Rachel—who sits at a respectfully lower level—being mercilessly teased. Impressed by her easy, hearty laughter, he asks how she has lived 60 years without seeing any trouble. Startled by this naive question, Rachel tells her story.

Born among slaves, she was raised in Virginia. Her mother, who was from Maryland, often went into tantrums, proclaiming, "I wa'nt bawn in the mash to be fool' by trash! I's one o' de ole Blue Hen's Chicken's, I is!" Rachel and her husband had seven children to whom they were devoted, but by and by, their mistress sold all her slaves at auction in Richmond. As Rachel says this, she rises to tower above the narrator. Chained and put on display for buyers, she watched her husband and most of her children being sold, then seized her young son Henry and threatened to kill anyone who touched him. Henry whispered for her not to worry, as he would escape to the North and return to buy her freedom. Since that day, 22 years ago Easter, Rachel has not seen her husband or six of her children.

Rachel's new owner took her to Newbern (New Bern, North Carolina?) and made her his family cook. Eventually, the war came and he fled before Union troops, who took the town and made his house their headquarters. While cooking for the Union officers, Rachel asked after her son Henry, in case they saw him in the North. Unbeknownst to her at the time, Henry had fled North and become a barber. Later, he hired himself out to Union officers and scoured the South looking for her.

One night a black regiment held a ball at the house. While Rachel was working, a spruce young man danced into her kitchen with his partner. When Rachel ordered him out, he shot her a surprised look. When more men came in, she straightened up to proclaim that she "wa'nt bawn in the mash to be fool' by trash," causing the young man to stare. The next morning, the young man returned to the kitchen early. As Rachel removed biscuits from the oven, the man leaned over to look in her face. Recognizing Henry by scars he had acquired as a child, Rachel realized that at last she had her own again.

CRITICAL COMMENTARY

In "A True Story," nobody suspects the trouble, anguish, and pain Aunt Rachel has experienced until, provoked by an unthinking comment, she tells her employer-family and the narrator her story asserting her humanity and individuality. The family likes, appreciates, and even cares for her while seeing only a living stereotype of the contented "darky." Targeting northern liberals and southern apologists, Clemens dashes that image with the force of Rachel's personality.

Clemens himself is the "thinks-he-knows-and-understands" liberal. Often a character in his stories, usually the butt of a joke, here he is the butt of a serious joke. Moved by the story of Mary Ann Cord, cook for his sister-in-law, SUSAN LANGDON CRANE, he wanted to tell it. "Misto C-" may not be Samuel Clemens any more than his persona in other stories, but he seems similar. Misto C-, an unthinking white man with unrealized prejudices about black people, respects Rachel and admires his perception of her happy disposition, believing she has experienced no trouble, suffering, or grief to upset that disposition. Not prejudiced against her, he views her as a simple creature caring for a white family who in turn cares for her. Resembling a paternalistic plantation owner, he is benevolent and not deliberately hateful or cruel but unable to see her humanity. She shows him.

With Rachel sitting "respectfully below our level" (befitting her station, the narrator observes),

teased by the family as one might tease a child, her strong reaction to his comment that she has known no trouble stuns him. Her response to his stammering is a story of more than words. It compares black/white family feelings, enhances immediacy, emphasizes commonality, equalizes.

Fictional, despite its title and subtitle, the story is true to the black experience. The subtitle implies authenticity. Rachel's name alludes to the biblical Rachel's grief over losing her children. Her movements while talking symbolize her altering status; initially "below our level," she "had gradually risen while she warmed to her subject, and now she towered above us, black against the stars," stressing the point at the end, "I jist straightened myself up so—jist as I is now, plum to de ceilin'. . . ." This elevation of her humanity implies superiority over those who judged only her appearance.

Clemens accentuates Rachel's humanity by revealing her flaws. Proud of her Maryland ancestry, Rachel repeats her mother's refrain that she is one of the "ole Blue Hen's Chickens." She is proud to be the Union officers' cook ("no small-fry officers . . . dey was de biggest dey is"). Rachel takes seriously the general's telling her to "boss dat kitchen." When a black regiment holds a dance, she becomes angry at the common soldiers cavorting in her kitchen and explodes when a young spruced soldier and "a yaller wench" laugh at her turban, actually her manner. This fortunate explosion results in the reunion with her son.

She is thankful for finding one of her seven lost children, as she understands that most displaced slaves never find anyone. Her dramatic monologue, preparation for the vernacular *Huckleberry Finn*, contains an untypical Clemens persona, not innocent or buffoonish but a humiliated stand-in for white America. Still, Rachel dominates the story. She carries the weight of her burdens and years with dignity, never outwardly complaining. Telling her story, she reveals more than a happy servant but a person with flaws and an eventful life beyond domestic duties—a fully realized human being.

Critical Commentary by John H. Davis

BIBLIOGRAPHY

Quirk, Tom. *Mark Twain: A Study of the Short Fiction.* New York: Twayne, 1997.

Twain, Mark. "A True Story: Repeated Word for Word as I Heard It." In *Mark Twain: Collected Tales, Sketches, Speeches, & Essays, 1852–1890,* edited by Louis J. Budd, 578–582. New York: Library of America, 1992.

"The Turning Point of My Life"

ESSAY published in 1910. An important adjunct to Clemens's AUTOBIOGRAPHY, this essay arises from the deterministic philosophy that he espouses in WHAT IS MAN? (1906). Though he submitted this piece in response to a magazine's invitation to write on the title subject, the essay is essentially a revision of a dictation that he made three years earlier, shortly after publishing *What Is Man?*

SYNOPSIS

Clemens begins by rejecting the idea of a single turning point in his life, arguing instead that a chain of 10,000 links has determined his life. He cites JULIUS CAESAR's crossing of the Rubicon—one of history's most celebrated turning points—as merely the last link of a long chain. As Caesar hesitated to cross the river, an impulsive act by his trumpeter suddenly moved him to decision. That tiny link affected virtually every event that has followed in Western history.

Since Clemens sees literature as the most important feature of his life, his own most important turning point must therefore be the link that turned him in that direction. To find that link, he goes back to when he was 12. At that time, a measles epidemic so scared him that he deliberately contracted the disease to end the suspense. After he got well, his mother—who was tired of trying to keep him out of mischief—took him out of school and apprenticed him to a printer; that was the first link. Later, his printing work took him to IOWA, where he read about the Amazon and planned to go there. His plan meant nothing by itself, however, until *circumstance* stepped in. When he found a $50 bill, he used it to go down the Mississippi River to NEW ORLEANS in order to ship out to SOUTH AMERICA. Since there were no ships to take him to the Amazon, he instead became a steamboat PILOT, until the CIVIL WAR intruded. This time, circumstance got his brother appointed secretary to NEVADA Territory; he followed his brother to the West, where he used what printing work had taught him about literature to become a reporter for the VIRGINIA CITY TERRITORIAL ENTERPRISE. Later, the SACRAMENTO UNION sent him to the SANDWICH ISLANDS. This gained him such notoriety that he took up LECTURING in SAN FRANCISCO and began earning the wherewithal to see the world and join the QUAKER CITY excursion. This, in turn, led to his writing *Innocents Abroad*, which made him a member of the literary guild. He can therefore truthfully state that he entered the literary profession because he had the measles when he was 12.

What interests Clemens about these details is that he foresaw none of them, while circumstance did his planning for him, with the help of his temperament. He sees little difference between a man and a watch, except that the man is conscious and the watch is not. He goes on to argue that the real turning point of his and everyone else's life was the Garden of Eden, where ADAM AND EVE forged the first link that would lead him into literature by eating the forbidden apple. He cannot help but wonder what would have happened if God had put Martin Luther and Joan of Arc in the Garden instead. If they had been ordered not to eat the apple, they would not have eaten it, and there would be no human race and he would never have gone into literature.

BACKGROUND AND PUBLISHING HISTORY

In October 1906, Clemens received a letter that moved him to dictate an autobiographical passage on the "accidents" in his life that became the basis for this essay (the passage appears in MARK TWAIN IN ERUPTION). After drafting the present 3,670-word essay twice in 1909, he published it in HARPER'S BAZAAR in February 1910, two months before he died. Seven years later, A. B. PAINE republished it in the *What Is Man? and Other Essays*. Paul Baender published a corrected version in the Mark Twain Papers (now the MARK TWAIN PROJECT) edition *What Is Man? and other Philosophical Writings* in 1973.

"Two Little Tales"

SHORT STORY that Clemens wrote while living in LONDON in fall 1900. The title alludes to its story-within-a-story structure. The first story is set in London in February 1900, when Britain was busy fighting in the South African (Boer) War. The unidentified narrator tells of a friend who has another friend who cannot get the attention of the War Office; this man has invented a boot that would be invaluable to British troops in South Africa. Even the narrator's friend, who is "not unknown," cannot get through to the director-general of the Shoe-Leather Department.

This story follows certain DIALOGUE conventions. As the friend explains his difficulties, the narrator exposes the fallacies of his arguments, asserting that he knows better because he is "very old and very wise." He explains how to break through the government bureaucracy by means of a parable: "How the Chimney-sweep Got the Ear of the Emperor." This second story concerns the emperor of an unnamed realm vexed by the "plague of dysentery" devastating his army. The emperor himself becomes afflicted; nothing can be done, despite the efforts of the greatest physicians of the land.

Meanwhile, Tommy, a lowly 16-year-old assistant cesspool cleaner, has a younger chimney-sweep friend, Jimmy, who says he can cure the emperor. He learned from an old ZULU man that eating a slice of ripe watermelon will quickly cure any case of dysentery. Tommy conveys the idea to the emperor by telling it to a butcher, who in turn tells a chestnut-seller, and so on. Finally, the message reaches the Lord High Chamberlain and the emperor himself. Tommy explains that everyone has a special friend willing to pass on a message; one only has to find the *first* friend to get the message started.

After the emperor is cured, he wants to give a suitable reward. Responsibility for the message is traced all the way back down to Jimmy. The emperor sends Jimmy his reward: a pair of his own boots. They are too big for Jimmy, so he gives them to the old Zulu. After the narrator finishes the story, his friend approaches a friend of the director-general. The army soon adopts his friend's boots.

BACKGROUND AND PUBLISHING HISTORY

Clemens's immediate inspiration for this 4,100-word short story appears to have been the success of the makers of PLASMON in getting the British army to adopt the diet supplement during the South African War. His point seems to be that bureaucracy is blind even to useful truths, unless it is penetrated by personal contacts. The story first appeared in London's *Century* magazine in November 1901.

"The United States of Lyncherdom"

Posthumously published ESSAY that Clemens wrote after reading a news story about an August 1901 lynching incident in southwestern Missouri. According to his account, a mob reacted to the murder of a young white woman in Pierce City by lynching three AFRICAN AMERICANS, including two who were very old, and driving 30 families into the woods. Although the lynching of African Americans in the South was occurring with increasing frequency around that time, Clemens was particularly upset by the Pierce City incident because it occurred in his home state, which would ever afterward be branded a land of lynchers. Clemens adds little more about the Pierce City incident and instead devotes the bulk of his 3,030-word essay to the nature of lynching in the United States, with a suggestion for its remedy.

The Missouri lynching incident to which Clemens alluded occurred in Pierce City, a small town southeast of Joplin, on the night of August

19, 1901. It may have been even more horrendous than what he described. About 300 people were driven out of Pierce City, and members of the lynch mob fired at least 600 rounds of ammunition at them with 50 rifles that they had borrowed from the local National Guard armory. Many evacuees settled in Springfield, Missouri, about 45 miles to the east, never to return. Missouri later experienced other lynchings, but the Pierce City incident appears to have been the worst.

Incidents of lynching, vigilantism, and TAR-AND-FEATHERING appear throughout Clemens's writings and provide evidence of his long aversion to all forms of injustice. "The United States of Lyncherdom" explicitly addresses a number of points that his earlier writings address implicitly. For example, his belief that a person with true moral courage can face down a lynch mob is expressed in *Huckleberry Finn* (1884) in chapter 22, when Colonel Sherburn relies only on the strength of his own character to turn away an angry mob that wants to hang him. The inspiration behind Clemens's creation of Sherburn was probably the "brave gentleman" mentioned in "The United States of Lyncherdom" whom Clemens had seen deride and drive away a mob when he was a boy. When Theodor Fischer, the narrator of "CHRONICLE OF YOUNG SATAN," reluctantly joins a mob throwing stones at a woman being hanged, Satan laughs and later reveals that, of the 68 people attending the hanging, 62 had no more desire to throw a stone than Theodore had (chapter 9).

SYNOPSIS

After expressing dismay that Missouri has lost its innocence to lawless assassins, Clemens attempts to explain why lynching is proliferating throughout the United States. First, he dismisses the notion that provocations of any kind might ever justify a lynching. So far as he is concerned, taking the law into one's own hands can never be justified. He then asks why lynching is becoming so popular as a method of dealing with cases of what he calls the "usual crime" (an evident reference to crimes against white women). He dismisses any suggestion that many people believe that "lurid and terrible" punishments provide more effective deterrents to

crime than ordinary punishments by arguing that strange and well-publicized events are always imitated. In fact, he suggests that lynchers are the "worst enemies of their women" because they help inspire the very crimes they ostensibly aim to prevent.

After pointing to more evidence of the widespread proliferation of lynching in the United States, Clemens suggests that the increase reflects the natural human tendency to imitate. He also blames a common weakness of human beings—moral cowardice, which encourages people to follow mobs in order to avoid incurring their neighbors' disapproval. After citing the heroism of two southern sheriffs who single-handedly stopped lynchings in Georgia and Indiana, he suggests that the remedy for lynching lies in finding other brave men to station in each affected community. In the absence of enough men in America to fill those stations, Clemens proposes recalling American missionaries from China. Being universally regarded as an already excellent people, the Chinese do not need Christian missionaries as much as Americans do. Moreover, the missionaries are already well trained in facing mobs without flinching.

BACKGROUND AND PUBLISHING HISTORY

Clemens evidently wrote this essay for the *NORTH AMERICAN REVIEW* in August 1901, and he also considered using it as the introduction for a book on lynching that he wanted to write. However, he decided against publication and abandoned the book project, and the essay was not published during his lifetime. It first appeared in *EUROPE AND ELSEWHERE* (1923), a collection of previously unpublished material assembled by ALBERT BIGELOW PAINE. Paine's text was used in *A Pen Warmed Up in Hell* (1972), edited by Frederick Anderson, and in *Collected Tales, Sketches, Speeches, & Essays, 1891–1910* (1992), edited by Louis J. Budd.

In 2001, L. Terry Ogel of Virginia Commonwealth University, with the assistance of the editors of the MARK TWAIN PROJECT, published a corrected version of "The United States of Lyncherdom" that established the hitherto unknown extent of Paine's tampering with Clemens's original text. Paine deleted nearly 400 words, softened several passages, and distorted Clemens's meaning significantly in several places.

The story of Pierce City's 1901 lynching again made headlines in mid-2005, when a descendant of one of the black families that had been run out of Pierce City located the grave of an ancestor who had been buried in the town's cemetery and made arrangements to have the body reinterred in Springfield, where other relatives had settled after being run out in 1901. The publicity surrounding this event called attention to another event that had occurred a few years earlier. At that time, a college student found a copy of the August 25, 1901, edition of the *St. Louis Post-Dispatch* that had a front-page story about the Pierce City lynching and included photographs of some of the families that had been run out of Pierce City. After this story came to the attention of Missouri congresswoman Lacy Clay, she and 13 other black Democrats introduced into the House of Representatives a bill titled the 1901 Missouri African American Expulsion Commission Act, which called for a federal investigation of the 1901 incident.

"Villagers of 1840–3"

Informal notes on Clemens's Hannibal neighbors. While summering in WEGGIS, Switzerland, in 1897, Clemens wrote roughly 8,000 words about everyone he could remember from his childhood, drawing on his memories and an 1884 book on MARION COUNTY containing biographical sketches. He recorded these notes largely for his own satisfaction around the same time that he began writing "Hellfire Hotchkiss" and "TOM SAWYER'S CONSPIRACY." "Villagers of 1840–3" is Clemens's own title, but he probably intended the second date to be "1853"— the year that he left Hannibal.

First published in the Mark Twain Papers (predecessor of the MARK TWAIN PROJECT) edition *HANNIBAL, HUCK AND TOM* (1969), edited by WALTER BLAIR, "Villagers" provides a trove of information on Clemens's early life and the people who inspired

many characters in his Tom Sawyer and Huckleberry Finn stories. His notes are particularly rich on the Clemens family. He calls his father "Judge Carpenter," his brother Orion "Oscar Carpenter," and himself "Simon Carpenter." A corrected version of "Villagers" was published in *HUCK FINN AND TOM SAWYER AMONG THE INDIANS AND OTHER UNFINISHED STORIES* (1989).

"Wapping Alice"

Posthumously published SHORT STORY. In 1877, while the Clemenses were living in Hartford, Lizzie Wells, a family maid, tripped their house's burglar alarm, revealing the fact that she was admitting a secret lover named Willie Taylor. When Clemens and JOSEPH TWICHELL later confronted Wells, she claimed that Taylor had made her pregnant, and they pressured him into marrying her. Over the next 30 years, Clemens wrote about this incident intermittently. After first using real names, he rewrote the story around 1897 as fiction and set it in LONDON's Wapping district. This version retained many real details of the Wells incident, but added a surprising twist: After the fictional Alice marries her lover, she announces that she is actually a man.

After failing to sell the story to HARPER'S MAGAZINE in 1907, Clemens set it aside. It was first published in 1981 by the Friends of the Bancroft Library—with which the MARK TWAIN PROJECT is affiliated. A special booklet edited by HAMLIN HILL includes all of Clemens's "Wapping Alice" manuscripts, several letters to his wife, and the text of "The McWilliamses and the Burglar Alarm" (see McWILLIAMS FAMILY STORIES).

"The War Prayer"

SHORT STORY written in early 1905 and published posthumously. An outgrowth of Clemens's increasing opposition to war and imperialism, "The War Prayer" expresses the horrible implications of war by spelling out the full meaning of military victory. The story's single incident may go back to a moment described in *Life on the Mississippi* (1883), in which an apparently deranged man delivers a speech that leaves his audience thinking that he is an archangel (chapter 57).

SYNOPSIS

The setting could be any Christian country during any war. Patriotism is rampant, soldiers are marching off, and churches everywhere are asking God to support their cause. The scene narrows to a single church packed with people whose young men will leave the next day. After the pastor delivers a long, eloquent prayer, asking God to bless their arms and grant them victory, a strange elderly man in a robe advances to the pulpit and motions him aside. Calling himself a messenger from the Throne, the stranger explains that the prayer just delivered is actually two prayers: one uttered, the other *unuttered*. God will grant the uttered prayer if the parishioners wish it, he promises—but only after he articulates for them the unuttered prayer behind their request for "victory." He then asks God to tear the enemy to bloody shreds, devastate his homes, leave his unoffending widows grief-stricken and his children homeless. After the man finishes, everyone concludes that he is a lunatic because there is no sense in what he has said.

PUBLISHING HISTORY

According to A. B. PAINE, Clemens had no intention of trying to publish this story in his lifetime; however, he did submit it to HARPER'S BAZAAR, which rejected it as unsuitable. Paine himself included a long extract in *Mark Twain: A Biography* (1912), and he published the entire story in EUROPE AND ELSEWHERE (1923). FREDERICK ANDERSON later included a corrected text in *A Pen Warmed Up in Hell* (1972).

The television play MARK TWAIN: BENEATH THE LAUGHTER (1979) depicts Clemens reading the manuscript of "The War Prayer" to his shocked daughter Jean. As he reads, the scene cuts to a 19th-century Protestant church, in which the story is acted out with Richard Moll as the stranger. Another dramatization of "The War Prayer" is

appended to the end of the television play THE PRIVATE HISTORY OF A CAMPAIGN THAT FAILED (1981).

CRITICAL COMMENTARY

Disturbed that a war of liberation he initially supported had become a war of imperialism and that, as is often true, partisans expected God to take their side in the war, Clemens wrote "The War Prayer" to illuminate the hypocrisy and horror of merging religion and war. He utilizes an archetypal figure to vivify the unspoken side of prayer. Resembling traditional representations of wise men, wizards, hermits, and prophets, as in depictions by William Blake, this mysterious figure walks into church as the pastor prays for God's aid in the war: "An aged stranger entered . . . his long body clothed in a robe that reached to his feet, his head bare, his white hair descending in a frothy cataract to his shoulders, his seamy face unnaturally pale, pale even to ghastliness." Those confusing the Creator with a destroyer hear what is said, without comprehending or conceiving the consequences of prayers, as the stranger comes to clarify.

The stranger's appearance is familiar but still striking. As a wizard, he evokes the awe of inexplicable forces, power beyond ordinary control, a dread that urges one to listen attentively. As a wise man, he is one who should be listened to, but ironically his wisdom is beyond his audience's understanding. As a prophet, he issues a dire warning.

To remove the bewitchments war enthusiasm has cast on his "spell-bound audience," the stranger shockingly announces, "I come from the Throne— bearing a message from Almighty God!" to explain the double consequences of their two-sided prayer. Their prayer was simple, a request for victory, but granting it entails unforeseen results, which he forces them to visualize: horrific death and suffering, a wasteland of homes paralleling their "wilderness of flags," starving and homeless innocents. Salvation for one side is destruction for another. Unaware of the consequences, the audience fails to realize the contradictions of praying to a God of Love to support hatred.

As in "To the Person Sitting in Darkness," "KING LEOPOLD'S SOLILOQUY," and other satires on war and imperialism, Clemens shows readers other sides of issues. One should be cautious for what one prays; the prayer might be granted. Hoping that they "ignorantly and unthinkingly" prayed for the outlined results, the stranger waits to hear if they still wish them. The final irony, however, is that the congregation sees not an emblematic wise man, prophet, or wrathful God in the stranger but a stereotypical Tom O'Bedlam, a lunatic. Rather than accept the insanity of war, the people consider the messenger insane.

Critical Commentary by John H. Davis

BIBLIOGRAPHY

Twain, Mark. "The War Prayer." In *A Pen Warmed Up in Hell: Mark Twain in Protest*, edited by Frederick Anderson, 88–91. New York: Harper & Row, 1972.

What Is Man?

Book published in 1906. In the last decades of his life, Clemens adopted a mechanistic and deterministic philosophy that he called his private "gospel," which he sums up in *What Is Man?* Published only anonymously during Clemens's lifetime, this 27,500-word volume is a Socratic DIALOGUE in which an "Old Man" spends several days converting a "Young Man" to his philosophy, whose essential idea is that man is a machine controlled by outside forces, such as heredity, environment, and training. Further, man creates nothing, acts only to satisfy his own needs, and should neither be praised for good acts nor be condemned for bad ones. Free will, heroism, genius, virtue, and vice are all merely man's delusions. While the origins of Clemens's ideas are complex, two particularly important sources may have been W. E. H. LECKY and a man named MACFARLANE whom Mark Twain claimed to know when he was younger.

Clemens began articulating his private gospel during the early 1880s and first gave it public expression in "What Is Happiness?," a paper delivered to Hartford's MONDAY EVENING CLUB in February 1883. His gospel received fuller expression in *Connecticut Yankee* (1889), a novel that builds to a grimly deterministic ending. Midway through its narrative, for example, its hero Hank Morgan decides that rea-

soning with Morgan le Fay is pointless because of her training. He explains that "training is all there is *to* a person. We speak of nature: it is folly: there is no such thing as nature; what we call by that misleading name is merely heredity and training. We have no thoughts of our own, no opinions of our own: they are transmitted to us, trained into us" (chapter 18).

Though Clemens never publicly acknowledged his authorship of *What Is Man?*, he expressed many of its core ideas in "THE TURNING POINT OF MY LIFE," which *HARPER'S BAZAAR* published three months before he died. Other writings that deal with similar themes include his MYSTERIOUS STRANGER stories, "CORN-PONE OPINIONS," and "THE DERVISH AND THE OFFENSIVE STRANGER."

SYNOPSIS

(Remarks within parentheses derive from sources outside this dialogue.)

Part 1

As an Old Man (O.M.) and a Young Man (Y.M.) converse, the O.M. asserts that a human being is merely a machine. Objecting to this, the Y.M. demands proof, thus beginning their dialogue. Prodded by the O.M., the Y.M. defines a "machine." The O.M. then demonstrates how this definition applies to human behavior, showing that man is an impersonal engine. Whatever a man is, is due to his make and the influences of his heredity, habitat and associations. Commanded by *exterior* influences, man *originates* nothing, not even a thought. The O.M. goes on to argue that even the first man, Adam, had no original thoughts. Only gods have them. Even WILLIAM SHAKESPEARE created nothing. He merely imitated people whom God had created.

Part 2

The O.M. dismisses acts of "self-sacrifice" that appear to demonstrate love, philanthropy, or patriotism as motivated solely by the desire for self-approval that is trained into man. We help others because it gratifies *us;* we regret hurting others only because the guilt disturbs *us.*

Part 3

To prove his Gospel of Self-Approval, the O.M. challenges the Y.M. to cite an example of a totally

Clemens in a pensive mood around the time he published *What Is Man?* (Courtesy, Mark Twain Memorial)

selfless act. The Y.M. suggests an example from a novel (Florence Wilkinson, *The Strength of the Hills*, 1901) in which a lumberman sacrifices his worldly interests to save souls for the glory of God and Christ, solely for duty's sake. The O.M. counters that the lumberman is acting only for self-approval; furthermore, he is indifferent to the hardships that his actions produce for his own family.

Later the Y.M. offers the sinking of the *Berkeley Castle* as an example of selfless sacrifice. At their colonel's command, a thousand unprotesting soldiers went down with the troopship so that women and children could be saved on its few lifeboats (an allusion to the H.M.S. *Birkenhead,* which sank off of South Africa in 1852, drowning about 450 people). The O.M. dismisses their heroism, however, as purely a product of their military training.

Part 4

The O.M. defines "training" as not merely formal instruction, but *all* outside influences that a person encounters from cradle to grave. To make his point,

he asks why people adhere to certain religious sects and not to others. The answer lies in the cultures with which a person is associated.

To challenge the O.M.'s assertion that a man always acts to please his interior master, the Y.M. asks why it is that he scolds a servant, even though he *wants* to control his temper. The O.M. explains that there are two kinds of pleasure: primary and secondary. Scolding gives the Y.M. short-term primary pleasure, which mastering his temper provides long-term secondary pleasure.

Part 5

To further his case that man is a machine, the O.M. reminds the Y.M. how the mind sometimes works by itself all night, keeping one awake and restless, despite one's trying to make it stop. He challenges the Y.M. to command his mind not to wander. Several days later, the Y.M. reports back, conceding that he could not control his mind even once in 10 experiments. In one instance, for example, he could not clear his head of the popular song "THE SWEET BYE AND BYE." Other examples of man's inability to control his own mind include moments when he blurts out words without knowing that they are coming.

To defend his assertion that no man ever originates or creates anything, the O.M. argues that those we call "inventors" are merely discoverers who observe things and add to what others have already seen. The process is the same even in the creation of a Shakespearean play. Men observe and combine, just as a rat does when his observation of a smell leads to his discovery of a cheese.

Part 6

The Y.M. dislikes the fact that the O.M.'s theories strip away man's dignities and grandeurs, which the O.M. calls mere shams. The Y.M.'s objection to having man reduced to the level of a rat leads to discussion of intellect and instinct. The O.M. argues that intellect works the same in both man and the animals; the difference is a matter only of capacity.

The O.M. flatly denies the existence of free will—untrammeled power to *act* as one pleases. He believes that there is only "free choice"—the ability to choose between options.

Conclusion

At their final meeting, the Y.M. asks the O.M. if he intends to publish his ideas. Challenged to answer this question himself, the Y.M. concedes that publishing this philosophy would be harmful. He finds it desolate and degrading, as it denies man glory, pride, or heroism, turning him into a mere coffee mill. While the Y.M. frets that this philosophy must make a person wretched, the O.M. points out that he himself has an inborn temperament to be cheerful, despite his convictions. And it is differences in temperament that explain why different people may respond so differently to the same experiences. The O.M. sees no point in publishing his philosophy, since mankind generally *feels* rather than *thinks* and would not respond to it.

BACKGROUND AND PUBLISHING HISTORY

After completing *Following the Equator* in 1897, Clemens began writing stories that seem to have helped him cope with the misfortunes that were befalling his family. He left most of these manuscripts—such as "Which Was the Dream?" and "THE GREAT DARK"—unfinished and was hesitant to express his opinions publicly. Between April and July 1898, while he was living in AUSTRIA, he wrote the first half of *What Is Man?* After setting the manuscript aside, he went back to it around late 1901 or early 1902, then tinkered with it over the next three or four years, while testing its ideas on members of his household and close friends. After deciding to publish the book, he deleted several chapters. One of them argues that man's "moral sense" places him below the animals because it enables him to do wrong; two others examine God's attitude toward man and argue that God is a cruel and vindictive being.

Clemens completed *What Is Man?* in the fall of 1905 and decided to publish it anonymously the following spring. To make it difficult for his authorship to be recognized, he deleted several passages that might be associated with him—such an allusion to the jingle in "PUNCH, BROTHERS, PUNCH!" He maintained his anonymity by having Frank N. Doubleday serve as his go-between with De Vinne Press, a New York City firm that published 250 copies of the book

in August 1906. Issued without an author's name, the book was copyrighted under the name of J. W. Bothwell, De Vinne's superintendent.

What Is Man? received little notice after it was published. The NEW YORK SUN and *New York Times* found merit in its wit and clarity but dismissed its arguments as old. Clemens later regretted publishing the book, since it attracted so little interest. His lack of confidence in the book may have been reflected in the fact that he never showed a copy to his close friend the Reverend JOSEPH TWICHELL.

Two days after Clemens died, the NEW YORK TRIBUNE revealed his authorship of the book in an article containing long extracts. Later that year, an unauthorized edition of *What Is Man?* with Clemens's name on it was published in England. The first authorized edition with his name appeared in 1917, when Harper's published *What Is Man? and Other Essays.* Edited by A. B. PAINE, this volume's 16 essays also include "At the Shrine of St. WAGNER," "THE DEATH OF JEAN," "ENGLISH AS SHE IS TAUGHT," "HOW TO MAKE HISTORY DATES STICK," *IS SHAKESPEARE DEAD?,* "A Scrap of Curious History," "SWITZERLAND, The Cradle of Liberty," "TAMING THE BICYCLE," "THE TURNING POINT OF MY LIFE," and "WILLIAM DEAN HOWELLS."

In 1973, the Mark Twain Papers (predecssor of the MARK TWAIN PROJECT) issued a corrected edition of *What Is Man?* edited by Paul Baender. Drawing on Clemens's original manuscripts—all of which survive—this edition shows Clemens's textual changes and incorporates his omitted chapters. The same volume also includes "CHRISTIAN SCIENCE," *LETTERS FROM THE EARTH,* and other, shorter writings relating to religion and philosophy.

The 1996 OXFORD MARK TWAIN edition includes a facsimile reprint of the original 1906 edition of *What Is Man?* This edition contains a new introduction by novelist Charles Johnson and an afterword by Linda Wagner-Martin.

CRITICAL COMMENTARY

Clemens prefaces *What Is Man?* with a note on the work's vintage; it was crafted over a period of 25 years and revised heavily during the last seven. With a several-decade gestation period, *What Is Man?* is in a sense a collaboration between early and later Mark Twains, mirroring the back-and-forth exchanges between the Socratic dialogue's naive Young Man and the wised-up Old Man. This revisiting of physical territory at different points in a psychological trajectory occurs in other areas of Clemens's work, such as his TRAVEL BOOKS, which moves from the puckish *The Innocents Abroad* (1869) through *A Tramp Abroad* (1880) to the world-weary *Following the Equator* (1897). If the absorption of experience by youth is a key theme throughout Clemens's body of work, *What Is Man?* stages this process explicitly by bringing divergent perspectives into collision in a scene of direct persuasion.

The examples that populate Clemens's dialogue constellate a freewheeling and imaginative intellect approaching its subject from several angles at once, including tidy thought experiments, representative scenes of Anglo-American history, and efficiently sketched thumbnail anecdotes. The Old Man's fast-shifting and wide-ranging examples include steam engines built of various metals, William Shakespeare's culture-bound genius, a man who gives his last quarter to a beggar on a snowy night, Alexander Hamilton's duel, and a Kentuckian seeking revenge. The Young Man's rebuttals include a lumberman who moves to the slums of New York to convert "half-civilized foreign paupers," tipping in Europe, and the stoic self-sacrifice of the crew of the sinking British ship the *Berkeley Castle*. One extended anecdote exhibits a deft and improbable symmetry reminiscent of Clemens's characteristic short yarns: an "infidel" convinces a dying Christian boy to give up his faith. He then becomes a Christian missionary and convinces a dying native boy to give up his traditional faith. Both boys die between belief systems, disillusioned and without faith; their mothers are not pleased and the recently christened missionary has done no apparent good in either case.

Clemens published *What is Man?* under a carefully engineered anonymity because he feared the public impact it would have and did not want it associated with his name. But *What Is Man?*, if a taut and readable exposition of Clemens's determinist "gospel," failed to make waves as a particularly novel or rigorous proposition. In many ways, it reflects an extreme version of views that had been

held among psychological circles since the mid-19th century. And, as Sherwood Cummings notes, its structure implicitly recapitulates the history of thinking on the subject over several hundred years from René Descartes through John Stuart Mill to the brink of William James. It has also received relatively little direct critical attention as a literary text.

Though *What Is Man?* takes the form of a dialogue, its diction and cadences generally have little in common with the breezy oral style associated with Clemens's work. Even in comparison to ancient Platonic dialogues in which Socrates questioned his interlocutors on their internal inconsistencies by asking probing and rhetorical questions, Clemens's Old Man aggressively propounds his mechanistic thesis and defies the Young Man to refute, or even wiggle free of, his assertions. As the Old Man and Young Man argue, the contour of their exchange is taut and manufactured, in stark contrast to the digressive style of Clemens's generally chattier narrators and interlocutors. In the dialogue, rather than aiming to entertain, Clemens's interest in simulating speech contracts in favor of advancing his case. At a broader generic level, Clemens never engaged with developments in naturalist fiction of the period, by writers such as Frank Norris, Stephen Crane, and Theodore Dreiser, who were also motivated by a parallel interest of determinism and explored human behavior as a function of circumstances and biology.

Clemens's reasoning, which he tightened over a quarter century, shifts much of its burden onto the cornerstone concept of temperament. According to the Old Man, a person can be understood as entirely the result of training and external influence—except for temperament, the irreducible black box in which human mystery and individuality resides. The differentiating spark labeled temperament plays for Clemens the same role that soul does in a religious worldview (which the old and young men agree is a mystery) or, in modern biological research, DNA. If, as Clemens insists, people function like machines, temperament is the inexplicable algorithm by which any given person will absorb and respond to external stimuli. This kernel of varied human reactions to the world, from laughter to despair, is the main blind spot of Clemens's model, the final displaced location of the human mysteries dispelled throughout the text and an obstinate source of wonder and hope.

Critical Commentary by Alex Feerst

BIBLIOGRAPHY

Cummings, Sherwood. "Man: Machine or Dreamer? In *Mark Twain and Science: Adventures of a Mind*, 201–218. Baton Rouge: Louisiana State University Press, 1988.

Johnson, Charles, "Introduction." In *What Is Man?* edited by Shelley Fisher Fishkin. New York: Oxford University Press, 1996.

Quirk, Tom. "The Late Years, 1891–1910: False Starts and Flights of Fancy." In *Mark Twain : A Study of the Short Fiction*, 86–128. New York: Twayne Publishers, 1997.

Tuckey, John S. "Mark Twain's Later Dialogue: The 'Me' and the Machine." *American Literature* 41, no. 4 (January 1970): 532–542. Reprinted in *On Mark Twain: The Best from American Literature*, edited by Louis J. Budd and Edwin H. Cady, 127–138. Durham: N.C.: Duke University Press, 1987.

Twain, Mark. *What Is Man?*, edited by Shelley Fisher Fishkin. New York: Oxford University Press, 1996.

Wagner-Martin, Linda. "Afterword." In *What Is Man?* edited by Shelley Fisher Fishkin. Oxford: Oxford University Press, 1996.

Which Was the Dream? and Other Symbolic Writings of the Later Years, Mark Twain's (1967)

Collection of unfinished stories edited by JOHN S. TUCKEY for the Mark Twain Papers (see MARK TWAIN PROJECT) and published by the University of California Press. Clemens wrote the volume's 11 stories between 1896 and 1905. Seven of the fragments are substantial pieces: "Which Was the Dream?," "THE ENCHANTED SEA WILDERNESS," "An Adventure in Remote Seas," "THE GREAT DARK," "Indiantown," "Which Was It?" and "THREE THOUSAND YEARS AMONG THE MICROBES." The four briefer fragments—placed in a appendix—are titled "The Passenger's Story." "The Mad Passenger," "Dying Deposition," and "Trial of the Squire." Aside from "The Great Dark" and a small part of "Three Thousand Years," all the stories in the volume were published in the volume for the first time.

Most of the stories are narrated by men similar to Clemens himself who have thought themselves lucky until they find themselves in the midst of nightmarish failures. Each narrator poses the same question: Is he living in a dark dream from which he will awaken, or is his nightmare the reality, with the happiness he previously knew the dream?

Tuckey's *THE DEVIL'S RACE-TRACK: MARK TWAIN'S GREAT DARK WRITINGS* (1980) is a popular edition selecting what Tuckey regards as the best stories from *Which Was the Dream?* and *FABLES OF MAN*.